Macmillan

Dic tion ary

for

Children

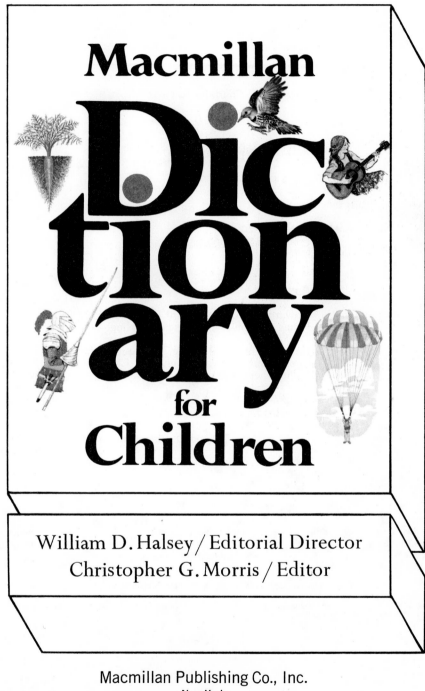

Macmillan

Dictionary

for Children

William D. Halsey / Editorial Director
Christopher G. Morris / Editor

Macmillan Publishing Co., Inc.
New York
Collier Macmillan Publishers
London

Editorial Staff

Supervising Editor	Phyllis R. Winant
Definers	Vesta K. Wells; Natalie Hilzen; Katherine A. Brodie; Robert K. Haycraft; Nancy B. Nightingale; Pamela M. Nugent; Deborah DiGiovanna
Art Editors	Patricia Bonder; Susan Strane
Pronunciation Editor	Robin Corey
Language Notes Editor	Ruth M. Allen
Copy Editors	Alison Bell; Charlotte R. Gross
Research Editor	Joseph P. McAteer, Jr.

Art Staff

Art Director	Zelda Haber
Associate Art Director	Trudy Veit
Assistant Art Director	Marvin Friedman
Designer	Lee Davidson

Artists

Principal Artists	Howard Berelson; Howard Friedman; Fred Irvin; James Gordon Irving; Erica Merkling; Dan Todd
Contributing Artists	Dorothea and Sy Barlowe; Kenneth Barr; Ann Brewster; George Buctel; Eva Cellini; Alex Ebel; Martin Eichtersheimer; Rene Martin; Maria Mizzaro; Harry McNaught

Consultants

Educational Consultants	Lee A. Block; William D. Flanagan; Sandra Maccarone
Editorial Consultants	John N. K. Young; Pete Shiflet; Kathleen Fischer
Readability Consultant	Milton D. Jacobson

This dictionary is also published in a text edition, with different front and back matter, under the title *Macmillan Beginning Dictionary*. Pages 1–724 of this book have been licensed to Field Enterprises Educational Corporation and appear in the *Childcraft Dictionary*.

Copyright © 1977, 1976, 1975 Macmillan Publishing Co., Inc.

Library of Congress Catalog Card Number 74-24661

Macmillan Publishing Co., Inc., 866 Third Avenue, New York, New York 10022
Collier-Macmillan Canada, Ltd.

Manufactured in the United States of America

Welcome To *Your* Dictionary

The *Macmillan Dictionary for Children* is a book about words. It can be the most important book that you own, because you use words in everything you do. This dictionary can answer any question you have about words. It will tell you what words mean and how they are used, how to spell them and how to say them, and many other things about them.

This dictionary has been made especially for *you*. It is different from the dictionaries that adults use, and also from the word books for younger children who have not really learned to read. This dictionary has pictures in full color, so that you can see things as they actually look. It is printed in large type for easy reading. And it is arranged so that the most important information, the word's meaning, comes right after the word itself.

This is a *real* dictionary, with all the same features that a dictionary for adults has. But it has been written so that it will be easy for you to understand. Words are explained in a clear, natural way, with language just like the kind you see in your everyday reading. Each definition includes a complete sentence showing how the word is used. We even used a computer to be sure that we always have the simplest words possible in our definitions. This computer told us whenever we were using a word that was too hard, so that we could change to an easier one.

A dictionary is first of all a book that you turn to for information, but we think that the *Macmillan Dictionary for Children* is also a book you will want to read just for fun. We're sure you'll enjoy looking at the colorful pictures. And we've included a special feature called *language notes*— short articles giving interesting information about our language. As you leaf through the book, you can spot these notes easily because they're set off by blue lines. Try them and find out how fascinating words can be.

We hope this dictionary will be a great help to you in understanding and using words. Knowing about words is one of the most important things you can ever learn.

A dictionary can be hard to handle if you're not sure how to use it. Turn the page to learn how.

How To Use Your Dictionary

All kinds of information about words is waiting for you in the pages of the *Macmillan Dictionary for Children.* You can learn the meaning of words you read or words you hear on radio and television. You can learn how to spell words, how to say them, and where they come from. But you can't make use of all this word information unless you know how to find it and how to understand it.

There really isn't anything difficult about learning how this dictionary works. But a dictionary is a special kind of book, and there are some special things you need to know in order to use this one. The following sections will show you how to use your dictionary.

How to Look Up Words

Because there are so many words in this dictionary, there would be no way that you could find the one you wanted if all the words were not arranged according to a system. This system is *alphabetical order*—the words are arranged in a long list following the order of the alphabet. All the words that start with the letter **a**, like **admit**, **afternoon**, and **awake**, come at the beginning of the book. Then come words that begin with **b**, then **c**, and so on through the rest of the alphabet to **z.**

Under each letter of the alphabet, the words that are listed there are also arranged in alphabetical order. Since all the words in the **a** section of your dictionary start with the same first letter, the second letter decides the order of words in the list. If the second letter, or even the third, is the same—as in **alligator** and **allow**—then a letter farther along in the word decides which comes first.

acrobat	asparagus
add	aspen
airplane	asphalt

How to Spell Words

When you look at the pages of your dictionary, you will see that all the words in the alphabetical list are printed in dark, heavy letters. This is so that you can easily find the word you want as you look down the page. When you get to the word you're after, you will see that it looks exactly the way it would look in any book, magazine, or newspaper you may be reading. If you want to write the word yourself, you should spell it *exactly* as you see it in the dictionary. Whenever you aren't sure how to spell a word, check your dictionary. That way your spelling will always be correct.

What Words Mean

This dictionary can answer any question that you have about a word, but the one you will most often ask is: "What does it mean?" That is why the meaning of a word in your dictionary comes right after the word itself.

> **baboon**   A large monkey that has a face like a dog. Baboons live in open country in different parts of Africa. They live together in large groups, and they travel great distances in search of food.

The meaning of a word is also called its *definition*. As you can see from the example above, the definition of the word **baboon** begins by telling you what it is—a large monkey with a face like a dog. Then as you read on, you can learn more things about a **baboon**—that it is found in open country in Africa, and that it lives with other baboons in large groups, and travels great distances in search of food.

Many words have more than one meaning. The different meanings of such words are listed separately and numbered in order. The first meaning given is the one that is most important, and it is followed by the second most important, and so on.

How Words Are Used

After the definition of a word in your dictionary, you will find an example of how the word is used. These examples are always complete sentences, because whenever you see or hear an unfamiliar word, it is always written or spoken as part of a sentence.

> **alone** Not near or with another or others. She enjoyed being *alone* on the beach. There was just one puppy all *alone* in the window of the pet store. Because all his friends were away, he went to the game *alone*.

As you can see from these examples, a sentence can often be even more helpful than a definition in understanding what a word means. If you think about it, you'll realize that learning what a word means from its use in a sentence is just what you do all the time yourself, even without a dictionary. Whenever you hear or read a certain word whose meaning you're not completely sure of, you can get an idea of what it means from the way it's used and the words it's used with. So this dictionary teaches you about words in the same way that you learn them on your own, when you can't check the dictionary.

How Words Are Spoken

After all the meanings of a word, you will see the word printed again in heavy black type, a little smaller than it is at the beginning of the entry. This marks the beginning of some special information about the word.

> **ra·di·o** (rā′dē ō) *noun, plural* **radios;** *verb* **radioed, radioing.**

First, the word is divided up into parts by large black dots. These parts of a word are called *syllables*. Sometimes when you want to write or say a word, it helps to be able to think of it as being divided in this way. This dividing of a word into parts also shows you how to break up the word when you are writing. You can divide the word any place where there is a dot. After the division of the word into syllables comes a special spelling of the word. This special spelling, called the *pronunciation,* tells you how to say the word. It does not always look like the regular spelling of the word, because it uses special symbols that are not found in ordinary writing and printing.

boat (bōt) **know** (nō)
buy (bī) **wade** (wād)

The letters and symbols used in the pronunciation stand for the sounds we make when we speak. At the bottom of each right-hand page is a *pronunciation key.* This key takes each of these letters and symbols and shows how it is used in a familiar word. When you see a certain symbol in a pronunciation, you should say it in the same way you say that letter in the word shown in the key. For example, when you see the symbol ē, you should say it as you do the letter **e** in the word **me**.

at; āpe; cär; end; mē; it; īce; hot; ōld;
fôrk; wood; fōol; oil; out; up; turn; sing;
thin; this; hw in white; zh in treasure.
ə stands for a in about, e in taken
i in pencil, o in lemon, and u in circus.

When we say a long word, we speak some parts of the word more loudly than we do others. In your dictionary, a heavy black mark (╱) after a part of a word shows that it is spoken the loudest of any part of the word. A lighter mark (╱) means that this part of the word is spoken loudly, but not so loud as a part with a heavy black mark. If there is no mark at all, that means this part of the word is spoken more softly than any part that has a mark.

bi·cy·cle (bi′si kəl)
black·board (blak′bôrd′)

The words we use when we speak are divided into different groups. These groups are called *parts of speech.* The part of speech of a word is determined by the way the word is used. The eight parts of speech are: *noun, verb, adjective, adverb, pronoun, preposition, conjunction,* and *interjection.* In your dictionary a word's part of speech is shown right after the pronunciation.

shark (shärk) *noun . . .*

After the part of speech, there is more special information about the word. You can see how to speak or write a word when you want to show the idea of more than one. This idea is called the word's *plural.*

> **class·room** . . . *noun, plural* **classrooms.**
> **ber·ry** . . . *noun, plural* **berries.**

You can also see how a word would be used if you are talking about action in the past or continuous action in the present, or if you want to express the idea of "more" or "most."

> **clean** . . . *adjective;* **cleaner, cleanest;** *verb,* **cleaned, cleaning.**

You would say "John *cleaned* his room yesterday" to show that something happened in the past or "Karen is *cleaning* out her desk." to show that something is now happening. And you would say "Tom's jacket is *cleaner* than Bill's" and "Ellen has the *cleanest* Girl Scout uniform" to show that something is *more clean* or *most clean.*

How to Learn About Words from Pictures

The old saying is "A picture is worth a thousand words." Your dictionary has just over 1000 pictures and more than half a million words, so even in a book of words a picture is worth a lot. The reason that pictures are so important is that they can often tell more about a word than a definition can. Why not prove this to yourself? Read the following definition.

> **balance** **1.** The condition of having all the parts of something exactly the same in weight, amount, or force. The two children kept the seesaw in *balance.*

Can you explain what *balance* is? If you can't, turn to page 50 in your dictionary and look at the picture there under the word *balance.* Do you have a better idea of what this word means now?

How to Learn More About Words

Where do our words come from? Why do we have the words we do in our language? How do words change over the years? Although you don't have to know the answers to such questions in order to speak, write and read English well, you've probably wondered about these things anyway, just out of curiosity.

Many of our words have interesting stories behind them that tell how they became part of our language and where they came from. These word stories appear in your dictionary as language notes. They are marked by a blue triangle and printed between two heavy blue lines.

When you use your dictionary to look up a word, see if there is a language note anywhere on the same page as your word. Take the time to read these notes—you'll be surprised at how much you can learn from them.

Now that you've finished reading this Guide, you should be ready to use your dictionary without any trouble. If there is anything in this book that you don't understand, or that you think is wrong, please write to us and let us know about it. We made this book for you, and we want to be sure that we've done all we can to help you learn about words.

Now that you know how to use it, your dictionary can really be your friend.

The Story of English

"This hamburger tastes great!" "What time does the next show start? "I think it's going to rain." "Watch out for that car!" "You did a good job of cleaning up."

Look at the five sentences above. How are they the same? They tell about different things. They are arranged in different ways. Each one has a different number of words. They are made up of 30 different words in all. Yet in one important way all these sentences are the same—they are all written in one *language*—**English**. But just what *is* a "language" and what is "English?"

What is Language?

When a lot of people live in the same place and talk the same way, the words they use are called a *language*. We use words all the time to tell other people what we are thinking, and we want to be sure that they can understand us. That is why we have languages. If each person had his own special words and his own special way of talking, no one would be able to understand what anybody else was saying. Suppose you made up a word—"teerow"—and decided that it meant "good." If you said "That is a *teerow* book," nobody would know whether you meant that the book was *good, bad, big, new, funny, heavy,* or whatever. So you would say that the book was "good," because that is a word other people know. We have to agree on what a word means and how to use it so that we can understand each other.

People who know a lot about languages think that very long ago there may have been just one language spoken on earth. But as time went on and people moved to different parts of the world, the way they spoke changed. This one language became many different languages. Today there are more than 3000 languages in the world. They include **French**, **Spanish**, **German**, **Russian**, **Chinese**, and also the language in this book—**English**

You learn to speak when you are very young, probably without even knowing that you are learning anything. The language that you speak is the one you hear around you as you are growing up—the one your family and friends speak. If you were born in the United States, the language is probably English. If you were born somewhere else, you might have learned a different language—in some countries two, three, or even more languages are spoken. A baby can learn any language; it all depends on which one he or she hears.

If you think about it, you can probably remember times when you have heard people speaking a different language. The way that you knew it was different was simple—you couldn't understand what was being said. And that is exactly what makes two languages different from one another—a person speaking one can't understand a person speaking the other. If you and a friend both speak English, you can understand each other even though both of you don't speak it in exactly the same way. But if you met a person who spoke only Chinese, you and that person could not understand each other at all.

How Language Started

Suppose that you were in the situation that is mentioned on the last page, where you spoke only English and you met someone who spoke only Chinese. How would you and that person talk to each other?

You would probably use the same kind of "language" that the first people who lived on earth used—*sign language.* To show you wanted something to eat, you might put your hand to your mouth and pretend to chew something, or you might point to your stomach.

For millions of years, people "talked" to each other in just this way. They did not use words at all. They may have made sounds, but these were just noises without meaning. Those early people could think, but they could not use words to tell what their thoughts were.

Nobody knows when or where people began to use words. Perhaps one day a person said "Ouch!" when he hurt himself, and other people who heard him then also began to say "Ouch!" when they were hurt. We do not know for sure. The first language was probably made up of short, simple sounds for things that were important to early people—*meat, rain, fire, stone,* and so on.

The reason that we do not know very much about the first languages is that they were never written down. Once people had words, they could tell each other what they were thinking. But as soon as a person said something, his idea would be gone, unless the other

person could remember what he had said. Then, about 5000 years ago, people learned how to write. This meant that a person's thoughts could be put down for others to see and remember, even when he was not there.

The first kind of writing did not use letters as we do today. Instead, each idea was shown by a picture that stood for the word. For example, "fish" was shown by a picture of a fish.

People were much better off with "picture writing" than when they had no writing at all, but there were certain things wrong with this system. First, a person could only write down something that could be seen—he could not draw a picture of words like *love, see, tired, true,* or *help.* Also, the person who drew a picture could never be sure that someone who saw it would know what he meant—did a picture of two men and three deer mean "Two men saw three deer" or "Two men chased three deer" or "Two men killed three deer" or what?

Then, about 3500 years ago, something very important happened. Someone—we do not know who the person was or exactly where he lived—invented the alphabet. Now, words could be written down just as we write them today—by putting together letters that stand for the sound of the word. This made writing much easier to understand. The invention of "letter writing" brought language to the form in which we use it today.

Languages Before English

We have said that there are many different languages spoken in the world. But more than half the people in the world today speak languages that come from one old language called **Indo-European.**

The Indo-Europeans were a group of people who lived in the northern part of the continent of Europe. There was not much food in the area where these people lived, and life was hard. So the Indo-European people began to leave their homes to live in other places. As they moved, they took their language with them. They settled down to live all over Europe and in other parts of the world.

As time went by, the Indo-European people who lived in different places began to speak in different ways. Over thousands of years the original Indo-European language changed to become many different languages. Some of these are no longer spoken, but many still are, including **Spanish, French, Russian, Portuguese**—and **English.** We know that all these languages come from Indo-European because they all have similar words for certain things, such as *mother, father, cow, house, wolf,* and *winter.*

England, the country from which English gets its name, is part of a group of islands called the **British Isles**. Up until about 1500 years ago, the people who lived in these islands did not speak English. They spoke a language called **Celtic**, which is very different from English.

Then, in about the year 450, several groups of people called *tribes* came to England by boat. These tribes fought a war with the Celtic people. The Celts lost the war, and they had to leave England and move to other parts of the British Isles. Today only a few people in the British Isles speak a Celtic language, and there are almost no words in English that came from Celtic.

The three tribes that took over England from the Celtic people came from a place that is now the country of **Germany**, in northern Europe. These tribes were named the **Angles**, the **Saxons**, and the **Jutes**. They all spoke the same language, but in slightly different ways, because they had lived in different parts of Germany. Once they had settled in one place—England—all the tribes began to speak the same way. This new language became known as **English**, after the tribe called the **Angles**. The Angles were the most important of the tribes, and they ruled the most land.

The Beginnings of English

Old English

We have said that the Anglo-Saxon tribes spoke English. But it was not the same as the English that is spoken today. The form of English that they spoke is called **Old English**.

There is no one alive today who speaks Old English, but if there were you would not be able to understand such a person. You would think he was speaking a foreign language. Many of the words of Old English have been passed down to modern English, but over the years they have changed greatly in what they mean and in the way they are spelled. Old English sounded very different from modern English, and people put words together in different ways.

Even though Old English would sound strange if you heard it today, most of the common words that you use every day came from Old English. When we speak about the most important things in life we use Old English words—words like *man*, *woman*, and *child*; *eat*, *drink*, and *sleep*; *morning*, *noon*, and *night*; *day*, *month*, and *year*, or *love*, *life*, and *death*.

When you first learned to talk, the words you used were probably from Old English, such as *eyes*, *nose*, *mouth*, *dog*, *cat*, *play*, *walk*, *house*, *go*, and *eat*. The names of the colors—*red*, *yellow*, and so on— came from Old English. So do the words we use when we count from one to a hundred. Old English also gives us the common words we use to put sentences together, like *at*, *in*, *by*, *out*, *from*, *of*, *to*, *a*, *an*, and *the*. In fact, if a word is short and simple and is used a lot, chances are that it comes from Old English.

The Angles, the Saxons, and Jutes were not the only groups to come to England in early times. Other tribes also *invaded* (came into the country to try to take over). Those tribes were known as **Vikings**. Like the other tribes, the Vikings came from northern Europe.

The Vikings were also known as **Scandinavians**, because the area they came from was called **Scandinavia**. This area is now the countries of **Denmark** and **Norway**. During the time from about the year 800 to the year 1000, the Scandinavians fought many battles with the English people. Kings from Denmark ruled the northern part of England for a long period of time. The part of England they ruled was called the *Danelaw*; this is where our English word *law* comes from.

The Scandinavians were related to the Anglo-Saxon tribes who already lived in the country. Because of this, the language that they spoke was very similar to English. So the Scandinavians did not change English in any important way when they began to use it. The Scandinavians did, however, add many new words to the English language. Scandinavian words include such important terms as *they*, *them*, and *their*; *dirt*, *knife*, *sky*, and *egg*; *cut*, *scare*, *take*, and *get*; and *happy*, *low*, *tight*, and *wrong*.

The 'War' Between English and French

England is separated from the continent of Europe by a small body of water called the **English Channel**. In the year 1066, another group of people invaded England, this time by sailing across the English Channel. These people lived in an area just on the other side of the Channel, called **Normandy**, and they were known as **Normans**.

Like the other groups that invaded England, the Normans originally came from northern Europe. (The word *Norman* meant "north man.") They had first lived in Scandinavia and were related to the Vikings. But they did not speak the same language. When the Normans settled in Normandy, they began to speak the language that the people there spoke. This language was **French**, because Normandy was part of the country of **France**.

When the Normans invaded England, the English army marched out to meet and fight them. At a place near the English Channel called **Hastings**, the Norman army and English army fought a great battle. The Normans won, and Harold, the English king, was killed. The Norman king, William the Conqueror, became king of England.

The Normans brought about the most important change in England since the English language was first spoken there. Because they ruled the country, their language—French—became the main language. All people who were rich or important spoke French. English was spoken only by poor country people.

The king and the people around him conducted the

affairs of the government in French. People spoke French when they were buying or selling something or carrying on other kinds of business. Men who held high positions in the army, the navy, or the church always spoke French. Poems and other kinds of writing were done in French, not English. For a time it seemed that people might stop speaking English altogether, because the language was thought to be so unimportant.

By the year 1362, however, English had again become the main language of the country. That was the first year that *Parliament*, the place where the laws of the country were made, had a rule that people who spoke there had to use English rather than French. By the middle of the 1500s, French was not used at all.

There were several different reasons why French "lost out" to English as the language of the country. First, the common people had continued to speak English and did not learn French. This meant that the only language everyone could understand was English. A court of law could not carry on its business in French if the person on trial spoke only English. Second, as time went on the Normans began to think of themselves as English, not French. Normandy, had come under the rule of the king of France, and England and France were now at war with one another. Finally, a *plague* (a very bad disease) called the *Black Death* killed thousands of people. Life in England changed because of this, and French-speaking people no longer held all the important jobs.

French Words In English

French did not become the language of England, but it did change the English language. Thousands of French words were added to English, including some of our most important words. The English people did not change the way they spoke or the way they put words together in a sentence because of French. But they now had many new words that were not in English before.

Because the French-speaking Normans had ruled the country, many French words having to do with government came into English. These include *president, congress, mayor, constitution, city, state,* and *nation.* We can see the areas where French-speaking people were important from the words themselves, which came from French—*religion, art, poetry, court, medicine, army, navy, dance, fashion,* and *society.*

Most jobs done by English people were simple and involved working outdoors with the hands. *Farmer, woodsman, fisherman, hunter,* and *shepherd* are Old English words. The French-speaking people on the other hand often had indoor jobs that called for more education or training—*tailor, physician, attorney, carpenter,* and *plumber* all came from French.

French-speaking and English-speaking people lived in

very different ways. This is shown by the words we get from each language. The English were farmers, so our words for farm animals came from Old English—*cow, calf, pig,* and *sheep.* But because the French were good at cooking, the words for these animals when they are cooked and served as food came from French—*beef, veal, pork,* and *mutton.*

Many of the French words in English were originally part of an older language called **Latin**. The French language comes from Latin, and words passed from Latin to French and then to English. Latin gets its name from a place called **Latium**, in what is now the country of **Italy**, in southern Europe. Latin was spoken by a group of people called the **Romans**. They went out from **Rome**, a large city in the center of Italy, to live in France and many other parts of the world.

There are not many words that came straight from Latin into English. The Romans did, however, live in England for a time. They came there about 2000 years ago. The Anglo-Saxon tribes had not yet invaded England and the Celts still ruled. The Roman soldiers fought the Celts and took over part of the country. But after some years the Roman soldiers left to fight in other wars. So Latin did not become the main language in England. Only a few Latin words, such as *camp, wine, bishop,* and *pope,* were added to English at this time. The coming of the Normans changed all this, and Latin has been important to English ever since.

Different Kinds of English

We have seen how language changes when people move over the water. This is what happened when the different groups—the Anglo-Saxons, the Normans, and so on—came to England by boat. The next great change in English also happened because of people moving over water. But it was the opposite kind of movement—this time people did not come to England by boat, they left it.

The first group of English-speaking people who came to live in North America arrived here in 1607. They were led by Captain John Smith, and they settled in what is now Virginia. As soon as they arrived, a new kind of language was born. It is called **American English**.

You might think that since those early settlers spoke English, they could have just gone on talking the same way that they had when they were back in England. But life in American was different. When a person saw something he had never seen in England, he had to have a new word to talk about it.

In 1608, only one year after he came to America, Captain John Smith wrote about a kind of boat called a *canoe*. This word had never been used in England, because there were no canoes there. By the year 1620, there were already many new American English words, such as *moose*, *raccoon*, and *opossum*.

Where did these new words come from? Most of them came from the people who were already here when the English settlers came—the American Indians. The Indians had to have words for the animals, plants, and other things that they saw. So the English settlers borrowed the words that the Indians used for these things. When an English person saw a North American animal for the first time—such as a *skunk*—he would find out what the Indians called it and start using that word. This was much easier than making up a new word.

People from England went to live in other places besides North America; in fact they settled all over the world. In each place they went, life was different from what it had been like in England. So the way they spoke changed.

Several kinds of English grew up. They were named after the places where the English people went to live. Besides American English, they include **Canadian English**, **South African English**, **Australian English**, and **Indian English**. The kind of English spoken by the people who stayed in England is called **British English**.

Today British English and American English are not really that different. If you met someone who came from England, you could tell from the way he said his words that he was not an American. But you would probably not have much trouble understanding what he was saying.

The one real difference between British and American English is in the names of certain things. For example, what we call an *elevator*, they call a *lift*. What we call a *truck* they call a *lorry*; what we call *gasoline* they call *petrol*. The reason for these differences is simple: these things have been invented since the English came here.

English Around the World

Throughout the years, people who speak English have in one way or another known or learned about people from all over the world. In early times, this happened because England was a place that people from many other countries came to. Later, it happened because people left England to go to many other countries.

It would take up too much room to list all the words that we get from other languages, but we can mention a few. From Europe, we have taken the **Spanish** words *cigar*, *mosquito*, *canyon*, *rodeo*, *alligator*, and *tornado*. We have also taken the **Italian** words *umbrella*, *pistol*, *balcony*, *piano*, and *balloon*. **Dutch** has given us *deck*, *dock*, *pump*, *boss*, and *cookie*, and from **German** we have *hamburger*, *pretzel*, and *kindergarten*. Other words from European languages include *ski*, *flamingo*, and *penguin*.

From the Middle East, we have *candy*, *cotton*, *coffee*, *giraffe*, *tiger*, *chess*, *sugar*, and *spinach*. Asia has given us *pepper*, *panther*, *shampoo*, *silk*, *tea*, *jungle*, and *ketchup*. *Kangaroo* is an Australian word. From Africa we get such words as *chimpanzee*.

We have said that there are more than 3000 languages in the world. Some of them are spoken by millions of people, and some by only a few thousand. English is the only language that is spoken in countries all over the world.

English is the language that about 350 million people in the world first spoke as they were growing up. Only one language—**Mandarin**, the main language of China—is the native language of more people. But Mandarin is not used in other countries the way English is. In many countries, all children have to study English as a foreign language in school. English is the language most often used by people from different countries who do not speak each other's language. For example, pilots flying from one country to another speak English over the radio, no matter where they are or where they come from.

There is no such thing as an "official" language of the world that a person uses when he is talking to someone from another country. In the past, this was not too important. There were no telephones, radios, or other modern forms of talking to people over long distances, and travel to other countries was something very few people did. A person might live his whole life without meeting someone from another country. Today, the world is very different, and there is much more need for people to have a common world language. If this ever happens, it is likely that the language will be English.

In the last 16 pages you have seen where English comes from and how important it is. Starting on the next page, your dictionary will tell you about 30,000 English words. We hope that after reading this you will want to learn as much as you can about them.

English— The World Language

Pronunciation Key

a	a as in **at, bad**
ā	a as in **ape**, ai as in **pain**, ay as in **day**
ä	a as in **father, car**
e	e as in **end, pet**
ē	e as in **me**, ee as in **feet**, ea as in **meat**, ie as in **piece**, y as in **finally**
i	i as in **it, pig**
ī	i as in **ice, fine**, ie as in **lie**, y as in **my**
o	o as in **odd, hot**
ō	o as in **old**, oa as in **oat**, ow as in **low**, oe as in **toe**
ô	o as in **coffee, fork**, au as in **author**, aw as in **law**, a as in **all**
oo	oo as in **wood**, u as in **put**
o͞o	oo as in **fool**, ue as in **true**
oi	oi as in **oil**, oy as in **boy**
ou	ou as in **out**, ow as in **cow**
u	u as in **up, mud**, o as in **oven, love**
ur	ur as in **turn**, er as in **term**, ir as in **bird**, or as in **word**
yo͞o	u as in **use**, ue as in **cue**, ew as in **few**, eu as in **feud**
ə	a as in **ago**, e as in **taken**, i as in **pencil**, o as in **lemon**, u as in **helpful**
b	b as in **bat, above, job**
ch	ch as in **chin, such**, tch as in **hatch**
d	d as in **dear, soda, bad**
f	f as in **five, defend, leaf**, ff as in **off**
g	g as in **game, ago, fog**
h	h as in **hit, ahead**
j	j as in **joke, enjoy**, g as in **gem**, dge as in **edge**
k	k as in **kit, baking, seek**, ck as in **tack**, c as in **cat**
l	l as in **lid, sailor, feel**, ll as in **ball, allow**
m	m as in **man, family, dream**
n	n as in **not, final, on**
ng	ng as in **singer, long**, n as in **sink**
p	p as in **pail, repair, soap**
r	r as in **ride, parent, four**
s	s as in **sat, aside, cats**, c as in **cent**, ss as in **pass**
sh	sh as in **shoe, wishing, fish**
t	t as in **tag, pretend, hat**
th	th as in **thin, ether, both**
<u>th</u>	th as in **this, mother, smooth**
v	v as in **very, favor, salve**
w	w as in **wet, reward**
y	y as in **yes**
z	z as in **zoo, gazing**, zz as in **jazz**, s as in **rose, dogs**
zh	s as in **treasure**, z as in **azure**, ge as in **garage**

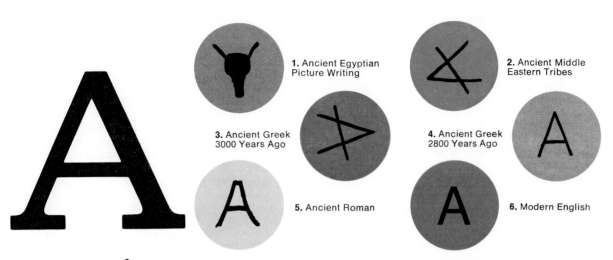

1. Ancient Egyptian Picture Writing

2. Ancient Middle Eastern Tribes

3. Ancient Greek 3000 Years Ago

4. Ancient Greek 2800 Years Ago

5. Ancient Roman

6. Modern English

A is the first letter of the alphabet. The oldest form of the letter **A** was a drawing that the ancient Egyptians (**1**) used in their picture writing nearly 5000 years ago. This drawing was borrowed by several ancient tribes (**2**) in the Middle East. They called it *aleph*, which meant "ox." If you turn the letter **A** upside-down, you will see a design that looks like the head and horns of an ox. The ancient Greeks (**3**) borrowed a form of this letter about 3000 years ago. At first they wrote it like an upside-down capital letter **A**. Several hundred years later, the Greeks turned their letter **A** around (**4**). This made it look like a modern capital letter **A**. The Romans (**5**) borrowed this letter from the Greeks about 2400 years ago. They wrote it almost the same way that we write the capital letter **A** today (**6**).

a, A The first letter of the alphabet.
 a, A (ā) *noun, plural* **a's, A's.**

a *A* dog would love that bone. She has *a* bicycle. He washes his car once *a* week. The orange is *a* fruit.
 a (ə *or* ā) *indefinite article.*

abacus A frame with beads that move along wires or rods. A person can add, subtract, multiply, or divide with an abacus. The abacus was first used thousands of years ago. It is used today in China, Japan, and some other countries.
 ab·a·cus (ab′ə kəs) *noun, plural* **abacuses.**

 ▲ Long ago in Greece and Rome, abacuses were made of a board covered with dust or sand. Marks could be made in the dust and then wiped away. The word **abacus** comes from a word that meant "dust."

abandon To give up completely; leave. The sailors *abandoned* the sinking ship. The man *abandoned* his wife and family.
 a·ban·don (ə ban′dən) *verb,* **abandoned, abandoning.**

abbey **1.** A building or buildings where monks or nuns live a religious life. **2.** A group of monks or nuns who live in an abbey.
 ab·bey (ab′ē) *noun, plural* **abbeys.**

abbreviate To make something shorter. We *abbreviate* the words "United States" as "U.S."
 ab·bre·vi·ate (ə brē′vē āt′) *verb,* **abbreviated, abbreviating.**

abbreviation A letter or group of letters that stands for a longer word or phrase. *Jan.* is the abbreviation for *January, Fri.* is the abbreviation for *Friday,* and *N.Y.* is the abbreviation for *New York.*
 ab·bre·vi·a·tion (ə brē′vē ā′shən) *noun, plural* **abbreviations.**

 ▲ People use **abbreviations** in writing when they do not want to write out the full word that the abbreviation stands for. Most abbreviations have a period at the end. For example, *in.* is the abbreviation for the word *inch.* This is so that a person who reads the abbreviation will know it is not a real word. Sometimes, though, an abbreviation looks so different from a real word that it does not need to have a period. For example, *UN* is the abbreviation for *United Nations.*

abdicate To give up power. The old king *abdicated,* and his son became king.
 ab·di·cate (ab′də kāt′) *verb,* **abdicated, abdicating.**

1

abdomen   **1.** The part of the body that holds the stomach. It is below the chest. The abdomen has many organs that are important in digestion, including the stomach, the intestines, the kidneys, and the liver. **2.** The rear part of the body of an insect.

Abdomen

ab·do·men (ab′də mən *or* ab dō′mən) *noun, plural* **abdomens.**

abide   To put up with a person or thing. Tom could not *abide* his sister's messy room.
a·bide (ə bīd′) *verb,* **abode** or **abided, abiding.**
to abide by. To obey. Jim always *abides by* the law.

ability   The power or skill to do something. Man is the only animal that has the *ability* to speak. Ruth has great *ability* as a singer.
a·bil·i·ty (ə bil′ə tē) *noun, plural* **abilities.**

able   Having the power or skill to do something. A deer is *able* to run very fast. Joan was *able* to read at an early age.
a·ble (ā′bəl) *adjective,* **abler, ablest.**

abolish   To put an end to; do away with. President Abraham Lincoln *abolished* slavery.
a·bol·ish (ə bol′ish) *verb,* **abolished, abolishing.**

abolition   The act of abolishing; doing away with. The town's goal was the *abolition* of water pollution.
ab·o·li·tion (ab′ə lish′ən) *noun.*

aborigine   One of the first people to live in a place. The Indians are the *aborigines* of America.
ab·o·rig·i·ne (ab′ə rij′ə nē) *noun, plural* **aborigines.**

abortion   The birth of a developing baby before it is old enough to be able to live on its own. A doctor can perform an operation that causes this to take place.
a·bor·tion (ə bôr′shən) *noun, plural* **abortions.**

abound   To be plentiful. Corn and wheat *abound* on that farm. Buffalo used to *abound* in North America.
a·bound (ə bound′) *verb,* **abounded, abounding.**

about   That book is *about* John F. Kennedy. Tim was *about* to leave for home. There were *about* twenty people waiting for the bus.
a·bout (ə bout′) *preposition; adverb.*

above   The kite flew *above* the trees. The stars glittered *above.*
a·bove (ə buv′) *preposition; adverb.*

aboveboard   Honest. He is open and *aboveboard* in his business dealings.
a·bove·board (ə buv′bôrd′) *adjective.*

▲ The word **aboveboard** comes from an old saying—"above the board." This expression was used in card games. A player who played with his hands "above the board" (the card table was then called a *board*) was thought to be honest. The idea was that if his hands were above the table, he could not cheat by hiding cards under the table.

abreast   Side by side. The students walked down the hall two *abreast.* The apple trees stood four *abreast* in the field.
a·breast (ə brest′) *adverb.*

The drummers are marching **abreast.**

abridge   To shorten by using fewer words. Because time was running out, Mr. Green had to *abridge* his speech.
a·bridge (ə brij′) *verb,* **abridged, abridging.**

abroad   Outside of one's country. Her parents went *abroad* to France for their vacation.
a·broad (ə brôd′) *adverb.*

abrupt   **1.** Without warning; sudden; unexpected. The bus made an *abrupt* stop at the corner. **2.** Not polite or gentle; blunt. The waiter gave her an *abrupt* answer.
a·brupt (ə brupt′) *adjective.*

abscess   A collection of pus in some part of the body. It usually comes from an infection.
ab·scess (ab′ses) *noun, plural* **abscesses.**

absence   **1.** A being away. In the teacher's *absence,* a substitute teacher took over the class. **2.** A lack; being without. *Absence* of rain caused the plants to die.
ab·sence (ab′səns) *noun, plural* **absences.**

absent **1.** Not present; away. When he caught a cold, he was *absent* from school for two days. **2.** Lacking. Leaves are *absent* on trees in winter.
ab·sent (ab′sənt) *adjective.*

absent-minded Forgetful; not paying attention to what is going on. She stared out the window in an *absent-minded* way. The *absent-minded* man was always losing things.
ab·sent-mind·ed (ab′sənt mīn′did) *adjective.*

absolute **1.** Complete; entire. She believes in telling the *absolute* truth. **2.** Having unlimited power. Long ago, kings were *absolute* rulers. **3.** Positive; sure. The family had *absolute* proof that the land belonged to them.
ab·so·lute (ab′sə lo͞ot′) *adjective.*

absolutely **1.** Completely. He is *absolutely* right about that. **2.** Positively. He was *absolutely* sure that he wanted to buy a dog.
ab·so·lute·ly (ab′sə lo͞ot′lē *or* ab′sə lo͞ot′ lē) *adverb.*

absorb **1.** To soak up or take in. A sponge *absorbs* water. Susan *absorbs* any new knowledge very quickly. **2.** To hold the interest of. The book about animals *absorbed* Jim.
ab·sorb (ab sôrb′ *or* ab zôrb′) *verb,* absorbed, absorbing.

absorption The ability to soak up or take in. A sponge is used in cleaning because it has great *absorption.*
ab·sorp·tion (ab sôrp′shən *or* ab zôrp′shən) *noun.*

abstain To keep oneself from doing something. Her mother asked her to *abstain* from eating candy.
ab·stain (ab stān′) *verb,* abstained, abstaining.

abstract Expressing a quality without naming the person or thing that has the quality. "Beauty" is an *abstract* word because it does not refer to a particular person or thing. "Butterfly" is not an *abstract* word because it does refer to a particular thing.
ab·stract (ab′strakt *or* ab strakt′) *adjective.*

absurd Definitely not true; silly; foolish. It is *absurd* to believe that the moon is made of green cheese.
ab·surd (ab surd′ *or* ab zurd′) *adjective.*

abundance A very large amount; a quantity that is more than enough. Because the farmer had an *abundance* of food, he gave some to a poor family that did not have enough.
a·bun·dance (ə bun′dəns) *noun.*

abundant More than enough; plentiful. Rockets need an *abundant* amount of fuel when they fly into space.
a·bun·dant (ə bun′dənt) *adjective.*

abuse **1.** To make bad or wrong use of. The children *abused* their free time by making a mess of the classroom. **2.** To treat cruelly or badly. The dog was *abused* by its owner. **3.** To put too much strain on. We *abuse* our health when we do not eat properly. *Verb.*
—**1.** Bad or wrong use. The ruler's *abuse* of power caused the people to hate him. **2.** Bad treatment. During the trip on the old, bumpy road our car took much *abuse.* **3.** Rude speech; insulting language. The boy suffered *abuse* from his friends after he got them in trouble. *Noun.*
a·buse (ə byo͞oz′ *for verb;* ə byo͞os′ *for noun*) *verb,* abused, abusing; *noun, plural* abuses.

abyss A large, deep hole in the earth; a bottomless hole.
a·byss (ə bis′) *noun, plural* abysses.

acacia A small tree or bush with leaves like ferns. This tree is found in warm areas throughout the world.
a·ca·cia (ə kā′shə) *noun, plural* acacias.

academy **1.** A private high school. **2.** A school that trains people for a special field of study. My brother attends the Air Force *Academy.*
a·cad·e·my (ə kad′ə mē) *noun, plural* academies.

▲ The word **academy** comes from the Greek name of a place near Athens. Plato, a famous Greek teacher, had a school there more than two thousand years ago. The Romans used this name for any school like this one.

accelerate To speed up; move faster. The car *accelerated* as it went down the hill.
ac·cel·er·ate (ak sel′ə rāt′) *verb,* accelerated, accelerating.

acceleration A moving faster or speeding up. Tom's *acceleration* of the car frightened the passengers.
ac·cel·er·a·tion (ak sel′ə rā′shən) *noun, plural* accelerations.

accelerator A pedal on an automobile or other machine that speeds up the motor. Nancy wanted the car to go faster, so she pressed down on the *accelerator.*
ac·cel·er·a·tor (ak sel′ə rā′tər) *noun, plural* accelerators.

at; āpe; cär; end; mē; it; īce; hot; ōld;
fôrk; wood; fo͞ol; oil; out; up; turn; sing;
thin; this; hw in white; zh in treasure.
ə stands for a in about, e in taken
i in pencil, o in lemon, and u in circus.

accent **1.** A stronger tone of voice given to a word or part of a word. In the word "happy," the *accent* is on the first syllable. In "forget," the *accent* is on the second syllable. **2.** A mark used on a word to show which syllable is spoken with an accent. In this dictionary, the mark ′ is used to show the syllable in the word spoken with the most force. The mark ′ is used to show a syllable with a weaker accent. In the word "abbreviate," we place the accents like this: ə brē′vē āt′. **3.** A certain way of saying words that is used by people in one part of a country. He has a Southern *accent* because he was born in Alabama. **4.** A mixing of a foreign way of speaking with the language of another country. Her grandmother speaks English with a German *accent. Noun.*
—To pronounce a word or syllable in a stronger way. You *accent* the first syllable of the word "apple." *Verb.*
ac·cent (ak′sent *for noun;* ak′sent *or* ak sent′ *for verb*) *noun, plural* **accents;** *verb,* **accented, accenting.**

accept **1.** To take or receive something that is given. She *accepted* the birthday gift from her aunt. The candidate *accepted* his party's nomination for senator. **2.** To agree to; answer "yes" to. The speaker *accepted* the club's invitation to talk about his new book. **3.** To believe to be true. His mother *accepted* his reason for being late.
ac·cept (ak sept′) *verb,* **accepted, accepting.**

acceptable Good enough to be accepted; satisfactory. Her book report was *acceptable.* The bank said that his check was not *acceptable* because he did not sign it.
ac·cept·a·ble (ak sep′tə bəl) *adjective.*

acceptance **1.** A taking of something given or offered. Sarah's *acceptance* of the present pleased her mother. **2.** A being accepted; approval. Her idea gained *acceptance* from the rest of the group.
ac·cept·ance (ak sep′təns) *noun, plural* **acceptances.**

access **1.** An entrance or approach. We had easy *access* into the abandoned house because the door was broken. **2.** A way or means of approach. The campers had *access* to the lake through the woods.
ac·cess (ak′ses) *noun, plural* **accesses.**

accessory **1.** Something that is added to help a more important thing. The green necklace was a pretty *accessory* to the woman's blue dress. **2.** A person who helps another person commit a crime. He was an *accessory* to the bank robbery because he drove the car that the robbers used to escape. *Noun.*
—Useful but not necessary; additional. The listing of street addresses is an *accessory* feature of a telephone book. *Adjective.*
ac·ces·so·ry (ak ses′ər ē) *noun, plural* **accessories;** *adjective.*

accident **1.** Something that happens for no apparent reason and is not expected. The discovery of an oil well on the farm was a happy *accident.* **2.** An unhappy event that is not expected. During the snowstorm there were many *accidents* on the highways. **3.** Chance; fortune. I found the missing watch by *accident* while I was looking for my comb.
ac·ci·dent (ak′sə dənt) *noun, plural* **accidents.**

accidental Happening by chance; not meant to happen. While the children were digging in the park, they made an *accidental* discovery of some old coins. The *accidental* fall caused an injury to his leg.
ac·ci·den·tal (ak′sə dent′əl) *adjective.*

accidentally By accident. I met her *accidentally* on the bus.
ac·ci·den·tal·ly (ak′sə den′təl ē *or* ak′sə-dent′lē) *adverb.*

acclaim To welcome with strong approval; applaud. The crowd *acclaimed* the astronauts. *Verb.*
—Great praise or welcome. The boxing champion was greeted with much *acclaim* by his fans. *Noun.*
ac·claim (ə klām′) *verb,* **acclaimed, acclaiming;** *noun, plural* **acclaims.**

acclimate To adjust or become adjusted to a new place or situation. John quickly *acclimated* himself to the new school. The fish *acclimated* easily to the new tank.
ac·cli·mate (ak′lə māt′ *or* ə klī′mit) *verb,* **acclimated, acclimating.**

accommodate **1.** To have room for; hold. That movie theater *accommodates* 600 people. **2.** To do a favor for; help out. The policeman *accommodated* us when we asked him for directions. **3.** To supply a place to stay or sleep. That motel *accommodates* 200 people each night.
ac·com·mo·date (ə kom′ə dāt′) *verb,* **accommodated, accommodating.**

accommodation **1.** A convenience or a help. Giving me a ride to school was a big *accommodation.* **2. accommodations.** A place to stay or sleep. When we were traveling, we always found good *accommodations.*
ac·com·mo·da·tion (ə kom′ə dā′shən) *noun, plural* **accommodations.**

accompaniment **1.** A thing that goes along with something else. Cranberry sauce is a delicious *accompaniment* to turkey. **2.** A musical part that is played as background for the main part. The girl sang with a piano *accompaniment*.
ac·com·pa·ni·ment (ə kum′pə ni mənt) *noun, plural* **accompaniments.**

accompany **1.** To go along with. I'll *accompany* you to the movies. **2.** To happen at the same time as. Wind often *accompanies* rain. **3.** To play an accompaniment for another musical instrument. While Beth played the flute, Ron *accompanied* her on the piano.
ac·com·pa·ny (ə kum′pə nē) *verb,* **accompanied, accompanying.**

accomplice A person who helps another person commit a crime. Because he supplied the guns the robbers used, the man was an *accomplice* to the robbery.
ac·com·plice (ə kom′plis) *noun, plural* **accomplices.**

accomplish To carry out or complete; perform. The pilot *accomplished* his mission and returned to the base.
ac·com·plish (ə kom′plish) *verb,* **accomplished, accomplishing.**

accomplishment **1.** The act of accomplishing; completion. The *accomplishment* of our goal will be very difficult. **2.** Something done successfully; achievement. The first moon landing was a great *accomplishment*. **3.** A special skill or ability that is usually gained by training. Playing the piano well is his greatest *accomplishment*.
ac·com·plish·ment (ə kom′plish mənt) *noun, plural* **accomplishments.**

accord Agreement; harmony. A longer vacation period is in *accord* with the demands of the workers. *Noun.*
—To agree or be in harmony with. His opinions on politics *accord* with hers. *Verb.*
ac·cord (ə kôrd′) *noun, plural* **accords;** *verb,* **accorded, according.**
of one's own accord. By a person's own choice; voluntarily. The boys cleaned their room *of their own accord.*

accordance Agreement. John acted in *accordance* with our wish that he take care of our dog while we were away.
ac·cord·ance (ə kôrd′əns) *noun.*

according According to. **1.** In agreement with. Everything went *according to* our plan. Each man was paid *according to* the amount of work he did. **2.** On the authority of. *According to* the weatherman, it will probably rain tomorrow.
ac·cord·ing (ə kôr′ding) *adjective.*

accordion A musical instrument with keys, metal reeds, and a bellows. The bellows pushes air through the reeds to make a note.
ac·cor·di·on (ə kôr′dē ən) *noun, plural* **accordions.**

Accordion

account **1.** A spoken or written statement; report. There was an *account* of the baseball game in the newspaper. **2.** A record of money spent or received. My mother takes care of the household *accounts*. Joan has five hundred dollars in her bank *account*. **3.** Importance; worth. The lonely old man felt he was of little *account. Noun.*
—To consider to be. I *account* him an honest man. *Verb.*
ac·count (ə kount′) *noun, plural* **accounts;** *verb,* **accounted, accounting.**
on account of. Because of. The game was delayed *on account of* rain.
to account for. To give an explanation or reason for. How do you *account for* your lateness? The heavy snowfall *accounts for* the closing of school today.

accountant Someone who is trained to take care of the money records of a person or a business.
ac·count·ant (ə kount′ənt) *noun, plural* **accountants.**

accumulate To gather or pile up; collect. He *accumulated* a large number of books while he was at college. A large pile of mail had *accumulated* while we were away on vacation.
ac·cu·mu·late (ə kyoo′myə lāt′) *verb,* **accumulated, accumulating.**

accumulation **1.** The act of accumulating; piling up. The *accumulation* of evidence against the defendant led to his being found guilty. **2.** Something accumulated; collection. There was an *accumulation* of dust in the corner of the room.

at; āpe; cär; end; mē; it; īce; hot; ōld;
fôrk; wood; fōol; oil; out; up; turn; sing;
thin; this; hw in white; zh in treasure.
ə stands for a in about, e in taken
i in pencil, o in lemon, and u in circus.

5

ac·cu·mu·la·tion (ə kyōō'myə lā'shən) *noun*, *plural* **accumulations.**

accuracy A being without mistakes; correctness. She did her work with *accuracy*.
ac·cu·ra·cy (ak'yər ə sē) *noun*.

accurate **1.** Making few or no errors or mistakes; exact. His new watch is very *accurate*. **2.** Without errors or mistakes; correct. The newspaper stories about the accident were not *accurate*.
ac·cu·rate (ak'yər it) *adjective*.

accusation A statement that a person has committed a crime; charge of doing something wrong.
ac·cu·sa·tion (ak'yə zā'shən) *noun*, *plural* **accusations.**

accuse To state that a person has committed a crime or has done something bad. The storekeeper *accused* the boy of stealing a watch.
ac·cuse (ə kyōōz') *verb*, **accused, accusing.**

accustom To make familiar by use, custom, or habit. She had to *accustom* herself to getting up early when she spent the summer on a farm.
ac·cus·tom (ə kus'təm) *verb*, **accustomed, accustoming.**

accustomed Usual. The dog lay in his *accustomed* place by the fire.
ac·cus·tomed (ə kus'təmd) *adjective*.
accustomed to. Used to; in the habit of. The policeman was *accustomed to* the noisy traffic.

ace **1.** A playing card having one mark in the center. **2.** A person who is an expert at something. Karen is an *ace* at tennis. *Noun*.
—Of the highest quality; expert. Bob is an *ace* pitcher. *Adjective*.
ace (ās) *noun*, *plural* **aces;** *adjective*.

ache **1.** To be in pain. His whole body *ached* after the rough football game. **2.** To be eager; long for. After a month away, he *ached* to get back home. *Verb*.
—A pain. After throwing the ball so much, he had an *ache* in his arm. *Noun*.
ache (āk) *verb*, **ached, aching:** *noun*, *plural* **aches.**

achieve **1.** To accomplish or succeed. She *achieved* her goal of winning the prize for the best essay. **2.** To gain or to reach by one's effort. Robert Frost *achieved* fame as a poet.
a·chieve (ə chēv') *verb*, **achieved, achieving.**

Ace of Hearts

achievement **1.** Something accomplished or achieved. The invention of the telephone was a great *achievement*. **2.** Something gained by effort. The *achievement* of the right to vote for women took a long time.
a·chieve·ment (ə chēv'mənt) *noun*, *plural* **achievements.**

acid **1.** Sour, sharp, or biting to the taste. A lemon has an *acid* taste. **2.** Sharp or biting in actions or speech. The man's *acid* remark hurt Jim's feelings. *Adjective*.
—A chemical that joins with a base to make a salt. Acids have a sour taste when dissolved in water. An acid will cause blue litmus paper to turn red. *Noun*.
ac·id (as'id) *adjective; noun*, *plural* **acids.**

acknowledge **1.** To admit that something is true. She *acknowledged* that she had made a mistake. **2.** To recognize the ability or authority of. The class *acknowledged* that Ann was the best speller. **3.** To say that something has been received. She *acknowledged* all her birthday gifts.
ac·knowl·edge (ak nol'ij) *verb*, **acknowledged, acknowledging.**

acknowledgment The act of acknowledging. Her *acknowledgment* that she had made a mistake made her feel better.
ac·knowl·edg·ment (ak nol'ij mənt) *noun*, *plural* **acknowledgments.**

acne A kind of skin disease in which a person has pimples, especially on the face. It is caused by infection in the oil glands under the skin. People most often get acne during their teenage years, when these glands are very active.
ac·ne (ak'nē) *noun*.

acorn The nut of the oak tree.
a·corn (ā'kôrn *or* ā'kərn) *noun*, *plural* **acorns.**

acquaint To make familiar. Each camper must *acquaint* himself with the rules of the swimming pool. I am *acquainted* with most of the people who live on our street.
ac·quaint (ə kwānt') *verb*, **acquainted, acquainting.**

acquaintance **1.** A person one knows only slightly. Helen met some *acquaintances* during her trip into town. **2.** Knowledge of some-

Acorns

thing gained from experience. Betty had some *acquaintance* with the game of chess because she had played it before.

ac·quaint·ance (ə kwānt'əns) *noun, plural* **acquaintances.**

acquire To get as one's own; obtain. When she went to the farm, she *acquired* a liking for horseback riding. He *acquired* the ability to speak Spanish while he lived in Mexico.

ac·quire (ə kwīr') *verb,* **acquired, acquiring.**

acquit To free from a charge of a crime; declare not guilty. The jury *acquitted* him because they believed that the evidence proved him innocent.

ac·quit (ə kwit') *verb,* **acquitted, acquitting.**

acre A way of measuring land. It is equal to 43,560 square feet. An acre of land is slightly smaller in size than a football field.

a·cre (ā'kər) *noun, plural* **acres.**

acreage An area of land measured in acres; number of acres.

a·cre·age (ā'kər ij) *noun.*

acrobat A person who performs stunts that require great physical ability. An acrobat most often works in a circus walking on a tightrope or swinging on a trapeze.

ac·ro·bat (ak'rə bat') *noun, plural* **acrobats.**

▲ The word **acrobat** comes from an old Greek word that meant "to walk on tiptoe" or "to climb up high."

across We came *across* in a rowboat. The cat walked *across* our path. She lives *across* the street from me.

a·cross (ə krôs') *adverb; preposition.*

act **1.** Something that is done; a deed. Saving the child's life was an *act* of bravery. **2.** The doing of something. The thief was caught in the *act* of opening the safe. **3.** A law. The United States can declare war only by an *act* of Congress. **4.** One of the parts of a play. "Hamlet" has five *acts. Noun.*
—**1.** To do something or move. After the accident she *acted* quickly to help the others. **2.** To perform before an audience or in a movie. The hero of the play *acted* so well that he got the main role in the next show. *Verb.*

act (akt) *noun, plural* **acts;** *verb,* **acted, acting.**

action **1.** The doing of something. Throwing a ball, jumping over a fence, and running down a hill are all *actions.* **2.** Something that is done; an act. Helping the blind man across the busy street was a kind *action.* **3.** A battle. My uncle was wounded in *action* during the war.

ac·tion (ak'shən) *noun, plural* **actions.**

activate To put into action; cause to work or operate. Pushing the button *activates* the machine.

ac·ti·vate (ak'tə vāt') *verb,* **activated, activating.**

active **1.** Full of action; moving around much of the time. Ellen was an *active* girl, and she always found something to keep her busy. **2.** In action; working. Hawaii has several *active* volcanoes.

ac·tive (ak'tiv) *adjective.*

activity **1.** The state of being active; movement. Building a house involves much *activity.* **2.** A thing to do or to be done. Jane takes part in many school *activities.*

ac·tiv·i·ty (ak tiv'ə tē) *noun, plural* **activities.**

actor A person who plays a part in a play, movie, or television program.

ac·tor (ak'tər) *noun, plural* **actors.**

actress A girl or woman actor.

ac·tress (ak'tris) *noun, plural* **actresses.**

actual Real; existing. That book is about *actual* people, not imaginary ones. The *actual* cause of the accident is not known.

ac·tu·al (ak'chōo əl) *adjective.*

actually In fact; really. He said that he stayed home because he was sick, but *actually* he wanted to watch the baseball game on television.

ac·tu·al·ly (ak'chōo ə lē) *adverb.*

acute **1.** Sharp and severe. Mary had an *acute* pain in her side after running so far. **2.** Quick in seeing and understanding. The bright girl had an *acute* mind, so she learned things easily. **3.** Very bad; serious; critical. The lack of rain this year has led to an *acute* water shortage.

a·cute (ə kyōōt') *adjective.*

acute angle An angle that has less than ninety degrees.

ad A short word for **advertisement.** A picture or message that tries to sell something is an ad. ▲ Another word that sounds like this is **add.**

ad (ad) *noun, plural* **ads.**

A.D. An abbreviation meaning "in the year of the Lord." It is used in giving dates since the birth of Christ. 1000 *A.D.* means 1000 years after the birth of Christ.

at; āpe; cär; end; mē; it; īce; hot; ōld;
fôrk; wood; fōol; oil; out; up; turn; sing;
thin; this; hw in white; zh in treasure.
ə stands for a in about, e in taken
i in pencil, o in lemon, and u in circus.

adage An old and familiar saying that is believed to be true; proverb. "The early bird catches the worm" is an adage.
ad·age (ad′ij) *noun, plural* **adages.**

adamant Refusing to change one's mind or position; firm. The senator was *adamant* in his support of equal rights for all people.
ad·a·mant (ad′ə mənt) *adjective.*

Adam's apple A lump in the throat just below the chin. It is made up of a kind of tissue called cartilage. All people have an Adam's apple, although it is easier to notice in men than in women.
Ad·am's apple (ad′əmz).

adapt To adjust to new conditions or surroundings. When the family moved to Florida, they had to *adapt* to the warm weather.
a·dapt (ə dapt′) *verb,* **adapted, adapting.**

add **1.** To find the sum of two or more numbers. If you *add* 2 and 7, you get 9. **2.** To put one thing with another. Mother *added* cream to her coffee. Wes *added* a new stamp to his collection. **3.** To put more onto something written or said. He thanked us for the gift and *added* that it was just what he wanted. ▲ Another word that sounds like this is **ad.**
add (ad) *verb,* **added, adding.**

addend Any number that can be added to another number. In the problem *5 + 3 = 8, 5* and *3* are the addends.
ad·dend (ad′end *or* ə dend′) *noun, plural* **addends.**

adder A kind of snake. The type of adder found in Europe is poisonous, while the kind found in North America is harmless.
ad·der (ad′ər) *noun, plural* **adders.**

Adder

addict A person who has let himself be taken over by a drug or habit. An addict has little control over himself because the drug or habit controls him. Doctors are trying to find a cure for heroin *addicts.*
ad·dict (ad′ikt) *noun, plural* **addicts.**

▲ The word **addict** used to mean "to deliver" or "to turn over." A judge could *addict* someone to prison. A person could be *addicted* to another person as a servant or slave. Our meaning of *addict* comes from the idea of a person's becoming a slave to a habit.

addition **1.** The adding of two or more numbers or things. *9 + 2 + 5 = 16* is an example of addition. **2.** The act of adding. The *addition* of salt helped give flavor to the soup. **3.** Something that is added. Mr. Jones built an *addition* to his house because he needed more room for his family.
ad·di·tion (ə dish′ən) *noun, plural* **additions.**
in addition or **in addition to.** As well as; also. *In addition to* being on the baseball team, he is also on the football team.

additional Added; extra. Frank got *additional* information for his report from the library.
ad·di·tion·al (ə dish′ən əl) *adjective.*

address **1.** The place at which a person lives or an organization is located. Carol's *address* is 90 Pine Lane. That store's *address* is 595 Main Street. **2.** The writing on a letter or package that tells where it is to be sent. I can't read the *address* on this letter. **3.** A speech. The President's *address* to the nation will be on television. *Noun.*
—1. To write on a letter or package the place to which it will be delivered. Father asked me to *address* this letter. **2.** To speak to a person or a group. The congressman *addressed* the audience in the town hall. *Verb.*
ad·dress (ə dres′ *or* ad′res *for noun;* ə dres′ *for verb*) *noun, plural* **addresses;** *verb,* **addressed, addressing.**

adenoids Small masses of flesh that grow at the top of the throat in back of the nose. Adenoids are glands, and if they become swollen it is hard to breathe and speak.
ad·e·noids (ad′ən oidz′) *noun plural.*

adept Being very good at doing something; skilled. Janet was an *adept* skater because she practiced every morning.
a·dept (ə dept′) *adjective.*

adequate As much as is needed; enough. Those plants will not grow without *adequate* rain. His grades were *adequate,* but not high enough for him to make the honor roll.
ad·e·quate (ad′ə kwət) *adjective.*

adhere **1.** To stick tight; become attached. The chewing gum *adhered* to his shoe. **2.** To follow closely; be faithful. If you *adhere* to the route on the map, you won't get lost.
ad·here (ad hēr′) *verb,* **adhered, adhering.**

adhesive A substance that makes things stick together. Glue and paste are *adhesives*. *Noun.*
—Having a sticky surface that will hold tight to other things. A postage stamp is *adhesive* on one side. The bandage was held on his skin with *adhesive* tape. *Adjective.*
ad·he·sive (ad hē′siv) *noun, plural* **adhesives;** *adjective.*

adios The Spanish word that means "good-by."
a·di·os (ä′dē ōs′) *interjection.*

adjacent Lying next to or near. The garage is *adjacent* to the house.
ad·ja·cent (ə jā′sənt) *adjective.*

adjective A word that tells something about a noun or a pronoun. An adjective describes a person, place, or thing. Some examples of adjectives are: We own a *red* car. Bill is *tall*. She was *sad*. That is *his* bat. Ann has *many* books. We own *two* dogs.
ad·jec·tive (aj′ik tiv) *noun, plural* **adjectives.**

adjoin To be next to. Things that adjoin are very close to each other. Our farm *adjoins* theirs.
ad·join (ə join′) *verb,* **adjoined, adjoining.**

adjourn To stop and put off something until a time in the future. The class president *adjourned* the meeting until next week. The Senate will *adjourn* for the summer.
ad·journ (ə jurn′) *verb,* **adjourned, adjourning.**

adjust 1. To change and make right or better; arrange in the best way. Helen *adjusted* the length of her new skirt. The mechanic had to *adjust* the brakes on the car. 2. To be comfortable or used to something; adapt. Ben found it hard to *adjust* to the new neighborhood.
ad·just (ə just′) *verb,* **adjusted, adjusting.**

adjustment 1. A change to make something right or better; correction. He spent an hour making the *adjustments* on the brakes. 2. The act of becoming used to or comfortable in a situation. It took Karen several weeks to make the *adjustment* to her new home in the country.
ad·just·ment (ə just′mənt) *noun, plural* **adjustments.**

ad-lib To do or say something that has not been planned or practiced before. He forgot part of his speech, so he had to *ad-lib* as he went along.
ad-lib (ad′lib′) *verb,* **ad-libbed, ad-libbing.**

administer 1. To control the operation of; manage; direct. Her uncle *administers* the company's sales department. 2. To give; pro-

vide. The Red Cross *administers* first aid. The judge *administered* the oath to the witness.
ad·min·is·ter (ad min′is tər) *verb,* **administered, administering.**

administration 1. The control of the operations of a business, a school, a government, or some other group. He has always worked for another person and has no experience in *administration*. 2. A group of people who are in charge of the operation of something. The principal is the head of the school *administration*. 3. **the Administration**. The President of the United States, together with his cabinet and the other officials who make up the executive branch of the government. 4. The period of time during which a government holds office. The first American space flight took place during the *administration* of President Kennedy.
ad·min·is·tra·tion (ad min′is trā′shən) *noun, plural* **administrations.**

admiral A navy officer of the highest rank. The four ranks of admirals are **rear admiral, vice admiral, admiral,** and **fleet admiral.** Fleet admiral is the highest rank of admiral.
ad·mi·ral (ad′mər əl) *noun, plural* **admirals.**

admiration A feeling of approval or respect. We feel *admiration* when we think that a person is very good or a thing is very beautiful.
ad·mi·ra·tion (ad′mə rā′shən) *noun.*

admire 1. To feel a great respect for. I *admire* a person who is always honest. 2. To look at or speak of with pleasure and approval. She *admired* her friend's new coat.
ad·mire (ad mīr′) *verb,* **admired, admiring.**

admission 1. The act of allowing to come in or enter. Her parents held a party to celebrate her *admission* to college. 2. The price that a person has to pay to come in. The *admission* to the baseball game was three dollars. 3. The act of saying that something is true; confession. She found it hard to make the *admission* that she had lost her friend's ring.
ad·mis·sion (ad mish′ən) *noun, plural* **admissions.**

admit 1. To allow to come in; let in. John was *admitted* to the club last week. 2. To

at; āpe; cär; end; mē; it; īce; hot; ōld;
fôrk; wood; fo͞ol; oil; out; up; turn; sing;
thin; this; hw in white; zh in treasure.
ə stands for a in about, e in taken
i in pencil, o in lemon, and u in circus.

confess the truth of. He *admitted* that he had broken the lamp.

ad·mit (ad mit′) *verb,* **admitted, admitting.**

admittance The right to come in; permission to enter. This ticket gives you *admittance* to the movie theater.

ad·mit·tance (ad mit′əns) *noun.*

adobe **1.** A brick made of a sandy kind of clay. Bits of straw are sometimes mixed with the clay, and the bricks are dried in the sun. **2.** A building made with adobe.

a·do·be (ə dō′bē) *noun, plural* **adobes.**

Adobe Building

adolescent A young person who is not yet an adult. A person between the ages of twelve and twenty-one is an adolescent.

ad·o·les·cent (ad′əl es′ənt) *noun, plural* **adolescents.**

adopt **1.** To take a child of other parents as a member of one's own family. The couple *adopted* a boy and a girl from an orphanage. **2.** To take and use as one's own. The tune for the "Star-Spangled Banner" was *adopted* from a British song. **3.** To accept or approve. The people of the town voted to *adopt* the plan for a new library.

a·dopt (ə dopt′) *verb,* **adopted, adopting.**

adoption The act of adopting. The *adoption* of the baby took two months.

a·dop·tion (ə dop′shən) *noun, plural* **adoptions.**

adore To love and admire greatly; worship. She *adores* her grandmother.

a·dore (ə dôr′) *verb,* **adored, adoring.**

adorn To add something beautiful to; decorate. She *adorned* the table with flowers.

a·dorn (ə dôrn′) *verb,* **adorned, adorning.**

adrift Moving freely with the current or wind; drifting. When something is adrift, it is not tied or anchored or held in any way. The boys set the canoe *adrift* by accident.

a·drift (ə drift′) *adverb; adjective.*

adult **1.** A person who is fully grown. A man or woman who is more than twenty-one years old is an adult. **2.** A plant or animal that is fully grown. *Noun.*

—Having grown to full size; mature. An *adult* butterfly develops from a caterpillar. *Adjective.*

a·dult (ə dult′ *or* ad′ult) *noun, plural* **adults;** *adjective.*

adulterate To make weaker or less good by adding something. The restaurant *adulterated* the orange juice by adding water.

a·dul·ter·ate (ə dul′tə rāt′) *verb,* **adulterated, adulterating.**

advance **1.** To move forward. He *advanced* the hands of the clock to the correct time. The army *advanced* to the gates of the enemy's city. **2.** To help the progress of; add to; improve. The scientist hoped that his experiments would *advance* man's knowledge of the sea. **3.** To offer; propose. The club's president *advanced* a new plan for a camping trip. **4.** To move up in position; promote. The hard-working student *advanced* to the head of his class. **5.** To give money before it is due. His mother said she would *advance* him his allowance for the next week so he could buy his friend a present. *Verb.*

—**1.** A move forward. The army made a steady *advance* toward the city. **2.** Progress; improvement. The development of the airplane was an *advance* in long-distance travel. **3.** A payment given before it is due. He received an *advance* on his next month's salary. **4. advances.** Attempts to gain the friendship of someone. Because he was shy, he was nervous when people made *advances*. *Noun.*

ad·vance (ad vans′) *verb,* **advanced, advancing;** *noun, plural* **advances.**

advancement **1.** Progress; improvement. Her *advancement* in reading ability pleased the teacher. **2.** A move up in position; promotion. That job offers great opportunities for *advancement*.

ad·vance·ment (ad vans′mənt) *noun, plural* **advancements.**

advantage Something that can be of extra help or of use in doing certain things. Being tall is an *advantage* for a basketball player. Her knowledge of typing was an *advantage* when she looked for a job.

ad·van·tage (ad van′tij) *noun, plural* **advantages.**

to take advantage of. 1. To make good use of. He *took advantage of* the opportunity to learn French. **2.** To make unfair use of.

She *took advantage of* her friend's generosity by borrowing her records too often.

advantageous Being of extra help; favorable. Capturing her brother's queen put Jean in an *advantageous* position in their chess game.
ad·van·ta·geous (ad′vən tā′jəs) *adjective.*

adventure 1. Something a person does that involves danger and difficulties. Columbus' voyage to the New World was a great *adventure.* That book is about the *adventures* of the pioneers. 2. An exciting or unusual experience. Their first trip by airplane was an *adventure* for the boys.
ad·ven·ture (ad ven′chər) *noun, plural* **adventures.**

adventurous 1. Eager to have exciting or dangerous experiences; bold. The *adventurous* campers set off on a canoe trip in the wilderness. 2. Full of danger; risky. The first voyages to the New World were *adventurous* journeys.
ad·ven·tur·ous (ad ven′chər əs) *adjective.*

adverb A word that tells something about a verb, an adjective, or another adverb. An adverb may tell how something is done (The boy walked *quickly.*). It may also tell where or when something is done (The ship sailed *away.*), (She went to bed *early.*). An adverb can also tell how much something is felt (I am *very* tired.).
ad·verb (ad′vurb′) *noun, plural* **adverbs.**

adversary A person or group that is on the other side in a contest or fight; opponent or enemy. Her *adversary* in the tennis match was two games ahead.
ad·ver·sar·y (ad′vər ser′ē) *noun, plural* **adversaries.**

adverse 1. Opposite to what is wanted; not favorable. The football game was played under *adverse* conditions because of the heavy rain. 2. Not friendly or agreeable. Her mother was *adverse* to the idea of a picnic that weekend.
ad·verse (ad vurs′ *or* ad′vurs) *adjective.*

adversity Misfortune, suffering, or difficulty. The shipwrecked sailor showed courage in the face of *adversity.*
ad·ver·si·ty (ad vur′sə tē) *noun, plural* **adversities.**

advertise To make known to the public. A business can advertise something by describing what is special or good about it, so that people will learn about it and want to buy it. That company *advertises* its toothpaste on television and in magazines. The school *advertised* the play by putting up posters. Her mother *advertised* for a baby-sitter in the town newspaper.
ad·ver·tise (ad′vər tīz′) *verb,* **advertised, advertising.**

advertisement A public announcement describing what is special or good about something. Some advertisements are made to get people to buy a product or use a service, or to support a person or cause. Other advertisements are made in order to find a thing that is wanted or a person to do something.
ad·ver·tise·ment (ad′vər tīz′mənt *or* ad-vur′tiz mənt) *noun, plural* **advertisements.**

advice An idea that is offered to a person telling him or her how to act in a certain situation. The father gave his daughter *advice* about how to take care of her new puppy.
ad·vice (əd vīs′) *noun.*

advisable Being a good or smart thing to do; wise; sensible. It is *advisable* to drive at a slower speed on wet roads.
ad·vis·a·ble (əd vī′zə bəl) *adjective.*

advise 1. To give advice. To advise someone is to suggest a good way to act or the right thing to do in a certain situation. His doctor *advised* him not to eat so much candy. 2. To give information to; notify. The letter *advised* Carol that she had won first prize in the contest.
ad·vise (əd vīz′) *verb,* **advised, advising.**

adviser A person who gives advice. High schools have *advisers* who help students make decisions about what to study.
ad·vis·er (əd vī′zər) *noun, plural* **advisers.**

advocate To speak in favor of; urge; support. The congressman *advocated* strict penalties against people who polluted the air and water. *Verb.*
—A person who speaks in favor of someone or something. Lawyers are *advocates* for people who go to court. *Noun.*
ad·vo·cate (ad′və kāt′ *for verb;* ad′və kit *for noun*) *verb,* **advocated, advocating;** *noun, plural* **advocates.**

adz A tool that looks like an ax. It has a curved blade and is used to shape logs and other large pieces of wood. This word is also spelled **adze.**
adz (adz) *noun, plural* **adzes.**

at; āpe; cär; end; mē; it; īce; hot; ōld;
fôrk; wood; fōōl; oil; out; up; turn; sing;
thin; this; hw in white; zh in treasure.
ə stands for a in about, e in taken
i in pencil, o in lemon, and u in circus.

aerial In the air. Trapeze artists do *aerial* acrobatics. The helicopter pilot took an *aerial* photograph of the city. *Adjective.*
—A radio or television antenna. *Noun.*
aer·i·al (er′ē əl) *adjective; noun, plural* **aerials.**

aeronautics The science that has to do with flight. Aeronautics is concerned with designing, building, and flying aircraft.
aer·o·nau·tics (er′ə nô′tiks) *noun plural.*

aerosol A mass of very fine particles of a solid or a liquid that are suspended in a gas.

Television Aerial

Smoke and fog are aerosols that occur in nature. There are also aerosols of paint and other materials that are sealed in cans and released in the form of a fine spray.
aer·o·sol (er′ə sôl′) *noun, plural* **aerosols.**

aerospace The earth's atmosphere and outer space. The entire region in which aircraft and spacecraft can be operated is called aerospace.
aer·o·space (er′ō spās′) *noun.*

aesthetic Having to do with art and beauty and things that are beautiful. We can judge a painting or a building from an *aesthetic* point of view.
aes·thet·ic (es thet′ik) *adjective.*

affable Easy to meet and talk to; friendly. The old country doctor was an *affable* man.
af·fa·ble (af′ə bəl) *adjective.*

affair **1.** A thing that is done or has to be done. Moving to a new home can be a confusing *affair.* He had to finish some business *affairs* before he went on vacation. **2.** Something that happens; event. The dance was going to be a formal *affair.*
af·fair (ə fer′) *noun, plural* **affairs.**

affect[1] **1.** To make something happen to; have an effect on. The lack of rain may *affect* the crops in a bad way this year. **2.** To make a person feel something in his heart. The photographs of the hungry children *affected* him very much and made him sad.
af·fect (ə fekt′) *verb,* **affected, affecting.**

▲ The words **affect** and **effect** sound the same and have the same basic meaning, but they cannot be used in the same way. **Affect** is a verb: A poor diet can *affect* your health. **Effect** is a noun: Daily exercise will have a good *effect* on your health.

affect[2] To pretend to have or feel. He *affected* bravery, but he was really afraid.
af·fect (ə fekt′) *verb,* **affected, affecting.**

affection A feeling of love. When you feel affection for people, you like them very much and care about what happens to them. He had a deep *affection* for his sister and brother.
af·fec·tion (ə fek′shən) *noun, plural* **affections.**

affectionate Full of or showing love. She gave her grandmother an *affectionate* hug.
af·fec·tion·ate (ə fek′shə nit) *adjective.*

affiliate To join or have something to do with. Our local television station is *affiliated* with the national network.
af·fil·i·ate (ə fil′ē āt′) *verb,* **affiliated, affiliating.**

affirmative Saying that something is true; saying "yes." He gave an *affirmative* answer to my question by nodding his head.
af·firm·a·tive (ə fur′mə tiv) *adjective.*

affix To attach to something. He *affixed* the picture to the wall with a thumbtack.
af·fix (ə fiks′) *verb,* **affixed, affixing.**

afflict To cause a person great pain or trouble; make miserable. Helen was *afflicted* by poison ivy for a week.
af·flict (ə flikt′) *verb,* **afflicted, afflicting.**

affliction **1.** A cause of pain or trouble. Blindness is a severe *affliction.* **2.** The condition of suffering pain or deep unhappiness. The neighbors were very kind to the sick woman during her *affliction.*
af·flic·tion (ə flik′shən) *noun, plural* **afflictions.**

affluent Having a large amount of money; rich; wealthy. The expensive jewelry store had many *affluent* customers.
af·flu·ent (af′lōō ənt) *adjective.*

afford **1.** To have enough money to pay for. He cannot *afford* a new car. **2.** To be able to do or spare without causing harm. I can only *afford* to watch television for an hour tonight because I have homework to do. **3.** To give or provide. A vacation *affords* us time to rest.
af·ford (ə fôrd′) *verb,* **afforded, affording.**

affront A deliberate insult. Her rude comment about my home was an *affront* to me.
af·front (ə frunt′) *noun, plural* **affronts.**

afire On fire; burning. The old house was *afire*. It was hard to set the damp log *afire*.
a·fire (ə fīr′) *adjective; adverb.*

afloat Floating on water. There are fallen leaves *afloat* on the pond. The life boat was made so that it would stay *afloat*.
a·float (ə flōt′) *adjective; adverb.*

afoot **1.** On foot; by walking. They left their bicycles and continued *afoot*. **2.** In action; going on. Secret plans for the attack were *afoot*.
a·foot (ə foot′) *adverb; adjective.*

afraid **1.** Feeling fear; frightened. Are you *afraid* of snakes? He is *afraid* to fly in an airplane. **2.** Feeling unhappy or sorry about. I'm *afraid* that I will not be able to spend the night at your house.
a·fraid (ə frād′) *adjective.*

Africa A continent south of Europe, between the Atlantic Ocean and the Indian Ocean.
Af·ri·ca (af′ri kə) *noun.*

African Of or having to do with Africa or its people. We saw an exhibit of *African* art. *Adjective.*
—1. A black person who was born in Africa. **2.** Any person who is a citizen of an African country. *Noun.*
Af·ri·can (af′ri kən) *adjective; noun, plural* **Africans.**

aft At or toward the rear of a boat or aircraft. The sailor walked *aft*.
aft (aft) *adverb.*

after The dog walked *after* his owner. The police went *after* the thieves. It is ten minutes *after* three o'clock. I came on Sunday and he came one day *after*. It happened *after* you left.
af·ter (af′tər) *preposition; adverb; conjunction.*

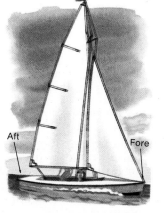
Aft — Fore

aftermath Something that comes as a result of something else. Often floods are the *aftermath* of a hurricane.
af·ter·math (af′tər math′) *noun, plural* **aftermaths.**

afternoon The part of the day between noon and evening.
af·ter·noon (af′tər noon′) *noun, plural* **afternoons.**

afterward At a later time. We chopped wood for an hour, and *afterward* we rested for an hour. ▲ This word is also spelled **afterwards.**
af·ter·ward (af′tər wərd) *adverb.*

again Once more; another time. She did not hear him the first time, so he called to her *again*.
a·gain (ə gen′) *adverb.*

▲ The word **again** used to mean "back" or "in the opposite direction." A ball that was thrown against a wall was said to bounce *again* to the person who had thrown it. The idea of doing something a second time came from this earlier English meaning.

against He threw the ball *against* the wall. The senator voted *against* the bill. The fish swam *against* the current of the river. She leaned her bicycle *against* the tree.
a·gainst (ə genst′) *preposition.*

agate **1.** A stone that is striped with different colors. It is a kind of quartz. **2.** A marble that is made of agate or looks like it, and is used for playing games.
ag·ate (ag′it) *noun, plural* **agates.**

Cross Section of an Agate

age **1.** The amount of time that a person, animal, or thing has lived or existed. Her *age* is ten years. He retired from his job at the *age* of sixty-five. **2.** A particular period of time. Her grandfather was enjoying his old *age*. Ed wrote a paper about the atomic *age*. **3.** A long time. We haven't been to visit them for *ages*. *Noun.*
—1. To make old. Having a hard life can *age* a person. **2.** To become old or mature. Some cheese tastes better when it *ages*. *Verb.*
age (āj) *noun, plural* **ages;** *verb,* **aged, aging** or **ageing.**

aged **1.** Having grown old. The young girl helped take care of her *aged* grandfather. **2.** Having the age of. She has a brother *aged* three.
a·ged (ā′jid *for definition 1;* ājd *for definition 2*) *adjective.*

at; āpe; cär; end; mē; it; īce; hot; ōld;
fôrk; wood; fool; oil; out; up; turn; sing;
thin; this; hw in white; zh in treasure.
ə stands for a in about, e in taken
i in pencil, o in lemon, and u in circus.

agency A company or a person that does certain work for other companies or people. An employment *agency* helps people to find jobs. An advertising *agency* prepares advertisements for companies that are its clients. The FBI is a law-enforcement *agency* of the federal government.
a·gen·cy (ā′jən sē) *noun, plural* **agencies.**

agent 1. A person who acts for some other person or company. The real estate *agent* sold the young couple a new house. The secret *agent* acted as a spy in a foreign country. 2. Something that does a certain thing. Soap is a cleaning *agent.*
a·gent (ā′jənt) *noun, plural* **agents.**

aggravate 1. To make worse. Being out in the rain *aggravated* his cold. 2. To make angry; annoy. His constant complaining *aggravates* her.
ag·gra·vate (ag′rə vāt′) *verb,* **aggravated, aggravating.**

aggression An attack or warlike action. Acts of aggression are often made against a person or country that has not done anything to cause such an attack. A country that sends an army to take over the land of another country is guilty of aggression.
ag·gres·sion (ə gresh′ən) *noun, plural* **aggressions.**

aggressive 1. Being warlike and ready to attack without a good reason. The *aggressive* nation sent its troops to attack a neighboring country. 2. Very forceful and bold. An *aggressive* salesman does not easily accept "no" for an answer.
ag·gres·sive (ə gres′iv) *adjective.*

aghast Feeling great surprise or shock. She was *aghast* at his cheating on the test.
a·ghast (ə gast′) *adjective.*

agile Able to move and react quickly and easily. A cat is an *agile* animal.
ag·ile (aj′əl) *adjective.*

agility Quickness and ease in moving and reacting. An acrobat must have *agility.*
a·gil·i·ty (ə jil′ə tē) *noun.*

agitate 1. To move back and forth; stir up. The wind *agitated* the water and made waves. A washing machine *agitates* clothes. 2. To disturb the feelings of; excite. The report that there might be an earthquake in the area *agitated* the people who lived there.
ag·i·tate (aj′ə tāt′) *verb,* **agitated, agitating.**

agitator A person or thing that stirs up or disturbs. The governor blamed the riot on *agitators* who aroused the people of the area.
ag·i·ta·tor (aj′ə tā′tər) *noun, plural* **agitators.**

aglow Bright with light or warmth; glowing. The Christmas tree was *aglow* with candles. The room was set *aglow* by the blazing logs in the fireplace.
a·glow (ə glō′) *adjective; adverb.*

agnostic A person who believes that it is not possible to know for sure whether or not God really exists.
ag·nos·tic (ag nos′tik) *noun, plural* **agnostics.**

ago Before the time it is now; past. He left ten minutes *ago.* Dinosaurs lived long *ago.*
a·go (ə gō′) *adjective; adverb.*

agony Great pain or suffering of the mind or body. He was in *agony* from the toothache. She suffered *agony* at the death of her pet.
ag·o·ny (ag′ə nē) *noun, plural* **agonies.**

agree 1. To have the same idea. A person who agrees, thinks or feels the same way about a thing as someone else does. His friends thought it was a good day to go to the beach, but Jim did not *agree.* 2. To say "yes" to something. He *agreed* to lend me his bicycle.
a·gree (ə grē′) *verb,* **agreed, agreeing.**
agree with. To be good for. When he has a stomach ache, cold drinks do not *agree with* him.

agreeable 1. Nice; pleasant. She is a very *agreeable* person. 2. Willing to say "yes." I will come to the party if my mother is *agreeable.*
a·gree·a·ble (ə grē′ə bəl) *adjective.*

agreement 1. An understanding between people or groups. The brothers made an *agreement* about dividing their chores. The two nations signed a peace *agreement* during the meeting. 2. The state of agreeing; having the same ideas. My father is in *agreement* with my mother about what color to paint the house.
a·gree·ment (ə grē′mənt) *noun, plural* **agreements.**

agricultural Having to do with farming or farms; of agriculture. Because of his interest in farming, the boy went to an *agricultural* college.
ag·ri·cul·tur·al (ag′rə kul′chər əl) *adjective.*

agriculture The raising of crops and farm animals; farming.
ag·ri·cul·ture (ag′rə kul′chər) *noun.*

ahead Jim was way *ahead* of the other runners in the race. Go *ahead* with your plans for the party. Our team is six points *ahead.* A person must work hard to get *ahead* in that company.
a·head (ə hed′) *adverb.*

ahoy An expression used by sailors as a greeting or to attract attention. When the sailors saw the other ship, they yelled "Ship *ahoy!*"

a·hoy (ə hoi′) *interjection.*

aid To give help or support. Jim *aided* the farmer in his search for the lost cattle. Two boy scouts *aided* us in putting up the tent. *Verb.*
—**1.** Help or support; assistance. The older boys came to my *aid* when I climbed too high in the tree. **2.** Something that is helpful. A dictionary is an *aid* in learning new words. *Noun.* ▲ Another word that sounds like this is **aide.**

aid (ād) *verb,* **aided, aiding;** *noun, plural* **aids.**

aide A helper or assistant. During the summer, she worked as a nurse's *aide.* ▲ Another word that sounds like this is **aid.**

aide (ād) *noun, plural* **aides.**

ail **1.** To cause illness or trouble for. What *ails* your brother? **2.** To be ill; feel sick. My aunt has been *ailing* for about a month now. ▲ Another word that sounds like this is **ale.**

ail (āl) *verb,* **ailed, ailing.**

ailanthus A tree that has leaves shaped like feathers and clusters of small green flowers. It grows well in city areas where other trees fail to grow.

ai·lan·thus (ā lan′thəs) *noun, plural* **ailanthuses.**

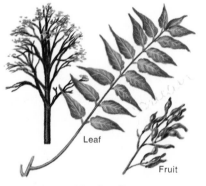

Leaf

Fruit

Ailanthus Tree

aileron A movable part on the back of an airplane wing. By moving up and down, the aileron controls the speed of the airplane in flight.

ai·le·ron (ā′lə ron′) *noun, plural* **ailerons.**

ailment An illness; sickness. His *ailment* was cured by a long rest.

ail·ment (āl′mənt) *noun, plural* **ailments.**

aim **1.** To direct or point a weapon or a blow. The boxer *aimed* a punch at the other fighter's jaw. The hunter *aimed* at the deer but missed him. **2.** To intend for; direct toward. The mayor *aimed* his speech at the young people who would vote in the next election. *Verb.*
—**1.** The act of pointing or directing a weapon or blow. His *aim* was not good enough to hit the bull's-eye. **2.** Goal; purpose. Her *aim* was to become the best player on the team. *Noun.*

aim (ām) *verb,* **aimed, aiming;** *noun, plural* **aims.**

aimless Without purpose or aim. They went on an *aimless* walk through the fields.

aim·less (ām′lis) *adjective.*

ain't **1.** Am not. **2.** Is not; are not. **3.** Has not; have not.

▲ *Ain't* is not considered to be good English. Because of this, careful speakers and writers avoid using *ain't.*

---

air **1.** What we breathe. Air is all around us, but we cannot see it, smell it, or taste it. Air is a mixture of many gases, but just two gases, nitrogen and oxygen, make up 99 percent of the air. **2.** The open space above us; the sky. He threw the ball into the *air.* **3.** Fresh air. Please open the window and let in some *air.* **4.** A song or tune. He whistled a cheerful *air* as he worked. **5.** A way, look, or manner. He has an *air* of mystery about him. **6. airs.** Showy manners used to impress others. She always puts on *airs* when her younger sister's friends are around. *Noun.*
—**1.** To let air through. Please open the windows and *air* out the room before you leave. **2.** To make known. The workers *aired* their complaints about having to work such long hours. *Verb.* ▲ Other words that sound like this are **ere** and **heir.**

air (er) *noun, plural* **airs;** *verb,* **aired, airing.**

on the air. Broadcasting or being broadcast. That program will be *on the air* at 6:30 tonight.

air conditioner A machine used to cool off and clean the air in a place. Air conditioners are used during the summer in homes,

at; āpe; cär; end; mē; it; īce; hot; ōld;
fôrk; wood; fo͞ol; oil; out; up; turn; sing;
thin; this; hw in white; zh in treasure.
ə stands for a in about, e in taken
i in pencil, o in lemon, and u in circus.

cars, stores, and other places to provide air that makes us more comfortable.

aircraft   Any machine made to fly in the air. Airplanes, helicopters, gliders, and balloons are all aircraft.
air·craft (er′kraft′) *noun, plural* **aircraft.**

airfield   The landing field of an airport.
air·field (er′fēld′) *noun, plural* **airfields.**

air force   The branch of a country's armed forces that uses aircraft, such as the United States Air Force.

airline   A system of carrying people and things from one place to another by airplane.
air·line (er′līn′) *noun, plural* **airlines.**

airliner   A large airplane that carries passengers from one place to another.
air·lin·er (er′lī′nər) *noun, plural* **airliners.**

air-mail   To send a letter by airplane. My mother is going to *air-mail* this letter to our congressman. *Verb.*
—Having to do with air mail. I sent an *air-mail* letter to my friend who lives very far from me. *Adjective.*
—By air mail. Please send this package *air-mail* so it will arrive more quickly. *Adverb.*
air-mail (er′māl′) *verb,* **air-mailed, air-mailing;** *adjective; adverb.*

air mail   Mail carried between cities by airplane.

airman   A man in the United States Air Force who is not an officer.
air·man (er′mən) *noun, plural* **airmen.**

airplane   A machine that flies in the air. An airplane has two wings. Because it is heavier than air, it has propellers or jet engines to make it fly.
air·plane (er′plān′) *noun, plural* **airplanes.**

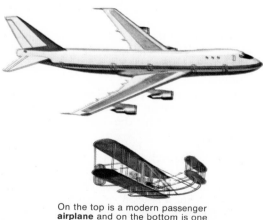

On the top is a modern passenger **airplane** and on the bottom is one of the first airplanes ever built.

airport   A place with fields for airplanes to land and take off. An airport has buildings for sheltering and fixing airplanes, and other buildings for people who are waiting to take an airplane flight.
air·port (er′pôrt′) *noun, plural* **airports.**

air pressure   The force that air puts on everything it touches. Air pressure is caused by the weight of the air high above the earth pressing down on the air below.

airship   An aircraft that is lighter than air, is driven by a motor, and can be steered.
air·ship (er′ship′) *noun, plural* **airships.**

airstrip   A paved or cleared area where aircraft can land and take off.
air·strip (er′strip′) *noun, plural* **airstrips.**

airtight   **1.** So tight that no air or gases can get in or out. The jelly was packed in an *airtight* jar so that it would stay fresh. **2.** Having no weak points that could be easily attacked. The police had an *airtight* case against the man who was accused of robbing the bank.
air·tight (er′tīt′) *adjective.*

airy   **1.** Light as air; delicate. She wore an *airy* gown that fluttered in the breeze. **2.** Open to the air; breezy. We bought the house because it was so *airy* and cheerful.
air·y (er′ē) *adjective,* **airier, airiest.**

aisle   The space between two rows or sections of something. We walked down the *aisle* between the counters in the grocery store. There were several *aisles* in the movie theater. ▲ Other words that sound like this are **I'll** and **isle.**
aisle (īl) *noun, plural* **aisles.**

ajar   Partly open. The front door was *ajar* and the cat ran out. The door to the safe was left *ajar.*
a·jar (ə jär′) *adjective; adverb.*

akimbo   Having one's hands on one's hips with the elbows turned outward.
a·kim·bo (ə kim′bō) *adjective.*

akin   **1.** Of the same kind; similar. Love and friendship are *akin.* **2.** Belonging to the same family; related. She and I are *akin* because our grandmothers were sisters.
a·kin (ə kin′) *adjective.*

Alabama   A state in the southeastern United States. Its capital is Montgomery.
Al·a·bam·a (al′ə bam′ə) *noun.*

The girl is standing with her arms **akimbo.**

▲ The name **Alabama** comes from two Indian words that mean "people who gather plants" or "people who clear land." The words were used first as the name of an Indian tribe that lived near the Alabama River. Then the tribe's name was used for the river, and the state of Alabama was later named for the river.

alabaster   A smooth, whitish stone. It is used mostly to make sculptures.
a·la·bas·ter (al′ə bas′tər) *noun.*

alarm   **1.** A bell, buzzer, or other thing used to wake people up or to warn them of danger. He set the *alarm* for seven o'clock before going to bed. The bank has an *alarm* that rings to alert the police if a robbery takes place. **2.** A sudden fear of danger. The loud thunder filled the child with *alarm.* **3.** A warning of danger. The dark clouds and strong winds were an *alarm* that a hurricane was approaching. *Noun.*
—To make afraid. The news that war might break out *alarmed* the people. *Verb.*
a·larm (ə lärm′) *noun, plural* **alarms;** *verb,* **alarmed, alarming.**

▲ The word **alarm** comes from an old Italian phrase that meant "to arms!" This phrase was used as a warning to tell soldiers to pick up their weapons, or *arms,* and be ready to fight.

alas   An expression used to show sorrow or disappointment.
a·las (ə las′) *interjection.*

Alaska   The largest state of the United States. It is located in the northwestern part of North America. The capital of Alaska is Juneau.
A·las·ka (ə las′kə) *noun.*

▲ The name **Alaska** comes from a word meaning "mainland" or "great land." This name was used by Eskimos who lived on islands off the coast of Alaska. The earlier name of this area was "Russian America" because it once belonged to Russia. The United States bought the land from Russia in 1867.

albatross   A large sea bird that has a long, hooked beak and webbed feet. The albatross has large wings and is able to fly for very long distances. It is usually found in the southern oceans of the world.
al·ba·tross (al′bə trôs′) *noun, plural* **albatrosses.**

▲ The name **albatross** is believed to come from a word that meant "bucket of water" or "water carrier." Because the albatross is able to fly for such a long time over the ocean, people once thought that it was somehow able to carry a supply of fresh water in its body to drink as it flew.

album   **1.** A book with blank pages. People use albums to hold photographs, pictures, or other things that they collect. My uncle has many *albums* filled with postage stamps. **2.** A long-playing phonograph record. Ann gave her brother an *album* by his favorite singer for his birthday.
al·bum (al′bəm) *noun, plural* **albums.**

alchemy   A kind of chemistry practiced during the Middle Ages. Men who studied alchemy attempted to turn common metals into gold. They also tried to discover a magic substance that could cure all diseases and help people to live longer.
al·che·my (al′kə mē) *noun.*

alcohol   A liquid that has no color or smell. It catches fire easily and evaporates very quickly. One kind of alcohol is used in making certain drinks that can cause a temporary change in a person's thoughts and behavior. Alcohol is also used in making medicines and chemicals, and for many other purposes. Some kinds of alcohol are very poisonous. Alcohol comes from certain grains and fruit. It also can be made from artificial substances.
al·co·hol (al′kə hôl′) *noun, plural* **alcohols.**

alcoholic   Containing alcohol. At the party Ted's father served *alcoholic* drinks to the adults and soda to the children. *Adjective.*
—A person who has a strong need for alcohol because he suffers from alcoholism. *Noun.*
al·co·hol·ic (al′kə hô′lik) *adjective; noun, plural* **alcoholics.**

alcoholism   A disease in which a person's need to drink alcoholic beverages is so strong that he cannot control it.
al·co·hol·ism (al′kə hô liz′əm) *noun.*

alcove   A small room or area that is partly closed off from a larger room.
al·cove (al′kōv′) *noun, plural* **alcoves.**

at; āpe; cär; end; mē; it; īce; hot; ōld;
fôrk; wood; fōol; oil; out; up; turn; sing;
thin; this; hw in white; zh in treasure.
ə stands for a in about, e in taken
i in pencil, o in lemon, and u in circus.

alder A tree or shrub that grows in cool and moist places. The alder is similar to the birch tree. It has rough bark and roundish leaves.
al·der (ôl′dər) *noun, plural* **alders.**

Leaf

Alder Tree

ale An alcoholic drink that is like beer, but stronger and more bitter. ▲ Another word that sounds like this is **ail.**
ale (āl) *noun, plural* **ales.**

alert **1.** Watching very carefully. An *alert* guard saw the robbers enter the building. **2.** Quick to act or learn; lively; active. Her good work shows that she has an *alert* mind. *Adjective.*
—A signal that warns of possible danger; alarm. The troops remained underground during the air raid *alert. Noun.*
—To make aware of; warn. The Coast Guard *alerted* the town to the coming hurricane. *Verb.*
a·lert (ə lurt′) *adjective; noun, plural* **alerts;** *verb,* **alerted, alerting.**

alfalfa A plant like clover. It has bluish-purple flowers. Alfalfa is grown as a food for cattle and other livestock.
al·fal·fa (al fal′fə) *noun.*

algae A large group of water plants that do not have roots or flowers. Seaweed is a kind of algae.
al·gae (al′jē) *noun plural.*

algebra A kind of mathematics in which letters are used along with numbers. The letters stand for numbers that are un-

Alfalfa

known. An example of an algebra problem is: $10x - 3 = 17$.
al·ge·bra (al′jə brə) *noun.*

alias Another name a person calls himself. A person usually uses an alias to hide his real identity. "Billy the Kid" was the *alias* of an outlaw named William H. Bonney. *Noun.*
—Otherwise called; also known as. Sam Jones, *alias* John Williams, was wanted by the police for questioning. *Adverb.*
a·li·as (ā′lē əs) *noun, plural* **aliases;** *adverb.*

alibi **1.** A claim or proof that one was somewhere else when a crime or other act was going on. When the police questioned the man about the robbery, he had a good *alibi,* so he was not arrested. **2.** An excuse. Do you have an *alibi* for being late?
al·i·bi (al′ə bī′) *noun, plural* **alibis.**

▲ The word **alibi** comes from a Latin word that means "somewhere else." When a person was accused of a crime, he would try to prove that he was in another place at the time of the crime. The claim or proof that a person was somewhere else became known as his *alibi.*

alien A person who is not a citizen of the country in which he lives; foreigner. That man is an *alien* in America because he is still a citizen of France. *Noun.*
—Not familiar; different. The customs of those people are *alien* to me. *Adjective.*
al·ien (āl′yən *or* ā′lē ən) *noun, plural* **aliens;** *adjective.*

alienate To make someone feel unfriendly or angry. The child's bad temper *alienated* some of his friends.
al·ien·ate (āl′yə nāt′ *or* ā′lē ə nāt′) *verb,* **alienated, alienating.**

alight[1] **1.** To get down; land. The girl *alighted* from her pony. **2.** To come down from the air; land. The bee *alighted* on the flower.
a·light (ə līt′) *verb,* **alighted** or **alit, alighting.**

alight[2] **1.** Lighted up; glowing. Her face was *alight* with joy. **2.** On fire; burning. During the fireworks, the sky seemed *alight* with color.
a·light (ə līt′) *adjective.*

align To bring into line; put in a line. The captain *aligned* his troops for the parade.
a·lign (ə līn′) *verb,* **aligned, aligning.**

alike In the same way; similarly. She and her twin sister often dress *alike. Adverb.*

—Like one another; similar. No two people have fingerprints that are exactly *alike*. *Adjective.*
a·like (ə līk´) *adverb; adjective.*

alimentary canal A long tube beginning at the mouth. Food moves through this as it is digested and then passed out of the body as waste matter.
al·i·men·ta·ry canal (al´ə men´tər ē *or* al´ə ment´rē).

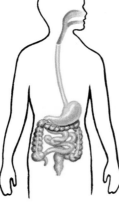
Alimentary Canal

alimony Money paid by a person to support his or her husband or wife after they have been divorced or legally separated.
al·i·mo·ny (al´ə-mō´nē) *noun, plural* **alimonies.**

alive 1. Having life; living. These flowers must be given water if you want them to stay *alive.* 2. Having power; active. They kept *alive* the memory of the dead hero by naming a school after him.
a·live (ə līve´) *adjective.*

all 1. The whole of. We ate *all* the ice cream. 2. Every one. Students from *all* the schools in town were in the swimming meet. *Adjective.*
—Everything or everyone. *All* were saved from the fire. *Noun.*
—The whole amount or number. *All* of us are going to the party. *Pronoun.*
—Completely. The work is *all* finished. *Adverb.* ▲ Another word that sounds like this is **awl.**
all (ôl) *adjective; noun; pronoun; adverb.*

allege To say or declare positively, but without final proof. It has been *alleged* that the man stole the jewels, but he has not yet been convicted of the crime.
al·lege (ə lej´) *verb,* **alleged, alleging.**

allegiance True and faithful feelings and behavior; loyalty. When a person gives his allegiance to someone or something, he promises not to harm that person or thing and to do everything he can to help.
al·le·giance (ə lē´jəns) *noun.*

allergic Having an allergy. When a person is allergic to something, his body reacts against it. Being in a dusty room makes him sneeze because he is *allergic* to dust.
al·ler·gic (ə lur´jik) *adjective.*

allergy A reaction of a person's body against certain foods, plants, or other things that don't bother most other people. A person who has an allergy to wool may get a rash if he wears clothes that are made with wool next to his skin.
al·ler·gy (al´ər jē) *noun, plural* **allergies.**

alley 1. A narrow street or passageway between buildings. There is an *alley* behind those apartments where people can park their cars. 2. A long, narrow path down which bowling balls are rolled. The pins to be knocked down by the ball are at the far end of the alley. This is also called a **bowling alley.**
al·ley (al´ē) *noun, plural* **alleys.**

alliance An agreement between two or more countries, groups, or people to work together in doing something. The two nations had an *alliance* by which each promised to help the other fight if a third country attacked one of them.
al·li·ance (ə lī´əns) *noun, plural* **alliances.**

allied Joined together to do or get something that both or all want. During World War II, the United States, Great Britain, and the Soviet Union were *allied* nations who fought against Germany, Italy, and Japan.
al·lied (ə līd´ *or* al´īd) *adjective.*

alligator An animal with a long head and tail and a thick, tough skin. It lives in rivers and marshes in America and China. Alligators look like crocodiles but have shorter, wider heads.
al·li·ga·tor (al´ə gā´tər) *noun, plural* **alligators**

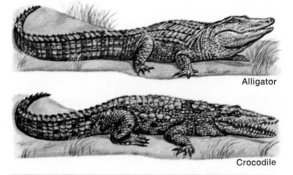
Alligator

Crocodile

at; āpe; cär; end; mē; it; īce; hot; ōld;
fôrk; wood; fōol; oil; out; up; turn; sing;
thin; this; hw in white; zh in treasure.
ə stands for a in about, e in taken
i in pencil, o in lemon, and u in circus.

19

allot To give out as a share. Mrs. Smith *allotted* one apple and one candy bar to each child who came to the house at Halloween.
al·lot (ə lot′) *verb,* **allotted, allotting.**

allow **1.** To give permission to do or have something; permit. His father does not *allow* him to ride his bicycle on the lawn. Smoking is not *allowed* in that theater. **2.** To add or take away an amount for a special reason. We *allowed* an extra hour to make the trip in case the traffic was heavy.
al·low (ə lou′) *verb,* **allowed, allowing.**

allowance **1.** A fixed amount of money given at certain regular times. Billy gets an *allowance* of one dollar a week for helping his father cut the grass. **2.** An amount added or taken away for a special reason. The salesman gave us an *allowance* of $600 on the price of a new car because we traded in our old one.
al·low·ance (ə lou′əns) *noun, plural* **allowances.**
to make allowance for. To take into consideration; allow for. The teacher *made allowance for* the boy's being new to the school, and did not blame him for not knowing the rules.

alloy A metal made by mixing two or more different metals and melting them together. Brass is an *alloy* of copper and zinc.
al·loy (al′oi *or* ə loi′) *noun, plural* **alloys.**

all right **1.** Acceptable; good enough. It is *all right* with me if you go. The book was not as good as she had hoped it would be, but it was *all right*. **2.** Not hurt or ill; safe; well. His friend asked him if he was *all right* after he fell off his bicycle. **3.** Yes. *All right*, I'll do it.

allude To mention briefly or refer to indirectly. Don't even *allude* to the mistake he made in the game; he feels very bad about it.
al·lude (ə lood′) *verb,* **alluded, alluding.**

ally To join together in order to do something. England and America *allied* themselves during World War II. *Verb.*
—A person, nation, or group who joins with another in order to do something. France was an *ally* of the American colonies during the Revolutionary War. *Noun.*
al·ly (ə lī′ *for verb;* al′ī *or* ə lī′ *for noun*) *verb,* **allied, allying;** *noun, plural* **allies.**

almanac A book that contains facts and figures on many different subjects. Most almanacs are published every year. Some almanacs are arranged like a calendar and give facts about the weather, the tides, and the rising and setting of the sun for each day of the year.

al·ma·nac (ôl′mə nak′) *noun, plural* **almanacs.**

almond An oval nut that can be eaten and is used in desserts and candy. It grows on a tree which is also called an almond.
al·mond (ä′mənd *or* am′ənd) *noun, plural* **almonds.**

Fruit

Nut   Kernel

Almond

almost Very close to; nearly. I am *almost* finished with the work. He is *almost* six years old.
al·most (ôl′mōst) *adverb.*

aloft **1.** Far above the ground; high up. There were many kites *aloft* at the beach last weekend. **2.** High up on the masts of a sailing ship. The sailors climbed *aloft* on ladders made of rope.
a·loft (ə lôft′) *adverb.*

aloha *Aloha* is the Hawaiian word that means "love," and it is used to say both "hello" and "good-by."
a·lo·ha (ə lō′ə *or* ä lō′hä) *noun, plural* **alohas;** *interjection.*

alone Not near or with another or others. She enjoyed being *alone* on the beach. There was just one puppy all *alone* in the window of the pet store. Because all his friends were away, he went to the game *alone*.
a·lone (ə lōn′) *adjective; adverb.*
to leave alone or **to let alone.** To leave undisturbed; not bother or interfere with in any way. Please *leave me alone* for an hour so I can finish reading this book.

along Flowers grew *along* the path. We walked *along* the highway. Don't forget to bring *along* your umbrella. The car moved *along* swiftly.
a·long (ə lông′) *preposition; adverb.*

alongside A police car pulled up *alongside* and then passed them. The truck was parked *alongside* the curb.
a·long·side (ə lông′sīd′) *adverb; preposition.*

aloof Not warm or friendly; reserved. The old queen had an *aloof* manner toward people. *Adjective.*
—At a distance; apart. When the two brothers argued, their older sister always tried to remain *aloof. Adverb.*
a·loof (ə loof′) *adjective; adverb.*

aloud So as to be heard; out loud. Each student will read his report *aloud* to the class. He shouted *aloud* from the mountaintop and heard the echo.
a·loud (ə loud´) *adverb.*

alpaca An animal that lives in the mountains of South America and has long, silky wool. The alpaca is related to the camel and the llama.
al·pac·a (al pak´ə) *noun, plural* **alpacas.**

alphabet The letters or symbols that are used to write a language, arranged in their proper order.
al·pha·bet (al´fə-bet´) *noun, plural* **alphabets.**

Alpaca

▲ The word **alphabet** comes from the Greek words *alpha* and *beta.* *Alpha* and *beta* are the names of the first two letters in the Greek alphabet.

alphabetical Arranged in the order of the letters of the alphabet. The words in a dictionary are listed in *alphabetical* order.
al·pha·bet·i·cal (al´fə bet´i kəl) *adjective.*

already He has *already* left. Are you finished *already?*
al·read·y (ôl red´ē) *adverb.*

also She swims well and is *also* a good tennis player.
al·so (ôl´sō) *adverb.*

altar A table or a raised place that is used for religious services. ▲ Another word that sounds like this is **alter.**
al·tar (ôl´tər) *noun, plural* **altars.**

alter To make or become different; change. The tailor *altered* her dress by making it smaller around the waist. ▲ Another word that sounds like this is **altar.**
al·ter (ôl´tər) *verb,* **altered, altering.**

alternate **1.** To take turns. My brother and I *alternate* at washing the car each week. **2.** To happen by turns, with one thing following another in a certain order. Red stripes *alternate* with white stripes on the American flag. *Verb.*
—**1.** First one, then the other; every other. I have piano lessons on *alternate* Mondays. **2.** Taking the place of another; substitute. Please think of an *alternate* plan in case the first plan doesn't work. *Adjective.*
—A person who takes the place of another; substitute. *Noun.*
al·ter·nate (ôl´tər nāt´ *for verb;* ôl´tər nit *for adjective and noun*) *verb,* **alternated, alternating;** *adjective; noun, plural* **alternates.**

alternating current An electric current that flows regularly first in one direction and then in another.

alternative A choice between two or more things. Betsy had the *alternative* of going to the beach with her friends or going on a picnic with her family.
al·ter·na·tive (ôl tur´nə tiv) *noun, plural* **alternatives.**

although *Although* I ate a big dinner, I was hungry again very soon.
al·though (ôl thō´) *conjunction.*

altimeter An instrument that shows how high above the ground or above sea level something is. An altimeter is used in an airplane to show the pilot how high above the ground he is.
al·tim·e·ter (al tim´ə tər *or* al´tə mē´tər) *noun, plural* **altimeters.**

altitude The height that something is above the ground or above sea level. The pilot flew the plane at an *altitude* of 8000 feet. As we drove up the mountain we saw a sign that said we were at an *altitude* of 4000 feet above sea level.
al·ti·tude (al´tə tood´ *or* al´tə tyood´) *noun, plural* **altitudes.**

alto **1.** The lowest female voice, or the highest male voice. **2.** A singer who has such a voice. **3.** A musical instrument that has the range of an alto voice.
al·to (al´tō) *noun, plural* **altos.**

altogether His arrow missed the target *altogether.* There were twelve of us *altogether* at the party.
al·to·geth·er (ôl´tə geth´ər) *adverb.*

aluminum A light, soft, silvery-white metal. Aluminum is the most common metal found in the earth. It is used in making many different things, such as pots and pans for cooking, trucks, airplanes, or machines. It is also used as a building material. Aluminum is a chemical element.
a·lu·mi·num (ə loo´mə nəm) *noun.*

---

at; āpe; cär; end; mē; it; īce; hot; ōld;
fôrk; wood; fool; oil; out; up; turn; sing;
thin; this; hw in white; zh in treasure.
ə stands for **a** in about, **e** in taken
i in pencil, **o** in lemon, and **u** in circus.

---

always All the time; every time. There is *always* snow and ice at the North Pole.
al·ways (ôl′wāz *or* ôl′wēz) *adverb.*

am I *am* happy that you can come to my birthday party. I *am* going to the circus tomorrow.
am (am *or* əm) *verb.*

A.M. The time of day between midnight and noon. She wakes up at 7:30 *A.M.* He met his friend for lunch at 11:30 *A.M.*

▲ A.M. comes from the first letters of the Latin words *ante meridiem. Ante meridiem* means "before noon."

amateur A person who does something just for the pleasure of doing it, not for money. Only *amateurs* in sports are allowed to take part in the Olympic games. *Noun.*
—Done by or made up of amateurs. He will run the mile in the *amateur* track meet. *Adjective.*
am·a·teur (am′ə chər *or* am′ə tər) *noun, plural* **amateurs;** *adjective.*

amaze To surprise greatly; astonish. The girl's speed at solving difficult mathematical problems *amazed* us all.
a·maze (ə māz′) *verb,* **amazed, amazing.**

amazement Great surprise or wonder; astonishment. The boy was filled with *amazement* as he watched the circus acrobats perform.
a·maze·ment (ə māz′mənt) *noun.*

ambassador A person in the government who is sent to represent his country in a foreign country.
am·bas·sa·dor (am bas′ə dər) *noun, plural* **ambassadors.**

amber A hard yellow-orange or yellow-brown material that is used to make jewelry. Amber is a fossil that is formed from the resin of pine trees that grew millions of years ago.
am·ber (am′bər) *noun.*

ambiguous Having more than one meaning; not clear. The sentence "Tom told Bill that his dog bit the mailman" is *ambiguous.* We cannot be sure which boy the dog belongs to, because we do not know whether "his" refers to Tom or to Bill.
am·big·u·ous (am big′yo͞o əs) *adjective.*

ambition A strong desire to succeed at something. My sister's *ambition* is to become a doctor.
am·bi·tion (am bish′ən) *noun, plural* **ambitions.**

ambitious Having a strong desire to succeed at something; having ambition. The *ambitious* young worker hoped to be president of the company someday.
am·bi·tious (am bish′əs) *adjective.*

▲ The word **ambitious** goes back to a Latin word. In ancient Rome, men who wanted to be elected to a government job wore white robes. Sometimes a man would walk all around the city in his white robes so that people would see him and know he was running for office. The Latin word originally meant "going around trying to get votes."

ambulance A special kind of car that is used to carry hurt or sick people to a hospital. An ambulance has medical equipment to help people until they can get to the hospital.
am·bu·lance (am′byə ləns) *noun, plural* **ambulances.**

ambush A surprise attack by people who are hidden. The troops did not want to march through the forest because they were afraid of an *ambush* by enemy soldiers. *Noun.*
—To make a surprise attack from a hidden place. The soldiers *ambushed* the enemy near the river. *Verb.*
am·bush (am′boosh) *noun, plural* **ambushes;** *verb,* **ambushed, ambushing.**

ameba A very tiny animal. An ameba is so small that it can only be seen through a microscope. Its body is made up of only one cell. An ameba is always moving and changing shape. This word is also spelled **amoeba.**
a·me·ba (ə mē′bə) *noun, plural* **amebas.**

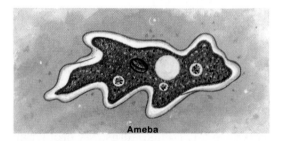
Ameba

amen May it be so. *Amen* is said after a prayer. People say *amen* to show that they agree with what has been said and hope it comes true.
a·men (ā′men′ *or* ä′men′) *interjection.*

amend To change something to make it better. In 1865 the Constitution was *amended* to outlaw slavery in the United States.
a·mend (ə mend′) *verb,* **amended, amending.**

amendment A change made to improve something. In 1920, women were given the right to vote by an *amendment* to the Constitution.
a·mend·ment (ə mend′mənt) *noun, plural* **amendments.**

amends To make amends. To make up for a wrong. He tried *to make amends* for his rude behavior by apologizing to his mother.
a·mends (ə mendz′) *noun plural.*

America 1. Another name for the **United States.** 2. Another name for **North America** or **South America.** 3. Another name for the **Western Hemisphere.** Look up those words for more information.
A·mer·i·ca (ə mer′i kə) *noun.*

▲ The name **America** comes from *Amerigo* Vespucci, an Italian explorer. It was once believed that he discovered America before Christopher Columbus.

American 1. Of the United States. The Fourth of July is an important date in *American* history. 2. Of North America or South America. The coyote is an *American* animal. *Adjective.*
—1. A person who was born or is living in the United States. 2. Any person who was born in North America or South America. *Noun.*
A·mer·i·can (ə mer′i kən) *adjective; noun, plural* **Americans.**

American English The language that is used by people who live in the United States.

▲ **American English** refers to the way the English language is used in the United States. We do not speak and write in exactly the same way as people who live in England. American English began to be used as soon as the first colonists from England arrived in the New World. For example, the word *canoe* had not been used in England. But it appears in a book written in 1608 by Captain John Smith. The colonists found many new things in America that they had not known about before. So they had to make up words that were not known in England in order to describe these things.

amiable Friendly and kind; good-natured. The owner of the bookstore was an *amiable* man who enjoyed having people come in just to look around and talk.
a·mi·a·ble (ā′mē ə bəl) *adjective.*

amid In the middle of. The house stood *amid* a grove of pine trees.
a·mid (ə mid′) *preposition.*

amigo A Spanish word that means "friend."
a·mi·go (ə mē′gō) *noun, plural* **amigos.**

amiss Not right or proper; wrong. I knew something was *amiss* when Bob said he didn't want to go to the baseball game.
a·miss (ə mis′) *adjective.*

ammonia A gas that is a mixture of nitrogen and hydrogen. It has no color but has a very sharp smell. A mixture of ammonia in water is used as a cleanser in many homes.
am·mo·nia (ə mōn′yə) *noun, plural* **ammonias.**

ammunition Bullets, shells, grenades, bombs, and other things that can be fired from guns or exploded in some other way.
am·mu·ni·tion (am′yə nish′ən) *noun.*

amnesia A loss of memory. Amnesia is caused by injury to a person's brain or by sickness or shock.
am·ne·sia (am nē′zhə) *noun.*

amoeba A very tiny animal. This word is usually spelled **ameba.** Look up **ameba** for more information.

among The campers pitched their tents *among* the trees. Elephants and whales are *among* the largest animals in the world. He divided the cake *among* his friends.
a·mong (ə mung′) *preposition.*

amount What something adds up to; total quantity. What is the *amount* of money you spent this week? We have a large *amount* of homework to do for tomorrow. *Noun.*
—To equal or add up to. The grocery bill *amounts* to thirty dollars. *Verb.*
a·mount (ə mount′) *noun, plural* **amounts;** *verb,* **amounted, amounting.**

amphibian 1. Any of a group of cold-blooded animals with backbones. Amphibians have moist skin without scales. They usually live in or near water. Frogs and toads are amphibians. 2. Any animal that lives both on the land and in the water. Alligators, seals, and otters are amphibians.
am·phib·i·an (am fib′ē ən) *noun, plural* **amphibians.**

at; āpe; cär; end; mē; it; īce; hot; ōld;
fôrk; wood; fool; oil; out; up; turn; sing;
thin; this; hw in white; zh in treasure.
ə stands for **a** in about, **e** in taken
i in pencil, **o** in lemon, and **u** in circus.

amphibious   Able to live on the land and in the water. The seal and the frog are *amphibious* animals.
   am·phib·i·ous (am fib′ē əs) *adjective.*

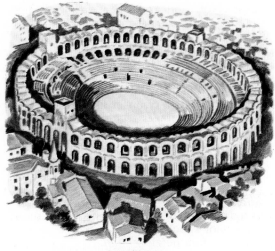
Amphitheater

amphitheater   A circular or oval building. An amphitheater has seats rising in rows around a central open space. Sports contests and plays take place in amphitheaters.
   am·phi·the·a·ter   (am′fə thē′ə tər)   *noun, plural* **amphitheaters.**

ample   Enough or more than enough. Our car has *ample* room for five people. We bought *ample* food for our camping trip.
   am·ple (am′pəl) *adjective,* **ampler, amplest.**

amplify   1. To add to; make larger. The teacher asked Ruth to *amplify* her short speech by giving more details. 2. To make sound stronger or louder. The microphone will *amplify* the speaker's voice so that the people in the back of the room can hear.
   am·pli·fy (am′plə fī′) *verb,* **amplified, amplifying.**

amputate   To cut off. The doctor had to *amputate* the soldier's wounded leg.
   am·pu·tate (am′pyə tāt′) *verb,* **amputated, amputating.**

amuse   To make pleased or happy. When something amuses us, we usually laugh or smile. The silly clowns at the circus *amused* the children.
   a·muse (ə myo͞oz′) *verb,* **amused, amusing.**

amusement   1. The condition of being amused and entertained. The magician did tricks for the *amusement* of the children. 2. Something that amuses or entertains. Fishing and playing baseball are Joe's favorite outdoor *amusements.*
   a·muse·ment (ə myo͞oz′mənt) *noun, plural* **amusements.**

an   He ate *an* apple. We saw *an* elephant at the zoo. She bought *an* umbrella. We will leave in *an* hour. ▲ **An** means the same thing as **a. An** is used instead of **a** in front of words that have *a, e, i, o,* or *u* as their first letter, or words that sound like they begin with one of these letters when you say them.
   an (an *or* ən) *indefinite article.*

anaconda   A very large snake found in South America. The anaconda can coil around and crush an animal to death.
   an·a·con·da   (an′ə kon′də)   *noun,   plural* **anacondas.**

Anaconda

analysis   A way of finding out what something is made of by separating it into parts. We made an *analysis* of the lake water and found it was very polluted.
   a·nal·y·sis (ə nal′ə sis) *noun, plural* **analyses.**

analyze   1. To find out what something is made of by separating it into parts. If we *analyze* air we find that it is made up mostly of nitrogen and oxygen. 2. To study something carefully. The detective *analyzed* the evidence in the robbery.
   an·a·lyze (an′əl īz′) *verb,* **analyzed, analyzing.**

anarchy   The condition of a country where there are no laws or government.
   an·ar·chy (an′ər kē) *noun.*

anatomy   1. A branch of science that deals with the structure of animals or plants. 2. The structure of an animal or plant or one of its parts. We are studying the *anatomy* of a frog in science class.
   a·nat·o·my (ə nat′ə mē) *noun, plural* **anatomies.**

ancestor   A person from whom one is descended. Your grandparents and great-grandparents are your *ancestors.*
   an·ces·tor (an′ses′tər) *noun, plural* **ancestors.**

anchor A very heavy piece of metal that keeps a boat or ship from drifting. *Noun.*
—To hold something in place with an anchor. We will *anchor* the boat while we fish. The sailboat *anchored* in the harbor. *Verb.*
 an·chor (ang′kər) *noun, plural* **anchors;** *verb,* **anchored, anchoring.**

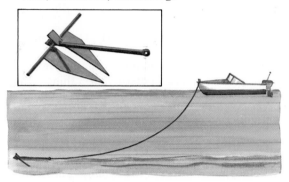

The **anchor** at the top is a close-up of the one in the water.

ancient Having to do with times very long ago; very old. The workers found the ruins of an *ancient* city when they were digging.
 an·cient (ān′shənt) *adjective.*

and He is tall *and* strong. Susan *and* Jane came to visit me. Two *and* two make four. Treat her fairly, *and* she'll be fair with you.
 and (and *or* ənd *or* ən) *conjunction.*

andiron Either of two metal supports that are used for holding wood in a fireplace.
 and·i·ron (and′ī-ərn) *noun, plural* **andirons.**

anecdote A short story about some event or incident. An anecdote is usually told by a speaker to amuse an audience or to make a point.
 an·ec·dote (an′ik-dōt′) *noun, plural* **anecdotes.**

Andirons

anemia A condition that occurs when the blood does not have enough red cells or when a person has lost blood. Often when a person has anemia, he is tired and weak.
 a·ne·mi·a (ə nē′mē ə) *noun.*

anemometer An instrument used to measure the speed of the wind.
 an·e·mom·e·ter (an′ə mom′ə tər) *noun, plural* **anemometers.**

anemone A plant that has white, red, or purple flowers that are shaped like cups.
 a·nem·o·ne (ə nem′ə nē) *noun, plural* **anemones.**

anesthetic A drug or other substance that causes a loss of feeling in the body. The doctor gave her an *anesthetic* before setting her broken arm.
 an·es·thet·ic (an′is thet′ik) *noun, plural* **anesthetics.**

angel **1.** A heavenly being who serves God as a helper and messenger. **2.** A person who is like an angel in goodness or beauty.
 an·gel (ān′jəl) *noun, plural* **angels.**

anger A strong feeling that a person has toward another person or a thing that opposes, insults, or hurts him. In a fit of *anger*, Joan threw a book at her brother. *Noun.*
—To make angry. Jack's rude answer *angered* his father. *Verb.*
 an·ger (ang′gər) *noun; verb,* **angered, angering.**

angle **1.** The space between two lines or surfaces that meet. When two walls meet in a corner they form an angle. **2.** A point of view. Jeff was having trouble solving the problem, so he tried to look at it from another *angle. Noun.*
—To move or bend at an angle. The road *angles* to the right as it goes up the mountain. *Verb.*
 an·gle (ang′gəl) *noun, plural* **angles;** *verb,* **angled, angling.**

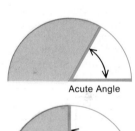

Acute Angle

Right Angle

angry **1.** Feeling or showing anger. Tom was *angry* with his sister for breaking his model airplane. **2.** Inflamed and painful. He had an *angry* sore on his knee.
 an·gry (ang′grē) *adjective,* **angrier, angriest.**

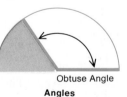

Obtuse Angle
Angles

at; āpe; cär; end; mē; it; īce; hot; ōld;
fôrk; wood; fool; oil; out; up; turn; sing;
thin; this; hw in white; zh in treasure.
ə stands for **a** in about, **e** in taken
i in pencil, **o** in lemon, and **u** in circus.

anguish   Very great suffering of the body or mind; agony. The child was in *anguish* over the death of his dog.
an·guish (ang′gwish) *noun.*

animal   Any living thing that is not a plant. A man, a cow, a bird, a fish, a snake, a fly, and a worm are all animals. Most animals can move about freely, use plants and other animals as food, and have sense organs.
an·i·mal (an′ə məl) *noun, plural* **animals.**

animosity   Deep hatred. The *animosity* between the two countries led to war.
an·i·mos·i·ty (an′ə mos′ə tē) *noun, plural* **animosities.**

ankle   The joint that connects the foot and the leg.
an·kle (ang′kəl) *noun, plural* **ankles.**

anklet   A short sock reaching just above the ankle.
an·klet (ang′klit) *noun, plural* **an·klets.**

Anklets

annex   To add or attach to something larger. The United States *annexed* the independent republic of Texas and made it a state in 1845. *Verb.*
—A building used as an addition to another building. The school was too small, so the school board built an *annex* for extra classrooms. *Noun.*
an·nex (ə neks′ *for verb;* an′eks *for noun*) *verb,* **annexed, annexing;** *noun, plural* **annexes.**

annihilate   To destroy completely; wipe out. The earthquake *annihilated* the town.
an·ni·hi·late (ə nī′ə lāt′) *verb,* **annihilated, annihilating.**

anniversary   The return each year of a special day. The *anniversary* of the day of your birth is your birthday. On February 15th the couple will celebrate the tenth *anniversary* of their wedding.
an·ni·ver·sa·ry (an′ə vur′sər ē) *noun, plural* **anniversaries.**

announce   To make something known. Mr. Jones *announced* that he would run for mayor in the next election.
an·nounce (ə nouns′) *verb,* **announced, announcing.**

announcement   A public notice that announces something. An *announcement* of the winners of the contest will be made soon.
an·nounce·ment (ə nouns′mənt) *noun, plural* **announcements.**

announcer   A person who announces something. The radio *announcer* gave the news every hour.
an·nounc·er (ə noun′sər) *noun, plural* **announcers.**

annoy   To bother or disturb. Her brother's teasing *annoys* her.
an·noy (ə noi′) *verb,* **annoyed, annoying.**

annoyance   **1.** A person or thing that bothers; nuisance. His constant complaining was an *annoyance* to her. **2.** The act of annoying or the state of being annoyed. Signs at the zoo warn against the *annoyance* of animals by visitors. Her angry remark showed her *annoyance* at his silly behavior.
an·noy·ance (ə noi′əns) *noun, plural* **annoyances.**

annual   **1.** Happening once a year; yearly. My father takes an *annual* vacation. The earth makes an *annual* orbit around the sun. **2.** Measured by the year. The doctor recorded the child's *annual* growth.
an·nu·al (an′yoo əl) *adjective.*

anoint   To put oil on during a religious ceremony. The priest *anointed* the king.
a·noint (ə noint′) *verb,* **anointed, anointing.**

anonymous   **1.** Written or done by someone whose name is not known. The police got an *anonymous* phone call telling them where the criminal was hiding. **2.** Keeping one's name a secret. The man who donated the money wanted to remain *anonymous.*
a·non·y·mous (ə non′ə məs) *adjective.*

another   I want *another* piece of cake. Joan saw *another* dress that she liked better than the first one. Tom finished his hamburger and then ordered *another.* That plan didn't work, so we'll use *another.*
an·oth·er (ə nuth′ər) *adjective; pronoun.*

answer   **1.** Something written, said, or done in reply. Did you get an *answer* to your letter? He would not give an *answer* to my question. **2.** The solution to a problem. To find the right *answer,* multiply by 12. *Noun.*
—**1.** To write or speak in reply to something. She *answered* her friend's long letter. **2.** To act in response to something. The two boys ran to *answer* the doorbell. **3.** To agree with; fit. That man *answers* to the description of the robber. *Verb.*
an·swer (an′sər) *noun, plural* **answers;** *verb;* **answered, answering.**

ant A small insect related to bees and wasps. Ants live together in large groups that are called colonies. ▲ Another word that sounds like this is **aunt**.
ant (ant) *noun, plural* **ants.**

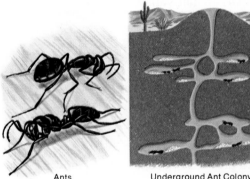

Ants   Underground Ant Colony

antagonism A strong feeling against a person or thing. After their quarrel, the two boys felt great *antagonism* toward each other.
an·tag·o·nism (an tag′ə niz′əm) *noun, plural* **antagonisms.**

antagonize To make someone feel dislike; irritate. The clerk's rude manner *antagonized* many customers.
an·tag·o·nize (an tag′ə nīz′) *verb,* **antagonized, antagonizing.**

Antarctica The continent at the South Pole. Antarctica is almost completely covered with ice all year long.
Ant·arc·ti·ca (ant ärk′ti kə *or* ant är′ti kə) *noun.*

Antarctic Ocean The water around Antarctica which is made up of the most southern parts of the Atlantic, Pacific, and Indian Oceans.
Ant·arc·tic (ant ärk′tik *or* ant är′tik).

anteater A toothless animal with a long, narrow head, long sticky tongue, and strong front claws. The anteater claws into ant hills and uses its tongue to capture ants and other insects for food.
ant·eat·er (ant′ē′tər) *noun, plural* **anteaters.**

Anteater

antelope A slender, swift animal that has long horns. Antelopes look like deer, but they are related to goats.
an·te·lope (ant′əl ōp′) *noun, plural* **antelopes.**

Antelope

antenna 1. A metal rod or wire used to send out or receive radio and television signals; aerial. 2. One of a pair of long, thin feelers on the head of an insect or a lobster.
an·ten·na (an ten′ə) *noun, plural* **antennas** (*definition 1*) or **antennae** (*definition 2*).

anthem A song of gladness, praise, or patriotism. The national *anthem* of the United States is "The Star-Spangled Banner."
an·them (an′thəm) *noun, plural* **anthems.**

anther The part of the stamen of a flower that contains the pollen.
an·ther (an′thər) *noun, plural* **anthers.**

anthology A book or other collection of poems, stories, or articles.
an·thol·o·gy (an thol′ə jē) *noun, plural* **anthologies.**

anthracite A very hard, shiny black coal that burns with a low, smokeless flame. This kind of coal is sometimes called **hard coal.**
an·thra·cite (an′thrə sīt′) *noun.*

anti- A *prefix* that means "opposed to or against." *Antiwar* means "opposed to war."

at; āpe; cär; end; mē; it; īce; hot; ōld;
fôrk; wood; fool; oil; out; up; turn; sing;
thin; this; hw in white; zh in treasure.
ə stands for a in about, e in taken
i in pencil, o in lemon, and u in circus.

antibiotic   A substance that is produced by molds or bacteria. Antibiotics are used in medicine to kill or slow the growth of germs that cause disease.
  an·ti·bi·ot·ic (an′tē bī ot′ik)   *noun, plural* **antibiotics.**

antibody   A substance produced by the blood that destroys or weakens germs. Antibodies help protect the body against certain diseases.
  an·ti·bod·y (an′ti bod′ē)   *noun, plural* **antibodies.**

anticipate   To look forward to; expect. I do not *anticipate* any trouble.
  an·tic·i·pate (an tis′ə pāt′)   *verb,* **anticipated, anticipating.**

anticipation   The act of anticipating; expectation. In *anticipation* of a hot summer ahead, we bought an air conditioner.
  an·tic·i·pa·tion   (an tis′ə pā′shən)   *noun, plural* **anticipations.**

antidote   A medicine that works against the effects of a poison. After the baby swallowed the poison, the doctor gave him an *antidote* to make him well.
  an·ti·dote (an′ti dōt′)   *noun, plural* **antidotes.**

antique   Of times long ago. We went to an exhibit of *antique* automobiles. *Adjective.*
—Something made very long ago. The museum has *antiques* from the time of colonial America. *Noun.*
  an·tique (an tēk′)   *adjective; noun, plural* **antiques.**

antiseptic   A substance that kills germs or stops their growth. Alcohol and iodine are antiseptics.
  an·ti·sep·tic (an′ti sep′tik)   *noun, plural* **antiseptics.**

antitoxin   An antibody produced by the body that protects a person from a particular disease.
  an·ti·tox·in (an′ti tok′sin)   *noun, plural* **antitoxins.**

antler   One of the two branched horns of a deer, elk, or moose. Antlers are shed each year and grow back again the next year.
  ant·ler (ant′lər) *noun, plural* **antlers.**

antonym   A word that has the opposite meaning of another word. *Sweet* and *sour, up* and *down,* and *hot* and *cold* are antonyms.
  an·to·nym (an′tə nim′) *noun, plural* **antonyms.**

Antlers

anvil   An iron or steel block on which metals are hammered into shape. Metals are usually softened by heating before they are placed on an anvil.
  an·vil   (an′vəl) *noun, plural* **anvils.**

Anvil

anxiety   **1.** A feeling of fearful worry or nervousness about what may happen. The mother was filled with *anxiety* because her child was lost. **2.** A strong desire; eagerness. His *anxiety* to please his teacher made him work very hard at school.
  anx·i·e·ty (ang zī′ə tē) *noun, plural* **anxieties.**

anxious   **1.** Nervous, worried, or fearful about what may happen. The mother was *anxious* about her children's safety when they were out after dark. **2.** Wanting something eagerly. The boy was *anxious* to make friends at his new school.
  anx·ious (angk′shəs) *adjective.*

any   Take *any* seat. Pick *any* book you want. Did you buy *any* apples? *Any* child can do this problem. He runs faster than *any* of the other boys. Stop before you go *any* farther.
  an·y (en′ē) *adjective; pronoun; adverb.*

anybody   Has *anybody* seen Jack?
  an·y·bod·y (en′ē bod′ē) *pronoun.*

anyhow   I didn't want to go to the movies *anyhow.* Our best player was hurt, but we won the game *anyhow.*
  an·y·how (en′ē hou′) *adverb.*

anyone   *Anyone* who lives in this town can go swimming in the town pool.
  an·y·one (en′ē wun′) *pronoun.*

anyplace   I couldn't find the book *anyplace.*
  an·y·place (en′ē plās′) *adverb.*

anything   I'll do *anything* you ask me to. Frank isn't *anything* like his brother.
  an·y·thing (en′ē thing′) *pronoun; adverb.*

anytime   You may leave for the beach *anytime* you want to.
  an·y·time (en′ē tīm′) *adverb.*

anyway   It's raining, but we are going for a walk *anyway.*
  an·y·way (en′ē wā′) *adverb.*

anywhere   Just put the books down *anywhere.*
  an·y·where (en′ē hwer′) *adverb.*

aorta The main artery of the body. The aorta carries blood from the upper left side of the heart to all parts of the body except the lungs.
a·or·ta (ā ôr′tə) *noun, plural* **aortas.**

apart **1.** Away from one another. The girls lived two miles *apart*. The trains left three hours *apart*. **2.** To pieces. The mechanic took the engine *apart* to find out what was wrong with it.
a·part (ə pärt′) *adverb.*
apart from. Besides. *Apart from* the bad weather, we had a good vacation.

apartment A room or set of rooms to live in. Apartments are usually in a large building.
a·part·ment (ə pärt′mənt) *noun, plural* **apartments.**

apathy A lack of interest or concern; indifference. We listened to the boring speaker with *apathy*.
ap·a·thy (ap′ə thē) *noun.*

ape A large animal that has no tail. An ape is a kind of monkey. It is able to stand and walk almost as straight as a person can. Chimpanzees, gorillas, and orangutans are all types of apes. *Noun.*
—To imitate someone. My brother Chuck is always *aping* people to make his friends laugh. *Verb.*
ape (āp) *noun, plural* **apes;** *verb,* **aped, aping.**

aphid A small insect that lives by sucking juices from plants.
a·phid (ā′fid *or* af′id) *noun, plural* **aphids.**

Aphid

apiece For each one; each. These candy bars are fifteen cents *apiece*. Mother gave the boys who raked up the leaves five dollars *apiece* for their work.
a·piece (ə pēs′) *adverb.*

apologize To say one is sorry; make an apology. I *apologized* to my sister when I broke her toy.
a·pol·o·gize (ə pol′ə jīz′) *verb,* **apologized, apologizing.**

apology A statement that one is sorry for having done something that is wrong or that hurts another person. Please accept my *apology* for being late.
a·pol·o·gy (ə pol′ə jē) *noun, plural* **apologies.**

Apostle An early follower of Christ. There were twelve Apostles chosen by Christ to preach the gospel.
A·pos·tle (ə pos′əl) *noun, plural* **Apostles.**

apostrophe A punctuation mark (') used in the following ways: **1.** To show that a letter or letters have been left out in a word or words. For example, "you're" means "you are." The apostrophe has taken the place of the *a* in *are*. **2.** To show that something belongs to a person or thing. "Paul's dog" means "the dog that belongs to Paul." **3.** To show the plural of letters or numbers. She got four *A's* on her report card.
a·pos·tro·phe (ə pos′trə fē) *noun, plural* **apostrophes.**

apothecary A person who makes and sells medicine; druggist.
a·poth·e·car·y (ə poth′ə ker′ē) *noun, plural* **apothecaries.**

appall To fill with horror or terror; shock. We were *appalled* by the news of the airplane crash.
ap·pall (ə pôl′) *verb,* **appalled, appalling.**

apparatus Anything that is used for a particular reason. Gymnasium equipment, chemistry sets, tools, and machinery are all different kinds of apparatus.
ap·pa·rat·us (ap′ə rat′əs *or* ap′ə rā′təs) *noun, plural* **apparatus** or **apparatuses.**

apparel Clothing; clothes. That store sells women's and children's *apparel*.
ap·par·el (ə par′əl) *noun.*

apparent **1.** Easily seen or understood. His black eye was *apparent* even though he wore dark glasses. It was *apparent* to us that she was telling the truth about what happened. **2.** Seeming real or true even though it may not be. The *apparent* size of a star in the sky is much smaller than its real size.
ap·par·ent (ə par′ənt) *adjective.*

apparently As far as one can tell; seemingly. *Apparently*, it is going to rain.
ap·par·ent·ly (ə par′ənt lē) *adverb.*

appeal **1.** A call for help or sympathy. Each year that church makes an *appeal* for money to aid the poor. **2.** The power to interest. Sports have a great *appeal* to many boys and girls. **3.** A request to have a case heard again by a higher court of law or judge. *Noun.*
—**1.** To call for help; request strongly. The people of the town *appealed* to the governor

at; āpe; cär; end; mē; it; īce; hot; ōld; fôrk; wood; fool; oil; out; up; turn; sing; thin; this; hw in white; zh in treasure.
ə stands for a in about, e in taken
i in pencil, o in lemon, and u in circus.

for help after the flood. **2.** To be attractive or interesting. Camping out in the woods does not *appeal* to her. **3.** To ask to have a case heard again before a higher court of law or judge. *Verb.*
　ap·peal (ə pēl′) *noun, plural* **appeals;** *verb,* **appealed, appealing.**

appear **1.** To come into sight; be seen. The snowy mountain peaks *appeared* in the distance. **2.** To seem. He *appeared* interested in the game, but he was really bored. **3.** To come before the public. That actor has often *appeared* on television.
　ap·pear (ə pēr′) *verb,* **appeared, appearing.**

appearance **1.** The act of appearing or coming into sight. The sun made a sudden *appearance* through the clouds. **2.** Outward look. In spite of his troubles, he gave the *appearance* of being happy. **3.** The act of coming before the public. That was her first *appearance* in the movies.
　ap·pear·ance (ə pēr′əns) *noun, plural* **appearances.**

appease To satisfy or calm. The owner of the business *appeased* the striking workers by giving in to their demands for more pay.
　ap·pease (ə pēz′) *verb,* **appeased, appeasing.**

appendicitis An inflammation of the appendix, that causes swelling and bad pain.
　ap·pen·di·ci·tis (ə pen′də sī′tis) *noun.*

appendix **1.** A thin growth shaped like a bag or pouch. It is attached to the large intestine. **2.** A part added to the end of a book. An appendix gives more facts about the subject of the book.
　ap·pen·dix (ə pen′diks) *noun, plural* **appendixes** or **appendices.**

appetite **1.** A desire for food. When Bill was sick he had no *appetite* at all. **2.** Any strong desire. Jim has an *appetite* for adventure and excitement.
　ap·pe·tite (ap′ə tīt′) *noun, plural* **appetites.**

Appendix

applaud To show approval or enjoyment by clapping the hands. The children *applauded* the clown's funny tricks.
　ap·plaud (ə plôd′) *verb,* **applauded, applauding.**

applause Approval or enjoyment shown by

clapping the hands. Everyone joined in the *applause* at the end of the magician's act.
　ap·plause (ə plôz′) *noun.*

apple A roundish fruit with red, yellow, or green skin. Apples have firm white flesh surrounding a core with small seeds.
　ap·ple (ap′əl) *noun, plural* **apples.**

Blossom

Fruit

Apple Tree

appliance A small machine that has a particular use. Most appliances are found in the home. Refrigerators, washing machines, toasters, and irons are appliances.
　ap·pli·ance (ə plī′əns) *noun, plural* **appliances.**

application **1.** The act of putting something to use. The *application* of scientific knowledge made it possible for men to walk on the moon. **2.** The act of putting something on. The *application* of paint made the old house look like new. **3.** A request. He made an *application* for the job of delivery boy.
　ap·pli·ca·tion (ap′lə kā′shən) *noun, plural* **applications.**

apply **1.** To use. He had to *apply* force to open the locked door. **2.** To put on. They *applied* two coats of paint to the wall. **3.** To ask or request something. He *applied* for a summer job at the grocery store. **4.** To devote oneself with effort. She tried to *apply* herself to her homework. **5.** To be suitable or have to do with. The law against speeding *applies* to all drivers.
　ap·ply (ə plī′) *verb,* **applied, applying.**

appoint To decide on something; select. The judge *appointed* the date of the trial. The President *appointed* Judge Smith to the Supreme Court.
　ap·point (ə point′) *verb,* **appointed, appointing.**

appointment **1.** The act of naming someone to an office or job. When the principal retired, his position was filled by the *appointment* of Mrs. Brown. **2.** An agreement to meet or see someone at a certain time and place. I have an *appointment* with the doctor at ten o'clock.

ap·point·ment (ə point′mənt) *noun, plural* **appointments.**

appraise To estimate or set the value of something. Mother asked the jeweler to *appraise* Grandmother's diamond ring because she wanted to sell it.

ap·praise (ə prāz′) *verb,* **appraised, appraising.**

appreciate **1.** To recognize the value of something. Everyone *appreciates* loyal friends. **2.** To be grateful for something. I *appreciate* your running these errands for me.

ap·pre·ci·ate (ə prē′shē āt′) *verb,* **appreciated, appreciating.**

appreciation **1.** The act of recognizing the value of something. The boy had an *appreciation* of good music. **2.** A being grateful or thankful. He wrote her a note of thanks in *appreciation* for her present.

ap·pre·ci·a·tion (ə prē′shē ā′shən) *noun.*

apprehend To capture and take to jail. The police *apprehended* the robber as he was running from the bank.

ap·pre·hend (ap′ri hend′) *verb,* **apprehended, apprehending.**

apprehension **1.** A fear of what may happen. The thought of going to the dentist filled me with *apprehension.* **2.** Arrest or capture. The chase ended with the *apprehension* of the criminal.

ap·pre·hen·sion (ap′ri hen′shən) *noun, plural* **apprehensions.**

apprentice A person who works for a skilled worker in order to learn a trade or skill. In earlier times, an apprentice worked for someone for a certain period of time in return for his training.

ap·pren·tice (ə pren′tis) *noun, plural* **apprentices.**

approach **1.** To come near or close to. The car *approached* at a high speed. **2.** To go to with a plan or request. He *approached* his father with the hope of getting a higher allowance. *Verb.*
—**1.** The act of coming closer. I always look forward to the *approach* of summer vacation. **2.** A way of doing something. His *approach* to training his dog was to be very patient. **3.** A way of reaching a place or person. The only *approach* to the town was blocked by snow. *Noun.*

ap·proach (ə prōch′) *verb,* **approached, approaching;** *noun, plural* **approaches.**

appropriate In keeping with a situation; correct or suitable. Warm clothes are *appropriate* for a cold day. *Adjective.*
—To set apart for a particular use. The principal *appropriated* money for new band uniforms. *Verb.*

ap·pro·pri·ate (ə prō′prē it *for adjective;* ə prō′prē āt′ *for verb*) *adjective; verb,* **appropriated, appropriating.**

approval **1.** A good opinion; approving. The mayor's decision was looked on with *approval* by most people. **2.** Permission or consent. We need Father's *approval* before we can use his power tools.

ap·prov·al (ə proo′vəl) *noun, plural* **approvals.**

approve **1.** To have or give a good opinion of something. My mother doesn't *approve* of my staying up late on school nights. **2.** To consent to something. The town *approved* the school budget for the new year.

ap·prove (ə proov′) *verb,* **approved, approving.**

approximate Nearly correct or exact. The *approximate* cost of the radio is twenty-five dollars. *Adjective.*
—To come near or close to; estimate. Dad asked the man to *approximate* the cost of the paint job. *Verb.*

ap·prox·i·mate (ə prok′sə mit *for adjective;* ə prok′sə māt′ *for verb*) *adjective; verb,* **approximated, approximating.**

approximately Nearly; about. We had *approximately* four inches of snow yesterday.

ap·prox·i·mate·ly (ə prok′sə mit lē) *adverb.*

apricot A roundish, orange-colored fruit that looks like a small peach. Apricots grow on trees in warm climates.

a·pri·cot (ā′prə kot′ *or* ap′rə kot′) *noun, plural* **apricots.**

April The fourth month of the year. April has thirty days.

A·pril (ā′prəl) *noun.*

Apricots

at; āpe; cär; end; mē; it; īce; hot; ōld; fôrk; wood; fool; oil; out; up; turn; sing; thin; this; hw in white; zh in treasure.
ə stands for a in about, e in taken i in pencil, o in lemon, and u in circus.

▲ **April** was named after the Greek goddess of love. This month is in the spring, and many people think of spring as a time of love.

apron A garment worn over the front of the body to protect one's clothing. Cooks and butchers wear aprons.
a·pron (ā′prən) *noun,* *plural* **aprons.**

apt 1. Likely; inclined. You're *apt* to hurt yourself if you're not more careful when you're riding your bicycle. 2. Quick to learn. He is an *apt* student in mathematics.
apt (apt) *adjective.*

aptitude 1. A natural ability or talent. It is often said that a person is born with an aptitude for a certain thing. Bill has an *aptitude* for music. 2. Quickness in learning. Joan was a student of great *aptitude.*
ap·ti·tude (ap′tə tōōd′ *or* ap′tə tyōōd′) *noun,* *plural* **aptitudes.**

aqualung A device used by a person to breathe underwater.
aq·ua·lung (ak′wə lung′) *noun, plural* **aqualungs.**

Apron

Aquarium

aquarium 1. A tank, bowl, or other container in which fish, water animals, and water plants are kept. An aquarium is usually made of glass or some other material that one can see through. 2. A building that holds collections of fish, water animals, and water plants.

People visit an aquarium for pleasure or to study the animals and plants kept there.
a·quar·i·um (ə kwer′ē əm) *noun, plural* **aquariums.**

aqueduct A pipe or other channel that carries water over a long distance.
aq·ue·duct (ak′wə dukt′) *noun, plural* **aqueducts.**

Arab 1. A member of a people who live in southwestern Asia and northern Africa. 2. A person who was born or is living in Arabia. *Noun.*
—Of the Arabs or Arabia. *Adjective.*
Ar·ab (ar′əb) *noun, plural* **Arabs;** *adjective.*

Arabia A large peninsula in southwestern Asia.
A·ra·bi·a (ə rā′bē ə) *noun.*

Arabian Having to do with Arabia or the people of Arabia. *Adjective.*
—A person who was born or is living in Arabia. *Noun.*
A·ra·bi·an (ə rā′bē ən) *adjective; noun, plural* **Arabians.**

Arabic Having to do with the Arabs or their language. *Adjective.*
—The language of the Arabs. *Noun.*
Ar·a·bic (ar′ə bik) *adjective; noun.*

Arabic numerals The number symbols 1, 2, 3, 4, 5, 6, 7, 8, 9, and 0. This numbering system is believed to have been developed in India about 2000 years ago. The numerals are called "Arabic" because they were introduced to Western Europe by the Arabs.

arbitrary Based on a person's own opinion or wishes rather than on a rule or law. A judge cannot make *arbitrary* decisions; they must be made according to the law.
ar·bi·trar·y (är′bə trer′ē) *adjective.*

arbitrate To settle a dispute or disagreement for someone else. The umpires *arbitrated* the argument between the two teams.
ar·bi·trate (är′bə trāt′) *verb,* **arbitrated, arbitrating.**

arbitration A way of settling a dispute or disagreement by agreeing to accept the decision of a person or group that is not involved.
ar·bi·tra·tion (är′bə trā′shən) *noun.*

arbor A place that is covered and shaded by trees or shrubs, or by vines growing on a frame. An arbor is usually found in a garden.
ar·bor (är′bər) *noun, plural* **arbors.**

arc 1. An unbroken curved line between any two points on a circle. 2. Any line curving in this way. The rainbow formed a colorful *arc* in the sky. ▲ Another word that sounds like this is **ark.**
arc (ärk) *noun, plural* **arcs.**

arch **1.** A curved structure that is built to support the weight of the material above it. Four *arches* supported the bridge across the river. **2.** Anything like an arch in shape or use. The curved part of the foot between the toes and the heel is called the arch. *Noun.*
—To form in an arch. The cat *arched* its back in anger. *Verb.*
arch (ärch) *noun, plural* **arches;** *verb,* **arched, arching.**

Arch

archaeology The study of the way man lived a very long time ago. The people who study archaeology are called **archaeologists.** They dig up the remains of ancient cities and towns and then study the tools, weapons, pottery, and other things they find.
ar·chae·ol·o·gy (är′kē ol′ə jē) *noun.*

archbishop A bishop of the highest rank.
arch·bish·op (ärch′bish′əp) *noun, plural* **archbishops.**

archer A person who shoots with a bow and arrow.
arch·er (är′chər) *noun, plural* **archers.**

archery The skill or sport of shooting with a bow and arrow.
arch·er·y (är′chər ē) *noun.*

Archery

archipelago **1.** A large group of islands. **2.** A large body of water having many islands in it.
ar·chi·pel·a·go (är′kə pel′ə gō′) *noun, plural* **archipelagos** or **archipelagoes.**

architect A person whose work is to design and draw plans for buildings. He then sees that the buildings are built according to his designs and plans. The *architect* made plans for building a large shopping center.
ar·chi·tect (är′kə tekt′) *noun, plural* **architects.**

architecture **1.** The science, art, or profession of designing and planning buildings. **2.** A particular style or method of building. Mark studied Greek *architecture* in his art class at college.
ar·chi·tec·ture (är′kə tek′chər) *noun.*

arctic At or near the North Pole; very far north. *Adjective.*
—the **Arctic.** An ice-covered region surrounding the North Pole. *Noun.*
arc·tic (ärk′tik *or* är′tik) *adjective; noun.*

Arctic Ocean The ocean surrounding the North Pole.

are You *are* late. We *are* glad you could come.
are (är) *verb.*

area **1.** The amount of surface within a given boundary. The *area* of our yard is 400 square feet. **2.** A particular space, region, or section. We eat in the dining *area* of the house. My aunt lives in the farming *area* of the state. **3.** A field of interest or study. My sister is going to study in the *area* of science at college.
ar·e·a (er′ē ə) *noun, plural* **areas.**

area code A set of three numbers that stands for one of the areas into which the United States is divided for telephone service. You dial these three numbers before the local number when you call from one area to another.

arena A space that is used for sports contests or entertainment. In the arenas of ancient Rome, men fought with lions. Today, circuses and sports events take place in arenas.
a·re·na (ə rē′nə) *noun, plural* **arenas.**

at; āpe; cär; end; mē; it; īce; hot; ōld; fôrk; wood; fōōl; oil; out; up; turn; sing; thin; this; hw in white; zh in treasure.
ə stands for a in about, e in taken i in pencil, o in lemon, and u in circus.

▲ The word **arena** comes from a Latin word that means "sand." The ancient Romans covered the ground in their arenas with sand.

aren't Why *aren't* you going with us? These shoes *aren't* new.
aren't (ärnt *or* är′ənt) contraction for "are not."

argue **1.** To have a disagreement; quarrel. My sister and brother often *argue* over who should walk the dog. **2.** To give reasons for or against something. He *argued* against going to the beach because it looked like rain.
ar·gue (är′gyōō) *verb,* **argued, arguing.**

argument **1.** A discussion of something by people who do not agree. They had an *argument* over whose turn it was to wash the dishes. **2.** A reason or reasons given for or against something. His *argument* for getting a bicycle was that he needed it for his job of delivering newspapers.
ar·gu·ment (är′gyə mənt) *noun, plural* **arguments.**

arid Getting very little rain; dry. A desert is an *arid* region.
ar·id (ar′id) *adjective.*

arise **1.** To get up; stand up. The audience *arose* and applauded at the end of the play. **2.** To move upward; rise. A mist is beginning to *arise* from the lake. **3.** To come into being; appear. Questions often *arise* in our minds as we read about new things.
a·rise (ə rīz′) *verb,* **arose, arisen, arising.**

aristocracy **1.** A class of persons who are born into a high social position; nobility. Kings, queens, princes, and dukes are members of the aristocracy. **2.** Any group of persons who are thought to be outstanding because of wealth, intelligence, or ability.
ar·is·toc·ra·cy (ar′is tok′rə sē) *noun, plural* **aristocracies.**

aristocrat **1.** A person who belongs to the aristocracy. **2.** A person who has the tastes and attitudes of the aristocracy. He was an *aristocrat* in his taste for expensive things.
a·ris·to·crat (ə ris′tə krat′) *noun, plural* **aristocrats.**

arithmetic **1.** The science of figuring with numbers. When you study arithmetic you learn how to add, subtract, multiply, and divide. **2.** The act of adding, subtracting, multiplying, or dividing. You must have made a mistake in your *arithmetic*.
a·rith·me·tic (ə rith′mə tik′) *noun.*

Arizona A state in the southwestern United States. Its capital is Phoenix.
Ar·i·zo·na (ar′ə zō′nə) *noun.*

▲ **Arizona** comes from an Indian word that means "a place where there is a little spring." This was the name of a part of the state where explorers found silver. The name became famous, and people began to use it for the whole area that became the state of Arizona.

ark The large ship that Noah built to save himself, his family, and two members of every kind of animal from the flood God sent to punish mankind. ▲ Another word that sounds like this is **arc**.
ark (ärk) *noun.*

Arkansas A state in the south-central United States. Its capital is Little Rock.
Ar·kan·sas (är′kən sô′) *noun.*

▲ **Arkansas** was an Indian name for a tribe that lived near the Arkansas River. It means "people who live down the river." French explorers used the word for the river near this tribe's village, and later it was used for the state.

arm¹ **1.** The part of the body between the shoulder and the wrist. **2.** Anything shaped or used like an arm. The *arms* of the green chair are loose. The *arm* of a phonograph contains the needle that touches the record.
arm (ärm) *noun, plural* **arms.**

arm² Any weapon. A gun is an arm. *Noun.* —**1.** To supply with weapons. The troops *armed* themselves for the battle. **2.** To supply with anything that protects or strengthens. A porcupine is *armed* with quills. *Verb.*
arm (ärm) *noun, plural* **arms;** *verb,* **armed, arming.**

armada A large group of warships. The Spanish *Armada* was defeated by the English in 1588.
ar·ma·da (är mä′də) *noun, plural* **armadas.**

armadillo A small, insect-eating animal that digs into the ground looking for food. It has a hard bony shell, a long snout, strong, sharp claws, and a long tail. The armadillo is

Armadillo

found in South America and parts of the southern United States.

ar·ma·dil·lo (är'mə dil'ō) *noun, plural* **armadillos.**

▲ The word **armadillo** comes from a Spanish word that means "little armored animal." Spanish explorers who found this animal in America thought that the armadillo's hard shell looked like armor.

---

armament The military forces, equipment, and supplies of a country.

ar·ma·ment (är'mə mənt) *noun, plural* **armaments.**

armchair A chair with parts on both sides that support a person's arms or elbows.

arm·chair (ärm'cher') *noun, plural* **armchairs.**

armistice A temporary stop in fighting agreed on by those who are fighting; truce.

ar·mi·stice (är'mi stis) *noun, plural* **armistices.**

Armor

armor **1.** A covering for the body, usually made from metal. In former times it was worn for protection during battle. **2.** Any protective covering. The metal plates on a tank or warship are armor. The hard shell of an armadillo is armor.

ar·mor (är'mər) *noun.*

armored Protected or equipped with armor. The President rode in an *armored* car so that he couldn't be hurt.

ar·mored (är'mərd) *adjective.*

armory A place where weapons are kept.

ar·mor·y (är'mər ē) *noun, plural* **armories.**

armpit The hollow part under the arm at the shoulder.

arm·pit (ärm'pit') *noun, plural* **armpits.**

arms Weapons. The defeated troops laid down their *arms.*

arms (ärmz) *noun plural.*

army **1.** A large, organized group of soldiers who are armed and trained for fighting on land. **2.** Any large group of people or things. An *army* of teenagers came to the concert to hear the famous singing group.

ar·my (är'mē) *noun, plural* **armies.**

aroma A pleasant or agreeable smell; fragrance. The cookies we were baking gave off a delicious *aroma.*

a·ro·ma (ə rō'mə) *noun, plural* **aromas.**

arose I *arose* at seven o'clock this morning. Look up **arise** for more information.

a·rose (ə rōz') *verb.*

around She wore a belt *around* her waist. We walked *around* the block. The horses wandered *around* in the field. I'll meet you *around* ten o'clock. The wheel spun *around* and *around.* We spread the news *around* so all our friends would know.

a·round (ə round') *preposition; adverb.*

arouse To excite or stir up. Her rudeness *aroused* everyone's anger.

a·rouse (ə rouz') *verb,* **aroused, arousing.**

arrange **1.** To put in some kind of order. The teacher *arranged* the names of the children in alphabetical order. **2.** To prepare for; plan. Who *arranged* this meeting? Can you *arrange* to meet us at the dance tonight? **3.** To adapt or fit a piece of music for instruments or voices for which it was not originally written.

ar·range (ə rānj') *verb,* **arranged, arranging.**

arrangement **1.** The act of putting in order. The *arrangement* of the books took two hours. **2.** Something arranged. They made a flower *arrangement* for the party. **3. arrangements.** Plans or preparations. We made *arrangements* for Joan's surprise birthday party.

ar·range·ment (ə rānj'mənt) *noun, plural* **arrangements.**

array An orderly grouping, arrangement, or display. This store carries a wide *array* of

---

at; āpe; cär; end; mē; it; īce; hot; ōld; fôrk; wood; fo͞ol; oil; out; up; turn; sing; thin; this; hw in white; zh in treasure. ə stands for a in about, e in taken i in pencil, o in lemon, and u in circus.

toys and games. The movie featured an *array* of famous stars. *Noun.*

—To put in order. The officer *arrayed* the troops for battle. *Verb.*

ar·ray (ə rā′) *noun, plural* **arrays;** *verb,* **arrayed, arraying.**

arrest **1.** To seize and hold by authority of the law. The policemen *arrested* the robber. **2.** To stop or hold. We hope to *arrest* pollution in this country. *Verb.*

—The act of seizing by authority of the law. There were ten *arrests* in the city yesterday. *Noun.*

ar·rest (ə rest′) *verb,* **arrested, arresting;** *noun, plural* **arrests.**

arrival **1.** The act of arriving. The reporters were waiting for the *arrival* of the President. **2.** A person or thing that arrives or has arrived. New *arrivals* waited in line for their baggage at the airport.

ar·riv·al (ə rī′vəl) *noun, plural* **arrivals.**

arrive To come to a place. We will *arrive* in Florida at midnight. I *arrived* at school on time. Has the jury in that case *arrived* at a decision yet?

ar·rive (ə rīv′) *verb,* **arrived, arriving.**

arrogant Having or showing too much pride or confidence. An arrogant person does not have any respect for other people or their opinions. The boy was quite *arrogant* because his family was very wealthy.

ar·ro·gant (ar′ə gənt) *adjective.*

arrow **1.** A slender stick that has a sharp point at one end and feathers at the other. An arrow is made to be shot from a bow. **2.** Something that is like an arrow. The road sign had an *arrow* to show which way traffic was supposed to go.

ar·row (ar′ō) *noun, plural* **arrows.**

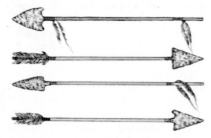

American Indian Arrows

arrowhead The pointed tip or head of an arrow.

ar·row·head (ar′ō hed′) *noun, plural* **arrowheads.**

arsenal A place for making or storing weapons and ammunition.

ar·se·nal (är′sə nəl) *noun, plural* **arsenals.**

arsenic A white, tasteless, very poisonous substance. It is used in rat, insect, and weed poisons.

ar·se·nic (är′sə nik) *noun.*

arson The crime of purposely setting fire to a building or other property.

ar·son (är′sən) *noun.*

art **1.** Painting, drawing, and sculpture. We study *art* at school. **2.** The works made by artists; paintings, drawings, and sculptures. We went to an exhibit of American Indian *art* at the museum. **3.** The making or doing of anything that has beauty or meaning. Poetry, music, and ballet dancing are *arts.* **4.** A special skill, ability, or craft. She has an *art* for making people feel at ease. The *art* of cooking came easily to him.

art (ärt) *noun, plural* **arts.**

artery **1.** One of the tubes that carry blood away from the heart to all parts of the body. **2.** A main road or channel. This highway is the major *artery* between the two cities.

ar·ter·y (är′tər ē) *noun, plural* **arteries.**

arthritis A painful inflammation of a joint or joints of the body.

ar·thri·tis (är thrī′tis) *noun.*

Artichoke

artichoke A plant like a thistle, with large leaves, greenish-yellow flower heads, and purple flowers. The flower head is cooked and eaten as a vegetable.

ar·ti·choke (är′tə chōk′) *noun, plural* **artichokes.**

article **1.** A composition written for a newspaper, magazine, or book. The scientist wrote an *article* on space travel for the encyclopedia. **2.** A particular thing or object; item. Several *articles* were stolen from the house. She bought some new *articles* of

clothing for the camping trip. **3.** A separate section of a formal document. There are articles in treaties, constitutions, and contracts. *Article* I of the United States Constitution has to do with the powers of Congress. **4.** The words *a, an,* and *the. A* and *an* are indefinite articles. *The* is a definite article.
 ar·ti·cle (är′ti kəl) *noun, plural* **articles.**

articulate Able to express oneself clearly. The professor was very *articulate* about the subject of his new book. *Adjective.*
—To express oneself clearly. He was so upset that he could not *articulate* his feelings about the argument. *Verb.*
 ar·tic·u·late (är tik′yə lit *for adjective;* är-tik′yə lāt′ *for verb*) *adjective; verb,* **articulated, articulating.**

artificial **1.** Made by people, not by nature; not natural. An electric lamp gives *artificial* light. The *artificial* flowers were made of plastic. **2.** Not sincere or true. His show of interest in the game was *artificial* because all sports really bored him.
 ar·ti·fi·cial (är′tə fish′əl) *adjective.*

artificial respiration The forcing of air into and out of the lungs of a person who has stopped breathing. This helps the person to start breathing normally again. Artificial respiration is used to save people who have almost drowned.

artillery **1.** Large, heavy firearms. Cannons are artillery. **2.** The part of the army that uses such firearms.
 ar·til·ler·y (är til′ər ē) *noun.*

artisan A person who is skilled in a particular craft; craftsman. Carpenters, plumbers, and electricians are artisans.
 ar·ti·san (är′tə zən) *noun, plural* **artisans.**

artist A person who is skilled in painting, music, literature, or any other form of art.
 art·ist (är′tist) *noun, plural* **artists.**

artistic Having to do with art or artists. My brother has *artistic* interests.
 ar·tis·tic (är tis′tik) *adjective.*

as The second movie was not *as* good *as* the first. I have dresses in many colors, such *as* red and blue. Bob arrived *as* we were leaving. I'm speaking to you *as* a friend. He goes to the same school *as* I do.
 as (az) *adverb; conjunction; preposition; pronoun.*

asbestos A grayish substance. Its fibers may be woven or pressed into material that does not burn or conduct electricity. The firemen's clothes were made from a material containing *asbestos.*
 as·bes·tos (as bes′təs *or* az bes′təs) *noun.*

ascend To move or go upward; climb. The elevator *ascended* quickly to the twentieth floor. The hikers *ascended* the hill and rested when they reached the top.
 as·cend (ə send′) *verb,* **ascended, ascending.**

ascent **1.** Movement upward. We watched the *ascent* of the kite high into the sky. **2.** The act of climbing or going up. A heavy snowstorm made an *ascent* of the mountain impossible.
 as·cent (ə sent′) *noun, plural* **ascents.**

ascertain To find out for sure; determine. The police were not able to *ascertain* the identity of the person who wrote the mysterious letter.
 as·cer·tain (as′ər tān′) *verb,* **ascertained, ascertaining.**

ash¹ A grayish-white powder left after something has been burned. An *ash* from Father's cigar fell on the floor.
 ash (ash) *noun, plural* **ashes.**

ash² A tree that has a strong wood. It is used in building. Some baseball bats are made from the wood of the ash.
 ash (ash) *noun, plural* **ashes.**

Leaf

Ash Tree

ashamed **1.** Feeling shame. A person who is ashamed is upset or uncomfortable because he has done something bad or silly. The boy was *ashamed* of the mistake he had made. **2.** Not wanting to do something be-

at; āpe; cär; end; mē; it; īce; hot; ōld;
fôrk; wood; fōōl; oil; out; up; turn; sing;
thin; this; hw in white; zh in treasure.
ə stands for a in about, e in taken
i in pencil, o in lemon, and u in circus.

cause of fear or shame. He was *ashamed* to tell his family that he had failed the test.

a·shamed (ə shāmd′) *adjective*.

ashes The grayish-white powder left after something has been burned. The campers poured water on the *ashes* of their fire.

ash·es (ash′iz) *noun plural*.

ashore On or to the shore or land. The children paddled the canoe *ashore*. Most of the sailors are *ashore* on leave.

a·shore (ə shôr′) *adverb; adjective*.

Asia The largest continent. Asia lies between the Pacific Ocean to the east and Europe and Africa to the west.

A·sia (ā′zhə) *noun*.

Asian Of Asia. He is studying *Asian* history. *Adjective*.
—A person who was born or is living in Asia. *Noun*.

A·sian (ā′zhən) *adjective; noun, plural* **Asians**.

aside On or to one side. Father turned *aside* to let the car behind us pass. Put your worries *aside* and have a good time!

a·side (ə sīd′) *adverb*.

ask **1.** To put a question about something; inquire. We *asked* how to get to town. **2.** To put a question to. He *asked* a policeman where the nearest post office was. **3.** To call for an answer to. He *asked* a question about the arithmetic problem. **4.** To make a request. She *asked* for a second piece of cake. May I *ask* for your help? **5.** To invite. Pam *asked* her friends to come to her party.

ask (ask) *verb*, **asked, asking**.

askew At or to one side; turned the wrong way. The picture was hung *askew* until she straightened it. Your hat is *askew*.

a·skew (ə skyo͞o′) *adverb; adjective*.

asleep **1.** Sleeping. Be very quiet because the baby is *asleep*. **2.** Without feeling; numb. His foot was *asleep* because he sat still for so long. *Adjective*.
—Into a condition of sleep. Grandfather fell *asleep* while he was watching television. *Adverb*.

a·sleep (ə slēp′) *adjective; adverb*.

The boy is wearing his cap **askew**.

asparagus The young green shoots of a garden plant. They are cooked and eaten as a vegetable. The shoots are shaped like spears. They grow from underground stems and have large, scaly leaves at the tip.

as·par·a·gus (əs par′ə gəs) *noun*.

Spears of Asparagus

aspect **1.** A particular way in which something can be looked at and thought about. The mayor's committee considered every *aspect* of the effect of pollution on the city. **2.** Look; appearance. The deserted old house had such a gloomy *aspect* that the children were afraid to go near it.

as·pect (as′pekt) *noun, plural* **aspects**.

aspen A tree whose leaves shake in the slightest breeze. An aspen is a kind of poplar.

as·pen (as′pən) *noun, plural* **aspens**.

Leaves in Autumn

Aspen Tree

asphalt A brown or black substance found in natural deposits or made from petroleum. Asphalt mixed with sand or gravel is used to pave roads.

as·phalt (as′fôlt) *noun*.

aspirin A white drug used to ease pain. Some people take *aspirin* when they have a cold or a headache.

as·pi·rin (as′pər in) *noun, plural* **aspirins**.

ass **1.** An animal that looks like a horse but is smaller and has longer ears; donkey. **2.** A stupid or silly person.

ass (as) *noun, plural* **asses**.

assassin A person who murders another person suddenly and by surprise. An assassin is someone who kills an important or famous person.

as·sas·sin (ə sas′in) *noun, plural* **assassins.**

assassinate To murder suddenly and by surprise. The police have captured the man who tried to *assassinate* the ambassador.

as·sas·si·nate (ə sas′ə nāt′) *verb,* **assassinated, assassinating.**

assault A sudden, violent attack. The troops gave way under the *assault* of the enemy. *Noun.*
—To make an assault on; attack. The soldiers *assaulted* the fort. *Verb.*

as·sault (ə sôlt′) *noun, plural* **assaults;** *verb,* **assaulted, assaulting.**

assemble 1. To gather or bring together. A crowd began to *assemble* outside the movie theater. Bob has *assembled* a large collection of foreign stamps. 2. To put or fit together. We had to *assemble* the parts of the bicycle.

as·sem·ble (ə sem′bəl) *verb,* **assembled, assembling.**

assembly 1. A group of people gathered together for some purpose. The school *assembly* was held in the auditorium. 2. A group of people who make laws. In some states of the United States, the lower house of the legislature is called the *Assembly.* 3. The act of putting or fitting together. Many workers take part in the *assembly* of one automobile.

as·sem·bly (ə sem′blē) *noun, plural* **assemblies.**

assert 1. To state strongly and clearly. The lawyers *assert* that their client is not guilty. 2. To insist on; claim. My little brother *asserted* his independence by demanding that he be allowed to walk to school by himself.

as·sert (ə surt′) *verb,* **asserted, asserting.**

assess 1. To set the value of property for taxation. Mr. Smith's farm is *assessed* at $50,000. 2. To charge or tax. Our library *assesses* a person five cents a day for each day that his book is overdue.

as·sess (ə ses′) *verb,* **assessed, assessing.**

asset 1. Something valuable or useful; advantage. Being tall is a great *asset* for a basketball player. 2. **assets.** Things that have money value. His *assets* include a house, a car, and a boat.

as·set (as′et) *noun, plural* **assets.**

assign 1. To give out. Our teacher will *assign* a different science project to each student. 2. To appoint. The mayor *assigned* her to the committee on education. 3. To fix definitely; name. The coach *assigned* the date for the game.

as·sign (ə sīn′) *verb,* **assigned, assigning.**

assignment 1. Something that is assigned. My arithmetic *assignment* is to do ten multiplication problems. 2. The act of assigning. The company's *assignment* of my father to a new job meant that we had to move to another city.

as·sign·ment (ə sīn′mənt) *noun, plural* **assignments.**

assist To help; aid. All the people in the town got together to *assist* the family whose house had burned down.

as·sist (ə sist′) *verb,* **assisted, assisting.**

assistance Help; aid. Father will need some *assistance* in carrying the packages.

as·sist·ance (ə sis′təns) *noun.*

assistant A person who helps. The man's *assistant* helps him to run the store. *Noun.*
—Helping. The head football coach has four *assistant* coaches on his staff. *Adjective.*

as·sist·ant (ə sis′tənt) *noun, plural* **assistants;** *adjective.*

associate 1. To connect in one's mind. I always *associate* ice cream and cake with birthday parties. 2. To join as a friend or partner. My brother *associates* mostly with boys who like sports as much as he does. *Verb.*
—A friend or partner. My father has two *associates* in his new business. *Noun.*

as·so·ci·ate (ə sō′shē āt′ *or* ə sō′sē āt′ *for verb;* ə sō′shē it *or* ə sō′sē it *for noun*) *verb,* **associated, associating;** *noun, plural* **associates.**

association 1. A group of people joined together for a common purpose. My friends and I belong to an *association* that helps preserve the natural forests of our state. 2. Friendship; companionship. Bob was proud of his *association* with the captain of the high school football team. 3. The connection made in the mind between thoughts and feelings. What *associations* do you have with the word "summer"?

as·so·ci·a·tion (ə sō′sē ā′shən *or* ə sō′shē-ā′shən) *noun, plural* **associations.**

assortment A collection of different kinds. That store carries a large *assortment* of sports equipment.

as·sort·ment (ə sôrt′mənt) *noun, plural* **assortments.**

at; āpe; cär; end; mē; it; īce; hot; ōld;
fôrk; wood; fōol; oil; out; up; turn; sing;
thin; this; hw in white; zh in treasure.
ə stands for a in about, e in taken
i in pencil, o in lemon, and u in circus.

assume **1.** To take for granted; suppose. I *assume* we will arrive at the station on time if we leave now. **2.** To take upon oneself; undertake. You will have to *assume* the responsibility of feeding the dog. **3.** To take for oneself; seize. The dictator *assumed* control of the country.
as·sume (ə soom′) *verb*, **assumed, assuming.**

assumption **1.** The act of assuming. A member of a jury must make the *assumption* that a defendant is innocent until he is proven guilty. **2.** Something that is assumed. Your *assumption* turned out to be wrong.
as·sump·tion (ə sump′shən) *noun, plural* **assumptions.**

assurance **1.** A statement that is supposed to make a person certain or sure. My father gave the shopkeeper his *assurance* that he would pay for the window I had broken. **2.** Confidence. We had every *assurance* that our team would win the championship.
as·sur·ance (ə shoor′əns) *noun, plural* **assurances.**

assure **1.** To tell positively. I *assure* you that I won't be late. **2.** To make certain or sure. He checked the car carefully to *assure* that it was in good condition.
as·sure (ə shoor′) *verb*, **assured, assuring.**

aster A flower that has white, pink, purple, or yellow petals around a yellow center. Asters bloom in the fall.
as·ter (as′tər) *noun, plural* **asters.**

▲ The name **aster** comes from the Latin word for "star." The flower's petals look like the rays of a star.

asterisk A star-shaped mark (*) used in printing or writing to tell the reader to look somewhere else on the page for more information.
as·ter·isk (as′tə-risk′) *noun, plural* **asterisks.**

astern **1.** At or toward the rear of a ship. The ship's crew all gathered *astern* to watch the astronauts' landing. **2.** Behind a ship. A sailboat followed *astern*. **3.** Backward; with the back of the ship forward. The ship pulled *astern* into the dock.
a·stern (ə sturn′) *adverb*.

Asters

asteroid Any of the thousands of small, rocky bodies that revolve around the sun. Most of them are between the orbits of the planets Mars and Jupiter.
as·ter·oid (as′tə roid′) *noun, plural* **asteroids.**

asthma A disease that causes wheezing and coughing and makes breathing difficult.
asth·ma (az′mə) *noun*.

astir In motion; active. Very few people were *astir* as dawn broke over the city.
a·stir (ə stur′) *adjective*.

astonish To surprise very much; amaze. The news that he has won the contest will *astonish* him. It is *astonishing* that such a small boy can throw a ball so far.
as·ton·ish (əs ton′ish) *verb*, **astonished, astonishing.**

astonishment Very great surprise; amazement. The child was filled with *astonishment* when she saw the magician pull a rabbit from his hat.
as·ton·ish·ment (əs ton′ish mənt) *noun*.

astound To surprise very much; amaze; astonish. The first flight in outer space *astounded* the whole world.
as·tound (əs tound′) *verb*, **astounded, astounding.**

astray Off the right way or path. The family was sad because their dog had gone *astray* and gotten lost.
a·stray (ə strā′) *adverb*.

astride With one leg on each side of. The cowboy sat *astride* his horse.
a·stride (ə strīd′) *preposition*.

The boy is sitting **astride** the fence.

astrology The study of the influence that the stars and planets are supposed to have on people and events. Some people use astrology to try to predict what will happen in the future.

as·trol·o·gy (əs trol′ə jē) *noun.*

astronaut A person who flies in a spacecraft. The *astronauts* landed safely on the moon.

as·tro·naut (as′trə nôt′) *noun, plural* **astronauts.**

▲ The word **astronaut** is made up of two Greek words that mean "star" and "sailor." An astronaut is thought of as sailing among the stars.

astronomer A person who knows a great deal about astronomy. An astronomer studies stars and planets by looking at them through a telescope.

as·tron·o·mer (əs tron′ə mər) *noun, plural* **astronomers.**

astronomical 1. Relating to astronomy. The astronauts have collected many important *astronomical* facts during their space flights. 2. Very great or large. For someone with a small allowance, the cost of a bicycle is *astronomical.*

as·tro·nom·i·cal (as′trə nom′i kəl) *adjective.*

astronomy The science that deals with the study of the sun, moon, stars, planets, and other heavenly bodies.

as·tron·o·my (əs tron′ə mē) *noun.*

asylum 1. A place that takes care of people who are not able to care for themselves. People who are mentally ill may live in an asylum. 2. A place of safety or protection. In earlier times, a church was an asylum where criminals were safe from arrest.

a·sy·lum (ə sī′ləm) *noun, plural* **asylums.**

at The race starts *at* the top of the hill. He looked *at* the picture. We eat lunch *at* noon. England and the Colonies were *at* war during the American Revolution. She bought the car *at* a low price.

at (at) *preposition.*

ate We *ate* all the pie. Look up **eat** for more information. ▲ Another word that sounds like this is **eight.**

ate (āt) *verb.*

atheist A person who does not believe in God.

a·the·ist (ā′thē ist) *noun, plural* **atheists.**

athlete A person who is good at and trained in sports or exercises that take strength, skill, and speed. Baseball players, hockey players, swimmers, and skiers are athletes.

ath·lete (ath′lēt) *noun, plural* **athletes.**

athletic 1. Relating to an athlete or athletes. Our school has just bought new basketballs, baseball bats, and other *athletic* equipment. 2. Good at sports. Linda is *athletic* and enjoys many outdoor sports.

ath·let·ic (ath let′ik) *adjective.*

Atlantic The ocean that separates Europe and Africa from North America and South America. *Noun.*
—Of the Atlantic Ocean. *Adjective.*

At·lan·tic (at lan′tik) *noun; adjective.*

atlas A book of maps.

at·las (at′ləs) *noun, plural* **atlases.**

▲ In very old stories, *Atlas* was a giant who was made to hold the sky on his shoulders. In the front of early books of maps, there was often a picture of Atlas holding up the sky. So people began to call a book of this kind an **atlas.**

atmosphere 1. The air that surrounds the earth. Before the first space flights, no person had ever traveled beyond the earth's *atmosphere.* 2. The mass of gases that surrounds any heavenly body. Scientists do not think people could live in the *atmosphere* on Mars. 3. The air in a particular place. This attic has a hot, stuffy *atmosphere.* 4. The mood or influence that surrounds a place. Our house has a happy *atmosphere* at holiday time.

at·mos·phere (at′məs fēr′) *noun, plural* **atmospheres.**

atmospheric Having to do with the atmosphere. *Atmospheric* pressure on the earth's surface at sea level is about 15 pounds per square inch.

at·mos·pher·ic (at′məs fer′ik) *adjective.*

atoll A ring-shaped coral island that surrounds a shallow body of water.

at·oll (at′ôl *or* ə tôl′) *noun, plural* **atolls.**

atom The smallest particle of a chemical element that has all the qualities of that element. An atom has a central nucleus of protons and neutrons that is surrounded by electrons. All matter in the universe is made up of atoms.

at·om (at′əm) *noun, plural* **atoms.**

atomic 1. Having to do with an atom or atoms. Those scientists are taking part in

at; āpe; cär; end; mē; it; īce; hot; ōld;
fôrk; wood; fōōl; oil; out; up; turn; sing;
thin; this; hw in white; zh in treasure.
ə stands for a in about, e in taken
i in pencil, o in lemon, and u in circus.

atomic research. **2.** Using atomic energy. An *atomic* submarine can stay underwater for long periods of time.
    a·tom·ic (ə tom′ik) *adjective.*

atomic bomb   A very powerful bomb. Its great force comes from the energy released by the splitting of atoms. This bomb is also called an **atom bomb.**

atomic energy   Energy that can be released from the nucleus of an atom. This kind of energy is usually called **nuclear energy.** Look up **nuclear energy** for more information.

atone   To make up for a wrong; make amends. She *atoned* for her rude behavior by apologizing to me.
    a·tone (ə tōn′) *verb,* **atoned, atoning.**

atop   On top of. There were ten candles *atop* my birthday cake.
    a·top (ə top′) *preposition.*

attach   **1.** To fasten. You can *attach* the sign to the wall with nails. Bob *attached* the leash to the dog's collar. **2.** To add or include. Thomas Jefferson *attached* his signature to the Declaration of Independence. **3.** To bind by a strong feeling. Tom is very *attached* to his family.
    at·tach (ə tach′) *verb,* **attached, attaching.**

attachment   **1.** The act of attaching. The *attachment* of the tow truck to the wrecked car was difficult. **2.** A strong feeling of affection or devotion. The child showed his *attachment* to his sister by hugging her. **3.** A part or device that is connected to a larger thing. The camera had a flash *attachment* for taking pictures indoors.
    at·tach·ment (ə tach′mənt) *noun, plural* **attachments.**

attack   **1.** To begin to fight against. The dog *attacked* the robber. **2.** To write or speak against. The newspapers *attacked* the mayor's speech. **3.** To begin to work on with energy. The boys *attacked* the job of setting up the tent. **4.** To act harmfully on. A plant disease *attacked* all the elm trees in our yard. *Verb.*
    —**1.** The act of attacking. The enemy's *attack* on the fort came without warning. **2.** A sudden fit of sickness. She drank the glass of soda so fast that she had an *attack* of hiccups. *Noun.*
    at·tack (ə tak′) *verb,* **attacked, attacking;** *noun, plural* **attacks.**

attain   **1.** To arrive at; reach. My great-grandfather *attained* the age of ninety. **2.** To get by hard work; achieve. Jim has finally

attained his ambition to be on the football team.
    at·tain (ə tān′) *verb,* **attained, attaining.**

attempt   To make an effort to do something; try. The prisoner *attempted* to escape from jail. *Verb.*
    —**1.** A try; effort. Bob made an *attempt* to learn how to ski, but he kept falling down. **2.** An attack. The traitor made an *attempt* on the king's life. *Noun.*
    at·tempt (ə tempt′) *verb,* **attempted, attempting;** *noun, plural* **attempts.**

attend   **1.** To be present at. She has to *attend* a club meeting this afternoon. **2.** To go with. Three bridesmaids *attended* the bride. **3.** To take care of; wait on. Doctors and nurses *attended* to the injured man.
    at·tend (ə tend′) *verb,* **attended, attending.**

attendance   **1.** The act of being present. Betty's *attendance* at school was poor last year. **2.** The number of people present. The *attendance* at the baseball game was over 500.
    at·ten·dance (ə ten′dəns) *noun.*

attention   **1.** Careful watching or listening. The magician had the children's *attention.* He called my *attention* to the airplane flying high above us. **2.** Notice or consideration. Pollution of our rivers and lakes calls for immediate *attention.* **3. attentions.** Kind or polite acts. The host's many *attentions* made every guest at the party feel welcome. **4.** A position in which a person stands very straight, with his arms at his sides, his feet together, and his eyes looking ahead. The band stood at *attention,* waiting for the parade to start.
    at·ten·tion (ə ten′shən) *noun, plural* **attentions.**

attest   To give proof of. The shelves full of books in his room *attest* to his enjoyment of reading.
    at·test (ə test′) *verb,* **attested, attesting.**

attic   The space just below the roof of a house. Our *attic* is filled with old clothes, toys, and many other things no one in the family really wants any more.
    at·tic (at′ik) *noun, plural* **attics.**

attire   Dress; clothing. The queen was clothed in rich *attire.*
    at·tire (ə tīr′) *noun.*

attitude   A way of thinking, acting, or feeling. Tom's *attitude* toward school is more enthusiastic than mine.
    at·ti·tude (at′ə tōōd′ *or* at′ə tyōōd′) *noun, plural* **attitudes.**

attorney   A person who has the legal power

to act for another person; lawyer. The prisoner's *attorney* presented his case to the judge and jury.

at·tor·ney (ə tur′nē) *noun, plural* **attorneys.**

attract To draw or pull. A magnet will *attract* an iron bar. The beautiful scenery in these mountains *attracts* many tourists.

at·tract (ə trakt′) *verb,* **attracted, attracting.**

attraction 1. The act or power of attracting. The *attraction* of the magnet drew the nails across the table. 2. A person or thing that attracts. The clowns were the main *attraction* at the circus.

at·trac·tion (ə trak′shən) *noun, plural* **attractions.**

attractive Having a pleasing quality that attracts people; charming. Mary is a very *attractive* girl.

at·trac·tive (ə trak′tiv) *adjective.*

attribute To think of as belonging to or coming from. The coach *attributed* the team's victory to training and practice. Air pollution in cities has been *attributed* partly to car exhaust. *Verb.*
—A quality that is thought of as belonging to a person or thing; characteristic. One of Frank's *attributes* is his friendliness. *Noun.*

at·trib·ute (ə trib′yo͞ot *for verb;* at′rə byo͞ot′ *for noun*) *verb,* **attributed, attributing;** *noun, plural* **attributes.**

auction A public sale at which things are sold to the person who offers the most money. My mother bid five dollars for a rocking chair at the church *auction. Noun.*
—To sell at an auction. When we bought our new house, my parents *auctioned* off some of our old furniture. *Verb.*

auc·tion (ôk′shən) *noun, plural* **auctions;** *verb,* **auctioned, auctioning.**

▲ The word **auction** goes back to a Latin word that means "to become bigger or higher." At an auction, the price of something gets higher and higher until someone offers the highest price and the article is sold to him.

audible Loud enough to be heard. The music was barely *audible* after Jim turned down the volume of the phonograph.

au·di·ble (ô′də bəl) *adjective.*

audience 1. A group of people gathered to hear or see something. The *audience* at the theater applauded the actors in the play. 2. All the people who give attention to something. That television program has a large *audience.* 3. A formal meeting with a person

of very high rank. The young man was granted an *audience* with the king.

au·di·ence (ô′dē əns) *noun, plural* **audiences.**

audio Relating to sound. He bought new *audio* equipment for his record player.

au·di·o (ô′dē ō′) *adjective.*

auditor A person who checks business accounts or records to see if they are correct.

au·di·tor (ô′də tər) *noun, plural* **auditors.**

auditorium A large room in a school, church, theater, or other building where a group of people can gather. We have student meetings in the school *auditorium* once a week.

au·di·to·ri·um (ô′də tôr′ē əm) *noun, plural* **auditoriums.**

auger A tool for boring holes in wood.

au·ger (ô′gər) *noun, plural* **augers.**

augment To make greater; increase. John tries to *augment* his income by working at night as well as during the day.

aug·ment (ôg ment′) *verb,* **augmented, augmenting.**

August The eighth month of the year. August has thirty-one days.

Au·gust (ô′gəst) *noun.*

▲ *Augustus,* who was the first emperor of Rome, named the month of **August** after himself.

auk A diving sea bird that lives along northern seacoasts. Auks have webbed feet, short wings that are used as paddles in swimming, and white feathers.

auk (ôk) *noun, plural* **auks.**

aunt 1. The sister of one's mother or father. 2. The wife of one's uncle. ▲ Another word that sounds like this is **ant.**

aunt (ant *or* änt) *noun, plural* **aunts.**

Auk

auricle Either of

at; āpe; cär; end; mē; it; īce; hot; ōld;
fôrk; wood; fo͞ol; oil; out; up; turn; sing;
thin; this; hw in white; zh in treasure.
ə stands for a in about, e in taken
i in pencil, o in lemon, and u in circus.

the two chambers of the heart. The auricles receive blood from the veins and send it to the ventricles.

au·ri·cle (ôr′i kəl) *noun, plural* **auricles.**

Australia **1.** A continent southeast of Asia, between the Indian Ocean and the Pacific Ocean. It is the smallest of the continents. **2.** A country made up of this continent and the island of Tasmania. Its capital is Canberra.

Aus·tra·lia (ôs trāl′yə) *noun.*

authentic Real; genuine; correct. The witness gave an *authentic* account of the accident. She collects *authentic* signatures of famous people.

au·then·tic (ô then′tik) *adjective.*

author A person who writes books, stories, plays, poems, or articles. Who is the *author* of this book?

au·thor (ô′thər) *noun, plural* **authors.**

authority **1.** The power or right to act, order, or make decisions. The captain has *authority* over the men on his ship. **2.** A person or group having this power or right. We reported the crime to the *authorities,* and they caught the burglar. **3.** A good source of information or facts. The dictionary is an *authority* on how to spell words. That professor is an *authority* on the life of Abraham Lincoln.

au·thor·i·ty (ə thôr′ə tē) *noun, plural* **authorities.**

authorize **1.** To give authority to. My father *authorized* the real estate agent to sell our house. **2.** To approve officially. The governor *authorized* the building of the new highway.

au·thor·ize (ô′thə rīz′) *verb,* **authorized, authorizing.**

auto Automobile. Look up **automobile** for more information.

au·to (ô′tō) *noun, plural* **autos.**

autobiography The story of a person's own life written by himself. The politician is writing his *autobiography.*

au·to·bi·og·ra·phy (ô′tə bī og′rə fē) *noun, plural* **autobiographies.**

autograph A person's name that he has written in his own handwriting. I got the singer's *autograph* after his performance. *Noun.*

—To write one's name in one's own handwriting. The writer *autographed* a copy of her book for me. *Verb.*

au·to·graph (ô′tə graf′) *noun, plural* **autographs;** *verb,* **autographed, autographing.**

automatic **1.** Acting, moving, or operating by itself. We have an *automatic* dishwasher. **2.** Done without a person's control. Breathing is an *automatic* action of the body during sleep. *Adjective.*

—A gun that keeps firing and reloading until the trigger is released. *Noun.*

au·to·mat·ic (ô′tə mat′ik) *adjective; noun, plural* **automatics.**

automation The development and use of machines to do jobs that used to be done by people. Machines that can pick cotton are an example of the use of automation as an aid in farming.

au·to·ma·tion (ô′tə mā′shən) *noun.*

automobile A vehicle that usually has four wheels and is powered by an engine that uses gasoline; car. An automobile is used mainly to carry passengers.

au·to·mo·bile (ô′tə mə bēl′) *noun, plural* **automobiles.**

On the top is an **automobile** that was made years ago. On the bottom is a modern one.

autopsy A medical examination of a dead body to find the cause of death.

au·top·sy (ô′top′sē) *noun, plural* **autopsies.**

autumn The season of the year coming between summer and winter; fall.

au·tumn (ô′təm) *noun, plural* **autumns.**

auxiliary **1.** Giving aid or extra support. This sailboat has an *auxiliary* engine in case there is no wind. **2.** Additional; extra. The mayor put *auxiliary* policemen on duty during the President's visit. *Adjective.*

—Something added to give help or support. My mother belongs to the woman's *auxiliary* of my father's club. *Noun.*

aux·il·ia·ry (ôg zil′yər ē) *adjective; noun, plural* **auxiliaries.**

available That can be gotten, had, or

used. This shirt is *available* in several different colors. There are still a few seats *available* for the game.
a·vail·a·ble (ə vā′lə bəl) *adjective.*

avalanche The swift, sudden fall of a mass of snow, ice, earth, or rocks down a mountain slope.
av·a·lanche (av′ə lanch′) *noun, plural* **avalanches.**

avenue A wide street. Trees line the *avenues* of the city.
av·e·nue (av′ə nyo͞o′ *or* av′ə no͞o′) *noun, plural* **avenues.**

average **1.** A number found by dividing the sum of two or more quantities by the number of quantities. The *average* of 2, 4, 6, and 8 is 5. **2.** The usual amount or kind. This year's rainfall came close to the *average. Noun.*
—Usual; typical; ordinary. He is of *average* height and weight. The *average* house in this country has at least one radio. *Adjective.*
—**1.** To find the average of. Jim *averaged* his three bowling scores and wound up with 126. **2.** To have as an average. That basketball player *averages* twenty points a game. *Verb.*
av·er·age (av′ər ij *or* av′rij) *noun, plural* **averages;** *adjective; verb,* **averaged, averaging.**

avert **1.** To turn away or aside. Jim *averted* his eyes from the glare of the sun. **2.** To prevent; avoid. Dad *averted* a crash by slamming on the car's brakes.
a·vert (ə vurt′) *verb,* **averted, averting.**

aviation The science or art of flying aircraft.
a·vi·a·tion (ā′vē ā′shən) *noun.*

aviator A person who flies an airplane or other aircraft; pilot.
a·vi·a·tor (ā′vē ā′tər) *noun, plural* **aviators.**

avocado A pear-shaped tropical fruit that grows on trees. It has a dark green skin and a pulp with a nutty taste. Avocados are eaten raw in salads.
av·o·ca·do (av′ə-kä′dō) *noun, plural* **avocados.**

avoid To keep away from. We took a back road to *avoid* the heavy traffic on the highway.
a·void (ə void′) *verb,* **avoided, avoiding.**

await **1.** To wait for. The parents had long *awaited* the day of

Avocado

their son's graduation from college. **2.** To be ready for. Many changes *await* her in her new school.
a·wait (ə wāt′) *verb,* **awaited, awaiting.**

awake To wake up. It is hard for Bill to *awake* in the morning. *Verb.*
—Not asleep. He was *awake* most of the night because of the noise outside. *Adjective.*
a·wake (ə wāk′) *verb,* **awoke** or **awaked, awaking;** *adjective.*

awaken To wake up. He *awakened* when the dog barked.
a·wak·en (ə wā′kən) *verb,* **awakened, awakening.**

award **1.** To give after careful thought. The judges *awarded* my dog first prize at the dog show. **2.** To give because of a legal decision. The jury *awarded* money to the woman who had been injured in the accident. *Verb.*
—Something that is given after careful thought. He received the *award* for being the best speller. *Noun.*
a·ward (ə wôrd′) *verb,* **awarded, awarding;** *noun, plural* **awards.**

aware Knowing or realizing. The girl was not *aware* that her family was planning a surprise party for her.
a·ware (ə wer′) *adjective.*

away The frightened rabbit hopped *away.* Put the tools *away.* The little boy turned *away* to hide his tears. The sounds of footsteps faded *away.* The town is three miles *away* from our house. My brother has been *away* for three weeks.
a·way (ə wā′) *adverb; adjective.*

awe Great wonder together with fear or deep respect. They read with *awe* the news of the astronauts' landing on the moon. *Noun.*
—To fill with awe. We were *awed* by the force of the thunderstorm. *Verb.*
awe (ô) *noun; verb,* **awed, awing.**

awful **1.** Causing fear, dread, or awe; terrible. The earthquake caused an *awful* disaster. **2.** Very bad. I thought that movie was *awful.* **3.** Very large; great. A million dollars is an *awful* lot of money.
aw·ful (ô′fəl) *adjective.*

awfully **1.** Terribly; dreadfully. Her knee hurt *awfully* where she had scraped it.

at; āpe; cär; end; mē; it; īce; hot; ōld;
fôrk; wood; fo͞ol; oil; out; up; turn; sing;
thin; this; hw in white; zh in treasure.
ə stands for a in about, e in taken
i in pencil, o in lemon, and u in circus.

2. Very. I am *awfully* glad that you won first prize.
aw·ful·ly (ô′fə lē *or* ôf′lē) *adverb.*

awhile For a short time. They rested *awhile* before playing another game of tennis.
a·while (ə hwīl′) *adverb.*

awkward 1. Not graceful; clumsy. The young colt was *awkward* and had trouble standing up. **2.** Difficult or embarrassing. It was an *awkward* moment for Bill when the teacher found out that he hadn't done his homework. **3.** Difficult to use or handle. The large piano was an *awkward* piece of furniture to move.
awk·ward (ôk′wərd) *adjective.*

awl A pointed tool used for making small holes in leather or wood. She used an *awl* to put her initials on the belt. ▲ Another word that sounds like this is **all.**
awl (ôl) *noun, plural* **awls.**

Azalea

awning A rooflike cover of canvas, metal, or other material over a door or window. An awning is used as a shelter from the sun or rain.
aw·ning (ô′ning) *noun, plural* **awnings.**

awoke I *awoke* at seven-thirty this morning. Look up **awake** for more information.
a·woke (ə wōk′) *verb.*

ax A tool that has a metal blade attached to a handle. An ax is used for cutting down trees and chopping wood. This word is also spelled **axe.**
ax (aks) *noun, plural* **axes.**

axis A straight line around which an object or body turns or seems to turn. The earth turns on an imaginary *axis* that runs from the North Pole through the South Pole.
ax·is (ak′sis) *noun, plural* **axes.**

axle A bar or shaft on which a wheel or pair of wheels turn. The mechanic is fixing the front *axle* of John's car.
ax·le (ak′səl) *noun, plural* **axles.**

Axis

aye Yes. All who are in favor of the plan say "*aye.*" *Adverb.*
—A vote of yes or a person who votes yes. The *ayes* won when we counted the votes. *Noun.* ▲ Other words that sound like this are **eye** and **I.**
aye (ī) *adverb; noun, plural* **ayes.**

azalea A small bush with dark green leaves and clusters of red, pink, or white flowers.
a·za·lea (ə zāl′yə) *noun, plural* **azaleas.**

▲ The name **azalea** goes back to a Latin word that means "dry." At one time it was thought that azaleas grow best in dry soil.

---

azure A clear blue color. *Noun.*
—Having a clear blue color. *Adjective.*
az·ure (azh′ər) *noun, plural* **azures;** *adjective.*

at; āpe; cär; end; mē; it; īce; hot; ōld;
fôrk; wood; fōol; oil; out; up; turn; sing;
thin; **th**is; **hw** in white; **zh** in treasure.
ə stands for **a** in about, **e** in taken
i in pencil, **o** in lemon, and **u** in circus.

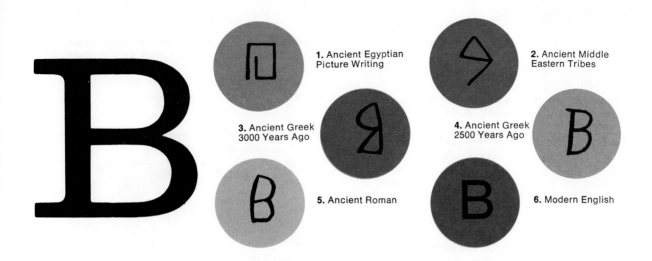

1. Ancient Egyptian Picture Writing

2. Ancient Middle Eastern Tribes

3. Ancient Greek 3000 Years Ago

4. Ancient Greek 2500 Years Ago

5. Ancient Roman

6. Modern English

B is the second letter of the alphabet. The oldest form of the letter **B** was a drawing that the ancient Egyptians (**1**) used in their picture writing nearly 5000 years ago. This drawing was borrowed by several ancient tribes (**2**) in the Middle East. They changed its shape and made it the second letter of their alphabet. The ancient Greeks (**3**) borrowed a form of this letter about 3000 years ago. At first they wrote it like a backwards capital letter **B**. Several hundred years later the Greeks turned their letter **B** around (**4**). This made it look more like a modern capital letter **B**. The Romans (**5**) borrowed this letter from the Greeks about 2400 years ago. They wrote it in almost the same way that we write the capital letter **B** today (**6**).

b, B The second letter of the alphabet.
b, B (bē) *noun, plural* **b's, B's.**

baa The sound that a sheep makes; bleat. *Noun.*
—To make such a sound. *Verb.*
baa (bä) *noun, plural* **baas;** *verb,* **baaed, baaing.**

babble **1.** To make sounds that have no meaning. The baby *babbles* because he hasn't learned to talk yet. **2.** To talk in a foolish way; chatter. The silly boy *babbled* on about his new bicycle. **3.** To make a low, murmuring sound. The brook *babbled* as it flowed over the pebbles. *Verb.*
—**1.** Sounds that have no meaning. There was a *babble* of voices in the classroom because everyone was talking at once. **2.** A low, murmuring sound. We could hear the *babble* of the brook. *Noun.*
bab·ble (bab′əl) *verb,* **babbled, babbling;** *noun, plural* **babbles.**

babe A baby.
babe (bāb) *noun, plural* **babes.**

baboon A large monkey that has a face like a dog. Baboons live in open country in different parts of Africa. They live together in large groups, and they travel great distances in search of food.
ba·boon (ba boon′) *noun, plural* **baboons.**

baby **1.** A very young child; infant. The *baby* is learning how to walk. **2.** The youngest person in a family or group. She is the *baby* of the family because her brothers and sisters are all older. **3.** A person who acts in a spoiled way. He is such a *baby* when he can't do what he wants. *Noun.*
—**1.** Of or for a baby. Mother put my little sister in the *baby* carriage. **2.** Very young. Dad bought Susy a *baby* turtle. *Adjective.*
—To treat like a baby. The mother *babied* her son by bringing him supper in bed even though he wasn't sick. *Verb.*
ba·by (bā′bē) *noun, plural* **babies;** *adjective; verb,* **babied, babying.**

baby-sit To take care of a child or children while the parents are away for a time. My

Baboon

older sister *baby-sits* for the neighbors on Friday nights.

ba·by·sit (bā′bē sit′) *verb,* **baby-sat, baby-sitting.**

bachelor A man who has not married.

bach·e·lor (bach′ə lər) *noun, plural* **bachelors.**

back **1.** The part of the body behind the chest. Johnny scratched his *back.* **2.** The upper part of the body of an animal. Alice petted the puppy on its *back.* **3.** The part of anything that is opposite the front part. The man signed his name on the *back* of the check. Jim sat in the *back* of the classroom. *Noun.*

—**1.** To help or support. He *backed* his friend in the quarrel with two other boys. **2.** To move backward. Mother *backed* the car into the garage. The frightened child *backed* away from the growling dog. *Verb.*

—**1.** Behind the front part. He went around the house to the *back* door. **2.** Past; old. Dad threw away some *back* copies of the magazine. *Adjective.*

—**1.** Toward the back; backward. Carol moved *back* to let the bicycle rider go past. **2.** In the place where something used to be. She put the keys *back* in her purse. *Adverb.*

back (bak) *noun, plural* **backs;** *verb,* **backed, backing;** *adjective; adverb.*

backboard The board to which the basket is attached in basketball.

back·board (bak′bôrd′) *noun, plural* **backboards.**

backbone The column of bones in the back; spine. People, dogs, birds, fish, frogs, and snakes all have backbones. The backbone supports the body.

back·bone (bak′bōn′) *noun, plural* **backbones.**

backfire An explosion in a gasoline engine that causes a loud noise. We heard the *backfire* of the old car.

back·fire (bak′fīr′) *noun, plural* **backfires.**

backgammon A game for two people that is played on a special board. The players throw dice to see how they may move their pieces.

back·gam·mon (bak′gam′ən) *noun.*

background **1.** The part of a picture or scene that seems to be in the distance. Look up the word **foreground** for a picture of this. **2.** A person's past experience. Because of his many years of playing baseball, he has a good *background* for the job as coach of the team.

back·ground (bak′ground′) *noun, plural* **backgrounds.**

backhand A stroke in tennis and other games. It is made with the back of the hand turned forward.

back·hand (bak′hand′) *noun, plural* **backhands.**

A Backhand Stroke

backward **1.** Toward the back. Mary looked *backward* when she heard the noise behind her. **2.** With the back first. Tom was walking *backward* and fell. Jerry wore his cap *backward.* This word is also spelled **backwards.** *Adverb.*

—Toward the back. She gave a *backward* glance. *Adjective.*

back·ward (bak′wərd) *adverb; adjective.*

bacon Meat from the back and sides of a pig. Bacon is flavored with salt and treated with smoke to preserve it.

ba·con (bā′kən) *noun.*

bacteria Very tiny plants. Bacteria are so small that they can only be seen through a powerful microscope. Some kinds of bacteria cause diseases. Other kinds do useful things, like making soil richer.

bac·te·ri·a (bak tēr′ē ə) *noun plural.*

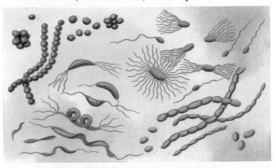

These are different types of **bacteria** as seen under a microscope.

bacterium One of the bacteria. Look up **bacteria** for more information.
bac·te·ri·um (bak tēr′ē əm) *noun, plural* **bac·teria.**

bad Not good. That was a *bad* television program. Stealing the money was a *bad* thing to do. It is *bad* for your teeth to eat too much candy. She felt *bad* because she had hurt her friend's feelings. The *bad* news about his accident upset his friends.
bad (bad) *adjective,* **worse, worst.**

badge Something worn to show that a person belongs to a certain group. The boy scout had a merit *badge* on his uniform that he had earned for a science project. The sheriff wore a *badge* on his shirt.
badge (baj) *noun, plural* **badges.**

badger A furry animal with short legs and long claws. Badgers live in holes in the ground which they dig with their claws. They hunt for food at night. *Noun.*
—To bother or annoy. My brother always *badgers* me by trying to borrow money. *Verb.*
badg·er (baj′ər) *noun, plural* **badgers;** *verb,* **badgered, badgering.**

Badger

badly **1.** In a bad way. The team played *badly* and lost the game. **2.** Very much. He needs new shoes *badly.*
bad·ly (bad′lē) *adverb.*

badminton A game for two or four players. In badminton, the players use rackets to hit a small object called a shuttlecock back and forth over a high net.
bad·min·ton (bad′min′tən) *noun.*

▲ The game of **badminton** was named after an English duke's estate where the game was first played.

baffle To be too confusing for someone to understand. The magician's trick of pulling a rabbit out of a hat *baffled* the children.
baf·fle (baf′əl) *verb,* **baffled, baffling.**

bag Something used to hold things. Bags are made of paper, cloth, plastic, or other material. She put the groceries in a *bag.* Dad bought a *bag* of grass seed. Edna put her keys in her *bag.* I ate a whole *bag* of popcorn.
bag (bag) *noun, plural* **bags.**

baggage The suitcases, trunks, and bags that a person takes with him when he goes on a trip.
bag·gage (bag′ij) *noun.*

baggy Hanging loosely; sagging. The old man wore *baggy* trousers.
bag·gy (bag′ē) *adjective,* **baggier, baggiest.**

bagpipe A musical instrument made of a leather bag and pipes. A person makes music by blowing air into the bag and then pressing the bag so that the air is forced out through the pipes. The bagpipe is often played in Scotland.
bag·pipe (bag′pīp′) *noun, plural* **bagpipes.**

Bagpipe

bail¹ Money given to a court of law to get a prisoner out of jail until the time of his trial. The money guarantees that the prisoner will appear for his trial. *Noun.*
—To get a prisoner out of jail until the time of his trial by giving bail. *Verb.* ▲ Another word that sounds like this is **bale.**
bail (bāl) *noun, plural* **bails;** *verb,* **bailed, bailing.**

bail² To take water out of a boat with a pail or other container. The boys will have to *bail* water out of their rowboat or it will sink. ▲ Another word that sounds like this is **bale.**
bail (bāl) *verb,* **bailed, bailing.**
to bail out. To jump out of an airplane with a parachute. The pilot *bailed out* when his plane caught fire.

at; āpe; cär; end; mē; it; īce; hot; ōld;
fôrk; wood; fōol; oil; out; up; turn; sing;
thin; this; hw in white; zh in treasure.
ə stands for **a** in about, **e** in taken
i in pencil, **o** in lemon, and **u** in circus.

bait Something that tempts or attracts. The fisherman used worms as *bait* to catch the fish. *Noun.*
—**1.** To put bait on. We *baited* the trap with cheese to catch the mouse. **2.** To tease in a mean way. The other boys tried to *bait* him by calling him a coward. *Verb.*
bait (bāt) *noun, plural* **baits;** *verb,* **baited, baiting.**

bake **1.** To cook by dry heat in an oven. Mother *baked* bread. The potatoes *baked* slowly. **2.** To harden or dry by heating. People *bake* bowls and dishes in ovens called kilns. The sun *baked* the grass until it turned brown.
bake (bāk) *verb,* **baked, baking.**

baker A person who bakes and sells bread, cakes, cookies, and pastries.
bak·er (bā′kər) *noun, plural* **bakers.**

bakery A place where bread, cakes, cookies, and pastries are baked or sold.
bak·er·y (bā′kər ē) *noun, plural* **bakeries.**

baking powder A powder used in baking to make dough or batter rise.

balance **1.** The condition of having all the parts of something exactly the same in weight, amount, or force. The two children kept the seesaw in *balance.* **2.** A steady position. He lost his *balance* and fell down the stairs. The tightrope walker kept her *balance.* **3.** An instrument for weighing things. The chemist weighed some powder on the *balance.* **4.** The part that is left over. He still has the *balance* of his homework to do after supper. *Noun.*
—To put or keep in a steady position. The girl *balanced* a book on her head. *Verb.*
bal·ance (bal′əns) *noun, plural* **balances;** *verb,* **balanced, balancing.**

The children are **balancing** on the seesaw.

balcony **1.** A platform that juts out from the wall of a building. A balcony has a low wall or railing on three sides. **2.** An upper floor that juts out into a large room or auditorium. Churches and theaters have balconies with seats.
bal·co·ny (bal′kə nē) *noun, plural* **balconies.**

bald **1.** Having little or no hair on the head. My father is getting *bald.* **2.** Without a natural covering. The *bald* hilltop had no trees or shrubs.
bald (bôld) *adjective,* **balder, baldest.**

▲ The first meaning of **bald** was "round like a ball." People probably started calling someone without hair *bald* because a smooth, hairless head looks something like a round ball.

bald eagle A large eagle of North America. The bald eagle is brown with a white head, neck, and tail. The bald eagle is the national symbol of the United States.

bale A large bundle of things tied together tightly for shipping or storing. The farmer stored the *bales* of hay in the barn for the winter. ▲ Another word that sounds like this is **bail.**
bale (bāl) *noun, plural* **bales.**

balk **1.** To stop short and refuse to go on. The mule *balked* and would not move. **2.** To keep from going on; hinder. The guards *balked* the prisoners' plans to escape from jail.
balk (bôk) *verb,* **balked, balking.**

ball¹ **1.** A round object. Bill wound the kite string into a *ball.* **2.** A roundish object used in various games. John brought his *ball* and bat for the baseball game. **3.** A game played with a ball. I play *ball* after school every day. **4.** A pitch in baseball that does not pass over home plate in the area between the batter's knees and shoulders and that he does not swing at. ▲ Another word that sounds like this is **bawl.**
ball (bôl) *noun, plural* **balls.**

ball² A large, formal party for dancing. The beautiful princess met the handsome prince at the *ball.* ▲ Another word that sounds like this is **bawl.**
ball (bôl) *noun, plural* **balls.**

ballad A simple poem or song that tells a story. The cowboy sang a *ballad* about the Old West.
bal·lad (bal′əd) *noun, plural* **ballads.**

ballast Something heavy used to give balance. Sand or rocks are used as ballast. Ballast is put in a ship to keep it steady in the water.
bal·last (bal′əst) *noun, plural* **ballasts.**

ball bearing A bearing made up of a number of metal balls, on which the moving part of a machine turns easily. The wheels of my roller skates turn on *ball bearings.*

ballerina A woman or girl who dances ballet.
bal·le·ri·na (bal′ə rē′nə) *noun, plural* **ballerinas.**

ballet A form of dance. Dancers use certain formal steps and movements when dancing ballet. A ballet usually tells a story.
bal·let (ba lā′ *or* bal′ā) *noun, plural* **ballets.**

balloon A bag filled with air or other gas. Small balloons are used as children's toys or for decoration. Large balloons are made to rise and float in the air. These balloons have cabins or baskets for carrying passengers or scientific instruments. *Noun.*
—To swell out or grow larger like a balloon. The parachute *ballooned* when it opened. *Verb.*
bal·loon (bə lōōn′) *noun, plural* **balloons;** *verb,* **ballooned, ballooning.**

Ballerina

ballot A printed form or other thing used in voting. A voter checks or writes down his choice on a paper ballot, and then puts the ballot into a box, or else he votes by means of a ballot in a special machine. Later the ballots are counted to see who has won the election. *Noun.*
—To use a ballot for voting. The students *balloted* to choose a class president. *Verb.*
bal·lot (bal′ət) *noun, plural* **ballots;** *verb,* **balloted, balloting.**

▲ In ancient Greece, people voted by putting a little ball into the voting box. A person used a white ball to vote for someone and a black ball to vote against someone. The word **ballot** comes from the word for these balls.

ball-point pen A pen whose point is a small metal ball that rolls the ink from a container inside the pen onto the paper.
ball-point pen (bôl′point′).

ballroom A large room where dances and other parties are given.
ball·room (bôl′rōōm′ *or* bôl′room′) *noun, plural* **ballrooms.**

balsa A strong and very light wood from a tropical American tree. Balsa is easy to cut and carve. It is used to make airplane and boat models.
bal·sa (bôl′sə) *noun.*

balsam An evergreen tree that grows in North America. Wood from the balsam is used to make boxes and crates.
bal·sam (bôl′səm) *noun, plural* **balsams.**

bamboo A tall, treelike plant that is related to grass. The bamboo has woody stems that are used to make fishing poles, canes, and furniture.
bam·boo (bam-bōō′) *noun, plural* **bamboos.**

ban To forbid; prohibit. The government *bans* the hunting of animals in that national park. *Verb.*
—An official order that forbids something. There is a *ban* on smoking in that theater. *Noun.*
ban (ban) *verb,* **banned, banning;** *noun, plural* **bans.**

Bamboo

banana A slightly curved fruit that has a yellow or red skin. Bananas grow in bunches on a treelike plant that has very large leaves. They grow in tropical regions of the world.
ba·nan·a (bə nan′ə) *noun, plural* **bananas.**

Fruit

Banana Tree

band¹ **1.** A group of persons or animals. A *band* of thieves held up the stagecoach. **2.** A group of musicians playing together. The

at; āpe; cär; end; mē; it; īce; hot; ōld; fôrk; wood; fōōl; oil; out; up; turn; sing; thin; this; hw in white; zh in treasure. ə stands for a in about, e in taken i in pencil, o in lemon, and u in circus.

school *band* played at the football game. *Noun.*

—To gather together in a group. The neighbors *banded* together to clean up litter in the vacant lot. *Verb.*
band (band) *noun, plural* **bands;** *verb,* **banded, banding.**

band² **1.** A strip of cloth or other material. Gail tied a red *band* in her hair. There were metal *bands* around the barrel. **2.** A stripe of color. The barber pole has *bands* of red and white around it. *Noun.*

—To put a band on. Jack *banded* the leg of the pigeon so he could identify it. *Verb.*
band (band) *noun, plural* **bands;** *verb,* **banded, banding.**

bandage A strip of cloth or other material used to cover or bind a wound or injury. Father put a *bandage* on Jerry's cut finger. *Noun.*

—To cover or bind with a bandage. The nurse *bandaged* Ann's scraped knee. *Verb.*
band·age (ban′dij) *noun, plural* **bandages;** *verb,* **bandaged, bandaging.**

Bandage

bandanna A large handkerchief with a bright pattern on it. The cowboy wore a red *bandanna* around his neck.
ban·dan·na (ban dan′ə) *noun, plural* **bandannas.**

bandit A robber or outlaw. *Bandits* held up the stagecoach.
ban·dit (ban′dit) *noun, plural* **bandits.**

bang A loud, sudden noise or blow. The door shut with a *bang. Noun.*

—**1.** To make a loud, sudden noise. The door *banged* shut. **2.** To strike or hit noisily. She *banged* the table with her fist. *Verb.*
bang (bang) *noun, plural* **bangs;** *verb,* **banged, banging.**

bangs Hair cut short and worn over the forehead. Carol wore her hair in *bangs* and pigtails.
bangs (bangz) *noun plural.*

banish **1.** To punish someone by making him leave his country. The king *banished* the man who had been a spy for the enemy. **2.** To send or drive away. The boys *banished* the player from the game for being a bad sport.
ban·ish (ban′ish) *verb,* **banished, banishing.**

banister A railing along a staircase, and the posts that support this railing.

ban·is·ter (ban′is tər) *noun, plural* **banisters.**

banjo A musical instrument that has a round body, a long neck, and five strings. A banjo is played by plucking the strings with the fingers or with a pick.
ban·jo (ban′jō) *noun, plural* **banjos** or **banjoes.**

Banjo

bank¹ **1.** A long mound or heap. The bulldozer dug up a *bank* of earth. **2.** The rising ground along a river or lake. We go fishing along the river's *bank. Noun.*

—To form into a bank; pile; heap. The plow *banked* the snow along the side of the road. *Verb.*
bank (bangk) *noun, plural* **banks;** *verb,* **banked, banking.**

bank² A place where people borrow or save money. Dad went to the *bank* to deposit one hundred dollars in his savings account. Johnny was given a toy *bank* to save his pennies in. *Noun.*

—To do business with a bank. She *banks* at the savings bank on Main Street. *Verb.*
bank (bangk) *noun, plural* **banks;** *verb,* **banked, banking.**

banker A person who helps run a bank.
bank·er (bang′kər) *noun, plural* **bankers.**

bankrupt Not able to pay what one owes. The businessman was *bankrupt* when his company failed. *Adjective.*

—To make bankrupt. The fire in his store *bankrupted* the owner. *Verb.*
bank·rupt (bangk′rupt′) *adjective; verb,* **bankrupted, bankrupting.**

▲ The word **bankrupt** comes from two Italian words that mean "broken bench." In the Middle Ages in Italy, each banker had a bench where he kept his money. Supposedly, when a banker could not pay people what he owed them, his bench was broken.

---

banner A flag or other piece of cloth that has a design and sometimes writing on it. The fans at the baseball game hung *banners* from the grandstand. *Noun.*
—Important; outstanding. It was a *banner* year for the high school football team because they won the county championship. *Adjective.*
ban·ner (ban′ər) *noun, plural* **banners;** *adjective.*

banquet A large formal dinner prepared for many people. A banquet is given for a special occasion. The school gave a *banquet* for the students who won scholarship awards.
ban·quet (bang′kwit) *noun, plural* **banquets.**

Banner

baptism A religious ceremony of dipping a person in water or sprinkling him with water. Baptism is a sign of being admitted into a Christian church.
bap·tism (bap′tiz′əm) *noun, plural* **baptisms.**

baptize To make a person a member of a Christian church by dipping him in water or sprinkling him with water. The minister *baptized* the baby.
bap·tize (bap tīz′ *or* bap′tīz) *verb,* **baptized, baptizing.**

bar **1.** A piece of metal, wood, soap, or other material that is longer than it is wide. There are *bars* on the windows of the jail. Ken ate a *bar* of candy. **2.** Something that blocks the way. The boy's small size was a *bar* to his being on the football team. **3.** A stripe or band of color. Andy's shirt has *bars* of blue and yellow on it. **4.** In music, an upright line placed on a staff to mark the division between two measures. **5.** A unit of music between two bars; measure. **6.** The profession of a lawyer. The young man passed the examination and was admitted to the *bar.* **7.** A place where alcoholic drinks are served or sold. *Noun.*
—**1.** To use a bar to fasten something. Dad *barred* the door with a heavy piece of wood. **2.** To keep out. Visitors are *barred* from the hospital in the morning. *Verb.*
bar (bär) *noun, plural* **bars;** *verb,* **barred, barring.**

barb A sharp point that curves backward. The *barb* of the fishhook caught in the fish's mouth.
barb (bärb) *noun, plural* **barbs.**

barbarian A person who belongs to a tribe or a people that is savage or uncivilized. *Barbarians* conquered Rome about 1500 years ago.
bar·bar·i·an (bär ber′ē ən) *noun, plural* **barbarians.**

barbecue A meal cooked outdoors over an open fire. *Noun.*
—To cook a meal outdoors over an open fire. Dad *barbecued* the chicken. *Verb.*
bar·be·cue (bär′bə kyoo̅′) *noun, plural* **barbecues;** *verb,* **barbecued, barbecuing.**

barbed wire Wire with barbs attached. It is used in fences.

barber A person whose work is cutting hair and trimming or shaving beards.
bar·ber (bär′bər) *noun, plural* **barbers.**

Barbed Wire Fence

bare **1.** Without covering or clothing; naked. Joey walked on the beach with *bare* feet. In winter the trees are *bare.* **2.** Empty. After we took all the books out, the shelves were *bare.* **3.** Just enough; mere. She receives only the *bare* minimum in salary for her work. *Adjective.*
—To uncover. He *bared* his chest by opening his shirt. The cat *bared* its claws. *Verb.*
▲ Another word that sounds like this is **bear.**
bare (ber) *adjective,* **barer, barest;** *verb,* **bared, baring.**

bareback On the back of a horse without a saddle. She is a *bareback* rider in the circus. *Adjective.*
—Without a saddle. The cowboy rode the horse *bareback.* *Adverb.*
bare·back (ber′bak′) *adjective; adverb.*

barefoot With the feet bare. The *barefoot* boy got a splinter in his toe. She walked *barefoot* on the grass.
bare·foot (ber′foot′) *adjective; adverb.*

at; āpe; cär; end; mē; it; īce; hot; ōld; fôrk; wood; fōōl; oil; out; up; turn; sing; thin; this; hw in white; zh in treasure.
ə stands for a in about, e in taken i in pencil, o in lemon, and u in circus.

barely Only just; scarcely. There was *barely* enough food to go around.
bare·ly (ber′lē) *adverb.*

bargain **1.** Something offered for sale or bought at a low price. At only ten cents, this ball-point pen is a *bargain*. **2.** An agreement. My brother and I made a *bargain* that I would wash the dishes if he would dry them. *Noun.*
—To try to reach a bargain. Betty *bargained* with the salesman in order to get a good price on the used bicycle. *Verb.*
bar·gain (bär′gin) *noun, plural* **bargains;** *verb,* **bargained, bargaining.**

barge A flat-bottomed boat. Barges are used to carry freight on canals and rivers.
barge (bärj) *noun, plural* **barges.**

baritone **1.** A man's singing voice that is lower than tenor and higher than bass. **2.** A singer who has such a voice.
bar·i·tone (bar′ə tōn′) *noun, plural* **baritones.**

bark¹ The outer covering of the trunk, branches, and roots of a tree. Bark is usually thick and rough. *Noun.*
—To scrape or rub the skin off. He *barked* his shins when he fell on the stairway. *Verb.*
bark (bärk) *noun, plural* **barks;** *verb,* **barked, barking.**

bark² The short, sharp sound that a dog makes. *Noun.*
—**1.** To make the short, sharp sound that a dog makes. The watchdog *barked* at the stranger. **2.** To speak loudly and sharply. The sheriff *barked* "Hands up!" at the outlaw. *Verb.*
bark (bärk) *noun, plural* **barks;** *verb,* **barked, barking.**

barley The grain of a plant that is like grass. Barley is often used as animal feed and to make malt.
bar·ley (bär′lē) *noun.*

barn A building on a farm. Barns are used to store hay and grain, and to house cows and horses.
barn (bärn) *noun, plural* **barns.**

Barn

barnyard A yard around a barn. The chickens pecked for food in the *barnyard*.
barn·yard (bärn′yärd′) *noun, plural* **barnyards.**

barometer An instrument for measuring the pressure of the atmosphere. A barometer shows changes in the weather.
ba·rom·e·ter (bə rom′ə tər) *noun, plural* **barometers.**

baron A nobleman of the lowest rank. ▲ Another word that sounds like this is **barren.**
bar·on (bar′ən) *noun, plural* **barons.**

barracks A building or group of buildings where soldiers live. Barracks are found on military bases.
bar·racks (bar′əks) *noun plural.*

barracuda A fierce fish that lives in warm seas. The barracuda has a long, narrow body and a large mouth with sharp teeth. Barracudas have been known to attack swimmers.
bar·ra·cu·da (bar′ə kōō′də) *noun, plural* **barracudas** or **barracuda.**

Barracuda

barrage A heavy amount of cannon, rocket, or gun fire to keep enemy soldiers from moving forward or attacking.
bar·rage (bə räzh′) *noun, plural* **barrages.**

barrel **1.** A large, round wooden container with curved sides. The farmer packed the apples in *barrels*. **2.** A metal tube that forms part of a gun. Bullets are fired through the barrel.
bar·rel (bar′əl) *noun, plural* **barrels.**

barren Not able to produce anything. No plants could grow in the sandy, *barren* soil. The apple tree is *barren* and cannot bear fruit. ▲ Another word that sounds like this is **baron.**
bar·ren (bar′ən) *adjective.*

Barrel

barricade Something that blocks the way. The police set up *barricades* to keep the crowds away from the accident. *Noun.*
—To block the way with a barricade. The settlers piled up logs to *barricade* the entrance to the fort. *Verb.*
  bar·ri·cade (bar′ə kād′) *noun, plural* **barricades;** *verb,* **barricaded, barricading.**

barrier Something that blocks the way. The fallen tree was a *barrier* to traffic on the road.
  bar·ri·er (bar′ē ər) *noun, plural* **barriers.**

barter To trade goods for other goods without using money. The early pioneers *bartered* seed for animal skins with the Indians. *Verb.*
—The trading of goods for other goods without the use of money. Among early settlers in this country much trade was carried on by *barter. Noun.*
  bar·ter (bär′tər) *verb,* **bartered, bartering;** *noun.*

base¹ **1.** The part that something rests or stands on; the lowest part. That lamp has a wooden *base.* The boys camped at the *base* of the mountain. **2.** The main part of something. Mother made soup with a chicken *base.* **3.** A starting place. The airplanes got back to the *base* safely. **4.** One of the four corners of a baseball diamond. The batter reached first *base.* **5.** A chemical that joins with an acid to make a salt. Bases have a bitter taste when dissolved in water. A base will cause red litmus paper to turn blue. *Noun.*
—To put on a base. The builders *based* the house on concrete. The famous writer *bases* his stories on his own experiences. *Verb.*
▲ Another word that sounds like this is **bass.**
  base (bās) *noun, plural* **bases;** *verb,* **based, basing.**

base² **1.** Not brave or honorable; cowardly, shameful, or bad. Telling lies about his friend was a *base* thing to do. **2.** Low in value when compared with something else. Iron is a *base* metal; gold is a precious metal. ▲ Another word that sounds like this is **bass.**
  base (bās) *adjective,* **baser, basest.**

baseball **1.** A game played with a ball and bat by two teams of nine players each. Baseball is played on a field with four bases that form a diamond. To score a run, you must reach home base by way of first, second, and third bases before you or your team are put out. Each team is allowed three outs in an inning, and a game is made up of nine innings. **2.** The ball used in this game.
  base·ball (bās′bôl′) *noun, plural* **baseballs.**

basement The lowest floor of a building. The basement is below or partly below the ground.
  base·ment (bās′mənt) *noun, plural* **basements.**

bashful Embarassed and shy around people. The *bashful* little boy hid behind his mother's skirt.
  bash·ful (bash′fəl) *adjective.*

basic Forming the most important part; fundamental. Food is a *basic* human need. The *basic* parts of a bicycle are the wheels, handlebars, and frame. A *basic* difference between the two friends is that Mike likes to play baseball and Bill likes to read.
  ba·sic (bā′sik) *adjective.*

basin **1.** A round or oval bowl for holding liquids. Johnny filled the *basin* of the sink with water. **2.** An area containing water. The harbor has a boat *basin.* **3.** All the land that is drained by a river and by all the streams flowing into the river.
  ba·sin (bā′sin) *noun, plural* **basins.**

basis The part that something rests or depends on; foundation. The *basis* for my opinion on the matter is something I read about it in a book.
  ba·sis (bā′sis) *noun, plural* **bases.**

bask To lie in and enjoy a pleasant warmth. The children *basked* in the sun on the beach. The boys *basked* in front of the campfire.
  bask (bask) *verb,* **basked, basking.**

Baseball

at; āpe; cär; end; mē; it; īce; hot; ōld;
fôrk; wood; fōol; oil; out; up; turn; sing;
thin; this; hw in white; zh in treasure.
ə stands for a in about, e in taken
i in pencil, o in lemon, and u in circus.

basket **1.** Something to hold things. Baskets are made of twigs, straw, strips of wood, or other material woven together. Phil picked apples and put them in a *basket.* Dad bought a *basket* of pears from the farmer. **2.** A metal hoop with a net hanging from it used in basketball. The ball is thrown through the basket to score a goal.
bas·ket (bas′kit) *noun, plural* **baskets.**

basketball **1.** A game played with a large, round ball on a rectangular court by two teams of five players each. To score a goal, a player must throw the ball through a raised basket at the opponent's end of the court. **2.** The ball used in this game.
bas·ket·ball (bas′kit bôl′) *noun, plural* **bas-ketballs.**

Basketball

bass¹ **1.** The lowest man's singing voice. **2.** A singer who has such a voice. **3.** A musical instrument that has a similar range. ▲ Another word that sounds like this is **base.**
bass (bās) *noun, plural* **basses.**

bass² Any of a number of North American fish. Bass are used for food. They can be found in streams and lakes, and in the sea.
bass (bas) *noun, plural* **bass** or **basses.**

bass drum A very large drum that gives a deep, booming sound when it is struck.
bass drum (bās).

bassoon A musical instrument that makes a low sound when it is played. The bassoon is made up of a long double wooden tube. It is played by blowing into a curved metal mouthpiece at one end.
bas·soon (bə-soon′) *noun, plural* **bassoons.**

Bassoon

bass viol The largest stringed musical instrument. It gives a very low sound when it is played. The bass viol is shaped like a violin, but it is played standing upright on the floor because it is very large. The musician plays it with a bow or by plucking with his fingers.
bass vi·ol (bās vī′əl).

baste¹ To pour melted butter, fat, gravy, or other liquid over food to keep it moist while it is roasting. Mother used a large spoon to *baste* the chicken.
baste (bāst) *verb,* **basted, basting.**

baste² To sew with long, loose stitches. She *basted* the seam of the dress in place before sewing it on the sewing machine.
baste (bāst) *verb,* **basted, basting.**

bat¹ **1.** A strong wooden stick or club. A bat is used to hit the ball in baseball and softball. **2.** A turn to hit the ball in baseball and softball. Our team is at *bat. Noun.*
—To hit the ball with a bat. Jack *batted* the ball out of the park. It is her turn to *bat. Verb.*
bat (bat) *noun, plural* **bats;** *verb,* **batted, batting.**

bat² A small, furry animal. A bat has a body like a mouse and wings of thin skin. Bats fly mostly at night.
bat (bat) *noun, plural* **bats.**

Bat

batch A group of things or persons. Susan baked a *batch* of cookies. We threw away a *batch* of old newspapers.
   batch (bach) *noun, plural* **batches.**

bath **1.** A washing of something in water. She took a warm *bath*. John gave his dog a *bath*. **2.** The water used for bathing. The *bath* was too hot. **3.** A place or room for bathing; bathroom. The house has two bedrooms and one *bath*.
   bath (bath) *noun, plural* **baths.**

bathe **1.** To wash something in water. Mary is going to *bathe* her puppy. He *bathes* each morning before breakfast. **2.** To go swimming. The children love to *bathe* in the ocean during the summer. **3.** To surround or cover with something. Sweat *bathed* his forehead. She turned on the lamps, and the room was *bathed* in light.
   bathe (bath) *verb*, **bathed, bathing.**

bathing suit A piece of clothing worn while swimming.

bathroom A room that has a sink, toilet, and a bathtub or shower.
   bath·room (bath′room′ *or* bath′room′) *noun, plural* **bathrooms.**

bathtub A large tub to bathe in.
   bath·tub (bath′tub′) *noun, plural* **bathtubs.**

baton A stick or rod. The conductor used a *baton* to direct the orchestra. The drum majorette twirled her *baton*.
   ba·ton (bə ton′) *noun, plural* **batons.**

battalion A large part of an army. A battalion forms part of a regiment.
   bat·tal·ion (bə tal′yən) *noun, plural* **battalions.**

Baton

batter¹ To hit over and over again with heavy blows. The sailor was afraid the high waves would *batter* the small boat to pieces.
   bat·ter (bat′ər) *verb*, **battered, battering.**

batter² A mixture of flour, milk or water, and other things. Batter is fried or baked to make pancakes, doughnuts, biscuits, or cakes.
   bat·ter (bat′ər) *noun, plural* **batters.**

batter³ A person whose turn it is to bat in a game of baseball or softball.
   bat·ter (bat′ər) *noun, plural* **batters.**

battering ram A heavy beam once used in war to batter down walls or gates.

Battering Ram

battery **1.** A device that produces an electric current by chemical changes in the materials inside it. Flashlights must have *batteries* to work. Her portable radio needs a new *battery*. **2.** A group of things that are alike or that work together. A *battery* of microphones stood in front of the astronaut as he gave his speech. The *battery* of guns was silent after the battle was over.
   bat·ter·y (bat′ər ē) *noun, plural* **batteries.**

battle A fight or struggle. The two armies fought a *battle*. Life in the Arctic is a constant *battle* against the cold. *Noun.*
   —To fight or struggle. The armies *battled* for control of the city. The ship *battled* the high waves. *Verb.*
   bat·tle (bat′əl) *noun, plural* **battles;** *verb,* **battled, battling.**

battle-ax A heavy ax with a wide blade. It was once used as a weapon in war.
   bat·tle-ax (bat′əl aks′) *noun, plural* **battle-axes.**

battlefield A place where a battle was fought or is being fought. Gettysburg is a famous *battlefield* of the Civil War.
   bat·tle·field (bat′əl fēld′) *noun, plural* **battlefields.**

battlement A low wall built along the top of a fort or tower. A battlement has a series of openings for soldiers to shoot through at someone attacking from outside.
   bat·tle·ment (bat′əl mənt) *noun, plural* **battlements.**

at; āpe; cär; end; mē; it; īce; hot; ōld; fôrk; wood; fool; oil; out; up; turn; sing; thin; this; hw in white; zh in treasure.
ə stands for a in about, e in taken i in pencil, o in lemon, and u in circus.

battleship A large warship with very powerful guns and thick, heavy armor.
   bat·tle·ship (bat′əl ship′) *noun, plural* **battleships.**

bawl To cry or shout loudly. The lost child *bawled* for his mother. *Verb.*
   —A loud cry or shout. *Noun.* ▲ Another word that sounds like this is **ball.**
   bawl (bôl) *verb,* **bawled, bawling;** *noun.*
   to bawl out. To scold loudly. Dad *bawled out* my brother for breaking the window.

bay¹ A part of a sea or lake that stretches into the land.
   bay (bā) *noun, plural* **bays.**

bay² The deep, long barking or howling of a dog. The hunter heard the *bay* of the hounds chasing a rabbit. *Noun.*
   —To bark or howl with deep, long sounds. The dog *bayed* at the moon. *Verb.*
   bay (bā) *noun, plural* **bays;** *verb,* **bayed, baying.**

bayonet A large knife that fits on the end of a rifle. A bayonet is used in fighting.
   bay·o·net (bā′ə net′) *noun, plural* **bayonets.**

Bayonet

bayou A stream that flows slowly through marshy land. Bayous are found in the southern United States.
   bay·ou (bī′o͞o *or* bī′ō) *noun, plural* **bayous.**

bazaar A sale of different things for some special purpose. Mother baked a cake for the church *bazaar.*
   ba·zaar (bə zär′) *noun, plural* **bazaars.**

B.C. An abbreviation meaning "before Christ." It is used in giving dates before the birth of Christ. 100 *B.C.* means 100 years before the birth of Christ.

be That house must *be* the largest one in town. Bill is going to *be* sixteen years old tomorrow. This game should *be* fun. She will *be* home soon. *Be* kind to him. The train may

be late. ▲ Another word that sounds like this is **bee.**
   be (bē) *verb,* **been, being.**

beach The land along the edge of an ocean. A beach is covered with sand or pebbles. We hunted for different kinds of shells along the *beach. Noun.*
   —To run a boat onto a beach. We *beached* our sailboat in order to paint it. *Verb.*
   ▲ Another word that sounds like this is **beech.**
   beach (bēch) *noun, plural* **beaches;** *verb,* **beached, beaching.**

beacon A light or other signal that warns or guides. The *beacon* from the lighthouse guided the ship through the fog.
   bea·con (bē′kən) *noun, plural* **beacons.**

bead **1.** A small round piece of glass, wood, plastic, or other material. A bead has a hole through it so that it can be strung on a wire or string with other pieces like it. Alice wore a necklace of red *beads.* **2.** Any small round thing. *Beads* of sweat rolled down the runner's face. *Noun.*
   —To decorate with beads. The woman's long dress was *beaded* with silver. *Verb.*
   bead (bēd) *noun, plural* **beads;** *verb,* **beaded, beading.**

beagle A small dog with short legs, a smooth coat, and drooping ears. Beagles are kept as pets and also are used to hunt squirrels, rabbits, and other small animals.
   bea·gle (bē′gəl) *noun, plural* **beagles.**

Beagle

beak The hard mouth part of a bird. Hawks and eagles have sharp, hooked beaks.
   beak (bēk) *noun, plural* **beaks.**

beaker A glass cup or container with a lip for pouring. Beakers are used in laboratories.
   beak·er (bē′kər) *noun, plural* **beakers.**

beam **1.** A long, strong piece of wood or metal. Beams are used in building to support floors or ceilings. **2.** A narrow ray of light. *Beams* of sunlight came through the window. The campers could see the path by the *beams* of their flashlights. *Noun.*
   —**1.** To shine brightly. The sun *beamed* down on the cornfield. **2.** To smile happily. The girl *beamed* with happiness when her parents gave her a bicycle. *Verb.*
   beam (bēm) *noun, plural* **beams;** *verb,* **beamed, beaming.**

bean **1.** A smooth, flat seed that is eaten as a vegetable. There are many different kinds of beans. Sometimes the long pods that these seeds grow in are also eaten. Some beans that people eat are the lima bean, string bean, and the kidney bean. **2.** Any seed that looks like a bean. Mother ground the coffee *beans*.
bean (bēn) *noun, plural* **beans**.

bear¹ **1.** To hold up; support or carry. Beams *bear* the weight of the roof of our house. Don't climb that tree because its branches won't *bear* your weight. **2.** To bring forth; give birth to. The peach tree *bears* fruit. Our dog will *bear* puppies soon. **3.** To put up with patiently; stand. My brother Tom cannot *bear* being teased. The little girl was able to *bear* the pain of her broken arm bravely. ▲ Another word that sounds like this is **bare**.
bear (ber) *verb,* **bore, borne** or **born, bearing**.

bear² A large, heavy animal with thick shaggy fur. A bear has sharp claws and a very short tail. There are many kinds of bears, including the black bear, brown bear, grizzly bear, and the polar bear. ▲ Another word that sounds like this is **bare**.
bear (ber) *noun, plural* **bears**.

Bear

beard **1.** The hair that grows on a man's face. **2.** Something that looks like a beard. That goat has a *beard* on its chin.
beard (bērd) *noun, plural* **beards**.

Beard

bearing **1.** The way that a person walks, stands, or acts. The young man has the *bearing* of an athlete. **2.** Connection in thought. Jack's silly remark had no *bearing* on what we were talking about. **3. bearings.** Knowledge of one's position or direction. The campers lost their *bearings* and wandered for hours before they found the right path again. **4.** A part of a machine that holds a moving part and allows it to move with less friction. Joe replaced a worn *bearing* in the automobile engine.
bear·ing (ber′ing) *noun, plural* **bearings**.

beast **1.** Any animal that has four feet. We went to the zoo to see the tigers, elephants, and other *beasts* of the jungle. **2.** A person who is coarse or cruel.
beast (bēst) *noun, plural* **beasts**.

beat **1.** To hit again and again; pound. He *beat* the drum during the parade. The wicked man *beat* his horse. The ocean waves *beat* against the side of the boat. **2.** To do better than; get the better of; defeat. Our baseball team *beat* their team. She *beat* her brother at checkers. **3.** To thump or throb. He could feel the kitten's heart *beat*. **4.** To move up and down; flap. The eagle *beat* its wings. **5.** To stir or mix with force. She *beat* the eggs for the cake. *Verb.*
—**1.** A blow made over and over again. We could hear the *beat* of the drum. **2.** A throb. He pressed his hand to his chest and felt the *beat* of his heart. **3.** A regular route or round. Jack saw a policeman patrolling his *beat*. **4.** The basic unit of time in music. Jill tapped her foot to the *beat* of the music. *Noun.* ▲ Another word that sounds like this is **beet**.
beat (bēt) *verb,* **beat, beaten** or **beat, beating;** *noun, plural* **beats**.

beaten Their basketball team has *beaten* ours every year. Look up **beat** for more information. *Verb.*
—**1.** Worn by use. The hunters followed a *beaten* path through the woods. **2.** Defeated. The *beaten* football team hoped to do better in the next game. *Adjective.*
beat·en (bēt′ən) *verb; adjective*.

beautiful Pleasing to look at or hear. She has a *beautiful* face. The band played some *beautiful* music. We had *beautiful* weather for our picnic.
beau·ti·ful (byōō′ti fəl) *adjective*.

beauty **1.** A quality that makes a person or thing pleasing to look at or hear. The garden is a place of *beauty* when all the flowers are in bloom. **2.** A person or thing that is beautiful. Steve's new bicycle is a *beauty*.
beau·ty (byōō′tē) *noun, plural* **beauties**.

at; āpe; cär; end; mē; it; īce; hot; ōld;
fôrk; wood; fōōl; oil; out; up; turn; sing;
thin; this; hw in white; zh in treasure.
ə stands for a in about, e in taken
i in pencil, o in lemon, and u in circus.

beaver A furry, brown animal that has a broad, flat tail and webbed hind feet to help it swim. The beaver lives in or near the water in a house built of branches, stones, and mud. It protects its house from the water by building a dam of these same materials.
bea·ver (bē′vər) *noun, plural* **beavers.**

Beaver

became My older sister *became* a lawyer. Look up **become** for more information.
be·came (bi kām′) *verb.*

because For the reason that. Phil is cold *because* he did not wear his sweater. She drank two glasses of water *because* she was thirsty.
be·cause (bi kôz′) *conjunction.*
because of. On account of. They were late to the party *because of* a flat tire.

beckon To make a sign or signal to someone. He *beckoned* to his friend to join him by waving his hand.
beck·on (bek′ən) *verb,* **beckoned, beckoning.**

become **1.** To grow to be; come to be. Tadpoles *become* frogs. I have *become* tired. **2.** To look well on; flatter; suit. A blue shirt *becomes* him.
be·come (bi kum′) *verb,* **became, become, becoming.**
become of. To happen to. What has *become of* my pencil?

becoming Looking well on; flattering. Jerry's new jacket is *becoming* to him.
be·com·ing (bi kum′ing) *adjective.*

bed **1.** Something used to sleep or rest on. Dad bought Philip a new *bed* with a thick mattress. The deer slept on a *bed* of leaves. **2.** A piece of ground used to grow plants in. Mother planted roses in the flower *bed*. **3.** The ground at the bottom of a river, stream, or lake. The stream had a *bed* of sand and pebbles. **4.** A foundation or support. The road was built on a *bed* of gravel. *Noun.*
—To give a place to sleep to. Johnny decided to *bed* his dog in the garage. *Verb.*

bed (bed) *noun, plural* **beds;** *verb,* **bedded, bedding.**

bedding Sheets, blankets, and other coverings used on a bed.
bed·ding (bed′ing) *noun, plural* **beddings.**

bedraggled Wet, limp, and dirty. We found a *bedraggled* kitten in the street.
be·drag·gled (bi drag′əld) *adjective.*

bedroom A room for sleeping. Our house has three *bedrooms*.
bed·room (bed′rōōm′ *or* bed′room′) *noun, plural* **bedrooms.**

bedside The space beside a bed. The mother waited at the sick little boy's *bedside* until he was asleep.
bed·side (bed′sīd′) *noun, plural* **bedsides.**

bedspread A top cover for a bed.
bed·spread (bed′spred′) *noun, plural* **bedspreads.**

bedtime The time for a person to go to bed. Her *bedtime* is nine o'clock.
bed·time (bed′tīm′) *noun, plural* **bedtimes.**

bee An insect that has a thick, hairy body, four wings, and a stinger. A bee feeds on nectar and pollen. Some bees live in colonies or hives, and make honey and beeswax. ▲ Another word that sounds like this is **be.**
bee (bē) *noun, plural* **bees.**

beech A tree that has smooth, light gray bark and small, sweet nuts. ▲ Another word that sounds like this is **beach.**
beech (bēch) *noun, plural* **beeches.**

Leaf
in Autumn

Beech Tree

beef The meat of a steer, cow, or bull used for food.
beef (bēf) *noun.*

beefsteak A slice of beef to be broiled or fried.
beef·steak (bēf′stāk′) *noun, plural* **beefsteaks.**

beehive   A hive or house for bees.
bee·hive (bē′hīv′) *noun, plural* **beehives.**

Beehive

Inside the Beehive

been   I have *been* sick with a cold. ▲ Another word that sounds like this is **bin.**
been (bin) *verb.*

beer   An alcoholic drink made from specially treated grains, called malt, and the fruit of a certain plant, called hops.
beer (bēr) *noun, plural* **beers.**

beeswax   The yellow wax given out by honeybees, used by them to make their honeycombs.
bees·wax (bēz′waks′) *noun.*

beet   A plant with long, thick roots. The leaves and roots of some beets are cooked and eaten as vegetables. ▲ Another word that sounds like this is **beat.**
beet (bēt) *noun, plural* **beets.**

beetle   An insect with hard front wings that protect the thin hind wings when folded. Beetles have biting mouth parts. Some beetles cause much damage to plants.
bee·tle (bēt′əl) *noun, plural* **beetles.**

Beetles

befall   To happen or happen to. The sailors were afraid that some harm might *befall* their ship in the storm.
be·fall (bi fôl′) *verb,* **befell, befallen, befalling.**

before   In front of; ahead of. Ed stood *before* me in line. The letter A comes *before* B. We arrived at the party *before* everyone else. *Preposition.*
—In front; ahead; already. I've seen that movie *before. Adverb.*
—Earlier than the time when. It grew dark *before* the boys finished the game. *Conjunction.*
be·fore (bi fôr′) *preposition; adverb; conjunction.*

beforehand   Ahead of time. Paul found out *beforehand* what his birthday present was.
be·fore·hand (bi fôr′hand′) *adverb.*

beg   To ask for; ask. A tramp in our neighborhood sometimes *begs* for a meal. I *beg* your pardon; I didn't mean to hurt your feelings.
beg (beg) *verb,* **begged, begging.**

began   The boy *began* to run. Look up **begin** for more information.
be·gan (bi gan′) *verb.*

beggar   A very poor person. Some beggars ask for money, food, or clothes in order to live.
beg·gar (beg′ər) *noun, plural* **beggars.**

begin   1. To do the first part of something; make a start. The builders will *begin* to build the house next month. *Begin* your homework now. 2. To come into being; start. The movie *begins* at two o'clock.
be·gin (bi gin′) *verb,* **began, begun, beginning.**

beginner   A person who is starting to do something for the first time. My little brother is in a swimming class for *beginners.*
be·gin·ner (bi gin′ər) *noun, plural* **beginners.**

beginning   1. The first part. The *beginning* of the story was exciting. 2. The time when something begins; start. Yesterday was the *beginning* of my vacation.
be·gin·ning (bi gin′ing) *noun, plural* **beginnings.**

at; āpe; cär; end; mē; it; īce; hot; ōld;
fôrk; wood; fool; oil; out; up; turn; sing;
thin; this; hw in white; zh in treasure.
ə stands for a in about, e in taken
i in pencil, o in lemon, and u in circus.

begonia   A tropical plant with large, bright flowers.
be·gon·ia (bi gōn′-yə) *noun, plural* **begonias.**

Begonia

begun   The game has *begun*. Look up **begin** for more information.
be·gun (bi gun′) *verb.*

behalf   On **behalf of** or **in behalf of**. For the good of; for. The church held a fair *on behalf of* the town hospital.
be·half (bi haf′) *noun.*

behave   1. To act; do. The little boy *behaved* bravely when he did not cry after he hurt his knee. 2. To act in a good way. My little brother promised to *behave* himself at the party.
be·have (bi hāv′) *verb*, **behaved, behaving.**

behavior   A way of behaving or acting. The children's *behavior* was good. The science class studied the *behavior* of the grasshopper.
be·hav·ior (bi hāv′yər) *noun.*

behead   To cut off someone's head.
be·head (bi hed′) *verb*, **beheaded, beheading.**

behind   1. At the back of. I sit *behind* my best friend in school. Jim hid *behind* a tree. 2. Later than; after. The second bus came ten minutes *behind* the first bus. 3. Not as good as. Our team was *behind* the other team by three points. *Preposition.*
—1. At the back. He sneaked up on his friend from *behind*. 2. In a place just left. In the race, Joe left the other runners far *behind*. 3. Not on time; late; slow. He is *behind* in his homework. *Adverb.*
be·hind (bi hīnd′) *preposition; adverb.*

behold   To look at; see. The campers stayed up late to *behold* the beauty of the stars.
be·hold (bi hōld′) *verb*, **beheld, beholding.**

beige   A pale-brown color. *Noun.*
—Having the color beige. *Adjective.*
beige (bāzh) *noun, plural* **beiges;** *adjective.*

being   The baby is *being* washed. *Verb.*
—1. Life. Many of our customs came into *being* years ago. 2. A person or animal. *Noun.*
be·ing (bē′ing) *verb; noun, plural* **beings.**

belated   Late. My aunt sent me a *belated* birthday present a week after my birthday.
be·lat·ed (bi lā′tid) *adjective.*

belfry   A tower or a room in a tower where bells are hung. Some churches have a belfry.
bel·fry (bel′frē) *noun, plural* **belfries.**

belief   1. Trust; faith. She has a *belief* in her brother's honesty. 2. Something that is believed to be true. Our country was founded on the *belief* that all men are created equal. It is my *belief* that she is honest.
be·lief (bi lēf′) *noun, plural* **beliefs.**

believe   1. To have trust or faith in the truth of. The police didn't *believe* the thief. Jack *believes* in ghosts. 2. To think; suppose. I *believe* that Chris went to the ball game.
be·lieve (bi lēv′) *verb*, **believed, believing.**

Belfry

belittle   To make seem less important. The boy *belittled* his younger brother's stamp collection because he was jealous.
be·lit·tle (bi lit′əl) *verb*, **belittled, belittling.**

bell   1. A hollow metal object that is shaped like a cup. A bell makes a ringing sound when struck.   2. Something that makes a ringing sound like a bell. He went up to the door and rang the *bell*.
bell (bel) *noun, plural* **bells.**

Bell

belligerent   1. Wanting to fight. That *belligerent* boy is a bully and always picks on other boys. 2. Busy fighting; at war. The two *belligerent* countries fought a long battle.
bel·lig·er·ent (bə lij′ər ənt) *adjective.*

bellow   To make a loud, deep sound; roar. The bull *bellowed* in the pasture. The angry man *bellowed* at the boys who had broken his window. *Verb.*
—A loud, deep sound; roar. *Noun.*
bel·low (bel′ō) *verb*, **bellowed, bellowing;** *noun, plural* **bellows.**

bellows   A device that makes a strong current of air when it is pumped open and closed. Some bellows are used to make fires burn faster. Some musical instruments, such as the accordion, are made to produce sound by means of a bellows.

bel·lows (bel′ōz) *noun, plural.*

Bellows

belly 1. The front part of the body below the chest and above the legs; abdomen. 2. The stomach. 3. A curved or bulging part of something. The airplane made an emergency landing on its *belly. Noun.*
—To swell or billow. The sails of the ship *bellied* out. *Verb.*

bel·ly (bel′ē) *noun, plural* **bellies;** *verb,* **bellied, bellying.**

belong 1. To have a special right or place. The lamp *belongs* on that table. The coat *belongs* in the closet, not on the floor. 2. To be owned by. The baseball cap *belongs* to Fred. 3. To be part of. Fran *belongs* to a stamp club.

be·long (bi lông′) *verb,* **belonged, belonging.**

belongings Things owned by a person; possessions. Mike packed his *belongings* in a large box.

be·long·ings (bi lông′ingz) *noun, plural.*

beloved Loved very much. The little boy has lost his *beloved* puppy.

be·lov·ed (bi luv′id *or* bi luvd′) *adjective.*

below From my window I could see the street *below.* Jerry's bunk bed is *below* his brother's.

be·low (bi lō′) *adverb; preposition.*

belt 1. A strip or band of cloth, leather, or other material. People wear belts around the waist to hold up clothing. 2. A region or area. We drove through the farm *belt* and saw many cows. 3. An endless band wound around two wheels or pulleys. A belt transfers power or motion from one wheel or pulley to another.

belt (belt) *noun, plural* **belts.**

bench 1. A long seat. We sat on the park *bench.* 2. A long table for working on. The carpenter repaired the broken chair at his *bench.* 3. A judge in a court of law. The thief was brought before the *bench. Noun.*
—To keep a player from playing. The coach *benched* the football player because he had played so badly in the last game. *Verb.*

bench (bench) *noun, plural* **benches;** *verb,* **benched, benching.**

bend 1. To change the shape of something by making it curved or crooked. Terry will *bend* the wire to make a hook. The stream *bends* to the left just beyond those trees. 2. To move the top part of the body forward and down; stoop; bow. Sam *bent* over to tie his shoe. *Verb.*
—Something bent. The boys' tent is just beyond the *bend* in the trail. *Noun.*

bend (bend) *verb,* **bent, bending;** *noun, plural* **bends.**

A Bend in a River

beneath He stood *beneath* the tree. Betty swept the dust *beneath* the rug. The house has an attic above and a basement *beneath.*

be·neath (bi nēth′) *preposition; adverb.*

benefit Something that helps a person or thing. Knowing how to speak Spanish is a great *benefit* if you visit Mexico. *Noun.*
—To be helpful to; be helped by. Rain will *benefit* the farmer's crops. *Verb.*

ben·e·fit (ben′ə fit) *noun, plural* **benefits;** *verb,* **benefited, benefiting.**

bent He *bent* the coat hanger. Look up **bend** for more information. *Verb.*
—1. Curved or crooked. He found a *bent* nail in his tool chest. 2. Determined; set. He was *bent* on going fishing. *Adjective.*

bent (bent) *verb; adjective.*

at; āpe; cär; end; mē; it; īce; hot; ōld;
fôrk; wood; fo͞ol; oil; out; up; turn; sing;
thin; this; hw in white; zh in treasure.
ə stands for a in about, e in taken
i in pencil, o in lemon, and u in circus.

beret A soft, round, flat cap.
be·ret (bə rā′) *noun, plural* **berets.**

berry A small, juicy, and fleshy fruit that can be eaten. A berry has many seeds. Blackberries, blueberries, and strawberries are berries. ▲ Another word that sounds like this is **bury.**
ber·ry (ber′ē) *noun, plural* **berries.**

Beret

berth **1.** A bed or bunk on a train or ship. I had the upper *berth* on our train trip. **2.** A place for a ship to dock. The freighter was in its *berth* in the harbor. ▲ Another word that sounds like this is **birth.**
berth (burth) *noun, plural* **berths.**

beseech To ask someone in a pleading way; beg. I *beseech* you to help me.
be·seech (bi sēch′) *verb,* **besought** or **beseeched, beseeching.**

beset To surround and attack. The hunter and his dogs *beset* the bear.
be·set (bi set′) *verb,* **beset, besetting.**

beside He sat *beside* his friend. The oak tree is *beside* the house.
be·side (bi sīd′) *preposition.*

besides He didn't want to go to the party; *besides,* he had work to do. There were many people at the park *besides* us.
be·sides (bi sīdz′) *adverb; preposition.*

besiege **1.** To surround in order to capture. The soldiers *besieged* the fort. **2.** To crowd around. The fans *besieged* the football player to get his autograph.
be·siege (bi sēj′) *verb,* **besieged, besieging.**

best He is the *best* hitter on the baseball team. I like chocolate ice cream *best.* She is the *best* on the tennis team.
best (best) *adjective; adverb; noun.*

bestow To give. The school *bestowed* a medal on the student.
be·stow (bi stō′) *verb,* **bestowed, bestowing.**

bet An agreement to pay money to another person if he is right about something and you are wrong. I made a *bet* with my friend that our team would win. The other team won, so I lost my *bet. Noun.*
—**1.** To agree to pay money to another person if he is right about something and you are wrong; make a bet. Paul *bet* George that he could beat him in tennis. **2.** To say with confidence; be certain. I *bet* that it won't rain tomorrow. *Verb.*

bet (bet) *noun, plural* **bets;** *verb,* **bet** or **betted, betting.**

betray **1.** To give help to the enemy of. The wicked man *betrayed* his country. **2.** To be unfaithful to. She will not *betray* her friend by telling others his secret.
be·tray (bi trā′) *verb,* **betrayed, betraying.**

better Our team is *better* than theirs. He is a *better* student than his friend. She swims *better* than I do. Which is the *better* of these two books?
bet·ter (bet′ər) *adjective; adverb; noun, plural* **betters.**

between The table is *between* the chairs. Terry does not eat *between* meals. During an eclipse, the moon is *between* the earth and the sun. There was a quarrel *between* the two brothers. There are two farms with a lake *between.*
be·tween (bi twēn′) *preposition; adverb.*

beverage A liquid for drinking. Orange juice, milk, and coffee are beverages.
bev·er·age (bev′ər ij) *noun, plural* **beverages.**

beware To be on one's guard; be careful. *Beware* of the traffic when you cross the street. *Beware* of that dog.
be·ware (bi wer′) *verb.*

bewilder To confuse or puzzle; mix up. The hard arithmetic problem *bewildered* the boy.
be·wil·der (bi wil′dər) *verb,* **bewildered, bewildering.**

bewitch **1.** To cast a spell over someone by witchcraft or magic. The wicked fairy *bewitched* the prince and turned him into a frog. **2.** To charm. The girl's beautiful smile *bewitched* everyone.
be·witch (bi wich′) *verb,* **bewitched, bewitching.**

beyond Our camp is *beyond* those trees. He stayed awake well *beyond* his bedtime. The toys cost far *beyond* what they should. What Dad told us about computers was *beyond* me. Look *beyond,* and you'll see the mountains in the distance.
be·yond (bē ond′) *preposition; adverb.*

bias A strong leaning for or against a person or thing when there is no reason for it. A good judge never shows *bias* when he tries a case in court. *Noun.*
—To cause to have or show bias. That boy's bragging about how smart he is has *biased* me against him even though I don't know him well. *Verb.*
bi·as (bī′əs) *noun, plural* **biases;** *verb,* **biased, biasing.**

Bible **1.** The sacred writings of the Christian

religion as contained in the Old Testament and the New Testament. **2.** The sacred writings of the Jewish religion as contained in the Old Testament.

Bi·ble (bī′bəl) *noun.*

biblical Found in the Bible; relating to the Bible. The story of Noah's ark is a *biblical* story.

bib·li·cal (bib′li kəl) *adjective.*

bibliography A list of books about a subject.

bib·li·og·ra·phy (bib′lē og′rə fē) *noun, plural* **bibliographies.**

biceps The large muscle in the top part of the upper arm.

bi·ceps (bī′seps) *noun, plural* **biceps** or **bicepses.**

bicker To quarrel in a noisy way about something that is not very important. The two brothers always *bicker* about whose turn it is to wash the dishes.

bick·er (bik′ər) *verb,* **bickered, bickering.**

bicuspid A tooth with two points. A grown person has eight bicuspids.

bi·cus·pid (bī kus′pid) *noun, plural* **bicuspids.**

bicycle A light vehicle to ride on. A bicycle has two wheels, one behind the other. It has a seat, handlebars to steer with, and two foot pedals to turn the wheels and make it go forward.

bi·cy·cle (bī′si kəl) *noun, plural* **bicycles.**

bid **1.** To give an order to; command. The judge *bid* the prisoner to step forward. **2.** To say when meeting or leaving someone. The children *bid* their aunt good-by. **3.** To offer to pay. Ted *bid* fifty dollars for the old desk at the auction. *Verb.*
—An offer to pay money. Mary made a *bid* for a lamp at the auction. *Noun.*

bid (bid) *verb* **bid, bidding;** *noun, plural* **bids.**

bidding **1.** An order; command. The boy mowed the lawn at his father's *bidding.* **2.** The making of bids. The *bidding* at the auction was noisy.

bid·ding (bid′ing) *noun, plural* **biddings.**

bide **To bide one's time.** To wait for the right moment or chance. She will *bide her time* until spring to buy a winter coat on sale.

bide (bīd) *verb,* **bided, biding.**

big Great in size or amount; large. New York is a *big* city. A redwood is a *big* tree. That was a *big* mistake. He is a *big* man in our town. Jack is a *big* talker.

big (big) *adjective,* **bigger, biggest.**

bike A bicycle.

bike (bīk) *noun, plural* **bikes.**

bile A bitter yellow or greenish liquid made in the liver. Bile helps the body to digest food.

bile (bīl) *noun.*

bill¹ **1.** A notice of money owed for something bought or for work done. Mom paid the telephone *bill.* Steve thought that the *bill* for repairs on his bike was too high. **2.** A piece of paper money. Nancy paid for the book with a one-dollar *bill.* **3.** A poster or sign with an advertisement. He placed some *bills* on the wall advertising a sale. **4.** A suggested law. The new tax *bill* was passed by Congress. *Noun.*
—To send a written notice of money owed to someone. The store will *bill* Susan for the dresses she bought. *Verb.*

bill (bil) *noun, plural* **bills;** *verb,* **billed, billing.**

bill² The hard mouth part of a bird; beak. The woodpecker has a heavy, pointed bill. The duck has a broad, flat bill.

bill (bil) *noun, plural* **bills.**

Bill

billboard A large board placed out of doors for displaying signs or advertisements. You see billboards along highways.

bill·board (bil′bôrd′) *noun, plural* **billboards.**

billfold A folding case for paper money. Many billfolds also have places for a driver's license, cards, and other things.

bill·fold (bil′fōld′) *noun, plural* **billfolds.**

billiards A game played with hard balls that are hit with a long stick called a cue. Billiards is played on a large table with a raised edge.

bil·liards (bil′yərdz) *noun.*

billion A thousand millions; 1,000,000,000.

bil·lion (bil′yən) *noun, plural* **billions;** *adjective.*

billow A great swelling wave of something. *Billows* of smoke poured out of the chimney. *Noun.*

at; āpe; cär; end; mē; it; īce; hot; ōld;
fôrk; wood; fōol; oil; out; up; turn; sing;
thin; this; hw in white; zh in treasure.
ə stands for a in about, e in taken
i in pencil, o in lemon, and u in circus.

—To rise or swell in billows. Smoke *billowed* from the burning house. The sail of the boat *billowed* in the wind. *Verb.*
bil·low (bil′ō) *noun, plural* **billows;** *verb,* **billowed, billowing.**

bin A closed place or box for holding or storing something. We keep the coal for the furnace in a *bin.* ▲ Another word that sounds like this is **been.**
bin (bin) *noun, plural* **bins.**

binary Having to do with a system of numbers in which any number may be expressed by 0 or 1, or by a combination of these. The ordinary number 2 is the same as the *binary* number 10. Many electronic computers use the *binary* system of numbering.
bi·na·ry (bī′nər ē) *adjective.*

bind **1.** To tie together; fasten. He will *bind* the package with string for mailing. Ann always *binds* her hair with ribbon. **2.** To tie a bandage around. The nurse will *bind* up Ed's sprained ankle. **3.** To fasten together between covers. We watched the machine *bind* the pages into a book.
bind (bīnd) *verb,* **bound, binding.**

bingo A game in which each player covers numbers on a card as they are called out. The winner is the first player to cover a row of numbers.
bin·go (bing′gō) *noun.*

binoculars A device that makes distant objects look larger and closer. Binoculars are made up of two telescopes joined together, so that a person can look at distant objects with both eyes.
bi·noc·u·lars (bə nok′yə lərz) *noun, plural.*

Binoculars

biography A true, written story about a person's life. We enjoyed reading the *biography* of Eleanor Roosevelt.
bi·og·ra·phy (bī og′rə fē) *noun, plural* **biographies.**

biologist A person who studies biology or who knows a great deal about biology.
bi·ol·o·gist (bī ol′ə jist) *noun, plural* **biologists.**

biology The study of plants and animals. Biology deals with how plants and animals live and grow, how they are made, and where they are found throughout the world.
bi·ol·o·gy (bī ol′ə jē) *noun.*

birch A tree that has hard wood and white bark that peels off easily in thin strips. The American Indians used the bark of the birch to make canoes.
birch (burch) *noun, plural* **birches.**

Leaves

Birch Tree in Autumn

bird An animal that has wings and a body covered with feathers. Birds have a backbone, are warm-blooded, and lay eggs. They walk on their two legs. Most birds can fly. Eagles, robins, chickens, and penguins are birds.
bird (burd) *noun, plural* **birds.**

birth **1.** The beginning of the life of a person or animal. The puppy's *birth* took place last week. My sister's baby was very small at *birth.* The cat gave *birth* to five kittens. **2.** The beginning of anything. The *birth* of the United States took place in 1776. ▲ Another word that sounds like this is **berth.**
birth (burth) *noun, plural* **births.**

birthday **1.** The day on which a person is born. Christopher's *birthday* is December 12, 1972. **2.** The return each year of this day. Mary's *birthday* is tomorrow.
birth·day (burth′dā′) *noun, plural* **birthdays.**

birthmark A mark on the skin that has been there since birth.
birth·mark (burth′märk′) *noun, plural* **birthmarks.**

birthplace The place where a person was born. Phil's *birthplace* is New Orleans.
birth·place (burth′plās′) *noun, plural* **birthplaces.**

biscuit A small cake of baked dough.
bis·cuit (bis′kit) *noun, plural* **biscuits.**

bishop **1.** A member of the clergy who has a high rank. The bishop is the head of a church district. **2.** A piece in the game of chess. You move the bishop in a slanting direction across the squares of the chessboard.
bish·op (bish′əp) *noun, plural* **bishops.**

bison A large animal that has a big shaggy head with short horns and a humped back; buffalo. A bison is a wild ox. Bison are found in North America.
bi·son (bī′sən *or* bī′zən) *noun, plural* **bison.**

Bison

bit¹ **1.** The metal piece of a bridle that goes into the horse's mouth. **2.** The part of a tool that makes holes or bores into wood or other material. A bit fits into the part of a tool called the brace.
bit (bit) *noun, plural* **bits.**

bit² **1.** A small piece or part. Carl threw a *bit* of meat to the dog. I dropped the glass and it broke into *bits*. **2.** A short while. Wait a *bit*.
bit (bit) *noun, plural* **bits.**
a bit. A little; slightly. I am *a bit* tired.

bit³ The girl *bit* into the sandwich.
bit (bit) *verb.*

Bit

bite **1.** To seize, cut into, or pierce with the teeth. Did he *bite* off a piece of your candy bar? **2.** To wound with teeth, fangs, or a stinger. I killed the mosquito before it could *bite* me. **3.** To make something sting. The icy wind will *bite* our cheeks. **4.** To take or swallow bait. The fish will not *bite* today. *Verb.*
—**1.** A seizing or cutting into something with the teeth. The dog's *bite* caused a bad sore. **2.** A wound made by biting. The cat scratched at the flea *bite*. **3.** A piece bitten off. Do you want a *bite* of my apple? **4.** A sting. When I went out I felt the *bite* of the cold air. *Noun.*
bite (bīt) *verb,* **bit, bitten** or **bit, biting;** *noun, plural* **bites.**

bitten He has already *bitten* into the sandwich.
bit·ten (bit′ən) *verb.*

bitter **1.** Having a biting, harsh, bad taste. The strong coffee tasted *bitter*. The boy did not like the *bitter* cough medicine. **2.** Causing or showing sorrow or pain. The children shivered in the *bitter* cold. **3.** Showing anger or hatred. The two men were *bitter* enemies.
bit·ter (bit′ər) *adjective.*

bituminous coal A soft black coal that burns with a smoky flame. This coal is also called **soft coal.**
bi·tu·mi·nous coal (bī tōō′mə nəs *or* bī-tyōō′mə nəs).

black **1.** The darkest of all colors; the opposite of white. **2.** A member of one of the major divisions of the human race. Black people generally have dark skin. *Noun.*
—**1.** Having the darkest of all colors; having the color of coal; opposite of white. **2.** Having no light; dark. When the lights went out the room was *black*. **3.** Of or having to do with black people. *Adjective.*
black (blak) *noun, plural* **blacks;** *adjective,* **blacker, blackest.**

blackberry A sweet, juicy, black berry. Blackberries grow on a bush.
black·ber·ry (blak′ber′ē) *noun, plural* **blackberries.**

blackbird Any of various birds that are mostly black. Some male blackbirds have bright markings, such as red patches on the wings. Female blackbirds have all black or brown feathers.
black·bird (blak′-burd′) *noun, plural* **blackbirds.**

Blackberries

blackboard A hard, smooth board made of slate or other material. Blackboards are used for writing or drawing on with chalk. Some kinds of blackboards are black, while others are green.
black·board (blak′bôrd′) *noun, plural* **blackboards.**

at; āpe; cär; end; mē; it; īce; hot; ōld; fôrk; wood; fool; oil; out; up; turn; sing; thin; this; hw in white; zh in treasure.
ə stands for a in about, e in taken i in pencil, o in lemon, and u in circus.

blacken 1. To make or become black. Smoke from the fireplace *blackened* the walls of the room. The white curtains may *blacken* from the smoke. 2. To do harm to. That nasty rumor will *blacken* his reputation.
black·en (blak′ən) *verb*, **blackened, blackening.**

blackmail The attempt to get money from someone by threatening to tell bad things about him. *Noun.*
—To try to get money from someone by threatening to tell bad things. The men tried to *blackmail* the senator by saying that they would make it known that he had once been in prison. *Verb.*
black·mail (blak′māl′) *noun; verb*, **blackmailed, blackmailing.**

blacksmith A person who makes things from iron. A blacksmith heats the iron in a forge and then hammers it into shape on an anvil. A blacksmith can make horseshoes.
black·smith (blak′smith′) *noun, plural* **blacksmiths.**

blacksnake A black snake of North America. Blacksnakes are harmless to people.
black·snake (blak′snāk′) *noun, plural* **blacksnakes.**

black widow A black spider. The female black widow is poisonous and has a red mark on her body. The female black widow is larger than the male, and often eats the male after mating.

bladder A small baglike part in the body. The bladder holds urine from the kidneys.
blad·der (blad′ər) *noun, plural* **bladders.**

blade 1. The sharp part of anything that cuts. He sharpened the *blade* of his knife. Dad put a new *blade* in his razor. 2. A leaf of grass. 3. The wide, flat part of something. He dipped the *blade* of the oar into the water. String caught in the *blades* of the fan.
blade (blād) *noun, plural* **blades.**

blame 1. To find fault with. Bill didn't *blame* his friend for getting angry. 2. To hold responsible for something wrong or bad. The neighbor *blamed* my brother for breaking the window. *Verb.*
—Responsibility for something wrong or bad. He took the *blame* for the accident. *Noun.*
blame (blām) *verb*, **blamed, blaming;** *noun.*

blank 1. Without writing or printing; unmarked. I turned to a *blank* page in my notebook. 2. With empty spaces to be filled in. Bill filled in the *blank* order form. 3. Without thought; vacant. The boy was daydreaming and gave me a *blank* stare. *Adjective.*
—1. An empty space to be filled in. Fill in the *blank* with your name and address. 2. A paper with spaces to be filled in. My friend gave me an application *blank* for joining the stamp club. 3. A cartridge with gunpowder but no bullet. *Noun.*
blank (blangk) *adjective*, **blanker, blankest;** *noun, plural* **blanks.**

blanket 1. A covering made of wool, nylon, or other material. Blankets are used on beds to keep people warm. 2. Anything that covers like a blanket. A *blanket* of fog lay over the town. *Noun.*
—To cover with a blanket. The snowstorm *blanketed* the city with snow. *Verb.*
blan·ket (blang′kit) *noun, plural* **blankets;** *verb*, **blanketed, blanketing.**

blare To make a loud, harsh sound. The car horns *blared* in the busy street. *Verb.*
—A loud, harsh sound. The *blare* of the siren hurt my ears. *Noun.*
blare (bler) *verb*, **blared, blaring,** *noun, plural* **blares.**

blast 1. A strong rush of wind or air. A *blast* of cold air blew into the room. 2. A loud noise made by a horn. We heard the *blast* of trumpets in the marching band. 3. An explosion. When the old building was blown up, the *blast* made the windows of our house rattle. *Noun.*
—1. To blow up with explosives. The workmen *blasted* a hole in the rock with dynamite. 2. To ruin. The rain *blasted* our hopes for a picnic. *Verb.*
blast (blast) *noun, plural* **blasts;** *verb*, **blasted, blasting.**
to blast off. To take off into flight propelled by rockets. The spacecraft will *blast off* in an hour.

blaze¹ 1. A bright flame; a glowing fire. We could see the *blaze* of the burning building. 2. A bright light. We shielded our eyes from the *blaze* of the sun. 3. A bright display. The circus parade was a *blaze* of color. *Noun.*
—1. To burn brightly. The campfire *blazed* all night. 2. To shine brightly. The tree will *blaze* with lights on Christmas. 3. To show strong feeling. Her eyes *blazed* with anger. *Verb.*
blaze (blāz) *noun, plural* **blazes;** *verb*, **blazed, blazing.**

blaze² A mark made on a tree to show a trail or boundary. You make a *blaze* by chipping off a piece of bark. *Noun.*
—To show a trail or boundary by putting marks on trees. The hikers will *blaze* a trail through the woods. *Verb.*
blaze (blāz) *noun, plural* **blazes;** *verb*, **blazed, blazing.**

bleach To make something white. The sun *bleached* the sheets. Mother will *bleach* the shirts when she washes them. *Verb.*
—A substance used for bleaching. She uses a chemical *bleach* in her wash. *Noun.*
  bleach (blēch) *verb,* **bleached, bleaching;** *noun, plural* **bleaches.**

bleak 1. Open and unprotected from the wind; bare. There were no trees growing on the *bleak* mountaintop. 2. Cold and gloomy. It was a *bleak* December day. Everyone thought that the *bleak* old house was haunted.
  bleak (blēk) *adjective,* **bleaker, bleakest.**

bled Her cut finger *bled.*
  bled (bled) *verb.*

bleed 1. To lose blood. If you cut yourself, you will *bleed.* 2. To lose sap or other liquid. A tree will *bleed* if you cut into its trunk.
  bleed (blēd) *verb,* **bled, bleeding.**

blemish Something that spoils beauty or perfection; flaw. The scar is a *blemish* on his face. One day's absence was the only *blemish* on his school attendance record. *Noun.*
—To spoil the beauty or perfection of something; mar. Worm holes *blemish* an apple. *Verb.*
  blem·ish (blem′ish) *noun, plural* **blemishes;** *verb,* **blemished, blemishing.**

blend 1. To mix together completely. She will *blend* flour, milk, and eggs to make pancakes. The voices in the choir *blend* well. 2. To shade into each other. The sea and sky seemed to *blend* on the horizon. *Verb.*
—A mixture. Dad smokes a strong *blend* of tobacco. *Noun.*
  blend (blend) *verb,* **blended, blending;** *noun, plural* **blends.**

bless 1. To make holy. The minister will *bless* the new chapel. 2. To ask God's help for. The little boy prayed that God would *bless* his mother and father. 3. To make happy or fortunate. Members of our family have been *blessed* with good teeth.
  bless (bles) *verb,* **blessed** or **blest, blessing.**

blessing 1. A prayer to God for His favor or to give thanks. The minister gave a *blessing* at the end of the church service. 2. A person or thing that brings happiness. The helpful child was a *blessing* to her sick grandmother. 3. A wish for happiness or success; good wishes. She sent her *blessings* for a happy new year.
  bless·ing (bles′ing) *noun, plural* **blessings.**

blew Jack *blew* on his hot soup to cool it. Look up **blow** for more information. ▲ Another word that sounds like this is **blue.**
  blew (blo͞o) *verb.*

blight 1. A disease of plants. Blight makes a plant wither and die. 2. Something that harms or ruins. Those dirty old buildings are a *blight* on our city.
  blight (blīt) *noun, plural* **blights.**

blind 1. Without sight; unable to see. The boy helped the *blind* man across the street. 2. Not easily seen; hidden. The sign warned of a *blind* driveway on the road ahead. 3. Done with instruments only and not with the eyes. The pilot of the airplane had to make a *blind* landing because of the storm. 4. Closed at one end. The thief ran into a *blind* alley and could not escape the police. 5. Without thought or good sense. Tom didn't know the answer to the problem so he made a *blind* guess. *Adjective.*
—1. To make unable to see. The sun will *blind* you if you look at it too long. 2. To take away thought or good sense. Fear *blinded* him. *Verb.*
—Something that blocks a person's sight or keeps the light out. Janet lowered the *blinds* of the window. *Noun.*
  blind (blīnd) *adjective,* **blinder, blindest;** *verb,* **blinded, blinding;** *noun, plural* **blinds.**

Blindfold

blindfold To cover someone's eyes. He *blindfolded* his little sister for the game. *Verb.*
—A cover for the eyes. The *blindfold* was a strip of cloth. *Noun.*
  blind·fold (blīnd′fōld′) *verb,* **blindfolded, blindfolding;** *noun, plural* **blindfolds.**

at; āpe; cär; end; mē; it; īce; hot; ōld; fôrk; wood; fo͞ol; oil; out; up; turn; sing; thin; this; hw in white; zh in treasure.
ə stands for a in about, e in taken
i in pencil, o in lemon, and u in circus.

blink 1. To close and open the eyes quickly. The child *blinked* when the photographer took the picture. 2. To flash on and off; twinkle. Stars *blinked* in the sky.
blink (blingk) *verb*, **blinked, blinking.**

bliss Great happiness. The little boy was filled with *bliss* at the thought of going to the circus.
bliss (blis) *noun*.

blister 1. A sore place on the skin that looks like a small bubble. A blister is filled with a watery substance. It is usually caused by rubbing or by a burn. Susan has a *blister* on her heel where her sneaker rubbed it. 2. Any small bubble or swelling. *Blisters* formed on the new coat of paint. *Noun*.
—To form a blister on; have blisters. Touching the hot iron made his finger *blister*. The hot sun *blistered* his nose. *Verb*.
blis·ter (blis′tər) *noun, plural* **blisters;** *verb*, **blistered, blistering.**

blizzard A heavy snowstorm with very strong winds.
bliz·zard (bliz′ərd) *noun, plural* **blizzards.**

bloat To make bigger; cause to swell. Drinking too much water *bloated* his stomach.
bloat (blōt) *verb*, **bloated, bloating.**

blob A drop or small lump of something soft. Sally got a *blob* of paint on her dress.
blob (blob) *noun, plural* **blobs.**

block 1. A piece of something hard and solid. The workmen built the church with *blocks* of stone. The children built a fort with wooden *blocks*. 2. An area in a town or city with four streets around it. Karen walks her dog around the *block* every morning. 3. The length of one side of a block in a town or city. Frank lives three *blocks* from the school. 4. A number of things that are alike. Bill bought a *block*

Blocks

of foreign stamps for his stamp collection. 5. Anything that stops something else. The fallen tree was a *block* to traffic. 6. A pulley in a frame. *Noun*.
—To get in the way of or stop. Patrick's bicycle *blocked* the sidewalk. The house next door *blocks* the view from my window. The football player *blocked* the pass. *Verb*.

block (blok) *noun, plural* **blocks;** *verb*, **blocked, blocking.**

blockade A shutting off of an area to keep people and supplies from going in or out. During a war an enemy may use ships to set up a blockade around the harbor or port of a city. *Noun*.
—To shut off with a blockade. Ships will *blockade* the enemy's harbor. *Verb*.
block·ade (blo kād′) *noun, plural* **blockades;** *verb*, **blockaded, blockading.**

blockhouse 1. A strong building made of wooden timbers or logs. It has holes in the walls to shoot weapons from. Blockhouses were formerly used as forts. 2. A strong building near the launching pad of a rocket. A blockhouse is used to protect people who are watching rocket launchings.
block·house (blok′hous′) *noun, plural* **block-houses.**

Blockhouse

blond 1. Light-yellow. He has *blond* hair like his mother. 2. Having light-yellow hair and light-colored eyes and skin. Most of the members of Noreen's family are *blond*. *Adjective*.
—A person with light-yellow hair and light-colored eyes and skin. *Noun*. This word is also spelled **blonde.**
blond (blond) *adjective*, **blonder, blondest;** *noun, plural* **blonds.**

blood 1. The bright red liquid that runs from a cut. Blood is pumped by the heart through the veins and arteries to all parts of the body. It carries oxygen and food to the body and takes away waste materials. 2. Family relationship. Susan and I are of the same *blood* because our mothers are sisters.
blood (blud) *noun*.

in cold blood. Without being at all sorry. The prisoner killed the guard *in cold blood* in order to escape.

bloodhound A large dog with long, drooping ears and a wrinkled face. Bloodhounds have such a good sense of smell that they are often used to track down escaped criminals or find people who are lost.
blood·hound (blud′hound′) *noun, plural* **bloodhounds.**

Bloodhound

bloodshed The loss of blood or life. The king's soldiers won the battle without much *bloodshed.*
blood·shed (blud′shed′) *noun.*

bloodstream The blood as it flows through the body.
blood·stream (blud′strēm′) *noun.*

bloodthirsty Eager to cause bloodshed; cruel.
blood·thirst·y (blud′thurs′tē) *adjective.*

blood vessel Any of the tubes in the body through which the blood flows. Arteries and veins are blood vessels.

bloody 1. Covered or stained with blood. The bandage on his cut knee was all *bloody.* 2. Causing much bloodshed. Many men were killed in the *bloody* battle.
blood·y (blud′ē) *adjective,* **bloodier, bloodiest.**

bloom The time of flowering. The roses are in *bloom. Noun.*
—To have flowers; blossom. Cherry trees *bloom* in the spring. *Verb.*
bloom (bloom) *noun, plural* **blooms;** *verb,* **bloomed, blooming.**

blossom 1. The flower of a plant or tree that produces fruit. We gathered *blossoms* from the apple trees in the orchard. 2. The time of flowering. The lilacs are in *blossom. Noun.*
—1. To have flowers or blossoms; bloom. The peach trees *blossom* in the spring. 2. To grow; develop. That young writer has *blos-*

somed into one of the country's best novelists. *Verb.*
blos·som (blos′əm) *noun, plural* **blossoms;** *verb,* **blossomed, blossoming.**

blot 1. A spot or stain. Betty got a *blot* of paint on her picture when her brush dripped. 2. Something that spoils or harms. Those billboards along the highway are a *blot* on the beautiful countryside. *Noun.*
—1. To spot or stain. The ink from my pen *blotted* my letter, and I had to copy it over. 2. To soak up or dry with a blotter. He *blotted* his signature carefully so the ink wouldn't smear. *Verb.*
blot (blot) *noun, plural* **blots;** *verb,* **blotted, blotting.**

blotch A large spot or stain. The jelly he spilled left a *blotch* on the tablecloth. The rash covered his arms with red *blotches. Noun.*
—To mark or cover with spots or stains. The hot sun *blotched* her back. *Verb.*
blotch (bloch) *noun, plural* **blotches;** *verb,* **blotched, blotching.**

blotter A piece of soft, thick paper used to soak up or dry wet ink. He used a *blotter* on his signature on the check.
blot·ter (blot′ər) *noun, plural* **blotters.**

blouse A piece of clothing for the upper part of the body. Girls and women wear blouses with skirts or slacks.
blouse (blous *or* blouz) *noun, plural* **blouses.**

Blouse

blow¹ 1. A hard hit or stroke. A blow may be made with the fist, a weapon, or some object. A sudden *blow* on the jaw knocked the champion out. 2. A sudden happening that causes great shock or unhappiness. The death of their dog was a *blow* to the whole family.
blow (blō) *noun, plural* **blows.**

blow² 1. To move with speed or force. The wind

began to *blow* against the sails of the boat. An autumn breeze *blew* the leaves across the yard. **2.** To send out a strong current of air. *Blow* on your hands to warm them. **3.** To move by a current of air. His hat *blew* off as he ran to catch the bus. **4.** To form or shape by a current of air. My little sister loves to *blow* soap bubbles. We are going to *blow* up balloons for my brother's birthday party. **5.** To sound by a blast of air. When the whistle *blows* the race will start. **6.** To break or destroy by an explosion. The soldiers *blew* up the enemy's bridge. **7.** To stop working properly. Our tire *blew* out, and we had to stop to change it.
blow (blō) *verb,* **blew, blown, blowing.**

blower A machine for making a current of air or for forcing air into a place. A *blower* cooled the mine shaft with fresh air.
blow·er (blō′ər) *noun, plural* **blowers.**

blown The wind has *blown* the snow into high drifts. Look up **blow** for more information.
blown (blōn) *verb.*

blowtorch A small torch that shoots out a very hot flame. Blowtorches are used to melt metal and to burn off old paint.
blow·torch (blō′tôrch′) *noun, plural* **blowtorches.**

Blowtorch

blubber A layer of fat under the skin of whales, seals, and some other sea animals. The oil made from whale blubber used to be burned in lamps. Now the oil is used in soaps and other products.
blub·ber (blub′ər) *noun, plural* **blubbers.**

blue The color of the clear sky in the daytime. The colors of the American flag are red, white, and *blue. Noun.*
—**1.** Having the color blue. **2.** Unhappy; sad; discouraged. Mike felt *blue* and lonely during his first week away at summer camp. *Adjective.* ▲ Another word that sounds like this is **blew.**
blue (blōo) *noun, plural* **blues;** *adjective,* **bluer, bluest.**

blueberry A small, dark-blue, sweet berry with tiny seeds. Blueberries grow on a shrub.
blue·ber·ry (blōo′ber′ē) *noun, plural* **blueberries.**

bluebird A small songbird of North America that has blue feathers on its back.
blue·bird (blōo′burd′) *noun, plural* **bluebirds.**

bluegrass A grass that has bluish-green stems. Bluegrass is raised as food for cattle and horses and is used for lawns.
blue·grass (blōo′gras′) *noun, plural* **bluegrasses.**

Blueberries

Bluebird

blue jay A bird of North America that has a crest on its head and blue feathers with black-and-white markings.

blue jeans Pants or overalls made of blue denim.

blueprint A paper printed with white lines on a blue background. It is used to show the plan for building something. The workmen looked at the *blueprints* so that they would know how the house should be built.
blue·print (blōo′print′) *noun, plural* **blueprints.**

blues **1.** Sadness; low spirits. Jerry has had the *blues* ever since his best friend moved away. **2.** Music that sounds sad and has a rhythm like jazz.
blues (blōoz) *noun plural.*

bluff[1] A high, steep bank or cliff. As the ship pulled closer to shore they saw the *bluffs* jutting up from the sea. *Noun.*
—Rough in a good-natured way; hearty. John's uncle greeted him with a *bluff* slap on the back. *Adjective.*
bluff (bluf) *noun, plural* **bluffs;** *adjective.*

bluff² To try to fool people about something. A person who bluffs tries to make people think he is braver than he really is or that he knows something that he really doesn't. George always tries to *bluff* the other boys into thinking he is the strongest. *Verb.*
—Something that is pretended in order to fool other people. All his boasting about being able to swim the fastest is just a big *bluff. Noun.*
 bluff (bluf) *verb,* **bluffed, bluffing;** *noun, plural* **bluffs.**

blunder A careless or stupid mistake. Forgetting his mother's birthday was an awful *blunder. Noun.*
—**1.** To make a careless or stupid mistake. You really *blundered* when you said that Abraham Lincoln was the first president of the United States. **2.** To move in a clumsy way. The lost campers *blundered* through the woods looking for the path. *Verb.*
 blun·der (blun′dər) *noun, plural* **blunders;** *verb,* **blundered, blundering.**

blunderbuss A short gun with a wide muzzle flared at the end. Blunderbusses were used for shooting things at close range without careful aim. They are no longer used.
 blun·der·buss (blun′dər bus′) *noun, plural* **blunderbusses.**

Blunderbuss

blunt **1.** Having a dull edge or point; not sharp. This pencil is *blunt* and needs to be sharpened. **2.** Very outspoken and frank about what one thinks. Tom's *blunt* criticism of his sister hurt her feelings. *Adjective.*
—To make less sharp; make dull. Ann *blunted* her mother's scissors by using them to cut the wire. *Verb.*
 blunt (blunt) *adjective,* **blunter, bluntest;** *verb,* **blunted, blunting.**

blur To make dim or hard to see; make less clear: Fog began to *blur* the outline of the city. *Verb.*
—Something that is dim or hard to see. The faces of the crowd were only a *blur* to the driver of the racing car. *Noun.*

 blur (blur) *verb,* **blurred, blurring;** *noun, plural* **blurs.**

blurt To say suddenly or without thinking. Ted was sorry after he *blurted* out the secret.
 blurt (blurt) *verb,* **blurted, blurting.**

blush To become red in the face. A person blushes because he is ashamed, embarrassed, or confused. Bill *blushed* every time the teacher called on him because he was so shy. *Verb.*
—A reddening of the face because of shame, embarrassment, or confusion. The little girl's *blush* showed how shy she was toward strangers. *Noun.*
 blush (blush) *verb,* **blushed, blushing;** *noun, plural* **blushes.**

bluster **1.** To blow in a noisy or violent way. The wind *blustered* through the trees. **2.** To talk in a loud or threatening way. When my brother gets angry, you can hear him *bluster* all over the house. *Verb.*
—**1.** A noisy, violent blowing. The *bluster* of the storm kept us awake all night. **2.** Loud, threatening talk. That boy is a bully who is full of *bluster* but scared to fight. *Noun.*
 blus·ter (blus′tər) *verb,* **blustered, blustering;** *noun.*

boa constrictor A large snake that is found in Mexico and in Central and South America. A boa constrictor is not poisonous. It kills other animals by wrapping itself around them and squeezing them to death.
 bo·a con·stric·tor (bō′ə kən strik′tər).

boar A wild pig or hog that has a hairy coat and a long snout. ▲ Another word that sounds like this is **bore.**
 boar (bôr) *noun, plural* **boars** or **boar.**

Boar

at; āpe; cär; end; mē; it; īce; hot; ōld;
fôrk; wood; fo̅o̅l; oil; out; up; turn; sing;
thin; this; hw in white; zh in treasure.
ə stands for a in about, e in taken
i in pencil, o in lemon, and u in circus.

board   **1.** A long, flat piece of sawed wood. Boards are used in building houses and other things. **2.** A flat piece of wood or other material used for some special purpose. Get the *board* and we'll play a game of checkers. **3.** A group of people who are chosen to manage or direct something. The school *board* helps to run the school. **4.** Meals served daily for pay. Frank found a good room with *board* near his college campus. *Noun.*
—**1.** To cover with boards. We always *board* up the windows of our summer cabin when we go home at the end of the summer. **2.** To get a room to sleep in and meals for pay. He *boarded* with a French family in Paris last summer. **3.** To get on a ship, plane, or train. We will *board* the plane in New York to fly to England. *Verb.*
   board (bôrd) *noun, plural* **boards;** *verb,* **boarded, boarding.**
   on board. On or in a ship, plane, or train; aboard. There were seventy-five people *on board* our plane.

boarding house   A house where a person can get a room to sleep in and meals for pay.

boast   **1.** To talk too much or with too much pride about oneself; brag. If Bob is going to *boast* all the time about being on the football team, his friends will begin to be angry with him. **2.** To be proud of having. Our town *boasts* a big new sports stadium. *Verb.*
—Talk that is too much about oneself. His *boast* that he is the best player on the team is not true. *Noun.*
   boast (bōst) *verb,* **boasted, boasting;** *noun, plural* **boasts.**

boat   **1.** A small vessel that is used for traveling on water. A boat is moved by using oars, paddles, sails, or a motor. A boat is usually open. **2.** Any kind of ship. An ocean liner is a boat. *Noun.*
—To go in a boat; carry in a boat. We want to spend the vacation *boating* and fishing. *Verb.*
   boat (bōt) *noun, plural* **boats;** *verb,* **boated, boating.**

boathouse   A house for sheltering or storing boats. We keep our sailboat in a *boathouse* during the winter.
   boat·house (bōt′hous′) *noun, plural* **boat-houses.**

bob[1]   To move up and down or back and forth with a jerky motion. The beach ball *bobbed* on the waves. The hen *bobbed* its head as it pecked its food. *Verb.*
—A jerky motion. Jim answered his mother's question with a *bob* of his head. *Noun.*
   bob (bob) *verb,* **bobbed, bobbing;** *noun, plural* **bobs.**

bob[2]   **1.** A short haircut for a woman or child. **2.** A float or cork at the end of a fishing line. The *bob* moved up and down when the fish bit at the bait. *Noun.*
—To cut hair short. The barber *bobbed* my sister's long hair. *Verb.*
   bob (bob) *noun, plural* **bobs;** *verb,* **bobbed, bobbing.**

bobbin   A spool around which yarn or thread is wound. A bobbin is used in weaving, spinning, or sewing on a sewing machine.
   bob·bin (bob′in) *noun, plural* **bobbins.**

bobcat   A small wild cat of North America. A bobcat has reddish-brown fur with dark spots and a short tail.
   bob·cat (bob′kat′) *noun, plural* **bobcats.**

Bobcat

bobolink   A songbird of North and South America that lives in fields. It is related to the blackbird.
   bob·o·link (bob′ə lingk′) *noun, plural* **bobo-links.**

bobsled   A long sled for racing. A bobsled has two sets of runners, a steering wheel, and brakes.
   bob·sled (bob′sled′) *noun, plural* **bobsleds.**

Bobsled

bobwhite An American bird that has a reddish-brown body with white, black, and tan markings. Its call sounds a little like its name. A bobwhite is a kind of quail.
bob·white (bob′hwīt′) *noun, plural* **bobwhites.**

Bobwhite

bode To be a sign of. The dark clouds *bode* a storm.
bode (bōd) *verb,* **boded, boding.**

bodily Of the body. The people who were in the automobile accident suffered almost no *bodily* harm, but they were very frightened.
bod·i·ly (bod′ə lē) *adjective.*

body 1. All of a person, animal, or plant. An athlete must have a strong *body*. 2. The main part of something. The *body* of the new jet airplane is very large. 3. A group of persons or things. The student *body* at the high school is headed by a president that the students elect. 4. A separate part or mass. The Atlantic Ocean is a huge *body* of water. The sun, the moon, and the stars are heavenly *bodies*.
bod·y (bod′ē) *noun, plural* **bodies.**

bodyguard A person or persons who protect someone from danger or attack. The king's *bodyguard* goes with him wherever he goes.
bod·y·guard (bod′ē gärd′) *noun, plural* **bodyguards.**

bog Wet, spongy ground; marsh; swamp. A bog is made up mainly of decayed plants. Cranberries grow in *bogs*. *Noun.*
—To become stuck. The car will *bog* down on those muddy roads. I got *bogged* down on the last arithmetic problem. *Verb.*
bog (bog) *noun, plural* **bogs;** *verb,* **bogged, bogging.**

boil¹ 1. To form bubbles and give off steam. Water will *boil* if you heat it enough. 2. To cause to boil. Mary *boiled* water for tea. 3. To cook by boiling. We *boiled* the potatoes for dinner. *Verb.*
—The condition of boiling. Bring the water to a *boil* and then turn off the heat. *Noun.*
boil (boil) *verb,* **boiled, boiling;** *noun.*

boil² A red swelling beneath the skin that hurts. A boil is caused by infection and it is full of pus.
boil (boil) *noun, plural* **boils.**

boiler 1. A large tank in which water is made into steam. The steam made in a boiler is used to heat buildings and to run engines. 2. A pan or pot in which something is heated or boiled. We cooked the ears of corn in a large *boiler*.
boil·er (boi′lər) *noun, plural* **boilers.**

boiling point The temperature at which a liquid begins to boil. The boiling point of water at sea level is 212 degrees on the Fahrenheit thermometer, or 100 degrees on the centigrade thermometer.

bold 1. Not afraid; brave. A person who is bold is willing to do dangerous things. The *bold* explorer pushed on into the deepest part of the jungle. The fireman's rescue of the child from the burning roof was a *bold* thing to do. 2. Not polite; rude; fresh. The *bold* child always talked back to his parents.
bold (bōld) *adjective,* **bolder, boldest.**

boll The seed pod of a cotton or flax plant.
▲ Another word that sounds like this is **bowl.**
boll (bōl) *noun, plural* **bolls.**

boll weevil A beetle that lays eggs in the seed pods of the cotton plant. Boll weevils cause a great deal of damage to cotton plants.
boll wee·vil (wē′vəl).

bolster A long pillow or cushion. *Noun.*
—To support. The beams *bolstered* the roof of the cabin. The good news *bolstered* Jack's low spirits. *Verb.*
bol·ster (bōl′stər) *noun, plural* **bolsters;** *verb,* **bolstered, bolstering.**

bolt 1. A rod used to hold things together. A bolt usually has a head at one end and screw threads for a nut at the other. 2. A sliding bar for fastening a door. She closed the door and slid the *bolt* shut. 3. The part of a lock that is moved by a key. 4. A sudden spring or start. The frightened deer made a *bolt* for the woods. 5. A flash of lightning; thunderbolt. 6. A roll of cloth or paper. *Noun.*
—1. To fasten with a bolt. *Bolt* the door for the night after you have let the dog in. 2. To start and run off. The horse *bolted* and its rider fell off. 3. To swallow quickly or without chewing. Mother is always telling us not to *bolt* our breakfast. *Verb.*
bolt (bōlt) *noun, plural* **bolts;** *verb,* **bolted, bolting.**

at; āpe; cär; end; mē; it; īce; hot; ōld;
fôrk; wood; fool; oil; out; up; turn; sing;
thin; this; hw in white; zh in treasure.
ə stands for a in about, e in taken
i in pencil, o in lemon, and u in circus.

bomb   A hollow case filled with something that can explode. It is used as a weapon. A bomb is exploded by dropping or throwing it, or by lighting a fuse. The airplanes dropped *bombs* on the enemy's cities. *Noun.*
—To throw or drop a bomb on. The planes *bombed* the bridge so the soldiers could not enter the city. *Verb.*
   bomb (bom) *noun, plural* **bombs;** *verb,* **bombed, bombing.**

bombard   1. To attack with bombs or heavy fire from big guns. The army *bombarded* the fort. 2. To attack again and again. The reporters *bombarded* the astronauts with questions.
   bom·bard (bom bärd′) *verb,* **bombarded, bombarding.**

bomber   An airplane used to drop bombs.
   bomb·er (bom′ər) *noun, plural* **bombers.**

bond   1. Something that fastens or holds together. The prisoner's *bonds* were made of rope. There is a *bond* of friendship between the two boys. 2. A written receipt given by a government or a business for a loan of money. A bond is a promise to pay back the money borrowed at a certain date with interest.
   bond (bond) *noun, plural* **bonds.**

bondage   Slavery; lack of freedom. Abraham Lincoln freed the slaves from *bondage.*
   bond·age (bon′dij) *noun.*

bone   One of the parts of the skeleton of an animal with a backbone. Bones are hard and stiff. Jack broke one of the *bones* in his ankle playing football. *Noun.*
—To take out the bones of. My father *boned* the fish we caught, and then we cooked it. *Verb.*
   bone (bōn) *noun, plural* **bones;** *verb,* **boned, boning.**

bonfire   A large fire built outdoors. We sat around the *bonfire* at camp and sang songs.
   bon·fire (bon′fīr′) *noun, plural* **bonfires.**

bongo drums   A pair of small drums played with the hands while being held between the knees.
   bon·go drums (bong′gō).

bonnet   1. A covering for the head. A bonnet is usually tied under the chin by ribbons or strings. Bonnets are worn by children and women. 2. A covering for the head made of feathers.

Bongo Drums

It is worn by North American Indians.
   bon·net (bon′it) *noun, plural* **bonnets.**

bonus   Something extra. A bonus is given or paid in addition to what is due or expected. At Christmas time, the grocer gave each of his delivery boys a twenty dollar *bonus* in addition to their salaries.
   bo·nus (bō′nəs) *noun, plural* **bonuses.**

bony   1. Made of bone. The skeleton is a *bony* structure. 2. Full of bones. The fish we caught was so *bony* that it was hard to eat. 3. Very thin. A *bony* old dog came to our back door begging for food.
   bon·y (bō′nē) *adjective,* **bonier, boniest.**

Bonnet

boo   A sound made to frighten or to show dislike. Tom's mother jumped when he leaped out of the closet and yelled *"Boo!" Interjection.*
—To show that one does not like something by shouting "boo." The crowd *booed* the baseball player when he struck out. *Verb.*
   boo (bōo) *interjection; verb,* **booed, booing.**

book   Sheets of paper fastened together between two covers. The pages of a book have writing or printing on them. Mother read to us from a *book* of fairy tales. I have to make a report on the *book* I've just read for school. We have *books* for arithmetic, science, and geography at school. *Noun.*
—To arrange for ahead of time. Father *booked* rooms at the motel before we left on our trip so we would be sure to have a place to stay for the night. *Verb.*
   book (book) *noun, plural* **books;** *verb,* **booked, booking.**

bookcase   A set of shelves for holding books. Put the book back in the *bookcase* neatly when you have finished reading it.
   book·case (book′kās′) *noun, plural* **book-cases.**

bookkeeper   A person who keeps the records of a business. The *bookkeeper* at the grocery store keeps a record of all the money the owner of the store makes from selling groceries.
   book·keep·er (book′kē′pər) *noun, plural* **bookkeepers.**

booklet   A small, thin book. Booklets usually have paper covers. A *booklet* came with the electric knife, telling how to use it.

book·let (book′lit) *noun, plural* **booklets.**

boom¹ **1.** A deep, hollow sound. A boom sounds like the noise an explosion makes. We heard the *boom* of thunder and knew that a storm was coming. **2.** A time of fast growth. The sale of overshoes at the store has had a *boom* ever since the heavy snowstorm. *Noun.*

—**1.** To make a deep, hollow sound. Our voices *boomed* in the empty house. **2.** To grow suddenly and rapidly. Business at the department store *booms* as Christmas comes closer. *Verb.*

boom (bōōm) *noun, plural* **booms;** *verb,* **boomed, booming.**

boom² **1.** A long pole or beam used to stretch the bottom of a sail. **2.** The long pole on a derrick that holds up the load that is being lifted.

boom (bōōm) *noun, plural* **booms.**

boomerang A flat curved piece of wood. A boomerang can be thrown so that it returns to the thrower. A boomerang is used as a weapon by the native tribes of Australia.

boom·er·ang (bōō′mə rang′) *noun, plural* **boomerangs.**

Boomerang

boon A help; benefit. The rain was a big *boon* to my vegetable garden after so much dry weather.

boon (bōōn) *noun, plural* **boons.**

boost A push or shove up. Give me a *boost* to help me climb up the tree. *Noun.*

—To push or shove up. I *boosted* my little brother over the fence. *Verb.*

boost (bōōst) *noun, plural* **boosts;** *verb,* **boosted, boosting.**

boot A covering for the foot and lower part of the leg. Boots are usually made of leather or rubber. Put on your *boots* if you are going out to play in the snow. *Noun.*

—To kick. The player *booted* the football. *Verb.*

boot (bōōt) *noun, plural* **boots;** *verb,* **booted, booting.**

booth **1.** A place where things are sold or shown. Everyone crowded around the refreshment *booth* at the fair. **2.** A small closed place. I made a telephone call from a tele-

phone *booth.* There was a long line of people at the ticket *booth* at the movie theater.

booth (booth) *noun, plural* **booths.**

Booth

border **1.** A boundary line. They crossed the *border* between the United States and Canada. **2.** A strip along the edge of anything. Sue's skirt has a pretty red *border. Noun.*

—**1.** To lie on the edge of. California *borders* Oregon. **2.** To put an edging on. She *bordered* the handkerchief with lace. *Verb.*

bor·der (bôr′dər) *noun, plural* **borders;** *verb,* **bordered, bordering.**

bore¹ **1.** To make by digging. Workmen *bored* a tunnel through the mountain. **2.** To make a hole in. The carpenter *bored* the wood with his drill. ▲ Another word that sounds like this is **boar.**

bore (bôr) *verb,* **bored, boring.**

bore² To make very tired by being uninteresting and dull. Bill always *bores* his friends by telling them the same jokes over and over again. *Verb.*

—A person or thing that is uninteresting and dull. That television program is a *bore. Noun.* ▲ Another word that sounds like this is **boar.**

bore (bôr) *verb,* **bored, boring;** *noun, plural* **bores.**

bore³ Tom *bore* his defeat in the spelling contest very well and congratulated the winner. Look up **bear** for more information.

bore (bôr) *verb.*

at; āpe; cär; end; mē; it; īce; hot; ōld; fôrk; wood; fōol; oil; out; up; turn; sing; thin; this; hw in white; zh in treasure. ə stands for a in about, e in taken i in pencil, o in lemon, and u in circus.

born 1. Brought into life or being. The cat has newly *born* kittens. 2. By birth; natural. Tom is a *born* athlete who plays almost every sport very well. *Adjective.*
—Our cat has *born* six kittens. Look up **bear** for more information. *Verb.* ▲ Another word that sounds like this is **borne.**
born (bôrn) *adjective; verb.*

borne Mary has *borne* the pain of her sprained ankle without crying at all. Look up **bear** for more information. ▲ Another word that sounds like this is **born.**
borne (bôrn) *verb.*

borough 1. In some states of the United States, a town or village that governs itself. 2. One of the five divisions of New York City. ▲ Other words that sound like this are **burro** and **burrow.**
bor·ough (bur′ō) *noun, plural* **boroughs.**

borrow 1. To take something from another person with the understanding that it must be given back. I'm allowed to *borrow* my brother's bicycle sometimes. We *borrow* books from the library. 2. To take something and use it as one's own. The name of the animal "chipmunk" was *borrowed* from the American Indians.
bor·row (bôr′ō *or* bor′ō) *verb,* **borrowed, borrowing.**

bosom The upper, front part of the chest. The mother hugged the frightened child to her *bosom. Noun.*
—Close and dear. Tom and Jack are *bosom* buddies. *Adjective.*
bos·om (booz′əm) *noun, plural* **bosoms;** *adjective.*

boss A person who watches over and plans the work of others. The *boss* hired three new people to help get the job done on time. *Noun.*
—To be the boss of. Jack gets mad at his older sister when she tries to *boss* him around. *Verb.*
boss (bôs) *noun, plural* **bosses;** *verb,* **bossed, bossing.**

botany The study of plants. When you study botany you learn about many different kinds of plants and the way they are formed. You also find out how plants grow and where they grow.
bot·a·ny (bot′ən ē) *noun.*

both *Both* boys made the basketball team. Why not invite *both* to the party? They were *both* tired and hungry after their long hike.
both (bōth) *adjective; pronoun; conjunction.*

bother 1. To trouble or annoy. Meeting new people *bothers* the shy boy. 2. To take the trouble. Don't *bother* to make lunch because I'm not hungry. *Verb.*
—A person or thing that troubles or annoys. I think making my bed every day is a *bother. Noun.*
both·er (both′ər) *verb,* **bothered, bothering;** *noun, plural* **bothers.**

bottle A container to hold liquids. A bottle has a narrow neck that can be closed with a cap or stopper. Bottles are usually made of glass or plastic. *Noun.*
—To put in bottles. That company *bottles* soft drinks. *Verb.*
bot·tle (bot′əl) *noun, plural* **bottles;** *verb,* **bottled, bottling.**

bottom 1. The lowest part. The ball rolled to the *bottom* of the hill. 2. The under or lower part. The *bottom* of the rowboat needs painting. 3. The ground under water. The *bottom* of the pond is sandy. 4. The most important part. The detective tried to get to the *bottom* of the mystery by asking questions. *Noun.*
—Lowest or last. I hid my money in the *bottom* drawer of my bureau. *Adjective.*
bot·tom (bot′əm) *noun, plural* **bottoms;** *adjective.*

bough A large branch of a tree. Father fastened the swing to a *bough* of the old tree in our backyard. ▲ Another word that sounds like this is **bow.**
bough (bou) *noun, plural* **boughs.**

bought We *bought* groceries at the store. Look up **buy** for more information.
bought (bôt) *verb.*

boulder A large rock that is rounded and smooth. The *boulder* fell off the cliff and blocked the road below.
boul·der (bōl′dər) *noun, plural* **boulders.**

boulevard A wide city street. A boulevard often has trees growing along its sides.
boul·e·vard (bool′ə värd′) *noun, plural* **boulevards.**

bounce 1. To spring back after hitting something. The ball *bounced* into the street. 2. To cause to spring back. He *bounced* the ball against the wall. *Verb.*
—A spring; bound. With one *bounce* the ball disappeared over the fence. *Noun.*
bounce (bouns) *verb,* **bounced, bouncing;** *noun, plural* **bounces.**

bound¹ 1. Fastened; tied. The bank robbers left the guard *bound* and gagged. 2. Certain; sure. The team is *bound* to lose the game if the players don't practice. 3. Having an obligation; obliged. I am *bound* by my promise to keep the secret. *Adjective.*

—We *bound* the box of books with rope. Look up **bind** for more information. *Verb.*
  bound (bound) *adjective; verb.*

bound² **1.** To leap; spring; jump. The rabbit *bounded* away into the woods. **2.** To spring back after hitting something. The ball *bounded* off the wall. *Verb.*
—A long or high leap. With one *bound* the deer was across the stream. *Noun.*
  bound (bound) *verb,* **bounded, bounding;** *noun, plural* **bounds.**

bound³ A line that marks the farthest edge; boundary. In the volleyball game, the ball went out of *bounds. Noun.*
—To form the boundary of. A road *bounds* the farmer's land on the north. *Verb.*
  bound (bound) *noun, plural* **bounds;** *verb,* **bounded, bounding.**

bound⁴ Going toward. The train is *bound* for New York.
  bound (bound) *adjective.*

boundary A line that marks the edge of an area of land; border. Dad built a fence along the *boundary* of our property.
  bound·a·ry (boun′dər ē *or* bound′rē) *noun, plural* **boundaries.**

bountiful More than enough; abundant. The farmer had a *bountiful* harvest.
  boun·ti·ful (boun′ti fəl) *adjective.*

bounty **1.** A reward for killing certain animals. The county government pays a *bounty* of five dollars for every coyote killed. **2.** Generosity; goodness. Many poor people were helped by the rich man's *bounty.*
  boun·ty (boun′tē) *noun, plural* **bounties.**

bouquet A bunch of flowers. The young man brought a *bouquet* of roses to his girlfriend.
  bou·quet (bō kā′ *or* bōō kā′) *noun, plural* **bouquets.**

Bouquet

bout **1.** A trial of skill; contest. The two men will wrestle in the second *bout.* **2.** An attack or outburst; fit; spell. The boy had a *bout* of coughing.
  bout (bout) *noun, plural* **bouts.**

bow¹ **1.** To bend forward. People bow to show respect or to greet someone. **2.** To give in; submit. The small boy *bowed* to his older sister's wishes. *Verb.*
—A bending forward of the head or body. The knight made a *bow* before the queen. *Noun.* ▲ Another word that sounds like this is **bough.**
  bow (bou) *verb,* **bowed, bowing;** *noun, plural* **bows.**

bow² **1.** A weapon for shooting arrows. A bow is made of a strip of wood that is bent by a string fastened to each end. **2.** A knot with two or more loops. Carol tied a pretty green *bow* on the package. **3.** A long piece of wood with horsehairs stretched from one end to the other. This bow is used to play the violin.
  bow (bō) *noun, plural* **bows.**

Bows

bow³ The front end of a boat. ▲ Another word that sounds like this is **bough.**
  bow (bou) *noun, plural* **bows.**

bowels **1.** A long tube in the body; intestines. Food passes from the stomach into the bowels. **2.** The deepest part of something. The coal mine was in the *bowels* of the earth.
  bow·els (bou′əlz) *noun plural.*

bowl¹ **1.** A rounded dish that holds things. Mother put lettuce in the salad *bowl.* Jerry poured milk into a *bowl* for the cat. **2.** Something shaped like a bowl. The round end of a spoon is called a bowl. A football stadium is sometimes called a bowl. ▲ Another word that sounds like this is **boll.**
  bowl (bōl) *noun, plural* **bowls.**

bowl² A wooden ball used in a game. *Noun.*
—**1.** To play the game of bowling. Tom likes to *bowl* on Saturday night. **2.** To roll a ball in bowling. It is your turn to *bowl. Verb.* ▲ Another word that sounds like this is **boll.**
  bowl (bōl) *noun, plural* **bowls;** *verb,* **bowled, bowling.**

bowlegged Having legs that curve outward. The cowboy was *bowlegged* from riding a horse for many years.
  bow·leg·ged (bō′leg′id) *adjective.*

at; āpe; cär; end; mē; it; īce; hot; ōld;
fôrk; wood; fōol; oil; out; up; turn; sing;
thin; this; hw in white; zh in treasure.
ə stands for a in about, e in taken
i in pencil, o in lemon, and u in circus.

bowling A game that you play by rolling a heavy ball down an alley to knock down wooden pins at the other end.
bowl·ing (bō′ling) *noun.*

bowman A person who shoots with a bow and arrow; archer.
bow·man (bō′mən) *noun, plural* **bowmen.**

bowstring A strong string fastened to the two ends of a bow for shooting arrows.
bow·string (bō′string′) *noun, plural* **bowstrings.**

box[1] **1.** A container used to hold things. A box is made of cardboard, wood, or another heavy material. It has four sides, a bottom, and sometimes a top. Phil put the books in a large *box*. Mother keeps her rings in a jewelry *box*. **2.** A closed-in area or place. He sat in a *box* at the theater. *Noun.*
—To put in a box. Andy helped his father *box* apples for the market. *Verb.*
box (boks) *noun, plural* **boxes;** *verb,* **boxed, boxing.**

box[2] A blow made with the open hand or the fist. The grouchy old man gave the boy a *box* on the ear. *Noun.*
—**1.** To hit with the open hand or the fist. Tom will *box* Bill's ears if he doesn't stop teasing him. **2.** To fight someone with the fists as a sport. The two men will *box* each other for the championship. *Verb.*
box (boks) *noun, plural* **boxes;** *verb,* **boxed, boxing.**

boxcar A car of a railroad train used to carry freight. A boxcar is enclosed on all sides. It is loaded through a sliding door on the side.
box·car (boks′kär′) *noun, plural* **boxcars.**

Boxcars

boxer **1.** A person who boxes. The *boxer* knocked out his opponent in the third round of the fight. **2.** A dog with short hair. The boxer has a tan or reddish-brown coat with white markings. Boxers are related to bulldogs, but are larger.
box·er (bok′sər) *noun, plural* **boxers.**

boxing The sport of fighting with the fists.
box·ing (bok′sing) *noun.*

Boxing

boy A male child from birth to the time he is a young man.
boy (boi) *noun, plural* **boys.**

boycott To join with others against a person, nation, or business. People sometimes boycott a store whose prices are too high by refusing to buy things from it. *Verb.*
—A planned joining together of people against a person, nation, or business. The people in our neighborhood led a *boycott* against the bus company because it raised its fares. *Noun.*
boy·cott (boi′kot) *verb,* **boycotted, boycotting;** *noun, plural* **boycotts.**

▲ About one hundred years ago a man named Captain Charles *Boycott* rented land to farmers in Ireland. The person who owned the land was English, and the Irish farmers thought they should own the land themselves, instead of someone from another country. So they refused to pay their rent to Captain Boycott. None of the people would talk to him or have anything to do with him. Captain Boycott finally had to give up his job and go back to England. Since that time, the word **boycott** has been used in talking about actions of this kind.

boyhood The time of being a boy. He spent his *boyhood* on a farm.
boy·hood (boi′hood′) *noun, plural* **boyhoods.**

boyish Of a boy; like a boy. Jeff and his friends played some *boyish* tricks on Halloween.
boy·ish (boi′ish) *adjective.*

boy scout A member of the Boy Scouts.

Boy Scouts An organization for boys. The

Boy Scouts teaches boys outdoor skills, physical fitness, and good citizenship.

brace **1.** Something that holds parts together or holds a thing steady. The roof of the old shack needs a *brace* to hold it up. **2. braces.** Metal wires used to make teeth straight. **3.** A tool that is like a handle. It is used to hold a drill or bit. **4.** A pair. The pirate held a *brace* of pistols. We saw a *brace* of geese. *Noun.*
—**1.** To hold steady; support. The boy *braced* the tree with wires so that the wind wouldn't blow it over. **2.** To prepare for a shock. *Brace* yourself for some bad news. **3.** To give energy to. The cold winter air *braced* us. *Verb.*
　brace (brās) *noun, plural* **braces;** *verb,* **braced, bracing.**

bracelet A band or chain worn around the wrist as an ornament. Some bracelets are made of gold and silver.
　brace·let (brās′lit) *noun, plural* **bracelets.**

bracket **1.** A piece of wood, metal, or stone fastened to a wall to support something. The shelf was held up by *brackets.* **2.** One of two marks, [ ], used to enclose words or numbers. **3.** Group. His father is in a high income *bracket. Noun.*
—**1.** To put words or numbers in brackets. **2.** To group together. The teacher will *bracket* the students according to their reading speeds. *Verb.*
　brack·et (brak′it) *noun, plural* **brackets;** *verb,* **bracketed, bracketing.**

brad A thin nail with a small head.
　brad (brad) *noun, plural* **brads.**

brag To speak too well of what one does or owns; boast. She *brags* about how smart she is. The boy *bragged* to his friends about his new bicycle.
　brag (brag) *verb,* **bragged, bragging.**

braid A strip made by weaving together three or more long pieces of hair, straw, or cloth. Carol wears her hair in *braids.* Henry's band uniform is decorated with gold *braid. Noun.*
—To weave together long pieces of hair, straw, or cloth. Ralph tried to *braid* a belt from strips of leather. *Verb.*
　braid (brād) *noun, plural* **braids;** *verb,* **braided, braiding.**

Braid

braille A system of printing for blind people. The letters of the alphabet in braille are formed by raised dots. Blind people read braille by touching the dots with their fingers.
　braille (brāl) *noun.*

▲ The word **braille** comes from the name of a blind Frenchman, Louis *Braille.* He was a teacher of other blind people, and he thought of this way to write for them.

brain **1.** The large mass of nerves and tissue that is inside the head of persons and animals. The brain is the main part of the nervous system. The brain controls the actions of the body. It also lets us think, learn, and remember. **2. brains.** Intelligence. My older sister has real *brains. Noun.*
—To hit on the head. The hunter *brained* the animal with a large club. *Verb.*
　brain (brān) *noun, plural* **brains;** *verb,* **brained, braining.**

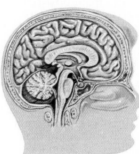
Brain

brake¹ Something used to stop or slow the movement of a wheel, or of a car, truck, bicycle, or other vehicle. Many brakes work by pressing against the wheel. *Noun.*
—To cause something to stop or slow down by using a brake. Tony *braked* his bicycle by pressing the pedals backward. *Verb.* ▲ Another word that sounds like this is **break.**
　brake (brāk) *noun, plural* **brakes;** *verb,* **braked, braking.**

brake² An area of ground covered with shrubs and bushes. ▲ Another word that sounds like this is **break.**
　brake (brāk) *noun, plural* **brakes.**

brakeman A person who helps the conductor of a railroad train. In the past, his job was to operate the train's brakes.
　brake·man (brāk′mən) *noun, plural* **brakemen.**

bramble A bush with thorny stems. The blackberry plant is a kind of bramble.
　bram·ble (bram′bəl) *noun, plural* **brambles.**

---

at; āpe; cär; end; mē; it; īce; hot; ōld; fôrk; wood; fōol; oil; out; up; turn; sing; thin; this; hw in white; zh in treasure. ə stands for a in about, e in taken i in pencil, o in lemon, and u in circus.

bran The ground-up outer covering of wheat or other grains. The bran is separated from the flour by sifting. Bran is used to feed cows and other livestock. It is also used in breakfast cereals.
bran (bran) *noun.*

branch **1.** A part of a tree or bush that grows out from the trunk. **2.** Anything that goes out from a main part. A *branch* of the river flows near town. Dad works at a *branch* of the main post office. *Noun.*
—To divide into branches. The tree *branched.* Turn left at the place where the path *branches. Verb.*
branch (branch) *noun, plural* **branches;** *verb,* **branched, branching.**

brand **1.** A kind or make of something. She likes that *brand* of ice cream. He bought a new *brand* of soap. **2.** A mark made on the skin of cattle or other animals. A brand is made with a hot iron. It shows who owns an animal. **3.** A mark of disgrace. In former times a brand was burned on the skin of criminals. *Noun.*
—To mark with a brand. The cowboys will *brand* the cattle. His stealing *brands* him as a criminal. *Verb.*
brand (brand) *noun, plural* **brands;** *verb,* **branded, branding.**

brand-new Completely new. My uncle bought a *brand-new* house that no one has ever lived in.
brand-new (brand′nо̄о̄′ *or* brand′nyо̄о̄′) *adjective.*

brandy An alcoholic drink. Brandy is made from fermented fruit juice or wine.
bran·dy (bran′dē) *noun, plural* **brandies.**

brass A yellow metal that is a mixture of copper and zinc melted together. Brass is used to make musical instruments, candlesticks, and dishes.
brass (bras) *noun.*

brave Having courage. A person who is brave can face danger or pain without being afraid. The *brave* girl jumped into the water to save the drowning child. *Adjective.*
—To face danger or pain without being afraid. The fireman *braved* the burning house to rescue the trapped child. *Verb.*
brave (brāv) *adjective,* **braver, bravest;** *verb,* **braved, braving.**

bravery The ability to face danger or pain without being afraid; courage.
brav·er·y (brā′vər ē) *noun.*

breach A break made in something. Water poured through the *breach* in the dam. *Noun.*
—To make a break in; break through. The soldiers *breached* the enemy's lines. *Verb.*
breach (brēch) *noun, plural* **breaches;** *verb,* **breached, breaching.**

bread **1.** A food made by mixing flour or meal with water or milk, and then baking it in an oven. **2.** The food and other things needed for a person to live. He earns his daily *bread* by writing. ▲ Another word that sounds like this is **bred.**
bread (bred) *noun, plural* **breads.**

breadth The wideness of something measured from one side to the other side; width.
breadth (bredth) *noun.*

break **1.** To make come to pieces by force. The clumsy boy may *break* the glass. The cup will *break* if you drop it. Joe did not *break* his ankle, but he has a bad sprain. **2.** To harm or damage. The baby will *break* the typewriter if he bangs on it. **3.** To fail to obey; fail to keep. Tom will *break* the law if he drives too fast on this road. She never *breaks* a promise. **4.** To come or change suddenly. She hopes to *break* the school record at the swimming meet. We are trying to *break* my little brother's habit of sucking his thumb. A rash *broke* out on Mary's back. **5.** To force one's way. The prisoner *broke* out of jail. A burglar *broke* into the house by the back door. **6.** To fill with sorrow. The little boy's heart will *break* if we do not find his lost kitten. *Verb.*
—**1.** A broken place; something broken. His arm has a bad *break.* The sun is shining through a *break* in the clouds. The men took a ten-minute *break* from their work. **2.** The act of breaking. The puppy made a *break* for the door. *Noun.* ▲ Another word that sounds like this is **brake.**
break (brāk) *verb,* **broke, broken, breaking;** *noun, plural* **breaks.**

breakdown A failing to work. Because of the *breakdown* of the car, we had to walk.
break·down (brāk′doun′) *noun, plural* **breakdowns.**

breaker A large wave that foams as it breaks on rocks or the shore.
break·er (brā′kər) *noun, plural* **breakers.**

Breaker

breakfast The first meal of the day. The children had *breakfast* before going to school.
   break·fast (brek′fəst) *noun, plural* **break-fasts.**

breast **1.** The front part of the body. The breast is found between the stomach and the neck. **2.** A gland that gives milk.
   breast (brest) *noun, plural* **breasts.**

breastbone The flat narrow bone in the center of the breast, to which the ribs are joined.
   breast·bone (brest′bōn′) *noun, plural* **breastbones.**

breath **1.** Air drawn into and forced out of the lungs when you breathe. **2.** The act of breathing. The swimmer held her *breath* under water. **3.** The ability to breathe easily. Racing up the stairs made him lose his *breath.* **4.** A slight flow of air. There was not a *breath* of fresh air in the room.
   breath (breth) *noun, plural* **breaths.**

breathe **1.** To draw air into the lungs and then force it out. **2.** To whisper. She promised not to *breathe* a word of the secret.
   breathe (brēth) *verb,* **breathed, breathing.**

breathless **1.** Out of breath. The boy was *breathless* after running all the way home. **2.** Excited or fearful. The children were *breathless* as they watched the acrobats at the circus.
   breath·less (breth′lis) *adjective.*

bred George *bred* puppies to sell. Look up **breed** for more information. ▲ Another word that sounds like this is **bread.**
   bred (bred) *verb.*

breeches Pants that reach to the knees. Men wore breeches in former times.
   breech·es (brich′iz) *noun plural.*

breed **1.** To raise. She *breeds* roses in her garden. Al *breeds* chickens to sell at the market. **2.** To bring forth young. Certain animals *breed* only in the winter.
   breed (brēd) *verb,* **bred, breeding.**

breeding The way someone is brought up; training. Her nice manners show good *breeding.*
   breed·ing (brē′ding) *noun.*

breeze A mild, gentle wind. The *breeze* caused the trees to sway. *Noun.*

Breeches

—To move in an easy or quick way. Arthur *breezed* into the room. Mary *breezed* through her homework. *Verb.*
   breeze (brēz) *noun, plural* **breezes;** *verb,* **breezed, breezing.**

brew **1.** To make beer or ale. Beer and ale are brewed by soaking, boiling, and fermenting malt and hops. **2.** To make tea or coffee by soaking in hot or boiling water. **3.** To bring about; cause. Those two boys always seem to be *brewing* mischief. **4.** To form; gather. A storm is *brewing. Verb.*
—A drink made by brewing. *Noun.*
   brew (broo) *verb,* **brewed, brewing;** *noun, plural* **brews.**

briar A thorny shrub. This word is usually spelled **brier.** Look up **brier** for more information.

bribe Money or gifts given to someone to get him to do something wrong or something he does not want to do. The crook offered the member of the jury a *bribe* to say he was innocent. *Noun.*
—To give a bribe to. The driver tried to *bribe* the policeman to let him go without a ticket for speeding. *Verb.*
   bribe (brīb) *noun, plural* **bribes;** *verb,* **bribed, bribing.**

brick A block of clay baked in an oven or in the sun. Bricks are used in building. The walls of my house are made of *bricks.*
   brick (brik) *noun, plural* **bricks.**

bride A woman who has just married or is about to be married.
   bride (brīd) *noun, plural* **brides.**

bridegroom A man who has just married or is about to be married.
   bride·groom (brīd′groom′) *noun, plural* **bridegrooms.**

bridge **1.** Anything built across a river, road, or railroad track so that people can get from one side to the other. **2.** The top bony part of a person's nose. **3.** A raised area on the deck of a ship. The captain or another officer steers the ship from the bridge. *Noun.*
—To build a bridge across. The workmen *bridged* the highway. *Verb.*
   bridge (brij) *noun, plural* **bridges;** *verb,* **bridged, bridging.**

at; āpe; cär; end; mē; it; īce; hot; ōld; fôrk; wood; fool; oil; out; up; turn; sing; thin; this; hw in white; zh in treasure. ə stands for a in about, e in taken i in pencil, o in lemon, and u in circus.

bridle The part of a horse's harness that fits over the animal's head. The bridle is used to guide or control the horse. *Noun.*
—**1.** To put a bridle on. Carol will *bridle* her horse. **2.** To hold back; control. John is trying hard to *bridle* his bad temper. *Verb.*
  bri·dle (brīd′əl) *noun, plural* **bridles;** *verb,* **bridled, bridling.**

Bridle

brief **1.** Short in time. Aunt Martha came for a *brief* visit. **2.** Using few words. Her letter was very *brief. Adjective.*
—To give last-minute directions or facts to. The commander *briefed* the pilots just before their mission. *Verb.*
  brief (brēf) *adjective,* **briefer, briefest;** *verb,* **briefed, briefing.**

brier A bushy plant with thorns. The raspberry plant and the blackberry plant are sometimes called briers. The thorns on these plants are also called briers. This word is also spelled **briar.**
  bri·er (brī′ər) *noun, plural* **briers.**

brig **1.** A sailing ship with two masts. **2.** A prison on a ship.
  brig (brig) *noun, plural* **brigs.**

Brig

brigade **1.** A part of the army. A brigade is made up of two or more battalions. **2.** A group of people organized for a special purpose. Dad belongs to the volunteer fire *brigade.*
  bri·gade (bri gād′) *noun, plural* **brigades.**

bright **1.** Giving much light; filled with light. The *bright* light of the sun hurt her eyes. The waxed floor has a *bright* shine. **2.** Clear; strong. Richard painted the chair a *bright* red. **3.** Smart; clever. Sarah is a *bright* student. Kicking that hornet's nest wasn't a very *bright* thing to do.
  bright (brīt) *adjective,* **brighter, brightest.**

brilliant **1.** Very bright; sparkling. A *brilliant* light was shining. **2.** Very fine; splendid. Our team won because of the boys' *brilliant* playing. **3.** Very intelligent. That woman is a *brilliant* scientist.
  bril·liant (bril′yənt) *adjective.*

brim An edge or rim. My glass is filled to the *brim.* Mary's beach hat has a wide *brim. Noun.*
—To be full to the brim. The bathtub was *brimming* with water. *Verb.*
  brim (brim) *noun, plural* **brims;** *verb,* **brimmed, brimming.**

brine Water that is full of salt. Brine is used for pickling foods.
  brine (brīn) *noun.*

bring **1.** To cause something or someone to come with you. Remember to *bring* your books home. Carl will *bring* his records to the party. **2.** To cause something to come or happen. The heavy rains will *bring* floods. The firemen will *bring* the fire under control quickly.
  bring (bring) *verb,* **brought, bringing.**
  to bring up. 1. To raise someone. My mother was *brought up* on a farm. **2.** To mention; suggest. Don't *bring up* the subject of cleaning my room again.

brink **1.** The edge at the top of a steep place. Joey stood on the *brink* of the cliff to look down at the valley below. **2.** The point just before something happens; verge. He is on the *brink* of tears. The two countries were on the *brink* of war.
  brink (bringk) *noun, plural* **brinks.**

brisk **1.** Quick and lively. The girls walked at a *brisk* pace. **2.** Refreshing; keen; sharp. We went out into the *brisk* winter air.
  brisk (brisk) *adjective,* **brisker, briskest.**

bristle A short, stiff hair. Hogs have bristles. My hairbrush and toothbrush are both made of *bristles. Noun.*
—**1.** To have the hairs on the neck or body rise. My dog will *bristle* if he sees your cat. **2.** To stand up stiffly. The porcupine's quills *bristled. Verb.*
  bris·tle (bris′əl) *noun, plural* **bristles;** *verb,* **bristled, bristling.**

Britain The countries of England, Scotland, and Wales; Great Britain.
  Brit·ain (brit′ən) *noun.*

84

British Of Great Britain. Drinking tea in the middle of the afternoon is a *British* custom. *Adjective.*
—**the British.** The people of Great Britain. *Noun.*
  Brit·ish (brit′ish) *adjective; noun.*

brittle Very easily broken. The *brittle* icicles snapped in two when I touched them. The glass is *brittle* and will break into many pieces if you drop it.
  brit·tle (brit′əl) *adjective.*

broad 1. Large from one side to the other side; wide. There is a *broad* driveway in front of the school. 2. Wide in range; not limited. John has a *broad* knowledge of foreign stamps and coins. 3. Clear and open. The thief tried to rob the bank in *broad* daylight.
  broad (brôd) *adjective,* **broader, broadest.**

broadcast 1. To send out music, news, or other kinds of programs by radio or television. That radio station *broadcasts* twenty-four hours a day. 2. To make widely known. You shouldn't *broadcast* that secret to the whole school. *Verb.*
—Something that is broadcast by radio or television. My parents listen to the news *broadcast* every evening. *Noun.*
  broad·cast (brôd′kast′) *verb,* **broadcast or broadcasted, broadcasting;** *noun, plural* **broadcasts.**

brocade A heavy cloth with patterns woven into it. The queen wore a robe of gold *brocade.*
  bro·cade (brō kād′) *noun, plural* **brocades.**

broccoli A plant whose thick green stems and flower buds are eaten as a vegetable.
  broc·co·li (brok′ə-lē) *noun, plural* **broccoli.**

Spears of Broccoli

broil 1. To cook over an open fire or under the flame in the broiler of a stove. We are going to *broil* the steak over our barbecue. 2. To be very hot. We *broiled* in the hot sun on the beach.
  broil (broil) *verb,* **broiled, broiling.**

broiler A pan, grill, or part of a stove that is used to broil food.
  broil·er (broi′lər) *noun, plural* **broilers.**

broke Jack *broke* the dish when he dropped it. Look up **break** for more information.
  broke (brōk) *verb.*

broken Mary has *broken* her watch. Look up **break** for more information. *Verb.*
—1. In pieces. You can throw away that *broken* dish. 2. Not kept. You ought to say you're sorry for your *broken* promise. 3. Not working; damaged. Our television set is *broken. Adjective.*
  bro·ken (brō′kən) *verb; adjective.*

bronchial tubes The branches of the windpipe. Air flows to and from the lungs through the bronchial tubes.
  bron·chi·al tubes (brong′kē əl).

bronchitis A sickness from a cold in the bronchial tubes. When you have bronchitis, you have a bad cough.
  bron·chi·tis (brong kī′tis) *noun.*

bronco A small, partly wild horse of the western United States.
  bron·co (brong′kō) *noun, plural* **broncos.**

bronze 1. A reddish-brown metal made by melting together copper and tin. Bronze is made into dishes, jewelry, and statues. 2. A reddish-brown color. *Noun.*
—Reddish-brown. *Adjective.*
—To make reddish-brown. The sun had *bronzed* the lifeguard's back. *Verb.*
  bronze (bronz) *noun, plural* **bronzes;** *adjective; verb,* **bronzed, bronzing.**

brooch A pin worn as an ornament. A brooch is fastened with a clasp. Mother wore a silver *brooch* on the collar of her dress.
  brooch (brōch *or* brooch) *noun, plural* **brooches.**

brood The young birds that are hatched from eggs at the same time. The hen took care of her *brood* of chicks. *Noun.*
—1. To sit on eggs in order to hatch them. Hens, robins, and other birds brood until the baby birds hatch from their eggs. 2. To think or worry about for a long time. Mary *brooded* over the loss of her kitten. *Verb.*
  brood (brood) *noun, plural* **broods;** *verb,* **brooded, brooding.**

Brooch

at; āpe; cär; end; mē; it; īce; hot; ōld;
fôrk; wood; fool; oil; out; up; turn; sing;
thin; this; hw in white; zh in treasure.
ə stands for a in about, e in taken
i in pencil, o in lemon, and u in circus.

brook   A small stream.
    brook (brŏŏk) *noun, plural* **brooks.**

broom   **1.** A brush with a long handle used for sweeping. **2.** A bush that has long, thin branches, small leaves, and yellow flowers.
    broom (brŏŏm *or* broom) *noun, plural* **brooms.**

broth   A thin soup. Broth is made by boiling meat, fish, or vegetables in water.
    broth (brôth) *noun, plural* **broths.**

brother   A boy or man having the same parents as another person.
    broth·er (bruth′ər) *noun, plural* **brothers.**

brotherhood   The close feeling between brothers.
    broth·er·hood (bruth′ər hood′) *noun.*

brother-in-law   **1.** The brother of one's husband or wife. **2.** The husband of one's sister.
    broth·er-in-law (bruth′ər in lô′) *noun, plural* **brothers-in-law.**

brought   Ted *brought* me a birthday present. Look up **bring** for more information.
    brought (brôt) *verb.*

brow   **1.** The part of the face above the eyes; forehead. Jack wrinkled his *brow* as he tried to remember the answer. **2.** The curved line of hair above the eye; eyebrow. **3.** The edge of a steep place. From the *brow* of the hill we could see for miles around.
    brow (brou) *noun, plural* **brows.**

brown   A dark color like that of chocolate or coffee. *Noun.*
    —Having the color brown. *Adjective.*
    —To make or become brown. The sun *browned* his skin. The rolls *browned* in the oven. *Verb.*
    brown (broun) *noun, plural* **browns;** *adjective,* **browner, brownest;** *verb,* **browned, browning.**

brownie   **1.** A kind of fairy. Brownies are supposed to do good things for people. **2.** A small, flat chocolate cake with nuts in it. **3. Brownie.** A girl who belongs to the junior division of the Girl Scouts.
    brown·ie (brou′nē) *noun, plural* **brownies.**

browse   To look here and there in a book, library, or store. Mary likes to *browse* through the books on the library shelf before picking one to take home and read.
    browse (brouz) *verb,* **browsed, browsing.**

bruise   **1.** An injury that does not break the skin, but makes a bluish or blackish mark on it. A bruise is caused by a fall, blow, or bump. **2.** A mark on the outside of a fruit, vegetable, or plant caused by a blow or bump. *Noun.*

—To cause a bruise on the skin of. Sara *bruised* her arm when she fell off her bicycle. *Verb.*
    bruise (brŏŏz) *noun, plural* **bruises;** *verb,* **bruised, bruising.**

brunette   **1.** Dark-brown. Eve has *brunette* hair. **2.** Having dark-brown hair and dark-colored eyes and skin. Many Spanish people are *brunette. Adjective.*
    —A person with dark-brown hair and dark-colored eyes and skin. Mary and her sisters are *brunettes. Noun.*
    bru·nette (brŏŏ net′) *adjective; noun, plural* **brunettes.**

brush¹   **1.** A tool that is used for scrubbing, smoothing, sweeping, or painting. A brush is made of bristles attached to a stiff back or to a handle. I used a clothes *brush* to get the cat hairs off my skirt. **2.** The act of using a brush. Give your hair a good *brush.* **3.** A light touch in passing. I felt a *brush* on my legs as the cat went by. *Noun.*
    —**1.** To scrub, smooth, sweep, or paint with a brush. *Brush* your teeth every day. Henry *brushed* the crumbs from his lap. **2.** To touch lightly in passing. Leaves and branches *brushed* my face as I walked through the heavy woods. *Verb.*
    brush (brush) *noun, plural* **brushes;** *verb,* **brushed, brushing.**

brush²   **1.** Shrubs, small trees, and bushes growing together. The frightened rabbit disappeared into the *brush.* **2.** Twigs or branches cut or broken off from trees.
    brush (brush) *noun.*

Brussels sprouts   Buds that grow along the thick stem of a leafy plant. Brussels sprouts are cooked and eaten as a vegetable.
    Brus·sels sprouts (brus′əlz).

brutal   Like a savage animal; cruel. The *brutal* man beat the dog.
    bru·tal (brŏŏt′əl) *adjective.*

brute   **1.** An animal. A *brute* cannot reason or feel the way a human does. **2.** A cruel person. I saw that *brute* kicking an old dog.
    brute (brŏŏt) *noun, plural* **brutes.**

Brussels Sprouts

bubble   A round thing formed from a liquid and filled with air or gas. There are *bubbles* in my ginger ale. The children blew soap *bubbles* with a pipe. *Noun.*
—To form bubbles. Water *bubbles* when it is boiling. *Verb.*
   bub·ble (bub′əl) *noun, plural* **bubbles;** *verb,* **bubbled, bubbling.**

buck   A male deer, antelope, rabbit, or goat. *Noun.*
—**1.** To jump into the air with the back arched and the head down. A horse can *buck* to throw off a rider. **2.** To work or push against. We had to *buck* heavy traffic on the highway. *Verb.*
   buck (buk) *noun, plural* **bucks;** *verb,* **bucked, bucking.**

bucket   A container used for carrying water, sand, or other things; pail.
   buck·et (buk′it) *noun, plural* **buckets.**

buckle   **1.** A fastening used to hold together the two ends of a belt or strap. My belt has a silver *buckle.* **2.** A bend or bulge. The heat caused a *buckle* in the surface of the road. *Noun.*
—**1.** To fasten with a buckle. The pilot told us to *buckle* our seat belts because the plane was about to land. **2.** To bend or bulge. The shelf began to *buckle* because I put too many books on it. *Verb.*
   buck·le (buk′əl) *noun, plural* **buckles;** *verb,* **buckled, buckling.**

buckskin   A yellowish-tan leather made from the skins of deer or sheep. Buckskin is strong and soft.
   buck·skin (buk′skin′) *noun, plural* **buckskins.**

buckwheat   A plant whose seeds are used as feed for animals or are ground into flour.
   buck·wheat (buk′-hwēt′) *noun, plural* **buckwheats.**

bud   A small swelling on a plant. A bud will later grow into a flower, a leaf, or a branch. The *buds* on the rosebush show that it will bloom soon. *Noun.*
—To form buds. The trees are beginning to *bud.* *Verb.*
   bud (bud) *noun, plural* **buds;** *verb,* **budded, budding.**

Buckwheat   Seed

buddy   A very close friend; pal. Jack is my *buddy.*
   bud·dy (bud′ē) *noun, plural* **buddies.**

budge   To move even a little. Harry wouldn't *budge* from bed when I woke him this morning. We couldn't *budge* the heavy box.
   budge (buj) *verb,* **budged, budging.**

budget   A plan for using money. A budget shows how much money a person will have and the ways it will be spent. Mother made a *budget* for household expenses for the month. The cost of building highways is a part of the *budget* of a state. *Noun.*
—To make a plan for the spending of money. Jay *budgets* his allowance very carefully and always has a little left over at the end of the week. *Verb.*
   budg·et (buj′it) *noun, plural* **budgets;** *verb,* **budgeted, budgeting.**

buff   **1.** A soft, strong, yellowish-brown leather. Buff was formeriy made from the skin of buffalo and is now made from the skin of oxen. **2.** A yellowish-brown color. *Noun.*
—Having the color buff; yellowish-brown. *Adjective.*
—To polish; shine. Mary *buffed* her shoes to make them shiny. *Verb.*
   buff (buf) *noun, plural* **buffs;** *adjective; verb,* **buffed, buffing.**

buffalo   **1.** A North American wild ox; bison. A buffalo has a big shaggy head with short horns and a humped back. **2.** Any of various oxen of Europe, Asia, and Africa. The water buffalo of Asia is used to draw heavy loads.
   buf·fa·lo (buf′ə lō′) *noun, plural* **buffaloes** or **buffalos** or **buffalo.**

buffet   **1.** A piece of furniture. A buffet has a flat top to serve food from and drawers or shelves for storing dishes, silver, and table linen. **2.** A meal laid out on a buffet or a table so that guests may serve themselves.
   buf·fet (bə fā′ *or* boo fā′) *noun, plural* **buffets.**

bug   **1.** Any of a group of insects with or without wings. Bugs have beaklike mouth parts for sucking. A bedbug is a bug. **2.** Any insect. Ants, spiders, and cockroaches are bugs. **3.** A germ that causes a disease. A lot of

at; āpe; cär; end; mē; it; īce; hot; ōld;
fôrk; wood; fōōl; oil; out; up; turn; sing;
thin; this; hw in white; zh in treasure.
ə stands for a in about, e in taken
i in pencil, o in lemon, and u in circus.

pupils missed school because of the flu *bug*. **4.** A fault in the working of a machine. There is some *bug* in the car engine that makes it stall. *Noun.*
—To hide a small microphone in. People sometimes *bug* rooms so that they can overhear other people's conversations without their knowing about it. *Verb.*
  bug (bug) *noun, plural* **bugs;** *verb,* **bugged, bugging.**

buggy   A light carriage with four wheels. A buggy is pulled by one horse.
  bug·gy (bug′ē) *noun, plural* **buggies.**

bugle   A brass musical instrument shaped like a trumpet. Bugles are used in the army and navy to sound signals.
  bu·gle (byo̅o̅′gəl) *noun, plural* **bugles.**

Bugle

bugler   A person who plays a bugle.
  bu·gler (byo̅o̅′glər) *noun, plural* **buglers.**

build   **1.** To make by putting parts or material together. John is going to *build* a bookcase with boards. The state will soon *build* a new highway near our farm. Beavers *build* dams. **2.** To form little by little; develop. That storekeeper is trying to *build* a successful business. *Verb.*
—The way in which something is put together. That football player has a strong *build. Noun.*
  build (bild) *verb,* **built, building;** *noun, plural* **builds.**

building   **1.** Something built. Houses, hotels, schools, stores, and garages are buildings. **2.** The act of making houses, stores, bridges, and similar things.
  build·ing (bil′ding) *noun, plural* **buildings.**

built   The boys *built* a tree hut. Look up **build** for more information.
  built (bilt) *verb.*

bulb   **1.** A round, underground part of a plant. The plant grows from the bulb. Onions, lilies, and tulips grow from bulbs. **2.** Any object with a rounded part. Put a new electric light *bulb* in the lamp.
  bulb (bulb) *noun, plural* **bulbs.**

bulge   A rounded part that swells out. The ball made a *bulge* in Tom's pocket. *Noun.*
—To swell out. The bag *bulged* with groceries. *Verb.*

bulge (bulj) *noun, plural* **bulges;** *verb,* **bulged, bulging.**

bulk   **1.** Large size. The *bulk* of the fat man in the circus made it hard for him to move around. **2.** The largest or main part. The farmer grew corn on the *bulk* of his land.
  bulk (bulk) *noun.*

bull   **1.** The full-grown male of cattle. **2.** The full-grown male of the elephant, moose, or seal.
  bull (bool) *noun, plural* **bulls.**

bulldog   A heavily built dog. A bulldog has a large head, square jaws, short legs, and a smooth coat. The bulldog is known for the strong, stubborn grip of its jaws.
  bull·dog (bool′dôg′) *noun, plural* **bulldogs.**

bulldozer   A tractor with a powerful motor. A bulldozer has a heavy metal blade in front. It is used for clearing land by moving earth and rocks.
  bull·doz·er (bool′dō′zər) *noun, plural* **bulldozers.**

Bulldozer

bullet   A small piece of rounded or pointed metal. A bullet is made to be shot from a gun.
  bul·let (bool′it) *noun, plural* **bullets.**

bulletin   **1.** A short announcement of the latest news. We heard a *bulletin* on the radio about the coming hurricane. **2.** A small newspaper or magazine published regularly. Our club *bulletin* lists the dates of meetings.
  bul·le·tin (bool′it ən) *noun, plural* **bulletins.**

bullfight   A sport in which a man fights a bull in an arena. Bullfights are popular in Spain, Mexico, and South America.
  bull·fight (bool′fīt′) *noun, plural* **bullfights.**

bullfrog   A large frog that has a loud, bellowing croak. The bullfrog is the largest frog in the United States.
  bull·frog (bool′frôg′ *or* bool′frog′) *noun, plural* **bullfrogs.**

bull's-eye   **1.** The center circle of a target. John's arrow hit the *bull's-eye.* **2.** A shot that hits this circle.
  bull's-eye (boolz′ī′) *noun, plural* **bull's-eyes.**

bully A person who is tough and likes to fight. A bully is always frightening or hurting people who are smaller or weaker than he is. *Noun.*
—To frighten into doing something. Mary *bullies* her little brother into running errands for her. *Verb.*
> **bul·ly** (bool′ē) *noun, plural* **bullies;** *verb,* **bullied, bullying.**

bumblebee A large bee with a thick, hairy body. Most bumblebees have yellow and black stripes across their backs.
> **bum·ble·bee** (bum′bəl bē′) *noun, plural* **bumblebees.**

bump 1. To strike or knock suddenly. The two cars *bumped* into each other. Tom *bumped* his knee on the chair. 2. To move with jerks and jolts. The wagon *bumped* along the dirt road. *Verb.*
—1. A heavy knock or blow. The *bump* on his head made him dizzy. 2. A swelling or lump. There is a *bump* on my knee where the baseball hit it. *Noun.*
> **bump** (bump) *verb,* **bumped, bumping;** *noun, plural* **bumps.**

Bumblebee

bumper A heavy metal bar across the front or back of a car or truck. A bumper protects the car or truck from damage if it bumps into something. *Noun.*
—Very large. The farmer had a *bumper* crop of wheat this year. *Adjective.*
> **bump·er** (bum′pər) *noun, plural* **bumpers;** *adjective.*

Bumper

bun A sweetened roll. A bun often has raisins in it.
> **bun** (bun) *noun, plural* **buns.**

bunch 1. A number of things fastened or growing together. We bought a *bunch* of grapes at the fruit store. Put that *bunch* of letters in the desk drawer. 2. A group of people. A *bunch* of us are going to the movies. *Noun.*
—To gather together. The kittens *bunched* together to keep warm. *Verb.*
> **bunch** (bunch) *noun, plural* **bunches;** *verb,* **bunched, bunching.**

bundle A number of things tied or wrapped together. Put that *bundle* of newspapers in the trash can. Mother's arms were full of *bundles* from the store. *Noun.*
—To tie or wrap together. Mary *bundled* some dirty clothes for the laundry. *Verb.*
> **bun·dle** (bund′əl) *noun, plural* **bundles;** *verb,* **bundled, bundling.**

bungalow A small house. A bungalow usually has only one story.
> **bun·ga·low** (bung′gə lō′) *noun, plural* **bungalows.**

bunk A narrow bed that is built against a wall like a shelf.
> **bunk** (bungk) *noun, plural* **bunks.**

Bunsen burner An instrument that uses a mixture of air and gas to make a very hot, blue flame. Bunsen burners are often used in science laboratories.
> **Bun·sen burner** (bun′sən).

bunt To tap a baseball so that it goes only a short distance. The batter *bunted* the ball. *Verb.*
—A baseball that has been bunted. *Noun.*
> **bunt** (bunt) *verb,* **bunted, bunting;** *noun, plural* **bunts.**

buoy 1. A floating object that is anchored. Buoys are used to warn ships of dangerous rocks or to show the safe way through a channel. 2. Something used by a person to keep floating in water; life buoy.
> **bu·oy** (bōō′ē *or* boi) *noun, plural* **buoys.**

bur A prickly covering of a seed. This word is usually spelled **burr.** Look up **burr** for more information.

burden 1. Something that is carried; load. The mule carried its *burden* of logs easily. 2. Something very hard to bear. He found it a *burden* to earn enough money to support his large family. *Noun.*

Buoy

—To put too heavy a load on. The heavy snow *burdened* the branches of the small tree. *Verb.*

bur·den (burd′ən) *noun, plural* **burdens;** *verb,* **burdened, burdening.**

bureau **1.** A chest of drawers. I keep my sweaters, shirts, and socks in my *bureau.* **2.** A department of a government. I listen to the reports from the weather *bureau* on the radio. **3.** An office or agency. Father bought our airplane tickets at the travel *bureau.*

bu·reau (byoor′ō) *noun, plural* **bureaus.**

burglar A person who breaks into a house, store, or other place to steal something. *Burglars* broke into the hotel room and stole some valuable jewels.

bur·glar (bur′glər) *noun, plural* **burglars.**

burial The act of putting a dead body in the earth, a tomb, or the sea. Many people were present at the *burial* of the famous general.

bur·i·al (ber′ē əl) *noun, plural* **burials.**

buried The dog has *buried* his favorite bone. Look up **bury** for more information.

bur·ied (ber′ēd) *verb.*

burlap A coarse cloth. Burlap is used for making bags, curtains, and wall coverings.

bur·lap (bur′lap) *noun, plural* **burlaps.**

burn **1.** To set on fire; be on fire. Joe will *burn* the pile of leaves he has raked in the yard. The damp wood *burned* slowly. **2.** To injure by fire or heat. The child *burned* her hand on the hot stove. **3.** To make by fire or heat. A spark from the campfire *burned* a hole in Jim's sweater. **4.** To feel or cause to feel hot. The child *burned* with fever. The pepper *burned* his tongue. **5.** To use for light or heat. Our furnace *burns* oil. *Verb.*

—An injury caused by fire or heat. She got a *burn* on her hand from the hot iron. *Noun.*

burn (burn) *verb,* **burned** or **burnt, burning;** *noun, plural* **burns.**

burner The part of a stove or furnace from which the flame comes. Put the pot on the back *burner* of the stove.

burn·er (bur′nər) *noun, plural* **burners.**

burnt The spark *burnt* a hole in the rug. Look up **burn** for more information.

burnt (burnt) *verb.*

burr **1.** A prickly covering of the seed of some plants. Burrs stick to cloth and fur. **2.** Any plant that has burrs. This word is also spelled **bur.**

burr (bur) *noun, plural* **burrs.**

burro A small donkey. Burros are used for riding and for carrying loads. ▲ Other words that sound like this are **borough** and **burrow.**

bur·ro (bur′ō) *noun, plural* **burros.**

burrow A hole dug in the ground by an animal. An animal uses its burrow to live in or hide in. *Noun.*

—**1.** To dig a hole in the ground. Moles and gophers *burrow.* **2.** To search. She *burrowed* in her purse for her keys. *Verb.* ▲ Other words that sound like this are **borough** and **burro.**

bur·row (bur′ō) *noun, plural* **burrows;** *verb,* **burrowed, burrowing.**

burst **1.** To break open suddenly. The balloon *burst* when I stuck it with a pin. The buds on the roses were ready to *burst* into bloom. **2.** To be very full. My closet is *bursting* with clothes. **3.** To come or go suddenly. Tom *burst* into my room. The child *burst* into tears when she broke her doll. *Verb.*

—**1.** The act of bursting; outbreak. There was a *burst* of laughter when he told the joke. **2.** A sudden effort. With a *burst* of speed, the runner won the race. *Noun.*

burst (burst) *verb,* **burst, bursting;** *noun, plural* **bursts.**

bury **1.** To put a dead body in the earth, a tomb, or the sea. The boys *buried* their dead dog in the yard. **2.** To cover up; hide. Our dog likes to *bury* its bones. ▲ Another word that sounds like this is **berry.**

bur·y (ber′ē) *verb,* **buried, burying.**

bus A large vehicle with a motor and rows of seats for carrying many passengers. Buses usually go along a regular route. She goes to school by *bus. Noun.*

—To carry or go in a bus. Our town *buses* pupils to school. *Verb.*

bus (bus) *noun, plural* **buses** or **busses;** *verb,* **bused** or **bussed, busing** or **bussing.**

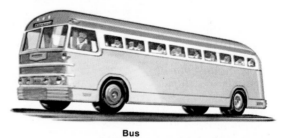

Bus

bush A woody plant; shrub. A bush is smaller than a tree and has many branches near the ground. Berries and roses grow on bushes.

bush (boosh) *noun, plural* **bushes.**

bushel A measure for grain, fruit, vegetables, and other dry things. A *bushel* is equal to 4 pecks, or 32 quarts. We bought a *bushel* of corn to roast for our picnic.

bush·el (boosh′əl) *noun, plural* **bushels.**

bushy Thick and spreading like a bush. A squirrel has a *bushy* tail.
bush·y (boosh′ē) *adjective*, **bushier, bushiest.**

business **1.** The work that a person does to earn a living. Mr. Brown's *business* is farming. **2.** A store, factory, or other similar thing. The owner of the gas station sold his *business* and moved to another town. **3.** The buying and selling of things; trade. The garage is doing a big *business* in snow tires this winter. **4.** Matter or affair. What *business* is it of yours how he wears his hair?
busi·ness (biz′nis) *noun, plural* **businesses.**

businessman A man who owns or works in a business. A man who manages a supermarket is a businessman.
busi·ness·man (biz′nis man′) *noun, plural* **businessmen.**

bust A statue of a person's head and shoulders. There is a *bust* of George Washington near the entrance to our post office.
bust (bust) *noun, plural* **busts.**

Bust

bustle To move or hurry in an excited or noisy way. Mother and Father *bustled* around getting everything ready for the birthday party. *Verb.*
—Noisy, excited activity. There was much *bustle* as the family packed to go away on vacation. *Noun.*
bus·tle (bus′əl) *verb,* **bustled, bustling;** *noun.*

busy **1.** Doing something; active. Mary is *busy* making plans to go to the circus. **2.** Full of activity. Today was a *busy* day. The airport is a *busy* place. **3.** In use. When I telephoned, her line was *busy. Adjective.*
—To make busy; keep busy. Betty *busied* herself with cleaning the room. *Verb.*
bus·y (biz′ē) *adjective,* **busier, busiest;** *verb,* **busied, busying.**

but Tom is tall, *but* his sister is short. Beth's bruised knee hurt, *but* she did not cry. Jack delivers newspapers every day of the week *but* Sunday. I saw your brother *but* a few minutes ago. ▲ Another word that sounds like this is **butt.**
but (but) *conjunction; preposition; adverb.*

butcher A person who cuts up and sells meat. Mother sent me to the *butcher* to buy some lamb chops.
butch·er (booch′ər) *noun, plural* **butchers.**

butler A male servant. A butler is the head servant in a household.
but·ler (but′lər) *noun, plural* **butlers.**

butt¹ **1.** The thicker or larger end of something. The boy held the *butt* of the rifle against his shoulder as he aimed at the target. **2.** An end that is left over. Please be sure to put your cigarette *butts* in the trash. ▲ Another word that sounds like this is **but.**
butt (but) *noun, plural* **butts.**

butt² A person or thing that people make fun of. The new boy was the *butt* of the other children's teasing. ▲ Another word that sounds like this is **but.**
butt (but) *noun, plural* **butts.**

butt³ To strike hard with the head or the horns. The goat *butted* the gate. *Verb.*
—A push or blow with the head or the horns. The calf gave its mother a playful *butt. Noun.* ▲ Another word that sounds like this is **but.**
butt (but) *verb,* **butted, butting;** *noun, plural* **butts.**

butter **1.** A solid yellowish fat. Butter is separated from cream or milk by churning. We use butter as a spread for bread and in cooking. **2.** A spread that is like butter. Butter can be made from apples or from ground-up peanuts. *Noun.*
—To spread with butter. Be sure to *butter* the bread for the sandwiches. *Verb.*
but·ter (but′ər) *noun, plural* **butters;** *verb,* **buttered, buttering.**

buttercup A common plant that has yellow flowers shaped like cups.
but·ter·cup (but′ər kup′) *noun, plural* **buttercups.**

butterfly An insect with a thin body and four large brightly-colored wings. Butterflies fly in the daytime.
but·ter·fly (but′ər flī′) *noun, plural* **butterflies.**

Butterfly

buttermilk The sour liquid that is left after milk or cream has been churned to make butter.
but·ter·milk (but′ər milk′) *noun, plural* **buttermilks.**

at; āpe; cär; end; mē; it; īce; hot; ōld;
fôrk; wood; fool; oil; out; up; turn; sing;
thin; this; hw in white; zh in treasure.
ə stands for a in about, e in taken
i in pencil, o in lemon, and u in circus.

butternut   The oily nut of a tree that is related to the·walnut.
   but·ter·nut (but'ər nut') *noun, plural* **butternuts.**

butterscotch   A candy made from brown sugar and butter.
   but·ter·scotch (but'ər skoch') *noun.*

button   **1.** A small, round flat thing. A button is used to fasten clothing or to ornament it. Will you please sew the *button* back on my coat? The waiter wore a red uniform with brass *buttons.* **2.** A knob that is turned or pushed to make something work. Press the elevator *button* if you want the elevator to stop at this floor. *Noun.*
   —To fasten with buttons. Jack *buttoned* his overcoat because it was cold out. *Verb.*
   but·ton (but'ən) *noun, plural* **buttons;** *verb,* **buttoned, buttoning.**

buttress   A strong, heavy thing built against a wall to hold it up or make it stronger. *Noun.*
   —To make something stronger with a buttress. The walls of the cathedral were *buttressed. Verb.*
   but·tress (but'ris) *noun, plural* **buttresses;** *verb,* **buttressed, buttressing.**

buy   To get something by paying money for it; purchase. John can *buy* an ice-cream cone for twenty-five cents. Our family *bought* a new car last year. *Verb.*
   —A bargain. That used car is a good *buy. Noun.* ▲ Another word that sounds like this is **by.**
   buy (bī) *verb,* **bought, buying;** *noun, plural* **buys.**

buyer   A person who buys. Tom put his car up for sale, but there have been no *buyers.*
   buy·er (bī'ər) *noun, plural* **buyers.**

buzz   A humming sound. A bee makes a buzz. The *buzz* of talking stopped when the teacher came into the room. *Noun.*
   —**1.** To make a humming sound. The mosquito *buzzed* in my ear all night. **2.** To fly an airplane low over something. The pilot *buzzed* the bridge. *Verb.*
   buzz (buz) *noun, plural* **buzzes;** *verb,* **buzzed, buzzing.**

buzzard   A very large bird that has a sharp, hooked beak and long, sharp claws. A buzzard is a kind of hawk. Buzzards are birds of prey.
   buz·zard (buz'ərd) *noun, plural* **buzzards.**

buzzer   A thing that makes a buzzing sound as a signal. It is worked by electricity. He pressed the *buzzer,* and Joan opened the front door.
   buzz·er (buz'ər) *noun, plural* **buzzers.**

by   There is a table *by* the bed. The bus went *by* us. He came *by* train. That book was written *by* Charles Dickens. We buy milk *by* the gallon. Please be here *by* eight o'clock. My friend's house is close *by.* A car passed *by.* ▲ Another word that sounds like this is **buy.**
   by (bī) *preposition; adverb.*

bygone   Gone by; past; former. The old man thought of his *bygone* school years. *Adjective.*
   —**bygones.** Something gone by or past. Let's make up our quarrel and let *bygones* be *bygones. Noun.*
   by·gone (bī'gôn') *adjective; noun plural.*

bypass   A road that turns off the main road. We took the *bypass* to avoid all the traffic in the center of town. *Noun.*
   —To go around by a bypass. The highway was built to *bypass* the town. *Verb.*
   by·pass (bī'pas') *noun, plural* **bypasses;** *verb,* **bypassed, bypassing.**

by-product   Something useful that comes from the making of something else. Buttermilk is a *by-product* of butter.
   by·prod·uct (bī'prod'əkt) *noun, plural* **by-products.**

bystander   A person who is at a place while something is happening but does not take part in it. Several *bystanders* watched the fight between the two boys.
   by·stand·er (bī'stan'dər) *noun, plural* **bystanders.**

Buzzard

at; āpe; cär; end; mē; it; īce; hot; ōld;
fôrk; wood; fōōl; oil; out; up; turn; sing;
thin; this; hw in white; zh in treasure.
ə stands for **a** in about, **e** in taken
i in pencil, **o** in lemon, and **u** in circus.

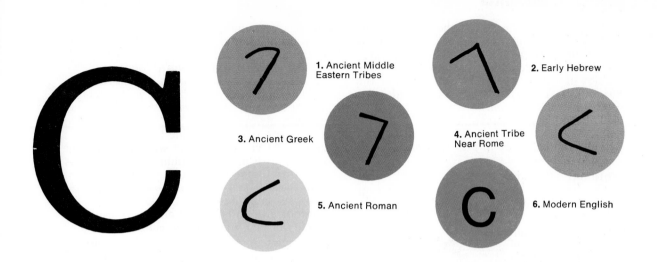

1. Ancient Middle Eastern Tribes

2. Early Hebrew

3. Ancient Greek

4. Ancient Tribe Near Rome

5. Ancient Roman

6. Modern English

C is the third letter of the alphabet. Although the letter **C**, as we pronounce it today, was not used before Roman times, the history of the letter goes back to the earliest alphabets. The oldest form of **C** was the third letter in the alphabet used by several ancient tribes (**1**) in the Middle East. In the early Hebrew alphabet (**2**) this letter was called *gimel* and was used to stand for the hard *g* sound, such as the *g* in *game*. The ancient Greeks (**3**) borrowed this letter about 3000 years ago. This letter was then borrowed by an ancient tribe (**4**) that settled north of Rome about 2800 years ago. These people made no distinction between the hard *g* sound and the *k* sound, such as the *k* in *king*. Because of this, they began to use this early form of **C** to stand for both sounds. When the Romans (**5**) borrowed the letter, they also used it to stand for both the hard *g* and *k* sounds. The *k* sound was used more often than the hard *g* sound in the language of the Romans. So the Roman letter **C** was used more and more to stand for the *k* sound and was used less and less to stand for the hard *g* sound. About 2200 years ago, the Romans began using **C** to stand for only the *k* sound and made up a new letter, **G**, to stand for the hard *g* sound. Since that time, the capital letter **C** has been written almost exactly as we write it today (**6**).

c, C   The third letter of the alphabet.
  c, C (sē) *noun, plural* c's, C's.

cab   **1.** An automobile that can be hired; taxicab. We took a *cab* to the airport. **2.** A carriage that can be hired. It has a driver and is pulled by one horse. **3.** The covered part of a truck, steam shovel, or other machine. The driver or the operator of the machine sits in the cab.
  cab (kab) *noun, plural* **cabs.**

cabbage   A plant that has thick green or reddish-purple leaves that form a round head. The leaves of the cabbage are eaten as a vegetable.
  cab·bage (kab′ij) *noun, plural* **cabbages.**

cabin   **1.** A small, simple house. Cabins are often built of rough boards or logs. Our family rented a *cabin* on the lake for the summer. **2.** A private room on a ship. They were seasick and spent most of the trip across the ocean in their *cabin*. **3.** A place in an aircraft for passengers, crew members, or cargo.
  cab·in (kab′in) *noun, plural* **cabins.**

cabinet   **1.** A piece of furniture that has shelves or drawers. Most cabinets have doors. The dishes and glasses are kept in the kitchen *cabinet*. She put the letter in the top drawer of the filing *cabinet*. **2.** A group of people who are chosen by the head of a nation to advise him. A cabinet is made up of the heads of the different departments of the government.
  cab·i·net (kab′ə nit) *noun, plural* **cabinets.**

cable   **1.** A strong, thick rope. Most cables are made up of wires that are twisted to-

Cabin

93

gether. The ship was held to the dock by huge *cables.* **2.** A bundle of wires that has a covering around it for protection. It is used to carry an electric current. Telegraph or telephone cables are often laid under the ocean or the ground. **3.** A message that is sent under the ocean by cable. *Noun.*
—To send a message under the ocean by cable. *Verb.*
ca·ble (kā′bəl) *noun, plural* **cables;** *verb,* **cabled, cabling.**

cable car A car drawn by an overhead cable. It is used to carry people or things up and down a steep hill.

caboose A railroad car that is at the end of a freight train. The trainmen or workmen live, rest, or work in the caboose.
ca·boose (kə-boos′) *noun, plural* **cabooses.**

cacao An evergreen tree found in warm tropical climates. The seeds of this tree are used in making cocoa and chocolate.
ca·ca·o (kə ka′ō *or* kə kā′ō) *noun, plural* **cacaos.**

Cable Car

cactus A plant that has a thick stem covered with spines instead of leaves. Cactuses are found in desert areas of North and South America. Many cactuses have beautiful flowers and fruit that can be eaten.
cac·tus (kak′təs) *noun, plural* **cactuses** or **cacti.**

Cactuses

cadet A young man who is a student in a military academy. Cadets train to be officers in the army, air force, navy, or coast guard.
ca·det (kə det′) *noun, plural* **cadets.**

▲ The first meaning of **cadet** was "younger son or brother." In the past, the oldest son in a family always inherited his father's land. So a younger son often joined the army as his career. After a while, the word for younger son came to mean "a young man who joins the army to become an officer."

café A small restaurant. They sat at the outdoor *café* to have something to drink.
ca·fé (ka fā′) *noun, plural* **cafés.**

cafeteria A restaurant where a customer buys food at a counter and carries it to his table himself.
caf·e·te·ri·a (kaf′ə tēr′ē ə) *noun, plural* **cafeterias.**

caffeine A bitter white substance found in coffee and tea. Caffeine stimulates the body and helps to keep a person from feeling tired and sleepy. This word is also spelled **caffein.**
caf·feine (ka fēn′) *noun.*

cage **1.** An open structure that is closed in with wooden or metal bars or with wire mesh. The lion at the circus was put into a *cage* after the show. **2.** Something that has the same shape or use as a cage. The cashier at the amusement park sat in a *cage. Noun.*
—To put or keep in a cage. The scientist will *cage* the mice during the experiment. *Verb.*
cage (kāj) *noun, plural* **cages;** *verb,* **caged, caging.**

cake **1.** A baked mixture of flour, eggs, sugar, and flavoring. Many cakes are covered with icing. **2.** A flat, thin mass of food that is baked or fried. A pancake is a kind of cake. **3.** A flattened or shaped mass of anything. Please give me a *cake* of soap. *Noun.*
—To make into or become a hard, solid mass. The mud on his boots *caked* as it dried. *Verb.*
cake (kāk) *noun, plural* **cakes;** *verb,* **caked, caking.**

calculate **1.** To find out by using addition, subtraction, multiplication, or division. Karen will *calculate* how much each person owes for the flowers we bought. **2.** To figure out beforehand; estimate. The campers *calculated* that they had packed enough food for five days. **3.** To plan; intend. The politician's speech was *calculated* to make people vote for him.
cal·cu·late (kal′kyə lāt′) *verb,* **calculated, calculating.**

calculation The act of calculating. By the *calculation* of scientists, the sun is about 93,000,000 miles away from the earth.
   cal·cu·la·tion (kal′kyə lā′shən) *noun, plural* **calculations.**

calculator A machine that can solve mathematical problems.
   cal·cu·la·tor (kal′kyə lā′tər) *noun, plural* **calculators.**

calendar **1.** A chart showing the days, weeks, and months of a year. The *calendar* shows that my birthday falls on a Wednesday this year. **2.** A schedule of events that will take place. In a court of law, cases to be tried are listed on a *calendar.*
   cal·en·dar (kal′ən dər) *noun, plural* **calendars.**

calf¹ **1.** A young cow or bull. **2.** A young seal, elephant, or whale. **3.** Leather that is made from the skin or hide of a calf.
   calf (kaf) *noun, plural* **calves.**

calf² The fleshy part of the back of the leg, between the knee and the ankle.
   calf (kaf) *noun, plural* **calves.**

calico A cotton material that has small, brightly colored designs printed on it. I have a bedspread made of *calico. Noun.*
   —**1.** Made of calico. Jane wore a *calico* dress. **2.** Having spots; spotted. Sara has a *calico* cat. *Adjective.*
   cal·i·co (kal′ə kō′) *noun, plural* **calicoes** or **calicos;** *adjective.*

Calico Cat

California A state in the western United States, on the Pacific Ocean. Its capital is Sacramento.
   Cal·i·for·nia (kal′ə forn′yə *or* kal′ə fôr′nē ə) *noun.*

▲ **California** was the name of a make-believe island in a very old Spanish story. When Spanish explorers landed on the southern end of California, they thought they were on an island. So they named it after the island in the story. Other Spanish explorers went farther north and took this name with them. The name was finally used for all the land that became the state of California.

call **1.** To speak or say in a loud voice. Please raise your hand when I *call* your name. **2.** To ask or order to come. The cat will come if you *call.* We will have to *call* a cab if the rain doesn't stop soon. **3.** To give a name to; name. She wants to *call* her new puppy "Daisy." **4.** To telephone. They will *call* us from the airport when they arrive. **5.** To make a short visit or stop. We will *call* at your house about one o'clock tomorrow afternoon. *Verb.*
   —**1.** A loud shout; cry. We heard Mother's *call* for someone to help her with the packages. **2.** A particular sound or cry made by a bird or animal. Jack can recognize many different bird *calls.* **3.** The act of getting in touch with someone by telephone. I will expect your *call* at about four o'clock. **4.** A short visit or stop. The family doctor made a *call* to look at my little sister, who was ill. *Noun.*
   call (kôl) *verb,* **called, calling;** *noun, plural* **calls.**

callus A hardened and thickened place on the skin. People get calluses on their hands and feet.
   cal·lus (kal′əs) *noun, plural* **calluses.**

calm **1.** Not moving; still. The sea was *calm* after the storm. **2.** Not excited or nervous; quiet. The people in the building stayed *calm* during the fire and got out safely. *Adjective.*
   —A time during which there is quiet or stillness. There was a *calm* before the storm struck the town. *Noun.*
   —To make or become calm. Mother sang to the baby to *calm* him after he was frightened. The noisy boys *calmed* down when the movie started. *Verb.*
   calm (käm) *adjective,* **calmer, calmest;** *noun, plural* **calms;** *verb,* **calmed, calming.**

calorie **1.** A unit that is used to measure the amount of heat in something. **2.** A unit that is used to measure the amount of energy produced by food. One slice of white bread has about sixty-five calories.
   cal·o·rie (kal′ər ē) *noun, plural* **calories.**

calves More than one calf. Look up **calf** for more information.
   calves (kavz) *noun plural.*

at; āpe; cär; end; mē; it; īce; hot; ōld;
fôrk; wood; fōol; oil; out; up; turn; sing;
thin; this; hw in white; zh in treasure.
ə stands for a in about, e in taken
i in pencil, o in lemon, and u in circus.

came My friend *came* to dinner last night. Look up **come** for more information.

came (kām) *verb.*

Camel

camel A large animal that has a humped back, long legs, and a long neck. Camels are found in deserts of northern Africa and central Asia. They are very strong and can go for days without water. They are used for riding and carrying loads. The camel of northern Africa has one hump, and the camel of central Asia has two humps.

cam·el (kam′əl) *noun, plural* **camels.**

camera A device for taking photographs or motion pictures. Most cameras consist of a box that has an opening at one end to let the light in.

cam·er·a (kam′ər ə *or* kam′rə) *noun, plural* **cameras.**

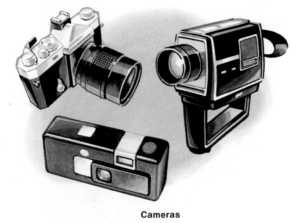

Cameras

camouflage A disguise or false appearance that is used to hide something. The camouflage of soldiers and military equipment with paint or leaves hides them from the enemy. The tan coat of a lion is a natural camouflage because it matches the color of the dry grasses where the lion lives. *Noun.*
—To change the appearance of something in order to hide or trick. The soldiers *camouflaged* the tank by covering it with bushes and branches. *Verb.*

cam·ou·flage (kam′ə fläzh′) *noun, plural* **camouflages;** *verb,* **camouflaged, camouflaging.**

camp An outdoor place with tents or cabins where people live or sleep for a time. The soldiers set up *camp* near the river. Sam will go to a boys' *camp* in the mountains this summer. *Noun.*
—To set up and live in a camp. We *camped* out on our trip through the southern part of the United States. *Verb.*

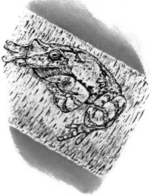

Camouflage

camp (kamp) *noun, plural* **camps;** *verb,* **camped, camping.**

campaign A series of actions that are carried on to bring about a special result. The general's *campaign* was aimed at getting control of the enemy's territory. My father worked on Mr. White's *campaign* for election as mayor. *Noun.*
—To carry on or take part in a campaign. Are you going to *campaign* for Jan for class president? *Verb.*

cam·paign (kam pān′) *noun, plural* **campaigns;** *verb,* **campaigned, campaigning.**

camper **1.** A person who stays at or lives in a camp. **2.** A car or trailer that is built or used for camping. Our family slept in the *camper* during our trip this summer.

camp·er (kam′pər) *noun, plural* **campers.**

campfire An outdoor fire that is used for cooking or keeping warm in a camp.

camp·fire (kamp′fīr′) *noun, plural* **campfires.**

camphor A white substance that has a strong odor. Camphor is used in mothballs, in some medicines, and in making plastics.

cam·phor (kam′fər) *noun.*

campus The grounds and buildings of a school, college, or university.

cam·pus (kam′pəs) *noun, plural* **campuses.**

▲ Although **campus** comes from a Latin word meaning "field," the word is only about two hundred years old. It was first used at an American college, Princeton University.

can¹ She *can* walk faster than you. The car *can* hold five people. He *can* speak French and Spanish. *Can* you fix the broken radio? Mother says we *can* go to the zoo tomorrow afternoon.
can (kan) *verb.*

can² A container made of metal. Most cans have lids or covers. Mother opened up a *can* of soup for lunch. Please put the old rags in the garbage *can.* You have to add one *can* of water to the soup mix. We bought six *cans* of soda. *Noun.*
—To put into or preserve in a can. We are going to *can* peaches this fall. *Verb.*
can (kan) *noun, plural* **cans;** *verb,* **canned, canning.**

Canada The country north of the United States of America. Its capital is Ottawa.
Can·a·da (kan′ə də) *noun.*

Canadian A person who was born or is living in Canada. *Noun.*
—Of Canada. Ice hockey is a *Canadian* sport. *Adjective.*
Can·a·di·an (kə nā′ dē ən) *noun, plural* **Canadians;** *adjective.*

canal A waterway dug across land. A canal is used for boats and ships to travel through, and for carrying water from lakes or rivers to places that need it.
ca·nal (kə nal′) *noun, plural* **canals.**

canary **1.** A small yellow songbird. Canaries are often kept as pets. **2.** A light, bright yellow color. *Noun.*
—Having the color canary; light, bright yellow. *Adjective.*
ca·nar·y (kə ner′ē) *noun, plural* **canaries;** *adjective.*

Canary

cancel **1.** To do away with or stop. Did you *cancel* your dentist appointment? The football game was *canceled* because of snow. **2.** To cross out or mark with a line or lines to show that it cannot be used again. The post office will *cancel* the stamp on the letter.
can·cel (kan′səl) *verb,* **canceled, canceling.**

cancer A disease in which a cell or group of cells begin to divide and grow more rapidly than is normal. Cancer destroys healthy tissues and organs and can cause death.
can·cer (kan′sər) *noun.*

candidate A person who seeks or is put forward by others for an office or honor. The senator is going to be the Democratic *candidate* for President.
can·di·date (kan′də dāt′) *noun, plural* **candidates.**

candle A stick of wax or tallow formed around a wick, or string that will burn. A candle is burned to give light.
can·dle (kand′əl) *noun, plural* **candles.**

candlestick A holder for a candle.
can·dle·stick (kand′əl stik′) *noun, plural* **candlesticks.**

candy A sweet food made of sugar or syrup with flavorings, nuts, or fruit. I love chocolate *candy.* Ray ate a lemon *candy. Noun.*
—To cover or cook with sugar. Mother is going to *candy* the fruit. *Verb.*
can·dy (kan′dē) *noun, plural* **candies;** *verb,* **candied, candying.**

cane **1.** A stick used to help someone walk. Most canes are made of wood. Jenny used a *cane* after she sprained her ankle. **2.** The long, woody, jointed stem of the bamboo, reed, and other tall grass plants. Cane is used in making furniture. **3.** A plant that has a long, woody, jointed stem. Bamboo is a cane.
cane (kān) *noun, plural* **canes.**

cannibal A person who eats human flesh.
can·ni·bal (kan′ə bəl) *noun, plural* **cannibals.**

cannon A large, heavy gun that is mounted on wheels or some other base.
can·non (kan′ən) *noun, plural* **cannons** or **cannon.**

Cannon

at; āpe; cär; end; mē; it; īce; hot; ōld; fôrk; wood; fo͞ol; oil; out; up; turn; sing; thin; this; hw in white; zh in treasure.
ə stands for a in about, e in taken i in pencil, o in lemon, and u in circus.

cannot Can not. I *cannot* come tomorrow.
can·not (kan′ot *or* ka not′) *verb.*

canoe A light, narrow boat that is moved by hand with a paddle. Most canoes are pointed at both ends. *Noun.*
—To paddle or go in a canoe. We will *canoe* around the lake after lunch. *Verb.*
ca·noe (kə nōō′) *noun, plural* **canoes;** *verb,* **canoed, canoeing.**

canopy A covering that is made of cloth or other material. A canopy is hung over a bed, throne, or entrance to a building.
can·o·py (kan′ə pē) *noun, plural* **canopies.**

can't I *can't* go with you; I have to study.
can't (kant) contraction for **cannot.**

cantaloupe A kind of melon that has a rough, pale green or yellow skin and sweet, yellowish-orange flesh.
can·ta·loupe (kan′tə lōp′) *noun, plural* **cantaloupes.**

canteen **1.** A small metal container for carrying water or other liquids to drink. **2.** A store in a school or factory that sells food, drinks, and other things.
can·teen (kan-tēn′) *noun, plural* **canteens.**

Canteen

canvas A strong, heavy cloth made of cotton, flax, or hemp. It is used to make things that must be strong and last for a long time. Tents, sails, certain pieces of clothing, and boat and truck covers are made of canvas. Oil paintings are painted on pieces of canvas.
can·vas (kan′vəs) *noun, plural* **canvases.**

canyon A deep valley with very high, steep sides. A canyon often has a stream running through it.
can·yon (kan′yən) *noun, plural* **canyons.**

cap **1.** A close-fitting covering for the head. Most caps have a short brim or no brim. Nurses and policemen wear caps. **2.** Something that is used or shaped like a cap. John took the *cap* off the bottle of soda. I lost the *cap* to my fountain pen. **3.** A paper wrapping or covering that contains a small amount of explosive. Caps are used in toy guns. *Noun.*
—To put a cap on; cover with a cap. Please *cap* the bottle when you're finished. *Verb.*
cap (kap) *noun, plural* **caps;** *verb,* **capped, capping.**

capable Having or showing ability; able. Joan is a very *capable* driver. Our team is *capable* of winning the championship.
ca·pa·ble (kā′pə bəl) *adjective.*

capacity The amount that can be held in a space. The car's gas tank has a *capacity* of twenty gallons.
ca·pac·i·ty (kə pas′ə tē) *noun, plural* **capacities.**

cape¹ A piece of clothing without sleeves. A cape is worn loosely over the shoulders. The nurse wore a *cape* over her uniform.
cape (kāp) *noun, plural* **capes.**

cape² A pointed piece of land that sticks out from the coastline into the sea or a lake.
cape (kāp) *noun, plural* **capes.**

capital¹ **1.** A city or town where the government of a country or state is located. Austin is the *capital* of Texas. Washington, D.C. is the *capital* of the United States. **2.** A large form of a letter of the alphabet. A, B, C, and D are *capitals.* **3.** The total amount of money or property that is owned by a company or person. My father has enough *capital* to start his own business. *Noun.*
—**1.** Being the most important; main; chief. Madrid is Spain's *capital* city. **2.** Having to do with the death penalty. Many countries have done away with *capital* punishment. *Adjective.* ▲ Another word that sounds like this is **Capitol.**
cap·i·tal (kap′it əl) *noun, plural* **capitals;** *adjective.*

Canyon

capital² The top part of a column or pillar. The columns of the building had carved *capitals.* ▲ Another word that sounds like this is **Capitol.**
cap·i·tal (kap′it əl) *noun, plural* **capitals.**

capitalism An economic system in which land, factories, and other means of producing goods are owned and controlled by individual people instead of by the government. The economic system of the United States is based on capitalism.
cap·i·tal·ism (kap′it əl·iz′əm) *noun.*

capitalize To write or print with a capital letter or letters, or begin with a capital letter. You should always *capitalize* proper names.
cap·i·tal·ize (kap′it əl īz′) *verb,* **capitalized, capitalizing.**

Capitol 1. The building in which the U.S. Congress meets in Washington, D.C. 2. The building in which a state legislature meets. ▲ Another word that sounds like this is **capital.**
Cap·i·tol (kap′it əl) *noun.*

capsize To turn upside down. The strong wind *capsized* the small sailboat. The sailors held on to the sides of the boat after it *capsized.*
cap·size (kap′sīz *or* kap sīz′) *verb,* **capsized, capsizing.**

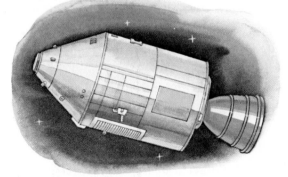
Space Capsule

capsule 1. A small case that holds a dose of medicine and can be swallowed whole. When you swallow a capsule, the case dissolves in your stomach and the medicine is used by

Capital

your body. 2. The part of a spacecraft that carries the astronauts. The capsule is the part that separates from the rocket after the spacecraft is launched.
cap·sule (kap′səl) *noun, plural* **capsules.**

captain 1. A person who is the leader of a group of people. Susan was *captain* of the girl's volleyball team. 2. A person who is in charge of a ship. My uncle is the *captain* of a fishing boat. 3. An officer in the army or navy. In the army, a captain is next below a major. In the navy, a captain is next below an admiral. *Noun.*
—To be the captain of; lead. John will *captain* the basketball team next year. *Verb.*
cap·tain (kap′tən) *noun, plural* **captains;** *verb,* **captained, captaining.**

caption The word or words under a picture that tell who or what it is. I wasn't sure who the man in the newspaper photograph was until I read the *caption* under it.
cap·tion (kap′shən) *noun, plural* **captions.**

captive A prisoner. The soldiers kept the *captives* in a jail inside the fort. *Noun.*
—Held prisoner. The *captive* lion was kept in a cage. *Adjective.*
cap·tive (kap′tiv) *noun, plural* **captives;** *adjective.*

capture To catch and hold a person, animal, or thing. The hunters *captured* a lion in the jungle. The exciting book *captured* Linda's interest, and she didn't hear her mother call her. *Verb.*
—The act of capturing a person, animal, or thing. The *capture* of the bank robber took place the day after the robbery. *Noun.*
cap·ture (kap′chər) *verb,* **captured, capturing;** *noun, plural* **captures.**

car 1. An automobile. A car is a vehicle with four wheels and an engine. 2. Any kind of vehicle that moves on wheels and is used to carry people or things from one place to another. A railroad train is made up of different cars that are joined together.
car (kär) *noun, plural* **cars.**

caramel 1. Sugar that is browned and melted by being heated slowly. Caramel is used in cooking to color and flavor gravy, cookies, and other foods. 2. A light-brown, soft candy flavored with caramel.

at; āpe; cär; end; mē; it; īce; hot; ōld;
fôrk; wood; fōol; oil; out; up; turn; sing;
thin; this; hw in white; zh in treasure.
ə stands for a in about, e in taken
i in pencil, o in lemon, and u in circus.

car·a·mel (kar′ə məl *or* kär′məl) *noun, plural* **caramels.**

carat A unit of weight for diamonds and other precious stones. A carat is the same weight as $1/5$ of a gram. ▲ Another word that sounds like this is **carrot.**
car·at (kar′ət) *noun, plural* **carats.**

caravan A group of people who travel together. A *caravan* of army trucks and soldiers moved slowly along the highway. The Arab merchants and their camels traveled in a *caravan* across the desert.
car·a·van (kar′ə van′) *noun, plural* **caravans.**

carbohydrate A compound made up of carbon, hydrogen, and oxygen. Carbohydrates are made by green plants. Starches and sugars are carbohydrates.
car·bo·hy·drate (kär′bō hī′drāt) *noun, plural* **carbohydrates.**

carbon A chemical element that is found in coal and charcoal. Diamonds and graphite are carbon in the form of crystals.
car·bon (kär′bən) *noun.*

carbon dioxide A gas that is made up of carbon and oxygen. Carbon dioxide has no color or odor. It is part of the air we breathe. When we breathe out, we put carbon dioxide in the air. Plants take in carbon dioxide from the air to make food. Carbon dioxide is used in soft drinks, fire extinguishers, and refrigerators.
carbon di·ox·ide (dī ok′sīd).

carbon monoxide A poisonous gas that has no color or odor. Carbon monoxide is formed when carbon burns but does not burn up completely. Carbon monoxide is found in the gases that come out of the exhaust pipes of automobiles.
carbon mon·ox·ide (mə nok′sīd).

carburetor The part of an engine in which gasoline is mixed with air to make a mixture that is explosive.
car·bu·re·tor (kär′bə rā′tər) *noun, plural* **carburetors.**

carcass The body of a dead animal.
car·cass (kär′kəs) *noun, plural* **carcasses.**

card A flat piece of stiff paper that has words or numbers or some kind of design on it. People have membership cards for libraries and for clubs they belong to. Schools give report cards and stores sell post cards. We play many games with decks of playing cards.
card (kärd) *noun, plural* **cards.**

cardboard A heavy, stiff paper. Cardboard is used to make boxes and posters.
card·board (kärd′bôrd′) *noun.*

cardinal 1. One of the group of important officials who rank just below the Pope in the Roman Catholic Church. They help the Pope govern the church and when he dies, they meet and elect the new Pope. Cardinals wear bright red robes and hats. 2. A songbird that has a crest of feathers on its head. The male cardinal has bright red feathers with a black patch around its bill. 3. A bright, deep red color. *Noun.*
—1. Of the greatest importance; chief. One of the *cardinal* issues in the town election was the vote on the new park and playground. 2. Having the color cardinal; bright, deep red. *Adjective.*
car·di·nal (kärd′ən əl) *noun, plural* **cardinals;** *adjective.*

Cardinal

cardinal number A number that tells how many. One, two, three, four, and so on are cardinal numbers.

care 1. A feeling of worry or unhappiness. The girls didn't have a *care* in the world as they ran down the beach splashing in the waves. 2. Close and serious attention. Don dried his mother's good dishes with great *care*. Take *care* when you cross the street. 3. Keeping or custody; protection. When he was on vacation, Brad left his cats in the *care* of his best friend. The sick child was under a doctor's *care*. *Noun.*
—1. To have an interest, liking, or concern about a person or thing. He doesn't *care* what people think of the way he dresses. 2. To have a feeling against; mind. Do you *care* if I borrow your bicycle? 3. To want or wish. Would you *care* to go to the movies with me? *Verb.*
care (ker) *noun, plural* **cares;** *verb,* **cared, caring.**

career The work that a person chooses to do through life. Eva chose a *career* as a nurse. Newspaper reporters meet many interesting people in their *career*.
ca·reer (kə rēr′) *noun, plural* **careers.**

carefree Happy and gay with nothing to worry about. Margaret and her friends felt absolutely *carefree* as they started off on their picnic.
care·free (ker′frē′) *adjective.*

careful Paying close attention; watchful. When a person is careful, he is alert and thinks about what he is doing or saying. If you're *careful* when you cross a street, you look both ways to be sure no cars are moving toward you.
care·ful (ker′fəl) *adjective.*

careless Not paying close enough attention to what one is doing or saying. Jean was *careless* when she ran down the stairs, and she tripped and fell. He did not get a good grade on his book report because he made many *careless* spelling mistakes.
care·less (ker′lis) *adjective.*

caress To touch or stroke gently and with love; pet. *Verb.*
—A gentle, loving touch or stroke. The *caress* of the boy's hand made the kitten purr. *Noun.*
ca·ress (kə res′) *verb,* **caressed, caressing;** *noun, plural* **caresses.**

cargo The goods carried by a ship, airplane, truck, or other vehicle. The ship unloaded a *cargo* of rice.
car·go (kär′gō) *noun, plural* **cargoes** or **cargos.**

caribou A large kind of deer that lives in northern regions. In Europe and Asia caribous are called reindeer. The female caribou is the only female deer that has antlers.
car·i·bou (kar′ə bōō′) *noun, plural* **caribous** or **caribou.**

carnation A red, pink, or white flower that has a spicy, fragrant smell. The carnation grows on a plant that has thin, pointed leaves.
car·na·tion (kär nā′shən) *noun, plural* **carnations.**

carnival A fair or festival that has games, rides, and other amusements.
car·ni·val (kär′nə vəl) *noun, plural* **carnivals.**

Carnations

carnivorous Eating the flesh of animals. Wolves, lions, dogs, and cats are carnivorous animals.
car·niv·o·rous (kär niv′ər əs) *adjective.*

carol A joyful song. We all sang Christmas *carols* around the tree. *Noun.*
—To sing joyously. The children went from house to house *caroling. Verb.*
car·ol (kar′əl) *noun, plural* **carols;** *verb,* **caroled, caroling.**

carp A fish that lives in fresh water and is used as food.
carp (kärp) *noun, plural* **carps** or **carp.**

carpenter A person who builds and repairs houses and other things made of wood.
car·pen·ter (kär′pən tər) *noun, plural* **carpenters.**

carpet 1. A covering for a floor, usually made of heavy woven fabric. Her mother bought a new *carpet* for their living room. 2. Anything like a carpet. The lawn was covered with a *carpet* of snow. *Noun.*
—To cover with a carpet. We are going to *carpet* the stairs in our house. *Verb.*
car·pet (kär′pit) *noun, plural* **carpets;** *verb,* **carpeted, carpeting.**

Baby Carriage

carriage 1. A vehicle that moves on wheels. Some carriages are used by people to travel from place to place and are pulled by horses. Baby carriages are small and light and are pushed by people. 2. A movable part of a machine that carries or holds up some other part. A carriage on a typewriter is the part that holds the paper and moves back and forth. Large, heavy guns have carriages that are frames with wheels and are used to move the guns from place to place.
car·riage (kar′ij) *noun, plural* **carriages.**

carrier A person or thing that carries something. Railroads are carriers.
car·ri·er (kar′ē ər) *noun, plural* **carriers.**

at; āpe; cär; end; mē; it; īce; hot; ōld; fôrk; wood; fōōl; oil; out; up; turn; sing; thin; this; hw in white; zh in treasure. ə stands for a in about, e in taken i in pencil, o in lemon, and u in circus.

carrot The long, orange-colored root of a plant. Carrots are eaten as a vegetable. ▲ Another word that sounds like this is **carat**.
car·rot (kar′ət) *noun, plural* **carrots.**

Carrot

carry **1.** To hold something while moving it. Evelyn said she would *carry* my suitcase when it got too heavy for me. The pipes in our house *carry* water. **2.** To have something. If you *carry* a pen, you have it in your pocket or pocketbook. If a store *carries* rubber boots, it has them there for you to buy. **3.** To keep doing something; continue. Sometimes her brother *carries* his teasing too far and makes her angry. **4.** To move a number from one column or place and add it where it belongs. When Mary added 23 and 39, she got 52 instead of 62 because she forgot to *carry* the 1 from the first column.
car·ry (kar′ē) *verb,* **carried, carrying.**

cart **1.** A strong wagon with two wheels that is used to carry a load. Carts are pulled by horses, mules, or oxen. **2.** A light vehicle with four wheels that is pushed by a person. We use carts in supermarkets to hold the groceries we take from the shelves. *Noun.*
—To move something in a cart. In many countries, farmers *cart* the vegetables they grow to the nearest town to sell them. *Verb.*
cart (kärt) *noun, plural* **carts;** *verb,* **carted, carting.**

Cart

cartilage A strong, flexible material that forms parts of the body of man and other animals that have a backbone. Cartilage is not as stiff or as hard as bone. Cartilage is the material that forms much of a person's nose.
car·ti·lage (kärt′əl ij) *noun.*

carton A box or container that is usually made of cardboard and comes in many shapes. Egg cartons are made to hold each egg separately. Milk sometimes comes in cartons. Our new television set was delivered in a strong *carton.* Chris drank a *carton* of orange juice.
car·ton (kärt′ən) *noun, plural* **cartons.**

cartoon A drawing that shows people or things in a way that makes you laugh. Some cartoons are put on movie film and seem to move. Comic strips are cartoons that appear in magazines and newspapers.
car·toon (kär tōōn′) *noun, plural* **cartoons.**

cartridge **1.** A small case that holds gunpowder and a bullet. Cartridges are made to be shot from a gun. **2.** Any small case that holds something. Some pens are loaded with cartridges full of ink. Some cameras have special cartridges that hold the film. The needle of a record player is held in a cartridge.
car·tridge (kär′trij) *noun, plural* **cartridges.**

Cartwheel

cartwheel **1.** The wheel of a cart. **2.** A kind of jump from one's feet to one's hands and back again. If a person keeps his arms and legs straight when doing a cartwheel, they look like the spokes of a wheel as it turns. Acrobats often do cartwheels.
cart·wheel (kärt′hwēl′) *noun, plural* **cartwheels.**

carve **1.** To cut meat into slices or pieces. Father will *carve* the turkey. **2.** To make something beautiful by cutting. Artists *carve* statues out of wood and stone. Some furniture is *carved* with designs of flowers and animals.

carve (kärv) *verb,* **carved, carving.**

cascade A small waterfall. *Noun.*
—To flow down in waves like a small waterfall. The water from the flooded stream will *cascade* over the hill. *Verb.*

cas·cade (kas kād′) *noun, plural* **cascades;** *verb,* **cascaded, cascading.**

Cascade

case¹ **1.** An example of something. The forest fire was an obvious *case* of carelessness. **2.** The real facts; state of affairs. He says he has forgotten his keys, and if that is the *case,* we are all locked out. **3.** A person who is sick or hurt; patient. The doctor said that Kate was the third *case* of flu he had treated that day. **4.** A matter to be investigated or decided by law. The police had no suspects in the *case* of the museum robbery. The judge will make his decision on the kidnap *case* tomorrow.

case (kās) *noun, plural* **cases.**
in any case. No matter what happens. *In any case,* you are never to run out into the street without looking first to see if any cars are coming.
in case. In the event that; if. *In case* anything happens, call me right away. Bring your bathing suit *in case* we go swimming.
in case of. If there is. *In case of* rain, we will go to the movies rather than playing a game of tennis.

case² A box or other container made to hold or cover something. Her new camera came in a leather *case.* We ordered a *case* of soft drinks for the picnic.

case (kās) *noun, plural* **cases.**

cash Money in the form of coins and paper bills. Instead of charging the dress, she paid *cash* for it. *Noun.*
—To get or give cash for. My father has to stop at the bank and *cash* a check before we can buy groceries. *Verb.*

cash (kash) *noun; verb,* **cashed, cashing.**
to cash in on. To take advantage of. The astronaut *cashed in on* his fame by running for election.

cashew A sweet nut that is shaped like a lima bean. It grows on an evergreen tree that is found in tropical countries.

cash·ew (kash′o͞o) *noun, plural* **cashews.**

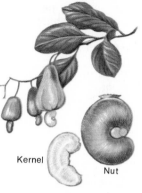

Kernel   Nut

Cashew

cashier A person whose job it is to take care of money. In a store or restaurant the cashier takes money from people who are paying for something.

cash·ier (ka shēr′) *noun, plural* **cashiers.**

cashmere A very soft woolen fabric. Cashmere is woven from the silky hair of goats that live in Asia.

cash·mere (kazh′mēr *or* kash′mēr) *noun, plural* **cashmeres.**

cask A large wooden barrel that is used to hold wine or other liquids.

cask (kask) *noun, plural* **casks.**

casket A box made of wood or metal, in which the body of a dead person is put to be buried; coffin.

cas·ket (kas′kit) *noun, plural* **caskets.**

casserole A deep dish in which food can be cooked and served. Mother took the lid off the *casserole* so the macaroni could get brown on top.

cas·se·role (kas′ə rōl′) *noun, plural* **casseroles.**

cast **1.** To throw through the air. We *cast* our fishing line into the stream, hoping to catch a fish. **2.** To cause to fall; throw off. The tree *cast* a long shadow on the ground. **3.** To send or put. She *cast* her vote for her best friend in the election for class president. **4.** To pick the actor or actors who will take different roles in a play. They *cast* Steve as the wicked prince in the class play. **5.** To shape by pouring a soft material into a mold to harden. The artist *cast* a statue of a horse by pouring melted bronze into a plaster mold. *Verb.*

at; āpe; cär; end; mē; it; īce; hot; ōld;
fôrk; wood; fo͞ol; oil; out; up; turn; sing;
thin; **this**; hw in white; zh in treasure.
ə stands for **a** in about, **e** in taken
i in pencil, **o** in lemon, and **u** in circus.

—**1.** The act of throwing something. Betty made a long *cast* with her fishing line. **2.** Something that is given shape in a mold. He made a plaster *cast* of a deer. **3.** The actors in a play or other show. The whole *cast* came on stage to take a bow together. **4.** A stiff form that is shaped around a part of the body to help a broken bone heal. The doctor put a plaster *cast* on Bill's broken arm. *Noun.*

  cast (kast) *verb,* **cast, casting;** *noun, plural* **casts.**

castanet One of a pair of small, wooden pieces that look like the two shells of a clam. They are clicked together in a person's hand in time to the rhythm of a dance.

  cas·ta·net (kas′tə net′) *noun, plural* **castanets.**

cast iron A hard, brittle kind of iron that is made by melting iron and pouring it into a mold.

castle **1.** A large building or group of buildings having high, thick walls with towers. Many castles had moats around them for defense against attack. Princes and nobles lived in castles in the Middle Ages. **2.** One of the pieces in a chess game; rook.

  cas·tle (kas′əl) *noun, plural* **castles.**

casual Done or happening without serious thought or planning. Our neighbors sometimes make a *casual* visit to our house without calling up beforehand.

  cas·u·al (kazh′ōō əl) *adjective.*

casualty A person who is injured or killed in an accident or a war. Soldiers who are captured by the enemy are also called casualties. The firemen reported 25 *casualties* in the fire.

  cas·u·al·ty (kazh′ōō əl te) *noun, plural* **casualties.**

cat **1.** A small furry animal that has short ears and a long tail. Cats are kept as pets and for catching mice and rats. **2.** Any animal of a group that includes lions, tigers, leopards, and also the kind of cats that are kept as pets in the home.

  cat (kat) *noun, plural* **cats.**

catalog A list. Libraries have catalogs of the titles, authors, and subject matter of all their books. Stores publish catalogs with pictures and prices of the things they have for sale. *Noun.*

—To make a list of; put in a list. I *cataloged* the stamps in my collection. *Verb.* This word is also spelled **catalogue.**

  cat·a·log (kat′əl ôg′ *or* kat′əl og′) *noun, plural* **catalogs;** *verb,* **cataloged, cataloging.**

cataract **1.** A large, steep waterfall. **2.** A strong flood or downpour of water. When the dam broke, *cataracts* of water rushed through the streets of the town.

  cat·a·ract (kat′ə rakt′) *noun, plural* **cataracts.**

catastrophe A great and sudden disaster. The plane crash was the worst *catastrophe* of the year.

  ca·tas·tro·phe (kə tas′trə fē′) *noun, plural* **catastrophes.**

catbird A dark gray songbird. Its call sounds like a cat meowing.

  cat·bird (kat′burd′) *noun, plural* **catbirds.**

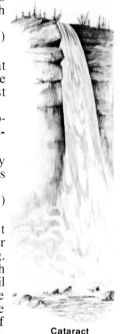

Cataract

catch **1.** To take or get hold of something or someone that is moving. Tom can *catch* a ball with one hand. We used a pail to *catch* water from the leaking roof. The police hoped to *catch* the thief before he got on the airplane. **2.** To be in time for. We will have to hurry to *catch* the school bus. **3.** To see or hear. He was able to *catch* sight of the rabbit before it hopped into the bushes. **4.** To become hooked or fastened. Bob's sweater *caught* on a branch. **5.** To come upon suddenly; surprise. My mother *caught* me eating before dinner. **6.** To get; receive. Dress warmly or you will *catch* cold. The logs *caught* fire. *Verb.*

—**1.** The act of catching something or someone. The first baseman made a great *catch*. **2.** Something that holds or fastens. The *catch* on the door was broken. **3.** Something that is taken hold of and held. Tommy's *catch* for the day was three fish. **4.** A game in which a ball is thrown back and forth between the players. **5.** A hidden reason or condition; trick. This arithmetic problem seems so easy that there must be a *catch* to it. *Noun.*

  catch (kach) *verb,* **caught, catching;** *noun, plural* **catches.**

catcher A person or thing that catches. In a baseball game the catcher is the player who stands behind home plate to catch balls that are thrown by the pitcher.

  catch·er (kach′ər) *noun, plural* **catchers.**

category A group or class of things. The books on that shelf are divided into two *categories*, history and geography.

cat·e·go·ry (kat′ə gôr′ē) *noun, plural* **categories.**

cater To provide food, supplies, and other services. A restaurant *catered* the wedding dinner.
ca·ter (kā′tər) *verb,* **catered, catering.**

caterpillar The furry, wormlike larva of a butterfly or moth. Look up the word **larva** for more information.
cat·er·pil·lar (kat′ər pil′ər) *noun, plural* **caterpillars.**

Caterpillar

▲ The word **caterpillar** probably comes from an old French word for this insect. The French word meant "hairy cat."

catfish A fish that does not have scales. A catfish has long feelers around its mouth that look like whiskers.
cat·fish (kat′fish′) *noun, plural* **catfish** or **catfishes.**

cathedral A large and important church. It is sometimes the official church of a bishop.
ca·the·dral (kə thē′drəl) *noun, plural* **cathedrals.**

Catholic Having to do with the Christian church that is headed by the Pope; Roman Catholic. *Adjective.*
—A person who is a member of the Catholic Church; Roman Catholic. *Noun.*
Cath·o·lic (kath′ə lik) *adjective; noun, plural* **Catholics.**

catsup A spicy red tomato sauce. This word is usually spelled **ketchup.** Look up **ketchup** for more information.
cat·sup (kat′səp *or* kech′əp) *noun, plural* **catsups.**

cattail A tall plant that grows in marshes. Cattails have long, furry brown tips.
cat·tail (kat′tāl′) *noun, plural* **cattails.**

cattle Cows, bulls, and steers that are raised for meat and milk products.
cat·tle (kat′əl) *noun.*

cattleman A man who owns or helps take care of cattle on a ranch.
cat·tle·man (kat′əl mən) *noun, plural* **cattlemen.**

caught I *caught* the butterfly in a net. Look up **catch** for more information.
caught (kôt) *verb.*

cauliflower A plant that has a round, white head with green leaves around it. The head of a cauliflower is eaten as a vegetable.
cau·li·flow·er (kô′li flou′ər *or* kol′ē flou′ər) *noun.*

Cauliflower

cause **1.** A person or thing that makes something happen. The hurricane was the *cause* of great damage to the town. **2.** Something a person or group believes in. Stopping the pollution of our air and water is a *cause* many people work for. *Noun.*
—To make something happen; result in. A heavy rainstorm *caused* us to cancel the picnic. *Verb.*
cause (kôz) *noun, plural* **causes;** *verb,* **caused, causing.**

caution **1.** Close care; watchfulness. Use *caution* when you leave a campfire, and be sure it is completely out. **2.** A warning about something. There was a sign saying "*caution*" on the road where rocks sometimes fell. *Noun.*
—To tell to do something with great care; warn. Mother *cautioned* us not to touch the pot when it was hot. *Verb.*
cau·tion (kô′shən) *noun, plural* **cautions;** *verb,* **cautioned, cautioning.**

cautious Using caution; very careful. Carol was very *cautious* the first time she tried to ski.
cau·tious (kô′shəs) *adjective.*

cavalry A group of soldiers fighting on horseback or from tanks and other armored vehicles.
cav·al·ry (kav′əl rē) *noun, plural* **cavalries.**

cave A natural hollow or hole that is underground or in the side of a mountain. *Noun.*
—To fall in or down. The walls of the old mine are about to *cave* in. *Verb.*
cave (kāv) *noun, plural* **caves;** *verb,* **caved, caving.**

at; āpe; cär; end; mē; it; īce; hot; ōld;
fôrk; wood; fo͞ol; oil; out; up; turn; sing;
thin; this; hw in white; zh in treasure.
ə stands for **a** in about, **e** in taken
i in pencil, **o** in lemon, and **u** in circus.

cave man A human being of the Stone Age who lived in a cave.

cavern A large cave that is underground.
cav·ern (kav′ərn) *noun, plural* **caverns.**

cavity A hollow place; hole. Decay causes *cavities* in the teeth. The explosion left a large *cavity* in the ground.
cav·i·ty (kav′ə tē) *noun, plural* **cavities.**

cease To stop. The rain *ceased* in the afternoon.
cease (sēs) *verb,* **ceased, ceasing.**

cedar An evergreen tree that has rough, dark-gray bark and many branches with needle-shaped leaves. The reddish wood of the cedar is very fragrant and strong and is used for making chests and cabinets and for lining closets.
ce·dar (sē′dər) *noun, plural* **cedars.**

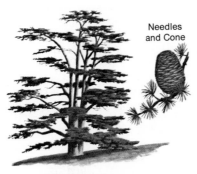

Needles and Cone

Cedar Tree

ceiling 1. The inside covering above a room. 2. The distance from the earth to the bottom of the lowest clouds. The airport canceled flights because there was a low *ceiling.* 3. The highest limit of anything. The government set a *ceiling* on food prices.
ceil·ing (sē′ling) *noun, plural* **ceilings.**

celebrate 1. To observe or honor a special day or event with ceremonies and other activities. We *celebrated* Ed's birthday by giving him a party. 2. To perform with the proper ceremonies. The new priest will *celebrate* Mass today.
cel·e·brate (sel′ə brāt′) *verb,* **celebrated, celebrating.**

celebration 1. The ceremonies and other activities that are carried on to observe or honor a special day or event. All the members of the winning team were at the victory *celebration.* 2. The act of celebrating. We were there for the *celebration* of her graduation from high school.
cel·e·bra·tion (sel′ə brā′shən) *noun, plural* **celebrations.**

celebrity A person who is well-known or often in the news. There were many *celebrities* at the opening of the new movie.
ce·leb·ri·ty (sə leb′rə tē) *noun, plural* **celebrities.**

celery The crisp, green or creamy-white stalks of a plant that is grown throughout the world. Celery is eaten raw or cooked.
cel·er·y (sel′ər ē) *noun.*

cell 1. A small, plain room in a prison, convent, or monastery. The monk lived in a stone *cell* with only a bed, a table, and a chair. 2. The very small, basic unit of living matter. All living things are made of cells. Cells consist of a mass of protoplasm with a nucleus near the center, surrounded by a cell membrane or wall. 3. A small hole or space. Honeycombs contain many cells. 4. A device that changes chemical energy into electrical energy. A battery is made up of one or more cells. ▲ Another word that sounds like this is **sell.**
cell (sel) *noun, plural* **cells.**

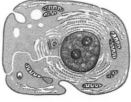

Cell

cellar A room or group of rooms built underground. Most cellars are under buildings and are used as storage places.
cel·lar (sel′ər) *noun, plural* **cellars.**

cello A musical instrument that is like a violin but is larger and lower in tone. A cello is held between the knees when it is played.
cel·lo (chel′ō) *noun, plural* **cellos.**

cellophane A thin, clear material made from cellulose. Cellophane is used as a wrapping to keep food fresh.
cel·lo·phane (sel′ə-fān′) *noun.*

celluloid A strong, clear plastic that burns easily. It is made from alcohol, camphor, and a mixture of cellulose and certain acids. The trademark for this plastic is **Celluloid.** It was the first plastic made in the United States.
cel·lu·loid (sel′yə loid′) *noun.*

Cello

cellulose A solid, white chemical substance

that forms the walls of plant cells. Cellulose makes up the woody part of trees and plants.

cel·lu·lose (sel′yə lōs′) *noun.*

Celsius scale The official name of the centigrade temperature scale. Look up **centigrade** for more information.

Cel·si·us scale (sel′sē əs skāl).

cement **1.** A powdery mixture that is made by burning limestone and clay. Cement is mixed with water to form a paste that becomes hard as rock when it dries. It is used in making sidewalks and streets and in holding bricks and stones together in buildings. **2.** Any soft substance that hardens to make things hold together. *Noun.*
—**1.** To cover with cement. The workmen *cemented* the sidewalk in front of our house. **2.** To fasten with cement. Rick *cemented* the wing to the model airplane. *Verb.*

ce·ment (sə ment′) *noun, plural* **cements;** *verb,* **cemented, cementing.**

cemetery A place for burying the dead.

cem·e·ter·y (sem′ə ter′ē) *noun, plural* **cemeteries.**

census An official count of the people living in a country or district. A census is taken in order to find out how many people there are, and their age, sex, and kind of work.

cen·sus (sen′səs) *noun, plural* **censuses.**

cent A coin of the United States and Canada. One hundred cents make a dollar. ▲ Other words that sound like this are **scent** and **sent.**

cent (sent) *noun, plural* **cents.**

centaur A creature in Greek legend that was part man and part horse.

cen·taur (sen′tôr) *noun, plural* **centaurs.**

center **1.** The middle point of a circle or sphere. It is the same distance from all points of the circumference of the circle or of the surface of the sphere. **2.** The middle point, part, or place of anything. The piece of candy had a chocolate *center.* We put the flowers in the *center* of the table. **3.** A main person, place, or thing. The new baby was the *center* of attention. Chicago is a leading trade *center* of the United States. **4.** A player on a team who has a position in the middle of the

Centaur

playing area. Dick plays *center* on the football team. *Noun.*
—To put in or at the center. We *centered* the picture on the wall. *Verb.*

cen·ter (sen′tər) *noun, plural* **centers;** *verb,* **centered, centering.**

centigrade Divided into one hundred degrees. On the *centigrade* temperature scale water freezes at zero degrees and boils at one and the boiling point of water is at one hundred degrees.

cen·ti·grade (sen′tə grād′) *adjective.*

centimeter A unit of length in the metric system. A centimeter is equal to one-hundredth of a meter, or .39 of an inch.

cen·ti·me·ter (sen′tə mē′tər) *noun, plural* **centimeters.**

centipede A small animal that has a long, flat body and many legs.

cen·ti·pede (sen′tə pēd′) *noun, plural* **centipedes.**

central **1.** In, at, or near the center or middle. The railroad station is in the *central* part of town. **2.** Very important; main; chief. She works in the *central* office of the bank. Who is the *central* character in that book?

cen·tral (sen′trəl) *adjective.*

Centipede

Central America The long, narrow strip of land that connects North and South America.

century A period of one hundred years. From 1650 to 1750 is a century. We are now living in the twentieth *century.*

cen·tu·ry (sen′chər ē) *noun, plural* **centuries.**

ceramics The art of making bowls, dishes, vases, and other things out of baked clay.

ce·ram·ics (sə ram′iks) *noun plural.*

cereal **1.** Any grass that produces grains that are used for food. Wheat, oats, rye, barley, and rice are cereals. **2.** A food that is made from this grain. Oatmeal is a cereal. ▲ Another word that sounds like this is **serial.**

ce·re·al (sēr′ē əl) *noun, plural* **cereals.**

at; āpe; cär; end; mē; it; īce; hot; ōld; fôrk; wood; fōōl; oil; out; up; turn; sing; thin; this; hw in white; zh in treasure. ə stands for a in about, e in taken i in pencil, o in lemon, and u in circus.

▲ The ancient Romans believed in a goddess of grain and farming named *Ceres.* The word **cereal** comes from her name.

ceremony 1. A formal act or set of acts done on a special or important occasion. The bride's mother cried during the wedding *ceremony.* 2. Very polite or formal behavior. The usher showed us to our seats with great *ceremony.*
cer·e·mo·ny (ser′ə mō′nē) *noun, plural* **ceremonies.**

certain 1. Sure; positive. I am *certain* that my answer is correct because I checked it. 2. Agreed upon; settled. I agreed to pay him a *certain* amount for his old bicycle. 3. Some; particular; known but not named. *Certain* animals hunt for food at night. *Certain* people already know who won the contest.
cer·tain (surt′ən) *adjective.*

certainty The state or quality of being sure or certain. There is no *certainty* that he will win the prize.
cer·tain·ty (surt′ən tē) *noun, plural* **certainties.**

certificate A written statement that proves certain facts to be true. Your birth *certificate* tells where and when you were born.
cer·tif·i·cate (sər tif′ə kit) *noun, plural* **certificates.**

chain 1. A row of rings or links that are connected to each other. Most chains are made of metal and are used to fasten, hold, or pull something. Joe fastened his bicycle to the fence with a *chain.* 2. A series of things that are connected or related to each other. The *chain* of mountains runs across the state. That man owns a *chain* of grocery stores. *Noun.*
—To fasten or hold with a chain. He *chained* his dog to the post so it couldn't run away. *Verb.*
chain (chān) *noun, plural* **chains;** *verb,* **chained, chaining.**

Chain

chair A piece of furniture for one person to sit on. A chair has a seat, legs, and a back. Some chairs have arms.
chair (cher) *noun, plural* **chairs.**

chairman A person who is in charge of a meeting or committee. The *chairman* called the meeting to order.

chair·man (cher′mən) *noun, plural* **chairmen.**

chalk 1. A soft, powdery white or gray limestone that is made up mostly of tiny seashells. Chalk is used to make lime and cement and as a fertilizer. 2. A piece of this substance or something like it. Chalk is used for writing and drawing on a blackboard. It is usually shaped like a crayon and is often colored. *Noun.*
—To mark, write, or draw with chalk. John *chalked* a circle on the sidewalk for a game of marbles. *Verb.*
chalk (chôk) *noun, plural* **chalks;** *verb,* **chalked, chalking.**

challenge 1. To ask or call to take part in a contest or fight. Fred *challenged* his friends to a race around the block. 2. To stop someone and order him to say who he is. The guard *challenged* anyone who tried to pass through the gate. *Verb.*
—1. A call to take part in a contest or fight. Our football team has accepted their team's *challenge.* 2. Something that calls for work, effort, and the use of one's talents. He found chemistry to be a real *challenge. Noun.*
chal·lenge (chal′ənj) *verb,* **challenged, challenging;** *noun, plural* **challenges.**

chamber 1. A bedroom. The *chamber* of the princess was in the tower of the castle. 2. A hall where a legislature or other lawmaking body meets. In Philadelphia, you can see the *chamber* where the Continental Congress met. 3. A legislature or other group of lawmakers. The Senate is the upper *chamber* of Congress. 4. An enclosed space in the body of an animal or plant. The heart has four *chambers.* 5. The part of the barrel of a gun into which the shell is put.
cham·ber (chām′bər) *noun, plural* **chambers.**

chameleon A small lizard that can change its color. When a chameleon is on the ground, it is brown. When it is on grass, it is greenish.
cha·me·leon (kə mēl′yən) *noun, plural* **chameleons.**

champion A person or thing that is the winner of first place in a contest or game. He is the state wrestling *champion.* Our school is the *champion* in basketball.
cham·pi·on (cham′pē ən) *noun, plural* **champions.**

championship The position of being a champion. She won the tennis *championship* last year.
cham·pi·on·ship (cham′pē ən ship′) *noun, plural* **championships.**

chance **1.** A good or favorable opportunity. The prisoner saw the *chance* to escape. She has a *chance* to visit Europe this summer. **2.** The likelihood of something happening; possibility. There's a *chance* that it may rain tomorrow. **3.** The happening of things by accident; fate; luck. He met her entirely by *chance.* **4.** A risk. She never takes *chances* when she is swimming alone. *Noun.*
—**1.** To risk. The prisoners decided to *chance* an escape. **2.** To happen accidentally. I *chanced* to meet her in the park. *Verb.*
—Happening accidentally; not expected. He learned about the surprise party through a *chance* remark. *Adjective.*
chance (chans) *noun, plural* **chances;** *verb,* **chanced, chancing;** *adjective.*

chancellor A very high official or head of government. In certain European countries the prime minister is called a chancellor.
chan·cel·lor (chan′sə lər) *noun, plural* **chancellors.**

chandelier A kind of light that hangs from the ceiling. Most chandeliers have several lights arranged on branches.
chan·de·lier (shand′əl ēr′) *noun, plural* **chandeliers.**

change **1.** To make or become different; alter. She *changed* the way she wore her hair. Joe *changed* his mind about going to the movies. The weather *changed* as we drove farther south. **2.** To replace with another or others; exchange. She went home and *changed* her wet clothes. Can you *change* a quarter for five nickels? The mechanic *changed* the oil in the car. Bob *changed* seats with Dick. *Verb.*
—**1.** The act or result of changing. We had a *change* in our plans for a picnic because of the bad weather. **2.** Something that may be put in place of another. He brought along a *change* of clothing on the camping trip. **3.** The money that is given back when the amount paid is more than the amount owed. She gave the clerk a five dollar bill and got forty cents in *change.* **4.** Coins. I have lots of *change* in my pocket. *Noun.*
change (chānj) *verb,* **changed, changing;** *noun, plural* **changes.**

channel **1.** The deepest part of a river, harbor, or other waterway. **2.** A body of water that connects two larger bodies of water. The Strait of Gibraltar is a narrow *channel* between the Atlantic Ocean and the Mediterranean Sea. **3.** A band of frequencies given to a radio or television station for the sending out of electronic signals. This old television set can only pick up one *channel. Noun.*

—To form a channel. The stream *channeled* its way down the mountain. *Verb.*
chan·nel (chan′əl) *noun, plural* **channels;** *verb,* **channeled, channeling.**

chant A singing or shouting of words over and over. Chants usually have a strong rhythm. The crowd broke into a *chant* before the basketball game began. *Noun.*
—To sing or shout a chant. The students *chanted* the school's name as the team came on the field. *Verb.*
chant (chant) *noun, plural* **chants;** *verb,* **chanted, chanting.**

chaos Complete confusion; great disorder. The village was in *chaos* after the earthquake struck.
cha·os (kā′os) *noun.*

chap¹ To split open, crack, or roughen. Her hands *chap* in the cold weather.
chap (chap) *verb,* **chapped, chapping.**

chap² A man or boy; fellow. Tom is a nice *chap.*
chap (chap) *noun, plural* **chaps.**

chapel A room, small building, or other place for worship.
chap·el (chap′əl) *noun, plural* **chapels.**

chaplain A clergyman for a prison, school, military unit, or other group.
chap·lain (chap′lin) *noun, plural* **chaplains.**

chaps Strong leather coverings worn over trousers. Chaps are sometimes worn by cowboys to protect their legs while riding horses.
chaps (chaps *or* shaps) *noun plural.*

chapter **1.** A main part of a book. My history book has fifteen *chapters.* **2.** A smaller division of a club or other organization. Dad's *chapter* of the business club meets once a month.
chap·ter (chap′tər) *noun, plural* **chapters.**

character **1.** All the qualities that make a person or thing what it is

Chaps

or make it different from others. That writer's stories all have a scary *character.* The countryside has a different *character* as you travel west. **2.** What a person really is. You can judge a person's character by the way he feels, thinks, and acts. **3.** Strength of mind, courage, and honesty taken together. That judge is a man of *character.* **4.** A person in a book, play, story, or motion picture. Who is your favorite *character* in that movie? **5.** A person who is different, funny, or strange. The old man was the town *character.* **6.** A mark or sign used in writing or printing to stand for something. The letters of the alphabet are characters.
char·ac·ter (kar′ik tər) *noun, plural* **characters.**

characteristic A quality or feature that makes a person or thing what it is or makes it different from others. Her kindness is her most outstanding *characteristic.* The ability to fly is a *characteristic* of most birds. *Noun.*
—Making a person or thing different from others. The *characteristic* taste of a lemon is sour. *Adjective.*
char·ac·ter·is·tic (kar′ik tə ris′tik) *noun, plural* **characteristics;** *adjective.*

characterize **1.** To make a person or thing different from others; distinguish. The kangaroo is *characterized* by its ability to hop great distances. **2.** To describe the character or qualities of. The author of the book *characterizes* the hero as a very kind man.
char·ac·ter·ize (kar′ik tə rīz′) *verb,* **characterized, characterizing.**

charcoal A soft, black substance that is a form of carbon. It is made by partly burning wood or other plant or animal matter. Charcoal is used as a fuel and as a pencil for drawing.
char·coal (chär′kōl′) *noun.*

charge **1.** To have or ask as a price. The shop *charged* ten dollars to repair the radio. **2.** To ask to pay for something. The neighbor *charged* the boys for the window that they broke. **3.** To put off paying for something until later. Mother *charged* the dress at the store and paid for it at the end of the month. **4.** To blame; accuse. The police *charged* him with robbery. **5.** To rush at; attack. The angry bull *charged* the farmer. The troops *charged* toward the fort. **6.** To fill or load. The soldier *charged* the cannon with shot. The mechanic *charged* the car's battery with electricity. *Verb.*
—**1.** The price asked for something. The *charge* for admission to the movie theater was two dollars. **2.** Care or responsibility.

She had *charge* of her brother while their mother was out. They are in *charge* of getting the food for the party. **3.** Blame; accusation. He was arrested on a *charge* of robbery. **4.** A rushing at; attack. The enemy's *charge* was turned back by the king's soldiers. *Noun.*
charge (chärj) *verb,* **charged, charging;** *noun, plural* **charges.**

chariot A two-wheeled vehicle drawn by horses. Chariots were used in ancient times in warfare, races, and processions.
char·i·ot (char′ē ət) *noun, plural* **chariots.**

Chariot

charity **1.** The giving of money or help to the poor or needy. The sick man had to depend on the *charity* of his friends until he was well enough to work. **2.** A fund or organization for helping the poor or needy. We always give money to a number of *charities* for orphans. **3.** Kindness or forgiveness in judging others. She shows *charity* even to those who are unkind to her.
char·i·ty (char′ə tē) *noun, plural* **charities.**

charm **1.** The power to attract or delight greatly. That fairy tale holds much *charm* for people of all ages. **2.** A small ornament or trinket worn on a bracelet or watch chain. She bought a silver *charm* for her bracelet. **3.** An act, saying, or thing that is supposed to have magic power. He carries a rabbit's foot as a *charm* for good luck. *Noun.*
—To attract or delight greatly. The story *charmed* the children. *Verb.*
charm (chärm) *noun, plural* **charms;** *verb,* **charmed, charming.**

charming Full of charm; attractive or delightful. She is a very *charming* person.
charm·ing (chär′ming) *adjective.*

chart **1.** A sheet of information arranged in lists, diagrams, tables, and graphs. He kept a *chart* of the weather during the year. **2.** A map. Sailors use *charts* that show how deep the water is and where rocks, harbors, and channels are. *Noun.*
—To make a map or chart of. The explorers *charted* the coastline. *Verb.*

chart (chärt) *noun, plural* **charts;** *verb,* **charted, charting.**

charter **1.** A written document giving certain rights and obligations. A charter is given by a government or ruler to a person, group of people, or company. The shipping company operated under a government *charter.* **2.** A leasing or renting of a bus, aircraft, or automobile. Those planes are available for *charter. Noun.*
—**1.** To lease or hire by charter. The school band *chartered* a bus for the trip. **2.** To give a charter to. The state *chartered* a new bank. *Verb.*
> **char·ter** (chär′tər) *noun, plural* **charters;** *verb,* **chartered, chartering.**

chase **1.** To go after and try to catch. The cat *chased* the mouse. The police *chased* the thief down the street. **2.** To cause to go away quickly; drive away. Mother *chased* the birds out of her garden. *Verb.*
—The act of going after and trying to catch. They caught the puppy after a long *chase. Noun.*
> **chase** (chās) *verb,* **chased, chasing;** *noun, plural* **chases.**

chasm A deep crack or opening in the earth's surface. Chasms are sometimes made by earthquakes.
> **chasm** (kaz′əm) *noun, plural* **chasms.**

chassis The main framework that supports the body of an automobile or airplane, or the parts of a radio or television set.
> **chas·sis** (shas′ē *or* chas′ē) *noun, plural* **chassis.**

chat To talk in a light, familiar, or informal way. The two friends *chatted* about the party they had been to. *Verb.*
—A light, familiar, or informal talk. *Noun.*
> **chat** (chat) *verb,* **chatted, chatting;** *noun, plural* **chats.**

chatter **1.** To talk quickly and foolishly. Jack *chattered* on and on about his new bicycle. **2.** To knock or click together quickly. My teeth *chattered* from the cold. *Verb.*
—**1.** Quick, foolish talk. We couldn't be heard above the *chatter* of the others. **2.** Quick, short sounds. We could hear the *chatter* of his teeth. *Noun.*

Chasm

chat·ter (chat′ər) *verb,* **chattered, chattering;** *noun, plural* **chatters.**

chauffeur A person whose work is driving an automobile.
> **chauf·feur** (shō′fər *or* shō fur′) *noun, plural* **chauffeurs.**

cheap **1.** Low in price; not costing much. Milk is *cheap* in that store. **2.** Charging low prices. That is a *cheap* restaurant. **3.** Having little value; not of good quality. The dress was made of very *cheap* material.
> **cheap** (chēp) *adjective,* **cheaper, cheapest.**

cheat To act or treat in a dishonest way. He *cheats* when we play cards. The crook *cheated* his partner out of his share of the money. *Verb.*
—A person who cheats; dishonest person. *Noun.*
> **cheat** (chēt) *verb,* **cheated, cheating;** *noun, plural* **cheats.**

▲ Long ago **cheat** meant "to take back." It was used to describe the way a landlord would take back land if the person who lived there died. Often there were people in the dead person's family who thought they should get the land. They felt that the land had been taken from them unfairly. So the word *cheat* came to mean "to take something from someone in a dishonest way."

---

check **1.** A sudden stop. Our lack of money put a *check* on our plans to go to the movies. **2.** A person or thing that stops, controls, or limits. The leash was a *check* on the dog. **3.** A test or other way of finding out if something is correct or as it should be. The teacher made a *check* of the classroom to see if everyone was present. **4.** A mark (✓) used to show that something has been approved or is correct. The club secretary put a *check* next to the name of each person who was present at the meeting. **5.** A written order directing a bank to pay a certain amount of money from the account of the person who signs it to the person named. She gave the store a *check* to pay for the new lamp. **6.** A slip of paper showing what is owed for food or drink in a restaurant. The *check* for our lunch was $4.00. **7.** A ticket, tag, or token given to a

at; āpe; cär; end; mē; it; īce; hot; ōld;
fôrk; wood; fool; oil; out; up; turn; sing;
thin; this; hw in white; zh in treasure.
ə stands for a in about, e in taken
i in pencil, o in lemon, and u in circus.

111

person who has left something so that he can get it back later. **8.** A pattern of squares. The skirt has black and white *checks. Noun.*
—**1.** To bring to a sudden stop. The army *checked* the attack of the enemy soldiers. **2.** To hold in control; curb. Joan *checked* her urge to laugh at the way her brother was dressed. **3.** To test or compare to find out if something is correct or as it should be. The mechanic *checked* the car's engine. I will *check* my answers with those in the back of the book. **4.** To mark with a check. Please *check* the right answer to each question. **5.** To leave something for a time. We *checked* our coats at the door. *Verb.*

> check (chek) *noun, plural* **checks;** *verb,* **checked, checking.**

checkerboard A square board marked off into sixty-four squares of two alternating colors. It is used in playing checkers and chess. Most checkerboards have red and black squares.

> check·er·board (chek′ər bôrd′) *noun, plural* **checkerboards.**

checkers A game for two people played on a checkerboard. Each player has twelve pieces. The game is won when one of the players cannot move a piece because all his pieces have been captured or blocked.

> check·ers (chek′ərz) *noun plural.*

cheek **1.** Either side of the face below the eye. **2.** A saucy way of acting or speaking. He had the *cheek* to tell me that I was lying.

> cheek (chēk) *noun, plural* **cheeks.**

cheer **1.** A shout of happiness, encouragement, or praise. Everyone had to learn the new school *cheer* in time for the game on Saturday. **2.** Good spirits; happiness. Summer vacation brings us all feelings of *cheer. Noun.*
—**1.** To give a shout of happiness, encouragement, or praise. The crowd *cheered* the batter when he hit a home run. **2.** To make or become happy. The news that he was well enough to leave the hospital *cheered* him up. *Verb.*

> cheer (chēr) *noun, plural* **cheers;** *verb,* **cheered, cheering.**

cheerful **1.** Showing or feeling happiness or good spirits. A cheerful person helps to make people around him happy. **2.** Bringing a feeling of happiness and good spirits. Our kitchen is a *cheerful* room.

> cheer·ful (chēr′fəl) *adjective.*

cheese A food made by pressing the curds of milk into a solid piece.

> cheese (chēz) *noun, plural* **cheeses.**

cheetah A wild cat that has spots like a leopard. Cheetahs live in Africa and southern Asia. They can run very fast.

> chee·tah (chē′tə) *noun, plural* **cheetahs.**

Cheetah

chef The head cook of a restaurant or hotel.

> chef (shef) *noun, plural* **chefs.**

chemical Having to do with or made by chemistry. *Adjective.*
—A substance made by or used in chemistry. Gases and acids are *chemicals. Noun.*

> chem·i·cal (kem′i kəl) *adjective; noun, plural* **chemicals.**

chemist A person who knows a great deal about chemistry.

> chem·ist (kem′ist) *noun, plural* **chemists.**

chemistry The science that studies all kinds of substances to learn what they are made of, of what characteristics they have, and what kinds of changes happen when they combine with other substances.

> chem·is·try (kem′is trē) *noun.*

cherish To love and treat tenderly; hold dear. Mary *cherishes* her kitten.

> cher·ish (cher′ish) *verb,* **cherished, cherishing.**

cherry **1.** A small, round red fruit with a smooth skin. Cherries have a pit in the center. They grow on a tree or shrub. Cherry trees have many clusters of white or pink flowers in the spring. **2.** A bright red color.

> cher·ry (cher′ē) *noun, plural* **cherries.**

Cherry

chess A game played by two people on a chessboard. Each player has sixteen pieces including one king. The object of the game is to put the other player's king out of action.
chess (ches) *noun.*

chessboard A square board marked with sixty-four squares of two alternating colors. It is used in playing chess and checkers.
chess·board (ches′bôrd′) *noun, plural* chess-boards.

chest 1. The upper, front part of the body of a person or other animal. The chest is enclosed by the ribs. The lungs and the heart are in the chest. 2. A large, strong box used for holding things.
chest (chest) *noun, plural* chests.

chestnut 1. A sweet-tasting nut that grows inside a large, prickly burr. 2. The tree that this nut grows on. It has long, leathery leaves and sweet-smelling flowers. 3. A reddish-brown color.
chest·nut (ches′nut′) *noun, plural* chestnuts.

chew To crush and grind something with the teeth. It's important to *chew* food thoroughly. The puppy *chewed* a hole in the slipper. *Verb.*
—Something that is chewed or is for chewing. *Noun.*
chew (chōo) *verb,* chewed, chewing; *noun, plural* chews.

chewing gum A sweet gum for chewing. Chewing gum comes in sticks or small candy-coated squares.

Chicano A term used to describe an American of Mexican birth or descent.
Chi·ca·no (chi kän′ō) *noun, plural* Chicanos.

chick A young chicken or other young bird.
chick (chik) *noun, plural* chicks.

chickadee A small bird that has gray feathers with black or white markings and a black head. The chickadee lives in North America. It has a call that sounds like its name.
chick·a·dee (chik′ə-dē′) *noun, plural* chickadees.

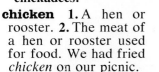
Chickadee

chicken 1. A hen or rooster. 2. The meat of a hen or rooster used for food. We had fried *chicken* on our picnic.
chick·en (chik′ən) *noun, plural* chickens.

chicken pox A mild disease that is easily passed from one person to another. When you have chicken pox you have a fever and you get a blotchy red rash on your body.

chief A person who is highest in rank or power; leader of a group. The *chief* of police will lead the parade. The Indian *chief* smoked the peace pipe first. *Noun.*
—1. Leading a group; highest in rank. Her older sister is *chief* counselor at that camp. 2. Most important; main. Your *chief* responsibility today is to cut the grass. *Adjective.*
chief (chēf) *noun, plural* chiefs; *adjective.*

chiefly 1. For the largest part; mostly. The house was made *chiefly* of wood. 2. More than anything; especially. Phil is *chiefly* interested in becoming a doctor.
chief·ly (chēf′lē) *adverb.*

chieftain A leader of a tribe or clan. The *chieftain* of the Scottish clan led his men into battle.
chief·tain (chēf′tən) *noun, plural* chieftains.

chihuahua A tiny dog that has big, pointed ears and usually a short tan coat. It is the smallest breed of dog.
chi·hua·hua (chi-wä′wə) *noun, plural* chihuahuas.

Chihuahua

child 1. A son or daughter. The parents were very proud of their only *child.* 2. A young boy or girl. That is a good book for a *child* of ten.
child (chīld) *noun, plural* children.

childhood The period of a person's life when he or she is a child. The children liked to hear their grandmother's stories about her *childhood.*
child·hood (chīld′hood′) *noun, plural* child-hoods.

childish Of, like, or suitable for a child. Refusing to try new kinds of food is *childish* behavior.
child·ish (chīl′dish) *adjective.*

children More than one child. Look up child for more information.
chil·dren (chil′drən) *noun plural.*

chili The dried pod of a plant, used to make

at; āpe; cär; end; mē; it; īce; hot; ōld;
fôrk; wood; fōol; oil; out; up; turn; sing;
thin; <u>th</u>is; hw in white; zh in treasure.
ə stands for a in about, e in taken
i in pencil, o in lemon, and u in circus.

a hot spice. ▲ Another word that sounds like this is **chilly.**

chil·i (chil′ē) *noun, plural* **chilies.**

chill 1. A mild but unpleasant coldness. Mother warmed the baby's bottle to take the *chill* off the milk. There was a *chill* in the air this morning. 2. A feeling of coldness in the body that makes a person shiver. He got a *chill* from sleeping without blankets. As she listened to the ghost story she felt a *chill* go through her. *Noun.*
—To make or become cold. We must *chill* the soda before serving it. *Verb.*
—Being unpleasantly cold; chilly. There was a *chill* wind blowing across the lake. *Adjective.*

chill (chil) *noun, plural* **chills;** *verb,* **chilled, chilling;** *adjective.*

chilly 1. Being unpleasantly cold; having a chill. It was a *chilly* morning so I put on an extra sweater. 2. Not warm and friendly. She was disappointed at the *chilly* welcome she got at the new school. ▲ Another word that sounds like this is **chili.**

chill·y (chil′ē) *adjective,* **chillier, chilliest.**

chime 1. One of a set of bells or pipes that are tuned to a musical scale. Chimes are usually played by being hit with small hammers. 2. The sound or sounds made by these bells or pipes when they are hit. We heard the *chime* of the church bells on Sunday morning. *Noun.*
—To make a musical sound by ringing. The church bells *chimed* in the steeple. *Verb.*

Chimney

chime (chīm) *noun, plural* **chimes;** *verb,* **chimed, chiming.**

chimney An upright, hollow structure that is connected to a fireplace or furnace. It carries away the smoke from the fire.

chim·ney (chim′nē) *noun, plural* **chimneys.**

chimpanzee A small African ape that has brownish-black hair. Chimpanzees live in trees.

chim·pan·zee (chim′pan zē′ *or* chim pan′zē) *noun, plural* **chimpanzees.**

chin The part of the face below the mouth and above the neck. The chin forms the front of the lower jaw. *Noun.*

—To lift oneself up to an overhead bar by pulling with the arms until the chin is level with or above the bar. *Verb.*

chin (chin) *noun, plural* **chins;** *verb,* **chinned, chinning.**

china 1. A fine pottery that is made of clay. 2. Dishes and other things made of china. We set the table with our best *china* for Sunday dinner.

chi·na (chī′nə) *noun.*

China A country in eastern Asia.

Chi·na (chī′nə) *noun.*

chinchilla A small South American animal that looks like a squirrel. A chinchilla has very thick, soft, silver-gray fur.

chin·chil·la (chin chil′ə) *noun, plural* **chinchillas.**

Chinese 1. A person who was born or is living in China. 2. The language spoken in China. *Noun.*
—Having to do with China. *Adjective.*

Chi·nese (chī nēz′) *noun, plural* **Chinese;** *adjective.*

chink A small, narrow opening; crack. Light came through *chinks* in the walls of the log cabin.

chink (chingk) *noun, plural* **chinks.**

chip 1. A very small piece of something that has been broken or cut off. There were *chips* of wood on the basement floor when Bob finished making the bookcase. 2. A place on an object where a small piece has been broken or cut off. The glass had a *chip* on the rim. *Noun.*
—To cut or break off a small piece or pieces of something. We had to *chip* the old paint off the window sill before repainting it. The cup *chipped* when I knocked it against the sink. *Verb.*

chip (chip) *noun, plural* **chips;** *verb,* **chipped, chipping.**

Chimpanzee

chipmunk A very small animal that has brown fur with dark stripes on its back and tail. A chipmunk is related to a squirrel.
chip·munk (chip′mungk′) *noun, plural* **chipmunks.**

Chipmunk

▲ The word **chipmunk** comes from the American Indian word for this animal, which means "head first." A chipmunk climbs down trees head first instead of feet first the way some animals do.

chirp A quick, sharp sound made by birds, insects, and other small animals. I heard the *chirp* of a cricket, but I couldn't find where it was hiding. *Noun.*
—To make a chirp. Our canary *chirps* when it is happy. *Verb.*
chirp (churp) *noun, plural* **chirps;** *verb,* **chirped, chirping.**

chisel A metal tool that has a sharp edge at the end of a blade. A chisel is used to cut or shape wood, stone, or metal. *Noun.*
—To cut or shape with a chisel. We *chiseled* the edge of the door so that it wouldn't stick. *Verb.*
chis·el (chiz′əl) *noun, plural* **chisels;** *verb,* **chiseled, chiseling.**

Chisel

chivalry The qualities that a good knight was supposed to have. Chivalry included politeness, bravery, honor, and the protecting of people who needed help.
chiv·al·ry (shiv′əl rē) *noun.*

chlorine A greenish-yellow poisonous gas that has a strong, unpleasant odor. Chlorine is used to kill germs and to bleach things. Chlorine is a chemical element.
chlo·rine (klôr′ēn) *noun, plural* **chlorines.**

chlorophyll The substance in plants that makes them green. Plants use chlorophyll to make food. They do this by changing the carbon dioxide and water that they take from the air and ground into sugar.
chlo·ro·phyll (klôr′ə fil′) *noun.*

chocolate **1.** A food substance that is made from cacao beans that are ground up and roasted. Chocolate is used to make drinks and candy. **2.** A drink made by dissolving chocolate in milk or water. The boys had some hot *chocolate* after they went ice skating. **3.** A candy made of or coated with chocolate. I gave my aunt a box of *chocolates.* **4.** A dark brown color. *Noun.*
—**1.** Made with chocolate. Mother made a *chocolate* cake for my birthday. **2.** Having a dark brown color. *Adjective.*
choc·o·late (chô′kə lit *or* chôk′lit) *noun, plural* **chocolates;** *adjective.*

choice **1.** The act of choosing. It took me a long time to make a *choice* between the two dresses I liked. **2.** The chance to choose. We were given a *choice* between going to the movies or visiting the zoo. **3.** A person or thing that is chosen. Strawberry ice cream was my *choice* for dessert. **4.** A variety or number of things from which to choose. The menu had a large *choice* of desserts. *Noun.*
—Of very good quality; excellent. We searched through the woods for a *choice* spot to have a picnic. *Adjective.*
choice (chois) *noun, plural* **choices;** *adjective,* **choicer, choicest.**

choir A group of singers who sing together in a church.
choir (kwīr) *noun, plural* **choirs.**

choke **1.** To stop or hold back the breathing of. The smoke from the fire *choked* us. **2.** To be unable to breathe easily. I *choked* on a bone. **3.** To stop up; fill up. Grease *choked* the kitchen drain. **4.** To hold back; check. Weeds *choked* the flowers in the garden. Tom tried to *choke* down his anger.
choke (chōk) *verb,* **choked, choking.**

at; āpe; cär; end; mē; it; īce; hot; ōld;
fôrk; wood; fōōl; oil; out; up; turn; sing;
thin; **this**; hw in white; zh in treasure.
ə stands for a in about, e in taken
i in pencil, o in lemon, and u in circus.

115

choose **1.** To pick one or more from all that there are. If you could have either a bicycle or a pair of ice skates, which one would you *choose?* **2.** To decide or prefer to do something. You can come to the game with us if you *choose.*
     choose (chōōz) *verb,* **chose, chosen, choosing.**

chop[1] **1.** To cut by a quick blow with something sharp. The fireman had to *chop* the door down with an ax. **2.** To cut into small pieces. They *chopped* onions to put in the stew. *Verb.*
—**1.** A quick blow with something sharp. It took many *chops* with the ax to cut down the tree. **2.** A small piece of meat that has a rib in it. We are having lamb *chops* for dinner. *Noun.*
     chop (chop) *verb,* **chopped, chopping;** *noun,* *plural* **chops.**

chop[2] The jaw or mouth of a person or animal. The dog licked his *chops* after chewing on the bone.
     chop (chop) *noun, plural* **chops.**

chopsticks A pair of long, thin sticks that are used to eat with. Chopsticks are held between the thumb and fingers of one hand. The Chinese and Japanese use chopsticks.
     chop·sticks (chop′stiks′) *noun plural.*

chord A combination of three or more notes of music that are sounded at the same time to produce a harmony. ▲ Another word that sounds like this is **cord.**
     chord (kôrd) *noun, plural* **chords.**

chore A small job. Feeding the chickens every morning was one of Tom's *chores* on the farm.
     chore (chôr) *noun, plural* **chores.**

chorus **1.** A group of people who sing or dance together. Bob is going to sing in the *chorus* of the musical play at school. **2.** A part of a song that is sung after each stanza. Most of the people couldn't remember the words of the hymn but they all knew the *chorus.* *Noun.*
—To sing or say at the same time. All the children *chorused* "yes" when they were asked if they wanted ice cream for dessert. *Verb.*
     cho·rus (kôr′əs) *noun, plural* **choruses;** *verb,* **chorused, chorusing.**

chose I *chose* a book on tennis for my sister's birthday gift. Look up **choose** for more information.
     chose (chōz) *verb.*

chosen The basketball team has *chosen* Ed as the new captain. Look up **choose** for more information.
     cho·sen (chō′zən) *verb.*

chowder A thick soup made with fish or clams and vegetables.
     chow·der (chou′dər) *noun, plural* **chowders.**

Christ Jesus, the founder of the Christian religion.
     Christ (krīst) *noun.*

christen **1.** To give a name to a person during baptism. The minister *christened* the baby "Mary Ann." **2.** To receive into a Christian church by baptism.
     chris·ten (kris′ən) *verb,* **christened, christening.**

Christian A person who believes in Jesus and follows His teachings. *Noun.*
—**1.** Having to do with Jesus or His teachings. **2.** Believing in Jesus and following His teachings. Easter is a holiday that is celebrated by all the *Christian* people of the world. *Adjective.*
     Chris·tian (kris′chən) *noun, plural* **Christians;** *adjective.*

Christianity The religion based on the teachings of Jesus.
     Chris·ti·an·i·ty (kris′chē an′ə tē) *noun.*

Christmas The celebration each year of the birth of Jesus. Christmas falls on December 25.
     Christ·mas (kris′məs) *noun, plural* **Christmases.**

Christmas tree A pine or other evergreen tree that is decorated with lights and ornaments at Christmas time.

chromium A hard silver-white metal that does not rust or become dull easily. Chromium is a chemical element. Many automobiles have chromium on the bumpers and other metal parts.
     chro·mi·um (krō′mē əm) *noun.*

chrysanthemum A round flower with many small petals.
     chry·san·the·mum (krə-san′thə məm) *noun, plural* **chrysanthemums.**

chubby Round and plump. The baby had *chubby* legs.
     chub·by (chub′ē) *adjective,* **chubbier, chubbiest.**

Chrysanthemum

chuckle To laugh in a quiet way. When we chuckle we are often laughing to ourselves. John *chuckled* when he read the letter from his brother. *Verb.*
—A quiet laugh. *Noun.*

chuck·le (chuk′əl) *verb,* **chuckled, chuckling;** *noun, plural* **chuckles.**

chunk A thick piece or lump. Ruth cut the cheese into big *chunks.*
chunk (chungk) *noun, plural* **chunks.**

church 1. A building where people gather together for Christian worship. I go to *church* on Sundays. 2. A group of Christians having the same beliefs; denomination. The Roman Catholic *Church* is in charge of many schools in our city.
church (church) *noun, plural* **churches.**

churn A container in which cream or milk is shaken or beaten to make butter. *Noun.*
—1. To shake or beat cream or milk in a special container to make butter. 2. To stir or move with a very rough motion. The water *churned* around the rocks at the bottom of the waterfall. A plow *churns* up the soil. *Verb.*
churn (churn) *noun, plural* **churns;** *verb,* **churned, churning.**

Churn

chute A steep passage or slide through which things may pass. There are chutes for mail so that it slides down into a mailbox. ▲ Another word that sounds like this is **shoot.**
chute (shoot) *noun, plural* **chutes.**

cider The juice that is pressed from apples. Cider is used as a drink and in making vinegar.
ci·der (sī′dər) *noun, plural* **ciders.**

cigar A roll of tobacco leaves that is used for smoking.
ci·gar (si gär′) *noun, plural* **cigars.**

cigarette A small roll of finely cut tobacco leaves wrapped in thin white paper that is used for smoking.
cig·a·rette (sig′ə ret′ *or* sig′ə ret′) *noun, plural* **cigarettes.**

cinder A bit of coal or wood that is burning but no longer flaming.
cin·der (sin′dər) *noun, plural* **cinders.**

cinnamon 1. A reddish-brown spice. Cinnamon is made from the dried inner bark of a tropical tree. 2. A light, reddish-brown color. *Noun.*
—Having a light, reddish-brown color. *Adjective.*
cin·na·mon (sin′ə mən) *noun; adjective.*

circle 1. A closed, curved line. Every point on the line is the same distance from a point inside called the center. 2. Anything that has a shape like a circle. A ring or a crown is a circle. We sat in a *circle* around the campfire. 3. A group of people who have interests that they share and enjoy together. Most of my *circle* of friends are interested in baseball. *Noun.*
—1. To make a circle around. We were told to *circle* the right answer on the page. 2. To move around in a circle. The airplane *circled* the airport. *Verb.*
cir·cle (sur′kəl) *noun, plural* **circles;** *verb,* **circled, circling.**

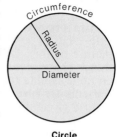

Circle

circuit 1. A going around. The earth takes one year to make its *circuit* around the sun. 2. The path of an electric current. Electricity in your house moves in a *circuit* that takes it from wires outside the house to the different wall sockets, switches, and appliances in the house.
cir·cuit (sur′kit) *noun, plural* **circuits.**

circular Having or making the shape of a circle; round. The skaters moved in a *circular* path around the ice rink. *Adjective.*
—A letter or an advertisement that is sent to many people. The store sent out *circulars* to announce the big sale. *Noun.*
cir·cu·lar (sur′kyə lər) *adjective; noun, plural* **circulars.**

circulate To move in a circle. The fan in the window *circulates* air around the room. The blood in our bodies *circulates* from the heart through the arteries of the body and then back through the veins to the heart, where it starts all over again.
cir·cu·late (sur′kyə lāt′) *verb,* **circulated, circulating.**

circulation 1. Movement around. The *circulation* of money starts at the mint where it is made, and passes from person to person until it goes back to the mint to be destroyed and new money is made to take its place. 2. The average number of copies of a news-

at; āpe; cär; end; mē; it; īce; hot; ōld;
fôrk; wood; fool; oil; out; up; turn; sing;
thin; this; hw in white; zh in treasure.
ə stands for a in about, e in taken
i in pencil, o in lemon, and u in circus.

paper or magazine that are sold in a given time. The *circulation* of our city's newspaper is over 100,000.

cir·cu·la·tion (sur′kyə lā′shən) *noun.*

circumference **1.** A line that forms the outside edge of a circle. Look up **circle** for a picture of this. **2.** The distance around something. The *circumference* of our round kitchen table is nine feet.

cir·cum·fer·ence (sər kum′fər əns) *noun, plural* **circumferences.**

circumstance A condition, act, or event that happens along with other things and has an effect on them. Good food and good music were two *circumstances* that helped make the party a success. Whether or not we have the beach party on Saturday depends on the weather, which is a *circumstance* beyond our control.

cir·cum·stance (sur′kəm stans′) *noun, plural* **circumstances.**

circus A show with trained animals and acrobats, clowns, and other people who do special things. A circus is often given in a huge tent and moves from town to town.

cir·cus (sur′kəs) *noun, plural* **circuses.**

cite **1.** To repeat the words of another person exactly; quote. He *cited* a paragraph in the encyclopedia that supported his theory. **2.** To mention as proof or support. The firemen *cited* the fire in the garage as an example of the danger of leaving oily rags lying around. ▲ Other words that sound like this are **sight** and **site.**

cite (sīt) *verb,* **cited, citing.**

citizen **1.** A person who was born in a country or who chooses to live in and become a member of a country. When you are a citizen of the United States, you have the right to vote for the people who run the government. You also have responsibilities, like paying taxes and obeying laws. **2.** Any person who lives in a town or city. The *citizens* of New York City voted against the new law.

cit·i·zen (sit′ə zən) *noun, plural* **citizens.**

citizenship The position of being a citizen of a country with all the rights, duties, and privileges that come with it. The immigrant had to pass a test to gain *citizenship* in the new country.

cit·i·zen·ship (sit′ə zən ship′) *noun, plural* **citizenships.**

citrus Any tree growing in warm regions that bears oranges, grapefruits, lemons, or limes.

cit·rus (sit′rəs) *noun, plural* **citruses.**

city A large area where many people live and work. A city is larger and more important than a town. Cities have their own local government, which is usually headed by a mayor and a council.

cit·y (sit′ē) *noun, plural* **cities.**

civic **1.** Having to do with a city. Keeping our streets and parks clean is a matter of *civic* pride. **2.** Having to do with a citizen or citizenship. It is a person's *civic* duty to vote.

civ·ic (siv′ik) *adjective.*

civil **1.** Having to do with a citizen or citizens. He was a leader in the movement for *civil* rights. **2.** Not connected with military or church affairs. The couple was married in a *civil* ceremony. **3.** Polite; courteous. Bob gave me a *civil* answer, even though he was angry at me.

civ·il (siv′əl) *adjective.*

civilian A person who is not in the armed forces. My brother is a *civilian* now that he has been discharged by the army. *Noun.*
—Relating to civilians. Father says it feels funny to be wearing *civilian* clothes again after being in the navy. *Adjective.*

ci·vil·ian (si vil′yən) *noun, plural* **civilians;** *adjective.*

civilization A condition of human society in which there is a highly developed knowledge of agriculture, trade, government, the arts, and science. Two of the main characteristics of civilization are writing and the growth of cities. In school we study the *civilization* of the ancient Egyptians.

civ·i·li·za·tion (siv′ə li zā′shən) *noun, plural* **civilizations.**

civilize To bring out of a primitive or ignorant condition. To civilize a people means to bring them knowledge of the arts, science, government, and agriculture.

civ·i·lize (siv′ə līz′) *verb,* **civilized, civilizing.**

civil service The branch of government service that is not part of the armed forces, the court system, or the legislature.

civil war A war between groups of citizens of the same country.

claim **1.** To demand as one's own. The settlers *claimed* the land along the river. Tom *claimed* the dollar Mary found in the hall, because he said he had dropped it. **2.** To say that something is true. Jim *claimed* that he had seen the robber run away. *Verb.*
—**1.** A demand for something as one's right. After the fire, Father filed a *claim* with the insurance company. **2.** A saying that something is true. John's *claim* that he is the fastest runner at school is not so. **3.** Something that is claimed. The miner's

claim is a piece of land in the hills. *Noun.*
claim (klām) *verb,* **claimed, claiming;** *noun,* *plural* **claims.**

clam An animal that has a soft body and a hinged shell in two parts. Clams are found in both salt and fresh water. Many kinds of clams are good to eat. *Noun.*
—To dig in the sand or mud for clams. *Verb.*
clam (klam) *noun,* *plural* **clams;** *verb,* **clammed, clamming.**

Clam

clamor 1. A loud continuous noise; uproar. The *clamor* of automobile horns filled the air on the crowded highway. 2. A loud protest or demand. The people made a *clamor* for less pollution in the town. *Noun.*
—To make a clamor. The crowd *clamored* for the umpire to change his decision. *Verb.*
clam·or (klam′ər) *noun,* *plural* **clamors;** *verb,* **clamored, clamoring.**

clamp A device used to hold things together tightly. Tom used a *clamp* to hold the two pieces of wood together until the glue dried. *Noun.*
—To fasten together with a clamp. Bill *clamped* the horn to the handlebar of his bicycle. *Verb.*
clamp (klamp) *noun,* *plural* **clamps;** *verb,* **clamped, clamping.**

Clamp

clan A group of families who all claim that they are descended from the same ancestor.
clan (klan) *noun,* *plural* **clans.**

clap 1. A sharp, sudden sound like two flat pieces of wood striking each other. There was a *clap* of thunder and then it began to rain. 2. A friendly slap. Bill gave his friend a *clap* on the shoulder. *Noun.*
—1. To strike together. The child *clapped* her hands with delight when she saw the birthday cake. 2. To applaud by clapping one's hands. The children all *clapped* when the magician's show was over. 3. To strike in a friendly way. Joe *clapped* Tom on the back and congratulated him for winning the prize. *Verb.*
clap (klap) *noun,* *plural* **claps;** *verb,* **clapped, clapping.**

clarify To make something easier to understand; explain clearly. The diagram helped to *clarify* the instructions for assembling the model airplane.
clar·i·fy (klar′ə fī′) *verb,* **clarified, clarifying.**

clarinet A musical instrument shaped like a tube. A clarinet is played by blowing into the mouthpiece and pressing keys or covering holes with the fingers to change the pitch.
clar·i·net (klar′ə-net′) *noun,* *plural* **clarinets.**

Clarinet

clarity Clearness. The directions for playing the game are written with great *clarity*.
clar·i·ty (klar′ə tē) *noun.*

clash 1. A loud, harsh sound like pieces of metal striking against each other. The band ended the parade music with a *clash* of cymbals. 2. A strong disagreement. There was a *clash* between the members of my family about where we'd go for our vacation. *Noun.*
—1. To come together with a clash. The pots and pans *clashed* when Betty dropped them on the kitchen floor. 2. To disagree strongly. Members of the team *clashed* over who should be the captain. *Verb.*
clash (klash) *noun,* *plural* **clashes;** *verb,* **clashed, clashing.**

clasp 1. A thing used to hold two parts or objects together. A hook or a buckle is a clasp. The *clasp* of my bracelet is broken. 2. A close or tight grasp. They said good-by with a *clasp* of hands. *Noun.*
—1. To fasten together with a clasp. Mary *clasped* her belt with a silver buckle. 2. To hold or grasp closely. The mother *clasped* the crying child in her arms. *Verb.*
clasp (klasp) *noun,* *plural* **clasps;** *verb,* **clasped, clasping.**

class 1. A group of persons or things alike in some way. A factory worker belongs to the working *class*. The mammals form one *class* of animals. 2. A group of students studying or

at; āpe; cär; end; mē; it; īce; hot; ōld;
fôrk; wood; fōōl; oil; out; up; turn; sing;
thin; this; hw in white; zh in treasure.
ə stands for a in about, e in taken
i in pencil, o in lemon, and u in circus.

meeting together. There are thirty students in my *class.* The science *class* took a field trip to the zoo. **3.** A grade or quality. That farmer grows a very high *class* of vegetables. *Noun.* —To group in a class; classify. Tom *classes* the stamps in his collection by the country from which they come. *Verb.*

class (klas) *noun, plural* **classes;** *verb,* **classed, classing.**

classic Of the highest quality; excellent. That new office building is a *classic* example of modern architecture. *Adjective.* —**1.** A very fine book or other work of art. That play by William Shakespeare is a *classic.* **2. the classics.** The writings of ancient Greece and Rome. *Noun.*

clas·sic (klas′ik) *adjective; noun, plural* **classics.**

classical **1.** Relating to the literature, art, and way of life of ancient Greece or Rome. That museum has a collection of *classical* statues. **2.** Very fine or excellent. The author has written a *classical* history of the American Revolution. **3.** Relating to music that follows a standard form. Classical music is different from popular music or folk music. A symphony is a piece of *classical* music.

clas·si·cal (klas′i kəl) *adjective.*

classification Arrangement in groups or classes. The *classification* of the stamps in the album is according to countries.

clas·si·fi·ca·tion (klas′ə fi kā′shən) *noun, plural* **classifications.**

classify To arrange in groups or classes. The librarian *classified* the books according to author.

clas·si·fy (klas′ə fī′) *verb,* **classified, classifying.**

classmate A member of the same class in school. I invited all my *classmates* to my birthday party.

class·mate (klas′māt′) *noun, plural* **class-mates.**

classroom A room in which classes are held.

class·room (klas′rōōm′ *or* klas′room′) *noun, plural* **classrooms.**

clatter A loud, rattling noise. The *clatter* of dishes from the kitchen was a sign that dinner was almost ready. *Noun.* —To make a loud, rattling noise. The pots *clattered* as she put them away. *Verb.*

clat·ter (klat′ər) *noun, plural* **clatters;** *verb,* **clattered, clattering.**

clause **1.** A part of a sentence. A clause has a subject and a verb. In the sentence "I watched television before I went to bed," "I

watched television" is an **independent clause** that can stand alone. "Before I went to bed" is a **dependent clause.** Its meaning depends on the main part of the sentence. **2.** A separate part of a law, treaty, or other formal agreement. There is a *clause* in our lease that says the landlord must keep our apartment warm enough in the winter.

clause (klôz) *noun, plural* **clauses.**

claw **1.** A sharp, curved nail on the foot of a bird or animal. A cat has very sharp *claws.* An eagle uses its *claws* to seize and kill its prey. **2.** One of the pincers of a lobster or crab. **3.** Anything like a claw. The forked end of the head of a hammer that is used to pull out nails is called a claw. *Noun.* —To scratch or tear with claws or hands. The puppy *clawed* the door because it wanted to come inside. *Verb.*

claw (klô) *noun, plural* **claws;** *verb,* **clawed, clawing.**

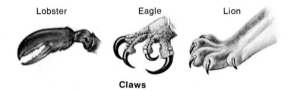

Lobster   Eagle   Lion

Claws

clay A kind of fine earth. Clay can be easily shaped when wet, but it becomes hard when it is dried or baked. Clay is used to make pottery and bricks.

clay (klā) *noun, plural* **clays.**

clean **1.** Free from dirt. After playing football, Jack changed into *clean* clothes. The air is not very *clean* in most big cities. **2.** Honorable or fair. That judge has led a *clean* life. The teams played *clean* football. **3.** Complete; thorough. The bank robbers made a *clean* escape. *Adjective.* —Completely. The arrow went *clean* through the target. *Adverb.* —To make clean. I have to *clean* my room today. Go and *clean* up for dinner. *Verb.*

clean (klēn) *adjective,* **cleaner, cleanest;** *adverb; verb,* **cleaned, cleaning.**

cleaner **1.** A person whose work or business is cleaning. Please take my dress to the *cleaner.* The window *cleaner* washed the windows of the apartment house. **2.** Something that removes dirt. Sally used a *cleaner* to get the coffee stain off the rug.

clean·er (klē′nər) *noun, plural* **cleaners.**

cleanliness The condition of being clean; the habit of always keeping clean. Cats are known for their *cleanliness.*

clean·li·ness (klen′lē nis) *noun.*

cleanly¹ Always clean or kept clean. A cat is a *cleanly* animal.
    clean·ly (klen′lē) *adjective,* **cleanlier, cleanliest.**

cleanly² In a clean way. The ax cut *cleanly* through the log.
    clean·ly (klēn′lē) *adverb.*

cleanse To make clean. The nurse *cleansed* the cut on my knee with soap.
    cleanse (klenz) *verb,* **cleansed, cleansing.**

cleanser Something that is used for cleaning. Mary scrubbed away the stains in the sink with a *cleanser.*
    cleans·er (klen′zər) *noun, plural* **cleansers.**

clear **1.** Free from anything that darkens; bright. The summer day was warm and *clear.* **2.** Easily seen through. The water of the pond was so *clear* that you could see the bottom. **3.** Easily seen, heard, or understood; plain; distinct. We had a *clear* view of the town from the top of the hill. His shout for help was loud and *clear.* The directions he gave us aren't very *clear. Adjective.*
    —In a clear way. Jack answered the question loud and *clear. Adverb.*
    —**1.** To make clear. Betty *cleared* the table after dinner. The detective *cleared* up the mystery of the missing necklace. **2.** To become clear. After the rain stopped, the sky *cleared.* **3.** To go by or over without touching. Sally *cleared* the fence with one leap. *Verb.*
    clear (klēr) *adjective,* **clearer, clearest;** *adverb; verb,* **cleared, clearing.**

clearing A piece of land that is free of trees or brush. The boys made a *clearing* in the woods for their camp.
    clear·ing (klēr′ing) *noun, plural* **clearings.**

cleaver A tool that has a short handle and a broad blade. A cleaver is used by butchers for cutting up meat.
    cleav·er (klē′vər) *noun, plural* **cleavers.**

clef A sign placed on a staff in music. A clef shows the pitch of the notes on the various lines and spaces.
    clef (klef) *noun, plural* **clefs.**

cleft A space or opening made by splitting; crack. Tom climbed the cliff by holding onto the *clefts* in the rocks. *Noun.*

Cleaver

—Divided. The baby has a *cleft* chin just like his father. *Adjective.*
    cleft (kleft) *noun, plural* **clefts;** *adjective.*

clench **1.** To close together tightly. John *clenched* his fists in anger. **2.** To grasp or grip tightly. The child *clenched* his mother's hand as they entered the doctor's office.
    clench (klench) *verb,* **clenched, clenching.**

clergy Ministers, priests, and rabbis. The clergy consists of all the people who are appointed to carry on religious work.
    cler·gy (klur′jē) *noun, plural* **clergies.**

clergyman A member of the clergy; minister, priest, or rabbi.
    cler·gy·man (klur′jē mən) *noun, plural* **clergymen.**

clerk **1.** A person who keeps records and files in an office. **2.** A person who sells goods to customers in a store. *Noun.*
    —To work as a clerk. Jack *clerks* in the grocery store on Saturdays. *Verb.*
    clerk (klurk) *noun, plural* **clerks;** *verb,* **clerked, clerking.**

▲ The word **clerk** comes from an Old English word that meant "priest or monk." Long ago priests and monks were almost the only people who could write and keep records. Later other people who kept written records were called clerks, too.

clever **1.** Bright and alert. Joe is a *clever* student. **2.** Showing skill and intelligence. The magician did some very *clever* tricks.
    clev·er (klev′ər) *adjective,* **cleverer, cleverest.**

click A light, sharp sound. We heard the *click* of Father's key in the lock. *Noun.*
    —To make a click. Her heels *clicked* on the pavement as she walked. *Verb.*
    click (klik) *noun, plural* **clicks;** *verb,* **clicked, clicking.**

client A person who uses the services of another person. The lawyer drew up a will for his *client.* That advertising agency has many *clients.*
    cli·ent (klī′ənt) *noun, plural* **clients.**

cliff A high, steep face of rock or earth. The valley was surrounded by *cliffs.*
    cliff (klif) *noun, plural* **cliffs.**

at; āpe; cär; end; mē; it; īce; hot; ōld;
fôrk; wood; fool; oil; out; up; turn; sing;
thin; this; hw in white; zh in treasure.
ə stands for a in about, e in taken
i in pencil, o in lemon, and u in circus.

climate The average weather conditions of a place or region. Climate includes average temperature, rainfall, humidity, and wind conditions. The *climate* in the mountains was cool and dry in the summer.
cli·mate (klī′mit) *noun, plural* **climates.**

climax The highest point. The *climax* of the movie came when the police chased the bank robbers and finally caught them.
cli·max (klī′maks) *noun, plural* **climaxes.**

climb To move or go upward. The boys *climbed* the big tree. Ivy *climbed* the side of the house. The prisoner *climbed* over the wall. Prices have *climbed* this month. *Verb.*
—**1.** The act of climbing. Their *climb* of the hill took an hour. **2.** A place to be climbed. That mountain is a dangerous *climb. Noun.*
climb (klīm) *verb,* **climbed, climbing;** *noun, plural* **climbs.**

cling To stick closely. Mud *clings* to your shoes. Little children sometimes *cling* to their mothers when they are frightened. He still *clings* to his belief in Santa Claus.
cling (kling) *verb,* **clung, clinging.**

clinic A place in a hospital, or connected with a hospital, where people come for medical help. He went to the dental *clinic* to have his teeth examined.
clin·ic (klin′ik) *noun, plural* **clinics.**

clip[1] To cut; cut short. Sally *clips* the loose ends of thread with her scissors when she is finished sewing. I tried to *clip* the hedge evenly. Tom *clipped* the article about the game out of the newspaper. *Verb.*
—A rate or pace. The bus moved along at a fast *clip. Noun.*
clip (klip) *verb,* **clipped, clipping;** *noun, plural* **clips.**

clip[2] A device used to hold things together. A *clip* for papers is made of bent wires. Tom held his tie in place with a *clip. Noun.*
—To fasten with a clip. Bill *clipped* the papers together. *Verb.*
clip (klip) *noun, plural* **clips;** *verb,* **clipped, clipping.**

clipper **1.** A tool used for cutting. The barber used a *clipper* to cut Frank's hair in the back. **2.** A fast sailing ship. American *clippers* were used as cargo ships during the 1800s and sailed all over the world.
clip·per (klip′ər) *noun, plural* **clippers.**

clipping A piece that is cut out of a magazine or newspaper. Betty keeps an album of *clippings* about her favorite baseball player.
clip·ping (klip′ing) *noun, plural* **clippings.**

cloak A loose outer piece of clothing, with or without sleeves. *Noun.*
—To cover or hide with a cloak. Fog *cloaked* the city. *Verb.*
cloak (klōk) *noun, plural* **cloaks;** *verb,* **cloaked, cloaking.**

clock A device used for measuring and showing the time. A clock usually has hands that pass over a dial marked to show hours and minutes. Clocks are not meant to be worn or carried about by a person as a watch is. *Noun.*
—To find out the speed of something by using a device like a clock. Jean *clocked* the runners in the race by using a stopwatch. *Verb.*
clock (klok) *noun, plural* **clocks;** *verb,* **clocked, clocking.**

Grandfather Clock

clockwise In the direction in which the hands of a clock move. Move the dial *clockwise* to turn on the radio. Look up **counterclockwise** for a picture of this.
clock·wise (klok′wīz′) *adverb; adjective.*

clog To block; stop up. Dirt will *clog* drains. Heavy traffic *clogged* the roads. *Verb.*
—A shoe with a thick wooden sole. *Noun.*
clog (klog) *verb,* **clogged, clogging;** *noun, plural* **clogs.**

cloister A covered walk along the wall of a building. A cloister is often built around the courtyard of a monastery, church, or college building.
clois·ter (klois′tər) *noun, plural* **cloisters.**

Cloister

close **1.** To shut. Please *close* the door. The grocery store *closed* for the night. **2.** To bring or come together. The dog's teeth *closed* on the bone. **3.** To bring or come to an end. He *closed* his letter with a promise to write again soon. *Verb.*
—**1.** Near. Our house is *close* to the school. Spring vacation is *close*. **2.** Near in affection; intimate. Sally and Bob are *close* friends. **3.** Lacking fresh air; stuffy. It is *close* in this room with the window shut. **4.** Nearly even; almost equal. It was a *close* race. *Adjective.*
—In a close position or way. Your car is not parked *close* enough to the curb. *Adverb.*
—End; finish. At the *close* of the day, we all went home. *Noun.* ▲ Another word that sounds like this is **clothes.**
close (klōz *for verb and noun;* klōs *for adjective and adverb*) *verb,* **closed, closing;** *adjective,* **closer, closest;** *adverb; noun.*

closet A small room for storing things. Hang your coat and dress in the clothes *closet*. Mother keeps the broom and the mop in a *closet* in the kitchen.
clos·et (kloz′it) *noun, plural* **closets.**

clot A soft lump. A *clot* of blood formed over the cut on Mary's finger. *Noun.*
—To form into clots. The bleeding stopped when the blood *clotted*. *Verb.*
clot (klot) *noun, plural* **clots;** *verb,* **clotted, clotting.**

cloth **1.** Material made by weaving or knitting fibers. Cloth is made from cotton, wool, silk, linen, or other fibers. **2.** A piece of cloth used for a particular purpose. Use this *cloth* to dust the living room.
cloth (klôth) *noun, plural* **cloths.**

clothe To put clothes on; Mother *clothed* us warmly because it was cold outdoors.
clothe (klō th) *verb,* **clothed** or **clad, clothing.**

clothes Things worn to cover the body. Betty hung her coat, dresses, skirts, and other *clothes* neatly in the closet. ▲ Another word that sounds like this is **close.**
clothes (klōz *or* klōthz) *noun plural.*

clothing Things worn to cover the body; clothes. The explorers wore very warm *clothing* when they went to the North Pole.
cloth·ing (klō′thing) *noun.*

cloud **1.** A gray or white mass of tiny drops of water or bits of ice floating high in the sky. **2.** Something like a cloud. The cowboys rode off in a *cloud* of dust. A *cloud* of birds filled the sky. *Noun.*
—**1.** To cover with a cloud or clouds. Smoke from the burning house *clouded* the whole street. **2.** To become cloudy. The sky sud-denly *clouded* over and it started to rain. *Verb.*
cloud (kloud) *noun, plural* **clouds;** *verb,* **clouded, clouding.**

cloudburst A sudden, heavy rainfall.
cloud·burst (kloud′burst′) *noun, plural* **cloudbursts.**

cloudy **1.** Covered with clouds. The sky was *cloudy* and dark. **2.** Not clear. The pond was so *cloudy* that you couldn't see the bottom.
cloud·y (klou′dē) *adjective,* **cloudier, cloudiest.**

clove¹ The dried flower bud of a tree that grows in the tropics. Cloves are used as a spice.
clove (klōv) *noun, plural* **cloves.**

clove² One of the sections of a garlic bulb.
clove (klōv) *noun, plural* **cloves.**

clover A plant having leaves made up of three leaflets and rounded, fragrant flower heads of white, red, or purple flowers. Clover is used as food for cows.
clo·ver (klō′vər) *noun, plural* **clovers.**

clown A person in a circus who makes people laugh by playing tricks or doing stunts. *Noun.*
—To act like a clown. Don't *clown* around when you are supposed to be doing your homework. *Verb.*
clown (kloun) *noun, plural* **clowns;** *verb,* **clowned, clowning.**

Clown

club **1.** A heavy stick that is thicker at one end. A club is used as a weapon. Some police officers carry clubs. **2.** A stick or bat used to hit a ball in various games. Clubs are used in the game of golf. **3.** A group of people who meet together for fun or some special purpose. Joe belongs to a swimming *club*. **4.** A playing card marked with one or more figures shaped like this: (♣) **5. clubs.**

at; āpe; cär; end; mē; it; īce; hot; ōld;
fôrk; wood; fool; oil; out; up; turn; sing;
thin; this; hw in white; zh in treasure.
ə stands for a in about, e in taken
i in pencil, o in lemon, and u in circus.

The suit of cards marked with this figure. *Noun.*

—To beat or strike with a club. The policeman *clubbed* the burglar as he climbed in the window. *Verb.*

  club (klub) *noun, plural* **clubs;** *verb,* **clubbed, clubbing.**

clue A hint that helps solve a problem or mystery. A fingerprint was the *clue* that solved the robbery. If you can't solve the riddle, I'll give you a *clue.*

  clue (klo͞o) *noun, plural* **clues.**

clump **1.** A group or bunch. The rabbit hopped out of a *clump* of bushes. **2.** A heavy, thumping sound. Betty fell out of the tree and landed with a *clump. Noun.*

—To walk heavily and noisily. The tired hikers *clumped* home. *Verb.*

  clump (klump) *noun, plural* **clumps;** *verb,* **clumped, clumping.**

clumsy Awkward; not graceful. My *clumsy* little brother is always knocking over his glass of milk.

  clum·sy (klum′zē) *adjective,* **clumsier, clumsiest.**

clung His wet shirt *clung* to his back. Look up **cling** for more information.

  clung (klung) *verb.*

cluster A number of things of the same kind that grow or are grouped together. Grapes grow in *clusters.* We could see a little *cluster* of houses in the distance. *Noun.*

—To grow or group in a cluster. We all *clustered* around the campfire and sang songs. *Verb.*

  clus·ter (klus′tər) *noun, plural* **clusters;** *verb,* **clustered, clustering.**

clutch To grasp tightly. The little boy *clutched* the money in his hand on the way to the grocery store. *Verb.*

—**1.** A tight grasp. I kept a *clutch* on my little sister's hand so she wouldn't get lost in the crowd. **2.** A device in a machine that connects or disconnects the motor that makes it run. *Noun.*

  clutch (kluch) *verb,* **clutched, clutching;** *noun, plural* **clutches.**

clutter A messy collection of things; litter. We all helped pick up the *clutter* of cans and bottles after the picnic. *Noun.*

—To litter or fill with a messy collection of things. Beth *cluttered* her closet with old, worn-out clothes. *Verb.*

  clut·ter (klut′ər) *noun, plural* **clutters;** *verb,* **cluttered, cluttering.**

coach **1.** A large, closed carriage drawn by horses. A coach has seats inside for passengers and a raised seat outside for the driver. **2.** A railroad car for passengers. **3.** A low-priced seat on a bus, airplane, or train. **4.** A teacher or trainer. The basketball *coach* runs the basketball team. *Noun.*

—To teach or train. Mr. Smith *coaches* the swimming team. *Verb.*

  coach (kōch) *noun, plural* **coaches;** *verb,* **coached, coaching.**

Coach

coal **1.** A black mineral that is used as a fuel. Coal is formed from decaying plants buried deep in the earth under great pressure. Coal is taken from the earth by mining. **2.** A piece of glowing or burned wood. We roasted hot dogs over the hot *coals* of the fire.

  coal (kōl) *noun, plural* **coals.**

coarse **1.** Made up of rather large parts; not fine. There is *coarse* sand on the bottom of the pond. **2.** Thick and rough. The *coarse* wool of the sweater made my skin itch. **3.** Crude; vulgar. Jack's father scolded him for his *coarse* table manners. ▲ Another word that sounds like this is **course.**

  coarse (kôrs) *adjective,* **coarser, coarsest.**

coast The land next to the sea; seashore. We saw a fleet of fishing boats just off the *coast. Noun.*

—To ride or slide along without effort or power. We *coasted* down the hill on our sleds. *Verb.*

  coast (kōst) *noun, plural* **coasts;** *verb,* **coasted, coasting.**

coastal Near or along a coast. There is good fishing in those *coastal* waters.

  coast·al (kōst′əl) *adjective.*

Coast Guard A military service that patrols and defends the coasts of the United States.

coastline The outline or shape of a coast. You can see on the map that the state of Florida has a long *coastline.*

  coast·line (kōst′līn′) *noun, plural* **coastlines.**

coat **1.** A piece of outer clothing with sleeves. I have a new winter *coat.* **2.** The outer covering of an animal. Our dog has a

brown *coat*. **3.** A layer. The painters put a new *coat* of paint on our house. *Noun.*
—To cover with a layer. Dust *coated* the furniture in the old house. I like nuts that are *coated* with sugar. *Verb.*
coat (kōt) *noun, plural* **coats;** *verb,* **coated, coating.**

coating A layer covering a surface. A thin *coating* of ice on the roads made driving dangerous.
coat·ing (kō′ting) *noun, plural* **coatings.**

coat of arms A design on and around a shield or on a drawing of a shield. A coat of arms can serve as the emblem of a person, family, country, or organization.

coax To persuade. My brother tried to *coax* Father into letting him borrow the family car by promising that he would drive very carefully and be home early.
coax (kōks) *verb,* **coaxed, coaxing.**

Coat of Arms

cob The center part of an ear of corn. The kernels grow on the cob in rows.
cob (kob) *noun, plural* **cobs.**

cobalt A silvery white metal. Cobalt is used in making alloys and paints. Cobalt is a chemical element.
co·balt (kō′bôlt) *noun.*

cobbler **1.** A person whose work is mending or making shoes. The *cobbler* put new heels on my shoes. **2.** A fruit pie baked in a deep dish.
cob·bler (kob′lər) *noun, plural* **cobblers.**

cobblestone A round stone. Cobblestones were formerly used to pave streets.
cob·ble·stone (kob′əl stōn′) *noun, plural* **cobblestones.**

Cobblestone Street

cobra A large, poisonous snake found in Africa and Asia. When a cobra becomes excited it spreads the skin about its neck so that it looks like a hood.
co·bra (kō′brə) *noun, plural* **cobras.**

Cobra

cock[1] **1.** A male chicken; rooster. **2.** The male of the turkey and other birds. *Noun.*
—To pull back the hammer of a gun so that it is ready for firing. He *cocked* his rifle. *Verb.*
cock (kok) *noun, plural* **cocks;** *verb,* **cocked, cocking.**

cock[2] To turn up; tip upward. My dog *cocks* his ears when he hears me whistle. *Verb.*
—An upward turn. With a *cock* of his arm, Joe threw the ball. *Noun.*
cock (kok) *verb,* **cocked, cocking;** *noun, plural* **cocks.**

cockatoo A parrot that has a crest. Cockatoos are found in Australia.
cock·a·too (kok′ə-tōō′) *noun, plural* **cockatoos.**

cockle A sea animal that has a hinged shell shaped like a heart. Cockles are used for food.
cock·le (kok′əl) *noun, plural* **cockles.**

cockpit The space in an airplane where the pilot sits.
cock·pit (kok′pit′) *noun, plural* **cockpits.**

cockroach A brown

Cockatoo

or black insect that has a long, flat body and long feelers. Cockroaches are common household pests.

cock·roach (kok′rōch′) *noun, plural* **cock-roaches.**

cocky Too sure of oneself. That bully is rude and *cocky.*

cock·y (kok′ē) *adjective,* **cockier, cockiest.**

cocoa **1.** A brown powder made by grinding up the dried seeds of the cacao tree and removing the fat. **2.** A drink made by mixing cocoa and milk or water. A cup of hot *cocoa* tasted good after walking outside in the snow.

co·coa (kō′kō) *noun, plural* **cocoas.**

coconut The large, round brown fruit of a palm tree. A coconut has a hard shell that is lined with a sweet, white meat. It is filled with a milky liquid that is good to drink.

co·co·nut (kō′kə nut′) *noun, plural* **coconuts.**

Whole Coconut

Split Coconut

Coconut Palm Tree

cocoon The silky case that a caterpillar spins around itself. Caterpillars live in their cocoons while they are growing into moths or butterflies.

co·coon (kə kōōn′) *noun, plural* **cocoons.**

cod A fish that is found in the cold, northern waters of the Atlantic Ocean. The cod is used for food.

cod (kod) *noun, plural* **cods** or **cod.**

code **1.** Any set of signals, words, or symbols used to send messages. Boy scouts learn to send messages by a *code* of signals made with flags. The *code* used in sending messages by telegraph uses long and short sounds that stand for letters. **2.** Any set of laws or rules that people live by. The building *code* in our town requires all apartment building to have fire escapes or fireproof staircases. *Noun.*
—To put into a code. Spies *code* secret information so the enemy will not understand it. *Verb.*

code (kōd) *noun, plural* **codes;** *verb,* **coded, coding.**

coeducation The education of both boys and girls in the same school.

co·ed·u·ca·tion (kō ej′ə kā′shən) *noun.*

coffee **1.** A dark brown drink. Coffee is made from the roasted and ground seeds of a small tropical tree. **2.** The beanlike seeds of the coffee tree.

cof·fee (kô′fē) *noun, plural* **coffees.**

coffin A box in which a dead person is put to be buried.

cof·fin (kô′fin) *noun, plural* **coffins.**

coil **1.** Anything wound in rings. Wind the hose into a *coil* when you finish watering the flowers. **2.** A wire wound into a spiral for carrying electricity. *Noun.*
—To wind round and round. Tom *coiled* the rope. The snake *coiled,* ready to strike. *Verb.*

coil (koil) *noun, plural* **coils;** *verb,* **coiled, coiling.**

coin A piece of metal used as money. A coin is stamped with official government markings to show how much it is worth. Pennies, nickels, dimes, and quarters are coins. *Noun.*
—**1.** To make money by stamping metal. The government *coins* money at the mint. **2.** To invent. Joe *coined* a new word. *Verb.*

coin (koin) *noun, plural* **coins;** *verb,* **coined, coining.**

coincide **1.** To happen at the same time. Jack doesn't know what to do, because football practice *coincides* with his appointment with the dentist. **2.** To be in the same place. The two roads *coincide* after you pass the town.

co·in·cide (kō′in sīd′) *verb,* **coincided, coinciding.**

coincidence The happening of two events at the same time or place. A coincidence seems remarkable because although it looks planned, it really is not. It was just a *coincidence* that the two girls wore the same dress to the party.

co·in·ci·dence (kō in′si dəns) *noun, plural* **coincidences.**

coke A gray-black substance used as fuel. Coke is made by heating coal with almost no air present.

coke (kōk) *noun.*

cold **1.** Having a low temperature; not warm. It is *cold* out today. My dinner was *cold* because I was late. **2.** Feeling a lack of warmth; chilly. The children were *cold* after playing outside in the snow. **3.** Not friendly or kind. Betty greeted me with a *cold* smile because she was angry at me. *Adjective.*

—**1.** A lack of warmth or heat. The *cold* made my teeth chatter. **2.** A common sickness that causes sneezing, coughing, and a running or stuffy nose. Tom was absent from school because he had a *cold. Noun.*
  cold (kōld) *adjective,* **colder, coldest;** *noun,* *plural* **colds.**

cold-blooded Having blood that changes in temperature with the temperature of the surrounding air or water. Snakes and turtles are cold-blooded animals. Cats and dogs are warm-blooded.
  cold-blood·ed (kōld′blud′id) *adjective.*

coliseum A large building or stadium used for sports or other entertainments. We went to an ice-skating show at the *coliseum.*
  col·i·se·um (kol′ə sē′əm) *noun, plural* **coliseums.**

collage A picture made by pasting paper, cloth, metal, and other things on a surface.
  col·lage (kə läzh′) *noun, plural* **collages.**

collapse **1.** To fall in; break down. The force of the explosion caused the walls of the house to *collapse.* The heat caused some of the marchers in the parade to *collapse.* **2.** To fold together. This cot *collapses* so that it can be stored easily. *Verb.*
—The act of falling in or breaking down. Many miners were injured in the *collapse* of the mine shaft. The *collapse* of the talks between the two countries threatened world peace. *Noun.*
  col·lapse (kə laps′) *verb,* **collapsed, collapsing;** *noun, plural* **collapses.**

collar A band or strap that is worn around the neck. Our dog has a leather *collar.* The *collar* of this dress is made of lace. *Noun.*
—**1.** To put a collar on. *Collar* the dog before you let him go outdoors. **2.** To seize. The police *collared* the thief as he ran down the street. *Verb.*
  col·lar (kol′ər) *noun, plural* **collars;** *verb,* **collared, collaring.**

collarbone The bone connecting the breastbone and the shoulder blade.
  col·lar·bone (kol′ər bōn′) *noun, plural* **collarbones.**

colleague A fellow worker. Dr. Smith's *colleagues* take care of his patients when he is away.
  col·league (kol′ēg) *noun, plural* **colleagues.**

collect **1.** To gather together. The boys *collected* wood for their campfire. Bob *collects* stamps as a hobby. Dust often *collects* under beds. **2.** To get payment for. The state *collects* tolls on this highway.
  col·lect (kə lekt′) *verb,* **collected, collecting.**

collection **1.** A gathering together. The *collection* of garbage is done by the city sanitation department. **2.** Money that is collected. We took up a *collection* to buy our teacher a present.
  col·lec·tion (kə lek′shən) *noun, plural* **collections.**

collector A person who collects. My brother is a *collector* of foreign coins.
  col·lec·tor (kə lek′tər) *noun, plural* **collectors.**

college A school that is higher than high school. A college gives degrees to show that a person has completed certain studies.
  col·lege (kol′ij) *noun, plural* **colleges.**

collide To crash against each other; clash. The car and the truck *collided* at the corner.
  col·lide (kə līd′) *verb,* **collided, colliding.**

collie A large, long-haired dog that has a long, narrow head. Collies were originally raised to herd sheep.
  col·lie (kol′ē) *noun, plural* **collies.**

Collie

collision The act of colliding; crash. The two bicycle riders had a *collision,* but neither one was hurt.
  col·li·sion (kə lizh′ən) *noun, plural* **collisions.**

colon[1] A mark of punctuation (:). A colon is used to draw attention to an explanation, a quotation, or a list.
  co·lon (kō′lən) *noun, plural* **colons.**

colon[2] The lower part of the large intestine.
  co·lon (kō′lən) *noun, plural* **colons.**

colonel An army officer. A colonel is below

at; āpe; cär; end; mē; it; īce; hot; ōld; fôrk; wood; fool; oil; out; up; turn; sing; thin; this; hw in white; zh in treasure.
ə stands for a in about, e in taken
i in pencil, o in lemon, and u in circus.

a general but above a major. ▲ Another word that sounds like this is **kernel**.

colo·nel (kurn′əl) *noun, plural* **colonels**.

colonial **1.** Relating to a colony. Great Britain was once a *colonial* power. **2.** Relating to the thirteen British colonies that became the United States of America.

col·o·ni·al (kə lō′nē əl) *adjective.*

colonist A person who lives in a colony.

col·o·nist (kol′ə nist) *noun, plural* **colonists**.

colonize To found a colony or colonies in. Spain *colonized* most of South America.

col·o·nize (kol′ə nīz′) *verb,* **colonized, colonizing**.

colonnade A row of columns. A colonnade is often used to support the roof of a building.

col·on·nade (kol′ə nād′) *noun, plural* **colonnades**.

Colonnade

colony **1.** A group of people who leave their own country and settle in another land. A *colony* of Puritans settled in America. **2.** A territory that is far away from the country that governs it. England once had many *colonies* under its rule. **3. the Colonies.** The thirteen British colonies that became the first states of the United States. **4.** A group of animals or plants of the same kind that live together. Sponges grow in *colonies*.

col·o·ny (kol′ə nē) *noun, plural* **colonies**.

color **1.** Red, blue, or yellow. All other colors are a combination or shade of red, blue, or yellow. The color of something comes from the way the light that the thing reflects strikes the eye. The *color* of grass is green. The *color* of my new winter coat is red. **2.** The coloring of the skin. Ellen has healthy *color* now that she is well again. That company hires workers without regard to race, creed, or *color. Noun.*
—To give color to. We all helped to *color* eggs for Easter. *Verb.*

col·or (kul′ər) *noun, plural* **colors;** *verb,* **colored, coloring**.

Colorado A state in the western United States. Its capital is Denver.

Col·o·rad·o (kol′ə rad′ō *or* kol′ə rä′dō) *noun.*

▲ **Colorado** was named after the Colorado River, which begins in this state. Spanish explorers first gave this name to another river which runs into the Colorado River. The water in the river looked red, and the Spanish name *Colorado* means "reddish."

colored **1.** Having color; not black and white. This book has *colored* pictures. **2.** Of the Negro race.

col·ored (kul′ərd) *adjective.*

colorful **1.** Full of color. Everyone admired Jack's *colorful* necktie. **2.** Interesting or vivid. The old man told us *colorful* stories of his life as a cowboy.

col·or·ful (kul′ər fəl) *adjective.*

coloring **1.** The way in which anything is colored. We drove into the country to see the brilliant *coloring* of the autumn leaves. **2.** Something used to give color. We used *coloring* to make the icing on the cake pink.

col·or·ing (kul′ər ing) *noun, plural* **colorings**.

colt A young horse.

colt (kōlt) *noun, plural* **colts**.

column **1.** A slender upright structure; pillar. A column is used as a support or ornament for part of a building. The roof of the porch on our house is held up by a row of *columns*. **2.** Anything like a column. Can you add up this long *column* of figures? A *column* of black smoke arose from the factory's chimney. **3.** A narrow, vertical section of printed words on a page. This page has two *columns*. **4.** A part of a newspaper written regularly by one person and about a special subject. My brother always reads the sports *column* in the evening paper. **5.** A long row or line. A *column* of soldiers marched down the road.

col·umn (kol′əm) *noun, plural* **columns**.

Column

comb **1.** A piece of plastic, metal, or other

material that has teeth. A comb is used to smooth, arrange, or fasten the hair. Another kind of comb is used to straighten out fibers of wool or cotton before spinning. **2.** A thick, fleshy red crest on the head of roosters and other fowl. *Noun.*
—**1.** To smooth or arrange with a comb. Betty *combed* the dog's fur to get the tangles out. **2.** To look everywhere in; search thoroughly. The police *combed* the woods looking for the lost child. *Verb.*

Comb of a Rooster

comb (kōm) *noun, plural* **combs;** *verb,* **combed, combing.**

combat Fight; battle. The soldier was wounded in *combat. Noun.*
—To fight against. Scientists invent new medicines to *combat* disease. *Verb.*

com·bat (kom′bat *for noun;* kəm bat′ *or* kom′bat *for verb*) *noun, plural* **combats;** *verb,* **combated, combating.**

combination **1.** Something that is formed by combining several things. Vanilla ice cream with chocolate sauce and whipped cream is a very good *combination.* **2.** A series of numbers or letters used to open certain locks. Only the owner of the store knew the *combination* of the safe.

com·bi·na·tion (kom′bə nā′shən) *noun, plural* **combinations.**

combine To join together; unite. Mary *combined* eggs, flour, and milk to make the batter for the pancakes. The thirteen colonies *combined* to form the United States. The two armies *combined* to defeat the enemy.

com·bine (kəm bīn′) *verb,* **combined, combining.**

combustion The act of burning. The car's engine runs by the *combustion* of gasoline.

com·bus·tion (kəm bus′chən) *noun, plural* **combustions.**

come **1.** To move toward. Does your dog *come* to you when you call it? Please *come* here a minute. **2.** To reach a place; arrive. All my friends say they will *come* to my party. The problem has *come* to my attention. The water *came* to a boil.

come (kum) *verb,* **came, come, coming.**

comedian A person who makes people laugh by telling funny jokes or acting out funny stories.

co·me·di·an (kə mē′dē ən) *noun, plural* **comedians.**

comedy A play or motion picture that is funny or has a happy ending.

com·e·dy (kom′ə dē) *noun, plural* **comedies.**

comet A bright heavenly body. A comet has a bright head and a long tail of light. A comet is made up of ice, frozen gases, and dust particles. A comet travels around the sun.

com·et (kom′it) *noun, plural* **comets.**

▲ The word **comet** comes from a Greek word that means "having long hair." The Greeks called a comet a "long-haired star" because a comet's tail looked like long hair flying behind it.

comfort **1.** A pleasant condition with freedom from worry, pain, or want. Although my family doesn't have a lot of money, we live in *comfort.* **2.** A person or thing that gives relief. When Mary was sick in bed, it was a real *comfort* to have her mother nearby. *Noun.*
—To ease the sorrow or pain of someone. We tried to *comfort* the lost child until we could find his mother. *Verb.*

com·fort (kum′fərt) *noun, plural* **comforts;** *verb,* **comforted, comforting.**

comfortable **1.** Giving ease or comfort. My own bed was so *comfortable* after all those nights I had spent in a sleeping bag on our camping trip. **2.** At ease. After a few weeks, the family began to feel very *comfortable* in their new home.

com·fort·a·ble (kum′fər tə bəl *or* kumf′tə bəl) *adjective.*

comic Funny; amusing. The tiny kitten hissing at the big dog was a *comic* sight. *Adjective.*
—**1.** A person who makes people laugh; comedian. That *comic* has a weekly show on television. **2. comics.** A group of comic strips. Our Sunday newspaper has colored *comics* in it. *Noun.*

com·ic (kom′ik) *adjective; noun, plural* **comics.**

comical Funny; amusing. We all laughed at the clown's *comical* tricks.

com·i·cal (kom′i kəl) *adjective.*

comic book A magazine or booklet of comic strips.

at; āpe; cär; end; mē; it; īce; hot; ōld;
fôrk; wood; fōōl; oil; out; up; turn; sing;
thin; this; hw in white; zh in treasure.
ə stands for a in about, e in taken
i in pencil, o in lemon, and u in circus.

comic strip A group of drawings that tell a story or part of a story. Comic strips usually tell stories that are funny or full of adventure.

©1974 UNITED FEATURE SYNDICATE, INC.

Comic Strip

comma A mark of punctuation (,). A comma is used to separate ideas or things in a series. Commas also help you to understand or read a sentence correctly.
com·ma (kom′ə) *noun, plural* **commas.**

command 1. To give an order to; direct. Jack *commanded* his dog to sit still. 2. To have power over; rule. The general *commands* the army. *Verb.*
—1. Order; direction. The soldiers obeyed the sergeant's *command.* 2. The power to command. The sheriff was in *command* of the search party. 3. The ability to use or control. Pierre has a good *command* of the English language even though he has only been in America a short time. *Noun.*
com·mand (kə mand′) *verb,* **commanded, commanding;** *noun, plural* **commands.**

commander 1. A person who is in command; leader. 2. A navy officer. A commander is below a captain but above a lieutenant. The two ranks of commander are **lieutenant commander** and **commander.**
com·mand·er (kə man′dər) *noun, plural* **commanders.**

commandment A law or command. "Thou shalt not steal" was one of the Ten *Commandments* given by God to Moses.
com·mand·ment (kə mand′mənt) *noun, plural* **commandments.**

commence To begin; start. The opening ceremonies for the game *commenced* with everyone singing the national anthem.

com·mence (kə mens′) *verb,* **commenced, commencing.**

commencement The day or ceremony of graduation. At commencement, a school or college gives diplomas or degrees to students who have completed a course of study.
com·mence·ment (kə mens′mənt) *noun, plural* **commencements.**

comment A remark or note. A comment explains or gives an opinion of a person or thing. After the game, the coach made a few *comments* in praise of the team's playing. *Noun.*
—To make a comment; remark. Mr. Brown would not *comment* on the rumor that he would run for governor. *Verb.*
com·ment (kom′ent) *noun, plural* **comments;** *verb,* **commented, commenting.**

commentator A person who comments on the news on radio or television.
com·men·ta·tor (kom′ən tā′tər) *noun, plural* **commentators.**

commerce The buying and selling of goods; trade; business. There is much *commerce* between states of the United States.
com·merce (kom′ərs) *noun.*

commercial Relating to business or trade. Jack is taking accounting and other *commercial* subjects in high school. *Adjective.*
—An advertising message on radio or television. The television show was interrupted every few minutes by a *commercial. Noun.*
com·mer·cial (kə mur′shəl) *adjective; noun, plural* **commercials.**

commission 1. A group of persons who are chosen to do certain work. The mayor named a *commission* to find out the causes of pollution in the city. 2. Money given for work done. The salesman receives a *commission* for every car he sells. 3. The act of committing. There has been a rise in the *commission* of crimes in the city. 4. A position of military rank. The soldiers received their *commissions* as lieutenants after completing a training course. 5. Working order. A dead battery has put our car out of *commission. Noun.*
—To give a person the right or power to do something. The school *commissioned* the architect to design a new gymnasium. *Verb.*
com·mis·sion (kə mish′ən) *noun, plural* **commissions;** *verb,* **commissioned, commissioning.**

commissioner A person who is in charge of a department of a government. The park *commissioner* has just announced plans to build a skating rink in the park.
com·mis·sion·er (kə mish′ə nər) *noun, plural* **commissioners.**

130

commit **1.** To do or perform. The man *committed* a crime when he robbed the bank. The baseball player *committed* two errors in the game. **2.** To devote; pledge. The town *committed* itself to raising money for the new hospital.
   com·mit (kə mit′) *verb*, **committed, committing.**

committee A group of persons chosen to do certain work. The decorations *committee* decorated the gym for the school dance.
   com·mit·tee (kə mit′ē) *noun, plural* **committees.**

commodity Something that can be bought and sold. Wheat, corn, and rice are agricultural *commodities.*
   com·mod·i·ty (kə mod′ə tē) *noun, plural* **commodities.**

common **1.** Happening often; familiar; usual. Where I live, snow is *common* in the winter. **2.** Belonging equally to all; shared by all alike. It is *common* knowledge that the earth is round. **3.** Ordinary; average. The dandelion is a *common* weed.
   com·mon (kom′ən) *adjective,* **commoner, commonest.**
   in common. Shared equally. The two friends had many interests *in common.*

commonplace Ordinary; not interesting, new, or remarkable. Snow is *commonplace* in Maine but not in Florida.
   com·mon·place (kom′ən plās′) *adjective.*

common sense Ordinary good judgment. A person learns common sense from experience, not from school or study. It is only *common sense* to make sure a campfire is completely out before leaving it.

commonwealth A nation or state that is governed by the people. The United States is a commonwealth. Certain states of the United States use Commonwealth instead of State as an official name.
   com·mon·wealth (kom′ən welth′) *noun, plural* **commonwealths.**

commotion A noisy confusion; disorder. There was a *commotion* at the ball park as the crowd booed the umpire's decision.
   com·mo·tion (kə mō′shən) *noun, plural* **commotions.**

communicate To exchange or pass along feelings, thoughts, or information. People communicate with each other by speaking or writing. When I was away at camp, I *communicated* with my family by writing letters and telephoning.
   com·mu·ni·cate (kə myoo′ni kāt′) *verb,* **communicated, communicating.**

communication **1.** An exchanging or sharing of feelings, thoughts, or information. The telephone makes *communication* over great distances possible. The Indians used smoke signals as a means of *communication.* **2. communications.** A system for sending messages by telephone, telegraph, radio, or television. *Communications* in the flooded town are still not working.
   com·mu·ni·ca·tion (kə myoo′ni kā′shən) *noun, plural* **communications.**

communion **1.** A sharing of feelings or thoughts. There was a close *communion* between the father and his son. **2. Communion.** A religious service commemorating the last meal of Jesus and His apostles on the night before the Crucifixion.
   com·mun·ion (kə myoon′yən) *noun, plural* **communions.**

communism A system of social organization in which all property and goods are owned by the government and are shared equally by all the people. The government of the Soviet Union is based on this system.
   com·mu·nism (kom′yə niz′əm) *noun.*

communist A person who believes in communism as a way of life or who belongs to a Communist Party.
   com·mu·nist (kom′yə nist) *noun, plural* **communists.**

Communist Party A political party that is in favor of communism.

community A group of people who live together in the same place. Our *community* voted to build a new library. She lives in a rural *community* that is quite far away from the nearest city.
   com·mu·ni·ty (kə myoo′nə tē) *noun, plural* **communities.**

commute To travel regularly to and from work over quite a long distance. Father *commutes* to the city every day by train.
   com·mute (kə myoot′) *verb,* **commuted, commuting.**

compact¹ **1.** Tightly packed together; dense. *Compact* snow is good for making snowballs. **2.** Taking up a small amount of space. We have very *compact* cooking equipment for camping. *Adjective.*

at; āpe; cär; end; mē; it; īce; hot; ōld;
fôrk; wood; fool; oil; out; up; turn; sing;
thin; this; hw in white; zh in treasure.
ə stands for a in about, e in taken
i in pencil, o in lemon, and u in circus.

—1. A small case for face powder. 2. An automobile that is smaller than a standard model. *Noun.*

  com·pact (kəm pakt′ *for adjective;* kom′pakt *for noun*) *adjective; noun, plural* **compacts.**

compact² An agreement. The Mayflower *Compact* was an agreement among the Pilgrims as to how their new colony would be governed.

  com·pact (kom′pakt) *noun, plural* **compacts.**

companion A person who often goes along with another; friend; comrade. Tom and Jack were constant *companions* at camp last summer.

  com·pan·ion (kəm pan′yən) *noun, plural* **companions.**

companionship The relation between good companions; friendship. Sue missed the *companionship* of her friends when she moved to a new town.

  com·pan·ion·ship (kəm pan′yən ship′) *noun.*

company 1. A guest or guests. We are having *company* for dinner. 2. A business firm or organization. My father works for a lumber *company.* 3. Companionship. When the rest of the family is away, I am grateful for my dog's *company.* 4. A group of performers. A *company* of musicians will present a concert at the town hall tonight.

  com·pa·ny (kum′pə nē) *noun, plural* **companies.**

comparative 1. That compares one thing with another. We made a *comparative* study of a frog and a worm in science class. 2. Measured or judged by comparing. Jack is a *comparative* stranger to me, because I've only met him once. *Adjective.*

—The form of an adjective or adverb that gives the idea of "more." For example, the comparative of "short" is "shorter": Mary is shorter (more short) than Sue. *Noun.*

  com·par·a·tive (kəm par′ə tiv) *adjective; noun, plural* **comparatives.**

compare 1. To study to find out how persons or things are alike or different. Tom and Jack *compared* their watches and saw that Jack's watch was five minutes ahead of Tom's. 2. To say or think that something is like something else; liken. The writer *compared* the sound of the thunder to the boom of big guns.

  com·pare (kəm per′) *verb,* **compared, comparing.**

comparison 1. The finding out of the likenesses and the differences between persons or things. A *comparison* of the two teams seems to show that Saturday's game will be close. 2. A likeness; similarity. There is no *comparison* between those two cars when it comes to speed.

  com·par·i·son (kəm par′ə sən) *noun, plural* **comparisons.**

compartment A separate division or section. My desk drawer has *compartments* for pencils, rubber bands, and paper clips.

  com·part·ment (kəm pärt′mənt) *noun, plural* **compartments.**

compass 1. An instrument for showing directions. A compass has a needle that points to the north. Airplane pilots, ship captains, and hikers all use a compass so they will always know in what direction they are going. 2. An instrument for drawing circles or measuring distances. A compass is made up of two arms joined together at the top. One of the arms ends in a point and the other one holds a pencil.

Compass

  com·pass (kum′pəs) *noun, plural* **compasses.**

compassion Sympathy for someone else's suffering or misfortune, together with the desire to help. Ruth had such *compassion* for the lonely old woman that she visited her in the hospital and brought her presents.

  com·pas·sion (kəm pash′ən) *noun.*

compel To force. The policemen *compelled* the crowds to stay away from the burning building.

  com·pel (kəm pel′) *verb,* **compelled, compelling.**

compensate 1. To pay. The company *compensated* Mary for the extra hours she worked. The government *compensated* the farmer for the land they took from him to build the highway. 2. To make up for something. The football player's speed *compensated* for his small size.

  com·pen·sate (kom′pən sāt′) *verb,* **compensated, compensating.**

compensation Something that makes up for something else. The company gave the worker money as a *compensation* for the extra work he had done.

  com·pen·sa·tion (kom′pən sā′shən) *noun, plural* **compensations.**

compete To try to win or gain something from another or others. The two girls *competed* against each other for first prize in the spelling contest.
com·pete (kəm pēt′) *verb*, **competed, competing.**

competent Able and capable. Only *competent* swimmers should use the deep end of the pool.
com·pe·tent (kom′pət ənt) *adjective.*

competition 1. The act of trying to win or gain something from another or others; rivalry. Our team was in *competition* with three others for the championship. 2. A contest. George is going to enter the swimming *competition.*
com·pe·ti·tion (kom′pə tish′ən) *noun, plural* **competitions.**

competitive Involving or using competition. Most sports are *competitive.*
com·pet·i·tive (kəm pet′ə tiv) *adjective.*

competitor A person or thing that tries to win or gain something from another or others. Sarah's main *competitor* in running for school president was her best friend. My father's gas station has two *competitors* within two blocks.
com·pet·i·tor (kəm pet′ə tər) *noun, plural* **competitors.**

compile To collect or put together in a list or report. Libraries *compile* facts about all the books they have on their shelves.
com·pile (kəm pīl′) *verb,* **compiled, compiling.**

complacent Pleased with oneself; satisfied. The boxing champion was so *complacent* that he did not even bother to train for his match with the challenger.
com·pla·cent (kəm plā′sənt) *adjective.*

complain 1. To say that something is wrong; find fault. My father *complains* that his train is never on time. My brother *complained* all day about a stomachache. 2. To make an accusation or charge. We *complained* to the police about our noisy neighbors.
com·plain (kəm plān′) *verb,* **complained, complaining.**

complaint 1. A finding fault. We took our *complaint* about the rude clerk to the store manager. 2. A cause for complaining. I have no *complaints* about the food in this restaurant. 3. An accusation or charge. The storekeeper made a *complaint* against the man that had robbed his store.
com·plaint (kəm plānt′) *noun, plural* **complaints.**

complement Something that makes complete. The football team now has its full *complement* of players. *Noun.*
—To make complete. The background music nicely *complements* the acting in the movie. *Verb.* ▲ Another word that sounds like this is **compliment.**
com·ple·ment (kom′plə mənt *for noun;* kom′plə ment′ *for verb*) *noun, plural* **complements;** *verb,* **complemented, complementing.**

complete 1. Having all its parts; whole; entire. Our school library has the *complete* writings of William Shakespeare. 2. Ended; finished. Rick promised his parents he would not go out and play until his homework was *complete.* 3. Thorough; perfect. The new play promised to be a *complete* success. *Adjective.*
—1. To make whole or perfect. Joe is trying to *complete* his collection of baseball cards. 2. To bring to an end; finish. Lucy wanted to *complete* the first chapter of her book before going to bed. *Verb.*
com·plete (kəm plēt′) *adjective; verb,* **completed, completing.**

completely 1. Wholly; entirely. Jill was being *completely* honest when she told the teacher that she had not tripped Pam on purpose. 2. Thoroughly; perfectly. Anne was *completely* exhausted after skiing all day.
com·plete·ly (kəm plēt′lē) *adverb.*

completion 1. The act of completing. The early *completion* of our house meant that we would be able to move in sooner. 2. The condition of being completed. Steve hoped to bring his science project to *completion* before spring vacation.
com·ple·tion (kəm plē′shən) *noun.*

complex 1. Hard or difficult to understand or do. I don't know how to solve this *complex* arithmetic problem. 2. Made up of many parts. My brother studied for months before he learned to fix such a *complex* machine as a computer.
com·plex (kəm pleks′) *adjective.*

complexion 1. The color and look of a person's skin. Alice has a lovely rosy *complexion.* 2. The general look or character of anything. The substitution of two new players on

at; āpe; cär; end; mē; it; īce; hot; ōld;
fôrk; wood; fōol; oil; out; up; turn; sing;
thin; this; hw in white; zh in treasure.
ə stands for a in about, e in taken
i in pencil, o in lemon, and u in circus.

our team changed the whole *complexion* of the game, and we won.
com·plex·ion (kəm plek′shən) *noun, plural* **complexions.**

complexity The quality of being complex. The *complexity* of the arithmetic problem puzzled all the students in the class.
com·plex·i·ty (kəm plek′sə tē) *noun, plural* **complexities.**

complicate To make harder to understand or do. His little brother's attempts to help only *complicated* John's job of washing the car.
com·pli·cate (kom′plə kāt′) *verb,* **complicated, complicating.**

complicated Hard to understand or do. The directions for putting together the bicycle were too *complicated* for me to follow.
com·pli·cat·ed (kom′plə kā′ tid) *adjective.*

complication A confused or difficult condition. The snowstorm that closed the airport caused a *complication* in our travel plans.
com·pli·ca·tion (kom′plə kā′shən) *noun, plural* **complications.**

compliment Something good that is said in praise or admiration. Joan receives many *compliments* on her cooking. *Noun.*
—To praise or admire. The teacher *complimented* Ellen on her well-written composition. *Verb.* ▲ Another word that sounds like this is **complement.**
com·pli·ment (kom′plə mənt *for noun;* kom′plə ment′ *for verb*) *noun, plural* **compliments;** *verb,* **complimented, complimenting.**

complimentary 1. Containing or expressing praise or admiration. The teacher made a *complimentary* remark to Mr. Smith about his daughter's work. 2. Without charge; free. The coach gave us two *complimentary* tickets to the football game.
com·pli·men·ta·ry (kom′plə men′tər ē *or* kom′plə men′trē) *adjective.*

comply To act in agreement with a request or rule. I *complied* with the doctor's orders and stayed home until my cold was better.
com·ply (kəm plī′) *verb,* **complied, complying.**

compose 1. To make up. The material in this dress is *composed* of cotton and rayon. Twelve people *compose* a jury. 2. To put together; create. Jack and Betty *composed* a new school cheer. The musician *composed* an opera. 3. To make quiet or calm. She tried to *compose* herself after hearing the sad news.
com·pose (kəm pōz′) *verb,* **composed, composing.**

composer A person who composes a musical work or anything else. Johann Sebastian Bach is a very famous *composer.*
com·pos·er (kəm pō′zər) *noun, plural* **composers.**

composite Made up of various parts. The photographer made a *composite* picture by putting together parts of a few old snapshots.
com·pos·ite (kəm poz′it) *adjective.*

composition 1. The making of anything. The *composition* of the musician's new opera took two years. 2. The parts that make up something. The scientist studied the moon rock to find out its *composition.* 3. Something that is put together or created. Steve wrote a *composition* for English class about life in colonial America.
com·po·si·tion (kom′pə zish′ən) *noun, plural* **compositions.**

composure Self-control; calmness. The mother's *composure* when the fire broke out helped her to save all her children.
com·po·sure (kəm pō′zhər) *noun.*

compound Made up of two or more parts. "Football" is a *compound* word. A grasshopper has *compound* eyes that allow it to see in almost all directions at once. *Adjective.*
—To mix or combine. A druggist's job is to *compound* medicines. *Verb.*
—1. A mixture or combination. Steel is a *compound* of iron and carbon. 2. A substance that is formed by the chemical combination of two or more elements. Water is a *compound* that is made of hydrogen and oxygen. *Noun.*
com·pound (kom′pound′ *for adjective and noun;* kəm pound′ *for verb*) *adjective; verb,* **compounded, compounding;** *noun, plural* **compounds.**

comprehend To understand. The teacher felt that her students still did not *comprehend* how to add and subtract fractions.
com·pre·hend (kom′pri hend′) *verb,* **comprehended, comprehending.**

▲ The word **comprehend** used to mean "to catch" or "to take hold of." For example, one horseman could ride fast enough to *comprehend* another. This led to our use of *comprehend* to mean "to take hold of with the mind" or "to understand."

comprehension The power of understanding. Pam said that a knowledge of how computers work was beyond her *comprehension.*
com·pre·hen·sion (kom′pri hen′shən) *noun, plural* **comprehensions.**

134

compress To press or squeeze together. The city has big machines that *compress* garbage so it will not take up so much room in the dump. *Verb.*
—A pad or cloth used to put pressure, heat, or cold on some part of the body. The mother put a cold *compress* on her child's head when he had a fever. *Noun.*
　com·press (kəm pres′ *for verb;* kom′pres′ *for noun*) *verb,* **compressed, compressing;** *noun, plural* **compresses.**

comprise To consist of. The state of Hawaii *comprises* eight main islands and many smaller ones.
　com·prise (kəm prīz′) *verb,* **comprised, comprising.**

compromise The settlement of an argument or disagreement. A compromise is reached by having each side give up part of its demands. When Rick refused to eat his spinach, his mother offered him a *compromise* and made him eat only half of it. *Noun.*
—To reach a settlement by agreeing that each side will give up some part of its demands. When the two boys wanted to watch different television programs, they *compromised* and watched parts of both. *Verb.*
　com·pro·mise (kom′prə mīz′) *noun, plural* **compromises;** *verb,* **compromised, compromising.**

compulsory Required by law or rules. Gym class is *compulsory* in this school unless a student has an excuse from a doctor.
　com·pul·so·ry (kəm pul′sər ē) *adjective.*

compute To find out or calculate by using mathematics; reckon. The builder *computed* the cost of a new garage. Scientists have *computed* how far away other planets are from the earth.
　com·pute (kəm pyo̅o̅t′) *verb,* **computed, computing.**

computer An electronic machine that can solve difficult and complicated mathematical problems at very high speeds.
　com·put·er (kəm pyo̅o̅′tər) *noun, plural* **computers.**

comrade A close friend who shares the same work or interests with another; companion.
　com·rade (kom′rad) *noun, plural* **comrades.**

▲ The word **comrade** comes from the Latin word for "room." *Comrade* first meant "someone who shares a room with another person."

---

concave Curving inward. The inside of a bowl is *concave.* The arch of a person's foot is *concave.*
　con·cave (kon kāv′ *or* kon′kāv) *adjective.*

conceal To put or keep out of sight; hide. Father *concealed* the car keys under the seat. Helen *concealed* her anger by smiling.
　con·ceal (kən sēl′) *verb,* **concealed, concealing.**

Concave　　Convex

concede To admit as true. The candidate for mayor would not *concede* that he had lost the election until all the votes were counted.
　con·cede (kən sēd′) *verb,* **conceded, conceding.**

conceited Having too high an opinion of oneself or of one's ability to do things. The *conceited* boy was always talking about how good-looking he was.
　con·ceit·ed (kən sē′tid) *adjective.*

conceive To think or imagine; think up. Scientists *conceived* the plan for the first spacecraft. It is hard to *conceive* of what life was like during the days of the cave men.
　con·ceive (kən sēv′) *verb,* **conceived, conceiving.**

concentrate 1. To bring together in one place. The population in our country is *concentrated* in the cities. The team *concentrated* their efforts on winning the game. 2. To make stronger or thicker. That company *concentrates* orange juice and sells it in small cans. 3. To pay attention. Bill could not *concentrate* on his homework because the room was too noisy.
　con·cen·trate (kon′sən trāt′) *verb,* **concentrated, concentrating.**

concentration 1. The act of concentrating or the state of being concentrated. Because of the shampoo's *concentration,* you don't have to use very much of it to get a lot of suds. 2. Close attention. Jim's *concentration* on the television program was so deep that he didn't hear the doorbell.
　con·cen·tra·tion (kon′sən trā′shən) *noun, plural* **concentrations.**

---

at; āpe; cär; end; mē; it; īce; hot; ōld; fôrk; wood; fo̅o̅l; oil; out; up; turn; sing; thin; this; hw in white; zh in treasure.
ə stands for **a** in about, **e** in taken **i** in pencil, **o** in lemon, and **u** in circus.

concept A general idea; thought. My cousin is always late for everything because he has no *concept* of what time it is.
con·cept (kon′sept) *noun, plural* **concepts.**

conception An idea; concept. Learning about travel in space gives you some *conception* of how enormous the universe must be.
con·cep·tion (kən sep′shən) *noun, plural* **conceptions.**

concern **1.** To be important to; have to do with. What Mother said about saving money *concerns* our whole family. **2.** To worry; trouble. Her bad cough *concerned* her friends. *Verb.*
—**1.** Something that is important to a person. Taking care of the puppy is my *concern.* **2.** Worried interest. He was full of *concern* for his sick brother. **3.** A business. Mr. Smith owns a clothing *concern. Noun.*
con·cern (kən surn′) *verb,* **concerned, concerning;** *noun, plural* **concerns.**

concerning About; regarding. Mike wrote me a long letter *concerning* his new school.
con·cern·ing (kən sur′ning) *preposition.*

concert A performance of music by a number of musicians. We went to a band *concert* in the park.
con·cert (kon′sərt) *noun, plural* **concerts.**

concerto A piece of music for one or more musical instruments accompanied by an orchestra.
con·cer·to (kən cher′tō) *noun, plural* **concertos.**

concession **1.** The act of conceding or granting. As a *concession,* Dad let Sally go camping with her older sisters. **2.** Something conceded. Father made a *concession* and let me stay up late on a school night so I could watch the football game. **3.** The right to something granted by a government or other authority. The town gave Mr. Alberts the *concession* to sell hot dogs in the park.
con·ces·sion (kən sesh′ən) *noun, plural* **concessions.**

conch The large, coiled shell of a sea animal.
conch (kongk *or* konch) *noun, plural* **conchs** or **conches.**

concise Saying much in few words. The coach's instructions to the team were clear and *concise.*
con·cise (kən sīs′) *adjective.*

conclude **1.** To bring to

Conch

an end; finish. When the band *concluded* the playing of the national anthem, the baseball game began. **2.** To decide after thinking. After hearing all the facts, he *concluded* that he had been wrong.
con·clude (kən klood′) *verb,* **concluded, concluding.**

conclusion **1.** The end of something. The *conclusion* of the movie was very happy. **2.** Arrangement; settlement. The *conclusion* of the treaty between the two countries took many months. **3.** Something decided after thinking. Tom came to the *conclusion* that he wanted to be a doctor when he grew older.
con·clu·sion (kən kloo′zhən) *noun, plural* **conclusions.**

concrete Able to be seen and touched; real. A chair is a *concrete* object. *Adjective.*
—A mixture of cement, pebbles, sand, and water. Concrete becomes very hard when it dries. Concrete is used in building office buildings and bridges and in paving roads and sidewalks. *Noun.*
con·crete (kon′krēt *or* kon krēt′) *adjective; noun.*

concussion **1.** A sudden, violent shaking. The house shook from the *concussion* of the explosion. **2.** An injury to the brain or spine caused by a fall or blow. Falling out of the tree on his head caused him to have a *concussion.*
con·cus·sion (kən kush′ən) *noun, plural* **concussions.**

condemn **1.** To be against; disapprove of. Many people *condemn* smoking. **2.** To find someone guilty. The judge *condemned* the thief to ten years in jail. **3.** To declare to be no longer safe or fit for use. The city government *condemned* the old building because it was falling down.
con·demn (kən dem′) *verb,* **condemned, condemning.**

condensation **1.** The act of condensing something. The *condensation* of steam causes it to change into water. **2.** Something condensed. Alice read a *condensation* of the long novel.
con·den·sa·tion (kon′den sā′shən) *noun, plural* **condensations.**

condense **1.** To make less; thicken; shorten. You can *condense* milk by boiling away much of the water in it. The writer *condensed* the long story to a short story. **2.** To change from a gas to a liquid or solid form. Steam *condenses* to water when cooled.
con·dense (kən dens′) *verb,* **condensed, condensing.**

condition **1.** The way that a person or thing is. That athlete keeps in good *condition* by doing exercises. **2.** Something needed for something else; a thing that something else depends on. Being a good skater is one of the *conditions* for getting on the hockey team. **3. conditions.** State of affairs; circumstances. Poor working *conditions* caused the employees to go on strike. *Noun.*
—**1.** To put in a healthy or good condition. Carl exercises to *condition* his body. **2.** To make used to something; accustom. Living at the North Pole soon *conditioned* the explorers to cold weather. *Verb.*
> **con·di·tion** (kən dish′ən) *noun, plural* **conditions;** *verb,* **conditioned, conditioning.**

condor A large bird with a hooked bill and a bare head and neck. A condor is a kind of vulture. It is found in the mountains of South America and California.
> **con·dor** (kon′dər) *noun, plural* **condors.**

Condor

conduct The way someone behaves. My mother was thankful for my little brother's good *conduct* in front of the guests. *Noun.*
—**1.** To behave. The spoiled child *conducted* himself badly. **2.** To direct or lead. Our music teacher will *conduct* the school orchestra. **3.** To take charge of; control; manage. Mrs. Smith *conducts* a successful hardware business. **4.** To carry or transmit. Cast iron *conducts* heat evenly. *Verb.*
> **con·duct** (kon′dukt *for noun;* kən dukt′ *for verb*) *noun, plural* **conducts;** *verb,* **conducted, conducting.**

conductor **1.** A person who conducts. Our music teacher is also the *conductor* of the school orchestra. **2.** A person on a train or bus who collects fares. The conductor also calls out the names of stops. **3.** Something that transmits heat, electricity, or sound. Plastic is a poor *conductor* of heat.
> **con·duc·tor** (kən duk′tər) *noun, plural* **conductors.**

cone **1.** A solid, pointed object that has a flat, round base. **2.** Something shaped like a cone. I like to eat ice cream in a *cone.* **3.** A fruit with scales, that grows on a pine tree or other evergreen tree. The cone bears the seeds.
> **cone** (kōn) *noun, plural* **cones.**

The teepee has the shape of a **cone.**

confederacy **1.** A group of countries, states, or people joined together for a common purpose. The five Indian tribes joined to form a *confederacy.* **2. the Confederacy.** The eleven southern states that left the Union in 1860 and 1861.
> **con·fed·er·a·cy** (kən fed′ər ə sē) *noun, plural* **confederacies.**

confederate **1.** A person or group that joins with another for a common purpose. The bank robber and his *confederates* were arrested by the police. **2. Confederate.** A person who fought for or supported the Confederacy. *Noun.*
—**Confederate.** Of the Confederacy. *Adjective.*
> **con·fed·er·ate** (kən fed′ər it) *noun, plural* **confederates;** *adjective.*

confederation **1.** The act of joining together to form a confederacy. The two small countries began plans for *confederation.* **2.** A group of countries or states that are joined together for a common purpose. From 1781 to 1789 the American states formed a *confederation.*
> **con·fed·er·a·tion** (kən fed′ə rā′shən) *noun, plural* **confederations.**

confer **1.** To meet and talk together. The coach of the football team will *confer* with his assistants about the new player. **2.** To give. The general will *confer* a medal on the brave soldier.
> **con·fer** (kən fur′) *verb,* **conferred, conferring.**

at; āpe; cär; end; mē; it; īce; hot; ōld;
fôrk; wood; fōol; oil; out; up; turn; sing;
thin; **th**is; **hw** in white; **zh** in treasure.
ə stands for **a** in about, **e** in taken
i in pencil, **o** in lemon, and **u** in circus.

conference A meeting. A *conference* of doctors from all over the state was held to discuss new ways to treat disease.
con·fer·ence (kon′fər əns) *noun, plural* conferences.

confess 1. To admit. The crook *confessed* his guilt. She *confessed* that she really liked him. 2. To tell a priest your sins.
con·fess (kən fes′) *verb,* confessed, confessing.

confession The confessing of something. The man made a full *confession* to the crime.
con·fes·sion (kən fesh′ən) *noun, plural* confessions.

confide To tell a secret to someone; trust. Janet always *confides* in her best friends. He *confided* his worries to his mother.
con·fide (kən fīd′) *verb,* confided, confiding.

confidence 1. Trust or faith. I have *confidence* in his honesty. 2. Faith in oneself. Mary gave the answer with *confidence*. 3. Trust that a person will not tell a secret. Sue told me her plans for the surprise party in *confidence*.
con·fi·dence (kon′fə dəns) *noun.*

confident Having trust or faith; sure. I am *confident* that our team will win the game.
con·fi·dent (kon′fə dənt) *adjective.*

confidential Secret. The President got a *confidential* letter from the ambassador.
con·fi·den·tial (kon′fə den′shəl) *adjective.*

confine To hold or keep in; limit. The sheriff *confined* the outlaw in a jail cell. Jean's bad cold *confined* her to her bed. *Verb.*
—A limit; boundary. The dog was not allowed to go outside the *confines* of the yard. *Noun.*
con·fine (kən fīn′ *for verb;* kon′fīn *for noun*) *verb,* confined, confining; *noun, plural* confines.

confirm 1. To show to be true or correct. The newspaper *confirmed* reports of a flood. 2. To consent to; approve. The Senate *confirmed* the trade agreement. 3. To admit a person to full membership in a church or synagogue.
con·firm (kən furm′) *verb,* confirmed, confirming.

confirmation 1. The act of confirming something. He called the hotel for *confirmation* of his reservation. 2. The ceremony of admitting a person to full membership in a church or synagogue.
con·fir·ma·tion (kon′fər mā′shən) *noun, plural* confirmations.

confiscate To take something by authority. The government *confiscated* the man's property when he couldn't pay his taxes.
con·fis·cate (kon′fis kāt′) *verb,* confiscated, confiscating.

conflict 1. A long fight; war. The War of 1812 was a *conflict* between America and England. 2. A strong disagreement. The two newspaper stories about the fire are in *conflict. Noun.*
—To disagree strongly. The two accounts of the accident *conflict. Verb.*
con·flict (kon′flikt *for noun;* kən flikt′ *for verb*) *noun, plural* conflicts; *verb,* conflicted, conflicting.

conform 1. To act or think in a way that agrees with a rule or a standard. New students were told that they must *conform* to the rules of the school. 2. To be the same; be like. The house *conformed* to the architect's plans.
con·form (kən fôrm′) *verb,* conformed, conforming.

confront To meet or face. The soldiers *confronted* the enemy soldiers. A hard problem *confronted* her.
con·front (kən frunt′) *verb,* confronted, confronting.

confuse 1. To mix up; bewilder. The hard rules for the game *confuse* me. The street signs *confused* the driver and he took a wrong turn. 2. To mistake one for another. People are always *confusing* the twins.
con·fuse (kən fyōōz′) *verb,* confused, confusing.

confusion 1. Disorder or bewilderment. Everything in my desk drawer was in *confusion*. In his *confusion*, he gave the wrong answer. 2. A mistaking of one person or thing for another. Mrs. Young's *confusion* of David with his brother embarrassed her.
con·fu·sion (kən fyōō′zhən) *noun, plural* confusions.

congratulate To give a person one's good wishes or praise for success or for something nice that has happened. We *congratulated* Ruth on doing such a good job on her science project.
con·grat·u·late (kən grach′ə lāt′) *verb,* congratulated, congratulating.

congratulations Good wishes or praise given for a person's success or for something nice that has happened. We offered *congratulations* to Phil when he won the race.
con·grat·u·la·tions (kən grach′ə lā′shənz) *noun plural.*

congregate To come together in a crowd. People *congregated* around the famous movie star to get her autograph.

con·gre·gate (kong′grə gāt′) *verb*, **congregated, congregating.**

congregation A gathering or crowd of people. There was a large *congregation* at church Sunday.
con·gre·ga·tion (kong′grə gā′shən) *noun, plural* **congregations.**

congress **1.** An assembly of people who make laws; lawmaking body. Many republics have a congress. **2. Congress.** A branch of the government of the United States that makes laws. Congress is made up of the Senate and the House of Representatives.
con·gress (kong′gris) *noun, plural* **congresses.**

congressman A member of Congress. When people say congressman, they usually mean a member of the House of Representatives.
con·gress·man (kong′gris mən) *noun, plural* **congressmen.**

conjunction **1.** A word used to connect words, phrases, clauses, and sentences. *And, or,* and *if* are conjunctions. In the sentence "He went fishing, but I stayed home," the word "but" is a conjunction. **2.** A joining together or combination. The President must act in *conjunction* with Congress to get laws passed.
con·junc·tion (kən jungk′shən) *noun, plural* **conjunctions.**

connect To fasten or join together. John and his father *connected* the trailer to the car. A highway *connects* the two towns.
con·nect (kə nekt′) *verb*, **connected, connecting.**

Connecticut A state in the northeastern United States. Its capital is Hartford.
Con·nect·i·cut (kə net′i kət) *noun.*

▲ The name **Connecticut** comes from an Indian word that means "a place beside the long river." Settlers then gave the name to the river, too. Soon they used it for villages near the Connecticut River. Later they used it for the state in which this river is located.

---

connection **1.** The act of fastening or joining things. The *connection* of the pipes under the sink was hard work. **2.** Relationship; association. The banker's *connection* with the bank lasted many years. The city is studying the *connection* between heavy traffic and air pollution. **3.** Something that connects. The repairman looked for the bad *connection* in the radio.
con·nec·tion (kə nek′shən) *noun, plural* **connections.**

conquer To overcome; defeat. The army

conquered the small country. He tried to *conquer* the habit of biting his nails.
con·quer (kong′kər) *verb*, **conquered, conquering.**

conqueror A person who conquers. In ancient times, Alexander the Great was a powerful *conqueror.*
con·quer·or (kong′kər ər) *noun, plural* **conquerors.**

conquest **1.** The act of conquering something. The *conquest* of the country took the invading army many months. **2.** Something conquered. Mexico was once a *conquest* of Spain.
con·quest (kon′kwest *or* kong′kwest) *noun, plural* **conquests.**

conscience A feeling about what is right and what is wrong. Your conscience tells you to do right and warns when you are doing something wrong. The lie that he told troubled his *conscience.*
con·science (kon′shəns) *noun, plural* **consciences.**

conscientious Showing honesty, thought, and care. Agnes does *conscientious* work at school.
con·sci·en·tious (kon′shē en′shəs) *adjective.*

conscious **1.** Knowing or realizing; aware. He was *conscious* of someone tapping his shoulder. **2.** Able to see and feel things; awake. He remained *conscious* even though he was hit hard on the head. **3.** Done on purpose. She made a *conscious* effort to stop laughing.
con·scious (kon′shəs) *adjective.*

consecutive Following one after another without a break. 1, 2, 3, and 4 are *consecutive* numbers.
con·sec·u·tive (kən sek′yə tiv) *adjective.*

consent To give permission; agree to. Mother would not *consent* to my going camping by myself. *Verb.*
—Permission. My parents had to give their *consent* before I could go on the field trip with my class. *Noun.*
con·sent (kən sent′) *verb*, **consented, consenting;** *noun, plural* **consents.**

consequence **1.** Outcome; result. He climbed over the barbed wire fence and as a

at; āpe; cär; end; mē; it; īce; hot; ōld;
fôrk; wood; fool; oil; out; up; turn; sing;
thin; this; hw in white; zh in treasure.
ə stands for a in about, e in taken
i in pencil, o in lemon, and u in circus.

consequence he ripped his pants. She suffered the *consequences* of her bad behavior. **2.** Importance. What he thinks is of little *consequence* to me.

con·se·quence (kon′sə kwens′) *noun, plural* **consequences.**

consequently As a result; therefore. The little boy did not wear his boots when it rained, and *consequently* he got his shoes wet.

con·se·quent·ly (kon′sə kwent′lē) *adverb.*

conservation The protection and wise use of the forests, rivers, minerals, and other natural resources of a country.

con·ser·va·tion (kon′sər vā′shən) *noun.*

conservative Wanting things to be as they used to be or to stay as they are; against change or new ideas. *Adjective.*
—A person who is conservative. *Noun.*

con·serv·a·tive (kən sur′və tiv) *adjective; noun, plural* **conservatives.**

conserve To keep and protect. Terry *conserved* his energy for the hike.

con·serve (kən surv′) *verb,* **conserved, conserving.**

consider **1.** To think carefully about before deciding. Tom's older sister will *consider* going to college. **2.** To think of as; believe to be. The boys *consider* Ed the best player on the team.

con·sid·er (kən sid′ər) *verb,* **considered, considering.**

considerate Thoughtful of other people and their feelings. The *considerate* boy offered his seat to the old man.

con·sid·er·ate (kən sid′ər it) *adjective.*

consideration **1.** Thoughtfulness for other people and their feelings. Jean shows *consideration* for the neighbors by not playing her record player too loudly. **2.** Careful thought before deciding about something. After much *consideration,* my brother decided to study to be a lawyer.

con·sid·er·a·tion (kən sid′ə rā′shən) *noun, plural* **considerations.**

consist To be made up. Bricks *consist* mostly of clay. A year *consists* of twelve months.

con·sist (kən sist′) *verb,* **consisted, consisting.**

consistency **1.** Thickness or stiffness. This paint has the *consistency* of glue. **2.** A keeping to one way of thinking or acting. Since he changes his mind so often, there is no *consistency* to what he says or believes.

con·sist·en·cy (kən sis′tən sē) *noun, plural* **consistencies.**

consistent **1.** Keeping to one way of thinking or acting. The boy remained *consistent* in his love of animals, and when he grew up he became a veterinarian. **2.** In agreement. What he said about the accident is not *consistent* with what really happened.

con·sist·ent (kən sis′tənt) *adjective.*

console[1] To comfort or cheer. You try to console a person when he is sad or disappointed about something. The mother tried to *console* the weeping child for the loss of her kitten.

con·sole (kən sōl′) *verb,* **consoled, consoling.**

console[2] The cabinet of a radio, television set, or phonograph that rests on the floor.

con·sole (kon′sōl) *noun, plural* **consoles.**

Console

consolidate To join together; combine. The two stores *consolidated* to form one large store.

con·sol·i·date (kən sol′ə dāt′) *verb,* **consolidated, consolidating.**

consonant A letter of the alphabet that is not a vowel. Consonants include the letters *b, d, f, g, m, p,* and *t.*

con·so·nant (kon′sə nənt) *noun, plural* **consonants.**

conspicuous Easily seen; attracting attention; striking. The blue ink left a *conspicuous* stain on the tablecloth.

con·spic·u·ous (kən spik′yoo əs) *adjective.*

conspiracy Secret planning together with others to do something wrong. The police arrested the leader of the *conspiracy* to rob the bank.

con·spir·a·cy (kən spir′ə sē) *noun, plural* **conspiracies.**

constable A member of the police force in England; policeman.

con·sta·ble (kon′stə bəl *or* kun′stə bəl) *noun, plural* **constables.**

constant Not changing; continuing. The nice weather has been *constant* all week. The boy's *constant* talking made the teacher angry.

con·stant (kon′stənt) *adjective.*

constellation   A group of stars. A constellation forms a pattern in the sky that looks like a picture. The Big Dipper and the Little Dipper are constellations.
   con·stel·la·tion (kon′stə lā′shən) *noun, plural* **constellations.**

constituent   Forming a needed part. Hydrogen and oxygen are the *constituent* parts of water. *Adjective.*
   —**1.** A needed part. Wood pulp is an important *constituent* of paper. **2.** A voter. The congressman always voted for laws that his *constituents* wanted. *Noun.*
   con·stit·u·ent (kən stich′o͞o ənt) *adjective; noun, plural* **constituents.**

constitute   To make up; form. Four quarts *constitute* a gallon.
   con·sti·tute (kon′stə to͞ot′ *or* kon′stə tyo͞ot′) *verb,* **constituted, constituting.**

constitution   **1.** The way in which a person or thing is made. The healthy boy has a strong *constitution.* **2.** The basic principles used to govern a state or country. The voters voted on changes in their state *constitution.* The *Constitution* of the United States has been our nation's plan of government since its adoption in 1789.
   con·sti·tu·tion (kon′stə to͞o′shən *or* kon′stə tyo͞o′shən) *noun, plural* **constitutions.**

constitutional   Having to do with a constitution. The United States has a *constitutional* form of government.
   con·sti·tu·tion·al (kon′stə to͞o′shən əl *or* kon′stə tyo͞o′shən əl) *adjective.*

constrict   To make smaller or narrower by pressing together. The dog's tight collar *constricted* its neck.
   con·strict (kən strikt′) *verb,* **constricted, constricting.**

constrictor   A large snake that can kill small animals by squeezing them in its coils. The python, anaconda, and boa constrictor are different kinds of constrictors.
   con·stric·tor (kən strik′tər) *noun, plural* **constrictors.**

Constrictor

construct   To make by putting parts together; build. Bob and his father *constructed* a tool shed in the back yard. The state will *construct* a new highway to the town.
   con·struct (kən strukt′) *verb,* **constructed, constructing.**

construction   The act of constructing something; building. The *construction* of the new gym was started last summer.
   con·struc·tion (kən struk′shən) *noun, plural* **constructions.**

constructive   Serving to make better; helpful. The coach always gives *constructive* criticism so that the players can improve their game.
   con·struc·tive (kən struk′tiv) *adjective.*

consul   A person appointed by a government to live in a foreign city. A consul protects his country's citizens and business there.
   con·sul (kon′səl) *noun, plural* **consuls.**

consult   To go to for advice or information. When you are ill, you *consult* a doctor. We *consulted* a map to find out where the town was located.
   con·sult (kən sult′) *verb,* **consulted, consulting.**

consume   To use up or destroy. A car *consumes* gasoline. He *consumes* too much time watching television.
   con·sume (kən so͞om′) *verb,* **consumed, consuming.**

consumer   A person who buys and uses up things. A housewife who shops for food in a grocery store is a consumer. People who buy radios, books, cars, and many other things are consumers.
   con·sum·er (kən so͞o′mər) *noun, plural* **consumers.**

consumption   The using up of something. The *consumption* of gasoline is greater in a big car than in a small car.
   con·sump·tion (kən sump′shən) *noun, plural* **consumptions.**

contact   A touching or meeting. When the baby came in *contact* with the hot stove, he burned his hand. Ann lost *contact* with her friends when she moved away. *Noun.*
   —To get in touch with; communicate with;

at; āpe; cär; end; mē; it; īce; hot; ōld;
fôrk; wood; fo͞ol; oil; out; up; turn; sing;
thin; this; hw in white; zh in treasure.
ə stands for a in about, e in taken
i in pencil, o in lemon, and u in circus.

reach. Mary tried to *contact* her friend by telephone. *Verb.*

con·tact (kon′takt) *noun, plural* **contacts;** *verb,* **contacted, contacting.**

contagious Spread from person to person. Everyone in the class caught chicken pox because it is so *contagious.*

con·ta·gious (kən tā′jəs) *adjective.*

contain 1. To hold. The jar *contains* candy. The shelf *contains* books. 2. To be made up of. Candy *contains* sugar. A quart *contains* two pints. 3. To keep or hold back. She tried to *contain* her laughter when the boy's chair tipped over backwards.

con·tain (kən tān′) *verb,* **contained, containing.**

container A box, can, or jar that holds something. I bought a *container* of milk at the grocery store.

con·tain·er (kən tā′nər) *noun, plural* **containers.**

contaminate To make dirty; pollute. If the town throws garbage in the river it will *contaminate* the water.

con·tam·i·nate (kən tam′ə nāt′) *verb,* **contaminated, contaminating.**

contemplate To think about something carefully for a long time. The young man sat and *contemplated* his future.

con·tem·plate (kon′təm plāt′) *verb,* **contemplated, contemplating.**

contemporary Belonging to the same time. George Washington and Thomas Jefferson were *contemporary* figures in our history. *Adjective.*

—A person who belongs to the same time as another person. *Noun.*

con·tem·po·rar·y (kən tem′pə rer′ē) *adjective; noun, plural* **contemporaries.**

contempt A feeling that a person or act is bad, mean, or worth nothing; scorn. He has *contempt* for people who are cruel to animals.

con·tempt (kən tempt′) *noun.*

contend 1. To compete. Sally and Mike *contended* for the swimming championship. 2. To argue. Tom *contended* that he could run the fastest. 3. To struggle. The explorers had to *contend* with very cold weather at the North Pole.

con·tend (kən tend′) *verb,* **contended, contending.**

content Happy and satisfied. Bill and Jane are not *content* to stay home and play games on rainy days. *Adjective.*

—To make happy; satisfy. A pat on the head and a kind word *contents* my dog. *Verb.*

—A feeling of being happy or satisfied. After eating, the baby went to sleep in complete *content. Noun.*

con·tent (kən tent′) *adjective; verb,* **contented, contenting;** *noun.*

contented Happy and satisfied. A contented person is happy with what he is and what he has. The *contented* kitten purred and rubbed against my leg.

con·tent·ed (kən ten′tid) *adjective.*

contents 1. What something holds. When the bag broke, its *contents* fell all over the floor. 2. What is written or spoken about. This book has a table of *contents* in the front.

con·tents (kon′tents) *noun plural.*

contest 1. A game or race that people try to win. Our team won the hurdles *contest.* Jim won the pie-eating *contest* at the church fair. 2. A struggle; fight. The American Civil War was a *contest* between the Northern states and the Southern states.

con·test (kon′test) *noun, plural* **contests.**

contestant A person who takes part in a contest. Barbara was a *contestant* in the swimming meet. The *contestant* on the television quiz show won a car and a trip to Hawaii.

con·test·ant (kən tes′tənt) *noun, plural* **contestants.**

continent One of the seven large land areas on the earth. The continents are Asia, Africa, North America, South America, Antarctica, Europe, and Australia.

con·ti·nent (kont′ən ənt) *noun, plural* **continents.**

continual Going on without stopping. The electric clock made a *continual* humming noise.

con·tin·u·al (kən tin′yo͞o əl) *adjective.*

continue To keep on happening or doing; go on without stopping. The snowfall *continued* for two days. Tom *continued* his work in spite of a bad headache.

con·tin·ue (kən tin′yo͞o) *verb,* **continued, continuing.**

continuous Going on without a break; unbroken. The river has a *continuous* flow of water.

con·tin·u·ous (kən tin′yo͞o əs) *adjective.*

contour The outline or shape of something. The astronauts could see the curved *contour* of the earth.

con·tour (kon′toor) *noun, plural* **contours.**

contract 1. To make or become shorter or smaller. A turtle can *contract* his neck so that his head can be drawn into its shell. We *contract* words like "are not" to form

"aren't" and "she had" to form "she'd."
2. To make an agreement. The workman *contracted* to paint the house for $600. *Verb.*
—An agreement. The singer signed a *contract* to make records for the record company. *Noun.*
> con·tract (kən trakt′ *for verb, definition 1;* kən trakt′ *or* kon′trakt *for verb, definition 2;* kon′trakt *for noun*) *verb,* **contracted, contracting;** *noun, plural* **contracts.**

contraction **1.** The act of contracting or the state of being contracted. The *contraction* of the heart forces blood into the arteries. **2.** A shortened form. "Wouldn't" is the contraction of "would not."
> con·trac·tion (kən trak′shən) *noun, plural* **contractions.**

contradict To say the opposite of; disagree with. The boy *contradicted* what he had said earlier about the accident.
> con·tra·dict (kon′trə dikt′) *verb,* **contradicted, contradicting.**

contralto **1.** The lowest female singing voice. **2.** A singer who has such a voice.
> con·tral·to (kən tral′tō) *noun, plural* **contraltos.**

contrary **1.** Entirely different; opposite. My brother's ideas about sports and music are *contrary* to my own. **2.** Liking to argue and oppose. That *contrary* boy never agrees with what other people say.
> con·trar·y (kon′trer ē *for definition 1;* kon′trer ē *or* kən trer′ē *for definition 2*) *adjective.*

contrast To show differences by comparing. The teacher *contrasted* life in a big city and life on a farm. *Verb.*
—A difference. There is a great *contrast* between the weather at the North Pole and the weather in the tropics. *Noun.*
> con·trast (kən trast′ *for verb;* kon′trast *for noun*) *verb,* **contrasted, contrasting;** *noun, plural* **contrasts.**

contribute To give. The townspeople *contributed* food and clothing to the family whose house had burned down. The children *contributed* ideas for the school picnic.
> con·trib·ute (kən trib′yōot) *verb,* **contributed, contributing.**

contribution **1.** The act of contributing; giving something. The wealthy man's *contribution* of money will help build a new hospital. **2.** Something contributed. We gave *contributions* to help hungry children in other countries.
> con·tri·bu·tion (kon′trə byōo′shən) *noun, plural* **contributions.**

control **1.** Power or authority. The dictator had complete *control* over the country. **2.** A holding back; check. She has no *control* over her temper. **3. controls.** Instruments for guiding a machine. An airplane or spacecraft has controls. *Noun.*
—**1.** To have power or authority over. In some countries, the government tries to *control* the way people act and think. **2.** To hold back; check. He tried to *control* his temper. *Verb.*
> con·trol (kən trōl′) *noun, plural* **controls;** *verb,* **controlled, controlling.**

control tower A tower on an airfield. The movement of airplanes landing or taking off is directed from the control tower.

controversial Causing an argument. Politics is often a *controversial* subject.
> con·tro·ver·sial (kon′trə vur′shəl) *adjective.*

controversy A disagreement; dispute. The new tax caused much *controversy.*
> con·tro·ver·sy (kon′trə vur′sē) *noun, plural* **controversies.**

Control Tower

convene To come or bring together for a meeting; assemble. Congress will *convene* again after the Christmas holidays.
> con·vene (kən vēn′) *verb,* **convened, convening.**

convenience Ease and comfort. The boys liked the *convenience* of canned foods when they went camping.
> con·ven·ience (kən vēn′yəns) *noun, plural* **conveniences.**

convenient Giving ease and comfort; useful; handy. A dishwasher is very *convenient* if you have lots of dishes to be washed.
> con·ven·ient (kən vēn′yənt) *adjective.*

convent A building where a group of nuns live.
> con·vent (kon′vent) *noun, plural* **convents.**

---

at; āpe; cär; end; mē; it; īce; hot; ōld;
fôrk; wood; fool; oil; out; up; turn; sing;
thin; this; hw in white; zh in treasure.
ə stands for a in about, e in taken
i in pencil, o in lemon, and u in circus.

convention 1. A formal meeting for some special purpose. Every four years the political parties hold *conventions* to choose candidates for President. 2. An accepted way of acting or doing something; custom. Shaking hands when you are introduced to someone is a *convention.*
con·ven·tion (kən ven′shən) *noun, plural* **conventions.**

conventional Following practices or customs. Saying "hello" is a *conventional* thing to do when you meet someone.
con·ven·tion·al (kən ven′shən əl) *adjective.*

conversation A friendly and informal talk. Joan and Sara had a long *conversation* about their summer vacations.
con·ver·sa·tion (kon′vər sā′shən) *noun, plural* **conversations.**

converse To talk together in a friendly and informal way. Mother and Aunt Ruth *conversed* by telephone about the day's events.
con·verse (kən vurs′) *verb,* **conversed, conversing.**

conversion The changing of something. The *conversion* of water into ice happens when the temperature of the water goes below 32° Fahrenheit.
con·ver·sion (kən vur′zhən) *noun, plural* **conversions.**

convert 1. To change something into something different. The new owner *converted* the large house into a hotel. 2. To cause a person to change a belief. The missionary tried to *convert* the tribe to the Christian faith.
con·vert (kən vurt′) *verb,* **converted, converting.**

convertible Able to be changed. The *convertible* sofa can be made into a bed. *Adjective.*
—An automobile with a roof that can be folded back. *Noun.*
con·vert·i·ble (kən vur′tə bəl) *adjective; noun, plural* **convertibles.**

convex Curving outward. The outside of a bowl is *convex.* Look up **concave** for a picture of this.
con·vex (kon veks′ *or* kon′veks) *adjective.*

convey 1. To take from one place to another; carry. These pipes *convey* water from the well to the house. 2. To make known; express. My older brother *conveys* his feelings about his life at college in the letters he writes home to the family.
con·vey (kən vā′) *verb,* **conveyed, conveying.**

convict To declare or prove that a person is guilty of a crime. The jury *convicted* the thief of robbery. *Verb.*
—A person who is serving a prison sentence. The police were looking for two *convicts* who had escaped from a nearby prison. *Noun.*
con·vict (kən vikt′ *for verb;* kon′vikt *for noun*) *verb,* **convicted, convicting;** *noun, plural* **convicts.**

conviction 1. The act of declaring or proving that a person is guilty of a crime. The jury's verdict resulted in the *conviction* of the thief. 2. The state of being found guilty of a crime. After his *conviction* for robbery, the man was sentenced to five years in jail. 3. A strong belief. Bill has the *conviction* that most people are good at heart.
con·vic·tion (kən vik′shən) *noun, plural* **convictions.**

convince To cause a person to believe something; persuade. She argued with her brother until she *convinced* him that she was right.
con·vince (kən vins′) *verb,* **convinced, convincing.**

▲ The word **convince** used to mean "to overcome or conquer." For example, one army could *convince* another army in battle. This meaning later led to the meaning "to overcome by persuading."

convulse To shake or disturb violently. The boy was *convulsed* with laughter by his friend's jokes.
con·vulse (kən vuls′) *verb,* **convulsed, convulsing.**

cook 1. To make food ready for eating by using heat. You can cook food by broiling, roasting, baking, boiling, or frying it. 2. To be cooked. The peas will *cook* quickly. *Verb.*
—A person who cooks. *Noun.*
cook (kook) *verb,* **cooked, cooking;** *noun, plural* **cooks.**

cookie A small, flat sweet cake. Mother baked raisin *cookies.* This word is also spelled **cooky.**
cook·ie (kook′ē) *noun, plural* **cookies.**

cool 1. Somewhat cold. The *cool* breeze felt good on the hot summer day. She brought us a *cool* drink of lemonade. 2. Not excited; calm. Everyone kept *cool* and got out of the burning building safely. 3. Not warm or friendly. She was very *cool* to him after he insulted her. *Adjective.*
—Something cool. We took a walk in the *cool* of the early morning. *Noun.*
—To make or become cool. Phil tried to *cool* his soup by blowing on it. *Verb.*
cool (kool) *adjective,* **cooler, coolest;** *noun; verb,* **cooled, cooling.**

coop A cage or pen for chickens or other small animals. Bob keeps his rabbits in a *coop* in the back yard. *Noun.*
—To put or keep in a coop or other small space. We *cooped* the dog up in the kitchen until the guests left. *Verb.*
   coop (ko͞op) *noun, plural* **coops;** *verb,* **cooped, cooping.**

cooperate To work together. The three classes *cooperated* in planning a picnic at the end of the school year.
   co·op·er·ate (kō op′ə rāt′) *verb,* **cooperated, cooperating.**

cooperation The act of working together. Keeping the streets of our town clean requires the *cooperation* of all the people who live here.
   co·op·er·a·tion (kō op′ə rā′shən) *noun.*

coordinate To work or cause to work well together; bring or put into proper working order. A good athlete's muscles *coordinate* well. In dancing, it is important to *coordinate* the movements of the feet to the beat of the music.
   co·or·di·nate (kō ôr′də nāt′) *verb,* **coordinated, coordinating.**

cope To struggle or handle with success. She had trouble *coping* with the extra homework.
   cope (kōp) *verb,* **coped, coping.**

copper 1. A reddish-brown metal. Copper is easy to form in different shapes, and it is an excellent conductor of heat and electricity. Copper is a chemical element. 2. A reddish-brown color. *Noun.*
—Having the color copper; reddish-brown. *Adjective.*
   cop·per (kop′ər) *noun; adjective.*

copperhead A poisonous snake found in the eastern part of the United States. It has a copper-colored head and a light brown body with dark brown markings.
   cop·per·head (kop′ər hed′) *noun, plural* **copperheads.**

Copperhead

copy 1. Something that is made to look exactly like something else; imitation; duplicate. He used carbon paper to make a *copy* of the letter he typed. 2. One of a number of books, magazines, or newspapers printed at the same time. He bought two *copies* of the new book on football. *Noun.*
—1. To make a copy of. *Copy* the book report neatly. 2. To make or do something that is exactly like something else. Mary *copied* her older sister's way of dressing. *Verb.*
   cop·y (kop′ē) *noun, plural* **copies;** *verb,* **copied, copying.**

copyright The sole right to print, sell, or copy a literary, musical, or artistic work. Copyrights are granted by law for a certain number of years. The writer has a *copyright* on the song he wrote.
   cop·y·right (kop′ē rīt′) *noun, plural* **copyrights.**

coral 1. A hard stony substance. Coral is made up of the skeletons of tiny sea animals. 2. The tiny sea animal that makes coral. 3. A pinkish-red color. *Noun.*
—Having the color coral; pinkish-red. *Adjective.*
   cor·al (kôr′əl) *noun, plural* **corals;** *adjective.*

Coral Snake

coral snake A poisonous American snake that has a narrow head and red, black, and yellow bands on its body.

cord 1. A string or thin rope. Cord is made of several strands twisted or woven together. She tied the books together with *cord.* 2. A covered wire that is used to connect a toaster, lamp, or other appliance to an electrical outlet. 3. A structure in the body that is like a cord. The spinal *cord* extends from the brain. 4. An amount of cut wood equaling

at; āpe; cär; end; mē; it; īce; hot; ōld;
fôrk; wood; fo͞ol; oil; out; up; turn; sing;
thin; this; hw in white; zh in treasure.
ə stands for a in about, e in taken
i in pencil, o in lemon, and u in circus.

128 cubic feet. A cord is a pile of wood that is 4 feet wide, 4 feet high, and 8 feet long. *Noun.*
—To fasten together with cord. He *corded* the boxes for easy handling. *Verb.* ▲ Another word that sounds like this is **chord.**

cord (kôrd) *noun, plural* **cords;** *verb,* **corded, cording.**

cordial Warm and friendly; hearty. He gave us a *cordial* greeting when we arrived.

cor·dial (kôr′jəl) *adjective.*

corduroy A cloth with rows of ribs. It is usually made of cotton and is used for clothing.

cor·du·roy (kôr′də roi′) *noun.*

core **1.** The hard, middle part of apples, pears, and certain other fruits. The seeds are in the core. **2.** The central, most important, or deepest part of anything. The *core* of the coach's talk was that the team needed more practice. *Noun.*
—To remove the core of. She *cored* the apples before baking them. *Verb.* ▲ Another word that sounds like this is **corps.**

core (kôr) *noun, plural* **cores;** *verb,* **cored, coring.**

cork **1.** The light, thick, outer bark of a kind of oak tree. Cork is used for such things as insulation, bottle stoppers, and floats for rafts. **2.** A stopper for a bottle or other thing made of cork. Please put the *cork* back in the bottle. *Noun.*
—To stop with a cork. She *corked* the thermos bottle. *Verb.*

cork (kôrk) *noun, plural* **corks;** *verb,* **corked, corking.**

The **corkscrew** on the right is a close-up of the one being used to open the bottle.

corkscrew A device for taking corks out of bottles.

cork·screw (kôrk′skroo′) *noun, plural* **corkscrews.**

corn **1.** A grain that grows in rows on the large ears of a tall plant. Corn is used for food. **2.** The plant that corn grows on.

corn (kôrn) *noun.*

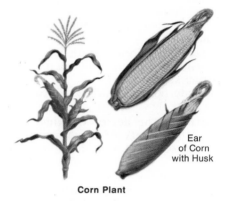

Ear
of Corn
with Husk

Corn Plant

corncob The woody core of an ear of corn. The corn kernels grow in rows on the corncob.

corn·cob (kôrn′kob′) *noun, plural* **corncobs.**

cornea The clear or transparent outer covering of the front of the eyeball. The cornea covers the iris and the pupil.

cor·ne·a (kôr′nē ə) *noun, plural* **corneas.**

corner **1.** The place or point where two lines or surfaces come together. She hit her leg on the sharp *corner* of the box. The table is in the *corner* of the room. **2.** The place where two streets come together. There is a mailbox on the *corner. Noun.*
—At or near a corner. Tom works at the *corner* drugstore after school. *Adjective.*
—To force or drive into a dangerous or difficult place or position. The dog *cornered* the cat under the bed. *Verb.*

cor·ner (kôr′nər) *noun, plural* **corners;** *adjective; verb,* **cornered, cornering.**

cornet A brass musical instrument that is like a trumpet.

cor·net (kôr net′) *noun, plural* **cornets.**

Cornet

coronation The ceremony of crowning a king or queen. Many important people were present for the *coronation* of the new queen.
cor·o·na·tion (kôr′ə nā′shən) *noun, plural* **coronations.**

corporal An army officer of the lowest rank. A corporal is below a sergeant but above a private.
cor·po·ral (kôr′pər əl *or* kôr′prəl) *noun, plural* **corporals.**

corporation An organization made up of a number of people who are allowed by law to act as a single person. A corporation is created by a government charter and has the right to buy and sell property, borrow and lend money, and to enter into contracts.
cor·po·ra·tion (kôr′pə rā′shən) *noun, plural* **corporations.**

corps **1.** A group of soldiers trained for special service. He belongs to the medical *corps.* **2.** A group of persons who act or work together. That restaurant has a large *corps* of waiters and waitresses. ▲ Another word that sounds like this is **core.**
corps (kôr) *noun, plural* **corps.**

corpse A dead human body.
corpse (kôrps) *noun, plural* **corpses.**

corpuscle A small cell that is part of the blood. Red and white blood cells are corpuscles.
cor·pus·cle (kôr′pus′əl) *noun, plural* **corpuscles.**

corral A space with a fence around it. A corral is used for cattle, horses, and other animals. *Noun.*
—**1.** To drive or put into a corral. The cowboys *corralled* the herd of horses. **2.** To capture by surrounding. The police *corralled* the gang of bank robbers. *Verb.*
cor·ral (kə ral′) *noun, plural* **corrals;** *verb,* **corralled, corralling.**

Corral

correct **1.** Not having any mistakes; accurate. This is the *correct* answer to the arithmetic problem. **2.** Proper. It is *correct* to thank people for gifts that they give you. *Adjective.*
—**1.** To mark the mistakes in; change to make right. The teacher *corrected* our spelling tests. **2.** To make agree with some standard. The doctor *corrected* my poor eyesight with glasses. *Verb.*
cor·rect (kə rekt′) *adjective; verb,* **corrected, correcting.**

correction **1.** The act of correcting. *Correction* of the trouble in the car's engine took the mechanic several hours. **2.** A change that is made to correct an error. I kept a list of the *corrections* I made in the report.
cor·rec·tion (kə rek′shən) *noun; plural* **corrections.**

correspond **1.** To agree; match. His answer to the question does not *correspond* with mine. **2.** To be similar. The gills of a fish *correspond* to the lungs of man. **3.** To write letters to one another. Jack and Bill *corresponded* when Bill was away at summer camp.
cor·re·spond (kôr′ə spond′) *verb,* **corresponded, corresponding.**

correspondence **1.** Agreement or similarity. The police found a close *correspondence* between the stories of the two witnesses. **2.** The writing of letters to one another. We kept up a *correspondence* for many years after he moved.
cor·re·spon·dence (kôr′ə spon′dəns) *noun.*

corridor A long hallway or passageway in a building. A corridor often has rooms opening onto it.
cor·ri·dor (kôr′ə dər) *noun, plural* **corridors.**

corrode To eat or wear away, little by little. Rust *corroded* our porch furniture.
cor·rode (kə rōd′) *verb,* **corroded, corroding.**

corrupt Able to be bribed; crooked; dishonest. The *corrupt* mayor was eventually found out and sent to jail. *Adjective.*
—To cause to be dishonest. That judge cannot be *corrupted. Verb.*
cor·rupt (kə rupt′) *adjective; verb,* **corrupted, corrupting.**

at; āpe; cär; end; mē; it; īce; hot; ōld;
fôrk; wood; fōōl; oil; out; up; turn; sing;
thin; this; hw in white; zh in treasure.
ə stands for a in about, e in taken
i in pencil, o in lemon, and u in circus.

corsage A flower or small bunch of flowers worn by a woman at the shoulder or waist, or on the wrist. He bought her a *corsage* to wear to the dance.
cor·sage (kôr säzh′) *noun, plural* **corsages.**

corset A close-fitting undergarment worn by women to shape and support the waist and hips.
cor·set (kôr′sit) *noun, plural* **corsets.**

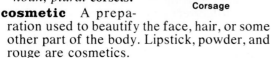

Corsage

cosmetic A preparation used to beautify the face, hair, or some other part of the body. Lipstick, powder, and rouge are cosmetics.
cos·met·ic (koz met′ik) *noun, plural* **cosmetics.**

cosmic Of or relating to the whole universe. *Cosmic* dust is very small particles of matter from outer space that fall to earth.
cos·mic (koz′mik) *adjective.*

cost **1.** An amount of money paid or charged for something; price. The *cost* of that book is five dollars. **2.** Something lost. The war was won at the *cost* of many lives. *Noun.*
—**1.** To be gotten or bought at the price of. The bicycle *cost* too much, so my father didn't buy it. **2.** To cause the loss of. The accident almost *cost* him his life. *Verb.*
cost (kôst) *noun, plural* **costs;** *verb,* **cost, costing.**

costly Costing much. Collecting rare stamps can be a *costly* hobby.
cost·ly (kôst′lē) *adjective,* **costlier, costliest.**

costume **1.** Clothes worn in order to look like someone or something else. She wore a ghost *costume* to the Halloween party. **2.** Clothes worn at a particular time or place or by particular people. She collects dolls dressed in the national *costumes* of every country in the world.
cos·tume (kos′tōōm *or* kos′tyōōm) *noun, plural* **costumes.**

cot A narrow bed. Cots are usually made of canvas stretched on a frame that can be folded.
cot (kot) *noun, plural* **cots.**

cottage A small house. We have a summer *cottage* at the beach.
cot·tage (kot′ij) *noun, plural* **cottages.**

cottage cheese A soft, white cheese. Cottage cheese is made from the curds of sour skim milk.

cotton A fluffy mass of soft white or gray fibers that grow in the large seed pod of a tall plant. Cotton is used to make thread or cloth.
cot·ton (kot′ən) *noun.*

cottontail An American rabbit that has brown or grayish fur and a short, fluffy, white tail.
cot·ton·tail (kot′ən tāl′) *noun, plural* **cottontails.**

cottonwood A tree that grows near rivers and streams in North America. It has tiny brown seeds covered with tufts of silky white hairs like cotton.
cot·ton·wood (kot′ən wood′) *noun, plural* **cottonwoods.**

Cotton Plant

couch A piece of furniture that two or more people can sit on at the same time. Couches usually have soft cushions.
couch (kouch) *noun, plural* **couches.**

cougar A golden-brown American animal that has a small head, long legs, and a slender, strong body. A cougar is a member of the cat family. A cougar is also called a **puma** and a **mountain lion.**
cou·gar (kōō′gər) *noun, plural* **cougars.**

Cougar

cough To force air from the lungs with a sudden, sharp sound. Beth stayed home today because she has a cold and *coughs* all the time. *Verb.*
—**1.** The sharp sound that is made when air is suddenly forced from the lungs. **2.** A sickness that causes a person to cough. *Noun.*
cough (kôf) *verb,* **coughed, coughing;** *noun, plural* **coughs.**

could I *could* tell that he was angry.
could (kood) *verb.*

couldn't The little boy *couldn't* reach the high shelf.

could·n't (kood′ənt) contraction for "could not."

council 1. A group of people called together. A council can give advice, discuss a problem, or make a decision. 2. A group of people elected to govern a city or town. Our town *council* discussed widening the main street at their meeting last night. ▲ Another word that sounds like this is **counsel**.

coun·cil (koun′səl) *noun, plural* **councils**.

counsel 1. Ideas or suggestions about what to do; advice. A good friend can often give you wise *counsel*. 2. A lawyer or group of lawyers who give legal advice. The *counsel* for the defense summed up the case for the jury. *Noun.*

—To give ideas or suggestions to; advise. Her brother *counseled* her to start working harder. *Verb.* ▲ Another word that sounds like this is **council**.

coun·sel (koun′səl) *noun, plural* **counsels**; *verb*, **counseled, counseling**.

counselor A person who helps or gives advice. Our *counselor* at summer camp taught us how to paddle a canoe.

coun·se·lor (koun′sə lər) *noun, plural* **counselors**.

count¹ 1. To find out how many of something there are; add up. *Count* the number of cookies in the box. 2. To say or write down numbers in order. He can *count* up to 100 really fast. 3. To include or be included when things are added up. There were forty people in the bus, *counting* the driver. 4. To depend; rely. Can I *count* on you if I need help? *Verb.*

—The number of things there are when you add them up; total. *Noun.*

count (kount) *verb*, **counted, counting**; *noun, plural* **counts**.

count² A European nobleman.

count (kount) *noun, plural* **counts**.

countdown The counting of time backward from a certain time to zero. This is done to tell people how much time is left before the start of something. The *countdown* for the launching of the spacecraft will begin soon.

count·down (kount′doun′) *noun, plural* **countdowns**.

counter¹ 1. A long table. Stores have counters on which things are sold. Some restaurants have counters on which meals are served. 2. Something used for counting. Some games have round, colored disks called counters to help keep score.

count·er (koun′tər) *noun, plural* **counters**.

counter² Opposite. He acted *counter* to instructions and wrote in pencil instead of ink. Your idea is *counter* to my idea. *Adverb, Adjective.*

—To go against; oppose. My friend *countered* my idea for a picnic and said he wanted to go to the movies instead. *Verb.*

coun·ter (koun′tər) *adverb; adjective; verb*, **countered, countering**.

counterclockwise In the direction opposite to the direction the hands of a clock move. You turn a screw *counterclockwise* if you want to take it out.

coun·ter·clock·wise (koun′tər klok′wīz′) *adverb; adjective.*

counterfeit To make a copy or imitation of something in order to cheat or fool other people. It is a crime to *counterfeit* money. *Verb.*

—A copy or imitation made in order to cheat or fool someone. The shopkeeper had a twenty dollar bill that was a *counterfeit. Noun.*

—Not genuine. The man was put in jail for making *counterfeit* money. *Adjective.*

coun·ter·feit (koun′tər fit′) *verb*, **counterfeited, counterfeiting**; *noun, plural* **counterfeits**; *adjective.*

counterpart A person or thing that is very much like or equal to another. The United States Congress is the *counterpart* of the British Parliament.

coun·ter·part (koun′tər pärt′) *noun, plural* **counterparts**.

country 1. Any area of land; region. We have a summer cabin in mountain *country*. 2. An area of land that has boundaries and has a government that is shared by all the people; nation. The United States and Canada are *countries*. 3. The land outside of cities and towns. We decided to go for a drive in the *country. Noun.*

—Having to do with land outside of cities and towns; rural. We drove along narrow *country* roads. *Adjective.*

coun·try (kun′trē) *noun, plural* **countries**; *adjective.*

at; āpe; cär; end; mē; it; īce; hot; ōld;
fôrk; wood; fōōl; oil; out; up; turn; sing;
thin; this; hw in white; zh in treasure.
ə stands for a in about, e in taken
i in pencil, o in lemon, and u in circus.

countryman A person who lives in one's own country.
coun·try·man (kun′trē mən) *noun, plural* **countrymen.**

countryside The land outside of cities and towns.
coun·try·side (kun′trē sīd′) *noun, plural* **countrysides.**

county One of the sections into which a state or country is divided. Counties have their own local government.
coun·ty (koun′tē) *noun, plural* **counties.**

couple 1. Two things that are the same or go together in some way; pair. She bought a *couple* of lamps to go on her dressing table. 2. A man and woman who are married, engaged, or partners in a dance or game. My father and mother are a happy *couple. Noun.*
—To join together. We *coupled* the trailer and the car. *Verb.*
cou·ple (kup′əl) *noun, plural* **couples;** *verb,* **coupled, coupling.**

coupon A ticket or part of a ticket. A coupon can be exchanged for a gift or for a discount on the price of something. The *coupon* in the box of cereal was good for ten cents toward the price of the next box.
cou·pon (kōō′pon *or* kyōō′pon) *noun, plural* **coupons.**

courage A strength that a person has that helps him to face danger without fear; bravery. She showed great *courage* in swimming out through the rough waves to save the drowning child.
cour·age (kur′ij) *noun.*

courageous Brave. A courageous person can face something that is dangerous, very hard, or painful without fear. The *courageous* fireman went into the burning building to save the old man.
cou·ra·geous (kə rā′jəs) *adjective.*

course 1. A moving onward from one point to the next; progress. He grew four inches in the *course* of a year. 2. A way; route; track. The airplane flew off its *course.* The river had a winding *course.* 3. A way of acting. The most sensible *course* would be to go home now before it starts to rain. 4. An area used for certain sports or games. We are going to the golf *course* this afternoon. 5. A series of classes or lessons. I am taking a *course* in cooking. 6. A part of a meal that is served at one time. Our first *course* was fruit cup and the second *course* was soup. ▲ Another word that sounds like this is **coarse.**
course (kôrs) *noun, plural* **courses.**
of course. Certainly; naturally. *Of course* I'll help you with your work.

court 1. An open space that is surrounded by walls or buildings; courtyard. Our apartment house is built around a *court.* 2. A space or area that is marked off for certain games. The gym has a basketball *court.* 3. The place where a king or queen and their attendants live. 4. A room or building where trials are held or where other matters are decided by law. *Noun.*
—To try to win the favor or love of a person. The politician *courted* the voters in his state. *Verb.*
court (kôrt) *noun, plural* **courts;** *verb,* **courted, courting.**

courteous Having good manners; polite. A courteous person is always thoughtful of the feelings of others.
cour·te·ous (kur′tē əs) *adjective.*

courtesy A way of behaving that shows good manners and a thoughtfulness toward other people; politeness. Everyone likes that grocery clerk because of his *courtesy* to all his customers.
cour·te·sy (kur′tə sē) *noun.*

courthouse 1. A building in which courts of law are held. 2. A building in which the offices of a county government are located.
court·house (kôrt′hous′) *noun, plural* **courthouses.**

courtyard An open area that is surrounded by walls or buildings. The rooms of the palace looked out onto the *courtyard.*
court·yard (kôrt′yärd′) *noun, plural* **courtyards.**

cousin The son or daughter of an aunt or uncle. **First cousins** have the same grandparents; **second cousins** have the same great-grandparents.
cou·sin (kuz′in) *noun, plural* **cousins.**

cove A small sheltered bay or inlet. The sailors anchored their boat in a *cove* where they were protected from the wind.
cove (kōv) *noun, plural* **coves.**

Cove

cover **1.** To put something over or on. The girl *covered* her hair with a bright red scarf. Snow *covered* the ground during the night. **2.** To hide. She tried to *cover* up her mistake with a lie. Darkness *covered* the hills. **3.** To travel over. Sally *covered* the distance from her house to mine in five minutes on her bicycle. **4.** To deal with; include. The book I'm reading *covers* the history of airplanes. That magazine *covers* sports. *Verb.*
—**1.** Something that is put on or over something else. Put a *cover* on the pot. What is the picture on the *cover* of that book? **2.** Something that hides or protects. The prisoner escaped from jail under the *cover* of darkness. The hikers took *cover* in a barn when the storm broke. *Noun.*
cov·er (kuv′ər) *verb*, **covered, covering;** *noun, plural* **covers.**

covered wagon A large wagon with a canvas top that is spread over hoops. American pioneers traveled in covered wagons when they moved westward.

Covered Wagon

covering Anything that covers. A rug is a *covering* for a floor. Our new car has plastic seat *coverings.*
cov·er·ing (kuv′ər ing) *noun, plural* **coverings.**

covet To want something very much that belongs to another person. Jack *coveted* his brother's new baseball glove.
cov·et (kuv′it) *verb*, **coveted, coveting.**

cow **1.** The full-grown female of cattle. Cows are raised for their milk. **2.** The female of some other large animals. A female moose, elephant, or whale is called a cow.
cow (kou) *noun, plural* **cows.**

coward A person who lacks courage. A coward is often shamefully afraid of anything that is dangerous or hard to do.
cow·ard (kou′ərd) *noun, plural* **cowards.**

cowardly Not courageous; showing fear in a shameful way. It was *cowardly* of him to run away from the injured man for fear that he would be blamed for the accident.
cow·ard·ly (kou′ərd lē) *adjective.*

cowboy A man who herds and takes care of cattle on a ranch. Cowboys ride on horseback to do their work.
cow·boy (kou′boi′) *noun, plural* **cowboys.**

Coyote

coyote An animal that looks like a wolf and lives in the prairies of North America.
coy·o·te (kī ō′tē *or* kī′ōt) *noun, plural* **coyotes** or **coyote.**

cozy Warm and comfortable; snug. The kitten slept in a *cozy* spot by the fire. We felt very *cozy* in the house when we heard the winter wind howling outside.
co·zy (kō′zē) *adjective*, **cozier, coziest.**

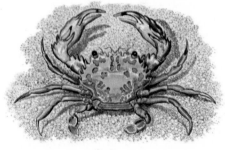
Crab

crab An animal that lives in the water and is covered by a hard shell. Crabs have a wide, flat body, four pairs of legs, and a pair of claws. Many kinds of crabs are good to eat.
crab (krab) *noun, plural* **crabs.**

crab apple A small, hard, sour-tasting

at; āpe; cär; end; mē; it; īce; hot; ōld;
fôrk; wood; fōol; oil; out; up; turn; sing;
thin; this; hw in white; zh in treasure.
ə stands for a in about, e in taken
i in pencil, o in lemon, and u in circus.

apple that is used to make jelly. Crab apples grow on trees that have many beautiful clusters of flowers in the spring.

crack **1.** A break or narrow opening between the parts of something. A crack does not make a thing fall into parts. The window has a *crack* in it where the ball hit it. There are *cracks* between the floor boards in my room. **2.** A sudden, sharp noise like that made by something breaking. When a bat hits a baseball you hear a crack. **3.** A sharp, hard blow. The swinging door gave him a painful *crack* on the head. *Noun.*
—**1.** To break without coming completely apart; split. The cup *cracked* when I hit it against the sink. The squirrel *cracked* the acorn with his teeth. **2.** To make a sudden, sharp noise. The cowboy showed us how he *cracked* the whip. **3.** To hit with a sharp, hard blow. He *cracked* his head on the door. *Verb.*
  crack (krak) *noun, plural* **cracks;** *verb,* **cracked, cracking.**

cracker A thin, crisp biscuit.
  crack·er (krak′ər) *noun, plural* **crackers.**

crackle To make slight, sharp snapping sounds. Dry leaves *crackle* when you walk on them. Some cold cereals *crackle* when you pour on milk. *Verb.*
—A slight, sharp snapping sound. The *crackle* of the burning logs was a pleasant sound. *Noun.*
  crack·le (krak′əl) *verb,* **crackled, crackling;** *noun, plural* **crackles.**

cradle **1.** A small bed for a baby. Most cradles are set on rockers so the baby can be rocked to sleep. **2.** Anything like a cradle in shape or use. A box on rockers used to wash gold from earth is a cradle. The part of a phone that holds the receiver is called a cradle. *Noun.*
—To hold in a cradle. Mother *cradled* the baby in her arms until he fell asleep. *Verb.*
  cra·dle (krād′əl) *noun, plural* **cradles;** *verb,* **cradled, cradling.**

Cradle

craft **1.** A special skill that a person has. The chair was carved with great *craft.* **2.** A trade or work that needs special skill. Carpentry is a *craft* that takes years to master. **3.** Skill in deceiving people; cunning. The thief showed great *craft* because he left no clues. **4.** A boat or airplane. The harbor was filled with small sailing *craft.*
  craft (kraft) *noun, plural* **crafts.**

craftsman A person who has a special skill in making or doing something. The man who made this beautiful antique furniture was a fine *craftsman.*
  crafts·man (krafts′mən) *noun, plural* **craftsmen.**

crag a steep, rugged rock or cliff. Eagles live on high mountain *crags.*
  crag (krag) *noun, plural* **crags.**

cramp¹ A sharp pain in a muscle that suddenly gets tight. She got a *cramp* in her leg when she was swimming, and had to be helped out of the water. *Noun.*
—To cause a sharp pain in a muscle. Holding the pencil tightly for so long *cramped* his hand. *Verb.*
  cramp (kramp) *noun, plural* **cramps;** *verb,* **cramped, cramping.**

Cranberries

cramp² To limit. We left too late and were very *cramped* for time.
  cramp (kramp) *verb,* **cramped, cramping.**

cranberry A sour, red berry that grows on low shrubs and bushes in bogs and swamps. Cranberries are used to make sauce, juice, and jelly.
  cran·ber·ry (kran′ber′ē) *noun, plural* **cranberries.**

crane **1.** A large bird that has very long thin legs and a long neck and bill. Cranes live near water, and wade along the shore looking for food in the water. **2.** A large machine with a long arm that can be moved up and down and in a circle. Cranes are used to lift and move heavy objects that are attached to cables at the end of the arm. *Noun.*
—To stretch out the neck in order to see better. The people standing in back of the crowd had to *crane* their necks to see the parade. *Verb.*

crane (krān) *noun, plural* **cranes;** *verb,* **craned, craning.**

Crane

crank **1.** A part of a machine that has a handle attached to a rod. When the handle is turned, the rod turns with it and makes the machine work. The storekeeper turned the *crank* of the store's awning to lower it. **2.** A person who has queer ideas. The police said that the strange telephone calls were the work of a *crank.* **3.** A person who is always grouchy or cross. She said that her brother was being a *crank* today and we should leave him alone. *Noun.*
—To turn a crank so that something will work. Years ago people had to *crank* the engine of a car to start it. *Verb.*
crank (krangk) *noun, plural* **cranks;** *verb,* **cranked, cranking.**

crash **1.** A sudden, loud noise like something breaking or smashing. There was a *crash* when the ball broke the window. **2.** A violent collision. We read about the terrible plane *crash. Noun.*
—**1.** To make a sudden, loud noise. The lamp *crashed* to the floor. **2.** To collide violently. The car *crashed* into a wall. *Verb.*
crash (krash) *noun, plural* **crashes;** *verb,* **crashed, crashing.**

crate A box made of slats of wood. Crates are used to hold and protect things that are being stored or moved. My uncle sent us a *crate* of oranges from Florida. *Noun.*
—To pack in a crate or crates. The farmer *crated* the lettuce before he shipped it to the market. *Verb.*
crate (krāt) *noun, plural* **crates;** *verb,* **crated, crating.**

crater A hollow area that looks like the inside of a bowl. There are many *craters* on the surface of the moon.
cra·ter (krā'tər) *noun, plural* **craters.**

crawl **1.** To move very slowly. Babies *crawl* by moving on their hands and knees. Worms *crawl* by pulling their bodies along the ground. Traffic *crawled* along the highway. **2.** To be covered with crawling things. The picnic table *crawled* with ants. *Verb.*
—**1.** A very slow movement. Traffic slowed to a *crawl* in the fog. **2.** A fast swimming stroke. When a person does the crawl his face is down, he lifts his arms over his head one after the other, and he keeps kicking his feet. *Noun.*
crawl (krôl) *verb,* **crawled, crawling;** *noun, plural* **crawls.**

Crayfish

crayfish A small animal that looks like a lobster and lives in fresh water. Crayfish are a kind of shellfish and are used as food.
cray·fish (krā'fish') *noun, plural* **crayfish** or **crayfishes.**

crayon A colored stick made of a waxy material used for drawing or writing. Crayons come in all different colors.
cray·on (krā'on *or* krā'ən) *noun, plural* **crayons.**

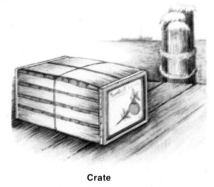

Crate

at; āpe; cär; end; mē; it; īce; hot; ōld;
fôrk; wood; fōōl; oil; out; up; turn; sing;
thin; **th**is; **hw** in white; **zh** in treasure.
ə stands for **a** in about, **e** in taken
i in pencil, **o** in lemon, and **u** in circus.

crazy **1.** Having a mind that is sick; insane; mentally ill. The prisoner almost became *crazy* after spending twenty years in an enemy prison. **2.** Foolish. Putting three dogs and two cats in the same room was a *crazy* thing to do. **3.** Very enthusiastic. My brother is *crazy* about fishing.
cra·zy (krā′zē) *adjective,* **crazier, craziest.**

creak To make a sharp, squeaking sound. The old stairs *creak* when you step on them. *Verb.*
—A sharp, squeaking sound. The rusty gate opened with a loud *creak. Noun.* ▲ Another word that sounds like this is **creek.**
creak (krēk) *verb,* **creaked, creaking;** *noun, plural* **creaks.**

cream **1.** The yellowish-white part of milk. Cream has fat in it and is thicker than milk. Butter is made from cream. **2.** A soft, thick lotion or foam that is put on the skin. My father uses shaving *cream* that smells like mint. My mother uses *cream* to keep her hands soft.
cream (krēm) *noun, plural* **creams.**

crease A line or mark made by folding or wrinkling something. The rain ruined the *crease* in my slacks. *Noun.*
—To make or get a line or mark in by folding or wrinkling. I *creased* my shirt badly when I packed it. *Verb.*
crease (krēs) *noun, plural* **creases;** *verb,* **creased, creasing.**

create To cause something new to exist or happen. The lack of rain that summer *created* a shortage of wheat the next winter. An author *creates* characters in his books.
cre·ate (krē āt′) *verb,* **created, creating.**

creation **1.** The act of causing something new to exist or happen. The *creation* of the motion picture took many months to complete. **2.** Anything that has been made. A sculpture, a painting, or a book is a creation.
cre·a·tion (krē ā′shən) *noun, plural* **creations.**

creative Having or showing ability to make something new. A poet must be *creative.*
cre·a·tive (krē ā′tiv) *adjective.*

creator **1.** A person who makes something new. That author is the *creator* of many novels. **2. the Creator.** God.
cre·a·tor (krē ā′tər) *noun, plural* **creators.**

creature A living person or animal. Deer, bears, and wolves are *creatures* of the forest.
crea·ture (krē′chər) *noun, plural* **creatures.**

credit **1.** Belief in the truth of something; faith. His friends gave full *credit* to his story. **2.** Reputation. His *credit* was not good at the store because he didn't pay his bills. **3.** Praise or honor. She deserves the *credit* for the dinner because she did most of the cooking. **4.** Something that is owed to a person. I have a five dollar *credit* at the bookstore. *Noun.*
—**1.** To believe; trust. I *credit* his story of the accident because he is always honest. **2.** To put an amount of money that is owed to someone into an account for him. The store *credited* his account with ten dollars when he returned the shirt. *Verb.*
cred·it (kred′it) *noun, plural* **credits;** *verb,* **credited, crediting.**

creed A statement of what a person or group of people believe in. Sandra has to learn the Girl Scout's *creed.*
creed (krēd) *noun, plural* **creeds.**

creek A small stream. A creek is bigger than a brook but smaller than a river. ▲ Another word that sounds like this is **creak.**
creek (krēk *or* krik) *noun, plural* **creeks.**

creep **1.** To move slowly and quietly; crawl. The baby *creeps* on his hands and knees. The last days before vacation seemed to *creep* by. **2.** To grow along the ground or over a surface. The ivy *creeps* over the fence in our yard. **3.** To feel as if things were crawling over one's skin. The howling of the dog made my flesh *creep.*
creep (krēp) *verb,* **crept, creeping.**

crepe A cloth that has a crinkled surface.
crepe (krāp) *noun, plural* **crepes.**

crepe paper A thin paper with a crinkled surface. Crepe paper can be stretched to take on different shapes and is used for decorating rooms for parties.

crept The crabs *crept* along the sand. Look up **creep** for more information.
crept (krept) *verb.*

crescent The shape the moon has when you can only see a thin, curved part of it.
cres·cent (kres′ənt) *noun, plural* **crescents.**

The moon has a **crescent** shape.

crest **1.** A bunch of feathers on the head of a bird. Bluejays have a *crest* on their head. **2.** A plume or other decoration on the top of a helmet. **3.** The highest part of something. We have a long way to climb before we reach the *crest* of the hill. We watched Susan on her surfboard riding the *crest* of the big wave.
crest (krest) *noun, plural* **crests.**

Crest

crew A group of people who work together to make something run. The people who work on a ship, airplane, or train are called the crew. A team of men who row a racing boat are its crew.
crew (kro͞o) *noun, plural* **crews.**

crib **1.** A small bed for a baby. Cribs have high sides that can be moved up and down. **2.** A box or rack that holds food for cattle and horses to eat from. **3.** A small building that grain or corn is stored in on a farm.
crib (krib) *noun, plural* **cribs.**

Crib

cricket¹ A black or brown insect that looks like a short grasshopper. Crickets have strong back legs that are used for hopping. The male makes a chirping noise by rubbing his front wings together.
crick·et (krik′it) *noun, plural* **crickets.**

cricket² A game like baseball played with a ball and bats on a grass field. Each team has eleven players and instead of home base, there is a goal, called a wicket, at each end of the field. Cricket is popular in England and in certain countries that were once ruled by England.
crick·et (krik′it) *noun.*

cried My baby sister *cried* when she fell and hurt her knee. Look up **cry** for more information.
cried (krīd) *verb.*

crime Something that is very wrong and against the law to do. Robbery is a crime, and a person who robs someone else can be sent to jail.
crime (krīm) *noun, plural* **crimes.**

criminal A person who does something that is a crime. The robber was a *criminal* and was sent to prison. *Noun.*
—Having to do with crime or the laws about crime. Linda is studying to be a *criminal* lawyer. *Adjective.*
crim·i·nal (krim′ən əl) *noun, plural* **criminals;** *adjective.*

crimson A deep red color. *Noun.*
—Having the color crimson. The setting sun was *crimson. Adjective.*
crim·son (krim′zən) *noun, plural* **crimsons;** *adjective.*

cripple A person or animal that cannot move some part of the body in the proper way because of an injury or a disease. The fox was a *cripple* after his leg was crushed in the trap. *Noun.*
—**1.** To badly injure a person or animal. Polio *crippled* many children years ago. **2.** To cause damage to something so that it cannot work properly. The heavy snowstorm *crippled* the airlines for several days. *Verb.*
crip·ple (krip′əl) *noun, plural* **cripples;** *verb,* **crippled, crippling.**

crisis **1.** A very important turning point that helps decide what will happen in the future. Having to decide whether or not to go to college was the first real *crisis* in his life. **2.** A difficult or dangerous situation. The murder of the prime minister caused a *crisis* in that country.
cri·sis (krī′sis) *noun, plural* **crises.**

crisp **1.** Hard but breaking easily into bits. Fresh lettuce, celery, and radishes should be *crisp. Crisp* bacon has most of the fat cooked out of it. **2.** Clear and cool; brisk. John likes to go fishing on *crisp* autumn days. **3.** Short and to the point. The coach gave *crisp* instructions to the team.
crisp (krisp) *adjective,* **crisper, crispest.**

at; āpe; cär; end; mē; it; īce; hot; ōld; fôrk; wood; fo͞ol; oil; out; up; turn; sing; thin; this; hw in white; zh in treasure.
ə stands for a in about, e in taken i in pencil, o in lemon, and u in circus.

crisscross Marked with lines that cross one another. The game of tic-tac-toe is played on a *crisscross* diagram. *Adjective.*
—A design made by crossing lines. A plaid is a *crisscross* of lines and colors. *Noun.*
—To mark with or make lines that cross one another. We could see where their footprints *crisscrossed* in the snow. *Verb.*
criss·cross (kris′krôs′) *adjective; noun, plural* **crisscrosses;** *verb,* **crisscrossed, crisscrossing.**

critic A person whose job is to say or write what he thinks is good or bad about books, motion pictures, music, art, or plays. We looked in the newspaper to see what the movie *critic* said about the new movie.
cri·tic (krit′ik) *noun, plural* **critics.**

critical **1.** Always finding something wrong with things. He was *critical* of every plan that we suggested. She is always *critical* of the way other people dress. **2.** Having to do with a person whose job is to be a critic. There is a good *critical* review of his new book in the newspaper. **3.** Dangerous or serious. There is a *critical* shortage of water in the town.
crit·i·cal (krit′i kəl) *adjective.*

criticism **1.** The act of saying what is good or bad about something. Don read with interest the newspaper's *criticism* of the artist's work. **2.** Disapproval. Her brother's *criticism* of the way she dressed made her angry.
crit·i·cism (krit′ə siz′əm) *noun, plural* **criticisms.**

criticize **1.** To say what is good or bad about something. His job on television is to *criticize* new movies. **2.** To find fault with something. Peggy *criticized* her brother's table manners.
crit·i·cize (krit′ə sīz′) *verb,* **criticized, criticizing.**

croak A deep, hoarse sound like one made by a frog or crow. *Noun.*
—To make a deep, hoarse sound. The frogs *croaked* in the pond. *Verb.*
croak (krōk) *noun, plural* **croaks;** *verb,* **croaked, croaking.**

Crochet

crochet To make something by looping thread or yarn into connected stitches with a needle that has a hook at one end. Aunt Agnes *crocheted* a beautiful blanket for the baby.
cro·chet (krō shā′) *verb,* **crocheted, crocheting.**

crocodile A long animal with short legs, thick, scaly skin, and a long, strong tail. A crocodile has strong jaws with long rows of teeth. Crocodiles live in and near water in Asia, Africa, and America. They look like and are related to alligators. Look up **alligator** for a picture of this animal.
croc·o·dile (krok′ə dīl′) *noun, plural* **crocodiles.**

crocus A small flower that grows from an underground bulb. Crocuses grow in many colors and have thin leaves like blades of grass. They are one of the first flowers to bloom in the spring.
cro·cus (krō′kəs) *noun, plural* **crocuses.**

Crocus

crook **1.** A bent part; curve. Barbara carried the umbrella in the *crook* of her arm. **2.** A person who is not honest. The *crook* broke into their house and stole the television set. *Noun.*
—To bend; curve; hook. Jean *crooked* her finger at us to tell us to come over. *Verb.*
crook (krook) *noun, plural* **crooks;** *verb,* **crooked, crooking.**

crooked **1.** Not straight; bent or curving. The path that we followed through the woods was very *crooked.* **2.** Not honest. The *crooked* man cheated at cards.
crook·ed (krook′id) *adjective.*

crop **1.** Plants that are grown to be used as food or to make something else. We harvested a huge *crop* of tomatoes this year. Cotton is an important *crop* in the South. **2.** A group of persons or things that come at the same time. We had a large *crop* of new students come to our school this fall. **3.** A pouch near the bottom of the throat of a bird. Food is held in the crop and is prepared for digestion. **4.** A short whip that has a loop at the end

instead of a lash. Some horseback riders use crops. *Noun.*
—To cut or bite off the top part of something. Dad *cropped* the row of bushes around our house. *Verb.*
crop (krop) *noun, plural* **crops;** *verb,* **cropped, cropping.**

croquet An outdoor game played with sticks called mallets that are used to hit wooden balls along the ground and through wire hoops called wickets.
cro·quet (krō kā′) *noun.*

Croquet

cross 1. A post or stake that has another bar across it. The cross is the symbol of Christianity because Christ died on a cross. 2. Anything shaped like a cross. On some tests you make a *cross* next to the right answer to a question. 3. A mixing of two or more animals or plants of different kinds. A mule is a *cross* between a horse and a donkey. *Noun.*
—1. To move or go from one side of something to the other. The ship *crossed* the ocean in seven days. She *crossed* the street when the light turned green. 2. To draw a line across. You *cross* a "t" in writing. Bill *crossed* out the mistake in his composition. 3. To put or lay one thing across another. She *crossed* her legs when she sat down. *Verb.*
—1. In a bad temper; grouchy. My sister gets *cross* when people criticize her. 2. Lying or going from one side of something to another. We met at the *cross* streets in the middle of town. *Adjective.*
cross (krôs) *noun, plural* **crosses;** *verb,* **crossed, crossing;** *adjective,* **crosser, crossest.**

crossbow A weapon that was used in the Middle Ages. A crossbow had a bow mounted across a wooden stock along which arrows could be shot.
cross·bow (krôs′bō′) *noun, plural* **crossbows.**

crossing 1. A place where two lines or other things cross each other. We stopped at the railroad *crossing* to let the train go through. 2. A place where a street or river may be crossed. There is a shallow *crossing* just down the stream.
cross·ing (krô′sing) *noun, plural* **crossings.**

crossroad 1. A road that crosses another road or a road that leads from one main road to another. 2. **crossroads.** The place where two or more roads cross each other. There was a traffic light at the *crossroads.*
cross·road (krôs′rōd′) *noun, plural* **crossroads.**

cross section 1. A slice or piece made by cutting straight across something. When you slice a banana you make cross sections. 2. A sample of people or things that is thought to show what the whole group of people or things is like. A poll of a *cross section* of voters in the state showed that the senator would probably be elected to another term in office.

crotch The place where the body divides into two legs, or where a branch of a tree divides from the trunk or from another branch.
crotch (kroch) *noun, plural* **crotches.**

crouch To stoop or bend low with the knees bent. The cat *crouched* in the bushes, ready to spring if a bird came close.
crouch (krouch) *verb,* **crouched, crouching.**

crow¹ 1. To make the loud, sharp cry of a rooster. The farmer's rooster *crows* every morning when the sun rises. 2. To make a happy yell or cry. Steve *crowed* with delight when he won the contest.
crow (krō) *verb,* **crowed, crowing.**

Crow

crow² A large bird with shiny, black feathers and a harsh cry.
crow (krō) *noun, plural* **crows.**

at; āpe; cär; end; mē; it; īce; hot; ōld;
fôrk; wood; fōol; oil; out; up; turn; sing;
thin; this; hw in white; zh in treasure.
ə stands for a in about, e in taken
i in pencil, o in lemon, and u in circus.

crowbar A heavy steel or iron bar that has one flattened end. A crowbar is used to lift things up or pry things apart.
crow·bar (krō′bär′) *noun, plural* **crowbars.**

Crowbar

crowd A large number of people gathered together. There was a *crowd* of people waiting to get into the theater. *Noun.*
—**1.** To put or force too many people or things into too small a space. Roberta *crowded* her shelf with books. **2.** To move by pushing or shoving. She asked the man behind her in line not to *crowd* her. *Verb.*
crowd (kroud) *noun, plural* **crowds;** *verb,* **crowded, crowding.**

crown **1.** A covering for the head worn by kings and queens. A crown is often made of gold and silver set with jewels. **2.** The highest or top part of anything. The hikers climbed to the *crown* of the hill. Betty squashed the *crown* of Father's hat when she accidentally sat on it. **3.** The part of a tooth that can be seen above the gums. *Noun.*
—To make a person a king or queen at a special ceremony during which a crown is put on his or her head. *Verb.*
crown (kroun) *noun, plural* **crowns;** *verb,* **crowned, crowning.**

Crown

crow's-nest A small platform near the top of a ship's mast. Sailors use it as a lookout tower.
crow's-nest (krōz′nest′) *noun, plural* **crow's-nests.**

crucial Very important; decisive. When a thing is crucial it means that it will decide whether something else succeeds or fails. The last inning of the baseball game was *crucial* to our team.
cru·cial (krōō′shəl) *adjective.*

crucifixion **1.** The act of crucifying a person. **2. Crucifixion.** The putting to death of Christ on a cross.
cru·ci·fix·ion (krōō′sə fik′shən) *noun, plural* **crucifixions.**

crucify To put a person to death by nailing or tying the hands and feet to a cross.
cru·ci·fy (krōō′sə fī′) *verb,* **crucified, crucifying.**

crude **1.** In a natural or raw state. *Crude* rubber is rubber as it is drained from the bark of rubber trees. **2.** Done or made without skill; rough. The boys built a *crude* shack in the woods out of odd bits of wood they had found. **3.** Not polite or in good taste; not refined; rude. It was *crude* of them to laugh at the girl when she lost her balance and fell off the chair.
crude (krōōd) *adjective,* **cruder, crudest.**

cruel **1.** Willing to cause pain or suffering to others. The *cruel* man beat his dog. **2.** Causing pain or suffering. A *cruel*, biting cold wind swept across the plains.
cru·el (krōō′əl) *adjective,* **crueler, cruelest.**

cruelty **1.** A being willing to cause pain or suffering to others. That man is hated because of his *cruelty* to animals. **2.** A cruel act. The prisoners suffered many *cruelties* in the enemy prison camp.
cru·el·ty (krōō′əl tē) *noun, plural* **cruelties.**

cruet A small glass bottle that vinegar, oil, or other dressings are served in.
cru·et (krōō′it) *noun, plural* **cruets.**

Cruets

cruise **1.** To sail from place to place. We *cruised* along the coast until we found a place to anchor for a while. **2.** To move or ride from place to place. A police car *cruises* through our neighborhood each night. *Verb.*
—A trip in a boat taken for pleasure. We would love to take a *cruise* to Hawaii. *Noun.*
cruise (krōōz) *verb,* **cruised, cruising;** *noun, plural* **cruises.**

cruiser **1.** A warship that is faster than a battleship and carries fewer guns. **2.** A motorboat with a cabin, that is used for pleasure.
cruis·er (krōō′zər) *noun, plural* **cruisers.**

crumb A tiny piece of bread, cake, cracker, or cookie. We put out *crumbs* for the birds.
crumb (krum) *noun, plural* **crumbs.**

crumble 1. To break into small pieces. The muffin *crumbled* when I tried to butter it. 2. To fall apart or be destroyed. The old house is slowly *crumbling.* The team's hopes for winning the game *crumbled* when the best player got sick.
crum·ble (krum′bəl) *verb,* **crumbled, crumbling.**

crumple 1. To press or crush into wrinkles or folds. We *crumpled* sheets of newspaper to start the fire. 2. To fall down or collapse. Susan *crumpled* to the ground when she hit her head on the low branch.
crum·ple (krum′pəl) *verb,* **crumpled, crumpling.**

crunch To chew or crush with a noisy, crushing sound. The rabbit *crunched* on a carrot. *Verb.*
—A crushing, crackling sound. We heard the *crunch* of the hiker's boots in the snow. *Noun.*
crunch (krunch) *verb,* **crunched, crunching;** *noun, plural* **crunches.**

crusade 1. Any of the military expeditions undertaken by the Christian people of Europe between the years 1095 and 1291 to take the Holy Land away from the Muslims. 2. A strong fight against something evil or for something good. We started a *crusade* to clean up the town parks. *Noun.*
—To fight in a crusade. He is *crusading* against the pollution of our nation's lakes and rivers. *Verb.*
cru·sade (kroō sād′) *noun, plural* **crusades;** *verb,* **crusaded, crusading.**

crusader A person who fights in a crusade. She is a *crusader* for civil rights.
cru·sad·er (kroō sā′dər) *noun, plural* **crusaders.**

crush 1. To squeeze very hard. When you crush something, it is broken, put out of shape, or hurt in some way. We have a machine that *crushes* ice into small bits. The garbage can was *crushed* when the truck ran over it. 2. To put down; subdue. Her hopes of going to the circus were *crushed* when she got sick and had to stay in bed. *Verb.*
—1. A very strong pressure or squeezing. The *crush* of the crowd pushed him against the door of the bus. 2. A sudden, strong liking for a person. My sister has a *crush* on a handsome movie actor. *Noun.*
crush (krush) *verb,* **crushed, crushing;** *noun, plural* **crushes.**

crust 1. The hard, crunchy outside part of bread, rolls, or other food. A pie has a *crust* of dough. We fed the birds *crusts* of bread. 2. Any hard outside part or coating. The pond was covered with a *crust* of ice. The *crust* of the earth is a layer of rock twenty miles deep. *Noun.*
—To cover with a crust. Ice *crusted* the pond. *Verb.*
crust (krust) *noun, plural* **crusts;** *verb,* **crusted, crusting.**

crustacean An animal that has a hard shell and lives mostly in water. Lobsters, crabs, shrimp, and barnacles are crustaceans.
crus·ta·cean (krus tā′shən) *noun, plural* **crustaceans.**

crutch A support that helps a lame person in walking. A crutch is a pole that usually has a padded part at the top that fits under the arm so a person can lean on it.
crutch (kruch) *noun, plural* **crutches.**

Crutches

cry 1. To shed tears; weep. The baby will *cry* when he is hungry. She *cried* when she lost her ring on the beach. 2. To call loudly; shout. The man in the burning building *cried* for help. *Verb.*
—1. A loud call or shout. Sarah gave a *cry* of joy when she saw the bicycle under the Christmas tree. The boys heard a *cry* for help from the lake. 2. The special sound that an animal or bird makes. Late at night we listened to the *cries* of the owls. *Noun.*
cry (krī) *verb,* **cried, crying;** *noun, plural* **cries.**

crystal 1. A clear kind of rock that has no color. Crystal is a kind of quartz. 2. A body that is formed by certain substances when they solidify. Crystals have flat surfaces. Salt forms in crystals. Snowflakes are crystals. 3. A very fine, clear glass used to make drinking glasses, bowls, plates, and vases. Crystal sparkles in the light.
crys·tal (krist′əl) *noun, plural* **crystals.**

at; āpe; cär; end; mē; it; īce; hot; ōld;
fôrk; wood; foōl; oil; out; up; turn; sing;
thin; <u>th</u>is; hw in white; zh in treasure.
ə stands for a in about, e in taken
i in pencil, o in lemon, and u in circus.

cub A very young bear, fox, wolf, lion, or tiger.
cub (kub) *noun, plural* **cubs.**

cube 1. A solid figure with six equal, square sides. 2. Something shaped like a cube. Put more ice *cubes* in my iced tea, please. 3. The product of a number that is multiplied by itself two times. The cube of 2 is 8 because $2 \times 2 \times 2 = 8$. *Noun.*
—To cut or make into cubes. Alan *cubed* potatoes to make potato salad. *Verb.*
cube (kyo͞ob) *noun, plural* **cubes;** *verb,* **cubed, cubing.**

The building block is a **cube.**

cubic 1. Shaped like a cube. These building blocks are *cubic*. 2. Having length, breadth, and thickness. The volume of a cube can be measured in *cubic* inches or *cubic* feet.
cu·bic (kyo͞o′bik) *adjective.*

cub scout A boy who is a junior member of the Boy Scouts.

cuckoo A bird that has a long tail and a call that sounds like its name. Most cuckoos have brown feathers and lay their eggs in the nests of other birds.
cuck·oo (ko͞o′ko͞o *or* kook′o͞o) *noun, plural* **cuckoos.**

Cuckoo

cucumber A long, green vegetable with white flesh and many seeds inside. The cucumber grows on a vine. Cucumbers are eaten raw in salads or made into pickles.
cu·cum·ber (kyo͞o′kum′bər) *noun, plural* **cucumbers.**

cud Food that comes back into the mouth from the first stomach of cows and some other animals so that they can chew it again.
cud (kud) *noun, plural* **cuds.**

cue[1] A signal that tells someone to begin to do something. The ring of the telephone was the actor's *cue* to walk on stage. *Noun.*
—To give a signal to someone to tell them to begin to do something. Betty's job was to stand backstage and *cue* the actors. *Verb.*
cue (kyo͞o) *noun, plural* **cues;** *verb,* **cued, cuing.**

cue[2] A long, thin stick that is used to strike the ball in playing pool or billiards.
cue (kyo͞o) *noun, plural* **cues.**

cuff[1] 1. A band of material at the bottom of a sleeve. 2. A turned-up fold of material at the bottom of a trouser leg.
cuff (kuf) *noun, plural* **cuffs.**

cuff[2] To hit with the hand. The grocer *cuffed* the boy on the head for stealing an apple. *Verb.*
—A hit with the hand; slap. She gave the dog a *cuff* when he snapped at her. *Noun.*
cuff (kuf) *verb,* **cuffed, cuffing;** *noun, plural* **cuffs.**

culprit A person who is guilty of doing something that is wrong. The woman identified the two men as the *culprits* who stole her purse.
cul·prit (kul′prit) *noun, plural* **culprits.**

cultivate 1. To prepare and use land for growing vegetables, flowers, or other crops. To cultivate land, you plow and fertilize it and get rid of weeds in it before you plant seeds. 2. To work hard to improve or develop. Tom tried to *cultivate* good study habits.
cul·ti·vate (kul′tə vāt′) *verb,* **cultivated, cultivating.**

cultivator A tool or machine used to loosen the soil and pull up weeds around growing plants.
cul·ti·va·tor (kul′tə vā′tər) *noun, plural* **cultivators.**

cultural Having to do with culture. We read a book about the *cultural* history of ancient Greece.
cul·tur·al (kul′chər əl) *adjective.*

culture 1. The arts, beliefs, and customs that make up a way of life for a group of people at a certain time. We are studying the *culture* of the North American Indian. 2. The good

Cultivator

taste and manners, and the knowledge and appreciation of the arts that come as a result of good education. The family sent their son to Europe to gain *culture.* **3.** The improvement and development of something. Gymnastics are a part of physical *culture.*

cul·ture (kul′chər) *noun, plural* **cultures.**

cunning **1.** Very clever at fooling or deceiving others. The *cunning* thief disguised herself as a maid and robbed people at the party. **2.** Very cute; charming. Everyone said that Katherine was such a *cunning* baby. *Adjective.*

—Cleverness at fooling or deceiving others. Foxes are said to show much *cunning* in escaping from hunters. *Noun.*

cun·ning (kun′iṅg) *adjective; noun.*

cup **1.** A small bowl with a handle that is used to drink from. **2.** Anything that has the shape of a cup. A silver *cup* was the prize for the winner of the sailing race. *Noun.*

—To shape like a cup. Dan *cupped* his hands under the hose to fill them with water to drink. *Verb.*

cup (kup) *noun, plural* **cups;** *verb,* **cupped, cupping.**

cupboard A closet with shelves to store dishes or food.

cup·board (kub′ərd) *noun, plural* **cupboards.**

cupcake A small cake. Cupcakes are baked in metal pans with several cup-shaped hollows.

cup·cake (kup′kāk′) *noun, plural* **cupcakes.**

Cupid The god of love. Cupid is usually pictured as a young boy who has wings and carries a bow and arrow. Valentines often have a picture of Cupid on them.

Cu·pid (kyoo′pid) *noun.*

Cupid

curb **1.** A border of concrete or stone along the side of a road or sidewalk. We were lucky to find a place to park along the *curb* in front of the restaurant. **2.** Anything that holds back or controls an action. We decided to put a *curb* on our spending by following a strict budget. **3.** A chain or strap that is fastened to a horse's bit. It is used to control the horse when the reins are pulled. *Noun.*

—To hold back or control. She *curbed* her anger at what he said by counting silently to ten before she answered him. *Verb.*

curb (kurb) *noun, plural* **curbs;** *verb,* **curbed, curbing.**

cure **1.** To make a person or animal healthy again. The veterinarian *cured* our dog. **2.** To get rid of. My mother says to *cure* a cold you have to stay in bed and rest. **3.** To preserve or prepare meat and fish for use by drying, smoking, or salting. Farmers *cure* the meat of pigs to make bacon. *Verb.*

—Something that makes a person or animal healthy again. Aspirin is the best *cure* for my headache. *Noun.*

cure (kyoor) *verb,* **cured, curing;** *noun, plural* **cures.**

curfew A fixed time at night when a person has to be indoors or at home. At camp we had a 10:00 *curfew* to be in bed.

cur·few (kur′fyoo) *noun, plural* **curfews.**

▲ The word **curfew** comes from two early French words that meant "cover" and "fire." In the Middle Ages, a bell rang at night to tell people that it was time for them to put out or cover their fires. This signal became known as the "cover-fire" or *curfew.*

---

curiosity **1.** A strong wish to learn about things that are new, strange, or interesting. The children had a great *curiosity* about what was in the locked closet. **2.** Something that is interesting because it is strange, rare, or unusual. A horse-drawn carriage is a *curiosity* today.

cu·ri·os·i·ty (kyoor′ē os′ə tē) *noun, plural* **curiosities.**

curious **1.** Eager to learn about things that are new, strange, or interesting. I was really *curious* to know more about the new girl in class. **2.** Strange or unusual. Tom has a collection of *curious* old coins.

cu·ri·ous (kyoor′ē əs) *adjective.*

curl To twist in curved rings or coils. She *curled* her hair for the party. The smoke *curled* from his pipe. The cat *curled* up for a nap. *Verb.*

—**1.** A curved lock of hair; ringlet. My little sister has *curls* all over her head. **2.** Something shaped like a ring or coil. A *curl* of smoke rose upward out of the chimney. *Noun.*

at; āpe; cär; end; mē; it; īce; hot; ōld;
fôrk; wood; fool; oil; out; up; turn; sing;
thin; this; hw in white; zh in treasure.
ə stands for a in about, e in taken
i in pencil, o in lemon, and u in circus.

curl (kurl) *verb,* **curled, curling;** *noun, plural* **curls.**

curly Forming or having curls. She has *curly* hair.
cur·ly (kur′lē) *adjective,* **curlier, curliest.**

currant **1.** A small, sour berry that grows in bunches on a bush. Currants are used to make jelly. **2.** A small seedless raisin used in cakes, pies, and buns. ▲ Another word that sounds like this is **current.**
cur·rant (kur′ənt) *noun, plural* **currants.**

currency **1.** The money that is used in a country. Dollar bills, quarters, and dimes are part of the currency of the United States. Pesos are part of the currency of Mexico. **2.** General use or acceptance. As more and more people use a new slang word, they begin to give it *currency.*
cur·ren·cy (kur′ən sē) *noun, plural* **currencies.**

current Being part of the present time. If something is happening, used, or believed in now it is current. My *current* address is on the envelope. The *current* belief is that there is probably no life on the planet Venus. *Adjective.*
—**1.** A part of the air or of a body of water that is moving along in a path. The rubber raft was caught in the *current* and carried out to sea. A cold *current* of air flowed through the room when she opened the door. **2.** A flow of electricity in a wire or through anything. When a fuse burns out it stops the electric *current* in the circuit. **3.** The way events or thoughts seem to move along a path. The *current* of public opinion today seems to be that the mayor should not run for reelection. *Noun.* ▲ Another word that sounds like this is **currant.**
cur·rent (kur′ənt) *adjective; noun, plural* **currents.**

curriculum All the different courses that are given in a school or college. My ninth grade *curriculum* will be made up of English, algebra, biology, history, and Spanish.
cur·ric·u·lum (kə rik′yə ləm) *noun, plural* **curriculums.**

curse **1.** A wish that something evil or harmful will happen to a person or thing. A curse is often made by calling on God or gods. **2.** A word or words used in swearing. A curse is usually said in anger. *Noun.*
—**1.** To wish that something evil or harmful will happen to a person or thing. The soldier *cursed* the enemy. **2.** To say a word or words that show hate or anger; swear. He *cursed* when he hit his thumb with the hammer. **3.** To cause evil, harm, or suffering to. He had been *cursed* with a weak back for years. *Verb.*
curse (kurs) *noun, plural* **curses;** *verb,* **cursed, cursing.**

curtain **1.** A piece of cloth hung across an open space. Curtains are hung at windows, in doorways, and across the front part of a stage. **2.** Anything like a curtain. A *curtain* of fog hid the tops of the tall buildings. *Noun.*
—To put a curtain over; screen. We *curtained* off a part of the basement as a workshop. *Verb.*
cur·tain (kur′tin) *noun, plural* **curtains;** *verb,* **curtained, curtaining.**

Curtsy

curtsy A bow showing respect made by bending the knees and lowering the body slightly. Women and girls curtsy and men and boys bow.
curt·sy (kurt′sē) *noun, plural* **curtsies.**

A **curve** in a road

curve **1.** A line that keeps bending in one direction. A curve has no straight parts or angles. **2.** Something that has the shape of a curve. The river has a *curve* in it further on. The baby rested his head in the *curve* of his mother's arm. *Noun.*
—To bend or move in a curved line. The road *curves* as you come off the bridge. The base-

ball *curved* to the left as it came near the batter. *Verb.*

curve (kurv) *noun, plural* **curves;** *verb,* **curved, curving.**

cushion **1.** A pillow or soft pad used to sit, lie, or rest on. Our couch has three *cushions* on the seat. **2.** Anything that softens a blow or protects against harm. A savings account in a bank can be a *cushion* if you lose your job. *Noun.*
—**1.** To make a pillow or soft pad for. We are going to *cushion* the rocking chair so that it is more comfortable. **2.** To soften a blow or shock. The pile of leaves *cushioned* my fall from the tree. *Verb.*
    cush·ion (koosh′ən) *noun, plural* **cushions;** *verb,* **cushioned, cushioning.**

custard A sweet dessert made of eggs, milk, and sugar that are cooked together into a pudding.
    cus·tard (kus′tərd) *noun, plural* **custards.**

custodian A person who is responsible for the care of a person or thing. The school *custodian* made sure the buildings were kept clean and in good repair.
    cus·to·di·an (kəs tō′dē ən) *noun, plural* **custodians.**

custody The care and keeping of a person or thing. She was in her grandmother's *custody* while her parents lived in China for a year. The suspected bank robber was taken into the *custody* of the police until bail was arranged.
    cus·to·dy (kus′tə dē) *noun, plural* **custodies.**

custom **1.** A way of acting that has become accepted by many people. Customs are learned and passed down from one generation to another. Decorating trees and giving presents at Christmas is a *custom* shared by many people in this country. **2.** The usual way that something is done; habit. It is my *custom* to walk to school every morning. **3. customs.** Taxes that a government collects on products that are brought in from a foreign country. We had to pay *customs* on the sweaters we had bought in Scotland.
    cus·tom (kus′təm) *noun, plural* **customs.**

customary Usual. It is *customary* in our family to have Thanksgiving dinner at our grandmother's house.
    cus·tom·ar·y (kus′tə mer′ē) *adjective.*

customer A person who buys something. That store thinks of us as regular *customers* because we shop there at least once a week.
    cus·tom·er (kus′tə mər) *noun, plural* **customers.**

cut **1.** To divide, pierce, open, or take away

a part with something sharp. We could not untie the knot, so we had to *cut* the string. Laura *cut* the pie into six slices. I *cut* my foot on the sharp rock. We have to *cut* the grass today. The cold wind *cut* through her light jacket. **2.** To make by using a sharp tool. We *cut* a hole in the door so the cat could come in and go out. **3.** To make shorter or smaller. He *cut* his speech because it was too long. The store will *cut* all its prices for the big sale. **4.** To cross or pass. The river *cuts* through the valley. Let's *cut* through the park instead of walking around it. *Verb.*
—**1.** An opening or slit made with something sharp. He got a *cut* on his hand from the broken glass. **2.** A decrease. Father asked if I would mind taking a *cut* in my allowance. *Noun.*
    cut (kut) *verb,* **cut, cutting;** *noun, plural* **cuts.**

cute Adorable; charming; appealing. All the puppies were so *cute* that it was hard to choose which one to buy.
    cute (kyo͞ot) *adjective,* **cuter, cutest.**

cuticle A tough layer of skin. We have cuticles around the edges of our fingernails.
    cu·ti·cle (kyo͞o′ti kəl) *noun, plural* **cuticles.**

cutlass A sword with a wide, flat, curved blade.
    cut·lass (kut′ləs) *noun, plural* **cutlasses.**

Cutlass

cutter **1.** A person whose job it is to cut out things. A diamond *cutter* cuts away bits of

at; āpe; cär; end; mē; it; īce; hot; ōld; fôrk; wood; fo͞ol; oil; out; up; turn; sing; thin; this; hw in white; zh in treasure.
ə stands for a in about, e in taken
i in pencil, o in lemon, and u in circus.

the stone to give a diamond a special shape. A dress *cutter* cuts out dresses from fabric. **2.** A tool or machine that is used to cut out things. It is fun to use cookie *cutters* to make different shapes. **3.** A small, fast ship. The Coast Guard uses *cutters* to rescue people who are having trouble at sea.
  cut·ter (kut′ər) *noun, plural* **cutters.**

cutting **1.** Able to make a slit or other opening in; sharp. The *cutting* edge of a knife is thinner than the other edge. **2.** Hurting a person's feelings. He made a *cutting* remark about his friend's new jacket, and then he was sorry. *Adjective.*
—**1.** A small part cut from a plant that is used to grow a new plant. If you take a *cutting* from ivy and put it in water, it will grow roots and can be planted. **2.** An article or picture cut out of a newspaper or magazine; clipping. *Noun.*
  cut·ting (kut′ing) *adjective; noun, plural* **cuttings.**

cycle A series of events that happen one after another in the same order, over and over again. Spring, summer, autumn, and winter are the *cycle* of the four seasons of the year. *Noun.*
—To ride a bicycle, tricycle, or motorcycle. We plan to *cycle* in the park. *Verb.*
  cy·cle (sī′kəl) *noun, plural* **cycles;** *verb,* **cycled, cycling.**

cyclone A very powerful windstorm. The winds in a cyclone move around and around and can cause much damage.
  cy·clone (sī′klōn) *noun, plural* **cyclones.**

cylinder A solid or hollow object that is shaped like a roller or a soup can.

cyl·in·der (sil′ən dər) *noun, plural* **cylinders.**

cymbal A metal musical instrument that is shaped like a plate. One cymbal is hit against another to make a ringing sound. ▲ Another word that sounds like this is **symbol.**
  cym·bal (sim′bəl) *noun, plural* **cymbals.**

Leaves and Cone

Cypress Tree

cypress Any of various evergreen trees that have small scalelike leaves. The wood of the cypress is very hard and is used for building.
  cy·press (sī′prəs) *noun, plural* **cypresses.**

czar One of the emperors who once ruled Russia.
  czar (zär) *noun, plural* **czars.**

at; āpe; cär; end; mē; it; īce; hot; ōld; fôrk; wood; fōol; oil; out; up; turn; sing; thin; this; hw in white; zh in treasure.
ə stands for a in about, e in taken i in pencil, o in lemon, and u in circus.

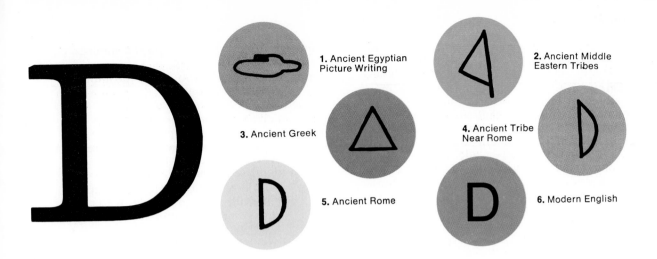

1. Ancient Egyptian Picture Writing

2. Ancient Middle Eastern Tribes

3. Ancient Greek

4. Ancient Tribe Near Rome

5. Ancient Rome

6. Modern English

D is the fourth letter of the alphabet. The oldest form of the letter **D** was a drawing that the ancient Egyptians (**1**) used in their picture writing nearly 5000 years ago. This drawing was borrowed by several ancient tribes (**2**) in the Middle East. They drew this letter like a triangle. The ancient Greeks (**3**) borrowed this letter and called it *delta*. We use the word "delta" for soil that builds up at the mouth of a river. The Greek letter was borrowed by an ancient tribe (**4**) that settled north of Rome about 2800 years ago. They changed the shape of *delta* by rounding two of the sides of the triangle. The Romans (**5**) borrowed this letter and, by about 2400 years ago, were writing it almost exactly the way we write the capital letter **D** today (**6**).

d, D The fourth letter of the alphabet.
   d, D (dē) *noun, plural* **d's, D's.**

dab **1.** To touch lightly and gently; tap. Tim's mother *dabbed* his cut knee with cotton. **2.** To put on lightly and gently. Betty *dabbed* lotion on her sunburn. *Verb.*
   —**1.** A small, moist mass of something. The girl formed a *dab* of clay into the shape of a bowl. **2.** A little bit. Alice wanted only a *dab* of butter on her mashed potatoes. *Noun.*
   dab (dab) *verb,* **dabbed, dabbing;** *noun, plural* **dabs.**

dabble **1.** To work at or do something a little, but not in a serious way. He only *dabbled* at playing the piano because he would never take the time to practice. **2.** To splash in and out of the water. The girls sat on the dock to *dabble* their feet in the water.
   dab·ble (dab'əl) *verb,* **dabbled, dabbling.**

dachshund A small dog with a long body, very short legs, and drooping ears.
   dachs·hund (däks'hoont' *or* däks'hoond') *noun, plural* **dachshunds.**

▲ The word **dachshund** comes from the German name for the dog, which means "badger dog." These dogs were first raised for hunting badgers.

dad Father. Children often call their father *Dad.*
   dad (dad) *noun, plural* **dads.**

daddy Father. Mary and Jack call their father *Daddy.*
   dad·dy (dad'ē) *noun, plural* **daddies.**

daddy-longlegs An animal that looks like a spider. It has a small round body and very long, thin legs.
   dad·dy-long·legs (dad'ē lông'legz') *noun, plural* **daddy-longlegs.**

daffodil A plant that has long, thin leaves and yellow or white flowers.
   daf·fo·dil (daf'ə dil') *noun, plural* **daffodils.**

dagger A small weapon that looks like a knife. A dagger is used for stabbing.
   dag·ger (dag'ər) *noun, plural* **daggers.**

daily Appearing, done, or happening every day. Mr. Smith reads the *daily* newspaper on his way to work. Peggy does her *daily* job of making her bed before she leaves for school. *Adjective.*
   —Day after day; every day. That train runs *daily. Adverb.*
   —A newspaper published every day or every weekday. *Noun.*
   dai·ly (dā'lē) *adjective; adverb; noun, plural* **dailies.**

dainty Delicate and pretty. Joan's older sis-

Daffodil

165

ter wore a *dainty* gold bracelet to the school dance.

dain·ty (dān′tē) *adjective,* **daintier, daintiest.**

dairy **1.** A place where milk and cream are stored or made into butter and cheese. **2.** A store or company that sells milk, cream, butter, and cheese. **3.** A farm where cows are raised, milk and cream are produced, and butter and cheese are made.

dair·y (der′ē) *noun, plural* **dairies.**

dais A slightly raised platform for a throne, a speaker's desk, or seats for guests of honor.

da·is (dā′is) *noun, plural* **daises.**

daisy A plant that has a flower of pink, white, or yellow petals around a yellow center.

dai·sy (dā′zē) *noun, plural* **daisies.**

Dalmatian A large dog that has a short-haired white coat covered with small black or brown spots.

Dal·ma·tian (dal-mā′shən) *noun, plural* **Dalmatians.**

Daisy

dam A wall built across a stream or river to hold back the water. *Noun.*
—To hold back by a dam. Beavers *dam* streams with mud and sticks. *Verb.* ▲ Another word that sounds like this is **damn.**

dam (dam) *noun, plural* **dams;** *verb,* **dammed, damming.**

Dam

damage Harm or injury that makes something less valuable or useful. The flood caused great *damage* to the farms in the area. *Noun.*
—To harm or injure. Rain came through the open window and *damaged* the books that were on the window sill. *Verb.*

dam·age (dam′ij) *noun, plural* **damages;** *verb,* **damaged, damaging.**

dame **1.** A woman who has a position of rank. **2.** An elderly woman.

dame (dām) *noun, plural* **dames.**

damn **1.** To say that something is very bad or of little worth. The critics *damned* the new movie. **2.** To curse or swear at. ▲ Another word that sounds like this is **dam.**

damn (dam) *verb,* **damned, damning.**

damp A little wet; moist. He wiped up the spilled milk with a *damp* sponge. Karen put on a warm sweater because it was such a *damp* and chilly day. *Adjective.*
—Slight wetness; moisture. *Noun.*

damp (damp) *adjective,* **damper, dampest;** *noun.*

dampen **1.** To make a little wet or moist. *Dampen* the rag before you wipe the table. **2.** To lessen the force or strength of. Losing the game *dampened* the team's spirits.

damp·en (dam′pən) *verb,* **dampened, dampening.**

dance **1.** To move the body or feet in time to music. Alice likes to *dance.* **2.** To move or jump about quickly or lightly. Waves *danced* on the lake. *Verb.*
—**1.** A particular set of steps or movements done in time to music. The waltz is a hard *dance* to learn. **2.** A party where people dance. There will be a *dance* Friday night at the high school. *Noun.*

dance (dans) *verb,* **danced, dancing;** *noun, plural* **dances.**

dancer A person who dances. Jill wants to study to be a *dancer.*

danc·er (dan′sər) *noun, plural* **dancers.**

dandelion A plant with a bright yellow flower and long leaves. Dandelion leaves are sometimes eaten in salads or cooked as a vegetable.

dan·de·li·on (dand′əl ī′ən) *noun, plural* **dandelions.**

▲ The word **dandelion** comes from the French name for this flower, which means "lion's teeth." The French probably called the plant by this name because its leaves have sharp edges like teeth.

dandruff Small white or gray pieces of dead skin that fall from the scalp.

dan·druff (dan′drəf) *noun.*

dandy A man who is too fussy about his clothes and the way he looks.

dan·dy (dan′dē) *noun, plural* **dandies.**

danger **1.** The chance that something bad or

harmful will happen. The children knew the *danger* in skating on thin ice. **2.** Something that may cause harm or injury. Icy roads are a *danger* to drivers.

dan·ger (dān′jər) *noun, plural* **dangers.**

dangerous Likely to cause something bad or harmful to happen. Driving too fast is *dangerous.*

dan·ger·ous (dān′jər əs) *adjective.*

dangle To hang or swing loosely. Paul sat down on the edge of the swimming pool to *dangle* his feet in the water.

dan·gle (dang′gəl) *verb,* **dangled, dangling.**

dare **1.** To challenge someone to do something. Bill *dared* Joe to jump off the high diving board. **2.** To be bold enough to try; have the courage for. The boys did not *dare* to skate on the thin ice. *Verb.*
—A challenge. Alice took her brother's *dare* and jumped across the stream. *Noun.*

dare (der) *verb,* **dared, daring;** *noun, plural* **dares.**

daring Courage or boldness; bravery. The first explorers of the North Pole are famous for their *daring. Noun.*
—Courageous and bold; brave; fearless. The girl was given a medal for her *daring* rescue of the drowning child. *Adjective.*

dar·ing (der′ing) *noun; adjective.*

dark **1.** Having little or no light. The night is very *dark* because the clouds are covering the moon. **2.** Not light in color; almost the color of black. Nancy has *dark* hair and brown eyes. *Adjective.*
—**1.** A lack of light. We keep a light on in my little brother's room at night because he is afraid of the *dark.* **2.** Night or nightfall; the end of daylight. Bob's mother told him to be home before *dark. Noun.*

dark (därk) *adjective,* **darker, darkest;** *noun.*
in the dark. Without knowledge; not aware. The teacher kept us *in the dark* about the party because she wanted to surprise us.

darken To make or become dark or darker. Janet watched the rain clouds *darken* the sky. The white paint had *darkened* with age.

dark·en (där′kən) *verb,* **darkened, darkening.**

darling A person who is loved very much. A husband and wife may call each other *darling. Noun.*
—**1.** Very much loved; dear. The mother wrote a letter to her daughter at camp that began with the words "My *darling* Amy." **2.** Cute and attractive; charming. Everyone thought the kittens were *darling. Adjective.*

dar·ling (där′ling) *noun, plural* **darlings;** *adjective.*

darn To mend by making stitches back and forth across a hole or tear. She *darned* the holes in her sweater.

darn (därn) *verb,* **darned, darning.**

dart A thin, pointed object that looks like a small arrow. Darts are thrown at targets in certain games. *Noun.*
—**1.** To jump or move suddenly and quickly. We watched the rabbit *dart* into the bushes. **2.** To throw or send suddenly and quickly. The frog *darted* out its tongue to catch the fly. She *darted* an angry look at her friend for giving away her secret. *Verb.*

dart (därt) *noun, plural* **darts;** *verb,* **darted, darting.**

Dart

dash **1.** To move fast; rush. We tried to teach our dog not to *dash* after cars. **2.** To hit or throw with force; smash. High waves *dashed* against the ship during the storm. **3.** To destroy or ruin. Spraining her ankle *dashed* her hopes of winning the race. *Verb.*
—**1.** A fast movement or sudden rush. The hikers made a *dash* for cover when the rain started. **2.** A small amount that is added or mixed in. Add another *dash* of salt to the beef stew. **3.** A short race. Both schools had runners in the 50-yard *dash. Noun.*

dash (dash) *verb,* **dashed, dashing;** *noun, plural* **dashes.**

dashboard A panel in front of the driver in an automobile. It has dials and instruments to help the driver operate the car. They tell how fast the car is going, how much gas there is in the gas tank, and other things.

dash·board (dash′bôrd′) *noun, plural* **dashboards.**

at; āpe; cär; end; mē; it; īce; hot; ōld;
fôrk; wood; fool; oil; out; up; turn; sing;
thin; this; **hw** in white; **zh** in treasure.
ə stands for **a** in about, **e** in taken
i in pencil, **o** in lemon, and **u** in circus.

data Facts, figures, and other information. The school kept records of the students' names, addresses, ages, and other *data*.
da·ta (dā′tə *or* dat′ə) *noun plural.*

date¹ **1.** The day, month, year, or time when something happened or happens. The *date* of Jane's birthday is June 3. The *date* that the thirteen colonies declared their independence from England is 1776. The post office stamps a *date* on the envelope of every letter that is mailed. **2.** An agreement to meet or be with someone at a certain time and place. The two friends made a *date* to meet for lunch on Thursday. **3.** A person with whom one has such an agreement. My brother doesn't have a *date* for the dance yet. *Noun.*
—**1.** To mark with a time or date. Jim *dated* his test paper. **2.** To find out or fix the time of. The scientists at the museum were able to *date* the dinosaur bones they found. **3.** To belong to or come from a certain time. The old chair in the living room *dates* from the late 1800s. *Verb.*
date (dāt) *noun, plural* **dates;** *verb,* **dated, dating.**
out of date. No longer in fashion or use. The old woman's dress was *out of date.*
up to date. In fashion or use; modern; current. This telephone book is *up to date.*

date² **1.** A sweet fruit that grows on a kind of palm tree. **2.** The tree that this fruit grows on. This tree is also called a **date palm.**
date (dāt) *noun, plural* **dates.**

Fruit

Date Palm Tree

daughter A female child. A girl or woman is the daughter of her mother and father.
daugh·ter (dô′tər) *noun, plural* **daughters.**

daughter-in-law The wife of a son.
daugh·ter-in-law (dô′tər in lô′) *noun, plural* **daughters-in-law.**

dawn **1.** The first light that appears in the morning; daybreak. **2.** The beginning or first sign. The *dawn* of civilization took place thousands and thousands of years ago. *Noun.*
—**1.** To begin to get light in the morning; become day. We sat on the beach and watched the day *dawn*. **2.** To begin to be clear or understood. It *dawned* on him that he was being tricked. *Verb.*
dawn (dôn) *noun, plural* **dawns;** *verb,* **dawned, dawning.**

day **1.** The period of light between the rising and setting of the sun; daylight. **2.** The 24 hours of one day and night. We have a vacation of ten *days* in the spring. **3.** The part of a day spent working. Jean's school *day* ends at three o'clock in the afternoon. **4.** A time or period. In the present *day*, more people live in cities than on farms.
day (dā) *noun, plural* **days.**

daybreak The time each morning when light first appears; dawn.
day·break (dā′brāk′) *noun, plural* **daybreaks.**

day care center A nursery school that takes care of and teaches small children during the day. Day care centers are most often used by children whose mothers are not home during the day because they go to work. This is also called a **day nursery.**

daydream Pleasant thinking or wishing about things one would like to do or have happen. Janet had a *daydream* of being a famous writer someday. *Noun.*
—To think about pleasant things in a dreamy way. Bill's father told him to get to work and not to *daydream* all day. *Verb.*
day·dream (dā′drēm′) *noun, plural* **daydreams;** *verb,* **daydreamed, daydreaming.**

daylight **1.** The light of day; daytime. **2.** The dawn; daybreak. The farmer was up doing his chores before *daylight.*
day·light (dā′līt′) *noun.*

daytime The time when it is day and not night; daylight.
day·time (dā′tīm′) *noun.*

daze To confuse or stun; bewilder. The fall from the tree *dazed* her. *Verb.*
—A confused or stunned condition. The car accident left him in a *daze*. *Noun.*
daze (dāz) *verb,* **dazed, dazing;** *noun, plural* **dazes.**

dazzle To daze or make almost blind by too much light. Tom always wears sunglasses when he goes to the beach so the sun will not *dazzle* his eyes. *Verb.*
—Something that dazzles. The *dazzle* of the city's lights excited the little boy. *Noun.*

daz·zle (daz′əl) *verb*, **dazzled, dazzling;** *noun, plural* **dazzles.**

D.C. **1.** An abbreviation for **District of Columbia. 2.** An abbreviation for **direct current.**

deacon **1.** A church officer who helps a minister. **2.** A member of the clergy who ranks just below a priest.
dea·con (dē′kən) *noun, plural* **deacons.**

dead **1.** No longer living or having life. The plant was *dead* because it had not gotten enough water and sun. **2.** Never having had life. Rocks are *dead* matter. **3.** Without power, usefulness, or interest. I can't call my mother because the telephone is *dead.* Summer is never a *dead* time for Jean because she visits her uncle's farm during July and August. **4.** Complete; total. The patients waited in the doctor's office in *dead* silence. **5.** Sure or certain; exact. He hit the target at *dead* center. *Adjective.*
—**1.** Completely. The hikers were *dead* tired. **2.** Directly; straight. The exit from the highway is *dead* ahead. *Adverb.*
—**1.** People who are no longer living. The minister led us in a prayer for the *dead.* **2.** The time of greatest darkness or coldness. Thunder woke him up in the *dead* of night. On long, cold nights in the *dead* of winter, Alice likes to sit by the fire with a good book. *Noun.*
dead (ded) *adjective*, **deader, deadest;** *adverb; noun.*

deaden To dull or weaken. The dentist gave John an injection to *deaden* the pain in his sore tooth.
dead·en (ded′ən) *verb*, **deadened, deadening.**

dead end A street or passage that is closed at one end.

deadline A set time by which something must be finished; time limit. The *deadline* for handing in our book reports is this Friday.
dead·line (ded′līn′) *noun, plural* **deadlines.**

deadly **1.** Causing or likely to cause death. The policeman took *deadly* aim at the fleeing murderer. **2.** Meaning to kill or destroy. The two countries became *deadly* enemies when they went to war.
dead·ly (ded′lē) *adjective*, **deadlier, deadliest.**

deaf **1.** Not able to hear, or not able to hear well. The *deaf* man knew what people were saying to him because he could read their lips. When you call our old dog you have to shout because she is *deaf.* **2.** Not willing to hear or listen. He was *deaf* to her call for help.
deaf (def) *adjective*, **deafer, deafest.**

deafen To make deaf. The noise of the machines in the factory *deafened* us for a moment.
deaf·en (def′ən) *verb*, **deafened, deafening.**

deal **1.** To have to do with; be about. Mary wanted to read a book that would *deal* with dogs and cats. **2.** To act or behave. The principal tried to *deal* fairly with the boys who had been making too much noise in the halls. **3.** To do business; trade. That store *deals* in candy, newspapers, and magazines. **4.** To give or deliver. Whose turn is it to *deal* the cards? *Verb.*
—A bargain or agreement. My uncle made a *deal* with a man from New York to sell his house. *Noun.*
deal (dēl) *verb*, **dealt, dealing;** *noun, plural* **deals.**
a great deal or **a good deal.** A large amount or quantity. Sally spent *a great deal* of time making her own Christmas cards.

dealer **1.** A person who buys or sells something for a living. We bought our new car from the car *dealer* in town. **2.** A person who gives out cards in a card game.
deal·er (dē′lər) *noun, plural* **dealers.**

dealt I read a book that *dealt* with the discovery of North America. Look up **deal** for more information.
dealt (delt) *verb.*

dear Much or greatly loved. Polly has been my *dear* friend ever since elementary school. When we write a letter we put *"Dear"* before a person's name. *Adjective.*
—A much loved person. You are such a *dear* to come over and help with the party. *Noun.*
—An exclamation of surprise, disappointment, or trouble. Oh *dear!* I've missed the bus. *Interjection.* ▲ Another word that sounds like this is **deer.**
dear (dēr) *adjective*, **dearer, dearest;** *noun, plural* **dears;** *interjection.*

dearly Very much; a great deal. Ruth *dearly* loves her mother.
dear·ly (dēr′lē) *adverb.*

death **1.** The end of life in people, plants, or animals. Highway accidents cause many *deaths.* **2.** Anything like death. The *death* of English rule in America came with the Revolutionary War.
death (deth) *noun, plural* **deaths.**

at; āpe; cär; end; mē; it; īce; hot; ōld;
fôrk; wood; fo͞ol; oil; out; up; turn; sing;
thin; this; hw in white; zh in treasure.
ə stands for a in about, e in taken
i in pencil, o in lemon, and u in circus.

debate A talk or argument. There was much *debate* in the state about whether to build a new highway. The television station asked the two candidates for mayor to have a *debate* on the campaign issues. *Noun.*
—**1.** To argue about or discuss at a public meeting. The two senators *debated* whether or not the Senate should pass the new tax bill. **2.** To think about; consider. They *debated* whether or not they would go to the movies. *Verb.*
  de·bate (di bāt′) *noun, plural* **debates;** *verb,* **debated, debating.**

debris The scattered remains of something that has been broken or destroyed; rubbish. The earthquake destroyed so many buildings that the streets were filled with *debris.*
  de·bris (di brē′) *noun.*

debt **1.** Something that is owed to another. After paying all his *debts,* he still has money in the bank. I owe you a *debt* of gratitude for all your help. **2.** The condition of owing. Father is in *debt* to the bank because he had to borrow money to buy our new house.
  debt (det) *noun, plural* **debts.**

decade A period of ten years. The period of time between 1970 and 1980 is a *decade.*
  dec·ade (dek′ād) *noun, plural* **decades.**

decanter A fancy glass bottle with a top that is used as a stopper. Decanters are usually used to hold wine or liquor.
  de·cant·er (di kan′tər) *noun, plural* **decanters.**

decay A slow rotting of plant and animal matter. The dentist told Bill to brush his teeth at least twice a day to prevent tooth *decay.* The wooden beams of the old house showed *decay. Noun.*

Decanter

—To rot slowly. The oranges we were storing in the cellar turned moldy and began to *decay. Verb.*
  de·cay (di kā′) *noun, plural* **decays;** *verb,* **decayed, decaying.**

deceased Dead. The children of the *deceased* man have already been told of his death. *Adjective.*
—**the deceased.** A dead person or persons. *Noun.*
  de·ceased (di sēst′) *adjective; noun.*

deceit **1.** The act of lying or cheating. The salesman was guilty of *deceit* when he told the customer that the used bicycle for sale was a new one. **2.** The quality that makes someone lie or cheat. The girl was full of *deceit* as she tried to put the blame for the missing money on someone else.
  de·ceit (di sēt′) *noun, plural* **deceits.**

deceive To make someone believe something that is not true. He *deceived* his parents by telling them he had no homework to do, because he wanted to watch television instead of studying.
  de·ceive (di sēv′) *verb,* **deceived, deceiving.**

December The twelfth and last month of the year. December has thirty-one days.
  De·cem·ber (di sem′bər) *noun.*

▲ In the early Roman calendar, March was the first month of the year, and **December** was the tenth month. The word *December* comes from the Latin word for "ten."

decent **1.** Proper and respectable. It is not *decent* to listen in on other people's private conversations. It was very *decent* of Nancy to help her brother with his homework. **2.** Fairly good; satisfactory. She'll never be an A student, but she gets *decent* grades in school.
  de·cent (dē′sənt) *adjective.*

deceptive Misleading; meant to trick. Ellen hid her anger with a *deceptive* smile.
  de·cep·tive (di sep′tiv) *adjective.*

decide **1.** To make up one's mind. Alice has *decided* to study to be a doctor. **2.** To settle or judge a question or argument. The judge *decided* in favor of the prisoner.
  de·cide (di sīd′) *verb,* **decided, deciding.**

decided Definite; sure. The taller basketball player had a *decided* advantage over the others.
  de·cid·ed (di sī′did) *adjective.*

decimal Based on the number 10. Money in the United States is based on the *decimal* system. *Adjective.*
—A fraction with a denominator of 10, or a multiple of 10 such as 100 or 1000. This is also called a **decimal fraction.** The decimal fraction .5 is another way of writing $^5/_{10}$. *Noun.*
  dec·i·mal (des′ə məl) *adjective; noun, plural* **decimals.**

decimal point A period put before a decimal fraction. The periods in .5, .30, and .052 are decimal points.

decipher 1. To make out the meaning of something difficult to understand. The teacher handed the spelling test back to Jim to write again because she could not *decipher* his handwriting. 2. To change secret writing into ordinary writing. The enemy knew about the plans for the attack because they had stolen and *deciphered* the general's secret message.
de·ci·pher (di sī′fər) *verb*, **deciphered, deciphering.**

decision The act or result of making up one's mind. John likes to think carefully about a problem before he makes a *decision*.
de·ci·sion (di sizh′ən) *noun, plural* **decisions.**

decisive 1. Deciding something finally and completely. The army suffered a *decisive* defeat and was forced to surrender to the enemy. 2. Showing firmness and determination. The boy defended his innocence in such a *decisive* manner that no one believed that he had stolen the money.
de·ci·sive (di sī′siv) *adjective.*

deck 1. The floor on a ship or boat. A deck may have a roof or covering over it or be completely open. 2. A platform that is like the deck of a ship or boat. Father built a *deck* onto the back of the house so we could sit out in the sun. 3. A set of playing cards. Bob shuffled the *deck* and then dealt the cards. *Noun.*
—To dress or decorate. We all *decked* ourselves out in funny costumes for Halloween. *Verb.*
deck (dek) *noun, plural* **decks;** *verb,* **decked, decking.**

declaration The act of announcing or of making something known. The *declaration* of war is a power given to the Congress by the Constitution of the United States.
dec·la·ra·tion (dek′lə rā′shən) *noun, plural* **declarations.**

Declaration of Independence A statement made on July 4, 1776, that the thirteen American colonies were independent of England.

declare 1. To announce or make something known. The two countries *declared* war. 2. To say strongly and firmly. She *declared* that she was right and nothing would change her mind.
de·clare (di kler′) *verb,* **declared, declaring.**

decline 1. To refuse politely. Alice wrote Jack a note to *decline* the invitation to his birthday party. 2. To grow less or weaker; decrease. The power of kings and queens has *declined* in modern times. Food prices *declined* again this week. *Verb.*
—A lessening or weakening of power, health, value, or amount. We've noticed a *decline* in the old man's health ever since his accident. *Noun.*
de·cline (di klīn′) *verb,* **declined, declining;** *noun, plural* **declines.**

decode To change secret writing into ordinary language. The spy *decoded* the secret message.
de·code (dē kōd′) *verb,* **decoded, decoding.**

decompose To rot or decay. Steve cut down the tree for firewood but left the stump behind to *decompose*.
de·com·pose (dē′kəm pōz′) *verb,* **decomposed, decomposing.**

decorate 1. To make more beautiful; ornament. The children *decorated* the Christmas tree with lights and ornaments. Mother *decorated* the living room by painting the walls and choosing a new rug and draperies. 2. To give a badge or medal to. The army *decorated* the soldier for bravery.
dec·o·rate (dek′ə rāt′) *verb,* **decorated, decorating.**

decoration 1. The act of making more beautiful; decorating. The *decoration* of the gym for the dance took all day. 2. Something that is used to decorate; ornament. We took down the balloons, crepe paper, and other *decorations* after the party was over. 3. A badge or medal. All the boys in the Boy Scout troop wore their *decorations* for the Fourth of July parade.
dec·o·ra·tion (dek′ə rā′shən) *noun, plural* **decorations.**

decoy 1. A model of a bird used to attract real birds into a trap or to within shooting distance of a hunter. The hunter floated a wooden *decoy* on the lake and waited in the bushes for it to attract a duck. 2. A person who leads another person into danger or into a trap. Police departments in big cities use policemen in everyday clothes as *decoys* for criminals in dangerous neighborhoods. *Noun.*
—To attract or lead into danger or into a trap. Jane tried to *decoy* the rabbit that was eating the lettuce in her garden. *Verb.*
de·coy (dē′koi *or* di koi′ *for noun;* di koi′ *for verb*) *noun, plural* **decoys;** *verb,* **decoyed, decoying.**

at; āpe; cär; end; mē; it; īce; hot; ōld;
fôrk; wood; fool; oil; out; up; turn; sing;
thin; this; hw in white; zh in treasure.
ə stands for a in about, e in taken
i in pencil, o in lemon, and u in circus.

171

decrease To make or become less. Father *decreased* the speed of the car as we came to our exit on the highway. We hope that the number of car accidents on our block will *decrease* because of the new stop sign at the end of the street. *Verb.*
—**1.** The act of becoming less. The *decrease* in Christmas shopping for this year will mean less money for the stores. **2.** The amount by which something becomes less. There was a *decrease* of ten degrees in the temperature during the night. *Noun.*
> **de·crease** (di krēs′ *for verb;* dē′krēs′ *or* di-krēs′ *for noun*) *verb,* **decreased, decreasing;** *noun, plural* **decreases.**

decree An official order or decision. The king sent out a *decree* that all taxes would be raised. *Noun.*
—To order or decide officially. The dictator *decreed* the arrest of all people who were against the government. *Verb.*
> **de·cree** (di krē′) *noun, plural* **decrees;** *verb,* **decreed, decreeing.**

dedicate To set apart for or devote to a special purpose or use. Two floors of the new hospital will be *dedicated* to medical research.
> **ded·i·cate** (ded′ə kāt′) *verb,* **dedicated, dedicating.**

dedication A setting apart for or devotion to a special purpose or use. All the teachers, students, and parents were invited to the *dedication* of the new school this Friday afternoon.
> **ded·i·ca·tion** (ded′ə kā′shən) *noun, plural* **dedications.**

deduct To take away or subtract from a total. The teacher told the class that she would *deduct* five points for each wrong answer on the test.
> **de·duct** (di dukt′) *verb,* **deducted, deducting.**

deduction The taking away from a total; subtraction. The store made a *deduction* of ten dollars from the regular price of fifty dollars for the radio.
> **de·duc·tion** (di duk′shən) *noun, plural* **deductions.**

deed **1.** Something done; act; action. Sue did a good *deed* by helping the blind woman across the street. **2.** A written, legal agreement. When Father bought our house, he got a *deed* to show that he owned it.
> **deed** (dēd) *noun, plural* **deeds.**

deep **1.** Far down from the top. Jane warned her little brother not to go near the *deep* end of the swimming pool where the water was over his head. **2.** Great in degree; intense; extreme. Ruth fell into a *deep* sleep. **3.** Difficult to understand. My sister's chemistry book is too *deep* for me. **4.** Completely taken up with something; occupied; absorbed. He didn't hear the doorbell ring because he was *deep* in thought. **5.** Low in pitch. Don could easily sing the low notes in the song because he had such a *deep* voice. *Adjective.*
—In, at, or to a great depth. The explorers went *deep* into the jungle. *Adverb.*
> **deep** (dēp) *adjective,* **deeper, deepest;** *adverb.*

deer An animal that has hoofs and chews its cud. A male deer has antlers that are shed every year and grow back the next year. Deer can run very fast. ▲ Another word that sounds like this is **dear.**
> **deer** (dēr) *noun, plural* **deer.**

Deer

deface To spoil or mar. The policeman made the boys wash their names off the statue and warned them never to *deface* public property again.
> **de·face** (di fās′) *verb,* **defaced, defacing.**

defeat To win a victory over; overcome in a contest of any kind. Our basketball coach told us he thought we could easily *defeat* the visiting team. The troops defending the fort *defeated* the attacking enemy. *Verb.*
—The state of being defeated in a contest of any kind. Our team's *defeat* ended our hopes of winning the championship. *Noun.*
> **de·feat** (di fēt′) *verb,* **defeated, defeating;** *noun, plural* **defeats.**

defect A flaw or weakness. These dishes are for sale cheap because they have *defects* in them.
> **de·fect** (dē′fekt *or* di fekt′) *noun, plural* **defects.**

defective Having a flaw or weakness; not perfect. *Defective* electrical wiring is the cause of many fires in people's homes.
> **de·fec·tive** (di fek′tiv) *adjective.*

defend **1.** To guard against attack or danger; protect. The soldiers did their best to *defend* the people in the town from the attacking army. **2.** To speak or act in support of. The lawyer agreed to *defend* the woman accused of robbery because he believed she was innocent.
de·fend (di fend′) *verb,* **defended, defending.**

defense **1.** The act of guarding against attack or danger. The country was not prepared for the *defense* of its borders against the enemy troops. **2.** A person or thing that protects. The dam was the city's only *defense* against floods. **3.** Support. The governor spoke in *defense* of his plan to give more state aid to public transportation. **4.** The defending team or players in a game. Our hockey team has a good *defense.*
de·fense (di fens′) *noun, plural* **defenses.**

defensive Guarding or protecting against attack. Knights used to put on *defensive* armor before going into battle.
de·fen·sive (di fen′siv) *adjective.*

defer[1] To put off to a future time; delay. The judge asked the jury to *defer* judgment in the case until they had heard all the facts.
de·fer (di fur′) *verb,* **deferred, deferring.**

defer[2] To yield in judgment or opinion. Bob thought he should *defer* to his father on what to buy his mother for a Christmas present.
de·fer (di fur′) *verb,* **deferred, deferring.**

defiance Bold refusal to obey or respect authority. The man showed his *defiance* by deliberately breaking the law.
de·fi·ance (di fī′əns) *noun, plural* **defiances.**

deficiency **1.** A lack of something needed or necessary. Diane takes vitamin pills every morning to help keep her healthy and prevent a vitamin *deficiency.* **2.** The amount by which something is lacking. The banker counted the money in the safe after the robbery and found a *deficiency* of $10,000.
de·fi·cien·cy (di fish′ən sē) *noun, plural* **deficiencies.**

define **1.** To give the meaning or meanings of. A dictionary *defines* words. **2.** To describe or fix exactly. The river *defines* the boundary between the two states.
de·fine (di fīn′) *verb,* **defined, defining.**

definite Certain; clear. It is *definite* that Mary is going to college next fall.
def·i·nite (def′ə nit) *adjective.*

definite article The word *the* is the definite article. *The* is used to point out one or more particular persons or things. *The* train is late. *The* boys are fighting.

definition An explanation of the meaning of a word or group of words. A definition for the word *family* is "a father, mother, and their children."
def·i·ni·tion (def′ə nish′ən) *noun, plural* **definitions.**

deform To spoil the form or shape of. Constant winds had *deformed* and bent the tree.
de·form (di fôrm′) *verb,* **deformed, deforming.**

defrost To make free of ice or frost; thaw. Mother has to *defrost* the refrigerator to keep the freezer free of ice.
de·frost (di frôst′) *verb,* **defrosted, defrosting.**

deft Skillful and clever; nimble. The girl's *deft* fingers raced over the piano keys.
deft (deft) *adjective.*

defy To oppose or challenge boldly. To *defy* his mother, Dick deliberately went outside without a jacket even though she had told him to wear one.
de·fy (di fī′) *verb,* **defied, defying.**

degrade To lower in character, quality, or rank. Telling lies *degrades* a person.
de·grade (di grād′) *verb,* **degraded, degrading.**

degree **1.** A stage or step in a process or series. A young child learns to walk by *degrees.* **2.** Amount or extent. To what *degree* is Bob interested in becoming a doctor? **3.** A unit for measuring temperature. A person's normal body temperature is 98.6 *degrees* Fahrenheit. **4.** A unit for measuring angles, or arcs of a circle. Two perpendicular lines form a 90 *degree* angle.
de·gree (di grē′) *noun, plural* **degrees.**

deity A god or goddess. Mars was the Roman *deity* of war.
de·i·ty (dē′ə tē) *noun, plural* **deities.**

The **degrees** are marked on the thermometer.

at; āpe; cär; end; mē; it; īce; hot; ōld; fôrk; wood; fool; oil; out; up; turn; sing; thin; this; hw in white; zh in treasure. ə stands for a in about, e in taken i in pencil, o in lemon, and u in circus.

dejected Depressed or sad. The basketball team felt *dejected* after losing the game.
de·ject·ed (di jek′tid) *adjective.*

Delaware A state in the eastern United States. Its capital is Dover.
Del·a·ware (del′ə wer′) *noun.*

▲ The name **Delaware** comes from the name of the first governor of Virginia, Lord *De La Warr.* An English sailor named a piece of land that sticks out into what is now called the Delaware Bay after this governor. Later, other English settlers used the name for the bay and the river running into it. The name was then given to the colony and the state.

delay 1. To put off to a later time; postpone. The officials had to *delay* the start of the football game because of the rain. 2. To make late. We would have come sooner, but we were *delayed* by a flat tire. 3. To slow down; linger. Jane will miss the bus if she *delays* any longer. *Verb.*
—The act of delaying or the state of being delayed. There will be a short *delay* of fifteen minutes before the train arrives. *Noun.*
de·lay (di lā′) *verb,* **delayed, delaying;** *noun,* plural **delays.**

delegate A person who is chosen to act for others. Each country that belongs to the United Nations is represented by a *delegate. Noun.*
—To choose or send as a delegate. The club *delegated* Bill to make arrangements for a Christmas party. *Verb.*
del·e·gate (del′ə gāt′ *or* del′ə git *for noun;* del′ə gāt′ *for verb*) *noun,* plural **delegates;** *verb,* **delegated, delegating.**

delegation A group of delegates or representatives. A *delegation* from the fire department marched in the Fourth of July parade.
del·e·ga·tion (del′ə gā′shən) *noun,* plural **delegations.**

deliberate 1. Done or said on purpose. He told his mother a *deliberate* lie and blamed the broken window on his brother. 2. Careful and slow; not hasty or rash. The judge was *deliberate* when he studied the evidence presented at the trial. The old man walked down the street with *deliberate* steps. *Adjective.*
—To think over or discuss carefully. The young man *deliberated* whether or not he should study to be a lawyer. *Verb.*
de·lib·er·ate (di lib′ər it *for adjective;* di lib′ə rāt′ *for verb*) *adjective; verb,* **deliberated, deliberating.**

delicacy 1. Fineness; daintiness. The *delicacy* of the lace made it look like a cobweb.

2. A rare or choice food. Snails are thought to be a *delicacy* by some people.
del·i·ca·cy (del′i kə sē) *noun,* plural **delicacies.**

delicate 1. Fine or dainty. The threads of a spider's web are *delicate.* 2. Pleasing in smell, taste, or color; mild or soft. There was a *delicate* scent of roses in the air. Mary's dress is a *delicate* shade of pink. 3. Easily damaged; fragile. Mother never puts her *delicate* wine glasses in the dishwasher because they break too easily. 4. Very sensitive. Scientists have *delicate* instruments that can detect an earthquake thousands of miles away.
del·i·cate (del′i kit) *adjective.*

delicatessen A store that sells food that is ready to eat. Cold meats, cheeses, and salads are sold in a delicatessen.
del·i·ca·tes·sen (del′i kə tes′ən) *noun,* plural **delicatessens.**

delicious Pleasing or delightful to the taste or smell. The stew cooking for dinner smelled *delicious* to the hungry boy.
de·li·cious (di lish′əs) *adjective.*

delight Great pleasure; joy. Joan beamed with *delight* as she watched the circus. *Noun.*
—1. To give great pleasure or joy to. The puppet show in the park *delighted* the children. 2. To have or take great pleasure. Tom was *delighted* to go fishing with his father. *Verb.*
de·light (di līt′) *noun,* plural **delights;** *verb,* **delighted, delighting.**

delightful Very pleasing. We all had a *delightful* time at the party.
de·light·ful (di līt′fəl) *adjective.*

delirious Wildly excited. Rick's high fever made him *delirious.* Betty was *delirious* with happiness when she won the prize.
de·lir·i·ous (di lēr′ē əs) *adjective.*

deliver 1. To carry or take. The department store promised it would *deliver* our new television set this week. 2. To say; utter. Father is going to *deliver* a speech to a meeting of businessmen. 3. To strike or throw. The pitcher *delivered* a curve ball that the batter swung at and missed.
de·liv·er (di liv′ər) *verb,* **delivered, delivering.**

delivery 1. The act of carrying or taking something to a place or person. The postman makes a mail *delivery* every day except Sundays and holidays. The eggs were missing from the grocery *delivery.* 2. A way of speaking or singing. The singer's *delivery* was excellent.
de·liv·er·y (di liv′ər ē) *noun,* plural **deliveries.**

delta An area of land at the mouth of a river. A delta is formed by deposits of earth, sand, and stone. A delta is usually shaped like a triangle.
del·ta (del′tə) *noun, plural* **deltas.**

▲ The word **delta** comes from the Greek name for the fourth letter in the Greek alphabet. The letter delta was drawn as a triangle, and deltas in rivers are often in the shape of a triangle.

---

demand **1.** To ask for urgently or forcefully; claim as a right. The angry customer asked to see the store manager to *demand* an apology from the rude clerk. The judge *demanded* silence in the courtroom. **2.** To call for; need. Bill's new job *demands* hard work. *Verb.*
—**1.** The act of demanding. The workers' *demand* for higher salaries was turned down. **2.** Something that is demanded. The butcher said that the *demand* for turkeys was very high at Thanksgiving time. *Noun.*
de·mand (di mand′) *verb,* **demanded, demanding;** *noun, plural* **demands.**

democracy **1.** A government that is run by the people who live under it. In a democracy, the people may run the government indirectly by electing representatives who govern for them. Or they may run it directly by having meetings which everyone can come to. The government of the United States is an indirect democracy because we elect representatives to do the work of a government for us. A New England town meeting is a direct democracy because all the people make decisions. **2.** A country in which the government is a democracy. Canada is a *democracy.*
de·moc·ra·cy (di mok′rə sē) *noun, plural* **democracies.**

democrat **1.** A person who believes that a government should be run by the people who live under it. **2. Democrat.** A person who belongs to the Democratic Party.
dem·o·crat (dem′ə krat′) *noun, plural* **democrats.**

democratic **1.** Of or supporting a democracy. The United States is a *democratic* country. **2.** Believing that all people should be treated as equals. Thomas Jefferson expressed *democratic* ideas when he wrote the Declaration of Independence.
dem·o·crat·ic (dem′ə krat′ik) *adjective.*

Democratic Party One of the two major political parties in the United States.

demolish To tear down or destroy. The workmen's job was to *demolish* the old fac-

tory to make way for a new office building.
de·mol·ish (di mol′ish) *verb,* **demolished, demolishing.**

demon **1.** An evil spirit; devil. **2.** A person who does something with great skill or energy. Henry is such a *demon* for work that he spends every weekend at the office.
de·mon (dē′mən) *noun, plural* **demons.**

demonstrate **1.** To explain, prove, or show clearly. The science teacher dropped a pencil out the window to *demonstrate* the law of gravity. A salesman *demonstrated* the new coffeepot at the department store. **2.** To take part in a public meeting or parade to protest something or make demands. An angry group of citizens *demonstrated* against pollution of the river by wastes from the factory.
dem·on·strate (dem′ən strāt′) *verb,* **demonstrated, demonstrating.**

demonstration **1.** Something that explains, proves, or shows clearly. The fireman's rescue of the child from the burning house was a *demonstration* of his bravery. **2.** A public meeting or parade to protest something or make demands. The workers held a *demonstration* to demand a raise in pay.
dem·on·stra·tion (dem′ən strā′shən) *noun, plural* **demonstrations.**

den **1.** A place where wild animals live. Bears use caves as a *den* during their long sleep in winter. **2.** A small, cozy room for reading or studying. **3.** A group of about eight cub scouts.
den (den) *noun, plural* **dens.**

denial The act of denying. The judge listened to the prisoner's *denial* of the charges against him.
de·ni·al (di nī′əl) *noun, plural* **denials.**

denim **1.** A heavy cotton cloth used for work or sports clothes. **2. denims.** Pants or overalls made of this cloth.
den·im (den′im) *noun, plural* **denims.**

denomination **1.** A religious group or sect. The Lutherans are a *denomination* of the Protestant church. **2.** One kind of unit. A dime and a nickel are coins of different *denominations.*
de·nom·i·na·tion (di nom′ə nā′shən) *noun, plural* **denominations.**

at; āpe; cär; end; mē; it; īce; hot; ōld; fôrk; wood; fool; oil; out; up; turn; sing; thin; this; hw in white; zh in treasure. ə stands for a in about, e in taken i in pencil, o in lemon, and u in circus.

denominator The number below the line in a fraction. The denominator shows the number of equal parts into which the whole is divided. In the fraction $1/2$, 2 is the denominator.
de·nom·i·na·tor (di nom′ə nā′tər) *noun, plural* **denominators.**

denote 1. To be a sign of; show. A dark sky and high winds usually *denote* the coming of a storm. 2. To be a name for; mean. The word "dentist" *denotes* a doctor who takes care of people's teeth.
de·note (di nōt′) *verb,* **denoted, denoting.**

denounce To speak against in public; accuse. The speaker *denounced* living conditions in the slums.
de·nounce (di nouns′) *verb,* **denounced, denouncing.**

dense Packed closely together; thick. The boys wandered away from the camp and got lost in the *dense* woods.
dense (dens) *adjective,* **denser, densest.**

density Closeness; thickness. Pea soup has a greater *density* than water. The *density* of population is greater in a big city than it is in the country.
den·si·ty (den′sə tē) *noun, plural* **densities.**

dent A small hollow made in the surface of something by a blow or pressure. Roy got a *dent* in the front of his bicycle when he hit the tree. *Noun.*
—To make a dent or hollow in. *Verb.*
dent (dent) *noun, plural* **dents;** *verb,* **dented, denting.**

dental 1. Having to do with the teeth. Good *dental* care helps prevent tooth decay. 2. Having to do with a dentist's work. Our dentist has an X-ray machine and other *dental* equipment in his office.
den·tal (dent′əl) *adjective.*

dentin The hard, bony material that forms the main part of the tooth. It is covered by the enamel.
den·tin (den′tin) *noun.*

dentist A doctor who takes care of people's teeth. A dentist cleans teeth, fills cavities, pulls teeth that are diseased, and makes teeth to take the place of real ones that have been pulled.
den·tist (den′tist) *noun, plural* **dentists.**

deny 1. To say that something is not true. The prisoner *denied* that he had robbed the bank. 2. To refuse to give or grant. The company *denied* the workers' request for longer vacations.
de·ny (di nī′) *verb,* **denied, denying.**

depart 1. To go away; leave. The train is due to *depart* from the station at ten o'clock. 2. To change or differ. Jim *departed* from his usual routine of getting up early and was late for school.
de·part (di pärt′) *verb,* **departed, departing.**

department A separate part; division. The English *department* at school will have three new teachers this fall. In the United States, the *Department* of the Treasury is in charge of printing paper money and making coins.
de·part·ment (di pärt′mənt) *noun, plural* **departments.**

department store A large store that sells many different kinds of goods in different departments.

departure The act of departing. The plane's *departure* was delayed two hours because of the thick fog that surrounded the airport. Sue's taking a bus to work was a *departure* from her habit of walking the whole way.
de·par·ture (di pär′chər) *noun, plural* **departures.**

depend 1. To rely or trust. You can always *depend* on Jane to be on time. 2. To get help or support. Children *depend* on their parents until they can earn their own living. 3. To be influenced or determined. Whether or not we go on the hike *depends* on the weather.
de·pend (di pend′) *verb,* **depended, depending.**

dependable Reliable or trustworthy. A person who is dependable can be trusted to do a job without being watched or checked.
de·pen·da·ble (di pen′də bəl) *adjective.*

dependence The state of being dependent. A baby's *dependence* on his mother grows less as he gets older.
de·pen·dence (di pen′dəns) *noun.*

dependent 1. Relying on someone else for what is needed or wanted. Jim was *dependent* on his parents to pay for his college education. 2. Influenced by something. Our plans for the picnic are *dependent* on the weather. *Adjective.*
—A person who relies on someone else for help or support. Most states in the United States consider children to be *dependents* until they are 18 or 21 years old. *Noun.*
de·pen·dent (di pen′dənt) *adjective; noun, plural* **dependents.**

depict To show by drawing or painting. The artist tried to *depict* the breaking of the ocean's waves on the beach.
de·pict (di pikt′) *verb,* **depicted, depicting.**

deposit 1. To put money or valuable things in a bank or other safe place. Ted *deposited*

twenty dollars in his savings account at the bank. **2.** To put or set down; place. Ruth *deposited* the groceries on the kitchen table. *Verb.*
—**1.** Something put in a bank or other safe place. Pat made a *deposit* of fifty dollars. **2.** Something given as part of a payment or promise to pay more later. Susan put down a *deposit* of twenty dollars on the new bicycle and planned to pay the rest by the end of the month. **3.** Something that has settled and is left as a layer. There was a thick *deposit* of dust in the house when we came back from our month's vacation. **4.** A large amount of mineral in rock or in the ground. Texas has large *deposits* of oil underground. *Noun.*
> **de·pos·it** (di poz′it) *verb*, **deposited, depositing**; *noun, plural* **deposits.**

depot   A railroad or bus terminal.
> **de·pot** (dē′pō) *noun, plural* **depots.**

depress   To make sad or gloomy. The death of their dog *depressed* the whole family.
> **de·press** (di pres′) *verb*, **depressed, depressing.**

depression   **1.** Sadness; gloom. Failing to make the team caused Jack to have a fit of *depression.* **2.** A low place or hollow. The car bumped over a *depression* in the road. **3.** A time when business is slow and people are out of work. Many people lost their jobs during the *Depression* of the 1930's.
> **de·pres·sion** (di presh′ən) *noun, plural* **depressions.**

deprive   To keep from having or doing. The dictator *deprived* the people of their right to vote. The new highway will *deprive* the children of their playground.
> **de·prive** (di prīv′) *verb*, **deprived, depriving.**

depth   **1.** The distance from top to bottom or from front to back. The *depth* of the pool was twelve feet at the deep end. The *depth* of our back yard is fifty feet. **2.** The quality of being deep. The mother's *depth* of understanding helped her son with his problems.
> **depth** (depth) *noun, plural* **depths.**

deputy   A person appointed to take the place of another. The sheriff appointed a *deputy* to help him keep order in the town.
> **dep·u·ty** (dep′yə tē) *noun, plural* **deputies.**

derby   A man's stiff round hat with a narrow rolled brim.
> **der·by** (dur′bē) *noun, plural* **derbies.**

derive   To get from a source; obtain. The word "democracy" is *derived* from a Greek word. That family *derives* pleasure from going camping together.
> **de·rive** (di rīv′) *verb*, **derived, deriving.**

derrick   **1.** A machine for lifting and moving heavy objects. It has a long arm attached to the base of an upright post. **2.** The framework over an oil well or other drill hole that supports the drilling machinery.
> **der·rick** (der′ik) *noun, plural* **derricks.**

descend   **1.** To move or come from a higher place to a lower one. They rode up the hill on horseback but *descended* on foot. **2.** To come down from an earlier source or ancestor. The farm *descended* from the father to his son.
> **de·scend** (di send′) *verb*, **descended, descending.**

Oil Derrick

descendant   A person who comes from a particular ancestor or group of ancestors. Jack is a *descendant* of the early Dutch settlers in New York.
> **de·scen·dant** (di sen′dənt) *noun, plural* **descendants.**

descent   **1.** A coming from a higher place to a lower one. The quick *descent* of the elevator made my stomach feel funny. **2.** A downward slope. There was a steep *descent* down the stairs of the old tower. **3.** Ancestry or birth. He is of Polish *descent.* ▲ Another word that sounds like this is **dissent.**
> **de·scent** (di sent′) *noun, plural* **descents.**

describe   To give a picture of something in words; tell or write about. The boy *described* his adventures at camp. Can you *describe* the man you saw at the window?
> **de·scribe** (di skrīb′) *verb*, **described, describing.**

▲   The word **describe** used to mean "to write down." When a person writes something down, he puts it in words. So *describe* came to mean "to tell about in words," whether the words are written or spoken.

---

at; āpe; cär; end; mē; it; īce; hot; ōld; fôrk; wood; fōōl; oil; out; up; turn; sing; thin; this; hw in white; zh in treasure. ə stands for a in about, e in taken i in pencil, o in lemon, and u in circus.

description 1. The act of giving a picture using words. Betty's *description* of the movie she had seen was very complete. 2. A statement that describes. My father sent a *description* of our lost dog to the newspaper. 3. Kind; sort; variety. There were cats of every *description* in the show.
de·scrip·tion (di skrip′shən) *noun, plural* descriptions.

descriptive Giving a picture in words. The tourists were given *descriptive* pamphlets about places to visit in the city.
de·scrip·tive (di skrip′tiv) *adjective.*

desegregate To do away with the system or practice of having separate schools and other facilities for different races. The government ordered the town to *desegregate* its public schools.
de·seg·re·gate (dē seg′rə gāt′) *verb,* desegregated, desegregating.

desert[1] A hot, dry sandy area of land with few or no plants growing on it. *Noun.*
—Not lived in or on; desolate. The man was shipwrecked on a *desert* island when his boat sank. *Adjective.*
des·ert (dez′ərt) *noun, plural* deserts; *adjective.*

desert[2] To go away and leave a person or thing that should not be left; abandon. The man *deserted* his wife and children. The soldier *deserted* his company. ▲ Another word that sounds like this is **dessert**.
de·sert (di zurt′) *verb,* deserted, deserting.

deserve To have a right to; be worthy of. The girl *deserves* praise for working so hard.
de·serve (di zurv′) *verb,* deserved, deserving.

design 1. A plan, drawing, or outline made to serve as a guide or pattern. Everyone liked the architect's *design* for the new school. 2. An arrangement of different parts or colors; pattern. The carpet in the living room has a blue and green *design. Noun.*
—To make a plan, drawing, or outline of; make a pattern for. She *designed* beautiful costumes for the play. *Verb.*
de·sign (di zīn′) *noun, plural* designs; *verb,* designed, designing.

The pillows have an American Indian **design**.

designate 1. To mark or point out; show. Jack used a blue pencil to *designate* rivers and lakes on the map he was drawing. 2. To call by a particular name or title. The head of the government of the United States is *designated* "President." 3. To choose; name. He was *designated* chairman of the fund drive.
des·ig·nate (dez′ig nāt′) *verb,* designated, designating.

desirable Worth having or wishing for; pleasing. That corner lot is a *desirable* place to lay out a baseball field.
de·sir·a·ble (di zīr′ə bəl) *adjective.*

desire To wish for; long for. Jack *desires* a college education. *Verb.*
—A longing; wish. The cold and hungry man had a *desire* for a bowl of hot soup. *Noun.*
de·sire (di zīr′) *verb,* desired, desiring; *noun, plural* desires.

desk A piece of furniture used for reading or writing. It has a flat or sloping top and usually drawers.
desk (desk) *noun, plural* desks.

Desk

desolate 1. Without people; deserted. In the winter, that beach is really *desolate.* 2. Destroyed; ruined. The fire left the forest *desolate.* 3. Miserable; cheerless. The lost child was *desolate* without his mother.
des·o·late (des′ə lit) *adjective.*

despair A complete loss of hope. The family was filled with *despair* when their house was destroyed by the fire. *Noun.*
—To give up or lose hope; be without hope. After three days, she *despaired* of ever finding her lost puppy. *Verb.*
de·spair (di sper′) *noun; verb,* despaired, despairing.

desperate 1. Reckless because of having no hope. A desperate person is ready or willing to take any risk. The *desperate* thief shot at the policeman who was chasing him. 2. Very bad or hopeless. The mountain climbers who were trapped by the snowstorm were in a *desperate* position.
des·per·ate (des′pər it) *adjective.*

desperation A reckless feeling coming from loss of hope. In *desperation,* the fireman tried to knock down the door to reach the trapped children.
des·per·a·tion (des′pə rā′shən) *noun.*

despise To look down on as hateful; scorn. She *despised* him because he had treated her so cruelly.
de·spise (di spīz′) *verb,* **despised, despising.**

despite In spite of. He went to school *despite* his bad cold.
de·spite (di spīt′) *preposition.*

dessert A sweet food served at the end of a meal. Cake, pie, fruit, pudding, and ice cream are desserts. ▲ Another word that sounds like this is **desert.**
des·sert (di zurt′) *noun, plural* **desserts.**

destination A place to which a person or thing is going or being sent. The airplane's *destination* is Paris.
des·ti·na·tion (des′tə nā′shən) *noun, plural* **destinations.**

destine 1. To set apart for a particular purpose or use; intend. That land is *destined* for a new hospital. 2. To be decided ahead of time. She is *destined* to become a musician.
des·tine (des′tin) *verb,* **destined, destining.**

destiny What happens to a person or thing; fortune. He felt that it was his *destiny* to become a great surgeon.
des·ti·ny (des′tə nē) *noun, plural* **destinies.**

destroy To ruin completely; wreck. The earthquake *destroyed* the city. Locusts *destroyed* the crops.
de·stroy (di stroi′) *verb,* **destroyed, destroying.**

destroyer A small, fast warship.
de·stroy·er (di stroi′ər) *noun, plural* **destroyers.**

destruction 1. The act of destroying. Chemical sprays are sometimes used for the *destruction* of the breeding places of mosquitoes. 2. Great damage or ruin. The earthquake caused the total *destruction* of the city.
de·struc·tion (di struk′shən) *noun, plural* **destructions.**

destructive Causing destruction. Moths are *destructive* to clothes made of wool.
de·struc·tive (di struk′tiv) *adjective.*

detach To unfasten and separate; take off. She *detached* the price tag from the gift before wrapping it.
de·tach (di tach′) *verb,* **detached, detaching.**

detached 1. Not attached; not connected. The *detached* house was surrounded by a large yard. 2. Not taking sides in an argument. The reporter was a *detached* observer at the murder trial.
de·tached (di tacht′) *adjective.*

detail 1. A small or less important part of a whole; item. The newspaper gave few *details* about the accident. 2. A dealing with matters one by one. He told us he spent the summer at camp, but he didn't have time to go into *detail.* 3. A small group of persons sent on some special duty. A *detail* of policemen patrols the park at night. *Noun.*
—1. To tell or describe item by item. She *detailed* her experiences as a writer to the students. 2. To assign to or send on special duty. The captain *detailed* soldiers to guard the gate. *Verb.*
de·tail (di tāl′ *or* dē′tāl) *noun, plural* **details;** *verb,* **detailed, detailing.**

detain 1. To keep from going; hold back; delay. A flat tire *detained* him on his way home. 2. To keep in custody. The police *detained* the man who was suspected of robbery.
de·tain (di tān′) *verb,* **detained, detaining.**

detect To find out; discover. I called the fire department after I *detected* smoke coming from the garage.
de·tect (di tekt′) *verb,* **detected, detecting.**

detective A policeman or other person who searches for information in order to solve a crime and catch a criminal. *Noun.*
—Having to do with detectives and their work. Bob likes to read *detective* stories. *Adjective.*
de·tec·tive (di tek′tiv) *noun, plural* **detectives;** *adjective.*

deter To discourage from doing something because of fear or doubt. The huge waves *deterred* him from going swimming.
de·ter (di tur′) *verb,* **deterred, deterring.**

detergent A chemical substance used for washing. A detergent acts like soap.
de·ter·gent (di tur′jənt) *noun, plural* **detergents.**

deteriorate To make or become worse. Nancy's car *deteriorated* as it got older.
de·te·ri·o·rate (di tēr′ē ə rāt′) *verb,* **deteriorated, deteriorating.**

determination 1. A definite and firm purpose. Her *determination* to become a doctor was encouraged by her parents. 2. The act of deciding or settling ahead of time. The campers' *determination* of what to take on their trip took a long time.

at; āpe; cär; end; mē; it; īce; hot; ōld;
fôrk; wood; fōol; oil; out; up; turn; sing;
thin; this; hw in white; zh in treasure.
ə stands for a in about, e in taken
i in pencil, o in lemon, and u in circus.

de·ter·mi·na·tion (di tur′mi nā′shən) *noun, plural* **determinations.**

determine **1.** To decide or settle definitely or ahead of time. The members of the club *determined* the date for their next meeting. **2.** To find out by watching or checking. She *determined* the name of the flower by looking for its picture in a book about plants. **3.** To be the cause of. The number of votes each candidate gets will *determine* who will be the class president.
de·ter·mine (di tur′min) *verb,* **determined, determining.**

determined Having one's mind made up; firm. The basketball team made a *determined* effort to win.
de·ter·mined (di tur′mind) *adjective.*

detest To dislike very much; hate. Bill *detests* being teased by his older brother.
de·test (di test′) *verb,* **detested, detesting.**

detour A roundabout or indirect way. We had to take a *detour* because the main highway was being repaired. *Noun.*
—To cause to make a detour. The police *detoured* the traffic because of the accident. *Verb.*
de·tour (dē′toor) *noun, plural* **detours;** *verb,* **detoured, detouring.**

detract To take away from the value or beauty of something. The ugly advertisements along the road *detracted* from the beauty of the countryside.
de·tract (di trakt′) *verb,* **detracted, detracting.**

devastate To destroy; ruin. The hurricane *devastated* the small towns along the coast.
dev·as·tate (dev′əs tāt′) *verb,* **devastated, devastating.**

develop **1.** To bring or come into being or activity; grow. She *developed* an interest in poetry at an early age. He *developed* his muscles by exercising. The widespread use of the automobile has *developed* the nation's highway system. **2.** To treat an exposed photographic film, plate, or print with a chemical so that the picture can be seen.
de·vel·op (di vel′əp) *verb,* **developed, developing.**

development **1.** The act or process of developing. The *development* of a spacecraft that could reach the moon took many years. **2.** An event or happening. The radio station reported new *developments* in the search for the missing child. **3.** A group of houses or other buildings on a large piece of land. The houses often look alike and are built by one builder.

de·vel·op·ment (di vel′əp mənt) *noun, plural* **developments.**

deviate To move or turn away from an action, thought, or statement. He *deviated* from the truth when he told the story of how we got home.
de·vi·ate (dē′vē āt′) *verb,* **deviated, deviating.**

device **1.** Something made or invented for a particular purpose. A can opener is a device. **2.** A plan or scheme; trick. She used the *device* of pretending to have a sore throat to stay home from school.
de·vice (di vīs′) *noun, plural* **devices.**

devil **1. the Devil.** The evil spirit that is thought to be the ruler of hell. **2.** A wicked, cruel, or mean person.
dev·il (dev′əl) *noun, plural* **devils.**

devise To think out; invent; plan. We *devised* a secret code so that no one else would know what we were saying to each other.
de·vise (di vīz′) *verb,* **devised, devising.**

devote To give effort, attention, or time to some person or purpose. She *devoted* all her energy to studying dancing.
de·vote (di vōt′) *verb,* **devoted, devoting.**

devoted Loyal; faithful. My *devoted* friend would do anything for me.
de·vot·ed (di vō′tid) *adjective.*

devotion A strong affection; loyalty; faithfulness. He felt great *devotion* to his parents.
de·vo·tion (di vō′shən) *noun, plural* **devotions.**

devour **1.** To eat; consume. The lion *devoured* the deer. The hungry boy *devoured* his dinner. **2.** To destroy. Fire *devoured* the house.
de·vour (di vour′) *verb,* **devoured, devouring.**

devout **1.** Very religious. The priest was a *devout* man. **2.** Sincere; earnest. You have my *devout* wishes for your success in the school play.
de·vout (di vout′) *adjective.*

dew Moisture from the air that forms drops on cool surfaces. Dew gathers on grass, plants, and trees during the night. ▲ Other words that sound like this are **do** and **due.**
dew (do͞o *or* dyo͞o) *noun, plural* **dews.**

dewlap The loose hanging skin under the throat of cattle and certain other animals.
dew·lap (do͞o′lap′ *or* dyo͞o′lap′) *noun, plural* **dewlaps.**

dexterous Having or showing skill in using the hands, body, or mind. Both magicians and surgeons are dexterous with their hands.
dex·ter·ous (deks′tər əs) *adjective.*

diabetes A disease in which there is not

enough of a certain substance called insulin in the blood. As a result of diabetes, there is too much sugar in the blood.

di·a·be·tes (dī′ə bē′tis *or* dī′ə bē′tēz) *noun.*

diacritical mark A mark or sign such as ¨ , ^ , ¯ , ′, or ′ placed over, under, or across a letter either as part of the spelling or to show pronunciation. The pronunciation of the word "skate" using a diacritical mark is *skāt.*

di·a·crit·i·cal mark (dī′ə krit′i kəl).

diagnosis The act of finding out what is wrong with a person or animal by examination and the study of symptoms. The doctor's *diagnosis* showed that Jane had chicken pox.

di·ag·no·sis (dī′əg nō′sis) *noun, plural* **diagnoses.**

diagonal Having a slanting direction. Her dress had a pattern of *diagonal* stripes. *Adjective.*
—A straight line that connects the opposite corners of a rectangle. *Noun.*

The necktie has **diagonal** stripes.

di·ag·o·nal (dī ag′ən əl) *adjective; noun, plural* **diagonals.**

diagram A plan or sketch that shows the parts of a thing. A diagram shows how something is put together or how it works. He had a *diagram* of the model airplane that showed how to put it together. *Noun.*
—To show by a diagram; make a diagram of. The engineer *diagramed* the parts of the automobile engine. *Verb.*

di·a·gram (dī′ə gram′) *noun, plural* **diagrams;** *verb,* **diagramed, diagraming.**

dial **1.** The face of an instrument. A dial is marked with numbers, letters, or other signs. A pointer moves over these markings and shows how much there is of something. A clock, compass, or meter has a dial. **2.** The disk on a radio or television set that tunes in a station or channel. **3.** The disk on some telephones that is turned to the numbers and letters of the number being called. *Noun.*
—**1.** To tune in by using a radio or television dial. *Dial* the channel that the movie is being shown on. **2.** To call by means of a telephone dial. My brother *dialed* a wrong number. *Verb.*

di·al (dī′əl *or* dīl) *noun, plural* **dials;** *verb,* **dialed, dialing.**

dialect A type of language that is spoken in a particular area or by a particular group of people. A dialect differs from other forms of the same language in the way some words are spoken, or in the way words are used in sentences, or in what certain words mean.

di·a·lect (dī′ə lekt′) *noun, plural* **dialects.**

dialogue A conversation. That play was full of funny *dialogue.*

di·a·logue (dī′ə lôg′ *or* dī′ə log′) *noun, plural* **dialogues.**

dial tone The steady humming sound in a telephone that tells the caller that he may dial his number.

The two lines on the sign are **diameters.**

diameter **1.** A straight line passing through the center of a circle or other round object, from one side to the other. **2.** The length of such a line; the width or thickness of something round. Scientists think that the *diameter* of the earth is about 8000 miles.

di·am·e·ter (dī am′ə tər) *noun, plural* **diameters.**

diamond **1.** A mineral that is usually colorless. A diamond comes from pure carbon in the form of a crystal. It is the hardest natural material known. Diamonds are used in industry for cutting and grinding. Cut and polished diamonds are used as jewels. **2.** A playing card marked with one or more figures shaped like this: ♦ . **3.** The suit of cards marked with this figure. **4.** The space on a baseball field that is inside the lines that connect the bases.

The sign has a **diamond** shape.

dia·mond (dī′mənd *or* dī′ə mənd) *noun, plural* **diamonds.**

diaper A baby's undergarment made of soft, folded cloth or other material.

dia·per (dī′pər *or* dī′ə pər) *noun, plural* **diapers.**

---

at; āpe; cär; end; mē; it; īce; hot; ōld;
fôrk; wood; fōol; oil; out; up; turn; sing;
thin; this; hw in white; zh in treasure.
ə stands for a in about, e in taken
i in pencil, o in lemon, and u in circus.

diaphragm **1.** A wall of muscle that divides the chest from the abdomen. It is used in breathing. **2.** A disk used to change sound into electrical signals, or to change electrical signals into sound. It is used in telephones and microphones.

di·a·phragm (dī′ə fram′) *noun, plural* diaphragms.

diary A written record of the things that one does each day. Mary kept a *diary* when she was away at summer camp.

di·a·ry (dī′ər ē) *noun, plural* diaries.

dice Small cubes of wood, plastic, or other material marked on each side with from one to six dots. Dice are used in some games. *Noun.*

—To cut into small cubes. Please help me *dice* the potatoes for the stew. *Verb.*

dice (dīs) *noun plural; verb,* diced, dicing.

A Pair of Dice

dictate **1.** To say or read something aloud to be written down or recorded by another. A businessman often *dictates* letters to his secretary. **2.** To order by authority. The victorious nation *dictated* the terms of the peace treaty. *Verb.*

—A rule or command that must be obeyed. He believes in following the *dictates* of the law. *Noun.*

dic·tate (dik′tāt) *verb,* dictated, dictating; *noun, plural* dictates.

dictator A person who has complete authority. The *dictator* took away the peoples' right to vote.

dic·ta·tor (dik′tā′tər) *noun, plural* dictators.

dictionary A book that has words of a language arranged in alphabetical order, together with information about them. This dictionary tells what words mean, how they are spelled, how they are used, how they are pronounced, and where they come from.

dic·tion·ar·y (dik′shə ner′ē) *noun, plural* dictionaries.

did *Did* you know that man? I *did* not see him. Look up **do** for more information.

did (did) *verb.*

didn't I *didn't* do my homework.

did·n't (did′ənt) contraction for "did not."

die¹ **1.** To stop living; become dead. Many soldiers *died* in the war. The flowers *died* during the cold spell. **2.** To lose force or strength; come to an end. The wind suddenly *died* as the sailboat neared the shore. The music *died* away in the distance. **3.** To want

very much. The hikers were *dying* for a cold drink of water. ▲ Another word that sounds like this is **dye.**

die (dī) *verb,* died, dying.

die² **1.** A small cube used in games. Look up the word **dice** for more information. **2.** A metal block or plate used to stamp designs or letters on coins. ▲ Another word that sounds like this is **dye.**

die (dī) *noun, plural* dice *(for definition 1)* or dies *(for definition 2).*

diesel engine An engine that burns fuel oil. The oil is set on fire by heat produced by the compression of air in the engine.

die·sel engine (dē′zəl).

diet **1.** The food and drink usually eaten by a person or animal. Her *diet* is made up of meat, vegetables, and fruit. A giraffe's *diet* is mostly leaves. **2.** A special selection of food and drink chosen by a person for reasons of health or for losing or gaining weight. Because he is too heavy, his doctor told him to go on a *diet. Noun.*

—To eat according to a special diet in order to be healthy or to lose or gain weight. She *dieted* for many weeks and lost twelve pounds. *Verb.*

di·et (dī′ət) *noun, plural* diets; *verb,* dieted, dieting.

dietitian A person who is trained to plan balanced meals. A dietitian usually works at a hospital or school.

di·e·ti·tian (dī′ə tish′ən) *noun, plural* dietitians.

differ **1.** To be unlike; not be the same. Michael and Edward *differ* greatly in looks, even though they are brothers. **2.** To have a different opinion; disagree. My sister *differs* with the rest of our family about where to go on our vacation.

dif·fer (dif′ər) *verb,* differed, differing.

difference **1.** The state or quality of being unlike or different. Was there a *difference* between her answer and his? **2.** A way of being unlike or different. One of the *differences* between the sisters is the color of their hair. **3.** The amount left after one quantity is subtracted from another. The *difference* between 16 and 12 is 4. **4.** A disagreement about something. They were able to settle their *differences* without a fight.

dif·fer·ence (dif′ər əns *or* dif′rəns) *noun, plural* differences.

different **1.** Not alike or similar. A bicycle and a motorcycle are *different.* **2.** Not the same; separate. It rained two *different* times this afternoon.

dif·fer·ent (dif′ər ənt *or* dif′rənt) *adjective.*

difficult **1.** Hard to do, solve, or understand; not easy. Carrying the heavy bed upstairs was a *difficult* job. This is a *difficult* arithmetic problem. **2.** Hard to get along with or please. He becomes very *difficult* when he can't have his own way.
dif·fi·cult (dif′ə kult′) *adjective.*

difficulty **1.** The fact of being difficult. The *difficulty* of learning how to ride a bicycle discouraged him. **2.** Something that is hard to do, understand, or deal with. Ruth had *difficulty* fitting everything into her small suitcase.
dif·fi·cul·ty (dif′ə kul′tē) *noun, plural* **difficulties.**

dig **1.** To break up or turn over the earth with a shovel, the hands, or claws. Our dog likes to *dig* in the yard for bones. I *dig* in the vegetable garden with a spade. **2.** To make or get by digging. The men had to *dig* a well for water. The workmen will *dig* through the mountain to finish the highway. We *dig* clams at the seashore when the tide is low. **3.** To find or discover by searching or by study. It took the reporter weeks to *dig* up enough facts to write a story on the jewel robbery. **4.** To poke or thrust. The cat loved to *dig* her claws into the tree and scratch.
dig (dig) *verb,* **dug, digging.**

digest To break down food in the mouth, stomach, and intestines. When we digest food, we change it into a form that can be taken in and used by the body. *Verb.*
—A summary of a longer book or document. I am reading a *digest* of that long novel. *Noun.*
di·gest (di jest′ *or* dī jest′ *for verb;* dī′jest *for noun) verb,* **digested, digesting;** *noun, plural* **digests.**

digestion The process of digesting. Digestion starts in the mouth and is completed in the small intestine.
di·ges·tion (di jes′chən *or* dī jes′chən) *noun, plural* **digestions.**

digestive Relating to or helping digestion. Saliva from the mouth is the first of the *digestive* juices that break down pieces of food.
di·ges·tive (di jes′tiv *or* dī jes′tiv) *adjective.*

digit One of the numerals 0, 1, 2, 3, 4, 5, 6, 7, 8, or 9. Sometimes 0 is not called a digit.
dig·it (dij′it) *noun, plural* **digits.**

dignified Having dignity; noble. The wedding party walked down the aisle of the church in a *dignified* manner.
dig·ni·fied (dig′nə fīd′) *adjective.*

dignity The state of being noble, worthy, or

honorable. Despite great hardship and poverty, their mother kept her *dignity.*
dig·ni·ty (dig′nə tē) *noun, plural* **dignities.**

dike A dam or high wall of earth built to hold back the waters of a sea or river.
dike (dīk) *noun, plural* **dikes.**

Dike

dilapidated Fallen into ruin or decay; broken down. Father is going to build a new tool shed to replace the *dilapidated* one we have now.
di·lap·i·dat·ed (di lap′ə dā′tid) *adjective.*

diligent Careful and hard-working. Janet is a *diligent* student.
dil·i·gent (dil′ə jənt) *adjective.*

dilute To make thin or weaker by adding a liquid. The directions on the can of frozen orange juice say to *dilute* the contents with three cans of cold water.
di·lute (di l̅o̅o̅t′ *or* dī l̅o̅o̅t′) *verb,* **diluted, diluting.**

dim **1.** Having or giving little light; not bright. There was only a *dim* light in the hallway. **2.** Not clear; indistinct. He could see a *dim* outline of the building through the fog. **3.** Not seeing, hearing, or understanding clearly. The old man's eyes were growing *dim. Adjective.*
—To make or become dim. Ann always *dimmed* her car headlights at night when she passed cars going in the other direction. *Verb.*
dim (dim) *adjective,* **dimmer, dimmest;** *verb,* **dimmed, dimming.**

at; āpe; cär; end; mē; it; īce; hot; ōld;
fôrk; wood; f̅o̅o̅l; oil; out; up; turn; sing;
thin; this; hw in white; zh in treasure.
ə stands for a in about, e in taken
i in pencil, o in lemon, and u in circus.

dime   A coin in the United States and Canada that is worth ten cents.
   dime (dīm) *noun, plural* **dimes.**

dimension   Measurement of length, width, or height. The *dimensions* of the room are 15 feet long, 12 feet wide, and 8 feet high.
   di·men·sion (di men′shən) *noun, plural* **dimensions.**

diminish   To make or become smaller. The camper's supply of food *diminished* as the days wore on.
   di·min·ish (di min′ish) *verb,* **diminished, diminishing.**

diminutive   Very small; tiny. A baby has *diminutive* hands and feet.
   di·min·u·tive (di min′yə tiv) *adjective.*

dimple   A small hollow on a person's cheek or chin. Linda had *dimples* in her cheeks whenever she smiled. *Noun.*
   —To mark with or form dimples. A smile *dimpled* the little boy's face. *Verb.*
   dim·ple (dim′pəl) *noun, plural* **dimples;** *verb,* **dimpled, dimpling.**

din   A loud noise that goes on for some time. The *din* of car horns kept us awake. *Noun.*
   —To say over and over. Mother *dinned* into our ears that we must try to stand up straight. *Verb.*
   din (din) *noun, plural* **dins;** *verb,* **dinned, dinning.**

dine   To eat dinner. Mom and Dad *dined* at a restaurant on their anniversary.
   dine (dīn) *verb,* **dined, dining.**

diner   **1.** A person who is eating dinner. The *diners* in the restaurant were not aware that a fire had broken out in the kitchen. **2.** A small restaurant that is in the shape of a railroad car. That *diner* is a favorite stop for truck drivers on their way through town.
   din·er (dī′nər) *noun, plural* **diners.**

dinghy   A small rowboat.
   din·ghy (ding′gē) *noun, plural* **dinghies.**

dingy   Having a dirty and dull appearance; not bright and cheery. The white curtains were *dingy* from the dirt and soot that came in through the window.
   din·gy (din′jē) *adjective,* **dingier, dingiest.**

dining room   A room where meals are served and eaten.

dinner   **1.** The main meal of the day. On Sunday we eat *dinner* at four o'clock in the afternoon. **2.** A formal meal in honor of some person or event. The school gave the members of the football team a *dinner* to celebrate their winning season.
   din·ner (din′ər) *noun, plural* **dinners.**

dinosaur   One of a large group of extinct reptiles that lived millions of years ago. Some dinosaurs were the largest land animals that have ever lived.
   din·o·saur (dī′nə sôr′) *noun, plural* **dinosaurs.**

Dinosaur

diocese   A church district that is under the authority of a bishop.
   di·o·cese (dī′ə sis *or* dī′ə sēs′) *noun, plural* **dioceses.**

dip   **1.** To put into water or another liquid for a moment. Nancy *dipped* her hand in the clear water of the stream. **2.** To go in water and come out quickly. Peter *dipped* in the swimming pool to cool off. **3.** To lower and raise again. The soldier *dipped* the flag in salute as the President of the United States rode by. **4.** To sink or go down. The sun *dipped* below the horizon as evening came. *Verb.*
   —**1.** The act of dipping. Ruth took one last *dip* in the ocean before she went home. **2.** A liquid into which something is dipped for cleaning or coloring. We put the eggs in a *dip* to color them for Easter. **3.** A sinking or drop. The car ahead of us suddenly disappeared because of a *dip* in the road. *Noun.*
   dip (dip) *verb,* **dipped, dipping;** *noun, plural* **dips.**

diphthong   Two vowel sounds in one syllable that are pronounced as one speech sound. The *oa* in *boat* and the *ie* in *pie* are diphthongs.
   diph·thong (dif′thông′ *or* dip′thông′) *noun, plural* **diphthongs.**

diploma   A printed piece of paper given by a school or college to a graduating student that says he or she has successfully finished a course of study.
   di·plo·ma (di plō′mə) *noun, plural* **diplomas.**

diplomat A person whose job is to handle relations between his country and other countries of the world. A diplomat must be very skillful in dealing with people.
  dip·lo·mat (dip′lə mat′) *noun, plural* **diplomats.**

dipper **1.** A cup with a long handle that is used to lift water or other liquids. **2. Dipper.** Either of two groups of stars in the northern sky that are in the shape of a dipper. The larger of these groups is called the **Big Dipper,** and the smaller is called the **Little Dipper.**
  dip·per (dip′ər) *noun, plural* **dippers.**

Dipper

direct **1.** To manage or control; guide. There is a policeman on each busy corner downtown to *direct* traffic. Our school drama club asked the music teacher to *direct* the Christmas play. **2.** To order; command. The general *directed* the troops to attack. **3.** To tell or show someone the way. Can you *direct* me to the nearest bus stop? **4.** To turn or send in a particular direction or to a particular place. Jim *directed* the hose at the flowers. *Verb.*
—**1.** Going in a straight line or by the shortest way. We are taking a *direct* flight to London. Main Street is a *direct* route between my house and Janet's. **2.** Honest; straightforward. The witness gave *direct* answers to all the lawyer's questions. *Adjective.*
—Directly. This plane goes *direct* to New York from Los Angeles. *Adverb.*
  di·rect (di rekt′ *or* dī rekt′) *verb,* **directed, directing;** *adjective; adverb.*

direct current An electric current that flows only in one direction. A flashlight and a radio with batteries run on direct current.

direction **1.** Management or control; guidance. The young doctor performed the operation under the *direction* of an older, more experienced doctor. **2.** The line or course along which something moves, faces, or lies. We decided to walk in the *direction* of the lake. **3.** An order or instruction on how to do something or how to act. Follow the doctor's *directions* and take the pills four times a day. The *directions* on the package are to cook the vegetables in boiling water.
  di·rec·tion (di rek′shən *or* dī rek′shən) *noun, plural* **directions.**

directly **1.** In a direct line or manner; straight. The third baseman threw the ball *directly* to his teammate covering first base. **2.** At once; without delay. Amy came home *directly* after the concert. **3.** Exactly; absolutely. Tim's likes and dislikes in music are *directly* opposite to his father's.
  di·rect·ly (di rekt′lē *or* dī rekt′lē) *adverb.*

director A person or thing that manages or controls. A person who directs a play, movie, or television show is called a director.
  di·rec·tor (di rek′tər *or* dī rek′tər) *noun, plural* **directors.**

directory A list of names and addresses. A telephone directory lists the telephone numbers of people living in a particular area.
  di·rec·to·ry (di rek′tər ē *or* dī rek′tər ē) *noun, plural* **directories.**

dirigible A large balloon that is in the shape of a cigar. It is driven by a motor and can be steered.
  dir·i·gi·ble (dir′ə jə bəl *or* də rij′ə bəl) *noun, plural* **dirigibles.**

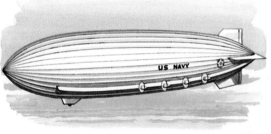
Dirigible

dirt **1.** Mud, dust, or other material that makes something unclean. Tommy washed the *dirt* off his hands before coming to dinner. **2.** Loose earth or soil. The gardener filled the pots with *dirt* before planting the flowers in them.
  dirt (durt) *noun.*

dirty Soiled; not clean. Fred put all his *dirty* clothes in a pile for the laundry. Cleaning out the garage was a hard and *dirty* job.
  dirt·y (dur′tē) *adjective,* **dirtier, dirtiest.**

disable To take away ability; cripple. A broken leg can *disable* a person for months.
  dis·a·ble (dis ā′bəl) *verb,* **disabled, disabling.**

disadvantage **1.** Something that makes it

at; āpe; cär; end; mē; it; īce; hot; ōld;
fôrk; wood; fōōl; oil; out; up; turn; sing;
thin; this; hw in white; zh in treasure.
ə stands for a in about, e in taken
i in pencil, o in lemon, and u in circus.

harder to succeed. Being short is a *disadvantage* to a basketball player. **2.** A loss or injury; harm. It will be to Ann's *disadvantage* if she turns down that offer for free skiing lessons.
> **dis·ad·van·tage** (dis′əd van′tij) *noun, plural* **disadvantages.**

disagree **1.** To differ in opinion; argue. Mike *disagreed* with his brother over which television show to watch at seven o'clock. **2.** To be different or unlike. The stories of the two witnesses *disagreed* so much that the policeman didn't know which one to believe. **3.** To be harmful. Hot, spicy foods *disagree* with me.
> **dis·a·gree** (dis′ə grē′) *verb,* **disagreed, disagreeing.**

disagreement A difference of opinion; argument. Mary had a *disagreement* with her father over whether or not she could use the family car for the weekend.
> **dis·a·gree·ment** (dis′ə grē′mənt) *noun, plural* **disagreements.**

disappear **1.** To go out of sight. We watched the sun *disappear* behind a cloud. **2.** To pass away; end. Dinosaurs *disappeared* from the earth millions of years ago.
> **dis·ap·pear** (dis′ə pēr′) *verb,* **disappeared, disappearing.**

disappearance The act or fact of disappearing. The *disappearance* of the two mountain climbers made everyone fear that they were dead.
> **dis·ap·pear·ance** (dis′ə pēr′əns) *noun, plural* **disappearances.**

disappoint To fail to live up to one's hopes. You will *disappoint* your sister if you do not take her to the movies as you promised.
> **dis·ap·point** (dis′ə point′) *verb,* **disappointed, disappointing.**

disappointment **1.** A feeling of being disappointed. Kate couldn't hide her *disappointment* when it rained and the picnic was called off. **2.** A person or thing that disappoints. The coach thought the new player would be very good, but he turned out to be a *disappointment.*
> **dis·ap·point·ment** (dis′ə point′mənt) *noun, plural* **disappointments.**

disapprove To have a feeling against. Jan's parents *disapprove* of smoking.
> **dis·ap·prove** (dis′ə prōōv′) *verb,* **disapproved, disapproving.**

disaster An event that causes much suffering or loss. Floods, fires, and earthquakes are disasters.
> **dis·as·ter** (di zas′tər) *noun, plural* **disasters.**

▲ The word **disaster** comes from two Greek words. One word means "against," and the other word means "star." Long ago, people believed that the stars had an effect on their lives. When the stars were "against" a person, something very bad would happen to him.

disbelief Lack of belief; refusal to believe. Helen's face showed *disbelief* when she heard that her experiment had been awarded first prize at the science fair.
> **dis·be·lief** (dis′bi lēf′) *noun, plural* **disbeliefs.**

discard To throw aside or give up as useless, worthless, or unwanted. Jane went through her closet and *discarded* all her worn-out clothes.
> **dis·card** (dis kärd′) *verb,* **discarded, discarding.**

discern To make out or recognize. We could barely *discern* the figure of a man in the fog.
> **dis·cern** (di surn′ *or* di zurn′) *verb,* **discerned, discerning.**

discharge **1.** To let go or release; dismiss. When the company went out of business it had to *discharge* all its workers. **2.** To unload or remove. The ship *discharged* its cargo of bananas and other fruits at the dock. **3.** To fire or shoot. The policeman *discharged* his gun into the air as a warning for the thief to stop. **4.** To send off or let out. The factory should not be allowed to *discharge* its wastes into the river. *Verb.*
—The act of discharging. The *discharge* of the airplane's passengers will be at gate ten. *Noun.*
> **dis·charge** (dis chärj′ *for verb;* dis′chärj′ *for noun) verb,* **discharged, discharging;** *noun, plural* **discharges.**

disciple **1.** A person who follows and believes in a leader or his teachings. The young doctor was a devoted *disciple* of the famous surgeon. **2.** One of the followers of Jesus.
> **dis·ci·ple** (di sī′pəl) *noun, plural* **disciples.**

discipline Training or punishment that develops orderly behavior. Those children have had no *discipline* from their parents. *Noun.*
—To train to be obedient. An officer in the army must be able to *discipline* the troops under his command. *Verb.*
> **dis·ci·pline** (dis′ə plin) *noun, plural* **disciplines;** *verb,* **disciplined, disciplining.**

disclose To make known. Mary promised her best friend that she would not *disclose* her secret to anyone.

dis·close (dis klōz′) *verb,* **disclosed, disclosing.**

disconnect To separate; undo. The repairman had to *disconnect* the television set before fixing it.
dis·con·nect (dis′kə nekt′) *verb,* **disconnected, disconnecting.**

discontented Unhappy and restless. Ann started looking for a new job because she was *discontented* with the one she had.
dis·con·tent·ed (dis′kən ten′tid) *adjective.*

discontinue To put an end to; stop. The owners of our town newspaper are going to *discontinue* publishing it because not enough people buy the paper.
dis·con·tin·ue (dis′kən tin′yōō) *verb,* **discontinued, discontinuing.**

discount The amount taken off the regular price. Nancy bought a dress on sale at a 25 percent *discount.*
dis·count (dis′kount′) *noun, plural* **discounts.**

discourage **1.** To cause to lose courage, hope, or confidence. Failing to have her first story published did not *discourage* Pam from wanting to become a writer. **2.** To try to keep a person from doing something. They *discouraged* us from starting out on our trip because of the heavy snowstorm.
dis·cour·age (dis kur′ij) *verb,* **discouraged, discouraging.**

discover To see or find out for the first time. Marie Curie and her husband *discovered* the chemical element radium. Dick *discovered* his mistake in the arithmetic problem and corrected it.
dis·cov·er (dis kuv′ər) *verb,* **discovered, discovering.**

discovery **1.** The act of seeing or finding out something for the first time. Christopher Columbus's *discovery* of America happened in 1492. **2.** Something that is seen or found out for the first time. Electricity was an important *discovery.*
dis·cov·er·y (dis kuv′ər ē) *noun, plural* **discoveries.**

discriminate To treat a person differently from others because of unfair feelings. It is against the law to *discriminate* against people because of their color, religion, sex, or age.
dis·crim·i·nate (dis krim′ə nāt′) *verb,* **discriminated, discriminating.**

discrimination An unfair difference in treatment. That company hires people without *discrimination.*
dis·crim·i·na·tion (dis krim′ə nā′shən) *noun.*

discuss To talk over; speak about. The city council held a meeting to *discuss* the building plans for the new hall.
dis·cuss (dis kus′) *verb,* **discussed, discussing.**

discussion The act of talking something over. Jane's question about the new school rules started a *discussion* that continued for half an hour.
dis·cus·sion (dis kush′ən) *noun, plural* **discussions.**

disdain A feeling of dislike or scorn for a person or thing. The older boy treated younger boys with *disdain. Noun.*
—To look down on. He *disdained* all help from his friends. *Verb.*
dis·dain (dis dān′) *noun; verb,* **disdained, disdaining.**

disease Sickness or illness. Chicken pox is a *disease* that many children have. That tree with brownish leaves is suffering from a *disease.*
dis·ease (di zēz′) *noun, plural* **diseases.**

disgrace **1.** The loss of honor or respect; shame. The president of the company resigned in *disgrace* when the police learned about the money he had stolen. **2.** A person or thing that causes a loss of honor or respect. Living conditions in that slum are a *disgrace* to our city. *Noun.*
—To bring shame to. He *disgraced* his family by cheating on the test. *Verb.*
dis·grace (dis grās′) *noun, plural* **disgraces;** *verb,* **disgraced, disgracing.**

disguise **1.** To change or hide the way one looks in order to look like someone or something else. The children wore animal costumes to *disguise* themselves on Halloween. **2.** To hide. Mother tried to *disguise* the bitter taste of the cough medicine by mixing it with orange juice. *Verb.*
—Something that changes or hides the way one looks. A mustache was part of the thief's *disguise. Noun.*
dis·guise (dis gīz′) *verb,* **disguised, disguising;** *noun, plural* **disguises.**

disgust A sickening feeling of strong dislike. She felt *disgust* when she saw the man beating his dog with a stick. *Noun.*
—To cause strong dislike in; sicken. The awful smell from the polluted river *disgusted* us. *Verb.*

at; āpe; cär; end; mē; it; īce; hot; ōld;
fôrk; wood; fōol; oil; out; up; turn; sing;
thin; this; hw in white; zh in treasure.
ə stands for a in about, e in taken
i in pencil, o in lemon, and u in circus.

dis·gust (dis gust′) *noun; verb,* **disgusted, disgusting.**

dish **1.** A plate or shallow bowl used for holding food. A dish can be made out of china, glass, or metal. **2.** Food made in a particular way. Spaghetti with tomato sauce is my brother's favorite *dish. Noun.*
—To put or serve in a dish. Mother *dished* up dinner as soon as everyone sat down. *Verb.*
dish (dish) *noun, plural* **dishes;** *verb,* **dished, dishing.**

dishonest Not fair or honest. A student who cheats on a test is being *dishonest.* The salesman used *dishonest* methods to sell used cars.
dis·hon·est (dis on′ist) *adjective.*

dishonor Loss of honor or reputation; disgrace; shame. It is no *dishonor* to admit you are wrong if you have made a mistake. *Noun.*
—To disgrace or shame. The player was such a poor sport that he *dishonored* the whole team. *Verb.*
dis·hon·or (dis on′ər) *noun, plural* **dishonors;** *verb,* **dishonored, dishonoring.**

dishwasher A machine that washes dishes, glasses, and pots.
dish·wash·er (dish′wô′shər *or* dish′wosh′ər) *noun, plural* **dishwashers.**

disinfect To destroy germs that cause disease. The nurse *disinfected* my cut before she bandaged it.
dis·in·fect (dis′in fekt′) *verb,* **disinfected, disinfecting.**

disintegrate To break up into many small pieces. A blow with the heavy hammer caused the stone to *disintegrate.*
dis·in·te·grate (dis in′tə grāt′) *verb,* **disintegrated, disintegrating.**

disinterested Free from selfish interest; fair. A judge should take a *disinterested* view of the cases that come before him.
dis·in·ter·est·ed (dis in′tər is tid *or* dis in′təres′tid *or* dis in′tris tid) *adjective.*

disk A flat, thin, round object that is shaped like a coin or phonograph record. The sun shone like a bright, golden *disk* in the sky.
disk (disk) *noun, plural* **disks.**

dislike A feeling of not liking or of being against something. My brother has a *dislike* of spinach. *Noun.*
—To have a feeling of not liking or of being against. Susan *dislikes* doing housework. *Verb.*
dis·like (dis līk′) *noun, plural* **dislikes;** *verb,* **disliked, disliking.**

dislocate To put a bone out of joint. The man *dislocated* his hip when he slipped and fell on the ice.
dis·lo·cate (dis′lō kāt′) *verb,* **dislocated, dislocating.**

dislodge To move or force out of a place or position. The flood threatened to *dislodge* two of the supports that held up the bridge.
dis·lodge (dis loj′) *verb,* **dislodged, dislodging.**

disloyal Not loyal; unfaithful. It was *disloyal* not to help your best friend.
dis·loy·al (dis loi′əl) *adjective.*

dismal Causing gloom or sadness; dreary; miserable. The weather this week has been so rainy and *dismal* that we haven't been outside to play.
dis·mal (diz′məl) *adjective.*

▲ The word **dismal** comes from two old French words that meant "unlucky days" or "evil days." In the Middle Ages, certain days on the calendar were marked "unlucky days" because people thought the position of the stars on those days would bring them bad luck. The two French words were put together to make the English word *dismal,* and the English called these days "dismal days." Later the word was used to talk about anything gloomy or unlucky.

dismay To make afraid or discouraged because of danger or trouble. The rising flood waters *dismayed* the people of the town. *Verb.*
—A feeling of fear or discouragement in the face of danger or trouble. The family was filled with *dismay* when they learned that the fire was near their house. *Noun.*
dis·may (dis mā′) *verb,* **dismayed, dismaying;** *noun.*

dismiss To send away or allow to leave. The teacher decided to *dismiss* the class early because it was the last day before summer vacation.
dis·miss (dis mis′) *verb,* **dismissed, dismissing.**

dismount To get off or down from. The cavalry officer gave the order to *dismount.*
dis·mount (dis mount′) *verb,* **dismounted, dismounting.**

disobedient Refusing or failing to obey. The *disobedient* child crossed the highway without his mother's permission.
dis·o·be·di·ent (dis′ə bē′dē ənt) *adjective.*

disobey To refuse or fail to obey. He *disobeyed* the traffic laws by driving through a red light.

dis·o·bey (dis′ə bā′) *verb,* **disobeyed, disobeying.**

disorder A lack of order; confusion. The room was in complete *disorder* after Timmy's birthday party. *Noun.*
—To disturb the order of; throw into confusion. The sudden downfall of rain *disordered* the parade. *Verb.*
dis·or·der (dis ôr′dər) *noun, plural* **disorders;** *verb,* **disordered, disordering.**

dispatch To send off quickly. He *dispatched* a telegram to announce his time of arrival. *Verb.*
—A written message or report. The newspaper received a *dispatch* from its reporter in London. *Noun.*
dis·patch (dis pach′) *verb,* **dispatched, dispatching;** *noun, plural* **dispatches.**

dispel To drive away or cause to disappear. The mother's kind words helped to *dispel* her child's fear of the dark.
dis·pel (dis pel′) *verb,* **dispelled, dispelling.**

dispense To give out. The town *dispensed* food and clothing to the people who were left homeless by the storm. There is a machine in the movie theater that *dispenses* candy and popcorn.
dis·pense (dis pens′) *verb,* **dispensed, dispensing.**

disperse To break up and scatter in different directions. The police *dispersed* the angry crowd before anyone got hurt.
dis·perse (dis purs′) *verb,* **dispersed, dispersing.**

displace 1. To take the place of. The airplane has *displaced* the train as the fastest means of transportation. 2. To move from the usual or proper place. The earthquake *displaced* many people from their homes.
dis·place (dis plās′) *verb,* **displaced, displacing.**

display To show or exhibit. The art museum was planning to *display* the new paintings it had bought. *Verb.*
—A show or exhibit. There has always been a *display* of affection between the two sisters. *Noun.*
dis·play (dis plā′) *verb,* **displayed, displaying;** *noun, plural* **displays.**

displease To offend or annoy. He *displeased* his mother when he didn't do his homework.
dis·please (dis plēz′) *verb,* **displeased, displeasing.**

disposal The act of disposing of something. The city is responsible for the *disposal* of garbage.

dis·pos·al (dis pō′zəl) *noun, plural* **disposals.**

dispose To dispose of. 1. To get rid of. My brother was able *to dispose of* his old car for $100 more than he had paid for it. 2. To deal with or settle. Mother quickly *disposed of* her work so that we could all go to the zoo for the afternoon.
dis·pose (dis pōz′) *verb,* **disposed, disposing.**

disposition A person's usual way of acting, thinking, or feeling. My sister always has a very cheerful *disposition,* even when she first wakes up in the morning.
dis·po·si·tion (dis′pə zish′ən) *noun, plural* **dispositions.**

dispute To argue against; disagree with. Jack *disputed* Bill's statement that he was a faster swimmer. *Verb.*
—An argument or quarrel. A judge had to settle the *dispute* between the two farmers over who owned the land. *Noun.*
dis·pute (dis pyo͞ot′) *verb,* **disputed, disputing;** *noun, plural* **disputes.**

disqualify To make or declare unfit or unable to do something. The judges had to *disqualify* the runner from the race for knocking down another runner.
dis·qual·i·fy (dis kwol′ə fī′) *verb,* **disqualified, disqualifying.**

disregard To pay no attention to; ignore. Tom tried to *disregard* the other children's mean comments about his new shirt. *Verb.*
—Lack of attention; neglect. Playing the radio very loudly late at night shows a *disregard* for other people. *Noun.*
dis·re·gard (dis′ri gärd′) *verb,* **disregarded, disregarding;** *noun.*

disrupt To break up or apart. The teacher told the two boys to stop talking because they were beginning to *disrupt* the whole class.
dis·rupt (dis rupt′) *verb,* **disrupted, disrupting.**

dissatisfied Not content; displeased. Ted took his new television set back to the store because he was *dissatisfied* with the picture he got.
dis·sat·is·fied (dis sat′is fīd′) *adjective.*

dissect To cut apart or divide in order to study or examine. Each biology student was

at; āpe; cär; end; mē; it; īce; hot; ōld;
fôrk; wood; fo͞ol; oil; out; up; turn; sing;
thin; this; hw in white; zh in treasure.
ə stands for a in about, e in taken
i in pencil, o in lemon, and u in circus.

given a frog to *dissect* in order to study its digestive system.

dis·sect (di sekt′ *or* dī sekt′) *verb,* **dissected, dissecting.**

dissent To differ strongly in opinion; disagree. The dictator did not allow anyone to *dissent* from the actions of the government. *Verb.*

—A strong difference of opinion; disagreement. John's suggestion to use the club's dues for a party met with *dissent. Noun.*

▲ Another word that sounds like this is **descent.**

dis·sent (di sent′) *verb,* **dissented, dissenting;** *noun.*

dissolve 1. To mix and make or become liquid. Sugar will *dissolve* in a cup of hot coffee. *Dissolve* the powder in milk to make the instant pudding. 2. To bring to an end. The club members voted to *dissolve* the dance committee once the dance was over.

dis·solve (di zolv′) *verb,* **dissolved, dissolving.**

distance 1. The amount of space between two things or points. The *distance* from Jane's house to the school is two blocks. 2. A far-off point or place. The driver slowed down because he saw a slow-moving truck in the *distance* ahead of him.

dis·tance (dis′təns) *noun, plural* **distances.**

distant 1. Far away in space or time; not near. Pluto is the most *distant* planet from the sun. Dinosaurs lived in the *distant* past. 2. Away. The farm was ten miles *distant* from the nearest town. 3. Not friendly. She has been very *distant* toward her best friend since their quarrel.

dis·tant (dis′tənt) *adjective.*

distill To make a liquid pure by heating it until it becomes a vapor and then cooling it until it becomes a liquid again. Gasoline is *distilled* from petroleum.

dis·till (dis til′) *verb,* **distilled, distilling.**

distinct 1. Not the same; separate; different. The letters were sorted into three *distinct* piles. 2. Easy to see, hear, or understand; clear. The words on the street sign became *distinct* when we walked closer. The sound of the drums was *distinct* even from a distance. The coach noticed a *distinct* improvement in the team's playing.

dis·tinct (dis tingkt′) *adjective.*

distinction 1. The act of making or noticing a difference between things. It is not always easy to make a *distinction* between poison ivy and other plants that look like it. 2. Something that makes a thing different from other things; difference. The ability to

fly is one of the *distinctions* between birds and other animals. 3. Excellence; worth. The senator was a man of *distinction.*

dis·tinc·tion (dis tingk′shən) *noun, plural* **distinctions.**

distinctive Making or showing a difference between things. I recognized the *distinctive* smell of roast turkey coming from the kitchen.

dis·tinc·tive (dis tingk′tiv) *adjective.*

distinguish 1. To know or show that there is a difference between certain things. The jeweler quickly *distinguished* the real diamond from the fake one. 2. To make something special or different. The cardinal's bright red feathers *distinguish* it from other birds. 3. To see or hear clearly. He could see three men walking toward him, but he could not *distinguish* their faces in the dark. 4. To make famous or deserving of special honor or attention; make well known. The doctor *distinguished* herself by her work in cancer research.

dis·tin·guish (dis ting′gwish) *verb,* **distinguished, distinguishing.**

distort To twist or bend out of shape. The curved mirror *distorted* the way she looked. The witness tried to *distort* the facts.

dis·tort (dis tôrt′) *verb,* **distorted, distorting.**

distract To draw someone's attention away from what he is doing or thinking. The noise *distracted* Tom from his homework.

dis·tract (dis trakt′) *verb,* **distracted, distracting.**

distraction Something that draws someone's attention away from what he is doing or thinking. I find telephone calls a *distraction* when I am trying to write a letter.

dis·trac·tion (dis trak′shən) *noun, plural* **distractions.**

distress 1. Great pain or sorrow; misery. My friend's illness was a great *distress* to me. 2. Danger, trouble, or great need. The sinking ship sent a message that it was in *distress. Noun.*

—To cause pain, sorrow, or misery. The bad news from home *distressed* the traveler. *Verb.*

dis·tress (dis tres′) *noun; verb,* **distressed, distressing.**

distribute 1. To give something out in shares; deal out. The teacher *distributed* new books to the class. 2. To spread something out over a large area; scatter. The farmer *distributed* seed over the plowed field. 3. To arrange or sort into groups. The post office *distributed* the letters according to which town they were going to.

dis·trib·ute (dis trib′yo͞ot) *verb*, **distributed, distributing.**

distribution The act of distributing. The Red Cross supervised the *distribution* of food and clothing to the flood victims.

dis·tri·bu·tion (dis′trə byo͞o′shən) *noun, plural* **distributions.**

district An area that is a special part of a larger area. That store is in the business *district* of the city. Jim had to go to a different school when his family moved to a new school *district*.

dis·trict (dis′trikt) *noun, plural* **districts.**

District of Columbia An area in the eastern United States between Maryland and Virginia. It is completely occupied by the city of Washington, the national capital. The District of Columbia is governed by the Federal government.

District of Co·lum·bi·a (kə lum′bē ə).

disturb 1. To make uneasy or nervous; worry. Having to take a test *disturbs* Richard, even though he is a good student. 2. To break in on; interrupt. The telephone call *disturbed* his sleep. 3. To upset or change the order or arrangement of things. The children *disturbed* the books on the shelf.

dis·turb (dis turb′) *verb*, **disturbed, disturbing.**

disturbance 1. A disturbing; interruption. The writer hoped that there would be no more *disturbance* of his work. 2. Something that disturbs. The noise was a *disturbance* to the students who were trying to concentrate. The policeman went to investigate the *disturbance*.

dis·turb·ance (dis tur′bəns) *noun, plural* **disturbances.**

ditch A long, narrow hole dug in the ground. Ditches are used to drain off water.

ditch (dich) *noun, plural* **ditches.**

dive 1. To plunge headfirst into water. At first, I was afraid to *dive* from the high board into the pool. 2. To plunge downward quickly and at a steep angle. We watched the eagle *dive* down from the sky. 3. To go, move, or drop suddenly and quickly. The sound of thunder made the frightened puppy *dive* under the bed. *Verb.*

—1. A headfirst plunge into water. Ellen did a *dive* from the rocks into the lake. 2. A quick, steep plunge. The plane went into a *dive* when it was hit by enemy fire. *Noun.*

dive (dīv) *verb*, **dived** or **dove, dived, diving;** *noun, plural* **dives.**

diver 1. A person who dives. 2. A person who works or explores underwater. Divers usually carry tanks of air on their backs or wear special suits and helmets with an air hose so that they can breathe underwater. 3. A bird that dives into water to get its food.

div·er (dī′vər) *noun, plural* **divers.**

Diver

diverse Not the same; different. The students in the class come from *diverse* backgrounds.

di·verse (di vurs′) *adjective.*

diversion 1. A changing of the direction in which something is going. The *diversion* of the train to a different track was necessary because the regular tracks were then being repaired. 2. Something that turns the attention in a different direction. The second robber created a *diversion* while the first picked the man's pocket. 3. Entertainment; amusement; pastime. Ronald's favorite *diversion* is fishing.

di·ver·sion (di vur′zhən) *noun, plural* **diversions.**

diversity Difference; unlikeness. The *diversity* of our interests makes it hard for my sister and me to agree on which television show to watch.

di·ver·si·ty (di vur′sə tē) *noun, plural* **diversities.**

divert 1. To change the direction in which something is going. The police *diverted* traffic from the street where the accident happened. 2. To turn the attention in a different direction. The ringing of the telephone *diverted* Tom from the book he was reading. 3. To entertain; amuse. The television show *diverted* me for a few minutes, but then I got bored.

di·vert (di vurt′) *verb*, **diverted, diverting.**

divide 1. To separate into parts, pieces, or

at; āpe; cär; end; mē; it; īce; hot; ōld;
fôrk; wood; fo͞ol; oil; out; up; turn; sing;
thin; this; hw in white; zh in treasure.
ə stands for a in about, e in taken
i in pencil, o in lemon, and u in circus.

groups. The baker *divided* the pie into ten slices. The class *divided* into two teams for the spelling contest. **2.** To separate into parts or pieces and give some to each; share. The three girls who found the lost dog *divided* the reward money. **3.** To show how many times one number contains another number. For example, when you *divide* 6 by 2 you get 3, because the number 6 contains the number 2 three times. **4.** To split up into opposing sides because of different feelings or ideas. The team *divided* on the choice of a new captain. *Verb.*

—A ridge of land that separates two areas that are drained by different rivers. *Noun.*
di·vide (di vīd') *verb,* **divided, dividing;** *noun, plural* **divides.**

dividend **1.** A number that is to be divided by another number. When you divide 6 by 3, the *dividend* is 6. **2.** Money that is earned by a business and is divided among the owners as their share of the profit.
div·i·dend (div'ə dend') *noun, plural* **dividends.**

divine **1.** Of or from God or a god. The old man prayed for *divine* mercy. **2.** Religious; sacred. The church bell called the people to *divine* worship.
di·vine (di vīn') *adjective.*

divisible Capable of being divided. The number 8 is *divisible* by the numbers 8, 4, 2, and 1.
di·vis·i·ble (di viz'ə bəl) *adjective.*

division **1.** The act of dividing or the state of being divided. The *division* of the house into apartments provided homes for five families. **2.** One of the parts into which something is divided. Asian history is one of the *divisions* of our social studies course. **3.** Something that divides or separates. The wooden fence formed a *division* between the farms. **4.** A unit of the army that is made up of different regiments.
di·vi·sion (di vizh'ən) *noun, plural* **divisions.**

divisor A number by which another number is to be divided. When you divide the number 6 by the number 3, the *divisor* is 3.
di·vi·sor (di vī'zər) *noun, plural* **divisors.**

divorce The legal ending of a marriage. *Noun.*
—To legally end a marriage. *Verb.*
di·vorce (di vôrs') *noun, plural* **divorces;** *verb,* **divorced, divorcing.**

dizzy Having the feeling of spinning and falling. The children ran in circles until they were *dizzy.*
diz·zy (diz'ē) *adjective,* **dizzier, dizziest.**

do **1.** The teacher helped Susan *do* the arithmetic problem. It was kind of Harry to *do* me a favor. It will *do* him good to take a vacation. **2.** *Do* is used to ask questions. *Do* you know John's last name? *Do* horses run faster than dogs? **3.** *Do* is used to make something that is said stronger. *Do* be quiet! **4.** *Do* is used with *not* to show that something is not real or true. I *do* not want to go. **5.** *Do* is used in place of a word or phrase that has already been used. Jan ice-skates as well as I *do.*
▲ Other words that sound like this are **dew** and **due.**
do (dōō) *verb,* **did, done, doing.**

Doberman Pinscher

Doberman pinscher A dog that has a long head, slender legs, and a shiny black or brown coat. Doberman pinschers were originally bred in Germany.
Do·ber·man pin·scher (dō'bər mən pin'shər).

docile Easy to teach, train, or handle. Jack has a *docile* pony that is easy to ride.
doc·ile (dos'əl) *adjective.*

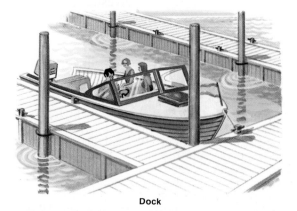
Dock

dock¹ **1.** A platform where boats or ships are tied up. A dock is built along the shore or out into the water. Docks are used for loading and unloading a ship's cargo and passengers. **2.** An area of water between two piers where

boats and ships tie up. The tugboat towed the ocean liner into the *dock. Noun.*
—**1.** To bring a boat or ship to a dock. The tanker *docked* and unloaded its cargo. **2.** To bring two spacecraft together in space. *Verb.*
dock (dok) *noun, plural* **docks;** *verb,* **docked, docking.**

dock² **1.** To take some away; make less. The company *docked* the man's salary because he missed two days of work. **2.** To make shorter by cutting off the end. The veterinarian *docked* the puppy's tail.
dock (dok) *verb,* **docked, docking.**

doctor **1.** A person who has been trained and licensed to treat sickness or injury. A physician or a dentist is a doctor. **2.** A person who has the highest degree from a university.
doc·tor (dok′tər) *noun, plural* **doctors.**

doctrine Something that is believed by a group of people. The beliefs of a religion and the ideals of a political party are doctrines.
doc·trine (dok′trin) *noun, plural* **doctrines.**

document A written or printed statement that gives official proof and information about something. A birth certificate, a deed to a house, and a diploma are documents.
doc·u·ment (dok′yə mənt) *noun, plural* **documents.**

dodge **1.** To keep away from something by moving aside quickly. Jane *dodged* the snowball that Jack threw at her. **2.** To get away from something in a tricky way. The witness *dodged* the lawyer's question by pretending that he didn't remember. *Verb.*
—**1.** A quick move to the side. The boxer avoided being hit by making a *dodge* to the left. **2.** A trick that is used to fool or cheat someone. The man used a clever *dodge* to keep from paying his taxes. *Noun.*
dodge (doj) *verb,* **dodged, dodging;** *noun, plural* **dodges.**

dodo A large bird that no longer exists. The dodo had a heavy hooked bill and a short tail of curly feathers. Its wings were so small that it was not able to fly.
do·do (dō′dō) *noun, plural* **dodos** or **dodoes.**

Dodo

doe **1.** A female deer. **2.** The female of several other animals, such as the antelope or hare.
▲ Another word that sounds like this is **dough.**
doe (dō) *noun, plural* **does.**

does She *does* beautiful paintings of flowers.
does (duz) *verb.*

doesn't Alan *doesn't* like cold weather.
does·n't (duz′ənt) contraction for "does not."

dog An animal that has four legs and makes a barking noise. There are more than 200 different kinds of dogs. Dogs can be as small as five inches tall or as big as three feet tall. People keep dogs in their homes as pets or guards. Dogs are closely related to wolves, foxes, and coyotes. *Noun.*
—To follow closely in the way a hunting dog would. Michael *dogged* his little sister's footsteps to make sure she didn't get lost. *Verb.*
dog (dog) *noun, plural* **dogs;** *verb,* **dogged, dogging.**

dogwood A tree that has flowers with a greenish-yellow center and pink or white leaves that look like petals.
dog·wood (dog′wood′) *noun, plural* **dogwoods.**

Blossom

Dogwood Tree

doily A small piece of linen, lace, paper, or some other material. Doilies are usually placed under something, such as a vase or plate, as a decoration or to protect furniture.
doi·ly (doi′lē) *noun, plural* **doilies.**

doll A toy that looks like a baby, a child, or a grown person.
doll (dol) *noun, plural* **dolls.**

dollar A unit of money in the United States. A dollar is worth one hundred cents.
dol·lar (dol′ər) *noun, plural* **dollars.**

at; āpe; cär; end; mē; it; īce; hot; ōld;
fôrk; wood; fōōl; oil; out; up; turn; sing;
thin; **th**is; hw in white; zh in treasure.
ə stands for **a** in about, **e** in taken
i in pencil, **o** in lemon, and **u** in circus.

193

dolphin　An animal that lives in the sea and is related to the whale. Dolphins have a snout that is like a beak, and two flippers. Although a dolphin looks like a fish, it is a mammal. Dolphins are very intelligent animals.
　dol·phin (dol′fin) *noun, plural* **dolphins.**

Dolphin

domain　All the land that is controlled by a ruler or government. The young knight was the bravest man in the king's *domain*.
　do·main (dō mān′) *noun, plural* **domains.**

dome　A round roof that looks something like an upside-down cup. Domes are built on a base that is circular or has many sides. Some state capital buildings have domes.
　dome (dōm) *noun, plural* **domes.**

domestic　**1.** Having to do with the home and family. Mr. and Mrs. Brown take turns doing the cleaning, cooking, and other *domestic* chores in their house. **2.** Not wild; tame. Dogs and cats are *domestic* animals. **3.** Having to do with one's own country; not foreign. The President of the United States must make decisions on both foreign and *domestic* affairs.
　do·mes·tic (də mes′tik) *adjective.*

domesticate　To train or change a wild animal so that it can live with or be used by people; tame. Man first *domesticated* wild horses to pull loads and help him in farming.
　do·mes·ti·cate (də mes′tə kāt′) *verb,* **domesticated, domesticating.**

dominant　Most powerful or important. England was the *dominant* country in the world for many years. Blue is the *dominant* color in our kitchen.
　dom·i·nant (dom′ə nənt) *adjective.*

dominate　To rule or control because of power, strength, or importance. The Roman Empire *dominated* a large part of the world 2000 years ago.
　dom·i·nate (dom′ə nāt′) *verb,* **dominated, dominating.**

dominion　A land or territory that is controlled by a ruler or government.
　do·min·ion (də min′yən) *noun, plural* **dominions.**

domino　**1.** One of a set of small black tiles marked with dots, that are used in playing a game. **2. dominoes.** The game that is played with these tiles.
　dom·i·no (dom′ə nō′) *noun, plural* **dominoes.**

donate　To give to; contribute. The family *donated* their old clothes to people who needed them.
　do·nate (dō′nāt) *verb,* **donated, donating.**

donation　A gift; contribution. The hospital fund received *donations* of more than $1000 from the businessmen in our town.
　do·na·tion (dō nā′shən) *noun, plural* **donations.**

done　The carpenters have *done* a very good job on our house. Look up **do** for more information. *Verb.*
　—Cooked. When the meat is *done,* we can start our dinner. *Adjective.*
　done (dun) *verb; adjective.*

donkey　An animal that looks very much like a small horse. Donkeys have longer ears and a shorter mane than horses do. They are often used to pull or carry loads.
　don·key (dong′kē *or* dung′kē) *noun, plural* **donkeys.**

Donkey

don't　Please *don't* tell anyone else the secret I told you.
　don't (dōnt) contraction for "do not."

doom　Something causing pain, ruin, or

death; a terrible fate. The mountain climber met his *doom* when the rope he was holding snapped. *Noun.*

—To fix the result of something before it happens, especially when the result is bad. Until his recent success, the writer felt that he was *doomed* to fail. *Verb.*

doom (do͞om) *noun, plural* **dooms;** *verb,* **doomed, dooming.**

door A movable part that is used to open or close an entrance in something. Doors are usually made of wood, metal, or glass.

door (dôr) *noun, plural* **doors.**

doorbell A bell or buzzer that someone who is outside a door rings to show that he wants to come in.

door·bell (dôr′bel′) *noun, plural* **doorbells.**

doorstep A step or flight of steps leading from the outside door of a building to the ground or sidewalk.

door·step (dôr′step′) *noun, plural* **doorsteps.**

doorway An opening in a wall that leads in and out of a room or building and is closed by a door.

door·way (dôr′wā′) *noun, plural* **doorways.**

dope 1. A very stupid person. 2. Opium, heroin, or some similar drug. ▲ These two meanings are used mostly in everyday conversation. 3. A varnish or similar liquid. Dope is used in building models of airplanes.

dope (dōp) *noun, plural* **dopes.**

dormant Not active for a period of time. The volcano which had been *dormant* for years suddenly erupted.

dor·mant (dôr′mənt) *adjective.*

dormitory A building in which there are many bedrooms. Many colleges have dormitories where students live.

dor·mi·to·ry (dôr′mə tôr′ē) *noun, plural* **dormitories.**

dormouse A small animal that is like a squirrel. Dormice have brown or gray fur. They go to sleep, or hibernate, in the winter.

dor·mouse (dôr′mous′) *noun, plural* **dormice.**

dory A rowboat that has a flat bottom and high sides. Fishermen often use dories.

do·ry (dôr′ē) *noun, plural* **dories.**

Dormouse

dose The amount of medicine that a person is given at one time. The doctor prescribed a small *dose* of aspirin for the boy who had a fever.

dose (dōs) *noun, plural* **doses.**

dot A small, round mark; small spot or speck. When the ink spattered, it left *dots* of ink on the desk. The *dot* on the map showed the exact location of the town. *Noun.*

—1. To mark with a dot or dots. In the summer, Michael's face is *dotted* with freckles. 2. To be scattered here and there. Small houses *dotted* the seashore. *Verb.*

dot (dot) *noun, plural* **dots;** *verb,* **dotted, dotting.**

dote To give too much affection. The grandparents *doted* on their only grandchild and spoiled him a little.

dote (dōt) *verb,* **doted, doting.**

double 1. Twice as many or as much; twice as large or as strong. A man who is six feet tall is *double* the height of a child who is three feet tall. 2. Having or made up of two parts. People stood in a *double* line in front of the theater. The man led a *double* life as a businessman and a spy. *Adjective.*

—Two instead of one; in pairs. The ride on the merry-go-round made Helen feel dizzy and see everything *double. Adverb.*

—1. Something that is twice as much. Ten is the *double* of five. 2. A person or thing that is very much or just like another. Christopher is the *double* of his father. 3. A hit in baseball in which the batter goes to second base. *Noun.*

—1. To make or become twice as many or as much. John's parents *doubled* his weekly allowance from twenty-five cents to fifty cents. 2. To bend, fold, or turn over or back. The funny story made Harry *double* over with laughter. 3. To hit a double in baseball. *Verb.*

dou·ble (dub′əl) *adjective; adverb; noun, plural* **doubles;** *verb,* **doubled, doubling.**

double-cross To cheat or betray someone by not doing what one has promised. The robber *double-crossed* his partner by running off with the money that they were supposed to share.

dou·ble-cross (dub′əl krôs′) *verb,* **double-crossed, double-crossing.**

at; āpe; cär; end; mē; it; īce; hot; ōld;
fôrk; wood; fo͞ol; oil; out; up; turn; sing;
thin; this; hw in white; zh in treasure.
ə stands for a in about, e in taken
i in pencil, o in lemon, and u in circus.

double-header Two games of baseball or another sport that are played one right after the other on the same day.
dou·ble-head·er (dub′əl hed′ər) *noun, plural* **double-headers.**

double play A play in baseball in which two runners are put out.

doubt To not believe or trust; be unsure. The judge *doubted* that the prisoner was telling the truth. I brought my umbrella with me, even though I *doubt* that it will rain. *Verb.*
—**1.** A feeling of not believing or trusting. Jim had *doubts* about the honesty of the man who was trying to sell him the car. **2.** A state of being undecided or unsure. The result of the race was in *doubt* until the horses reached the finish line. *Noun.*
doubt (dout) *verb,* **doubted, doubting;** *noun, plural* **doubts.**

doubtful Feeling, showing, or causing doubt; not sure or certain. The team was *doubtful* about its chances of winning the big game.
doubt·ful (dout′fəl) *adjective.*

doubtless Without doubt; certainly. Maria draws so well that she will *doubtless* become an artist someday.
doubt·less (dout′lis) *adverb.*

dough A thick mixture of flour, liquid, and other ingredients that is used to make bread, cookies, pie crusts, and other food. ▲ Another word that sounds like this is **doe.**
dough (dō) *noun, plural* **doughs.**

doughnut A small, round cake that usually has a hole in the middle. A doughnut is cooked in fat.
dough·nut (dō′nut′) *noun, plural* **doughnuts.**

dove¹ A bird that has a thick body and short legs. It makes a cooing sound. A dove is a kind of pigeon. A white dove is sometimes used as a symbol of peace.
dove (duv) *noun, plural* **doves.**

Dove

dove² The girl *dove* from the rocks into the lake. Look up **dive** for more information.
dove (dōv) *verb.*

down¹ From a higher to a lower place. The painter climbed *down* from the ladder. The noisy crowd quieted *down.* The price of milk has gone *down. Adverb.*
—Down along, through, or into something. Jeff met a friend of his as he walked *down* the street. *Preposition.*
—To bring or put down. The policeman tackled the escaping thief and *downed* him. *Verb.*
—One of four chances that a football team gets to move the ball ten yards. If it does not move the ball that far, the other team gets possession of the ball. *Noun.*
down (doun) *adverb; preposition; verb,* **downed, downing;** *noun, plural* **downs.**

down² Fine, soft feathers. Baby birds have *down* until their regular feathers grow in.
down (doun) *noun.*

downpour A very heavy rain.
down·pour (doun′pôr′) *noun, plural* **downpours.**

downright Thorough; complete. The rumor about him is a *downright* lie. *Adjective.*
—Thoroughly; completely. She was *downright* nasty when I asked her to help me. *Adverb.*
down·right (doun′rīt′) *adjective; adverb.*

downstairs **1.** Down the stairs. Andy tripped and fell *downstairs.* **2.** On or to a lower floor. While Sandy was in her room, she could hear her parents talking *downstairs.*
down·stairs (doun′sterz′) *adverb.*

downstream In the direction in which a stream flows. Dick didn't have to paddle the canoe as it drifted *downstream.* The *downstream* current is very strong.
down·stream (doun′strēm′) *adverb; adjective.*

downtown To or in the main part or business district of a town. Peter went *downtown* to see a movie. The *downtown* stores are larger than the ones in our neighborhood.
down·town (doun′toun′) *adverb; adjective.*

downward From a higher to a lower place. The road is level and then goes *downward* into the valley. This word is also spelled **downwards.** *Adverb.*
—Moving from a higher place to a lower place. The hikers followed the *downward* course of the stream from the mountain top. *Adjective.*
down·ward (doun′wərd) *adverb; adjective.*

dowry The money or property that a woman brings to her husband when she gets married.

dow·ry (dour′ē) *noun, plural* **dowries.**

doze To sleep lightly or for a short time; take a nap. The truck driver pulled off the road when he realized that he was starting to *doze.*

doze (dōz) *verb,* **dozed, dozing.**

Dragon

dozen A group of twelve. The grocery store sells eggs by the *dozen.* She bought three *dozen* doughnuts.

doz·en (duz′ən) *noun, plural* **dozens** or **dozen.**

drab Not cheerful or bright; dull. The dark, *drab* room was much nicer after we put up new curtains.

drab (drab) *adjective,* **drabber, drabbest.**

draft **1.** A current of air in an enclosed space. Emily felt a cold *draft* from the open window. **2.** A device that controls the flow of air in something. Furnaces, fireplaces, and some stoves have drafts. **3.** A sketch, plan, or rough copy of something. The author wrote three different *drafts* of his novel. **4.** The selecting of a person or persons for some special purpose. My father is not eligible for the *draft* because he has already served in the army. *Noun.*
—**1.** To make a sketch, plan, or rough copy of something. David *drafted* the letter in pencil and then typed it. **2.** To select a person or persons for some special purpose. The politician was *drafted* by his party to run for mayor. *Verb.*
—Used for pulling loads. Elephants are used as *draft* animals in some countries. *Adjective.*

draft (draft) *noun, plural* **drafts;** *verb,* **drafted, drafting;** *adjective.*

draftsman A person who draws or designs plans for machinery, buildings, and other things.

drafts·man (drafts′mən) *noun, plural* **draftsmen.**

drag **1.** To pull or move along slowly or heavily. He *dragged* the heavy trunk across the room. Time *dragged* on while we waited for the train that was late. **2.** To search the bottom of a body of water with a hook or net. The fisherman *dragged* the bottom of the lake for the sunken rowboat. *Verb.*

drag (drag) *verb,* **dragged, dragging.**

dragon An imaginary beast that is supposed to look something like a giant lizard with claws and wings.

drag·on (drag′ən) *noun, plural* **dragons.**

dragonfly A large insect that has a thin body and two pairs of wings. Dragonflies eat mosquitoes and other insects. They live near fresh water.

drag·on·fly (drag′ən-flī′) *noun, plural* **dragonflies.**

Dragonfly

drain **1.** To empty water or other liquid from something. The workers *drained* the water from the swimming pool at the end of the summer. **2.** To tire or use up; exhaust. The long hike *drained* our energy. *Verb.*
—**1.** An opening, pipe, or other device that draws off water or another liquid. The *drain* in the sink is clogged. **2.** Something that uses up or exhausts. Buying the bicycle was a *drain* on my savings. *Noun.*

drain (drān) *verb,* **drained, draining;** *noun, plural* **drains.**

drainage A drawing off or emptying of water or other liquid. The *drainage* of the swamp land made it possible for the farmer to plant crops there.

drain·age (drā′nij) *noun.*

drake A male duck.

drake (drāk) *noun, plural* **drakes.**

drama **1.** A story that is written for actors to perform on the stage; play. **2.** A happening that is as exciting or interesting as a play. The newspaper story reported the *drama* of the

at; āpe; cär; end; mē; it; īce; hot; ōld; fôrk; wood; fo͞ol; oil; out; up; turn; sing; thin; this; hw in white; zh in treasure.
ə stands for a in about, e in taken i in pencil, o in lemon, and u in circus.

firemen's rescue of the family from the burning building.

dra·ma (drä′mə *or* dram′ə) *noun, plural* **dramas.**

dramatic **1.** Of or having to do with plays or acting. My older brother is taking *dramatic* lessons. **2.** As exciting and interesting as a play. Our team won a *dramatic* victory by tying the score and then going ahead in the last minutes of the game.

dra·mat·ic (drə mat′ik) *adjective.*

dramatist A person who writes plays.

dram·a·tist (dram′ə tist) *noun, plural* **dramatists.**

dramatize **1.** To write or perform something as a play. The members of the Sunday school class *dramatized* several stories from the Bible. **2.** To make something seem very exciting. Pat *dramatized* what happened on her vacation so that it sounded like a real adventure.

dram·a·tize (dram′ə tīz′) *verb,* **dramatized, dramatizing.**

drank Mark *drank* three glasses of water. Look up **drink** for more information.

drank (drangk) *verb.*

drape To cover or decorate with cloth that hangs loosely. The woman *draped* a shawl over her shoulders. *Verb.*
—Cloth that is hung at a window; drapery. Christine opened the *drapes* to let sunlight into the room. *Noun.*

drape (drāp) *verb,* **draped, draping;** *noun, plural* **drapes.**

drapery Cloth that is hung in loose folds. Draperies are usually used as window curtains.

dra·per·y (drā′pər ē) *noun, plural* **draperies.**

drastic Very strong or harsh; extreme. Forbidding automobiles on the main street was the *drastic* measure that the town took to stop air pollution.

dras·tic (dras′tik) *adjective.*

draw **1.** To bring or move in a particular direction or to a particular position. The farmer used horses to *draw* his wagon. The cowboy *drew* his gun and fired. I will have to *draw* money from my savings to pay for my brother's birthday present. The popular singer always *draws* a large crowd to his concerts. **2.** To make a picture of something. People usually *draw* with a pencil, pen, or crayons. **3.** To cause or allow a current of air to pass. The chimney does not *draw* well because it is blocked with dead leaves. *Verb.*
—**1.** The act of drawing. The cowboy was quick on the *draw* and fired first. **2.** A game or contest in which the players or teams have the same score; tie. The chess game ended in a *draw. Noun.*

draw (drô) *verb,* **drew, drawn, drawing;** *noun, plural* **draws.**

drawback A thing that makes something more difficult or unpleasant; disadvantage. The main *drawback* of our new house is that it is so far away from my school.

draw·back (drô′bak′) *noun, plural* **drawbacks.**

drawbridge A kind of bridge that can be raised or lowered, or moved to one side. Drawbridges are sometimes used over water so that tall boats or ships can pass through when the bridge is raised. In olden times, castles had drawbridges which could be raised to keep enemies from crossing the water around the castle.

draw·bridge (drô′brij′) *noun, plural* **drawbridges.**

Drawbridge

drawer A box that fits into a piece of furniture and can be pulled out and pushed in. Bureaus, desks, and cabinets have drawers.

drawer (drôr) *noun, plural* **drawers.**

drawing **1.** A picture or design made with a pencil, pen, crayon, or similar thing. **2.** The choosing of a winning chance or ticket in a lottery or raffle. The *drawing* for the winning number will be next Saturday night.

draw·ing (drô′ing) *noun, plural* **drawings.**

drawl To speak in a slow or lazy way. The sleepy boy *drawled* his answer to the question. *Verb.*
—A slow way of speaking. Many people from the southern part of the United States speak with a *drawl. Noun.*

drawl (drôl) *verb,* **drawled, drawling;** *noun, plural* **drawls.**

drawn The artist has *drawn* many sketches of the church. Look up **draw** for more information.

drawn (drôn) *verb.*

dread To look forward to with fear; be afraid about something that has not happened yet. Walter *dreaded* going to the dentist. *Verb.*
—A feeling of fear about what may happen. Jimmy thought of the airplane trip with *dread* because he was scared of flying. *Noun.*
—Causing fear; dreadful. Polio is one of the *dread* diseases that modern medicine has almost completely wiped out. *Adjective.*

dread (dred) *verb,* **dreaded, dreading;** *adjective.*

dreadful **1.** Very frightening; terrible. The *dreadful* storm caused floods that destroyed many homes. **2.** Very bad; awful. I saw a *dreadful* movie on television last night.

dread·ful (dred′fəl) *adjective.*

dream **1.** A series of thoughts or feelings that a person has while asleep. Linda had a *dream* last night that she was able to fly. **2.** An idea that is like a dream but is thought by a person who is awake; daydream. Peter's great *dream* is to become an actor someday. *Noun.*
—**1.** To see, feel, or think about in a dream. Alfred dozed off and *dreamed* about riding a white horse. **2.** To imagine. I didn't take an umbrella because I never *dreamed* it would rain. *Verb.*

dream (drēm) *noun, plural* **dreams;** *verb,* **dreamed** or **dreamt, dreaming.**

▲ The word **dream** probably comes from an old German word that means "to fool or trick." Often dreams are so real that they fool us and make us think that something that was only a dream really did happen.

dreamt Robin *dreamt* that she and Jack had a fight.

dreamt (dremt) *verb.*

dreary Sad or dull; gloomy. Painting the small, dark room a bright yellow made it less *dreary.*

drear·y (drēr′ē) *adjective,* **drearier, dreariest.**

dredge A large machine that scoops up mud, sand, and other material from the bottom of a body of water. The engineers used a *dredge* to make the canal deeper. *Noun.*
—To clean out or deepen with a dredge. The machine *dredged* mud from the river. *Verb.*

dredge (drej) *noun, plural* **dredges;** *verb,* **dredged, dredging.**

dregs Small pieces that settle at the bottom of a liquid. There was nothing left of the coffee but the *dregs* at the bottom of the cup.

dregs (dregz) *noun plural.*

drench To make something completely wet; soak. The big wave *drenched* the boys on the raft.

drench (drench) *verb,* **drenched, drenching.**

dress **1.** A garment for a woman or girl. A dress usually looks like a blouse and skirt that have been sewn together. **2.** Clothing or a particular style of clothing. The guests at the ball were all wearing formal *dress. Noun.*
—**1.** To put clothes on. Lisa *dressed* quickly because she was late for school. **2.** To arrange, prepare, or treat something. The butcher *dressed* the turkey for us so that it would be easier to cook. The doctor *dressed* the boy's wound and bandaged it. *Verb.*

dress (dres) *noun, plural* **dresses;** *verb,* **dressed, dressing.**

dresser A piece of furniture that has drawers for storing clothes and other things. A dresser often has a large mirror attached to it.

dress·er (dres′ər) *noun, plural* **dressers.**

dressing **1.** A sauce that is put on salads and some other foods. **2.** A mixture of bread crumbs and seasonings used to stuff turkey or chicken. **3.** A medicine or bandage that is put on a wound or sore.

dress·ing (dres′ing) *noun, plural* **dressings.**

drew Mitchell *drew* a funny picture of his uncle. Look up **draw** for more information.

drew (dro̅o̅) *verb.*

dribble **1.** To flow or let flow in small drops; trickle. Rain *dribbled* through the cracks in the roof. **2.** To move a ball along by bouncing or kicking it. Players *dribble* the ball in basketball and soccer. *Verb.*
—A dripping; trickle. A *dribble* of juice from the plum ran down Kevin's chin. *Noun.*

drib·ble (drib′əl) *verb,* **dribbled, dribbling;** *noun, plural* **dribbles.**

dried Mary washed her hair and then *dried* it. Look up **dry** for more information.

dried (drīd) *verb.*

at; āpe; cär; end; mē; it; īce; hot; ōld; fôrk; wood; fo̅o̅l; oil; out; up; turn; sing; thin; this; hw in white; zh in treasure. ə stands for a in about, e in taken i in pencil, o in lemon, and u in circus.

drier The clothes were *drier* after they had been hanging on the line for an hour. Look up **dry** for more information. *Adjective.*

—A machine that dries something. This word is usually spelled **dryer**. Look up **dryer** for more information. *Noun.*

dri·er (drī′ər) *adjective; noun, plural* **driers.**

dries Short hair *dries* faster than long hair.
dries (drīz) *verb.*

driest The cave was the *driest* place we could find during the storm. Look up **dry** for more information.
dri·est (drī′ist) *adjective.*

drift To move or pile up because of a current of air or water. The fisherman stopped rowing and let his boat *drift* downstream. Smoke from the fire *drifted* up into the sky. *Verb.*

—Something that has been moved along or piled up by air or water currents. The storm caused *drifts* of snow more than ten feet deep. *Noun.*

drift (drift) *verb,* **drifted, drifting;** *noun, plural* **drifts.**

driftwood Wood that floats on water or is brought to the shore by water.
drift·wood (drift′wood′) *noun, plural* **drift-woods.**

Drill

drill 1. A tool that is used to cut holes in wood, plastic, and other hard material. A drill usually has a long, pointed end that is turned with a crank or by an electric motor. 2. Training or teaching by making someone do something again and again; practice. For our social studies *drill*, the teacher asked us to name the capital of each state. *Noun.*

—1. To make a hole in something with a drill; use a drill. The carpenter *drilled* a hole in the wood. The company *drilled* for oil in Texas. 2. To train or teach a person by having him do something again and again. The school band *drilled* by marching back and forth. *Verb.*

drill (dril) *noun, plural* **drills;** *verb,* **drilled, drilling.**

drink 1. To swallow a liquid. I *drink* a glass of milk with every meal. 2. To soak up. The plants *drank* in the rain. 3. To drink an alcoholic beverage. *Verb.*

—1. A liquid for drinking. Lemonade is my favorite *drink* in the summer. 2. A portion of liquid. The tennis players stopped to have a *drink* of orange juice. 3. An alcoholic beverage. *Noun.*

drink (dringk) *verb,* **drank, drunk, drinking;** *noun, plural* **drinks.**

drip To fall or let fall in drops. Raindrops *dripped* from the trees. He *dripped* paint from the brush onto his shirt. *Verb.*

—A falling of liquid in drops. There was a *drip* of water from the broken pipe. *Noun.*

drip (drip) *verb,* **dripped, dripping;** *noun, plural* **drips.**

drive 1. To use and steer a car or other vehicle. My father says he will teach me to *drive* when I am sixteen years old. The farmer *drove* his truck to the market. 2. To go or be carried in a car or other vehicle. We plan to *drive* to the city on Saturday. 3. To cause to move, work, or go. Strong winds *drove* the sailboat onto the rocks. The carpenter used a hammer to *drive* the nail into the board. The baseball player tried to *drive* the ball over the fence for a home run. My brother's constant teasing *drives* me crazy. *Verb.*

—1. A trip in a car or other vehicle. The *drive* to the city was unpleasant because there was so much traffic. 2. A road or driveway. She parked the car in the *drive* and walked to the front door. 3. A strong hit. In the golf tournament, Johnny hit a *drive* more than 250 yards. 4. A special effort to do something. The town started a *drive* to raise money for a new hospital. *Noun.*

drive (drīv) *verb,* **drove, driven, driving;** *noun, plural* **drives.**

drive-in A restaurant, movie theater, or bank that can take care of customers in their cars.
drive-in (drīv′in′) *noun, plural* **drive-ins.**

driver A person who drives an automobile, truck, or other vehicle.
driv·er (drī′vər) *noun, plural* **drivers.**

driveway A private road that leads to a house, garage, or other building from a road or street.
drive·way (drīv′wā′) *noun, plural* **drive-ways.**

dromedary   A kind of camel that has one hump. Dromedaries live in Arabia and North Africa.

drom·e·dar·y (drom′ə der′ē) *noun, plural* **dromedaries.**

Dromedary

drone¹   A male bee that does no work.

drone (drōn) *noun, plural* **drones.**

drone²   **1.** To make a low, continuous humming sound. The small airplane *droned* as it climbed higher. **2.** To talk in a dull, boring way. People began to leave when the speaker *droned* on and on about his experiences. *Verb.*
—A low, continuous humming sound. The *drone* of the car's engine could be heard down the road. *Noun.*

drone (drōn) *verb,* **droned, droning;** *noun, plural* **drones.**

drool   To let saliva drip from the mouth. The baby *drooled* on his bib.

drool (drool) *verb,* **drooled, drooling.**

droop   To hang or sink down; sag. The little girl's eyelids *drooped* and she was soon asleep.

droop (droop) *verb,* **drooped, drooping.**

drop   **1.** To fall or cause to fall to a lower position; move or fall down. The wet dish *dropped* from Kathy's hand. Philip tripped and *dropped* the book he was carrying. The temperature *dropped* to below freezing on Christmas Eve. **2.** To stop doing something. Ricky decided to *drop* out of school and get a job. **3.** To do or give something in a casual way. My aunt *dropped* in to see us last week. Natalie always *drops* a hint about what she wants for her birthday. **4.** To leave out. Although Susan knits carefully, she sometimes accidentally *drops* a stitch. *Verb.*
—**1.** A very small amount of liquid. A drop is usually shaped like a tiny ball. There was a *drop* of blood on Margaret's hand where the cat had scratched her. **2.** The act of dropping

or falling. The weatherman said there would be a *drop* in temperature tonight. **3.** The distance between one thing and another thing that is below it. From the tree branch to the ground was a *drop* of ten feet. *Noun.*

drop (drop) *verb,* **dropped** or **dropt, dropping;** *noun, plural* **drops.**

drought   A long period of time when there is very little rain or no rain at all.

drought (drout) *noun, plural* **droughts.**

drove¹   We *drove* downtown in the car. Look up **drive** for more information.

drove (drōv) *verb.*

drove²   **1.** A group of animals that move or are driven along together. The cowboys brought a *drove* of cattle to the ranch. **2.** A large number of people; crowd. People went to the beach in *droves* on the hot summer day.

drove (drōv) *noun, plural* **droves.**

drown   **1.** To die in water because there is no air to breathe. The lifeguard saved the girl as she was about to *drown*. **2.** To kill by keeping under water or another liquid. Two people were *drowned* in the flood. **3.** To cover up the sound of something by a louder sound. We tried to say good-by, but the roar of the airplane engines *drowned* out our words.

drown (droun) *verb,* **drowned, drowning.**

drowsy   Half asleep; sleepy. George felt *drowsy* after dinner and decided to take a nap.

drow·sy (drou′zē) *adjective,* **drowsier, drowsiest.**

drug   **1.** A chemical or other substance that makes a change in a person's body. Most drugs are used to treat or cure diseases. **2.** A substance to which a person can become addicted. Heroin is a drug. *Noun.*
—To give a drug to a person. The nurse *drugged* the patient so that he would sleep. *Verb.*

drug (drug) *noun, plural* **drugs;** *verb,* **drugged, drugging.**

druggist   **1.** A person who has a license to make and sell medicine; pharmacist. **2.** A person who owns or runs a drugstore.

drug·gist (drug′ist) *noun, plural* **druggists.**

drugstore   A store where medicines and drugs are sold. Drugstores often also sell

at; āpe; cär; end; mē; it; īce; hot; ōld;
fôrk; wood; fool; oil; out; up; turn; sing;
thin; this; hw in white; zh in treasure.
ə stands for a in about, e in taken
i in pencil, o in lemon, and u in circus.

201

cosmetics, candy, cigarettes, magazines, and various other things.

drug·store (drug'stôr') *noun, plural* **drug-stores.**

drum **1.** A musical instrument that makes a sound when it is beaten. A drum is a hollow object that is covered at the top and at the bottom with material that is stretched very tight. A person who plays a drum hits the material with a stick or with his hand. **2.** Something that is shaped like a drum. The oil was stored in large metal *drums. Noun.*
—**1.** To beat or play on a drum. **2.** To make a sound like a drum. The bored student *drummed* on the desk with his fingers. **3.** To force into a person's head by repeating. He finally *drummed* the idea into her head that he didn't like to be called by his nickname. *Verb.*
drum (drum) *noun, plural* **drums;** *verb,* **drummed, drumming.**

A Set of Drums

drum major A person who leads a marching band.

drum majorette A girl who twirls a baton while marching with a band in a parade.
drum ma·jor·ette (mā'jə ret').

drumstick **1.** A stick used for beating a drum. **2.** The lower part of the leg of a cooked chicken or turkey.
drum·stick (drum'stik') *noun, plural* **drum-sticks.**

drunk Have you *drunk* your milk yet? Look up **drink** for more information. *Verb.*
—Having had too much alcoholic liquor to drink. *Adjective.*
—A person who has had or often has too much alcoholic liquor to drink. *Noun.*
drunk (drungk) *verb; adjective,* **drunker, drunkest;** *noun, plural* **drunks.**

dry **1.** Not wet or damp; with very little or no water or other liquid. The farmer had to bring water from the stream because the well was *dry.* Cactus plants grow well in a *dry* desert climate. **2.** Not in or under water. After the long voyage, the sailors were happy to be back on *dry* land again. **3.** Thirsty. Frank was so *dry* after playing tennis that he drank three glasses of water. **4.** Not interesting; dull. The book was so *dry* that Janet fell asleep while reading it. *Adjective.*
—To make or become dry. If you wash the dishes, I'll *dry* them. *Verb.*
dry (drī) *adjective,* **drier, driest;** *verb,* **dried, drying.**

dry cell An electric cell in which the substance that conducts the electrical current is made of a paste so that it will not spill.

dry-clean To clean clothes by using chemicals instead of water.
dry-clean (drī'klēn') *verb,* **dry-cleaned, dry-cleaning.**

dryer A machine or device for drying something. Jim put the wet laundry in the clothes *dryer.* This word is also spelled **drier.**
dry·er (drī'ər) *noun, plural* **dryers.**

dry goods Cloth, thread, lace, ribbons, and the like.

dual Made up of or having two parts. The driving instructor used a car that had *dual* controls so that he could stop the car if a student made a bad mistake in driving. ▲ Another word that sounds like this is **duel.**
du·al (dōō'əl *or* dyōō'əl) *adjective.*

duchess The wife or widow of a duke.
duch·ess (duch'is) *noun, plural* **duchesses.**

duck¹ **1.** A bird that has a broad, flat bill and webbed feet that help it to swim. There are both wild and tame ducks. Tame ducks are often raised for food. **2.** A female duck. The male is often called a drake.
duck (duk) *noun, plural* **ducks.**

Duck

duck² **1.** To push someone under water suddenly. Jake swam behind Don and playfully *ducked* him. **2.** To lower the head or bend down quickly. Jerry *ducked* his head to keep from being hit by the ball.
duck (duk) *verb,* **ducked, ducking.**

duckling   A young duck.
   duck·ling (duk′ling) *noun, plural* **ducklings.**

duct   A tube, pipe, or channel that carries a liquid or air. Tears are formed in glands behind the eyes and are carried to the eyes by tiny ducts. Ducts are used in some buildings to carry hot or cold air to control the temperature in rooms.
   duct (dukt) *noun, plural* **ducts.**

due   **1.** Owed or owing. The rent for the apartment is *due* on the first day of each month. If you don't return your library book when it is *due,* you will have to pay a fine. **2.** Expected or supposed to arrive or be ready. The train is *due* at noon. *Adjective.*
   —**1.** Something that is owed. You should give him his *due* and congratulate him for beating you in the contest. **2. dues.** A fee that a person pays to a club for the right of being a member. *Noun.*
   —Straight; directly. The explorers walked *due* west toward the setting sun. *Adverb.* ▲ Other words that sound like this are **dew** and **do.**
   due (dōō *or* dyōō) *adjective; noun, plural* **dues;** *adverb.*

duel   A formal fight between two people with swords or pistols. A duel is held to settle an argument or to decide a question of honor. Duels are usually fought in the presence of two witnesses who are called seconds. *Noun.*
   —To fight a duel. *Verb.* ▲ Another word that sounds like this is **dual.**
   du·el (dōō′əl *or* dyōō′əl) *noun, plural* **duels;** *verb,* **dueled, dueling.**

duet   A piece of music written for two singers or two musical instruments.
   du·et (dōō et′ *or* dyōō et′) *noun, plural* **duets.**

dug   The men *dug* a hole and planted a tree in it. Look up **dig** for more information.
   dug (dug) *verb.*

dugout   **1.** A long shelter in which baseball players sit when they are not playing. Dugouts are built at the side of the field and usually have a roof and three sides. **2.** A rough shelter that is made by digging a hole in the ground or in the side of a hill. **3.** A canoe or boat that is made by hollowing out a large log.
   dug·out (dug′out′) *noun, plural* **dugouts.**

duke   A nobleman who has the highest rank below a prince.
   duke (dōōk *or* dyōōk) *noun, plural* **dukes.**

dull   **1.** Not sharp or pointed; blunt. The knife was so *dull* that Matthew could not cut the steak. **2.** Not interesting; plain or boring. The movie was so *dull* that Keith left before it was over. **3.** Slow to learn or understand; not intelligent. A person would have to be very *dull* not to understand that joke. **4.** Not bright, clear, or distinct. The barn was painted a *dull* red. Marcia felt a *dull* ache in her legs for several days after the long hike. *Adjective.*
   —To make or become dull. Using the kitchen scissors for cutting wire *dulled* them. *Verb.*
   dull (dul) *adjective,* **duller, dullest;** *verb,* **dulled, dulling.**

dumb   **1.** Not able to speak. Although she was born deaf and *dumb,* she learned to communicate through sign language. We were struck *dumb* by the surprising news. **2.** Stupid. You have to be really *dumb* to fall for such a silly trick.
   dumb (dum) *adjective,* **dumber, dumbest.**

dummy   **1.** A figure that is made to look like a person. The *dummy* in the department store window was dressed in a wedding dress. **2.** Something that is made to look like something else that is real. The actor's gun was a *dummy.*
   dum·my (dum′ē) *noun, plural* **dummies.**

dump   To drop, unload, or empty. The truck *dumped* the gravel on the sidewalk. Michael *dumped* his books on the table. *Verb.*
   —A place where garbage and trash are dumped. At the end of the day, the garbage trucks unloaded at the city *dump. Noun.*
   dump (dump) *verb,* **dumped, dumping;** *noun, plural* **dumps.**

dune   A mound or ridge of sand that has been piled up by the wind.
   dune (dōōn *or* dyōōn) *noun, plural* **dunes.**

Dune

dungaree   **1.** A heavy cotton cloth that is used to make work clothes, sportswear, and sails. **2. dungarees.** Pants or work clothes that are made from this cloth.

at; āpe; cär; end; mē; it; īce; hot; ōld;
fôrk; wood; fōōl; oil; out; up; turn; sing;
thin; this; hw in white; zh in treasure.
ə stands for a in about, e in taken
i in pencil, o in lemon, and u in circus.

dun·ga·ree (dung'gə rē') *noun, plural* **dungarees.**

dungeon A dark prison or cell that is built underground. The king's guards captured the traitor and put him in the *dungeon* of the castle.
dun·geon (dun'jən) *noun, plural* **dungeons.**

duplicate Just like something else. My parents gave me a *duplicate* key to our front door. *Adjective.*
—Something that is just like something else; exact copy. William liked the snapshot so much that I had a *duplicate* made for him. *Noun.*
—To make an exact copy of something. The secretary *duplicated* the letter so that she would have a copy after she mailed it. *Verb.*
du·pli·cate (dōō'pli kit *or* dyōō'pli kit *for adjective and noun;* dōō'pli kāt' *or* dyōō'pli kāt' *for verb*) *adjective; noun, plural* **duplicates;** *verb,* **duplicated, duplicating.**

durable Able to last a long time in spite of much use or wear. My mother bought my brother *durable* shoes with heavy soles.
du·ra·ble (door'ə bəl *or* dyoor'ə bəl) *adjective.*

duration The length of time during which something continues. The doctor said that Nancy should stay in bed for the *duration* of her illness.
du·ra·tion (doo rā'shən *or* dyoo rā'shən) *noun, plural* **durations.**

during My grandparents always go away to the country *during* the summer. Joseph was awakened by a telephone call *during* the night.
dur·ing (door'ing *or* dyoor'ing) *preposition.*

dusk The time of day just before the sun goes down; twilight. The farmer worked in the fields from dawn to *dusk.*
dusk (dusk) *noun.*

dust Tiny pieces of earth, dirt, or other matter. The horse kicked up a cloud of *dust* as it galloped along the dirt road. *Noun.*
—1. To remove the dust from something by brushing or wiping. I *dusted* the table and then polished it with wax. 2. To cover or sprinkle. The baker *dusted* the doughnuts with sugar. The farmer *dusted* his crops with a chemical that killed insects. *Verb.*
dust (dust) *noun; verb,* **dusted, dusting.**

Dutch Of or relating to the Netherlands, its people, or their language. *Adjective.*
—1. the Dutch. The people of the Netherlands. 2. The language of the Netherlands. *Noun.*
Dutch (duch) *adjective; noun.*

duty 1. Something that a person is supposed to do. Mr. Robinson said it was his *duty* as a citizen to vote in every election. Locking up the store at night was one of the manager's *duties.* 2. A tax that is paid on goods that are brought into or taken out of a country.
du·ty (dōō'tē *or* dyōō'tē) *noun, plural* **duties.**

dwarf 1. A person, animal, or plant that is much smaller than the normal size. 2. A little man in fairy tales who has magical powers. *Noun.*
—To make seem small. The skyscraper *dwarfed* the buildings around it. *Verb.*
dwarf (dwôrf) *noun, plural* **dwarfs** or **dwarves;** *verb,* **dwarfed, dwarfing.**

dwell To live in. After living in the country for many years, they decided to *dwell* in the city.
dwell (dwel) *verb,* **dwelt** or **dwelled, dwelling.**

dwelling A place where a person lives. We live in a two-family *dwelling.*
dwell·ing (dwel'ing) *noun, plural* **dwellings.**

dwindle To become less or smaller; shrink slowly. The crowd began to *dwindle* after the parade passed by.
dwin·dle (dwind'əl) *verb,* **dwindled, dwindling.**

dye A substance that is used to give a particular color to cloth, hair, food, or other materials. *Noun.*
—To color or stain something with a dye. When the blue curtains faded, my mother *dyed* them red. *Verb.* ▲ Another word that sounds like this is **die.**
dye (dī) *noun, plural* **dyes;** *verb,* **dyed, dyeing.**

dying Our sailboat slowed because the wind was *dying* down. Look up **die** for more information.
dy·ing (dī'ing) *verb.*

dynamic Having or showing a lot of energy; active; forceful. That *dynamic* young woman is sure to become a leader.
dy·nam·ic (dī nam'ik) *adjective.*

dynamite A substance that explodes with great force. Dynamite is used to blow up rocks. *Noun.*
—To blow something up with dynamite. The builders *dynamited* the rocks so that they could put a road through. *Verb.*
dy·na·mite (dī'nə mīt') *noun; verb,* **dynamited, dynamiting.**

dynamo An electric motor or generator. Dynamos usually produce a direct current.
dy·na·mo (dī'nə mō') *noun, plural* **dynamos.**

dynasty A series of rulers who belong to the same family.
dy·nas·ty (dī'nəs tē) *noun, plural* **dynasties.**

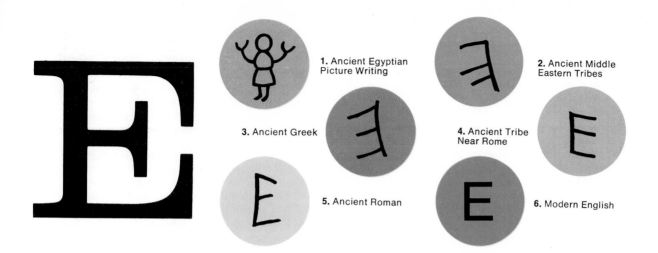

1. Ancient Egyptian Picture Writing

2. Ancient Middle Eastern Tribes

3. Ancient Greek

4. Ancient Tribe Near Rome

5. Ancient Roman

6. Modern English

E is the fifth letter of the alphabet. The oldest form of the letter **E** was a drawing that the ancient Egyptians (**1**) used in their picture writing nearly 5000 years ago. The drawing showed a person with his arms stretched out. Several ancient tribes (**2**) in the Middle East borrowed the drawing for their alphabet. They changed its shape by drawing it as a tall line with three or, sometimes, four short lines on the left side. This letter was used to stand for the *h* sound. When the ancient Greeks (**3**) borrowed this letter, they used it to stand for both the *h* sound and the *e* sound. Because they had another letter that stood for the *h* sound, the Greeks began to use this letter to stand for only the *e* sound. This Greek letter was borrowed by an ancient tribe (**4**) that settled north of Rome about 2800 years ago. They gave this letter its modern shape by turning the Greek letter around. The Romans (**5**) borrowed this new form of **E.** By about 2400 years ago, they were writing it almost the same way that we write the capital letter **E** today (**6**).

e, E The fifth letter of the alphabet.
e, E (ē) *noun, plural* **e's, E's.**

each *Each* player gets a turn to hit the ball. My aunt gave *each* of us a piece of pie. These candies are ten cents *each.*
each (ēch) *adjective; pronoun; adverb.*

each other. One another. We see *each other* every day.

eager Wanting very much to do something. A person who is eager is full of interest and enthusiasm. The boys were *eager* to go to the ball game.
ea·ger (ē′gər) *adjective.*

eagle A large, powerful bird. Eagles hunt and feed on small animals. They are known for their sharp eyesight and have strong claws. One kind of eagle, the bald eagle, is the national symbol of the United States.
ea·gle (ē′gəl) *noun, plural* **eagles.**

ear¹ **1.** The part of the body with which people and animals hear. **2.** The sense of hearing. Her voice is soft and pleasing to the *ear.*
ear (ēr) *noun, plural* **ears.**

ear² The part of certain plants on which the grains or seeds grow. The grains of corn and wheat grow on ears.
ear (ēr) *noun, plural* **ears.**

eardrum The thin layer of tissue between the outer and middle parts of the ear. It moves back and forth when sound waves strike it.
ear·drum (ēr′drum′) *noun, plural* **eardrums.**

earl A nobleman in Great Britain.
earl (url) *noun, plural* **earls.**

Eagle

205

early **1.** In or near the beginning. We started out on the hike in the *early* morning. Linda's birthday is *early* in March. **2.** Before the usual time. We had an *early* dinner so we all could watch the movie on TV.
ear·ly (ur′lē) *adjective,* **earlier, earliest;** *adverb.*

earn **1.** To get as pay for work done. Larry *earned* fifty dollars mowing lawns. **2.** To deserve or win because of hard work. Leslie *earned* her high marks by studying hard. ▲ Another word that sounds like this is **urn.**
earn (urn) *verb,* **earned, earning.**

earnest Not joking or fooling about something. An earnest person is sincere and serious about what he says and does. John was being *earnest* when he said he was sorry for what he did.
ear·nest (ur′nist) *adjective.*

earnings Money that has been earned; pay. Charlie put all his *earnings* in the bank to save up for a car.
earn·ings (ur′ningz) *noun plural.*

earphone A part of a machine that receives sound. Earphones are placed over or held at a person's ear so that he can listen.
ear·phone (ēr′fōn′) *noun, plural* **earphones.**

earring A piece of jewelry worn on the ear.
ear·ring (ēr′ring′) *noun, plural* **earrings.**

earth **1.** The planet that we live on. The earth is the fifth largest planet in the solar system. It is the third in order of distance from the sun. **2.** Dry land; the ground. After many weeks at sea, the sailors were glad to feel the *earth* under their feet again. **3.** Soil; dirt. Tom planted the seeds in the *earth.*
earth (urth) *noun, plural* **earths.**

earthen **1.** Made out of earth. The log cabin had an *earthen* floor. **2.** Made out of clay that has been baked and made hard. In the museum we saw *earthen* bowls made by Indians.
earth·en (ur′thən) *adjective.*

earthly **1.** Having to do with the earth or this world, rather than with heaven. The old man left all his *earthly* goods to his grandchildren. **2.** Possible; imaginable. These shoes are so old that they're of no *earthly* use to anyone.
earth·ly (urth′lē) *adjective.*

earthquake A shaking or trembling of the ground. Earthquakes are caused by rock, lava, or hot gases moving deep inside the earth. Some earthquakes are so large that they cause the ground to split and buildings to fall down.
earth·quake (urth′kwāk′) *noun, plural* **earthquakes.**

earthworm A worm that has a long body and lives in the soil.
earth·worm (urth′wurm′) *noun, plural* **earthworms.**

ease Freedom from trouble, pain, or hard work; comfort. After working for many years, my grandfather sold his business and lived a life of *ease.* Michael rides a bicycle with *ease. Noun.*
—**1.** To make free from trouble, pain, or worry. The news that Paul's plane had landed safely *eased* his mother's mind. **2.** To move slowly or carefully. Norma *eased* the car into the small parking space. *Verb.*
ease (ēz) *noun; verb,* **eased, easing.**

easel A tall stand or rack. Easels are used to hold blackboards, signs, and artists' paintings.
ea·sel (ē′zel) *noun, plural* **easels.**

Easel

easily **1.** Without trying hard. I can touch my toes *easily.* **2.** Without any doubt; for sure. Warren is *easily* the best player on the team. **3.** Very likely; possibly. If the books are too heavy, you could *easily* drop them.
eas·i·ly (ē′zə lē) *adverb.*

east **1.** The direction a person faces when he watches the sun rise in the morning. East is one of the four main points of the compass. It is directly opposite west. **2. East.** Any area or place that is in the east. **3. the East.** The eastern part of the United States, along the Atlantic coast. **4. the East.** Asia and the islands close to it. *Noun.*
—**1.** Toward or in the east. Our school is on the *east* side of town. **2.** Coming from the east. An *east* wind was blowing. *Adjective.*
—Toward the east. We bicycled *east* to get to the park. *Adverb.*
east (ēst) *noun; adjective; adverb.*

Easter A Christian holy day that celebrates the rising of Christ from the grave. Easter is on a Sunday between March 22 and April 25, but it does not come on the same date each year. It falls on the Sunday after the first full moon on or following March 21.
East·er (ēs′tər) *noun, plural* **Easters.**

eastern 1. In or toward the east. There is a large river in the *eastern* part of that state. 2. Coming from the east. An *eastern* breeze was blowing. 3. **Eastern.** Of or in the part of the United States that is in the east. 4. **Eastern.** Of or in Asia and the islands close to it.
east·ern (ēs′tərn) *adjective.*

easterner 1. A person living in the east. 2. **Easterner.** A person living in the eastern part of the United States.
east·ern·er (ēs′tər nər) *noun, plural* **easterners.**

Eastern Hemisphere The eastern half of the earth. It includes Europe, Asia, Africa, and Australia.

eastward Toward the east. The river flows *eastward* through the state.
east·ward (ēst′wərd) *adverb; adjective.*

easy 1. Needing only a little work; not hard to do. The math problems were *easy.* 2. Without pain, trouble, or worry. The clerk felt *easy* in his mind once the money was locked in the safe. 3. Not strict. She is an *easy* teacher.
eas·y (ē′zē) *adjective,* **easier, easiest.**

eat 1. To chew on and swallow. I like to *eat* popcorn when I'm at the movies. 2. To have a meal. Our family usually *eats* at six o'clock. 3. To wear away or use up. Rust has *eaten* away the surface of the metal porch furniture.
eat (ēt) *verb,* **ate, eaten, eating.**

eaves The under part of a roof that hangs over the side of a building.
eaves (ēvz) *noun plural.*

eavesdrop To listen to other people talking and not let them know about it. The girl learned about her own surprise party by *eavesdropping* as her friends planned it.
eaves·drop (ēvz′drop′) *verb,* **eavesdropped, eavesdropping.**

▲ The word **eavesdrop** once meant the area at the side of a house, where rainwater on the roof would *drop* from the *eaves* to the ground. A person who stood in this place to listen in secret to people talking inside the house was said to be *eavesdropping.*

ebb The flowing out of the ocean from the shore. The beach was covered with seaweed and shells at the tide's *ebb. Noun.*
—1. To flow out. We sat on the beach and watched the tide *ebb.* 2. To become less or weaker. Hope of finding the lost plane began to *ebb. Verb.*
ebb (eb) *noun, plural* **ebbs;** *verb,* **ebbed, ebbing.**

ebony A hard, black wood. It comes from trees that grow in Africa and Asia. Ebony is used to make black piano keys.
eb·on·y (eb′ə nē) *noun, plural* **ebonies.**

eccentric Not like other people; different and odd. Everyone thought the man was *eccentric* because he used to go swimming in the middle of winter.
ec·cen·tric (ek sen′trik) *adjective.*

echo The repeating of a sound. Echoes are caused when sound waves strike a surface that blocks them and they are thrown back. We shouted "hello" toward the hill and soon heard the *echo* of our own voices. *Noun.*
—1. To send back the sound of something. The walls of the cave *echoed* with voices and footsteps. 2. To be heard again. His warning *echoed* in her ears. *Verb.*
ech·o (ek′ō) *noun, plural* **echoes;** *verb,* **echoed, echoing.**

eclipse A darkening or hiding of the sun or the moon. In an eclipse of the sun, the moon passes between the sun and the earth. In an eclipse of the moon, the earth passes between the sun and the moon.
e·clipse (i klips′) *noun, plural* **eclipses.**

ecology A science that is part of biology. Ecology studies how plants and animals live in relation to each other and to their environment.
e·col·o·gy (ē kol′ə jē) *noun.*

economic Having to do with economics. The President spoke on television about his new *economic* programs.
ec·o·nom·ic (ek′ə nom′ik *or* ē′kə nom′ik) *adjective.*

economical Using only a small amount of something; not wasting anything. A person who is economical is very careful about spending money. A car that is economical

at; āpe; cär; end; mē; it; īce; hot; ōld; fôrk; wood; fōōl; oil; out; up; turn; sing; thin; this; hw in white; zh in treasure.
ə stands for a in about, e in taken i in pencil, o in lemon, and u in circus.

doesn't use very much gasoline and doesn't cost a lot of money to run.
ec·o·nom·i·cal (ek′ə nom′i kəl *or* ē′kə nom′i-kəl) *adjective.*

economics The science that studies how money and goods are produced, how they are divided up among people, and how they are used.
ec·o·nom·ics (ek′ə nom′iks *or* ē′kə nom′iks) *noun plural.*

economist A person who knows a great deal about economics.
e·con·o·mist (i kon′ə mist) *noun, plural* **economists.**

economize 1. To cut down on spending money; save. Our family has to *economize* because prices are so high. 2. To be careful to use only a small amount of something; not waste any. Everyone had to *economize* on water because there was a shortage.
e·con·o·mize (i kon′ə mīz′) *verb,* **economized, economizing.**

economy 1. The way a country produces, divides up, and uses its money and goods. The *economy* of the United States is different from that of China. 2. The careful use of money and other things to cut down on waste and to save. He tries to practice *economy* in buying groceries.
e·con·o·my (i kon′ə mē) *noun, plural* **economies.**

ecstasy A feeling of being so happy that you are thrilled. The children were in *ecstasy* when their mother brought the puppy home.
ec·sta·sy (ek′stə sē) *noun, plural* **ecstasies.**

-ed A *suffix* that is added to a verb to show that an action is in the past. The word *walked* in "He walked to work yesterday" is the past tense of *walk.* The word *walked* in "She has walked to work every day this week" is the past participle of *walk.*

edge 1. A line or place where something ends; side. Ron wrote his name along the *edge* of his notebook. The pencil rolled off the *edge* of the desk. The lake is over by the *edge* of the woods. 2. The side of a tool that cuts. That knife has a sharp *edge. Noun.*
—1. To move slowly or carefully, little by little. Sally *edged* toward the door, hoping that no one would see her leave. 2. To put an edge on; form an edge on. Jane *edged* the handkerchief with lace. *Verb.*
edge (ej) *noun, plural* **edges;** *verb,* **edged, edging.**

edible Fit or safe to eat. Not all kinds of berries are *edible.*
ed·i·ble (ed′ə bəl) *adjective.*

edit To correct and check something written so that it is ready to be printed. Before that story can be put in a book, it must be *edited.* Henry's father *edits* the town newspaper.
ed·it (ed′it) *verb,* **edited, editing.**

edition 1. The form in which a book is printed. That dictionary is now for sale in a paperback *edition.* 2. One of the copies of a book, newspaper, or magazine printed at one time. Jim bought the morning *edition* of the newspaper.
e·di·tion (i dish′ən) *noun, plural* **editions.**

editor A person who edits. The newspaper *editor* wrote an article in favor of raising city taxes.
ed·i·tor (ed′ə tər) *noun, plural* **editors.**

editorial 1. An article in a newspaper or magazine written by the editor. An editorial gives an opinion on some subject. The *editorial* praised Congress for passing the new law. 2. A statement on a television or radio program that gives the opinion of the management of the station. *Noun.*
—Of or having to do with editors or their work. The article is on the *editorial* page of the newspaper. *Adjective.*
ed·i·to·ri·al (ed′ə tôr′ē əl) *noun, plural* **editorials;** *adjective.*

educate 1. To teach or train. Teachers *educate* children. 2. To send to school. The cost of *educating* children at college is very high today.
ed·u·cate (ej′ə kāt′) *verb,* **educated, educating.**

education 1. The act or process of gaining knowledge. A person's *education* at college usually takes four years. 2. The knowledge gained. He has little *education* in science.
ed·u·ca·tion (ej′ə kā′shən) *noun, plural* **educations.**

educational 1. Of or having to do with education. This state's *educational* system is one of the largest in the country. 2. That is meant to teach something; giving knowledge. Our class saw an *educational* film about how steel is made.
ed·u·ca·tion·al (ej′ə kā′shən əl) *adjective.*

eel A long, thin fish that looks like a snake.
eel (ēl) *noun, plural* **eels** or **eel.**

Eel

eerie Strange in a scary way; making people frightened or nervous. It was *eerie* that a black cat wandered into our yard on Halloween.
ee·rie (ēr′ē) *adjective,* **eerier, eeriest.**

effect **1.** Something that happens as a result of something else. One *effect* of prices going up was that people began to buy less. **2.** The power to change something or to make something happen; influence. Punishment has no *effect* on that naughty child. That new traffic law doesn't go into *effect* until next month. *Noun.*
—To make happen; bring about; cause. The medicine *effected* a cure of her sore throat. *Verb.* Look up the word **affect** for more information.
ef·fect (i fekt′) *noun, plural* **effects;** *verb,* **effected, effecting.**

effective Able to change something or to make something happen. Rhoda used very *effective* arguments and got everyone to agree with her. The medicine was not *effective* in bringing his fever down.
ef·fec·tive (i fek′tiv) *adjective.*

efficient Able to get the results wanted without wasting time or effort. With our *efficient* new washing machine, the laundry gets done much faster.
ef·fi·cient (i fish′ənt) *adjective.*

effort **1.** Hard work. Climbing the steep hill took much *effort.* **2.** A hard try. Make an *effort* to get there on time.
ef·fort (ef′ərt) *noun, plural* **efforts.**

egg¹ **1.** A round or roundish body out of which young animals hatch. Eggs are laid by female birds, insects, fish, and snakes. **2.** The inside of a hen's egg that is used for food. I like bacon and *eggs* for breakfast. **3.** A cell that is produced in the bodies of female animals. Human beings, horses, dogs, and many kinds of other animals grow from these cells.
egg (eg) *noun, plural* **eggs.**

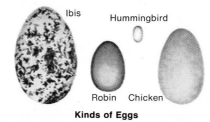

Ibis
Hummingbird
Robin Chicken
Kinds of Eggs

egg² To urge. The two boys began to fight after they were *egged* on by the others in the playground.
egg (eg) *verb,* **egged, egging.**

eggplant A vegetable that has a shiny, purple skin. Eggplants have a shape similar to the shape of an egg.
egg·plant (eg′plant′) *noun, plural* **eggplants.**

ego **1.** All of one's own thoughts and feelings; one's own self. The ego is the inner part of a person that makes him or her different from other people. **2.** Great liking or admiration for oneself; conceit. That famous actor is known for his *ego.*
e·go (ē′gō) *noun, plural* **egos.**

Eggplant

Egypt A country in northeastern Africa. Ancient Egypt was the center of one of the world's earliest and greatest civilizations.
E·gypt (ē′jipt) *noun.*

Egyptian **1.** A person who was born or is living in Egypt. **2.** The language of the people of Egypt in ancient times. *Noun.*
—Of or having to do with Egypt or its people. *Adjective.*
E·gyp·tian (i jip′shən) *noun, plural* **Egyptians;** *adjective.*

eight One more than seven; 8. ▲ Another word that sounds like this is **ate.**
eight (āt) *noun, plural* **eights;** *adjective.*

eighteen Eight more than ten; 18.
eight·een (ā′tēn′) *noun, plural* **eighteens;** *adjective.*

eighteenth **1.** Next after the seventeenth. **2.** One of eighteen equal parts; 1/18.
eight·eenth (ā′tēnth′) *adjective; noun, plural* **eighteenths.**

eighth **1.** Next after the seventh. **2.** One of eight equal parts; 1/8.
eighth (āth) *adjective; noun, plural* **eighths.**

eightieth **1.** Next after the seventy-ninth. **2.** One of eighty equal parts; 1/80.
eight·i·eth (ā′tē ith) *adjective; noun, plural* **eightieths.**

eighty Eight times ten; 80.
eight·y (ā′tē) *noun, plural* **eighties;** *adjective.*

either She didn't want *either* dress. There were no houses on *either* side of the road.

at; āpe; cär; end; mē; it; īce; hot; ōld;
fôrk; wood; fool; oil; out; up; turn; sing;
thin; this; hw in white; zh in treasure.
ə stands for a in about, e in taken
i in pencil, o in lemon, and u in circus.

Either is fine with me. *Either* be quiet or leave the library. He didn't see what happened and she didn't *either*.

ei·ther (ē′t͟hər *or* ī′t͟hər) *adjective; pronoun; conjunction; adverb.*

elaborate Worked out or made with great care and in great detail. *Elaborate* plans were made for the wedding. *Adjective.*
—To work out with great care; add details to. The reporter asked the President to *elaborate* on what he had said in answer to an earlier question. *Verb.*

e·lab·o·rate (i lab′ər it *for adjective;* i lab′ə-rāt′ *for verb*) *adjective; verb,* **elaborated, elaborating.**

elapse To go by; pass. Three years *elapsed* before they saw each other again.

e·lapse (i laps′) *verb,* **elapsed, elapsing.**

elastic Able to go back to its own shape soon after being stretched, squeezed, or pressed together. Rubber bands, balloons, and metal springs are elastic. *Adjective.*
—A tape or fabric that can stretch. Her skirt had *elastic* around the waist. *Noun.*

e·las·tic (i las′tik) *adjective; noun, plural* **elastics.**

elbow **1.** The part of the arm where the bones of the lower arm joins the bone of the upper arm. **2.** Something having the same shape as a bent elbow. A pipe that curves at a sharp angle is sometimes called an elbow. *Noun.*
—To push with the elbows; shove. Chuck tried to *elbow* me off the line in the lunchroom. *Verb.*

el·bow (el′bō) *noun, plural* **elbows;** *verb,* **elbowed, elbowing.**

elder Born earlier; older. My *elder* sister wants to be a lawyer. *Adjective.*
—A person who is older. She has great respect for her *elders. Noun.*

eld·er (el′dər) *adjective; noun, plural* **elders.**

elderly Rather old. That *elderly* man uses a cane.

eld·er·ly (el′dər lē) *adjective.*

eldest Born first; oldest. Matthew is the *eldest* of three children.

eld·est (el′dist) *adjective.*

elect **1.** To choose by voting. The people of the town *elected* a new mayor. **2.** To make a choice; choose; decide. John *elected* history as his main study in college.

e·lect (i lekt′) *verb,* **elected, electing.**

election The act of electing. There is an *election* for President every four years in this country.

e·lec·tion (i lek′shən) *noun, plural* **elections.**

electric Having to do with electricity; run

or produced by electricity. An *electric* clock keeps good time. I have a set of *electric* trains. Joel got an *electric* shock when he plugged in the lamp.

e·lec·tric (i lek′trik) *adjective.*

electrical Having to do with electricity; electric. Irons and other *electrical* appliances are now on sale at that store.

e·lec·tri·cal (i lek′tri kəl) *adjective.*

electric eel A long fish that looks like an eel. It is able to give off electric shocks to protect itself and to catch small fish for food.

Electric eel

electrician A person who works with or repairs things that are electric.

e·lec·tri·cian (i lek′trish′ən) *noun, plural* **electricians.**

electricity **1.** One of the basic forms of energy in our world. Electricity can run motors and produce light and heat. It makes radios, televisions, and telephones work. Electricity is carried by electrons and protons. **2.** Electric current. *Electricity* is running through those wires.

e·lec·tric·i·ty (i lek tris′ə tē) *noun.*

electrocute To kill by means of a very strong electric shock.

e·lec·tro·cute (i lek′trə kyo͞ot′) *verb,* **electrocuted, electrocuting.**

electrode A place where electric current enters or leaves a battery or other electrical device.

e·lec·trode (i lek′trōd) *noun, plural* **electrodes.**

electromagnet A piece of iron with wire wound around it. It becomes a magnet when an electric current is passed through the wire.

e·lec·tro·mag·net (i lek′trō mag′nit) *noun, plural* **electromagnets.**

electron A very tiny particle that is too small to be seen. An electron is one of the basic pieces of all matter. An electron carries a negative electrical charge and forms the part of an atom outside the nucleus. An electric current is really a flow of a large number of electrons.
e·lec·tron (i lek′tron) *noun, plural* **electrons.**

electronics The science that studies electrons and how they act and move. The study of electrons has led to the development of radio, television, and computers.
e·lec·tron·ics (i lek tron′iks) *noun plural.*

elegant Rich and fine in quality. The queen was dressed in *elegant* robes.
el·e·gant (el′ə gənt) *adjective.*

element 1. One of the materials out of which all other things are made up. Iron, oxygen, gold, and carbon are elements. Every element is made up of only one kind of atom, so it cannot be broken down into simpler materials by chemicals. There are more than 100 known elements. 2. One of the parts that something is made of. Words are the *elements* used to build sentences. This story is exciting and has all the *elements* of a good mystery. 3. The natural or most comfortable place to be. The ocean is the whale's *element.* 4. **the elements.** Rain, wind, snow, and other forces of nature. The explorers struggled against *the elements* to make their way across the mountains.
el·e·ment (el′ə mənt) *noun, plural* **elements.**

elementary Dealing with the simple parts or beginnings of something. We learned about addition and subtraction when we studied *elementary* arithmetic.
el·e·men·ta·ry (el′ə men′tər ē *or* el′ə-men′trē) *adjective.*

elementary school A school for children from the ages of about six to twelve or fourteen. Elementary schools usually cover the first six or eight grades. An elementary school is sometimes also called a **grade school** or a **grammar school.**

elephant A huge gray animal. An elephant has a long trunk, large, floppy ears, and two ivory tusks. It makes a sound like a trumpet. Elephants come from parts of Asia and Africa. They are the largest and strongest land animals.
el·e·phant (el′ə fənt) *noun, plural* **elephants** or **elephant.**

elevate To raise to a higher level; lift up. The worker in the garage *elevated* the car so that he could repair the wheel.
el·e·vate (el′ə vāt′) *verb,* **elevated, elevating.**

elevation 1. A raising or lifting up. The cranes beside those docks are used for the *elevation* of boats from the water. 2. A raised thing or place. The cabin is on a slight *elevation* that looks over the lake. 3. The height above the earth's surface or above sea level. The plane flew at an *elevation* of 30,000 feet.
el·e·va·tion (el′ə vā′shən) *noun, plural* **elevations.**

elevator 1. A small room or cage that can be raised or lowered. It is used for carrying people and things from one floor to another in a building, mine, or other place. 2. A building for storing grain.
el·e·va·tor (el′ə vā′tər) *noun, plural* **elevators.**

eleven One more than ten; 11.
e·lev·en (i lev′ən) *noun, plural* **elevens;** *adjective.*

eleventh 1. Next after the tenth. 2. One of eleven equal parts; $^{1}/_{11}$.
e·lev·enth (i lev′ənth) *adjective; noun, plural* **elevenths.**

elf A kind of fairy who has magical powers. In legends and folk tales, elves are usually small and full of mischief.
elf (elf) *noun, plural* **elves.**

eligible Having the qualities needed for something; fit to be chosen. A person must be thirty-five years old to be *eligible* to run for President of the United States.
el·i·gi·ble (el′i jə bəl) *adjective.*

Elephant

at; āpe; cär; end; mē; it; īce; hot; ōld; fôrk; wood; fool; oil; out; up; turn; sing; thin; this; hw in white; zh in treasure. ə stands for a in about, e in taken i in pencil, o in lemon, and u in circus.

eliminate To get rid of; remove or leave out. The city is trying to *eliminate* pollution. When the family was deciding which house to buy, they *eliminated* all those that didn't have a back yard.
e·lim·i·nate (i lim′ə nāt′) *verb,* **eliminated, eliminating.**

Elk

elk A large deer of North America. The male elk has very large antlers.
elk (elk) *noun, plural* **elk** or **elks.**

ellipse A figure that looks like a narrow or flattened circle.
el·lipse (i lips′) *noun, plural* **ellipses.**

elm A tall tree. Elms are often planted to shade streets and lawns. The hard, heavy wood of this tree is used to make boxes and crates.
elm (elm) *noun, plural* **elms.**

Leaves

Elm Tree

eloquent Having or showing an ability to use words well. The mayor is an *eloquent* speaker. The lawyer made an *eloquent* plea to the jury to find his client innocent of the crime.
el·o·quent (el′ə kwənt) *adjective.*

else He looks just like someone *else* I know. If anyone *else* comes, we won't have enough chairs. Where *else* did you go on Saturday? Dress warmly when you go out, or *else* you'll catch cold.
else (els) *adjective; adverb.*

elsewhere The librarian said we'd have to look *elsewhere* for that book because the school library did not have it.
else·where (els′hwer′) *adverb.*

elude To avoid or escape by being clever or quick. The bandit *eluded* the police by hiding in an abandoned building.
e·lude (i lo͞od′) *verb,* **eluded, eluding.**

elves More than one elf. Look up **elf** for more information.
elves (elvz) *noun plural.*

emancipate To set free from slavery or control. President Lincoln's proclamation *emancipated* the slaves.
e·man·ci·pate (i man′sə pāt′) *verb,* **emancipated, emancipating.**

embankment A mound of earth, stones, or bricks used to hold up a road or to hold back water.
em·bank·ment (em bangk′mənt) *noun, plural* **embankments.**

Embankment

embargo An order by a government that forbids certain ships from entering or leaving its ports. During the war, the prime minister placed an *embargo* on the ships of those countries that had helped the enemy.
em·bar·go (em bär′gō) *noun, plural* **embargoes.**

212

embark   **1.** To go on board a ship for a trip. The passengers *embarked* at New York. **2.** To start out or set out. The explorers *embarked* upon a dangerous journey. Doug *embarked* on a career in business after he finished college.
em·bark (em bärk′) *verb,* **embarked, embarking.**

embarrass   To make someone feel shy, uncomfortable, or ashamed. Her foolish mistake *embarrassed* her.
em·bar·rass (em bar′əs) *verb,* **embarrassed, embarrassing.**

embarrassment   A feeling of shyness or being ashamed. He turned red with *embarrassment* when he realized what a silly thing he had said.
em·bar·rass·ment (em bar′əs mənt) *noun,* **plural embarrassments.**

embassy   The official home and office in a foreign country of an ambassador and the people who work for him.
em·bas·sy (em′bə sē) *noun, plural* **embassies.**

embed   To place or set firmly in something. The workmen *embedded* the flagpole in cement.
em·bed (em bed′) *verb,* **embedded, embedding.**

ember   A piece of wood or coal that is glowing in the ashes of a fire. The campers put water on the *embers* of their fire before they left.
em·ber (em′bər) *noun, plural* **embers.**

embezzle   To steal money or goods that one was supposed to take care of. The teller *embezzled* thousands of dollars from the bank.
em·bez·zle (em bez′əl) *verb,* **embezzled, embezzling.**

emblem   A sign or figure that stands for something. The shamrock is the *emblem* of Ireland. A country's flag is an *emblem* of the nation.
em·blem (em′bləm) *noun, plural* **emblems.**

emboss   To decorate or cover a surface with a design that is raised. Susan's stationery was *embossed* with her initials.
em·boss (em bôs′) *verb,* **embossed, embossing.**

embrace   To take or hold in the arms as a sign of love or friendship; hug. The returning soldier *embraced* his parents as soon as he got off the plane. *Verb.*
—A holding in the arms; hug. The puppy wiggled out of the child's *embrace. Noun.*
em·brace (em brās′) *verb,* **embraced, embracing;** *noun, plural* **embraces.**

embroider   **1.** To decorate cloth with designs sewn on with thread. Donna *embroidered* the napkins with flowers. **2.** To make a story more interesting by adding parts that have been made up. Uncle Henry always *embroiders* his stories about his childhood to make us laugh.
em·broi·der (em broi′dər) *verb,* **embroidered, embroidering.**

Embroider

embroidery   Designs that have been sewn on cloth with thread. The *embroidery* on her wedding dress was beautiful.
em·broi·der·y (em broi′dər ē) *noun, plural* **embroideries.**

embryo   An animal or plant that is just starting to live and grow, before its birth. A baby inside its mother, a chicken inside an egg, and a plant inside a seed are embryos.
em·bry·o (em′brē ō′) *noun, plural* **embryos.**

emerald   **1.** A bright-green, clear stone that is very valuable. Emeralds are often used in jewelry. **2.** A bright-green color. *Noun.*
—Having a bright-green color. *Adjective.*
em·er·ald (em′ər əld) *noun, plural* **emeralds;** *adjective.*

emerge   To come into view, come out, or come up. The sun *emerged* from behind a cloud. Ten people *emerged* from the elevator. New facts about the case *emerged* during the trial.
e·merge (i murj′) *verb,* **emerged, emerging.**

emergency   Something serious that comes without warning and calls for fast action. In case of an *emergency*, the doctor can be reached at his home. *Noun.*
—Having to do with an emergency; used during an emergency. There is an *emergency* exit at the back of the theater. *Adjective.*
e·mer·gen·cy (i mur′jən sē) *noun, plural* **emergencies;** *adjective.*

at; āpe; cär; end; mē; it; īce; hot; ōld;
fôrk; wood; fool; oil; out; up; turn; sing;
thin; this; hw in white; zh in treasure.
ə stands for a in about, e in taken
i in pencil, o in lemon, and u in circus.

213

emery A hard black or brown mineral in the form of a powder. Emery is used for grinding and polishing metals or stones. It is also put on pieces of cardboard to be used in filing the fingernails.
em·er·y (em′ər ē) *noun.*

emigrant A person who leaves his own country to live in another. Peggy's parents were *emigrants* from Ireland.
em·i·grant (em′ə grənt) *noun, plural* emigrants.

emigrate To leave one's own country to live in another. Her family plans to *emigrate* from the United States to England.
em·i·grate (em′ə grāt′) *verb,* emigrated, emigrating.

eminent Above others in rank, power, or achievement; outstanding. George Washington was *eminent* both as soldier and as President. Mrs. Lewis is an *eminent* lawyer in our town.
em·i·nent (em′ə nənt) *adjective.*

emit To send forth or give out. The sun *emits* heat and light. Boiling water *emits* steam.
e·mit (i mit′) *verb,* emitted, emitting.

emotion A strong feeling. Love, hate, happiness, sorrow, and fear are emotions. The talented actress was able to act out any *emotion.*
e·mo·tion (i mō′shən) *noun, plural* emotions.

emotional 1. Having to do with the emotions or feelings a person has. *Emotional* problems kept him from doing as good a job as he usually did. 2. Easily moved by emotion. My aunt is an *emotional* person who always cries during sad movies. 3. That moves or touches the emotions. The general made an *emotional* speech at the ceremony honoring men who had died in battle.
e·mo·tion·al (i mō′shən əl) *adjective.*

emperor A man who is the ruler of an empire.
em·per·or (em′pər ər) *noun, plural* emperors.

emphasis 1. Special attention or importance given to something. Father always placed much *emphasis* on telling the truth. There is an *emphasis* on reading and arithmetic in elementary school. 2. Special force used when saying a particular word or syllable; stress. The *emphasis* is on the first syllable in the word "empty" and on the second syllable in the word "employ."
em·pha·sis (em′fə sis) *noun, plural* emphases.

emphasize To put emphasis on; stress. The mayor's speech *emphasized* the need for a new hospital.
em·pha·size (em′fə sīz′) *verb,* emphasized, emphasizing.

empire A group of countries, lands, or peoples under one government or ruler. The *empire* of ancient Rome was powerful.
em·pire (em′pīr) *noun, plural* empires.

employ 1. To pay someone to do work; hire. The store *employed* extra workers at Christmas. 2. To make use of; use. The gardener *employed* a shovel and a hoe in his work. *Verb.*
—Service for pay; employment. George is in the *employ* of a large shipping company. *Noun.*
em·ploy (em ploi′) *verb,* employed, emloying; *noun.*

employee A person who works for some person or business for pay. The store gives its *employees* a raise twice a year.
em·ploy·ee (em ploi′ē *or* em′ploi ē′) *noun, plural* employees.

employer A person or business that pays a person or group of people to work. Mr. Green's *employer* promoted him to a higher position.
em·ploy·er (em ploi′ər) *noun, plural* employers.

employment 1. The act of employing or the state of being employed. The automobile company's *employment* of more men made it possible to manufacture cars faster. 2. The work that a person does; job. After the factory closed, it was hard for many of the workers to find new *employment.*
em·ploy·ment (em ploi′mənt) *noun, plural* employments.

empress A woman who is the ruler of an empire.
em·press (em′pris) *noun, plural* empresses.

empty Having nothing in it; without what is usually inside. The bottom drawer of the dresser is *empty,* and you can use it for your shirts. The house was *empty* in August because the whole family was away on vacation. *Adjective.*
—1. To take out the contents of; make empty. Steve *emptied* out his pockets. Janet *emptied* the glass of milk. 2. To become empty. The theater *emptied* when the movie was over. 3. To take out all that is in something. Joan *emptied* the water out of the bathtub. 4. To pour or flow out. That river *empties* into the sea. *Verb.*
emp·ty (emp′tē) *adjective,* emptier, emptiest; *verb,* emptied, emptying.

emu A bird of Australia that is like an ostrich. An emu cannot fly, but it can run very fast.
e·mu (ē′myo͞o) *noun, plural* **emus.**

Emu

enable To make able. The school raised enough money to *enable* the library to buy many new books.
en·a·ble (i nā′bəl) *verb,* **enabled, enabling.**

enact **1.** To make into law. Congress *enacted* a new bill on education this year. **2.** To act out on stage; play. Sandra *enacted* the part of the queen in this year's class play.
en·act (i nakt′) *verb,* **enacted, enacting.**

enamel **1.** A smooth, hard coating like glass. Enamel is put on metal, glass, or other material to protect or decorate it. **2.** A paint that dries to form a hard, glossy surface. They painted the kitchen with white *enamel.* **3.** The hard, white outer layer of the teeth. Decay can eat through a tooth's *enamel.*
e·nam·el (i nam′əl) *noun, plural* **enamels.**

-ence A *suffix* that means "the state of being." *Independence* means "the state of being independent."

enchant **1.** To put a magical spell on. The witch had *enchanted* the handsome prince and turned him into a frog. **2.** To delight; charm. The children were *enchanted* by the beautiful costumes the dancers wore in the play.
en·chant (en chant′) *verb,* **enchanted, enchanting.**

encircle **1.** To form a circle around; surround. The soldiers *encircled* the enemy's camp. **2.** To move in a circle around. Many satellites *encircle* the earth.
en·cir·cle (en sur′kəl) *verb,* **encircled, encircling.**

enclose **1.** To shut in or surround on all sides. The back yard was *enclosed* by a picket fence. **2.** To put inside something. Aunt Jean *enclosed* pictures of the children with her letter.
en·close (en klōz′) *verb,* **enclosed, enclosing.**

encompass To form a circle around; surround. A stone wall *encompasses* the castle.
en·com·pass (en kum′pəs) *verb,* **encompassed, encompassing.**

encore **1.** A demand made by an audience to a performer to go on performing. People usually clap for a long time to call for an encore. The singer received four *encores* at the end of her performance. **2.** Something that is performed in answer to such a demand. As an *encore,* he sang the song that had made him famous.
en·core (äng′kôr) *noun, plural* **encores.**

encounter To meet; come upon or against. The soldiers *encountered* the enemy and defeated them. The sailors *encountered* stormy weather on their voyage. *Verb.*
—A coming upon or against; meeting. Susan's *encounter* with the movie star was the talk of the neighborhood. *Noun.*
en·coun·ter (en koun′tər) *verb,* **encountered, encountering;** *noun, plural* **encounters.**

encourage **1.** To give courage, hope, or confidence to; urge on. The coach *encouraged* Jack to try out for the swimming team. **2.** To give help to; help bring about. The low price of homes *encouraged* many people to settle in that town.
en·cour·age (en kur′ij) *verb,* **encouraged, encouraging.**

encouragement Something that encourages. His father's praise of his marks at school was an *encouragement* to Al.
en·cour·age·ment (en kur′ij mənt) *noun, plural* **encouragements.**

encyclopedia A book or set of books giving a great deal of information about many things. An encyclopedia is usually made up of a large number of articles about various subjects.
en·cy·clo·pe·di·a (en sī′klə pē′dē ə) *noun, plural* **encyclopedias.**

end **1.** The last part. The *end* of the movie was happy. **2.** The part where something starts or stops. They each held an *end* of the rope. Make a left turn at the *end* of the road.

at; āpe; cär; end; mē; it; īce; hot; ōld;
fôrk; wood; fo͞ol; oil; out; up; turn; sing;
thin; this; hw in white; zh in treasure.
ə stands for a in about, e in taken
i in pencil, o in lemon, and u in circus.

My vacation is at an *end.* **3.** Purpose; goal; outcome. The *end* of all his hard studying is to get into college. *Noun.*
—To bring or come to an end. The heavy rain *ended* their picnic. The ball game *ended* at ten o'clock. *Verb.*

end (end) *noun, plural* **ends;** *verb,* **ended, ending.**

endanger To put in danger. The flood *endangered* the lives of hundreds of people.

en·dan·ger (en dān′jər) *verb,* **endangered, endangering.**

endeavor To make an effort; try. The judge always *endeavored* to be fair and just. *Verb.*
—A serious effort to do or achieve something. His *endeavors* to do well on the test were rewarded with a high mark. *Noun.*

en·deav·or (en dev′ər) *verb,* **endeavored, endeavoring;** *noun, plural* **endeavors.**

ending The last or final part. I like stories that have happy *endings.*

end·ing (en′ding) *noun, plural* **endings.**

endless **1.** Having no limit or end; going on forever. There were *endless* miles of desert as far as the eye could see. Our teacher has *endless* patience and never loses her temper. **2.** Without ends. A circle is *endless.*

end·less (end′lis) *adjective.*

endorse **1.** To sign one's name on the back of a check or similar paper. You have to *endorse* the check or the bank won't cash it. ·**2.** To give support or approval to. The senator *endorsed* the President's statement.

en·dorse (en dôrs′) *verb,* **endorsed, endorsing.**

endow **1.** To give money or property to. Many wealthy people have *endowed* that museum with valuable paintings. **2.** To give an ability, a talent, or some other good quality to at birth. The ballerina was *endowed* with natural grace.

en·dow (en dou′) *verb,* **endowed, endowing.**

endurance The power to stand anything. The pioneers who crossed this country in covered wagons had much *endurance.*

en·dur·ance (en door′əns *or* en dyoor′əns) *noun.*

endure **1.** To bear; stand; put up with. The first explorers of the North Pole had to *endure* many hardships. **2.** To continue; last. That great artist's name is sure to *endure* forever.

en·dure (en door′ *or* en dyoor′) *verb,* **endured, enduring.**

enemy **1.** A person who hates or wishes to harm another. The dictator's cruelty caused him to have many *enemies.* **2.** A country that is at war with another country. France and Germany were *enemies* in World War II. **3.** Something that is dangerous or harmful. A lack of rain can be a farmer's *enemy.*

en·e·my (en′ə mē) *noun, plural* **enemies.**

energetic Full of energy. An energetic person is eager and ready to work or do things. After a good rest, the hikers felt *energetic* enough to go on.

en·er·get·ic (en′ər jet′ik) *adjective.*

energy **1.** The strength or eagerness to work or do things. Carol has so much *energy* that she gets up early to do exercises. **2.** The capacity for doing work. Some forms of energy are light, heat, and electricity.

en·er·gy (en′ər jē) *noun, plural* **energies.**

enforce To make certain that a law or rule is carried out; put or keep in force. The police in that town *enforce* the traffic laws strictly.

en·force (en fôrs′) *verb,* **enforced, enforcing.**

engage **1.** To hire. The automobile factory *engaged* more workers. **2.** To take up the time or attention of. A stranger *engaged* him in a conversation at the bus stop. Practicing the piano *engages* much of her time. **3.** To promise; pledge. Dennis and Linda are *engaged* to be married.

en·gage (en gāj′) *verb,* **engaged, engaging.**

engagement **1.** The act of engaging or the state of being engaged. The *engagement* of workers at the printing plant was the job of the foreman. **2.** A promise to marry. That young couple's *engagement* was announced last week by their parents. **3.** A meeting with someone at a certain time; appointment. My parents have an *engagement* for dinner this evening.

en·gage·ment (en gāj′mənt) *noun, plural* **engagements.**

Automobile Engine

engine **1.** A machine that uses energy to run other machines. Engines can get their energy from the burning of oil or gasoline or from steam. The part of a car that makes it go is the engine. **2.** A machine that pulls a railroad train; locomotive.

en·gine (en′jin) *noun, plural* **engines.**

engineer **1.** A person who is trained in engineering. An engineer may plan and build bridges, roads, or airplanes. **2.** A person who drives a locomotive. The *engineer* blew the train's whistle as it neared the station.

en·gi·neer (en′jə nēr′) *noun, plural* **engineers.**

engineering The work that uses scientific knowledge for such things as building bridges and dams, drilling for oil, or designing machines.

en·gi·neer·ing (en′jə nēr′ing) *noun.*

England The largest part of the island of Great Britain, in the soutern part.

Eng·land (ing′glənd) *noun.*

English **1.** The language spoken in England, the United States, Canada, Australia, New Zealand, and some other places. **2. the English.** The people of England. *Noun.*
—1. Of England or its people. Jan's report tells about various *English* customs. **2.** Of the English language. The book was written in French, but you can buy an *English* translation of it. *Adjective.*

Eng·lish (ing′glish) *noun; adjective.*

English horn A long, thin musical instrument.

Englishman A person who was born or is living in England.

Eng·lish·man (ing′-glish mən) *noun, plural* **Englishmen.**

English Horn

engrave **1.** To cut or carve letters, figures, or designs into a surface. The jeweler *engraved* her name on the back of her watch. **2.** To print something from a metal plate or other material that has been cut with letters or figures. The printer *engraved* the invitations to the wedding.

en·grave (en grāv′) *verb,* **engraved, engraving.**

engulf To flow over and fill or cover completely. The waves *engulfed* the small boat.

en·gulf (en gulf′) *verb,* **engulfed, engulfing.**

enhance To make greater; add to. The rose bushes by the front door *enhance* the beauty of the house.

en·hance (en hans′) *verb,* **enhanced, enhancing.**

enjoy **1.** To get joy or pleasure from; be happy with. The whole family *enjoys* going to the beach. **2.** To have as an advantage. That city *enjoys* warm weather the year round.

en·joy (en joi′) *verb,* **enjoyed, enjoying.**
to enjoy oneself. To have a good time. We all *enjoyed ourselves* at the movies.

enjoyable Giving joy or happiness; pleasant. The class had an *enjoyable* time at the museum.

en·joy·a·ble (en joi′ə bəl) *adjective.*

enjoyment Pleasure; joy. Many people find *enjoyment* in collecting stamps.

en·joy·ment (en joi′mənt) *noun, plural* **enjoyments.**

enlarge To make or become larger. We are *enlarging* our house by adding an extra bedroom.

en·large (en lärj′) *verb,* **enlarged, enlarging.**

enlighten To give knowledge or wisdom to. The news reports *enlightened* us about what was really happening.

en·light·en (en līt′ən) *verb,* **enlightened, enlightening.**

enlist **1.** To join the army, navy, or some other part of the armed forces. He *enlisted* in the navy as soon as the war broke out. **2.** To get the help or support of. The mayor *enlisted* the entire town in the drive to clean up the streets.

en·list (en list′) *verb,* **enlisted, enlisting.**

enormous Much greater than the usual size or amount; very large. Some dinosaurs were *enormous.* The flood caused an *enormous* amount of damage.

e·nor·mous (i nôr′məs) *adjective.*

enough As much or as many as needed. There is not *enough* room for all of us in the car. There were *enough* players for a game of baseball. *Adjective.*
—An amount that is as much or as many as

at; āpe; cär; end; mē; it; īce; hot; ōld;
fôrk; wood; fōol; oil; out; up; turn; sing;
thin; **th**is; **hw** in **wh**ite; **zh** in treasure.
ə stands for **a** in about, **e** in taken
i in pencil, **o** in lemon, and **u** in circus.

needed. There is *enough* here to feed the whole family. *Noun.*
—**1.** To an amount or degree big enough to fill a need. The meat is not cooked *enough.* Is he feeling well *enough* to go out? **2.** Quite; very. The path up the mountain is certainly steep *enough. Adverb.*
> **e·nough** (i nuf′) *adjective; noun; adverb.*

enrage To make very angry; put into a rage. My father was *enraged* when he realized we'd been cheated.
> **en·rage** (en rāj′) *verb,* **enraged, enraging.**

enrich To improve or make better by adding something. They *enrich* bread at this bakery by adding vitamins to it.
> **en·rich** (en rich′) *verb,* **enriched, enriching.**

enroll To make or become a member. The teacher *enrolled* seven new students in the class.
> **en·roll** (en rōl′) *verb,* **enrolled, enrolling.**

enrollment **1.** The act of enrolling. *Enrollment* at the school takes place the first week in September. **2.** The number of persons enrolled. The class has an *enrollment* of 25.
> **en·roll·ment** (en rōl′mənt) *noun, plural* **enrollments.**

ensign **1.** A flag or banner. The *ensign* of the United States was flying on the boat. **2.** A navy officer of the lowest rank. An ensign is next below a lieutenant.
> **en·sign** (en′sīn *or* en′sən *for definition 1;* en′sən *for definition 2*) *noun, plural* **ensigns.**

Ensign

ensure **1.** To make sure or certain; guarantee. Careful planning helped to *ensure* the success of the project. **2.** To make safe; protect. A shot of vaccine will *ensure* you against getting that disease.
> **en·sure** (en shoor′) *verb,* **ensured, ensuring.**

entangle To catch in a tangle or net. The kitten *entangled* its claws in the yarn.
> **en·tan·gle** (en tang′gəl) *verb,* **entangled, entangling.**

enter **1.** To go or come into or in. The train *entered* the tunnel. A sudden thought *entered* his mind. **2.** To pass through something; pierce. The rusty nail *entered* the bottom of his foot. **3.** To become a member or part of; join. Frances will *enter* high school next year. **4.** To enroll; register. Vic *entered* his dog in the contest. **5.** To put down in writing; make a record of. The bank *enters* in your bankbook the amount of money you put in or take out.
> **en·ter** (en′tər) *verb,* **entered, entering.**

enterprise Something that a person plans or tries to do. An enterprise is often something difficult or important. Our space program is an exciting *enterprise.*
> **en·ter·prise** (en′tər prīz′) *noun, plural* **enterprises.**

entertain **1.** To keep interested and amused. The clown *entertained* the children. **2.** To have as a guest. On the weekends, they often *entertain* people in their house in the country. **3.** To keep in mind; consider. Harry is *entertaining* an offer for a new job.
> **en·ter·tain** (en′tər tān′) *verb,* **entertained, entertaining.**

entertainer Someone who entertains people for a living. Singers, dancers, and comedians are entertainers.
> **en·ter·tain·er** (en′tər tā′nər) *noun, plural* **entertainers.**

entertainment **1.** The act of entertaining. The *entertainment* of guests is something Mother does very well. **2.** Something that interests and amuses. The *entertainment* at the party was a puppet show.
> **en·ter·tain·ment** (en′tər tān′mənt) *noun, plural* **entertainments.**

enthrall To hold the attention and interest of someone completely. The audience was *enthralled* as they watched the lion tamer's act.
> **en·thrall** (en thrôl′) *verb,* **enthralled, enthralling.**

enthusiasm A strong feeling of excitement and interest about something. The whole class looked forward to the puppet show with *enthusiasm.*
> **en·thu·si·asm** (en thoo′zē az′əm) *noun.*

enthusiastic Full of enthusiasm. A person who is enthusiastic is very excited, interested, and eager about something. We were all *enthusiastic* about going on a picnic.
> **en·thu·si·as·tic** (en thoo′zē as′tik) *adjective.*

entire Having all the parts; with nothing left out; whole. Joe ate the *entire* box of cookies. It took an *entire* morning to clean the attic.
> **en·tire** (en tīr′) *adjective.*

entirely Completely; totally. It will be *entirely* your fault if you don't get there on time.
> **en·tire·ly** (en tīr′lē) *adverb.*

entitle **1.** To give a right to. Buying a ticket to the amusement park *entitles* you to one free ride. **2.** To give the title of; call. Charles Dickens *entitled* the book "David Copperfield."
> **en·ti·tle** (en tīt′əl) *verb,* **entitled, entitling.**

entrance¹ **1.** A place through which one enters. The *entrance* to the building is in the middle of the block. Only one *entrance* to the park was open. **2.** The act of entering. Everyone stood up at the judge's *entrance*. **3.** The power, right, or permission to enter. Students were given free *entrance* to the game.
en·trance (en′trəns) *noun, plural* **entrances.**

entrance² To fill with delight or wonder. The children were *entranced* by the clown and his trick dog.
en·trance (en trans′) *verb,* **entranced, entrancing.**

entreat To ask earnestly; beg. The prisoner *entreated* the king to let him go.
en·treat (en trēt′) *verb,* **entreated, entreating.**

entry **1.** The act of entering. At the President's *entry* into the hall, the band began to play. **2.** A place through which one enters; entrance. The workman's ladder blocked the *entry* to the building. **3.** Something written in a book, list, diary, or other record. Sam made an *entry* in his diary. Each word explained in this dictionary is an *entry*. **4.** Something that is entered in a contest or race. The judges must have all *entries* for the art show by next Friday.
en·try (en′trē) *noun, plural* **entries.**

enunciate To speak or pronounce words. It is difficult to understand someone who does not *enunciate* his words clearly.
e·nun·ci·ate (i nun′sē āt′) *verb,* **enunciated, enunciating.**

envelop To wrap or cover completely. Fog *enveloped* the city.
en·vel·op (en vel′əp) *verb,* **enveloped, enveloping.**

envelope A flat covering or container made of paper. Envelopes are used for mailing letters and other papers. Envelopes can usually be folded over and sealed up.
en·ve·lope (en′və lōp′ *or* än′və lōp′) *noun, plural* **envelopes.**

envious Feeling or showing envy; jealous. When people are envious, they often feel dislike for a person who has something they would like to have. All the girls on the block were *envious* of Lynn's new bicycle.
en·vi·ous (en′vē əs) *adjective.*

environment The surrounding in which a person, animal, or plant lives. Environment can affect the growth of a person, animal, or plant. The zoo in our city tries to make each animal's cage like its natural *environment*.
en·vi·ron·ment (en vī′rən mənt) *noun, plural* **environments.**

envy **1.** A feeling of jealousy and not being happy about someone else's good luck. He was filled with *envy* when he saw his friend's birthday presents. **2.** A person or thing that makes one feel envy. Andy's new bicycle made him the *envy* of his friends. *Noun.*
—To feel envy toward or because of. Everyone in the class *envies* her because of her good grades. He *envies* his friend's new camera. *Verb.*
en·vy (en′vē) *noun, plural* **envies;** *verb,* **envied, envying.**

eon A very long period of time. That deposit of coal was formed *eons* ago.
e·on (ē′ən *or* ē′on) *noun, plural* **eons.**

epic A long poem. It tells of the adventures and deeds of a great hero in legend or history. *Noun.*
—**1.** Being an epic. The class read an *epic* poem about a great king and his knights. **2.** Like something in an epic; great. We admire the *epic* courage of the pioneers who settled the far west of the United States. *Adjective.*
ep·ic (ep′ik) *noun, plural* **epics;** *adjective.*

epidemic The very fast spread of a disease. During an epidemic, many people have the same disease at the same time. We had an *epidemic* of chicken pox in our town.
ep·i·dem·ic (ep′ə dem′ik) *noun, plural* **epidemics.**

▲ The word **epidemic** goes back to a Greek word that means "among the people." An epidemic is a very fast spreading of a disease among many people.

episode One part of a series of events in a story or real life. I watched the third *episode* of that television series.
ep·i·sode (ep′ə sōd′) *noun, plural* **episodes.**

epoch A period of time during which something developed or took place. The first airplane flight marked a new *epoch* in travel.
ep·och (ep′ək) *noun, plural* **epochs.**

equal **1.** That is the same in amount, number, size, or value. Four quarts are *equal* to one gallon. Both girls have an *equal* chance to win the tennis match because they are both good players. **2.** Having enough strength or

at; āpe; cär; end; mē; it; īce; hot; ōld;
fôrk; wood; fool; oil; out; up; turn; sing;
thin; this; hw in white; zh in treasure.
ə stands for a in about, e in taken
i in pencil, o in lemon, and u in circus.

ability to do something. Artie was not *equal* to running in the race after he hurt his foot. *Adjective.*

—A person that is equal. Joan is Kevin's *equal* in softball because she plays as well as he does. *Noun.*

—To be equal to. Two plus two *equals* four. *Verb.*

e·qual (ē′kwəl) *adjective; noun, plural* **equals;** *verb,* **equaled, equaling.**

equality The quality of being equal. The Constitution of the United States provides for the *equality* of all Americans under the law.

e·qual·i·ty (i kwol′ə tē) *noun.*

equation A statement in mathematics that two quantities are equal. $5 + 4 = 9$ is an equation.

e·qua·tion (i kwā′zhən) *noun, plural* **equations.**

equator An imaginary line around the earth. It is halfway between the North and South Poles. The United States and Canada are north of the equator. Most of South America is south of the equator.

e·qua·tor (i kwā′tər) *noun, plural* **equators.**

The dotted line represents the **equator.**

▲ In the Middle Ages, people used a Latin name for the **equator** that meant "something that makes night and day equal." On the days each year when the sun is exactly over the equator, night and day are the same length.

equatorial At or near the equator. All the countries in Central America are equatorial countries.

e·qua·to·ri·al (ē′kwə tôr′ē əl) *adjective.*

equilibrium Balance. The tightrope walker carried a pole to help him keep his *equilibrium.*

e·qui·lib·ri·um (ē′kwə lib′rē əm) *noun.*

equinox One of the two times of the year when day and night are equal in length all over the earth. During these two times the sun is exactly above the equator. The equinoxes take place about March 21 and September 23.

e·qui·nox (ē′kwə noks′) *noun, plural* **equinoxes.**

equip To provide with whatever is needed. The ship was *equipped* with hoses to be used in case of fire.

e·quip (i kwip′) *verb,* **equipped, equipping.**

equipment 1. Anything that is provided for a particular purpose or use; supplies. Jed bought a tent, a sleeping bag, and other camping *equipment.* 2. The act of equipping. The *equipment* of the entire football team with new uniforms cost the school a lot of money.

e·quip·ment (i kwip′mənt) *noun.*

equivalent Equal. A quarter is *equivalent* to five nickels. Shaking your head from side to side is *equivalent* to saying "no." *Adjective.*

—Something that is equal. Ten dimes are the *equivalent* of one dollar. *Noun.*

e·quiv·a·lent (i kwiv′ə lənt) *adjective; noun, plural* **equivalents.**

-er[1] A *suffix* that means "a person or thing that does something." *Teacher* means "a person who teaches." *Opener* means "a thing that opens."

-er[2] A *suffix* that means "more." *Colder* means "more cold." It shows that an adjective or adverb is in its comparative form. The word *colder* is the comparative form of *cold.* The word *faster* is the comparative form of *fast.*

era A period of time or of history. Our class is studying the colonial *era* in American history.

e·ra (er′ə) *noun, plural* **eras.**

erase To rub out; scratch or wipe off. He *erased* the word that was spelled wrong and wrote in the correct spelling. Would you please *erase* the blackboard?

e·rase (i rās′) *verb,* **erased, erasing.**

eraser Something used to rub out or remove marks. This pencil has a rubber *eraser* on one end.

e·ras·er (i rā′sər) *noun, plural* **erasers.**

ere Before. ▲ This word is used mainly in poetry and other writing. ▲ Other words that sound like this are **air** and **heir.**

ere (er) *preposition; conjunction.*

erect Upright; raised. The dog's ears became *erect* when its owner whistled. *Adjective.*

—1. To build. A new apartment house will be *erected* on that lot. 2. To put or raise into an upright position. They hurried to *erect* the tent so they could get inside before the rain began. *Verb.*

e·rect (i rekt′) *adjective; verb,* **erected, erecting.**

ermine   An animal that is valued for its fur. It has brown fur that changes to white in the winter.
er·mine (ur′min) *noun, plural* **ermines** or **ermine.**

Ermine

erode   To wear or wash away slowly; eat away. Ocean waves *eroded* the shore. Rust had *eroded* the tin roof of the shed.
e·rode (i rōd′) *verb,* **eroded, eroding.**

erosion   A slow wearing, washing, or eating away. The trees and grass helped prevent the *erosion* of soil on the hill by protecting it from the wind and rain.
e·ro·sion (i rō′zhən) *noun.*

errand   A short trip to do something. I have to go to the grocery store, stop at the cleaners, and do several other *errands* this morning.
er·rand (er′ənd) *noun, plural* **errands.**

error   **1.** Something that is wrong; mistake. There were five spelling *errors* on his test paper. **2.** A wrong play made by a fielder in baseball. An error lets a base runner get to base safely or lets a batter remain at bat when he would have been put out if the play had been made correctly.
er·ror (er′ər) *noun, plural* **errors.**

erupt   To break out suddenly and with force. The volcano *erupted* and covered the land around it with lava. A fight *erupted* between the two hockey teams.
e·rupt (i rupt′) *verb,* **erupted, erupting.**

escalator   A moving stairway. It is made of a series of steps pulled by a continuous chain. An escalator is used to carry people from one floor to another.
es·ca·la·tor (es′kə lā′tər) *noun, plural* **escalators.**

escape   To get away; get free. The bird *escaped* from the cage and flew into the woods. The bicycle rider *escaped* getting hurt when he avoided the truck that was coming toward him. *Verb.*
—1. The act of escaping. The rabbit made its *escape* when its owner forgot to lock the cage door. **2.** A way of escaping. A rope ladder served as an *escape* from the burning house. *Noun.*
es·cape (es kāp′) *verb,* **escaped, escaping;** *noun, plural* **escapes.**

escort   A person or persons who go along with others. An escort does this to be polite or to honor or protect someone. The President's car had a police *escort*. My *escort* to the party made sure I got home safely. *Noun.*
—To act as an escort. John *escorted* Ann to the dance. *Verb.*
es·cort (es′kôrt *for noun;* es kôrt′ *for verb*) *noun, plural* **escorts;** *verb,* **escorted, escorting.**

Eskimo   **1.** A member of a people living in Alaska, northern Canada, and other arctic regions. **2.** The language spoken by these people. *Noun.*
—Having to do with the Eskimos or their language. *Adjective.*
Es·ki·mo (es′kə mō′) *noun, plural* **Eskimos** or **Eskimo;** *adjective.*

esophagus   A tube through which food passes from the mouth to the stomach.
e·soph·a·gus (i-sof′ə gəs) *noun.*

especially   More than usually; particularly. Kathy came over *especially* to see my new dress. Be *especially* careful not to slip on the icy sidewalk.
es·pe·cial·ly (es-pesh′ə lē) *adverb.*

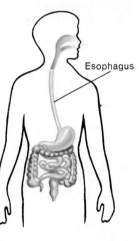
Esophagus

essay   A short written composition on a subject. Sally wrote an *essay* about the need for world peace.
es·say (es′ā) *noun, plural* **essays.**

at; āpe; cär; end; mē; it; īce; hot; ōld;
fôrk; wood; fōōl; oil; out; up; turn; sing;
thin; th**i**s; hw in white; zh in treasure.
ə stands for a in about, e in taken
i in pencil, o in lemon, and u in circus.

essence 1. Something that makes a thing what it is; necessary and basic part. Love of others is the *essence* of brotherhood. 2. A concentrated substance or solution. We used *essence* of peppermint to add flavoring to the candy we made.
es·sence (es′əns) *noun, plural* essences.

essential Very important or necessary. It is *essential* that we leave now or we'll miss the last train. *Adjective.*
—A necessary or basic part. We brought food, sleeping bags, a tent, and other *essentials* for our camping trip. *Noun.*
es·sen·tial (i sen′shəl) *adjective; noun, plural* essentials.

-est A *suffix* that means "most." *Coldest* means "most cold." It shows that an adjective or adverb is in its superlative form. The word *coldest* is the superlative of *cold.* The word *fastest* is the superlative of *fast.*

establish 1. To set up. The college *established* a new course for students interested in computers. The young doctor *established* himself in his new offices. 2. To show or prove to be true. The lawyer *established* the fact that his client was innocent by showing that he was out of town on the day of the crime.
es·tab·lish (es tab′lish) *verb,* established, establishing.

establishment 1. An establishing. The *establishment* of a new health center for the town took longer than was planned. 2. Something established. A department store, a school, a business, and a household are establishments.
es·tab·lish·ment (es tab′lish mənt) *noun, plural* establishments.

estate 1. A piece of land in the country with a large house. That rich man owns a fine *estate* with a swimming pool, tennis courts, and stables. 2. Everything that a person owns. The woman left her entire *estate* to her children.
es·tate (es tāt′) *noun, plural* estates.

esteem To think highly of. The captain's men *esteemed* him for his bravery. *Verb.*
—High respect and admiration. Everyone in town had great *esteem* for the judge's honesty. *Noun.*
es·teem (es tēm′) *verb,* esteemed, esteeming; *noun, plural* esteems.

estimate An opinion of the value, quality, or cost of something. The repairman gave an *estimate* on what it would cost to patch the roof. *Noun.*
—To form an opinion. We *estimated* that

the trip would take an hour, but it took longer because of heavy traffic. *Verb.*
es·ti·mate (es′tə mit *for noun;* es′tə māt′ *for verb*) *noun, plural* estimates; *verb,* estimated, estimating.

estimation An opinion or judgment. In her *estimation,* the project will be finished in two weeks.
es·ti·ma·tion (es′tə mā′shən) *noun, plural* estimations.

etc. An abbreviation that means "and so forth" or "and the rest." We saw a film about animals that live in Africa, such as elephants, lions, monkeys, *etc.*

etch To engrave a picture or design on metal by letting acid burn into parts of it. The artist *etched* a portrait of an old man.
etch (ech) *verb,* etched, etching.

eternal 1. Lasting forever. The laws of nature are *eternal.* 2. That seems to last or go on forever. She complained about the *eternal* noise that her neighbors made.
e·ter·nal (i turn′əl) *adjective.*

eternity Time without beginning or end; all time.
e·ter·ni·ty (i tur′nə tē) *noun, plural* eternities.

ether A colorless liquid that burns easily and has a strong smell. It is used in medicine to put people to sleep during operations.
e·ther (ē′thər) *noun.*

ethnic Having to do with a group of people who have the same language and culture. There are many different *ethnic* groups in New York City.
eth·nic (eth′nik) *adjective.*

etiquette Rules of correct behavior. Eating peas with a knife is not considered good *etiquette.*
et·i·quette (et′i kit *or* et′i ket′) *noun, plural* etiquettes.

etymology The history of a word from its beginning to its present form. An etymology tells what other language a word has come from. It also tells about any changes in spelling or meaning that have taken place in the word over the years. An example of an etymology is as follows. The word *pigeon* originally came from the Latin word *pipire,* which meant "to chirp." This word later passed into the French language as *pijon,* which meant "a young chirping bird." By the time it came into English, it was spelled *pejon* and meant "a young dove." The way we now spell it is the same way it is spelled in French today, *pigeon.*
et·y·mol·o·gy (et′ə mol′ə jē) *noun, plural* etymologies.

eucalyptus   A tall tree that grows in warm climates. Its hard wood is used to make floors, ships, and buildings. Oil made from its leaves is used in medicine.
  eu·ca·lyp·tus (yo͞o′kə lip′təs) *noun, plural* **eucalyptuses.**

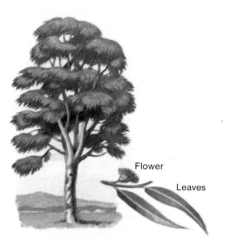

Eucalyptus Tree

Europe   The continent that is between Asia and the Atlantic Ocean.
  Eu·rope (yoor′əp) *noun.*

European   Of Europe. *Adjective.*
—A person who was born or is living in Europe. *Noun.*
  Eu·ro·pe·an (yoor′ə pē′ən) *adjective; noun, plural* **Europeans.**

evacuate   To leave or cause to leave; empty or remove. Firemen *evacuated* the tenants from the burning building.
  e·vac·u·ate (i vak′yo͞o āt′) *verb,* **evacuated, evacuating.**

evade   To get away from by clever planning. The escaped prisoner *evaded* the police by hiding on the roof of an old building. The man tried to *evade* paying his income taxes.
  e·vade (i vād′) *verb,* **evaded, evading.**

evaluate   To judge or discover the value of. That test is used to *evaluate* how well students are doing in the reading program.
  e·val·u·ate (i val′yo͞o āt′) *verb,* **evaluated, evaluating.**

evaporate   To change from a liquid or solid into a gas. Water evaporates when it is boiled and becomes steam.
  e·vap·o·rate (i vap′ə rāt′) *verb,* **evaporated, evaporating.**

eve   The evening or day before a holiday or other important day. On Christmas *Eve* we all wrapped presents. On the *eve* of the school elections, John seemed likely to be elected class president.
  eve (ēv) *noun, plural* **eves.**

even   **1.** Completely flat. Our house is built on a piece of *even* ground. **2.** At the same height. The snow drifts were *even* with the tops of the parked cars. **3.** Free from changes; regular. We were able to keep up an *even* speed on the highway. Sally has an *even* temper. **4.** That is the same or equal. At the end of the fifth inning the score in the game was *even*. **5.** Able to be divided by 2 without a remainder. 4, 28, and 72 are *even* numbers. *Adjective.*
—**1.** As a matter of fact; actually. She was willing, *even* eager, to help us. **2.** Though it may seem unlikely. He was always friendly, *even* to strangers. **3.** Still; yet. Her grade on the test was *even* better than his. *Adverb.*
—To make even. The workers *evened* the bumpy road by filling in the holes with gravel. That last goal *evened* the score of the hockey game. *Verb.*
  e·ven (ē′vən) *adjective; adverb; verb,* **evened, evening.**

evening   The late afternoon and early nighttime. *Noun.*
—Having to do with evening. The family eats its *evening* meal at seven o'clock. *Adjective.*
  eve·ning (ēv′ning) *noun, plural* **evenings;** *adjective.*

event   **1.** Anything that happens that is important. We studied the *events* leading up to the American Revolution. The first time he went to the circus was a real *event* in his life. **2.** A contest in a program of sports. The mile run was the main *event* at the track meet.
  e·vent (i vent′) *noun, plural* **events.**
  in the event of. If something should happen; in case of. *In the event of* rain, the baseball game will be played tomorrow.

eventual   Happening in the end; final. The *eventual* decision on whether to build a public swimming pool depends on how much money the town can raise.
  e·ven·tu·al (i ven′cho͞o əl) *adjective.*

eventually   In the end; finally. We waited and waited for Lisa, but *eventually* we went to the movies without her.
  e·ven·tu·al·ly (i ven′cho͞o ə lē) *adverb.*

at; āpe; cär; end; mē; it; īce; hot; ōld;
fôrk; wood; fo͞ol; oil; out; up; turn; sing;
thin; **th**is; **hw** in white; **zh** in treasure.
ə stands for **a** in about, **e** in taken
i in pencil, **o** in lemon, and **u** in circus.

ever Has she *ever* visited Florida before? They lived happily *ever* after. How did you *ever* lift that heavy trunk by yourself?
ev·er (ev′ər) *adverb.*

evergreen Having green leaves or needles all year long. We have three *evergreen* trees in our back yard. *Adjective.*
—An evergreen shrub, tree, or other plant. Pine trees, spruce trees, and holly trees are evergreens. Evergreens are used for Christmas trees because they stay green and don't lose their needles in the winter. *Noun.*
ev·er·green (ev′ər grēn′) *adjective; noun, plural* **evergreens.**

every *Every* student in the class is here today.
eve·ry (ev′rē) *adjective.*
every other. Each second one; skipping one. The garbage collector comes to our house *every other* day.

everybody *Everybody* in the family went next door to meet the new neighbors.
eve·ry·bod·y (ev′rē bod′ē) *pronoun.*

everyday **1.** Having to do with every day; daily. Walking the dog is an *everyday* chore for me. Saving people's lives is an *everyday* happening for a fireman. **2.** Fit for regular days; not special. Most people get dressed up to go to a party instead of wearing their *everyday* clothes.
eve·ry·day (ev′rē dā′) *adjective.*

everyone He bought ice cream for *everyone* who was at the party.
eve·ry·one (ev′rē wun′) *pronoun.*

everything She showed her mother *everything* she had bought.
eve·ry·thing (ev′rē thing′) *pronoun.*

everywhere They want to travel *everywhere* in the United States before they visit any other country.
eve·ry·where (ev′rē hwer′) *adverb.*

evidence Proof of something. The footprints were used by the police as *evidence* that the suspect had been near the scene of the crime.
ev·i·dence (ev′ə dəns) *noun.*

evident Easily seen or understood; clear. It was *evident* that they didn't like the movie since they walked out before the end.
ev·i·dent (ev′ə dənt) *adjective.*

evil Bad, wicked, or harmful. The *evil* witch turned the prince into a frog. *Adjective.*
—Wickedness. The minister's sermon spoke out against *evil*. War is a great *evil* of mankind. *Noun.*
e·vil (ē′vəl) *adjective; noun, plural* **evils.**

evolution **1.** A very slow development, growth, or change. The *evolution* of the automobile was shown at the museum with pictures of early cars and pictures of cars of today. **2.** The idea that all living animals and plants slowly developed over millions of years from much earlier and simpler forms of life.
ev·o·lu·tion (ev′ə lōō′shən) *noun, plural* **evolutions.**

evolve To develop or grow gradually. Elephants *evolved* from huge animals called mammoths that lived during the time that dinosaurs were alive.
e·volve (i volv′) *verb,* **evolved, evolving.**

ewe A female sheep. ▲ Other words that sound like this are **yew** and **you.**
ewe (yōō) *noun, plural* **ewes.**

ex- A *prefix* that means "former." *Ex-president* means "a former president."

exact Without anything wrong; very accurate. This clock gives the *exact* time.
ex·act (eg zakt′) *adjective.*

exactly **1.** Without any mistake; accurately. He measured the boards for the bookcase *exactly*. **2.** In the exact way; quite. The accident happened *exactly* as I told him.
ex·act·ly (eg zakt′lē) *adverb.*

exaggerate To make something seem larger or greater than it is. The fisherman *exaggerated* the size of the fish he had caught. She *exaggerated* when she said she had eaten five gallons of ice cream yesterday.
ex·ag·ger·ate (eg zaj′ə rāt′) *verb,* **exaggerated, exaggerating.**

examination **1.** The act of examining. The dentist's *examination* of my teeth showed that I had no cavities. **2.** A test. My sister in college has many *examinations* at the end of the year.
ex·am·in·a·tion (eg zam′ə nā′shən) *noun, plural* **examinations.**

examine **1.** To look at closely and carefully; check. Tony *examined* the baseball bat before buying it to be sure it wasn't cracked. The doctor *examined* the child to see if she had the flu. **2.** To test. The teacher said she would *examine* the class in arithmetic the next day.
ex·am·ine (eg zam′in) *verb,* **examined, examining.**

example **1.** One thing that is used to show what other similar things are like. Sherry's picture was hung up as an *example* of the work the class was doing in art. **2.** A problem. The arithmetic *example* on the blackboard was hard to understand.

ex·am·ple (eg zam′pəl) *noun, plural* **examples.**

to set an example. To serve as a model for others. John's hard work in class *set an example* for the other students.

exasperate To annoy greatly; make angry. She always became *exasperated* when her brother teased her.
ex·as·per·ate (eg zas′pə rāt′) *verb,* **exasperated, exasperating.**

excavate **1.** To remove by digging. The workmen *excavated* dirt and rocks with a steam shovel. **2.** To uncover by digging. The museum sent a group of men to *excavate* the ruins of the ancient city. **3.** To make by digging. The miners *excavated* a tunnel in the side of the mountain.
ex·ca·vate (eks′kə vāt′) *verb,* **excavated, excavating.**

excavator A large machine used for digging.
ex·ca·va·tor (eks′kə vā′tər) *noun, plural* **excavators.**

Excavator

exceed To go ahead of; be greater than. The driver *exceeded* the speed limit because he was in a hurry. Gloria's skill as a speller *exceeds* everyone else's in the class.
ex·ceed (ek sēd′) *verb,* **exceeded, exceeding.**

excel To be better or greater than others. Pete *excels* as a football player.
ex·cel (ek sel′) *verb,* **excelled, excelling.**

excellence The state of being better or greater. His *excellence* as a pitcher was known by the whole school.
ex·cel·lence (ek′sə ləns) *noun.*

excellent Very, very good; outstanding. The teacher told Jim's parents that his work in arithmetic was *excellent.*
ex·cel·lent (ek′sə lənt) *adjective.*

except The store is open every day *except* Sunday. He would go with us, *except* he has work to do.
ex·cept (ek sept′) *preposition; conjunction.*

exception **1.** The state of being left out. Everyone went on the picnic with the *exception* of Mary, who was sick. **2.** A person or thing that is left out or that is different from others. Most birds can fly, but the penguin is an *exception.*
ex·cep·tion (ek sep′shən) *noun, plural* **exceptions.**

exceptional Not ordinary; unusual; extraordinary. Doris is an *exceptional* piano player.
ex·cep·tion·al (ek sep′shən əl) *adjective.*

excess An amount greater than what is needed or usual; extra amount or degree. An *excess* of water in the fish tank caused it to overflow. Linda's savings were in *excess* of $300. *Noun.*
—Greater than what is needed or usual; extra. When you travel on an airplane you have to pay for *excess* luggage. *Adjective.*
ex·cess (ek′ses *or* ek ses′) *noun, plural* **excesses;** *adjective.*

excessive More than is necessary or usual. He spends an *excessive* amount of money on candy.
ex·ces·sive (ek ses′iv) *adjective.*

exchange To give or give up for something else; change. He *exchanged* the shirt he had been given as a present and got a belt instead. Jerry *exchanged* baseball cards with his friend. *Verb.*
—**1.** The act of giving one thing in return for another. The two friends enjoyed their *exchange* of letters. **2.** A place where things are bought, sold, or traded. Stocks are bought and sold at the Stock *Exchange* in New York. **3.** A central office where telephone lines are connected for a town or part of a large city. *Noun.*
ex·change (eks chānj′) *verb,* **exchanged, exchanging;** *noun, plural* **exchanges.**

excite To stir up; arouse. The home team's great play *excited* the fans. The old, deserted house *excited* the children's curiosity.
ex·cite (ek sīt′) *verb,* **excited, exciting.**

excitement **1.** The state of being excited. Tom could hardly sleep because of his *excitement* over being made captain of the team. **2.** Something that stirs up or excites. Winning the contest was an *excitement* she would never forget.
ex·cite·ment (ek sīt′mənt) *noun.*

exciting Causing excitement; thrilling. For

at; āpe; cär; end; mē; it; īce; hot; ōld;
fôrk; wood; fool; oil; out; up; turn; sing;
thin; this; hw in white; zh in treasure.
ə stands for a in about, e in taken
i in pencil, o in lemon, and u in circus.

me, the tightrope walkers are the most *exciting* part of the circus.
ex·cit·ing (ek sī′ting) *adjective.*

exclaim To speak or cry out suddenly. A person usually exclaims because he is angry, excited, or surprised. "You took my baseball bat without asking me!" Phil *exclaimed* angrily to his brother.
ex·claim (eks klām′) *verb,* **exclaimed, exclaiming.**

exclamation Something exclaimed. In the sentence "Hurray, our team won again!" "Hurray" is an exclamation.
ex·cla·ma·tion (eks′klə mā′shən) *noun, plural* **exclamations.**

exclamation point A punctuation mark (!). It is used after a word, group of words, or sentence to show an exclamation of anger, surprise, or excitement. This mark of punctuation is also called an **exclamation mark.**

exclude To keep from entering; shut out. All those who aren't eighteen or over are *excluded* from voting.
ex·clude (eks klood′) *verb,* **excluded, excluding.**

exclusive 1. Belonging to a single person or group. She has *exclusive* ownership of the house and property. 2. Open to a certain kind of person or group only. That is an *exclusive* club for lawyers only.
ex·clu·sive (eks kloo′siv) *adjective.*

excuse 1. To forgive; pardon; overlook. Please *excuse* me for stepping on your toe. We *excused* her rude remark because we knew she was very tired. 2. To let off from duty. He was *excused* from football practice because he had hurt his knee. 3. To serve as a reason or explanation for. Her being sick *excused* her absence from school yesterday. *Verb.*
—A reason given to explain something. Oversleeping is not a good *excuse* for being late to school. *Noun.*
ex·cuse (eks kyooz′ *for verb;* eks kyoos′ *for noun*) *verb,* **excused, excusing;** *noun, plural* **excuses.**

execute 1. To carry out; put into effect. The captain *executed* the colonel's orders. 2. To put to death by order of the law. The murderer was *executed* for his crime.
ex·e·cute (ek′sə kyoot′) *verb,* **executed, executing.**

execution 1. The act of executing. The *execution* of the plan to clean up the neighborhood will call for everyone's help. 2. The act of putting to death by order of the law.

ex·e·cu·tion (ek′sə kyoo′shən) *noun, plural* **executions.**

executive Having to do with directing or managing matters in business or government. Mr. Carter had an *executive* position as vice-president of the company. *Adjective.*
—1. A person who directs or manages. All the *executives* of the company met to discuss ways of selling their new product. 2. The branch of government that manages the affairs of a nation and sees that the laws are carried out. *Noun.*
ex·ec·u·tive (eg zek′yə tiv) *adjective; noun, plural* **executives.**

exempt To excuse. He was *exempted* from taking the final test because of his good marks during the year. *Verb.*
—Freed from doing or giving something; excused. Church land is usually *exempt* from real estate taxes. *Adjective.*
ex·empt (eg zempt′) *verb,* **exempted, exempting;** *adjective.*

exercise 1. Activity that trains or improves the body or the mind. Walking is good *exercise.* That book has arithmetic *exercises* at the end of each chapter. 2. Use or practice. The dictator's *exercise* of power made him many enemies. 3. A ceremony or program. Graduation *exercises* included speeches by teachers and students. *Noun.*
—1. To put or go through exercises. I *exercise* my dog in the park. He *exercises* by walking two miles every day. 2. To make use of. A person should *exercise* his rights as a citizen by voting. *Verb.*
ex·er·cise (ek′sər sīz′) *noun, plural* **exercises;** *verb,* **exercised, exercising.**

exert To make use of; use. The firemen had to *exert* all their strength to break down the door.
ex·ert (eg zurt′) *verb,* **exerted, exerting.**

exhale To breathe out. His doctor listened to his heart as he inhaled and *exhaled.*
ex·hale (eks hāl′) *verb,* **exhaled, exhaling.**

exhaust 1. To make very weak or tired. The long, hot hike *exhausted* us. 2. To use up completely. The campers *exhausted* their supply of water. *Verb.*
—The used steam or gases that escape from an engine. An automobile has a pipe at the rear to let out the *exhaust. Noun.*
ex·haust (eg zôst′) *verb,* **exhausted, exhausting;** *noun, plural* **exhausts.**

exhaustion An exhausting or being exhausted. Jack's *exhaustion* was caused by his three-mile run.
ex·haus·tion (eg zôs′chən) *noun.*

exhibit To show. The school *exhibited* the best art work of the students for all the parents to see. Donna *exhibited* great talent in playing the piano. *Verb.*
—Something shown. We went to see the *exhibit* of African art at the museum. Jack's science *exhibit* won first prize. *Noun.*
   ex·hib·it (eg zib′it) *verb*, **exhibited, exhibiting;** *noun, plural* **exhibits.**

exhibition 1. The act of exhibiting; showing. Her being rude to the guests was an *exhibition* of bad manners. 2. A public show. The class went to an *exhibition* of rare books shown at the town library.
   ex·hi·bi·tion (ek′sə bish′ən) *noun, plural* **exhibitions.**

exhilarate To make cheerful, lively, or excited. The brisk air of the mountains *exhilarated* the hikers as they walked along the trail.
   ex·hil·a·rate (eg zil′ə rāt′) *verb*, **exhilarated, exhilarating.**

exile To send a person away from his country or home as a punishment. His country *exiled* him for being a spy. *Verb.*
—1. The state of being exiled. The government decided that *exile* would be the punishment for the traitors. 2. A person who is sent away from his country or home. *Noun.*
   ex·ile (eg′zīl *or* ek′sīl) *verb*, **exiled, exiling;** *noun, plural* **exiles.**

exist 1. To be real. He does not believe that ghosts *exist*. 2. To have life; live. Man cannot *exist* for long without water. 3. To be found. Outside of zoos, polar bears *exist* only in arctic regions.
   ex·ist (eg zist′) *verb*, **existed, existing.**

existence 1. The fact of being alive. The *existence* of some wild animals is in danger because so many of them are killed for sport. 2. A way of living; life. The early colonists in America led a dangerous *existence*.
   ex·ist·ence (eg zis′təns) *noun, plural* **existences.**

exit 1. The way out. We left the movies by the *exit* on the left. 2. The act of leaving. His *exit* from the room was not noticed. *Noun.*
—To go out; leave; depart. We *exited* by the side door during the fire drill. *Verb.*
   ex·it (eg′zit *or* ek′sit) *noun, plural* **exits;** *verb*, **exited, exiting.**

exotic Foreign; strange; unusual. These *exotic* flowers come from Hawaii.
   ex·ot·ic (eg zot′ik) *adjective.*

expand To make or grow larger; stretch out. Heat *expands* metal. The bird *expanded* its wings and flew away.

ex·pand (eks pand′) *verb*, **expanded, expanding.**

expanse A wide, open area. The stagecoach had to cross a large *expanse* of desert to reach the closest town.
   ex·panse (eks pans′) *noun, plural* **expanses.**

expansion 1. The act of expanding or the state of being expanded. After its *expansion*, the school had thirty new classrooms. 2. The amount that something expands.
   ex·pan·sion (eks pan′shən) *noun, plural* **expansions.**

expect 1. To look forward to. He *expects* to get a new bicycle for his birthday. 2. To want something because it is right or necessary. The teacher *expected* an apology from the rude child. 3. To think; suppose. I *expect* he won't be coming to school because he has a cold.
   ex·pect (eks pekt′) *verb*, **expected, expecting.**

expectation The act of expecting. The man anchored his boat securely in *expectation* of the coming storm.
   ex·pec·ta·tion (eks′pek tā′shən) *noun, plural* **expectations.**

expedition A journey made for a particular reason. The scientists made an *expedition* to Alaska to study the animals in the area.
   ex·pe·di·tion (eks′pə dish′ən) *noun, plural* **expeditions.**

expel To drive or force out. They will *expel* her from school if she continues to disobey everyone.
   ex·pel (eks pel′) *verb*, **expelled, expelling.**

expenditure The spending of time, money, or energy. Building a new house requires the *expenditure* of a great deal of money.
   ex·pend·i·ture (eks pen′di chər) *noun, plural* **expenditures.**

expense 1. Money spent to buy or do something; cost. My father cannot afford the *expense* of a new car. 2. A cause or reason for spending money. Building the swimming pool was a big *expense*.
   ex·pense (eks pens′) *noun, plural* **expenses.**

expensive Having a high price; very costly. Charlie bought an *expensive* new radio.
   ex·pen·sive (eks pen′siv) *adjective.*

experience 1. Something that a person has

at; āpe; cär; end; mē; it; īce; hot; ōld;
fôrk; wood; fōōl; oil; out; up; turn; sing;
thin; this; hw in white; zh in treasure.
ə stands for a in about, e in taken
i in pencil, o in lemon, and u in circus.

done, seen, or taken part in. Their *experience* with the bear in the national park is something they won't soon forget. The old man told us about his *experiences* as a soldier. **2.** The knowledge or skill a person gains from doing something. Jack has three years' *experience* as a salesman. Ken is the only one on the football team with *experience* because all the other players are new. *Noun.*
—To have something happen to one; feel; undergo. I didn't *experience* much pain when the dentist drilled my tooth. *Verb.*
ex·pe·ri·ence (eks pēr′ē əns) *noun, plural* **experiences;** *verb,* **experienced, experiencing.**

experiment A test that is used to discover or prove something. We did an *experiment* in class to show that a fire needs oxygen to burn. *Noun.*
—To make an experiment or experiments. Scientists tested the new drug by *experimenting* with mice. *Verb.*
ex·per·i·ment (eks per′ə mənt *for noun;* eks per′ə ment′ *for verb*) *noun, plural* **experiments;** *verb,* **experimented, experimenting.**

experimental Having to do with experiments. There is *experimental* proof that water becomes steam when it is heated.
ex·per·i·men·tal (eks per′ə ment′əl) *adjective.*

expert A person who knows a great deal about some special thing. That professor is an *expert* on American history. *Noun.*
—Having or showing a great deal of knowledge. The swimming coach gave me *expert* advice about how to learn how to dive. *Adjective.*
ex·pert (eks′purt *for noun;* eks′purt *or* eks purt′ *for adjective*) *noun, plural* **experts;** *adjective.*

expire To come to an end. Your library card will *expire* at the end of the month if you don't renew it.
ex·pire (eks pīr′) *verb,* **expired, expiring.**

explain **1.** To make something plain or clear; tell the meaning of. Can you *explain* how you got your answer to this math problem? **2.** To give or have a reason for. Can she *explain* why she was late for school?
ex·plain (eks plān′) *verb,* **explained, explaining.**

explanation **1.** The act of making something plain or clear. My brother's *explanation* of how to make a kite helped me understand how to do it. **2.** A reason or meaning. Mother wanted an *explanation* for the broken vase.
ex·pla·na·tion (eks′plə nā′shən) *noun, plural* **explanations.**

explicit Stated or shown clearly. He gave *explicit* instructions on how we should do the work.
ex·plic·it (eks plis′it) *adjective.*

explode **1.** To burst suddenly and with a loud noise; blow up. The soda bottle *exploded* because of the heat. The amusement park *exploded* firecrackers to celebrate the Fourth of July. **2.** To break forth noisily or with force. He *exploded* with anger when he saw that his bicycle had been stolen.
ex·plode (eks plōd′) *verb,* **exploded, exploding.**

exploit A brave deed or act. The story is about the exciting *exploits* of a knight who saves the life of his king.
ex·ploit (eks′ploit) *noun, plural* **exploits.**

exploration The act of exploring. Columbus's *explorations* led to his discovery of America.
ex·plo·ra·tion (eks′plə rā′shən) *noun, plural* **explorations.**

explore **1.** To travel in unknown lands for the purpose of discovery. Astronauts *explored* the moon to learn what it is like. **2.** To look through closely; examine. Jack and his friends *explored* the deserted house. Doctors *explore* the causes of disease.
ex·plore (eks plôr′) *verb,* **explored, exploring.**

explorer A person who explores.
ex·plor·er (eks plôr′ər) *noun, plural* **explorers.**

explosion **1.** The act of bursting or expanding suddenly and noisily. The *explosion* of the bomb broke windows in all the buildings nearby. **2.** A sudden outburst. We didn't know what had caused his *explosion* of anger.
ex·plo·sion (eks plō′zhən) *noun, plural* **explosions.**

explosive Likely to explode or cause an explosion. A bomb is an *explosive* device. His *explosive* temper frightens me. *Adjective.*
—Something that can explode or cause an explosion. Dynamite is an *explosive. Noun.*
ex·plo·sive (eks plō′siv) *adjective; noun, plural* **explosives.**

export To send goods to other countries to be sold or traded. Some South American countries *export* coffee to the United States. *Verb.*
—Something that is sold or traded to another country. Wheat is an *export* of this country. *Noun.*
ex·port (eks pôrt′ *or* eks′pôrt′ *for verb;* eks′pôrt′ *for noun*) *verb,* **exported, exporting;** *noun, plural* **exports.**

expose **1.** To leave open or without protection. She was *exposed* to the mumps when her best friend had them. He *exposed* himself to the laughter of his classmates when he made such a foolish mistake. **2.** To make something known; reveal. The police *exposed* a gang of thieves who were stealing cars. **3.** To allow light to reach a photographic film or plate. I *exposed* the film of my camera when I loaded it under the lamp.
ex·pose (eks pōz′) *verb,* **exposed, exposing.**

exposition A large public display. There was an *exposition* of camping equipment at the trade center.
ex·po·si·tion (eks′pə zish′ən) *noun, plural* **expositions.**

exposure **1.** The act of exposing. The government's *exposure* of the plot to kill the king shocked the public. **2.** The condition of being exposed. The mountain climbers were suffering from *exposure* after the climb in the terrible cold and wind. **3.** A position in relation to the sun or wind. This room has a southern *exposure*, so it gets a lot of sunlight. **4.** The act of exposing a photographic film to light.
ex·po·sure (eks pō′zhər) *noun, plural* **exposures.**

express To say or show. He *expressed* his happiness by smiling. The artist's paintings of plants and animals *express* her love of nature. *Verb.*
—**1.** Special or particular. He came here for the *express* purpose of seeing her. **2.** Having to do with fast transportation or delivery. We took an *express* bus into the city. *Adjective.*
—**1.** A system of fast transportation or delivery. I sent my trunk to camp by *express*. **2.** A train, bus, or elevator that is fast and makes few stops. *Noun.*
ex·press (eks pres′) *verb,* **expressed, expressing;** *adjective; noun, plural* **expresses.**

expression **1.** The act of putting thoughts or feelings into words or actions. The letter was an *expression* of his thanks to us. **2.** An outward show; look. Robin had a disappointed *expression* on her face when the kitten jumped out of her arms. **3.** A common word or group of words. "Look before you leap" and "He who hesitates is lost" are well-known *expressions*.
ex·pres·sion (eks presh′ən) *noun, plural* **expressions.**

expressive Full of expression. The poet read his poem to the audience in a very *expressive* voice.
ex·pres·sive (eks pres′iv) *adjective.*

expressway A wide highway built for fast and direct traveling.
ex·press·way (eks pres′wā′) *noun, plural* **expressways.**

Expressway

extend **1.** To make or be longer; stretch out. The bird *extended* its wings and flew away. The driveway *extends* from the house to the street. **2.** To offer or give. We *extended* our welcome to the new neighbors.
ex·tend (eks tend′) *verb,* **extended, extending.**

extension **1.** A stretching out; addition. They built an *extension* to the house so they would have a room for the new baby. **2.** An extra telephone added to the same line as the main telephone.
ex·ten·sion (eks ten′shən) *noun, plural* **extensions.**

extensive Large; broad. The flood caused *extensive* damage to the farms in the area.
ex·ten·sive (eks ten′siv) *adjective.*

extent The space, amount, degree, or limit to which something extends. Betty would go to any *extent* to help a friend. The manager explained the *extent* of their duties to the new workers.
ex·tent (eks tent′) *noun, plural* **extents.**

exterior The outer part; outward look or manner. The *exterior* of the building is made of brick. Although he has a calm *exterior*, Jack often feels nervous. *Noun.*
—Having to do with the outside; outer. The *exterior* walls were painted white. *Adjective.*

at; āpe; cär; end; mē; it; īce; hot; ōld;
fôrk; wood; fool; oil; out; up; turn; sing;
thin; this; hw in white; zh in treasure.
ə stands for a in about, e in taken
i in pencil, o in lemon, and u in circus.

229

ex·te·ri·or (eks tēr′ē ər) *noun, plural* **exteriors;** *adjective.*

exterminate To wipe out; destroy. Dad used a spray to *exterminate* the bugs.
ex·ter·mi·nate (eks tur′mə nāt′) *verb,* **exterminated, exterminating.**

external Having to do with the outside; outer. The skin of a banana is its *external* covering.
ex·ter·nal (eks turn′əl) *adjective.*

extinct 1. No longer existing. Leopards will become *extinct* if people keep killing them to make fur coats. 2. No longer active or burning. The village is built on an *extinct* volcano.
ex·tinct (eks tingkt′) *adjective.*

extinguish To put out. The firemen *extinguished* the fire in about twenty minutes.
ex·tin·guish (eks ting′gwish) *verb,* **extinguished, extinguishing.**

extra More than what is usual, expected, or needed; additional. I spent *extra* time studying to get a better grade on that test. She did *extra* work to get more pay. *Adjective.*
—1. Something added to what is usual, expected, or needed. That car has many *extras,* such as a clock, a radio, and air conditioning. 2. A special edition of a newspaper that is printed to report something important. The paper printed an *extra* to announce that the war was over. *Noun.*
—Unusually. My mother bought an *extra* large cake for my birthday party. *Adverb.*
ex·tra (eks′trə) *adjective; noun, plural* **extras;** *adverb.*

extract To take or pull out. The dentist *extracted* her tooth. Scientists have found a way to *extract* salt from sea water. *Verb.*
—Something that is extracted. The cake was flavored with *extract* of vanilla. *Noun.*
ex·tract (eks trakt′ *for verb;* eks′trakt *for noun*) *verb,* **extracted, extracting;** *noun, plural* **extracts.**

extraordinary Very unusual; remarkable. Ann's art teacher said that she had *extraordinary* talent.
ex·traor·di·nar·y (eks trôr′də ner′ē *or* eks′trə ôr′də ner′ē) *adjective.*

extravagance The spending of too much money. When Mother goes shopping, she avoids all *extravagance* and only buys what she needs.
ex·trav·a·gance (eks trav′ə gəns) *noun, plural* **extravagances.**

extravagant Spending too much money; spending in a careless way. The *extravagant* man bought only very expensive clothes.
ex·trav·a·gant (eks trav′ə gənt) *adjective.*

extreme 1. Going beyond what is usual; very great or severe. Vic and Mike were in *extreme* danger when they were caught in the rock slide. 2. Very far; farthest. She lives at the *extreme* end of the block. *Adjective.*
—1. The greatest or highest degree of something. Starvation is the *extreme* of hunger. 2. **extremes.** Complete opposites. Hot and cold are *extremes* of each other. *Noun.*
ex·treme (eks trēm′) *adjective; noun, plural* **extremes.**

extremely Very. He was *extremely* happy when he won the contest.
ex·treme·ly (eks trēm′lē) *adverb.*

eye 1. The part of the body by which people and animals see. 2. The colored part of the eye; iris. Joe has brown *eyes.* 3. The part of the face around the eye. When he fell, he got a black *eye.* 4. A look. She cast a shy *eye* at the new neighbors. 5. Something like an eye in shape, position, or use. The bud of a potato and the hole in a needle are called *eyes.* *Noun.*
—To watch carefully or closely. The detective *eyed* every move the suspect made. *Verb.*
▲ Other words that sound like this are **aye** and **I.**
eye (ī) *noun, plural* **eyes;** *verb,* **eyed, eying** or **eyeing.**

eyeball The part of the eye that the eyelids close over.
eye·ball (ī′bôl′) *noun, plural* **eyeballs.**

eyebrow The hair that grows on the bony part of the face above the eye.
eye·brow (ī′brou′) *noun, plural* **eyebrows.**

eyeglasses A pair of lenses in a frame that help make a person's eyesight better.
eye·glass·es (ī′glas′iz) *noun plural.*

eyelash One of the small, stiff hairs growing on the edge of the eyelid. The baby has very long *eyelashes.*
eye·lash (ī′lash′) *noun, plural* **eyelashes.**

eyelet A small hole in a material for a cord or lace to go through. Shoe laces are put through eyelets. ▲ Another word that sounds like this is **islet.**
eye·let (ī′lit) *noun, plural* **eyelets.**

eyelid The fold of skin that can open and close over the eye.
eye·lid (ī′lid′) *noun, plural* **eyelids.**

eyesight The ability to see; vision. They tested our *eyesight* in school by asking us to read a chart.
eye·sight (ī′sīt′) *noun.*

eyetooth Either of the two pointed teeth in the upper, front part of the mouth.
eye·tooth (ī′tōōth′) *noun, plural* **eyeteeth.**

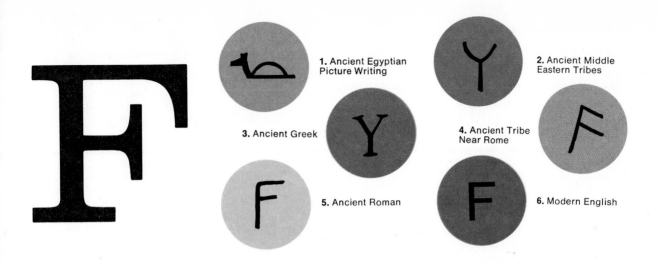

1. Ancient Egyptian Picture Writing

2. Ancient Middle Eastern Tribes

3. Ancient Greek

4. Ancient Tribe Near Rome

5. Ancient Roman

6. Modern English

F is the sixth letter of the alphabet. The oldest form of the letter **F** was a drawing that the ancient Egyptians (**1**) used in their picture writing nearly 5000 years ago. This drawing was borrowed by several ancient tribes (**2**) in the Middle East. They used it to stand for both the consonant sound *w*, as the *w* in *water*, and the vowel sound *u*, as the *u* in *rude*. The ancient Greeks (**3**) borrowed this letter, writing it very much like a modern capital letter *Y*. They used it to stand for the *u* sound only. Another letter, which was called *digamma*, was used to stand for the *w* sound. *Digamma* looked very much like a modern capital letter *F*. These letters were borrowed by an ancient tribe (**4**) that settled north of Rome about 2800 years ago. They used both the letter that looked like a capital *Y* and the letter called *digamma* to stand for the *f* sound. This was probably the first time in the history of the alphabet that the *f* sound was used. The Romans (**5**) borrowed the letter called *digamma* to stand for the *f* sound in their alphabet. By about 2400 years ago the Roman letter **F** was written in almost the same way that we write the capital letter **F** today (**6**).

f, F The sixth letter of the alphabet.
f, F (ef) *noun, plural* **f's, F's.**

fable A story that is meant to teach a lesson. The characters in fables are usually animals that talk and act like people.
fa·ble (fā′bəl) *noun, plural* **fables.**

fabric A material that is woven or knitted; cloth. Fabric is made from natural or man-made fibers. Cotton, silk, flannel, and felt are fabrics.
fab·ric (fab′rik) *noun, plural* **fabrics.**

fabulous Too much to believe; seeming impossible; amazing. He read a story about dragons and other *fabulous* creatures. She spent *fabulous* amounts of money on books and records.
fab·u·lous (fab′yə ləs) *adjective.*

face **1.** The front of the head. The eyes, nose, and mouth are parts of the face. **2.** A look on the face; expression. The boy's *face* was happy when he saw his friends. The children made funny *faces* in the mirror. **3.** The front, main, or outward part of something. We could see many people skiing down the *face* of the mountain. There are numbers on the *face* of a clock. *Noun.*
—1. To have or turn the face toward. Please *face* the camera. The school *faces* the park.

2. To meet openly and with courage. He always *faces* his problems. *Verb.*
face (fās) *noun, plural* **faces;** *verb,* **faced, facing.**

facet One of the small, polished flat surfaces of a cut gem.
fac·et (fas′it) *noun, plural* **facets.**

facial Of or for the face. A smile is a happy *facial* expression.
fa·cial (fā′shəl) *adjective.*

Facets

facilitate To make easier; help in the doing of. Zip Codes are used to *facilitate* mail service.
fa·cil·i·tate (fə sil′ə tāt′) *verb,* **facilitated, facilitating.**

facility **1.** Ease or skill in doing something. He rides his new bicycle with great *facility*. **2. facilities.** Something that makes a job easier to do or serves a particular purpose. The kitchen *facilities* in our summer cabin consist of a stove, refrigerator, and sink. There are very good playground *facilities* in our town.
fa·cil·i·ty (fə sil′ə tē) *noun, plural* **facilities.**

fact Something that is known to be true or real; something that has really happened. Is it a *fact* that you won first prize? The police were interested in finding out the *facts* of the accident. It is a scientific *fact* that the earth revolves around the sun.

fact (fakt) *noun, plural* **facts.**

factor **1.** One of the things that causes something else. Sunny weather and good food were important *factors* in the success of the picnic. **2.** Any of the numbers that form a product when multiplied together. The *factors* of 12 are 12 and 1, 6 and 2, and 3 and 4.

fac·tor (fak′tər) *noun, plural* **factors.**

factory A building or group of buildings where things are manufactured. Automobiles are made in factories.

fac·to·ry (fak′tər ē) *noun, plural* **factories.**

factual Containing or having to do with facts. The witness gave a *factual* account of the accident.

fac·tu·al (fak′chōo əl) *adjective.*

faculty **1.** A natural power of the mind or body. Hearing and speaking are two human *faculties.* **2.** A special talent or skill for doing something. She has a great *faculty* for making friends. **3.** All the teachers of a school, college, or university. The *faculty* had a meeting before the school year began.

fac·ul·ty (fak′əl tē) *noun, plural* **faculties.**

fad Something that is very popular for a short period of time. My sister and her friends don't do that dance anymore; it was last year's *fad.*

fad (fad) *noun, plural* **fads.**

fade **1.** To lose color or brightness. Some colored materials will *fade* when they are washed. The strong sunlight *faded* the curtains. **2.** To lose strength or energy; disappear gradually. The sound of footsteps *faded* away.

fade (fād) *verb,* **faded, fading.**

Fahrenheit Of or according to the temperature scale on which 32 degrees is the freezing point of water and 212 degrees is the boiling point of water.

Fahr·en·heit (far′ən hīt′) *adjective.*

▲ The word **Fahrenheit** comes from the name of Gabriel Daniel *Fahrenheit.* He was the German scientist who figured out this scale for measuring temperature.

---

fail **1.** To not succeed in doing or getting something. He *failed* the test the first time he took it. We *failed* to get to the station in time to catch our train. **2.** To be of no use or help to; disappoint. Her friends *failed* her when she needed their help. **3.** To not be enough;

run out. The water supply *failed* during the emergency. **4.** To become weaker in strength or health. My grandfather's eyesight is beginning to *fail.* **5.** To not be able to pay what one owes; go bankrupt. Her father's small store *failed* when the new department store opened nearby.

fail (fāl) *verb,* **failed, failing.**

failure **1.** The act of not succeeding in doing or getting something. She was disappointed at her *failure* to get on the swimming team. **2.** A person or thing that does not succeed. The school play will not be a *failure* if everyone works hard. **3.** The condition of not being enough. The bad weather caused a crop *failure.*

fail·ure (fāl′yər) *noun, plural* **failures.**

faint **1.** Not clear or strong; weak. We heard the *faint* cry of a puppy from the basement. There was a *faint* light at the end of the road. **2.** Weak and dizzy. After playing all morning, the children were *faint* with hunger by noon. *Adjective.*
—A condition in which a person seems to be asleep and does not know what is going on around him. *Noun.*
—To be as if asleep and not know what is going on around one. He *fainted* when he heard the news of his wife's accident. *Verb.* ▲ Another word that sounds like this is **feint.**

faint (fānt) *adjective,* **fainter, faintest;** *noun, plural* **faints;** *verb,* **fainted, fainting.**

fair¹ **1.** Not in favor of any one more than another or others; just. The judges made a *fair* decision in choosing Jim the winner of the race. **2.** According to the rules. The referee said it was a *fair* tackle. **3.** Neither too good nor too bad; average. She has a *fair* chance of winning the tennis match. **4.** Light in coloring; not dark. He has *fair* hair. **5.** Not cloudy; clear; sunny. The weather for the weekend will be *fair.* **6.** Pleasing to the eye; attractive; beautiful. The prince married the *fair* young princess. *Adjective.*
—In a fair manner; according to the rules. Jack always plays *fair. Adverb.* ▲ Another word that sounds like this is **fare.**

fair (fer) *adjective,* **fairer, fairest;** *adverb.*

fair² **1.** A public showing of farm products. Fairs are held to show and judge crops and cows, pigs, and other livestock. Fairs often have shows, contests, and entertainment. **2.** Any large showing of products or objects. Father took us to see the Canadian exhibit at the World's *Fair.* **3.** The showing and selling of things for a particular cause or reason. Our school book *fair* is going to raise money for a

new playground. ▲ Another word that sounds like this is **fare**.
> **fair** (fer) *noun, plural* **fairs**.

fairly **1.** In a fair manner; honestly; justly. That teacher always treats each pupil *fairly*. **2.** Somewhat; rather. John has saved a *fairly* large amount of money.
> **fair·ly** (fer′lē) *adverb*.

fairy A tiny being in stories who is supposed to have magic powers.
> **fair·y** (fer′ē) *noun, plural* **fairies**.

faith **1.** Belief or trust. I have great *faith* in her honesty. **2.** A religion. There are people of many different *faiths* in our city.
> **faith** (fāth) *noun, plural* **faiths**.

faithful **1.** Loyal and devoted. She has always been a *faithful* friend. **2.** Honest and accurate; true. He made a *faithful* copy of the drawing.
> **faith·ful** (fāth′fəl) *adjective*.

fake A person or thing that is not what it should be or claims to be. That is not a real fireplace; it's a *fake*. *Noun*.
—**1.** To take on the appearance of; pretend. He *faked* illness in order to stay home from school. **2.** To make something seem true or real in order to fool. The dishonest clerk stole the money and *faked* the records so that no one would know. *Verb*.
> **fake** (fāk) *noun, plural* **fakes**; *verb*, **faked**, **faking**.

Falcon

falcon A bird that looks like a hawk. Falcons have short, hooked bills and long toes with strong, hooked claws. A falcon can fly very fast. Falcons are good hunters and many have been trained by man to hunt birds and small animals.
> **fal·con** (fôl′kən *or* fal′kən) *noun, plural* **falcons**.

fall **1.** To come down from a higher place; drop. The lamp will *fall* off the table if the baby keeps playing with it. The mountain climber held the rope tightly so that he would not *fall*. The weather report says snow will *fall* tonight. **2.** To become lower or less. Their voices *fell* to a whisper when the band started to play. The price of eggs has *fallen* by five cents. **3.** To take place; happen. Christmas *falls* on December 25. **4.** To pass into a particular state or condition; become. He *fell* in love with her. She couldn't come to the party because she *fell* ill. **5.** To be defeated, captured, or overthrown. The city *fell* after a long battle. **6.** To hang down. The dress *fell* in soft folds. *Verb*.
—**1.** A coming down from a higher place. He hurt himself in the *fall* from the ladder. The skater took a *fall* on the ice. **2.** The amount of anything that comes down. We had a six-inch *fall* of rain on Saturday. **3.** A loss of power; capture or defeat. The whole country was in confusion after the *fall* of the government. **4.** A lowering or lessening. There was a *fall* in the price of apples last month. **5.** The season of the year coming between summer and winter; autumn. The weather begins to get cooler in the fall. **6.** **falls.** A fall of water from a higher place; waterfall. *Noun*.
—Having to do with the fall season. We went shopping for new *fall* clothes. *Adjective*.
> **fall** (fôl) *verb*, **fell**, **fallen**, **falling**; *noun, plural* **falls**; *adjective*.

fallen The leaves of the trees have *fallen*.
> **fall·en** (fô′lən) *verb*.

fallout The radioactive material that falls to the earth after a nuclear bomb explodes.
> **fall·out** (fôl′out′) *noun*.

false **1.** Not true or correct; wrong. The witness swore not to make a *false* statement. **2.** Not real; artificial. Her grandmother wears *false* teeth. **3.** Used to fool or trick. He gave a *false* impression when he acted as if the bicycle belonged to him.
> **false** (fôls) *adjective*, **falser**, **falsest**.

falter To act or speak as if one is not certain; hesitate. The baby *faltered* for a moment before trying to take a step. The man *faltered* every time he spoke of the accident.
> **fal·ter** (fôl′tər) *verb*, **faltered**, **faltering**.

at; āpe; cär; end; mē; it; īce; hot; ōld; fôrk; wood; fool; oil; out; up; turn; sing; thin; this; hw in white; zh in treasure. ə stands for a in about, e in taken i in pencil, o in lemon, and u in circus.

fame The quality of being famous or well-known. The tennis player's *fame* spread across the country.
fame (fām) *noun*.

familiar **1.** Often heard or seen. I can't remember the name of the song, but the tune is *familiar*. Fog is a *familiar* sight near the sea. **2.** Knowing something well. I am *familiar* with that story. **3.** Friendly or close. She is on *familiar* terms with all her neighbors.
fa·mil·iar (fə mil′yər) *adjective*.

family **1.** A father and mother and their children. Twenty *families* live on our street. **2.** The children of a father and mother. My parents raised a large *family*. **3.** A group of people who are related to each other; relatives. The whole *family* will get together for the Christmas holidays. **4.** A group of related animals or plants. Zebras and donkeys belong to the horse *family*. **5.** Any group of things that are the same or similar. English and German belong to the same *family* of languages.
fam·i·ly (fam′ə lē *or* fam′lē) *noun, plural* **families**.

famine A very great lack of food in an area or country. Many people died of starvation during the *famine* in that country.
fam·ine (fam′in) *noun, plural* **famines**.

famous Very well-known; having great fame. Thomas Edison is *famous* for having invented the electric light. A crowd of boys gathered around the *famous* baseball player.
fa·mous (fā′məs) *adjective*.

fan¹ **1.** A device shaped like part of a circle that is held in the hand and waved back and forth to make air move. **2.** A mechanical device having several blades that are turned by an electric motor. Fans are used to make air move for cooling or heating. **3.** Anything that looks like a fan. The open tail of the peacock is called a fan. *Noun.*
—To move air toward or on. He *fanned* the flames of the fire to make it burn more. She *fanned* herself with a newspaper in the hot, stuffy room. *Verb.*
fan (fan) *noun, plural* **fans;** *verb,* **fanned, fanning**.

Fan

fan² A person who is very enthusiastic about something. My brother is a real football *fan* who watches the games on television every Sunday.
fan (fan) *noun, plural* **fans**.

fanatic A person who is much too devoted to a cause or too enthusiastic about something. That man is such a *fanatic* about being clean that he will not shake hands with other people for fear of getting their germs. Mike is a sports *fanatic* who can watch one game on television while listening to another on the radio. *Noun.*
—Much too devoted or enthusiastic. She is a *fanatic* follower of that political leader. *Adjective.*
fa·nat·ic (fə nat′ik) *noun, plural* **fanatics;** *adjective*.

fancy **1.** The power to picture something in the mind; imagination. A unicorn is a creature of *fancy*. **2.** Something that is imagined. Being a princess was the little girl's favorite *fancy*. **3.** A liking or fondness. Andrew has a *fancy* for cowboy movies. The two girls took a *fancy* to each other. *Noun.*
—Not plain; very decorated. Nancy wore a *fancy* dress to the party. *Adjective.*
—**1.** To imagine. Tom likes to *fancy* himself as a famous baseball player. **2.** To be fond of; like. Which of the dresses do you *fancy* the most? *Verb.*
fan·cy (fan′sē) *noun, plural* **fancies;** *adjective,* **fancier, fanciest;** *verb,* **fancied, fancying**.

fang A long, pointed tooth. The fangs of certain snakes contain poison.
fang (fang) *noun, plural* **fangs**.

fantastic **1.** Very strange; odd. The wood in the fireplace took on *fantastic* shapes as it burned. **2.** Very good; excellent. The hikers had a *fantastic* view of the town from the top of the mountain.
fan·tas·tic (fan tas′tik) *adjective*.

fantasy Something that is imagined or not real. The author wrote *fantasies* about life on other planets.
fan·ta·sy (fan′tə sē) *noun, plural* **fantasies**.

far **1.** At a great distance; not near. She traveled *far* from home to visit her uncle. **2.** To or at a certain place, distance, or time. Read as *far* as chapter two for tomorrow. As *far* as I can tell, she's right. The meeting lasted *far* into the afternoon. **3.** Very much. It would be *far* better if you waited to leave until the rain stops. *Adverb.*
—**1.** At a great distance; distant. He lives in the *far* northern part of the country. **2.** More distant; farther away. The spacecraft landed on the *far* side of the moon. *Adjective.*

far (fär) *adverb*, **farther** or **further**, **farthest** or **furthest**; *adjective*, **farther** or **further**, **farthest** or **furthest**.

fare **1.** The cost of a ride on a bus, train, airplane, ship, or taxi. The bus driver collected the *fares*. **2.** A passenger who pays a fare. *Noun.*
—To get along; do. He is *faring* well at his new school. *Verb.* ▲ Another word that sounds like this is **fair**.
  fare (fer) *noun*, *plural* **fares**; *verb*, **fared**, **faring**.

farewell Good-by and good luck. The guests said their *farewells* and left.
  fare·well (fer′wel′) *interjection*; *noun*, *plural* **farewells**.

farm A piece of land that is used to raise crops and animals for food. *Noun.*
—To raise crops and animals on a farm. Most of the people in this valley *farm* for a living. *Verb.*
  farm (färm) *noun*, *plural* **farms**; *verb*, **farmed**, **farming**.

farmer A person who lives on and runs a farm.
  farm·er (fär′mər) *noun*, *plural* **farmers**.

farming The business of raising crops or animals on a farm; agriculture. Most of the people in that area make a living by *farming*.
  farm·ing (fär′ming) *noun*.

farsighted Able to see things that are far away more clearly than things that are close. Grandmother is *farsighted* and must wear glasses to read.
  far·sight·ed (fär′sī′tid) *adjective*.

farther The little boat drifted *farther* and *farther* from the dock. They live at the *farther* side of town. Look up **far** for more information.
  far·ther (fär′t͟hər) *adverb*; *adjective*.

farthest Jane sat *farthest* from the front of the room. He lives *farthest* away from school. The town lies just over the *farthest* hill. Look up **far** for more information.
  far·thest (fär′t͟hist) *adverb*; *adjective*.

fascinate To attract and hold the interest of; charm. The magician's tricks *fascinated* the children in the audience.
  fas·ci·nate (fas′ə nāt′) *verb*, **fascinated**, **fascinating**.

fascism A form of government in which a dictator rules. Under fascism there is strict government control of labor and business, a great stress on national interests, and the putting down by force of all opposition to the government.
  fas·cism (fash′iz′əm) *noun*.

fashion **1.** The newest custom or style in dress or behavior. He always bought the latest *fashion* in men's clothing. **2.** Manner or way. She decorated her room in her own *fashion*. *Noun.*
—To give form to; make; shape. Grandfather *fashioned* a little boat out of a block of wood. *Verb.*
  fash·ion (fash′ən) *noun*, *plural* **fashions**; *verb*, **fashioned**, **fashioning**.

fast¹ **1.** Acting, moving, or done very quickly; rapid. Ice hockey is a very *fast* game. If she catches a *fast* train, she will be here in an hour. He is a very *fast* thinker who can make decisions quickly. **2.** Ahead of the correct time. My watch is ten minutes *fast*. **3.** Faithful; loyal. Those two men have been *fast* friends since they were in college. **4.** Not easily faded. Are the colors in this material *fast*? *Adjective.*
—**1.** In a firm way; tightly; securely. The tent was held *fast* by poles driven into the ground. **2.** Soundly; deeply. He has been *fast* asleep since nine o'clock. **3.** With speed; quickly. The horse ran *fast*. *Adverb.*
  fast (fast) *adjective*, **faster**, **fastest**; *adverb*.

fast² To eat little or no food, or only certain kinds of food. In many religions, people *fast* on certain holy days. *Verb.*
—A day or period of fasting. Many Roman Catholics observe a *fast* each year on Good Friday. *Noun.*
  fast (fast) *verb*, **fasted**, **fasting**; *noun*, *plural* **fasts**.

fasten To attach, close, or put firmly. Mother *fastened* the gold pin to her dress. Please *fasten* the door when you leave. She *fastened* her attention on the book she was reading.
  fas·ten (fas′ən) *verb*, **fastened**, **fastening**.

fat A yellow or white oily substance. Fat is found mainly in certain body tissues of animals and in some plants. *Noun.*
—**1.** Having much fat or flesh on the body. That *fat* man weighs 300 pounds. We had a *fat* 20-pound turkey for Thanksgiving. **2.** Having much in it; full. All that money made his wallet *fat*. *Adjective.*
  fat (fat) *noun*, *plural* **fats**; *adjective*, **fatter**, **fattest**.

at; āpe; cär; end; mē; it; īce; hot; ōld;
fôrk; wood; fo͞ol; oil; out; up; turn; sing;
thin; t͟his; hw in white; zh in treasure.
ə stands for a in about, e in taken
i in pencil, o in lemon, and u in circus.

fatal 1. Causing death. There are many *fatal* accidents on highways. 2. Causing harm; very bad. He broke his arm when he made the *fatal* mistake of jumping out of the tree.
fa·tal (fāt′əl) *adjective.*

fate The power that is believed to control what is going to happen or how things will turn out. People have no control over fate. The team blamed its failure to win the game on *fate.*
fate (fāt) *noun, plural* **fates.**

father 1. The male parent of a child. 2. A priest.
fa·ther (fä′thər) *noun, plural* **fathers.**

father-in-law The father of one's husband or wife.
fa·ther-in-law (fä′thər in lô′) *noun, plural* **fathers-in-law.**

fathom A measure equal to six feet. Fathoms are used mainly in measuring the depth of the ocean.
fath·om (fath′əm) *noun, plural* **fathoms.**

fatigue A being tired. Fatigue can be caused by working too hard. *Noun.*
—To cause to be tired. The long hours of studying *fatigued* him. *Verb.*
fa·tigue (fə tēg′) *noun; verb,* **fatigued, fatiguing.**

fatten To make or become fat. The farmer *fattened* the turkeys for Thanksgiving.
fat·ten (fat′ən) *verb,* **fattened, fattening.**

faucet A thing for turning on or off the flow of water or another liquid from a pipe or container.
fau·cet (fô′sit) *noun, plural* **faucets.**

fault 1. Something that is wrong with and spoils something else. The roof of the house fell in because of a *fault* in the beams. His bad temper is his main *fault.* 2. The responsibility for a mistake. It was her *fault* that I was late. The driver of the speeding car was at *fault* in the accident. 3. A mistake; error. He corrected the *faults* in his spelling.
fault (fôlt) *noun, plural* **faults.**

faun A god of the woods and fields in Roman myths. A faun had the body of a man and the ears, horns, legs, and tail of a goat. ▲ Another word that sounds like this is **fawn.**
faun (fôn) *noun, plural* **fauns.**

favor 1. An act of kindness. He did her a *favor* by giving her a ride to school. 2. Friendliness or approval; liking. The candidate won the *favor* of the voters and was elected. 3. A small gift. All the children at the party were given horns, balloons, and other *favors. Noun.*

—1. To show kindness or favor to; oblige. Please *favor* us with an answer to our letter. 2. To approve of; like. She *favors* the color red. 3. To show special treatment or kindness. The mother cat *favored* the sick kitten over the others. 4. To look like; resemble. The baby *favors* his father. *Verb.*
fa·vor (fā′vər) *noun, plural* **favors;** *verb,* **favored, favoring.**
in one's favor. To one's advantage. The score was three to nothing *in our favor.*

favorable 1. Showing approval or liking; approving. I hoped she would give me a *favorable* answer and say she could come to the party. 2. In one's favor; benefiting. If the weather is *favorable,* we'll go on a picnic.
fa·vor·a·ble (fā′vər ə bəl) *adjective.*

favorite Liked best. Which is your *favorite* baseball team? Summer is her *favorite* time of year. *Adjective.*
—A person or thing that is liked best. Mystery stories are my *favorites. Noun.*
fa·vor·ite (fā′vər it) *adjective; noun, plural* **favorites.**

fawn A young deer. ▲ Another word that sounds like this is **faun.**
fawn (fôn) *noun, plural* **fawns.**

Fawn

fear A strong feeling caused by knowing that danger, pain, or evil is near. The man felt great *fear* when he saw the escaped lion. *Noun.*
—1. To be afraid of. My brother *fears* the dark. He *fears* snakes. 2. To be worried or anxious. She *feared* that we would be late for the show if we didn't hurry. *Verb.*
fear (fēr) *noun, plural* **fears;** *verb,* **feared, fearing.**

fearful 1. Feeling or showing fear; afraid. The cat was *fearful* of the barking dog. 2. Causing fear; frightening; scary. The thunder and lightning were *fearful.*
fear·ful (fēr′fəl) *adjective.*

feast A large, rich meal for many people on a special occasion. The king invited his knights to a *feast. Noun.*
—To have a feast; eat richly. We *feasted* on turkey and stuffing on Thanksgiving. *Verb.*
 feast (fēst) *noun, plural* **feasts;** *verb,* **feasted, feasting.**

feat An act or deed that shows great courage, strength, or skill. Climbing that mountain was quite a *feat.*
▲ Another word that sounds like this is **feet.**
 feat (fēt) *noun, plural* **feats.**

feather One of the light growths that cover a bird's skin. Feathers protect the bird's skin from injury and help keep the bird warm.
 feath·er (feth′ər) *noun, plural* **feathers.**
 feather in one's cap. An act to be proud of. Winning the spelling contest was a *feather in his cap.*

▲ Long ago when a soldier was very brave in battle, he was awarded a feather to wear in his cap or helmet. Wearing a **feather in one's cap** was a great honor. After a while, people began to use a *feather in one's cap* for anything that a person should be proud of.

feature 1. An important or outstanding part or quality of something. One of the most important *features* of the camel is its ability to go for days without water. Among the *features* of that new house are air conditioning in every room and a swimming pool in the back yard. 2. A part of the face. The eyes, nose, mouth, and chin are *features.* 3. A full-length motion picture. *Noun.*
—To give an important place to. The concert *features* a singing group and a guitar player. *Verb.*
 fea·ture (fē′chər) *noun, plural* **features;** *verb,* **featured, featuring.**

February The second month of the year. February has twenty-eight days except in leap year, when it has twenty-nine.
 Feb·ru·ar·y (feb′roo er′ē *or* feb′yoo er′ē) *noun.*

▲ The word **February** comes from the Latin name of a religious holiday that the ancient Romans used to hold in the middle of this month.

fed The dog has not been *fed* its dinner yet. Look up **feed** for more information.
 fed (fed) *verb.*

federal 1. Formed by an agreement between states to join together as one nation. The United States has a *federal* government. 2. Having to do with the central government of the United States, thought of as separate from the government of each state. The power to conduct foreign affairs and provide for defense are *federal* powers.
 fed·er·al (fed′ər əl) *adjective.*

federation A union formed by agreement between states, nations, or other groups. The various nations formed a *federation* to work for world peace.
 fed·er·a·tion (fed′ə rā′shən) *noun, plural* **federations.**

fee Money asked or paid for some service or right. We paid a *fee* of two dollars for a license for our dog. The admission *fee* to the circus is four dollars.
 fee (fē) *noun, plural* **fees.**

feeble Not strong; weak. The *feeble* old woman walked with a cane. We heard the *feeble* cry of a cat from the basement.
 fee·ble (fē′bəl) *adjective,* **feebler, feeblest.**

feed 1. To give food to. Can I *feed* the baby? The mother lion *fed* her baby cubs. 2. To give as food. She *fed* oats to the horse. 3. To supply with something necessary or important. Melting snow from the mountains *feeds* the rivers each spring. My sister is learning how to *feed* information into a computer at school. 4. To eat. The cows are *feeding* in the pasture. Frogs *feed* on flies. *Verb.*
—Food for farm animals. Grass, hay, and grains are *feed* for cattle. *Noun.*
 feed (fēd) *verb,* **fed, feeding;** *noun, plural* **feeds.**

feel 1. To find out about by touching or handling; touch. I can *feel* the difference between wool and cotton. 2. To be aware of by touch. She could *feel* the rain on her face. 3. To have or cause the sense of being something. The water *feels* warm. He *feels* happy when he thinks of his new bicycle. 4. To think; believe. Many people *feel* that our team should have won the game. 5. To try to find by touching. She *felt* her way up the stairs in the dark. *Verb.*
—The way that something seems to the touch. I like the warm *feel* of wool against my skin. *Noun.*
 feel (fēl) *verb,* **felt, feeling;** *noun, plural* **feels.**

at; āpe; cär; end; mē; it; īce; hot; ōld;
fôrk; wood; fōol; oil; out; up; turn; sing;
thin; this; hw in white; zh in treasure.
ə stands for a in about, e in taken
i in pencil, o in lemon, and u in circus.

237

feeler A part of an animal's body that is used for touch. An insect has feelers.
feel·er (fē′lər) *noun, plural* **feelers.**

feeling **1.** The ability to feel by touching; sense of touch. He rubbed his cold hands to bring back the *feeling.* **2.** A being aware of; sense of being. Having missed breakfast, I had a *feeling* of hunger around noon. **3.** An emotion. Joy, fear, and anger are feelings. **4. feelings.** The tender or sensitive part of a person's nature. She hurt his *feelings* when she didn't even say hello to him. **5.** A way of thinking; opinion; belief. It is my *feeling* that you are right about what happened.
feel·ing (fē′ling) *noun, plural* **feelings.**

feet More than one foot. Look up **foot** for more information. ▲ Another word that sounds like this is **feat.**
feet (fēt) *noun plural.*

feign To put on a false show of; pretend. She *feigned* sickness so that she wouldn't have to go to the dentist.
feign (fān) *verb,* **feigned, feigning.**

feint A blow or movement meant to trick or take away attention from the main point of attack. *Noun.*
—To make a feint. The boxer *feinted* with his left hand and then hit with his right. *Verb.* ▲ Another word that sounds like this is **faint.**
feint (fānt) *noun, plural* **feints;** *verb,* **feinted, feinting.**

fell[1] She slipped on the ice and *fell.* Look up **fall** for more information.
fell (fel) *verb.*

fell[2] **1.** To hit and knock down; cause to fall. The fighter *felled* his opponent. **2.** To cut down. The·lumberjack *felled* the tree.
fell (fel) *verb,* **felled, felling.**

fellow **1.** A man or boy. He is certainly a clever *fellow* to come up with such a good idea. **2.** A person who is like another; companion; associate. *Noun.*
—Being the same or very much alike. He got along well with his *fellow* classmates. *Adjective.*
fel·low (fel′ō) *noun, plural* **fellows;** *adjective.*

felt[1] I *felt* the cold wind against my face. Look up **feel** for more information.
felt (felt) *verb.*

felt[2] A material made of wool, hair, or fur that is pressed together in layers instead of being woven or knitted. Felt is used to make hats.
felt (felt) *noun, plural* **felts.**

female **1.** Of or having to do with the sex that gives birth to young or produces eggs. A mare is a *female* horse. **2.** Having to do with women or girls; feminine. *Adjective.*
—A female person or animal. Her dog is a *female.* There was an even number of *females* and males in the class. *Noun.*
fe·male (fē′māl) *adjective; noun, plural* **females.**

feminine Of or having to do with women or girls.
fem·i·nine (fem′ə nin) *adjective.*

fence **1.** A structure that is used to surround, protect, or mark off an area. A fence may be made of wire or wood. There was a white picket *fence* in front of the house. The farmer put up a *fence* around the pasture to keep the cows from straying. **2.** A person who buys and sells stolen goods. The thief took the stolen diamonds to a *fence. Noun.*
—**1.** To put a fence around. Mother *fenced* her vegetable garden to keep the rabbits out. In the spring, part of the park is *fenced* off for a ball field. **2.** To fight with a sword or foil; take part in the sport of fencing. The two boys *fenced* as the other members of the class watched. *Verb.*
fence (fens) *noun, plural* **fences;** *verb,* **fenced, fencing.**

fencing The art or sport of fighting with a sword or foil.
fenc·ing (fen′sing) *noun.*

Fencing

fender **1.** A metal piece that sticks out over the wheel of an automobile or bicycle for protection against splashed water or mud. **2.** A metal screen in front of a fireplace to protect against sparks.
fend·er (fen′dər) *noun, plural* **fenders.**

ferment **1.** To go through or cause a chemical change that results in the forming of bubbles of gas. When milk *ferments,* it turns sour. When the juice of grapes *ferments,* it turns into wine. **2.** To cause by stirring up or exciting feelings. The rebel leaders tried to *ferment* a revolution by blaming the government for the lack of food in the country. *Verb.*

—Something that causes a substance to ferment. Certain bacteria and molds are used as ferments in making some cheeses. *Noun.*

fer·ment (fər ment′ *for verb;* fur′ment *for noun*) *verb,* **fermented, fermenting;** *noun, plural* **ferments.**

fern A plant that has large feathery leaves and no flowers. Ferns reproduce from spores instead of seeds.

fern (furn) *noun, plural* **ferns.**

ferocious Extremely cruel or mean; savage; fierce. A hungry lion can be *ferocious.*

fe·ro·cious (fə-rō′shəs) *adjective.*

ferret An animal that looks like a weasel. Ferrets have yellowish-white fur and pink eyes. They are sometimes trained to hunt rats, mice, and rabbits. *Noun.*
—**1.** To hunt with ferrets. **2.** To look for; search. He *ferreted* through his drawers looking for the missing sock. *Verb.*

fer·ret (fer′it) *noun, plural* **ferrets;** *verb,* **ferreted, ferreting.**

Fern

Ferret

Ferris wheel A large, revolving wheel with seats hung from its rim. It is used at fairs and amusement parks to give people rides.

Fer·ris wheel (fer′is).

ferry A boat used to carry people, cars, and goods across a river, channel, or other narrow body of water. This is also called a **ferryboat.** *Noun.*
—To go or carry in a ferry. The rescue workers *ferried* the storm victims to land. *Verb.*

fer·ry (fer′ē) *noun, plural* **ferries;** *verb,* **ferried, ferrying.**

fertile **1.** Able to produce crops and plants easily and plentifully. There is very *fertile* soil in this valley. **2.** Able to produce eggs, seeds, pollen, or young. An animal is *fertile* when it is able to give birth to young. **3.** Able to develop into or become a new person or animal. An egg must be *fertile* in order for a chick to hatch from it.

fer·tile (furt′əl) *adjective.*

fertilize **1.** To make fertile. A chick hatched from the *fertilized* egg. **2.** To put fertilizer on. The farmer *fertilized* the field with manure.

fer·ti·lize (furt′əl īz′) *verb,* **fertilized, fertilizing.**

fertilizer A substance that is added to soil to make it better for the growing of crops. Manure and certain chemicals are used as fertilizers.

fer·ti·liz·er (furt′əl ī′zər) *noun, plural* **fertilizers.**

festival A celebration or holiday. Many religious *festivals,* such as Christmas and Easter, take place every year. Ten new movies are being shown at this year's film *festival.*

fes·ti·val (fes′tə vəl) *noun, plural* **festivals.**

fetch To go after and bring back; get. Please *fetch* two more chairs from the other room.

fetch (fech) *verb,* **fetched, fetching.**

fetter A chain or piece of iron put on the feet to prevent movement.

fet·ter (fet′ər) *noun, plural* **fetters.**

feud A bitter, violent quarrel between two persons, families, or groups. A feud lasts for many years. The *feud* between the two tribes resulted in the deaths of many people.

feud (fyood) *noun, plural* **feuds.**

feudalism A political system in the western part of Europe during the Middle Ages. Under feudalism, a lord provided land and protection for people under his rule, who were known as vassals. In return they promised loyalty and service to the lord.

feu·dal·ism (fyood′əl iz′əm) *noun.*

fever A body temperature that is higher than normal. A person has a fever if his temperature is more than 98.6 degrees. The sick boy had a *fever* of 102 degrees.

fe·ver (fē′vər) *noun, plural* **fevers.**

at; āpe; cär; end; mē; it; īce; hot; ōld;
fôrk; wood; fool; oil; out; up; turn; sing;
thin; this; hw in white; zh in treasure.
ə stands for a in about, e in taken
i in pencil, o in lemon, and u in circus.

few Not many. *Few* people came to the meeting. *Adjective.*
—Not many persons or things. Many people were invited to the party, but *few* came. He sold only a *few* of the newspapers. *Noun.*
few (fyo͞o) *adjective,* **fewer, fewest;** *noun.*

fez A round, red felt hat that has a tassel. Fezzes used to be commonly worn by men in Turkey.
fez (fez) *noun, plural* **fezzes.**

fiancé A man to whom a woman is engaged to be married.
fi·an·cé (fē′än sā′) *noun, plural* **fiancés.**

fiancée A woman to whom a man is engaged to be married.
fi·an·cée (fē′än sā′) *noun, plural* **fiancées.**

fiber A fine, threadlike part. Cotton *fibers* can be spun into thread. The rope was made of hemp *fibers.*
fi·ber (fī′bər) *noun, plural* **fibers.**

fiberglass A strong material that is made of fine threads of glass. Fiberglass will not burn easily. It is used for insulation and in the making of boats.
fi·ber·glass (fī′bər glas′) *noun.*

fiction A written work that tells a story about characters and events that are not real. Novels and short stories are fiction.
fic·tion (fik′shən) *noun.*

fiddle A violin. *Noun.*
—To play a violin. *Verb.*
fid·dle (fid′əl) *noun, plural* **fiddles;** *verb,* **fiddled, fiddling.**

field 1. A piece of open or cleared land. We could see the farmer in the wheat *field.* 2. Land that contains or gives a natural resource. There were about ten oil wells in the oil *field.* 3. An area or piece of land on which certain games are played. The players have just come out on the football *field.* 4. An area of interest or activity. Jack hopes to work in the *field* of medicine when he gets out of college. *Noun.*
—To catch, stop, or pick up a ball that has been hit in baseball. The shortstop *fielded* the ball and threw it to first base. *Verb.*
field (fēld) *noun, plural* **fields;** *verb,* **fielded, fielding.**

fielder A baseball player in the field who tries to field the ball and put out the team at bat.
field·er (fēl′dər) *noun, plural* **fielders.**

field glasses A pair of small binoculars used outdoors.

field trip A trip away from the classroom to see things that have been studied. The class took a *field trip* to the ocean to study the plants along the seashore.

fierce 1. Cruel or dangerous; savage. The hungry animal was *fierce.* 2. Very strong or violent; raging. There was a *fierce* storm last night that blew down several trees.
fierce (fērs) *adjective,* **fiercer, fiercest.**

fiesta A festival or celebration. In many Latin American countries, fiestas are held in honor of certain saints.
fi·es·ta (fē es′tə) *noun, plural* **fiestas.**

fife A musical instrument like a flute. The fife makes a shrill tone and is most often used with drums in a marching band.
fife (fīf) *noun, plural* **fifes.**

fifteen Five more than ten; 15.
fif·teen (fif′tēn′) *noun, plural* **fifteens;** *adjective.*

fifteenth 1. Next after the fourteenth. 2. One of fifteen equal parts; 1/15.
fif·teenth (fif′tēnth′) *adjective; noun, plural* **fifteenths.**

fifth 1. Next after the fourth. 2. One of five equal parts; 1/5.
fifth (fifth) *adjective; noun, plural* **fifths.**

fiftieth 1. Next after the forty-ninth. 2. One of fifty equal parts; 1/50.
fif·ti·eth (fif′tē ith) *adjective; noun, plural* **fiftieths.**

fifty Five times ten; 50.
fif·ty (fif′tē) *noun, plural* **fifties;** *adjective.*

fig The sweet fruit of a shrub or small tree that grows in warm regions. Figs have many tiny seeds.
fig (fig) *noun, plural* **figs.**

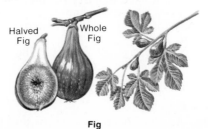

Halved Fig   Whole Fig

Fife

Fig

fight 1. A battle or struggle. There was a *fight* between the two armies. The two boys had a fist *fight*. 2. A quarrel. The two sisters had a *fight* over which television program to watch. *Noun.*
—1. To take part in a battle with. The British *fought* the American colonists in 1776. The policeman *fought* with the thief. 2. To struggle against; try to overcome. The firemen *fought* the blaze for hours. 3. To carry on a battle, contest, or struggle. The sick man *fought* for his life. *Verb.*
fight (fīt) *noun, plural* **fights;** *verb,* **fought, fighting.**

fighter 1. A person who fights. 2. A person who boxes for a living.
fight·er (fī′tər) *noun, plural* **fighters.**

figurative Using words in a way that is different from their actual meanings. *Her head is in the clouds* is a figurative expression because her "head" is not really in the "clouds;" she's only daydreaming.
fig·ur·a·tive (fig′yər ə tiv) *adjective.*

figure 1. A symbol that stands for a number. 0, 1, 2, 3, 4, and 5 are figures. 2. An amount given in figures. The population *figures* of the cities and towns are given on the back of the map. 3. A form or outline; shape. He saw the *figure* of a dog in the moonlight. 4. A person; character. The mayor is a public *figure.* 5. A design; pattern. The cloth had bright red *figures* on it. *Noun.*
—1. To find an answer by using numbers. Father and Mother *figured* the cost of the trip. 2. To stand out; have importance; appear. Several well-known people *figured* in the news today. *Verb.*
fig·ure (fig′yər) *noun, plural* **figures;** *verb,* **figured, figuring.**
to figure out. To come to know or understand. She *figured out* who the murderer was before she got to the end of the book.

figurehead 1. A carved wooden figure placed on the bow of a ship for decoration. 2. A person who has a position of authority but who has no real power or responsibility. The queen of England is a *figurehead;* Parliament runs the government.
fig·ure·head (fig′yər hed′) *noun, plural* **figureheads.**

figure of speech An expression in which words are used in a way that is different from their actual meanings. Figures of speech are used to make writing or speaking fresher and more expressive. "When she saw she was late, she flew out of the house" is a *figure of speech.*

filament A very fine thread, or a part that is like a thread. The filament in an electric light bulb is a fine wire that gives off light when an electric current passes through it.
fil·a·ment (fil′ə mənt) *noun, plural* **filaments.**

file¹ 1. A folder, drawer, cabinet, or other container in which papers, cards, or records are arranged in order. 2. A set of papers, cards, or records arranged in order. Mother keeps a *file* of recipes. 3. A line of persons, animals, or things placed one behind the other. *Noun.*
—1. To keep papers, cards, or records arranged in order. The secretary *filed* the letters in alphabetical order. 2. To hand in or put on a record. The policeman *filed* a report of the accident. Father must *file* his income tax return. 3. To march or move in a file. The passengers *filed* off the airplane. *Verb.*
file (fīl) *noun, plural* **files;** *verb,* **filed, filing.**

file² A steel tool having many tiny ridges on one or two sides. A file is used to cut, smooth, or grind down a hard substance. *Noun.*
—To cut, smooth, or grind down with a file. I *filed* my fingernails. *Verb.*
file (fīl) *noun, plural* **files;** *verb,* **filed, filing.**

filings Small bits that have been removed by a file. A magnet attracts iron *filings.*
fil·ings (fī′lingz) *noun plural.*

Figurehead

fill 1. To make or become full. Please *fill* the bucket with water. He will *fill* the box with books. The room *filled* with fresh air when we opened the window. 2. To take up the whole space of. The students *filled* the auditorium. The smell of roses *filled* the room. 3. To give or have whatever is asked for or needed. The grocery store *filled* our order. 4. To stop up or close up by putting something in. The painter *filled* the hole in the wall with plaster before painting. The dentist *filled* a cavity in my tooth. 5. To have or hold a position or office. Mr. Smith will *fill* the office of company treasurer after my father retires. *Verb.*
—Something used to fill. Gravel was used as *fill* for the hole in the road. *Noun.*
fill (fil) *verb,* **filled, filling;** *noun, plural* **fills.**

fillet A slice of meat or fish without bones or fat. *Noun.* This word is also spelled **filet.**
—To cut meat or fish into fillets. *Verb.*
fil·let (fi lā′ *or* fil′ā) *noun, plural* **fillets;** *verb,* **filleted, filleting.**

filling A thing used to fill something. Mother used cherries as a pie *filling.* He broke the *filling* in one of his teeth when he bit into the hard candy.
fill·ing (fil′ing) *noun, plural* **fillings.**

filly A female colt.
fil·ly (fil′ē) *noun, plural* **fillies.**

film 1. A very thin layer or covering. The windows were covered with a *film* of dirt. 2. A thin roll or strip of material coated with a substance that is sensitive to light. It is used to take photographs. 3. A motion picture. *Noun.*
—1. To cover or become covered with a thin layer of something. The windows of the car were *filmed* with dust from the road. 2. To take pictures of with a motion-picture camera. He *filmed* the football game. *Verb.*
film (film) *noun, plural* **films;** *verb,* **filmed, filming.**

filter 1. A device through which a liquid or air is passed in order to clean out any dirt or other unclean matter. Our swimming pool at school has a *filter.* 2. A material through which a liquid or air passes in a filter. Paper, sand, cloth, and charcoal are often used as filters. *Noun.*
—1. To pass a liquid or air through a filter; strain. The water was *filtered* through charcoal. 2. To take out or separate by a filter. The solid pieces of dirt were *filtered* from the water. 3. To go through slowly. The sunlight *filtered* through the trees. *Verb.*
fil·ter (fil′tər) *noun, plural* **filters;** *verb,* **filtered, filtering.**

filth Disgusting or sickening dirt. The water in the pond was filled with garbage and other *filth.*
filth (filth) *noun.*

filthy Extremely dirty; foul. The streets were *filthy.*
filth·y (fil′thē) *adjective,* **filthier, filthiest.**

fin 1. One of the movable parts that look like wings, sticking out from the body of a fish. A fish uses its fins to swim and balance itself in the water. Certain other water animals, such as whales and porpoises, have fins. 2. Something that has the same shape or use as a fin. Rockets often have fins to give them balance during flight.
fin (fin) *noun, plural* **fins.**

final 1. Coming at the end; last. I just finished reading the *final* chapter of the book. What was the *final* score of the game? 2. Deciding completely. The decision of the judges is *final. Adjective.*
—1. The last examination of a school or college course of study. My brother Jim is studying for his history *final.* 2. The last or deciding game or match in a series. Our team reached the *finals* of the basketball tournament. *Noun.*
fi·nal (fīn′əl) *adjective; noun, plural* **finals.**

finale The last part of something; conclusion. The music program included a piano solo as its *finale.*
fi·na·le (fi nä′lē) *noun, plural* **finales.**

finally At the end; at last. We *finally* finished our homework.
fi·nal·ly (fīn′əl ē) *adverb.*

finance 1. The management of money matters for people, businesses, or governments. The president of that bank is an expert in *finance.* 2. **finances.** The amount of money had by a person, business, or government; funds. The company's *finances* were very low. *Noun.*
—To provide money for. His parents *financed* his college education. *Verb.*
fi·nance (fi nans′ *or* fī′nans) *noun, plural* **finances;** *verb,* **financed, financing.**

financial Having to do with money matters. Banks, stock exchanges, and insurance companies handle *financial* dealings. Newspapers often have a *financial* section.
fi·nan·cial (fi nan′shəl *or* fī nan′shəl) *adjective.*

finch A small songbird. The sparrow, canary, and cardinal are kinds of finches.
finch (finch) *noun, plural* **finches.**

find 1. To come upon by accident; happen on. Where did you *find* that four-leaf clover?

She *found* a wallet on the sidewalk. **2.** To get or learn by adding, subtracting, multiplying, or dividing. Please *find* the sum of this column of numbers. **3.** To learn or discover. I *found* that I could not study well with the radio on. **4.** To look for and get something lost or left. The police *found* the missing money in an old warehouse. **5.** To come to a decision about and declare. The jury *found* the man guilty. *Verb.*
—Something that is found. She came up with some great *finds* when she looked through the attic. *Noun.*
> **find** (fīnd) *verb,* **found, finding;** *noun, plural* **finds.**
> **to find out.** To learn; discover. Try to *find out* what time the meeting is.

fine¹ **1.** Of very high quality; very good; excellent. John is a *fine* musician. **2.** Very small or thin. Betty used a *fine* thread to sew on the button. That book has *fine* print. *Adjective.*
—Very well. He is doing *fine* in school. *Adverb.*
> **fine** (fīn) *adjective,* **finer, finest;** *adverb.*

fine² An amount of money paid as a punishment for breaking a rule or law. There is a *fine* of fifty dollars for littering. *Noun.*
—To punish by making pay a fine. The judge *fined* the driver for going through a red light. *Verb.*
> **fine** (fīn) *noun, plural* **fines;** *verb,* **fined, fining.**

finger **1.** One of the five separate parts at the end of the hand. Usually, a person is said to have four fingers and a thumb. **2.** Anything that has the same shape or use as a finger. *Fingers* of sunlight came through the window. *Noun.*
—To touch, handle, or play with the fingers. The witness *fingered* his handkerchief nervously as the lawyer questioned him. *Verb.*
> **fin·ger** (fing′gər) *noun, plural* **fingers;** *verb,* **fingered, fingering.**

fingernail A hard layer on the end of a finger.
> **fin·ger·nail** (fing′gər nāl′) *noun, plural* **fingernails.**

fingerprint An impression of the markings on the inner surface of the tip of a finger. Fingerprints help to identify people because no two people have the same fingerprints. *Noun.*
—To take the fingerprints of. The police *fingerprinted* the suspected thief. *Verb.*
> **fin·ger·print** (fing′gər print′) *noun, plural* **fingerprints;** *verb,* **fingerprinted, fingerprinting.**

finish **1.** To bring to an end; come to the end of; complete. When will you *finish* your homework? When he *finished* speaking, we all applauded. **2.** To use up completely. We *finished* the jar of peanut butter. **3.** To treat the surface of in some way. He used clear varnish to *finish* the cabinet. *Verb.*
—**1.** The last part of anything; end. We watched the *finish* of the race. **2.** The surface of something. The table has a shiny *finish.* *Noun.*
> **fin·ish** (fin′ish) *verb,* **finished, finishing;** *noun, plural* **finishes.**

fiord A deep, narrow inlet of the sea between high, steep cliffs. The country of Norway has many fiords.
> **fiord** (fyôrd) *noun, plural* **fiords.**

fir An evergreen tree that is related to the pine. Firs have cones and are often used as Christmas trees. ▲ Another word that sounds like this is **fur.**
> **fir** (fur) *noun, plural* **firs.**

Needles and Cone

Fir Tree

fire **1.** The flame, heat, and light given off in burning. **2.** Something burning. He added another log to the *fire.* **3.** Burning that destroys or causes damage. The bad wiring in the old house started a *fire.* **4.** A very strong emotion or feeling; passion. The angry man's eyes were full of *fire.* **5.** The shooting of guns. We heard the sound of rifle *fire* in the distance. *Noun.*
—**1.** To set on fire; cause to burn. We *fired* the heap of dead leaves. **2.** To dismiss from a job. The company *fired* seven employees. **3.** To

at; āpe; cär; end; mē; it; īce; hot; ōld;
fôrk; wood; fōol; oil; out; up; turn; sing;
thin; this; hw in white; zh in treasure.
ə stands for **a** in about, **e** in taken
i in pencil, **o** in lemon, and **u** in circus.

cause to be excited or stirred up. Stories about pirates *fired* the child's imagination. **4.** To shoot a firearm. He *fired* the gun once. *Verb.*
fire (fīr) *noun, plural* **fires;** *verb,* **fired, firing.**

firearm A weapon used for shooting. A firearm is usually a weapon that can be carried and fired by one person. Rifles, pistols, and shotguns are firearms.
fire·arm (fīr′ärm′) *noun, plural* **firearms.**

firecracker A paper tube containing gunpowder and a fuse. Firecrackers are often exploded on holidays and at celebrations.
fire·crack·er (fīr′krak′ər) *noun, plural* **firecrackers.**

fire engine A truck that carries equipment for fighting and putting out fires. Most fire engines have a machine that pumps water or chemicals on a fire to put it out.

fire escape A metal stairway attached to the outside of a building. It is used for escape in case of fire.

fire extinguisher A device containing chemicals that can be sprayed on a fire to put it out.
fire ex·tin·guish·er (eks ting′gwish ər).

firefly A small beetle that gives off short flashes of light.
fire·fly (fīr′flī′) *noun, plural* **fireflies.**

Fire Escape

firehouse A building for firemen and trucks and equipment for putting out fires.
fire·house (fīr′hous′) *noun, plural* **firehouses.**

fireman **1.** A man whose work is to put out and prevent fires. He is also called a **firefighter. 2.** A man who takes care of the fire in a furnace or steam engine.
fire·man (fīr′mən) *noun, plural* **firemen.**

fireplace **1.** An opening in a room with a chimney leading up from it. Fires are built in fireplaces. **2.** A structure outdoors in which a fire is built.
fire·place (fīr′plās′) *noun, plural* **fireplaces.**

fireproof That will not burn or will not burn easily. The new hospital is *fireproof.*
fire·proof (fīr′prōōf′) *adjective.*

fireside **1.** The area around a fireplace; hearth. **2.** The home or family life.
fire·side (fīr′sīd′) *noun, plural* **firesides.**

firewood Wood that is used in making a fire.
fire·wood (fīr′wood′) *noun.*

fireworks Firecrackers and other such devices that are burned or exploded to make loud noises or brilliant shows of light. Fireworks are used in many Fourth of July celebrations.
fire·works (fīr′wurks′) *noun plural.*

firm[1] **1.** Not giving in to pressure; solid. This is a very *firm* mattress. **2.** Not easily moved; secure. We made sure the fence posts were *firm* in the ground. **3.** Not changing; staying the same. It is my *firm* belief that he is honest. They had a *firm* friendship for many years. **4.** Steady or strong. Mary spoke with a *firm* voice when she made her speech. *Adjective.*
—So as not to move or change. The post was stuck *firm* in the ground. She stayed *firm* in her belief that he was wrong. *Adverb.*
firm (furm) *adjective,* **firmer, firmest;** *adverb.*

firm[2] A company in which two or more people go into business together. There are five partners in my father's law *firm.*
firm (furm) *noun, plural* **firms.**

first Before all others. Our team finished in *first* place. George Washington was the *first* President of the United States. *Adjective.*
—**1.** Before all others. She was ranked *first* in her class in mathematics. **2.** For the first time. I *first* heard the news yesterday. *Adverb.*
—**1.** A person or thing that is first. This invention is the *first* of its kind. **2.** The beginning. I liked the new boy from the *first. Noun.*
first (furst) *adjective; adverb; noun, plural* **firsts.**

Fireplace

244

first aid Emergency treatment that is given to a sick or injured person before a doctor comes.

first-class **1.** Of the highest rank or best quality. The singer gave a *first-class* performance. **2.** Having to do with a class of mail that includes mainly letters, packages, and other written or sealed matter. **3.** Having to do with the best and most expensive seats or rooms on a ship, train, or airplane. We bought *first-class* tickets for our plane trip. *Adjective.*
—By first-class mail or travel seats or rooms. I sent the package *first-class. Adverb.*
  first-class (furst′klas′) *adjective; adverb.*

first-hand Direct from the first or original source. He has *first-hand* knowledge of the accident. I learned of the argument *first-hand.*
  first-hand (furst′hand′) *adjective; adverb.*

fish **1.** An animal that lives in the water. Fish have backbones, gills for breathing, fins, and, usually, an outer covering of thin bony scales for protection. Fish are cold-blooded animals and are found in almost all fresh and salt waters of the world. **2.** The flesh of fish used as food. Are we having meat or *fish* for dinner? *Noun.*
—**1.** To catch or try to catch fish. We *fished* for trout. **2.** To look or search. He *fished* around in his pocket for the key. *Verb.*
  fish (fish) *noun, plural* **fish** or **fishes;** *verb,* **fished, fishing.**

fisherman A person who fishes for a living or for sport.
  fish·er·man (fish′ər mən) *noun, plural* **fishermen.**

fishery **1.** A place for catching fish. **2.** A place where fish are bred.
  fish·er·y (fish′ər ē) *noun, plural* **fisheries.**

fishing rod A long pole made of wood, metal, or fiberglass. It has a hook, line, and usually a reel attached to it and is used for catching fish.

fishy **1.** Like a fish in odor or taste. His hands smelled *fishy* after cleaning the fish. **2.** Not likely to be true. He gave us a *fishy* excuse for being late.
  fish·y (fish′ē) *adjective,* **fishier, fishiest.**

fission The splitting or breaking apart of an atomic nucleus into two parts. Large amounts of energy are released during fission.
  fis·sion (fish′ən) *noun.*

fist A hand that is tightly closed with the fingers doubled into the palm.
  fist (fist) *noun, plural* **fists.**

fit¹ **1.** Suitable, right, or proper. This water is not *fit* to drink. She is *fit* for the job. **2.** In good health; healthy. A person should exercise to keep *fit. Adjective.*
—**1.** To be suitable, right, or proper for. The part of the witch in the play does not *fit* her. **2.** To be the right or correct size or shape for. That coat *fits* you well. **3.** To make right, proper, or suitable. He *fit* his speech to the serious nature of the occasion. **4.** To supply with what is necessary or suitable; equip. The campers were *fitted* with all the supplies needed for the trip. **5.** To join, adjust, or put in. We *fitted* the pieces of the jigsaw puzzle together. *Verb.*
—The way in which something fits. The jacket has a tight *fit. Noun.*
  fit (fit) *adjective,* **fitter, fittest;** *verb,* **fitted, fitting;** *noun, plural* **fits.**

fit² **1.** A sudden, sharp attack of something. She had a *fit* of coughing. **2.** A sudden burst. He yelled at us in a *fit* of anger.
  fit (fit) *noun, plural* **fits.**

five One more than four; 5.
  five (fīv) *noun, plural* **fives;** *adjective.*

fix **1.** To make firm or secure; fasten tightly. The campers *fixed* the pegs for the tent in the ground. **2.** To arrange definitely; settle. He *fixed* the price for the used car at $1000. Have they *fixed* the date for their wedding? **3.** To direct or hold steadily. He *fixed* his eyes straight ahead. **4.** To place; put. The police *fixed* the responsibility for the accident on the driver of the blue car. **5.** To repair; mend. Can you *fix* the broken chair? **6.** To get ready or arrange; prepare. I will *fix* dinner tonight. She *fixed* up the room before the guests arrived. **7.** To try to get something to come out the way one wants. The dishonest man tried to *fix* the boxing match by bribing one of the boxers to lose on purpose. *Verb.*
—Trouble; difficulty. My sister got herself into quite a *fix* by accepting two dates for the same dance. *Noun.*
  fix (fiks) *verb,* **fixed, fixing;** *noun, plural* **fixes.**

fixture Something that is firmly fastened into place to stay. A bathtub, a toilet, and a washbowl are bathroom fixtures.
  fix·ture (fiks′chər) *noun, plural* **fixtures.**

at; āpe; cär; end; mē; it; īce; hot; ōld;
fôrk; wood; fo͞ol; oil; out; up; turn; sing;
thin; this; hw in white; zh in treasure.
ə stands for a in about, e in taken
i in pencil, o in lemon, and u in circus.

flag A piece of cloth having different colors and designs on it. Flags are used as symbols of countries or of organizations. Flags are also sometimes used for giving signals. *Noun.*
—To stop or signal. She *flagged* a taxicab by waving her hand. *Verb.*
flag (flag) *noun, plural* **flags;** *verb,* **flagged, flagging.**

U.S. Flag

flair A natural talent. Monty has a *flair* for acting. ▲ Another word that sounds like this is **flare.**
flair (fler) *noun, plural* **flairs.**

flake A small, thin flat piece. Large *flakes* of snow covered the window sill. *Noun.*
—To chip or peel off in flakes. The painter *flaked* the old paint off the wall. *Verb.*
flake (flāk) *noun, plural* **flakes;** *verb,* **flaked, flaking.**

flame 1. One of the tongues of light given off by a fire. The *flames* from the burning house could be seen from miles away. 2. Gas or vapor that has been set on fire to give off light or heat. She lowered the *flame* under the frying pan on the stove. 3. The condition of burning. The house burst into *flame. Noun.*
—1. To burn with flames; blaze. The fire *flamed* for hours. 2. To light up or glow. His face *flamed* with anger at his sister's rude remark. *Verb.*
flame (flām) *noun, plural* **flames;** *verb,* **flamed, flaming.**

flamingo A pink or red bird that has a long thin neck and legs, and webbed feet. Flamingos live near shallow lakes and lagoons in tropical areas throughout the world.
fla·min·go (flə ming′gō) *noun, plural* **flamingos** or **flamingoes.**

flammable Able to be set on fire easily. Some gases are very *flammable.*
flam·ma·ble (flam′ə bəl) *adjective.*

flank The part between the ribs and the hip on either side of the body of a person or an animal. *Noun.*

Flamingo

—1. To be at the side of. Two statues of lions *flanked* the entrance to the library. 2. To attack or move around the side of. Our ships *flanked* the enemy fleet. *Verb.*
flank (flangk) *noun, plural* **flanks;** *verb,* **flanked, flanking.**

flannel A soft cotton or woolen material. Flannel is used for such things as nightgowns, babies' clothes, and shirts.
flan·nel (flan′əl) *noun, plural* **flannels.**

flap 1. To move up and down. The bird *flapped* its wings. 2. To swing or wave loosely and with noise. The curtain *flapped* in the breeze. *Verb.*
—1. The motion or the noise made by something when it flaps. We could hear the *flap* of the shutters against the house. 2. Something that is attached at only one edge so that it may move. The cover over the opening of a pocket is called a flap. The part of an envelope that is folded down in closing it is a flap. *Noun.*
flap (flap) *verb,* **flapped, flapping;** *noun, plural* **flaps.**

flare 1. To burn with a sudden, very bright light. The match *flared* in the darkness and went out. 2. To break out with sudden or violent feeling. Her temper *flared* at the insulting remark he made. 3. To open or spread outward. Mary's new skirt *flares* from the waist. *Verb.*
—1. A sudden bright light. A flare usually lasts only a short time. 2. A fire or burst of light used as a signal or to give light. The captain of the ship in trouble sent up *flares* as a signal for help. *Noun.* ▲ Another word that sounds like this is **flair.**
flare (fler) *verb,* **flared, flaring;** *noun, plural* **flares.**

flash 1. A sudden, short burst of light or flame. The *flash* of lightning scared the puppy. 2. A very short period of time; instant. The fire engines were at the scene of the fire in a *flash. Noun.*
—1. To burst out in sudden light or fire. Lightning *flashed* in the sky. 2. To show suddenly and for a short time. Her eyes *flashed* with anger. 3. To come or move suddenly or quickly. The ambulance *flashed* by. The answer to the riddle *flashed* into his mind. *Verb.*
flash (flash) *noun, plural* **flashes;** *verb,* **flashed, flashing.**

flashlight An electric light that is powered by batteries and is small enough to be carried around.
flash·light (flash′līt′) *noun, plural* **flashlights.**

flask A small bottle that is used to hold liquids.
　flask (flask) *noun,* *plural* **flasks.**

flat¹ **1.** Smooth or even; level. It is easy to ride a bicycle on a *flat* road. The field is *flat* in some parts. **2.** Lying, placed, or stretched at full length; spread out. He was still *flat* on his back. **3.** Not very deep or thick; shallow. The food was served on a large *flat* tray. **4.** That cannot

Flask

be changed. The bus charges a *flat* rate for the trip. **5.** Without much interest or energy; dull. The singer gave a *flat* performance. **6.** Containing little or no air. We got a *flat* tire riding over the broken glass. *Adjective.*
—**1.** A flat part or surface. He hit the table with the *flat* of his hand. **2.** A tire that has little or no air. **3.** In music, a tone or note that is one half note below its natural pitch. **4.** A symbol (♭) that shows this tone or note. *Noun.*
—**1.** In a flat manner. The cat lay *flat* on the ground. **2.** Exactly; precisely. He ran the race in four minutes *flat.* **3.** Below the true pitch in music. She sang *flat. Adverb.*
　flat (flat) *adjective,* **flatter, flattest;** *noun,* *plural* **flats;** *adverb.*

flat² An apartment or set of rooms on one floor of a building.
　flat (flat) *noun,* *plural* **flats.**

flatcar A railroad car that has a floor but no roof or sides. It is used for carrying freight.
　flat·car (flat′kär′) *noun,* *plural* **flatcars.**

flatfish A fish that has a flattened body. A flatfish has both eyes on the upper side of the body. Flounder, sole, and halibut are flatfish.
　flat·fish (flat′fish′) *noun,* *plural* **flatfish** or **flatfishes.**

Flatfish

flatten To make or become flat or flatter. The cloth *flattened* out when it was ironed.
　flat·ten (flat′ən) *verb,* **flattened, flattening.**

flatter **1.** To praise too much or insincerely. He *flattered* her by saying that she was the most beautiful girl in the world. **2.** To show as more attractive than is actually true. That picture *flatters* him.
　flat·ter (flat′ər) *verb,* **flattered, flattering.**

flavor **1.** A particular taste. Adding pepper to the stew will give it a spicy *flavor.* **2.** A special or main quality. The speaker's personal experiences as a policeman added *flavor* to the lecture. *Noun.*
—To give flavor or taste to. Mother *flavored* the apple pie with cinnamon. *Verb.*
　fla·vor (flā′vər) *noun,* *plural* **flavors;** *verb,* **flavored, flavoring.**

flavoring Something added to food or drink to give flavor. Jane added lemon *flavoring* to the cookies.
　fla·vor·ing (flā′vər ing) *noun,* *plural* **flavorings.**

flaw A scratch, crack, or other defect. There is a *flaw* in that glass vase. That young man's selfishness is a *flaw* in his character.
　flaw (flô) *noun,* *plural* **flaws.**

flax A fiber that comes from the stem of a certain plant. This fiber is spun into thread, and the thread is used to make linen cloth. Flax can also be used to make rope and rugs.
　flax (flaks) *noun.*

flea An insect without wings. Fleas feed on the blood of human beings, dogs, cats, and other animals. A flea can sometimes carry disease by giving it to the person or animal it is living on. ▲ Another word that sounds like this is **flee.**
　flea (flē) *noun,* *plural* **fleas.**

Flax

fled The thief stole the jewelry and *fled* from the house.
　fled (fled) *verb.*

at; āpe; cär; end; mē; it; īce; hot; ōld;
fôrk; wood; fōōl; oil; out; up; turn; sing;
thin; **this;** **hw** in white; **zh** in treasure.
ə stands for **a** in about, **e** in taken
i in pencil, **o** in lemon, and **u** in circus.

flee **1.** To run away. The robbers tried to *flee* across the park with the woman's purse. The family *fled* from the burning house. **2.** To move or pass away quickly. The days of my vacation *fled* by. ▲ Another word that sounds like this is **flea**.
flee (flē) *verb,* **fled, fleeing.**

fleece The coat of wool covering a sheep. *Noun.*
—To cut the fleece from. The farm hand used a pair of electric clippers to *fleece* the sheep. *Verb.*
fleece (flēs) *noun; verb,* **fleeced, fleecing.**

fleet¹ **1.** A group of warships under one command. The admiral ordered the *fleet* to sail. **2.** Any group of ships, airplanes, or cars. My uncle owns a *fleet* of taxicabs. The *fleet* of fishing boats left port before dawn for the day's work.
fleet (flēt) *noun, plural* **fleets.**

fleet² Fast; swift. The deer is a very *fleet* animal.
fleet (flēt) *adjective,* **fleeter, fleetest.**

fleeting Passing very quickly; very brief. The woman had only a *fleeting* look at the car because it drove by her so fast.
fleet·ing (flē′ting) *adjective.*

flesh **1.** The soft part of the body that covers the bones and is covered by skin. **2.** The soft part of fruit or vegetables that can be eaten.
flesh (flesh) *noun.*

fleshy Plump; fat. We eat the *fleshy* part of a banana.
flesh·y (flesh′ē) *adjective,* **fleshier, fleshiest.**

flew The bird *flew* away as soon as it saw the cat creeping up on it. Look up **fly** for more information. ▲ Other words that sound like this are **flu** and **flue**.
flew (flo͞o) *verb.*

flex To bend. The baseball pitcher *flexed* his throwing arm often to keep it loose.
flex (fleks) *verb,* **flexed, flexing.**

flexible Able to bend without breaking; not stiff. Rubber is a *flexible* material.
flex·i·ble (flek′sə bəl) *adjective.*

flick A light, quick snap. Jim turned the lock on the front door with a *flick* of the wrist. *Noun.*
—**1.** To hit or remove with a quick, light snap. She *flicked* the crumbs off the table before serving the dessert. **2.** To make a light, quick movement. Bob *flicked* a string in front of the cat to get her to chase it. *Verb.*
flick (flik) *noun, plural* **flicks;** *verb,* **flicked, flicking.**

flicker¹ **1.** To burn with an unsteady or wavering light. The candles *flickered* in the breeze from the open window. **2.** To move back and forth with a quick, unsteady movement. Shadows from the leaves of the trees *flickered* on the barn door. *Verb.*
—**1.** An unsteady or wavering light. The *flicker* of the firelight made strange shadows on the wall. **2.** A quick, unsteady movement. We watched the *flicker* of the snake's tongue. *Noun.*
flick·er (flik′ər) *verb,* **flickered, flickering;** *noun, plural* **flickers.**

flicker² A North American woodpecker. It has yellow markings on its wings and tail.
flick·er (flik′ər) *noun, plural* **flickers.**

flied The batter *flied* to left field. Look up **fly** for more information.
flied (flīd) *verb.*

flier A person or thing that flies. The eagle is a powerful *flier.* This word is also spelled **flyer**.
fli·er (flī′ər) *noun, plural* **fliers.**

flies More than one fly. Look up **fly** for more information.
flies (flīz) *noun plural.*

Flicker

flight¹ **1.** Movement through the air with the use of wings; flying. We watched the graceful *flight* of the gull. **2.** The distance or course traveled by a bird or aircraft. It is a long *flight* from the United States to the Soviet Union. **3.** A group of things flying through the air together. We watched a *flight* of birds heading south for the winter. **4.** A trip in an airplane. The senator has a ticket on the five o'clock *flight* to Washington, D.C. **5.** A set of stairs or steps between floors or landings of a building. Steve had to walk up four *flights* of stairs to get to his apartment because the elevator wasn't working.
flight (flīt) *noun, plural* **flights.**

flight² The act of running away; escape. Our shouts put the robber to *flight*.
flight (flīt) *noun, plural* **flights.**

flimsy Without strength; light and thin; frail. Helen felt cold in the cool night air because she had on a *flimsy* summer blouse. Bill's parents didn't believe his *flimsy* excuse for being late.
flim·sy (flim′zē) *adjective,* **flimsier, flimsiest.**

flinch To draw back from something that is painful, dangerous, or unpleasant. Charlie *flinched* when the doctor gave him the flu shot.
flinch (flinch) *verb,* **flinched, flinching.**

fling To throw or move suddenly and with force. Jack always *flings* his books and coat on his bed. *Verb.*
—**1.** A throw. The boy gave the pebble a *fling* and it landed in the pond. **2.** A time of doing exactly what one pleases. After graduating from college, Mary went to Europe and had a *fling* before looking for a job at home. *Noun.*
fling (fling) *verb,* **flung, flinging;** *noun, plural* **flings.**

flint A very hard, gray stone that makes sparks when struck against steel. Before the invention of matches, flint was used to light fires.
flint (flint) *noun, plural* **flints.**

flintlock An old-fashioned gun. In a flint-lock, flint is struck against steel to make sparks that set the gunpowder on fire.
flint·lock (flint′lok′) *noun, plural* **flintlocks.**

Flintlock

flip To toss or move with a quick, jerking motion. Tom and Nat decided to *flip* a coin to see who would go first. Ed *flipped* the pages of the book until he came to the part he was looking for. *Verb.*
—A toss. The argument between the boys was decided by a *flip* of a coin. *Noun.*
flip (flip) *verb,* **flipped, flipping;** *noun, plural* **flips.**

flipper **1.** A broad, flat limb on a seal, turtle, penguin, or other animal. Flippers are used for swimming and moving along on land. **2.** One of a pair of rubber shoes shaped like a duck's feet. Flippers are worn to make swimming or skin diving easier.
flip·per (flip′ər) *noun, plural* **flippers.**

flirt To act romantic in a playful way. The

pretty girl liked to *flirt* with every boy she met.
flirt (flurt) *verb,* **flirted, flirting.**

flit To move quickly and lightly. We watched the butterflies *flit* among the flowers.
flit (flit) *verb,* **flitted, flitting.**

Float

float **1.** To rest on top of water or other liquid. In swimming class Lucy learned how to *float* on her back. **2.** To move along slowly in the air or on water. They *floated* down the river on a raft. *Verb.*
—**1.** Anything that rests on top of water. A raft anchored on the edge of the swimming area in a lake is a float. **2.** A low, flat platform on wheels that carries an exhibit in a parade. *Noun.*
float (flōt) *verb,* **floated, floating;** *noun, plural* **floats.**

flock **1.** A group of animals of one kind that is herded or gathered together. The farmer tends his *flock* of sheep. We saw a *flock* of geese flying south. **2.** A large number or group. A *flock* of newspaper reporters crowded around the President after he gave his speech. The minister gave a sermon every Sunday morning to the faithful members of his *flock. Noun.*
—To move or gather as a group. People always *flock* to the beaches during the hot summer weather. *Verb.*
flock (flok) *noun, plural* **flocks;** *verb,* **flocked, flocking.**

at; āpe; cär; end; mē; it; īce; hot; ōld;
fôrk; wood; fo͞ol; oil; out; up; turn; sing;
thin; this; hw in white; zh in treasure.
ə stands for a in about, e in taken
i in pencil, o in lemon, and u in circus.

249

floe A mass or sheet of floating ice. ▲ Another word that sounds like this is **flow**.
floe (flō) *noun, plural* **floes.**

Floe

flood **1.** A great flow of water over dry land. The people who lived in the river valley feared a *flood* because there was a lot of heavy rain. **2.** A great flow of anything. The girl told all her problems to her friend in a *flood* of words mixed with tears. *Noun.*
—**1.** To cover with water. The town was *flooded* when the dam broke. **2.** To fill or overwhelm. The baseball field was *flooded* with light for the night game. *Verb.*
flood (flud) *noun, plural* **floods;** *verb,* **flooded, flooding.**

floor **1.** The part of a room that a person walks or stands on. The kitchen *floor* is covered with tiles. **2.** Any surface that is like a floor. The ship sank to the ocean *floor.* **3.** The story of a building. Mother's office is on the second *floor* of the building. *Noun.*
—**1.** To cover with a floor. Dad decided to *floor* the basement with cement. **2.** To knock down. The boxer *floored* the other fighter in the sixth round. *Verb.*
floor (flôr) *noun, plural* **floors;** *verb,* **floored, flooring.**

flop **1.** To drop or fall heavily. John was so tired he couldn't wait to get home and *flop* into bed. **2.** To move around or flap loosely. The dog's ears *flopped* around its face when it ran. **3.** To fail completely. The new restaurant *flopped* after being open for only a month. *Verb.*
—**1.** The act or sound of dropping or falling heavily. The seal jumped up to catch a fish and landed in the water with a *flop.* **2.** A complete failure. The new play was such a

flop it closed after the first performance. *Noun.*
flop (flop) *verb,* **flopped, flopping;** *noun, plural* **flops.**

Florida A state in the southeastern United States. Its capital is Tallahassee.
Flor·i·da (flôr′ə də *or* flor′ə də) *noun.*

▲ **Florida** is a Spanish word that means "flowery." Ponce de Leon landed in Florida during the Spanish holiday of flowers. He named the place from the name of the holiday.

florist A person who sells flowers and indoor plants.
flo·rist (flôr′ist) *noun, plural* **florists.**

flounder[1] To struggle or stumble about. Henry and his friends went hiking and had to *flounder* about in mud that came way above their ankles.
floun·der (floun′dər) *verb,* **floundered, floundering.**

flounder[2] A flatfish that lives in salt water. It is eaten as food.
floun·der (floun′dər) *noun, plural* **flounders** or **flounder.**

flour A fine meal that is made by grinding and sifting wheat, rye, or other grains. Flour is used to make bread and cake.
flour (flour) *noun, plural* **flours.**

flourish **1.** To grow or develop strongly and with vigor. Tomatoes will *flourish* in a very sunny garden if they are given lots of water. A highly developed civilization *flourished* in Greece thousands of years ago. **2.** To wave in the air boldly. The guard *flourished* a gun at the escaping prisoners. *Verb.*
—A showy or bold action or sound. The leading actor walked on stage with a *flourish.* The trumpets announced the coming of the king with a *flourish. Noun.*
flour·ish (flur′ish) *verb,* **flourished, flourishing;** *noun, plural* **flourishes.**

flow **1.** To move along steadily in a stream. A stream *flows* past the back of our house. Electricity *flows* through wires. The crowd *flowed* out of the football stadium when the game was over. **2.** To hang or fall loosely. Mary's long hair *flowed* to her waist. *Verb.*
—**1.** The act of flowing. The *flow* of a river can be controlled by building a dam. **2.** Something that flows. Every morning the highways going into the city are filled with a steady *flow* of cars. *Noun.* ▲ Another word that sounds like this is **floe.**
flow (flō) *verb,* **flowed, flowing;** *noun, plural* **flows.**

flower 1. The part of a plant that has colored petals; blossom. The flower contains seeds that are able to produce new plants. 2. The finest part or time. The adventures of King Arthur and his knights took place when knighthood was in *flower. Noun.*
—To produce flowers; blossom. Cherry trees *flower* in the early spring. *Verb.*
flow·er (flou′ər) *noun, plural* **flowers;** *verb,* **flowered, flowering.**

flown The bird had *flown* out of the cage. Look up **fly** for more information.
flown (flōn) *verb.*

flu A disease that is like a very bad cold. It is caused by a virus and can easily spread from one person to another. This word is a short form of **influenza,** which is the full name for this disease. ▲ Other words that sound like this are **flew** and **flue.**
flu (flo͞o) *noun, plural* **flus.**

flue A passage in a chimney that draws the smoke from a fireplace out of the room and into the outside air. ▲ Other words that sound like this are **flew** and **flu.**
flue (flo͞o) *noun, plural* **flues.**

fluff A soft, light material. The baby's hair is just like *fluff. Noun.*
—To pat or puff into a soft, light mass. Alice *fluffed* up the cushions on the couch before the guests arrived. *Verb.*
fluff (fluf) *noun; verb,* **fluffed, fluffing.**

fluffy Covered with or like fluff. Dad took us to the farm to see the *fluffy* baby chicks.
fluff·y (fluf′ē) *adjective,* **fluffier, fluffiest.**

fluid A gas or liquid. Fluids can flow easily. Air and water are fluids. *Noun.*
—Flowing; not solid. Water is *fluid. Adjective.*
flu·id (flo͞o′id) *noun, plural* **fluids;** *adjective.*

flung Peter *flung* the glass against the wall in anger. Look up **fling** for more information.
flung (flung) *verb.*

flurry A sudden outburst or stir. There is always a *flurry* of excitement on Christmas morning when the children come down to open their presents. Today's weather report calls for snow *flurries.*
flur·ry (flur′ē) *noun, plural* **flurries.**

flush¹ 1. To turn red or cause to turn red; blush. The woman's face *flushed* when she could not remember her guest's last name. 2. To flow or rush suddenly. Water *flushed* through the pipes. 3. To empty or wash with a sudden rush of water. The city sent some workmen to *flush* out the drain on the corner that was clogged with leaves and litter. *Verb.*
—1. A reddish color or glow. Ruth came in from skiing with a healthy *flush* on her cheeks. 2. A sudden rush or flow. Ted turned on the water for the garden hose and a *flush* of water poured all over the walk. *Noun.*
flush (flush) *verb,* **flushed, flushing;** *noun,* **plural flushes.**

flush² Even or level. The orange juice was *flush* with the rim of the glass. We tried to hang the second picture on the wall *flush* with the first one.
flush (flush) *adjective; adverb.*

fluster To make embarrassed or nervous; confuse. It *flustered* Tim and Sarah to be the only couple on the dance floor. *Verb.*
—Nervous confusion. The bridegroom was in a *fluster* the morning of the wedding. *Noun.*
flus·ter (flus′tər) *verb,* **flustered, flustering;** *noun.*

flute A long, thin musical instrument. A person plays a flute by holding it out to one side and blowing across a hole at one end. The player makes different notes by covering the holes with his fingers or by pushing down keys that cover the holes.
flute (flo͞ot) *noun, plural* **flutes.**

Flute

flutter To move or fly with quick, light movements. The flag *fluttered* in the breeze. Butterflies *fluttered* among the flowers. *Verb.*
—1. A quick, light movement. We heard a *flutter* of wings and hoped it might be the wild geese returning to their nests. 2. A state of excitement or confusion. The appearance of the movie star caused a *flutter* among his fans. *Noun.*
flut·ter (flut′ər) *verb,* **fluttered, fluttering;** *noun, plural* **flutters.**

at; āpe; cär; end; mē; it; īce; hot; ōld; fôrk; wood; fo͞ol; oil; out; up; turn; sing; thin; this; hw in white; zh in treasure.
ə stands for a in about, e in taken i in pencil, o in lemon, and u in circus.

fly¹ One of a large group of insects that have two wings. Houseflies, mosquitoes, and gnats are flies.
fly (flī) *noun, plural* **flies.**

fly² **1.** To move through the air with wings. Some birds that live in cold areas *fly* south for the winter. **2.** To pilot or travel in an aircraft. My uncle *flew* a bomber during the war. Arthur *flew* to Los Angeles last night to visit his grandmother. **3.** To move or float in the air. The ocean spray *flew* into our faces. The boy went to the park to *fly* his kite. A flag *flew* from the ship's mast. **4.** To go swiftly. The mother *flew* up the stairs when she heard her baby crying. **5.** To hit a ball high into the air in baseball. The batter *flied* to left field. *Verb.*
—**1.** A flap of material that covers buttons or a zipper on a piece of clothing. Men's trousers have a *fly* in front. **2.** A baseball hit high into the air. The batter hit a *fly* to center field. *Noun.*
fly (flī) *verb,* **flew, flown, flying** (*for definitions 1–4*) or **flied, flying** (*for definition 5*); *noun, plural* **flies.**

flycatcher A bird that flies after insects and catches them for food.
fly·catch·er (flī′-kach′ər) *noun, plural* **flycatchers.**

flyer A person or thing that flies. This word is usually spelled **flier.** Look up **flier** for more information.

flying fish A saltwater fish that has fins like wings. The flying fish uses its fins to leap into the air and glide above the surface of the water.

Flycatcher

Flying Fish

flying saucer An unidentified flying object that is in the shape of a saucer. Some people think that flying saucers come from outer space.

flywheel A heavy wheel that keeps an engine running at an even speed.
fly·wheel (flī′hwēl′) *noun, plural* **flywheels.**

foal A young horse, donkey, zebra, or similar animal.
foal (fōl) *noun, plural* **foals.**

foam A mass of bubbles. *Foam* forms on waves as they break against the shore. *Noun.*
—To form or flow in a mass of bubbles. The beer *foamed* when it was poured into the glass. The rushing stream *foamed* over the rocks. *Verb.*
foam (fōm) *noun; verb,* **foamed, foaming.**

foam rubber A firm, spongy rubber that is used for seats, mattresses, and pillows.

focus **1.** The point at which light rays meet after being bent by a lens. **2.** The distance from the lens to the point where the rays meet. The eye of a farsighted person has a longer *focus* than the eye of a person with normal eyesight. **3.** A center of activity or interest. The speaker was the *focus* of attention for the audience. *Noun.*
—**1.** To bring to a meeting point or focus. A magnifying glass can be used to *focus* the sun's rays on a piece of paper and start a fire. **2.** To bring into focus so as to make a clear image. The photographer *focused* the camera before taking the picture. **3.** To fix or direct. The wedding guests *focused* all their attention on the bride and groom. *Verb.*
fo·cus (fō′kəs) *noun, plural* **focuses;** *verb,* **focused, focusing.**

fodder Food for horses, cows, and other farm animals. Hay and cornstalks are fodder.
fod·der (fod′ər) *noun, plural* **fodders.**

foe An enemy. The knight said to the stranger, "Are you friend or *foe?*"
foe (fō) *noun, plural* **foes.**

fog **1.** A cloud of small drops of water close to the earth's surface. The thick *fog* made driving dangerous. **2.** A state of confusion. Before Father has his coffee in the morning, he walks around the house in a *fog. Noun.*
—To cover or become covered with fog. We had trouble driving home because the heavy mist had *fogged* the road. *Verb.*
fog (fôg) *noun, plural* **fogs;** *verb,* **fogged, fogging.**

foggy **1.** Full of or hidden by fog; misty. It was such a *foggy* evening we could not see the tops of the tallest buildings. **2.** Confused or unclear. John had only a *foggy* idea of what was wrong with his car.
fog·gy (fôg′ē) *adjective,* **foggier, foggiest.**

person or thing. The sheriff dragged the out-law off by *force*. Ruth had to use *force* to open the jar. **3.** A group of people who work together. The police *force* in this city is one of the best in the country. **4.** Something that moves a body or stops or changes its motion. The *force* of gravity causes things to fall when they are dropped. *Noun.*
—**1.** To make do something. The robber *forced* the banker to open the safe and give him the money. **2.** To break open. Jim *forced* the lock on his suitcase because he had lost the key. *Verb.*
> **force** (fôrs) *noun, plural* **forces;** *verb,* **forced, forcing.**

forceps A small tool for gripping and holding things. Forceps are used by doctors and dentists in operations.
> **for·ceps** (fôr′seps) *noun, plural* **forceps.**

ford A shallow place where a river, stream, or other body of water may be crossed. *Noun.*
—To cross at a shallow place. The riders *forded* the river. *Verb.*
> **ford** (fôrd) *noun, plural* **fords;** *verb,* **forded, fording.**

fore At or toward the front. He stood at the *fore* part of the ship. Look up the word **aft** for a picture of this. ▲ Other words that sound like this are **for** and **four.**
> **fore** (fôr) *adjective.*

forearm The part of the arm between the elbow and the wrist.
> **fore·arm** (fôr′ärm′) *noun, plural* **forearms.**

forecast To tell what will or may happen; predict. The gypsy said that she had the power to *forecast* the future. *Verb.*
—A statement that tells what will or may happen; prediction. Let's listen to the weath-er *forecast* to find out if it's going to rain tomorrow. *Noun.*
> **fore·cast** (fôr′kast′) *verb,* **forecast** or **forecasted, forecasting;** *noun, plural* **forecasts.**

forefather An ancestor. His *forefathers* came to America during colonial times.
> **fore·fa·ther** (fôr′fä′thər) *noun, plural* **forefathers.**

forefinger The finger next to the thumb.
> **fore·fin·ger** (fôr′fing′gər) *noun, plural* **forefingers.**

forefoot One of the front feet of an animal that has four feet.
> **fore·foot** (fôr′foot′) *noun, plural* **forefeet.**

foregone Known or decided ahead of time. Carl's election as captain of the basketball team was a *foregone* conclusion.
> **fore·gone** (fôr′gôn) *adjective.*

foreground The part of a picture or view nearest to a person's eye. That painting shows a small village in the *foreground* and snow-covered mountains in the background.
> **fore·ground** (fôr′ground′) *noun, plural* **fore-grounds.**

The boy is in the **foreground** and the buildings are in the background.

forehead The part of the face above the eyes.
> **fore·head** (fôr′id *or* fôr′hed′) *noun, plural* **foreheads.**

foreign **1.** Of or from another country. My neighbor from France speaks English with a *foreign* accent. **2.** Outside a person's own country. Have you ever visited any *foreign* countries? **3.** Having to do with other coun-tries. The President has many people to ad-vise him on what the country's *foreign* policy should be.
> **for·eign** (fôr′ən) *adjective.*

foreigner A person who is from another country.
> **for·eign·er** (fôr′ə nər) *noun, plural* **foreign-ers.**

foreleg One of the front legs of an animal that has four legs.
> **fore·leg** (fôr′leg′) *noun, plural* **forelegs.**

foreman **1.** A workman who is in charge of a group of workers. Ron is the *foreman* at the factory. **2.** The chairman of a jury. The *fore-man* announced the verdict of the jury.
> **fore·man** (fôr′mən) *noun, plural* **foremen.**

foremost First in position or importance. The judge was considered the *foremost* citi-zen of the town.
> **fore·most** (fôr′mōst′) *adjective.*

---

at; āpe; cär; end; mē; it; īce; hot; ōld;
fôrk; wood; fōōl; oil; out; up; turn; sing;
thin; **th**is; **hw** in white; **zh** in treasure.
ə stands for **a** in about, **e** in taken
i in pencil, **o** in lemon, and **u** in circus.

forerunner A person or thing that comes before. A brisk wind and a dark sky are often *forerunners* of a storm.
fore·run·ner (fôr′run′ər) *noun, plural* **fore-runners.**

foresaw We *foresaw* the difficulty of climbing the mountain.
fore·saw (fôr sô′) *verb.*

foresee To know or see ahead of time. No one can really *foresee* what the world will be like one hundred years from now.
fore·see (fôr sē′) *verb,* **foresaw, foreseen, foreseeing.**

foreseen We should have *foreseen* that we did not have enough gasoline for the trip.
fore·seen (fôr sēn′) *verb.*

foresight Care or thought for the future. Emily showed *foresight* in bringing along an umbrella.
fore·sight (fôr′sīt′) *noun.*

forest Many trees and plants covering a large area of land; woods.
for·est (fôr′ist) *noun, plural* **forests.**

foretell To tell ahead of time; predict. The old woman said she could *foretell* a person's future by looking at the stars.
fore·tell (fôr tel′) *verb,* **foretold, foretelling.**

foretold The prophet *foretold* the king's death.
fore·told (fôr tōld′) *verb.*

forever **1.** Throughout all time; without ever coming to an end. No one can expect to live *forever.* **2.** Without letting up; always; constantly. That girl is *forever* complaining about something.
for·ev·er (fə rev′ər) *adverb.*

forfeit To lose or have to give up because of some fault or mistake. Jane *forfeited* the tennis match because she was sick and couldn't play. *Verb.*
—Something lost because of some fault or mistake. *Noun.*
for·feit (fôr′fit) *verb,* **forfeited, forfeiting;** *noun, plural* **forfeits.**

forgave Tom's grandmother *forgave* him for accidentally breaking her vase.
for·gave (fər gāv′) *verb.*

forge¹ A furnace or hearth in which metal is heated. The fire softens the metal so that it can be hammered into shape. A blacksmith uses a forge to make horseshoes. *Noun.*
—**1.** To heat in a forge until very hot and then hammer into shape. Blacksmiths used to *forge* iron into tools as well as horseshoes. **2.** To make or form. The United Nations *forged* a peace agreement between the two

countries that were at war. **3.** To copy in order to trick or cheat. The police caught the man trying to *forge* someone else's signature on the check. *Verb.*
forge (fôrj) *noun, plural* **forges;** *verb,* **forged, forging.**

Forge

forge² To move forward slowly but steadily. The ferry *forged* through the rough waters of the bay.
forge (fôrj) *verb,* **forged, forging.**

forget **1.** To not be able to remember. Harry wrote down Joan's telephone number so he would not *forget* it. **2.** To fail to think of or do. I *forgot* to tell my parents that I would be late for dinner.
for·get (fər get′) *verb,* **forgot, forgotten** or **forgot, forgetting.**

forgetful Likely to forget; having a poor memory. Tom is so *forgetful* that he can never remember where he has left his glasses.
for·get·ful (fər get′fəl) *adjective.*

forget-me-not A small blue or white flower. The forget-me-not grows in clusters on a low plant.
for·get-me-not (fər-get′mē not′) *noun, plural* **forget-me-nots.**

forgive To stop blaming or feeling anger toward; pardon or excuse. John knew his father would *forgive* him for breaking the window. After Kate apologized, her mother *forgave* her rude remark.
for·give (fər giv′) *verb,* **forgave, forgiven, forgiving.**

Forget-me-not

forgiven Margaret has *forgiven* her brother for tearing her sweater.
for·giv·en (fər giv′ən) *verb.*

forgot Phyllis was late for school because she *forgot* to set the alarm clock to wake her up. Look up **forget** for more information.
for·got (fər got′) *verb.*

forgotten Ruth realized that she had *forgotten* her keys. Look up **forget** for more information.
for·got·ten (fər got′ən) *verb.*

fork 1. A tool with a handle at one end and two or more thin pointed parts at the other. One kind of fork is used for eating food. Another very large fork is used for pitching hay. 2. The place where something divides. Turn left at the *fork* in the road. *Noun.*
—1. To lift or pitch with a fork. The farmer *forked* hay into the wagon. 2. To divide into branches. The river *forks* two miles upstream. *Verb.*
fork (fôrk) *noun, plural* **forks;** *verb,* **forked, forking.**

form 1. The outside of something; shape. Ed could see the dim *form* of the bridge through the fog. 2. Kind or type. The tree is one *form* of plant. 3. A way of behaving or of doing something. Dick worked to improve his *form* in diving. 4. A sheet of paper with blanks that are to be filled in. The man who was applying for a job filled out a *form. Noun.*
—1. To make or shape. The artist *formed* a woman's head out of clay. The robbers *formed* a plan to rob the bank. 2. To take shape. The water dripping from the roof *formed* into icicles. 3. To make up. Students *formed* the biggest part of the crowd waiting to get into the concert. *Verb.*
form (fôrm) *noun, plural* **forms;** *verb,* **formed, forming.**

formal 1. Very stiff and proper. The teacher's manner was so *formal* that the students were a little afraid of him. 2. Following strict custom or ceremony. The President gave the ambassador a *formal* welcome. 3. Done or made with authority; official. A lawyer had to write a *formal* contract when we bought our house. *Adjective.*
—A formal dress or a formal dance or other event. *Noun.*
for·mal (fôr′məl) *adjective; noun, plural* **formals.**

formation 1. The process of forming or making. The *formation* of ice from water requires a temperature of less than thirty-two degrees. 2. Something formed or made.

Scientists agree that some rock *formations* are billions of years old. 3. The way something is formed. The school band was told to line up in parade *formation.*
for·ma·tion (fôr mā′shən) *noun, plural* **formations.**

former 1. The first of two. Jack and Bill are both on the football team; the *former* (Jack) is a guard and the latter (Bill) is a tackle. 2. Belonging to or happening in the past; earlier. In *former* times, people used fireplaces to heat their houses.
for·mer (fôr′mər) *adjective.*

formerly In time past; once. Trains were *formerly* pulled by steam locomotives.
for·mer·ly (fôr′mər lē) *adverb.*

formula 1. A set method of doing something. There is no real *formula* for making friends. 2. A set order of letters, symbols, or numbers that is used to express a rule or principle. H_2O is the *formula* for water.
for·mu·la (fôr′myə lə) *noun, plural* **formulas.**

forsake To give up or leave. He has decided to *forsake* the city and live on a farm.
for·sake (fôr sāk′) *verb,* **forsook, forsaken, forsaking.**

forsaken Bob took in a stray puppy whose owners had *forsaken* it.
for·sak·en (fôr sā′kən) *verb.*

forsook Jill's friends *forsook* her just when she needed them most.
for·sook (fôr sook′) *verb.*

forsythia A shrub that has yellow flowers shaped like little bells. The flowers grow in clusters along the stem and bloom in the early spring.
for·syth·i·a (fôr sith′ē ə) *noun, plural* **forsythias.**

fort A strong building or area that can be defended against an enemy.
fort (fôrt) *noun, plural* **forts.**

forth 1. Forward. From that day *forth*, the man was never lonely again. 2. Out into view. The buds on our rosebush burst

Forsythia

at; āpe; cär; end; mē; it; īce; hot; ōld; fôrk; wood; fōōl; oil; out; up; turn; sing; thin; this; hw in white; zh in treasure. ə stands for **a** in about, **e** in taken **i** in pencil, **o** in lemon, and **u** in circus.

257

forth all at once. ▲ Another word that sounds like this is **fourth.**
forth (fôrth) *adverb.*

fortieth **1.** Next after the thirty-ninth. **2.** One of forty equal parts; ¹/₄₀.
for·ti·eth (fôr′tē ith) *adjective; noun, plural* **fortieths.**

fortify **1.** To protect. Two thousand years ago the Chinese built a wall on their northern border to *fortify* themselves against invaders. **2.** To make strong or stronger. This breakfast cereal is *fortified* with vitamins and iron.
for·ti·fy (fôr′tə fī′) *verb,* **fortified, fortifying.**

fortress A strong place that can be defended against attack; fort.
for·tress (fôr′tris) *noun, plural* **fortresses.**

fortunate Lucky. Sarah is very *fortunate* to have won first prize in the contest.
for·tu·nate (fôr′chə nit) *adjective.*

fortune **1.** Something either good or bad that will happen to a person. The gypsy in the circus said she could tell my *fortune.* **2.** Luck. It was Donna's good *fortune* to find a summer job she liked at the first place she looked. **3.** Great wealth; riches. The queen has a *fortune* in jewels.
for·tune (fôr′chən) *noun, plural* **fortunes.**

fortuneteller A person who claims to be able to tell another person's fortune.
for·tune·tell·er (fôr′chən tel′ər) *noun, plural* **fortunetellers.**

forty Four times ten; 40.
for·ty (fôr′tē) *noun, plural* **forties;** *adjective.*

forum **1.** The public square of an ancient Roman city. All business and other important activities took place in the forum. **2.** A meeting to discuss issues or questions of public interest. An open *forum* was held at the school to discuss the plans for the new library.
fo·rum (fôr′əm) *noun, plural* **forums.**

forward Toward what is in front or ahead. The soldier stepped *forward* to receive the medal. We are looking *forward* to our vacation. This word is also spelled **forwards.** *Adverb.*
—**1.** At or toward the front. John had a *forward* seat on the plane. The football player made a *forward* pass. **2.** Bold or rude. Linda is a *forward* girl who talks back to her teacher. *Adjective.*
—To send ahead to a new address. Jane's parents *forwarded* the mail she got during the summer to her address at camp. *Verb.*
—A player whose position is near the front lines in certain games. Dave played *forward* on the basketball team. *Noun.*

for·ward (fôr′wərd) *adverb; adjective; verb,* **forwarded, forwarding;** *noun, plural* **forwards.**

fossil The remains or traces of an animal or plant that lived long ago. The boys found *fossils* of ancient sea animals in some rocks.
fos·sil (fos′əl) *noun, plural* **fossils.**

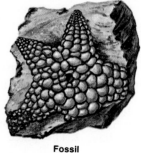
Fossil

foster To help the growth or development of. Tom's parents tried to *foster* his interest in music by giving him piano lessons. *Verb.*
—Giving or receiving care in a family without being related by birth or adoption. The city has a special department that tries to find *foster* parents for children who have no homes of their own. *Adjective.*
fos·ter (fôs′tər) *verb,* **fostered, fostering;** *adjective.*

fought Bob *fought* in a boxing match. Look up **fight** for more information.
fought (fôt) *verb.*

foul **1.** Very unpleasant or dirty. There was a *foul* odor in the air when the sewer pipes broke. I would never go swimming in that river because the water is *foul.* **2.** Cloudy, rainy, or stormy. *Foul* weather delayed the ship. **3.** Very bad; evil. The police are investigating a *foul* crime that occurred in our neighborhood last night. **4.** Breaking the rules; unfair. An umpire or referee is used in sports to apply the rules and prevent any *foul* play. **5.** Outside the foul line in a baseball game. The batter hit a *foul* ball. *Adjective.*
—**1.** A breaking of rules. The basketball player committed a *foul* by knocking down another player. **2.** A baseball that is hit outside the foul line. *Noun.*
—**1.** To make dirty. The factory *fouled* the lake by pumping all its garbage and waste into it. **2.** To tangle or become tangled. The boy *fouled* the fishing line in the bushes along the shore. **3.** To hit a foul ball in baseball. The batter *fouled* the ball to the right of first base. *Verb.* ▲ Another word that sounds like this is **fowl.**
foul (foul) *adjective,* **fouler, foulest;** *noun, plural* **fouls;** *verb,* **fouled, fouling.**

foul line Either of the two lines in baseball that go from home plate through first or third base to the limits of the playing field.

found¹   Janet *found* the watch she thought she had lost. Look up **find** for more information.
　found (found) *verb.*

found²   To start or bring into being; establish. The students worked together to *found* a science club.
　found (found) *verb,* **founded, founding.**

foundation   Something that serves as a base or support. The *foundation* of the old house was made of brick.
　foun·da·tion (foun dā′shən) *noun, plural* **foundations.**

foundry   A place where metal is melted and formed into different shapes.
　found·ry (foun′drē) *noun, plural* **foundries.**

fountain   **1.** A stream of water that is made to shoot up. Some fountains are used to drink from, and others are used only as decoration. **2.** The source of anything. That teacher is a real *fountain* of knowledge about American history.
　foun·tain (fount′ən) *noun, plural* **fountains.**

Fountain

fountain pen   A pen that has a little tube inside to hold and feed ink to the writing point.

four   One more than three; 4. ▲ Another word that sounds like this is **for.**
　four (fôr) *noun, plural* **fours;** *adjective.*

Four-H clubs   A group of organizations for young people. It teaches skill in farming and homemaking.
　Four-H clubs (fôr′āch′).

fourteen   Four more than ten; 14.
　four·teen (fôr′tēn′) *noun, plural* **fourteens;** *adjective.*

fourteenth   **1.** Next after the thirteenth. **2.** One of fourteen equal parts; ¹/₁₄.
　four·teenth (fôr′tēnth′) *adjective; noun, plural* **fourteenths.**

fourth   **1.** Next after the third. **2.** One of four equal parts; ¹/₄. ▲ Another word that sounds like this is **forth.**
　fourth (fôrth) *adjective; noun, plural* **fourths.**

fowl   **1.** One of a group of birds that are used for food. The chicken, turkey, and duck are kinds of fowl. **2.** Any bird. Andy likes to hunt pheasant and other wild *fowl.* ▲ Another word that sounds like this is **foul.**
　fowl (foul) *noun, plural* **fowl** or **fowls.**

fox   A wild animal that is something like a dog. A fox has a pointed nose and ears, a bushy tail, and thick fur.
　fox (foks) *noun, plural* **foxes.**

Fox

foxhound   A hound with a very sharp sense of smell. It is trained to hunt foxes. A foxhound has a tan, black, and white coat.
　fox·hound (foks′hound′) *noun, plural* **foxhounds.**

fraction   **1.** A part of a whole; small part. Only a *fraction* of the people watching the football game left before it was over. **2.** A number that is one or more of the equal parts of a whole. A fraction shows the division of one number by a second number.   ²/₃, ³/₄, and ¹/₁₆ are fractions.
　frac·tion (frak′shən) *noun, plural* **fractions.**

fracture   To crack or break. Steve *fractured* his ankle playing ice hockey. *Verb.*
　—A crack or break. Mary's *fracture* kept her in the hospital for two weeks. *Noun.*
　frac·ture (frak′chər) *verb,* **fractured, fracturing;** *noun, plural* **fractures.**

fragile   Easily broken; delicate. That china cup is very *fragile.*
　frag·ile (fraj′əl) *adjective.*

fragment   A part that is broken off; small piece. The boys found some *fragments* of Indian arrowheads in the woods behind our house.

at; āpe; cär; end; mē; it; īce; hot; ōld;
fôrk; wood; fōol; oil; out; up; turn; sing;
thin; this; hw in white; zh in treasure.
ə stands for a in about, e in taken
i in pencil, o in lemon, and u in circus.

frag·ment (frag′mənt) *noun, plural* **fragments.**

fragrance A sweet or pleasing smell. Roses have a beautiful *fragrance.*
  fra·grance (frā′grəns) *noun, plural* **fragrances.**

fragrant Having a sweet or pleasing smell. Ann was wearing a *fragrant* perfume.
  fra·grant (frā′grənt) *adjective.*

frail 1. Lacking in strength; weak. The child was too *frail* to take part in gym classes. 2. Easily broken or torn; delicate. That lace is very old and *frail.*
  frail (frāl) *adjective,* **frailer, frailest.**

frame 1. A structure that borders or supports something. The window *frame* needs painting. We put the painting in a *frame.* The *frame* of our house is made out of heavy wooden beams. 2. The way a person's body is formed. Joe has such a big *frame* he has trouble finding clothes to fit him. *Noun.*
—1. To set in a border. The painter *framed* his picture and sold it at an art show. 2. To draw up or make. The teacher *framed* his questions so that the pupils could easily understand them. *Verb.*
  frame (frām) *noun, plural* **frames;** *verb,* **framed, framing.**

framework A structure that gives shape or support to something. The *framework* of the building is steel.
  frame·work (frām′wurk′) *noun, plural* **frameworks.**

franc A coin of France, Belgium, Switzerland, and some other countries. ▲ Another word that sounds like this is **frank.**
  franc (frangk) *noun, plural* **francs.**

France A country in western Europe. Its capital is Paris.
  France (frans) *noun.*

frank Honest and open in expressing one's real thoughts and feelings. Let me be *frank* with you and tell you what I really think. ▲ Another word that sounds like this is **franc.**
  frank (frangk) *adjective,* **franker, frankest.**

frankfurter A reddish sausage made of beef or beef and pork. It is often served on a long roll with mustard and relish.
  frank·furt·er (frangk′fər tər) *noun, plural* **frankfurters.**

▲ The word **frankfurter** comes from a German word that means "of or from Frankfurt." Frankfurt is a city in Germany, and it is possible that this kind of sausage was first made in Frankfurt.

---

frantic Wildly excited by worry or fear. The mother was *frantic* when she lost her child in the crowded department store.
  fran·tic (fran′tik) *adjective.*

fraternity A social organization or club for men or boys. Some students at the university pay dues to belong to a *fraternity.*
  fra·ter·ni·ty (frə tur′nə tē) *noun, plural* **fraternities.**

fraud 1. A tricking of someone in order to cheat him. The salesman tried to sell fake diamonds and was arrested for *fraud.* 2. A person or thing that tricks or cheats. A man is a *fraud* if he practices medicine when he really isn't a doctor.
  fraud (frôd) *noun, plural* **frauds.**

fray To separate into loose threads. Many years of wear had *frayed* the cuffs of Sam's coat.
  fray (frā) *verb,* **frayed, fraying.**

freak 1. A person, animal, or plant that has not developed normally. A mouse with two tails would be a *freak.* 2. Anything odd or unusual. Heavy rain in a desert would be a real *freak.*
  freak (frēk) *noun, plural* **freaks.**

freckle A small brownish spot on the skin. Helen has bright red hair and *freckles.*
  freck·le (frek′əl) *noun, plural* **freckles.**

free 1. Having one's liberty; not under another's control. America became a *free* country in 1776 when it fought off English rule. 2. Not held back or confined. You are *free* to come and go as you like in the library. 3. Not troubled by something. My aunt lives a life that is *free* from care or worry. 4. Without cost. We received *free* tickets to the show. *Adjective.*
—Without cost. Children were admitted *free* to the theater. *Adverb.*
—To make or set free. The child *freed* the trapped animal. *Verb.*
  free (frē) *adjective,* **freer, freest;** *adverb;* *verb,* **freed, freeing.**

freedom 1. The condition of being free; liberty. The American colonists struggled for their *freedom.* 2. The condition of being able to move or act without being held back. Our dog has complete *freedom* of the house.
  free·dom (frē′dəm) *noun, plural* **freedoms.**

freeway A highway with more than two lanes and no toll charges. A freeway is used for fast and direct driving.
  free·way (frē′wā′) *noun, plural* **freeways.**

freeze 1. To harden because of the cold. When water *freezes,* it becomes ice. 2. To cover or become covered with ice; block with

ice. The cold weather *froze* the pipes in our house while we were on vacation. **3.** To make or become very cold. I almost *froze* last night waiting for the bus. **4.** To become fixed or motionless. Jack *froze* when he saw the snake two feet away from him. **5.** To damage or be damaged by cold or frost. The orange crop in Florida *froze* this winter.
    freeze (frēz) *verb,* **froze, frozen, freezing.**

freezer A refrigerator or part of a refrigerator used to freeze food quickly or to store food that is already frozen.
    freez·er (frē′zər) *noun, plural* **freezers.**

freight **1.** The carrying of goods by land, air, or water. **2.** The goods carried in this way; cargo. It took five hours to unload all the *freight* from the train.
    freight (frāt) *noun.*

freighter A ship used for carrying cargo.
    freight·er (frā′tər) *noun, plural* **freighters.**

French **1.** The people of France. **2.** The language of France. *Noun.*
    —Having to do with France, its people, or their language. *Adjective.*
    French (french) *noun; adjective.*

French fries Potatoes that are cut into thin strips and fried in deep fat until they are brown and crisp.

French horn A brass musical instrument. A French horn has a long, coiled tube that widens into the shape of a bell.

Frenchman A person who was born or is living in France.
    French·man (french′mən) *noun, plural* **Frenchmen.**

French Horn

frenzy Wild excitement. The people were in a *frenzy* to escape from the burning building.
    fren·zy (fren′zē) *noun, plural* **frenzies.**

frequency **1.** A happening again and again. The people were afraid to go out at night because of the *frequency* of robberies on the streets. **2.** The number of times something happens or takes place during a period of time. The *frequency* of a person's heartbeat is usually between sixty and ninety beats a minute.
    fre·quen·cy (frē′kwən sē) *noun, plural* **frequencies.**

frequent Happening often; taking place again and again. There are *frequent* thunder-storms in this area every summer. The campers made *frequent* visits to town to buy food and supplies.
    fre·quent (frē′kwənt) *adjective.*

fresh **1.** Newly done, made, or gathered. We put on a *fresh* coat of paint in the kitchen. I always buy *fresh* vegetables instead of canned or frozen ones. **2.** New; another. Don moved to South America to get a *fresh* start in life. **3.** Clean or refreshing. It was very stuffy in the room so we stepped outside for a breath of *fresh* air. **4.** Not salty. A lake has *fresh* water. **5.** Rude; impudent. She was kept after school for being *fresh* to the teacher.
    fresh (fresh) *adjective,* **fresher, freshest.**

freshman A student in the first year of high school or college.
    fresh·man (fresh′mən) *noun, plural* **fresh-men.**

freshwater Living in fresh water. The trout is a *freshwater* fish.
    fresh·wa·ter (fresh′wô′tər) *adjective.*

friar A man who belongs to a religious order of the Roman Catholic Church.
    fri·ar (frī′ər) *noun, plural* **friars.**

friction **1.** The rubbing of one thing against another. The *friction* of the rope in Mike's hand gave him a burn. **2.** A force that resists movement between two surfaces that are touching one another. The *friction* between two parts of a machine can be reduced by oiling them. **3.** Anger or ill will. There was much *friction* between the two nations.
    fric·tion (frik′shən) *noun.*

Friday The sixth day of the week.
    Fri·day (frī′dē *or* frī′dā) *noun, plural* **Fridays.**

▲ **Friday** comes from an earlier English word that meant "Frigg's day." People who lived in England long ago believed that Frigg was the queen of the gods of the sky.

---

fried I *fried* an egg for my breakfast this morning. Look up **fry** for more information.
    fried (frīd) *verb.*

friend A person whom one knows and likes well. The two boys have been good *friends* since they met at school last year.
    friend (frend) *noun, plural* **friends.**

at; āpe; cär; end; mē; it; īce; hot; ōld;
fôrk; wood; fool; oil; out; up; turn; sing;
thin; this; hw in white; zh in treasure.
ə stands for a in about, e in taken
i in pencil, o in lemon, and u in circus.

friendly 1. Like a friend; showing friendship. The teacher was always ready to give her students *friendly* advice whenever they needed it. 2. Not angry or fighting; not hostile. Those two countries are on *friendly* terms with each other.
friend·ly (frend′lē) *adjective,* **friendlier, friendliest.**

friendship The warm feeling between friends. The two boys' *friendship* started when they used to play baseball together.
friend·ship (frend′ship′) *noun, plural* **friendships.**

fright 1. A sudden fear or alarm. The people in the burning building were seized with *fright.* 2. A person or thing that is ugly or shocking. That witch costume you wore on Halloween made you look a *fright.*
fright (frīt) *noun, plural* **frights.**

frighten 1. To make or become suddenly afraid or alarmed. The loud explosion *frightened* everyone. 2. To drive away by scaring. The dog *frightened* away the squirrels.
fright·en (frīt′ən) *verb,* **frightened, frightening.**

frigid 1. Very cold. The Eskimos have to know how to live in a *frigid* climate. 2. Cold in feeling; unfriendly. The political candidate gave his opponent a *frigid* greeting when they met on the street.
frig·id (frij′id) *adjective.*

fringe 1. A border of hanging threads or cord. The bedspread has a *fringe* all the way around the edge. 2. Anything like a fringe. A *fringe* of bushes lined the driveway. *Noun.*
—To make a fringe for. Mother *fringed* the towels when she finished sewing them. Daisies *fringed* the path to the house. *Verb.*
fringe (frinj) *noun, plural* **fringes;** *verb,* **fringed, fringing.**

Fringe

frivolous Lacking seriousness or sense; silly. That girl is so *frivolous* that she can't seem to keep her mind on anything for very long.
friv·o·lous (friv′ə ləs) *adjective.*

frog A small animal with webbed feet and no tail, that lives in or near water. A frog has strong back legs that it uses for hopping.
frog (frôg *or* frog) *noun, plural* **frogs.**

Frog

frogman A swimmer who is specially trained and equipped to work underwater.
frog·man (frôg′man′ *or* frog′man′) *noun, plural* **frogmen.**

frolic To play about happily and gaily. We liked to watch the colts *frolic* in the field.
frol·ic (frol′ik) *verb,* **frolicked, frolicking.**

from We flew *from* New York to Chicago. I go to school *from* nine o'clock to three. Two *from* five leaves three. Bob shivered *from* the cold. It's easy to tell lions *from* tigers.
from (from *or* frum *or* frəm) *preposition.*

frond The leaf of a fern.
frond (frond) *noun, plural* **fronds.**

front 1. The part that faces forward or comes first. This jacket has a zipper in the *front.* Jane sits in *front* of me in history class. 2. The land that lies along a street or body of water. We rented a cabin on the lake *front* for the summer. 3. A place where fighting is going on between two enemy forces. The general rode all along the *front* to encourage his men. 4. The boundary line between two air masses of different temperatures. The weatherman says we will have a drop in temperature tonight as the cold *front* moves into the area. *Noun.*
—On or near the front. The important news stories are printed on the *front* page of the newspaper. *Adjective.*
—To face toward. Our house *fronts* on a busy street. *Verb.*
front (frunt) *noun, plural* **fronts;** *adjective;* *verb,* **fronted, fronting.**

frontier 1. The last settled area of a country before the part that is not settled or developed begins. The development of the railroad helped to move the American *frontier* further west. 2. The border between two countries. We crossed the *frontier* between Canada and the United States on our automobile trip. 3. Any new area. Doctors are constantly exploring the *frontiers* of medicine.
fron·tier (frun tēr′) *noun, plural* **frontiers.**

frost **1.** Tiny crystals that form on a surface when the temperature is below freezing. Frost is formed by the freezing of water vapor in the air. There was *frost* on the windowpanes this morning. **2.** Very cold weather. *Frost* destroyed the orange crop in Florida this winter. *Noun.*
—To cover with frost or something like frost. Ruth *frosted* the birthday cake with chocolate icing. *Verb.*
  frost (frôst) *noun, plural* **frosts;** *verb,* **frosted, frosting.**

frostbite The freezing of some part of the body caused by exposure to extreme cold. *Noun.*
—To injure by exposure to extreme cold. The explorer's fingers and toes were *frostbitten* by the cold. *Verb.*
  frost·bite (frôst′bīt′) *noun; verb,* **frostbit, frostbitten, frostbiting.**

frosting A mixture of sugar, butter, and flavoring used to cover a cake or cookies; icing.
  frost·ing (frôs′ting) *noun, plural* **frostings.**

frosty Cold enough for frost; freezing. Our family loves to take walks on crisp, *frosty* evenings.
  frost·y (frôs′tē) *adjective,* **frostier, frostiest.**

froth A mass of bubbles formed in or on a liquid; foam. The *froth* on top of the ice cream soda tickled Janet's nose when she drank it. *Noun.*
—To form froth. The tired horse *frothed* at the mouth. *Verb.*
  froth (frôth) *noun, plural* **froths;** *verb,* **frothed, frothing.**

frown A wrinkling of the forehead. A person makes a frown because he is thinking hard or is angry or worried about something. A *frown* came to Linda's face when she tried to think of an answer to the riddle. *Noun.*
—**1.** To wrinkle the forehead in thought, anger, or worry. Mike *frowned* when his father made him stay home on Saturday to do his homework. **2.** To look with anger or disapproval. Louise's parents *frown* on her staying out late at night. *Verb.*
  frown (froun) *noun, plural* **frowns;** *verb,* **frowned, frowning.**

froze The lake *froze* last night, so we went ice-skating today. Look up **freeze** for more information.
  froze (frōz) *verb.*

frozen The water dripping from the roof had *frozen* and formed icicles. Look up **freeze** for more information.
  fro·zen (frō′zən) *verb.*

frugal **1.** Not wasteful; saving. A person who is frugal is very careful not to spend money on things that are not needed. **2.** Costing little. He ate a *frugal* meal of beans and bread.
  fru·gal (froo′gəl) *adjective.*

fruit The part of a plant that contains the seeds. Oranges, apples, and nuts are fruits that can be eaten.
  fruit (froot) *noun, plural* **fruit** or **fruits.**

frustrate To discourage or prevent. Joe was *frustrated* by his bad luck in trying to find a summer job. The rainy weather threatened to *frustrate* our plans for a camping trip.
  frus·trate (frus′trāt) *verb,* **frustrated, frustrating.**

fry To cook in hot fat. Andy *fried* bacon and eggs for his breakfast.
  fry (frī) *verb,* **fried, frying.**

fudge A soft candy made out of sugar, milk, butter, and flavoring.
  fudge (fuj) *noun, plural* **fudges.**

fuel Something that is burned to provide heat or power. Coal, wood, and oil are fuels.
  fu·el (fyoo′əl) *noun, plural* **fuels.**

fugitive A person who runs away or tries to escape. A person who runs away from the police is a fugitive from the law.
  fu·gi·tive (fyoo′jə tiv) *noun, plural* **fugitives.**

fulcrum The support on which a lever turns when it is moving or lifting something. The farmer used a rock as a *fulcrum* to move the heavy boulder.
  ful·crum (fool′krəm) *noun, plural* **fulcrums.**

fulfill **1.** To carry out or finish. Jim quickly *fulfilled* his chores for the day and went home early. **2.** To meet or satisfy. Jack was not hired for the job because he did not *fulfill* all the requirements.
  ful·fill (fool fil′) *verb,* **fulfilled, fulfilling.**

full **1.** Holding as much or as many as possible. Henry poured himself a *full* glass of milk. Janet's parents had a house *full* of guests for the party. **2.** Complete; entire. Each of these soup bowls holds a *full* cup. We have a *full* two weeks of vacation. **3.** Having a rounded outline; plump. That girl has a *full*, round face. **4.** Having a lot of cloth. The dress has a *full* skirt. *Adjective.*

at; āpe; cär; end; mē; it; īce; hot; ōld; fôrk; wood; fool; oil; out; up; turn; sing; thin; this; hw in white; zh in treasure. ə stands for a in about, e in taken i in pencil, o in lemon, and u in circus.

—Completely; entirely. He filled the pitcher *full* with lemonade. *Adverb.*

full (fool) *adjective,* **fuller, fullest;** *adverb.*

fullback A football player who stands farthest behind the front line.

full·back (fool′bak′) *noun, plural* **fullbacks.**

full moon The moon when all of the side that faces the earth is shining.

fully 1. Completely; entirely. I don't *fully* understand that arithmetic problem. 2. At least; not less than. The train was *fully* an hour late.

ful·ly (fool′ē) *adverb.*

fumble 1. To look for in a clumsy way. Jill *fumbled* around in her purse looking for her keys. 2. To handle clumsily or drop. Bob *fumbled* the football and made it possible for the other team to score. *Verb.*

—The act of fumbling. The quarterback's *fumble* helped the other team to get a touchdown. *Noun.*

fum·ble (fum′bəl) *verb,* **fumbled, fumbling;** *noun, plural* **fumbles.**

fume A smoke or gas that is harmful or has a bad smell. The *fumes* from automobiles make the city's air harmful to breathe. *Noun.*

—To be filled with anger or irritation. The driver *fumed* as he waited in the heavy traffic jam. *Verb.*

fume (fyoom) *noun, plural* **fumes;** *verb,* **fumed, fuming.**

fun Enjoyment or playfulness. We had *fun* riding our sleds down the hill. Harry is always full of *fun.*

fun (fun) *noun.*

to make fun of. To laugh at; ridicule. Jane *made fun of* her brother when he tried to cook breakfast.

function 1. Use or purpose. What is Susan's *function* in the club? The *function* of the heart is to pump blood through the body. 2. A formal gathering. All the friends and supporters of the art museum went to a *function* to celebrate its fiftieth anniversary. *Noun.*

—To work or serve. A motor *functions* best when it is kept well oiled. *Verb.*

func·tion (fungk′shən) *noun, plural* **functions;** *verb,* **functioned, functioning.**

fund 1. A sum of money set aside for a specific purpose. Mr. and Mrs. Black set up a *fund* for their children's college education. 2. A supply. This book has a *fund* of information on American Indians. 3. **funds.** Money that is ready for use. The state does not have the *funds* to repair the highway.

fund (fund) *noun, plural* **funds.**

fundamental Serving as a basis; essential; basic. Learning the rules is a *fundamental* part of any game. *Adjective.*

—An essential part. Addition and subtraction are two of the *fundamentals* of arithmetic. *Noun.*

fun·da·men·tal (fun′də ment′əl) *adjective; noun, plural* **fundamentals.**

funeral The ceremony and services held before the burial of a dead person. A funeral is often held in a church or temple.

fu·ner·al (fyoo′nər əl) *noun, plural* **funerals.**

fungi More than one fungus.

fun·gi (fun′jī) *noun plural.*

fungus One of a large group of plants that does not have flowers or leaves. Fungi do not have green coloring matter and therefore must live on other plants. Mushrooms, mildews, and molds are fungi.

fun·gus (fung′gəs) *noun, plural* **fungi** or **funguses.**

Fungus

funnel 1. A utensil that has a wide cone at one end and a thin tube at the other. When a funnel is used, something can be poured into a container with a small opening without spilling. 2. A round chimney or smokestack on a steamship or steam engine.

fun·nel (fun′əl) *noun, plural* **funnels.**

funny 1. Causing laughter. Tina told us a very *funny* joke. 2. Strange; odd. It seems *funny* that he never told us his name.

fun·ny (fun′ē) *adjective,* **funnier, funniest.**

fur 1. The soft, thick, hairy coat of certain animals. The mink has soft, dark-brown fur. 2. The skin of an animal that has fur. Fur is used in making clothing, rugs, and many other things. ▲ Another word that sounds like this is **fir.**

fur (fur) *noun, plural* **furs.**

furious 1. Very angry. Father was *furious* when he missed the train by one minute. 2. Violent; fierce. Summer is often a time of *furious* thunderstorms.

fu·ri·ous (fyoor′ē əs) *adjective.*

furlong A measure of distance equal to one-eighth of a mile, or 220 yards.

fur·long (fur′lông) *noun, plural* **furlongs.**

furnace An enclosed place where heat is produced. We use a furnace to heat a house or other building.
fur·nace (fur′nis) *noun, plural* **furnaces.**

furnish 1. To supply with furniture. Debbie's parents *furnished* a playroom in their basement. 2. To supply or provide. The book *furnished* us with facts about the American Revolution.
fur·nish (fur′nish) *verb,* **furnished, furnishing.**

furniture Tables, chairs, beds, and other movable articles used in a home or office.
fur·ni·ture (fur′ni chər) *noun.*

furrow A long, narrow groove. Farmers plant seeds in the *furrows* they dig. The cars made *furrows* in the dusty road.
fur·row (fur′ō) *noun, plural* **furrows.**

Furrows

furry Like fur or covered with fur. The new rug in the living room is soft and *furry.* A hamster is a *furry* little animal that many children have as pets.
fur·ry (fur′ē) *adjective,* **furrier, furriest.**

further The student went to the encyclopedia for *further* information on the subject of space travel. Look up **far** for more information. *Adjective, Adverb.*
—To help forward; support. The United Nations was formed to *further* the cause of peace. *Verb.*
fur·ther (fur′thər) *adjective; adverb; verb,* **furthered, furthering.**

furthermore In addition; moreover; besides. I don't want to go to bed yet, and *furthermore* I still have some homework to do.
fur·ther·more (fur′thər môr′) *adverb.*

furthest John threw the ball *furthest* of all the players. Going to Canada for a visit is the *furthest* distance Carol has ever been from home. Look up **far** for more information.
fur·thest (fur′thist) *adverb; adjective.*

fury 1. Violent anger; rage. The man flew into a *fury* when his store was robbed. 2. Violence; fierceness. The *fury* of the storm raged all night.
fu·ry (fyoor′ē) *noun, plural* **furies.**

fuse¹ 1. A strip of metal in an electric circuit. The fuse melts and breaks the circuit if the current becomes too strong. Fuses are used to prevent fire that can result from overloaded wires. 2. A piece of cord that can burn. A fuse is used to set off a bomb or other explosive.
fuse (fyōōz) *noun, plural* **fuses.**

fuse² 1. To melt by heating. He *fused* the metal by intense heat. 2. To blend or unite. Because gold is such a soft metal, it is *fused* with silver or copper to harden it.
fuse (fyōōz) *verb,* **fused, fusing.**

fuselage The main body of an airplane that holds the passengers, cargo, and crew.
fu·se·lage (fyōō′sə läzh′ *or* fyōō′sə lij) *noun, plural* **fuselages.**

fuss An unnecessary stir or bother over small or unimportant things. Ralph's mother always makes a *fuss* over him when he comes home from summer camp. There was a big *fuss* over which team would be up at bat first. *Noun.*
—To make an unnecessary stir or bother over small or unimportant things. Father *fussed* because his necktie had a stain on it. *Verb.*
fuss (fus) *noun, plural* **fusses;** *verb,* **fussed, fussing.**

future That will be or will happen; coming. Jim's teacher said she hoped that his *future* work would be better. *Adjective.*
—The time that is to come. In the *future,* please call if you are going to be late for dinner. *Noun.*
fu·ture (fyōō′chər) *adjective; noun.*

fuzz Fine, loose fibers or hair. A peach is covered with *fuzz.*
fuzz (fuz) *noun.*

fuzzy 1. Covered with or like fuzz. Caterpillars are *fuzzy.* The blanket was soft and *fuzzy.* 2. Not clear; blurred. That would be a good photograph except that it's too *fuzzy.*
fuzz·y (fuz′ē) *adjective,* **fuzzier, fuzziest.**

at; āpe; cär; end; mē; it; īce; hot; ōld;
fôrk; wood; fōōl; oil; out; up; turn; sing;
thin; this; hw in white; zh in treasure.
ə stands for a in about, e in taken
i in pencil, o in lemon, and u in circus.

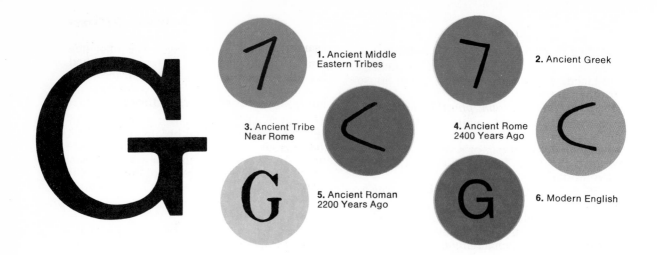

1. Ancient Middle Eastern Tribes

2. Ancient Greek

3. Ancient Tribe Near Rome

4. Ancient Rome 2400 Years Ago

5. Ancient Roman 2200 Years Ago

6. Modern English

G is the seventh letter of the alphabet. Although the modern letter **G** was invented by the Romans, its history goes back to the earliest alphabets. The oldest form of the letter **G** was the third letter of the alphabet used by several ancient tribes (**1**) in the Middle East. The Greeks (**2**) borrowed this letter about 3000 years ago. It was pronounced as a hard *g*, such as the *g* in *game*. This letter was then borrowed by an ancient tribe (**3**) that settled north of Rome about 2800 years ago. These people made no distinction between the hard *g* sound and the *k* sound, such as the *k* in *king*. Because of this, they began to use the letter to stand for both sounds. The Romans (**4**) borrowed the letter from them and also used it to stand for both the hard *g* and *k* sounds. The *k* sound was used more often than the hard *g* sound in the language of the Romans. So this letter, which had once been used for only the hard *g* sound, came to be used for only the *k* sound. About 2200 years ago, the Romans (**5**) invented a new letter to stand for the hard *g* sound. This letter, which was made by adding a short line to the letter **C,** was written in almost the same way that we write the capital letter **G** today (**6**).

g, G The seventh letter of the alphabet.
g, G (jē) *noun, plural* **g's, G's.**

gable The end of a sloping roof, along with the part between the sides of the roof.
ga·ble (gā′bəl) *noun, plural* **gables.**

gadget A small, unusual tool or device. A bottle opener with a penknife at one end is a *gadget.*
gad·get (gaj′it) *noun, plural* **gadgets.**

gag **1.** Something put in the mouth to keep a person from talking or shouting. **2.** A joke. The comedian on television told many *gags. Noun.*
—**1.** To keep someone from talking or shouting by using a gag. The robbers tied up and *gagged* the shopkeeper. **2.** To choke. The boy always *gags* when he takes that bitter medicine. *Verb.*
gag (gag) *noun, plural* **gags;** *verb,* **gagged, gagging.**

gaiety Joy and fun; being merry; cheerfulness. She loves the *gaiety* of Christmas. The *gaiety* of the clown made us smile.
gai·e·ty (gā′ə tē) *noun, plural* **gaieties.**

gaily In a gay manner; happily; cheerfully. The campers sang *gaily* around the campfire.
gai·ly (gā′lē) *adverb.*

gain To get or win. Our team *gained* control of the ball. Ann will *gain* experience by working at the store. The army *gained* a victory. The car *gained* speed as it moved down the hill. *Verb.*
—Something gained. The football player made a *gain* of ten yards. Eating too much food can cause a *gain* in weight. *Noun.*
gain (gān) *verb,* **gained, gaining;** *noun, plural* **gains.**

gait A way of moving on foot. The boy walked with a slow *gait.* ▲ Another word that sounds like this is **gate.**
gait (gāt) *noun, plural* **gaits.**

galaxy A very large group of stars. There are many galaxies in the universe. The Milky Way is a galaxy.
gal·ax·y (gal′ək sē) *noun, plural* **galaxies.**

gale **1.** A very strong wind. The *gale* drove the ship against the rocks. **2.** A sudden, loud bursting out or bursting forth. The clown's funny tricks sent the children into *gales* of laughter.
gale (gāl) *noun, plural* **gales.**

gallant Good and brave. The *gallant* knight died for his king.
gal·lant (gal′ənt) *adjective.*

gallery **1.** The highest balcony of a theater or large hall. **2.** A room or building where paintings and statues are shown or sold.
gal·ler·y (gal′ər ē) *noun, plural* **galleries.**

galley **1.** A long, low ship used in early times. A galley had sails and oars. **2.** The kitchen of a ship or airplane.
gal·ley (gal′ē) *noun, plural* **galleys.**

gallon A unit of measure for liquids. A gallon equals four quarts.
gal·lon (gal′ən) *noun, plural* **gallons.**

gallop The fastest gait of a horse or other four-footed animal. *Noun.*
—To move or ride at a gallop. The racehorses *galloped* to the finish line. *Verb.*
gal·lop (gal′əp) *noun, plural* **gallops;** *verb,* **galloped, galloping.**

gallows A frame from which criminals are hanged.
gal·lows (gal′ōz) *noun, plural* **gallowses** or **gallows.**

galoshes Overshoes made of rubber or plastic. Galoshes are worn in snowy or rainy weather.
ga·losh·es (gə losh′iz) *noun plural.*

gamble **1.** To play a game for money; bet. The men *gambled* with dice. He *gambled* his money on the horse race. **2.** To take a chance. The coach *gambled* when he used the new player in an important game. *Verb.*
—A risk. Buying a used car without trying it out is a big *gamble. Noun.*
gam·ble (gam′bəl) *verb,* **gambled, gambling;** *noun, plural* **gambles.**

Galoshes

game **1.** A way of playing. Let's play a *game* of ball. **2.** A sport or contest with certain rules. Are you going to the football *game?* Jeff likes the *game* of checkers. In the third inning the *game* was tied. **3.** Wild animals, birds, or fish hunted or caught for sport or food. The men went hunting for deer and other *game. Noun.*
—Full of spirit and courage. Are you *game* for a swim in the cold water? *Adjective.*
game (gām) *noun, plural* **games;** *adjective,* **gamer, gamest.**

gander A grown male goose.

gan·der (gan′dər) *noun, plural* **ganders.**

gang A group of people who do things together. Hank went fishing with a *gang* of his friends. The men on the road *gang* are building a new highway. A *gang* of thieves robbed the bank.
gang (gang) *noun, plural* **gangs.**

gangplank A movable board or bridge used for getting on and off a boat or ship.
gang·plank (gang′plangk′) *noun, plural* **gangplanks.**

Gangplank

gangster A member of a gang of criminals.
gang·ster (gang′stər) *noun, plural* **gangsters.**

gangway A passageway on either side of a ship's deck.
gang·way (gang′wā′) *noun, plural* **gangways.**

gap A break, crack, or opening. Our dog got out of the yard through a *gap* in the fence.
gap (gap) *noun, plural* **gaps.**

garage A building where cars and trucks are parked or repaired.
ga·rage (gə räzh′ *or* gə räj′) *noun, plural* **garages.**

garbage Food and other things that are thrown out from a kitchen.
gar·bage (gär′bij) *noun.*

▲ The word **garbage** first meant "the insides of an animal used as food." These were usually eaten only by people who could not afford to eat more expensive meat, and other people threw them out. So the word *garbage* came to mean "food that is thrown out."

at; āpe; cär; end; mē; it; īce; hot; ōld; fôrk; wood; fōōl; oil; out; up; turn; sing; thin; this; hw in white; zh in treasure.
ə stands for a in about, e in taken i in pencil, o in lemon, and u in circus.

garden A piece of ground where flowers or vegetables are grown. Mother planted a rose *garden* in the yard. The farmer grows peas, tomatoes, and beets in his *garden. Noun.*
—To work in a garden. Mr. Edwards *gardens* every day after work. *Verb.*
gar·den (gärd′ən) *noun, plural* **gardens;** *verb,* **gardened, gardening.**

Gardenia

gardenia A yellow or white flower with waxy petals. Gardenias have a sweet smell.
gar·de·nia (gär dēn′yə) *noun, plural* **gardenias.**

gargoyle A waterspout in the form of an odd or ugly person or animal. Gargoyles stick out from the roof of a building and carry off rain water.
gar·goyle (gär′goil) *noun, plural* **gargoyles.**

Gargoyle

garlic A plant that is related to the onion. The bulb of the plant is used for flavoring in cooking.
gar·lic (gär′lik) *noun, plural* **garlics.**

garment A piece of clothing. A coat, a sweater, or a shirt are garments.
gar·ment (gär′mənt) *noun, plural* **garments.**

garnet A deep-red gem that is used in jewelry.
gar·net (gär′nit) *noun, plural* **garnets.**

garnish To decorate. The cook *garnished* the fish with slices of lemon.
gar·nish (gär′nish) *verb,* **garnished, garnishing.**

garrison A place where soldiers are stationed. A *garrison* protected the town from enemy troops.
gar·ri·son (gar′ə sen) *noun, plural* **garrisons.**

garter A strap or band that holds up a stocking or stock. A garter is usually made of elastic.
gar·ter (gär′tər) *noun, plural* **garters.**

garter snake A snake that is green or brown with yellow stripes. It is harmless to people.

gas 1. A form of matter that is not solid or liquid. Gas can move about freely and does not have a definite shape. The air we breathe is made of gases. Some kinds of gases burn and are used for heating or cooking. 2. Gasoline. We filled the car's tank with *gas.* Look up **gasoline** for more information.
gas (gas) *noun, plural* **gases.**

gaseous In the form of gas; like gas. The air we breathe is *gaseous.*
gas·e·ous (gas′ē əs *or* gash′əs) *adjective.*

gas mask A mask worn over the nose and mouth. It has a filter that keeps a person from breathing poisonous gases and other harmful substances.

gasoline A liquid that burns easily. It is made mostly from petroleum. Gasoline is used as a fuel to make cars, trucks, and airplanes go.
gas·o·line (gas′ə lēn′ *or* gas′ə lēn′) *noun, plural* **gasolines.**

gasp To draw in air suddenly or with effort. She *gasped* for breath after running in the race. *Verb.*
—The act or sound of gasping. We heard a *gasp* from the frightened man. *Noun.*
gasp (gasp) *verb,* **gasped, gasping;** *noun, plural* **gasps.**

gate A movable part like a door that is put in an opening in a fence or wall. ▲ Another word that sounds like this is **gait.**
gate (gāt) *noun, plural* **gates.**

gateway 1. An open place in a fence or wall where a gate is put. 2. The way to get someplace or do something. The city of St. Louis is called the *gateway* to the West.
gate·way (gāt′wā′) *noun, plural* **gateways.**

gather 1. To come or bring together. Billy *gathered* his books off the table and put them

away. The bird *gathered* twigs for its nest. A crowd *gathered* at the scene of the accident. **2.** To reach an opinion; conclude. We *gathered* from the dark clouds that a storm was coming. **3.** To bring cloth together in folds. She *gathered* the skirt at the waist.
> **gath·er** (ga<u>th</u>′ər) *verb,* **gathered, gathering.**

gaudy Too bright and showy. The yellow and pink coat with green buttons looked *gaudy.*
> **gaud·y** (gô′dē) *adjective,* **gaudier, gaudiest.**

gauge **1.** A standard of measurement. There is a *gauge* for measuring the barrel of a shotgun. There is also a *gauge* for measuring the distance between two rails on a railroad track. **2.** An instrument for measuring. A barometer is a *gauge* that measures the pressure of the atmosphere. *Noun.*
—To measure. Scientists can *gauge* the exact amount of rain that falls during a storm. *Verb.*
> **gauge** (gāj) *noun, plural* **gauges;** *verb,* **gauged, gauging.**

gaunt Very thin. The man was *gaunt* and bony from hunger.
> **gaunt** (gônt) *adjective,* **gaunter, gauntest.**

gauze A very thin cloth that you can see through. It is used mostly for making bandages.
> **gauze** (gôz) *noun.*

gave Nancy *gave* her boyfriend a gift. Look up **give** for more information.
> **gave** (gāv) *verb.*

gavel A small wooden hammer. It is used by the person in charge of a meeting or trial to call for order or attention.
> **gav·el** (gav′əl) *noun, plural* **gavels.**

gay Full of joy and fun; merry; cheerful. The children were *gay* at the birthday party. Ruth wore a *gay* dress with many pink ribbons.
> **gay** (gā) *adjective,* **gayer, gayest.**

Gavel

gaze To look at something a long time without looking away. Ken *gazed* at the beautiful sunset. *Verb.*
—A long, steady look. Her *gaze* rested on her friend's new bicycle. *Noun.*
> **gaze** (gāz) *verb,* **gazed, gazing;** *noun, plural* **gazes.**

gazelle A graceful animal that can run very fast. It is found in Africa and Asia.
> **ga·zelle** (gə zel′) *noun, plural* **gazelles** or **gazelle.**

Gazelle

gear **1.** A wheel with teeth on the edge. The teeth are made to fit in between the teeth of another gear, so that one gear can cause the other to turn. **2.** Equipment for a particular purpose. My hiking *gear* includes a knapsack, sleeping bag, and cooking kit. *Noun.*
—To fit. The school was *geared* to meet the needs of bright students. *Verb.*
> **gear** (gēr) *noun, plural* **gears;** *verb,* **geared, gearing.**

gearshift A part that joins a set of gears to a motor. An automobile has a gearshift.
> **gear·shift** (gēr′shift′) *noun, plural* **gearshifts.**

geese More than one goose. Look up **goose** for more information.
> **geese** (gēs) *noun plural.*

Geiger counter A device used to discover and measure the strength of rays from a radioactive substance.
> **Gei·ger counter** (gī′gər).

▲ The **Geiger counter** was named after Hans *Geiger.* He was a German scientist who helped invent this device.

at; āpe; cär; end; mē; it; īce; hot; ōld; fôrk; wood; fōol; oil; out; up; turn; sing; thin; <u>th</u>is; hw in white; zh in treasure. ə stands for a in about, e in taken i in pencil, o in lemon, and u in circus.

gelatin A substance like jelly. It is made from the skin, bones, and other parts of animals. Gelatin is used in jellies and desserts and in making glue.
gel·a·tin (jel′ət ən) *noun.*

gem A precious stone that has been cut and polished; jewel. The queen wore rubies, diamonds, and other *gems.*
gem (jem) *noun, plural* **gems.**

Kinds of Gems

Sapphire · Jade · Ruby · Diamond · Turquoise · Topaz · Emerald · Opal

gene One of the tiny units of a cell of an animal or plant that determines the characteristics that an offspring inherits from its parent or parents.
gene (jēn) *noun, plural* **genes.**

general 1. For all; for the whole. A *general* meeting of the club was held to discuss the new rules. That exhibit is open to the *general* public. 2. By all or many. There was a *general* panic during the earthquake. *Adjective.*
—An army officer of the highest rank. The five ranks of general are **brigadier general, major general, lieutenant general, general,** and **general of the army.** *Noun.*
gen·er·al (jen′ər əl) *adjective; noun, plural* **generals.**

generally 1. Usually. I *generally* walk to school. 2. Without going into detail. *Generally* speaking, the book was good.
gen·er·al·ly (jen′ər ə lē) *adverb.*

generate To bring about or produce. That machine *generates* electricity.
gen·er·ate (jen′ə rāt′) *verb,* **generated, generating.**

generation 1. A group of persons born around the same time. My parents call me and my friends the younger *generation.* 2. One step in the line of descent of a family. A grandfather, father, and son make up three *generations.*
gen·er·a·tion (jen′ə rā′shən) *noun, plural* **generations.**

generator A machine that produces electricity, steam, or other energy.
gen·er·a·tor (jen′ə rā′tər) *noun, plural* **generators.**

generous 1. Unselfish. A generous person is willing and happy to share with others. Bill is *generous* with his new bicycle and lets his friends ride it. 2. Large; abundant. She gave him a *generous* helping of cake.
gen·er·ous (jen′ər əs) *adjective.*

genie A spirit with magic powers in Arab fairy tales.
ge·nie (jē′nē) *noun, plural* **genies.**

genius 1. Great ability to think and to invent or create things. The artist who painted those great paintings in the art musuem was a person of *genius.* 2. A person who has this ability. A great scientist, musician, or artist is a *genius.*
gen·ius (jēn′yəs) *noun, plural* **geniuses.**

gentle 1. Mild and kindly. She gave the baby a *gentle* hug. The teacher criticized the boy's work in a *gentle* way. 2. Soft or low. We heard the *gentle* tapping of the rain on the window. She spoke in a *gentle* voice. 3. Gradual; not steep. The children slid down the *gentle* slope on their sleds.
gen·tle (jent′əl) *adjective,* **gentler, gentlest.**

▲ The word **gentle** was used first to mean "noble" or "born of a good family." Being kind was thought of as a quality of people of noble birth. So we began to use *gentle* to mean "kind and friendly."

gentleman 1. A man who is polite, kind, and honorable. The judge was a real *gentleman* and was admired by all the people in town. 2. A man of high social position. 3. Any man. "A *gentleman* is at the door to see you," Bill said.
gen·tle·man (jent′əl mən) *noun, plural* **gentlemen.**

gently In a gentle way. The snow fell *gently.* He petted the kitten *gently.*
gent·ly (jent′lē) *adverb.*

genuine 1. Real. This belt is made of *genuine* leather. 2. Sincere; honest. She made a *genuine* effort to help us.
gen·u·ine (jen′yo͞o in) *adjective.*

geographical Having to do with geography.
ge·o·graph·i·cal (jē′ə graf′i kəl) *adjective.*

geography The study of the surface of the earth and the plant, animal, and human life on it. When you study geography, you learn about the earth's countries and people, and about its climate, oceans and rivers, mountains, and natural resources.

ge·og·ra·phy (jē og′rə fē) *noun, plural* **geographies.**

geological Having to do with geology.

ge·o·log·i·cal (jē′ə loj′i kəl) *adjective.*

geology The study of the history of the earth. When you study geology, you study rocks and minerals to find out what the earth is made of and what changes have taken place on the earth's surface.

ge·ol·o·gy (jē ol′ə jē) *noun, plural* **geologies.**

geometric Having to do with geometry. A triangle is a *geometric* form. The rug has a *geometric* design of circles and squares.

ge·o·met·ric (jē′ə met′rik) *adjective.*

geometry The part of mathematics that has to do with the measurement and comparison of points, lines, angles, plane figures, and solids.

ge·om·e·try (jē om′ə trē) *noun.*

Georgia A state in the southeastern United States. Its capital is Atlanta.

Geor·gia (jôr′jə) *noun.*

▲ **Georgia** was named after King *George* II of England. George II gave some men the right to start a colony in part of what is now this state.

---

geranium A plant with bright red, pink, or white flowers.

ge·ra·ni·um (jə rā′nē əm) *noun, plural* **geraniums.**

germ A tiny plant or animal. Germs are so small that they can be seen only through a microscope. Many germs cause disease.

germ (jurm) *noun, plural* **germs.**

Geraniums

German 1. A person who was born or is living in Germany. 2. The language of Germany. *Noun.* —Having to do with Germany, its people, or their language. *Adjective.*

Ger·man (jur′mən) *noun, plural* **Germans;** *adjective.*

Germany A country in north-central Europe. It is divided into **West Germany** and **East Germany.**

Ger·ma·ny (jur′mə nē) *noun.*

gesture 1. A movement of the hands, head, or other part of the body that shows what a person is thinking or feeling. Holding out your hand with the palm up is a *gesture* that you want something. 2. Something done to express a feeling or for effect. Going to visit her sick classmate was a kind *gesture. Noun.* —To make or use gestures. The policeman *gestured* for the driver to stop. *Verb.*

ges·ture (jes′chər) *noun, plural* **gestures;** *verb,* **gestured, gesturing.**

get 1. To receive or take as one's own; gain; earn. Alice hopes to *get* a new bicycle for Christmas. Stephen thinks he will *get* an A on the test. 2. To cause to do, be, or become; bring about or happen. He will *get* lunch ready. When will we *get* home? I'm afraid I'll *get* a cold. The boys may *get* lost in the woods. I *get* up at seven o'clock. Hold the dog or he will *get* away.

get (get) *verb,* **got, got** or **gotten, getting.**

Geyser

geyser A hot spring from which steam and hot water shoot into the air.

gey·ser (gī′zər) *noun, plural* **geysers.**

ghastly Terrible; horrible. The story was a *ghastly* tale of murder.

ghast·ly (gast′lē) *adjective,* **ghastlier, ghastliest.**

---

at; āpe; cär; end; mē; it; īce; hot; ōld;
fôrk; wood; fōol; oil; out; up; turn; sing;
thin; this; hw in white; zh in treasure.
ə stands for a in about, e in taken
i in pencil, o in lemon, and u in circus.

---

ghetto   A part of a city where members of a certain race or religion live because they are poor or because they are discriminated against. Ghettos often are very crowded and have old, rundown buildings.
ghet·to (get′ō) *noun, plural* **ghettos** or **ghettoes.**

ghost   The supposed spirit of a dead person.
ghost (gōst) *noun, plural* **ghosts.**

ghostly   Of a ghost; like a ghost. He thought he heard *ghostly* sounds coming from the old house. The statue had a *ghostly* appearance in the dim light.
ghost·ly (gōst′lē) *adjective,* **ghostlier, ghostliest.**

giant   **1.** An imaginary creature like a huge man. A giant has great strength. **2.** A person or thing that is very large, powerful, or important. That man is a *giant* in the field of medicine. That company is a *giant* in automobile manufacturing. *Noun.*
—Very large. The scientist looked through a *giant* telescope. *Adjective.*
gi·ant (jī′ənt) *noun, plural* **giants;** *adjective.*

gibbon   A small animal that lives in trees. A gibbon has long arms and no tail. It is a kind of ape.
gib·bon (gib′ən) *noun, plural* **gibbons.**

giddy   **1.** Having a spinning feeling in the head; dizzy. Nancy felt *giddy* after swinging high on the swing. **2.** Playful; silly. That *giddy* girl spends most of her time going to dances and parties.
gid·dy (gid′ē) *adjective,* **giddier, giddiest.**

Gibbon

gift   **1.** Something given; present. Jean could hardly wait to open her birthday *gifts.* **2.** Talent; ability. He has a *gift* for music.
gift (gift) *noun, plural* **gifts.**

gigantic   Like a giant; huge and powerful. A *gigantic* whale swam under the ship.
gi·gan·tic (jī gan′tik) *adjective.*

giggle   To laugh in a high, silly way. The boy *giggled* at the funny joke. *Verb.*
—A high, silly laugh. The girl gave a *giggle* when she saw the clown. *Noun.*
gig·gle (gig′əl) *verb,* **giggled, giggling;** *noun, plural* **giggles.**

gild   To cover with a thin layer of gold or golden color. The artist *gilded* the picture frame. ▲ Another word that sounds like this is **guild.**
gild (gild) *verb,* **gilded, gilding.**

gill   The part of a fish and most other water animals used for breathing. A gill takes in oxygen from the water.
gill (gil) *noun, plural* **gills.**

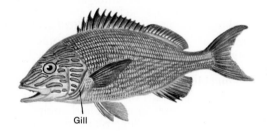
Gill

gin¹   A colorless alcoholic drink that is flavored with juniper berries.
gin (jin) *noun, plural* **gins.**

gin²   A machine for separating cotton from its seeds.
gin (jin) *noun, plural* **gins.**

ginger   A hot spice that comes from the root of a tropical plant. Ginger is used in food and medicine.
gin·ger (jin′jər) *noun, plural* **gingers.**

gingerbread   A dark, sweet cake or cookie flavored with ginger.
gin·ger·bread (jin′jər bred′) *noun, plural* **gingerbreads.**

gingham   A strong cotton fabric. It usually has a pattern of checks, stripes, or plaid.
ging·ham (ging′-əm) *noun, plural* **ginghams.**

giraffe   A large animal that lives in Africa. The giraffe has a very long neck, long, thin legs, and a coat with brown patches. Giraffes are the tallest living animals.
gi·raffe (jə raf′) *noun, plural* **giraffes.**

Giraffe

girder A large, heavy beam. Girders are used to support floors and the frameworks of buildings and bridges.
gird·er (gur′dər) *noun, plural* **girders.**

girl A female child from birth to the time she is a young woman.
girl (gurl) *noun, plural* **girls.**

▲ The word **girl** used to mean "a child or young person." The word was used for both boys and girls, and boys were sometimes called "knave girls." Later people began to use *girl* for female children only.

girl scout A member of the Girl Scouts.

Girl Scouts An organization for girls. It helps girls to develop character and physical fitness.

give **1.** To hand over or grant to another or others. Ellen's parents will *give* her a bicycle for Christmas. *Give* the kitten a bowl of milk. Mr. Smith will *give* Frank three dollars for mowing the lawn. The teacher *gave* them permission to leave the room. The thief *gave* himself up to the police. **2.** To make or do; bring about; cause. Tim *gave* a shout when he found the cave. The puppy will not *give* you any trouble. The noise *gives* me a headache. **3.** To break down; yield. If the dam *gives*, the town will be flooded. She would not *give* in and admit she was wrong.
give (giv) *verb,* **gave, given, giving.**

given Ann has *given* her brother a present.
giv·en (giv′ən) *verb.*

glacier A large mass of ice. A glacier is formed by snow that does not melt. It moves slowly across land or down a valley. Long ago, glaciers covered much of North America, Europe, and Russia.
gla·cier (glā′shər) *noun, plural* **glaciers.**

Glacier

glad Happy; pleased. Alan is *glad* to be home. I am *glad* to meet you.
glad (glad) *adjective,* **gladder, gladdest.**

▲ The word **glad** used to mean "bright and shining." For example, someone might have said, "This gold is *glad*." Often when people are happy, their faces are bright. So the word *glad* came to mean "very happy."

gladiator In ancient Rome, a man who fought another man for public entertainment.
glad·i·a·tor (glad′ē ā′tər) *noun, plural* **gladiators.**

gladiolus A flower shaped like a funnel that grows in clusters along a long stem.
glad·i·o·lus (glad′ē ō′-ləs) *noun, plural* **gladioli** or **gladioluses.**

glance A quick look. She gave me an angry *glance* over her shoulder. *Noun.*
—**1.** To take a quick look. He *glanced* in the mirror. **2.** To hit something and move off at a slant. The sword *glanced* off the knight's armor. *Verb.*
glance (glans) *noun, plural* **glances;** *verb,* **glanced, glancing.**

Gladiolus

gland A part inside the body that makes a substance that the body uses or gives off. Glands near the eyes make tears. Another kind of gland makes a substance that helps control the growth of the body.
gland (gland) *noun, plural* **glands.**

glare **1.** A strong, unpleasant light. The *glare* of the car's headlights hurt my eyes. **2.** An angry look or stare. Sue gave Jack a *glare* when he stepped on her foot. *Noun.*
—**1.** To shine with a strong, unpleasant light. The sunlight *glared* on the sand of the beach. **2.** To give an angry look. The old man *glared* at the noisy children. *Verb.*
glare (gler) *noun, plural* **glares;** *verb,* **glared, glaring.**

at; āpe; cär; end; mē; it; īce; hot; ōld;
fôrk; wood; fo͞ol; oil; out; up; turn; sing;
thin; this; hw in white; zh in treasure.
ə stands for a in about, e in taken
i in pencil, o in lemon, and u in circus.

glass **1.** A hard material that breaks easily. Glass can be seen through. **2.** A container made of glass that is used for drinking. She filled the *glass* with milk. He drank three *glasses* of water. **3. glasses.** A pair of lenses made of glass, used to help a person see better; eyeglasses.
　glass (glas) *noun, plural* **glasses.**

gleam A flash or beam of bright light. I could see the *gleam* of a flashlight. The polished silver has a nice *gleam. Noun.*
—To shine; glow. The new car *gleamed* in the sunlight. *Verb.*
　gleam (glēm) *noun, plural* **gleams;** *verb,* **gleamed, gleaming.**

glee Joy or delight. The little boy laughed with *glee* when he opened his presents.
　glee (glē) *noun.*

glen A small, narrow valley. The hikers rested in a *glen* between the hills.
　glen (glen) *noun, plural* **glens.**

glide To move smoothly along without any effort. The skater *glided* across the ice. The sailboat *glided* along on the lake.
　glide (glīd) *verb,* **glided, gliding.**

glider An aircraft that flies without a motor. Rising air currents keep a glider in the air.
　glid·er (glī′dər) *noun, plural* **gliders.**

glimmer **1.** A dim, unsteady light. We could see the *glimmer* of a distant star. **2.** A weak sign; hint. There was not even a *glimmer* of hope that we would find the lost dog. *Noun.*
—To shine with a dim, unsteady light; flicker. The lights on the airplane *glimmered* in the night sky. *Verb.*
　glim·mer (glim′ər) *noun, plural* **glimmers;** *verb,* **glimmered, glimmering.**

glimpse A quick look; glance. He caught a *glimpse* of his friend in the crowd. *Noun.*
—To look quickly; see for a moment; glance. I *glimpsed* the famous actor as he drove by in his car. *Verb.*
　glimpse (glimps) *noun, plural* **glimpses;** *verb,* **glimpsed, glimpsing.**

glisten To shine with bright flashes; sparkle. The snow *glistened* in the sun. Tears *glistened* on the little boy's cheeks.
　glis·ten (glis′ən) *verb,* **glistened, glistening.**

glitter To shine with bright flashes; sparkle. The gold ring *glittered* on her finger. Stars *glittered* in the sky.
　glit·ter (glit′ər) *verb,* **glittered, glittering.**

gloat To look at or think about something with great satisfaction. The gambler *gloated* over all the money he had won.
　gloat (glōt) *verb,* **gloated, gloating.**

globe **1.** The world. Fred traveled around the *globe* and saw many new and interesting things. **2.** A round ball with a map of the world on it. We studied the oceans and continents on a *globe* in our classroom. **3.** Anything shaped like a ball. Mother placed a glass *globe* over the light bulb in the hall.
　globe (glōb) *noun, plural* **globes.**

Globe

gloom **1.** Dim light or darkness. She could not see anything in the *gloom* of the forest at night. **2.** Low spirits; sorrow; sadness. He was filled with *gloom* when his best friend moved away.
　gloom (glōōm) *noun.*

gloomy **1.** Sad. Joan felt *gloomy* because she couldn't go to the party. **2.** Dim; dark. He was scared to go into the *gloomy* hallway. It was a *gloomy*, rainy day.
　gloom·y (glōō′mē) *adjective,* **gloomier, gloomiest.**

glorify To praise or worship. The people will *glorify* the great hero.
　glo·ri·fy (glôr′ə fī′) *verb,* **glorified, glorifying.**

glorious Full of glory; grand; magnificent. A *glorious* sunset filled the sky.
　glo·ri·ous (glôr′ē əs) *adjective.*

glory **1.** Great praise; honor; fame. John did all the work, but his brother got the *glory.* **2.** Great beauty; splendor; magnificence. The sun shone in all its *glory.*
　glo·ry (glôr′ē) *noun, plural* **glories.**

gloss A smooth, bright look; shine; luster. Stephen waxed the floor to give it a nice *gloss.*
　gloss (glôs) *noun, plural* **glosses.**

glossary A list of hard words and their meanings. The words in a glossary are in alphabetical order. Some books have a glossary at the end.
　glos·sa·ry (glos′ər ē) *noun, plural* **glossaries.**

glossy Having a smooth, bright look; shiny. The photograph has a *glossy* surface. My cat has *glossy* fur.
　gloss·y (glô′sē) *adjective,* **glossier, glossiest.**

glove A covering for the hand. Most gloves have separate parts for each of the four fingers and for the thumb. However, boxing gloves and some baseball gloves hold the four fingers together in one part.
　glove (gluv) *noun, plural* **gloves.**

glow A light or shine. At sunrise, the sky has an orange *glow*. A firefly gives off a *glow*. Her face has the *glow* of good health. *Noun.*
—To shine. The light bulb *glows* brightly. Karen's face *glowed* with health. *Verb.*
  glow (glō) *noun, plural* **glows;** *verb,* **glowed, glowing.**

glue A substance for sticking things together. *Noun.*
—**1.** To stick things together with glue. Jack *glued* the broken vase together. **2.** To fasten or hold tightly. She *glued* her eyes to the television screen. *Verb.*
  glue (glōō) *noun, plural* **glues;** *verb,* **glued, gluing.**

gnarled Having a rough, twisted look. There is a *gnarled* old oak tree beside our house. The old sailor has *gnarled* hands.
  gnarled (närld) *adjective.*

gnat A small fly. Some gnats bite and suck blood from people and animals. Others feed on plants.
  gnat (nat) *noun, plural* **gnats.**

gnaw To bite again and again so as to wear away little by little. The dog *gnawed* the bone. A rat had *gnawed* a hole through the fence.
  gnaw (nô) *verb,* **gnawed, gnawing.**

gnome A kind of dwarf in fairy tales.
  gnome (nōm) *noun, plural* **gnomes.**

▲ The word **gnome** is said to go back to the Greek word for "intelligence." People used to believe that gnomes knew all about the minerals and riches that could be found under the ground.

---

gnu A large animal that lives in Africa. A gnu is a kind of antelope. ▲ Other words that sound like this are **knew** and **new.**
  gnu (nōō *or* nyōō) *noun, plural* **gnus** or **gnu.**

Gnu

go **1.** To move from one place to another; move along, ahead, or away. They plan to *go* to the beach today. I have to *go* now, or I'll be late. **2.** To pass. Time *goes* quickly when you're busy. **3.** To reach; lead. The road *goes* east from here. The lamp cord isn't long enough to *go* from the wall to the table. **4.** To be, become, or continue. Ellen always *goes* to sleep early on school nights. **5.** To work; run. Our car won't *go*. **6.** To have as a result; turn out. The game didn't *go* well for our team. **7.** To be given. First prize *goes* to Holly. **8.** To have a place; belong. That chair *goes* in the kitchen.
  go (gō) *verb,* **went, gone, going.**

goal **1.** Something that a person wants and tries to get or become; aim; purpose. Gail's *goal* in life is to become a doctor. **2.** A place in certain games where players must get the ball or puck in order to score. The hockey player shot the puck into the *goal*.
  goal (gōl) *noun, plural* **goals.**

goat An animal that is related to the sheep. Goats have short horns and a tuft of hair under their chins that looks like a beard. They are raised in many parts of the world for their milk, hair, meat, and skin.
  goat (gōt) *noun, plural* **goats** or **goat.**

Goat

goatee A small pointed beard. It is only large enough to cover the chin and ends in a point just below the chin.
  goat·ee (gō tē′) *noun, plural* **goatees.**

gobble¹ To eat something quickly and in large chunks. The boys *gobbled* their food and then ran out to play.
  gob·ble (gob′əl) *verb,* **gobbled, gobbling.**

gobble² To make the sound that a turkey makes. *Verb.*
—The sound that a turkey makes. *Noun.*
  gob·ble (gob′əl) *verb,* **gobbled, gobbling;** *noun, plural* **gobbles.**

at; āpe; cär; end; mē; it; īce; hot; ōld; fôrk; wood; fōōl; oil; out; up; turn; sing; thin; this; hw in white; zh in treasure.
ə stands for a in about, e in taken i in pencil, o in lemon, and u in circus.

goblet A kind of drinking glass. A goblet is tall and is set on a long stem.
gob·let (gob′lit) *noun, plural* **goblets.**

God The being that people worship as the maker and ruler of the world.
God (god) *noun.*

god A being who is supposed to have special powers over the lives and doings of people. The myths of ancient Greece and Rome tell stories about *gods* and goddesses.
god (god) *noun, plural* **gods.**

goddess A female god. Gods and *goddesses* ruled the world in Greek myths.
god·dess (god′is) *noun, plural* **goddesses.**

goes Tom *goes* to football practice after school.
goes (gōz) *verb.*

gold **1.** A heavy yellow metal used to make jewelry and coins. Gold is a chemical element. **2.** The yellow color of this metal. *Noun.*
—Having the color gold. The leaves are red and *gold* in the fall. *Adjective.*
gold (gōld) *noun, plural* **golds;** *adjective.*

golden **1.** Made of or containing gold. Susan owns a pair of *golden* earrings that once belonged to her grandmother. **2.** Having the color or shine of gold; bright or shining. The field of *golden* wheat swayed in the wind. **3.** Very good or valuable; excellent. If he takes that job, it will be a *golden* opportunity for him to become successful.
gold·en (gōld′ən) *adjective.*

Goldenrod

goldenrod A tall plant that has long stalks of yellow flowers.
gold·en·rod (gōld′ən rod′) *noun, plural* **goldenrods.**

goldfinch An American bird that is yellow with black markings.
gold·finch (gōld′finch′) *noun, plural* **goldfinches.**

Goldfinch

goldfish A small fish that is usually orange-gold in color. Goldfish are often raised in home aquariums.
gold·fish (gōld′fish′) *noun, plural* **goldfish** or **goldfishes.**

Golf

golf A game played outdoors on a special course. It is played with a small, hard ball and a set of long, thin clubs with iron or wooden heads. The object of the game is to hit the ball into each of a series of holes with as few strokes at the ball as possible. *Noun.*
—To play the game of golf. *Verb.*
golf (golf) *noun; verb,* **golfed, golfing.**

gondola **1.** A long, narrow boat with a high peak at each end. It is rowed at its stern by one person with an oar or pole. Gondolas are used to carry passengers on the canals of Venice, Italy. **2.** A compartment under a dirigible or large balloon. It is used to carry passengers and equipment.
gon·do·la (gon′də lə) *noun, plural* **gondolas.**

Gondola

gone Stan had already *gone* home when we arrived. Look up **go** for more information. *Verb.*

—Used up or spent. The cake is all *gone.* *Adjective.*
gone (gôn) *verb; adjective.*

gong A piece of metal shaped like a plate that is used as a musical instrument. It is played with a stick that looks like a small hammer. A gong makes a deep sound when it is struck.
gong (gông *or* gong) *noun, plural* **gongs.**

Goose

good Of high quality; not bad or poor. The food at this restaurant is *good.* I thought the movie was very *good.* Paul is a *good* swimmer. Her health has always been *good.* It's a *good* day for a picnic. We had a *good* time at the party. The children were *good* all afternoon. *Adjective.*
—**1.** Benefit; advantage. I'm telling you this for your own *good.* **2.** Kindness or honesty. She feels there is some *good* in everybody. *Noun.*
good (good) *adjective,* **better, best;** *noun.*
for good. Forever; permanently. Joan said she was leaving *for good.*

good-by Farewell. *"Good-by!"* she called, as we drove down the driveway. After saying our *good-bys,* we left the party. This word is also spelled **good-bye.**
good-by (good′bī′) *interjection; noun, plural* **good-bys.**

Good Friday The Friday before Easter. It is set aside as the anniversary of the day Jesus died.

good-natured Pleasant, kindly, and cheerful toward others. She's very *good-natured* and never minds when people drop in without being invited.
good-na·tured (good′nā′chərd) *adjective.*

goodness A being good; kindness or generosity. He helped us out of the *goodness* of his heart. *Noun.*
—A word used to express surprise. My *goodness,* I never thought she'd say such a thing! *Interjection.*
good·ness (good′nis) *noun; interjection.*

goods **1.** Things that are sold; merchandise. All of the store's *goods* are on sale. **2.** Things that belong to someone; belongings. The family lost all their household *goods* in the fire.
goods (goodz) *noun plural.*

goose **1.** A bird that looks like a duck but is larger and has a longer neck. Geese can swim and they have webbed feet. Many kinds of geese are wild, but others are tame and are raised for food. **2.** A female goose. A male goose is called a gander.
goose (goos) *noun, plural* **geese.**

gopher A small animal that looks like a chipmunk but is larger. Gophers have large pouches in their cheeks. They burrow under the ground to build long tunnels in which they live. Gophers are found throughout North America.
go·pher (gō′fər) *noun, plural* **gophers.**

Gopher

gorge A deep, narrow valley or canyon that has steep, rocky walls. *Noun.*
—To eat a very large amount of food; stuff with food. She *gorged* herself with four helpings of spaghetti. *Verb.*
gorge (gôrj) *noun, plural* **gorges;** *verb,* **gorged, gorging.**

gorgeous Very beautiful to look at. We took a drive in the country and saw the *gorgeous* colors of the autumn leaves.
gor·geous (gôr′jəs) *adjective.*

at; āpe; cär; end; mē; it; īce; hot; ōld;
fôrk; wood; fool; oil; out; up; turn; sing;
thin; this; hw in white; zh in treasure.
ə stands for a in about, e in taken
i in pencil, o in lemon, and u in circus.

gorilla A large, very strong animal that is a kind of monkey. Gorillas have big, heavy bodies, short legs, and long arms. They live in Africa. ▲ Another word that sounds like this is **guerrilla**.
go·ril·la (gə ril′ə) *noun, plural* **gorillas.**

▲ The word **gorilla** comes from a Greek word that means "wild, hairy person." Some early explorers in Africa thought that the gorillas were wild people instead of animals.

Gorilla

gospel 1. The teachings of Jesus and the Apostles. 2. **Gospel.** In the Bible, any one of the first four books of the New Testament. They are about the life and teachings of Jesus. 3. Anything believed as absolutely true. The old woman took her doctor's advice as *gospel.*
gos·pel (gos′pəl) *noun, plural* **gospels.**

gossip 1. Talk or rumors about other people. Gossip is talk that is often untrue and unkind. There's a lot of *gossip* going around about why he is leaving town. 2. A person who repeats rumors to others and who enjoys talking about other people. She's nothing but a *gossip,* and I'd never trust her to keep a secret. *Noun.*
—To repeat what one knows or is told about other people; spread gossip. My uncle likes to *gossip* about his neighbors. *Verb.*
gos·sip (gos′ip) *noun, plural* **gossips;** *verb,* **gossiped, gossiping.**

got I *got* a new jacket last week. Look up **get** for more information.
got (got) *verb.*

gotten We had already *gotten* a letter from her when she called. Look up **get** for more information.
got·ten (got′ən) *verb.*

gouge 1. A tool with a curved, hollow blade. A gouge is used for making holes or grooves in wood. 2. A hole, groove, or cut. Ben got a long *gouge* in his hand when he fell against the nail. *Noun.*
—To cut or scoop out. The carpenter *gouged* the wood for the shelves. *Verb.*
gouge (gouj) *noun, plural* **gouges;** *verb,* **gouged, gouging.**

Gourds

gourd A rounded fruit related to the pumpkin or squash. Gourds grow on vines and have a hard outer rind. They are used to make bowls, jugs, and dippers. Gourds are also hung for decoration.
gourd (gôrd) *noun, plural* **gourds.**

gourmet A person who loves fine food and knows a great deal about it. My uncle is a *gourmet* who has written a cookbook, and he does most of the cooking for his family.
gour·met (goor mā′ *or* goor′mā) *noun, plural* **gourmets.**

gout A disease that causes painful swellings of the joints in the body. Gout usually affects the joints in the big toe.
gout (gout) *noun.*

govern To rule, control, or manage. The President and the Congress *govern* the nation. The man's actions were *governed* by his desire to make money.
gov·ern (guv′ərn) *verb,* **governed, governing.**

government 1. The group of people in charge of ruling or managing a country, state, city, or other place. The *government* in this country is elected by the people. 2. A way of ruling or governing. The English people have a democratic *government.*
gov·ern·ment (guv′ərn mənt *or* guv′ər mənt) *noun, plural* **governments.**

governor 1. The person elected to be the head of government of a state of the United States. 2. A device that controls the speed of an engine.
gov·er·nor (guv′ər nər) *noun, plural* **governors.**

gown 1. A woman's dress. Gowns are usually worn to parties and other special occasions. 2. A long, loose robe. Students at graduation ceremonies wear gowns.

gown (goun) *noun, plural* **gowns.**

grab To take hold of suddenly; seize; snatch. Danny had to *grab* his jacket and run to get the bus because he was late. The painter *grabbed* at the window sill as the ladder began to sway. *Verb.*

—A sudden, snatching movement. The pitcher made a *grab* for the ball, but it flew over his head. *Noun.*

grab (grab) *verb,* **grabbed, grabbing;** *noun, plural* **grabs.**

Gown

grace 1. Smooth, beautiful motion or action. The ballerina danced with *grace.* 2. A short prayer said before or after a meal. 3. Kindness and courtesy to others; manners. He had the *grace* to apologize for being so rude. *Noun.*

—To add honor or beauty to. A bouquet of roses *graced* the table. The queen *graced* the dinner with her presence. *Verb.*

grace (grās) *noun, plural* **graces;** *verb,* **graced, gracing.**

graceful Smooth and beautiful in motion or action. The dancer made a *graceful* bow to the audience.

grace·ful (grās′fəl) *adjective.*

gracious Showing kindness and courtesy; full of grace and charm. The man was a *gracious* host who made his guests feel welcome.

gra·cious (grā′shəs) *adjective.*

grackle A kind of blackbird. It has a long tail and shiny black feathers.

grack·le (grak′əl) *noun, plural* **grackles.**

Grackle

grade 1. A year or level of work in school. My brother is in the first *grade.* 2. A number or letter showing how well a student has done in work at school; mark. Barbara's *grade* on her geography paper was A. 3. A degree or step in value, quality, or rank. This beef is of the highest *grade.* 4. The slope of a road or a railroad track. There was a steep *grade* on the road that went up the side of the mountain. *Noun.*

—1. To place or arrange in grades; sort. The farmer *graded* the eggs by size and color. 2. To give a grade to; mark. The teacher *graded* the spelling tests. 3. To make ground more level; make less steep. The bulldozer *graded* the new road. *Verb.*

grade (grād) *noun, plural* **grades;** *verb,* **graded, grading.**

grade school A school for children from the ages of about six to twelve or fourteen. This school is often called an **elementary school.**

gradual Happening little by little; moving or changing slowly. Tom watched the *gradual* growth of the seeds into plants in his vegetable garden.

grad·u·al (graj′o͞o əl) *adjective.*

graduate 1. To finish studying at a school or college and be given a diploma. My sister Vivian *graduated* from high school last year. 2. To mark off in equal spaces for measuring. This thermometer is *graduated* in degrees. *Verb.*

—A person who has finished studying at a school or college and has been given a diploma. *Noun.*

grad·u·ate (graj′o͞o āt′ *for verb;* graj′o͞o it *for noun*) *verb,* **graduated, graduating;** *noun, plural* **graduates.**

graduation 1. The act of graduating. Certain subjects must be taken for *graduation* at that college. 2. The ceremony of graduating from a school or college. Susan's whole family went to her *graduation.*

grad·u·a·tion (graj′o͞o ā′shən) *noun, plural* **graduations.**

graft 1. To put a shoot, bud, or branch from one plant into a cut or slit in another plant so that the two pieces will grow together and form one plant. 2. To transfer a piece of skin

at; āpe; cär; end; mē; it; īce; hot; ōld;
fôrk; wood; fo͞ol; oil; out; up; turn; sing;
thin; this; hw in white; zh in treasure.
ə stands for a in about, e in taken
i in pencil, o in lemon, and u in circus.

or bone from one part of the body to another, or from one person to another. The doctors *grafted* skin from the patient's leg onto his burned arm. *Verb.*

—Something that has been grafted. *Noun.*

graft (graft) *verb,* **grafted, grafting;** *noun, plural* **grafts.**

grain 1. The seed of wheat, corn, rice, oats, and other cereal plants. That breakfast cereal is made from *grains* of rice. 2. A tiny, hard piece of something. *Grains* of sand ran through Jesse's fingers as he dug a hole near the shore. 3. The lines and other marks that run through wood, stone, and other things.

grain (grān) *noun, plural* **grains.**

gram A unit of weight in the metric system. One gram is equal to .035 ounces.

gram (gram) *noun, plural* **grams.**

grammar 1. A system of arranging words in sentences so that the meaning of what is said is clearly communicated. Grammar is based on a series of rules. Most of these rules come naturally to us as we use our language or as we hear it used by other people. 2. The use of words in a way that is thought of as correct. Many people think that the word "ain't" is bad *grammar.*

gram·mar (gram′ər) *noun.*

grammar school A school for children from the ages of about six to twelve or fourteen.

grammatical 1. Following the rules of grammar. The sentence "Bought I a shirt white" is not *grammatical,* while "I bought a white shirt" is. 2. Having to do with grammar. His book report has several *grammatical* errors.

gram·mat·i·cal (grə mat′i kəl) *adjective.*

grand 1. Large and splendid. The king lived in a *grand* palace. 2. Including everything; complete. The *grand* total of his winnings in the contest was five thousand dollars. 3. Most important; main. The dance was held in the *grand* ballroom. 4. Very good or excellent. We all had a *grand* time at the birthday party.

grand (grand) *adjective,* **grander, grandest.**

grandchild The child of one's son or daughter.

grand·child (grand′chīld′) *noun, plural* **grandchildren.**

granddaughter The daughter of one's son or daughter.

grand·daugh·ter (gran′dô′tər) *noun, plural* **granddaughters.**

grandfather The father of one's mother or father.

grand·fa·ther (grand′fä′thər *or* gran′fä′thər) *noun, plural* **grandfathers.**

grandfather clock A clock that is in a tall, narrow cabinet that stands on the floor.

grand jury A special kind of jury. It is chosen to hear charges about a crime and decide if there is enough evidence for a trial in a court of law.

grandmother The mother of one's mother or father.

grand·moth·er (grand′muth′ər *or* gran′-muth′ər) *noun, plural* **grandmothers.**

grandparent The parent of one's mother or father. A grandparent is either a grandmother or a grandfather.

grand·par·ent (grand′par′ənt) *noun, plural* **grandparents.**

grandson The son of one's son or daughter.

grand·son (grand′sun′ *or* gran′sun′) *noun, plural* **grandsons.**

grandstand The place where people sit when watching a parade or sports event. It is made up of raised rows of seats that are sometimes covered by a roof.

grand·stand (grand′stand′) *noun, plural* **grandstands.**

Grandstand

granite A hard kind of rock. Granite is used to build monuments and buildings.

gran·ite (gran′it) *noun.*

grant 1. To give or allow. The teacher *granted* him permission to go home early. 2. To admit to be true. I'll *grant* that your argument makes sense. *Verb.*

—Something that is granted; a gift. The farmer got a *grant* of land from the government. *Noun.*

grant (grant) *verb,* **granted, granting;** *noun, plural* **grants.**

to take for granted. To suppose something to be true without question. We *took it for granted* that you wanted to sleep late, so we turned off the alarm clock.

grape   A small, juicy, round fruit that grows in bunches on vines. Grapes have a smooth, thin skin that is usually green or purple in color. They are eaten raw or used to make raisins, jelly, jam, and wine.
grape (grāp) *noun, plural* **grapes.**

grapefruit   A round, pale-yellow fruit. It is like an orange, but larger and more sour.
grape·fruit (grāp′frōōt′) *noun, plural* **grape-fruits.**

Grapes

▲   This fruit is called **grapefruit** because it grows in bunches the way grapes do.

grapevine   **1.** A vine that grapes grow on. **2.** A secret or informal way of spreading news or rumors from person to person. We heard it through the *grapevine* that he asked her to the dance weeks ago.
grape·vine (grāp′vīn′) *noun, plural* **grape-vines.**

graph   A drawing that shows the relationship between changing things. The class drew a *graph* to show how the population of the United States has grown over the past one hundred years.
graph (graf) *noun, plural* **graphs.**

graphite   A soft, black mineral that is a form of the element carbon. It is used as the writing lead in pencils.
graph·ite (graf′īt) *noun.*

▲   The word **graphite** goes back to the Greek word "to write" because graphite is used for lead in pencils.

grasp   **1.** To take hold of firmly with the hand. Chuck *grasped* the handle of the bat tightly and swung at the ball. **2.** To see the meaning of; understand. I had a hard time *grasping* the meaning of that poem. *Verb.*
—1. The act of grasping. His *grasp* on the railing slipped, and he fell down the stairs. **2.** Knowledge; understanding. Julie has a good *grasp* of the problem. *Noun.*
grasp (grasp) *verb,* **grasped, grasping;** *noun, plural* **grasps.**

grass   Any of a large number of plants that have narrow leaves called blades. Grasses grow in lawns, fields, and pastures. Horses, cows, and sheep eat grass. Wheat, rye, oats, corn, sugarcane, rice, and bamboo are grasses.
grass (gras) *noun, plural* **grasses.**

grasshopper   An insect that has long, powerful legs which it uses for jumping. It also has wings. Grasshoppers make a chirping sound.
grass·hop·per (gras′hop′ər) *noun, plural* **grasshoppers.**

Grasshopper

grassland   Land that is covered mainly with grass and has few trees on it. It is often used as pasture for animals.
grass·land (gras′land′) *noun, plural* **grass-lands.**

grassy   Covered with grass. They had a picnic in the *grassy* meadow.
grass·y (gras′ē) *adjective,* **grassier, grassiest.**

grate¹   **1.** A frame of iron bars set over a window or other opening. It is used as a cover, guard, or screen. **2.** A frame of iron bars for holding burning fuel in a fireplace or furnace. ▲ Another word that sounds like this is **great.**
grate (grāt) *noun, plural* **grates.**

grate²   **1.** To make into small pieces or shreds by rubbing against a rough surface. Karen *grated* some cheese to sprinkle on top of the spaghetti. **2.** To rub or scrape with a harsh, grinding noise. The chalk *grated* on the blackboard. **3.** To be annoying, irritating, or unpleasant. Her shrill laugh really *grates* on my nerves. ▲ Another word that sounds like this is **great.**
grate (grāt) *verb,* **grated, grating.**

grateful   Full of thanks or warm feelings for a favor that one has received or for something that makes one happy. We were *grateful* to be inside on such a cold, stormy night.
grate·ful (grāt′fəl) *adjective.*

gratify   To give pleasure or satisfaction to; please. Sally was *gratified* when her teacher praised her report.
grat·i·fy (grat′ə fī′) *verb,* **gratified, gratifying.**

at; āpe; cär; end; mē; it; īce; hot; ōld;
fôrk; wood; fōōl; oil; out; up; turn; sing;
thin; this; hw in white; zh in treasure.
ə stands for a in about, e in taken
i in pencil, o in lemon, and u in circus.

grating¹ A frame of iron bars set over a window or other opening. It is used as a cover, guard, or screen. Windows in banks and post offices often have gratings over them.
grat·ing (grā′ting) *noun, plural* **gratings.**

Grating

grating² **1.** Making a harsh, grinding sound. There was a loud *grating* noise as we pulled the rusty lid open. **2.** Not pleasant; annoying. I find his habit of cracking his knuckles very *grating.*
grat·ing (grā′ting) *adjective.*

gratitude A feeling of thanks for a favor one has received or for something that makes one happy. She was full of *gratitude* for the help that we gave her.
grat·i·tude (grat′ə to̅o̅d′ *or* grat′ə tyo̅o̅d′) *noun.*

grave¹ A hole dug in the ground where a dead body is buried.
grave (grāv) *noun, plural* **graves.**

grave² **1.** Thoughtful and solemn; serious. The doctor's face was *grave* as he described the child's operation to her family. **2.** Very important. The general had to make *grave* decisions when the war broke out.
grave (grāv) *adjective,* **graver, gravest.**

gravel Pebbles and small pieces of rock. It is used for making driveways and roads.
grav·el (grav′əl) *noun.*

graveyard A place where people are buried; cemetery.
grave·yard (grāv′yärd′) *noun, plural* **grave-yards.**

gravitation The force or pull that draws all the bodies in the universe toward one another. Gravitation is the force that keeps the planets in their orbit around the sun. It also keeps objects on the surface of the earth.
grav·i·ta·tion (grav′ə tā′shən) *noun.*

gravity **1.** The force that pulls things toward the center of the earth. Gravity is the force that causes objects to fall when they are dropped. It also pulls them back to earth when they are thrown upward. Gravity also causes objects to have weight. **2.** Serious nature. Because of the *gravity* of the situa-tion, troops were sent to guard against an enemy attack.
grav·i·ty (grav′ə tē) *noun, plural* **gravities.**

gravy A sauce made from the juices that come from meat during cooking.
gra·vy (grā′vē) *noun, plural* **gravies.**

gray A color made by mixing black and white. *Noun.*
—Having the color gray. Jill has *gray* eyes. *Adjective.* This word is also spelled **grey.**
gray (grā) *noun, plural* **grays;** *adjective,* **grayer, grayest.**

graze¹ To feed on growing grass. The flock of sheep *grazed* on the hillside.
graze (grāz) *verb,* **grazed, grazing.**

graze² To scrape lightly. He *grazed* his knee when he fell.
graze (grāz) *verb,* **grazed, grazing.**

grease **1.** Melted animal fat. Bacon *grease* can be used in cooking. **2.** A thick oil. *Grease* is put on the parts of an automobile engine that move against one another. *Noun.*
—To rub or put grease on. *Grease* the baking pan so that the cake won't stick. *Verb.*
grease (grēs *for noun;* grēs *or* grēz *for verb*) *noun, plural* **greases;** *verb,* **greased, greasing.**

greasy **1.** Soiled with grease. The mechanic's overalls were *greasy* after he repaired the car. **2.** Containing much grease or fat. This fried chicken is *greasy.*
greas·y (grē′sē *or* grē′zē) *adjective,* **greasier, greasiest.**

great **1.** Very large in size, number, or amount. A *great* crowd gathered to welcome the astronauts to the city. **2.** Very important, excellent, or remarkable. The scientist's cure for this disease was a *great* discovery. William Shakespeare was a *great* writer. **3.** More than is usual; much. We'll never forget her *great* kindness to us when our mother was ill.
▲ Another word that sounds like this is **grate.**
great (grāt) *adjective,* **greater, greatest.**

Great Britain An island off the western coast of Europe. It is made up of England, Scotland, and Wales.

Great Dane A large, powerful dog. It has a smooth, short coat.
Great Dane (dān).

greatly Very much; highly. We *greatly* appreciated the beautiful gift you gave us.
great·ly (grāt′lē) *adverb.*

Greece A country in southeastern Europe, on the Mediterranean Sea. Its capital is Athens. Ancient Greece was a great center of learning and the arts.
Greece (grēs) *noun.*

greed A very great and selfish desire for

more than one's share of something. Because of his *greed* for money, the grocer tried to cheat everyone who came into his store.

greed (grēd) *noun, plural* **greeds.**

greedy   Having a great and selfish desire for more than one's share of something. The king was *greedy* for power, and he was eager to go to war to get more land.

greed·y (grē′dē) *adjective,* **greedier, greediest.**

Greek   Having to do with ancient or modern Greece, its people, or their language or culture. *Adjective.*

—**1.** A person who was born or is living in Greece. **2.** A person who lived in ancient Greece. **3.** The language of Greece. *Noun.*

Greek (grēk) *adjective; noun, plural* **Greeks.**

green   **1.** The color of growing grass and of leaves in the spring and summer. It is made by mixing blue and yellow. **2.** Ground covered with grass. The meeting took place near the village *green*. **3.** On a golf course, the area around the hole for the ball. It has very thick, closely cut grass. **4. greens.** Green leaves and stems of plants that are used for food. *Noun.*

—**1.** Having the color green. Mother bought a *green* coat. **2.** Covered with growing plants, grass, or leaves. The cows grazed over *green* pastures. **3.** Not full-grown; not ripe. I won't eat those *green* tomatoes. **4.** Having little or no training or experience. Mark was *green* compared to the other boys on the team. *Adjective.*

green (grēn) *noun, plural* **greens;** *adjective,* **greener, greenest.**

greenhouse   A building for growing plants.

green·house (grēn′hous′) *noun, plural* **greenhouses.**

Greenhouse

greet   **1.** To speak to or welcome in a friendly or polite way. Sharon *greeted* her guests at the door. **2.** To respond to; meet; receive. The principal's announcement that school would end early was *greeted* with cheers by the students.

greet (grēt) *verb,* **greeted, greeting.**

greeting   **1.** The act or words of a person who greets others. His *greeting* to us was a wave of his hand. **2. greetings.** A friendly message that is sent by someone. My friend sends *greetings* to me on my birthday every year.

greet·ing (grē′ting) *noun, plural* **greetings.**

grenade   A small bomb that can be thrown by hand.

gre·nade (gri nād′) *noun, plural* **grenades.**

grew   He *grew* tomatoes on his farm. Look up **grow** for more information.

grew (grōō) *verb.*

grey   A color made by mixing black and white. This word is usually spelled **gray.** Look up **gray** for more information.

greyhound   A slender dog with a smooth coat and a long nose. Greyhounds can run very fast.

grey·hound (grā′hound′) *noun, plural* **greyhounds.**

Greyhound

griddle   A heavy, flat metal plate with a handle. It is like a frying pan and is used for cooking pancakes and other food.

grid·dle (grid′əl) *noun, plural* **griddles.**

grief   Very great sadness or pain. His *grief* at the death of his grandfather was something he never forgot.

grief (grēf) *noun, plural* **griefs.**

at; āpe; cär; end; mē; it; īce; hot; ōld;
fôrk; wood; fōol; oil; out; up; turn; sing;
thin; this; hw in white; zh in treasure.
ə stands for a in about, e in taken
i in pencil, o in lemon, and u in circus.

grieve 1. To feel grief; mourn. The entire nation *grieved* at the death of the President. 2. To make someone feel grief or sorrow. His unkind words *grieved* his parents.
  grieve (grēv) *verb*, **grieved, grieving.**

Grill

grill A framework of metal bars for broiling meat or other food over an open fire. My father broiled hot dogs on the *grill* in the backyard. *Noun.*
—1. To broil on a grill. The campers *grilled* hamburgers for supper. 2. To question closely, harshly, and for a long time. The police *grilled* the bank robber until he told them where he had hidden the money. *Verb.*
  grill (gril) *noun, plural* **grills;** *verb,* **grilled, grilling.**

grim 1. Stern, frightening, and harsh. Her face had a cold, *grim* expression. 2. Refusing to give up; very stubborn. The soldiers fought with *grim* determination.
  grim (grim) *adjective,* **grimmer, grimmest.**

grimace A twisting of the face. People often make a grimace when they are not comfortable, pleased, or happy about something. *Noun.*
—To make a grimace. Eileen *grimaced* when she tasted the bitter medicine. *Verb.*
  gri·mace (grim′əs *or* gri mās′) *noun, plural* **grimaces;** *verb,* **grimaced, grimacing.**

grime Dirt that is covering or rubbed into a surface. The windows were covered with *grime.*
  grime (grīm) *noun.*

grin To smile very broadly and happily. Jack *grinned* when his father gave him his birthday present. *Verb.*
—A very broad, happy smile. Judy had a big *grin* on her face as she accepted first prize in the spelling contest. *Noun.*
  grin (grin) *verb,* **grinned, grinning;** *noun, plural* **grins.**

grind 1. To crush or chop into small pieces or into a fine powder. We watched the butcher *grind* the meat. 2. To make something smooth or sharp by rubbing it against something rough. The farmer *ground* his ax on the grindstone. 3. To rub or press down in a harsh or noisy way. She *grinds* her teeth whenever she gets very angry.
  grind (grīnd) *verb,* **ground, grinding.**

grindstone A round, flat stone that is set in a frame. By turning it around and around, a person can use it to sharpen knives, axes, and other tools or to polish or smooth things.
  grind·stone (grīnd′stōn′) *noun, plural* **grindstones.**

Grindstone

grip 1. A firm hold; tight grasp. I kept a good *grip* on the dog's collar when he tried to run after the cat. 2. Firm control or power. The city was in the *grip* of a heavy snowstorm. *Noun.*
—To take hold of firmly and tightly. Mickey *gripped* the bat and swung at the ball as hard as he could. *Verb.*
  grip (grip) *noun, plural* **grips;** *verb,* **gripped, gripping.**

grit 1. Very small bits of sand or stone. The strong wind at the beach blew *grit* in my eyes and my hair. 2. Bravery; courage. Jennifer showed real *grit* when she found her way back to camp alone after getting lost in the woods. *Noun.*
—To press together hard. Doug *gritted* his teeth and then held out his arm for the doctor to give him the flu shot. *Verb.*
  grit (grit) *noun; verb,* **gritted, gritting.**

grizzled Gray or mixed with gray. The old man had a *grizzled* beard.
  griz·zled (griz′əld) *adjective.*

grizzly bear A very large, powerful bear. It has long claws and usually brown or gray fur. Grizzly bears live in western North America.
griz·zly bear (griz′lē).

Grizzly Bear

groan A deep, sad sound that people sometimes make when they are unhappy, annoyed, or in pain. Mother let out a *groan* when the dog left muddy footprints all over the floor she had just washed. *Noun.*
—To make a deep, sad sound. Michael *groaned* when he tried to move his twisted ankle. *Verb.* ▲ Another word that sounds like this is **grown**.
groan (grōn) *noun, plural* **groans;** *verb,* **groaned, groaning.**

grocer A person who sells food and household supplies.
gro·cer (grō′sər) *noun, plural* **grocers.**

grocery 1. A store that sells food and household supplies. 2. **groceries.** Food and other things sold by a grocer. Mother sent Sam out to buy some *groceries.*
gro·cer·y (grō′sər ē) *noun, plural* **groceries.**

groom 1. A man who has just been married. 2. A person whose work is taking care of horses. *Noun.*
—1. To wash, brush, and take care of horses. Eddie knows about *grooming* horses because he worked on a farm last summer. 2. To make neat and pleasant in appearance. She *groomed* her hair for the party. *Verb.*
groom (groom) *noun, plural* **grooms;** *verb,* **groomed, grooming.**

groove A long, narrow cut or dent. The wheels of the car made *grooves* in the dirt road. A phonograph record has *grooves* in it for the needle of the record player. *Noun.*
—To make a groove or grooves in. The carpenter *grooved* the sides of the bookcase

so that the shelves would fit into place. *Verb.*
groove (groov) *noun, plural* **grooves;** *verb,* **grooved, grooving.**

grope 1. To feel about with the hands. As he entered the dark room, Jerry *groped* for the light switch. 2. To search about in the mind for something. He *groped* for the right answer as everyone waited for him to speak. 3. To find one's way by feeling about with the hands. The audience *groped* its way to the door as the theater filled with smoke.
grope (grōp) *verb,* **groped, groping.**

gross 1. With nothing taken out; total; entire. A person's *gross* income is all the money he or she earns before taxes are taken out of it. 2. Very bad or wrong; terrible. It is a *gross* injustice that this innocent man was sent to prison. 3. Coarse; vulgar. His *gross* jokes annoyed everyone at dinner. *Adjective.*
—1. The total amount. The company's *gross* for the year was five million dollars. 2. Twelve dozen; 144. The tennis coach ordered a *gross* of balls. *Noun.*
gross (grōs) *adjective,* **grosser, grossest;** *noun, plural* **grosses** (*for definition 1*) or **gross** (*for definition 2*).

grotesque Strange, ugly, or not natural. There were *grotesque* monsters in the movie.
gro·tesque (grō tesk′) *adjective.*

▲ The word that **grotesque** comes from was first used for paintings of strange beings that were part man and part animal. These paintings were found in caves in Italy hundreds of years ago, and the word for them came from the word for "cave." Now it is used for anything that is strange and ugly.

---

grouch A person who is cross and bad-tempered. A grouch usually complains a great deal.
grouch (grouch) *noun, plural* **grouches.**

ground¹ 1. The part of the earth that is solid; soil; land. The *ground* was covered with snow. 2. **grounds.** The land around a house or other building. The school *grounds* were planted with trees and flowers. 3. An area or piece of land used for some special purpose. A brook runs through the picnic *grounds.* 4. The cause for something said,

at; āpe; cär; end; mē; it; īce; hot; ōld; fôrk; wood; fool; oil; out; up; turn; sing; thin; this; hw in white; zh in treasure. ə stands for a in about, e in taken i in pencil, o in lemon, and u in circus.

done, or thought: reason. What *grounds* do the police have for thinking that he is the thief? **5.** grounds. The bits of coffee that settle at the bottom of a cup or that are left over in the coffeepot. *Noun.*
—**1.** To force or stay on the ground or to come down to the ground. The airport *grounded* the plane for three hours because of bad weather. **2.** To cause to hit the bottom of a river or other body of water. The captain *grounded* his ship on the sand bar. **3.** To hit a baseball so that it rolls or bounces along the ground. The batter *grounded* to the first baseman. **4.** To fix or base firmly. You must *ground* an argument on facts. **5.** To connect with the ground. These electric wires are dangerous if they aren't *grounded. Verb.*
ground (ground) *noun, plural* **grounds;** *verb,* **grounded, grounding.**

ground² The wheat was *ground* into flour. Look up **grind** for more information.
ground (ground) *verb.*

groundhog A small animal that has a plump body, short legs, and a bushy tail. It is usually called a **woodchuck.** Look up **woodchuck** for more information.
ground·hog (ground′hog′) *noun, plural* **groundhogs.**

group **1.** A number of persons or things together. A *group* of people gathered on the corner to watch the firemen put out the fire. **2.** A number of persons or things that belong together or that are put together. The teacher divided the class into *groups* who would read different stories. *Noun.*
—To form into a group. Our camp counselor *grouped* us by age. The boys *grouped* around the famous baseball player. *Verb.*
group (grōōp) *noun, plural* **groups;** *verb,* **grouped, grouping.**

grouse A bird that looks like a plump chicken. Grouse have brown, black, or gray feathers and are hunted as game.
grouse (grous) *noun, plural* **grouse** or **grouses.**

Grouse

grove A group of trees standing together. Oranges grow in *groves.*
grove (grōv) *noun, plural* **groves.**

grow **1.** To become bigger; increase. That plant will *grow* quickly. Joan *grew* two inches last year. **2.** To come into being and live; exist. Cactuses don't *grow* in this part of the country. **3.** To cause to grow. That farmer *grows* corn. **4.** To become. It *grew* cold as the sun went down. He *grew* rich as his business became successful.
grow (grō) *verb,* **grew, grown, growing.**
to grow up. To become an adult. Susan said she wants to become a lawyer when she *grows up.*

growl To make a deep, harsh, rumbling sound in the throat. Dogs and other animals often growl when they are angry. The bear *growled* when we got too close to its cage. *Verb.*
—A deep, harsh, rumbling sound made in the throat. He greeted us with a *growl* when he had to get out of the shower to open the door for us. *Noun.*
growl (groul) *verb,* **growled, growling;** *noun, plural* **growls.**

grown Sandra has *grown* very pretty. These trees have *grown* very tall. Look up **grow** for more information. ▲ Another word that sounds like this is **groan.**
grown (grōn) *verb.*

grown-up **1.** Having come to full growth; adult. He's a *grown-up* person now. **2.** Of or like an adult. Maria's *grown-up* manners make you think she's older than she is. *Adjective.*
—A person who has come to full growth; an adult. The *grown-ups* watched as the children swam in the pool. *Noun.*
grown-up (grōn′up′ *for adjective;* grōn′up′ *for noun*) *adjective; noun, plural* **grown-ups.**

growth **1.** The process of growing. Jim planted some seeds in his back yard and then watched their *growth.* The *growth* of Mr. Jackson's business has been very rapid. **2.** Something that has grown. A thick *growth* of weeds covered the path leading to the old house.
growth (grōth) *noun, plural* **growths.**

grub A beetle or other insect in an early stage of growth, when it looks like a worm. *Noun.*
—To dig in the ground; dig up from the ground. Pigs *grub* for food with their hooves and snouts. *Verb.*
grub (grub) *noun, plural* **grubs;** *verb,* **grubbed, grubbing.**

grudge Dislike or anger that has been felt for a long time. He's held a *grudge* against her ever since she ran against him for class president. *Noun.*
—To be unwilling to give or allow. Even though you don't like her, don't *grudge* her first prize if she deserves it. *Verb.*
grudge (gruj) *noun, plural* **grudges;** *verb,* **grudged, grudging.**

grueling Very difficult or exhausting. The cross-country bicycle race was *grueling.*
gru·el·ing (grōō′ə ling) *adjective.*

gruesome Causing disgust or fear; horrible. When we walked past the cemetery, we remembered all those *gruesome* stories about ghosts.
grue·some (grōō′səm) *adjective.*

gruff **1.** Deep and rough-sounding. The guard asked us in a *gruff* voice what we were doing in the building so late. **2.** Not friendly, warm, or polite. His manner is *gruff,* but he's really very kind.
gruff (gruf) *adjective,* **gruffer, gruffest.**

grumble To complain in a low voice; mutter in an unhappy way. Ted got out of bed and *grumbled* about having to wake up so early. *Verb.*
—**1.** Unhappy complaining or muttering. She answered with a *grumble* that she was tired of having to walk the dog and that it was Larry's turn. **2.** A low, rumbling sound. We could hear the *grumble* of thunder in the distance. *Noun.*
grum·ble (grum′bəl) *verb,* **grumbled, grumbling;** *noun, plural* **grumbles.**

grumpy In a bad mood; cross or grouchy. He's often *grumpy* when his older brother teases him.
grump·y (grum′pē) *adjective,* **grumpier, grumpiest.**

grunt A short, deep sound. The hog finished eating and lay down with a *grunt.* *Noun.*
—To make a short, deep sound. The man *grunted* in pain as the woman's umbrella poked him in the ribs. *Verb.*
grunt (grunt) *noun, plural* **grunts;** *verb,* **grunted, grunting.**

guarantee A promise to repair or replace something or to give back the money for it, if anything goes wrong with it before a certain time has passed. This toaster comes with a *guarantee* of one year. *Noun.*
—**1.** To give a guarantee for. The company *guarantees* this dishwasher for one year. **2.** To make sure or certain. Having that singer perform will *guarantee* that the dance will be a success. **3.** To promise something. The plumber *guaranteed* the work would be finished on time. *Verb.*
guar·an·tee (gar′ən tē′) *noun, plural* **guarantees;** *verb,* **guaranteed, guaranteeing.**

guard **1.** To keep safe from harm or danger; protect. The dog *guarded* the house. **2.** To watch over or control. The policeman *guarded* the prisoner. **3.** To try to prevent a player on another team from scoring. Jack *guarded* the other team's star player during the game. *Verb.*
—**1.** A person or group of persons that guards. The museum *guard* collected our tickets at the door. **2.** A close watch. A sentry kept *guard* at the army camp. **3.** Something that protects. Patrick's chin *guard* slipped during the football game, and he got cut in the mouth. **4.** A player at either side of the center in football. **5.** In basketball, either of two players whose position is toward the back of the court. *Noun.*
guard (gärd) *verb,* **guarded, guarding;** *noun, plural* **guards.**

guardian A person chosen by law to take care of someone who is young or who is not able to care for himself. After the baby's parents died, her uncle became her *guardian.*
guard·i·an (gär′dē ən) *noun, plural* **guardians.**

guerrilla A member of a small band of soldiers. Guerrillas are not part of the regular army of a country. They often fight the enemy by making quick, surprise attacks. ▲ Another word that sounds like this is **gorilla.**
guer·ril·la (gə ril′ə) *noun, plural* **guerrillas.**

guess **1.** To form an opinion without having enough knowledge or facts to be sure. Without a watch, he could only *guess* what time it was. **2.** To get the correct answer by guessing. I *guessed* the end of the mystery story. **3.** To think; believe; suppose. I *guess* he forgot her birthday because he didn't send her a card. *Verb.*
—An opinion formed without having enough knowledge or facts to be sure. His *guess* is that Ellen will be home by now. *Noun.*
guess (ges) *verb,* **guessed, guessing;** *noun, plural* **guesses.**

at; āpe; cär; end; mē; it; īce; hot; ōld; fôrk; wood; fōōl; oil; out; up; turn; sing; thin; this; hw in white; zh in treasure. ə stands for a in about, e in taken i in pencil, o in lemon, and u in circus.

guest 1. A person who is at another's house for a meal or a visit. We are having *guests* for dinner tonight. 2. A customer in a restaurant, hotel, or similar place. This motel has room for fifty *guests*.
guest (gest) *noun, plural* **guests.**

guide To show the way; direct. The boy scout *guided* the other campers through the woods. *Verb.*
—A person or thing that shows the way or directs. When my aunt and uncle were in Europe, their *guide* took them through the museums. *Noun.*
guide (gīd) *verb*, **guided, guiding;** *noun, plural* **guides.**

guided missile A missile that is guided along a certain course throughout its flight. It is guided by an automatic control inside it or by radio signals that it receives from the ground.

guide word One of the words that appear at the top of a page in dictionaries and some other books. Guide words show the first and last things that appear on a page. The guide words on this page of your dictionary are **guest** and **gulf.**

guild 1. In the Middle Ages, a group of people in the same trade or craft who joined together. Guilds were set up to see that the quality of work done was good and to look out for the interests of their members. 2. An organization of people with the same interests or aims. The women's *guild* of our church is holding a cake sale to raise money. ▲ Another word that sounds like this is **gild.**
guild (gild) *noun, plural* **guilds.**

guillotine A machine for executing a person by cutting off his head. It is made of a heavy blade that is dropped between two posts.
guil·lo·tine (gil′ə tēn′) *noun, plural* **guillotines.**

▲ The **guillotine** was named after Joseph I. *Guillotin.* He was a French doctor who is supposed to have urged the use of this machine as a fast and less painful way of executing people.

---

guilt 1. The state or fact of having done wrong or broken the law. The lawyer said that the new evidence proved the man's *guilt* in the robbery. 2. A feeling of having done something wrong; regret; shame. He felt a good deal of *guilt* after he'd been rude to the old woman.
guilt (gilt) *noun, plural* **guilts.**

guilty 1. Having done wrong; deserving to be blamed or punished. The jury found him *guilty* of armed robbery. We're all *guilty* of losing our temper sometimes. 2. Feeling or showing guilt or shame. She had a *guilty* conscience for days after she told the lie.
guilt·y (gil′tē) *adjective,* **guiltier, guiltiest.**

Guinea Fowl

guinea fowl A bird that has dark-gray feathers with small, white spots. It comes from Africa. Guinea fowl are raised as food in many parts of the world. A guinea fowl is sometimes also called a **guinea hen.**
guin·ea fowl (gin′ē).

guinea pig A small, plump animal with short ears, short legs, and no tail. It is often used in scientific experiments. Guinea pigs are very gentle and are often kept as pets.

Guinea Pig

guitar A musical instrument with a long neck and six or more strings. It is played by plucking or strumming the strings. Some kinds of guitars use electricity to make their sound louder.
gui·tar (gi tär′) *noun, plural* **guitars.**

Guitar

gulf A part of an ocean or sea that is partly enclosed by land. A gulf is usually larger and deeper than a bay.
gulf (gulf) *noun, plural* **gulfs.**

gull   A bird with gray and white feathers. It lives on or near bodies of water. It has long wings and a thick, slightly hooked beak. It is also called a **sea gull**.
   gull (gul) *noun, plural* **gulls.**

Gull

gullible   Believing or trusting in almost anything; easily fooled, tricked, or cheated. Everyone always plays jokes on him because he's *gullible* enough to believe any story you tell him.
   gul·li·ble (gul′ə bəl) *adjective.*

gully   A narrow ditch. After the rainstorm, there were *gullies* along the sides of the road.
   gul·ly (gul′ē) *noun, plural* **gullies.**

gulp   **1.** To swallow quickly, greedily, or in large amounts. Robin *gulped* a glass of milk and ran out to catch the bus. **2.** To draw in or swallow air; gasp. When her father asked her who had broken the window, Joyce *gulped* and said nothing. *Verb.*
   —The act of gulping. Frank finished the lemonade in two *gulps. Noun.*
   gulp (gulp) *verb,* **gulped, gulping;** *noun, plural* **gulps.**

gum¹   **1.** A thick, sticky juice that comes from various trees and plants. Gum hardens when it is dry. It is used for sticking paper and other things together. **2.** Gum that is made sweet and thick for chewing.
   gum (gum) *noun, plural* **gums.**

gum²   The pink, tough flesh around the teeth.
   gum (gum) *noun, plural* **gums.**

gumdrop   A small piece of candy that is like jelly coated with sugar.
   gum·drop (gum′drop′) *noun, plural* **gumdrops.**

gun   **1.** A weapon made up of a metal tube through which a bullet or something similar is shot. Pistols, rifles, and cannons are guns. **2.** Something that is like a gun in shape or use. Keith used a spray *gun* to paint the bookcase. *Noun.*
   —To shoot or hunt with a gun. The outlaw in the movie tried to *gun* down the sheriff. *Verb.*
   gun (gun) *noun, plural* **guns;** *verb,* **gunned, gunning.**

▲ The word **gun** is probably a short form of the name *Gunnhildr. Gunnhildr* was a common name for women in an old Scandinavian language. Men often gave women's names to their weapons, and the name *Gunnhildr* may have been chosen for a weapon because it was made up of two words that meant "war" and "battle."

gunner   A soldier or other person in the armed forces who handles and fires cannons and other large guns.
   gun·ner (gun′ər) *noun, plural* **gunners.**

gunpowder   A powder that burns and explodes when set on fire. It is used in guns, fireworks, and blasting.
   gun·pow·der (gun′pou′dər) *noun, plural* **gunpowders.**

gunwale   The upper edge of the side of a ship or boat.
   gun·wale (gun′əl) *noun, plural* **gunwales.**

guppy   A very small fish. The male is brightly colored. The guppy is often kept as a pet.
   gup·py (gup′ē) *noun, plural* **guppies.**

Guppies

▲ The word **guppy** comes from the name of R. J. L. *Guppy.* He was an English minister who knew a great deal about these fish and gave samples of them to a museum.

at; āpe; cär; end; mē; it; īce; hot; ōld;
fôrk; wood; fo͞ol; oil; out; up; turn; sing;
thin; **th**is; **hw** in white; **zh** in treasure.
ə stands for **a** in about, **e** in taken
i in pencil, **o** in lemon, and **u** in circus.

gurgle **1.** To flow or run with a bubbling sound. The stream *gurgled* around the rocks. **2.** To make a sound like this. The baby *gurgled* in her crib.
gur·gle (gur′gəl) *verb,* **gurgled, gurgling.**

gush **1.** To pour out suddenly and in large amounts. Water *gushed* from the broken pipe. His cut finger *gushed* blood until it was bandaged. **2.** To talk with so much feeling and eagerness that it seems silly. Our neighbor is always *gushing* about how smart her grandchildren are. *Verb.*
—A sudden, heavy flow. Oil poured out of the well in a *gush. Noun.*
gush (gush) *verb,* **gushed, gushing;** *noun, plural* **gushes.**

gust **1.** A sudden, strong rush of wind or air. A *gust* of wind lifted Paul's cap off his head and carried it across the street. **2.** A short or sudden bursting out of feeling. *Gusts* of laughter greeted the comedian as he danced out on stage.
gust (gust) *noun, plural* **gusts.**

gutter **1.** A channel or ditch along the side of a street or road to carry off water. Julie's ball rolled off the sidewalk into the *gutter.* **2.** A pipe or trough along the lower edge of a roof. It carries off rain water.
gut·ter (gut′ər) *noun, plural* **gutters.**

Gutter

Gutter

guy¹ A rope, chain, or wire used to steady or fasten something. Guys are used to steady a tent.
guy (gī) *noun, plural* **guys.**

guy² A boy or man; fellow. Marty is a very nice *guy.* ▲ This word is used only in everyday conversation.
guy (gī) *noun, plural* **guys.**

gym **1.** A room or building that is used for physical exercise; gymnasium. The school basketball team practices in the *gym* almost every day after classes. **2.** A course in physical education that is given in a school or college.
gym (jim) *noun, plural* **gyms.**

gymnasium A room or building with equipment for physical exercise or training and for indoor sports.
gym·na·si·um (jim nā′zē əm) *noun, plural* **gymnasiums.**

gymnastics Exercises done to develop the body.
gym·nas·tics (jim nas′tiks) *noun plural.*

Gymnastics

Gypsy A person belonging to a group of people who came to Europe from India long ago. Gypsies are a wandering people and they now live scattered throughout the world.
Gyp·sy (jip′sē) *noun, plural* **Gypsies.**

▲ The word **Gypsy** is short for "Egyptian." People used to think that Gypsies came from Egypt.

gyroscope A wheel that is mounted so that its axis can point in any direction. A gyroscope is used as a compass and to keep airplanes and ships steady.
gy·ro·scope (jī′rə skōp′) *noun, plural* **gyroscopes.**

at; āpe; cär; end; mē; it; īce; hot; ōld; fôrk; wood; fōōl; oil; out; up; turn; sing; thin; this; hw in white; zh in treasure.
ə stands for **a** in about, **e** in taken
i in pencil, **o** in lemon, and **u** in circus.

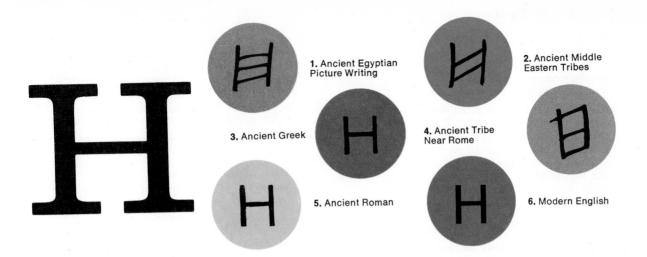

1. Ancient Egyptian Picture Writing

2. Ancient Middle Eastern Tribes

3. Ancient Greek

4. Ancient Tribe Near Rome

5. Ancient Roman

6. Modern English

H is the eighth letter of the alphabet. The oldest form of the letter **H** was probably a drawing that the ancient Egyptians (**1**) used in their picture writing more than 5000 years ago. This drawing, which meant "fence," was borrowed by several ancient tribes (**2**) in the Middle East. They used this letter to stand for an *h* sound made at the back of the throat. When the ancient Greeks (**3**) borrowed this letter they wrote it, at first, in the shape of two squares, one on top of the other. Later, the Greeks gave the letter its modern form of two tall lines connected by a short bar. The earlier form of **H** was borrowed by a tribe (**4**) that settled north of Rome about 2800 years ago. But the Romans (**5**) used the later Greek form of the letter. By about 2400 years ago, the Romans were writing this letter in almost the same way that we write the capital letter **H** today (**6**).

h, H   The eighth letter of the alphabet.
  h, H (āch) *noun, plural* **h's, H's.**

ha   **1.** A word used to show surprise, joy, or victory. "*Ha!* I've found the treasure!" cried the pirate. **2.** A word used to express laughter. "*Ha, ha, ha,*" laughed the boys at the funny joke.
  ha (hä) *interjection.*

habit   **1.** An action that you do so often or for so long that you do it without thinking. A habit is hard to stop or control. He has the bad *habit* of biting his fingernails. It is my dad's *habit* to read the paper at breakfast. **2.** A certain kind of dress. The nun's *habit* was black.
  hab·it (hab′it) *noun, plural* **habits.**

Habit

habitat   The place where an animal or plant naturally lives and grows. The natural *habitat* of fish is water. The desert is the *habitat* of the cactus.
  hab·i·tat (hab′ə tat′) *noun, plural* **habitats.**

hacienda   A large country estate used for farming or for raising cattle. There are haciendas in the southwestern United States and Mexico.
  ha·ci·en·da (hä′sē en′də) *noun, plural* **haciendas.**

hack   **1.** To cut or chop unevenly with heavy blows. This is often done with a hatchet or cleaver. The explorers *hacked* their way through the thick forest. **2.** To cough with short, harsh sounds.
  hack (hak) *verb,* **hacked, hacking.**

had   He *had* fun at the party. Look up **have** for more information.
  had (had *or* həd *or* əd) *verb.*

hadn't   I *hadn't* met her until yesterday.
  had·n't (had′ənt) contraction for "had not."

hail¹   To greet or attract the attention of by calling or shouting. He *hailed* his friend across the street by calling to him. She *hailed* a taxi by waving her arm. *Verb.*
  —A motion or call used as a greeting or to attract attention. *Noun.*
  hail (hāl) *verb,* **hailed, hailing;** *noun, plural* **hails.**
  to hail from. To come from. He *hails from* Florida.

hail²   **1.** Small roundish pieces of ice that fall in a shower like rain. The *hail* came down so hard that it crushed many of the flowers in the garden. **2.** A heavy shower of anything.

The married couple ran off in a *hail* of rice thrown by the guests. *Noun.*
—To pour down like hail. The bully *hailed* punches on the smaller boy. *Verb.*
hail (hāl) *noun; verb,* **hailed, hailing.**

hair **1.** A very thin, threadlike growth on the skin of people and animals. **2.** A mass of such growths. The girl's *hair* is brown and wavy. **3.** A very thin, threadlike growth on the outer layer of plants. ▲ Another word that sounds like this is **hare.**
hair (her) *noun, plural* **hairs.**

haircut The act or style of cutting the hair.
hair·cut (her′kut′) *noun, plural* **haircuts.**

hairy Covered with hair; having a lot of hair. An ape is a *hairy* animal.
hair·y (her′ē) *adjective,* **hairier, hairiest.**

half **1.** One of two equal parts of something. A pint is *half* a quart. We ate *half* the pie. She will be away at camp for a month and a *half.* **2.** Either of two time periods in certain sports. A football game or a basketball game is divided into two *halves. Noun.*
—Being one of two equal parts. We bought a *half* gallon of ice cream. *Adjective.*
—Not completely; partly. I was *half* asleep by the time the movie ended. *Adverb.*
half (haf) *noun, plural* **halves;** *adjective; adverb.*

half-mast The position of a flag when it is halfway down from the top of a pole. It is used as a sign of mourning for someone who has died or as a signal of distress.
half-mast (haf′mast′) *noun.*

halfway **1.** Half the distance; midway. We climbed *halfway* up the mountain. **2.** Not completely; partly. The movie is *halfway* over. *Adverb.*
—**1.** Half the way between two points. Ann was winning the sailboat race as her boat reached the *halfway* mark. **2.** Not finished; incomplete. *Halfway* measures will not solve the problem of pollution. *Adjective.*
half·way (haf′wā′) *adverb; adjective.*

halibut A large fish with a flat body. It may weigh several hundred pounds. This fish is found in the northern waters of the Atlantic and Pacific Oceans.
hal·i·but (hal′ə bət) *noun, plural* **halibut** or **halibuts.**

▲ The word **halibut** comes from two earlier English words that meant "holy" and "flat-fish." This fish was called "holy" because it was eaten on holy days when Christians were not allowed to eat meat.

hall **1.** A passageway onto which rooms open in a house or other building. The students lined up in the *hall* before they went into the auditorium. **2.** A room at the entrance to a building; lobby. We left our wet umbrellas in the *hall.* **3.** A building or room used for a particular purpose. We went to the concert *hall.* The dining *hall* of our school is in the basement. ▲ Another word that sounds like this is **haul.**
hall (hôl) *noun, plural* **halls.**

Halloween The evening of October 31. Halloween is celebrated by dressing up in costumes and playing tricks.
Hal·low·een (hal′ə wēn′ *or* hal′ō ēn′) *noun, plural* **Halloweens.**

hallway A hall or passageway.
hall·way (hôl′wā′) *noun, plural* **hallways.**

halo **1.** A ring of light painted by an artist around the head of a saint or angel. **2.** A circle of light that seems to surround the sun, the moon, or another heavenly body. The planet Saturn has two *halos.*
ha·lo (hā′lō) *noun, plural* **halos** or **haloes.**

halt A stop for a short time. The car came to a *halt* at the red light. *Noun.*
—To stop. The troops will *halt* when the sergeant gives the order. *Verb.*
halt (hôlt) *noun, plural* **halts;** *verb,* **halted, halting.**

halter A rope or strap used for leading or tying an animal. It fits over the animal's nose and over or behind its ears.
hal·ter (hôl′tər) *noun, plural* **halters.**

Halter

halve **1.** To divide into two equal parts. I *halved* an apple so that I could share it with my sister. **2.** To make less by half. Susan *halved* the recipe so there would be enough for two instead of four. ▲ Another word that sounds like this is **have.**
halve (hav) *verb,* **halved, halving.**

halves More than one half. Look up **half** for more information.
halves (havz) *noun plural.*

ham **1.** The meat from the back leg or shoulder of a hog. It is usually salted or smoked. **2.** An amateur radio operator.
ham (ham) *noun, plural* **hams.**

hamburger **1.** Ground beef. The recipe

calls for a pound of *hamburger*. **2.** A flat cake of ground beef. It is broiled or fried and usually served on a bun or roll.
ham·burg·er (ham′bur′gər) *noun, plural* **hamburgers.**

▲ The word **hamburger** comes from *Hamburger steak* or *Hamburg steak.* These names were first used in the beginning of the 1900s and came from the city of Hamburg, Germany. No one knows exactly why it is that hamburgers came to be named after this German city.

hammer **1.** A tool with a heavy metal head on a long handle. A hammer is used for driving nails and for beating or shaping metals. **2.** Anything that is like a hammer in shape or use. The *hammer* of a gun causes it to fire when the trigger is pulled. *Noun.*
—**1.** To strike again and again; pound. He *hammered* nails into the wall. The angry man *hammered* at the door with his fist. **2.** To pound into shape with a hammer. In camp, we learned to *hammer* a bowl out of copper. *Verb.*
ham·mer (ham′ər) *noun, plural* **hammers;** *verb,* **hammered, hammering.**

hammock A swinging bed that is hung between two trees or poles. It is made from a long piece of canvas or netting.
ham·mock (ham′ək) *noun, plural* **hammocks.**

Hammock

hamper[1] To get in the way of action or progress. Stalled cars *hampered* efforts to remove the snow from the streets.
ham·per (ham′pər) *verb,* **hampered, hampering.**
hamper[2] A large basket or container with a

cover. There are food *hampers* for picnics and clothes *hampers* for dirty laundry.
ham·per (ham′pər) *noun, plural* **hampers.**

hamster An animal that is like a mouse. It has a plump body, a short tail, and large cheek pouches. A hamster is a rodent.
ham·ster (ham′stər) *noun, plural* **hamsters.**

Hamster

hand **1.** The end part of the arm from the wrist down. It is made up of the palm, four fingers, and a thumb. We use our hands to pick up and hold onto things. **2.** Anything like a hand in shape or use. The *hands* of the clock pointed to three o'clock. **3. hands.** Control or possession. The town is in enemy *hands*. The decision is in your *hands*. **4.** A member of a group or crew; workman. The *hands* on the farm get up early to start their work. **5.** A way of doing something. Richard has such a quick *hand* at doing magic tricks that he always fools us. **6.** A part in something; share; role. Each student had a *hand* in planning the class dance. **7.** Help; aid. Ann gave me a *hand* in cleaning the blackboard. **8.** A round of applause; clapping. The audience gave the actors a big *hand*. **9.** One round of a card game. **10.** The cards a player holds in one round of a card game. **11.** A measurement equal to four inches. It is used to tell the height of a horse. *Noun.*
—To give or pass with the hand. He *handed* the book to the librarian. Please *hand* me the salt. *Verb.*
hand (hand) *noun, plural* **hands;** *verb,* **handed, handing.**
on hand. Ready or available for use. We always keep canned foods *on hand.*
on the other hand. From another point of view. That player is not very fast, but *on the other hand* he is very strong.
to hand down. To pass along. That gold watch was *handed down* to my father from his grandfather.

at; āpe; cär; end; mē; it; īce; hot; ōld;
fôrk; wood; fōōl; oil; out; up; turn; sing;
thin; this; hw in white; zh in treasure.
ə stands for a in about, e in taken
i in pencil, o in lemon, and u in circus.

handbag   A bag or case used by women; pocketbook. Women carry a wallet, keys, or cosmetics in it.
   hand·bag (hand′bag′) *noun, plural* **handbags.**

handball   **1.** A game in which players·take turns hitting a small rubber ball against a wall with the hand. **2.** The ball that is used in this game.
   hand·ball (hand′bôl′) *noun, plural* **handballs.**

handbook   A book that has information or instructions about a subject. We bought a *handbook* about New York City when we went there for a visit.
   hand·book (hand′book′) *noun, plural* **hand-books.**

handcuff   One of two metal rings joined by a chain. Handcuffs are locked around the wrists of a prisoner to keep him from using his hands. *Noun.*
   —To put handcuffs on. The policeman *hand-cuffed* the suspected thief and led him away. *Verb.*
   hand·cuff (hand′kuf′) *noun, plural* **hand-cuffs;** *verb,* **handcuffed, handcuffing.**

handful   **1.** The amount the hand can hold at one time. She took a *handful* of peanuts from the jar. **2.** A small amount or amount. Only a *handful* of people showed up for the club meeting.
   hand·ful (hand′fool′) *noun, plural* **handfuls.**

handicap   Anything that makes it harder for a person to do well or get ahead. Being short can be a *handicap* in playing basketball. *Noun.*
   —To put at a disadvantage; hinder. His poor eyesight *handicaps* him in his work. *Verb.*
   hand·i·cap (han′dē kap′) *noun, plural* **handi-caps;** *verb,* **handicapped, handicapping.**

handicraft   A trade, work, or art in which skill with the hands is needed. Making pottery and weaving are handicrafts.
   hand·i·craft (han′dē kraft′) *noun, plural* **handicrafts.**

handkerchief   A square, soft piece of cloth. It is usually used to wipe the nose or face.
   hand·ker·chief (hang′kər chif) *noun, plural* **handkerchiefs.**

handle   The part of an object that is made to be grasped by the hands. A frying pan, a suitcase, a tennis racket, a knife, and a broom have handles. *Noun.*
   —**1.** To touch or hold with the hand. Please *handle* the glass carefully so that it won't fall and break. **2.** To manage, control, or deal with. She knows how to *handle* dogs so they will obey her. Tom *handled* the problem well. *Verb.*

han·dle (hand′əl) *noun, plural* **handles;** *verb,* **handled, handling.**

handlebars   The curved bar on the front of a bicycle or motorcycle. The rider grips the ends of the bars and uses them to steer.
   han·dle·bars (hand′əl bärz′) *noun plural.*

handsome   **1.** Having a pleasing appearance; good-looking. He is a *handsome* man. That old desk is very *handsome.* **2.** Fairly large or generous. The family gave Sue a *handsome* reward for finding their pet dog.
   hand·some (han′səm) *adjective,* **handsomer, handsomest.**

handspring   A leap in which a person springs onto his hands with his feet over his head and then lands back on his feet again.
   hand·spring (hand′spring′) *noun, plural* **handsprings.**

Handspring

handwriting   Writing done by hand. It is writing done with a pen or pencil, not with a machine. Her *handwriting* is very hard to read.
   hand·writ·ing (hand′rī′ting) *noun, plural* **handwritings.**

handy   **1.** Within reach; nearby. Bob always keeps a handkerchief *handy.* **2.** Working well with one's hands; skillful. Mike is *handy* with tools. **3.** Easy to use or handle. My parents bought me a *handy* carrying case for all my school books.
   hand·y (han′dē) *adjective,* **handier, handiest.**

hang   **1.** To fasten something from above only, without support from below. We will *hang* our wet bathing suits on the line. Please *hang* the pictures on that empty wall. **2.** To attach something so it moves freely back and forth. We *hung* the gate on hinges. **3.** To put a person to death by hanging by a rope tied around the neck. *Verb.*
   —**1.** The way something hangs or falls. Kathy did not like the *hang* of her new dress. **2.** A way of doing something; knack. It takes a while to get the *hang* of riding a bicycle. *Noun.*

hang (hang) *verb,* **hung** *(for definitions 1 and 2)* or **hanged** *(for definition 3),* **hanging;** *noun.*

hangar A building or shed to keep airplanes in. ▲ Another word that sounds like this is **hanger.**
han·gar (hang′ər) *noun, plural* **hangars.**

hanger A device on which something is hung. I hung my coat on a *hanger.* ▲ Another word that sounds like this is **hangar.**
hang·er (hang′ər) *noun, plural* **hangers.**

hangnail A piece of skin that hangs loosely at the side or bottom of a fingernail.
hang·nail (hang′nāl′) *noun, plural* **hangnails.**

happen **1.** To take place; occur. The accident *happened* last week. **2.** To take place without plan or reason; occur by chance. Her birthday just *happens* to be the same day as mine. **3.** To come or go by chance. A policeman *happened* along just after the robbery. **4.** To be done. Something must have *happened* to the telephone, because it isn't working.
hap·pen (hap′ən) *verb,* **happened, happening.**

happening Something that happens; event. George told us about some of the *happenings* in the neighborhood while we were away.
hap·pen·ing (hap′ə ning) *noun, plural* **happenings.**

happily **1.** With pleasure or gladness. After the teacher praised her work, Ann walked *happily* home. **2.** Luckily. *Happily,* no one was hurt in the fire.
hap·pi·ly (hap′ə lē) *adverb.*

happiness The state of being glad or content. Their vacation on the farm was full of *happiness.*
hap·pi·ness (hap′ē nis) *noun.*

happy Feeling or showing pleasure or gladness. The children were *happy* when they got a new dog.
hap·py (hap′ē) *adjective,* **happier, happiest.**

harass To bother or annoy again and again. The bully *harassed* the younger children by teasing them.
har·ass (har′əs *or* hə ras′) *verb,* **harassed, harassing.**

harbor A sheltered place along a coast. Ships and boats often anchor in a harbor. *Noun.*
—**1.** To give protection or shelter to. It is against the law to *harbor* a criminal in your house. **2.** To keep in one's mind. Paul *harbored* a grudge against the boy who had been rude to him. *Verb.*
har·bor (här′bər) *noun, plural* **harbors;** *verb,* **harbored, harboring.**

hard **1.** Solid and firm to the touch; not soft. Rocks are *hard.* **2.** Needing or using much effort. Chopping wood is a *hard* job. This is a *hard* arithmetic problem. Bob is a *hard* worker. **3.** Full of sorrow, pain, or worry. Life was *hard* for the man after he lost his job. **4.** Having great force or strength. The fighter hit his opponent with a *hard* blow. *Adjective.*
—**1.** With effort or energy. Alan works *hard* on his farm. **2.** With force or strength. It rained so *hard* yesterday that the roads were flooded. **3.** With difficulty. The runner breathed *hard* after he had finished the race. *Adverb.*
hard (härd) *adjective,* **harder, hardest;** *adverb.*

hard-boiled Boiled until hard. A *hard-boiled* egg is boiled until its yoke and white are solid.
hard-boiled (härd′boild′) *adjective.*

harden To make or become hard. Joan made a clay bowl and put it in the sun to *harden.*
hard·en (härd′ən) *verb,* **hardened, hardening.**

hardly **1.** Just about; barely. We could *hardly* see the path in the dim light. **2.** Not likely; not quite. Since she is sick in bed, she will *hardly* be able to come to the party tonight.
hard·ly (härd′lē) *adverb.*

hardship Something that causes difficulty, pain, or suffering. The flood was a great *hardship* to the people of the town.
hard·ship (härd′ship′) *noun, plural* **hardships.**

hardware Metal articles used for making and fixing things. Tools, nails, and screws are hardware.
hard·ware (härd′wer′) *noun.*

hardwood The strong, heavy wood of certain trees. Oaks, beeches, and maples are hardwoods. Hardwood is used for furniture, floors, and sports equipment.
hard·wood (härd′wood′) *noun, plural* **hardwoods.**

hardy Strong and healthy. Henry is a *hardy* boy who loves being outdoors. Ivy is a *hardy* plant.
har·dy (här′dē) *adjective,* **hardier, hardiest.**

at; āpe; cär; end; mē; it; īce; hot; ōld; fôrk; wood; fōol; oil; out; up; turn; sing; thin; this; hw in white; zh in treasure. ə stands for a in about, e in taken i in pencil, o in lemon, and u in circus.

hare An animal that is like a rabbit, but larger. It has very long ears, strong back legs and feet, and a short tail. ▲ Another word that sounds like this is **hair.**
hare (her) *noun, plural* **hares** or **hare.**

Hare

harm **1.** Injury or hurt. To make sure no *harm* would come to the children, their mother made them wear life jackets when they went sailing. **2.** An evil; wrong. The bad child saw no *harm* in lying to his mother about stealing a candy bar. *Noun.*
—To do damage to; hurt. The dog looks fierce, but it will not *harm* you. *Verb.*
harm (härm) *noun, plural* **harms;** *verb,* **harmed, harming.**

harmful Causing harm; damaging. A poor diet is *harmful* to your health.
harm·ful (härm′fəl) *adjective.*

harmless Not able to cause harm; not damaging. That snake is *harmless.* They played a *harmless* joke on their friend.
harm·less (härm′lis) *adjective.*

harmonica A musical instrument. It is a small case with slots that contain a series of metal reeds. It is played by blowing in and out through the slots.
har·mon·i·ca (här mon′i kə) *noun, plural* **harmonicas.**

Harmonica

harmonize **1.** To arrange, sing, or play in harmony. The voices of the church choir *harmonized* in song. **2.** To go together in a pleasing way. The colors of the curtains and the rug *harmonize* well. **3.** To add notes to a melody to form chords in music.
har·mo·nize (här′mə nīz′) *verb,* **harmonized, harmonizing.**

harmony **1.** A combination of musical notes to form chords. **2.** A going well together. The *harmony* of the colors of the rainbow is very beautiful.
har·mo·ny (här′mə nē) *noun, plural* **harmonies.**

harness The straps, bands, and other fastenings used to attach a work animal to a cart, plow, or wagon. *Noun.*
—**1.** To put a harness on. The farmer *harnessed* his horses. **2.** To control and make use of. At that dam water power is *harnessed* to generate electricity. *Verb.*
har·ness (här′nis) *noun, plural* **harnesses;** *verb,* **harnessed, harnessing.**

harp A large, stringed musical instrument. The strings are set in an upright, triangle-shaped frame with a curved top. It is played by plucking the strings with the fingers.
harp (härp) *noun, plural* **harps.**

harpoon A weapon similar to a spear with a rope attached. A harpoon is used to kill or capture whales and other sea animals. It is shot from a gun or thrown by hand. *Noun.*
—To strike, catch, or kill with a harpoon. The sailors *harpooned* the whale after a long chase. *Verb.*
har·poon (här pōōn′) *noun, plural* **harpoons;** *verb,* **harpooned, harpooning.**

Harp

harpsichord A stringed musical instrument with a keyboard. It looks like a piano.
harp·si·chord (härp′sə kôrd′) *noun, plural* **harpsichords.**

harrow A heavy frame with upright disks or teeth. It is used to break up and level plowed land.
har·row (har′ō) *noun, plural* **harrows.**

harsh **1.** Rough or unpleasant to the ear, eye, taste, or touch. The towel felt *harsh* against my sunburned skin. **2.** Very cruel.

The prisoners got *harsh* treatment from the guards if they did not obey.

harsh (härsh) *adjective,* **harsher, harshest.**

harvest **1.** The gathering in of a crop when it is ripe. The men soon finished the *harvest* of the wheat. **2.** The crop that is gathered. The farmer has a large *harvest* of potatoes. *Noun.*
—To gather in a crop. We have to *harvest* the fruit now that it is ripe. *Verb.*

har·vest (här′vist) *noun, plural* **harvests;** *verb,* **harvested, harvesting.**

has Betty *has* a new bicycle.

has (haz) *verb.*

hash **1.** A cooked mixture of chopped meat, potatoes, and other vegetables. **2.** A mess; jumble. He made such a *hash* of the model airplane that it had to be done over.

hash (hash) *noun, plural* **hashes.**

hasn't She *hasn't* done any work at all today.

has·n't (haz′ənt) contraction for "has not."

haste Quickness in moving or in acting; speed; hurry. Ruth left the house in great *haste* so she wouldn't miss the bus.

haste (hāst) *noun.*

hasten To move quickly; speed up; hurry. The medicine *hastened* the recovery of the sick boy.

has·ten (hās′ən) *verb,* **hastened, hastening.**

hasty **1.** Quick; hurried. We ate a *hasty* breakfast because we were already late for school. **2.** Too quick; careless or reckless. Alice made a *hasty* decision that she was sorry for later.

hast·y (hās′tē) *adjective,* **hastier, hastiest.**

hat A covering for the head. It often has a brim and crown.

hat (hat) *noun, plural* **hats.**

hatch¹ **1.** To cause young to come from an egg. The mother robin *hatched* her eggs. The hen *hatched* her chicks. **2.** To come from an egg. The chicks *hatched* by pecking through their shells.

hatch (hach) *verb,* **hatched, hatching.**

hatch² **1.** An opening in the deck of a ship. It leads to lower decks. **2.** A cover or trap door for such an opening.

hatch (hach) *noun, plural* **hatches.**

hatchet A small ax with a short handle. It is made to be used with one hand.

hatch·et (hach′it) *noun, plural* **hatchets.**

hate To have very strong feelings against; dislike very much. She *hates* people who treat animals cruelly. I *hate* to clean the house.

hate (hāt) *verb,* **hated, hating.**

hatred A strong feeling against a person or thing. The people felt *hatred* toward the cruel dictator.

ha·tred (hā′trid) *noun, plural* **hatreds.**

haughty Having or showing too much pride in oneself. The *haughty* queen thought she was the most beautiful person in all the kingdom.

haugh·ty (hô′tē) *adjective,* **haughtier, haughtiest.**

haul **1.** To pull or move with force; drag. It took three of us to *haul* the heavy trunk up the stairs. **2.** To carry; transport. Railroads *haul* freight across the country. *Verb.*
—**1.** The act of hauling. Give the rope a *haul.* **2.** Something that is gotten by catching or winning. The fishermen came home with a big *haul* of fish. **3.** The distance something is hauled. It's a long *haul* from our farm to the town. *Noun.* ▲ Another word that sounds like this is **hall.**

haul (hôl) *verb,* **hauled, hauling;** *noun, plural* **hauls.**

haunch A part of the body of an animal around its hind leg. The lion sat on its *haunches* and roared.

haunch (hônch) *noun, plural* **haunches.**

haunt To visit or live in. People say that ghosts *haunt* the old house on the corner.

haunt (hônt) *verb,* **haunted, haunting.**

have **1.** They *have* a house in the country. Do you *have* any questions? I hope to *have* a good time at Lucy's party. My brother might *have* the chicken pox. Mother told me I *have* to clean my room before I can play. My cat will *have* kittens in about a week. **2.** *Have* is also used as a helping verb. It shows that the action of the main verb is finished. We *have* done the work. They *have* written a story. ▲ Another word that sounds like this is **halve.**

have (hav) *verb,* **had, having.**

haven A place of safety or shelter. The cool woods were a *haven* for the hot and tired hikers. A harbor is a *haven* for boats.

ha·ven (hā′vən) *noun, plural* **havens.**

haven't I *haven't* gone shopping for a new pair of shoes yet.

have·n't (hav′ənt) contraction for "have not."

---

at; āpe; cär; end; mē; it; īce; hot; ōld;
fôrk; wood; fōōl; oil; out; up; turn; sing;
thin; this; hw in white; zh in treasure.
ə stands for a in about, e in taken
i in pencil, o in lemon, and u in circus.

Hawaii An island state of the United States in the Pacific Ocean. Its capital is Honolulu. **Ha·wai·i** (hə wī′ē) *noun.*

▲ **Hawaii** was originally the name for the biggest island of the state. It may come from the name for a place in a very old story. This story says that this island was the early home of the first people to come to Hawaii.

hawk¹ A bird of prey. It has a sharp, hooked beak, strong claws, and short rounded wings.
hawk (hôk) *noun, plural* **hawks.**

hawk² To offer goods for sale by calling out. The peddler *hawked* fruit in the street.
hawk (hôk) *verb,* **hawked, hawking.**

hawthorn A thorny shrub or tree. It is similar to the rose. The hawthorn has small red, yellow, or black berries.
haw·thorn (hô′thôrn′) *noun, plural* **hawthorns.**

Hawk

hay Grass, alfalfa, or clover. Hay is cut and dried for use as feed for livestock. ▲ Another word that sounds like this is **hey.**
hay (hā) *noun, plural* **hays.**

hay fever A condition that causes a stuffy nose, itching eyes, and sneezing. Hay fever is an allergy that is caused by breathing the pollen of plants.

haystack A pile of hay stacked outdoors.
hay·stack (hā′stak′) *noun, plural* **haystacks.**

hazard Something that can cause harm or injury; risk; danger. Icy roads are a *hazard* to drivers.
haz·ard (haz′ərd) *noun, plural* **hazards.**

haze Mist, smoke, or dust in the air. The morning *haze* hid the bridge from us.
haze (hāz) *noun, plural* **hazes.**

hazel **1.** A tree or shrub that has light-brown nuts that can be eaten. **2.** A light-brown color like the color of this nut. *Noun.*
—Having the color hazel; light-brown. Nancy has beautiful *hazel* eyes. *Adjective.*
ha·zel (hā′zəl) *noun, plural* **hazels;** *adjective.*

hazy Not clear; blurred or confused. On a *hazy* day, we can see only a dim outline of the mountains. Bob's understanding of how a computer works is *hazy.*
ha·zy (hā′zē) *adjective,* **hazier, haziest.**

H-bomb A powerful bomb. It is also called a **hydrogen bomb.** Look up **hydrogen bomb** for more information.
H-bomb (āch′bom′) *noun, plural* **H-bombs.**

he Bob promised that *he* would be on time. Is your puppy a *he* or a she?
he (hē) *pronoun; noun, plural* **he's.**

head **1.** The top part of a person's body. The head is where the eyes, ears, nose, and mouth are. The brain is inside the head. **2.** The part of any other animal that is like a human head. Dogs, fish, and birds have heads. **3.** Anything that is like a head in shape or position. I walked up to the *head* of the stairs. Hit the nail on the *head.* Please buy a *head* of lettuce. Billy was at the *head* of the class. **4.** A person who is above the others; chief. The President is the *head* of our country's government. **5.** A single person or animal. The cowboys rounded up forty *head* of cattle. *Noun.*
—Top, chief, or front. Ed is the *head* lifeguard at the pool. *Adjective.*
—**1.** To be or go to the top or front of. The scout leader *headed* his troop in the parade. **2.** To be in charge of. Frank *heads* the school newspaper. **3.** To direct or move in a direction. The captain *headed* the ship northward. Dan *heads* for the beach on hot days. *Verb.*
head (hed) *noun, plural* **heads** *(for definitions 1-4)* or **head** *(for definition 5); adjective; verb,* **headed, heading.**

headache A pain in the head.
head·ache (hed′āk′) *noun, plural* **headaches.**

headdress A covering or decoration for the head. The Indian wore a *headdress* of feathers.
head·dress (hed′dres′) *noun, plural* **headdresses.**

headfirst With the head going in front. He dove *headfirst* into the water.
head·first (hed′fûrst′) *adverb.*

heading A title for a page or chapter.
head·ing (hed′ing) *noun, plural* **headings.**

Headdress

headland A point of land that sticks out into the water; cape.
head·land (hed′lənd) *noun, plural* **headlands.**

headlight A bright light on the front of an automobile or other vehicle. It got dark during the drive home, so Mother put on the car's *headlights.*
head·light (hed′līt′) *noun, plural* **headlights.**

headline A line printed at the top of a newspaper or magazine article. A headline tells what the article is about. It is printed in large or heavy type. *Noun.*
—To be the main attraction of a show. A magic act *headlined* the show. *Verb.*
> **head·line** (hed′līn′) *noun, plural* **headlines;** *verb,* **headlined, headlining.**

headlong 1. With the head first. He ran *headlong* into the kitchen door in the darkness. 2. In a reckless way; rashly. He rushed *headlong* into buying the used bicycle without noticing that it was damaged. *Adverb.*
—With the head first. She made a *headlong* dive into the lake. *Adjective.*
> **head·long** (hed′lông′) *adverb; adjective.*

head-on With the head or front end first. The car hit the pole *head-on.* The two cars were in a *head-on* crash.
> **head-on** (hed′ôn′ *or* hed′on′) *adverb; adjective.*

headphone A radio or telephone receiver held against the ear. It is held in place by a band that fits over the head.
> **head·phone** (hed′fōn′) *noun, plural* **headphones.**

headquarters Any center of operations or business. The general issued orders from his *headquarters.* That company's *headquarters* are in Chicago.
> **head·quar·ters** (hed′kwôr′tərz) *noun, plural* **headquarters.**

headstone A stone set at the head of a grave; tombstone.
> **head·stone** (hed′stōn′) *noun, plural* **headstones.**

headwaters The small streams at the beginning of a river. They all come together to form the river.
> **head·wa·ters** (hed′wô′tərz) *noun plural.*

headway Forward movement or progress. It was hard for the small ship to make any *headway* through the high waves. I can't make much *headway* with this problem.
> **head·way** (hed′wā′) *noun.*

heal To make or become well. The doctor *healed* the sick child with medicine. Her sprained ankle *healed* quickly, and she was soon skiing again. ▲ Other words that sound like this are **heel** and **he'll.**
> **heal** (hēl) *verb,* **healed, healing.**

health 1. Freedom from illness. You will lose your *health* if you don't eat the proper foods. 2. The condition of the body or mind. The doctor told Claire that she was in very good *health.*
> **health** (helth) *noun.*

healthful Helping one have good health. Exercise is *healthful.*
> **health·ful** (helth′fəl) *adjective.*

healthy Having, showing, or giving good health. The young farm boy had a *healthy* look. Walking is a *healthy* exercise.
> **health·y** (hel′thē) *adjective,* **healthier, healthiest.**

heap A collection of things piled together. Lisa left a *heap* of books lying in the middle of her bed. *Noun.*
—1. To make into a pile. We *heaped* the fallen leaves. 2. To give in large amounts. Mother *heaped* my plate with mashed potatoes. *Verb.*
> **heap** (hēp) *noun, plural* **heaps;** *verb,* **heaped, heaping.**

hear 1. To receive sound through the ears. I *hear* someone calling my name. My grandfather can't *hear* very well, so please speak loudly. 2. To listen to. Dad will *hear* both sides of our quarrel. 3. To get information about. The winner of the contest will *hear* the good news soon. Have you *heard* from Dick lately? ▲ Another word that sounds like this is **here.**
> **hear** (hēr) *verb,* **heard, hearing.**

heard I *heard* my brother coming home late last night. ▲ Another word that sounds like this is **herd.**
> **heard** (hurd) *verb.*

hearing 1. The ability to hear. Tina has very good *hearing.* 2. The act of listening or getting information. *Hearing* that her sister had won the contest made Ann very happy. 3. The chance to be heard. The mayor gave both sides a fair *hearing* before making a decision.
> **hear·ing** (hēr′ing) *noun, plural* **hearings.**

hearing aid A small device that makes sounds louder. It is worn in or near the ear to make poor hearing better.

heart 1. The part of the body that pumps blood. 2. The heart thought of as the center of a person's feelings. The happy boy spoke from his *heart* when he thanked us for finding his puppy. 3. Spirit; courage. The team lost *heart* after their defeat. 4. The center or middle of anything. We got lost in the *heart*

---

at; āpe; cär; end; mē; it; īce; hot; ōld;
fôrk; wood; fool; oil; out; up; turn; sing;
thin; this; hw in white; zh in treasure.
ə stands for a in about, e in taken
i in pencil, o in lemon, and u in circus.

of the forest. Let's get to the *heart* of the problem. **5.** A playing card marked with one or more red figures like this: (♥). **6.** Anything shaped like a heart. The children cut out paper *hearts* to make Valentine's Day cards.

> **heart** (härt) *noun, plural* **hearts.**

by heart. From or by memory. Susan learned her lines for the play *by heart.*

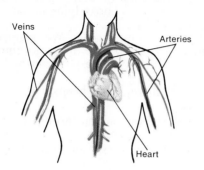

Veins
Arteries
Heart

heartbroken Filled with sorrow or grief. She was *heartbroken* when her dog died.

> **heart·bro·ken** (härt′brō′kən) *adjective.*

hearth The floor of a fireplace.

> **hearth** (härth) *noun, plural* **hearths.**

hearty **1.** Full of warmth, kindness, or enthusiasm. My uncle gave us a *hearty* welcome. **2.** Big and satisfying. Thanksgiving dinner is a *hearty* meal at our house.

> **heart·y** (här′tē) *adjective,* **heartier, heartiest.**

heat **1.** The state of being hot; high temperature; warmth. Heat is a form of energy. The sun gives off *heat.* The *heat* of the fire warmed the whole room. **2.** Strong feeling; excitement. He slammed the door in the *heat* of anger. *Noun.*
—To make or become hot or warm. Mom *heated* the milk before giving it to my baby sister. *Verb.*

> **heat** (hēt) *noun; verb,* **heated, heating.**

heater A device that gives heat. A radiator or a furnace is a kind of heater. We put an electric *heater* in the cold room.

> **heat·er** (hē′tər) *noun, plural* **heaters.**

heath A flat, open piece of land. It is covered with heather or low bushes.

> **heath** (hēth) *noun, plural* **heaths.**

heathen A person who does not believe in the God of the Christians, Jews, or Muslims. *Noun.*
—Having to do with heathens. Ancient *heathen* tribes worshiped many gods. *Adjective.*

> **hea·then** (hē′thən) *noun, plural* **heathens** or **heathen;** *adjective.*

▲ The word **heathen** comes from an Old English word that meant "a person who lives on the heath." *On the heath* meant "in the country." Most people who lived in the country at that time were not Christians. So calling someone a *heathen,* or country person, was the same as saying that he was not a Christian.

heather A low shrub that has purple and pink flowers. It grows wild in Scotland and England.

> **heath·er** (heth′ər) *noun, plural* **heathers.**

heave **1.** To lift, raise, or throw using force or effort. The men *heaved* bales of hay onto the truck. Jack *heaved* a rock across the stream. **2.** To give out with much force. Joey *heaved* a sigh of relief when he saw that his brother was not hurt. **3.** To rise and fall. The runner's chest *heaved* after the race.

> **heave** (hēv) *verb,* **heaved, heaving.**

Heather

heaven **1.** In the Christian religion, the place where God and the angels live. **2. heavens.** The space above and around the earth; sky. You can see many stars in the *heavens* on a clear, dark night.

> **heav·en** (hev′ən) *noun, plural* **heavens.**

heavenly **1.** Having to do with heaven; divine. Angels are *heavenly* beings. **2.** Having to do with the sky. The sun, the moon, and the stars are *heavenly* bodies. **3.** Happy, pleasing, or beautiful. This quiet, shaded place is a *heavenly* spot for a picnic.

> **heav·en·ly** (hev′ən lē) *adjective.*

heavily In a heavy way. The snow fell *heavily* on the ground during the blizzard.

> **heav·i·ly** (hev′əl ē) *adverb.*

heavy **1.** Having great weight; hard to lift or move. The desk was too *heavy* for Brad to move by himself. **2.** Having more than the usual weight. It's so cold that I need a *heavy* blanket to keep me warm. **3.** Large in size or amount. We were late because we got stuck in *heavy* traffic. We had a *heavy* rainfall last night.

> **heav·y** (hev′ē) *adjective,* **heavier, heaviest.**

Hebrew **1.** A member of one of the Jewish tribes of ancient times. **2.** The language spoken by the ancient Jews. The people of Israel speak a form of this language.

He·brew (hē′brōō) *noun, plural* **Hebrews.**

he'd *He'd* better hurry. *He'd* do it if he could. ▲ Another word that sounds like this is **heed.**

he'd (hēd) contraction for "he had" and "he would."

Hedge

hedge A row of shrubs or small trees planted close together. A hedge is used as a fence. *Noun.*
—**1.** To surround, close in, or separate with a hedge. All the people in our block *hedged* their front yards with bushes. **2.** To avoid answering a question directly. Johnny *hedged* the teacher's question because he hadn't done his homework. *Verb.*

hedge (hej) *noun, plural* **hedges;** *verb,* **hedged, hedging.**

hedgehog An animal that eats insects. It has a pointed snout and sharp, hard spines on its back and sides. When it is frightened or attacked, it rolls up into a ball with only its spines showing.

Hedgehog

hedge·hog (hej′-hog′) *noun, plural* **hedgehogs.**

heed To pay careful attention to; listen or mind. *Heed* my advice. ▲ Another word that sounds like this is **he'd.**

heed (hēd) *verb,* **heeded, heeding.**

heel¹ **1.** The rounded back part of the human foot below the ankle. **2.** Anything like a heel in shape, use, or position. The heel of the hand is the part of the palm near the wrist. I have to have the *heels* on these shoes fixed. *Noun.*
—To follow closely. The dog was taught to *heel* at his master's side. *Verb.* ▲ Other words that sound like this are **heal** and **he'll.**

heel (hēl) *noun, plural* **heels;** *verb,* **heeled, heeling.**

heel² To lean to one side. The strong winds forced the small sailboat to *heel* to the left. ▲ Other words that sound like this are **heal** and **he'll.**

heel (hēl) *verb,* **heeled, heeling.**

heifer A young cow.

heif·er (hef′ər) *noun, plural* **heifers.**

height **1.** The distance from bottom to top. The *height* of the statue is eleven feet. Paul's *height* is five feet ten inches. The mountain stands at a *height* of one mile above sea level. **2.** A high place. The little boy was afraid of *heights* and would never climb a tree. **3.** The highest point. The singer retired at the *height* of his career.

height (hīt) *noun, plural* **heights.**

heighten To make or become high or higher. The carpenter *heightened* the house by adding a third story to it.

height·en (hīt′ən) *verb,* **heightened, heightening.**

heir A person who has the right to the money or property of a person after that person is dead. ▲ Other words that sound like this are **air** and **ere.**

heir (er) *noun, plural* **heirs.**

held She *held* the ball in her hand. Look up **hold** for more information.

held (held) *verb.*

helicopter An aircraft that is kept in the air by blades that rotate above the craft.

hel·i·cop·ter (hel′ə kop′tər) *noun, plural* **helicopters.**

Helicopter

at; āpe; cär; end; mē; it; īce; hot; ōld;
fôrk; wood; fōol; oil; out; up; turn; sing;
thin; this; hw in white; zh in treasure.
ə stands for a in about, e in taken
i in pencil, o in lemon, and u in circus.

301

helium A light gas that has no color or odor. Helium is a chemical element.
he·li·um (hē′lē əm) *noun.*

▲ The word **helium** comes from the Greek word for "sun." Helium was first discovered by people who were studying the rays of light that come from the sun.

hell In the Christian religion, the place where Satan lives and where wicked people will be punished after death.
hell (hel) *noun.*

he'll *He'll* come to see us when he has time. *He'll* clean his room if I have anything to say about it! ▲ Other words that sound like this are **heal** and **heel.**
he'll (hēl) contraction for "he will" and "he shall."

hello A word used as a greeting. *"Hello,"* he called, when he met us on the street. They gave us a warm *hello* when we arrived.
hel·lo (he lō′ *or* hə lō′) *interjection; noun, plural* **hellos.**

helm The part of a ship used for steering. It is usually a wheel or tiller.
helm (helm) *noun, plural* **helms.**

helmet A covering for the head that is worn for protection. Soldiers, firemen, football players, and astronauts wear helmets.
hel·met (hel′mit) *noun, plural* **helmets.**

help 1. To give or do something that is useful, wanted, or needed; aid; assist. Barbara *helped* the blind woman across the street. Rick *helped* his brother paint the room. The coach's advice *helped* the team to win. Please *help* yourself to more potatoes. 2. To stop or avoid. I couldn't *help* laughing when I heard the story. *Verb.*
—1. The act of helping. Do you need *help?* 2. A person or thing that helps. Ruth is a big *help* to her mother around the house. *Noun.*
help (help) *verb,* **helped, helping;** *noun, plural* **helps.**

helpful Giving help; useful. A dictionary is *helpful* in spelling words correctly.
help·ful (help′fəl) *adjective.*

Helmet

helping A serving of food for one person. Would you like a second *helping* of turkey?
help·ing (hel′ping) *noun, plural* **helpings.**

helpless Not able to take care of oneself. He was made almost *helpless* by his broken ankle. A newborn kitten is *helpless.*
help·less (help′lis) *adjective.*

hem The border of a garment or piece of cloth. It is made by folding over the edge and sewing it down. Dresses, pillowcases, and curtains have hems. *Noun.*
—To fold over the edge of a piece of cloth and sew it down. Mother *hemmed* the dress. *Verb.*
hem (hem) *noun, plural* **hems;** *verb,* **hemmed, hemming.**
to hem in. To close in; surround. John felt *hemmed in* by the crowd of people who were watching the parade.

hemisphere One-half of the earth. The equator divides the earth into the Northern Hemisphere and the Southern Hemisphere. The earth is also divided into the Eastern Hemisphere and the Western Hemisphere. Europe, Africa, and Asia are in the Eastern Hemisphere. North and South America are in the Western Hemisphere.
hem·i·sphere (hem′is fēr′) *noun, plural* **hemispheres.**

hemlock 1. A tall evergreen tree similar to the pine. It has reddish bark and flat needles. 2. A poisonous plant that has spotted, hollow stems and clusters of white flowers.
hem·lock (hem′lok′) *noun, plural* **hemlocks.**

Needles

Cone

Hemlock Tree

hemp A strong, tough fiber made from the stem of a tall plant. It is used to make rope.
hemp (hemp) *noun, plural* **hemps.**

hen 1. The adult female of fowl on farms. 2. The female of various other birds.
hen (hen) *noun, plural* **hens.**

hence 1. As a result; therefore. Joan lived with a family in Spain last summer and *hence* learned to speak Spanish quite well. 2. From this time or place. The friends agreed to meet two weeks *hence* at the same place.
hence (hens) *adverb.*

her I gave *her* the book. *Her* coat is on the chair.
her (hur) *pronoun; adjective.*

herb 1. Any plant whose leaves, stems, seeds, or roots are used in cooking for flavoring or in medicines. Mint and parsley are herbs. 2. Any flowering plant that dies at the end of one growing season and does not form a woody stem.
herb (hurb *or* urb) *noun, plural* **herbs.**

herbivorous Feeding mainly on plants. A cow is a *herbivorous* animal.
her·biv·o·rous (hur biv′ər əs) *adjective.*

herd A group of animals. A *herd* of cattle grazed in the pasture. *Noun.*
—To group or lead in a herd. The cowboys *herded* the cattle and drove them to market. Our tour guide *herded* us into the bus. *Verb.*
▲ Another word that sounds like this is **heard.**
herd (hurd) *noun, plural* **herds;** *verb,* **herded, herding.**

here At, in, or to this place. I have been waiting *here* for an hour. Bring the book *here* and I'll read it to you. *Adverb.*
—This place. Can you show me how to get home from *here? Noun.*
—A word used in answering a roll call, calling an animal, or attracting attention. *Interjection.* ▲ Another word that sounds like this is **hear.**
here (hēr) *adverb; noun; interjection.*

hereditary Passed on or able to be passed on from an animal or plant to its offspring. Blue eyes are *hereditary.*
he·red·i·tar·y (hə red′ə ter′ē) *adjective.*

heredity The passing on of characteristics from an animal or plant to its offspring.
he·red·i·ty (hə red′ə tē) *noun, plural* **heredities.**

here's *Here's* the book I was telling you about.
here's (hērz) contraction for "here is."

heritage Something that is handed down from earlier generations or from the past; tradition. The right to vote is part of the American *heritage.*
her·it·age (her′ə tij) *noun, plural* **heritages.**

hermit A person who lives alone and away from other people. A hermit often lives like this for religious reasons.
her·mit (hur′mit) *noun, plural* **hermits.**

hero 1. A man or boy who is looked up to by others because he has done something brave or outstanding. The man who saved the boy from drowning was a *hero.* 2. The main male character in a play, story, or poem. The *hero* in the story killed the dragon and made the kingdom safe again.
he·ro (hēr′ō) *noun, plural* **heroes.**

heroic Having to do with a hero. The fireman made a *heroic* attempt to save the child.
he·ro·ic (hi rō′ik) *adjective.*

heroin A habit-forming drug. ▲ Another word that sounds like this is **heroine.**
her·o·in (her′ō in) *noun.*

heroine 1. A woman or girl who is looked up to by others because she has done something brave or outstanding. Dr. Smith is my *heroine,* because I want to be a doctor like her some day. 2. The main female character in a play, story, or poem. ▲ Another word that sounds like this is **heroin.**
her·o·ine (her′ō in) *noun, plural* **heroines.**

heron A bird with a long slender neck, a long pointed bill, and long thin legs.
her·on (her′ən) *noun, plural* **herons.**

Heron

herring A bony, saltwater fish of the northern Atlantic Ocean. It is used as food.
her·ring (her′ing) *noun, plural* **herring** or **herrings.**

hers This is my coat and that is *hers.*
hers (hurz) *pronoun.*

herself She *herself* knitted the sweater. Mary cut *herself.* Betty has not been *herself* lately.
her·self (hur self′) *pronoun.*

he's *He's* going to come with us. *He's* seen that movie three times.
he's (hēz) contraction for "he is" and "he has."

---

at; āpe; cär; end; mē; it; īce; hot; ōld;
fôrk; wood; fōōl; oil; out; up; turn; sing;
thin; **th**is; **hw** in white; **zh** in treasure.
ə stands for **a** in about, **e** in taken
i in pencil, **o** in lemon, and **u** in circus.

hesitant Doubtful; uncertain. Beth was *hesitant* about jumping into the cold lake.
hes·i·tant (hez′ət ənt) *adjective.*

hesitate **1.** To wait or stop a moment. The speaker *hesitated* and then went on with his speech. **2.** To fail to do because of doubt or fear. Tom *hesitated* to ask Doris to the dance because he was afraid that she'd say no.
hes·i·tate (hez′ə tāt′) *verb,* **hesitated, hesitating.**

hesitation The act of hesitating. Wendy accepted the job of class president without *hesitation.*
hes·i·ta·tion (hez′ə tā′shən) *noun, plural* **hesitations.**

hey A word used to attract attention or to show surprise or pleasure. "*Hey!* Watch where you're going when you're crossing the street!" ▲ Another word that sounds like this is **hay.**
hey (hā) *interjection.*

hi A word used to say "hello." ▲ Another word that sounds like this is **high.**
hi (hī) *interjection.*

hibernate To spend the winter sleeping. Bears and squirrels hibernate.
hi·ber·nate (hī′bər nāt′) *verb,* **hibernated, hibernating.**

hiccup **1.** A quick catching of the breath that one cannot control. **2. hiccups.** The condition of having one hiccup after another. You'll get the *hiccups* if you drink your milk too fast. *Noun.*
—To have hiccups. *Verb.*
hic·cup (hik′up) *noun, plural* **hiccups;** *verb,* **hiccupped, hiccupping.**

hickory A tall tree of North America. The hickory has nuts that are good to eat and strong, hard wood.
hick·o·ry (hik′ər ē) *noun, plural* **hickories.**

Leaves

Hickory Tree

hid The squirrel *hid* the acorns in a tree.
hid (hid) *verb.*

hidden The dog has *hidden* his bone.
hid·den (hid′ən) *verb.*

hide¹ **1.** To put or keep out of sight. Maria *hides* the money she saves in her bureau drawer. Jack tried to *hide* behind a tree, but the others found him. The heavy snowfall *hid* the deer's tracks. **2.** To keep secret. The lost little boy tried to *hide* his fears.
hide (hīd) *verb,* **hid, hidden** or **hid, hiding.**

hide² The skin of an animal. Leather shoes are made from hides.
hide (hīd) *noun, plural* **hides.**

hide-and-seek A children's game in which one player has to find all of the other players who are hiding.
hide-and-seek (hīd′ən sēk′) *noun.*

hideous Very ugly; horrible. Tom dressed up as a *hideous* monster for Halloween.
hid·e·ous (hid′ē əs) *adjective.*

hideout A place where one can hide. The thieves used a cave as their *hideout* from the police.
hide·out (hīd′out′) *noun, plural* **hideouts.**

hieroglyphic A picture or symbol that stands for a word, sound, or idea. The ancient Egyptians used hieroglyphics in their writing.
hi·er·o·glyph·ic (hī′ər ə glif′ik) *noun, plural* **hieroglyphics.**

Hieroglyphics

hi-fi A radio or phonograph that can reproduce sound almost exactly like the original sound.
hi-fi (hī′fī′) *noun, plural* **hi-fis.**

high **1.** Tall. That mountain is very *high.* The building is forty stories *high.* **2.** At a great distance from the ground. The bird was *high* in the sky. **3.** Above or more important than others. He had a *high* rank in the army. **4.** Greater than others. *High* winds swept the snow into drifts. The racing car was going at a *high* speed. She is trying to sell her bicycle for a *high* price. **5.** Shrill; sharp. The soprano sang a *high* note. *Adjective.*

—At or to a high place. He climbed *high* up the hill. *Adverb.*
—**1.** A high place or point. The temperature today reached a new *high* for the year. **2.** The arrangement of gears in an automobile that gives the greatest speed. *Noun.* ▲ Another word that sounds like this is **hi.**
   high (hī) *adjective,* **higher, highest;** *adverb; noun, plural* **highs.**

high jump A contest in which a person jumps as high as he can over a bar set between two upright poles.

High Jump

highland A part of a country that is high or hilly.
   high·land (hī′lənd) *noun, plural* **highlands.**

highly **1.** Very much; very. A cool swim in the ocean is *highly* pleasant on a hot summer day. **2.** With much praise or approval. The students think *highly* of their teacher. **3.** At a high price. Tom was not *highly* paid for mowing his neighbor's lawn.
   high·ly (hī′lē) *adverb.*

Highness A title of respect used when speaking to or about a member of a royal family. A king is spoken of as "His *Highness,*" and a queen is spoken of as "Her *Highness.*"
   High·ness (hī′nis) *noun, plural* **Highnesses.**

high school A school attended after elementary school or junior high school.

high seas The open waters of an ocean. The high seas are not under the control of any country.

high tide The tide when the level of the ocean is at its highest.

highway A main road. The state has built a new *highway* between the two cities.
   high·way (hī′wā′) *noun, plural* **highways.**

highwayman A robber who holds up travelers on a road.
   high·way·man (hī′wā′mən) *noun, plural* **highwaymen.**

hijack To take by force. Two armed men *hijacked* the airplane.
   hi·jack (hī′jak′) *verb,* **hijacked, hijacking.**

hike To take a long walk. The boy scout troop *hiked* to their camp by the lake. *Verb.*
—A long walk. We took a long *hike* in the woods. *Noun.*
   hike (hīk) *verb,* **hiked, hiking;** *noun, plural* **hikes.**

hilarious Very funny or gay. Jack told a *hilarious* story that made us all laugh.
   hi·lar·i·ous (hi ler′ē əs) *adjective.*

hill **1.** A raised, rounded part of the earth's surface. A hill is not as high as a mountain. **2.** A small heap or mound. Ants have made a *hill* in our backyard.
   hill (hil) *noun, plural* **hills.**

hillside The side or slope of a hill. Cattle grazed on the *hillside* near the farm.
   hill·side (hil′sīd′) *noun, plural* **hillsides.**

hilltop The top of a hill. We climbed to the *hilltop* to find a place for our picnic.
   hill·top (hil′top′) *noun, plural* **hilltops.**

hilly Having many hills. He lives in a *hilly* part of town.
   hill·y (hil′ē) *adjective,* **hillier, hilliest.**

hilt The handle of a sword or dagger.
   hilt (hilt) *noun, plural* **hilts.**

him We saw *him* yesterday at the game. I lent my bicycle to *him.* ▲ Another word that sounds like this is **hymn.**
   him (him *or* im) *pronoun.*

himself My father *himself* could not solve my arithmetic problem. That man has the habit of talking to *himself.* Tom has not been *himself* since he caught that bad cold.
   him·self (him self′) *pronoun.*

hind At the back; rear. Our dog hurt one of his *hind* legs.
   hind (hīnd) *adjective.*

hinder To hold back. The snowstorm *hindered* the search for the missing child. Mary's rudeness *hinders* her friendships with people.
   hin·der (hin′dər) *verb,* **hindered, hindering.**

at; āpe; cär; end; mē; it; īce; hot; ōld; fôrk; wood; fōōl; oil; out; up; turn; sing; thin; this; hw in white; zh in treasure. ə stands for a in about, e in taken i in pencil, o in lemon, and u in circus.

hinge   A jointed piece on which a door, gate, or lid moves back and forth or up and down. The *hinges* on the old gate squeak when you open or close it. *Noun.*
—**1.** To put hinges on; attach by hinges. The carpenter *hinged* the cupboard doors. **2.** To depend. The team's chances of winning the championship *hinge* on next week's game. *Verb.*
   hinge (hinj) *noun, plural* **hinges;** *verb,* **hinged, hinging.**

hint   A slight sign or suggestion. If you can't guess the answer to the riddle, I'll give you a *hint.* There is a *hint* of spring in the air this morning. *Noun.*
—To give a slight sign or suggestion. Mother *hinted* that I might be getting a bicycle for my birthday. *Verb.*
   hint (hint) *noun, plural* **hints;** *verb,* **hinted, hinting.**

hip   The bony part that sticks out on each side of the body just below the waist.
   hip (hip) *noun, plural* **hips.**

hippopotamus   A very large, heavy animal that eats plants. It lives in and near rivers and lakes in Africa. Hippopotamuses have short legs and thick skin with no hair.
   hip·po·pot·a·mus   (hip′ə pot′ə məs)   *noun, plural* **hippopotamuses.**

Hippopotamus

▲   The word **hippopotamus** comes from the Greek name for this animal. The Greek name meant "river horse."

---

hire   To pay for the work of a person or for the use of a thing. The school *hired* three new teachers this year. Ronnie's sister *hired* a car to drive to Florida. *Verb.*
—The act of hiring. That man has fishing boats for *hire. Noun.*
   hire (hīr) *verb,* **hired, hiring;** *noun.*

his   This is my book and that one is *his. His* dog has floppy ears.
   his (hiz) *pronoun; adjective.*

hiss   **1.** To make a sound like a long *s.* The frightened snake *hissed* at us. An angry cat *hisses.* **2.** To make this sound to show disapproval. The fans *hissed* when the umpire called a strike. *Verb.*
—A sound like a long *s.* We heard the *hiss* of steam from the radiator. *Noun.*
   hiss (his) *verb,* **hissed, hissing;** *noun, plural* **hisses.**

historian   A person who knows a great deal about history. Historians write history books.
   his·to·ri·an (his tôr′ē ən) *noun, plural* **historians.**

historic   Important in history. The committee tried to preserve all the *historic* old houses in town.
   his·tor·ic (his tôr′ik) *adjective.*

historical   Having to do with history. I am reading a *historical* book.
   his·tor·i·cal (his tôr′i kəl) *adjective.*

history   The story or record of what has happened in the past. The *history* of the United States as a nation can be thought of as beginning with the Revolutionary War.
   his·to·ry (his′tər ē) *noun, plural* **histories.**

hit   **1.** To give a blow to; strike. Jerry *hit* his brother. Lou *hit* the ball over the fence. **2.** To come against. The ball *hit* the fence. **3.** To come to; reach. The car *hit* ninety miles per hour. We finally *hit* upon the answer. **4.** To have a bad effect on. The unhappy news *hit* her hard. *Verb.*
—**1.** A blow or strike. The *hit* on her head stunned her. **2.** A person or thing that is successful or popular. His guitar playing made him the *hit* of the party. The new movie is a big *hit.* **3.** The hitting of a baseball by the batter in a way that allows him to get on base. *Noun.*
   hit (hit) *verb,* **hit, hitting;** *noun, plural* **hits.**

hitch   **1.** To fasten with a rope, strap, or hook. The farmer *hitched* the horse to the wagon. **2.** To move or lift with a jerk. The boy *hitched* up his trousers. *Verb.*
—**1.** A fastening. The *hitch* between the car and the trailer broke. **2.** An unexpected delay or problem. A sudden storm put a *hitch* in their plans to leave that day. **3.** A quick, jerky movement. He straightened his tie and gave his trousers a *hitch.* **4.** A kind of knot used to attach things together temporarily. *Noun.*
   hitch (hich) *verb,* **hitched, hitching;** *noun, plural* **hitches.**

hitchhike   To travel by walking along a road and getting free rides from cars or trucks that are passing by. Alan and Ricky *hitchhiked* into town.

hitch·hike (hich′hīk′) *verb,* **hitchhiked, hitch-hiking.**

hive **1.** A box or house for bees to live in. **2.** All the bees that live together in the same hive.
hive (hīv) *noun, plural* **hives.**

hives An itchy rash on the skin.
hives (hīvz) *noun plural.*

hoard To save and store or hide away. Jack *hoarded* his allowance until he had enough money to buy a camera. *Verb.*
—Something that is stored or hidden away. Susan had a *hoard* of candy bars in her desk drawer. *Noun.* ▲ Another word that sounds like this is **horde.**
hoard (hôrd) *verb,* **hoarded, hoarding;** *noun, plural* **hoards.**

hoarse **1.** Having a harsh, deep sound. Alice's voice was *hoarse* because of her bad cold. **2.** Having a harsh voice. Bill was *hoarse* after all the shouting he did at the game. ▲ Another word that sounds like this is **horse.**
hoarse (hôrs) *adjective,* **hoarser, hoarsest.**

hoax A trick meant to fool people. The report that a sea monster was seen in the bay was a *hoax.*
hoax (hōks) *noun, plural* **hoaxes.**

hobble **1.** To move or walk awkwardly with a limp. Judy *hobbled* around with a sprained ankle for two weeks.

Hobble

2. To keep from moving easily or freely. You *hobble* a horse by tying his front legs or his back legs together. *Verb.*
—A rope, strap, or other thing used to hobble a horse or other animal. *Noun.*
hob·ble (hob′əl) *verb,* **hobbled, hobbling;** *noun, plural* **hobbles.**

hobby Something that a person does regularly in his spare time because he enjoys it. Raising tropical fish is my *hobby.* Bob's *hobby* is collecting stamps.
hob·by (hob′ē) *noun, plural* **hobbies.**

▲ The word **hobby** comes from an earlier English word that once meant "toy horse." People used this word for a grown person's pastime because they thought that having a hobby was like playing with a toy horse.

hockey **1.** A game played on ice by two teams of six players each. The players wear ice skates and hit a rubber disk, called a puck, with curved sticks. Each team tries to get the puck into the other team's goal. **2.** A game played on a field by two teams of eleven players each. Curved sticks are used to hit a ball along the ground into the other team's goal.
hock·ey (hok′ē) *noun.*

Hockey

hoe A tool with a wide, thin blade set across the end of a long handle. Hoes are used to loosen the soil around plants and dig up weeds. *Noun.*
—To dig with a hoe. We *hoe* the garden once a week to keep the soil loose. *Verb.*
hoe (hō) *noun, plural* **hoes;** *verb,* **hoed, hoeing.**

hog **1.** A full-grown pig. Hogs are raised for their meat. **2.** A greedy or dirty person. *Noun.*
—To take more than one's share. The truck *hogged* the narrow road so that no cars could pass. *Verb.*
hog (hog) *noun, plural* **hogs;** *verb,* **hogged, hogging.**

Hog

at; āpe; cär; end; mē; it; īce; hot; ōld; fôrk; wood; fōol; oil; out; up; turn; sing; thin; **th**is; **hw** in **wh**ite; **zh** in treasure. ə stands for **a** in about, **e** in taken **i** in pencil, **o** in lemon, and **u** in circus.

307

hogan A house made of stones or logs with a roof of branches covered with earth. Some Navaho Indians live in hogans.
  ho·gan (hō′gän) *noun, plural* **hogans.**

Hogan

hoist To lift or pull up. The sailors *hoisted* the cargo onto the ship's deck with a crane. We *hoisted* the flag up the pole. *Verb.*
  —**1.** A device used to lift or pull up something heavy. The workman at the garage put the car on a *hoist* to raise it. **2.** A lift. Tom gave me a *hoist* up the tree. *Noun.*
  hoist (hoist) *verb,* **hoisted, hoisting;** *noun, plural* **hoists.**

hold¹ **1.** To take and keep in the hands or arms; grasp; grip. If you will *hold* the packages, I will unlock the door. She had to *hold* tightly to the railing as she came down the steep stairs. **2.** To keep in a certain place or position. The little boy would not *hold* still. The dam *held* back the flooding river. A good book *holds* your attention. **3.** To contain. This bottle *holds* two quarts. The bus will *hold* fifty people. **4.** To take part in; carry on. We were *holding* an interesting conversation when the phone rang. The club will *hold* its next meeting on Saturday. **5.** To believe to be; think. The judge *held* him responsible for the accident. *Verb.*
  —**1.** A grasp; grip. He didn't have a good *hold* on the heavy lamp, and he dropped it. **2.** Something that can be gripped. The boys couldn't find enough *holds* to climb the side of the cliff. **3.** A mark or symbol in music that shows a pause. *Noun.*
  hold (hōld) *verb,* **held, holding;** *noun, plural* **holds.**

hold² A space in a ship or airplane where cargo is stored.
  hold (hōld) *noun, plural* **holds.**

holdup **1.** A robbery by someone who is armed. There was a *holdup* in the jewelry store last week. **2.** A stopping or delay. There was a *holdup* of traffic because of the snowstorm.
  hold·up (hōld′up′) *noun, plural* **holdups.**

hole **1.** A hollow place in something solid. There was a big *hole* in the street after the heavy rain. The dog dug a *hole* in the ground to hide his bone. **2.** An opening through something. I wore a *hole* in the elbow of my old sweater. **3.** A small hollow place on the green of a golf course. The ball is hit into the hole. ▲ Another word that sounds like this is **whole.**
  hole (hōl) *noun, plural* **holes.**

holiday A day or days on which most people do not work. The Fourth of July and Thanksgiving Day are American holidays. My brother is home from college for the spring *holidays.*
  hol·i·day (hol′ə dā′) *noun, plural* **holidays.**

▲ The word **holiday** comes from an Old English word that meant "holy day." In England long ago, the only days when people did not work were ones that were set aside as special religious feast days.

hollow **1.** Having a hole or an empty space inside; not solid. A water pipe is *hollow.* **2.** Curved in like a cup or bowl; sunken. The thin woman had *hollow* cheeks. **3.** Deep and dull. The miners' footsteps made a *hollow* sound as they walked through the empty tunnel. *Adjective.*
  —**1.** A hole or empty space. The car bounced over a *hollow* in the dirt road. **2.** A valley. The farm nestled in the hollow between the hills. *Noun.*
  —To make an empty space inside. The rabbits *hollowed* out a burrow in the ground. *Verb.*
  hol·low (hol′ō) *adjective,* **hollower, hollowest;** *noun, plural* **hollows;** *verb,* **hollowed, hollowing.**

Holly

holly An evergreen tree. Holly has very shiny leaves with sharp, pointed edges and bright red berries. Its leaves and berries are often used as Christmas decorations.
  hol·ly (hol′ē) *noun, plural* **hollies.**

hollyhock A tall plant that has stalks of large, brightly colored flowers. It grows on a tall plant that has wrinkled leaves.
  hol·ly·hock (hol′ē hok′) *noun, plural* **hollyhocks.**

holster A leather case for carrying a gun. Holsters for pistols are worn on a belt around a person's waist.
hol·ster (hōl′stər) *noun, plural* **holsters.**

holy 1. Belonging to God; sacred. The priest stood at the *holy* altar. 2. Free from sin; like a saint. The nuns led a *holy* life. ▲ Another word that sounds like this is **wholly.**
ho·ly (hō′lē) *adjective,* **holier, holiest.**

Holster

home 1. The place in which a person lives. Steve's *home* is in an apartment house. Betty's *home* is that house up the road. 2. A person's family. Tommy, his sister Paula, and their parents have a happy *home.* 3. The place that a person comes from. Colorado has always been my *home.* 4. The goal or place of safety in some sports and games. 5. A place for the care of persons unable to care for themselves. *Noun.*
—1. At or to the place a person lives. My brother will come *home* for Christmas. 2. To the place or mark aimed at. She aimed at the tree and the arrow hit *home. Adverb.*
home (hōm) *noun, plural* **homes;** *adverb.*

homeland A country where a person was born or has his home. His *homeland* is Sweden, although he has been living in New York for three years.
home·land (hōm′land′) *noun, plural* **homelands.**

homely 1. Having a plain appearance; not good-looking. The dog he found was *homely,* but he loved it. 2. Simple and for every day; not fancy or special. The campers gave us a good, *homely* meal.
home·ly (hōm′lē) *adjective,* **homelier, homeliest.**

homemade Made at home in a person's own kitchen or by hand. Mother bakes *homemade* bread on Saturdays. We have a *homemade* swing on a tree in the yard.
home·made (hōm′mād′) *adjective.*

home plate The place where a baseball player stands to hit a pitched ball. A runner must touch home plate after rounding the bases in order to score a run.

homer A hit that scores a run. Look up **home run** for more information.
hom·er (hō′mər) *noun, plural* **homers.**

homeroom A classroom to which all the pupils in a class go in the mornings. Attendance is checked and special announcements are made there.
home·room (hōm′rōōm′ *or* hōm′room′) *noun, plural* **homerooms.**

home run A hit made by a baseball player that lets him go around all the bases to home plate and score a run.

homesick Sad or sick because of being away from one's home or family. The soldier was *homesick* during his first few months in the army.
home·sick (hōm′sik′) *adjective.*

homespun A cloth that is woven by hand at home, instead of in a factory by big machines.
home·spun (hōm′spun′) *noun.*

homestead 1. A farm with its house and other buildings. 2. A piece of land that was given by the United States government to a settler for farming.
home·stead (hōm′sted′) *noun, plural* **homesteads.**

homeward Toward home. The hikers turned *homeward* for the walk back.
home·ward (hōm′wərd) *adverb; adjective.*

homework A school lesson that is meant to be done at home, not in the classroom.
home·work (hōm′wurk′) *noun.*

hominy Kernels of white corn that are hulled and ground up. Hominy is mixed with water and boiled before it is eaten.
hom·i·ny (hom′ə nē) *noun.*

homogenized milk Milk in which the cream has been spread evenly throughout and will not separate and rise to the top.
ho·mog·e·nized milk (hə moj′ə nīzd′).

homograph A word with the same spelling as another, but with a different origin and meaning and, sometimes, a different pronunciation. *Bow* meaning "to bend forward" and *bow* meaning "a weapon for shooting arrows" are homographs.
hom·o·graph (hom′ə graf′) *noun, plural* **homographs.**

homonym A word with the same pronunciation as another, but with a different meaning and, often, a different spelling. *Lean* meaning

at; āpe; cär; end; mē; it; īce; hot; ōld; fôrk; wood; fōōl; oil; out; up; turn; sing; thin; **th**is; **hw** in white; **zh** in treasure. **ə** stands for **a** in about, **e** in taken **i** in pencil, **o** in lemon, and **u** in circus.

"to bend" and *lean* meaning "thin" are homonyms.

hom·o·nym (hom′ə nim′) *noun, plural* **homonyms.**

homophone A word with the same pronunciation as another, but with a different meaning and spelling. *Know* and *no* are homophones.

hom·o·phone (hom′ə fōn′) *noun, plural* **homophones.**

honest Truthful, fair, or trustworthy. An honest person does not cheat, lie, or steal. That farmer earns an *honest* living.

hon·est (on′ist) *adjective.*

honesty The quality of being honest; truthfulness; fairness. He answered all the questions with *honesty.*

hon·es·ty (on′is tē) *noun.*

honey 1. A thick, sweet liquid made by bees. Bees collect nectar from flowers and make honey, which they store in honeycombs. 2. A person or thing that is very dear and sweet; darling.

hon·ey (hun′ē) *noun, plural* **honeys.**

honeybee A bee that makes and stores honey.

hon·ey·bee (hun′ē bē′) *noun, plural* **honeybees.**

honeycomb 1. A wax structure made by bees to store their honey in. A honeycomb is made up of layers of six-sided cells. 2. Something that looks like a bee's honeycomb. There was a *honeycomb* of subway tunnels under the city. *Noun.*
—To make full of tunnels or cells like a bee's honeycomb. Secret passages *honeycombed* the castle. *Verb.*

hon·ey·comb (hun′ē kōm′) *noun, plural* **honeycombs;** *verb,* **honeycombed, honeycombing.**

honeymoon A vacation taken by a man and a woman who have just been married. *Noun.*
—To be or go on a honeymoon. *Verb.*

hon·ey·moon (hun′ē mōōn′) *noun, plural* **honeymoons;** *verb,* **honeymooned, honeymooning.**

▲ There was an old custom of having newly married people drink wine with honey in it for the first month of their marriage. A month was sometimes called a *moon,* and this early part of a marriage became known as the "honey month" or "honey moon." Now the word **honeymoon** is also used for the trip people take at the beginning of their marriage.

---

honeysuckle A climbing plant that has many small, sweet-smelling flowers.

hon·ey·suck·le (hun′ē-suk′əl) *noun, plural* **honeysuckles.**

honk 1. The cry of a goose. 2. Any sound like the cry of a goose. The *honk* of the automobile horn scared the deer. *Noun.*
—To make the cry of a goose or any sound like it. We heard the geese *honk* as they flew overhead. *Verb.*

honk (hongk) *noun, plural* **honks;** *verb,* **honked, honking.**

Honeysuckle

honor 1. A sense of what is right or honest. As a man of *honor,* he would not do business with the person who cheated those poor people. 2. A good name or reputation. When the bully called him a coward, Jack felt his *honor* was at stake. 3. A cause of respect, pride, or glory. It was a great *honor* for her to receive the scholarship award. 4. **Honor.** A title of respect used in speaking to or of a judge, mayor, or other official. *Noun.*
—To show great respect for a person or thing. The town *honored* the astronauts with a parade. *Verb.*

hon·or (on′ər) *noun, plural* **honors;** *verb,* **honored, honoring.**

honorable 1. Having or showing a sense of what is right or honest. The judge is an *honorable* man. 2. Worthy of or bringing honor or respect. Winning a prize at the science fair was an *honorable* achievement.

hon·or·a·ble (on′ər ə bəl) *adjective.*

hood 1. A covering for the head and neck. A hood is often attached to the collar of a coat. 2. The metal cover that is over the engine of an automobile. 3. Something that looks like a hood or is used as a cover. There is a metal *hood* over our stove. A cobra has a fold of loose skin called a *hood* that it can stretch open around its head.

Hood

hood (hood) *noun, plural* **hoods.**

hoodlum A rough and nasty person who causes trouble for other people. Several teenage *hoodlums* were caught stealing lunch money from the younger children in the school.
  hood·lum (hōōd′ləm) *noun, plural* **hoodlums.**

hoof The hard covering on the feet of horses, cattle, deer, and other animals.
  hoof (hoof *or* hōōf) *noun, plural* **hooves** or **hoofs.**

hook 1. A bent piece of metal, wood, or other strong material that is used to hold or fasten something. There is a row of coat *hooks* in the closet in our classroom. My dress has a *hook* on the collar. 2. Anything bent or shaped like a hook. A curved piece of wire with a barb at one end used for catching fish is a hook. *Noun.*
  —1. To hang, fasten, or attach with a hook. We *hooked* the wire picture hanger over the nail. 2. To catch with or on a hook. The fisherman *hooked* three fish. 3. To have or make into the shape of a hook. Bob *hooked* his leg over the arm of the chair. *Verb.*
  hook (hook) *noun, plural* **hooks;** *verb,* **hooked, hooking.**

hoop A ring made of wood, metal, or other material. Metal *hoops* hold together the staves of a barrel. Plastic *hoops* are a toy that can be spun around your body. Lions leap through flaming *hoops* in the circus. ▲ Another word that sounds like this is **whoop.**
  hoop (hōōp *or* hoop) *noun, plural* **hoops.**

Hoop

hoot 1. The sound that an owl makes. 2. A sound like the cry of an owl. People make a hoot when they do not like or do not believe something. John's friends gave a *hoot* when he said he saw a ghost in the old house. *Noun.*
  —To make the sound of an owl or any sound like this. The fans *hooted* when the other team made an error. *Verb.*
  hoot (hōōt) *noun, plural* **hoots;** *verb,* **hooted, hooting.**

hooves More than one hoof. Look up **hoof** for more information.
  hooves (hoovz *or* hōōvz) *noun plural.*

hop[1] 1. To make a short jump on one foot. When you play hopscotch, you have to *hop* from one square to another. 2. To move by jumping on both feet or all feet at once. Rabbits and frogs *hop.* 3. To jump over. We *hopped* the fence instead of walking around to the gate. *Verb.*
  —A short jump or leap. She went down the street with a *hop* and a skip. *Noun.*
  hop (hop) *verb,* **hopped, hopping;** *noun, plural* **hops.**

hop[2] A greenish-yellow fruit shaped like a cone that grows on a vine. Hops are used to flavor beer.
  hop (hop) *noun, plural* **hops.**

hope To want or wish for something very much. I *hope* Susan will feel better soon. The girls *hoped* for a sunny day so that they could go to the beach. *Verb.*
  —1. A strong wish and belief that a thing will happen. Alex is full of *hope* that he will go to college. 2. Something that is wished for. His *hope* is that he will be elected captain of the team. *Noun.*
  hope (hōp) *verb,* **hoped, hoping;** *noun, plural* **hopes.**

hopeful 1. Having or showing hope. She was *hopeful* that they would be able to get tickets for the movie. 2. Giving promise that what is wished for will happen. Ginny thought that her mother's smile was a *hopeful* sign that she could go to the party.
  hope·ful (hōp′fəl) *adjective.*

hopeless Having or giving no hope. When he failed the test after studying so hard, he felt *hopeless.*
  hope·less (hōp′lis) *adjective.*

hopper 1. A person or an animal that hops. Grasshoppers and kangaroos are hoppers. 2. A holder for grain, coal, or other things. Hoppers are wide open at the top with a small opening at the bottom. They are used to empty something into a container.
  hop·per (hop′ər) *noun, plural* **hoppers.**

hopscotch A children's game on numbered squares that are drawn on the ground. The players hop into the squares in a certain order and try to pick up a stone or other object that has been tossed into one of the squares.
  hop·scotch (hop′scoch′) *noun.*

horde A very large group. A *horde* of ants came out of the anthill. A *horde* of people

at; āpe; cär; end; mē; it; īce; hot; ōld; fôrk; wood; fōōl; oil; out; up; turn; sing; thin; this; hw in white; zh in treasure.
ə stands for a in about, e in taken i in pencil, o in lemon, and u in circus.

311

pushed their way into the baseball park. ▲ Another word that sounds like this is **hoard**.
horde (hôrd) *noun, plural* **hordes.**

horizon 1. The line where the sky and the ground or the sea seem to meet. We could see a huge ship on the *horizon.* 2. The limit of a person's knowledge, interests, or experience. He widened his *horizons* by reading many books.
ho·ri·zon (hə rī′zən) *noun, plural* **horizons.**

horizontal Flat and straight across; parallel to the horizon. The workmen put the *horizontal* beams of the house in place.
hor·i·zon·tal (hôr′ə zont′əl) *adjective.*

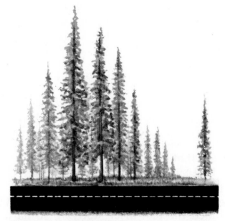

The road is **horizontal**. The trees are vertical.

hormone A substance made in the body that helps it grow or stay healthy. Hormones are made in certain glands and enter into the bloodstream. The blood carries them to the parts of the body where they are needed.
hor·mone (hôr′mōn) *noun, plural* **hormones.**

horn 1. A hard, pointed growth on the head of some animals. Deer, sheep, and rhinoceroses have horns. 2. Something that looks like the horn of an animal. Some owls have tufts of feathers on their heads called horns. 3. A brass musical instrument. Horns have a narrow end that you blow into to play them. 4. A device used to make a warning signal. The bus driver honked his *horn* at the children in the street.
horn (hôrn) *noun, plural* **horns.**

Horns

horned toad A lizard that has spiny horns on its head and scales on its body. Horned toads live in dry areas in the western United States.
horned toad (hôrnd).

Horned Toad

hornet A large wasp that can give a very painful sting.
hor·net (hôr′nit) *noun, plural* **hornets.**

horny Made of horn or something that is hard like a horn. A deer's antlers are a *horny* growth.
horn·y (hôr′nē) *adjective,* **hornier, horniest.**

horrible 1. Causing great fear or shock. It was *horrible* to see the house burn to the ground. Murder is a *horrible* crime. 2. Very bad, ugly, or unpleasant. There was a *horrible* smell by the garbage heap.
hor·ri·ble (hôr′ə bəl) *adjective.*

horrid 1. Causing great fear or shock; horrible. She thought the monster movie was so *horrid* that she left before it was over. 2. Very bad, ugly, or unpleasant. My brother thinks spinach tastes *horrid*, but I like it.
hor·rid (hôr′id) *adjective.*

horrify To cause great fear or shock. Seeing the two cars crash *horrified* him.
hor·ri·fy (hôr′ə fī′) *verb,* **horrified, horrifying.**

horror 1. A feeling of great fear and dread. They watched with *horror* as the ship burned and sank. He has a *horror* of being alone in the dark. 2. A strong feeling of dislike or shock. She looked around the dirty old house with *horror.* 3. A person or thing that causes great fear, shock, or dislike. They all felt that war was a *horror.*
hor·ror (hôr′ər) *noun, plural* **horrors.**

horse 1. A large animal with four legs with hooves and a long, flowing mane and tail. Horses are used for riding and pulling heavy loads. 2. A frame with legs. Some horses have soft, leather pads on top and are used in gym for doing exercises. Others are plain and are used with a board across them as work tables. ▲ Another word that sounds like this is **hoarse.**

horse (hôrs) *noun, plural* **horses.**

horseback   On the back of a horse. Don and Linda are going to ride *horseback* to the campsite.

horse·back (hôrs′bak′) *adverb.*

horsefly   A large fly with a fat body. The female gives a painful bite to horses and other animals and to people.

horse·fly (hôrs′flī′) *noun, plural* **horseflies.**

horseman   **1.** A man who rides on a horse. **2.** A man who is skilled in riding or handling horses. Her uncle is a fine *horseman.*

horse·man (hôrs′mən) *noun, plural* **horse-men.**

horsepower   A unit for measuring the power of an engine.

horse·pow·er (hôrs′pou′ər) *noun.*

horseshoe   **1.** A U-shaped piece of metal curved to fit the shape of a horse's hoof. A horseshoe is nailed onto the hoof to protect it. **2. horseshoes.** A game played by throwing a U-shaped piece toward a post so that it will land around the post.

horse·shoe (hôrs′shoo′) *noun, plural* **horse-shoes.**

hose   **1.** A tube of rubber or other material that will bend easily. Hoses are used to carry water or other fluids from one place to another. The boy watered the garden with a *hose.* Gasoline is pumped through a *hose* into a car, truck, or airplane. **2.** Stockings or socks. *Noun.*
—To wash or water with a hose. We *hosed* down the car before we waxed it. Will you *hose* off the front porch? *Verb.*

hose (hōz) *noun, plural* **hoses** *(for definition 1)* or **hose** *(for definition 2); verb,* **hosed, hosing.**

Hose

hospitable   Making a guest or visitor feel welcome and comfortable; friendly. The lady who owned the small hotel was very *hospita-ble,* even though we arrived late at night.

hos·pi·ta·ble (hos′pi tə bəl *or* hos pit′ə bəl) *adjective.*

hospital   A place where doctors and nurses take care of people who are sick or hurt.

hos·pi·tal (hos′pit əl) *noun, plural* **hospitals.**

▲   The first meaning of **hospital** was "a place where travelers can find rest and food." These places often took care of poor people who could not pay to stay at other places, and eventually the word *hospital* was used for any place that took care of poor sick people. This last use of *hospital* led to our meaning, "a place for the care of sick people."

hospitality   A friendly welcome and treatment of guests or visitors. We thanked our friends for their *hospitality* to us last weekend.

hos·pi·tal·i·ty (hos′pə tal′ə tē) *noun, plural* **hospitalities.**

hospitalize   To put a person in a hospital so that he will get the care he needs. The skier was *hospitalized* for weeks with a broken leg.

hos·pi·tal·ize (hos′pit əl īz′) *verb,* **hospital-ized, hospitalizing.**

host¹   A man who invites people to come to his home as his guests. We thanked our *host* for a wonderful party.

host (hōst) *noun, plural* **hosts.**

host²   A large number. On a clear night, you can see a *host* of stars in the sky.

host (hōst) *noun, plural* **hosts.**

hostage   A person who is held as a prisoner by someone until money is paid or promises are kept. The passengers and crew of the hijacked plane were held as *hostages* until a ransom was paid.

hos·tage (hos′tij) *noun, plural* **hostages.**

hostel   A place that gives cheap lodging to young people on bicycle tours or hikes. ▲ Another word that sounds like this is **hos-tile.**

hos·tel (host′əl) *noun, plural* **hostels.**

hostess   **1.** A woman who invites people to

at; āpe; cär; end; mē; it; īce; hot; ōld;
fôrk; wood; fool; oil; out; up; turn; sing;
thin; this; hw in white; zh in treasure.
ə stands for a in about, e in taken
i in pencil, o in lemon, and u in circus.

come to her home as her guests. Mrs. Davis was the *hostess* at a large dinner party. **2.** A woman who serves food and greets people in a restaurant or on an airplane.
host·ess (hōs′tis) *noun, plural* **hostesses.**

hostile Feeling or showing hatred or dislike. After their fight, the boys wouldn't talk to each other for a week, and just gave each other *hostile* looks. ▲ Another word that sounds like this is **hostel.**
hos·tile (host′əl) *adjective.*

hot **1.** Having a high temperature. I burned my hand when I touched the *hot* iron. We were *hot* after sitting in the sun for an hour. **2.** Having a burning, sharp taste. We put *hot* mustard on our frankfurters. **3.** Violent; raging. Jack has a *hot* temper. **4.** Following very closely. The police were in *hot* pursuit of the robbers.
hot (hot) *adjective,* **hotter, hottest.**

hot dog A long, thin sausage; frankfurter. It is often served on a long roll with mustard and relish.

hotel A building with many rooms that people pay to sleep in. Most hotels serve meals.
ho·tel (hō tel′) *noun, plural* **hotels.**

hothouse A heated building made mainly of glass where plants are grown; greenhouse.
hot·house (hot′hous′) *noun, plural* **hot·houses.**

Houseboat

hound A dog that has been raised and trained to hunt. Beagles and bloodhounds are two kinds of hounds. *Noun.*
—To keep urging; pester. Father *hounded* me about cleaning up my room. *Verb.*
hound (hound) *noun, plural* **hounds;** *verb,* **hounded, hounding.**

hour **1.** A unit of time equal to sixty minutes. There are twenty-four hours in a day. We waited for one *hour,* from four o'clock to five o'clock, for Tom to meet us. **2.** A time of the day that is shown on a clock or watch. At what *hour* should we leave for the station? **3.** The time for anything. The doctor's office *hours* are from nine o'clock to four o'clock. Our lunch *hour* starts at twelve o'clock. ▲ Another word that sounds like this is **our.**
hour (our) *noun, plural* **hours.**

hourglass A device for measuring time. It is a glass tube with a narrow middle. A quantity of sand runs from the top part to the bottom part in exactly one hour.
hour·glass (our′glas′) *noun, plural* **hourglasses.**

hourly Done or happening every hour. There are *hourly* airplane flights to Washington, D.C. from New York City. *Adjective.*
—Every hour. The weather is reported *hourly* on the radio. *Adverb.*
Hourglass
hour·ly (our′lē) *adjective; adverb.*

house **1.** A building in which people live; home. Dave asked us to come to his *house* for dinner. **2.** The people who live in a house. Our whole *house* was awakened when the fire engines went by. **3.** Any building used for a special purpose. The town has a new movie *house.* **4.** A group of people who make laws. The United States Congress is made up of the House of Representatives, which is the lower *house,* and the Senate, which is the upper *house.* **5.** An audience. There was a full *house* for the opening of the new show. *Noun.*
—To give someone a place to live. We *housed* our friends for a month until their new home was ready. The horses are *housed* in a barn. *Verb.*
house (hous *for noun;* houz *for verb*) *noun, plural* **houses;** *verb,* **housed, housing.**

houseboat A big boat that people can live on.
house·boat (hous′bōt′) *noun, plural* **house·boats.**

housefly A fly that lives in and near people's houses. It eats food and garbage.
house·fly (hous′flī′) *noun, plural* **houseflies.**

household All the people who live in a house. Our *household* was very busy the week before Christmas. *Noun.*
—Having to do with a household. On Saturday, we all helped with cleaning, ironing, and other *household* chores. *Adjective.*

house·hold (hous′hōld′) *noun, plural* **house-holds;** *adjective.*

House of Commons The lower house of the British or Canadian Parliament. The members of the House of Commons are elected.

House of Lords The upper house of the British Parliament.

House of Representatives One of the two houses of the United States Congress.

housewife A woman who takes care of a house and the needs of a family.
house·wife (hous′wīf′) *noun, plural* **house-wives.**

housework Washing, ironing, cleaning, cooking, and other work that has to be done in taking care of a house and the people who live in it.
house·work (hous′wurk′) *noun.*

housing **1.** A number of houses. There is a lot of new *housing* being built in our town. **2.** A covering for the moving parts of a machine. The *housing* on Dad's drill gets very hot when the drill is used for a long time.
hous·ing (hou′zing) *noun, plural* **housings.**

hover To stay in the air, flying right above one place. The bird *hovered* over its nest. The helicopter *hovered* above the airport until there was room for it to land.
hov·er (huv′ər *or* hov′ər) *verb,* **hovered, hovering.**

how *How* will we get home from school today? *How* cold is it outside? *How* did you like the movie? *How* tall is he? *How* are you today? *How* did he happen to be so late?
how (hou) *adverb.*

however It is the middle of winter; *however,* it is very warm outside. *However* did you get such a bad cut on your arm?
how·ev·er (hou ev′ər) *conjunction; adverb.*

howl To make a loud, wailing cry. A dog and a wolf both howl. The wind howls when it blows hard. Jack *howled* when he hurt his toe. We *howled* with laughter. *Verb.*
—A loud, wailing cry. We heard the *howl* of the wind through the rafters of the old barn. *Noun.*
howl (houl) *verb,* **howled, howling;** *noun, plural* **howls.**

hub **1.** The middle part of a wheel. The spokes of the bicycle wheel go between the rim and the *hub.* **2.** A center of interest or movement. The gym was the *hub* of activity when the team practiced for a game.
hub (hub) *noun, plural* **hubs.**

huckleberry A small, shiny, dark-blue berry. Huckleberries grow on small, low shrubs. They are like blueberries but are smaller and darker.
huck·le·ber·ry (huk′əl-ber′ē) *noun, plural* **huckleberries.**

Huckleberries

huddle To gather close together in a bunch. The boys and girls *huddled* around the campfire. The hen *huddled* her baby chicks under her wings at night. *Verb.*
—A group of people or animals that are gathered close together. Bill joined the *huddle* of football players on the field. *Noun.*
hud·dle (hud′əl) *verb,* **huddled, huddling;** *noun, plural* **huddles.**

hue A color or a shade of a color. The sunset had an orange *hue.*
hue (hyo͞o) *noun, plural* **hues.**

hug **1.** To put the arms around a person or thing and hold close and tightly. He *hugged* his grandmother because he was so glad to see her. **2.** To keep close to. He *hugged* the curb when he rode his bicycle along the busy street. *Verb.*
—A close, tight clasp with the arms. He gave his dog a big *hug* when he came home. *Noun.*
hug (hug) *verb,* **hugged, hugging;** *noun, plural* **hugs.**

huge Very big; enormous. An elephant is a *huge* animal. Richard took such a *huge* helping of ice cream that he couldn't eat it all.
huge (hyo͞oj) *adjective,* **huger, hugest.**

hull **1.** The outer covering of a nut, grain, or other seed. **2.** The small leaves around the stem of a strawberry and certain other fruits. **3.** The sides and bottom of a boat or ship. *Noun.*
—To remove the hull from a seed or fruit. I *hulled* the strawberries and Susan sliced them. *Verb.*
hull (hul) *noun, plural* **hulls;** *verb,* **hulled, hulling.**

Hull

at; āpe; cär; end; mē; it; īce; hot; ōld; fôrk; wood; fo͞ol; oil; out; up; turn; sing; thin; <u>th</u>is; hw in white; zh in treasure. ə stands for a in about, e in taken i in pencil, o in lemon, and u in circus.

315

hum **1.** To make a soft, murmuring sound for a long time, like a bee. If you are trying to say "m" with your mouth closed, you are humming. The bumblebees were *humming* in the garden. **2.** To sing with the lips closed and without saying words. Mother was *humming* softly to herself while she was cooking dinner. *Verb.*
—A soft, murmuring sound that keeps going. The *hum* of the air conditioner seemed loud in the small room. *Noun.*
  hum (hum) *verb,* **hummed, humming;** *noun,* *plural* **hums.**

human Having to do with a person or persons; being a person or persons. Men, women, and children are *human* beings. *Human* nature is the way people think and behave. *Adjective.*
—A person. Every man, woman, and child is a *human. Noun.*
  hu·man (hyo͞o′mən) *adjective; noun, plural* **humans.**

humane Kind; not cruel. It was not *humane* to lock the big dog in the little cage for such a long time.
  hu·mane (hyo͞o mān′) *adjective.*

humanity **1.** People; mankind. Keeping our air and water clean will help all *humanity.* **2.** Kindness. The doctor treated his patients with great *humanity.*
  hu·man·i·ty (hyo͞o man′ə tē) *noun.*

humble **1.** Not proud; modest. A humble person does not think he is better than other people. The writer remained a *humble* man even after his books became very famous. **2.** Not big or important. They lived in a *humble* cottage on a farm. *Adjective.*
—To make humble. He was *humbled* when he saw what good work the others had done without his help. *Verb.*
  hum·ble (hum′bəl) *adjective,* **humbler, humblest;** *verb,* **humbled, humbling.**

humid Damp; moist. It was a hot, *humid* summer day.
  hu·mid (hyo͞o′mid) *adjective.*

humidity Water vapor in the air; dampness. The high *humidity* of the day made us feel warm and uncomfortable. An air conditioner is designed to take *humidity* out of the air.
  hu·mid·i·ty (hyo͞o mid′ə tē) *noun.*

humiliate To make a person feel very ashamed. He was *humiliated* when he failed the test after bragging that he was the best student.
  hu·mil·i·ate (hyo͞o mil′ē āt′) *verb,* **humiliated, humiliating.**

hummingbird A small bird with brightly colored feathers and a long, narrow bill. The hummingbird beats its wings so fast that they make a humming sound. It can fly backwards or sideways, and can hover above flowers while it drinks their nectar.
  hum·ming·bird (hum′ing burd′) *noun, plural* **hummingbirds.**

Hummingbird

humor **1.** The funny part of something. Humor is what makes a person laugh. The *humor* in the story came from the silly dog who thought he was a cat. **2.** The ability to make people laugh and to enjoy funny things. John has a good sense of *humor.* **3.** The mood that a person is in. Dick was in a good *humor* after having such a nice day fishing. *Noun.*
—To give in to what a person wants. When she was sick, her mother *humored* her by reading her favorite story over and over again. *Verb.*
  hu·mor (hyo͞o′mər) *noun, plural* **humors;** *verb,* **humored, humoring.**

humorous Making people laugh; funny; comical. They saw a *humorous* movie about a lady who thought she could fly.
  hu·mor·ous (hyo͞o′mər əs) *adjective.*

hump A rounded lump or bump. Some camels have two *humps* on their backs.
  hump (hump) *noun, plural* **humps.**

humus A dark part of the soil. Humus comes from dead plants.
  hu·mus (hyo͞o′məs) *noun.*

hunch To draw up or bend. The cold wind made him *hunch* his shoulders. *Verb.*
—A guess or sudden thought about something. I had a *hunch* my friend might visit, so I made a pitcher of lemonade. *Noun.*
  hunch (hunch) *verb,* **hunched, hunching;** *noun, plural* **hunches.**

hundred Ten times ten; 100.
  hun·dred (hun′drid) *noun, plural* **hundreds;** *adjective.*

hundredth **1.** Next after the ninety-ninth. **2.** One of a hundred equal parts; $1/100$.
  hun·dredth (hun′dridth) *adjective; noun, plural* **hundredths.**

hung We *hung* new curtains last night. Look up **hang** for more information.
  hung (hung) *verb.*

hunger 1. Pain or weakness caused by not eating enough food. During a long, cold winter many wild animals die of *hunger*. 2. The feeling of wanting or needing food. Karen's *hunger* made her gobble her lunch. 3. A strong wish or need for anything. The dictator had a *hunger* for power. *Noun.*
—To have a strong wish or need for something. I *hungered* for a hamburger with French fried potatoes. She *hungered* for words of praise from her teacher. *Verb.*
  hun·ger (hung′gər) *noun, plural* **hungers;** *verb,* **hungered, hungering.**

hungry 1. Wanting or needing food. Fred was *hungry* all morning because he didn't have time to eat breakfast. 2. Having a strong wish or need for anything. The orphans were *hungry* for love.
  hun·gry (hung′grē) *adjective,* **hungrier, hungriest.**

hunt 1. To chase in order to catch or kill. The hunters *hunted* deer. The police *hunted* the bank robbers. 2. To look hard to try to find something. We *hunted* all over the house for Mother's car keys. *Verb.*
—1. A chase made to catch or kill. The Indians went on a buffalo *hunt*. 2. A search to try to find something. The best part of the party was the *hunt* for the hidden presents. *Noun.*
  hunt (hunt) *verb,* **hunted, hunting;** *noun, plural* **hunts.**

hurdle 1. A fence or other barrier that has to be jumped over in a race. The horse cleared the *hurdle*. 2. **hurdles.** A race in which the runners must jump over fences while they keep running. 3. A difficulty or problem. Passing his final exams was the last *hurdle* before graduating from high school. *Noun.*
—To jump over. Jim *hurdled* the first fence ahead of the other runners. *Verb.*
  hur·dle (hurd′əl) *noun, plural* **hurdles;** *verb,* **hurdled, hurdling.**

hurl To throw hard and fast; fling. The pitcher turned and *hurled* the ball to the first baseman. We *hurled* the pebbles far out into the water.
  hurl (hurl) *verb,* **hurled, hurling.**

hurrah A shout of great happiness or praise. "Let's hear a big *hurrah* for our team!" yelled the cheerleader.
  hur·rah (hə rä′) *noun, plural* **hurrahs;** *interjection.*

hurricane A storm with very strong winds and heavy rain.
  hur·ri·cane (hur′ə kān′) *noun, plural* **hurricanes.**

hurried Done or made quickly or too quickly. She wrote a *hurried* note to tell her family where she was going and then ran for the bus.
  hur·ried (hur′ēd) *adjective.*

hurry To move faster than is usual; rush; speed. If we don't *hurry* we'll miss the train. We *hurried* our parents along so we could be first in line. *Verb.*
—1. The act of moving very quickly. In his *hurry* to pack, he forgot his toothbrush. 2. The wish or need to act or move very quickly. The children were in a *hurry* to go outside and play. *Noun.*
  hur·ry (hur′ē) *verb,* **hurried, hurrying;** *noun, plural* **hurries.**

hurt 1. To cause pain or injury. He fell on the rocks and *hurt* his arm. The doctor said the needle would not *hurt*. She *hurt* his feelings when she laughed at him. 2. To feel pain. My knee *hurts* because I twisted it. 3. To be bad for; harm. Being sick so often *hurt* his chances of making the team. *Verb.*
—A pain or injury. Betty had a *hurt* on her knee where she scraped it. *Noun.*
  hurt (hurt) *verb,* **hurt, hurting;** *noun, plural* **hurts.**

husband A man who is married.
  hus·band (huz′bənd) *noun, plural* **husbands.**

hush A silence or stillness. A hush comes when noise suddenly stops and everything is very quiet. *Noun.*

Hurdle

at; āpe; cär; end; mē; it; īce; hot; ōld;
fôrk; wood; fōol; oil; out; up; turn; sing;
thin; this; hw in white; zh in treasure.
ə stands for a in about, e in taken
i in pencil, o in lemon, and u in circus.

—**1.** To make quiet or silent. The dimming of the lights *hushed* the audience. **2.** To keep secret. They all agreed to *hush* up about the party so they could surprise her. *Verb.*
—Be quiet. "*Hush*," their mother said, "or you will wake the baby." *Interjection.*
hush (hush) *noun, plural* **hushes;** *verb,* **hushed, hushing;** *interjection.*

husk The dry, outside covering of some vegetables and fruits. We take the *husk* off corn before we cook it. *Noun.*
—To take off the husk from. If you *husk* the corn, I will peel the potatoes. *Verb.*
husk (husk) *noun, plural* **husks;** *verb,* **husked, husking.**

husky[1] **1.** Big and strong. The football player was a *husky* boy. **2.** Rough and deep in sound. His voice was *husky* when he had a cold.
husk·y (hus′kē) *adjective,* **huskier, huskiest.**

husky[2] A strong dog with a thick coat of hair and a bushy tail.
husk·y (hus′kē) *noun, plural* **huskies.**

hustle To move or do something very quickly and with energy. We had to *hustle* to finish all our work in an hour.
hus·tle (hus′əl) *verb,* **hustled, hustling.**

hut A small, roughly built house or shelter. There is a *hut* on the beach that we use to keep our fishing equipment in.
hut (hut) *noun, plural* **huts.**

hutch A house for rabbits or other small animals.
hutch (huch) *noun, plural* **hutches.**

hyacinth A sweet-smelling flower that has a thick stem with small flowers growing up and down it. Hyacinths grow from bulbs and have long leaves that grow up from the ground.
hy·a·cinth (hī′ə sinth′) *noun, plural* **hyacinths.**

Hyacinth

hybrid A plant or animal that is a mixture of two different kinds of plants or animals. A mule is a hybrid because its father is a donkey and its mother is a horse. *Noun.*
—Having to do with or being a hybrid. Dad raises *hybrid* roses. *Adjective.*
hy·brid (hī′brid) *noun, plural* **hybrids;** *adjective.*

hydrant A wide, covered pipe that sticks out of the ground and is attached to a water main. Fire hoses are attached to hydrants to get water to put out fires.
hy·drant (hī′drənt) *noun, plural* **hydrants.**

hydrogen A gas that burns very easily. It has no color, taste, or odor. Hydrogen is a chemical element.
hy·dro·gen (hī′drə jən) *noun.*

hydrogen bomb A very powerful bomb that explodes with great force. The fusion of atoms of hydrogen to form atoms of helium causes the explosion. The hydrogen bomb is more powerful than the atomic bomb.

hyena An animal that looks like a wolf. A hyena has a large head and front legs that are longer than the back legs. Hyenas live in Africa and Asia and hunt other animals for food.
hy·e·na (hī ē′nə) *noun, plural* **hyenas.**

Hyena

hygiene Things that must be done to keep people and places healthy and clean. Washing yourself and brushing your teeth are part of your personal *hygiene.*
hy·giene (hī′jēn) *noun.*

hymn A song of praise to God. ▲ Another word that sounds like this is **him.**
hymn (him) *noun, plural* **hymns.**

hyphen A mark (-) used to connect two or more parts of a word or two or more words. The word "merry-go-round" has two *hyphens* in it.
hy·phen (hī′fən) *noun, plural* **hyphens.**

hyphenate To put a hyphen or hyphens in a word. In the definition of *hygiene* on this page, the word *washing* is hyphenated.
hy·phen·ate (hī′fə nāt′) *verb,* **hyphenated, hyphenating.**

hypnotize To put someone in a trance that is like sleep. Someone who has been hypnotized can hear what the person who has hypnotized him says, and does what he is told to do by that person.
hyp·no·tize (hip′nə tīz′) *verb,* **hypnotized, hypnotizing.**

hysterical Caused by a very strong fear or sorrow. She burst into *hysterical* crying when she heard that her house had burned to the ground.
hys·ter·i·cal (his ter′i kəl) *adjective.*

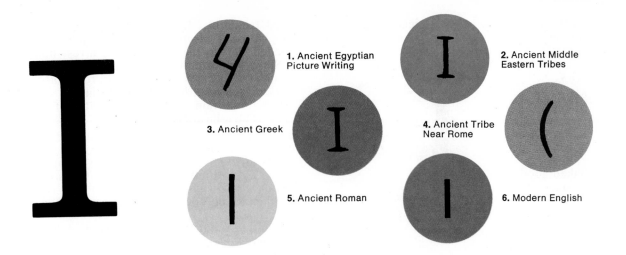

1. Ancient Egyptian Picture Writing

2. Ancient Middle Eastern Tribes

3. Ancient Greek

4. Ancient Tribe Near Rome

5. Ancient Roman

6. Modern English

I is the ninth letter of the alphabet. The oldest form of the letter I was a drawing that the ancient Egyptians (**1**) used in their picture writing nearly 5000 years ago. This drawing was borrowed by several ancient tribes (**2**) in the Middle East. They gave the letter its modern shape, writing it as a tall line with a short bar at the top and bottom. The ancient Greeks (**3**) borrowed this letter without changing its shape. The letter was then borrowed by an ancient tribe (**4**) that settled north of Rome about 2800 years ago. They changed its shape by not writing the short line at the top and bottom of the letter. The Romans (**5**) borrowed this form of I from them. Our modern capital letter I (**6**) looks very much like the ancient Greek letter.

i, I   The ninth letter of the alphabet.
  i, I (ī) *noun, plural* **i's, I's.**

I   *I* have a dog and a cat. ▲ Other words that sound like this are **aye** and **eye.**
  I (ī) *pronoun.*

ice   **1.** Water that has been made solid by cold; frozen water. The fisherman cut a hole through the *ice* on the lake. **2.** A frozen dessert made with sweetened water and fruit flavors. It was such a hot day that I bought a strawberry *ice* to cool me off. *Noun.*
  —**1.** To become covered with ice. The lake *ices* over in the winter. **2.** To keep or make cold. We *iced* the lemonade before we drank it. **3.** To decorate with icing. Sally and Tim *iced* a cake for their father's birthday. *Verb.*
  ice (īs) *noun, plural* **ices;** *verb,* **iced, icing.**

iceberg   A very large piece of floating ice. It comes from a glacier. The ship was damaged when it hit an *iceberg* in the stormy seas.
  ice·berg (īs′burg′) *noun, plural* **icebergs.**

icebox   **1.** A box or chest cooled with blocks of ice. It is used for storing food and drinks. **2.** A refrigerator.
  ice·box (īs′boks′) *noun, plural* **iceboxes.**

icecap   A sheet of ice with a high center. It covers an area of land and moves out from the center in all directions as it becomes larger.
  ice·cap (īs′kap′) *noun, plural* **icecaps.**

ice cream   A frozen dessert. It is made from milk products, sweeteners, and flavoring.

ice-skate   To skate on ice.
  ice-skate (īs′skāt′) *verb,* **ice-skated, ice-skating.**

ice skate   A shoe with a metal blade on the bottom. It is used for ice-skating.

Iceberg

icicle A pointed, hanging piece of ice. It is formed by water that freezes as it drips.
i·ci·cle (ī'si kəl) *noun, plural* **icicles.**

icing A mixture of sugar, eggs, butter, and flavoring. Icing is used to cover or decorate cakes or other baked goods.
ic·ing (ī'sing) *noun, plural* **icings.**

Icicles

icy **1.** Made of or covered with ice. Lynn slipped on the *icy* sidewalk. **2.** Very cold. When the *icy* winds blew, it grew cold in the house. **3.** Cold and unfriendly. Jane gave me an *icy* stare the next time I saw her after our big argument.
i·cy (ī'sē) *adjective,* **icier, iciest.**

I'd She asked if *I'd* borrowed her book. *I'd* go if you would. *I'd* think you would enjoy that movie.
I'd (īd) contraction for "I had," "I would," and "I should."

Idaho A state in the western United States. Its capital is Boise.
I·da·ho (ī'də hō) *noun.*

▲ **Idaho** probably comes from an Apache Indian name for another Indian tribe. The name was first used in what is now Colorado, but when Idaho became a state, the United States Senate gave it this name.

idea **1.** A thought, belief, or opinion formed in the mind. The author had an *idea* for a new novel. John has some very good *ideas* for the party decorations. **2.** The purpose of something. The *idea* of the game of baseball is to score runs for your team.
i·de·a (ī dē'ə) *noun, plural* **ideas.**

ideal A person or thing thought of as perfect. The famous football player was the *ideal* of many boys. *Noun.*
—Being exactly what one would hope for; perfect. The breeze makes it an *ideal* day for going sailing. *Adjective.*
i·de·al (ī dē'əl) *noun, plural* **ideals;** *adjective.*

identical **1.** The very same. Her birthday is on the *identical* day as mine. **2.** Exactly alike. The twins always wore *identical* clothes.
i·den·ti·cal (ī den'ti kəl) *adjective.*

identification **1.** The act of identifying. The woman's *identification* of the robber was needed before the police could arrest him. **2.** Something used to prove who a person is. John's father carried his passport for *identification* because it had his picture in it.
i·den·ti·fi·ca·tion (ī den'tə fi kā'shən) *noun, plural* **identifications.**

identify **1.** To show or prove that a person or thing is who or what you say it is. Mrs. Jones *identified* the robber by the scar on his face. **2.** To think of or treat as the same. Randy is always *identified* with his twin brother Ralph because no one can tell them apart.
i·den·ti·fy (ī den'tə fī') *verb,* **identified, identifying.**

identity **1.** What or who a person or thing is. His driver's license gave his *identity* as Mr. Brown. The famous actress tried to hide her *identity* by wearing a wig. **2.** The condition of being exactly the same. The *identity* of the twins made it hard for their friends to tell them apart.
i·den·ti·ty (ī den'tə tē) *noun, plural* **identities.**

idiom A phrase or expression whose meaning cannot be understood from the ordinary meanings of the separate words in it. "To pull a person's leg" is an idiom that means "to trick or tease."
id·i·om (id'ē əm) *noun, plural* **idioms.**

▲ Because **idioms** are a part of our everyday speaking and writing, we don't often think of the fact that they don't make sense according to the meanings of their separate words. It is only because we learn to speak our own language naturally as young children that the idioms in English don't seem strange or foolish to us. Try to imagine what a foreign boy learning English would think the first time he heard someone say, "I don't believe you; you're just pulling my leg!"

idiot **1.** A person who is mentally retarded. Even after he grows up, an idiot cannot ever learn how to feed himself or take care of himself. **2.** A very silly or foolish person. I was an *idiot* for not remembering that today was your birthday!
id·i·ot (id'ē ət) *noun, plural* **idiots.**

idle **1.** Not working or being used; not busy. The piano in our house is *idle* because two keys are broken and it can't be played. **2.** Lazy. She is an *idle* person who never does her share of work around the house. **3.** Having little worth or usefulness. Gossip is just *idle* talk. *Adjective.*

—**1.** To spend time doing nothing. He *idled* around the house all evening and did not do his homework. **2.** To run slowly and out of gear. When a machine *idles,* it does not produce any power. He left the car *idling* in the driveway while we went back into the house. **3.** To waste. He *idled* away the morning lying in bed. *Verb.* ▲ Another word that sounds like this is **idol.**

i·dle (īd′əl) *adjective,* **idler, idlest;** *verb,* **idled, idling.**

idol **1.** Something that is worshiped as a god. An idol is often a statue of a god. **2.** A person who is greatly loved or admired. Mrs. Sterling was an *idol* to many of her students. ▲ Another word that sounds like this is **idle.**

i·dol (īd′əl) *noun, plural* **idols.**

if *If* I hurt your feelings, I'm sorry. Even *if* it rains, the game will still be played. I will go *if* you do. I don't know *if* he will be there.

if (if) *conjunction.*

igloo A dome-shaped hut used by Eskimos to live in. It is usually built from blocks of hardened snow.

ig·loo (ig′lōō) *noun, plural* **igloos.**

Igloo

igneous Produced with great heat or by a volcano. An *igneous* rock is formed when lava from a volcano hardens.

ig·ne·ous (ig′nē əs) *adjective.*

ignite **1.** To burn or set on fire. We *ignited* the dead leaves with a match. **2.** To begin to burn; catch on fire. You must be careful with oily rags because they *ignite* easily.

ig·nite (ig nīt′) *verb,* **ignited, igniting.**

ignition **1.** The act of igniting. The *ignition* of the rockets sent the spacecraft on its way to the moon. **2.** A system for starting a car, a boat, or some other vehicle. The ignition starts the fuel and air burning in the engine.

ig·ni·tion (ig nish′ən) *noun, plural* **ignitions.**

ignorance A lack of knowledge; being ignorant. He hurt his leg skiing because of his *ignorance* of how to turn on the slopes.

ig·no·rance (ig′nər əns) *noun.*

ignorant Having or showing a lack of education or knowledge. He made the *ignorant* remark that all people who have brown eyes are smart.

ig·no·rant (ig′nər ənt) *adjective.*

ignore To pay no attention to. Ann was angry with Jerry, so she *ignored* him when he spoke to her.

ig·nore (ig nôr′) *verb,* **ignored, ignoring.**

▲ The first meaning of **ignore** was "not to know." Long ago someone could have said, "The young maiden *ignored* (did not know) how to thank the knight for saving her." If a person refuses to look at or will not talk to another person, he pretends he does not know the other person is there. So *ignore* came to mean "to refuse to pay attention to."

iguana A large greenish-brown lizard. It is found in the very warm parts of America. The iguana lives in trees.

i·gua·na (i gwä′nə) *noun, plural* **iguanas.**

Iguana

ill **1.** Not healthy or well. He is absent from school because he is *ill* with a cold. **2.** Bad or evil. The destruction of homes and crops were two *ill* results of the flood. *Adjective.*
—Unkindly; badly. Don't speak *ill* of him because he really is a nice boy. *Adverb.*
—**1.** Trouble, evil, or misfortune. War is one of the *ills* of mankind. **2.** A sickness. Chicken pox is a common *ill* among young children. *Noun.*

ill (il) *adjective,* **worse, worst;** *adverb; noun, plural* **ills.**

ill at ease. Uncomfortable. The shy girl was *ill at ease* among strangers.

I'll *I'll* win the contest no matter what it takes. *I'll* go if you will. ▲ Other words that sound like this are **aisle** and **isle.**

I'll (īl) contraction for "I will" and "I shall."

at; āpe; cär; end; mē; it; īce; hot; ōld; fôrk; wood; fōol; oil; out; up; turn; sing; thin; this; hw in white; zh in treasure. ə stands for **a** in about, **e** in taken **i** in pencil, **o** in lemon, and **u** in circus.

illegal   Not legal; against laws or rules. It is *illegal* to shoot off fireworks in that town. He made an *illegal* block in the football game and a penalty was called.
il·le·gal (i lē′gəl) *adjective.*

Illinois   A state in the north-central United States. Its capital is Springfield.
Il·li·nois (il′ə noi′ *or* il′ə noiz′) *noun.*

▲ **Illinois** is the way French explorers wrote the Indian name for a tribe that used to live in the place that is now the state of Illinois. The Indian word means "men" or "tribe of great men."

illiterate   Not able to read or write; lacking education. The young boy was *illiterate* because he had never gone to school.
il·lit·er·ate (i lit′ər it) *adjective.*

illness   A sickness or disease. Many illnesses can be cured by taking the right medicine.
ill·ness (il′nis) *noun, plural* **illnesses.**

illuminate   To light up; give light to. A lamp *illuminated* one corner of the dark room.
il·lu·mi·nate (i lo͞o′mə nāt′) *verb,* **illuminated, illuminating.**

illusion   A false idea or belief; misleading idea. If you put a straw in a glass of water, you have the *illusion* that the part in the water is larger than the part out of the water, though they're really the same size. We were under the *illusion* that the party was on Friday and not Saturday.

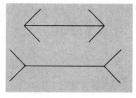

This **illusion** makes the bottom line seem longer.

il·lu·sion (i lo͞o′zhən) *noun, plural* **illusions.**

illustrate   **1.** To make clear or explain. The teacher *illustrated* how the human eye works by comparing it to a camera, which works in a similar way. **2.** To draw a picture or diagram to explain or decorate something written. The famous artist *illustrated* a book about tropical birds.
il·lus·trate (il′əs trāt′ *or* i lus′trāt′) *verb,* **illustrated, illustrating.**

illustration   **1.** Something used to make clear or explain. The teacher showed us how to solve the arithmetic problem as an *illustration* of how to do other problems of the same kind. **2.** A picture or diagram used to explain or decorate something written. The *illustrations* in this dictionary help to explain words that have been defined.

il·lus·tra·tion (il′əs trā′shən) *noun, plural* **illustrations.**

ill will   Unfriendly feeling. After the fight, the two boys felt *ill will* toward each other.

I'm   *I'm* going to the zoo today.
I'm (īm) contraction for "I am."

im-   A *prefix* that means "not." *Imperfect* means "not perfect." *Impractical* means "not practical."

image   **1.** A picture, idea, or likeness of a person or thing. A penny has an *image* of Abraham Lincoln on one side of it. Christopher is the *image* of his father. **2.** A typical example; picture. That athlete is the *image* of good health.
im·age (im′ij) *noun, plural* **images.**

imaginary   Existing only in the mind; unreal. Most people believe that ghosts are *imaginary.*
i·mag·i·nar·y (i maj′ə ner′ē) *adjective.*

imagination   **1.** The forming of pictures in the mind of things that are not really there. She pictured her summer vacation over and over in her *imagination* because it had been such fun. **2.** The ability or power to create or form new images or ideas. It took great *imagination* to write such a clever story.
i·mag·i·na·tion (i maj′ə nā′shən) *noun, plural* **imaginations.**

imaginative   **1.** Having a good imagination. The *imaginative* child made up stories to tell the younger children. **2.** Showing imagination. Bill wrote an *imaginative* story about a boy who could turn into anything he wanted to be.
i·mag·i·na·tive (i maj′ə nə tiv) *adjective.*

imagine   **1.** To picture a person or thing in the mind. Nancy tried to *imagine* life on the moon. The ending of the book was different from what I had *imagined.* **2.** To suppose; guess. I don't *imagine* we will go on a picnic if it rains.
i·mag·ine (i maj′in) *verb,* **imagined, imagining.**

imitate   **1.** To try to act or behave like another person does; copy. Joan *imitates* her older sister by dressing like her. Tony *imitated* the popular singer for his friends. **2.** To look like; resemble. The wooden floors were painted to *imitate* marble.
im·i·tate (im′ə tāt′) *verb,* **imitated, imitating.**

imitation   **1.** The act of copying. Russ does a great *imitation* of his teacher's voice. **2.** Something that is a copy of something else. We bought an *imitation* of a famous painting to hang in the den. *Noun.*
—Made to look like something real; not real.

My sister bought an *imitation* diamond ring that was really made of glass. *Adjective.*

im·i·ta·tion (im′ə tā′shən) *noun, plural* **imitations;** *adjective.*

immature Not having reached full growth; not mature. *Immature* corn is not ready to pick and eat.

im·ma·ture (im′ə choor′ *or* im′ə toor′ *or* im′ə tyoor′) *adjective.*

immediate **1.** Done or happening right away; without delay. When he asks his teacher a question, David gets an *immediate* answer. **2.** Close in time or space; near. Paul's parents said they won't get him a dog in the *immediate* future, but he may get one when he is older. He has no *immediate* plans for after graduation.

im·me·di·ate (i mē′dē it) *adjective.*

immediately Right away; now. If we leave *immediately,* we can get to the movie in time.

im·me·di·ate·ly (i mē′dē it lē) *adverb.*

immense Of great size; very large; huge. The whale is an *immense* animal that can grow as long as seventy feet.

im·mense (i mens′) *adjective.*

immigrant A person who comes to live in a country in which he or she was not born. My grandfather was an *immigrant* to the United States from Italy.

im·mi·grant (im′ə grənt) *noun, plural* **immigrants.**

immigrate To go to live in a country in which one was not born. My grandparents *immigrated* to the United States from Poland.

im·mi·grate (im′ə grāt′) *verb,* **immigrated, immigrating.**

immoral Wicked; evil; not moral. Lying about his friend was an *immoral* thing to do.

im·mor·al (i môr′əl) *adjective.*

immortal Living, lasting, or remembered forever. The ancient Greeks believed that their gods were *immortal.*

im·mor·tal (i môrt′əl) *adjective.*

immune Protected from a disease. The doctor gave me a vaccination that made me *immune* to smallpox.

im·mune (i myoon′) *adjective.*

impact The action of one object striking against another. The *impact* of the car crashing into the pole smashed the front fender of the car.

im·pact (im′pakt) *noun, plural* **impacts.**

impair To weaken; lessen the quality or strength of. The heavy fog *impaired* the driver's vision.

im·pair (im per′) *verb,* **impaired, impairing.**

impala A small, slender African antelope. It has a reddish or golden-brown coat. The impala can leap great distances.

im·pal·a (im pal′ə) *noun, plural* **impalas.**

impartial Not favoring one more than others; fair; just. A judge must be *impartial.*

im·par·tial (im·pär′shəl) *adjective.*

Impala

impatience A not being able to put up with delay or opposition calmly and without anger. Dad's *impatience* with George was caused by George's not keeping his room clean. Mother could sense the children's *impatience* for summer vacation to begin.

im·pa·tience (im pā′shəns) *noun.*

impatient Not able to put up with delay or opposition calmly and without anger. Joan became *impatient* when people were late for her party.

im·pa·tient (im pā′shənt) *adjective.*

impeach To bring formal charges of wrong conduct against a public official. An official may be removed from his office if he is found guilty of the charges.

im·peach (im pēch′) *verb,* **impeached, impeaching.**

▲ The word **impeach** used to mean "to prevent or hinder." For example, a person could say, "No one will *impeach* me from living where I want." People sometimes tried to prevent, or *impeach,* someone from doing something or holding some position by accusing him of doing something wrong. This led to the use of *impeach* to mean "to accuse formally of committing a crime while holding a government office."

imperial **1.** Having to do with an empire or an emperor or empress. The *imperial* palace

at; āpe; cär; end; mē; it; īce; hot; ōld; fôrk; wood; fōol; oil; out; up; turn; sing; thin; this; hw in white; zh in treasure.
ə stands for a in about, e in taken
i in pencil, o in lemon, and u in circus.

was the home of the emperor of the country. **2.** Having to do with one country's control over another or others. The United States started out as a group of colonies under the *imperial* rule of England.

im·pe·ri·al (im pēr′ē əl) *adjective.*

impersonate To copy the appearance and actions of. The man was arrested for *impersonating* a policeman.

im·per·son·ate (im pur′sə nāt′) *verb,* **impersonated, impersonating.**

implement Something used to do a particular job; tool. Hoes, rakes, and spades are gardening *implements.*

im·ple·ment (im′plə mənt) *noun, plural* **implements.**

imply To suggest without saying directly. Did you *imply* that I'm old-fashioned when you said my clothes were out of style?

im·ply (im plī′) *verb,* **implied, implying.**

import To bring in goods from another country for sale or use. We *import* tea from India. *Verb.*
—Something that is imported for sale or use. Oil is a valuable *import* for countries that do not have enough of it in their own land. *Noun.*

im·port (im pôrt′ *for verb;* im′pôrt′ *for noun*) *verb,* **imported, importing;** *noun, plural* **imports.**

importance The state of being important. Rain is of great *importance* to farmers since crops can't grow without water.

im·por·tance (im pôrt′əns) *noun.*

important Having great value or meaning. A proper diet is *important* to good health. Grain is an *important* crop in the United States.

im·por·tant (im pôrt′ənt) *adjective.*

impose To put or set on a person. The judge *imposed* a sentence of three years in jail on the thief. The city *imposed* a new tax on cigarettes.

im·pose (im pōz′) *verb,* **imposed, imposing.**

impossible **1.** Not able to happen or be done. It is *impossible* for a man to live forever. **2.** Not able to be put up with. He is an *impossible* person to work with.

im·pos·si·ble (im pos′ə bəl) *adjective.*

impress **1.** To have a strong effect on the mind or feelings. She *impressed* me as being a very nice person. **2.** To fix in the mind. Mother tried to *impress* a sense of right and wrong in all the children.

im·press (im pres′) *verb,* **impressed, impressing.**

impression **1.** An effect on the mind or feelings. What was your *impression* of the new girl in our class? **2.** A belief. I had the *impression* that they were brothers, but I was wrong. **3.** A mark or design produced by pressing or stamping. We made *impressions* of our hands in the wet concrete. **4.** Imitation. He did a very funny *impression* of a monkey.

im·pres·sion (im presh′ən) *noun, plural* **impressions.**

impressive Making a strong impression. His last dive was so *impressive* that the judges awarded him the gold medal.

im·pres·sive (im pres′iv) *adjective.*

imprint **1.** A mark made by pressing or stamping. Your boots have made *imprints* in the snow. **2.** A mark or effect. Age has left its *imprint* on my grandmother's face. *Noun.*
—To mark by pressing or stamping. The store *imprinted* envelopes with my name and address. *Verb.*

im·print (im′print′ *for noun;* im print′ *for verb*) *noun, plural* **imprints;** *verb,* **imprinted, imprinting.**

imprison To put or keep in prison; lock up. The convicted murderer was *imprisoned* after the trial.

im·pris·on (im priz′ən) *verb,* **imprisoned, imprisoning.**

impromptu Made or done without preparation or previous thought. When a person gives an *impromptu* speech, he has had no time to write or practice it.

im·promp·tu (im promp′tōō *or* im promp′tyōō) *adjective.*

improper **1.** Not correct. A screwdriver is an *improper* tool for driving nails. **2.** Showing bad manners or bad taste. It is *improper* to talk with food in your mouth.

im·prop·er (im prop′ər) *adjective.*

improper fraction A fraction that is equal to or greater than 1. $^8/_5$ and $^6/_6$ are both improper fractions because $^8/_5$ is equal to $1^3/_5$ and $^6/_6$ is equal to 1.

improve To make or become better. I am taking lessons to *improve* my singing. Her tennis has *improved* greatly since she has been practicing more.

im·prove (im prōōv′) *verb,* **improved, improving.**

improvement **1.** The act of improving or the state of being improved. A balanced diet and exercise will lead to *improvement* of your health. **2.** A change or a thing added that improves something. The new yellow curtains are an *improvement* to the room because they make it more cheerful. **3.** A person or thing that is better than another.

This new car is an *improvement* over our old broken-down one.

im·prove·ment (im prōōv′mənt) *noun, plural* **improvements.**

improvise **1.** To make up and perform without planning beforehand. The class *improvised* a welcome speech for the visiting parents. **2.** To make out of whatever materials are around. The children *improvised* bookcases out of wooden crates.

im·pro·vise (im′prə vīz′) *verb,* **improvised, improvising.**

impudent Bold and rude. The *impudent* boy talked back to the teacher.

im·pu·dent (im′pyə dənt) *adjective.*

impulse **1.** A sudden feeling that makes a person act without thinking. A sudden *impulse* made him give the new baseball mitt to his brother. **2.** A sudden force that causes motion; push. The *impulse* of the falling water turned the water wheel.

im·pulse (im′puls) *noun, plural* **impulses.**

impure Not clean; dirty. The dumping of garbage into the river has made it *impure.*

im·pure (im pyoor′) *adjective.*

in The cat is *in* the house. Go *in* the door on your left. The weather here is cold *in* the winter. My sister is the girl *in* the pink dress. Please come *in* out of the cold. ▲ Another word that sounds like this is **inn.**

in (in) *preposition; adverb.*

in- A *prefix* that means "not." *Inactive* means "not active." *Inexpensive* means "not expensive."

inaugurate **1.** To put a person in office with a formal ceremony. John F. Kennedy was *inaugurated* as President in 1961. **2.** To open or begin to use formally. The governor *inaugurated* the new bridge by being in the first car to drive across it.

in·au·gu·rate (in ô′gyə rāt′) *verb,* **inaugurated, inaugurating.**

inauguration **1.** The ceremony of putting a person in office with ceremony. Thousands of people watched the *inauguration* of the President on television. **2.** A formal beginning or opening. We went to the *inauguration* of the city's new public swimming pool.

in·au·gu·ra·tion (in ô′gyə rā′shən) *noun, plural* **inaugurations.**

inborn Born in a person; natural. Sandy has an *inborn* talent for playing the piano.

in·born (in′bôrn′) *adjective.*

incense¹ A substance that has a fragrant smell when it is burned. After the *incense* was lighted, it gave off a spicy smell.

in·cense (in′sens′) *noun, plural* **incenses.**

incense² To make very angry. It *incensed* her when she found out he had lied to her.

in·cense (in sens′) *verb,* **incensed, incensing.**

incentive Something that urges a person on. The possibility of a higher allowance was an *incentive* for Paul to do extra chores.

in·cen·tive (in sen′tiv) *noun, plural* **incentives.**

inch A measure of length that equals ¹/₁₂ of a foot. Twelve inches equal one foot. One inch is the same as 2.54 centimeters. *Noun.* —To move very slowly. She *inched* her way toward the door. *Verb.*

inch (inch) *noun, plural* **inches;** *verb,* **inched, inching.**

inchworm A kind of caterpillar. It moves by pulling the rear of its body up toward the front and then stretching the front end forward.

inch·worm (inch′wurm′) *noun, plural* **inchworms.**

Inchworm

incident Something that happens; event. Linda told us some of the funny *incidents* of her trip to Florida.

in·ci·dent (in′sə dənt) *noun, plural* **incidents.**

incidentally By the way. *Incidentally,* did Evelyn tell you she won first prize at the art show?

in·ci·den·tal·ly (in′sə dent′əl ē *or* in′sə dent′lē) *adverb.*

incinerator A furnace that burns garbage or trash.

in·cin·er·a·tor (in sin′ə rā′tər) *noun, plural* **incinerators.**

inclination **1.** A liking. I have an *inclination* to go to the movies rather than stay home. **2.** A natural tendency. She has an *inclination* toward being overweight, no matter how little she eats. **3.** A slope; slant. The

at; āpe; cär; end; mē; it; īce; hot; ōld; fôrk; wood; fōōl; oil; out; up; turn; sing; thin; <u>th</u>is; hw in white; zh in treasure. ə stands for a in about, e in taken i in pencil, o in lemon, and u in circus.

steep *inclination* of the hill makes it great for sledding.

in·cli·na·tion (in′klə nā′shən) *noun, plural* **inclinations.**

incline To slope or slant. The road is hard to walk on because it *inclines* upward. *Verb.*
—A surface that slopes. The ball rolled down the *incline* to the bottom of the hill. *Noun.*

in·cline (in klīn′ *for verb;* in′klīn′ *or* in klīn′ *for noun*) *verb,* **inclined, inclining;** *noun, plural* **inclines.**

Incline

include **1.** To have as part of the whole; contain. You don't have to buy batteries with that toy because they are already *included* in the box. **2.** To put in a group. Besides his friends, he *included* some of his sister's friends in the list of people he would invite to the party.

in·clude (in klo̅o̅d′) *verb,* **included, including.**

income Money received for work or from property or other things that are owned.

in·come (in′kum′) *noun, plural* **incomes.**

income tax A tax on a person's income.

incomplete Not complete; not finished. The boy's picture was *incomplete* because he ran out of paint.

in·com·plete (in′kəm plēt′) *adjective.*

incorporate To include something as part of something else. Let's *incorporate* her idea into our plan for the camping trip.

in·cor·po·rate (in kôr′pə rāt′) *verb,* **incorporated, incorporating.**

incorrect Not right or correct; not proper. You must do this problem over because your answer is *incorrect.*

in·cor·rect (in′kə rekt′) *adjective.*

increase To make or become greater in number or size. The library has *increased* its collection of mystery books. The number of

students trying out for the band has *increased* this year. *Verb.*
—The amount by which something is increased. He got an *increase* of fifty cents in his allowance. *Noun.*

in·crease (in krēs′ *for verb;* in′krēs′ *for noun*) *verb,* **increased, increasing;** *noun, plural* **increases.**

increasingly More and more. As the day wore on it became *increasingly* hotter.

in·creas·ing·ly (in krē′sing lē) *adverb.*

incredible Hard or impossible to believe. Do you think Bob's *incredible* story of helping to stop a bank robbery is true?

in·cred·i·ble (in kred′ə bəl) *adjective.*

incredulous Not able to believe something. Many people were *incredulous* when the men said they had found gold in the mountains.

in·cred·u·lous (in krej′ə ləs) *adjective.*

incubate To sit on eggs and keep them warm for hatching. A hen *incubates* her eggs.

in·cu·bate (ing′kyə bāt′) *verb,* **incubated, incubating.**

incubator A heated container. Some incubators are used for babies who are born too early. Others are used to hatch eggs.

in·cu·ba·tor (ing′kyə bā′tər) *noun, plural* **incubators.**

indeed Really; truly. He was *indeed* grateful to her for helping him.

in·deed (in dēd′) *adverb.*

indefinite **1.** Not clear, set, or exact; vague. His plans for the summer are still *indefinite.* **2.** Having no limits; not fixed. Jack will be away for an *indefinite* number of days.

in·def·i·nite (in def′ə nit) *adjective.*

indefinite article The indefinite article is *a* or *an.* *A* or *an* is used to show that the noun before which it comes is not a particular person or thing. *A* boy ran across the street. Is there *an* apple in the box?

indent To start a written line farther in than the other lines. We always *indent* the first sentence of a paragraph.

in·dent (in dent′) *verb,* **indented, indenting.**

independence Freedom from the control of another or others. The American colonies fought to win *independence* from England.

in·de·pend·ence (in′di pen′dəns) *noun.*

independent Free from the control or rule of another or others; separate. The American colonies fought with England to become an *independent* country. Jane moved out of town because she wanted to be *independent* of her family. He does what he wants, *independent* of anyone's wishes.

in·de·pend·ent (in′di pen′dənt) *adjective.*

326

index An alphabetical list at the end of a book. An index tells on what page a particular subject or name may be found. Joan looked in the *index* of her book on birds to find out on what page to look for information about the robin. *Noun.*
—To make an index for. The author *indexed* his book about Indians so the reader could look up the information he needed. *Verb.*
in·dex (in′deks) *noun, plural* **indexes;** *verb,* **indexed, indexing.**

▲ The word **index** comes from a Latin word that means "to show or point out." In Latin, the word *index* was first used to mean "forefinger," which is the finger we use to point at something.

index finger The finger next to the thumb; forefinger.

India A country in southern Asia. Its capital is New Delhi.
In·di·a (in′dē ə) *noun.*

Indian **1.** A member of one of the tribes living in North and South America before the Europeans discovered the continents. **2.** A person who was born or is living in India. *Noun.*
—**1.** Having to do with American Indians. **2.** Having to do with India or its people. *Adjective.*
In·di·an (in′dē ən) *noun, plural* **Indians;** *adjective.*

Indiana A state in the north-central United States. Its capital is Indianapolis.
In·di·an·a (in′dē an′ə) *noun.*

▲ The name **Indiana** comes from a Modern Latin word meaning "Indian." When the name was first used for this area, it still belonged to the Indians.

Indian corn A plant whose grain grows on large ears. Look up **corn** for more information.

Indian Ocean An ocean south of Asia, between Africa and Australia.

indicate **1.** To be a sign of; show. A high fever *indicates* that a person is sick. **2.** To point out. The guide *indicated* the best path for us to take.
in·di·cate (in′di kāt′) *verb,* **indicated, indicating.**

indication Something that indicates; a sign. Her good grades this year are an *indication* that she will do well next year.
in·di·ca·tion (in′di kā′shən) *noun, plural* **indications.**

indict To accuse and charge a person with committing a crime. A person must be indicted before he is given a trial. The man was *indicted* on charges of robbery, but he was found not guilty at his trial.
in·dict (in dīt′) *verb,* **indicted, indicting.**

indifference Lack of interest, concern, or care. His *indifference* to the feelings of other people made him very unpopular.
in·dif·fer·ence (in dif′ər əns *or* in dif′rəns) *noun.*

indifferent Having or showing a lack of interest, concern, or care. The football game was so exciting that the fans were *indifferent* to the rain that was pouring down.
in·dif·fer·ent (in dif′ər ənt *or* in dif′rənt) *adjective.*

indigestion Difficulty or discomfort in digesting foods. Food that is very spicy often causes *indigestion.*
in·di·ges·tion (in′di jes′chən *or* in′dī jes′chən) *noun.*

indignant Filled with anger about something unfair, cruel, or bad. The salesman became *indignant* when the customer accused him of cheating her.
in·dig·nant (in dig′nənt) *adjective.*

indigo **1.** A very dark blue dye. It can be obtained from various plants, but is now usually made by man. **2.** A plant from which this dye is obtained. **3.** A deep violet-blue color. *Noun.*
—Having the color indigo; violet-blue. *Adjective.*
in·di·go (in′di gō′) *noun, plural* **indigos** *or* **indigoes;** *adjective.*

Indigo

indirect **1.** Not in a straight line; roundabout. We took the *indirect* route through small towns in order to avoid the traffic on the main highway. **2.** Not straight to the point. Dad gave me an *indirect* answer when I asked if we could go to the circus.

at; āpe; cär; end; mē; it; īce; hot; ōld;
fôrk; wood; fŏŏl; oil; out; up; turn; sing;
thin; this; hw in white; zh in treasure.
ə stands for a in about, e in taken
i in pencil, o in lemon, and u in circus.

3. Not directly connected. An *indirect* result of my going to the new shopping center was meeting an old friend.
in·di·rect (in′də rekt′ *or* in′dī rekt′) *adjective.*

individual **1.** Single; separate. Each *individual* house has a back yard. **2.** Characteristic of a particular person or thing. She has an *individual* way of laughing. *Adjective.* —A single person or thing. He is a strange *individual. Noun.*
in·di·vid·u·al (in′də vij′ōō əl) *adjective; noun, plural* **individuals.**

individuality A quality that makes one person or thing different from others. He expresses his *individuality* in the way he dresses.
in·di·vid·u·al·i·ty (in′də vij′ōō al′ə tē) *noun, plural* **individualities.**

individually One at a time. My father taught each of us *individually* how to swim.
in·di·vid·u·al·ly (in′də vij′ōō ə lē) *adverb.*

indivisible Not able to be divided without leaving a remainder. 5 is *indivisible* by 2 because the answer has a remainder of 1.
in·di·vis·i·ble (in′də viz′ə bəl) *adjective.*

indoor Used or done within a house or building. The school had an *indoor* swimming pool.
in·door (in′dôr′) *adjective.*

indoors In or into a house or building. We went *indoors* when it began to rain.
in·doors (in′dôrz′) *adverb.*

indulge **1.** To allow oneself to have, do, or enjoy something. I *indulged* in some ice cream when I finished dieting. **2.** To give into the wishes of. Joey's grandparents *indulge* him by giving him anything he asks for.
in·dulge (in dulj′) *verb,* **indulged, indulging.**

industrial **1.** Having to do with or produced by industry. *Industrial* waste material flowed into the river and polluted it. **2.** Having highly-developed industry. The United States is an *industrial* country.
in·dus·tri·al (in dus′trē əl) *adjective.*

industrialize To set up or develop industry in an area or country. The governor wanted to *industrialize* the state to provide more jobs.
in·dus·tri·al·ize (in dus′trē ə līz′) *verb,* **industrialized, industrializing.**

industrious Working hard. The *industrious* student finished the report a week before it was due.
in·dus·tri·ous (in dus′trē əs) *adjective.*

industry **1.** Manufacturing plants and other businesses. The people want to bring *industry* to their town so that there will be more jobs. **2.** A branch of business, trade, or manufacturing. Some areas of the country depend on the tourist *industry* to bring in money. **3.** Hard work; steady effort. He shows much *industry* in preparing his homework.
in·dus·try (in′dəs trē) *noun, plural* **industries.**

inedible Not fit as food; not suitable for eating. Some mushrooms are *inedible.* The burned meat was *inedible.*
in·ed·i·ble (in ed′ə bəl) *adjective.*

inequality The condition of not being equal. There should not be an *inequality* between the salaries of a woman and a man who both do the same work.
in·e·qual·i·ty (in′i kwol′ə tē) *noun, plural* **inequalities.**

inert Not able to move or act; not moving. A mountain is *inert.*
in·ert (i nurt′) *adjective.*

inevitable Not able to be avoided; bound to happen. An *inevitable* result of closing your eyes is not being able to see.
in·ev·i·ta·ble (i nev′ə tə bəl) *adjective.*

infant A child during the earliest period of life; baby.
in·fant (in′fənt) *noun, plural* **infants.**

infantile paralysis A disease that can cause paralysis. It occurs mainly in children. It is also called **poliomyelitis.**
in·fan·tile pa·ral·y·sis (in′fən tīl′ pə ral′ə sis).

infantry Soldiers trained and equipped to fight on foot.
in·fan·try (in′fən trē) *noun, plural* **infantries.**

▲ The word **infantry** comes from the Italian word for "child." At first an infantry was made up of young boys who were the servants of knights. We use the same word for foot soldiers because when knights rode into battle on horseback, their young servants followed them on foot.

---

infect To cause disease in by allowing germs to enter. A dirty bandage can *infect* a cut.
in·fect (in fekt′) *verb,* **infected, infecting.**

infection A disease that is caused by germs entering the body. He got an *infection* in his foot after stepping on an old rusty nail.
in·fec·tion (in fek′shən) *noun, plural* **infections.**

infectious Spread by infection. Mumps is an *infectious* disease.
in·fec·tious (in fek′shəs) *adjective.*

inferior **1.** Of poor quality; below average. The food at that restaurant is *inferior.* **2.** Low or lower in quality, importance, or value. She always felt that her schoolwork was *inferior* to her sister's. The rank of sergeant is *inferior* to the rank of lieutenant.
in·fe·ri·or (in fēr′ē ər) *adjective.*

infield **1.** The area of a baseball field marked off by the paths connecting the bases. **2.** In baseball, the first, second, and third basemen and the shortstop.
in·field (in′fēld′) *noun, plural* **infields.**

infinite **1.** Without limits or an end. Outer space seems to be *infinite.* **2.** Very great. She takes *infinite* care to do good work.
in·fi·nite (in′fə nit) *adjective.*

infinitive A simple verb form. An infinitive is often preceded by "to." In the sentence "He likes to swim," "to swim" is an infinitive.
in·fin·i·tive (in fin′ə tiv) *noun, plural* **infinitives.**

inflame **1.** To excite greatly; stir up. The plan to turn the park into a parking lot *inflamed* the whole town. **2.** To make hot, red, or swollen. The infection in the cut *inflamed* his finger.
in·flame (in flām′) *verb,* **inflamed, inflaming.**

inflammable Easily set on fire. Gasoline is an *inflammable* liquid.
in·flam·ma·ble (in flam′ə bəl) *adjective.*

inflammation A condition of a part of the body in which there is heat, redness, swelling, and pain.
in·flam·ma·tion (in′flə mā′shən) *noun, plural* **inflammations.**

inflate **1.** To cause to swell by filling with air or gas. She used a pump to *inflate* the bicycle tire. The boy *inflated* the beach ball by blowing into it. **2.** To increase. Food prices have *inflated.*
in·flate (in flāt′) *verb,* **inflated, inflating.**

inflation **1.** The act of inflating. The *inflation* of the balloons for the party took all morning. **2.** An increase or rise in the usual or normal prices of goods and services.
in·fla·tion (in flā′shən) *noun, plural* **inflations.**

Inflate

influence **1.** The power of a person or thing to produce an effect on others. Use your *influence* to persuade your brother to study harder. **2.** A person or thing that has the power to produce an effect on others. Her friends were a good *influence* on her. *Noun.* —To change or have an effect on. The lawyer tried to *influence* the jury to say that the prisoner was innocent. *Verb.*
in·flu·ence (in′floo əns) *noun, plural* **influences;** *verb,* **influenced, influencing.**

influential Having or using influence. He is a very *influential* man in town.
in·flu·en·tial (in′floo en′shəl) *adjective.*

influenza A disease that causes fever, coughing, and muscle pains. Influenza can be spread easily from one person to another. This disease is also called **flu.**
in·flu·en·za (in′floo en′zə) *noun.*

inform **1.** To give information to; tell. Please *inform* us of the date you will arrive. **2.** To tell secret or harmful things about. The leader of the gang *informed* on his friends when he was caught.
in·form (in fôrm′) *verb,* **informed, informing.**

informal Without ceremony; not formal; casual. She gave a very *informal* party where everyone wore old clothes.
in·for·mal (in fôr′məl) *adjective.*

information **1.** Knowledge or facts about something. He asked for *information* about the bus schedule. You can get the *information* for your report from the encyclopedia. **2.** A service that answers questions and gives facts. She called *information* for the telephone number of the school.
in·for·ma·tion (in′fər mā′shən) *noun.*

infuriate To make very angry; make furious. My brother's constant teasing *infuriates* me.
in·fu·ri·ate (in fyoor′ē āt′) *verb,* **infuriated, infuriating.**

-ing A *suffix* that forms the present participle of verbs. The word *talking* is the present participle of *talk.*

ingenuity The quality of being clever and imaginative. She showed great *ingenuity* in making bookcases out of orange crates.
in·ge·nu·i·ty (in′jə noo′ə tē) *noun.*

at; āpe; cär; end; mē; it; īce; hot; ōld;
fôrk; wood; fool; oil; out; up; turn; sing;
thin; this; hw in white; zh in treasure.
ə stands for a in about, e in taken
i in pencil, o in lemon, and u in circus.

ingredient Any one of the parts that go into a mixture. Flour, eggs, sugar, and butter are the main *ingredients* of this cake.
in·gre·di·ent (in grē′dē ənt) *noun, plural* ingredients.

inhabit To live in or on. Many birds *inhabit* the woods. Man *inhabits* the earth.
in·hab·it (in hab′it) *verb,* inhabited, inhabiting.

inhabitant A person or animal that lives in a place. Most of the *inhabitants* of the town work at the nearby factory.
in·hab·it·ant (in hab′ət ənt) *noun, plural* inhabitants.

inhale To take into the lungs; breathe in. She *inhaled* the fresh, clean mountain air.
in·hale (in hāl′) *verb,* inhaled, inhaling.

inherent Forming a basic quality of a person or thing. Her *inherent* honesty kept her from keeping the money she found.
in·her·ent (in hēr′ənt *or* in her′ənt) *adjective.*

inherit 1. To get the property or money of a person who has died. Betty *inherited* the watch from her aunt. 2. To get from one's parent or parents. The little boy *inherited* his mother's black hair.
in·her·it (in her′it) *verb,* inherited, inheriting.

inheritance Something that is inherited. She received an *inheritance* of one thousand dollars from her grandfather.
in·her·it·ance (in her′it əns) *noun, plural* inheritances.

inhuman Without kindness, pity, or mercy; cruel; brutal. Beating the tired old horse was *inhuman.*
in·hu·man (in hyoō′mən) *adjective.*

initial Coming at the beginning; first. The *initial* letter of the word "ring" is "r." His *initial* response to the question was "no." *Adjective.*
—The first letter of a word or a name. "W.S." are the *initials* of William Shakespeare. *Noun.*
—To mark or sign with one's initial or initials. The teacher *initialed* the report after reading it. *Verb.*
i·ni·tial (i nish′əl) *adjective; noun, plural* initials; *verb,* initialed, initialing.

initiate 1. To be the first to do; begin; start. The new librarian *initiated* the practice of lending books for a month. 2. To make a person a member of an organization or group. The new members of the club were *initiated* into the club by the president at a special ceremony.
i·ni·ti·ate (i nish′ē āt′) *verb,* initiated, initiating.

initiative 1. The first step in doing or beginning something. Jean took the *initiative* at the party by introducing herself to the people she didn't know. 2. The ability or willingness to take a first step in doing or learning something. The lazy boy did not have much *initiative.*
i·ni·tia·tive (i nish′ə tiv) *noun.*

injection The forcing of a liquid through the skin into a muscle, vein, or the like. The doctor gave the boy an *injection* with a needle.
in·jec·tion (in jek′shən) *noun, plural* injections.

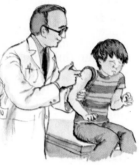
Injection

injure To cause harm to; damage or hurt. He *injured* himself when he fell off his bicycle. Failing the test *injured* her pride.
in·jure (in′jər) *verb,* injured, injuring.

injury Harm or damage done to a person or thing. The accident caused an *injury* to his leg.
in·ju·ry (in′jər ē) *noun, plural* injuries.

injustice 1. The lack of justice; unfairness. The lawyer protested against the *injustice* of the jury's decision. 2. Something unjust. He did his friend an *injustice* by calling him a liar when he really didn't know for sure whether he had lied or not.
in·jus·tice (in jus′tis) *noun, plural* injustices.

ink A colored liquid used for writing, drawing, or printing.
ink (ingk) *noun, plural* inks.

inkwell A container for ink. She had an *inkwell* on her desk.
ink·well (ingk′wel′) *noun, plural* inkwells.

inland Away from the coast or border. Kansas is an *inland* state. *Adjective.*
—In or toward the inner part of a country or region. He drove *inland* from the coast for many miles. *Adverb.*
in·land (in′lənd) *adjective; adverb.*

Inkwell

inlet A narrow body of water between islands, or leading into land from a larger body of water.

in·let (in′let′) *noun, plural* **inlets.**

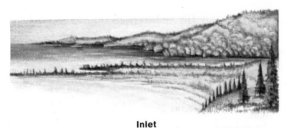

Inlet

inn A small hotel. An inn is usually in the country. ▲ Another word that sounds like this is **in.**

inn (in) *noun, plural* **inns.**

inner **1.** Farther in. The principal's office is in the *inner* room. **2.** More private; personal. Sally hid her *inner* feelings of disappointment at having lost the contest.

in·ner (in′ər) *adjective.*

inner ear The part of the ear that is behind the middle ear. It is the innermost part of the ear and contains organs that receive sound.

inning One of the parts into which a baseball game is divided. Both teams bat during an inning until three men on each team are put out.

in·ning (in′ing) *noun, plural* **innings.**

innkeeper A person who owns or manages an inn.

inn·keep·er (in′kē′pər) *noun, plural* **innkeepers.**

innocence The state or quality of being innocent. The *innocence* of the prisoner was proven during his trial.

in·no·cence (in′ə səns) *noun.*

innocent **1.** Free from guilt or wrong. The prisoner claimed that he was *innocent.* **2.** Not doing harm; harmless. The children hid from their mother as an *innocent* joke.

in·no·cent (in′ə sənt) *adjective.*

innovation Something new; change. The development of the X ray was a great *innovation* in medicine.

in·no·va·tion (in′ə vā′shən) *noun, plural* **innovations.**

innumerable Too many to be counted. There are *innumerable* stars in the sky.

in·nu·mer·a·ble (i nōō′mər ə bəl *or* i nyōō′-mər ə bəl) *adjective.*

inoculate To give a healthy person or animal a substance that contains germs that cause disease. This produces the disease in a mild form and prevents a more serious attack. A person can be inoculated against smallpox or typhoid fever.

in·oc·u·late (in ok′yə lāt′) *verb,* **inoculated, inoculating.**

inquire To try to get information or knowledge about by asking questions. She stopped at a gas station to *inquire* the way to get to the state park.

in·quire (in kwīr′) *verb,* **inquired, inquiring.**

inquiry **1.** A looking for information or knowledge. The fire department is making an *inquiry* into the cause of the fire. **2.** A question. There were many *inquiries* about the ad for the summer job.

in·quir·y (in kwīr′ē *or* in′kwər ē) *noun, plural* **inquiries.**

inquisitive Eager to know; curious. He is an *inquisitive* student who always asks questions.

in·quis·i·tive (in kwiz′ə tiv) *adjective.*

insane **1.** Not having a healthy mind; not sane; crazy. **2.** Of or for insane people. The state runs that *insane* asylum. **3.** Very foolish. It was *insane* to think that he could lift the car off the ground.

in·sane (in sān′) *adjective.*

inscribe To write, carve, engrave, or mark words or letters on something. The locket was *inscribed* with her initials.

in·scribe (in skrīb′) *verb,* **inscribed, inscribing.**

insect **1.** Any of a group of small animals without a backbone. The body of an insect is divided into three parts. Insects have three pairs of legs and usually two pairs of wings. Flies, ants, grasshoppers, and beetles are insects. **2.** Any animal that is similar to an insect. Ticks and spiders are sometimes called insects.

in·sect (in′sekt) *noun, plural* **insects.**

▲ The word **insect** comes from a Latin word that means "cut into." In Latin, an insect was called "an animal that has been cut into" because an insect's body is divided into three different sections.

insecticide A chemical for killing insects and other pests.

at; āpe; cär; end; mē; it; īce; hot; ōld;
fôrk; wood; fōol; oil; out; up; turn; sing;
thin; this; hw in white; zh in treasure.
ə stands for a in about, e in taken
i in pencil, o in lemon, and u in circus.

in·sec·ti·cide (in sek′tə sīd′) *noun, plural* **insecticides.**

insert To put, set, or place in. She *inserted* a piece of paper in the book to mark her place. Please *insert* the cork in the bottle. *Verb.*
—Something inserted. The Sunday edition of the newspaper has a four-page color *insert* on vacations. *Noun.*
in·sert (in surt′ *for verb;* in′surt *for noun*) *verb,* **inserted, inserting;** *noun, plural* **inserts.**

inside The inner side or part; interior. The *inside* of the car is blue. *Noun.*
—**1.** On or in the inside. I took an *inside* seat on the train. **2.** Known to only a few; not public. The reporter got the *inside* story on the robbery. *Adjective.*
—**1.** On, in, or toward the inside; within. She opened the door of the house and stepped *inside.* **2.** Indoors. The children played *inside* because of the rain. *Adverb.*
—In or into the inside of. I looked *inside* the closet for my coat. *Preposition.*
in·side (in′sīd′ *or* in′sīd′ *for noun and adjective;* in′sīd′ *for adverb and preposition*) *noun, plural* **insides;** *adjective; adverb; preposition.*

insignia A badge, medal, or other mark showing an honor or position. The policeman wore the *insignia* of a captain.
in·sig·ni·a (in sig′nē ə) *noun, plural* **insignias.**

Insignia

insignificant Having little or no importance or meaning. The evidence against the suspected thief was *insignificant.* She spent an *insignificant* amount of money on the decorations for the party.
in·sig·nif·i·cant (in′sig nif′i·kənt) *adjective.*

insincere Not sincere; dishonest. It is *insincere* to say that you like a person when you really don't.
in·sin·cere (in′sin sēr′) *adjective.*

insist To demand or say in a strong, firm manner. The doctor *insisted* that the sick man get plenty of rest. She *insisted* that she was right.
in·sist (in sist′) *verb,* **insisted, insisting.**

inspect **1.** To look at closely and carefully. The repairman *inspected* the tubes of the television set. **2.** To look at formally or officially. The general *inspected* the troops.
in·spect (in spekt′) *verb,* **inspected, inspecting.**

inspection **1.** The act of inspecting. The mechanic's *inspection* of the car took an hour. **2.** A formal or official examination. The soldiers' tents passed the sergeant's *inspection.*
in·spec·tion (in spek′shən) *noun, plural* **inspections.**

inspiration **1.** A person or thing that stirs the mind, feelings, or imagination. The writer's family was the *inspiration* for all his characters. **2.** A sudden, bright idea. Her plan for a surprise birthday party was an *inspiration.*
in·spi·ra·tion (in′spə rā′shən) *noun, plural* **inspirations.**

inspire **1.** To stir the mind, feelings, or imagination of. The senator's speech *inspired* the audience. **2.** To cause a person to have a particular thought or feeling. His success in school *inspired* him with hope for the future.
in·spire (in spīr′) *verb,* **inspired, inspiring.**

install **1.** To put in place for use or service. We had a new air conditioner *installed* today. **2.** To place a person in an office with a ceremony. The new club president will be *installed* at the next meeting.
in·stall (in stôl′) *verb,* **installed, installing.**

installment **1.** One of the parts of a sum of money that is owed and is to be paid at particular times. Father paid for our new car in thirty monthly *installments.* **2.** Any of several parts of a story that are issued or shown at particular times. The book was published in a magazine in weekly *installments.*
in·stall·ment (in stôl′mənt) *noun, plural* **installments.**

instance An example; case. The fireman's rescue of the man from the burning building was an *instance* of great courage.
in·stance (in′stəns) *noun, plural* **instances.**
for instance. For example. He enjoys team sports, *for instance,* baseball, football, and basketball.

instant **1.** A very short period of time; moment. We saw him for just an *instant* before he got on the plane. **2.** A particular moment or point in time. I want to leave this *instant. Noun.*
—**1.** Without delay; immediate. She gave us an *instant* reply to our question. **2.** Very important or necessary; urgent. The town had an *instant* need for help during the flood. **3.** Needing only additional liquid to prepare. Most instant foods are packaged in powder form. I made some *instant* mashed potatoes for dinner. *Adjective.*
in·stant (in′stənt) *noun, plural* **instants;** *adjective.*

instantly At once; without delay. He came *instantly* to the rescue of the kitten that was trapped in the tree.
in·stant·ly (in′stənt lē) *adverb.*

instead In place of another person or thing. We asked her brother to come to the movies, but she came *instead.*
in·stead (in sted′) *adverb.*
instead of. In place of; rather than. We went for a walk *instead of* going straight home after school.

instep The arched upper part of the human foot between the toes and the ankle.
in·step (in′step′) *noun, plural* **insteps.**

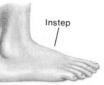

Instep

instinct A way of acting or behaving that a person or animal is born with and does not have to learn. Birds build nests by *instinct.*
in·stinct (in′stingkt) *noun, plural* **instincts.**

institute A school or other organization that is set up for a special purpose. She is studying piano at the music *institute.* Both her parents are doctors at the *institute* for cancer research.
in·sti·tute (in′stə tōōt′ *or* in′stə tyōōt′) *noun, plural* **institutes.**

institution **1.** An organization that is set up for a special purpose. A school is an *institution* of learning. **2.** A custom or law that has been followed for a long time. Having Thanksgiving dinner at my grandmother's house is an *institution* in our family.
in·sti·tu·tion (in′stə tōō′shən *or* in′stə tyōō′shən) *noun, plural* **institutions.**

instruct **1.** To show how to do or use; teach. My father *instructed* me in the correct use of the tool. **2.** To give directions or orders to. Mother *instructed* us to lock the door when we left.
in·struct (in strukt′) *verb,* **instructed, instructing.**

instruction **1.** The act of teaching. She learned how to skate through her brother's *instruction.* **2. instructions.** Directions, orders, or explanations. If you follow the *instructions,* you can put the model airplane together easily.
in·struc·tion (in struk′shən) *noun, plural* **instructions.**

instructor A person who instructs; teacher. My brother is a swimming *instructor* at the town pool.
in·struc·tor (in struk′tər) *noun, plural* **instructors.**

instrument **1.** A device used for doing a certain kind of work; tool. A drill is an *instrument* used by dentists. **2.** A device for producing musical sounds. She plays the guitar, flute, and several other *instruments.*
in·stru·ment (in′strə mənt) *noun, plural* **instruments.**

insulate To cover or surround with a material that slows or stops the flow of electricity, heat, or sound. The electrician *insulated* the electric wire with rubber. Our house is *insulated* so that it keeps warm inside in winter.
in·su·late (in′sə lāt′) *verb,* **insulated, insulating.**

insult To speak to or treat in a way that hurts or angers. He *insulted* his friend when he accused him of stealing. *Verb.*
—A remark or action that hurts or angers. Calling him a liar was a great *insult. Noun.*
in·sult (in sult′ *for verb;* in′sult *for noun*) *verb,* **insulted, insulting;** *noun, plural* **insults.**

insurance Protection against loss or damage. A person who wants insurance agrees to pay a small amount of money at regular times to a company. In exchange, the company promises to pay a certain amount in case of death, accident, fire, or theft. Mr. Baxter has $50,000 fire *insurance* on his house.
in·sur·ance (in shoor′əns) *noun.*

insure To protect by insurance. Dad's car is *insured* against accident or theft.
in·sure (in shoor′) *verb,* **insured, insuring.**

intake **1.** The amount of something taken in. The doctor told him to increase his *intake* of liquids while he had a cold. **2.** A place in a channel or pipe where a liquid or gas is taken in.
in·take (in′tāk′) *noun, plural* **intakes.**

integrate **1.** To make open to people of all races. The town *integrated* all its schools. **2.** To bring parts together into a whole. The reporter tried to *integrate* all the different accounts of the accident into his story.
in·te·grate (in′tə grāt′) *verb,* **integrated, integrating.**

integration The act of making something open to people of all races. In 1954 the Supreme Court ruled that there should

at; āpe; cär; end; mē; it; īce; hot; ōld;
fôrk; wood; fōol; oil; out; up; turn; sing;
thin; this; hw in white; zh in treasure.
ə stands for a in about, e in taken
i in pencil, o in lemon, and u in circus.

be *integration* in the public schools of this country.

in·te·gra·tion (in′tə grā′shən) *noun.*

integrity Complete honesty and sincerity. A person who lies has no *integrity.*

in·teg·ri·ty (in teg′rə tē) *noun.*

intellect The power of the mind to know, understand, and reason; intelligence. That scientist was a woman of great *intellect.*

in·tel·lect (int′əl ekt′) *noun, plural* **intellects.**

intellectual 1. Having to do with the intellect. He showed great *intellectual* ability in solving the mathematical problem. 2. Having intelligence. Albert Einstein was an *intellectual* person. *Adjective.*
—A person who has great intelligence. The person who wrote that book was one of the great *intellectuals* of his time. *Noun.*

in·tel·lec·tu·al (int′əl ek′chōō əl) *adjective; noun, plural* **intellectuals.**

intelligence 1. The ability to know, understand, and reason. She is a woman of great *intelligence.* 2. Secret information. The army's *intelligence* showed that the enemy was going to attack at dawn.

in·tel·li·gence (in tel′ə jəns) *noun.*

intelligent Having or showing intelligence; bright. That was an *intelligent* question to ask.

in·tel·li·gent (in tel′ə jənt) *adjective.*

intend 1. To have in mind as a purpose; plan. He *intends* to leave for summer camp next week. Do you *intend* to come to the party? 2. To mean for a particular person or purpose. That present is *intended* for you.

in·tend (in tend′) *verb,* **intended, intending.**

intense 1. Very great or strong. The heat from the iron was so *intense* that it burned a hole in the cloth. 2. Having or showing strong or true feeling. The worried woman had an *intense* look on her face as she waited for news of her sick child.

in·tense (in tens′) *adjective.*

intensity 1. The state or quality of being intense. The light from the searchlight shone with great *intensity.* 2. The amount of force or feeling. The pain from the broken bone increased in *intensity.* 3. The amount of strength of heat, light, or other energy per unit of area, volume, or mass.

in·ten·si·ty (in ten′sə tē) *noun, plural* **intensities.**

intent¹ 1. Something that is intended; purpose; aim. Her *intent* has always been to go to college. 2. Meaning; significance. What was the *intent* of what he said?

in·tent (in tent′) *noun, plural* **intents.**

intent² Having the mind firmly fixed on something. Is he *intent* on leaving now? She was *intent* on the book she was reading.

in·tent (in tent′) *adjective.*

intention Something that is intended; purpose; plan. I have no *intention* of going to her party.

in·ten·tion (in ten′shən) *noun, plural* **intentions.**

intentional Done on purpose; planned; meant. His bumping into me was *intentional.*

in·ten·tion·al (in ten′shən əl) *adjective.*

intercept To stop or take something on its way from one person or place to another. Johnny *intercepted* the ball as it was being passed from Joe to Fred. The teacher *intercepted* the note that June tried to give me.

in·ter·cept (in′tər sept′) *verb,* **intercepted, intercepting.**

intercom A radio or telephone system between different parts of a building, airplane, or ship.

in·ter·com (in′tər kom′) *noun, plural* **intercoms.**

interest 1. A desire or eagerness to know about or take part in something. He has a great *interest* in football. 2. Something that causes such a desire. Collecting records is Joan's main *interest* now. 3. The power to cause such a desire. That book about horses had little *interest* for him. 4. Advantage; benefit. A selfish person cares only about his own *interests.* 5. Money that is paid for the use of a larger sum of money. When a person borrows money from a bank, he must pay a certain amount of interest on the loan. 6. A right or share. He has an *interest* in his brother's business. *Noun.*
—1. To cause to want to know about or take part in. Mother *interested* me in gardening by giving me my own plants to take care of. 2. To hold the attention of. His story about his trip to Europe *interested* me. *Verb.*

in·ter·est (in′tər ist *or* in′trist) *noun, plural* **interests;** *verb,* **interested, interesting.**

interesting Causing or holding interest or attention. That was an *interesting* movie.

in·ter·est·ing (in′tə res′ting *or* in′tris ting) *adjective.*

interfere 1. To take part in the affairs of others without having been asked; meddle. Our nosy neighbor is always *interfering* by giving advice on everything. 2. To disturb or interrupt. That loud music *interferes* with my studying.

in·ter·fere (in′tər fēr′) *verb,* **interfered, interfering.**

interior 1. The inner side, surface, or part. The *interior* of the cave was dark. 2. The part of a country or region that is away from the coast or border. The *interior* of that country is mostly jungle. *Noun.*
—1. Having to do with or on the inside. The *interior* offices of the building are empty. 2. Away from the coast or border. Colorado is an *interior* state of the United States. *Adjective.*
in·te·ri·or (in tēr′ē ər) *noun, plural* **interiors;** *adjective.*

interjection A word or phrase that shows strong feeling. An interjection can be used alone. "Oh!," "Hey!," and "Ouch!" are interjections.
in·ter·jec·tion (in′ter jek′shən) *noun, plural* **interjections.**

intermediate In the middle; being between. Jack is in the *intermediate* class of swimmers at school.
in·ter·me·di·ate (in′tər mē′dē it) *adjective.*

intermission A time of rest or stopping between periods of activity. There was an *intermission* of ten minutes between the first and second acts of the play.
in·ter·mis·sion (in′tər mish′ən) *noun, plural* **intermissions.**

intern A doctor who has just graduated from medical school and is working in a hospital under more experienced doctors.
in·tern (in′turn′) *noun, plural* **interns.**

internal 1. Having to do with or on the inside; interior. The stomach and kidneys are *internal* organs of the body. 2. Having to do with matters within a country; domestic. The Congress passes laws having to do with the *internal* affairs of the United States.
in·ter·nal (in turn′əl) *adjective.*

international Having to do with or made up of two or more countries. The United Nations is an *international* organization. Boy scouts from all over the world attended the *international* gathering.
in·ter·na·tion·al (in′tər nash′ən əl) *adjective.*

interpret 1. To make clear or easy to understand. The teacher *interpreted* what the author meant in his poem. 2. To change from one language to another; translate. He *interpreted* in English what his cousin from Spain was saying. 3. To take as meaning; understand. I *interpreted* his nod as meaning "yes." 4. To perform so as to bring out the meaning. The pianist *interpreted* the musical piece with great feeling.
in·ter·pret (in tur′prit) *verb,* **interpreted, interpreting.**

interrogative Having the form of a question. "Who is it?" is an *interrogative* sentence. *Adjective.*
—A word or form used in asking a question. In the sentence "Who is it?," the word "who" is an *interrogative. Noun.*
in·ter·rog·a·tive (in′tə rog′ə tiv) *adjective; noun, plural* **interrogatives.**

interrupt 1. To break in upon or stop a person who is acting or speaking. Please do not *interrupt* me when i'm talking. 2. To stop or break off. She *interrupted* her work to answer the telephone. 3. To make a break in; stop. A special announcement *interrupted* the television show.
in·ter·rupt (in′tə rupt′) *verb,* **interrupted, interrupting.**

interruption 1. The state of being interrupted. There was an *interruption* in the radio program for a special report. 2. Something that interrupts. My little brother's questions were a constant *interruption.*
in·ter·rup·tion (in′tə rup′shən) *noun, plural* **interruptions.**

intersect 1. To divide by passing through or cutting across. The river *intersects* the valley. 2. To meet and cross each other. The two roads *intersect* in about a mile.
in·ter·sect (in′tər sekt′) *verb,* **intersected, intersecting.**

intersection The place where two or more things meet and cross each other. There was a traffic light at the *intersection* of the roads.
in·ter·sec·tion (in′tər sek′shən *or* in′tər-sek′shən) *noun, plural* **intersections.**

Intersection

at; āpe; cär; end; mē; it; īce; hot; ōld;
fôrk; wood; fōōl; oil; out; up; turn; sing;
thin; this; hw in white; zh in treasure.
ə stands for a in about, e in taken
i in pencil, o in lemon, and u in circus.

335

interval Time or space between. An *interval* of a year has passed since we saw her.
    in·ter·val (in′tər vəl) *noun, plural* **intervals.**

interview A meeting for a special purpose. The reporter arranged for an *interview* with the famous actress for the local newspaper. He is going to an *interview* for a summer job with that company. *Noun.*
    —To have an interview with. The author was *interviewed* about his newest book. *Verb.*
    in·ter·view (in′tər vyo͞o′) *noun, plural* **interviews;** *verb,* **interviewed, interviewing.**

intestine A long tube that extends down from the stomach. The intestine is part of the alimentary canal and is important in the digestion of food. It is divided into the large intestine and the small intestine.
    in·tes·tine (in tes′tin) *noun, plural* **intestines.**

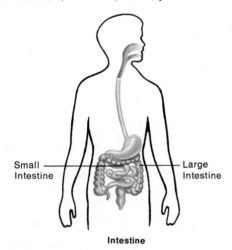

Small Intestine

Large Intestine

Intestine

intimate 1. Close and familiar; well-acquainted. They have been *intimate* friends for years. 2. Very personal; private. She kept a diary of her *intimate* thoughts.
    in·ti·mate (in′tə mit) *adjective.*

into She walked *into* the house. She put her suitcase *into* the closet. He bit *into* the apple. He bumped *into* the door. The water turned *into* ice. The dish broke *into* pieces.
    in·to (in′too *or* in′tə) *preposition.*

intolerant Not willing to allow people to think and act in a way that is different from one's own; not tolerant. He was very *intolerant* of people who disagreed with him.
    in·tol·er·ant (in tol′ər ənt) *adjective.*

intoxicate To make drunk. Too much liquor *intoxicated* him.
    in·tox·i·cate (in tok′sə kāt′) *verb,* **intoxicated, intoxicating.**

intricate Very hard to understand, explain, or do; complicated. He could not solve the *intricate* puzzle. The instructions for making the model boat were too *intricate* to follow.
    in·tri·cate (in′tri kit) *adjective.*

intrigue To make curious or interested; fascinate. The story of the sailor's adventures *intrigued* the boys.
    in·trigue (in trēg′) *verb,* **intrigued, intriguing.**

introduce 1. To make known or acquainted. Jane *introduced* us to her cousins. 2. To bring into use, knowledge, or notice. The singer *introduced* a new song that he had written. The farmer *introduced* a new breed of cattle to his area. 3. To begin; start. She *introduced* her speech with a funny joke.
    in·tro·duce (in′trə do͞os′ *or* in′trə dyo͞os′) *verb,* **introduced, introducing.**

introduction 1. The act of introducing or the state of being introduced. We shook hands after our *introduction.* 2. Something that introduces. The book has a short *introduction* written by the author.
    in·tro·duc·tion (in′trə duk′shən) *noun, plural* **introductions.**

invade 1. To go in and attack in order to conquer. Enemy troops *invaded* the country. 2. To interfere with. She *invaded* my privacy when she read my mail without asking.
    in·vade (in vād′) *verb,* **invaded, invading.**

invalid A person who is not able to take care of himself because of a sickness or injury. A broken leg made Kate an *invalid* for a while.
    in·va·lid (in′və lid) *noun, plural* **invalids.**

invent 1. To make or think of for the first time; create. Samuel Morse *invented* the telegraph. 2. To make up. Tom always *invents* excuses for being late.
    in·vent (in vent′) *verb,* **invented, inventing.**

▲ The first meaning of **invent** was "to find." For example, someone might have said, "The girl would not go home until she had *invented* her lost watch." The idea of finding something led to our use of *invent* to mean "to think of or make for the first time."

invention 1. The act of inventing. The *invention* of the airplane had a great effect on travel. 2. Something that is invented. The phonograph was one of Thomas Edison's most important *inventions.* 3. A false or untrue story. His story about seeing a monster is nothing but *invention.*
    in·ven·tion (in ven′chən) *noun, plural* **inventions.**

inventor A person who invents. Alfred Nobel was the *inventor* of dynamite.
    in·ven·tor (in ven′tər) *noun, plural* **inventors.**

inventory 1. A detailed list of articles on hand. The *inventory* showed exactly what goods the clothing store had and the price of each item. 2. The articles that are on such a list. The store has a large *inventory* of sports equipment.
in·ven·to·ry (in′vən tôr′ē) *noun, plural* in·ventories.

invert 1. To turn upside down. He *inverted* the box of coins and they all fell on the table. 2. To change the order or position of. If you *invert* the letters of the word "star," you have the word "rats."
in·vert (in vurt′) *verb,* inverted, inverting.

invertebrate Having to do with an animal that does not have a backbone. *Adjective.*
—An animal that does not have a backbone; invertebrate animal. Sponges, worms, lobsters, and insects are invertebrates. *Noun.*
in·ver·te·brate (in vur′tə brit *or* in vur′tə-brāt′) *adjective; noun, plural* invertebrates.

invest 1. To use money to buy something that will make more money. Dad *invested* his savings in the stock market. 2. To give or spend time or effort. She *invested* many hours in planning the class trip.
in·vest (in vest′) *verb,* invested, investing.

investigate To look into carefully in order to find facts and get information. The police *investigated* the robbery.
in·ves·ti·gate (in ves′tə gāt′) *verb,* investigated, investigating.

investigation The act of investigating. The police continued their *investigation* of the jewel theft.
in·ves·ti·ga·tion (in ves′tə gā′shən) *noun, plural* investigations.

investment 1. The act of investing money, time, or effort. He made a lot of money on his *investment* in real estate. 2. The amount of money that is invested. She has a thousand dollar *investment* in her friend's business. 3. Something in which money is invested. Buying that house was a good *investment.*
in·vest·ment (in vest′mənt) *noun, plural* investments.

invisible Not able to be seen; not visible. The children believed that an *invisible* ghost lived in the old house.
in·vis·i·ble (in viz′ə bəl) *adjective.*

invitation A written or spoken request to do something. We accepted her *invitation* to dinner. Have you received a wedding *invitation* from Susan's sister?
in·vi·ta·tion (in′və tā′shən) *noun, plural* invitations.

invite 1. To ask someone to go somewhere or to do something. Paul *invited* his friends to the movies. They *invited* us to have dinner with them. 2. To ask for; request. The teacher *invited* questions from the students on the library lesson. 3. To attract; tempt. On a hot summer's day the pool *invites* us to swim.
in·vite (in vīt′) *verb,* invited, inviting.

involuntary 1. Not done willingly or by choice; not voluntary. Mother let out an *involuntary* cry when she accidentally stuck herself with the pin. 2. Happening without a person's control. Breathing is an *involuntary* action.
in·vol·un·tar·y (in vol′ən ter′ē) *adjective.*

involve 1. To have as a necessary part; include. His job as a salesman *involves* a great deal of traveling. 2. To bring into difficulty. The man's remark *involved* him in an argument with the stranger. 3. To take up completely; absorb. He was *involved* all day in reading the book.
in·volve (in volv′) *verb,* involved, involving.

inward Toward the inside or center. The front gate opens *inward.* He opened the heavy door with an *inward* push.
in·ward (in′wərd) *adverb; adjective.*

iodine 1. A substance that is made up of shiny grayish crystals. Iodine is used in medicine and in photography. Iodine is a chemical element. 2. A brown medicine that contains iodine. It is put on cuts to protect against infection.
i·o·dine (ī′ə dīn′ *or* ī′ə dēn′) *noun.*

-ion A *suffix* that means: 1. "The act of." *Discussion* means "the act of discussing." 2. "The state of being." *Location* means "the state of being located."

Iowa A state in the north-central United States. Its capital is Des Moines.
I·o·wa (ī′ə wə) *noun.*

▲ **Iowa** comes from an Indian word that means "sleepy people." It was one Indian tribe's name for another tribe. Pioneers used the name for the biggest river in the area, and later it was chosen for the state's name.

Ireland A large island west of England. Ireland is one of the British Isles.
Ire·land (īr′lənd) *noun.*

at; āpe; cär; end; mē; it; īce; hot; ōld;
fôrk; wood; fōōl; oil; out; up; turn; sing;
thin; this; hw in white; zh in treasure.
ə stands for a in about, e in taken
i in pencil, o in lemon, and u in circus.

iris **1.** The round, colored part of the eye. The iris is between the cornea and the lens. It controls the amount of light that enters the eye. **2.** A plant that has long leaves shaped like a sword and purple, blue, or white flowers.
  i·ris (ī′ris) *noun, plural* **irises.**

Iris

Irish **1.** The people of Ireland or the people who are descended from them. **2.** The language of the people of Ireland.
  I·rish (ī′rish) *noun.*

Irish setter A dog that originally came from Ireland. It has a coat of silky, reddish hair.

iron **1.** A grayish-white metal. Iron is the most important of all metals and is used in making steel. Iron is a good conductor of heat and electricity. It is a chemical element. **2.** Something that is made from iron. The cowboy branded the cattle with a hot *iron.* **3.** An appliance with a flat surface that is heated and used to press or smooth clothes and materials. *Noun.*
  —**1.** Made of iron. The lion's cage has *iron* bars. **2.** Strong and hard. She has an *iron* will once she makes up her mind to do something. *Adjective.*
  —To press or smooth with a heated iron. John *ironed* his shirt. *Verb.*
  i·ron (ī′ərn) *noun, plural* **irons;** *adjective; verb,* **ironed, ironing.**

irony A way of speaking or writing in which what a person says is the opposite of what he really means or feels. To say "Oh, wonderful!" when you hear bad news is irony.
  i·ro·ny (ī′rə nē) *noun.*

irregular **1.** Not in the usual or normal way; unusual. His hours of work are very *irregular;* some days he works for ten hours and some for only two. **2.** Not smooth; uneven. The astronauts landed on the *irregular* surface of the moon.
  ir·reg·u·lar (i reg′yə lər) *adjective.*

irresistible That cannot be resisted or opposed. Mother's chocolate cake was *irresistible* to the children.
  ir·re·sist·i·ble (ir′i zis′tə bəl) *adjective.*

irrigate To supply land with water through streams, channels, or pipes. The farmer *irrigated* the dry land so that crops could be grown.
  ir·ri·gate (ir′ə gāt′) *verb,* **irrigated, irrigating.**

irrigation The act of supplying land with water. *Irrigation* made it possible for crops to grow in the desert.
  ir·ri·ga·tion (ir′ə gā′shən) *noun.*

Irrigation

irritate **1.** To make angry or impatient. Her brother's constant teasing *irritated* her. **2.** To make sore or sensitive. The smoke *irritated* my eyes.
  ir·ri·tate (ir′ə tāt′) *verb,* **irritated, irritating.**

is She *is* not home. He *is* four years old. Who *is* at the door? Today *is* Friday.
  is (iz) *verb.*

island **1.** A body of land that is completely surrounded by water. An island is smaller than a continent. Great Britain is an island. **2.** Something that looks like an island. There was an *island* of floating ice in the lake.
  is·land (ī′lənd) *noun, plural* **islands.**

Traffic Island

isle An island. Isles are usually small islands. ▲ Other words that sound like this are **aisle** and **I'll.**
  isle (īl) *noun, plural* **isles.**

islet A little island. ▲ Another word that sounds like this is **eyelet.**
  is·let (ī′lit) *noun, plural* **islets.**

isn't She *isn't* home yet.
  is·n't (iz′ənt) contraction for "is not."

isolate To place or set apart; separate from others. He was *isolated* from his sisters and brothers when he had the mumps so that they wouldn't get it.
i·so·late (ī′sə lāt′) *verb,* **isolated, isolating.**

Israel A country in southwestern Asia. Its capital is Jerusalem.
Is·ra·el (iz′rē əl) *noun.*

Israeli A person who was born or is living in Israel. *Noun.*
—Having to do with Israel. *Adjective.*
Is·rae·li (iz rā′lē) *noun, plural* **Israelis;** *adjective.*

issue 1. The act of sending or giving out. John was in charge of the *issue* of supplies for the camping trip. 2. Something that is sent or given out. Henry bought the morning *issue* of the newspaper. Do you have the latest *issue* of the magazine? 3. A subject that is being discussed or considered. The city council debated the *issue* of raising property taxes. *Noun.*
—To send or give out. The Department of the Treasury *issues* money. The teacher *issued* books to all the students. *Verb.*
is·sue (ish′o͞o) *noun, plural* **issues;** *verb,* **issued, issuing.**

isthmus A narrow strip of land that connects two larger pieces of land. An isthmus has water on two sides. North America and South America are connected by the Isthmus of Panama.
isth·mus (is′məs) *noun, plural* **isthmuses.**

it He threw the ball to me and I caught *it*. *It* snowed last night. Give *it* to me.
it (it) *pronoun.*

Italian 1. A person who was born or is living in Italy. 2. The language of Italy. *Noun.*
—Of or having to do with Italy, its people, or their language. *Adjective.*
I·tal·ian (i tal′yən) *noun, plural* **Italians;** *adjective.*

italic Of or having to do with a style of type whose letters slant to the right. *This sentence is printed in italic type. Adjective.*
—**italics.** Italic type. He printed the sentence in *italics. Noun.*
i·tal·ic (i tal′ik) *adjective; noun, plural* **italics.**

Italy A country in southern Europe. Its capital is Rome.
It·a·ly (it′əl ē) *noun.*

itch 1. A tickling or stinging feeling in the skin. An itch is relieved by scratching or rubbing. 2. A restless, uneasy feeling or longing. He had an *itch* to travel across the country. *Noun.*

—1. To have or cause a tickling or stinging feeling in the skin. This rough wool sweater *itches* my skin. The rash on my hand *itches*. 2. To have a restless, uneasy feeling or wanting. The bully was *itching* for a fight. *Verb.*
itch (ich) *noun, plural* **itches;** *verb,* **itched, itching.**

item 1. A single thing in a group or list. There are many rare *items* in his stamp collection. The shopping list has ten *items* on it. 2. A bit of news. There was an *item* in the newspaper about the football team's victory.
i·tem (ī′təm) *noun, plural* **items.**

it'll *It'll* soon be spring. *It'll* take me an hour to get home.
it'll (it′əl) contraction for "it will" and "it shall."

its The cat licked *its* paw. ▲ Another word that sounds like this is **it's.**
its (its) *adjective.*

it's *It's* cold today. *It's* been nice to see you. ▲ Another word that sounds like this is **its.**
it's (its) contraction for "it is" and "it has."

itself The yard is full of weeds, but the house *itself* is in good condition. The cat can wash *itself*.
it·self (it self′) *pronoun.*

-ity A *suffix* that means "the state of being." *Equality* means "the state of being equal."

I've *I've* no money. *I've* been home all day.
I've (īv) contraction for "I have."

-ive A *suffix* that means: 1. "Tending to do something." *Destructive* means "tending to destroy." 2. "Relating to." *Instinctive* means "relating to instinct."

ivory 1. A smooth, hard white substance. It forms the tusks of elephants, walruses, and certain other animals. Piano keys and buttons are often made of ivory. 2. A creamy white color. *Noun.*
—1. Made of or like ivory. The piano has *ivory* keys. 2. Having the color ivory. She wore an *ivory* dress. *Adjective.*
i·vo·ry (ī′vər ē) *noun, plural* **ivories;** *adjective.*

ivy A vine with shiny leaves. Ivy can climb up walls or grow along the ground.
i·vy (ī′vē) *noun, plural* **ivies.**

at; āpe; cär; end; mē; it; īce; hot; ōld; fôrk; wood; fo͞ol; oil; out; up; turn; sing; thin; this; hw in white; zh in treasure. ə stands for a in about, e in taken i in pencil, o in lemon, and u in circus.

J

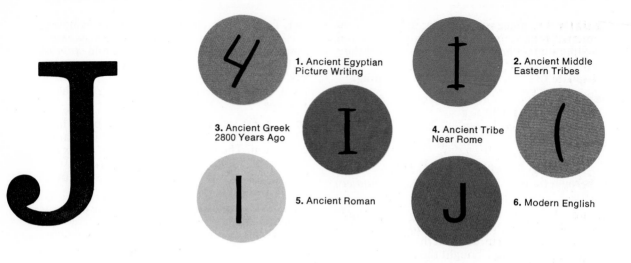

1. Ancient Egyptian Picture Writing

2. Ancient Middle Eastern Tribes

3. Ancient Greek 2800 Years Ago

4. Ancient Tribe Near Rome

5. Ancient Roman

6. Modern English

J is the tenth letter of the alphabet. It is one of only three letters that we use today that did not come from the Roman alphabet or an earlier alphabet. Because the letter **J** began as a form of the letter **I**, they have the same early history. The oldest form of the letters **I** and **J** was a drawing that the ancient Egyptians (**1**) used in their picture writing nearly 5000 years ago. This drawing was borrowed by several ancient tribes (**2**) in the Middle East. They wrote it as a tall line with a short bar at the top and bottom. The ancient Greeks (**3**) borrowed this letter without changing its shape. The letter was borrowed by an ancient tribe (**4**) that lived north of Rome about 2800 years ago. They changed its shape by not writing the short line at the top and bottom of the letter. The Romans (**5**) borrowed this form from them. In the Roman alphabet, the letter **I**, like our modern letter **Y**, stood for both a vowel sound and a consonant sound. In the Middle Ages, people began to lengthen the small letter **i** below the line when it was the first letter of a word. Two forms of the letter **I** were soon used. The new form was written almost exactly the way the small letter **j** is written today (**6**). By about 400 years ago the older letter **I** was used for only the vowel sound, and the new letter **J** was used for only the consonant sound.

j, J The tenth letter of the alphabet.
j, J (jā) *noun, plural* **j's, J's.**

jab To poke with something pointed. Ann accidentally *jabbed* her finger with a pin while she was sewing. *Verb.*
—A poke with something pointed. John fell asleep during the movie, so his brother gave him a *jab* in the ribs to wake him up. *Noun.*
jab (jab) *verb,* **jabbed, jabbing;** *noun, plural* **jabs.**

jack **1.** A tool that is used for lifting heavy objects a short distance. Carl raised the front end of his car off the ground with a *jack* so he could change the flat tire. **2.** A playing card with a picture of a young man on it. **3. jacks.** A game that is played with a small rubber ball and little pieces of metal that are also called "jacks." A player has to pick up a number of the metal jacks while bouncing and catching the ball with the same hand. *Noun.*
—To lift with a jack. The man at the gas station *jacked* the car up so he could look underneath. *Verb.*
jack (jak) *noun, plural* **jacks;** *verb,* **jacked, jacking.**

jackal An animal that looks something like a dog. A jackal has a pointed face, a bushy tail, and ears that point straight up. Jackals live on plains in Africa and Asia. They often eat the remains of another animal's prey.
jack·al (jak′əl) *noun, plural* **jackals.**

Jackal

jacket **1.** A short coat. The boy wore a *jacket* with the name of his high school across the back. **2.** An outer covering for a record or book. On the back of this book *jacket* there is a picture of the author.
jack·et (jak′it) *noun, plural* **jackets.**

jack-in-the-box A toy that is made up of a

box that a doll pops out of when the lid is opened.
jack-in-the-box (jak′in′thə boks′) *noun, plural* **jack-in-the-boxes.**

jackknife A large pocketknife with blades that fold into the handle.
jack·knife (jak′nīf′) *noun, plural* **jackknives.**

jack-o'-lantern A pumpkin that has been hollowed out and carved to look like a face. Jack-o'-lanterns are used at Halloween.
jack-o'-lan·tern (jak′ə-lan′tərn) *noun, plural* **jack-o'-lanterns.**

Jack-O'-Lantern

jackpot The top prize in a game or contest. That quiz show has a *jackpot* of $100,000.
jack·pot (jak′pot′) *noun, plural* **jackpots.**

jack rabbit A hare that has a thin body and very long ears. Jack rabbits use their strong back legs for leaping, and are one of the fastest of all animals.

jade A hard, green stone that is used for jewelry and carved ornaments.
jade (jād) *noun, plural* **jades.**

jagged Having sharp points that stick out. Eagles build their nests on high, *jagged* cliffs.
jag·ged (jag′id) *adjective.*

jaguar A large animal that belongs to the cat family. The short fur of a jaguar is golden with black spots. Jaguars are found in the southeastern United States, Mexico, and Central and South America.
jag·uar (jag′wär) *noun, plural* **jaguars.**

Jaguar

jail A building where people who are waiting for a trial or who have been found guilty of breaking the law are kept; prison. *Noun.*
—To put or keep in jail. The police *jailed* the men they caught robbing the bank. *Verb.*

jail (jāl) *noun, plural* **jails;** *verb,* **jailed, jailing.**

jam¹ **1.** To press or squeeze into a tight space. Ed tried to *jam* all his clothes into one small suitcase. People *jammed* onto the bus to get to work. **2.** To become or cause to become stuck so as not to work. The soldier's gun *jammed* when he tried to fire it. Rust and dirt *jammed* the lock on the gate. **3.** To push hard. Jim *jammed* on the brakes to stop the car. **4.** To bruise or crush. The girl *jammed* her hand when she closed the drawer on it. *Verb.*
—**1.** A mass of people or things so crowded together that it is difficult to move. Bill was three hours late because he was stuck in a traffic *jam.* **2.** A difficult situation. The man was in a real *jam* when the police found the stolen money in his room. *Noun.*
jam (jam) *verb,* **jammed, jamming;** *noun, plural* **jams.**

jam² A sweet food made by boiling fruit and sugar together until it is thick. Jam is used to spread on bread or other foods. Helen's grandmother makes strawberry *jam* every summer.
jam (jam) *noun, plural* **jams.**

janitor A person whose job is to take care of and clean a building.
jan·i·tor (jan′ə tər) *noun, plural* **janitors.**

January The first month of the year. January has thirty-one days.
Jan·u·ar·y (jan′yo͞o er′ē) *noun.*

▲ The Romans named **January** after *Janus,* their god of doors and gates. A holiday in his honor was held during this month. Janus was shown with two faces that looked in opposite directions. His holiday was probably held in January because this month looks in two directions—back on the year that has passed and ahead to the year to come.

Japan An island country in the Pacific Ocean. It is off the eastern coast of Asia. Its capital is Tokyo.
Ja·pan (jə pan′) *noun.*

Japanese **1.** A person who was born or is living in Japan. **2.** The language of Japan. *Noun.*

at; āpe; cär; end; mē; it; īce; hot; ōld;
fôrk; wood; fo͞ol; oil; out; up; turn; sing;
thin; this; hw in white; zh in treasure.
ə stands for a in about, e in taken
i in pencil, o in lemon, and u in circus.

—Having to do with Japan, its people, or their language. *Adjective.*

Jap·a·nese (jap'ə nēz') *noun, plural* **Japanese;** *adjective.*

Japanese beetle A beetle that came to the United States from Japan. It feeds on the leaves of plants.

jar¹ A container that has a wide mouth. A jar is usually made out of glass or pottery. Peanut butter, pickles, and jelly often come in jars. We bought two *jars* of strawberry jam at the county fair.

Japanese Beetle

jar (jär) *noun, plural* **jars.**

jar² **1.** To shake or vibrate. The explosion *jarred* the building. **2.** To have a harsh, unpleasant effect on. The sudden clatter of dishes *jarred* my nerves. *Verb.*
—A shake or sudden movement; shock. Lee wrapped the glass bowl up well so all the *jars* and bumps it would get in the mail would not break it. *Noun.*

jar (jär) *verb,* **jarred, jarring;** *noun, plural* **jars.**

javelin **1.** A light spear that was once used as a weapon. **2.** A long, thin shaft of metal that is thrown for distance in athletic contests.

jave·lin (jav'lin) *noun, plural* **javelins.**

Javelin

jaw **1.** The lower or upper bony part of the mouth. The jaws give shape to the mouth and hold the teeth in place. **2.** One of two parts of a tool that can be closed to grasp or hold something. The *jaws* of the vise held the piece of wood firm while Bob sanded it.

jaw (jô) *noun, plural* **jaws.**

jay Any of various noisy birds that have a crest and brightly colored feathers. One of the most common jays is a blue jay, which has blue feathers.

jay (jā) *noun, plural* **jays.**

Jay

jaywalk To cross the street without paying attention to the traffic lights or laws.

jay·walk (jā'wôk') *verb,* **jaywalked, jaywalking.**

jazz Music that has strong rhythm and accented notes that fall in unexpected places. Jazz originated in America. Musicians frequently make up and add notes of their own as they are playing a jazz piece.

jazz (jaz) *noun.*

jealous **1.** Fearful of losing someone's love to another person. Carol tried not to be *jealous* of her new baby brother. **2.** Having envy of a person, or what a person has or can do. Roy was *jealous* of his friend's ability to play football so well.

jeal·ous (jel'əs) *adjective.*

jealousy A jealous feeling; envy. There is often *jealousy* between brothers and sisters.

jeal·ous·y (jel'ə sē) *noun, plural* **jealousies.**

jean **1.** A strong cotton cloth used to make work clothes and other kinds of sport clothes. **2. jeans.** Trousers or overalls made out of this cloth.

jean (jēn) *noun, plural* **jeans.**

jeep A small, powerful automobile. A jeep is most often used by soldiers, but it is very useful to anyone who has to travel over land that does not have good roads.

jeep (jēp) *noun, plural* **jeeps.**

jelly A soft, firm food that is most often made from fruit juice boiled with sugar. It is frequently eaten at breakfast with toast or muffins. *Noun.*

—To make into jelly. My grandmother *jellies* plums every fall. *Verb.*

jel·ly (jel′ē) *noun, plural* **jellies;** *verb,* **jellied, jellying.**

jellyfish A sea animal with a body that is soft and firm like jelly, and is in the shape of an umbrella. There are many long, slender growths, called tentacles, hanging down from this body. The jellyfish uses its tentacles to catch and put food into its mouth.

jel·ly·fish (jel′ē fish′) *noun, plural* **jellyfish** or **jellyfishes.**

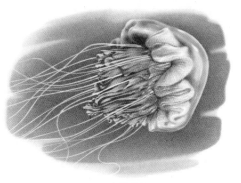

Jellyfish

jerk A sudden, sharp pull or twist; start. Joe gave the rope a *jerk.* The car started forward with a *jerk. Noun.*

—To move with a sudden, sharp motion. Susan *jerked* her head around when she heard the loud noise. *Verb.*

jerk (jurk) *noun, plural* **jerks;** *verb,* **jerked, jerking.**

jerkin A short, tight jacket that does not have sleeves. Jerkins were worn by men and boys in the 1500s and 1600s.

jer·kin (jur′kin) *noun, plural* **jerkins.**

jersey 1. A cloth that is knitted by machine out of wool, cotton, or other materials. Jersey is very soft and is used to make clothing. 2. A sweater made out of this cloth. It is put on over the head.

jer·sey (jur′zē) *noun, plural* **jerseys.**

Jerkin

jest A playful joke; prank. Bill meant his remark as a *jest,* but instead it hurt his friend's feelings. *Noun.*

—To speak or act in a playful way. You must be *jesting;* I can't believe what you say is true. *Verb.*

jest (jest) *noun, plural* **jests;** *verb,* **jested, jesting.**

Jesus The founder of the Christian religion. He was born in about 4 B.C. and died in about 29 A.D.

Je·sus (jē′zəs).

jet 1. A stream of liquid, gas, or vapor that is sent with force through a small opening. When Dick turned on the garden hose, a *jet* of water shot out. 2. A plane that is driven by a stream of hot gas. *Noun.*

—To shoot forth in a stream; spurt. Water *jetted* onto the street from the break in the water pipe. *Verb.*

jet (jet) *noun, plural* **jets;** *verb,* **jetted, jetting.**

jet-propelled Driven by a stream or jet of hot gas. The *jet-propelled* rocket was launched into orbit around the earth.

jet-pro·pelled (jet′prə peld′) *adjective.*

jet propulsion A method of moving an airplane, rocket, or other vehicle in one direction by using a stream or jet of hot gas forced out in the opposite direction.

jetty A wall that is built out into a body of water. Jetties can be built of rocks, wood, concrete, or steel. They are used to control the flow of a river or to protect the coast from breaking waves.

jet·ty (jet′ē) *noun, plural* **jetties.**

Jetty

at; āpe; cär; end; mē; it; īce; hot; ōld;
fôrk; wood; fo͞ol; oil; out; up; turn; sing;
thin; this; hw in white; zh in treasure.
ə stands for a in about, e in taken
i in pencil, o in lemon, and u in circus.

Jew **1.** A person who is descended from the ancient Hebrews. **2.** A person whose religion is Judaism.
Jew (jo͞o) *noun, plural* **Jews.**

jewel **1.** A precious stone; gem. Jewels are used in jewelry because of their beauty. They are also used in watches or machines because they are very hard and last a long time. **2.** A valuable necklace, pin, bracelet, or other ornament that is set with precious stones.
jew·el (jo͞o′əl) *noun, plural* **jewels.**

jeweler A person who makes, repairs, or sells jewelry or watches.
jew·el·er (jo͞o′ə lər) *noun, plural* **jewelers.**

jewelry Necklaces, pins, bracelets, or other ornaments. Jewelry is very often set with precious stones.
jew·el·ry (jo͞o′əl rē) *noun.*

Jewish Having to do with Jews, their religion, or their culture.
Jew·ish (jo͞o′ish) *adjective.*

jib A sail in the shape of a triangle that is in front of the mast.
jib (jib) *noun, plural* **jibs.**

jigsaw A saw that has a narrow blade and is set in a frame. A jigsaw is used to cut along wavy or curved lines.
jig·saw (jig′sô′) *noun, plural* **jigsaws.**

jigsaw puzzle A puzzle made up of small, curved cardboard or wooden pieces that can be fitted together to make a picture.

Jigsaw Puzzle

jingle To make or cause to make a tinkling or ringing sound. The bell on the cat's collar *jingled* whenever it moved. *Verb.*
—**1.** A tinkling or ringing sound. Whenever the cowboy walked you could hear the *jingle* of his spurs. **2.** A light, little tune that is easy to remember. Tim went to work humming the *jingle* he had heard on the radio. *Noun.*
jin·gle (jing′gəl) *verb,* **jingled, jingling;** *noun, plural* **jingles.**

job **1.** A position of work; employment. Alice took a *job* in the grocery store for the summer. **2.** Something that has to be done; piece of work. It is Dave's *job* to feed and walk the dog. The repair *job* on the television set will cost fifty dollars.
job (job) *noun, plural* **jobs.**

jockey A person whose job is to ride horses in races.
jock·ey (jok′ē) *noun, plural* **jockeys.**

Jockey

jog To run or move at a slow, steady pace. My father *jogs* in the park every morning for exercise. *Verb.*
—A slow, steady pace. The runner moved at a *jog. Noun.*
jog (jog) *verb,* **jogged, jogging;** *noun, plural* **jogs.**

join **1.** To put or fasten together so as to become one. Joan tied a knot to *join* the two ends of the rope. We all *joined* hands and formed a circle. **2.** To come together, or come together with. At what point do the two rivers *join*? This road *joins* the main highway just ahead. **3.** To become a member of. When Bill graduated from high school he *joined* the army. **4.** To come into the company of. Our friends at the other table came over to *join* us after they had finished eating.
join (join) *verb,* **joined, joining.**

joint **1.** The place or part where two or more bones meet or come together. The knee and the elbow are joints. Most joints move freely. **2.** The place or part where any two or more things meet or come together. The old chair was very unsteady because the *joint* in one of the legs was coming loose. *Noun.*
—Belonging to or done by two or more people. My father and his brothers are *joint* owners of the gas station. *Adjective.*
joint (joint) *noun, plural* **joints;** *adjective.*

joke Something that is said or done to make people laugh. John started to tell a *joke* but forgot the funny line at the end. Linda hid her sister's pajamas as a *joke. Noun.*

—To tell or make jokes. At school he spends more time laughing and *joking* with his friends than he does studying. *Verb.*

joke (jōk) *noun, plural* **jokes;** *verb,* **joked, joking.**

jolly Full of fun; merry and cheerful. The man who dressed up as Santa Claus was a big, *jolly* person. We sat around the campfire singing songs and having a *jolly* time.

jol·ly (jol′ē) *adjective,* **jollier, jolliest.**

jolt To move or cause to move with sudden, rough jerks. The jeep *jolted* along the dirt road. Hitting the car ahead of us *jolted* us right out of our seats. *Verb.*

—**1.** A jerk or jar. The bus stopped with a *jolt.* **2.** A surprise or shock. The news gave us quite a *jolt. Noun.*

jolt (jōlt) *verb,* **jolted, jolting;** *noun, plural* **jolts.**

jonquil A yellow or white flower that looks like a daffodil. A jonquil has a center petal shaped like a cup that is surrounded by six flat petals.

jon·quil (jong′-kwil) *noun, plural* **jonquils.**

Jonquils

jostle To bump or push roughly. Tim had to *jostle* his way across the crowded room. *Verb.*

—A bump or push. Ruth accidentally gave the lady next to her a *jostle* as she tried to get to the back of the bus. *Noun.*

jos·tle (jos′əl) *verb,* **jostled, jostling;** *noun, plural* **jostles.**

jot To make a short and quick note of something. The owner of the store *jotted* down the license number of the robber's car as it sped away.

jot (jot) *verb,* **jotted, jotting.**

journal **1.** A daily record or account. Linda kept a *journal* during the summer she spent at camp. At the end of each day the shopkeeper recorded in his *journal* how much money he had made. **2.** A magazine or newspaper. The medical *journal* published a report on the doctor's discovery.

jour·nal (jurn′əl) *noun, plural* **journals.**

journalist A person whose job is writing for a newspaper or magazine.

jour·nal·ist (jurn′əl ist) *noun, plural* **journalists.**

journey A long trip. The Pilgrims made a *journey* to the New World. *Noun.*

—To make a trip; travel. My brother wants to *journey* through Africa after graduating from college. *Verb.*

jour·ney (jur′nē) *noun, plural* **journeys;** *verb,* **journeyed, journeying.**

joust A formal contest or combat between two knights on horseback. Each knight was armed with a lance and wore armor. *Noun.*

—To fight or take part in a joust. The two knights *jousted* to win the hand of the beautiful princess. *Verb.*

joust (joust) *noun, plural* **jousts;** *verb,* **jousted, jousting.**

Joust

jovial Full of fun; merry; jolly. John is in a *jovial* mood today because it's his birthday.

jo·vi·al (jō′vē əl) *adjective.*

▲ The word **jovial** comes from *Jove,* which is the Latin name for the god Jupiter. People once thought that anyone who was born under the sign of the planet Jupiter would be a jolly, happy person.

jowl Heavy, loose flesh hanging from or under the lower jaw.

jowl (joul) *noun, plural* **jowls.**

joy **1.** A strong feeling of happiness or delight. The little boy jumped with *joy* when he saw his father coming home. **2.** A person or thing that causes a strong feeling of happiness. Nancy is so helpful around the house that she is a *joy* to her parents.

joy (joi) *noun, plural* **joys.**

at; āpe; cär; end; mē; it; īce; hot; ōld;
fôrk; wood; fool; oil; out; up; turn; sing;
thin; this; hw in white; zh in treasure.
ə stands for a in about, e in taken
i in pencil, o in lemon, and u in circus.

joyful Feeling, showing, or causing happiness; glad. The mother had a *joyful* look on her face when she saw that her son had not been hurt in the accident. The couple's fiftieth wedding anniversary was a *joyful* occasion.
joy·ful (joi′fəl) *adjective.*

joyous Joyful or happy. Beth's marriage was a *joyous* occasion for her and her family.
joy·ous (joi′əs) *adjective.*

Judaism The religion of the Jews. It is based on a belief in one God and the teachings of the Old Testament.
Ju·da·ism (jōō′dē iz′əm) *noun.*

judge **1.** To hear and decide in a court of law. The court has the power to *judge* cases that come before it. It is the job of the jury to *judge* that man innocent or guilty. **2.** To settle or decide. Three men and three women have been chosen to *judge* the beauty contest. **3.** To form an opinion of. *Judge* the movie by seeing it yourself; don't listen to what other people say about it. *Verb.*
—**1.** A person who decides on questions and disagreements in a court of law. A judge can be chosen by a government official or elected by the voters. **2.** A person who decides the winner in any contest. The *judges* at the dog show gave first prize to a collie. **3.** A person who knows enough about a subject to give an opinion about it. My uncle is a good *judge* of horses. *Noun.*
judge (juj) *verb,* **judged, judging;** *noun, plural* **judges.**

judgment **1.** The ability to decide or judge wisely; good sense. My mother has good *judgment* in handling money matters. **2.** An opinion. In my *judgment*, Michael is very good at drawing and painting. **3.** A verdict or decision handed down by a court of law. It was the *judgment* of the court that the man was guilty.
judg·ment (juj′mənt) *noun, plural* **judgments.**

judicial Having to do with courts of law or judges. It is the responsibility of the *judicial* branch of government to make the meaning of the law clear.
ju·di·cial (jōō·dish′əl) *adjective.*

judo A way of fighting and defending oneself without weapons.
ju·do (jōō′dō) *noun.*

▲ The word **judo** comes from a Japanese word that means "gentle way." This method of fighting is not so rough as other ways of fighting.

jug A rounded container that has a handle and a narrow neck. A jug is used for holding liquids, and is usually made out of pottery or glass.
jug (jug) *noun, plural* **jugs.**

juggle To keep balls or other objects in continuous motion from the hands into the air by skillful tossing and catching. My brother can *juggle* three oranges at once without letting one drop to the floor.
jug·gle (jug′əl) *verb,* **juggled, juggling.**

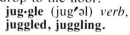
Jug

juice The liquid from vegetables, fruits, or meats. I love to drink fresh orange *juice* for breakfast. Mother let the roast beef cook in its own *juice.*
juice (jōōs) *noun, plural* **juices.**

July The seventh month of the year. July has thirty-one days.
Ju·ly (jōō lī′) *noun.*

▲ The word **July** comes from the Latin name for this month. The Romans named July after *Julius* Caesar because he was born in this month.

jumble To mix or throw into confusion. All the toys were *jumbled* together in a box. *Verb.*
—A confused mixture or condition; mess. Lucy threw everything in her closet into a *jumble* in trying to find her missing shoe. *Noun.*
jum·ble (jum′bəl) *verb,* **jumbled, jumbling;** *noun, plural* **jumbles.**

jump **1.** To leap into the air. Bob had to *jump* to catch the ball. Jean *jumped* off the high diving board. **2.** To move or get up suddenly. The students *jumped* to their feet when they heard the fire alarm ring. **3.** To leap or pass over. The boys had a contest to see who could *jump* the high fence. *Verb.*
—**1.** A leap; spring. The girl took a running *jump* across the puddle. **2.** A sudden move or start. Mother gave a *jump* when my sister and I scared her from behind the door. **3.** A sudden increase or rise. My father complained about the *jump* in the price of milk. *Noun.*
jump (jump) *verb,* **jumped, jumping;** *noun, plural* **jumps.**

jumper¹ A dress that is in one piece and does not have sleeves. A jumper is usually worn over a blouse or sweater.
jump·er (jum′pər) *noun, plural* **jumpers.**

jumper² A person or thing that jumps. David is the best *jumper* on the school basketball team.
jump·er (jum′pər) *noun, plural* **jumpers.**

junction A place where things meet or cross. A place where railroad ties meet is called a junction.
junc·tion (jungk′shən) *noun, plural* **junctions.**

June The sixth month of the year. June has thirty days.
June (jo͞on) *noun.*

Jumper

▲ The word **June** comes from the Latin name for the month. The ancient Romans believed that there was a queen of the gods named *Juno,* and they named this month in honor of her.

jungle Land in tropical areas that is covered with a thick mass of trees, vines, and bushes.
jun·gle (jung′gəl) *noun, plural* **jungles.**

junior **1.** The younger of two. The word "junior" is used after the name of a son who has the same name as his father. Robert Edwards, *Junior* is the son of Robert Edwards, Senior. **2.** Having a lower position or rank. A *junior* vice-president does not have as important a job as a senior vice-president. **3.** Having to do with the next-to-last year in high school or college. *Adjective.*
—**1.** A person who is younger than another. Alice is my *junior* by three years. **2.** A student who is in the next-to-last year of high school or college. *Noun.*
jun·ior (jo͞on′yər) *adjective; noun, plural* **juniors.**

juniper An evergreen shrub or tree. Junipers have purple cones that look like berries.
ju·ni·per (jo͞o′nə pər) *noun, plural* **junipers.**

junk¹ Old pieces of metal, wood, rags, or other things that are thrown away; trash.
junk (jungk) *noun.*

junk² A Chinese sailing ship.
junk (jungk) *noun, plural* **junks.**

Jupiter The largest planet. It is the fifth closest planet to the sun.
Ju·pi·ter (jo͞o′pə tər) *noun.*

juror A member of a jury. The *jurors* left the courtroom to decide on their verdict.
ju·ror (joor′ər) *noun, plural* **jurors.**

jury A group of people chosen to hear the facts in a matter that has been brought before a court of law. The jury makes a decision on this matter based on the facts they hear and on the law.
ju·ry (joor′ē) *noun, plural* **juries.**

just Fair and right; honest. The king was a stern but *just* ruler. Mrs. Smith thought ten dollars was a *just* reward to give the boy for finding her lost kitten. *Adjective.*
—**1.** Exactly; precisely. You said *just* what I was going to say. **2.** A little while ago. If you're looking for Father, I *just* saw him in the garage. **3.** By very little; barely. Because of all the traffic, Diane *just* made her plane in time. **4.** Only; merely, I'm not really hurt; it's *just* a scratch. *Adverb.*
just (just) *adjective; adverb.*

justice **1.** The quality of being fair and right. *Justice* demands that all people be treated as equals in a court of law. **2.** A judge of the Supreme Court of the United States. There are nine justices of the Supreme Court.
jus·tice (jus′tis) *noun, plural* **justices.**

justify **1.** To show to be fair or reasonable. Tom *justified* his teacher's faith in him by winning the scholarship. **2.** To prove to be blameless or without guilt. The lawyer tried to *justify* the suspect's action.
jus·ti·fy (jus′tə fī′) *verb,* **justified, justifying.**

jut To stick out. The lighthouse is on a piece of land that *juts* out into the sea.
jut (jut) *verb,* **jutted, jutting.**

jute A strong fiber that is used to make heavy cord or a coarse material called burlap. Jute comes from a plant that is grown mostly in tropical areas of Asia.
jute (jo͞ot) *noun, plural* **jutes.**

juvenile Of or for children or young people. The library keeps its collection of *juvenile* books on the second floor. *Adjective.*
—A young person. Our youth center offers many activities for *juveniles* in the neighborhood. *Noun.*
ju·ve·nile (jo͞o′vən əl *or* joo′və nīl′) *adjective; noun, plural* **juveniles.**

at; āpe; cär; end; mē; it; īce; hot; ōld; fôrk; wood; fo͞ol; oil; out; up; turn; sing; thin; this; hw in white; zh in treasure. ə stands for a in about, e in taken i in pencil, o in lemon, and u in circus.

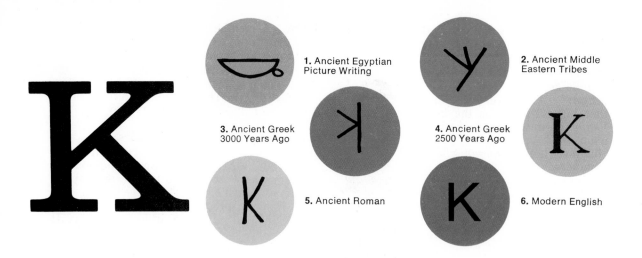

1. Ancient Egyptian Picture Writing

2. Ancient Middle Eastern Tribes

3. Ancient Greek 3000 Years Ago

4. Ancient Greek 2500 Years Ago

5. Ancient Roman

6. Modern English

K is the eleventh letter of the alphabet. The oldest form of the letter **K** was a drawing that the ancient Egyptians (**1**) used in their picture writing nearly 5000 years ago. This drawing looked something like a bowl or a cupped hand. When this drawing was borrowed by several ancient tribes (**2**) in the Middle East, its shape was changed so that it looked something like a hand with the fingers stretched out. The ancient Greeks (**3**) borrowed this letter about 3000 years ago. They wrote it very much like a backwards capital letter **K**. Several hundred years later, the Greeks reversed this letter (**4**). This new form of **K** was borrowed by the Romans (**5**) who, by about 2400 years ago, were writing it almost the same way that we write the capital letter **K** today (**6**).

k, K The eleventh letter of the alphabet.
  k, K (kā) *noun, plural* **k's, K's.**

kaleidoscope A tube that contains small pieces of colored glass or other objects at one end. When the other end of the tube is held up to the eye and turned, mirrors reflect a series of continually changing patterns.
  ka·lei·do·scope (kə lī′də skōp′) *noun, plural* **kaleidoscopes.**

Kangaroo

kangaroo An Australian animal that has small front legs and very strong back legs which it uses for leaping. A kangaroo also has a long, powerful tail that is used for balance. A female kangaroo carries her young in a pouch for about six months after birth.

kan·ga·roo (kang′gə rōō′) *noun, plural* **kangaroos** or **kangaroo.**

Kansas A state in the west-central United States. Its capital is Topeka.
  Kan·sas (kan′zəs) *noun.*

▲ **Kansas** was named for the biggest river in the state. The word was an Indian name for a tribe that used to live near this river.

katydid A large, green grasshopper. By rubbing its two wings together, the male katydid can make a shrill noise that sounds like its name.
  ka·ty·did (kā′tē did′) *noun, plural* **katydids.**

kayak **1.** An Eskimo canoe. It is made of animal skins stretched over a wooden or bone frame. A hole is left in the middle for one person to sit. **2.** A light canoe that looks like this.
  kay·ak (kī′ak) *noun, plural* **kayaks.**

Kayak

348

keel A wooden or steel piece that runs along the center of the bottom of a ship or boat. The keel supports the whole structure of the boat. *Noun.*
—**1.** To turn bottom up; capsize. The little sailboat *keeled* over in the strong wind. **2.** To fall over suddenly. The heat in the overcrowded subway was too much for the old man and he *keeled* over in a faint. *Verb.*
keel (kēl) *noun, plural* **keels;** *verb,* **keeled, keeling.**

keen **1.** Having a sharp cutting edge or point. A *keen* knife is an important tool in any kitchen. **2.** Sharp or quick in seeing, hearing, or thinking. That hound has a *keen* sense of smell. There is no doubt that the student who won the science prize has a *keen* mind. **3.** Full of enthusiasm; eager. Liz is *keen* about sports of any kind.
keen (kēn) *adjective,* **keener, keenest.**

Keep

keep **1.** To continue to have, hold, or do. Pam's mother let her *keep* the kitten that followed her home. **2.** To continue or cause to continue in a certain place or condition. The teacher asked the class to *keep* quiet. The mother *kept* her sick child in bed. A refrigerator *keeps* meat fresh. **3.** To store or put. Jerry *keeps* his toys in the bottom of the closet. **4.** To hold back; prevent. The cold weather may *keep* the plants from budding. Ruth couldn't *keep* from crying at the sad movie. **5.** To be faithful to; fulfill. The boy *kept* his promise and mowed the lawn for his father. **6.** To take care of. We all help my mother *keep* house. *Verb.*
—**1.** Food and a place to live. When the children grew up, they all left home and started earning their own *keep.* **2.** The strongest part in a castle or fort. *Noun.*
keep (kēp) *verb,* **kept, keeping;** *noun, plural* **keeps.**

keeping **1.** Care or charge. We left the key to our house in our neighbor's *keeping* while we were on vacation. **2.** Agreement or harmony. Greg's noisy jokes were not in *keeping* with the serious nature of the occasion.
keep·ing (kē′ping) *noun.*

keg A small barrel. Beer is put in kegs.
keg (keg) *noun, plural* **kegs.**

kelp A large, brown seaweed that grows along the coasts of the Atlantic and Pacific Oceans. Kelp is mostly used as a fertilizer.
kelp (kelp) *noun.*

kennel **1.** A house for a dog. The hunting dogs on the estate were kept in a *kennel.* **2.** A place where dogs are raised and trained. We bought this puppy from a well-known *kennel.*
ken·nel (ken′əl) *noun, plural* **kennels.**

Kentucky A state in the east-central United States. Its capital is Frankfort.
Ken·tuck·y (kən tuk′ē) *noun.*

▲ **Kentucky** comes from an Indian name for this area that probably meant "meadowland" or "flat land." After a while, the name was used for the river running through this flat land south of the Ohio River. When Virginia started a county in this area in 1776, it used the name *Kentucky.* When the county was later made a state, it kept the same name.

kept Jane *kept* the ball that she found in the playground. Look up **keep** for more information.
kept (kept) *verb.*

kerchief A piece of cloth that is worn over the head or around the neck.
ker·chief (kur′chif) *noun, plural* **kerchiefs.**

Kerchief

kernel **1.** The whole grain or seed of wheat or corn. When we eat corn on the cob, we are eating the kernels. **2.** The soft part inside the hard outer part of a seed, fruit, or nut. ▲ Another word that sounds like this is **colonel.**
ker·nel (kurn′əl) *noun, plural* **kernels.**

kerosene A thin, colorless oil that is made

at; āpe; cär; end; mē; it; īce; hot; ōld; fôrk; wood; fōōl; oil; out; up; turn; sing; thin; this; hw in white; zh in treasure. ə stands for a in about, e in taken i in pencil, o in lemon, and u in circus.

from petroleum. Kerosene was once used as a fuel for lamps before electricity was invented. Today it is used in fuel for jet engines.

ker·o·sene (ker′ə sēn′) *noun.*

ketchup A thick red sauce that is made of tomatoes, onions, salt, sugar, and spices. Ketchup is used to give flavor to hamburgers and many other foods. This word is also spelled **catsup.**

ketch·up (kech′əp) *noun.*

kettle A metal pot used for boiling liquids or for cooking foods.

ket·tle (ket′əl) *noun, plural* **kettles.**

kettledrum A drum that is made of copper or brass with a thin material called parchment stretched over the top.

ket·tle·drum (ket′əl·drum′) *noun, plural* **kettledrums.**

key¹ **1.** A shaped piece of metal that can open a lock on a door, drawer, or any other thing. Ellen lost the *key* so she could not unlock the front door. **2.** Anything that has a similar use. Susan used a roller skate *key* to tighten the skates on her shoes. **3.** Something that solves or explains. The detective found the *key* to the mystery. There is a *key* to the pronunciations in this dictionary at the bottom of the opposite page. **4.** Something that leads to or is a way of getting something. Hard work can sometimes be the *key* to success. **5.** The part that is pressed down to work a machine or musical instrument. The *keys* of a typewriter are marked with different numbers and letters of the alphabet. A piano has black and white *keys.* **6.** A musical scale in which all the notes are related to each other and are based on one basic note. The scale gets its name from this basic note. That song is written in the *key* of F. *Noun.*
—Very important; chief. The quarterback holds the *key* position on a football team. *Adjective.*
—To regulate or adjust the musical pitch of. The musicians in the orchestra have to *key* their instruments before a performance. *Verb.* ▲ Another word that sounds like this is **quay.**

Kettledrum

key (kē) *noun, plural* **keys;** *adjective; verb,* **keyed, keying.**

key² A low island or reef. There are keys along the southern tip of Florida. ▲ Another word that sounds like this is **quay.**

key (kē) *noun, plural* **keys.**

keyboard A set or row of keys. A piano or a typewriter has a keyboard.

key·board (kē′bôrd′) *noun, plural* **keyboards.**

keyhole The hole in a lock where a key is put.

key·hole (kē′hōl′) *noun, plural* **keyholes.**

keystone The top stone in the middle of an arch. The keystone holds the other stones of the arch together.

key·stone (kē′stōn′) *noun, plural* **keystones.**

khaki **1.** A dull, yellowish-brown color. **2.** A heavy cotton cloth of this color. Khaki is most often used to make military uniforms. *Noun.*
—Of the color khaki. *Adjective.*

khak·i (kak′ē *or* kä′kē) *noun, plural* **khakis;** *adjective.*

Keystone

kick **1.** To hit or strike out with the foot. Knowing how to *kick* correctly is very important when you are learning how to swim. **2.** To move by hitting with the foot. The boy *kicked* a tin can along on his way home from school. **3.** To spring back when fired. The rifle *kicked* so hard that it hurt Michael's shoulder. *Verb.*
—**1.** A hit or blow with the foot. Pete shut the door with a *kick.* **2.** The sudden springing back of a gun when it is fired. **3.** A feeling of excitement; thrill. Mary got a real *kick* out of going for her first ride in an airplane. *Noun.*

kick (kik) *verb,* **kicked, kicking;** *noun, plural* **kicks.**

kickoff A kick in football that puts the ball into play. The crowd in the stands stood up to watch the *kickoff.*

kick·off (kik′ôf′) *noun, plural* **kickoffs.**

kid **1.** A young goat. **2.** A child. ▲ This meaning is used mostly in everyday conversation. **3.** A kind of leather that is made from the skin of a young goat. Mother's handbag is made of black *kid. Noun.*
—To make fun of or tease. Jim's friends

kidded him about his new haircut. You should never take anything my brother says seriously because he is always *kidding. Verb.*

kid (kid) *noun, plural* **kids;** *verb,* **kidded, kidding.**

kidnap To seize or hold a person by force. Three men *kidnapped* the rich woman's daughter and demanded one million dollars before they would return her.

kid·nap (kid′nap′) *verb,* **kidnaped** or **kidnapped, kidnaping** or **kidnapping.**

kidney Either of two organs in the body that are shaped like a bean. The kidneys are found in the abdomen. They filter out waste from the bloodstream and pass it out in the form of urine.

kid·ney (kid′nē) *noun, plural* **kidneys.**

kill **1.** To take away the life of; put to death. Automobile accidents *kill* thousands of Americans every year. Many deer are *killed* every year during the hunting season. **2.** To put an end to; destroy. Failing the test *killed* the girl's chances of getting an A in the course. **3.** To use up. Ed *killed* an hour looking in store windows while he was waiting to meet his friend. *Verb.*
—**1.** The act of killing. Once the dogs had cornered the animal up a tree the hunters moved in for the *kill.* **2.** An animal that is killed. The wolf dragged its *kill* back to its den to feed its family. *Noun.*

kill (kil) *verb,* **killed, killing;** *noun, plural* **kills.**

killdeer A noisy bird that lives in fields along the coast of North America. Killdeers have brownish feathers with two black stripes along the breast.

kill·deer (kil′dēr′) *noun, plural* **killdeers** or **killdeer.**

Killdeer

kiln A furnace or oven for burning, baking, or drying. A kiln is used in making bricks, pottery, and charcoal.

kiln (kiln *or* kil) *noun, plural* **kilns.**

kilogram The basic unit of weight and mass in the metric system. A kilogram is equal to 1000 grams, or about two pounds and three ounces.

kil·o·gram (kil′ə gram′) *noun, plural* **kilograms.**

kilometer A unit of length in the metric system. A kilometer is equal to 1000 meters, or about .62 of a mile.

ki·lom·e·ter (ki lom′ə tər *or* kil′ə mē′tər) *noun, plural* **kilometers.**

kilowatt A unit of electrical power. A kilowatt is equal to 1000 watts.

kil·o·watt (kil′ə wot′) *noun, plural* **kilowatts.**

kilt A pleated, plaid skirt that reaches to the knees. A kilt is worn by men in Scotland.

kilt (kilt) *noun, plural* **kilts.**

Kilt

kimono A loose robe or gown that is tied with a sash. A kimono is worn by men and women in Japan.

ki·mo·no (ki mō′nə) *noun, plural* **kimonos.**

kin A person's whole family; relatives. All of Sarah's *kin* live in Alabama.

kin (kin) *noun.*

kind¹ Gentle, generous, and friendly. A kind person is always thoughtful of others. The boy was always *kind* to animals. It was *kind* of you to help me.

kind (kīnd) *adjective,* **kinder, kindest.**

kind² A type or class. The whale is a *kind* of mammal. That store has many different *kinds* of sports equipment.

kind (kīnd) *noun, plural* **kinds.**

kindergarten A class in school for children between the ages of four and six. It comes before first grade.

Kimono

at; āpe; cär; end; mē; it; īce; hot; ōld;
fôrk; wood; fōōl; oil; out; up; turn; sing;
thin; **th**is; hw in white; zh in treasure.
ə stands for a in about, e in taken
i in pencil, o in lemon, and u in circus.

kin·der·gar·ten (kin′dər gärt′ən) *noun, plural* **kindergartens.**

▲ The word **kindergarten** comes from a German word that means "children's garden."

---

kindle **1.** To set or catch on fire. The campers *kindled* the logs of the campfire. **2.** To stir up or excite. The factory's pollution of the river *kindled* the townspeople's anger.
kin·dle (kind′əl) *verb,* **kindled, kindling.**

kindly Having or showing kindness. The boys were not afraid of the principal because he had a *kindly* face. *Adjective.*
—**1.** In a kind or gentle manner. The stranger spoke *kindly* to the lost child. **2.** As a favor. *Kindly* mail this letter for me. **3.** Sincerely. Thank you *kindly* for your help. *Adverb.*
kind·ly (kīnd′lē) *adjective,* **kindlier, kindliest;** *adverb.*

kindness **1.** The quality of being kind. The *kindness* of Mike's friends when he was sick made him very grateful. **2.** A thoughtful, friendly act; favor. The guests thanked their hostess for her many *kindnesses.*
kind·ness (kīnd′nis) *noun, plural* **kindnesses.**

Kiosk

king **1.** A man who rules a country. **2.** A person or thing that is the best of its class. That man owns so many oil wells that he is known as an oil *king.* The lion is often thought of as the *king* of the jungle. **3.** A playing card with the picture of a king on it. **4.** An important piece in a game of chess or checkers.
king (king) *noun, plural* **kings.**

kingdom **1.** A country that is ruled by a king or queen. **2.** One of the three main divisions in nature. These divisions are the animal kingdom, the vegetable kingdom, and the mineral kingdom.

king·dom (king′dəm) *noun, plural* **kingdoms.**

kingfisher A brightly colored bird. A kingfisher has a crested head and a long, pointed bill. It eats fish, insects, and sometimes even small animals and birds.
king·fish·er (king′fish′ər) *noun, plural* **kingfishers.**

Kingfisher

kink **1.** A tight curl of hair, wire, or rope. The wind made Jane's hair full of *kinks.* **2.** A pain in a muscle; cramp. Dad got a *kink* in his back after he tried to move the heavy piano by himself. *Noun.*
—To form a kink or kinks. The thread *kinked* as Ann was sewing on the button. *Verb.*
kink (kingk) *noun, plural* **kinks;** *verb,* **kinked, kinking.**

kiosk A small building with one or more open sides. A kiosk is used especially as a newsstand, telephone booth, or subway entrance.
ki·osk (kē′osk *or* kē osk′) *noun, plural* **kiosks.**

kiss To touch with the lips as a sign of greeting or affection. The mother *kissed* her child. *Verb.*
—**1.** A touch with the lips as a sign of greeting or affection. Jill gave her father a *kiss* as she ran out the door. **2.** A small chocolate candy that is wrapped in tin foil. *Noun.*
kiss (kis) *verb,* **kissed, kissing;** *noun, plural* **kisses.**

kit **1.** A collection of tools or equipment for a particular purpose. The campers took along a first-aid *kit* in case of an accident. **2.** A set of parts or materials to be put together. Jack built a model of a rocket from a *kit.*
kit (kit) *noun, plural* **kits.**

kitchen A room where food is cooked.
kitch·en (kich′ən) *noun, plural* **kitchens.**

kitchenette A very small kitchen.
kitch·en·ette (kich′ə net′) *noun, plural* **kitchenettes.**

kite **1.** A light wooden frame that is covered with paper, plastic, or cloth. A kite is flown in the air at the end of a long string. **2.** A hawk that has a hooked bill, a forked tail, and long, narrow wings.
kite (kīt) *noun, plural* **kites.**

kitten A young cat. Robin's cat gave birth to four *kittens.*
kit·ten (kit′ən) *noun, plural* **kittens.**

knack A special ability or skill for doing something easily. My uncle has a *knack* for repairing things.
knack (nak) *noun.*

knapsack A bag made of canvas or leather that is used for carrying clothes, equipment, or other supplies. A knapsack is strapped over the shoulders and carried on the back.
knap·sack (nap′sak′) *noun, plural* **knapsacks.**

Kite

Knapsacks

knead To mix or work over with the hands. The baker had to *knead* the bread dough before baking it. ▲ Another word that sounds like this is **need.**
knead (nēd) *verb,* **kneaded, kneading.**

knee The joint of the leg between the thigh and the lower leg.
knee (nē) *noun, plural* **knees.**

kneecap A flat, movable bone in front of the knee. The kneecap protects the knee joint from getting injured.
knee·cap (nē′kap′) *noun, plural* **kneecaps.**

kneel To go down on a bent knee or knees. The knights had to *kneel* before the king.
kneel (nēl) *verb,* **knelt** or **kneeled, kneeling.**

knelt The little girl *knelt* beside her bed to say her prayers.
knelt (nelt) *verb.*

knew Sally *knew* the answer to the question. Look up **know** for more information. ▲ Other words that sound like this are **gnu** and **new.**
knew (no͞o *or* nyo͞o) *verb.*

knife **1.** A tool that is used for cutting. A knife has a sharp blade attached to a handle. **2.** The cutting blade of a tool or machine. *Noun.*
—To cut or stab with a knife. *Verb.*
knife (nīf) *noun, plural* **knives;** *verb,* **knifed, knifing.**

knight **1.** A soldier in the Middle Ages. A knight gave his loyalty to a king or lord and in return was given the right to hold land. A man had to serve as a page and squire before he could become a knight. **2.** A man who holds this title today as an honor for service to his country. In Great Britain, a knight uses the word "Sir" before his name. **3.** One of the pieces in a game of chess. A knight is in the shape of a horse's head. *Noun.*
—To raise to the rank of knight. The king *knighted* the soldier for his courage and loyalty. *Verb.* ▲ Another word that sounds like this is **night.**
knight (nīt) *noun, plural* **knights;** *verb,* **knighted, knighting.**

knit **1.** To make by looping yarn together, either by hand with long needles, or by a machine. The woman was *knitting* a sweater for her granddaughter **2.** To join or come together closely and securely. The broken bone in Nick's leg *knitted* well in six months.
knit (nit) *verb,* **knitted** or **knit, knitting.**

knives More than

Knitting

at; āpe; cär; end; mē; it; īce; hot; ōld; fôrk; wood; fo͞ol; oil; out; up; turn; sing; thin; this; hw in white; zh in treasure.
ə stands for a in about, e in taken i in pencil, o in lemon, and u in circus.

one knife. Look up **knife** for more information.

knives (nīvz) *noun plural.*

knob 1. A rounded handle for opening a door or drawer, or for working a radio or television. The *knob* on the drawer came off, so we had to pry it open. 2. A rounded lump. The squirrel hid its nuts in a *knob* of the trunk of an old tree.

knob (nob) *noun, plural* **knobs.**

knock 1. To strike with a sharp, hard blow or blows; hit. The falling branch *knocked* Jim on the head. I *knocked* on the door but no one answered. Dan *knocked* his leg against the table in his hurry to run out the door. 2. To push and cause to fall. The cat jumped on the table and *knocked* over the lamp. 3. To make a pounding or clanking noise. The engine of the old car *knocked. Verb.*

—1. A sharp, hard blow; hit. Bill got a *knock* on his head in the football game. I heard a *knock* on the door. 2. A pounding or clanking noise. Our old car had a *knock* in the engine. *Noun.*

knock (nok) *verb,* **knocked, knocking;** *noun, plural* **knocks.**

to knock out. To hit so hard as to make unconscious. The blow on his head *knocked out* the football player.

knocker A small metal knob or ring that is attached to a door with a hinge. A knocker is used for knocking on a door to let people inside know that you would like to come in.

knock·er (nok′ər) *noun, plural* **knock·ers.**

Knocker

knoll A small, rounded hill. We decided to have a picnic on a *knoll* at one end of the field.

knoll (nōl) *noun, plural* **knolls.**

knot 1. A fastening made by tying together pieces of thread, string, or cord. Mother tied the clothesline around the tree with a *knot.* 2. A tangle or lump. The wind had made so many *knots* in Nancy's hair that she had trouble combing it. 3. A small group of people or things. A *knot* of people waited on the platform for the train. 4. A dark, round spot in a board. A knot is the spot where a branch grew out of the trunk of a tree. 5. A measurement of speed used on ships and boats. A knot is the same as one nautical mile, which equals 6080 feet per hour. *Noun.*

—To tie in or with a knot. Carol *knotted* the string around the package. *Verb.* ▲ Another word that sounds like this is **not.**

knot (not) *noun, plural* **knots;** *verb,* **knotted, knotting.**

know 1. To understand clearly; be certain of the facts or truth of. The police *know* how the accident happened. Do you *know* what causes lightning? 2. To be acquainted or familiar with. I am a friend of Alice's, but I don't *know* her older brother. 3. To have skill or experience with. Dick *knows* how to type very well. ▲ Another word that sounds like this is **no.**

know (nō) *verb,* **knew, known, knowing.**

knowledge 1. What is known from understanding, experience, or study. Pam has enough *knowledge* of football to be able to follow a game on television. Ted has very little *knowledge* of Latin. 2. The fact of knowing. The *knowledge* that the car might slide on the icy road made Bill drive more slowly.

knowl·edge (nol′ij) *noun.*

known It is *known* that Christopher Columbus first reached America in 1492. Look up **know** for more information.

knuckle A joint of a finger.

knuck·le (nuk′əl) *noun, plural* **knuckles.**

Koala

koala A furry, chubby animal that lives in Australia. It has large bushy ears, a black nose, and no tail. Koalas live in trees, and the female carries her young in a pouch.

ko·a·la (kō ä′lə) *noun, plural* **koalas.**

at; āpe; cär; end; mē; it; īce; hot; ōld; fôrk; wood; fool; oil; out; up; turn; sing; thin; this; hw in white; zh in treasure. ə stands for a in about, e in taken i in pencil, o in lemon, and u in circus.

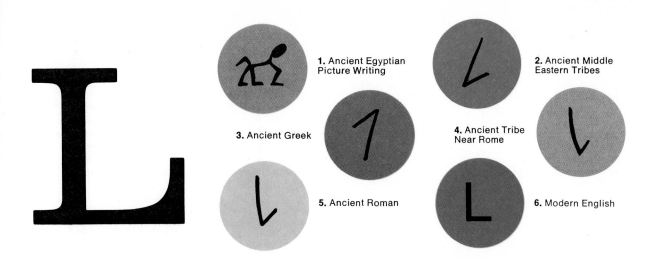

1. Ancient Egyptian Picture Writing

2. Ancient Middle Eastern Tribes

3. Ancient Greek

4. Ancient Tribe Near Rome

5. Ancient Roman

6. Modern English

L is the twelfth letter of the alphabet. The oldest form of the letter **L** was a drawing that the ancient Egyptians (**1**) used in their picture writing nearly 5000 years ago. This drawing was borrowed by several ancient tribes (**2**) in the Middle East. They simplified the drawing and gave it the shape that it has had throughout most of the history of the alphabet. The ancient Greeks (**3**) borrowed this letter, but changed its shape by reversing it and turning it upside-down. The older form of **L** was borrowed by an ancient tribe (**4**) that settled north of Rome about 2800 years ago. The Romans (**5**), who borrowed much of their alphabet from this tribe, also used this older form. By about 2400 years ago, the Romans were writing this letter in almost the same way that we write the capital letter **L** today (**6**).

l, L The twelfth letter of the alphabet.
l, L (el) *noun, plural* **l's, L's.**

lab A room for teaching science; laboratory.
lab (lab) *noun, plural* **labs.**

label A piece of cloth or paper fastened to something. The shirt has a *label* inside the collar with the maker's name on it. *Noun.*
—To put a label on. Jean will *label* the Christmas presents. *Verb.*
la·bel (lā′bəl) *noun, plural* **labels;** *verb,* **labeled, labeling.**

labor **1.** Hard work; toil. The farmer was tired after his *labor* in the corn field. **2.** People who do hard work for a living; workers as a group. *Labor* supported the senator when he ran for a new term. *Noun.*
—**1.** To do hard work. The men *labored* all day in the coal mine. **2.** To move slowly and with difficulty. The boy *labored* up the steep hill on his bicycle. *Verb.*
la·bor (lā′bər) *noun, plural* **labors;** *verb,* **labored, laboring.**

laboratory A room for teaching science or for doing scientific experiments.
lab·o·ra·to·ry (lab′ər ə tôr′ē *or* lab′rə tôr′ē) *noun, plural* **laboratories.**

laborer A person who does hard work; worker. That law was passed to protect *laborers* from poor working conditions.
la·bor·er (lā′bər ər) *noun, plural* **laborers.**

lace **1.** A string or cord used to pull or hold parts together. The *lace* on Carl's shoe broke. **2.** An open pattern of fine threads. The dress was trimmed with *lace. Noun.*
—To pull or hold together with a string or cord. Tim *laced* up his shoes. *Verb.*
lace (lās) *noun, plural* **laces;** *verb,* **laced, lacing.**

lack To be without; need. The town *lacks* a good park. The selfish boy *lacks* concern for other people. *Verb.*
—**1.** The needing of something. The *lack* of rain caused the farmer's crop to fail. **2.** Something needed. The most serious *lack* in his character is honesty. *Noun.*
lack (lak) *verb,* **lacked, lacking;** *noun, plural* **lacks.**

Lace

lacquer A substance that is put on wood or metal. It dries quickly to form a shiny coat.
lac·quer (lak′ər) *noun, plural* **lacquers.**

lacrosse A game played with a ball and a special racket that has a net on the end. Two teams of ten players each play the game. The object is to get the ball into a goal.
la·crosse (lə krôs′) *noun.*

355

▲ The name **lacrosse** comes from the French word for the staff that a bishop carries. French explorers first saw lacrosse played by Indians in Canada. Supposedly, they thought that the Indians' lacrosse sticks looked like a bishop's staff.

Lacrosse

lad A young fellow; boy. The proud man said his grandson was a fine *lad*.
lad (lad) *noun, plural* **lads.**

ladder A thing used for climbing. A ladder is made of two long poles with rungs fastened to them.
lad·der (lad′ər) *noun, plural* **ladders.**

Ladder

laden Filled; loaded. The pirate's chest was *laden* with jewels.
lad·en (lād′ən) *adjective.*

ladle A spoon with a long handle. A ladle has a bowl shaped like a cup. It is used to scoop out liquids.
la·dle (lād′əl) *noun, plural* **ladles.**

lady 1. Any woman. "There is a *lady* at the door to see you," Mark said. 2. A woman of high social position. 3. A girl or woman who is polite or has good manners. 4. **Lady.** In Great Britain, a woman of noble rank.
la·dy (lā′dē) *noun, plural* **ladies.**

▲ The word **lady** comes from an Old English word that meant "someone who kneads a loaf of bread." In former times, one of the jobs that a woman had was to make bread.

ladybug A small, round insect. It is bright red or orange with black spots. It eats insects that are harmful to plants.
la·dy·bug (lā′dē-bug′) *noun, plural* **ladybugs.**

Ladybug

lag To fall behind; move too slowly. The little boy always *lags* behind his older brothers, who can walk faster. *Verb.*
—A falling behind. After we saw the lightning, there was a *lag* of a few seconds before we heard the thunder. *Noun.*
lag (lag) *verb,* **lagged, lagging;** *noun, plural* **lags.**

lagoon A shallow body of water partly cut off from a larger body of water. A lagoon sometimes has a narrow strip of land or a coral reef going part way around it.
la·goon (lə gōōn′) *noun, plural* **lagoons.**

laid Martha *laid* the book on the table. Look up **lay** for more information.
laid (lād) *verb.*

lain The toys have *lain* on the floor all day. Look up **lie** for more information. ▲ Another word that sounds like this is **lane.**
lain (lān) *verb.*

lair A place where a wild animal lives or rests; den. The fox's *lair* was in a hole under the ground.
lair (ler) *noun, plural* **lairs.**

lake A body of water surrounded by land.
lake (lāk) *noun, plural* **lakes.**

lamb 1. A young sheep. 2. The meat from a lamb.
lamb (lam) *noun, plural* **lambs.**

lame 1. Not able to walk well. She was *lame* because she had hurt her leg. The *lame* man has to walk with a cane. 2. Stiff and painful. My back is *lame* from moving the heavy chest. 3. Poor or weak. He gave a *lame* excuse for not doing his homework. *Adjective.*
—To make lame. The accident had *lamed* him. *Verb.*

lame (lām) *adjective,* **lamer, lamest;** *verb,* **lamed, laming.**

lamp An object that gives off light. Some lamps hold light bulbs and work by electricity. Other lamps burn oil, kerosene, or gas to provide light.
lamp (lamp) *noun, plural* **lamps.**

lance A long spear. A lance is made of a wooden pole with a sharp metal point at one end. The knights were armed with *lances. Noun.*
—To cut open with a sharp instrument. The doctor *lanced* the boil on her arm so that the infection could drain. *Verb.*
lance (lans) *noun, plural* **lances;** *verb,* **lanced, lancing.**

Lance

land 1. The part of the earth's surface that is not under water; ground. The sailors were happy to stand on *land* after many weeks at sea. The *land* around our house is low and rocky. 2. A country or region. She went to Europe to visit foreign *lands. Noun.*
—1. To reach land; come to the ground. The ship *landed* at the dock. The airplane *landed* safely at the airport. 2. To come or bring ashore. The troops have *landed.* 3. To end up or cause to end up. Stealing apples from the store may *land* him in trouble. *Verb.*
land (land) *noun, plural* **lands;** *verb,* **landed, landing.**

landing 1. The act of reaching land; coming to the ground. The war started with the *landing* of the enemy soldiers. The airplane had a smooth *landing.* 2. The place on a dock or pier where people and goods are brought ashore. Crates were piled on the *landing* to be loaded onto the waiting trucks. 3. An area at the end of a flight of stairs. Steve went up the stairs and stopped on the *landing* to wait for his friend.
land·ing (lan′ding) *noun, plural* **landings.**

landlady 1. A woman who owns houses or apartments that she rents to other people.
2. A woman who runs an inn or boarding house.
land·la·dy (land′lā′dē) *noun, plural* **landladies.**

landlord 1. A man who owns houses or apartments that he rents to other people. 2. A man who runs an inn or boarding house.
land·lord (land′lôrd′) *noun, plural* **landlords.**

landmark 1. An object that is familiar and serves as a guide. The church steeple is a well-known *landmark* in our town. 2. An important event. The first landing of men on the moon was a *landmark* in history.
land·mark (land′märk′) *noun, plural* **landmarks.**

landscape 1. A scene or view on land. Joan watched the passing *landscape* from the train window. 2. A picture of such a scene. The artist painted a *landscape. Noun.*
—To make an area of land more beautiful by planting trees, shrubs, and gardens. Dad *landscaped* the yard around our house. *Verb.*
land·scape (land′skāp′) *noun, plural* **landscapes;** *verb,* **landscaped, landscaping.**

landslide 1. The sliding down of rocks and soil. We could hear the rumble of a *landslide* on the mountainside. 2. A great victory in an election. The mayor won by a *landslide.*
land·slide (land′slīd′) *noun, plural* **landslides.**

lane 1. A narrow way or road. The boy walked down the country *lane.* 2. A route for traffic going in one direction. The cars kept in the right-hand *lane* on the highway. ▲ Another word that sounds like this is **lain.**
lane (lān) *noun, plural* **lanes.**

language 1. Human speech; spoken or written words. We are able to express our thoughts and feelings by means of language. 2. The speech of a country or group. In Mexico, people speak the Spanish *language.* Different tribes of American Indians spoke different *languages.* 3. A way of expressing thoughts and feelings without words. Many deaf people use sign *language.*
lan·guage (lang′gwij) *noun, plural* **languages.**

▲ The word **language** comes from a Latin word that means "tongue," probably because we use the tongue to speak.

at; āpe; cär; end; mē; it; īce; hot; ōld;
fôrk; wood; fōōl; oil; out; up; turn; sing;
thin; <u>th</u>is; **hw** in white; **zh** in treasure.
ə stands for **a** in about, **e** in taken
i in pencil, **o** in lemon, and **u** in circus.

lantern A covering for a light. Some lanterns are made of metal with sides of glass. Most lanterns can be carried. The boy took the *lantern* with him to light up the tent.
lan·tern (lan′tərn) *noun, plural* **lanterns.**

Lantern

lap¹ The front part of a seated person between the waist and the knees.
lap (lap) *noun, plural* **laps.**

lap² To lie partly over another; extend over. She arranged the magazines on the table so that they would *lap* over each other. *Verb.*
—A going over the entire length of something. The boy ran three *laps* around the track. *Noun.*
lap (lap) *verb,* **lapped, lapping;** *noun, plural* **laps.**

lap³ **1.** To drink a liquid by lifting it up with the tongue. The kitten *lapped* her milk. **2.** To wash or move against gently. Waves *lap* against the shore.
lap (lap) *verb,* **lapped, lapping.**

lapel The front part of a coat or jacket that is folded back. Michael's new jacket has wide *lapels.*
la·pel (lə pel′) *noun, plural* **lapels.**

larch A tall tree that is like the pine. It sheds its needles and cones in the fall.
larch (lärch) *noun, plural* **larches.**

lard A soft, white fat. Lard comes from pigs and hogs. It is used in cooking.
lard (lärd) *noun, plural* **lards.**

large Big in size or amount. Carol lives in a *large* house. Toby has a *large* stamp collection.
large (lärj) *adjective,* **larger, largest.**

Lapel

large intestine The lower part of the intestines. Food matter goes from the small intestine into the large intestine.
large in·tes·tine (in tes′tin).

largely Mostly. The houses on that street are *largely* made of wood.
large·ly (lärj′lē) *adverb.*

lariat A long rope with a loop at one end. It is used to rope animals. The cowboy roped the calf with a *lariat.*
lar·i·at (lar′ē ət) *noun, plural* **lariats.**

▲ The word **lariat** comes from two Spanish words that mean "the rope."

lark¹ A small songbird with gray-brown feathers. Larks live in most parts of the world. The lark is known for its beautiful song.
lark (lärk) *noun, plural* **larks.**

lark² Something done for fun. The children went running through the snow for a *lark.*
lark (lärk) *noun, plural* **larks.**

larkspur A plant that has tall stalks of blue, purple, or white flowers.
lark·spur (lärk′spur′) *noun, plural* **larkspurs.**

Larkspur

larva The form of an insect in which it looks like a worm. It hatches from an egg and spends all its time eating. The caterpillar is the larva of a moth or butterfly, and the grub is the larva of a beetle.
lar·va (lär′və) *noun, plural* **larvae.**

▲ The word **larva** comes from a Latin word that means "mask." People used to think that this stage in an insect's growth hid or "masked" the way the insect would finally look.

larynx The top part of a person's windpipe. The larynx holds the vocal cords.
lar·ynx (lar′ingks) *noun, plural* **larynxes.**

laser A device that makes a very strong beam of light. The laser is used in medicine and in certain industries.
la·ser (lā′zər) *noun, plural* **lasers.**

lash¹ **1.** A blow with a whip. The cruel man gave the horse a *lash* with his whip. **2.** A small, stiff hair that grows on the edge of the eyelid; eyelash. *Noun.*

—**1.** To beat with a whip. The farmer *lashed* the stubborn mule. **2.** To strike against with force. Violent winds *lashed* the trees and houses on the island. **3.** To move back and forth quickly. The tiger *lashed* its tail in anger. *Verb.*

lash (lash) *noun, plural* **lashes;** *verb,* **lashed, lashing.**

lash² To tie with a rope. Bob and Joe *lashed* the boards together to make a raft.

lash (lash) *verb,* **lashed, lashing.**

lasso A long rope with a loop. It is used to rope animals. The cowboy used the *lasso* to capture the wild horse. *Noun.*
—To rope with a lasso. The cowboys will *lasso* the steer. *Verb.*

las·so (las′ō *or* la so͞o′) *noun, plural* **lassos** or **lassoes;** *verb,* **lassoed, lassoing.**

Lasso

last¹ **1.** Coming at the end; final. December is the *last* month of the year. Tom spent his *last* dollar on a present for his friend. **2.** Most recent; latest. Joel was nine years old on his *last* birthday. We watched television *last* night. **3.** Most unlikely. A giraffe is the *last* thing you would expect to see in the middle of Main Street. *Adjective.*
—**1.** At the end. We ate the ice cream *last* at the party. **2.** Most recently. When did Aunt Mary *last* write to us? I *last* saw Jane yesterday morning. *Adverb.*
—A person or thing that is last. I was the *last* in line in the lunchroom. *Noun.*

last (last) *adjective; adverb; noun.*

last² **1.** To go on; continue. The television show will *last* an hour. **2.** To stay in good condition. That coat will *last* if you take care of it.

last (last) *verb,* **lasted, lasting.**

lasting That lasts; continuing; permanent. That statue is a *lasting* monument to Abraham Lincoln.

last·ing (las′ting) *adjective.*

latch A fastening for holding a door, window, or gate closed. A latch is a piece of metal or wood that fits into place in a notch or groove. Sara lifted the *latch* to open the gate. *Noun.*
—To fasten or close the latch of something. George forgot to *latch* the door to the cabinet. *Verb.*

latch (lach) *noun, plural* **latches;** *verb,* **latched, latching.**

late **1.** Coming after the usual time. She was *late* to school today. Al had a *late* lunch. **2.** Coming near the end. It was *late* in the afternoon when we started our trip. **3.** Most recent; last. Dad bought a *late* model car. **4.** Recently dead. Jack's *late* uncle was a judge. *Adjective.*
—After the usual time. We arrived *late* at the party. They stayed up *late* last night. *Adverb.*

late (lāt) *adjective,* **later, latest;** *adverb.*

lately Not long ago; recently. Have you seen Paul *lately?*

late·ly (lāt′lē) *adverb.*

lateral On the side; to the side. A *lateral* pass in football is a pass made to one side rather than forward or backward.

lat·er·al (lat′ər əl) *adjective.*

lathe A machine that holds a long piece of wood or metal and spins it around, while a cutting tool is pressed against the spinning wood or metal to shape it. The table leg was shaped on a *lathe.*

lathe (lāth) *noun, plural* **lathes.**

lather **1.** Foam made by mixing soap and water. This shampoo makes a rich *lather.* **2.** Foam caused by sweating. The horse was covered with *lather* from pulling the plow. *Noun.*
—**1.** To form a lather. This soap does not *lather* well in cold water. **2.** To cover with lather. Bill *lathered* his face with soap before shaving. *Verb.*

lath·er (la*th*′ər) *noun, plural* **lathers;** *verb,* **lathered, lathering.**

at; āpe; cär; end; mē; it; īce; hot; ōld;
fôrk; wood; fo͞ol; oil; out; up; turn; sing;
thin; *th*is; hw in white; zh in treasure.
ə stands for a in about, e in taken
i in pencil, o in lemon, and u in circus.

Latin **1.** The language of the ancient Romans. **2.** A person who speaks a language that comes from Latin. The Italians, Spanish, French, and Portuguese are Latins. *Noun.*
—**1.** Having to do with Latin. She is studying *Latin* grammar. **2.** Having to do with the people or countries that use languages coming from Latin, Spain and Mexico are Latin countries. *Adjective.*
Lat·in (lat′in) *noun, plural* **Latins;** *adjective.*

latitude Distance measured on the earth's surface north and south of the equator. On a map or globe, lines of latitude are drawn running east and west. Latitude is expressed in degrees. Each degree is equal to around sixty-nine miles.
lat·i·tude (lat′ə-tōōd′ *or* lat′ə-tyōōd′) *noun, plural* **latitudes.**

Lines of Latitude

latter **1.** The second of two things mentioned. Of baseball and football, I like the *latter* sport best. **2.** Near the end; later. He spends the *latter* part of each day doing his homework.
lat·ter (lat′ər) *adjective.*

lattice A framework of thin strips of wood or metal placed across each other with open spaces between them. There were *lattices* on the windows of the cottage.
lat·tice (lat′is) *noun, plural* **lattices.**

laugh To make sounds that show amusement or happiness. The boys *laughed* at the joke. The children *laughed* at the silly monkeys in the zoo. *Verb.*
—The act or sound of laughing. The *laughs* of the audience filled the theater. *Noun.*
laugh (laf) *verb,* **laughed, laughing;** *noun, plural* **laughs.**

laughter The act or sound of laughing. The children's *laughter* showed that they were having fun at the party. We could hear *laughter* coming from the playground.
laugh·ter (laf′tər) *noun.*

launch¹ **1.** To start in motion; send off. The men at the space center will *launch* a rocket ship. **2.** To put into the water. The sailors *launched* the sailboat. **3.** To start something. The woman *launched* her political career by running for the city council.
launch (lônch) *verb,* **launched, launching.**

launch² A small, partly open motorboat.
launch (lônch) *noun, plural* **launches.**

launching pad A platform from which a rocket or missile is launched.

laundry **1.** A place where clothes, sheets, and other things are washed. We sent the shirts to the *laundry.* **2.** Things that have been washed or are to be washed. I put the *laundry* in the washing machine.
laun·dry (lôn′drē) *noun, plural* **laundries.**

laurel An evergreen tree that has stiff, pointed leaves. In ancient times, people placed wreathes made of laurel leaves on the heads of heroes.
lau·rel (lôr′əl) *noun, plural* **laurels.**

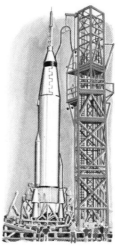
Launching Pad

lava **1.** Melted rock that comes out of a volcano when it erupts. **2.** Rock formed by lava that has cooled and hardened.
la·va (lä′və *or* lav′ə) *noun.*

lavender **1.** A plant that has pleasant-smelling light-purple flowers. The dried leaves and flowers of the lavender are used in chests or closets to give a pleasant odor to clothes and sheets. Oil from the flowers is used in perfumes. **2.** A light-purple color. *Noun.*
—Having the color lavender; light-purple. *Adjective.*
lav·en·der (lav′ən-dər) *noun, plural* **lavenders;** *adjective.*

Lavender

law **1.** A rule made by a government for all the people in a town, state, or country. Our state has *laws* against driving too fast. **2.** A set or system of such rules. The *law* of America is based on the system used in England. Robbery, kidnaping, and murder are against the *law.* **3.** The profession of a lawyer. My older brother is interested in *law* as a career. **4.** Any rule. This science book tells us about the *law* of gravity.
law (lô) *noun, plural* **laws.**

lawn An area with mowed grass around a house or other building.

lawn (lôn) *noun, plural* **lawns.**

lawn mower A machine with blades for cutting grass.

lawyer A person who knows a great deal about law. A lawyer gives legal advice and represents people in court.

law·yer (lô′yər) *noun, plural* **law-yers.**

Lawn Mower

lay¹ **1.** To put or place. Dan always *lays* his coat over the chair. *Lay* the plates on the table. **2.** To put down and fasten in place. The workman will *lay* the new carpet. **3.** To produce an egg or eggs. The chickens *lay* every day. ▲ Another word that sounds like this is **lei.**

lay (lā) *verb,* **laid, laying.**

lay² When he came home, he *lay* down to rest. Look up **lie** for more information. ▲ Another word that sounds like this is **lei.**

lay (lā) *verb.*

layer **1.** One thickness of something. A *layer* of dust covered the table. The wall has several *layers* of paint. **2.** A chicken that lays eggs.

lay·er (lā′ər) *noun, plural* **layers.**

lazy Not willing to work. The *lazy* boy would not put away his clothes.

la·zy (lā′zē) *adjective,* **lazier, laziest.**

lead¹ **1.** To show the way. The dog *leads* the blind man across streets. **2.** To go or be first; be ahead of others. The general will *lead* the parade. Our team *leads* by a score of three to nothing. Carol *leads* the class in arithmetic. **3.** To be a way; go. This hall *leads* to the cafeteria. **4.** To be the head of; direct. That teacher *leads* the school orchestra. **5.** To live. Our doctor *leads* a busy life. *Verb.*
—**1.** The first position; being ahead. Hank took the *lead* in the race. **2.** Clue. The detective had a good *lead* as to who stole the money. *Noun.*

lead (lēd) *verb,* **led, leading;** *noun, plural* **leads.**

lead² **1.** A heavy, soft, gray metal. Lead is easy to bend and melt. It is used to make pipes and solder. Lead is a chemical element. **2.** A thin piece of a soft, black substance in a pencil. ▲ Another word that sounds like this is **led.**

lead (led) *noun, plural* **leads.**

leader A person who leads. My brother is the *leader* of the school band. Sue was the *leader* in the swimming race.

lead·er (lē′dər) *noun, plural* **leaders.**

leaf **1.** One of the flat, green parts of a plant. A leaf grows from a stem. **2.** A sheet of paper. Al tore a *leaf* out of his notebook. *Noun.*
—**1.** To grow leaves. Many trees *leaf* in the spring. **2.** To turn pages and glance at them quickly. Ann *leafed* through a magazine while waiting in the dentist's office. *Verb.*

leaf (lēf) *noun, plural* **leaves;** *verb,* **leafed, leafing.**

Compound Leaf

Simple Leaf

leaflet A small printed sheet. This game comes with a *leaflet* that gives the rules. The candidate for office handed out *leaflets* to people on the street.

leaf·let (lēf′lit) *noun, plural* **leaflets.**

league¹ A number of people, groups, or countries joined together for a common purpose. Those two baseball teams belong to the same *league.*

league (lēg) *noun, plural* **leagues.**

league² A measure of distance that was used in former times. A league is equal to three miles.

league (lēg) *noun, plural* **leagues.**

leak A hole or tear that lets something pass through by accident. The *leak* in the milk carton let the milk drip out on the table. The tire went flat because of a *leak. Noun.*
—**1.** To have a leak. The roof of that old

at; āpe; cär; end; mē; it; īce; hot; ōld;
fôrk; wood; fool; oil; out; up; turn; sing;
thin; this; hw in white; zh in treasure.
ə stands for a in about, e in taken
i in pencil, o in lemon, and u in circus.

house *leaks*. **2.** To pass through a hole or tear. All the air *leaked* out of the tire. **3.** To let something secret become known. The man *leaked* the government secret to the newspapers. *Verb.* ▲ Another word that sounds like this is **leek.**

leak (lēk) *noun, plural* **leaks;** *verb,* **leaked, leaking.**

lean¹ **1.** To be at a slant; bend. The walls of the old shed *lean* out. **2.** To rest on a person or thing for support. *Lean* on my arm. She *leaned* on the chair. Tom *leans* on his older brother for help. **3.** To put something at a slant. Ed *leaned* the fishing pole against the wall.

lean (lēn) *verb,* **leaned, leaning.**

lean² **1.** Having little or no fat; not fat. That boy is tall and *lean*. She buys *lean* meat at the butcher shop. **2.** Not producing much; poor. That was a *lean* year for farmers.

lean (lēn) *adjective,* **leaner, leanest.**

leap To jump. Philip *leaped* to his feet. The horse *leaped* the fence. *Verb.*
—A jump. The cat made a *leap* from the open window. *Noun.*

leap (lēp) *verb,* **leaped** or **leapt, leaping;** *noun, plural* **leaps.**

leapfrog A game in which players take turns leaping over the backs of other players.

leap·frog (lēp′- frôg′ *or* lēp′frog′) *noun.*

leap year A year that has an extra day, February 29. Leap year comes every four years.

learn **1.** To get to know something by study or practice; gain knowledge or skill. He wants to *learn* to speak French. Annette *learned* how to swim this summer. **2.** To memorize. Jack

Leapfrog

learned his lines for the school play quickly. **3.** To find out about something. He never *learned* who had taken his bicycle.

learn (lurn) *verb,* **learned, learning.**

learned Having or showing knowledge. Our teacher is a *learned* person.

learn·ed (lur′nid) *adjective.*

learning Knowledge gained by careful study or practice. This book about ancient Rome was written by a man of *learning*.

learn·ing (lur′ning) *noun, plural* **learnings.**

lease A written agreement for renting a house, apartment, or land. Mr. Barton signed a *lease* for the apartment for three years and agreed to pay $200 per month rent. *Noun.*
—To rent. The family *leased* a house for the summer. *Verb.*

lease (lēs) *noun, plural* **leases;** *verb,* **leased, leasing.**

leash A strap or chain for holding or tying an animal. Jean fastened a *leash* to the dog's collar. *Noun.*
—To hold or tie with a leash. She *leashed* her puppy to take it for a walk. *Verb.*

leash (lēsh) *noun, plural* **leashes;** *verb,* **leashed, leashing.**

Leash

least Smallest. A second is the *least* amount of time that is shown on a watch. Jack did the *least* amount of work of any of the boys. *Adjective.*
—Something that is least. Saying he is sorry for breaking the vase is the *least* he can do. *Noun.*
—In the smallest degree. That boy is the *least* friendly person in the class. *Adverb.*

least (lēst) *adjective; noun; adverb.*

leather A material made from an animal skin that has been tanned. Leather is used for making shoes, gloves, jackets, and many other things.

leath·er (leth′ər) *noun, plural* **leathers.**

leave¹ **1.** To go from one place to another place; go away. She has to *leave* and go home. The plane *leaves* at six o'clock. You may *leave* the table if you have finished eating. **2.** To withdraw from; quit. He will *leave* the softball team. My older sister may *leave* her job. **3.** To let something stay behind. He *left* a note on his friend's desk. Dad will *leave* his suit at the cleaners. Sam *left* his notebook at school. **4.** To let stay in a certain way. He often *leaves* his work unfinished. *Leave* her alone. The good news *left* her feeling happy. **5.** To let another do something. Jerry told her to *leave* the cleaning to him. **6.** To give in a will. He will *leave* the house to his wife. **7.** To have left over. 10 minus 3 *leaves* 7.

leave (lēv) *verb,* **left, leaving.**

leave² **1.** Permission; consent. Dad gave us

leave to go camping overnight. **2.** Permission to be absent. The soldier asked for a *leave* so he could visit his sick mother.
leave (lēv) *noun, plural* **leaves.**

leaves More than one leaf. Look up **leaf** for more information.
leaves (lēvz) *noun plural.*

lecture **1.** A talk given to an audience. The famous writer gave a *lecture* on his travels in Japan. **2.** A scolding. Dad gave Mark a *lecture* for breaking the window. *Noun.*
—**1.** To give a lecture. Mr. Brown *lectures* on science at the college. **2.** To scold. The teacher *lectured* us for not doing our homework. *Verb.*
lec·ture (lek′chər) *noun, plural* **lectures;** *verb,* **lectured, lecturing.**

led The guide *led* the hunters through the forest. Look up **lead** for more information. ▲ Another word that sounds like this is **lead.**
led (led) *verb.*

ledge A narrow shelf. A window *ledge* juts out from the wall of a building. The climbers rested on a *ledge* of the mountain.
ledge (lej) *noun, plural* **ledges.**

lee A side of a ship sheltered from the wind. *Noun.*
—Sheltered from the wind. The sailors stayed on the *lee* side of the ship. *Adjective.*
lee (lē) *noun, plural* **lees;** *adjective.*

leech A worm that sucks blood. Leeches are found in ponds, rivers, and damp soil.
leech (lēch) *noun, plural* **leeches.**

leek A plant with long, thick leaves. It tastes like a mild onion. The leaves and bulb of the leek are eaten as vegetables. ▲ Another word that sounds like this is **leak.**
leek (lēk) *noun, plural* **leeks.**

left¹ On the west side of your body when you face north. Carl writes with his *left* hand. Nancy walked on the *left* side of the road. *Adjective.*
—The left side. His brother is standing on his *left* in the photograph. *Noun.*
—Toward the left. Turn *left* at the next corner. *Adverb.*
left (left) *adjective; noun; adverb.*

left² I *left* my books at home. Look up **leave** for more information.
left (left) *verb.*

left-hand **1.** On the left. Look in the *left-hand* drawer. **2.** For the left hand. She lost her *left-hand* glove.
left-hand (left′hand′) *adjective.*

left-handed **1.** Using the left hand more easily than the right hand. My sister is *left-handed*. **2.** Done with the left hand. Ken made a *left-handed* pass to the halfback.
left-hand·ed (left′han′did) *adjective.*

leftover Something that is left. Mother used the *leftovers* from last night's turkey dinner for our lunch.
left·o·ver (left′ō′vər) *noun, plural* **leftovers.**

leg **1.** One of the parts of the body that a person or animal stands and walks on. **2.** Something like a leg. The *leg* of the chair is broken.
leg (leg) *noun, plural* **legs.**
to pull one's leg. To trick or tease. Gail was only *pulling your leg* when she told you she was going to run away from home.

legal **1.** Having to do with law. He went to a lawyer for *legal* help. **2.** Allowed by law; lawful. He is the *legal* owner of the farm.
le·gal (lē′gəl) *adjective.*

legend A story passed down through the years that many people have believed, but that is not entirely true. There are many *legends* about the adventures of Robin Hood.
leg·end (lej′ənd) *noun, plural* **legends.**

legendary Of or having to do with legends. Paul Bunyan is a *legendary* character.
leg·end·ar·y (lej′ən der′ē) *adjective.*

leggings Coverings of cloth or leather for the legs. My little brother wears *leggings* when he goes out to play in the snow.
leg·gings (leg′ingz) *noun plural.*

Leggings

legible Easily read. His writing is not *legible* because it is so sloppy.
leg·i·ble (lej′ə bəl) *adjective.*

legion **1.** A unit of the army of ancient Rome. A legion had several thousand soldiers and several hundred men on horseback. **2.** An army. The enemy sent its *legions* to conquer the small country.
le·gion (lē′jən) *noun, plural* **legions.**

legislation **1.** The making or passing of laws. The work of the Senate and House of

at; āpe; cär; end; mē; it; īce; hot; ōld;
fôrk; wood; fool; oil; out; up; turn; sing;
thin; this; hw in white; zh in treasure.
ə stands for a in about, e in taken
i in pencil, o in lemon, and u in circus.

Representatives is *legislation*. **2.** The laws that are made. Congress passed new *legislation* dealing with housing.

leg·is·la·tion (lej′is lā′shən) *noun*.

legislative **1.** Of or having to do with making or passing laws. Senators and Congressmen have *legislative* duties. **2.** Having the power to make or pass laws. Congress is the *legislative* branch of the federal government.

leg·is·la·tive (lej′is lā′tiv) *adjective*.

legislature A body of persons elected to make or pass laws. The state *legislature* voted on a new tax bill.

leg·is·la·ture (lej′is-lā′chər) *noun*, *plural* **legislatures.**

Lei

legitimate According to what is right or lawful. The judge ruled that Mr. Goodwin was the *legitimate* owner of the house. The boy could not give a *legitimate* excuse for being late.

le·git·i·mate (li jit′ə mit) *adjective*.

lei A wreath of flowers or leaves. Leis are often worn around the neck in Hawaii. ▲ Another word that sounds like this is **lay.**

lei (lā) *noun*, *plural* **leis.**

leisure The time to do what you like; free time. The busy farmer did not have much *leisure. Noun.*
—Free. Kathy spends much of her *leisure* time playing tennis. *Adjective.*

lei·sure (lē′zhər *or* lezh′ər) *noun; adjective.*

lemon A yellow fruit with a sour taste. Lemons grow on small, thorny trees in warm regions. *Noun.*
—Made from lemon; flavored with lemon. Mother baked a *lemon* pie. *Adjective.*

lem·on (lem′ən) *noun, plural* **lemons;** *adjective.*

Lemons

lemonade A kind of drink made from lemon juice, water, and sugar.

lem·on·ade (lem′ə nād′) *noun, plural* **lemonades.**

lend **1.** To let someone have or use something for awhile. Please *lend* me your baseball glove for the game. **2.** To give someone money to use for a certain period of time at a set rate of interest. The bank will *lend* Mr. Brown $5000 to buy a car. **3.** To provide; give. The bright lights *lend* an air of excitement to the city.

lend (lend) *verb,* **lent, lending.**

length **1.** The distance from one end to the other end. The *length* of the room is ten feet. The *length* of the football field is one hundred yards. **2.** The amount of time from beginning to end. My vacation was three months in *length.* The *length* of the movie is two hours. **3.** A piece of something. Greg bought a *length* of rope.

length (lengkth *or* length) *noun, plural* **lengths.**

lengthen To make or become longer. Mother will *lengthen* Sue's dress. The days *lengthened* as summer grew near.

length·en (lengk′thən *or* leng′thən) *verb,* **lengthened, lengthening.**

lengthwise In the direction of the length. Jack split the log *lengthwise.* She gave the towel a *lengthwise* fold.

length·wise (lengkth′wīz′ *or* length′wīz′) *adverb; adjective.*

lens **1.** A piece of glass or other clear material that is curved to make light rays move apart or come together. A lens can make an object look larger or closer. Lenses are used in eyeglasses, telescopes, and microscopes. A magnifying glass is a lens. **2.** The part of the eye that focuses light rays onto the retina.

lens (lenz) *noun, plural* **lenses.**

lent I *lent* Jerry a pencil for the test. Look up **lend** for more information.

lent (lent) *verb.*

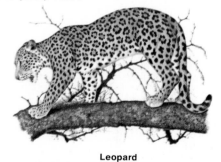

Leopard

leopard A large animal that lives in Africa and Asia. It is a member of the cat family. Leopards have a brownish-yellow coat with black spots.

leop·ard (lep′ərd) *noun, plural* **leopards.**

▲ The word **leopard** comes from two Greek words that mean "lion" and "panther." The ancient Greeks thought that a leopard was a cross between a lion and a panther.

less Ed has *less* work to do today than he had yesterday. She has *less* money than her sister has. Phil decided to eat *less* candy because he wanted to lose weight. This watch is *less* expensive than that one. I finished *less* of the work than I had planned. 10 *less* 7 is 3.
less (les) *adjective; adverb; noun; preposition.*

-less A *suffix* that means: **1.** "Without; having no." *Hopeless* means "having no hope." **2.** "That does not." *Endless* means "that does not end." **3.** "That cannot be." *Countless* means "that cannot be counted."

lessen To make or become less. The teacher *lessened* the amount of homework we had to do. The pain of his sprained ankle *lessened* after he soaked it in water. ▲ Another word that sounds like this is **lesson.**
less·en (les'ən) *verb,* **lessened, lessening.**

lesser Smaller or less. Of an inch and a foot, a foot is the larger distance and an inch is the *lesser.*
less·er (les'ər) *adjective.*

lesson **1.** Something that is learned or to be learned. Did you understand today's arithmetic *lesson?* We have five more *lessons* to study in our social studies book. **2.** A class or course of study. Ed has a piano *lesson* today. Carol is taking skating *lessons.* ▲ Another word that sounds like this is **lessen.**
les·son (les'ən) *noun, plural* **lessons.**

lest For fear that. He walked carefully on the icy street *lest* he slip and fall.
lest (lest) *conjunction.*

let **1.** To allow; permit. Mother *let* Fran go to the party. He *lets* his sister ride his bicycle. *Let* him alone! **2.** To allow to pass or go. The hole in the roof *lets* in the rain. Martha opened the cage and *let* the bird out. **3.** To cause or make. I will *let* Mom know what I want for my birthday. **4.** To rent. Mr. Brown *let* a summer house.
let (let) *verb,* **let, letting.**
to let down. To disappoint. He *let down* his friends when he didn't help them.
to let up. To lessen or stop. It seemed the rain would never *let up.*

let's *Let's* go for a walk.
let's (lets) contraction for "let us."

letter **1.** A mark that stands for a speech sound. The word "run" has three *letters.* **2.** A written message. Philip wrote a *letter* to his friend.
let·ter (let'ər) *noun, plural* **letters.**

lettuce A plant with large green leaves. Lettuce is eaten in salads.
let·tuce (let'is) *noun, plural* **lettuces.**

Lettuce

level **1.** Having a flat surface; even. The airport was built on *level* ground. **2.** At the same height. The top of the tree is *level* with the roof of the house. *Adjective.*
—**1.** A level surface. The hill is 100 feet above sea *level.* Dad parked the car on a lower *level* of the garage. **2.** Height. The flood in the basement rose to a *level* of two feet. **3.** A device used to show whether a surface is flat or not. The carpenter put a *level* on the shelf to make sure it was straight. *Noun.*
—To make flat. The men *leveled* the hilly land with a bulldozer. The fire *leveled* the house. *Verb.*
lev·el (lev'əl) *adjective; noun, plural* **levels;** *verb,* **leveled, leveling.**

lever **1.** A rod or bar used to lift things and pry things open. A crowbar is a kind of lever. **2.** A rod or bar attached to a machine. Carol pulled the *lever* on the gum machine to make the gum come out.
lev·er (lev'ər *or* lē'vər) *noun, plural* **levers.**

levy To collect by authority. The county plans to *levy* new taxes.
lev·y (lev'ē) *verb,* **levied, levying.**

liable **1.** Likely; apt. You are *liable* to catch cold if you don't dress warmly. **2.** Responsible by law. The owner of the car was *liable* for damages done to the other car.
li·a·ble (lī'ə bəl) *adjective.*

liar A person who tells lies.
li·ar (lī'ər) *noun, plural* **liars.**

liberal **1.** Generous. The rich man was *liberal* with his money. **2.** More than enough; plentiful. The school has a *liberal* supply of chalk.

at; āpe; cär; end; mē; it; īce; hot; ōld;
fôrk; wood; fōol; oil; out; up; turn; sing;
thin; this; hw in white; zh in treasure.
ə stands for a in about, e in taken
i in pencil, o in lemon, and u in circus.

3. Not narrow in one's thinking; broad-minded; tolerant. **4.** Wanting change for the better in political and social matters; favoring progress and reform. *Adjective.*
—A person who is liberal. *Noun.*
lib·er·al (lib′ər əl) *adjective; noun, plural* **liberals.**

liberate To set free. The soldiers *liberated* the prisoners.
lib·er·ate (lib′ə rāt′) *verb,* **liberated, liberating.**

liberty **1.** The ability to act, speak, or think the way one pleases. People have *liberty* in a free country. **2.** Freedom from another's control. England was forced to give the American colonies their *liberty.*
lib·er·ty (lib′ər tē) *noun, plural* **liberties.**

librarian A person who is in charge of a library.
li·brar·i·an (lī brer′ē ən) *noun, plural* **librarians.**

library **1.** A collection of books and magazines. Aunt Ruth gave Tom some books for his *library.* **2.** A room or building for such a collection. Mary went to the school *library* to study. I took out a book from the public *library.*
li·brar·y (lī′brer′ē) *noun, plural* **libraries.**

lice More than one louse. Look up **louse** for more information.
lice (līs) *noun plural.*

license A card, paper, or other object showing that a person has legal permission to do or have something. Sue's older sister has a driver's *license.* We must buy a dog *license* for our puppy. *Noun.*
—To give a license to a person. He is *licensed* to drive a bus. *Verb.*
li·cense (lī′səns) *noun, plural* **licenses;** *verb,* **licensed, licensing.**

lichen A plant without flowers that grows on tree trunks, rocks, or on the ground.
li·chen (lī′kən) *noun, plural* **lichens.**

lick **1.** To move the tongue over something. The kitten *licked* its paw. John *licked* the envelope to seal it. **2.** To eat or drink something by taking it up with the tongue. Alice *licked* the ice-cream cone. **3.** To defeat. Our football team *licked* their team. *Verb.*
—**1.** A movement of the tongue over something. She gave her lollipop a *lick.* **2.** Salt that animals can lick. The farmer put a block of salt in the pasture as a *lick* for the cows. **3.** A small amount; bit. The boy wouldn't do a *lick* of work. *Noun.*
lick (lik) *verb,* **licked, licking;** *noun, plural* **licks.**

licorice A sweet, black candy flavored with the juice from the root of a certain plant.
lic·o·rice (lik′ər is *or* lik′ər ish) *noun.*

▲ The word **licorice** comes from a Greek word that means "sweet root."

lid **1.** A movable cover. Mother lifted the *lid* off the garbage can. Jerry put the *lid* on the box. **2.** A fold of skin that can close over the eye; eyelid.
lid (lid) *noun, plural* **lids.**

lie[1] Something a person says that he knows is not true. A lie is told to fool people. She told a *lie* when she said she was at school today. *Noun.*
—To say something that is not true; tell a lie. That boy always *lies,* so you can't believe anything he says. *Verb.* ▲ Another word that sounds like this is **lye.**
lie (lī) *noun, plural* **lies;** *verb,* **lied, lying.**

lie[2] **1.** To put oneself in a flat position on a surface. I like to *lie* on the grass and watch the clouds. **2.** To be or rest on something. The book *lies* on the table. **3.** To stay in a certain place or condition. The treasure *lies* hidden at the bottom of the ocean. **4.** To be located or placed. Mexico *lies* south of the United States. **5.** To be found; exist. The future of our country *lies* in the hands of its young people. ▲ Another word that sounds like this is **lye.**
lie (lī) *verb,* **lay, lain, lying.**

lieutenant An army or navy officer. In the army, a lieutenant is next below a captain. The two ranks of lieutenant in the army are **second lieutenant** and **first lieutenant.** In the navy, a lieutenant is next below a commander. The two ranks of lieutenant in the navy are **lieutenant junior grade** and **lieutenant.**
lieu·ten·ant (l$\overline{oo}$ ten′ənt) *noun, plural* **lieutenants.**

▲ The word **lieutenant** comes from two French words that mean "taking the place of." At first, a lieutenant was someone who took the place of a person who held a higher rank or office.

life **1.** The quality that only plants and animals have. The quality of life makes it possible for them to grow and reproduce. Rocks do not have life. **2.** A living being; person. Firemen save many *lives* every year. **3.** The period from birth to death. His grandmother has had a long and happy *life.* **4.** The period during which something lasts or works. Poor

driving can shorten the *life* of a car. **5.** A way of living. City *life* can be exciting. **6.** A story of a person's life. I am reading a *life* of George Washington. **7.** Energy; spirit. Jim is always full of *life*.
　　life (līf) *noun, plural* **lives.**

lifeboat　A strong boat used for saving lives at sea. A lifeboat is usually carried on a larger ship.
　　life·boat (līf′bōt′) *noun, plural* **lifeboats.**

lifeguard　A person who works at a beach or swimming pool. A lifeguard is hired to protect and help swimmers.
　　life·guard (līf′gärd′) *noun, plural* **lifeguards.**

lifelike　Like life; copying real life. The doll was so *lifelike* that for a moment Jane thought it was a real baby.
　　life·like (līf′līk′) *adjective.*

life preserver　A device used to keep a person floating in water. A life preserver can be a belt, a jacket, or a round tube. It is usually made of cork or filled with air.

The man in the boat is wearing one kind of **life preserver** and he is throwing another kind to the man in the water.

lifetime　The period of time that a person lives or a thing lasts. That man has spent most of his *lifetime* as a teacher. The *lifetime* of a television set is about ten years.
　　life·time (līf′tīm′) *noun, plural* **lifetimes.**

lift　**1.** To raise or be raised; pick up. I can't *lift* this heavy suitcase. The team's spirits *lifted* after their victory over the league champions. **2.** To rise or seem to rise and go; disappear. When the fog *lifted,* we had a beautiful, clear day. *Verb.*
　　—1. The act of lifting. Give me a *lift* up into the tree. **2.** A free ride given to a person. Barbara's neighbor gave her a *lift* into town. **3.** A happy feeling. Jeff's compliment about her dress gave her a *lift. Noun.*
　　lift (lift) *verb,* **lifted, lifting;** *noun, plural* **lifts.**

lift-off　The action of a rocket or spacecraft as it rises from its launching pad. After the *lift-off,* the rocket started on its way to the moon.
　　lift-off (lift′ôf′) *noun, plural* **lift-offs.**

ligament　A band of strong tissue. A ligament connects bones or holds an organ of the body in place.
　　lig·a·ment (lig′ə mənt) *noun, plural* **ligaments.**

light¹　**1.** The form of energy that makes it possible for us to see. The sun gives off light. **2.** Something that gives off light or brightness. Candles and lamps are lights. Turn off the *light* when you leave the room. We could see the dim *lights* of a town in the distance. **3.** Something used to set fire to something else. A flame and a spark are lights. Give me a *light* so I can start the logs burning. **4.** Knowledge or information; understanding. The scientist's study shed new *light* on ways to prevent pollution. **5.** Public knowledge. Some new clues to the mystery have come to *light. Noun.*
　　—1. To burn or cause to burn. We will *light* candles if the electricity goes off. Wet wood will not *light* easily. **2.** To cause to give off light. When you *light* that lamp, it brightens up the whole room. **3.** To give brightness to. One large bulb *lights* the long hallway. **4.** To make or become bright or lively. Her face *lighted* up when she heard she had won the contest. **5.** To show the way by means of a light or lights. Please *light* our way up these dark steps with your flashlight. *Verb.*
　　—1. Bright; not dark. The room was *light* and airy. **2.** Pale in color. She has a *light* complexion and sunburns easily. *Adjective.*
　　light (līt) *noun, plural* **lights;** *verb,* **lighted** or **lit, lighting;** *adjective,* **lighter, lightest.**

light²　**1.** Having little weight; not heavy. The empty box was *light.* A *light* rain fell. **2.** Easy to do or bear; not hard. Rod's father gave him only a *light* punishment for staying out late. **3.** Moving easily; graceful; nimble. Good dancers are *light* on their feet. **4.** Entertaining; amusing; not serious. When I feel sad, I read something *light* to cheer me up. **5.** Few or slight. The army suffered *light* losses in the battle.
　　light (līt) *adjective,* **lighter, lightest.**

lighten¹　To make or become lighter or brighter. The sky *lightened* after the thunderstorm was over.
　　light·en (līt′ən) *verb,* **lightened, lightening.**

at; āpe; cär; end; mē; it; īce; hot; ōld; fôrk; wood; fo͞ol; oil; out; up; turn; sing; thin; **th**is; hw in white; zh in treasure. ə stands for a in about, e in taken i in pencil, o in lemon, and u in circus.

lighten² **1.** To make the weight or load of something less. The teacher *lightened* their homework assignment because she felt she had given them too much work. **2.** To make more cheerful. Dan's spirits were *lightened* when he was told he had passed the test.
light·en (līt′ən) *verb,* **lightened, lightening.**

light-hearted Cheerful; gay. The *light-hearted* boy always had a smile on his face.
light-heart·ed (līt′här′tid) *adjective.*

Lighthouse

lighthouse A tower with a strong light. It is built near a dangerous place in the water to warn or guide ships.
light·house (līt′hous′) *noun, plural* **lighthouses.**

lightning A flash of light in the sky. It is caused by electricity between clouds or between a cloud and the ground.
light·ning (līt′ning) *noun.*

Lightning

like¹ He looks *like* his brother. An airplane is *like* a bird because both can fly. She does well in subjects *like* arithmetic and science. It was just *like* him to forget to send me a birthday card. It looks *like* rain. The twin sisters wore *like* dresses. We bought tomatoes, celery, lettuce, and the *like.*
like (līk) *preposition; adjective; noun.*

like² To be fond of; enjoy. He *likes* sports. I *like* her more than I did when I first met her. *Verb.*
—likes. The things a person enjoys or prefers. She has strong *likes* and dislikes in clothes. *Noun.*
like (līk) *verb,* **liked, liking;** *noun plural.*

-like A *suffix* that means "similar to or resembling." *Catlike* means "similar to a cat."

likelihood Something likely to happen. In all *likelihood,* I will leave tomorrow.
like·li·hood (līk′lē hood′) *noun.*

likely **1.** Seeming to be true; probable. She gave us a *likely* reason for arriving late, so we did not blame her. **2.** To be expected. The weatherman says that it is *likely* to rain tomorrow. **3.** Right for the time or purpose; suitable. William is a *likely* candidate for school president because he has many good ideas. *Adjective.*
—Probably. Judging from her good grades, she's most *likely* very smart. *Adverb.*
like·ly (līk′lē) *adjective,* **likelier, likeliest;** *adverb.*

likeness **1.** A being alike; resemblance. The two brothers' *likeness* was very close. **2.** A picture. A dollar bill has a *likeness* of George Washington on it.
like·ness (līk′nis) *noun, plural* **likenesses.**

likewise In a like way; similarly. Watch what the swimming teacher does and then do *likewise.*
like·wise (līk′wīz′) *adverb.*

liking A choosing of one thing over another. My sister Karen has a special *liking* for folk music.
lik·ing (lī′king) *noun, plural* **likings.**

lilac **1.** A bush that has clusters of purple, pink, or white flowers. **2.** A pale pinkish-purple color. *Noun.*
—Having a pale pinkish-purple color. *Adjective.*
li·lac (lī′lək) *noun, plural* **lilacs;** *adjective.*

lily **1.** A large flower that is shaped like a trumpet. The lily grows from a bulb and has narrow leaves. **2.** Any plant like a lily. A water lily grows in the water.
lil·y (lil′ē) *noun, plural* **lilies.**

lily of the valley A plant that has tiny sweet-smelling, bell-shaped flowers growing down one side of its stem.

lima bean A pale green, flat bean that is cooked and eaten as a vegetable.
li·ma bean (lī′mə).

limb 1. A part of the body that is used in moving or grasping. Arms, legs, wings, and flippers are limbs. 2. One of the large branches of a tree. We hung a swing from a *limb* of the old tree.
limb (lim) *noun, plural* **limbs.**

Lily of the Valley

lime¹ A white, powdery substance made up of calcium and oxygen. It is made by burning limestone. Lime is used in making cement and as a fertilizer.
lime (līm) *noun.*

lime² A small, yellowish-green fruit. The lime has an oval or round shape, a thin rind, and a juicy pulp. It grows on a thorny evergreen tree.
lime (līm) *noun, plural* **limes.**

Lime

limerick A funny poem five lines long. An example of a limerick is: There once was a man named Paul/Who went to a masquerade ball./He decided to risk it/And go as a biscuit/But a dog ate him up in the hall.
lim·er·ick (lim′ər ik) *noun, plural* **limericks.**

▲ The word **limerick** comes from the name of a place in Ireland. It was an old Irish custom for people to take turns making up funny poems at parties. At the end of a poem, everyone would sing the words "Will you come up to Limerick?" This may be how we came to use *limerick* as the name for these funny poems.

limestone A rock used for building and for making lime.
lime·stone (līm′stōn′) *noun.*

limit The point at which something ends. Stay inside the *limits* of the park. He drove faster than the speed *limit*. Mother reached the *limit* of her patience with my little brother, so she sent him to his room. *Noun.*
—To keep within a bound or bounds; restrict. I have to *limit* my spending because I'm trying to save money. *Verb.*
lim·it (lim′it) *noun, plural* **limits;** *verb,* **limited, limiting.**

limp¹ To walk slowly or with difficulty. The dog with the hurt leg *limped* home. *Verb.*
—A lame walk or movement. Judy walks with a *limp* because she sprained her ankle playing tennis. *Noun.*
limp (limp) *verb,* **limped, limping;** *noun, plural* **limps.**

limp² Not stiff or firm. After three days, the flowers became *limp* and died.
limp (limp) *adjective,* **limper, limpest.**

line¹ 1. A long, thin mark or stroke. A line is usually made by a pen, pencil, or tool. White *lines* divide the lanes of the highway. 2. Anything like a line. His forehead was full of *lines* from frowning. 3. A limit or boundary; edge. That row of trees marks the *line* of our property. 4. A number of persons or things arranged one after the other; row. We waited in a long *line* outside the movie theater. 5. A row of words or letters on a page. Jack wrote a column of thirty *lines* for the school newspaper. 6. A short letter, note, or verse. She dropped me a *line* thanking me for the gift I gave her. 7. **lines.** The spoken words of an actor or actress. Bob was so scared of acting in front of a large audience that he forgot his *lines*. 8. A kind of goods. That store is selling a new *line* of bicycles. 9. A system of transportation in which vehicles travel over a route on a regular schedule. The bus *line* runs buses on most of the main streets of the city. 10. A cord, rope, wire, or cable that is used for a special purpose. Mother hung the wash on the *line* to dry. I called Dick on the telephone, but his *line* was busy. *Noun.*
—1. To mark or cover with lines. I always *line* blank paper that I'm going to write on.

at; āpe; cär; end; mē; it; īce; hot; ōld;
fôrk; wood; fool; oil; out; up; turn; sing;
thin; this; hw in white; zh in treasure.
ə stands for a in about, e in taken
i in pencil, o in lemon, and u in circus.

2. To place or arrange in a line. The teacher *lined* the pupils up according to height. **3.** To form a line. We *lined* up for lunch in the school cafeteria. *Verb.*
line (līn) *noun, plural* **lines;** *verb,* **lined, lining.**

line² **1.** To cover the inside of. The tailor *lined* the wool suit with silk. **2.** To be used as a lining or covering for. Paintings *lined* the walls of the museum.
line (līn) *verb,* **lined, lining.**

linear **1.** Having to do with or made up of a line or lines. The builder made a *linear* drawing of the house. **2.** Having to do with length. Feet, miles, centimeters, and inches are *linear* measurements.
lin·e·ar (lin′ē ər) *adjective.*

linen **1.** A strong cloth woven from fibers of flax. It is used for dresses, suits, and tablecloths. **2. linens.** Household things made of linen or a similar cloth. Sheets, tablecloths, towels, and napkins are linens.
lin·en (lin′ən) *noun, plural* **linens.**

liner A ship or airplane that belongs to a transportation line. Mary sailed to Europe on an ocean *liner.*
lin·er (lī′nər) *noun, plural* **liners.**

linger To stay on as if not wanting to leave; move slowly. The fans *lingered* outside the locker room after the game to see the players on the winning team.
lin·ger (ling′gər) *verb,* **lingered, lingering.**

lining The layer or coating that covers the inside of something. The fur *lining* of the jacket made it very warm.
lin·ing (lī′ning) *noun, plural* **linings.**

link One of the rings or loops of a chain. *Noun.*
—To join or be joined like a link; connect. Everyone *linked* arms and formed a circle. *Verb.*
link (lingk) *noun, plural* **links;** *verb,* **linked, linking.**

linoleum A floor covering. It is made with a hardened mixture of linseed oil and finely ground cork or wood put on a canvas back.
li·no·le·um (li nō′lē əm) *noun, plural* **linoleums.**

linseed oil A yellow or brown oil. It comes from the seed of certain flax plants. Linseed oil is used to make paints, varnish, ink, patent leather, and linoleum.
lin·seed oil (lin′sēd′).

lintel A piece set above a door or window to support the structure above it.
lin·tel (lint′əl) *noun, plural* **lintels.**

lion A large, strong animal of the cat family. The lion lives mainly in Africa and southern Asia. It has a yellowish-brown coat of short, coarse hair and a tufted tail. The male has long, shaggy hair around its neck, head, and shoulders.
li·on (lī′ən) *noun, plural* **lions.**

Lion

lioness A female lion.
li·on·ess (lī′ə nis) *noun, plural* **lionesses.**

lip **1.** Either of the two folds of flesh that form the opening to the mouth. **2.** The edge or rim of an opening. I chipped the *lip* of the pitcher.
lip (lip) *noun, plural* **lips.**

lipstick A stick of wax used as a cosmetic for coloring the lips.
lip·stick (lip′stik′) *noun, plural* **lipsticks.**

liquid A form of matter that is not a solid or a gas. A liquid can flow freely. It can take on the shape of any container into which it is poured, but will not necessarily fill it. Water is a liquid. *Noun.*
—In the form of a liquid; not solid or gaseous. That cough medicine comes in *liquid* form. *Adjective.*
liq·uid (lik′wid) *noun, plural* **liquids;** *adjective.*

liquor An alcoholic drink. Whiskey, gin, and scotch are liquors.
liq·uor (lik′ər) *noun, plural* **liquors.**

lisp A way of speaking in which a person says the sound of *s* as the sound of *th* in *thing.* He also says the sound of *z* as the sound of *th* in *them.* *Noun.*
—To speak with a lisp. *Verb.*
lisp (lisp) *noun, plural* **lisps;** *verb,* **lisped, lisping.**

list¹ A series of names, numbers, or other things. He made a *list* of the groceries he needed for the week. *Noun.*
—To make a list of or enter in a list. She *listed* the students in her class. His name is *listed* in the telephone book. *Verb.*
list (list) *noun, plural* **lists;** *verb,* **listed, listing.**

list² A leaning to one side. The *list* of the sailboat was caused by the strong wind. *Noun.*
—To lean to one side; tilt. The ship *listed* sharply in the bad storm. *Verb.*
list (list) *noun, plural* **lists;** *verb,* **listed, listing.**

listen To try to hear; pay attention in order to hear. Each morning we *listen* for the sound of the school bus coming up the hill. My brother *listened* in on my conversation with Betsy.
lis·ten (lis′ən) *verb,* **listened, listening.**

lit¹ Have you *lit* the fire yet? Look up **light** for more information.
lit (lit) *verb.*

lit² The bird *lit* on the branch of the tree.
lit (lit) *verb.*

liter A basic unit of measurement in the metric system. A liter is equal to about 1.05 quarts of liquid.
lit·er (lē′tər) *noun, plural* **liters.**

literally **1.** Word for word. He translated the story from Spanish into English *literally.* **2.** Really; actually. The city was *literally* destroyed by the earthquake.
lit·er·al·ly (lit′ər ə lē) *adverb.*

literature **1.** Writing that has lasting value. Literature includes plays, poems, and novels. My sister studies American *literature* in college. **2.** Printed matter of any kind. The salesman gave her some *literature* on the new automobile.
lit·er·a·ture (lit′ər ə chər *or* lit′ər ə choor′) *noun.*

litmus paper A paper soaked in a dye. It turns blue in a base solution and red in an acid solution.
lit·mus paper (lit′məs).

litter **1.** Bits or scraps of paper or other rubbish; mess. Broken bottles and other *litter* filled the empty lot. **2.** Young animals born at one time. The mother cat gave birth to a *litter* of five kittens. **3.** A stretcher for carrying a sick or injured person. *Noun.*
—To scatter bits of rubbish around carelessly; make dirty with litter. There is a fine of fifty dollars for *littering* the public beaches. *Verb.*
lit·ter (lit′ər) *noun, plural* **litters;** *verb,* **littered, littering.**

little **1.** Small in size or amount. A pebble is a *little* stone. Put a *little* water on the plant. **2.** Short in time or distance. We will be home in a *little* while. *Adjective.*
—Not much; slightly. Snow is *little* known in very warm, southern places. *Adverb.*

—**1.** A small amount. I ate only a *little* because I wasn't hungry. **2.** A short time or distance. Step back a *little* so that I can get by. *Noun.*
lit·tle (lit′əl) *adjective,* **less** or **lesser** or **littler, least** or **littlest;** *adverb,* **less, least;** *noun.*

live¹ **1.** To be alive; have life. Dinosaurs *lived* on earth millions of years ago. **2.** To stay alive. The oldest woman in the town *lived* for one hundred years. **3.** To support oneself. That family *lives* on a small income. **4.** To feed. Some birds *live* on bugs and worms. **5.** To make one's home. Ann and Susan *live* on the east side of town. He has *lived* in France for many years.
live (liv) *verb,* **lived, living.**

live² **1.** Having life; living. The hunter brought back a *live* elephant to the zoo. **2.** Burning. Be careful because there are still *live* coals in the fireplace. **3.** Carrying an electric current. After the thunderstorm, we had to be careful of *live* wires that were blown down across the road. **4.** Seen while actually happening; not on tape. We saw a *live* television show.
live (līv) *adjective.*

livelihood The way a person supports himself. He earned his *livelihood* by selling newspapers.
live·li·hood (līv′lē hood′) *noun, plural* **livelihoods.**

lively Full of life or energy; gay or cheerful. The *lively* kitten played with the ball of string. The band played a *lively* tune that made everyone want to dance. *Adjective.*
—In a lively manner; vigorously. The horses stepped *lively. Adverb.*
live·ly (līv′lē) *adjective,* **livelier, liveliest;** *adverb.*

Litter of Kittens

at; āpe; cär; end; mē; it; īce; hot; ōld;
fôrk; wood; fool; oil; out; up; turn; sing;
thin; this; hw in white; zh in treasure.
ə stands for a in about, e in taken
i in pencil, o in lemon, and u in circus.

live·ly (līv′lē) *adjective,* **livelier, liveliest;** *adverb.*

liver 1. A large, reddish-brown organ in the body. The liver makes bile and helps the body absorb food. 2. The liver of certain animals when used as food.
  liv·er (liv′ər) *noun, plural* **livers.**

livery 1. A uniform worn by servants. The *livery* of the doorman had a trimming of gold braid. 2. A stable where horses are cared for and rented out.
  liv·er·y (liv′ər ē) *noun, plural* **liveries.**

lives More than one life. Look up **life** for more information.
  lives (līvz) *noun plural.*

livestock Animals raised on a farm or ranch. Cows, horses, sheep, and pigs are livestock.
  live·stock (līv′stok′) *noun.*

livid 1. Having a pale, usually bluish color. His face was *livid* with anger. 2. Changed in color because of a bruise. Joel had a *livid* mark on his arm where the ball hit him.
  liv·id (liv′id) *adjective.*

living 1. Having life; alive. All animals are *living* creatures. Jeff read a book on famous *living* artists. 2. Of or for life. *Living* conditions in the town were bad after the flood. 3. Still active or in use. English is a *living* language. *Adjective.*
—1. The state or fact of being alive. 2. A means of support; livelihood. Dad earns his *living* as a fireman. 3. A way of life. The athlete believed in healthy *living. Noun.*
  liv·ing (liv′ing) *adjective; noun, plural* **livings.**

living room A room in a home for the general use of the family.

Lizard

lizard An animal that has a long, scaly body, four legs, and a long tail. Lizards are related to snakes and alligators. They are found in warm climates.
  liz·ard (liz′ərd) *noun, plural* **lizards.**

llama A large animal that lives in South America. It has a thick, woolly coat. Llamas are used for carrying heavy loads. The llama is related to the camel.
  lla·ma (lä′mə) *noun, plural* **llamas** or **llama.**

Llama

load 1. Something carried. The wagon has a *load* of hay. The boy is carrying a *load* of books. 2. Something that burdens the mind or heart. After the exam was over, Jill felt there was a *load* off her mind. *Noun.*
—1. To put a load in or on something. Jean *loaded* the box with old clothes. The men *loaded* the rocks onto the truck. 2. To put something needed into a device. Carol *loaded* the camera with film. 3. To put a charge of gunpowder or ammunition into a gun. The hunter *loaded* his rifle. *Verb.* ▲ Another word that sounds like this is **lode.**
  load (lōd) *noun, plural* **loads;** *verb,* **loaded, loading.**

loaf¹ 1. Bread baked in one piece. 2. Any mass of food in the shape of a loaf of bread. Mom made a meat *loaf* for dinner.
  loaf (lōf) *noun, plural* **loaves.**

loaf² To spend time doing little or nothing. I like to *loaf* on Sundays.
  loaf (lōf) *verb,* **loafed, loafing.**

loan 1. The act of lending something. John asked Sue for a *loan* of her pencil. 2. Something that is lent. Mr. Martin received a *loan* of five hundred dollars from the bank. *Noun.*
—To lend. Ed *loaned* Sam his baseball glove. I *loaned* my brother a dollar. *Verb.* ▲ Another word that sounds like this is **lone.**
  loan (lōn) *noun, plural* **loans;** *verb,* **loaned, loaning.**

loaves More than one loaf. Look up **loaf** for more information.
  loaves (lōvz) *noun plural.*

lobby 1. An entrance hall. The movie theater had a large *lobby.* 2. A person or group that tries to make lawmakers vote in a certain way. *Noun.*
—To try to make lawmakers vote in a certain way. A group of citizens *lobbied* against the bill to build a new highway. *Verb.*
  lob·by (lob′ē) *noun, plural* **lobbies;** *verb,* **lobbied, lobbying.**

lobster A small animal that has a hard shell and five pairs of legs with large claws on the front pair of legs. Lobsters are found in the ocean and are eaten as food.
lob·ster (lob′stər) *noun, plural* **lobsters.**

Lobster

local **1.** Having to do with a particular place. We went to the *local* library. My father writes for the *local* newspaper. **2.** Stopping at all the stops. We rode the *local* train. *Adjective.*
—A train, bus, or subway that stops at all the stops. *Noun.*
lo·cal (lō′kəl) *adjective; noun, plural* **locals.**

locality A place and the places near it. Terry liked the *locality* of the summer camp because it was in the woods and on a lake.
lo·cal·i·ty (lō kal′ə tē) *noun, plural* **localities.**

locate **1.** To find the place or position of. He could not *locate* his lost book. She *located* Kansas on the map. **2.** To settle in a particular place. The baker *located* his bakery in the new shopping center. The family left the large city to *locate* in a small town.
lo·cate (lō′kāt) *verb,* **located, locating.**

location **1.** The act of locating something. His *location* of the North Pole on the map was correct. **2.** The place where something is located; site. Where is the *location* of your school? Their new house has a beautiful *location* on top of a hill.
lo·ca·tion (lō kā′shən) *noun, plural* **locations.**

lock¹ **1.** A fastener for a door, window, chest, and many other things. A lock needs a key with a special shape to open it. **2.** A part of a canal or other waterway in which the water level can be changed to raise or lower ships. Ships use a lock to pass from one body of water to another that is at a different level. *Noun.*
—**1.** To fasten with a lock. Be sure to *lock* the front door. **2.** To shut in a place. The zoo keeper *locked* the monkey in the cage. Dad *locked* up the money in a metal box. **3.** To join or hold firmly. The two cars *locked* bumpers. *Verb.*
lock (lok) *noun, plural* **locks;** *verb,* **locked, locking.**

lock² A piece of hair, cotton, or wool.
lock (lok) *noun, plural* **locks.**

locker A small closet, cabinet, or chest that can be locked. At school, we have metal *lockers* to keep our coats, books, and other belongings in.
lock·er (lok′ər) *noun, plural* **lockers.**

locket A small case for holding a picture of someone. It is usually worn on a chain around the neck.
lock·et (lok′it) *noun, plural* **lockets.**

lockjaw A disease caused by germs that enter the body through a wound. This disease is also called **tetanus.** Look up **tetanus** for more information.
lock·jaw (lok′jô′) *noun.*

locksmith A person who makes or fixes locks.
lock·smith (lok′smith′) *noun, plural* **locksmiths.**

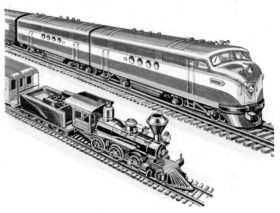

On the top is a modern **locomotive** and on the bottom is one used years ago.

locomotive An engine that moves on its own power. It is used to pull the cars of a railroad train.
lo·co·mo·tive (lō′kə mō′tiv) *noun, plural* **locomotives.**

▲ The word **locomotive** comes from two Latin words that mean "place" and "moving." *Locomotive* first meant "moving from place to place."

at; āpe; cär; end; mē; it; īce; hot; ōld; fôrk; wood; fōol; oil; out; up; turn; sing; thin; this; hw in white; zh in treasure. ə stands for a in about, e in taken i in pencil, o in lemon, and u in circus.

locust   **1.** A grasshopper that travels in huge swarms and destroys crops. **2.** A tree that has small, feathery leaves and white flowers.
lo·cust (lō′kəst) *noun, plural* **locusts.**

Leaf

Locust Tree

lode   A deposit of a metal in the earth. The prospector found a *lode* of silver. ▲ Another word that sounds like this is **load.**
lode (lōd) *noun, plural* **lodes.**

lodge   **1.** A small house, cottage, or cabin. The hunters stayed at a *lodge* in the mountains. **2.** A branch of a club or secret society. *Noun.*
—**1.** To live in a place for a while. People *lodged* in the school during the bad flood. **2.** To provide with a place to live for a while; rent rooms to. That woman *lodges* tourists in her home. **3.** To be stuck or fixed in a place. A pebble *lodged* in Tim's shoe. **4.** To bring to someone in authority. He *lodged* a complaint with his landlord about his noisy neighbors. *Verb.*
lodge (loj) *noun, plural* **lodges;** *verb,* **lodged, lodging.**

lodging   **1.** A place to live for a while. The family wanted *lodging* for the weekend. **2. lodgings.** A rented room or rooms in someone else's home.
lodg·ing (loj′ing) *noun, plural* **lodgings.**

loft   **1.** The upper floor, room, or space in a building. Lofts in office buildings are used as workrooms or storage areas. Lofts in stables and barns are used for storing hay. **2.** An upper floor or balcony in a large hall or church. The choir sang in the choir *loft.*
loft (lôft) *noun, plural* **lofts.**

lofty   **1.** Very high; towering. Ted saw many *lofty* skyscrapers in the city. The hikers climbed to the *lofty* mountaintop. **2.** High and noble. The knights of olden times believed in *lofty* ideals.
loft·y (lôf′tē) *adjective,* **loftier, loftiest.**

log   **1.** A long piece of a tree cut with the bark still on. The pioneer family cut *logs* to build a cabin. **2.** The record of the voyage of a ship or the flight of an airplane. The captain of the ship kept a *log. Noun.*
—**1.** To chop down trees in a forest and cut them into logs. **2.** To make a record of a ship's voyage or an airplane's flight in a log. *Verb.*
log (lôg *or* log) *noun, plural* **logs;** *verb,* **logged, logging.**

loganberry   The reddish-purple fruit of a thorny shrub. It has a sharp taste.
lo·gan·ber·ry (lō′gən-ber′ē) *noun, plural* **loganberries.**

logger   A person who logs trees; lumberjack.
log·ger (lô′gər *or* log′ər) *noun, plural* **loggers.**

logic   Correct thinking; sound reasoning. There is much *logic* in her argument.
log·ic (loj′ik) *noun.*

Loganberries

logical   **1.** Having to do with sound reasoning. Jean gave a *logical* explanation for what happened. **2.** Naturally to be expected. It is *logical* that if you make fun of him, you will hurt his feelings.
log·i·cal (loj′i kəl) *adjective.*

loin   **1.** The part of a person or animal that is on each side of the body, between the ribs and hip. **2.** A cut of meat from this part of an animal.
loin (loin) *noun, plural* **loins.**

loiter   **1.** To stand around; be idle. A group of boys *loitered* in the hall. **2.** To move slowly. Terry always *loiters* on her way to the dentist.
loi·ter (loi′tər) *verb,* **loitered, loitering.**

lollipop   A piece of hard candy on the end of a stick.
lol·li·pop (lol′ē pop′) *noun, plural* **lollipops.**

▲ The word **lollipop** probably comes from *lolly*, which is used in parts of England to mean "tongue." A lollipop is a candy that you lick with your tongue.

lone   **1.** Away from others; alone; solitary. A *lone* man walked along the road. A *lone* star twinkled in the early evening sky. **2.** Only; sole. The men rescued the *lone* passenger who survived the airplane crash. ▲ Another word that sounds like this is **loan.**
lone (lōn) *adjective.*

lonely **1.** Unhappy from being alone. Bob felt *lonely* at the new school. **2.** Away from others; alone. A *lonely* house stood by itself on the hill. **3.** Not often visited by people; deserted. We were the only ones on the *lonely* beach.
    lone·ly (lōn′lē) *adjective,* **lonelier, loneliest.**

lonesome **1.** Unhappy from being alone. Claire felt *lonesome* when her best friend went away for the summer. **2.** Not often visited by people; deserted. The car drove along the *lonesome* road.
    lone·some (lōn′səm) *adjective.*

long¹ **1.** Having great length; not short. It's a *long* way from Steve's house to school. The building has a *long* hallway. There was a *long* wait before the movie started. **2.** Having a certain length. The room is ten feet *long*. The program was an hour *long*. **3.** Taking more time to pronounce. The "e" in the word "be" is a *long* vowel. *Adjective.*
  —**1.** For a long time. Jack did not stay *long*. **2.** Throughout. It snowed all morning *long*. **3.** At a time in the far past. That castle was built *long* ago. *Adverb.*
  —A long time. She should be back before *long*. *Noun.*
    long (lông) *adjective,* **longer, longest;** *adverb; noun.*

long² To want very much; yearn. She *longed* to see her friends again.
    long (lông) *verb,* **longed, longing.**

longhand Writing that is done by hand. When you write in longhand, you write the words out in full.
    long·hand (lông′hand′) *noun.*

Longhorn

longhorn A breed of cattle with very long horns. Longhorns were once common in the southwestern United States.
    long·horn (lông′hôrn′) *noun, plural* **longhorns.**

longing A strong desire; yearning. The children have a *longing* to visit the zoo. *Noun.*
—Feeling a strong desire. Jeff cast *longing* glances at the cookies. *Adjective.*
    long·ing (lông′ing) *noun, plural* **longings;** *adjective.*

longitude Distance measured on the earth's surface east and west of an imaginary line. On a map or globe, lines of longitude are drawn from the North Pole to the South Pole. Longitude is expressed in degrees.
    lon·gi·tude (lôn′jə-to͞od′ *or* lôn′jə-tyo͞od′) *noun, plural* **longitudes.**

Lines of Longitude

look **1.** To use the eyes; see. Raymond *looked* at his friend's stamp collection. *Look* carefully before you cross the street. **2.** To make a search. Grace *looked* for her comb. Bill *looked* through the magazine to find the article on fishing. **3.** To appear; seem. She *looks* tired. *Verb.*
  —**1.** A glance. Take a *look* at Ken's new bicycle. **2.** Appearance. Nancy has a cheerful *look*. The new car has a shiny *look*. *Noun.*
    look (look) *verb,* **looked, looking;** *noun, plural* **looks.**
    to look after. To take care of. Bob *looked after* the neighbors' dog while they were away.
    to look forward to. To wait for eagerly. Steve *looks forward to* his birthday.
    to look up to. To respect. She *looks up to* her older sister.

looking glass A glass that reflects light; mirror. You can see yourself in a looking glass.

lookout **1.** A careful watch for someone or something. When crossing the street, be on the *lookout* for cars. **2.** A place from which to keep a careful watch. The high tower of the castle served as a *lookout*. **3.** A person who keeps a careful watch. The *lookout* in the tower called out a warning when enemy soldiers appeared.
    look·out (look′out′) *noun, plural* **lookouts.**

at; āpe; cär; end; mē; it; īce; hot; ōld;
fôrk; wood; fo͞ol; oil; out; up; turn; sing;
thin; <u>th</u>is; **hw** in white; **zh** in treasure.
ə stands for **a** in about, **e** in taken
i in pencil, **o** in lemon, and **u** in circus.

loom¹ A machine for weaving thread into cloth.

loom (lo͞om) *noun, plural* **looms.**

Loom

loom² To appear as large and dangerous. A ship *loomed* in the fog. His final exams *loomed* ahead.

loom (lo͞om) *verb,* **loomed, looming.**

loon A bird with short legs and webbed feet that dives into the water for fish. The loon has a loud, laughing call.

loon (lo͞on) *noun, plural* **loons.**

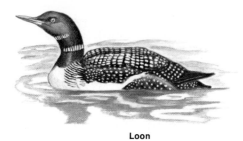

Loon

loop **1.** The rounded shape formed by the part of a string, wire, or rope that crosses itself. **2.** Anything that looks like this. You make a *loop* when you write the letter "g." Jerry put his belt through the *loops* of his pants. *Noun.*
—To make a loop in something; form a loop. Bill *looped* his shoestring while tying his shoe. *Verb.*

loop (lo͞op) *noun, plural* **loops;** *verb,* **looped, looping.**

loose **1.** Not fastened or attached firmly. A page was *loose* in the book. The doorknob is *loose.* A *loose* wire caused the radio to stop

playing. **2.** Free. The canary is *loose* in the house. **3.** Not tight. He wore a *loose* jacket. **4.** Not tied or joined together. She carries *loose* keys in her purse. **5.** Not in a package or container. Jack bought some *loose* candy at the store. **6.** Not packed or pressed tightly together. The workmen put *loose* gravel on the driveway. The tablecloth has a *loose* weave. *Adjective.*
—**1.** To set free; let go. He *loosed* the dog in the field. **2.** To make less tight; loosen or unfasten. She *loosed* the knot. *Verb.*

loose (lo͞os) *adjective,* **looser, loosest;** *verb,* **loosed, loosing.**

loosen To make or become loose or looser. Jack *loosened* his necktie. George *loosened* his hold on the rope.

loos·en (lo͞o′sən) *verb,* **loosened, loosening.**

loot Things stolen. The robbers hid their *loot* in a barn. *Noun.*
—To rob by force; plunder. Thieves *looted* the house. *Verb.* ▲ Another word that sounds like this is **lute.**

loot (lo͞ot) *noun; verb,* **looted, looting.**

lord **1.** A person who has power over others. In the Middle Ages, a lord was a powerful man who lived in a castle and had many people under him. **2. Lord.** In Great Britain, a man of noble rank. **3. Lord. a.** God. **b.** Christ.

lord (lôrd) *noun, plural* **lords.**

▲ The word **lord** comes from an Old English word that meant "keeper of the loaf." The lady of the house made the bread, and the lord, or man who was the head of the home, kept the bread and gave it out to the others in the household.

lose **1.** To have no longer; be without. The family will *lose* all their belongings if the firemen can't save their house. I *lost* my pencil. Ann doesn't want to *lose* Carol's friendship. **2.** To fail to keep. He *loses* his temper easily. That acrobat never *loses* his balance. **3.** To fail to win. The team *lost* the game. **4.** To fail to use; waste. The travelers will *lose* time if the bus breaks down.

lose (lo͞oz) *verb,* **lost, losing.**

loss **1.** The act of losing something. The *loss* of the game was a disappointment to the team. He was not worried about the *loss* of his pen. **2.** Something lost. The car was a total *loss* after the accident. Mr. Brown suffered great *losses* in the fire in his store.

loss (lôs) *noun, plural* **losses.**

lost Nancy *lost* her gloves. The team has *lost* the game. Look up **lose** for more information. *Verb.*

—1. That cannot be found; missing. Steve looked for his *lost* dog. **2.** No longer possessed. He thought sadly about his *lost* fortune. **3.** Not won. The team played well, but the game was *lost.* **4.** Not used; wasted. He drove all night to make up for *lost* time. **5.** Ruined; destroyed. Many lives were *lost* in the fire. *Adjective.*
  lost (lôst) *verb; adjective.*

lot **1.** A bit of paper, wood, straw, or other material used to decide something by chance. The boys drew *lots* to decide who would be first at bat in the game. **2.** This way of deciding something. The girls chose the captain of their team by *lot.* **3.** Fate or fortune. It was his *lot* in life to be poor. **4.** A plot of land. We play baseball on an empty *lot.* **5.** A number or group of persons or things. This is a poor *lot* of vegetables. **6.** A great amount. There are a *lot* of cars on the street. She ate *lots* of candy and got sick. *Noun.*
  —A great deal; much. She is a *lot* smarter than her brother. *Adverb.*
  lot (lot) *noun, plural* **lots;** *adverb.*

lotion A liquid used on the skin. A lotion heals, soothes, softens, or cleans the skin.
  lo·tion (lō′shən) *noun, plural* **lotions.**

lotus The large flower of a plant whose leaves float in the water.
  lo·tus (lō′təs) *noun, plural* **lotuses.**

loud Having a strong sound; not quiet. The jet plane made a *loud* noise. We could hear the *loud* trumpets in the marching band. *Adjective.*
  —In a loud way. Fred shouted *loud* and clear. *Adverb.*
  loud (loud) *adjective,* **louder, loudest;** *adverb.*

Lotus

loudspeaker A device that can change electrical signals into sounds and make the sounds louder. Loudspeakers are used in radios and phonographs.
  loud·speak·er (loud′spē′kər) *noun, plural* **loudspeakers.**

Louisiana A state in the southern United States. Its capital is Baton Rouge.
  Lou·i·si·an·a (lōō ē′zē an′ə *or* lōō′ə zē an′ə) *noun.*

▲ A French explorer named the Mississippi Valley **Louisiana** after King *Louis* XIV of France. When the land was divided up into states, Louisiana became the name of one of the states.

lounge To stand, sit, or lie down in a comfortable, lazy way. Bill *lounged* on the sofa. *Verb.*
  —A place where a person may lounge. The hotel has a *lounge* where guests may relax. *Noun.*
  lounge (lounj) *verb,* **lounged, lounging;** *noun, plural* **lounges.**

louse A tiny insect without wings. It lives on people and animals and sucks their blood.
  louse (lous) *noun, plural* **lice.**

love **1.** A strong, warm feeling for another; deep affection. **2.** A strong liking for something. She goes to concerts because of her *love* of music. *Noun.*
  —1. To have a strong, warm feeling for another. The mother and father *love* their children. **2.** To have a strong liking for something. He *loves* to read. She *loves* vanilla ice cream. *Verb.*
  love (luv) *noun, plural* **loves;** *verb,* **loved, loving.**

lovely **1.** Having a beautiful appearance or character. Brenda is a *lovely* person. **2.** Enjoyable. She had a *lovely* time at the party.
  love·ly (luv′lē) *adjective,* **lovelier, loveliest.**

low¹ **1.** Not high or tall. A *low* wall surrounds the yard. The branches of the tree are *low* enough for me to reach. The room has a *low* ceiling. **2.** Below the usual level. The river was *low.* The car drove at a *low* speed. **3.** Below others. He gets *low* grades in school. That meat is *low* in quality. **4.** Not favorable; bad. She has a *low* opinion of people who are cruel to animals. **5.** Not having enough. Our car is *low* on gasoline. **6.** Not loud; soft. He spoke in a *low* voice. **7.** Deep in pitch. He can sing very *low* notes. *Adjective.*
  —At or to a low place or level. The airplane flew *low* over the town. The campers' supplies ran *low* after they had been in the woods for two weeks. *Adverb.*

at; āpe; cär; end; mē; it; īce; hot; ōld; fôrk; wood; fōōl; oil; out; up; turn; sing; thin; this; hw in white; zh in treasure. ə stands for a in about, e in taken i in pencil, o in lemon, and u in circus.

—**1.** A low place or point. The temperature reached a new *low* during the night. **2.** The arrangement of gears in an automobile that gives the lowest speed and greatest power. The driver of the car shifted into *low* as he went up the steep hill. *Noun.*
> **low** (lō) *adjective*, **lower, lowest;** *adverb; noun, plural* **lows.**

lower He lives on a *lower* floor of the apartment house. Our supply of heating oil is *lower* than it should be. *Adjective.*
—**1.** To take down; bring down. The boys will *lower* the flag at dusk. Ellen *lowered* her arm when the teacher called her name. **2.** To make less; lessen. *Lower* your voice. *Verb.*
> **low·er** (lō′ər) *adjective; verb,* **lowered, lowering.**

low tide The tide when the level of the ocean or lake is at its lowest.

loyal Faithful and true. Tim is a *loyal* friend. She is *loyal* to her family.
> **loy·al** (loi′əl) *adjective.*

loyalty A being faithful and true. We can show our *loyalty* to our friends by helping them when they are in need.
> **loy·al·ty** (loi′əl tē) *noun, plural* **loyalties.**

lubricate To put oil or grease on the parts of a machine that move against each other so that they will move easily. Jeff *lubricated* the reel on his fishing pole with oil.
> **lu·bri·cate** (lōō′brə kāt′) *verb,* **lubricated, lubricating.**

luck **1.** What seems to happen to a person by chance. It was good playing and not *luck* that caused the team to win. She blamed all her troubles on bad *luck.* **2.** Good fortune. She had no *luck* in looking for her lost ring.
> **luck** (luk) *noun.*

luckily With luck; by luck. *Luckily,* Fred found his missing wallet.
> **luck·i·ly** (luk′ə lē) *adverb.*

lucky Having or bringing good luck. Pat was very *lucky* to win the prize. Ed always carries his *lucky* rabbit's foot.
> **luck·y** (luk′ē) *adjective,* **luckier, luckiest.**

lug To carry or drag with much trouble or effort. Fred had to *lug* his heavy suitcase upstairs.
> **lug** (lug) *verb,* **lugged, lugging.**

luggage The suitcases, trunks, and bags that a traveler takes along on a trip; baggage.
> **lug·gage** (lug′ij) *noun.*

lull To make or become calm. The sound of rain on the roof at night always *lulls* me to sleep. The storm finally *lulled. Verb.*
—A short period of calm or quiet. There was no *lull* in the heavy traffic. *Noun.*
> **lull** (lul) *verb,* **lulled, lulling;** *noun, plural* **lulls.**

lullaby A song that is sung to lull a baby to sleep.
> **lul·la·by** (lul′ə bī′) *noun, plural* **lullabies.**

lumber¹ Boards cut from logs. Dad bought *lumber* to build a shed.
> **lum·ber** (lum′bər) *noun.*

lumber² To move about in a clumsy, noisy way. The wagon *lumbered* down the dirt road. The elephant *lumbered* along the trail.
> **lum·ber** (lum′bər) *verb,* **lumbered, lumbering.**

lumberjack A person who cuts down trees and gets logs ready for the sawmill.
> **lum·ber·jack** (lum′bər jak′) *noun, plural* **lumberjacks.**

luminous Full of light; shining. We could see the *luminous* glow of a campfire through the trees.
> **lu·mi·nous** (lōō′mə nəs) *adjective.*

lump **1.** A shapeless piece of something; chunk. Joe took the *lump* of clay and made a figure of a man out of it. **2.** A swollen place; bump. He has a *lump* on his head where the ball hit him. *Noun.*
—**1.** To put or bring together. The brothers *lumped* their allowances to buy a camera. **2.** To form lumps. Oatmeal sometimes *lumps* when it cools. *Verb.*
> **lump** (lump) *noun, plural* **lumps;** *verb,* **lumped, lumping.**

lunar Of or having to do with the moon. The astronauts who went to the moon brought back *lunar* rocks for study. A *lunar* eclipse is the darkening of the moon when the earth moves between the sun and the moon.
> **lu·nar** (lōō′nər) *adjective.*

lunch A meal eaten between breakfast and dinner. *Noun.*
—To eat lunch. We *lunched* at noon. *Verb.*
> **lunch** (lunch) *noun, plural* **lunches;** *verb,* **lunched, lunching.**

luncheon A lunch. Mother went to a formal *luncheon* given by her club.
> **lunch·eon** (lun′chən) *noun, plural* **luncheons.**

lung One of two organs for breathing in the chest of man and other animals. The lungs supply the blood with oxygen and rid the blood of carbon dioxide.
> **lung** (lung) *noun, plural* **lungs.**

lunge A sudden movement forward. The catcher made a *lunge* for the ball. *Noun.*
—To move forward suddenly. The bear *lunged* at the campers. *Verb.*
> **lunge** (lunj) *noun, plural* **lunges;** *verb,* **lunged, lunging.**

lure 1. A strong attraction. The explorer felt the *lure* of adventure in the unknown land. 2. Bait used in fishing. Ted used a worm as a *lure* to catch the fish. *Noun.*
—To attract strongly. The boy was *lured* to the kitchen by the smell of freshly baked cookies. *Verb.*
  lure (loor) *noun, plural* **lures;** *verb,* **lured, luring.**

lush Thick, rich, and abundant. *Lush* plants grow in the jungle.
  lush (lush) *adjective,* **lusher, lushest.**

luster A bright shine; glow; sheen. He gave the table a nice *luster* by waxing it.
  lus·ter (lus′tər) *noun, plural* **lusters.**

lute A stringed musical instrument used in former times. It is played by plucking the strings. ▲ Another word that sounds like this is **loot.**
  lute (lo͞ot) *noun, plural* **lutes.**

luxurious 1. Fond of luxury. She has a *luxurious* taste for jewels and furs. 2. Giving luxury and much comfort. The family stayed at a *luxurious* hotel on the beach.
  lux·u·ri·ous (luk-shoor′ē əs *or* lug-zhoor′ē əs) *adjective.*

Lute

luxury 1. Something that gives much comfort and pleasure but is not really necessary. A color television set is a *luxury.* 2. A way of life that gives comfort and pleasure. The famous movie star makes a great deal of money and is used to *luxury.*
  lux·u·ry (luk′shər ē *or* lug′zhər ē) *noun, plural* **luxuries.**

-ly¹ A *suffix* that means "in a certain way or manner." *Gladly* means "in a glad way." *Greatly* means "in a great manner."

-ly² A *suffix* that means: 1. "Like." *Princely* means "like a prince." *Brotherly* means "like a brother." 2. "Happening at a certain period of time." *Weekly* means "happening every week."

lye A strong substance used in making soap and detergents. Lye is obtained by soaking wood ashes in water. ▲ Another word that sounds like this is **lie.**
  lye (lī) *noun.*

lying¹ He is *lying* if he says he doesn't know what happened. Look up **lie¹** for more information.
  ly·ing (lī′ing) *verb.*

lying² The dog is *lying* on the rug. Look up **lie²** for more information.
  ly·ing (lī′ing) *verb.*

lymph A clear liquid in the tissues of the body. Lymph brings food and oxygen to the cells of the body and carries away wastes.
  lymph (limf) *noun.*

Lynx

lynx A wildcat with long legs and a short tail.
  lynx (lingks) *noun, plural* **lynx** or **lynxes.**

lyre A stringed musical instrument of ancient times. The lyre was played by ancient Egyptians, Hebrews, and Greeks.
  lyre (līr) *noun, plural* **lyres.**

lyric Expressing strong emotion. The poet wrote *lyric* poems about nature. *Adjective.*
—1. A lyric poem. 2. **lyrics.** The words written for a song. The children learned both the *lyrics* and the melody of the song. *Noun.*
  lyr·ic (lir′ik) *adjective; noun, plural* **lyrics.**

lyrical Expressing strong emotion; lyric.

Lyre

at; āpe; cär; end; mē; it; īce; hot; ōld; fôrk; wood; fo͞ol; oil; out; up; turn; sing; thin; <u>th</u>is; hw in white; zh in treasure. ə stands for a in about, e in taken i in pencil, o in lemon, and u in circus.

1. Ancient Egyptian Picture Writing
2. Ancient Middle Eastern Tribes
3. Ancient Greek
4. Ancient Tribe Near Rome
5. Ancient Roman
6. Modern English

M is the thirteenth letter of the alphabet. The way we write the capital letter **M** today is very much like the way that it has been written since the earliest alphabets. The oldest form of the letter **M** was a drawing that the ancient Egyptians (**1**) used in their picture writing nearly 5000 years ago. This drawing was borrowed by several ancient tribes (**2**) in the Middle East. They used this letter to mean "water," and the shape of this early form of **M** looked something like waves. The ancient Greeks (**3**) borrowed this letter about 3000 years ago. The older, Middle Eastern form of **M** was borrowed by an ancient tribe (**4**) that settled north of Rome about 2800 years ago. But the Romans (**5**) did not borrow this form. They used the Greek form of **M**. By about 2400 years ago the Romans were writing it in almost the same way that we write the capital letter **M** today (**6**).

m, M The thirteenth letter of the alphabet.
m, M (em) *noun, plural* **m's, M's.**

ma'am Madam. ▲ This word is used mostly in everyday conversation.
ma'am (mam) *noun, plural* **ma'ams.**

macaroni A food made from flour paste or dough. It is usually shaped like short, hollow tubes. Macaroni is cooked by boiling it in water.
mac·a·ro·ni (mak′ə rō′nē) *noun, plural* **macaronis** or **macaronies.**

machine **1.** A device that does some particular job. It is made up of a number of moving or fixed parts that work together. A lawn mower, a hair dryer, and a printing press are machines. **2.** A simple device that is used to do work. A lever and a pulley are simple machines.
ma·chine (mə shēn′) *noun, plural* **machines.**

machine gun A rifle that keeps firing bullets as long as the trigger is pressed.

machinery **1.** Machines or parts of machines. The farmer's work was made easier by tractors and other *machinery*. The mechanics fixed the *machinery* of the elevator. **2.** A group of things or people that make something work. The President and the Congress are part of the *machinery* of the federal government.
ma·chin·er·y (mə shē′nər ē) *noun.*

mackerel A fish that lives in salt water and is caught for food. It has a silvery body with black markings on its back. The mackerel is related to the tuna.
mack·er·el (mak′ər əl) *noun, plural* **mackerels** or **mackerel.**

Mackerel

macron A short line (¯) that is placed over a vowel to show that it has a long sound.
ma·cron (mā′kron) *noun, plural* **macrons.**

mad **1.** Feeling or showing anger; angry. Roger was *mad* at me for borrowing his bicycle without asking him. **2.** Out of one's mind; crazy; insane. **3.** Very foolish or reckless; not wise or sensible. The two boys had the *mad* idea of building their own airplane and flying to Europe. **4.** Very enthusiastic. Don is *mad* about old movies and watches them every chance he gets. **5.** Wild and excited. We had to make a *mad* dash to the airport so we wouldn't miss the plane. **6.** Sick

380

with rabies. The police searched the neighborhood for the *mad* dog.

mad (mad) *adjective,* **madder, maddest.**

madam   A word used as a polite form of address to a woman.
mad·am (mad′əm) *noun, plural* **madams.**

made   Tom *made* a map of his neighborhood. Look up **make** for more information. ▲ Another word that sounds like this is **maid.**
made (mād) *verb.*

made-up   Not real or true. The man used a *made-up* name so that the police would not be able to find him.
made-up (mād′up′) *adjective.*

magazine   **1.** A printed collection of stories, articles, and pictures. A magazine is usually bound in a paper cover. Most magazines come out every week or every month. **2.** The part of a gun or rifle that holds the bullets.
mag·a·zine (mag′ə zēn′ *or* mag′ə zēn′) *noun, plural* **magazines.**

maggot   A fly that has just come out of its egg. It looks something like a worm and has a thick body with no legs.
mag·got (mag′ət) *noun, plural* **maggots.**

magic   **1.** The art of pretending to be able to do something that is not usually possible by using special charms or spells. In the story, the wicked witch used *magic* to turn the prince into a frog. **2.** The art or skill of doing tricks to entertain people. The magician made a rabbit appear from a hat and did other feats of *magic. Noun.*
—Using, done by, or for magic. The audience could not understand how the *magic* trick was done. *Adjective.*
mag·ic (maj′ik) *noun; adjective.*

magical   Using or done by magic. The wizard used his *magical* powers to turn straw into gold.
mag·i·cal (maj′i kəl) *adjective.*

magician   **1.** A person who entertains people by doing magic tricks. **2.** A man who has magical powers; wizard.
ma·gi·cian (mə jish′ən) *noun, plural* **magicians.**

magnesium   A silvery-white metal. It is tough and very light and is often mixed with other metals to make alloys. Magnesium is a chemical element.
mag·ne·si·um   (mag nē′zē əm   *or*   mag-nē′zhəm) *noun.*

magnet   A piece of stone, metal, or ore that has the power to attract iron or steel. Magnets are often made in the shape of a bar or horseshoe.
mag·net (mag′nit) *noun, plural* **magnets.**

magnetic   Having the power of a magnet. The *magnetic* needle of a compass points to the earth's *magnetic* poles.
mag·net·ic (mag net′ik) *adjective.*

magnetic pole   **1.** Either of the two points of a magnet where its magnetic force seems to be strongest. **2.** Either of the two points on the earth's surface toward which the needle of a compass points. One of these points is near the North Pole and the other is near the South Pole. They are the points where the earth's magnetic field is strongest.

magnetism   The power to attract iron, steel, and certain other materials. Some stones and metals and all electric currents have magnetism.
mag·net·ism (mag′nə tiz′əm) *noun.*

magnificent   Very beautiful and grand; splendid. The house on the top of the hill has a *magnificent* view of the valley. The queen wore a *magnificent* robe decorated with silver and gold.
mag·nif·i·cent (mag nif′ə sənt) *adjective.*

magnify   **1.** To make something look bigger than it really is. The microscope *magnified* the cell 100 times. **2.** To make something seem more important than it really is; exaggerate. Jack always *magnifies* his health problems.
mag·ni·fy   (mag′nə fī′)   *verb,*   **magnified, magnifying.**

magnifying glass   A lens or combination of lenses that make things look bigger than they really are.

magnitude   **1.** A greatness of size. We could only guess at the *magnitude* of the mountain. **2.** Importance. Christopher Columbus's discovery of America was an event of great *magnitude.*
mag·ni·tude (mag′nə tood′ *or* mag′nə tyood′) *noun.*

Magnifying Glass

at; āpe; cär; end; mē; it; īce; hot; ōld;
fôrk; wood; fool; oil; out; up; turn; sing;
thin; **this**; hw in white; zh in treasure.
ə stands for **a** in about, **e** in taken
i in pencil, **o** in lemon, and **u** in circus.

magnolia A tree that has long leaves and large, beautiful flowers. The flowers may be white, pink, purple, or yellow.
mag·no·lia (mag nōl′yə) *noun, plural* **magnolias.**

Blossom

Magnolia Tree

▲ The word **magnolia** comes from the name of Pierre *Magnol.* He was a French scientist who studied plants many years ago.

magpie A bird that has a long tail and a thick bill. Magpies are noisy and sometimes learn to imitate human speech. They are related to crows.
mag·pie (mag′pī) *noun, plural* **magpies.**

Magpie

mahogany **1.** An evergreen tree that grows in warm parts of North America and Latin America. The reddish-brown wood of this tree is strong and hard. It is often used in making furniture and musical instruments. **2.** A dark reddish-brown color. *Noun.*
—Having the color mahogany; dark reddish-brown. *Adjective.*
ma·hog·a·ny (mə hog′ə nē) *noun, plural* **mahoganies;** *adjective.*

maid **1.** A woman servant who does housework. The *maid* comes once a week to help Mother clean our house. **2.** A girl or young woman who is not married. The knight said she was a pretty young *maid.* ▲ Another word that sounds like this is **made.**
maid (mād) *noun, plural* **maids.**

maiden A girl or young woman who is not married. *Noun.*
—First or earliest. That ship's *maiden* voyage was from England to New York. *Adjective.*
maid·en (mād′ən) *noun, plural* **maidens;** *adjective.*

maiden name A woman's last name before she is married.

maid of honor An unmarried woman who is the main female attendant of the bride at a wedding.

mail **1.** Letters, packages, and papers that are sent or received through the post office. Ted received three birthday cards in yesterday's *mail.* **2.** The system by which mail is sent, moved, or delivered. It is usually run by the government of a country. We received an invitation to my cousin's wedding by *mail.* *Noun.*
—To send by mail. Roberta *mailed* her grandmother a letter. *Verb.* ▲ Another word that sounds like this is **male.**
mail (māl) *noun, plural* **mails;** *verb,* **mailed, mailing.**

mailbox **1.** A box in which letters are put so that they can be picked up by a mailman. **2.** A box into which a person's mail is put when it is delivered.
mail·box (māl′boks′) *noun, plural* **mailboxes.**

mailman A person whose job is carrying and delivering the mail. A mailman is also called a **postman.**
mail·man (māl′man′) *noun, plural* **mailmen.**

main The greatest in size or importance. The *main* branch of the library is in the center of the city. The *main* idea of the story was the young woman's bravery. Mrs. Hopkins served chicken as the *main* course of the meal. *Adjective.*
—A large pipe or cable. Mains are used to carry water, gas, and electricity. *Noun.* ▲ Another word that sounds like this is **mane.**
main (mān) *adjective; noun, plural* **mains.**

Maine A state in the northeastern United States, on the Atlantic Ocean. Its capital is Augusta.
Maine (mān) *noun.*

▲ The name **Maine** comes from the earlier English words "the *maine,*" which meant "mainland." Men who explored this region used these words to show the difference between the North American continent and the many islands along the coast in this area.

mainland The land that is the largest land mass of an area, country, or continent. Hong Kong is an·island located off the *mainland* of China.
main·land (mān′land′ *or* mān′lənd) *noun.*

mainly For the most part; chiefly. Although Lisa is interested *mainly* in popular music, she sometimes listens to classical music too. **main·ly** (mān'lē) *adverb.*

maintain **1.** To continue to have or do; go on with; keep. The truck *maintained* a speed of fifty miles an hour on the highway. It was hard for the skier to *maintain* his balance on the icy hill. **2.** To take care of. The town hired gardeners to *maintain* the park. The man found it difficult to *maintain* a large family on his small salary. **3.** To say in a firm and sure way. No matter what other people said, Bill *maintained* that he was right. **main·tain** (mān tān') *verb,* **maintained, maintaining.**

maintenance **1.** A maintaining or being maintained. The city government takes care of the *maintenance* of streets and sidewalks. **2.** Money, food, and shelter needed for living; means of support. The man made just enough money for the *maintenance* of his family. **main·te·nance** (mān'tə nəns) *noun.*

maize A grain that grows in rows on large ears on a tall plant. This grain is usually called **corn.** Look up **corn** for more information. ▲ Another word that sounds like this is **maze.** **maize** (māz) *noun.*

majestic Very grand and noble. The *majestic* mountains rose thousands of feet above the valley. **ma·jes·tic** (mə jes'tik) *adjective.*

majesty **1.** Great dignity; grandness. The crowds along the streets were thrilled by the *majesty* of the royal procession. **2. Majesty.** A title used in speaking to or about a king, queen, or other royal ruler. **maj·es·ty** (maj'is tē) *noun, plural* **majesties.**

major Bigger or more important. The *major* expense in my vacation was the cost of the airplane ticket. My father spent the *major* part of the day cleaning out the garage. *Adjective.*
—An army officer. A major ranks below a colonel but above a captain. *Noun.* **ma·jor** (mā'jər) *adjective; noun, plural* **majors.**

majority **1.** The larger number or part of something; more than half. The *majority* of the students voted for Martin for class president. **2.** The amount by which a larger number is bigger than a smaller number. The mayor won the election by 10,000 votes to 6,000, so he had a *majority* of 4,000 votes. **ma·jor·i·ty** (mə jôr'ə tē) *noun, plural* **majorities.**

make **1.** To cause something to be, become, or happen. A robin has begun to *make* a nest in the tree outside my window. Slamming a door *makes* a loud noise. A funny movie always *makes* him laugh. Bob *made* a speech to the class. The smell of food *made* me hungry. **2.** To add to; amount to; be the parts of. Ten and three *make* thirteen. Thirty-six inches *make* a yard. Fifty separate states *make* up the United States of America. **3.** To earn. Rachel *makes* a dollar an hour when she baby-sits for her neighbor's children. Mrs. Johnson *makes* her living by writing books. **4.** To go or get to. I woke up late and had to rush to *make* the bus on time. **5.** To win a place or position on. Lewis hopes to *make* the school basketball team this year. *Verb.*
—The style or type of something that is made and sold; brand. Our new car is the same *make* as our old car. *Noun.* **make** (māk) *verb,* **made, making;** *noun, plural* **makes.**
to make believe. To pretend. My little brother likes *to make believe* that he is a cowboy.
to make up. 1. To become friends again. The two friends argue all the time, but they always *make up* afterwards. **2.** To put cosmetics on. The actor *made up* before going on stage. **3.** To invent in the mind. Ed *made up* a funny story to amuse his sister.

make-believe Imagination. The book contained stories of ghosts and witches and other tales of *make-believe. Noun.*
—Not real; imaginary. The attic became the children's *make-believe* castle. *Adjective.* **make-be·lieve** (māk'bi lēv') *noun; adjective.*

make-up **1.** Lipstick, rouge, and other cosmetics that are put on the face. **2.** The way in which something is put together. The *make-up* of the class is half boys and half girls. **3.** A person's nature; personality. Marion is a friendly person, and it is not in her *make-up* to be rude to anyone. **make-up** (māk'up') *noun, plural* **make-ups.**

malaria A disease that causes chills, a high fever, and sweating. People get malaria when they are bitten by certain kinds of mosquitoes that carry the disease. **ma·lar·i·a** (mə ler'ē ə) *noun.*

at; āpe; cär; end; mē; it; īce; hot; ōld; fôrk; wood; fōol; oil; out; up; turn; sing; thin; this; hw in white; zh in treasure.
ə stands for a in about, e in taken i in pencil, o in lemon, and u in circus.

▲ The word **malaria** comes from two Italian words that mean "bad air." People used to think that the damp air from swamps caused this disease.

male **1.** Of or having to do with men or boys. *It seemed unfair to her that only* male *students were allowed to play on the baseball team.* **2.** Having to do with or belonging to the sex that can father young. *A* male *deer is called a buck. Adjective.*
—A male person or animal. *The* male *of cattle is a bull. Noun.* ▲ Another word that sounds like this is **mail.**
   mail (māl) *adjective; noun, plural* **males.**

malice The wish to cause harm or pain to someone. *It was* malice *that made the boy spread the nasty rumor about the new student.*
   mal·ice (mal′is) *noun.*

mallard A wild duck. The male mallard has a green head, a white band around the neck, a reddish-brown chest, and a grayish back.
   mal·lard (mal′ərd) *noun, plural* **mallards** or **mallard.**

Mallard

mallet A hammer that is made of wood. Mallets with short handles are usually used as tools. In some sports, such as croquet or polo, mallets with long handles are used to hit the ball.
   mal·let (mal′it) *noun, plural* **mallets.**

malt A grain that is soaked in warm water until it begins to grow and then is dried. It is usually made from barley. Malt is used in making beer and ale.
   malt (môlt) *noun.*

malted milk A drink made by mixing milk and sometimes ice cream with a powder made of malt.

mama Mother. *My little brother calls our mother* Mama.
   ma·ma (mä′mə) *noun, plural* **mamas.**

mammal A kind of animal that is warm-blooded and has a backbone. Most mammals are covered with fur or have some hair.

Female mammals have glands that produce milk, which they feed to their young. People, cattle, dogs, and whales are mammals.
   mam·mal (mam′əl) *noun, plural* **mammals.**

Mammoth

mammoth A kind of elephant that lived long ago. Mammoths had long, curving tusks and shaggy, brown hair. They were larger than elephants that live today. The last mammoths on earth died about 10,000 years ago. *Noun.*
—Very large; gigantic; huge. *The exploding bomb left a* mammoth *hole in the ground. Adjective.*
   mam·moth (mam′əth) *noun, plural* **mammoths;** *adjective.*

man **1.** An adult male person. *The boy grew up to be a handsome* man. *Until 1920, only* men *were allowed to vote.* **2.** A human being or the human race; a person or all people. Man *is the only animal that can speak. All* men *are created equal.* **3.** One of the pieces used in playing chess, checkers, and other games. *Noun.*
—To supply with men who do a certain job. *Ten sailors* manned *the lifeboats and saved the lives of many passengers. Verb.*
   man (man) *noun, plural* **men;** *verb,* **manned, manning.**

▲ At first the word **man** meant "any person." Long ago, if there were a father, a mother, and a small child in a room, someone could have said that there were three *men* in the room. Later people began to use the word only for a grown male person.

manage **1.** To direct or control. *The president of the company* managed *its business dealings. Only a very good rider could* manage *such a wild horse.* **2.** To succeed at doing something; be able to. *Our team* managed *to* win the game, even though our best player was sick.

man·age (man′ij) *verb,* **managed, managing.**

manager A person who manages something. The *manager* of the baseball team decided which player would pitch.

man·ag·er (man′i jər) *noun, plural* **managers.**

mandolin A musical instrument that is like a guitar. It has a pear-shaped body and metal strings.

man·do·lin (man′dəl in′ *or* mand′əl in′) *noun, plural* **mandolins.**

mane The long, thick hair on the neck of certain animals. Horses and male lions have manes. ▲ Another word that sounds like this is **main.**

mane (mān) *noun, plural* **manes.**

maneuver **1.** A planned movement of soldiers or ships. The generals discussed a *maneuver* to capture the enemy's supplies. **2.** A skillful or clever move or plan. Using a false name was one of the *maneuvers* the man used to keep from being caught by the police.

ma·neu·ver (mə nōō′vər) *noun, plural* **maneuvers.**

manganese A brittle, silver-gray metal. It is used in making steel. Manganese is a chemical element.

man·ga·nese (mang′gə nēz′) *noun.*

manger A large box in which food for horses and cattle is kept.

man·ger (mān′jər) *noun, plural* **mangers.**

mango A yellowish-red fruit that has a sweet, spicy taste. It grows on a tropical evergreen tree.

man·go (mang′gō) *noun, plural* **mangoes** or **mangos.**

manhole A large opening through which a workman can go to build or repair a sewer,

Manger

wires, pipes, or the like. Manholes are usually made in the street and have lids that can be removed.

man·hole (man′hōl′) *noun, plural* **manholes.**

manicure A cleaning, shaping, and, sometimes, polishing of the fingernails. *Noun.*
—To give a manicure to. *Verb.*

man·i·cure (man′ə kyoor′) *noun, plural* **manicures;** *verb,* **manicured, manicuring.**

mankind The human race; all people. War is one of the greatest evils of *mankind.*

man·kind (man′kīnd′) *noun.*

man-made Made by people, rather than by nature. Glass, steel, and plastic are *man-made;* water, coal, and wood are not.

man-made (man′mād′) *adjective.*

Mandolin

manner **1.** The way in which something is done. Jack came in and dropped his jacket on the floor in a careless *manner.* **2.** A way of acting or behaving. The old woman had a warm and friendly *manner.* **3. manners.** Polite ways of behaving or acting. My little brother is too young to have good table *manners.* ▲ Another word that sounds like this is **manor.**

man·ner (man′ər) *noun, plural* **manners.**

manor **1.** A large estate belonging to a lord in the Middle Ages. The lord lived on part of the land and the rest was divided among peasants, who paid rent to the lord in goods or work. **2.** A mansion. ▲ Another word that sounds like this is **manner.**

man·or (man′ər) *noun, plural* **manors.**

mansion A very large and grand home. The rich man lived in a beautiful old *mansion* by the ocean.

man·sion (man′shən) *noun, plural* **mansions.**

manslaughter The unlawful killing of one person by another. Manslaughter results from an accident and is not planned.

man·slaugh·ter (man′slô′tər) *noun.*

mantel The shelf above a fireplace. This is also called a **mantelpiece.**

man·tel (mant′əl) *noun, plural* **mantels.**

at; āpe; cär; end; mē; it; īce; hot; ōld;
fôrk; wood; fōol; oil; out; up; turn; sing;
thin; this; hw in white; zh in treasure.
ə stands for a in about, e in taken
i in pencil, o in lemon, and u in circus.

manual Done with or using the hands. You can see from the bookcases she built that Rosa has *manual* skill. All the children on the farm were used to doing *manual* labor. *Adjective.*
—A book that gives instructions or information about something. Rob had to study the drivers' *manual* before he took the test to get his drivers' license. *Noun.*
   man·u·al (man′yo͞o əl) *adjective; noun, plural* **manuals.**

manufacture **1.** To make or process something by machinery. That company *manufactures* bicycles. The mill *manufactured* wool into cloth. **2.** To make up; invent. He *manufactured* an excuse for forgetting her birthday. *Verb.*
—The act or process of manufacturing. The city of Detroit is famous for the *manufacture* of automobiles. *Noun.*
   man·u·fac·ture (man′yə fak′chər) *verb,* **manufactured, manufacturing;** *noun.*

manure Waste matter from animals that is used to fertilize land.
   ma·nure (mə noor′ *or* mə nyoor′) *noun.*

manuscript A book that is handwritten or typed. Before the invention of printing, all books were written manuscripts. Nowadays, an author sends his manuscript to a publisher or printer so that it can be made into a printed book.
   man·u·script (man′yə skript′) *noun, plural* **manuscripts.**

many Made up of a large number. There are *many* books on American history in that library. *Adjective.*
—A large number. The meeting of the club was called off because *many* of the members could not be there. *Noun.*
—A large number of people or things. *Many* were late for school because of the bad weather. *Pronoun.*
   man·y (men′ē) *adjective,* **more, most;** *noun; pronoun.*

map A drawing that shows all or part of the earth's surface. Maps of large areas usually show cities, rivers, oceans, and other features. *Noun.*
—**1.** To make a map of; show on a map. The explorers *mapped* the wilderness as they traveled through it. **2.** To plan in detail; arrange. The committee *mapped* out a campaign to raise money for a new hospital. *Verb.*
   map (map) *noun, plural* **maps;** *verb,* **mapped, mapping.**

maple A tree that has leaves with deep notches. Its seeds are contained in a small fruit that looks as though it has two wings. Its wood is used in making furniture.
   ma·ple (mā′pəl) *noun, plural* **maples.**

Maple Tree in Autumn

maple syrup A syrup made by boiling the sap of a certain kind of maple tree.

marble **1.** A hard, smooth stone. Marble is white, or streaked with different colors. It is often used in building and sculpture. **2.** A small, hard ball of glass used in games.
   mar·ble (mär′bəl) *noun, plural* **marbles.**

march **1.** To walk with regular steps as soldiers do. People who march walk in step with others in an orderly group. Firemen and policemen from our town *marched* in the parade. **2.** To move forward steadily. Time *marches* on. *Verb.*
—**1.** The act of marching. The parade started its *march* at noon. **2.** A musical piece that has a strong rhythm and is suitable for marching. The band played a military *march. Noun.*
   march (märch) *verb,* **marched, marching;** *noun, plural* **marches.**

March The third month of the year. March has thirty-one days.
   March (märch) *noun.*

▲ The word **March** comes from a Latin word that meant "of *Mars.*" The Romans often started wars in March so they named this month "the month of Mars" in honor of Mars, who was their god of war.

mare The female of the horse, donkey, zebra, or certain other animals.
   mare (mer) *noun, plural* **mares.**

margarine A food that is used in place of butter. It is made of animal or vegetable oil, milk, water, and salt. Another word for this is **oleomargarine.**
   mar·ga·rine (mär′jər in) *noun, plural* **margarines.**

margin **1.** The blank space around the written or printed part of a page. Judy wrote a note in the *margin* of her science book. **2.** An extra amount; amount in addition to what is necessary. You'd better allow a *margin* of an extra half hour for your trip in case the traffic is heavy. Our team won the game by a very small *margin*.

Marigolds

mar·gin (mär′jin) *noun, plural* **margins.**

marigold A plant that bears yellow, orange, or red flowers.
mar·i·gold (mar′ə gōld′) *noun, plural* **marigolds.**

marine **1.** Having to do with or living in the sea. Whales are *marine* animals. **2.** Having to do with ships. Several stores in the harbor sold *marine* supplies. *Adjective.*
—**Marine.** A member of the Marine Corps. *Noun.*
ma·rine (mə rēn′) *adjective; noun, plural* **Marines.**

Marine Corps A branch of the United States armed forces.

marionette A doll or puppet moved by strings or wires. It is usually made of wood.
mar·i·o·nette (mar′ē-ə net′) *noun, plural* **marionettes.**

mark **1.** A spot or trace made on one thing by another. A line, scratch, stain, or scar is a mark. The only *mark* on the car was a small scratch on the fender. **2.** A sign or symbol. Marion put her initials on her notebook cover as an identification *mark*. Does this sentence end with a question *mark?* **3.** A letter or number that shows how good a person's work is. I get better *marks* in history than in arithmetic. **4.** A line or object that shows position. The white pole was the halfway *mark* on the race track. **5.** Something that is aimed at; target or goal.

Marionette

The arrow fell short of the *mark. Noun.*
—**1.** To make or put a mark or marks on. My muddy boots *marked* the kitchen floor. **2.** To show clearly. A stone wall *marks* the end of the farmer's land. **3.** To be a sign or feature of. Sadness *marked* our moving away and having to say good-by to our friends. **4.** To give a mark to; grade. The teacher *marked* the spelling tests. *Verb.*
mark (märk) *noun, plural* **marks;** *verb,* **marked, marking.**

market **1.** A place or store where food or goods are sold. They bought shrimp at the fish *market*. **2.** A demand for something that is for sale. There is a very large *market* for television sets in this country. *Noun.*
—**1.** To buy food and other things at a market. Every Saturday my parents *market* for the week. **2.** To sell or put up for sale. The rancher *marketed* his cattle in town. *Verb.*
mar·ket (mär′kit) *noun, plural* **markets;** *verb,* **marketed, marketing.**

marmalade Jam made by boiling fresh fruit with sugar. It is most often made with oranges.
mar·ma·lade (mär′mə lād′) *noun, plural* **marmalades.**

maroon¹ A dark brownish-red color. *Noun.*
—Having the color maroon. *Adjective.*
ma·roon (mə rōōn′) *noun, plural* **maroons;** *adjective.*

maroon² To put a person ashore and leave him on a lonely island or coast. The pirates *marooned* their prisoner on a tiny, deserted island.
ma·roon (mə rōōn′) *verb,* **marooned, marooning.**

marquis A nobleman ranking next below a duke and above an earl or count.
mar·quis (mär′kwis *or* mär kē′) *noun, plural* **marquises** *or* **marquis.**

marriage **1.** The state of being married. My grandparents' *marriage* was a happy one. **2.** The act of marrying. That couple's *marriage* took place in June.
mar·riage (mar′ij) *noun, plural* **marriages.**

marrow The soft substance that fills the hollow parts of bones.
mar·row (mar′ō) *noun.*

at; āpe; cär; end; mē; it; īce; hot; ōld;
fôrk; wood; fōōl; oil; out; up; turn; sing;
thin; this; hw in white; zh in treasure.
ə stands for a in about, e in taken
i in pencil, o in lemon, and u in circus.

387

marry **1.** To take as a husband or wife; wed. They plan to *marry* when they finish college. **2.** To join as husband and wife. The minister *married* them in a church.
mar·ry (mar′ē) *verb*, **married, marrying.**

Mars The seventh largest planet. It is the fourth closest planet to the sun and has two moons.
Mars (märz) *noun.*

marsh Low, wet land. Grasses and reeds grow in marshes.
marsh (märsh) *noun, plural* **marshes.**

marshal **1.** An officer of a federal court who has the duties of a sheriff. **2.** A person who arranges certain ceremonies. People who wanted to march in the parade had to get permission from the parade *marshal. Noun.*
—To arrange in proper order. She tried to *marshal* her thoughts before making the speech. The general *marshaled* his troops for battle. *Verb.*
mar·shal (mär′shəl) *noun, plural* **marshals;** *verb,* **marshaled, marshaling.**

marshmallow A soft, white candy covered with powdered sugar.
marsh·mal·low (märsh′mel′ō *or* märsh′-mal′ō) *noun, plural* **marshmallows.**

marsupial A kind of animal. The female has a pouch in which she carries her young. Kangaroos and opossums are marsupials.
mar·su·pi·al (mär sōō′pē əl) *noun, plural* **marsupials.**

martin A kind of swallow that has dark feathers. Martins live throughout the world.
mar·tin (märt′ən) *noun, plural* **mar·tins.**

martyr A person who chooses to suffer or die rather than give up something he believes in. Many saints were martyrs.
mar·tyr (mär′tər) *noun, plural* **martyrs.**

Martin

marvel A wonderful or astonishing thing. Landing men on the moon is one of the *marvels* of modern science. *Noun.*
—To feel wonder and astonishment. Barbara *marveled* at the acrobat's skill. *Verb.*
mar·vel (mär′vəl) *noun, plural* **marvels;** *verb,* **marveled, marveling.**

marvelous Causing wonder or astonishment. The painter tried to show the *marvelous* beauty of the sunset.
mar·vel·ous (mär′və ləs) *adjective.*

Maryland A state in the eastern United States. Its capital is Annapolis.
Mar·y·land (mer′ə lənd) *noun.*

▲ **Maryland** was named for Queen Henrietta *Maria* of England. The man who started the colony of Maryland got the land from Queen Henrietta Maria's husband, King Charles I.

mascot An animal, person, or thing that is supposed to bring good luck. Sports teams often keep a pet animal as a *mascot.*
mas·cot (mas′kot) *noun, plural* **mascots.**

masculine Having to do with or like a man. My brother has a deep, *masculine* voice.
mas·cu·line (mas′kyə lin) *adjective.*

mash A mixture of grains that is fed to livestock or poultry. *Noun.*
—To make into a soft mass. After George boiled the potatoes, he *mashed* them. *Verb.*
mash (mash) *noun, plural* **mashes;** *verb,* **mashed, mashing.**

mask **1.** A covering worn to hide or protect the face. The children wore *masks* to the Halloween party. The baseball bounced off of the catcher's *mask.* **2.** Anything that hides or covers up something. He hid his sadness with a *mask* of happiness. *Noun.*
—**1.** To cover with a mask. The thief *masked* his face so no one would recognize him. **2.** To hide or cover up. A high stone wall *masked* the house from the road. Tony tried to *mask* his disappointment with a smile. *Verb.*
mask (mask) *noun, plural* **masks;** *verb,* **masked, masking.**

Masks

mason A person whose work is building with stone, bricks, or concrete.
　ma·son (mā′sən) *noun, plural* **masons.**

masquerade A party at which masks and costumes are worn.
　mas·quer·ade (mas′kə rād′) *noun, plural* **masquerades.**

mass **1.** A body of matter that has no particular shape. A *mass* of snow piled up along the fence. **2.** A large quantity or number. A *mass* of people showed up for the football game. **3.** Size or bulk. An elephant has great *mass*. **4.** The main or larger part. The *mass* of voters turned out for the election. **5.** The quantity of matter that a body contains. *Noun.*
　—To gather or form into a mass. The police *massed* the crowds along the sidewalk so that the parade could pass through. *Verb.*
　mass (mas) *noun, plural* **masses;** *verb,* **massed, massing.**

Mass The main religious ceremony in the Roman Catholic Church and certain other churches.
　Mass (mas) *noun, plural* **Masses.**

Massachusetts A state in the northeastern United States. Its capital is Boston.
　Mas·sa·chu·setts (mas′ə chōo′sits) *noun.*

▲ **Massachusetts** was the name of an Indian village by some hills near Boston. The word means "at the big hill." English settlers used the name for the tribe that lived in the village, and then later for the colony and the state.

massacre A brutal, bloody killing of many people or animals. *Noun.*
　—To kill many people or animals in a brutal, bloody way. *Verb.*
　mas·sa·cre (mas′ə kər) *noun, plural* **massacres;** *verb,* **massacred, massacring.**

massage The rubbing or kneading of the muscles and joints of the body. A massage relaxes the muscles and helps the circulation of the blood. *Noun.*
　—To give a massage to. The trainer *massaged* the athlete's sprained back. *Verb.*
　mas·sage (mə säzh′) *noun, plural* **massages;** *verb,* **massaged, massaging.**

massive Of great size; very big; large and solid. The safe in the bank has *massive* steel doors.
　mas·sive (mas′iv) *adjective.*

mast A tall pole on a sailing ship or boat that supports the sails and rigging. Masts are usually made of wood or steel.
　mast (mast) *noun, plural* **masts.**

master **1.** A person who has power or control over something. The *master* set his slaves free. The dog came when his *master* called him. **2.** A person who has great skill or knowledge about something. The museum has many works by *masters* of painting. **3.** A male teacher. Teachers in private schools are often called *masters*. **4. Master.** A form of address used before the name of a young boy. *Noun.*
　—**1.** Very skillful in an art or trade. The work on the new house was done by a *master* carpenter. **2.** Most important; main. The *master* bedroom was larger than the other bedrooms. All the lights in the building were controlled by a *master* switch. *Adjective.*
　—**1.** To gain control over. Elaine *mastered* her fears and dove from the high board into the pool. **2.** To become expert in. Keith *mastered* French easily. *Verb.*
　mas·ter (mas′tər) *noun, plural* **masters;** *adjective; verb,* **mastered, mastering.**

masterpiece Something that is done with great skill and craftsmanship. Several *masterpieces* were sold at the art auction.
　mas·ter·piece (mas′tər pēs′) *noun, plural* **masterpieces.**

mat **1.** A small, flat piece of material used as a floor covering or placed in front of a door. Mats are usually made of rubber or woven straw. **2.** A small, flat piece of material that is put under a dish, vase, or other object. It is used for decoration or to protect a surface. **3.** A large, thick pad or covering that is put on the floor to protect wrestlers or boxers. **4.** A thick, tangled mass. There was a *mat* of hair on the dog's back. *Noun.*
　—To become tangled in a thick mass. The wind *matted* her hair. *Verb.*
　mat (mat) *noun, plural* **mats;** *verb,* **matted, matting.**

match¹ A short, thin piece of wood or cardboard. It is coated on one end with a chemical substance that makes a flame when it is struck against something.
　match (mach) *noun, plural* **matches.**

match² **1.** A person or thing that is exactly equal to or very much like another. I bought a pocketbook that was a perfect *match* for my shoes. Bobby is a good tennis player, but he's

at; āpe; cär; end; mē; it; īce; hot; ōld;
fôrk; wood; fōol; oil; out; up; turn; sing;
thin; this; hw in white; zh in treasure.
ə stands for a in about, e in taken
i in pencil, o in lemon, and u in circus.

no *match* for Jack. **2.** A game or contest. Arthur challenged me to a bowling *match*. *Noun.*
—**1.** To be exactly equal to or like something. The new curtains *match* the rug very well. These gloves don't *match*. **2.** To find or make things that are exactly equal to or like one another. After Tony washed the socks, he *matched* them in pairs. **3.** To compete with as an equal. No one on the team could *match* Tom as a pitcher. *Verb.*

match (mach) *noun, plural* **matches;** *verb,* **matched, matching.**

mate **1.** One of a pair. I've lost the *mate* to this sock. **2.** A husband or wife. **3.** The male or female of a pair of animals. The lion guarded its *mate* and their cubs. **4.** An officer on a ship. *Noun.*
—To join in a pair for breeding. Birds *mate* in the spring. *Verb.*

mate (māt) *noun, plural* **mates;** *verb,* **mated, mating.**

material What something is made of or used for. Her winter coat is made of heavy *material*. Stone, wood, bricks, and cement are building *materials*. The woman used her experiences as a lawyer as *material* for her book.

ma·te·ri·al (mə tēr′ē əl) *noun, plural* **materials.**

maternal **1.** Of or like a mother. The cat's *maternal* instinct made her protect her kittens. **2.** Related through one's mother. Your *maternal* grandparents are your mother's parents.

ma·ter·nal (mə turn′əl) *adjective.*

mathematical Having to do with or using mathematics. My brother helped me solve the *mathematical* problem.

math·e·mat·i·cal (math′ə mat′i kəl) *adjective.*

mathematician A person who knows a great deal about mathematics.

math·e·ma·ti·cian (math′ə mə tish′ən) *noun, plural* **mathematicians.**

mathematics The study of numbers, quantities, measurements, and shapes, and how they relate to each other. Arithmetic, algebra, and geometry are parts of mathematics.

math·e·mat·ics (math′ə mat′iks) *noun plural.*

matinee A play or other performance given in the afternoon.

mat·i·nee (mat′ən ā′) *noun, plural* **matinees.**

matter **1.** Anything that has weight and takes up space. All things are made of matter. Matter can be a solid, liquid, or gas. **2.** A subject of discussion, interest, or action. My

father talked on the telephone about a business *matter*. This is a personal *matter* and doesn't concern you. **3.** Problem; trouble. Phyllis went to the dentist to find out what was the *matter* with her tooth. **4.** Written or printed material. The store sells books, newspapers, and other reading *matter*. **5.** An amount or quantity. It's only a *matter* of minutes before the train arrives. *Noun.*
—To be of importance. It doesn't *matter* to me which movie we go to see. *Verb.*

mat·ter (mat′ər) *noun, plural* **matters;** *verb,* **mattered, mattering.**

mattress A thick pad that is used as a bed or part of a bed. It is usually covered with cloth and stuffed with cotton, rubber, or hair. Most mattresses are made to fit on the frame of a bed.

mat·tress (mat′ris) *noun, plural* **mattresses.**

mature Having reached full growth; adult. When a puppy becomes *mature* it is called a dog. The farmer harvested the corn when it was *mature*. *Adjective.*
—To become fully grown or developed. The tomatoes are *maturing* fast. *Verb.*

ma·ture (mə choor′ *or* mə toor′ *or* mə-tyoor′) *adjective; verb,* **matured, maturing.**

maximum The greatest or highest number or point. It will take a *maximum* of three hours to finish the job. The temperature reached a *maximum* of ninety degrees yesterday. *Noun.*
—Greatest possible; highest. The *maximum* speed on this road is forty-five miles per hour. *Adjective.*

max·i·mum (mak′sə məm) *noun, plural* **maximums;** *adjective.*

may *May* I borrow your bicycle? Yes, you *may*. The newspaper said it *may* snow tomorrow. *May* you have a long, happy life.

may (mā) *verb.*

May The fifth month of the year. May has thirty-one days.

May (mā) *noun.*

▲ The word **May** comes from an old French word that meant "of *Maia*." Maia was the earth goddess in ancient Roman religion, and the Romans named this month "the month of Maia" in honor of her.

maybe I don't agree with you, but *maybe* you are right.

may·be (mā′bē) *adverb.*

mayonnaise A thick, creamy sauce or dressing. It is made of egg yolks, oil, and vinegar or lemon juice.

may·on·naise (mā′ə nāz′ *or* mā′ə nāz′) *noun.*

mayor The person who is the official head of a city or town government.
may·or (mā′ər) *noun, plural* **mayors.**

maze A confusing series of paths or passageways through which a person may have a hard time finding his way. Alice got lost in the *maze* of hallways in her new school. ▲ Another word that sounds like this is **maize.**
maze (māz) *noun, plural* **mazes.**

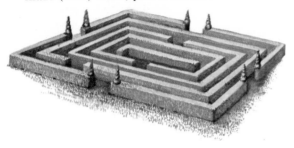

Maze

me The bus takes *me* to school. My cousin sent *me* a birthday card.
me (mē) *pronoun.*

meadow A field of grassy land. It is often used for growing hay or as a pasture for animals.
mead·ow (med′ō) *noun, plural* **meadows.**

meadowlark A songbird that has a yellow breast with a black bar across it. It has a pointed bill and a short tail. Meadowlarks live in North America.
mead·ow·lark (med′ō lärk′) *noun, plural* **meadowlarks.**

Meadowlark

meager Very little; hardly enough. The sick boy ate a *meager* meal of tea and toast.
mea·ger (mē′gər) *adjective.*

meal¹ The food served or eaten at one time. Breakfast is the first *meal* of the day.
meal (mēl) *noun, plural* **meals.**

meal² Grain that has been ground up.
meal (mēl) *noun, plural* **meals.**

mean¹ **1.** To have in mind; want to do or say. He did not *mean* to hurt your feelings. I do not know what you *mean* by that remark. **2.** To be defined as; have a particular sense. "To start" *means* "to begin."
mean (mēn) *verb,* **meant, meaning.**

mean² **1.** Not kind; not nice. It was *mean* of them to tease the little boy. **2.** Low in quality or rank. The poor old man lived in a *mean* shack. **3.** Hard to deal with; difficult. You'd better drive slowly because there's a *mean* curve in the road just ahead.
mean (mēn) *adjective,* **meaner, meanest.**

mean³ **1.** Something that is halfway between two extremes. Warmth is a happy *mean* between freezing cold and great heat. **2. means.** The way that something is or may be done. The man got the money through dishonest *means.* He used the back door as a *means* of escape. **3. means.** Money or property. The money for the new hospital was donated by a man of *means. Noun.*
—Halfway between two extremes; average. The *mean* temperature for last Saturday was sixty degrees. *Adjective.*
mean (mēn) *noun, plural* **means;** *adjective.*

meaning Something that is meant or intended. Do you understand the *meaning* of that poem? The word "run" has many *meanings.*
mean·ing (mē′ning) *noun, plural* **meanings.**

meant Sam *meant* to bring his umbrella with him, but he forgot. Look up **mean** for more information.
meant (ment) *verb.*

meantime The time between. I'll be gone for an hour; in the *meantime,* please answer the telephone if it rings.
mean·time (mēn′tīm′) *noun.*

meanwhile **1.** In or during the time between. The train doesn't leave for an hour; *meanwhile,* I'm going to read a book. **2.** At the same time. Father washed the car; *meanwhile* I mowed the lawn.
mean·while (mēn′hwīl′) *adverb.*

measles A disease that causes a rash of small red spots, a fever, and the symptoms of a bad cold. It is caused by a virus.
mea·sles (mē′zəlz) *noun plural.*

measure **1.** To find or show the size, weight, or amount of something. The doctor *measured* Richard and found that he had grown two inches in a year. My father *measured* the room before buying a new rug for it. The thermometer *measured* the tempera-

at; āpe; cär; end; mē; it; īce; hot; ōld;
fôrk; wood; fool; oil; out; up; turn; sing;
thin; this; hw in white; zh in treasure.
ə stands for a in about, e in taken
i in pencil, o in lemon, and u in circus.

ture in the house. **2.** To have as a measurement. The painting *measured* three feet long and two feet high. **3.** To mark off or set apart by measuring. I *measured* out two cups of flour for the cake. *Verb.*
—**1.** The size, weight, or amount of something. Without a ruler, I could only guess at the *measure* of the piece of wood. **2.** A unit, standard, or system of measurement. Inches and meters are *measures* of length. Good marks are not always a true *measure* of a student's intelligence. **3.** An instrument, container, or other device used for measuring. Bill used a cup *measure* to add milk to the pancake batter. **4.** An amount that can be measured. Our success was due in large *measure* to your help. **5.** Something that is done to make something else happen. The police took harsh *measures* to stop crime in the town. **6.** A bill or law. The Senate and the House of Representatives have passed the *measure.* **7.** A bar of music. *Noun.*

meas·ure (mezh′ər) *verb,* **measured, measuring;** *noun, plural* **measures.**

measurement **1.** The act of measuring. Rulers and scales are used for *measurement.* **2.** Something found or shown by measuring; the size, height, or amount of something. Fred used a ruler to get the *measurements* of the shelf. **3.** A system of measuring. Metric *measurement* is used in many countries of the world.

meas·ure·ment (mezh′ər mənt) *noun, plural* **measurements.**

meat **1.** The parts of an animal used as food. The flesh of a cow, pig, or lamb is meat. **2.** The soft part of anything that can be eaten. The soft, white part of a coconut is called the *meat.* **3.** The most important part of something. The story of the author's life as a soldier was the *meat* of the book. ▲ Another word that sounds like this is **meet.**

meat (mēt) *noun, plural* **meats.**

mechanic A person who is skilled in repairing and using machines. Jack works as an automobile *mechanic* at the garage.

me·chan·ic (mi kan′ik) *noun, plural* **mechanics.**

mechanical Using or having to do with machines. The *mechanical* toy was run by a small motor.

me·chan·i·cal (mi kan′i kəl) *adjective.*

mechanism The working parts of a machine. The jeweler said that the only thing wrong with the *mechanism* of my watch was a broken spring.

mech·a·nism (mek′ə niz′əm) *noun, plural* **mechanisms.**

medal A flat piece of metal that is often shaped like a coin. Medals are often given as a reward for bravery or achievement. ▲ Another word that sounds like this is **meddle.**

med·al (med′əl) *noun, plural* **medals.**

Medal

meddle To take part in another person's business without being asked or wanted. Bob told Jane not to *meddle* in his personal affairs. ▲ Another word that sounds like this is **medal.**

med·dle (med′əl) *verb,* **meddled, meddling.**

media More than one medium. The President's trip abroad was reported on television and in other news *media.*

me·di·a (mē′dē ə) *noun plural.*

medical Having to do with doctors and medicine. Doctors are trained in *medical* schools. The woman went to the hospital for *medical* treatment.

med·i·cal (med′i kəl) *adjective.*

medicine **1.** A drug or other substance used to prevent or cure disease or to relieve pain. She took the cough *medicine* every three hours. **2.** The science or practice of treating and curing disease or injury. Lisa is planning to have a career in *medicine.*

med·i·cine (med′ə sin) *noun, plural* **medicines.**

medicine man A person in certain North American Indian tribes who was believed to have magic powers.

medieval Having to do with or belonging in the Middle Ages.

me·di·e·val (mē′dē ē′vəl *or* mid ē′vəl) *adjective.*

Mediterranean A large sea between southern Europe, western Asia, and northern Africa. *Noun.*
—Of the Mediterranean Sea. *Adjective.*

Med·i·ter·ra·ne·an (med′ə tə rā′nē ən) *noun; adjective.*

medium **1.** Something that is in the middle. Pat tried to find a happy *medium* between working too hard and not doing anything. **2.** A substance or thing through which something acts or is done. The newspaper is a *medium* of communication. The air is a *medium* for sound waves. *Noun.*
—Having a middle position in size, amount, quality, or degree. Although her parents are both short, June is of *medium* height. *Adjective.*

me·di·um (mē′dē əm) *noun, plural* **mediums** or **media** *(for definition 2); adjective.*

meet **1.** To come face to face with; come upon. While walking downtown, Bill *met* a friend he hadn't seen in months. **2.** To be introduced to. I hope to *meet* your parents some day soon. **3.** To keep an appointment with. Jack asked Robin to *meet* him outside of school at three o'clock. **4.** To have enough for. Jim had to borrow money to *meet* his expenses. **5.** To come into contact with; join. The Hudson River *meets* the Atlantic Ocean at New York City. *Verb.*
—A meeting or contest. Our school placed first in the swimming *meet. Noun.* ▲ Another word that sounds like this is **meat.**
meet (mēt) *verb,* **met, meeting;** *noun, plural* **meets.**

meeting **1.** A gathering of people. All the members of the club came to the *meeting.* **2.** The act of coming together. We had a chance *meeting* with some old friends. **3.** The place where things meet. The town was located at the *meeting* of two rivers.
meet·ing (mē′ting) *noun, plural* **meetings.**

megaphone A device used to increase the sound of the voice. It is usually shaped something like a funnel.
meg·a·phone (meg′ə fōn′) *noun, plural* **mega-phones.**

melancholy **1.** Low in spirits; sad; gloomy. Susan had *melancholy* thoughts about what would happen if she failed the test. **2.** Causing low spirits or sadness. The old deserted house was a *melan-choly* sight. *Adjec-tive.*
—Low spirits; sad-ness. Chris was in a fit of *melancholy* when he found out that the camping trip had been called off. *Noun.*
mel·an·chol·y (mel′ən kol′ē) *adjective; noun.*

Megaphone

mellow **1.** Made wise and understanding by age. He used to be an impatient man, but he is *mellow* in his old age. **2.** Full, soft, and rich. The room echoed with the *mellow* sound of the violin.
mel·low (mel′ō) *adjective,* **mellower, mel-lowest.**

melody A series of musical notes that make up a tune. That song has a gay *melody.*
mel·o·dy (mel′ə dē) *noun, plural* **melodies.**

melon A large fruit that grows on a vine. Melons have a sweet, soft pulp that can be eaten. Cantaloupes are melons.
mel·on (mel′ən) *noun, plural* **melons.**

melt **1.** To change from a solid to a liquid by heating. The warm sun *melted* the ice on the pond. **2.** To slowly become a liquid; dissolve. The lump of sugar *melted* in the coffee. **3.** To disappear or change gradually. The clouds *melted* away. **4.** To become gentle or under-standing. His heart *melted* when the child began to cry.
melt (melt) *verb,* **melted, melting.**

member **1.** A person, animal, or thing that belongs to a group. The *members* of the club elected Ruth president. The lion is a *member* of the cat family. **2.** A part of the body of a person or an animal. A leg or arm is a member.
mem·ber (mem′bər) *noun, plural* **members.**

membrane A thin layer of skin or tissue. Membranes line parts of the body.
mem·brane (mem′brān) *noun, plural* **mem-branes.**

memo A short note. Mother wrote a *memo* of the errands she wanted me to do.
mem·o (mem′ō) *noun, plural* **memos.**

memorial Something that is a reminder of a person or event. Monuments and statues are often used as memorials. The town built a *memorial* to honor men who had died in the war.
me·mo·ri·al (mə môr′ē əl) *noun, plural* **memorials.**

Memorial Day A holiday in memory of servicemen who died in all American wars. It comes on the last Monday in May.

memorize To learn by heart; fix in the memory. The singer *memorized* the song so that he would not have to look at the music while he sang.
mem·o·rize (mem′ə rīz′) *verb,* **memorized, memorizing.**

memory **1.** The ability to remember things. Sally is a good student in history because she has a very good *memory* for facts and dates.

at; āpe; cär; end; mē; it; īce; hot; ōld;
fôrk; wood; fool; oil; out; up; turn; sing;
thin; this; hw in white; zh in treasure.
ə stands for a in about, e in taken
i in pencil, o in lemon, and u in circus.

2. All that a person can remember. Peter recited the poem from *memory*. **3.** A person or thing that is remembered. The trip to Canada was one of her happiest *memories*. The statue was put up to honor the *memory* of George Washington.

mem·o·ry (mem′ər ē) *noun, plural* **memories.**

men More than one man. Look up **man** for more information.

men (men) *noun plural.*

menace A person or thing that is a threat. Careless drivers are a *menace* to everyone else on the road. *Noun.*

—To threaten something; put in danger. The sudden storm *menaced* the small fishing boat. *Verb.*

men·ace (men′is) *noun, plural* **menaces;** *verb,* **menaced, menacing.**

mend To put in good condition again; fix or repair. Rachel used glue to *mend* the broken cup. Mother *mended* my torn baseball uniform. *Verb.*

—A mended place. You could see the *mend* where the hole in the sock had been sewed up. *Noun.*

mend (mend) *verb,* **mended, mending;** *noun, plural* **mends.**

-ment A *suffix* that means: **1.** "The act of doing something." *Development* means "the act of developing." **2.** "The state of being." *Amazement* means "the state of being amazed." **3.** "The result of." *Improvement* means "the result of improving."

mental **1.** Done by or having to do with the mind. Learning to speak is one stage of a child's *mental* development. **2.** Having to do with or for people who have a disease of the mind. The hospital treated many *mental* patients.

men·tal (ment′əl) *adjective.*

mention To speak about or refer to. David *mentioned* you in the letter he wrote to me. *Verb.*

—A short remark or statement. There was no *mention* of the robbery in this morning's newspaper. *Noun.*

men·tion (men′shən) *verb,* **mentioned, mentioning;** *noun.*

menu A list of the food that is available in a restaurant or other eating place. We wanted to order fried chicken but it wasn't on the *menu*.

men·u (men′yoo′) *noun, plural* **menus.**

meow The sound that a cat or kitten makes. *Noun.*

—To make this sound. The cat *meowed* because it was hungry. *Verb.*

me·ow (mē ou′) *noun, plural* **meows;** *verb,* **meowed, meowing.**

merchandise Things that are bought and sold. The hardware store sold tools, paint, and other *merchandise*.

mer·chan·dise (mur′chən dīz′ *or* mur′chən-dīs′) *noun.*

merchant **1.** A person whose business is buying and selling things. Mr. Brooks is a clothing *merchant*. **2.** A person who owns or runs a store. All the *merchants* in our town decorated their store windows at Christmas time.

mer·chant (mur′chənt) *noun, plural* **merchants.**

merchant marine The ships of a nation that are used in trade and commerce.

mercury A heavy, silver-colored metal. Mercury is a liquid at normal temperatures. It is used in thermometers and barometers. Mercury is a chemical element.

mer·cu·ry (mur′kyər ē) *noun.*

Mercury The smallest planet. It is the closest planet to the sun.

Mer·cu·ry (mur′kyər ē) *noun.*

mercy **1.** More kindness or forgiveness than is expected or deserved. The guilty man begged the judge for *mercy*. **2.** Something to be thankful for; blessing. It's a *mercy* that no one was hurt in the accident.

mer·cy (mur′sē) *noun, plural* **mercies.**

mere Nothing more than; only. The *mere* thought of having to do all that work made him feel tired.

mere (mēr) *adjective.*

merge To join and become one; come together. The two paths *merged* at the foot of the hill. The two businesses *merged* to become one large company.

merge (murj) *verb,* **merged, merging.**

meridian **1.** An imaginary circle on the earth's surface. It passes through the North and South Poles. **2.** The highest point that the sun or a star reaches in the sky. The sun's meridian is reached at about noon.

me·rid·i·an (mə rid′ē ən) *noun, plural* **meridians.**

merit **1.** Goodness, worth, or value. Your idea has great *merit*. **2. merits.** The actual facts of a matter. A fair judge will always decide a case on its *merits*. *Noun.*

—To deserve. The politician *merited* the huge number of votes he was given. *Verb.*

mer·it (mer′it) *noun, plural* **merits;** *verb,* **merited, meriting.**

mermaid An imaginary creature that was believed to live in the sea. It had the head and body of a beautiful woman and the tail of a fish.

mer·maid (mur′mād′) *noun, plural* **mermaids.**

merry Cheerful and gay; full of fun. The old man had a twinkle in his eye and a *merry* smile.

mer·ry (mer′ē) *adjective,* **merrier, merriest.**

merry-go-round A round platform that has wooden animals and seats on which people ride while the platform turns.

mer·ry-go-round (mer′ē gō round′) *noun, plural* **merry-go-rounds.**

Merry-go-round

mesh A net made of laced threads or wires. The metal screen on a window is a kind of mesh.

mesh (mesh) *noun, plural* **meshes.**

mess **1.** A dirty or disorderly state; untidy group of things. Please clean up the *mess* in your room. **2.** An unpleasant, difficult, or confusing state. The car accident made a *mess* of our vacation. **3.** A group of people in the army or navy who eat their meals together. *Noun.*
—**1.** To make dirty or disorderly. Our muddy boots *messed* the clean kitchen floor. **2.** To spoil or confuse. The rain *messed* up our plans for a picnic. *Verb.*

mess (mes) *noun, plural* **messes;** *verb,* **messed, messing.**

message Words sent from one person or group to another. I left a *message* for Jane to call me when she got home. The President's Memorial Day *message* was broadcast on television.

mes·sage (mes′ij) *noun, plural* **messages.**

messenger A person who delivers messages or runs errands. A *messenger* brought the telegram to our house.

mes·sen·ger (mes′ən jər) *noun, plural* **messengers.**

met Barbara and Ed *met* in front of the school. Look up **meet** for more information.

met (met) *verb.*

metabolism All of the chemical and biological processes that take place in a living thing. Metabolism is the means by which our bodies use the food we eat.

me·tab·o·lism (mə tab′ə liz′əm) *noun, plural* **metabolisms.**

metal A substance that has a shiny surface, can be melted, and can conduct heat and electricity. Iron, silver, copper, lead, brass, and bronze are metals.

met·al (met′əl) *noun, plural* **metals.**

metallic Of or containing a metal. The box was made of a *metallic* substance. The bell rang with a *metallic* sound.

me·tal·lic (mə tal′ik) *adjective.*

metamorphosis The series of changes in shape and function that certain animals go through as they develop from an immature form to an adult. Caterpillars become butterflies and tadpoles become frogs through metamorphosis.

met·a·mor·pho·sis (met′ə môr′fə sis) *noun, plural* **metamorphoses.**

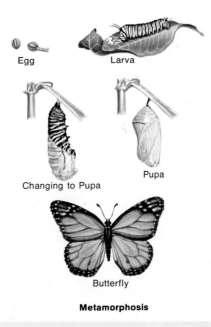

Egg　Larva

Changing to Pupa　Pupa

Butterfly

Metamorphosis

at; āpe; cär; end; mē; it; īce; hot; ōld;
fôrk; wood; fōōl; oil; out; up; turn; sing;
thin; **th**is; **hw** in white; **zh** in treasure.
ə stands for **a** in about, **e** in taken
i in pencil, **o** in lemon, and **u** in circus.

metaphor   A statement in which one thing is compared to another to suggest that they are smilar. Metaphors are often used in writing, especially poetry. "All the world's a stage" and "The Lord is my shepherd" are examples of metaphors.
   met·a·phor (met′ə fôr′) *noun, plural* **metaphors.**

meteor   A mass of metal or stone that comes into the earth's atmosphere from space. As it passes through the atmosphere at high speed, it becomes very hot and burns with a bright light as it falls to the earth.
   me·te·or (mē′tē ər) *noun, plural* **meteors.**

meteorite   A meteor that has fallen to the earth.
   me·te·or·ite (mē′tē ə rīt′) *noun, plural* **meteorites.**

meteorologist   A person who studies meteorology or who knows a great deal about meteorology.
   me·te·or·ol·o·gist (mē′tē ə rol′ə jist) *noun, plural* **meteorologists.**

meteorology   The science that studies the earth's atmosphere and the changes that take place within it. One important branch of meteorology is the study of the weather.
   me·te·or·ol·o·gy (mē′tē ə rol′ə jē) *noun.*

meter[1]   The basic unit of length in the metric system. A meter is equal to 39.37 inches, or slightly more than 3¼ feet.
   me·ter (mē′tər) *noun, plural* **meters.**

meter[2]   **1.** The regular pattern of rhythm that accented and unaccented syllables give to a line of poetry. **2.** The basic pattern of rhythm that accented notes or beats give to a piece of music.
   me·ter (mē′tər) *noun, plural* **meters.**

meter[3]   A device that measures or records something. Instruments that show how much electricity, water, or gas is used in a house or building or how fast a car is moving are kinds of meters.
   me·ter (mē′tər) *noun, plural* **meters.**

method   **1.** A way of doing something. Speaking on the telephone and writing a letter are two *methods* of communicating with another person. The doctor discovered a new *method* for treating the disease. **2.** Order or system. It was hard to find the one book we wanted because the books had been put on the shelves without *method*.
   meth·od (meth′əd) *noun, plural* **methods.**

metric   Of or having to do with the metric system. I bought a *metric* ruler. The gram is a *metric* measurement.
   met·ric (met′rik) *adjective.*

metric system   A system of measurement by tens. The meter is the basic unit of length, the kilogram is the basic unit of weight, and the liter is the basic unit of capacity.

metropolis   A large city. It is usually the largest or most important city in a country, state, or area.
   me·trop·o·lis (mə trop′ə lis) *noun, plural* **metropolises.**

metropolitan   Belonging to or having to do with a metropolis. There were 5000 persons on the *metropolitan* police force. A *metropolitan* area is made up of the city and the smaller towns around it.
   met·ro·pol·i·tan (met′rə pol′ə tən) *adjective.*

Mexican   A person who was born in Mexico or is a citizen of Mexico. *Noun.*
   —Of or having to do with Mexico or its people. *Adjective.*
   Mex·i·can (mek′si kən) *noun, plural* **Mexicans;** *adjective.*

Mexico   A country in North America that borders the southwestern United States. Its capital is Mexico City.
   Mex·i·co (mek′si kō′) *noun.*

mice   More than one mouse. Look up **mouse** for more information.
   mice (mīs) *noun plural.*

Michigan   A state in the north-central United States. Its capital is Lansing.
   Mich·i·gan (mish′ə gən) *noun.*

▲ **Michigan** is the way French explorers wrote an Indian name for Lake Michigan that meant "big water." The state was named for Lake Michigan.

microbe   A very tiny living thing. Some microbes cause disease.
   mi·crobe (mī′krōb) *noun, plural* **microbes.**

microorganism   A living thing that is too small to be seen with the naked eye. A virus is a microorganism.
   mi·cro·or·gan·ism (mī′krō ôr′gə niz′əm) *noun, plural* **microorganisms.**

microphone   A device that is used to transmit sound or to make it louder. A microphone changes sound waves into electrical signals.
   mi·cro·phone (mī′krə fōn′) *noun, plural* **microphones.**

microscope   A device that is used to look at things that are too small to be seen with the naked eye. It has a lens or combination of lenses that produce an enlarged image of anything seen through it.
   mi·cro·scope (mī′ krə skōp′) *noun, plural* **microscopes.**

The Metric System

How Long?

A **meter** (m) is a unit of length. In the picture, the baseball bat is about one *meter* long.

A **millimeter** and a **centimeter** are units of length used to measure smaller objects. A millimeter (mm) is

equal to one-thousandth of a meter. A centimeter (cm) is equal to one-hundredth of a meter. This needle is about one *millimeter* thick and four *centimeters* long.

A **kilometer** (km) is used to measure long distances. It is equal to 1000 meters. The Empire State Building is about one-half *kilometer* tall.

How Heavy?

A **kilogram** (kg) is a unit of weight. In the picture, the book weighs about two *kilograms*.

A **gram** (g) is a unit of weight used to measure lighter objects. A gram is equal to one-thousandth of a kilogram. Each of these peas weighs one *gram*.

How Much?

A **liter** (l) is a unit used to measure how much something holds, or its *capacity*. In the picture, the pitcher holds about one *liter* of liquid.

A **milliliter** (ml) is a unit of capacity used to measure smaller

amounts. A milliliter is equal to one-thousandth of a liter. This thermometer holds about two *milliliters* of liquid.

How Hot or Cold?

The **Celsius scale** (also sometimes called the **Centigrade scale**) is used to measure temperature. Water freezes at a temperature of zero degrees Celsius (0°C) and boils at a temperature of one hundred degrees Celsius (100°C). As an example, when water is 20°C, it is warm enough for swimming.

mid Being at or near the middle. My brother was born in the *mid* 1960s.
mid (mid) *adjective.*

midday The middle of the day; noon. We ate our lunch at *midday.*
mid·day (mid′dā′) *noun.*

middle Halfway between two things, sides, times, or the like. We sat in the *middle* row of the class. Ellen is the *middle* child in a family of three girls. *Adjective.*
—Something that is halfway between two things, sides, times, or the like. There is a white line down the *middle* of the street. *Noun.*
mid·dle (mid′əl) *adjective; noun, plural* mid·dles.

middle-aged In the time of life between youth and old age; between about forty and sixty years old. The bride's parents were *middle-aged.*
mid·dle-aged (mid′əl ājd′) *adjective.*

Middle Ages The period of European history from about 400 A.D. to 1450.

middle ear The hollow space between the eardrum and the inner ear. In human beings, the middle ear contains three very small bones that pass sound waves from the eardrum to the inner ear.

Middle East A region that is made up of Israel, Egypt, Syria, Turkey, Iran, and other countries between Europe and India.

Middle West A region of the north-central United States.

midget A very small person. A midget is much smaller than, but has the same proportions as, a normal adult.
midg·et (mij′it) *noun, plural* midgets.

midnight Twelve o'clock at night; the middle of the night.
mid·night (mid′nīt′) *noun.*

midst 1. The middle; center. Lesley got lost in the *midst* of the crowd. The telephone call came in the *midst* of a very important meeting. 2. A group of people. The soldiers were afraid that there was a spy in their *midst.*
midst (midst) *noun.*

midway In the middle; halfway. The sailors reached the *midway* point in their voyage. His house is *midway* between my house and yours. *Adjective, Adverb.*
—A place for games, rides, and other amusements at a circus, carnival, or fair. *Noun.*
mid·way (mid′wā′) *adjective; adverb; noun, plural* midways.

Midwest A region of the north-central United States.
Mid·west (mid′west′) *noun.*

might¹ We *might* have made the train if we had left sooner. ▲ Another word that sounds like this is **mite.**
might (mīt) *verb.*

might² Power or strength. He slammed the door with all his *might.* She tried with all her *might* not to cry. ▲ Another word that sounds like this is **mite.**
might (mīt) *noun.*

mighty Great in power, size, or amount. That nation has a *mighty* army. The Pacific is a *mighty* ocean.
might·y (mī′tē) *adjective,* **mightier, mightiest.**

migrate To move from one place to another. The pioneers in the United States *migrated* to the West to find land to settle on. Many birds *migrate* to the south in the fall.
mi·grate (mī′grāt) *verb,* **migrated, migrating.**

migration The act of moving from one place to another. During their *migration,* geese from Canada stop at a pond near our house.
mi·gra·tion (mī grā′shən) *noun, plural* migrations.

mild Gentle or calm; not harsh or sharp. A *mild* winter is one that is not very cold and snowy. A *mild* headache does not hurt too much. A *mild* cheese does not have a strong taste. A *mild* scolding is not an angry one.
mild (mīld) *adjective,* **milder, mildest.**

mile A measure of distance equal to 5280 feet.
mile (mīl) *noun, plural* miles.

mileage The number of miles traveled. The *mileage* on our car is 50,000 miles.
mile·age (mī′lij) *noun.*

military Having to do with an army, soldiers, or war. George wanted to follow a *military* career in the Marines. His *military* uniform was tan.
mil·i·tar·y (mil′ə ter′ē) *adjective.*

militia A group of citizens who are trained to fight and help in emergencies. Each state in the United States has a militia called the National Guard.
mi·li·tia (mi lish′ə) *noun, plural* militias.

milk 1. A white liquid food produced by glands in female mammals. The milk of cows is used as food by people. The milk of all mammals is used to feed their young. 2. A white liquid like this that is made in plants. The fruits of coconuts have milk that people use as food. *Noun.*
—To take milk from a cow or goat. It was the oldest son's job to *milk* the cows early each evening. *Verb.*
milk (milk) *noun, plural* milks; *verb,* **milked, milking.**

Milky Way A cloudy white path that stretches across the sky at night. It is made up of thousands of stars. It is a galaxy.

mill **1.** A building where there are machines to grind grain into flour or meal. **2.** A machine that grinds corn or other seeds. A coffee *mill* grinds coffee beans. **3.** A building where there are machines to make special materials. Steel *mills* make steel. *Noun.*
—**1.** To grind. The machines *milled* the grain into flour. **2.** To move around in a confused way. The frightened sheep *milled* around in the pen. *Verb.*
mill (mil) *noun, plural* **mills;** *verb,* **milled, milling.**

million One thousand times one thousand; 1,000,000.
mil·lion (mil′yən) *noun, plural* **millions;** *adjective.*

millionaire A person who has money or property worth a million or more dollars.
mil·lion·aire (mil′yə ner′) *noun, plural* **millionaires.**

mimeograph A machine that makes copies of written pages. Our teacher made copies of our test questions on the *mimeograph.*
mim·e·o·graph (mim′ē ə graf′) *noun, plural* **mimeographs.**

mimic To imitate, especially in order to make fun of. Bob likes to *mimic* his teachers. Some parrots *mimic* people's voices. *Verb.*
—A person or thing that imitates. *Noun.*
mim·ic (mim′ik) *verb,* **mimicked, mimicking;** *noun, plural* **mimics.**

minaret A tall, slender tower on top of a mosque. A crier calls people to prayer from a balcony near the top of a minaret.
min·a·ret (min′ə ret′) *noun, plural* **minarets.**

mince To chop into very small pieces. We *minced* onions to put in the meat loaf.
mince (mins) *verb,* **minced, mincing.**

mincemeat A filling for pies. Mincemeat is a mixture of finely chopped apples, raisins, currants, sugar and other spices, and sometimes meat.
mince·meat (mins′mēt′) *noun.*

Minaret

mind **1.** The part of a person that thinks, knows, learns, remembers, understands, and feels. Lorraine's high marks in school show that she has a good *mind.* I'll keep your invitation to visit in *mind* when I go to New York. Keep your *mind* on what you're doing. **2.** A wish or opinion. I changed my *mind* about visiting them when I heard she was sick. *Noun.*
—**1.** To pay attention to or worry about. *Mind* your manners at the dinner table. **2.** To take care of. A baby-sitter *minds* my little brother when our parents go out. **3.** To not like something; object to. Do you *mind* going to the movies alone? *Verb.*
mind (mīnd) *noun, plural* **minds;** *verb,* **minded, minding.**

mine[1] The bicycle that used to belong to my older sister is now *mine.*
mine (mīn) *pronoun.*

mine[2] **1.** A large open space dug under the ground. Coal, gold, diamonds, and other materials are dug out of mines. **2.** Any rich source or supply. The book was a *mine* of information about life under the sea. **3.** A bomb that is put underground or underwater. *Noun.*
—**1.** To take from under the ground. People *mine* coal in Pennsylvania. **2.** To put bombs in. The navy divers *mined* the harbor during the war. *Verb.*
mine (mīn) *noun, plural* **mines;** *verb,* **mined, mining.**

mineral A substance found in nature that is not an animal or a plant. Salt, coal, and gold are minerals. *Noun.*
—Containing minerals. *Mineral* water is water that has natural salts in it. *Adjective.*
min·er·al (min′ər əl) *noun, plural* **minerals;** *adjective.*

miniature Very small. Kathy made *miniature* furniture for her doll house. *Adjective.*
—Something made in a very small size. We bought a *miniature* of the Statue of Liberty as a souvenir of our trip to New York. *Noun.*
min·i·a·ture (min′ē ə chər *or* min′ə chər) *adjective; noun, plural* **miniatures.**

minimum The smallest or lowest amount. I will need a *minimum* of two weeks to finish

at; āpe; cär; end; mē; it; īce; hot; ōld; fôrk; wood; fo͞ol; oil; out; up; turn; sing; thin; this; hw in white; zh in treasure.
ə stands for a in about, e in taken
i in pencil, o in lemon, and u in circus.

my report. The temperature reached a *min-imum* of 20 degrees today. *Noun.*
—Lowest; smallest. The *minimum* pay for the job was $2.50 an hour. *Adjective.*
min·i·mum (min′ə məm) *noun, plural* **min-imums;** *adjective.*

minister **1.** A person who is authorized to conduct religious services; clergyman; pastor. **2.** A person who is in charge of a department of a government. *Noun.*
—To take care of. Nurses *minister* to sick people. *Verb.*
min·is·ter (min′is tər) *noun, plural* **ministers;** *verb,* **ministered, ministering.**

mink A small animal with soft, thick fur. Minks live in woods near water.
mink (mingk) *noun, plural* **minks** or **mink.**

Mink

Minnesota A state in the north-central United States. Its capital is St. Paul.
Min·ne·so·ta (min′ə sō′tə) *noun.*

▲ **Minnesota** was an Indian name for the Minnesota River. It means "water the color of the sky" or "cloudy water." Congress gave this name to the area that became the state of Minnesota.

---

minnow A very small, freshwater fish.
min·now (min′ō) *noun, plural* **minnows.**

minor Small in importance or size. The only mistake on her paper was a *minor* error in spelling. *Adjective.*
—A person who is not old enough to vote or be legally responsible for himself. *Noun.*
mi·nor (mī′nər) *adjective; noun, plural* **minors.**

minority **1.** The smaller part of a group or whole. John was elected class president because only a *minority* of students voted for the other candidate. **2.** A group of people that is thought of as different from the larger group of which it is a part because of race, religion, politics, or nationality.
mi·nor·i·ty (mə nôr′ə tē *or* mī nôr′ə tē) *noun, plural* **minorities.**

mint¹ **1.** A plant that has leaves that are used as flavoring. Peppermint and spearmint are kinds of mint. **2.** A candy flavored with mint.
mint (mint) *noun, plural* **mints.**

mint² **1.** A place where money in the form of coins is made by the government. **2.** A large amount of money. His big new car cost a *mint. Noun.*
—To make coins. The government *minted* new half dollars this year. *Verb.*
mint (mint) *noun, plural* **mints;** *verb,* **minted, minting.**

minuend The number from which another number is subtracted. In 6 − 2 = 4, the minuend is 6.
min·u·end (min′yoo end′) *noun, plural* **minuends.**

minus Decreased by; less. Ten *minus* seven is three. *Preposition.*
—**1.** Less than zero. It was *minus* four degrees this morning. **2.** Lower or less than. He got a grade of A *minus* on his paper. **3.** Showing that something is to be or has been taken away. A *minus* sign means that the number following it is to be subtracted. *Adjective.*
—A sign (−) that shows something is to be or has been subtracted. *Noun.*
mi·nus (mī′nəs) *preposition; adjective; noun, plural* **minuses.**

minute¹ **1.** A unit of time equal to sixty seconds. There are sixty minutes in an hour. **2.** A moment in time; instant. I knew who she was the *minute* she walked into the room. May I speak to you for a *minute?* **3. minutes.** A written report of what was said and done at a meeting. The secretary of our class took *minutes* of our meeting and read them to us the next time we met.
min·ute (min′it) *noun, plural* **minutes.**

minute² **1.** Very small; tiny. A *minute* piece of dust blew into my eye and the doctor had to take it out. **2.** Paying close attention to details; very careful and thorough. The detective made a *minute* examination of the desk for fingerprints.
mi·nute (mī noot′ *or* mī nyoot′) *adjective.*

minuteman A volunteer soldier who was not part of the regular army during the American Revolution, but was ready to fight at a minute's notice.
min·ute·man (min′it man′) *noun, plural* **minutemen.**

miracle **1.** Something amazing or wonderful that cannot be explained by the laws of nature. When the man who had been blind all his life could suddenly see, people said it was a *miracle*. **2.** An amazing or wonderful thing. It was a *miracle* that he escaped from the burning house.

mir·a·cle (mir′ə kəl) *noun, plural* **miracles.**

mirage Something that makes a person think he sees something that is not really there. Mirages are sometimes seen at sea or in the desert. A mirage is caused by light rays that are bent by layers of air at different temperatures. A common mirage is a sheet of water that you see ahead of you on a highway during a hot summer day.

mi·rage (mi räzh′) *noun, plural* **mirages.**

mirror A smooth, polished surface that shows the image of the person or thing in front of it by reflecting light. Most mirrors are made of glass with an aluminum or silver coating on the back. *Noun.*
—To reflect a picture or image. She could see herself *mirrored* in his dark glasses. *Verb.*

mir·ror (mir′ər) *noun, plural* **mirrors;** *verb,* **mirrored, mirroring.**

misbehave To do something that is wrong; behave badly. The child knew she was *misbehaving* when she drew pictures on the wall with her crayons.

mis·be·have (mis′bi hāv′) *verb,* **misbehaved, misbehaving.**

miscellaneous Made up of different kinds of things. There was a *miscellaneous* collection of papers, toys, and clothes in his top dresser drawer.

mis·cel·la·ne·ous (mis′ə lā′nē əs) *adjective.*

mischief Something a person does that is playful but often causes harm or trouble. The little boy did a lot of *mischief* when he was left alone with the crayons.

mis·chief (mis′chif) *noun.*

mischievous Full of mischief; playful or naughty. The *mischievous* child hid his brother's favorite toy.

mis·chie·vous (mis′chə vəs) *adjective.*

miser A person who loves money in a greedy way, and is stingy and selfish about spending it.

mi·ser (mī′zər) *noun, plural* **misers.**

miserable **1.** Very unhappy; wretched. Jane felt *miserable* about losing her dog. **2.** Very bad and uncomfortable. He had a *miserable* cold. **3.** Of little or no value; poor. He did such a *miserable* job of fixing the chair that it broke again the first time someone sat down on it.

mis·er·a·ble (miz′ər ə bəl) *adjective.*

misery Great unhappiness or pain. The bad flood caused *misery* for many people.

mis·er·y (miz′ər ē) *noun, plural* **miseries.**

misfortune **1.** Bad luck. It was Jack's *misfortune* to lose his new watch. **2.** An unlucky event or happening. The fire was a great *misfortune* to the family because most of their belongings were burned.

mis·for·tune (mis fôr′chən) *noun, plural* **misfortunes.**

misleading Causing a mistake or wrong idea. The witness told the police a *misleading* story because he did not want them to know what had really happened.

mis·lead·ing (mis lē′ding) *adjective.*

misplace **1.** To put something in a place and forget where it is; lose. Bob *misplaced* his hammer and had to buy a new one. **2.** To put in the wrong place. In the sentence "If you go please, tell me first," the comma after "please" is *misplaced*. It should be after "go."

mis·place (mis plās′) *verb,* **misplaced, misplacing.**

mispronounce To pronounce a word or sound in the wrong way. If you pronounce "write" as (rit) instead of (rīt), you are *mispronouncing* it.

mis·pro·nounce (mis′prə nouns′) *verb,* **mispronounced, mispronouncing.**

miss¹ **1.** To fail to do or get. Ben swung his bat and *missed* the ball. Jack *missed* the bus. Caroline *missed* her dentist appointment. Dad *missed* the exit on the highway and had to turn around. **2.** To notice or feel the absence or loss of a person or thing. I *missed* my sister when she went away for the summer. Mother didn't *miss* her watch until that evening when she wanted to wind it. **3.** To get away from; escape. We just *missed* being hit by the falling rock. *Verb.*
—A failure to hit or reach something. The rifleman hit the target five times without a *miss. Noun.*

miss (mis) *verb,* **missed, missing;** *noun, plural* **misses.**

miss² A title used for a girl or a woman who is not married. When "miss" is used with a person's name, it is written with a capital "M." Our friend, *Miss* Lane, will be visiting

at; āpe; cär; end; mē; it; īce; hot; ōld;
fôrk; wood; fōol; oil; out; up; turn; sing;
thin; this; hw in white; zh in treasure.
ə stands for a in about, e in taken
i in pencil, o in lemon, and u in circus.

this weekend. "Yes, *miss*, can I help you?" asked the sales clerk.

miss (mis) *noun, plural* **misses.**

missile Anything that is thrown or shot through the air. An arrow, a bullet, and a rock are missiles. A guided *missile* can be directed toward a target while it is in the air.

mis·sile (mis′əl) *noun, plural* **missiles.**

missing **1.** That is or was lost. The *missing* sock was found under the bed. **2.** Not there; absent or lacking. The puzzle was *missing* one piece.

miss·ing (mis′ing) *adjective.*

mission **1.** A group of people who are sent somewhere to do a special job. Four men formed a rescue *mission* to search for the lost boy. **2.** A special job or task. The astronauts went on a *mission* to the moon. **3.** A church or other place where a group of missionaries work.

mis·sion (mish′ən) *noun, plural* **missions.**

missionary A person who is sent by his church to teach his religion in another country. Our priest was a *missionary* in India for ten years.

mis·sion·ar·y (mish′ə ner′ē) *noun, plural* **missionaries.**

Mississippi A state in the southern United States. Its capital is Jackson.

Mis·sis·sip·pi (mis′ə sip′ē) *noun.*

▲ **Mississippi** comes from two Indian words that mean "big river," "great water," or "father of the waters." The name was first used in the northern part of the country for what is now called the Mississippi River, but French explorers carried it down the river. Congress gave the name to the area at the southern end of the river that became the state of Mississippi.

Missouri A state in the central United States. Its capital is Jefferson City.

Mis·sou·ri (mi zoor′ē *or* mi zoor′ə) *noun.*

▲ **Missouri** is an Indian word that means "people with the big canoes." It was the name of a tribe that lived near the mouth of the Missouri River when French explorers first went there. Later the name was used for the river near this tribe's home, and finally it was given to the state.

misspell To spell a word incorrectly. I *misspelled* "until" on the test because I spelled it with two l's at the end.

mis·spell (mis spel′) *verb,* **misspelled** or **misspelt, misspelling.**

mist A cloud of tiny drops of water or other liquid in the air. Early this morning, there was a heavy *mist* over the lake. The campers sprayed a *mist* of insecticide inside their tent. *Noun.*

—**1.** To be or become covered with a mist. Her eyes *misted* with tears. **2.** To rain in fine drops; drizzle. It *misted* in the morning, but by noon the sky was clear. *Verb.*

mist (mist) *noun; verb,* **misted, misting.**

mistake Something that is not correctly done, said, or thought; error. I made two spelling *mistakes* on the test. It was a *mistake* to tell her about the surprise party, since she can't keep a secret. *Noun.*

—To make an error about something. It is easy to *mistake* one twin for the other because they look exactly alike. *Verb.*

mis·take (mis tāk′) *noun, plural* **mistakes;** *verb,* **mistook, mistaken, mistaking.**

mistaken In error; wrong. Bob had a *mistaken* idea about what time the party was to begin. *Adjective.*

—Betty was *mistaken* for her sister. *Verb.*

mis·tak·en (mis tā′kən) *adjective; verb.*

mister A title used for a man. When mister is used with a man's name, it is written with a capital "M" and usually abbreviated as "Mr." *Mr.* Jackson lives next door to us. "Excuse me, *mister,* can you help me?," he asked.

mis·ter (mis′tər) *noun, plural* **misters.**

mistletoe A plant that has small, yellowish-green leaves and bunches of little white berries. Mistletoe grows on the branches of trees. Mistletoe is used as a Christmas decoration.

mis·tle·toe (mis′əl-tō′) *noun, plural* **mistletoes.**

Mistletoe

mistook I *mistook* Ruth for her twin sister. Look up **mistake** for more information.

mis·took (mis-took′) *verb.*

mistreat To be cruel, rough, or unkind to; treat badly. The child *mistreated* the cat by pulling its tail.

mis·treat (mis trēt′) *verb,* **mistreated, mistreating.**

mistress A woman who is in charge of something. A woman who has a home is mistress of her household. A woman who owns a dog is its mistress.

mis·tress (mis′tris) *noun, plural* **mistresses.**

misty **1.** Covered or clouded with mist. His eyes were *misty* with tears. **2.** Not clear; vague. I have only a *misty* idea of what she looked like.

mist·y (mis′tē) *adjective,* **mistier, mistiest.**

misunderstand To understand someone or something incorrectly. She *misunderstood* the instructions and wrote her test in pencil instead of ink.

mis·un·der·stand (mis′un dər stand′) *verb,* **misunderstood, misunderstanding.**

misunderstood We *misunderstood* the policeman's directions and got lost.

mis·un·der·stood (mis′un dər stood′) *verb.*

mite A tiny animal that looks like a spider. Mites live in foods, on plants, or on other animals. ▲ Another word that sounds like this is **might.**

mite (mīt) *noun, plural* **mites.**

mitt **1.** A baseball glove. Mitts have padding to protect a person's hand when a ball is caught. **2.** A glove that covers the palm of the hand but not the fingers.

mitt (mit) *noun, plural* **mitts.**

mitten A warm covering for the hand. A mitten covers four fingers together and the thumb separately.

mit·ten (mit′ən) *noun, plural* **mittens.**

mix **1.** To put two or more different things together. We *mixed* yellow roses and white roses in the bouquet. Grandmother *mixed* lemon juice, sugar, and water to make lemonade. **2.** To become mixed. Oil and water will not *mix.* **3.** To get along with other people. It was a great party because all the guests *mixed* well. *Verb.*
—Something that is made by mixing; mixture. We bought a pancake *mix* at the store. *Noun.*

mix (miks) *verb,* **mixed, mixing;** *noun, plural* **mixes.**

to mix up. To confuse. Henry said to do it one way, Don said to do it another way, and I got *mixed up* because I listened to both of them.

mixed number A number made up of a whole number and a fraction. The number 4⁷/₈ is a mixed number.

mixer A machine for mixing different things together. A cement *mixer* mixes cement, water, and sand to make concrete. We have a *mixer* in the kitchen that mixes batter for cakes.

mix·er (mik′sər) *noun, plural* **mixers.**

mixture Something made up of different things that are put together. The pancake batter is made up of a *mixture* of eggs, milk, and flour.

mix·ture (miks′chər) *noun, plural* **mixtures.**

moan A low, sad sound. A moan usually shows that a person feels pain or grief. She heard his *moan* and knew his tooth was hurting him again. *Noun.*
—To make or say with a low, sad sound. He *moaned* when I accidentally hit his sore arm. *Verb.* ▲ Another word that sounds like this is **mown.**

moan (mōn) *noun, plural* **moans;** *verb,* **moaned, moaning.**

moat A deep, wide ditch that was dug around a castle or town in former times for protection against an enemy. Moats were usually filled with water. A drawbridge had to be lowered over the moat so that people could cross it.

moat (mōt) *noun, plural* **moats.**

Moat

mob A large number of people; crowd. A mob is sometimes made up of people who are so angry or upset about something that they break the law and cause damage. An angry *mob* gathered in front of the jail to demand that the prisoner be set free. *Noun.*
—To crowd around in excitement or anger. Shoppers *mobbed* the store during the big sale. *Verb.*

mob (mob) *noun, plural* **mobs;** *verb,* **mobbed, mobbing.**

at; āpe; cär; end; mē; it; īce; hot; ōld; fôrk; wood; fōōl; oil; out; up; turn; sing; thin; this; hw in white; zh in treasure. ə stands for a in about, e in taken i in pencil, o in lemon, and u in circus.

403

moccasin A soft leather shoe. Moccasins were first worn by American Indians.
moc·ca·sin (mok′-ə sin) *noun, plural* **moccasins.**

Moccasins

mock 1. To make fun of in a mean way. He *mocked* her new hat by comparing it to a lamp shade. 2. To imitate or copy in a joking or rude way. It was not nice of him to *mock* the way the lame man walked. *Verb.*
—Not real; imitation. The boys had a *mock* battle with cardboard shields and wooden swords. *Adjective.*
mock (mok) *verb,* **mocked, mocking;** *adjective.*

mockingbird A bird that can imitate the calls of other birds. Mockingbirds live in North and South America. Most of them have dark-gray feathers with white markings.
mock·ing·bird (mok′ing burd′) *noun, plural* **mockingbirds.**

Mockingbird

mode¹ A way of doing something. Automobiles are a popular *mode* of transportation.
mode (mōd) *noun, plural* **modes.**

mode² A style of dress, fashion, or behavior that is popular at a particular time. Slacks for women have been the *mode* in recent years.
mode (mōd) *noun, plural* **modes.**

model 1. A small-sized copy of something. Don makes car *models* from kits. 2. A person or thing that is a good example of something and is copied. John is a *model* of a good student. 3. A person whose job is to wear new clothes so that customers can see what they look like. Models may work in stores or in fashion shows, or be photographed for magazines. 4. A style or type of thing. That car is a very old *model. Noun.*
—1. To make or design something. Linda *modeled* a pony in clay. 2. To follow or copy someone or something. Steve hopes to *model* his career after his grandfather's. 3. To work as a model. Ellen *modeled* at a fashion show. *Verb.*
mod·el (mod′əl) *noun, plural* **models;** *verb,* **modeled, modeling.**

moderate Not too much or too little; not extreme. The price of this coat was *moderate.* We have had *moderate* temperatures this winter. *Adjective.*
—To become or make less extreme or violent. The heavy winds *moderated* during the night. *Verb.*
mod·er·ate (mod′ər it *for adjective;* mod′ə-rāt′ *for verb*) *adjective; verb,* **moderated, moderating.**

modern 1. Having to do with the present time or recent time. Large jet planes are a *modern* means of transportation. Nuclear energy as a source of power is a *modern* development. 2. Having to do with history from about the year 1400 to the present. Last year, we studied ancient history; now we are learning about *modern* history.
mod·ern (mod′ərn) *adjective.*

modest 1. Not thinking too highly of oneself. A modest person does not brag about himself or show off. 2. Within reason; not extreme. We spent only a *modest* amount of money on the trip.
mod·est (mod′ist) *adjective.*

modify 1. To change in some way. We *modified* our plan for the new kitchen and added a small dining area at one end. 2. To limit the meaning of a word. In the sentence "He lives in a white house," the adjective "white" *modifies* the noun "house."
mod·i·fy (mod′ə fī′) *verb,* **modified, modifying.**

module A part of a spacecraft that has a special use and can be separated from the rest of the craft. A lunar module is the small craft in which astronauts land on the moon.
mod·ule (moj′ōol *or* mod′yōol) *noun, plural* **modules.**

moist Slightly wet; damp. We wiped the shelves with a *moist* cloth. The air was *moist* and chilly this morning.
moist (moist) *adjective,* **moister, moistest.**

moisten To make or become slightly wet. I *moistened* the soil around the plant.
moist·en (moi′sən) *verb,* **moistened, moistening.**

moisture Water or other liquid in the air or on a surface; slight wetness. There was *moisture* on the window from the steam in the kitchen.
mois·ture (mois′chər) *noun.*

molar Any one of the large teeth at the back of the mouth. Molars have broad surfaces for grinding food. A person has twelve molars.
mo·lar (mō′lər) *noun, plural* **molars.**

molasses A sweet, thick, yellowish-brown syrup that is made from sugarcane.
mo·las·ses (mə las′iz) *noun.*

mold[1] An empty form that is made in a special shape. A liquid or soft material is poured into a mold. When it hardens, it takes the shape of the mold. Mother put the ice cream into a *mold* shaped like a heart. *Noun.*
—**1.** To make into a special shape; form. We *mold* clay with our hands. **2.** To influence and give form to. Our parents help *mold* our habits. *Verb.*
mold (mōld) *noun, plural* **molds;** *verb,* **molded, molding.**

mold[2] A furry-looking green plant that grows on food and damp surfaces. Mold is a fungus. *Noun.*
—To become covered with mold. Bread often *molds* on hot summer days. *Verb.*
mold (mōld) *noun, plural* **molds;** *verb,* **molded, molding.**

molding A strip of wood, plaster, or other material that is used along the edges of walls, windows, or doorways.
mold·ing (mōl′ding) *noun, plural* **moldings.**

mole[1] A brown spot on the skin.
mole (mōl) *noun, plural* **moles.**

mole[2] A small animal with grayish, velvety fur that lives underground. Moles have long claws to dig their tunnels under the ground.
mole (mōl) *noun, plural* **moles.**

Mole

molecule The smallest particle into which a substance can be divided and not be changed chemically. A molecule is made up of two or more atoms that are joined by a pair of shared electrons.
mol·e·cule (mol′ə kyōōl′) *noun, plural* **molecules.**

mollusk An animal that lives in salt water and has no backbone. Most mollusks have a hard shell that protects their soft bodies. Clams, snails, and oysters are mollusks.

mol·lusk (mol′əsk) *noun, plural* **mollusks.**

molt To shed the hair, feathers, skin, or shell and grow a new covering. Birds and snakes molt.
molt (mōlt) *verb,* **molted, molting.**

molten Melted by heat. Lava from a volcano is *molten* rock.
mol·ten (mōlt′ən) *adjective.*

mom Mother. My sister and I call our mother *Mom.*
mom (mom) *noun, plural* **moms.**

moment **1.** A short period of time. I'll answer your question in just a *moment.* **2.** A particular point in time. Come home the *moment* I call you.
mo·ment (mō′mənt) *noun, plural* **moments.**

momentary Lasting only a short time. There was a *momentary* lull in the storm and then it rained heavily again.
mo·men·tar·y (mō′mən ter′ē) *adjective.*

momentous Having great importance. The end of the war was a *momentous* event.
mo·men·tous (mō men′təs) *adjective.*

momentum The force or speed that an object has when it is moving. A rock gains *momentum* as it rolls down a hill.
mo·men·tum (mō men′təm) *noun, plural* **momentums.**

monarch **1.** A king, queen, or other ruler of a state or country. **2.** A large orange and black butterfly found in North America.
mon·arch (mon′ərk) *noun, plural* **monarchs.**

monarchy **1.** Government by a king, queen, or other monarch. **2.** A nation or state that is ruled by a monarch.
mon·ar·chy (mon′ər kē) *noun, plural* **monarchies.**

monastery A place where monks live and work together.
mon·as·ter·y (mon′əs ter′ē) *noun, plural* **monasteries.**

Monday The second day of the week.
Mon·day (mun′dē *or* mun′dā) *noun, plural* **Mondays.**

▲ The Romans called this day "the day of the moon." The word **Monday** comes from an Old English word that meant "moon's day."

at; āpe; cär; end; mē; it; īce; hot; ōld; fôrk; wood; fōōl; oil; out; up; turn; sing; thin; this; hw in white; zh in treasure.
ə stands for a in about, e in taken i in pencil, o in lemon, and u in circus.

money The coins and paper currency of a country. Money is used to buy goods and pay people for services. Nickels, dimes, and dollar bills are money.
mon·ey (mun′ē) *noun, plural* **moneys.**

mongoose A slender animal that has a pointed face, a long tail, and rough, shaggy fur. Mongooses can kill poisonous snakes.
mon·goose (mong′gōōs′) *noun, plural* **mongooses.**

Mongoose

mongrel A dog or other animal that is a mixture of breeds.
mon·grel (mung′grəl *or* mong′grəl) *noun, plural* **mongrels.**

monitor **1.** A student who is given a special duty to do. Some monitors help take attendance and others help keep order. **2.** Any person that warns or keeps watch. The sailor's job was to be *monitor* of the radar screen. *Noun.*
—To watch over a group of things. She was picked to *monitor* the fire drill. *Verb.*
mon·i·tor (mon′ə tər) *noun, plural* **monitors;** *verb,* **monitored, monitoring.**

monk A man who has joined a religious order, lives in a monastery, and is bound by religious vows.
monk (mungk) *noun, plural* **monks.**

monkey A furry animal that has long arms and legs, and hands and feet that are used for grasping and climbing. Monkeys are intelligent and can learn quickly. *Noun.*
—To fool around or play. Don't *monkey* with the stove or you might get burned. *Verb.*
mon·key (mung′kē) *noun, plural* **monkeys;** *verb,* **monkeyed, monkeying.**

Monkey

monkey wrench A wrench with one

jaw that can be moved to fit different sized nuts and bolts.

monopoly The sole control of a product or service by a person or company. That bus company has a *monopoly* on public transportation in our town.
mo·nop·o·ly (mə nop′ə lē) *noun, plural* **monopolies.**

monotonous Tiring or not interesting because it does not change in any way. His *monotonous* voice never changes in tone. His job was *monotonous* because he did the same thing over and over.
mo·not·o·nous (mə not′ən əs) *adjective.*

monsieur Mister; sir. Monsieur is the French form of address for a man.
mon·sieur (mə syur′) *noun, plural* **messieurs.**

monsoon A very strong wind that blows in the Indian Ocean and southern Asia. In the summer, it blows from the ocean toward the land and brings very heavy rains. In the winter, it blows from the land toward the ocean.
mon·soon (mon sōōn′) *noun, plural* **monsoons.**

monster **1.** An imaginary creature that is huge and frightening. In fairy tales, there is sometimes a dragon or other terrible *monster.* **2.** A person who is so wicked that he does not seem like a human being. **3.** An animal or plant that is not normal. A turtle with two heads is a monster.
mon·ster (mon′stər) *noun, plural* **monsters.**

monstrous **1.** Horrible or frightening. The dragon in the story was a *monstrous* creature. **2.** Very, very large; enormous. The little girl thought the elephant she saw at the zoo was a *monstrous* animal. **3.** Very evil. Murder is a *monstrous* crime.
mon·strous (mon′strəs) *adjective.*

Montana A state in the northwestern United States. Its capital is Helena.
Mon·tan·a (mon tan′ə) *noun.*

▲ **Montana** comes either from a Latin word that means "covered with mountains" or from a Spanish word that means "mountain." *Montana* was first suggested as the name for Idaho, which has many mountains. That state was named *Idaho* instead, and the name *Montana* was given to this state even though there are not many mountains in Montana.

month One of the twelve parts of a year.
month (munth) *noun, plural* **months.**

monthly **1.** Done or happening once a month. We subscribe to a *monthly* sports

magazine. Our camera club has *monthly* meetings. **2.** Of or for a month. The *monthly* rainfall for April was twelve inches. *Monthly* sales for the store were $10,000. *Adjective.*
—Once a month; every month. The bill from the grocery store arrives *monthly. Adverb.*
—A magazine that is published once a month. *Noun.*

month·ly (munth′lē) *adjective; adverb; noun, plural* **monthlies.**

monument A building, statue, or other object that is made to honor a person or event. The Washington *Monument* in Washington, D.C., was built in honor of George Washington.

mon·u·ment (mon′-yə mənt) *noun, plural* **monuments.**

Monument

moo The sound that a cow makes. *Noun.*
—To make the sound that a cow makes. *Verb.*

moo (mo͞o) *noun, plural* **moos;** *verb,* **mooed, mooing.**

mood The way that a person feels at a certain time; state of mind. Our moods change; sometimes we are happy and other times we are sad. Getting an A on the test put him in a very good *mood.*

mood (mo͞od) *noun, plural* **moods.**

moon **1.** A heavenly body that revolves around the earth from west to east once every 29½ days. The moon seems to shine because it reflects light from the sun. The moon is the earth's satellite. **2.** A satellite of any planet. Mars has two *moons.*

moon (mo͞on) *noun, plural* **moons.**

moonlight The light that shines from the moon.

moon·light (mo͞on′līt′) *noun.*

moor¹ To fasten or tie a boat in place. We *moored* the sailboat at the dock with a rope.

moor (moor) *verb,* **moored, mooring.**

moor² An open area of wild land with few trees. There are moors in England and Scotland that are usually covered with heather and have wet, marshy ground.

moor (moor) *noun, plural* **moors.**

moose A large, heavy animal related to the deer that lives in forests in the northern United States and Canada. The male moose has enormous, broad antlers.

moose (mo͞os) *noun, plural* **moose.**

Moose

mop A bundle of yarn, cloth, or sponge attached to a long handle and used for cleaning. *Noun.*
—To clean or dry with a mop, towel, or sponge. We *mopped* the kitchen floor. I *mopped* up the spilled milk with a paper towel. *Verb.*

mop (mop) *noun, plural* **mops;** *verb,* **mopped, mopping.**

moral **1.** Good and honest in behavior and character. He is a *moral* man. **2.** Having to do with what is right and wrong. Whether or not to report that his friend had cheated was a *moral* question he had to answer for himself. *Adjective.*
—**1.** A lesson about right and wrong that is taught in a story, event, or fable. The *moral* of the story was "Don't put off until tomorrow what you can do today." **2. morals.** The beliefs that a person has about what is right and what is wrong. *Noun.*

mor·al (môr′əl) *adjective; noun, plural* **morals.**

morale The way a person or a group of people feel about what they are doing. The baseball team's *morale* was low after they lost their fifth game in a row.

mo·rale (mə ral′) *noun.*

more **1.** Greater in number, amount, or degree. A gallon is *more* than a quart.

at; āpe; cär; end; mē; it; īce; hot; ōld; fôrk; wood; fo͞ol; oil; out; up; turn; sing; thin; this; hw in white; zh in treasure.
ə stands for a in about, e in taken i in pencil, o in lemon, and u in circus.

407

2. Additional; further. I need *more* charcoal for the fire. *Adjective.*
—**1.** To a greater amount or degree. Be *more* careful. **2.** In addition; again. I will only tell you once *more. Adverb.*
—An extra amount. Our dogs always want *more* to eat. *Noun.*
more (môr) *adjective; adverb; noun.*

▲ **More** is used to make the comparative form of some adjectives and adverbs. Most English comparatives are formed by adding *-er* to the end of a word. For example, *tall* + *-er* forms the comparative *taller.* But many words, especially long ones, would sound awkward if we added *-er* to the end of the word. So instead we simply put the word "more" in front of it. We would say "more familiar," not "familiarer."

moreover Not only that; also. It's dark and cold, and *moreover* it's raining.
more·o·ver (môr ō′vər) *adverb.*

morning The first part of the day. Morning ends at noon. ▲ Another word that sounds like this is **mourning.**
morn·ing (môr′ning) *noun, plural* **mornings.**

morning glory A white, purple, or blue flower that is shaped like a trumpet and grows on a vine. The morning glory opens in the early morning and then closes for the rest of the day.

morsel A small bite of food or piece of something. The birds ate every *morsel* of bread we put out for them.
mor·sel (môr′səl) *noun, plural* **morsels.**

Morning Glories

mortal **1.** Certain to die. All things that live are *mortal.* **2.** Causing death. He was given a *mortal* wound by the enemy. *Adjective.*
—A person; human being. *Noun.*
mor·tal (môrt′əl) *adjective; noun, plural* **mortals.**

mortar[1] A material made of sand, water, and lime. Mortar is used like cement to hold bricks or stones together.
mor·tar (môr′tər) *noun.*

mortar[2] A thick heavy bowl in which something is crushed to a powder with a pestle.
mor·tar (môr′tər) *noun, plural* **mortars.**

mosaic A picture or design made by fitting together bits of stone, glass, or tile of different colors, and cementing them in place. Mosaics are used on the tops of tables, and to cover floors and walls.
mo·sa·ic (mō zā′ik) *noun, plural* **mosaics.**

Mosaic

mosque A Muslim temple or place of worship.
mosque (mosk) *noun, plural* **mosques.**

Mosque

mosquito A small insect with two wings. The female gives a sharp sting or bite that itches. Some mosquitoes carry malaria and other diseases.
mos·qui·to (məs kē′tō) *noun, plural* **mosquitoes** or **mosquitos.**

moss A small green plant that grows in groups to form a soft, thick mat on the ground, on rocks, or on trees. Mosses grow in shady places where it is damp.
moss (môs) *noun, plural* **mosses.**

most **1.** Greatest in number, amount, or degree. Who received the *most* votes in the election? **2.** Nearly all. *Most* children like to play games. *Adjective.*
—The greatest number, amount, or degree. One dollar is the *most* I can give you now. *Noun.*
—**1.** Very. She is a *most* unusual person. **2.** To the greatest degree. That was the *most* interesting book I have ever read. *Adverb.*
　most (mōst) *adjective; noun; adverb.*

▲ **Most** is used to make the superlative form of some adjectives and adverbs. Most English superlatives are formed by adding -*est* to the end of a word. For example, *fast* + -*est* forms the superlative *fastest.* But many words, especially long ones, would sound awkward if we added -*est* to the end of the word. So instead we simply put the word "most" in front of it. We would say "most famous" not "famousest."

mostly For the largest part; mainly; chiefly. It has been *mostly* cloudy today. The dress is *mostly* blue with only a little white trim.
　most·ly (mōst′lē) *adverb.*

motel A kind of hotel that is built near a main road. Travelers can drive up to it easily and park their cars near their rooms.
　mo·tel (mō tel′) *noun, plural* **motels.**

moth An insect that looks like a butterfly but flies mostly at night. The larvae of some moths eat holes in wool and other fabrics.
　moth (môth) *noun, plural* **moths.**

mother The female parent of a child.
　moth·er (muth′ər) *noun, plural* **mothers.**

mother-in-law The mother of one's husband or wife.
　moth·er-in-law (muth′ər in lô′) *noun, plural* **mothers-in-law.**

motion **1.** The act of changing place or position; movement. The steady *motion* of the boat made him feel sick. The policeman waved us on with a *motion* of his arm. **2.** A formal suggestion made at a meeting. I made a *motion* to have the secretary read the minutes of the last meeting. *Noun.*
—To move the hand or another part of the body as a sign of something. The teacher *motioned* for everyone to sit down. *Verb.*
　mo·tion (mō′shən) *noun, plural* **motions;** *verb,* **motioned, motioning.**

motion picture A series of pictures on a film. They are projected onto a white screen at such a high speed that it appears to the viewer that the people and things in the pictures are moving. This is also called a **moving picture.**

motive The reason that a person does something. A desire to go to college was his *motive* for trying to get good marks. Police looked for the *motive* for the crime to help them find the person who did it.
　mo·tive (mō′tiv) *noun, plural* **motives.**

motor A machine that makes other machines work. Some motors use electricity and others burn gasoline. The *motor* of a fan makes the fan blades turn. The gasoline *motor* of a car makes the car go. *Noun.*
—**1.** Having to do with a motor or something run by a motor. A car is a *motor* vehicle. Jerry has a *motor* scooter. We are going on a *motor* trip in Canada. **2.** Having to do with the nerves of a person's body that control motion. Pulling your hand back from a hot object is a *motor* action. *Adjective.*
—To travel by car. We *motored* through New England. *Verb.*
　mo·tor (mō′tər) *noun, plural* **motors;** *adjective; verb,* **motored, motoring.**

motorboat A boat that is run by a motor. Some motorboats have outboard motors. Others have larger inboard engines.
　mo·tor·boat (mō′tər bōt′) *noun, plural* **motorboats.**

motorcycle A two-wheeled vehicle that looks like a bicycle but is bigger and heavier and is run by an engine.
　mo·tor·cy·cle (mō′tər sī′kəl) *noun, plural* **motorcycles.**

motto A short sentence or phrase that says what someone believes or what something stands for. The Latin phrase, "E pluribus unum," which means "out of many, one," is the *motto* on the seal of the United States.
　mot·to (mot′ō) *noun, plural* **mottoes** or **mottos.**

mound **1.** A hill or heap of earth, stones, or other material. There are *mounds* of garbage in the dump. **2.** A slightly higher area in the center of a baseball diamond that the pitcher stands on to pitch the ball. *Noun.*
—To pile in a hill or heap. Bill likes to *mound* ice cream on top of his pie. *Verb.*
　mound (mound) *noun, plural* **mounds;** *verb,* **mounded, mounding.**

at; āpe; cär; end; mē; it; īce; hot; ōld; fôrk; wood; fōol; oil; out; up; turn; sing; thin; this; hw in white; zh in treasure.
ə stands for a in about, e in taken
i in pencil, o in lemon, and u in circus.

mount¹　**1.** To go up; climb. Alan *mounted* the stairs two at a time. **2.** To get up on. Have you ever *mounted* a horse? The cowboys *mounted* and rode off. **3.** To set in place. Ted *mounted* the stamps in his new album. **4.** To rise or increase. The cost of meat has been *mounting* steadily this year. *Verb.*
　—**1.** A horse or other animal for riding. **2.** A stand, frame, or other object used to hold something. We bought a wooden frame as a *mount* for the picture. *Noun.*
　mount (mount) *verb*, **mounted, mounting;** *noun, plural* **mounts.**

mount²　A hill or mountain.
　mount (mount) *noun, plural* **mounts.**

mountain　**1.** A mass of land that rises very high above the land around it. **2.** A very large pile or amount of something. There was a *mountain* of trash at the dump.
　moun·tain (mount′ən) *noun, plural* **moun·tains.**

mountain lion　A large wild cat that lives in the mountains of North and South America. This animal is usually called a **cougar.** Look up **cougar** for more information.

mountainous　**1.** Having many mountains. There is good skiing in that *mountainous* area. **2.** Very big; huge. The storm piled up *mountainous* drifts of snow.
　moun·tain·ous (mount′ən əs) *adjective.*

mountain range　A series of mountains that form a group.

mourn　To feel or show sorrow or grief. We *mourned* for all the men who died in the war.
　mourn (môrn) *verb*, **mourned, mourning.**

mourning　**1.** The act of showing sorrow or grief. He was in *mourning* for his grandfather, who had just died. **2.** Black clothing worn to show grief over a person's death. The widow wore *mourning.* ▲ Another word that sounds like this is **morning.**
　mourn·ing (môr′ning) *noun.*

mouse　A small, furry animal with a pointed nose, small ears, and a long, thin tail. Mice that live in houses are often gray. A field mouse is often brown and white.
　mouse (mous) *noun, plural* **mice.**

moustache　Hair that is grown above the upper lip. This word is usually spelled **mustache.** Look up **mustache** for more information.

Mouse

mouth　**1.** The opening through which people and animals take in food and through which sounds are made. The mouth contains the tongue and the teeth. **2.** Any opening that is like a mouth. We entered the *mouth* of the cave. The *mouth* of a river is where it empties into another body of water.
　mouth (mouth) *noun, plural* **mouths.**

mouthpiece　The part of a musical instrument, telephone, or other object that is put between or near the lips.
　mouth·piece (mouth′pēs′) *noun, plural* **mouthpieces.**

move　**1.** To change the place or direction of something. We had to *move* to different seats to get a good view of the movie screen. *Move* the chair near the window. Our family is going to *move* to the city. *Move* away from the fireplace if it's too hot. **2.** To go forward; advance. Time *moves* quickly when you are having fun. **3.** To put in motion. Wind *moves* a windmill. **4.** To cause someone to do something. Judy was *moved* by curiosity to open the package. **5.** To stir a person's feelings. Ted was *moved* to tears when he found the starving puppies. **6.** To make a suggestion at a meeting. Edward *moved* that the meeting be ended. *Verb.*
　—**1.** The act of moving. He was so frightened that he couldn't make a *move.* **2.** A person's turn to move a playing piece in certain games. *Noun.*
　move (mo͞ov) *verb*, **moved, moving;** *noun, plural* **moves.**

movement　**1.** The act of moving. A fan causes *movement* of air in a room. **2.** A group of moving parts that makes something work. The *movement* of a watch turns the hands. **3.** The actions of a group of people to reach some goal. The civil rights *movement* is working for equal opportunities for people of all races.
　move·ment (mo͞ov′mənt) *noun, plural* **movements.**

mover　A person whose job is to move people's furniture and other things from one house or office to another.
　mov·er (mo͞o′vər) *noun, plural* **movers.**

movie　**1.** A series of pictures on a film that is projected onto a screen; motion picture. **2. movies.** A building where movies are shown.
　mov·ie (mo͞o′vē) *noun, plural* **movies.**

mow　To cut grass, grain, or hay with a sharp blade or machine. Jack has to *mow* the lawn this afternoon.
　mow (mō) *verb*, **mowed, mowed** or **mown, mowing.**

mown After the grass was *mown,* we raked it into piles. ▲ Another word that sounds like this is **moan.**
  mown (mōn) *verb.*

Mr. A short way to write "Mister" when it is used with a man's name. "Dear *Mr.* Andrews," she wrote.
  Mr. (mis′tər) *plural,* **Messrs.**

Mrs. A title that is put before a married woman's name. *Mrs.* Whitney was my kindergarten teacher.
  Mrs. (mis′iz) *plural,* **Mmes.**

Ms. A title that is put before a woman's name. *Ms.* Simpson is the school librarian.
  Ms. (miz *or* em′es′) *plural,* **Mses.**

much Great in amount or degree. I don't have *much* money today. We had too *much* rain this week. *Adjective.*
—**1.** To a great degree; very. Dad was very *much* upset when he heard about the accident. **2.** Just about; nearly. We feel *much* the same as you do. *Adverb.*
—**1.** A great amount. *Much* has been written about Abraham Lincoln. **2.** Anything important. He's not *much* of a tennis player. *Noun.*
  much (much) *adjective,* **more, most;** *adverb,* **more, most;** *noun.*

mucus A slimy fluid that coats and protects the inside of the mouth, throat, and other parts of the body.
  mu·cus (myoo′kəs) *noun.*

mud Soft, wet, sticky earth or dirt. We tracked *mud* in the house after it rained.
  mud (mud) *noun.*

muff A roll of fur that is made so a person can put one hand in each end. Muffs keep your hands warm.
  muff (muf) *noun, plural* **muffs.**

muffin A small, fluffy bread that looks like a little cake.
  muf·fin (muf′in) *noun, plural* **muffins.**

muffle To soften the sound that something makes. The carpet *muffled* our footsteps. She *muffled* her laughter by burying her face in a pillow.
  muf·fle (muf′əl) *verb,* **muffled, muffling.**

Muff

muffler **1.** A warm scarf that is wrapped around the neck in cold weather. **2.** A device that reduces the noise made by an engine. Cars have mufflers.
  muf·fler (muf′lər) *noun, plural* **mufflers.**

mug A heavy drinking cup with a handle. Mugs are often made of pottery or metal. *Noun.*
—To attack a person with the intent to rob. The gang *mugged* him and stole his bicycle. *Verb.*
  mug (mug) *noun, plural* **mugs;** *verb,* **mugged, mugging.**

muggy Warm and damp. It was a *muggy* day with no breeze.
  mug·gy (mug′ē) *adjective,* **muggier, muggiest.**

Muhammad An Arab religious leader. He was the founder of the Muslim religion. It is believed that he was born in 570. He died in 632.
  Mu·ham·mad (moo ham′əd).

mulberry A tree with sweet, dark reddish-purple berries that look like blackberries and can be eaten. The leaves of some mulberry trees are fed to silkworms.
  mul·ber·ry (mul′ber′ē) *noun, plural* **mulberries.**

Mule

mule An animal that is produced by a female horse and a male donkey. A mule is as large as a horse, but it has longer ears and a tail like a donkey. Mules are used to carry and pull things.
  mule (myool) *noun, plural* **mules.**

multiple Having or involving many parts. He got *multiple* cuts and bruises when he fell off his bicycle. *Adjective.*
—A number that is multiplied a certain number of times. The numbers 8 and 12 are *multiples* of 4. *Noun.*

at; āpe; cär; end; mē; it; īce; hot; ōld;
fôrk; wood; fool; oil; out; up; turn; sing;
thin; this; hw in white; zh in treasure.
ə stands for a in about, e in taken
i in pencil, o in lemon, and u in circus.

mul·ti·ple (mul′tə pəl) *adjective; noun, plural* **multiples.**

multiplicand A number that is to be multiplied by another number. If you multiply 2 times 4, the *multiplicand* is 4.
mul·ti·pli·cand (mul′tə plə kand′) *noun, plural* **multiplicands.**

multiplication The act of taking a number and adding it to itself a certain number of times. In the multiplication of 2 times 4, you are adding 2 sets of 4, which equals 8.
mul·ti·pli·ca·tion (mul′tə pli kā′shən) *noun.*

multiplier A number that tells how many times to multiply another number. If you multiply 2 times 4, the *multiplier* is 2.
mul·ti·pli·er (mul′tə plī′ər) *noun, plural* **multipliers.**

multiply 1. To add a number to itself a certain number of times. If we *multiply* 2 times 4, we get 8. 2. To grow in number. The longer he waited to ask for help, the more his problems *multiplied.*
mul·ti·ply (mul′tə plī′) *verb,* **multiplied, multiplying.**

multitude A great number of people or things. A *multitude* of people came to the outdoor music festival.
mul·ti·tude (mul′tə tood′ *or* mul′tə tyood′) *noun, plural* **multitudes.**

mumble To speak low and unclearly. The shy boy *mumbled* his name.
mum·ble (mum′bəl) *verb,* **mumbled, mumbling.**

mummy A dead body that has been wrapped in cloth and preserved. Many mummies are found in ancient Egyptian tombs.
mum·my (mum′ē) *noun, plural* **mummies.**

mumps A contagious disease that causes the glands at the sides of the face to become swollen and sore.
mumps (mumps) *noun.*

munch To chew something in a noisy way. My pet rabbit *munches* his carrots.
munch (munch) *verb,* **munched, munching.**

municipal Having to do with the government and affairs of a city or town. We are having a *municipal* election this week to elect a new town sheriff.
mu·nic·i·pal (myoo nis′ə pəl) *adjective.*

mural A picture painted on a wall or ceiling. A mural usually covers a large part of the wall.
mu·ral (myoor′əl) *noun, plural* **murals.**

murder The deliberate and unlawful killing of a person. *Noun.*
—To kill a person deliberately and unlawfully. The robber *murdered* the store owner during the robbery. *Verb.*
mur·der (mur′dər) *noun, plural* **murders;** *verb,* **murdered, murdering.**

murky Dark and gloomy. We couldn't see beneath the surface of the *murky* water in the pond.
murk·y (mur′kē) *adjective,* **murkier, murkiest.**

murmur A low, soft sound. We heard the *murmur* of the brook in the distance. *Noun.*
—To make or say with a low, soft sound. The baby *murmured* in her sleep. *Verb.*
mur·mur (mur′mər) *noun, plural* **murmurs;** *verb,* **murmured, murmuring.**

muscle A tissue in the body of a person or animal, that is made up of strong fibers. Muscles can be tightened or relaxed to make the body move. Our muscles give us strength to lift and carry heavy things. He lifts weights to strengthen the *muscles* in his arms. ▲ Another word that sounds like this is **mussel.**
mus·cle (mus′əl) *noun, plural* **muscles.**

▲ The word **muscle** comes from a Latin word that first meant "little mouse." Later, the Romans used the same word for "muscle" because they thought some muscles were shaped like little mice.

muscular Having strong or well-developed muscles. The football player was a *muscular* man.
mus·cu·lar (mus′kyə lər) *adjective.*

museum A building where objects of art, science, or history are kept and displayed for people to see.
mu·se·um (myoo zē′əm) *noun, plural* **museums.**

mushroom Any of various plants that are shaped like a small umbrella. A mushroom is a fungus. Some mushrooms can be eaten, but others are poisonous. *Noun.*
—To grow or appear suddenly and quickly. New office buildings *mushroomed* all over the city. *Verb.*
mush·room (mush′room′ *or* mush′room′) *noun, plural* **mushrooms;** *verb,* **mushroomed, mushrooming.**

Mushrooms

music **1.** A pleasing or beautiful combination of sounds. **2.** A musical composition. Does the pianist know the *music* to that song? **3.** The written or printed signs that tell a person what sounds are used for a musical composition. Do you know how to read *music?*
mu·sic (myoo′zik) *noun.*

musical Having to do with or producing music. The trombone is a *musical* instrument. She has a *musical* voice. *Adjective.*
—A play that has songs and dancing in it. *Noun.*
mu·si·cal (myoo′zi kəl) *adjective; noun, plural* **musicals.**

musician A person who is skilled in playing a musical instrument, composing music, or singing.
mu·si·cian (myoo zish′ən) *noun, plural* **musicians.**

musket A gun with a long barrel like a rifle. It was used in warfare before modern rifles were invented.
mus·ket (mus′kit) *noun, plural* **muskets.**

Musket

muskmelon A large, sweet fruit. Cantaloupes are muskmelons.
musk·mel·on (musk′mel′ən) *noun, plural* **muskmelons.**

musk ox A shaggy, dark-brown animal that has large, curving horns, Musk oxen live in northern Canada.
musk ox (musk).

muskrat A small North American animal with dark-brown fur. Muskrats live in and near the water. A muskrat has webbed back legs and a flat tail that help it to swim.
musk·rat (musk′rat′) *noun, plural* **muskrat** or **muskrats.**

Muslim Having to do with the religion founded by Muhammad. *Adjective.*
—A person who follows the religion founded by Muhammad. *Noun.*
Mus·lim (muz′lim) *adjective; noun, plural* **Muslims.**

muslin A cotton cloth that is used to make sheets and some clothing.
mus·lin (muz′lin) *noun.*

mussel A kind of clam that has a narrow, bluish-black shell. Mussels are good to eat. ▲ Another word that sounds like this is **muscle.**
mus·sel (mus′əl) *noun, plural* **mussels.**

must You *must* return a book you borrow from the library. People *must* eat to live. It *must* be noon, because I'm hungry.
must (must) *verb.*

mustache Hair that is grown above a man's upper lip. My grandfather has a big *mustache* that curls up at each end. This word is also spelled **moustache.**
mus·tache (mus′tash *or* məs tash′) *noun, plural* **mustaches.**

Mustache

mustang A wild horse that lives on the American plains.
mus·tang (mus′tang) *noun, plural* **mustangs.**

mustard A sharp-tasting yellow paste or powder that is made from the seeds of a plant. Mustard is used to flavor food. The mustard plant has bunches of small, yellow flowers.
mus·tard (mus′tərd) *noun, plural* **mustards.**

muster **1.** To bring or call together; assemble. The captain *mustered* his troops for the day's march. **2.** To gather from within oneself. He *mustered* up his courage to face his punishment.
mus·ter (mus′tər) *verb,* **mustered, mustering.**

Muskrat

at; āpe; cär; end; mē; it; īce; hot; ōld;
fôrk; wood; fool; oil; out; up; turn; sing;
thin; this; hw in white; zh in treasure.
ə stands for a in about, e in taken
i in pencil, o in lemon, and u in circus.

mustn't We *mustn't* run through the hall.
must·n't (mus′ənt) contraction for "must not."

mute 1. Not able to speak because of an illness, birth defect, or injury. 2. Not willing to speak; silent. The accused man stood *mute* and would not defend himself. 3. Not pronounced. The "b" in "lamb" is *mute*. *Adjective.*
—1. A person who cannot speak. 2. A device put on a musical instrument to soften the tone. Mutes are usually used with trumpets and other brass instruments. *Noun.*
mute (myo͞ot) *adjective; noun, plural* **mutes.**

mutiny An open rebellion against authority. The sailors that took part in the *mutiny* were punished. *Noun.*
—To take part in an open rebellion; revolt. The sailors *mutinied* against their captain. *Verb.*
mu·ti·ny (myo͞o′tə nē) *noun, plural* **mutinies;** *verb,* **mutinied, mutinying.**

mutter To speak in a low, unclear way with the mouth almost closed. The boys were *muttering* complaints about the food at school when the teacher walked in. *Verb.*
—Words spoken in a low, unclear way. There was a *mutter* of disapproval when the girls kept giggling during the movie. *Noun.*
mut·ter (mut′ər) *verb,* **muttered, muttering;** *noun.*

mutton Meat from an adult sheep.
mut·ton (mut′ən) *noun.*

mutual Done or felt together; shared. The two men had a *mutual* dislike for each other.
mu·tu·al (myo͞o′cho͞o əl) *adjective.*

muzzle 1. The part of the head of an animal made up of the nose, mouth, and jaws. A collie has a long *muzzle*. 2. A set of straps that are made to fit over the muzzle of an animal to keep it from biting. 3. The opening at the front end of a gun. The bullet comes out through the muzzle. *Noun.*
—To put a muzzle on an animal. She *muzzled* the guard dog before she took him out for a walk. *Verb.*
muz·zle (muz′əl) *noun, plural* **muzzles;** *verb,* **muzzled, muzzling.**

my Alan is *my* brother. That is *my* pencil.
my (mī) *adjective.*

myrtle 1. An evergreen tree that has sweet-smelling white or pink flowers and shiny leaves. 2. A vine that grows along the ground in thick beds and has shiny leaves and blue flowers.
myr·tle (murt′əl) *noun, plural* **myrtles.**

Leaf

Myrtle Tree

myself I baked the cake *myself.* I cut *myself.* I haven't been *myself* since I had that terrible cold.
my·self (mī self′) *pronoun.*

mysterious Very hard or impossible to explain or understand; full of mystery. We heard *mysterious* sounds from the attic.
mys·te·ri·ous (mis tēr′ē əs) *adjective.*

mystery 1. Something that is not or cannot be known, explained, or understood. The identity of the murderer is a *mystery.* It is a *mystery* to us how he can be so alert when he has had so little sleep. 2. A book, play, or other story about a crime that is puzzling.
mys·ter·y (mis′tər ē) *noun, plural* **mysteries.**

myth 1. A story that tells about a belief of a group of people. Myths often tell about gods and heroes. They were made up when people tried to find an explanation or reason for something that happens in nature. Long ago people explained thunder by the *myth* that it was the noise made by the chariot of the god Thor as he rode across the skies. 2. A person or thing that is not real or true. The idea that a person gets warts from touching a frog is a *myth.*
myth (mith) *noun, plural* **myths.**

mythical Having to do with myths. A unicorn is a *mythical* creature. Apollo was a *mythical* god.
myth·i·cal (mith′i kəl) *adjective.*

mythology Myths and legends. Greek *mythology* is all the myths that were told and written in ancient Greece.
my·thol·o·gy (mi thol′ə jē) *noun, plural* **mythologies.**

1. Ancient Egyptian Picture Writing
2. Ancient Middle Eastern Tribes
3. Ancient Greek 3000 Years Ago
4. Ancient Greek 2500 Years Ago
5. Ancient Roman
6. Modern English

N is the fourteenth letter of the alphabet. The oldest form of the letter **N** was a drawing that the ancient Egyptians (**1**) used in their picture writing nearly 5000 years ago. This drawing, which was a wavy line that meant "water," was borrowed by several ancient tribes (**2**) in the Middle East. The ancient Greeks (**3**) borrowed this letter about 3000 years ago. They made a change in the shape of the letter by writing the middle line on a slant rather than straight. Several hundred years later, the Greeks (**4**) reversed the slant of the middle line, giving the letter **N** its modern shape. The Romans (**5**) borrowed this new form of the letter. By about 2400 years ago, the Romans were writing it in almost the same way that we write the capital letter **N** today (**6**).

n, N The fourteenth letter of the alphabet.
n, N (en) *noun, plural* **n's, N's.**

nag To bother by finding fault with and scolding all the time. Tim's sister is always *nagging* him about the way he dresses.
nag (nag) *verb,* **nagged, nagging.**

nail **1.** A thin piece of metal that is pointed at one end and flat at the other. A nail is hammered into pieces of wood to hold them together. **2.** The thin, hard layer at the end of a finger or toe. *Noun.*
—To hold together with a nail or nails. Tom *nailed* pieces of wood together to make a bookcase. *Verb.*
nail (nāl) *noun, plural* **nails;** *verb,* **nailed, nailing.**

naked **1.** Without clothing or covering of any kind. A person is *naked* when he takes a bath or shower. **2.** Without anything added. You do not need a telescope to see that star; you can see it with the *naked* eye.
na·ked (nā′kid) *adjective.*

name **1.** The word or words by which a person, animal, place, or thing is known. Her *name* is Debbie Taylor. Salmon is the *name* of a kind of fish. Denver is the *name* of the city where I was born. **2.** A bad or insulting word or phrase. The bully called the little boy *names.* **3.** Reputation or character. The girl's constant lying gave her a bad *name* around school. *Noun.*
—**1.** To give a name or names to. The couple *named* their first child Mark. **2.** To speak of; mention. The newspaper article *named* the people who won the awards. **3.** To appoint or choose. The President *named* Senator Brown to head the commission. *Verb.*
name (nām) *noun, plural* **names;** *verb,* **named, naming.**

namely That is to say. We visited two southern states, *namely* Mississippi and Georgia.
name·ly (nām′lē) *adverb.*

nap¹ A short sleep. The baby is taking her afternoon *nap. Noun.*
—To sleep for a short while. Mother *napped* for an hour before the guests came. *Verb.*
nap (nap) *noun, plural* **naps;** *verb,* **napped, napping.**

nap² The soft, fuzzy surface of cloth. This coat is so old that all the *nap* has worn off.
nap (nap) *noun.*

napkin A piece of cloth or paper used at meals for protecting clothing and for wiping the lips and hands.
nap·kin (nap′kin) *noun, plural* **napkins.**

narcissus A plant that has yellow or white flowers and long, thin leaves. The daffodil is a kind of narcissus.
nar·cis·sus (när sis′əs) *noun, plural* **narcissuses.**

narcotic A drug that dulls the senses, pro-

duces sleep, and eases pain when used in small doses. In large amounts, a narcotic becomes a poison. Opium is a *narcotic* that is made from poppy seeds.
nar·cot·ic (när kot′ik) *noun, plural* **narcotics.**

narrate To tell or relate. The newspaper reporter *narrated* an interesting story of his experiences and travels in the Soviet Union.
nar·rate (nar′āt *or* na rāt′) *verb,* **narrated, narrating.**

narrow 1. Not wide or broad. He jumped across the *narrow* stream. 2. Limited or small. Mike has a *narrow* range of interest in reading and likes only books about sports. 3. Barely successful; close. The fireman saved the child, but it was a *narrow* escape. *Adjective.*
—To make or become narrow. The workmen *narrowed* the sidewalk so that the street could be made wider. The river *narrows* at the bridge. *Verb.*
—**narrows.** The narrow part of a body of water. The bridge was built across the *narrows. Noun.*
nar·row (nar′ō) *adjective,* **narrower, narrowest;** *verb,* **narrowed, narrowing;** *noun plural.*

nasal Having to do with the nose. A cold usually stuffs up the *nasal* passages and makes it hard to breathe through the nose.
na·sal (nā′zəl) *adjective.*

nasturtium A plant that has yellow, orange, or red flowers. Nasturtiums have
sharp-tasting flower buds and seeds that are sometimes used in salads and pickles.
na·stur·tium (nə-stur′shəm) *noun, plural* **nasturtiums.**

Nasturtium

nasty 1. Coming from hate or spite; mean. That *nasty* rumor about my friend is not true. 2. Disagreeable or unpleasant. The weather today is very cold and *nasty.* 3. Harmful or severe. Sandy took a *nasty* fall when he was skiing last weekend.
nas·ty (nas′tē) *adjective,* **nastier, nastiest.**

nation A particular land where a group of people live together under one government and share the same language, culture, and history. The United States is a *nation.*
na·tion (na′shən) *noun, plural* **nations.**

national Having to do with a nation. Each of our two major political parties holds a *national* convention every four years to choose a candidate for President.
na·tion·al (nash′ən əl) *adjective.*

nationalism A feeling of deep loyalty to one's country.
na·tion·al·ism (nash′ən əl iz′əm) *noun.*

nationality 1. The fact or state of belonging to a particular nation. Pierre's *nationality* is French. 2. A group of people who share the same language, culture, and history. People of many different *nationalities* work at the United Nations.
na·tion·al·i·ty (nash′ə nal′ə tē) *noun, plural* **nationalities.**

native 1. A person who was born in a particular country or place. Uncle Karl is a *native* of Germany. Sarah is a *native* of Chicago. 2. One of the original people, animals, or plants growing in a region or country. The *natives* of the United States are American Indians. The kangaroo is a *native* of Australia. *Noun.*
—1. Born in a particular country or place. Tom is a *native* American. 2. Belonging to a person by birth. Maria's *native* language is Italian. Chris has a lot of *native* intelligence. 3. Originally living or growing in a region or country. Cactuses are *native* to desert regions. *Adjective.*
na·tive (nā′tiv) *noun, plural* **natives;** *adjective.*

natural 1. Found in nature; not made by people; not artificial. The *natural* rock formations overlooking the river rise 200 feet above the ground. 2. Having to do with nature. Biology is a *natural* science. 3. Belonging to from birth. Kathy has *natural* beauty. 4. Happening in the normal course of things. Grandfather died of *natural* causes when he was ninety years old. 5. Closely following nature; lifelike. This painting of Mother is very *natural. Adjective.*
—A person who is good at something because of a special talent or ability. Jerry is a *natural* at basketball. *Noun.*
nat·u·ral (nach′ər əl) *adjective; noun, plural* **naturals.**

naturalist A person who knows a great deal about animals or plants.
nat·u·ral·ist (nach′ər ə list) *noun, plural* **naturalists.**

naturally 1. As would be expected; of course. *Naturally* I'll help you. 2. By nature. He is *naturally* shy. 3. In a normal manner. Linda was too nervous to act *naturally.*
nat·u·ral·ly (nach′ər ə lē) *adverb.*

natural resources Materials found in nature that are useful or necessary for people to live. Water, forests, and minerals are natural resources.

nature **1.** The basic character and quality of a person or thing. Tom has a kindly *nature.* It is the *nature* of fire to be hot. **2.** The physical universe; all the things that are not made by people. The mountains, the forests, and the oceans are some of the wonders of *nature.* **3.** Sort or kind; variety. Bob enjoys reading books about camping, hiking, and things of that *nature.*
　　na·ture (nā′chər) *noun, plural* **natures.**

naught **1.** Nothing. All our plans came to *naught* in the end. **2.** Zero. Five plus *naught* equals five.
　　naught (nôt) *noun.*

naughty Behaving badly; mischievous or disobedient. The teacher is making Ned stay after school because he was very *naughty* today.
　　naugh·ty (nô′tē) *adjective,* **naughtier, naughtiest.**

nausea A sick feeling in the stomach. I take special pills to prevent *nausea* whenever I go on a long car drive.
　　nau·sea (nô′shə *or* nô′zē ə) *noun.*

nautical Having to do with ships, sailors, or navigation. The captain had many *nautical* maps and charts in his cabin.
　　nau·ti·cal (nô′ti kəl) *adjective.*

nautical mile A measurement of distance that is used by ships. It is equal to about 6076 feet.

naval Having to do with the navy. England was once the greatest *naval* power in the world. ▲ Another word that sounds like this is **navel.**
　　na·val (nā′vəl) *adjective.*

navel A round mark in the middle of the abdomen. The navel results from cutting the cord that connects a newborn baby to its mother. ▲ Another word that sounds like this is **naval.**
　　na·vel (nā′vəl) *noun, plural* **navels.**

navigate **1.** To sail or steer. The captain *navigated* the ship through the storm. **2.** To sail on or across. Modern ocean liners can *navigate* the Atlantic Ocean in less than a week.
　　nav·i·gate (nav′i gāt′) *verb,* **navigated, navigating.**

navigation **1.** The act of sailing or steering a ship. The captain found *navigation* almost impossible in the high waves. **2.** The art or science of figuring out the position and course of boats, ships, and aircraft. Bill's brother studied *navigation* when he was in the navy.
　　nav·i·ga·tion (nav′i gā′shən) *noun.*

navigator **1.** A person on a boat, ship, or airplane who is in charge of steering a course. **2.** A person who explores by ship. Ferdinand Magellan was a famous Portuguese *navigator* who organized the first voyage to sail around the world.
　　nav·i·ga·tor (nav′i gā′tər) *noun, plural* **navigators.**

navy **1.** All the warships of a country. The United States has one of the most powerful *navies* in the world. **2.** The men, supplies, and equipment that make up the entire sea force of a country. My brother is a lieutenant in the *navy.* **3.** A very dark-blue color; navy blue. *Noun.*
　—Having the color navy. *Adjective.*
　　na·vy (nā′vē) *noun, plural* **navies;** *adjective.*

navy blue A very dark-blue color.

nay No. "*Nay,*" said the knight to the traveler, "I do not know the way to Westwood Castle." ▲ This word was common in olden times, but it is not used often today. *Adverb.*
　—A vote or voter against. The chairman of the club counted the *nays* against the proposal. *Noun.* ▲ Another word that sounds like this is **neigh.**
　　nay (nā) *adverb; noun, plural* **nays.**

near Not far or distant. Night is drawing *near. Adverb.*
　—**1.** Not far or distant. Will I see you in the *near* future? **2.** Done or missed by only a small amount; narrow. The people in that building had a *near* escape from the fire. **3.** Close in feeling. She is a *near* and dear friend of mine. *Adjective.*
　—Close to or by. My grandparents live in a house *near* the beach. *Preposition.*
　—To come or draw near. The airplane *neared* the landing field. The wild animals ran the other way as the hunters *neared. Verb.*
　　near (nēr) *adverb; adjective,* **nearer, nearest;** *preposition; verb,* **neared, nearing.**

nearby A short distance away; not far off. My mother works in a *nearby* town. My brother and I go to school *nearby.*
　　near·by (nēr′bī′) *adjective; adverb.*

---

at; āpe; cär; end; mē; it; īce; hot; ōld;
fôrk; wood; fo͞ol; oil; out; up; turn; sing;
thin; this; hw in white; zh in treasure.
ə stands for a in about, e in taken
i in pencil, o in lemon, and u in circus.

nearly   All but; almost. I *nearly* forgot your birthday. It is *nearly* midnight.
near·ly (nēr′lē) *adverb.*

nearsighted   Able to see objects that are close by more clearly than those that are far away. Because my father is *nearsighted*, he needs to wear eyeglasses whenever he drives a car.
near·sight·ed (nēr′sī′tid) *adjective.*

neat   **1.** Clean and orderly; tidy. My sister always has a *neat* room, but mine is usually messy. Our teacher wants us to have *neat* handwriting. **2.** Done in a clever way. Robin learned a *neat* trick in school today. **3.** Wonderful or fine. We had a *neat* time at the party.
neat (nēt) *adjective,* **neater, neatest.**

Nebraska   A state in the central United States. Its capital is Lincoln.
Ne·bras·ka (ni bras′kə) *noun.*

▲ **Nebraska** was an Indian name for the Platte River. It means "flat water." The name of the river was changed later, but the Indian name was kept for the state.

necessarily   As a certain result. Tall people are not *necessarily* good basketball players.
nec·es·sar·i·ly (nes′ə ser′ə lē) *adverb.*

necessary   **1.** That cannot be done without; needed; required. Proper food and rest are *necessary* for good health. **2.** That cannot be avoided; certain. Low grades were a *necessary* result of the student's poor work.
nec·es·sar·y (nes′ə ser′ē) *adjective.*

necessity   **1.** Something that cannot be done without; requirement. Food, clothing, and shelter are the *necessities* of life. **2.** The fact of being necessary. Tom realized the *necessity* of finishing school if he wanted to be a doctor.
ne·ces·si·ty (ni ses′ə tē) *noun, plural* **necessities.**

neck   **1.** The part of the body of a person or animal that connects the head and the shoulders. **2.** The part of a piece of clothing that fits around the neck. Mike likes to leave the *neck* of his shirt open in hot weather. **3.** A narrow part that is like a neck in shape or position. This old bottle has a glass stopper that fits into its *neck*. We have a summer cottage on a little *neck* of land that juts out into the lake.
neck (nek) *noun, plural* **necks.**
neck and neck. At an equal pace; even. The two horses were running *neck and neck* in the race.

neckerchief   A scarf or kerchief that is worn around the neck.
neck·er·chief (nek′ər chif) *noun, plural* **neckerchiefs.**

necklace   A string of beads or other piece of jewelry that is worn around the neck for decoration. Ruth wore a red *necklace* with her blue dress.
neck·lace (nek′lis) *noun, plural* **necklaces.**

Neckerchief

necktie   A piece of cloth that is worn around the neck by putting it under a shirt collar and knotting it in front. Men and boys usually wear a necktie when they wear a suit.
neck·tie (nek′tī′) *noun, plural* **neckties.**

nectar   The sweet liquid formed in flowers. Bees use nectar to make honey.
nec·tar (nek′tər) *noun, plural* **nectars.**

need   **1.** The lack of something necessary, useful, or desired. The team's defeat showed their *need* for practice. **2.** Something that is necessary, useful, or desired. What are the *needs* for our camping trip? **3.** A necessity or obligation. There is no *need* to stay any longer. **4.** A time of trouble or difficulty. When Tom sprained his ankle, Carl was truly a friend in *need* and helped him get home. *Noun.*
—**1.** To have need of; require. I *need* a new pair of shoes. The town *needs* a larger hospital. **2.** To have to. *Need* she wait for him? No, she *need* not wait. *Verb.* ▲ Another word that sounds like this is **knead.**
need (nēd) *noun, plural* **needs;** *verb,* **needed, needing.**

needle   **1.** A thin, pointed instrument with a hole in one end. It is used in sewing. The thread is passed through the hole and the needle carries the thread through the cloth. **2.** A pointer on a compass or dial. The *needle* on the compass shows that we are walking north. **3.** A sharp, thin, hollow tube that is used for forcing fluid into the body. The doctor stuck a *needle* in John's arm when he gave him a flu shot. **4.** A thin rod that is used in knitting. Pat knitted the baby's sweater on very small *needles*. **5.** The thin, pointed leaves on a fir tree or pine tree. The *needles* of the pine tree do not fall off when winter comes. **6.** Anything that is thin and pointed like a needle. The *needle* on our record player is wearing down.
nee·dle (nēd′əl) *noun, plural* **needles.**

needless   Not needed; unnecessary. Buying

a new stove would be a *needless* expense because the one we have works perfectly well.

need·less (nēd′lis) *adjective.*

needn't You *needn't* hurry because we have plenty of time.

need·n't (nēd′ənt) contraction for "need not."

needy Very poor. The church collected old clothes and gave them to *needy* families.

need·y (nē′dē) *adjective,* **needier, neediest.**

negative 1. Saying "no." The man's answer to the question was *negative.* Lucy gave a *negative* shake of her head. 2. Not helpful. The girl had such a *negative* attitude toward learning French that she never was very good at speaking it. 3. Less than zero. −3 is a *negative* number. 4. Having a certain kind of electric charge. Magnets have a *negative* charge at one end and a positive charge at the other. 5. Not showing a certain disease or condition. The doctor knew that the injured boy did not have a broken leg because the X rays were *negative. Adjective.*
—1. A photographic image in which the areas that were light in the original subject are dark and those that were dark are light. Prints can be made from a negative. 2. A word or phrase that expresses a denial or says "no." "Not" is a negative. *Noun.*

neg·a·tive (neg′ə tiv) *adjective; noun, plural* **negatives.**

neglect 1. To fail to give proper attention or care to. The boy *neglected* his plants and they all died. 2. To fail to do. Mary cleaned her room, but *neglected* to make her bed. *Verb.*
—1. A failure to give proper attention; lack of care. Henry's *neglect* of his pet fish caused some of them to die. 2. The condition of not being cared for. No one lived there any more, and the old house had fallen into *neglect. Noun.*

neg·lect (ni glekt′) *verb,* **neglected, neglecting;** *noun.*

negotiate 1. To talk over and arrange the terms of. The factory owners met with the workers to *negotiate* the end of the strike. 2. To have a discussion in order to bring about an agreement. The two warring countries refused to *negotiate.*

ne·go·ti·ate (ni gō′shē āt′) *verb,* **negotiated, negotiating.**

negotiation A discussion for the purpose of bringing about an agreement. The *negotiations* to end the war between the two countries are going well.

ne·go·ti·a·tion (ni gō′shē ā′shən) *noun, plural* **negotiations.**

Negro A member of one of the major divisions of the human race. The native peoples of southern and central Africa are Negroes. *Noun.*
—Having to do with Negroes. *Adjective.*

Ne·gro (nē′grō) *noun, plural* **Negroes;** *adjective.*

neigh The sound that a horse makes. *Noun.*
—To make the sound that is made by a horse. *Verb.* ▲ Another word that sounds like this is **nay.**

neigh (nā) *noun, plural* **neighs;** *verb,* **neighed, neighing.**

neighbor 1. A person who lives in the house or apartment next to or near one's own. Our *neighbor* down the street took care of our dog while we were away on vacation. 2. A person, place, or thing that is next to or near another. Mexico is a *neighbor* of the United States.

neigh·bor (nā′bər) *noun, plural* **neighbors.**

▲ The word **neighbor** goes back to two Old English words that meant "near" and "farmer." Long ago, almost everyone lived on farms, and a farmer who lived next door to another person was called a "near farmer." The word *neighbor* was made by putting the words for "near" and "farmer" together.

---

neighborhood 1. A small area or district in a town or city where people live. The *neighborhood* near the river is one of the oldest in town. 2. The people living in the same area or district. The whole *neighborhood* is talking about the fire last night.

neigh·bor·hood (nā′bər hood′) *noun, plural* **neighborhoods.**

neither When I was sick, I could *neither* eat nor drink. Dad doesn't want to go to the movies; *neither* does Mom. *Neither* team played well in the game. Lucy tried on two dresses, but *neither* fit her.

nei·ther (nē′thər *or* nī′thər) *conjunction; adjective; pronoun.*

neon A colorless, odorless gas that makes up a very small part of the air. Tubes filled with neon are used in electric signs. Neon is a chemical element.

ne·on (nē′on) *noun.*

---

at; āpe; cär; end; mē; it; īce; hot; ōld;
fôrk; wood; fool; oil; out; up; turn; sing;
thin; this; hw in white; zh in treasure.
ə stands for a in about, e in taken
i in pencil, o in lemon, and u in circus.

nephew   **1.** The son of one's brother or sister. **2.** The son of one's brother-in-law or sister-in-law.
neph·ew (nef′yo͞o) *noun, plural* **nephews.**

Neptune   The fourth largest planet. It is the eighth closest planet to the sun. Neptune can only be seen from earth with the aid of a telescope.
Nep·tune (nep′to͞on *or* nep′tyo͞on) *noun.*

nerve   **1.** A bundle of fibers that carries messages between the brain and spinal cord and other parts of the body. If a person touches a hot stove, the brain receives a message of pain from the nerves in the hand. The brain then sends a message through the nerves to the hand that makes the person pull his hand away from the stove. **2.** Courage or bravery. The little boy did not have the *nerve* to jump off the high diving board.
nerve (nurv) *noun, plural* **nerves.**

nervous   **1.** Tense or upset. Loud noises make me *nervous.* **2.** Fearful or timid. I am very *nervous* about taking the exam.
nerv·ous (nur′vəs) *adjective.*

nervous system   The system in the body that includes the brain, spinal cord, and nerves. The nervous system controls all the activities of the body.

-ness   A *suffix* that means "the state of being." *Lightness* means "the state of being light." *Emptiness* means "the state of being empty."

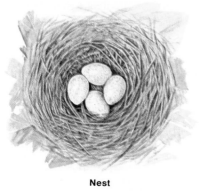

Nest

nest   **1.** A place built by a bird for laying its eggs and raising its young. A nest can be made out of grass, twigs, mud, or many other materials. **2.** A place made by insects, fish, turtles, or other animals for laying their eggs or raising their young. Some fish make nests by making a hole in the mud or sand with their tails. **3.** A group of birds, insects, or other animals living in a nest. There was a *nest* of robins in the maple tree by the barn. **4.** A cozy place or shelter. The kitten made a *nest* among the rags in the closet and fell asleep. *Noun.*
—To build or live in a nest. Every spring the sparrows *nest* under the roof of our garage. *Verb.*
nest (nest) *noun, plural* **nests;** *verb,* **nested, nesting.**

net¹   An open fabric that is made of threads, cords, or ropes. These materials are knotted or woven together so as to leave evenly spaced holes. Carl used a *net* to pull the fish that Jane caught into the boat. Susan hit the tennis ball into the *net. Noun.*
—To catch with a net. Ruth *netted* three large fish on her first day of fishing in the lake. *Verb.*
net (net) *noun, plural* **nets;** *verb,* **netted, netting.**

Net

net²   Remaining after all costs and deductions have been made. A storekeeper's *net* profit is the money left over after he buys the groceries he will sell and pays the rent and the other costs of running his business. The *net* weight of a can of corn is only the weight of the corn itself. *Adjective.*
—To earn or get as a profit. The sale of a car *nets* the automobile dealer a good profit. *Verb.*
net (net) *adjective; verb,* **netted, netting.**

network   **1.** A system of lines or structures that cross. The electric system for this building is a *network* of wires. A railroad yard is a *network* of tracks. **2.** A group of radio or television stations that work together so that they can all broadcast the same program at the same time.
net·work (net′wurk′) *noun, plural* **networks.**

neutral   **1.** Not taking or belonging to either side in a fight or argument. During the war the family left their home and fled to a *neutral*

country. **2.** Having no particular shade or tint. Gray is a *neutral* color. **3.** Neither an acid nor a base in chemistry. The right mixture of an acid and a base will produce a *neutral* salt. *Adjective.*
—A position of gears in an automobile. When a car is in neutral, the engine cannot send power to the wheels to make the car move. *Noun.*
   neu·tral (nōo′trəl *or* nyōo′trəl) *adjective; noun.*

neutron A small particle that is part of the nucleus, or center, of an atom. A neutron has no electric charge. It is a little heavier than a proton.
   neu·tron (nōo′tron *or* nyōo′tron) *noun, plural* **neutrons.**

Nevada A state in the western United States. Its capital is Carson City.
   Ne·vad·a (nə vad′ə *or* nə vä′də) *noun.*

▲ The name **Nevada** comes from the Sierra Nevada mountains in eastern California and the southwestern corner of Nevada. Spanish explorers named these mountains. The name means "snowy mountain range."

never He has *never* been to China. We *never* thought this work would be so hard. You *never* told me you and my cousin Dan were old friends.
   nev·er (nev′ər) *adverb.*

nevertheless It was a cloudy day; *nevertheless,* we went to the beach.
   nev·er·the·less (nev′ər <u>th</u>ə les′) *conjunction; adverb.*

new **1.** Recently grown or made; not old. Each spring the tree has *new* buds. Have you read this *new* book yet? That store sells both *new* and used furniture. **2.** Seen, known, made, or thought of for the first time. John found a *new* rock for his collection. Roger made many *new* friends during his stay at camp this summer. **3.** Not yet experienced. Doug was slow doing his job because he was still *new* at it. **4.** Coming or beginning again. Monday is the start of a *new* school week. ▲ Other words that sound like this are **gnu** and **knew.**
   new (nōo *or* nyōo) *adjective,* **newer, newest.**

newborn Born very recently. A *newborn* baby sleeps most of the time.
   new·born (nōo′bôrn′ *or* nyōo′bôrn′) *adjective.*

newcomer A person who has recently arrived. Mr. Edwards is a *newcomer* in town and hasn't made many friends yet.

   new·com·er (nōo′kum′ər *or* nyōo′kum′ər) *noun, plural* **newcomers.**

New England A region of the northeastern United States. Maine, Vermont, New Hampshire, Massachusetts, Rhode Island, and Connecticut are the New England states.

New Hampshire A state in the northeastern United States. Its capital is Concord.
   New Hamp·shire (hamp′shər).

▲ **New Hampshire** was named after the county of Hampshire, in England. The English county was the home of one of the men who started the American colony of New Hampshire.

New Jersey A state in the eastern United States. Its capital is Trenton.
   New Jer·sey (jur′zē′).

▲ **New Jersey** was named after the island of Jersey, in the English Channel. One of the first owners of the American colony was born on this island.

newly Lately; recently. That man is the *newly* elected governor of our state.
   new·ly (nōo′lē *or* nyōo′lē) *adverb.*

New Mexico A state in the southwestern United States. Its capital is Santa Fe.
   New Mex·i·co (mek′si kō′).

▲ A Spanish explorer who had been in Mexico named this area **New Mexico.** The name *Mexico* comes from the name of an Indian god.

new moon The moon when it cannot be seen or when it appears as a thin crescent with the hollow part on the right side.

news A report or information of something that happened recently. The soldier had heard no *news* from home in about a month. We watched a television program that gave the day's *news.*
   news (nōoz *or* nyōoz) *noun.*

newscast A radio or television program that presents the news.
   news·cast (nōoz′kast′ *or* nyōoz′kast′) *noun, plural* **newscasts.**

---

at; āpe; cär; end; mē; it; īce; hot; ōld; fôrk; wood; fōol; oil; out; up; turn; sing; thin; <u>th</u>is; hw in white; zh in treasure.
ə stands for **a** in about, **e** in taken
i in pencil, **o** in lemon, and **u** in circus.

newspaper Printed sheets of paper that contain news, interesting stories, opinions on local and national happenings, and advertising.

news·pa·per (nōōz′pā′pər *or* nyōōz′pā′pər) *noun, plural* **newspapers.**

newt A small, brightly colored salamander that lives in or around water.

newt (nōōt *or* nyōōt) *noun, plural* **newts.**

New Testament The second part of the Bible. It contains the life and teachings of Christ and His followers.

New World North and South America.

New York A state in the eastern United States. Its capital is Albany.

New York (yôrk).

Newt

▲ **New York** was named after the Duke of York and Albany, who later became King James II of England. The Duke of York and Albany was given the colony of New York by his brother, King Charles II.

next I'll see you *next* week. My friend lives in the *next* house. She is *next* in line. Barbara will sing *next.* Please visit us when you *next* come to town.

next (nekst) *adjective; adverb.*

next-door In the nearest building, house, or apartment. Our *next-door* neighbors share a driveway with us.

next-door (nekst′dôr′) *adjective.*

next door In the building, house, or apartment that is nearest. Jack lives *next door* to me.

nibble To eat or bite quickly and gently. The mouse *nibbled* the cheese. *Verb.*
—A small bite. The fish took a *nibble* at our bait but swam away. *Noun.*

nib·ble (nib′əl) *verb,* **nibbled, nibbling;** *noun, plural* **nibbles.**

nice 1. Pleasant or agreeable. The weather was *nice* yesterday. We had a *nice* time at the dance. 2. Kind and thoughtful. It was *nice* of Julie to ask us to the party. 3. Showing or needing care and skill; fine. Those wooden cabinets are a *nice* piece of work.

nice (nīs) *adjective,* **nicer, nicest.**

niche A hollow or recess in a wall. It is used as a setting for statues or vases.

niche (nich) *noun, plural* **niches.**

nick A place on a surface or edge that has been cut or chipped. The razor blade made a *nick* on Dad's face. When the mirror fell off the wall, it made some *nicks* in the table underneath it. *Noun.*
—To make a cut or chip on the surface or edge of. Mary *nicked* the side of the car on the garage door. *Verb.*

nick (nik) *noun, plural* **nicks;** *verb,* **nicked, nicking.**

in the nick of time. At the last moment; just in time. The lifeguard reached the drowning man just *in the nick of time.*

Niche

nickel 1. A hard, silvery metal. Nickel is very strong and is not easily worn away. Nickel is a chemical element. 2. A coin of the United States that is equal to five cents.

nick·el (nik′əl) *noun, plural* **nickels.**

nickname A name that is used instead of or in addition to a person's real name. Walter's *nickname* is "Butch." "Dan" is a *nickname* for Daniel. *Noun.*
—To give a nickname to. Bill was *nicknamed* "Red" by his friends because of his bright red hair. *Verb.*

nick·name (nik′nām′) *noun, plural* **nicknames;** *verb,* **nicknamed, nicknaming.**

nicotine A poisonous, oily substance that is found in the leaves, roots, and seeds of the tobacco plant.

nic·o·tine (nik′ə tēn′) *noun.*

niece 1. The daughter of one's brother or sister. 2. The daughter of one's brother-in-law or sister-in-law.

niece (nēs) *noun, plural* **nieces.**

night 1. The time when it is dark; time between the setting and rising of the sun. The baby slept quietly in her crib all *night* long. Friday is the *night* when our family goes out to dinner. 2. The darkness of night. The soldier slipped behind the enemy's lines under the cover of *night.* ▲ Another word that sounds like this is **knight.**

night (nīt) *noun, plural* **nights.**

nightfall The beginning of night; the end of the day.
night·fall (nīt′fôl′) *noun.*

nightgown A loose gown that is worn to bed by women or children.
night·gown (nīt′goun′) *noun, plural* night·gowns.

nightingale A small bird that lives in Europe. Nightingales have yellowish-brown feathers with a whitish crest. They are known for their beautiful song.
night·in·gale (nīt′ən gāl′ *or* nī′ting gāl′) *noun, plural* nightingales.

Nightingale

nightly Done or happening every night. My parents watch the *nightly* news show before they go to bed. *Adjective.*
—Every night. When my father is away on business, he calls home *nightly* to see how we are. *Adverb.*
night·ly (nīt′lē) *adjective; adverb.*

nightmare 1. A bad or frightening dream. Victor had a *nightmare* about being chased by a lion. 2. Any bad or frightening experience. Being lost in the big city was a *nightmare* for the boys.
night·mare (nīt′mer′) *noun, plural* night·mares.

▲ The word **nightmare** is made up of the word *night* and an old English word for a kind of monster. The word was first used for an imaginary creature that people once thought sat on a person while he was asleep and made him feel that he could not breathe.

nighttime The time when it is dark; night. Mother didn't like us going out alone at *nighttime.*
night·time (nīt′tīm′) *noun.*

nimble Light and quick in movement. The circus has *nimble* acrobats.
nim·ble (nim′bəl) *adjective,* nimbler, nimblest.

nine One more than eight; 9.
nine (nīn) *noun, plural* nines; *adjective.*

nineteen Nine more than ten; 19.
nine·teen (nīn′tēn′) *noun, plural* nineteens; *adjective.*

nineteenth 1. Next after the eighteenth. 2. One of nineteen equal parts; $1/19$.
nine·teenth (nīn′tēnth′) *adjective; noun, plural* nineteenths.

ninetieth 1. Next after the eighty-ninth. 2. One of ninety equal parts; $1/90$.
nine·ti·eth (nīn′tē ith) *adjective; noun, plural* ninetieths.

ninety Nine times ten; 90.
nine·ty (nīn′tē) *noun, plural* nineties; *adjective.*

ninth 1. Next after the eighth. 2. One of nine equal parts; $1/9$.
ninth (nīnth) *adjective; noun, plural* ninths.

nip 1. To catch hold of and bite or pinch. The parrot *nipped* the girl's finger. 2. To cut by pinching. The gardener *nipped* the dead leaves off the branch. 3. To cause to smart or sting. The cold night air *nipped* our faces. *Verb.*
—1. A bite or pinch. Tom pulled his foot away when he felt the *nip* of a crab on his toe. 2. A sharp, biting cold. There is a *nip* in the air today. *Noun.*
nip (nip) *verb,* nipped, nipping; *noun, plural* nips.

nipple 1. The small rounded tip in the center of a breast or udder. A baby or newly born animal sucks milk from its mother's nipple. 2. The rubber tip or mouthpiece of a baby's bottle. A baby sucks on the nipple to get milk or other liquids.
nip·ple (nip′əl) *noun, plural* nipples.

nitrate One of many compounds that are made from nitric acid. Nitrates are most often used in fertilizers and explosives.
ni·trate (nī′trāt) *noun, plural* nitrates.

nitric acid A colorless acid that contains nitrogen. Nitric acid is one of the strongest acids known.
ni·tric acid (nī′trik).

nitrogen A gas that has no color and no smell. It makes up almost four-fifths of the air on earth. Nitrogen is a chemical element.
ni·tro·gen (nī′trə jən) *noun.*

no *No,* I don't want to go to the movies tonight. *No,* that's not what I said. The sick woman is *no* better today than she was yesterday. Don't just give me *no* for an

at; āpe; cär; end; mē; it; īce; hot; ōld;
fôrk; wood; fo͞ol; oil; out; up; turn; sing;
thin; this; hw in white; zh in treasure.
ə stands for **a** in about, **e** in taken
i in pencil, **o** in lemon, and **u** in circus.

answer. There were *no* mistakes in her spelling test. Dinner will be ready in *no* time. He is *no* great baseball player. ▲ Another word that sounds like this is **know.**
no (nō) *adverb; noun, plural* **noes;** *adjective.*

nobility 1. People who have a high rank or title. Dukes, earls, and counts belong to the nobility. 2. Greatness of character. My grandfather is a kindly man of great *nobility.*
no·bil·i·ty (nō bil′ə tē) *noun, plural* **nobilities.**

noble 1. Having high rank or title. The Duke of Marlborough comes from a *noble* family. 2. Having or showing greatness of character; worthy. The fight for freedom is a *noble* cause. *Adjective.*
—A person of high rank or title. A duke is a *noble. Noun.*
no·ble (nō′bəl) *adjective,* **nobler, noblest;** *noun, plural* **nobles.**

nobleman A man of high rank or title.
no·ble·man (nō′bəl mən) *noun, plural* **noblemen.**

noblewoman A woman of high rank or title.
no·ble·wom·an (nō′bəl woom′ən) *noun, plural* **noblewomen.**

nobody I rang the doorbell, but *nobody* answered.
no·bod·y (nō′bod′ē) *pronoun.*

nocturnal 1. Happening at night. We sat quietly on our porch and listened to the *nocturnal* sounds of the country. 2. Active at night. The raccoon is a *nocturnal* animal that spends a large part of the day sleeping.
noc·tur·nal (nok turn′əl) *adjective.*

nod 1. To move the head quickly up and down. Jim *nodded* to show that he understood. 2. To let the head fall forward with a quick motion. The student sat *nodding* over the dull book and finally fell asleep. 3. To show by quickly moving the head up and down. Father *nodded* approval of our request. *Verb.*
—A quick up-and-down movement of the head. My friend greeted me with a *nod. Noun.*
nod (nod) *verb,* **nodded, nodding;** *noun, plural* **nods.**

noise 1. A sound that is loud and harsh. The *noise* of the traffic outside the window made it hard to sleep. 2. Any sound. I heard a *noise* in the bushes.
noise (noiz) *noun, plural* **noises.**

noisy Making much noise. The teacher told the *noisy* children in the hall to return to their own classroom.
nois·y (noi′zē) *adjective,* **noisier, noisiest.**

nomad A member of a group or tribe that does not have a permanent home. Nomads wander from place to place looking for food or for land where they can find food for their animals.
no·mad (nō′mad) *noun, plural* **nomads.**

nomadic Wandering from place to place. Many Eskimos are *nomadic.*
no·mad·ic (nō mad′ik) *adjective.*

nominate To choose as a candidate or appoint to an office. The Democrats *nominated* John F. Kennedy for President in 1960. The mayor *nominated* Mr. Smith as police chief.
nom·i·nate (nom′ə nāt′) *verb,* **nominated, nominating.**

nomination 1. The act of choosing a person to run for an office. The *nominations* for President of the United States take place in the summer before the election. 2. The appointment of a person to an office. The Senate has to approve the President's *nomination* for the Secretary of the Treasury.
nom·i·na·tion (nom′ə nā′shən) *noun, plural* **nominations.**

nominee A person who is chosen as a candidate for office. The Democratic *nominee* for President was a well-known senator.
nom·i·nee (nom′ə nē′) *noun, plural* **nominees.**

non- A *prefix* that means "not."

▲ There are many words beginning with **non-** that you will not find in this dictionary. You can understand the meaning of these words by putting the word "not" in front of the part of the word that follows *non-*. For example, the word *nonliving* means "not living," and the word *nonviolent* means "not violent."

none All the boys tried to catch the rabbit, but *none* could run fast enough. *None* of the stolen money was ever found. Help came *none* too soon. ▲ Another word that sounds like this is **nun.**
none (nun) *pronoun; adverb.*

nonsense A way of talking or acting that is silly and makes no sense. A little baby talks *nonsense.* Mother said she would not put up with any more *nonsense* from the children.
non·sense (non′sens) *noun.*

noodle A flat strip of dried dough. Noodles are made out of flour, water, and eggs.
noo·dle (nood′əl) *noun, plural* **noodles.**

noon Twelve o'clock in the daytime; the middle of the day.
noon (noon) *noun.*

no one   *No one* had any questions about the homework. I thought I heard the doorbell ring, but *no one* was there.

noose   A loop of rope with a special knot that lets the loop tighten when the end of the rope is pulled.
  noose (noos) *noun, plural* **nooses.**

nor   Neither my sister *nor* I have seen the movie that is playing downtown. Robin was not at school today, *nor* will she be here tomorrow.
  nor (nôr) *conjunction.*

normal   Like most others; usual or typical; regular. The baby's height and weight are *normal* for a child of his age. A person's *normal* temperature is 98.6 degrees. *Adjective.*
—The usual or regular condition or level. There was much more rain than *normal* during the last month. *Noun.*
  nor·mal (nôr′məl) *adjective; noun.*

north   **1.** The direction to your right as you watch the sun set in the evening. North is one of the four main points of the compass. It is located directly opposite south. **2. North.** Any region or place that is in this direction. **3. the North.** The region of the United States that is north of Maryland, the Ohio River, and Missouri. *Noun.*
—**1.** Toward or in the north. The oak tree is in the *north* part of the schoolyard. **2.** Coming from the north. A *north* wind was blowing. *Adjective.*
—Toward the north. We hiked *north* for a mile and then rested. *Adverb.*
  north (nôrth) *noun; adjective; adverb.*

North America   A continent in the western hemisphere. North America lies between the Atlantic Ocean and the Pacific Ocean. North America contains the countries of Mexico, the United States, and Canada. It is the third largest continent.

North American   **1.** A person who was born or is living in North America. **2.** Having to do with North America or its people.

North Carolina   A state in the United States, on the Atlantic Ocean. Its capital is Raleigh.
  North Car·o·li·na (kar′ə lī′nə).

▲   **North Carolina** was made from the northern part of the colony of Carolina. King Charles I of England named the colony *Carolana,* which means "from Charles" or "belonging to Charles." Later King Charles II changed the name to *Carolina.*

North Dakota   A state in the north-central United States. Its capital is Bismarck.
  North Da·ko·ta (də kō′tə).

▲   **North Dakota** was made from the northern part of the Dakota Territory. The territory was named after the Dakota Indians, who lived there. Their name is an Indian word that means "friendly tribes."

northeast   The direction halfway between north and east. *Noun.*
—**1.** Toward or in the northeast. He lives in the *northeast* section of town. **2.** Coming from the northeast. A *northeast* wind was blowing. *Adjective.*
—Toward the northeast. *Adverb.*
  north·east (nôrth′ēst′) *noun; adjective; adverb.*

northern   **1.** In or toward the north. There is a large lake in the *northern* part of that state. **2.** Coming from the north. A cold *northern* breeze was blowing. **3. Northern.** Of or in the part of the United States that is in the north.
  north·ern (nôr′thərn) *adjective.*

northerner   **1.** A person living in the north. **2. Northerner.** A person living in the northern part of the United States.
  north·ern·er (nôr′thər nər) *noun, plural* **northerners.**

northern lights   Shining bands or streams of light appearing in the northern sky.

Northern Lights

North Pole The point on earth that is farthest north. It is the northern end of the earth's axis.

North Star A bright star that is in the northern sky above the North Pole.

northwest The direction halfway between north and west. *Noun.*
—**1.** Toward or in the northwest. We drove to the *northwest* part of town. **2.** Coming from the northwest. A *northwest* wind was blowing. *Adjective.*
—Toward the northwest. Turn *northwest* at the next corner. *Adverb.*
   north·west (nôrth′west′) *noun; adjective; adverb.*

nose **1.** The part of the face or head that is used for breathing and smelling. Air comes into and goes out of the nose through the nostrils. **2.** The sense of smell. Dogs have good *noses.* **3.** The point or front of something that sticks out. The pilot headed the *nose* of the plane slightly downward when he prepared to land. *Noun.*
—**1.** To find or notice by smell. The dog *nosed* out the rabbit in the bushes. **2.** To push slowly and gently. Our dog *nosed* the back door open and followed us into the yard. *Verb.*
   by a nose. By a very small amount. He won the race *by a nose.*
   nose (nōz) *noun, plural* **noses;** *verb,* **nosed, nosing.**

nose cone The front part of a rocket that is in the shape of a cone. The nose cone often has a special shield that protects it from the enormous heat that builds up when it comes back into the earth's atmosphere. The nose cone separates from the rest of the rocket during flight.

Nose cone after its return from space

nostril One of two outer openings in the nose. Air is taken in and let out through the nostrils.
   nos·tril (nos′trəl) *noun, plural* **nostrils.**

not My mother is *not* home. He does *not* know how to swim. It did *not* rain at all this week. ▲ Another word that sounds like this is **knot.**
   not (not) *adverb.*

notable Worthy of being noticed; important or remarkable. The author's first book was a *notable* success. *Adjective.*
—A person who is important. The mayor and other *notables* of our town led the parade. *Noun.*
   no·ta·ble (nō′tə bəl) *adjective; noun, plural* **notables.**

notation **1.** A system of signs or symbols that are used to represent numbers, words, or other information. The sign ÷ is a *notation* in arithmetic. **2.** A quick note. Jim made *notations* in the margin of the book he was reading.
   no·ta·tion (nō tā′shən) *noun, plural* **notations.**

notch A nick or cut on the edge or surface of something. The hikers made *notches* in the trees as they went along so they could find their way back to camp. *Noun.*
—To make a notch or notches in. Dad used to measure how tall we were every year by having us stand next to a post and *notching* it. *Verb.*
   notch (noch) *noun, plural* **notches;** *verb,* **notched, notching.**

note **1.** A word, phrase, or short sentence that is written down to help a person remember what was in a talk or book. Lucy took *notes* during the history class. **2.** A comment that explains a word or part of a book. Our poetry book has *notes* at the bottom of the pages that give the meaning of words that are no longer used today. **3.** A short message or letter. Janet sent her aunt a *note* thanking her for the birthday present. **4.** Careful notice; regard. Take *note* of how long it takes you to get to Joe's house. **5.** Importance. A judge is a man of *note.* **6.** A hint or suggestion. John thought he heard a *note* of jealousy in his brother's voice. **7.** A single sound in music, or a sign that represents such a sound. **8.** The key of a piano. A piano has white and black *notes. Noun.*
—**1.** To put down in writing. Amy *noted* her friend's telephone number in her address book. **2.** To take careful notice of; regard. Please *note* the enclosed newspaper article. *Verb.*

note (nōt) *noun, plural* **notes;** *verb,* **noted, noting.**

notebook A book with pages for notes. Susan has a *notebook* for each of the five subjects she takes at school.
note·book (nōt′book′) *noun, plural* **notebooks.**

noted Well-known; famous. Joseph's grandfather is a *noted* businessman in our town.
not·ed (nō′tid) *adjective.*

nothing **1.** No thing; not anything. We bought *nothing* at the store. The girl was so shy she usually sat in a corner and said *nothing.* **2.** A person or thing that is of no importance. One dollar is *nothing* to a rich person. **3.** Zero. The final score in the game was two to *nothing. Noun.*
—In no way; not at all. You look *nothing* like your sister. *Adverb.*
noth·ing (nuth′ing) *noun; adverb.*

notice **1.** Attention or observation. The thief sneaked out the back door of the shop to escape *notice.* **2.** A warning. The enemy attacked the fort without *notice.* **3.** A printed or written announcement. There were *notices* about the circus posted up all over town. *Noun.*
—To become aware of; observe. He *noticed* that the room was getting cooler. I *noticed* Fred's car parked outside. *Verb.*
no·tice (nō′tis) *noun, plural* **notices;** *verb,* **noticed, noticing.**

notify To make known to; inform. A driver who has an accident with his car should *notify* the police.
no·ti·fy (nō′tə fī′) *verb,* **notified, notifying.**

notion **1.** An idea or belief. I haven't the slightest *notion* of what he's talking about. My older sister says that believing in ghosts is a silly *notion.* **2.** A desire or whim. Alan had a sudden *notion* to go skiing this weekend. **3. notions.** Ribbons, pins, needles, and other small, useful items.
no·tion (nō′shən) *noun, plural* **notions.**

notorious Well-known for something bad. Jesse James was one of the most *notorious* outlaws the West has ever known.
no·to·ri·ous (nō tôr′ē əs) *adjective.*

noun A word that names a person, place, or thing. A noun acts as the subject or object of a verb, or the object of a preposition. Most nouns have a plural that is formed by adding *-s* or *-es.* Such words as *Mary, child, river, antelope, house, courage,* and *society* are nouns.
noun (noun) *noun, plural* **nouns.**

nourish To provide food and other things needed for life and growth. Milk *nourishes* a baby or newborn animal. Sun, rain, and good soil *nourish* plants and trees.
nour·ish (nur′ish) *verb,* **nourished, nourishing.**

nourishment Something that is needed for life and growth. It is very important that children who are still growing get good *nourishment.*
nour·ish·ment (nur′ish mənt) *noun, plural* **nourishments.**

novel[1] A long story about imaginary people and events. A novel usually tells about events that might really take place and people like those in real life.
nov·el (nov′əl) *noun, plural* **novels.**

novel[2] New and unusual. Susan has come up with a really *novel* idea for a booth at the school fair.
nov·el (nov′əl) *adjective.*

novelist A person who writes novels. Charles Dickens was a famous English *novelist.*
nov·el·ist (nov′ə list) *noun, plural* **novelists.**

novelty **1.** A being new. Once the *novelty* of mowing the lawn wore off, John quickly got bored with it. **2.** Something that is new or unusual. Riding the city's subway trains was a *novelty* for the boy who lived on a farm. **3. novelties.** Small, cheap toys and decorations.
nov·el·ty (nov′əl tē) *noun, plural* **novelties.**

November The eleventh month of the year. November has thirty days.
No·vem·ber (nō vem′bər) *noun.*

▲ The name **November** comes from the Latin word for "nine." The early Roman calendar began with March, and November was the ninth month.

novice **1.** A person who is new to something; beginner. Ann was still a *novice* at swimming. **2.** A person who is taken into a religious order for a trial period of time before taking vows for that order. Before a woman becomes a nun, she becomes a novice.
nov·ice (nov′is) *noun, plural* **novices.**

at; āpe; cär; end; mē; it; īce; hot; ōld;
fôrk; wood; fool; oil; out; up; turn; sing;
thin; this; hw in white; zh in treasure.
ə stands for a in about, e in taken
i in pencil, o in lemon, and u in circus.

now I really have to go *now*. Jane arrived just *now*. *Now* that we are alone, I can tell you what I really think. Bob should be home by *now*.
  now (nou) *adverb; conjunction; noun.*

nowadays At the present time. Most people travel by airplane *nowadays* if they are going a long distance.
  now·a·days (nou′ə dāz′) *adverb.*

nowhere I've looked all over the house, but the cat is *nowhere* to be found.
  no·where (nō′hwer′) *adverb.*

nozzle A spout at the end of a hose or pipe. By turning the *nozzle* on the hose, the firefighters made the water come out in a fast stream.
  noz·zle (noz′əl) *noun, plural* **nozzles.**

Nozzle

nuclear **1.** Of or forming a nucleus. Protons and neutrons are *nuclear* particles. The *nuclear* membrane is a thin layer that surrounds the nucleus. **2.** Coming from or having to do with an atomic nucleus or atomic energy. The country exploded a *nuclear* weapon on an island in the ocean.
  nu·cle·ar (nōō′klē ər *or* nyōō′klē ər) *adjective.*

nuclear energy Energy that can be released from the nucleus of an atom. The release of this energy may be uncontrolled, as in the explosion of the atomic bomb. It may also be controlled and used to produce electric power, to run ships, and to treat certain diseases. This is also called **atomic energy.**

nuclei More than one nucleus.
  nu·cle·i (nōō′klē ī′ *or* nyōō′klē ī′) *noun plural.*

nucleus **1.** The small oval center of a plant or animal cell. The nucleus controls all the important activities of the cell, such as growth. It is also very important in the process by which one cell divides and becomes two cells. **2.** The center of an atom. The nucleus of an atom is made up of protons and neutrons. The nucleus carries a positive charge of electricity.
  nu·cle·us (nōō′klē əs *or* nyōō′klē əs) *noun, plural* **nuclei** *or* **nucleuses.**

nudge To push or touch gently in order to attract attention. Michael *nudged* me with his elbow when the teacher called my name. *Verb.*
  —A gentle push or touch. My sister gave me a *nudge* to get my attention. *Noun.*
  nudge (nuj) *verb,* **nudged, nudging;** *noun, plural* **nudges.**

nugget A lump of gold as it is found in nature.
  nug·get (nug′it) *noun, plural* **nuggets.**

nuisance A person, thing, or action that annoys. The little boy next door is a *nuisance* with his water pistol. Mother won't let us get a dog because she thinks having to walk it twice a day is a *nuisance.*
  nui·sance (nōō′səns *or* nyōō′səns) *noun, plural* **nuisances.**

numb Having lost feeling or movement. The skier's face was *numb* with cold. The young soldier was *numb* with fear the first time he was in a battle. *Adjective.*
  —To make or become numb. The cold *numbed* Tom's fingers. *Verb.*
  numb (num) *adjective,* **number, numbest;** *verb,* **numbed, numbing.**

number **1.** The total amount of things in a group; how many there are of something. The *number* of children in our family is three. **2.** A symbol or word that tells how many or which one. 2, 5, 77, and 396 are *numbers.* Fred's apartment *number* is 2D. Do you have Robin's telephone *number?* **3.** A total or sum. The person who guesses the right *number* of peanuts in the jar will win a prize. **4.** A large quantity or group. A *number* of people gathered outside the store before the sale started. **5. numbers.** Arithmetic. My brother Bob has always been very good at *numbers. Noun.*
  —**1.** To find out the number of; count. The policemen *numbered* the crowd at about 1000. **2.** To give a number or numbers to. The teacher told us to *number* the pages of our book reports before turning them in. **3.** To amount to or include; contain. The sixth grade *numbered* fifty-two students. **4.** To limit. The days are *numbered* before summer vacation ends. *Verb.*
  num·ber (num′bər) *noun, plural* **numbers;** *verb,* **numbered, numbering.**

number line A line on which points are marked with numbers.

numeral A figure or group of figures that stand for a number. 7 and VII are both *numerals* for seven.
nu·mer·al (nōō′mər əl *or* nyōō′mər əl) *noun*, *plural* **numerals.**

numerator The number above or to the left of the line in a fraction. In the fraction ½, 1 is the numerator.
nu·mer·a·tor (nōō′mə rā′tər *or* nyōō′mə-rā′tər) *noun*, *plural* **numerators.**

numerical Having to do with or expressed by a number or numbers. 2 + 3 = 5 is a *numerical* equation; a + b = c is not.
nu·mer·i·cal (nōō mer′i kəl *or* nyōō mer′i-kəl) *adjective.*

numerous 1. Forming a large number; many. Our parents have *numerous* friends in this neighborhood. 2. Containing a large number; large. The crowd was *numerous*.
nu·mer·ous (nōō′mər əs *or* nyōō′mər əs) *adjective.*

nun A woman who belongs to a religious order. ▲ Another word that sounds like this is **none.**
nun (nun) *noun*, *plural* **nuns.**

nurse 1. A person who is trained to take care of sick people. Nurses work with doctors in hospitals. 2. A woman who is hired to take care of children. *Noun.*
—1. To take care of. My grandmother *nursed* the sick kitten. 2. To feed milk to a baby or young animal from a nipple. A mother cat *nurses* its kittens until they are able to eat other food by themselves. *Verb.*
nurse (nurs) *noun*, *plural* **nurses;** *verb*, **nursed, nursing.**

nursery 1. A baby's bedroom. 2. A place where plants and trees are raised and sold.
nurs·er·y (nur′sər ē) *noun*, *plural* **nurseries.**

nursery school A school for children who are too young to go to kindergarten.

nut 1. The dry fruit of a plant. Nuts have a hard outer shell and a softer inside that can be eaten. 2. A piece of metal with a hole in the center. The nut screws onto a bolt and helps keep the bolt in place.
nut (nut) *noun*, *plural* **nuts.**

nutcracker 1. A tool that is used for breaking open the hard outer shell of a nut. 2. A bird that feeds on nuts. It is related to the crow.
nut·crack·er (nut′krak′ər) *noun*, *plural* **nut-crackers.**

nutmeg The hard seed of an evergreen tree. Nutmeg is dried and is then ground or made in a powder for use in flavoring foods.
nut·meg (nut′meg′) *noun*, *plural* **nutmegs.**

nutrient Something that is needed by people, animals, and plants for life and growth. The protein in meat is a nutrient for people and many animals. Plants use the nutrients in water and in the air to grow.
nu·tri·ent (nōō′trē ənt *or* nyōō′trē ənt) *noun*, *plural* **nutrients.**

nutrition 1. Food; nourishment. The child was sick because he had not had proper *nutrition*. 2. The process by which food is taken in and used by a person, animal, or plant. We are studying plant *nutrition* in science this month.
nu·tri·tion (nōō trish′ən *or* nyōō trish′ən) *noun.*

nutritious Giving nourishment; useful as a food. The mother was careful to give her child *nutritious* food.
nu·tri·tious (nōō trish′əs *or* nyōō trish′əs) *adjective.*

nuzzle 1. To touch or rub with the nose. The dog *nuzzled* his master when he wanted to be fed. 2. To lie close; cuddle. The little girl *nuzzled* against her mother's shoulder.
nuz·zle (nuz′əl) *verb*, **nuzzled, nuzzling.**

nylon A strong, man-made fabric. Nylon is used to make thread, clothes, stockings, tires for automobiles, tents for camping, and many other things.
ny·lon (nī′lon) *noun.*

nymph 1. In old legends, a goddess that lived in forests, hills, or rivers. Nymphs usually took the form of beautiful young women. 2. A young insect before it becomes an adult. The nymph of a butterfly is usually called a caterpillar.
nymph (nimf) *noun*, *plural* **nymphs.**

Nutcracker

at; āpe; cär; end; mē; it; īce; hot; ōld;
fôrk; wood; fōol; oil; out; up; turn; sing;
thin; this; hw in white; zh in treasure.
ə stands for a in about, e in taken
i in pencil, o in lemon, and u in circus.

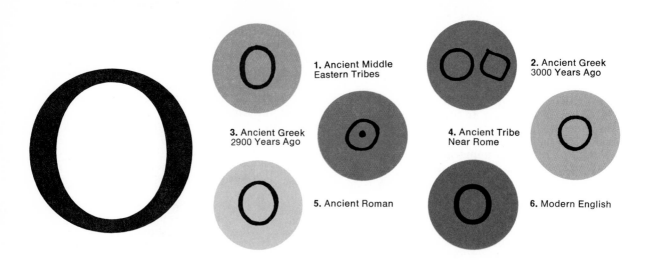

1. Ancient Middle Eastern Tribes

2. Ancient Greek 3000 Years Ago

3. Ancient Greek 2900 Years Ago

4. Ancient Tribe Near Rome

5. Ancient Roman

6. Modern English

O is the fifteenth letter of the alphabet. It is one of the very few letters whose shape has hardly changed throughout the entire history of the alphabet. The oldest form of the letter **O** was a letter used in the alphabet of several ancient tribes (**1**) in the Middle East. This letter was borrowed by the ancient Greeks (**2**) about 3000 years ago. About 100 years later, the Greeks (**3**) started to use a new form of **O**. They wrote it as a circle with a dot in the middle. The older form of **O**, without the dot, was borrowed by an ancient tribe (**4**) that settled north of Rome about 2800 years ago. The Romans (**5**) also used the older Greek form of **O**, writing it in almost the same way that we write the capital letter **O** today (**6**).

o, O The fifteenth letter of the alphabet.
  o, O (ō) *noun, plural* **o's, O's.**

oak Any of a large group of trees or shrubs that bear acorns. Oaks have a strong, heavy wood that is used in making furniture and boats and for covering floors.
  oak (ōk) *noun, plural* **oaks.**

Acorn

Leaf

Oak Tree

oar **1.** A long pole with a flat or curved blade at one end. Oars are usually made of wood. Oars are used to row or steer a boat. **2.** A person who rows a boat. ▲ Other words that sound like this are **or** and **ore.**
  oar (ôr) *noun, plural* **oars.**

oasis A place in a desert where trees, shrubs, and other plants can grow because there is a supply of water.
  o·a·sis (ō ā′sis) *noun, plural* **oases.**

Oasis

oat The grain of a plant that is related to grass. Oats are used as food by man and as feed for horses, cattle, and other animals.
  oat (ōt) *noun, plural* **oats.**

oath **1.** A statement or promise that a person swears is true. The witness put his hand on the Bible and made an *oath* that he would tell the truth about the accident. **2.** A word used in swearing; curse.
  oath (ōth) *noun, plural* **oaths.**

oatmeal **1.** A meal that is made by grinding or rolling oats. **2.** A cooked cereal that is made from this meal.
  oat·meal (ōt′mēl′) *noun, plural* **oatmeals.**

obedience The act of obeying or the state of being obedient. The umpire insisted on strict *obedience* to the rules of the game. The dog was rewarded with a biscuit for his *obedience*.

o·be·di·ence (ō bē′dē əns) *noun.*

obedient Tending or willing to obey. He was an *obedient* child who always did as he was told.

o·be·di·ent (ō bē′dē ənt) *adjective.*

obey 1. To carry out the orders, wishes, or instructions of. The boy *obeyed* his parents and came home before dark. 2. To carry out. He *obeyed* the law and didn't drive faster than the speed limit. The soldier was punished because he did not *obey* orders.

o·bey (ō bā′) *verb,* **obeyed, obeying.**

obi A wide sash worn with a Japanese kimono.

o·bi (ō′bē) *noun, plural* **obis.**

Obi

object 1. Anything that can be seen and touched; thing. She held a large round *object* in her hand. 2. A person or thing toward which feeling, thought, or action is directed. She was the *object* of his love. His rude behavior was the *object* of his parents' anger. 3. A thing that is wanted or aimed at; purpose; goal. The *object* of his telephone call was to invite me to the party. 4. The person or thing that receives the action of a verb or follows a preposition. In the sentence "I hit the ball," "ball" is the *object* of "hit." *Noun.*
—To be against; have or raise an objection. I *objected* to my brother's using my baseball glove without asking me first. *Verb.*

ob·ject (ob′jikt *for noun;* əb jekt′ *for verb*) *noun, plural* **objects;** *verb,* **objected, object-ing.**

objection A cause or reason for not liking or approving of something. Mother's *objection* to our going out was that it was too late.

ob·jec·tion (əb jek′shən) *noun, plural* **objec-tions.**

objective Not influenced by one's own personal feelings or opinions. The witness to the accident tried to be *objective* in the story she told the police. *Adjective.*
—Something that is wanted or aimed at. What was your *objective* in going to see her? *Noun.*

ob·jec·tive (əb jek′tiv) *adjective; noun, plural* **objectives.**

obligate To make a person do something because of a law, promise, or sense of duty. A driver is *obligated* to obey the traffic laws.

ob·li·gate (ob′lə gāt′) *verb,* **obligated, obli-gating.**

obligation Something a person must do; duty; responsibility. It is the *obligation* of all citizens to vote. We are under an *obligation* to pay him back the money he lent us.

ob·li·ga·tion (ob′lə gā′shən) *noun, plural* **obligations.**

oblige 1. To make a person do something by a law, promise, or sense of duty. Mr. Jones was *obliged* to pay for the window his son broke. 2. To make thankful for a service or favor. I am *obliged* to you for the help you have given me.

o·blige (ə blīj′) *verb,* **obliged, obliging.**

oblique angle Any angle that is not a right angle.

ob·lique angle (ə blēk′).

oblong Longer than wide. The necktie was in an *oblong* box.

ob·long (ob′lông′) *adjective.*

oboe A musical instrument that makes a high tone. The oboe is played by blowing into a mouthpiece.

o·boe (ō′bō) *noun, plural* **oboes.**

Oboe

obscure 1. Hard to understand; not clearly expressed. His explanation of the way the machine works was very *obscure*. 2. Not clearly seen, felt, or heard. She could not recognize the *obscure* figure in the faded picture. *Adjective.*
—To hide; conceal. Fog *obscured* the moon. *Verb.*

ob·scure (əb skyoor′) *adjective; verb,* **ob-scured, obscuring.**

---

at; āpe; cär; end; mē; it; īce; hot; ōld;
fôrk; wood; fool; oil; out; up; turn; sing;
thin; this; hw in white; zh in treasure.
ə stands for a in about, e in taken
i in pencil, o in lemon, and u in circus.

observation **1.** The act or power of noticing. The detective's careful *observation* helped him to solve the crime. **2.** The fact of being seen; notice. The thief escaped *observation* in the darkness. **3.** Something said; comment; remark. She made an *observation* about the weather.
ob·ser·va·tion (ob′zər vā′shən) *noun, plural* **observations.**

observatory A place or building that has telescopes for observing and studying the sun, moon, planets, and stars.
ob·serv·a·to·ry (əb zur′və tôr′ē) *noun, plural* **observatories.**

Observatory

observe **1.** To see or notice. She *observed* a delivery man coming up to the front door of her neighbor's house. **2.** To make a careful study of. The scientist *observed* how the mice acted after they were given the medicine. **3.** To follow, obey, or celebrate. The driver of the car *observed* the speed limit. We *observe* Thanksgiving with my grandparents.
ob·serve (əb zurv′) *verb,* **observed, observing.**

obsolete No longer in use or practice. Stagecoaches are *obsolete.*
ob·so·lete (ob′sə lēt′ *or* ob′sə lēt′) *adjective.*

obstacle A person or thing that stands in the way of or blocks progress. The heavy snowstorm was an *obstacle* to traffic.
ob·sta·cle (ob′stə kəl) *noun, plural* **obstacles.**

obstruct **1.** To fill with something that blocks. Fallen trees *obstructed* the road after the storm. **2.** To stand or be in the way of. The woman's large hat *obstructed* my view of the stage.
ob·struct (əb strukt′) *verb,* **obstructed, obstructing.**

obtain To get through effort; gain. In order to *obtain* the information I need for my report, I have to go to the library.
ob·tain (əb tān′) *verb,* **obtained, obtaining.**

obtuse angle Any angle that is greater than a right angle.
ob·tuse angle (əb tōōs′ *or* əb tyōōs′).

obvious Easily seen or understood. She made it *obvious* that she didn't want to go with us. It is *obvious* that you are wrong.
ob·vi·ous (ob′vē əs) *adjective.*

occasion **1.** The time when something happens. I cannot remember the *occasion*, but I have met her before. **2.** An important or special event. The baby's first birthday was an *occasion*. **3.** A suitable time; good opportunity. I haven't had many *occasions* to talk to him since he moved.
oc·ca·sion (ə kā′zhən) *noun, plural* **occasions.**

occasional Happening now and then; not frequent. The weatherman said there will be *occasional* showers today.
oc·ca·sion·al (ə kā′zhən əl) *adjective.*

occasionally Once in a while; at times. We see my aunt and uncle *occasionally.*
oc·ca·sion·al·ly (ə kā′zhən əl ē) *adverb.*

occupant A person who occupies a place or position. The *occupant* of the house is away for the day.
oc·cu·pant (ok′yə pənt) *noun, plural* **occupants.**

occupation **1.** The work that a person does in order to earn a living; profession. My father's *occupation* is teaching school. **2.** The act of occupying or the state of being occupied. The enemy soldiers' *occupation* of the town lasted for months.
oc·cu·pa·tion (ok′yə pā′shən) *noun, plural* **occupations.**

occupy **1.** To take up time or space; fill. Running errands for his mother *occupied* most of the morning. **2.** To take and keep control of. Enemy soldiers *occupied* the fort. **3.** To live in. They *occupy* the house just down the street. **4.** To keep busy. The children *occupied* themselves by working on model airplanes. **5.** To have as one's own; possess. Her mother *occupies* a position in the government.
oc·cu·py (ok′yə pī′) *verb,* **occupied, occupying.**

occur **1.** To take place; happen. The fire *occurred* in the middle of the night. **2.** To be found; appear. How many times does the word "to" *occur* on this page? **3.** To come to mind. It did not *occur* to me to take my umbrella.
oc·cur (ə kur′) *verb,* **occurred, occurring.**

occurrence **1.** The act of occurring. The *occurrence* of snow at this time of year is rare. **2.** Something that takes place or happens. Rain is an unusual *occurrence* in the desert.
oc·cur·rence (ə kur′əns) *noun, plural* **occurrences.**

ocean **1.** The whole body of salt water that covers nearly three-fourths of the earth's surface. **2.** Any one of the four main parts of this body of water: the Atlantic, Pacific, Indian, or Arctic Ocean.
o·cean (ō′shən) *noun, plural* **oceans.**

oceanography The science that has to do with the study of the ocean and the animals and plants that live in it.
o·cean·og·ra·phy (ō′shə nog′rə fē) *noun.*

ocelot A wildcat with a yellowish coat that is marked with black spots, rings, and stripes.
o·ce·lot (os′ə lot′ *or* ō′sə lot′) *noun, plural* **ocelots.**

Ocelot

o'clock Of or according to the clock. They will meet us at two *o'clock.*
o'clock (ə klok′) *adverb.*

octagon A figure having eight sides and eight angles.
oc·ta·gon (ok′tə gon′) *noun, plural* **octagons.**

octave **1.** The musical interval between the first and last notes of a scale. From middle C to the C below it is an octave. **2.** All the notes or keys of an instrument that make up this interval. Most pianos have a range of seven and one half octaves.
oc·tave (ok′tiv) *noun, plural* **octaves.**

October The tenth month of the year. October has thirty-one days.
Oc·to·ber (ok tō′bər) *noun.*

▲ **October** comes from the Latin word for "eight." In the early Roman calendar, March was the first month of the year, and October was the eighth month.

octopus An animal that lives in salt water and has a soft, rounded body and eight arms. There are suckers on the arms to help the octopus move along the ocean bottom and catch food.
oc·to·pus (ok′tə pəs) *noun, plural* **octopuses.**

▲ The word **octopus** comes from a Greek word that means "having eight feet."

Octopus

odd **1.** Different from the usual or normal; strange; peculiar. She has an *odd* way of dressing. It is *odd* that he never answered my letter. **2.** Not one of a pair or set. She has an *odd* glove and can't find its mate. I found an *odd* plate left from the set of old dishes. **3.** Happening or appearing now and then; occasional. He does *odd* jobs after school. **4.** Leaving a remainder of one when divided by two. 5, 7, and 19 are *odd* numbers.
odd (od) *adjective,* **odder, oddest.**

odds The difference in favor of or against something being true or happening. The *odds* are ten to one against that horse's winning the race. The *odds* are in favor of his being elected class president.
odds (odz) *noun plural.*

odor Smell; scent. The *odor* of flowers filled the room. The *odor* of garbage bothered the people who lived near the town dump.
o·dor (ō′dər) *noun, plural* **odors.**

of The cover *of* the book is red. She is a member *of* the club. The house is made *of* stone. The plant died *of* the cold. We met at five minutes *of* twelve. He is a man *of* honor. He said that he was not guilty *of* the crime.
of (ov *or* uv *or* əv) *preposition.*

at; āpe; cär; end; mē; it; īce; hot; ōld; fôrk; wood; fōōl; oil; out; up; turn; sing; thin; this; hw in white; zh in treasure.
ə stands for a in about, e in taken
i in pencil, o in lemon, and u in circus.

off He took the book *off* the shelf. She jumped *off* the horse. Please take *off* your coat and stay awhile. Please turn the radio *off*. He took the day *off* from work. We started *off* on our trip early in the morning. The lights in the house are *off*.
> **off** (ôf) *preposition; adverb; adjective.*

offend To cause to be angry or unhappy. His rude remark *offended* me.
> **of·fend** (ə fend′) *verb,* **offended, offending.**

offense **1.** The act of breaking the law or a rule. The thief will be punished for his *offense*. **2.** The act of causing anger or unhappiness. I meant no *offense* when I said that you aren't a good dancer. **3.** The attacking team or players in a game. Our football team has a good *offense*.
> **of·fense** (ə fens′ *for definitions 1 and 2;* ô′fəns *for definition 3*) *noun, plural* **offenses.**

offensive **1.** Causing anger or unhappiness. They got into an argument over his *offensive* remarks. **2.** Not pleasing; unpleasant; disagreeable. There was an *offensive* smell in the garbage can. **3.** Used for attack. A knife is an *offensive* weapon. *Adjective.*
> —A position or course of attack. The enemy took the *offensive* and surrounded the fort. *Noun.*
> **of·fen·sive** (ə fen′siv) *adjective; noun, plural* **offensives.**

offer **1.** To present to be accepted or turned down. She *offered* an apology for being late. He *offered* his suggestions for the party. **2.** To show a desire to do or give something; volunteer. She *offered* to help me with the ironing. **3.** To make a show of. The enemy *offered* little resistance when our soldiers attacked. *Verb.*
> —**1.** The act of offering. We accepted his *offer* of help. **2.** Something offered. The salesman turned down our *offer* of $500 for the old car. *Noun.*
> **of·fer** (ô′fər) *verb,* **offered, offering;** *noun, plural* **offers.**

office **1.** A place where the work of a business or profession is done. The door to her *office* was open. That company's *office* is upstairs. **2.** All the people who work in such a place. The *office* gave her a party before she got married. **3.** A position of authority, trust, or responsibility. He is going to run for the *office* of mayor.
> **of·fice** (ô′fis) *noun, plural* **offices.**

officer **1.** A person who has the power to command and lead others in the army or navy. Captains, generals, and admirals are officers. **2.** A person who has a position of authority, trust, or responsibility. The president and vice-president of the company are its *officers*. **3.** A policeman. We asked the *officer* for directions.
> **of·fi·cer** (ô′fə sər) *noun, plural* **officers.**

official A person who holds a certain office or position. The President and Vice-President are the two highest public *officials* in this country. *Noun.*
> —**1.** Of or having to do with an office or position of authority. Taking notes at each meeting is one of the *official* duties of the club secretary. **2.** Having the authority to do a specific job. Mr. Howard was the *official* scorekeeper at the basketball game. *Adjective.*
> **of·fi·cial** (ə fish′əl) *noun, plural* **officials;** *adjective.*

offset To make up for. Her kindness *offset* her bad temper.
> **off·set** (ôf′set′) *verb,* **offset, offsetting.**

offshoot Something that develops or grows from something else. A shoot or stem that grows from the main stem of a plant is an offshoot.
> **off·shoot** (ôf′sho͞ot′) *noun, plural* **offshoots.**

offshore Moving or in a direction away from the shore. We saw some people doing *offshore* fishing from their boats. *Adjective.*
> —Away from the shore. The storm has moved *offshore. Adverb.*
> **off·shore** (ôf′shôr′) *adjective; adverb.*

offspring The young of a person, animal, or plant. We went to the zoo and saw a female lion and her three *offspring*.
> **off·spring** (ôf′spring′) *noun, plural* **offspring** or **offsprings.**

often Many times; frequently. We went swimming *often* this summer.
> **of·ten** (ô′fən) *adverb.*

oh A word used to express surprise, happiness, sadness, pain, or other feeling. *Oh!* I didn't hear you come into the room! ▲ Another word that sounds like this is **owe.**
> **oh** (ō) *interjection.*

Ohio A state in the north-central United States. Its capital is Columbus.
> **O·hi·o** (ō hī′ō) *noun.*

▲ **Ohio** was an Indian name for the Ohio River that means "fine, great, beautiful river." Settlers used the name for the land around the river. When this land was made a county of Virginia, it was called *Ohio*, too. When the county became a separate state, it kept the same name.

oil Any one of a large group of substances that are greasy and will dissolve in alcohol but not in water. Oils are usually liquid or will easily become liquid when warmed. Oil is gotten from animals, vegetables, and minerals. *Noun.*
—To cover, polish, or supply with oil. Mother *oiled* the furniture. Father *oiled* the rusty hinges of the old gate so that it wouldn't creak when it was opened. *Verb.*
oil (oil) *noun, plural* **oils;** *verb,* **oiled, oiling.**

oil paint A paint that is made by mixing ground coloring matter with oil.

oil well A well that is dug or drilled in the earth to get oil or petroleum.

oily **1.** Of or like oil. The suntan lotion was *oily.* **2.** Containing, covered, or soaked with oil. We threw away the *oily* rags.
oil·y (oi′lē) *adjective,* **oilier, oiliest.**

ointment A soft substance that is put on the skin to heal, protect, or soften it. Ointments are usually greasy and often contain medicine. She put *ointment* on the burn to keep it from blistering.
oint·ment (oint′mənt) *noun, plural* **ointments.**

OK All right. Everything is *OK.* Is it *OK* if I borrow your book? *OK!* I'll do it!
OK (ō′kā′) *adjective; adverb; interjection.*

Oklahoma A state in the south-central United States. Its capital is Oklahoma City.
O·kla·ho·ma (ō′klə hō′mə) *noun.*

▲ In an Indian treaty of 1866, one tribe used the name **Oklahoma** for its lands. This Indian word means "red people." The name was given to a railroad station that used to be where Oklahoma City is today. Later it was chosen as the name for the state.

okra The soft, sticky green pods of a plant. Okra is used in soups and is eaten as a vegetable.
o·kra (ō′krə) *noun.*

old **1.** Having lived or existed for a long period of time. My grandfather is an *old* man. That church is a very *old* building. **2.** Of a certain age. Our car is three years *old.* **3.** From the past; not new or recent. That is an *old* song. She told us an *old* joke. **4.** Known for a long time; familiar.

Cross Section

Okra

We are *old* friends. **5.** Former. She is my *old* teacher from grammar school. That is my *old* neighborhood. **6.** Worn-out; used. We gave away all our *old* clothes. *Adjective.*
—A time in the past; former times. We read a story of the knights of *old. Noun.*
old (ōld) *adjective,* **older** or **elder, oldest** or **eldest;** *noun.*

olden Very old or ancient. Chariots were used in *olden* days.
old·en (ōld′ən) *adjective.*

old-fashioned **1.** Keeping to old ways, ideas, or customs. My aunt is very *old-fashioned* in the way she thinks. **2.** Out-of-date; no longer in fashion. She found an *old-fashioned* hat in the attic.
old-fash·ioned (ōld′fash′ənd) *adjective.*

Old Testament A collection of writings that make up the Jewish Bible and form the first part of the Christian Bible.

Old World The part of the world that includes Europe, Asia, and Africa. Columbus sailed from the *Old World* to the New World.

oleomargarine A substitute for butter. This is also called **margarine.** Look up **margarine** for more information.
o·le·o·mar·ga·rine (ō′lē ō mär′jər in) *noun, plural* **oleomargarines.**

olive **1.** The small, oily fruit of an evergreen tree. Olives have a single hard seed and firm flesh. They are often eaten pickled and are used to make olive oil. **2.** A dull yellowish-green color. *Noun.*
—Having the color olive; dull yellowish-green. *Adjective.*
ol·ive (ol′iv) *noun, plural* **olives;** *adjective.*

Olives

olive oil A clear yellow oil that is obtained from olives. It is used in salads and in cooking.

Olympic games **1.** An ancient Greek festival during which a series of competitions in athletics, poetry, and dancing were held. **2.** A

at; āpe; cär; end; mē; it; īce; hot; ōld;
fôrk; wood; fool; oil; out; up; turn; sing;
thin; this; hw in white; zh in treasure.
ə stands for a in about, e in taken
i in pencil, o in lemon, and u in circus.

modern series of athletic contests in which athletes from many countries take part. The Olympic games are held every four years in a different country. These games are also called the **Olympics.**

O·lym·pic games (ō lim′pik).

omelet   A food that is made of eggs that have been beaten, cooked in a pan, and then folded over.

om·e·let (om′ə lit *or* om′lit) *noun, plural* **omelets.**

omen   Something that is supposed to be a sign of good or bad luck. Breaking a mirror is thought to be a bad *omen.*

o·men (ō′mən) *noun, plural* **omens.**

ominous   Telling of trouble or bad luck to come; threatening. There were *ominous* black storm clouds coming in from the sea.

om·i·nous (om′ə nəs) *adjective.*

omit   To leave out; not include. Mother *omitted* butter from the shopping list.

o·mit (ō mit′) *verb,* **omitted, omitting.**

on   Your coat is *on* the bed. The plates are *on* the table. She put the hat *on* her head. Their house is *on* a lake. We left for camp *on* Wednesday. Harry is *on* the football team. She put her shoes *on.* Please move *on* so others can pass by. Turn the water *on.* If you don't hang *on,* you'll fall. The radio is *on.*

on (ôn *or* on) *preposition; adverb; adjective.*

once   **1.** One time. He has a piano lesson *once* a week. **2.** In time past; before. Parents were *once* children. *Adverb.*
—One single time. May I borrow your bicycle just this *once? Noun.*
—As soon as; when. The game is easy, *once* you learn the rules. *Conjunction.*

once (wuns) *adverb; noun; conjunction.*

one   **1.** The first and lowest number; 1. **2.** A single person or thing. Someone's been eating the cookies; there's only *one* left. *Noun.*
—**1.** Being a single person or thing. I only have *one* pencil. **2.** Some. Her practical jokes will get her in trouble *one* day. *Adjective.*
—**1.** A particular person or thing. *One* of the boys was left behind. **2.** Any person. *One* could see that Jack was very upset. *Pronoun.*
▲ Another word that sound like this is **won.**

one (wun) *noun, plural* **ones;** *adjective; pronoun.*

oneself   Seeing *oneself* on television would be exciting.

one·self (wun self′) *pronoun.*

one-sided   **1.** For or showing only one side; unfair; partial. The man's story of the argument was very *one-sided.* **2.** Not even or equal. The basketball game was very *one-*

sided, with our team losing by forty points.

one-sid·ed (wun′sī′did) *adjective.*

one-way   Moving or allowing movement in one direction only. That is a *one-way* street.

one-way (wun′wā′) *adjective.*

onion   The round or oval bulb of a plant. Onions have a strong, sharp taste and smell. They are eaten as a vegetable either raw or cooked.

on·ion (un′yən) *noun, plural* **onions.**

Kinds of Onions

only   Tom is an *only* child; he has no brothers and sisters. She is the *only* person who saw what happened. I have *only* two dollars. *Only* Jan remembered that today is my birthday. I would have gone to the game, *only* it was raining.

on·ly (ōn′lē) *adjective; adverb; conjunction.*

onto   The door opens *onto* the back yard. The actress walked *onto* the stage.

on·to (ôn′tōō *or* on′tōō) *preposition.*

onward   Toward the front; forward. They climbed *onward* toward the top of the hill. The men tried to stop the *onward* flow of the flood waters with bags of sand piled on top of one another.

on·ward (ôn′wərd *or* on′wərd) *adverb; adjective.*

ooze   To leak or pass out slowly through small holes or openings; seep. The mud *oozed* between my fingers when I tried to hold it in my hands.

ooze (ōōz) *verb,* **oozed, oozing.**

opal   A mineral that is used as a gem. Opals are white, milky blue, yellow, or black and show a slight change in color when they are moved in the light.

o·pal (ō′pəl) *noun, plural* **opals.**

opaque   **1.** Not letting light through; not transparent. The *opaque* window shades kept the sunlight out. **2.** Not shining; dull. The table was painted an *opaque* black color.

o·paque (ō pāk′) *adjective.*

open   **1.** Allowing movement in or out; not shut. She went through the *open* door. The

bird flew in through the *open* window. **2.** Not having its lid, door, or other covering closed. There was an *open* bottle of soda in the refrigerator. The drawer was *open.* **3.** Not closed in or covered. They rode their horses across the *open* meadow. **4.** Free to be used, taken, entered, or attended; available. The job of school secretary is still *open.* The meeting of the city council is *open* to the public. **5.** Able or ready to take in new ideas, facts, or beliefs. She is always *open* to suggestions. Janet has a very *open* mind. **6.** Honest; frank. She was very *open* with her friend about her problems. **7.** Ready to do business. That store is *open* every day but Sunday. *Adjective.*
—**1.** To make or become open. She *opened* the envelope and read the letter. The door creaked as it *opened.* **2.** To spread out; unfold. She *opened* the newspaper on the table. The petals of the flower *opened.* **3.** To set up or become available. They are *opening* a new dress shop in town. The pool *opens* in June. **4.** To begin; start. He *opened* his speech with a joke. *Verb.*
—Any space or area that is not closed in. The party was held in the *open. Noun.*
o·pen (ō′pən) *adjective; verb,* **opened, opening;** *noun.*

opener **1.** A thing that is used to open closed or sealed containers. Cans and bottles can be opened with an opener. **2.** The first thing or part in a series. Our baseball team won the *opener* of the baseball season.
o·pen·er (ō′pə nər) *noun, plural* **openers.**

opening **1.** An empty or clear space. We squeezed through an *opening* in the fence. **2.** The first part; beginning. The *opening* of the book was not too interesting. **3.** A job that is not filled. There is an *opening* for a delivery boy at the grocery store. **4.** The first time something is performed or open for business. The *opening* of the school play is tomorrow.
o·pen·ing (ō′pə ning) *noun, plural* **openings.**

opera A play having all or most of its words sung. Operas are presented with costumes, scenery, acting, and, sometimes, dancing. An orchestra usually plays music throughout the opera.
op·er·a (op′ər ə) *noun, plural* **operas.**

operate **1.** To go or run; work; function. The car's motor *operates* well. **2.** To cause to work. He knows how to *operate* the elevator. **3.** To perform surgery on the body of a sick or hurt person. The doctors *operated* on Janet to remove her appendix.
op·er·ate (op′ə rāt′) *verb,* **operated, operating.**

operation **1.** The act or way of working or directing. The *operation* of his business took up a lot of his time. My brother is learning about the *operation* of car engines. **2.** The state of being at work. The machine is in *operation.* **3.** Treatment that is performed on the body of a sick or hurt person by surgery. Bob had an *operation* to remove his tonsils.
op·er·a·tion (op′ə rā′shən) *noun, plural* **operations.**

operator A person who operates a machine or other device. My aunt is a telephone *operator.* The elevator *operator* is Mr. Lewis.
op·er·a·tor (op′ə rā′tər) *noun, plural* **operators.**

operetta A short opera that is funny. An operetta includes music and song combined with spoken parts and dancing.
op·er·et·ta (op′ə ret′ə) *noun, plural* **operettas.**

opinion **1.** A belief that is based on what a person thinks rather than on what is proved or known to be true. It is my *opinion* that he will win the race. What is your *opinion* of that movie? **2.** A formal judgment made by an expert. Father wanted to get his lawyer's *opinion* before he signed the contract.
o·pin·ion (ə pin′yən) *noun, plural* **opinions.**

opium A powerful drug that is habit-forming. Opium is made from a poppy plant. It is used to relieve pain and to cause sleep.
o·pi·um (ō′pē əm) *noun.*

opossum A small, furry animal that lives in trees. Female opossums carry their young in a pouch. When frightened, the opossum lies still as if it were dead. This animal is also called a **possum.**
o·pos·sum (ə pos′əm) *noun, plural* **opossums.**

Opossum

at; āpe; cär; end; mē; it; īce; hot; ōld; fôrk; wood; fōol; oil; out; up; turn; sing; thin; this; hw in white; zh in treasure.
ə stands for a in about, e in taken
i in pencil, o in lemon, and u in circus.

437

opponent   A person who is against another in a fight, contest, or discussion. The boxer beat his *opponent* and won the championship.
op·po·nent (ə pō′nənt) *noun, plural* **opponents.**

opportunity   A good chance; favorable time. When the pond froze, we had an *opportunity* to go ice skating.
op·por·tu·ni·ty (op′ər tōō′nə tē *or* op′ər-tyōō′nə tē) *noun, plural* **opportunities.**

oppose   **1.** To be against; resist. The people in the town *opposed* the plan to raise taxes. **2.** To be the opposite of; contrast. Good is *opposed* to evil.
op·pose (ə pōz′) *verb,* **opposed, opposing.**

opposite   **1.** On the other side of or across from another person or thing; facing. She lives on the *opposite* side of the street from me. He sat *opposite* me. **2.** Turned or moving the other way. We passed a red car going in the *opposite* direction from us. **3.** Completely different. Hot is *opposite* to cold. *Adjective.*
—A person or thing that is completely different from another. Summer and winter are *opposites.* White is the *opposite* of black. *Noun.*
op·po·site (op′ə zit) *adjective; noun, plural* **opposites.**

opposition   **1.** Action against. His *opposition* to the plan surprised his friends. **2.** A political party that is opposed to the party in power.
op·po·si·tion (op′ə zish′ən) *noun, plural* **oppositions.**

oppress   **1.** To control or rule by cruel and unjust means. The ruler's secret police *oppressed* the people of the country. **2.** To be a burden to; trouble or depress. His failure on the test *oppressed* him.
op·press (ə pres′) *verb,* **oppressed, oppressing.**

optical   **1.** Having to do with the sense of sight. A mirage is an *optical* illusion. **2.** Helping to see. A microscope is an *optical* instrument.
op·ti·cal (op′ti kəl) *adjective.*

optimistic   Tending to look on the bright side of things and believe that everything will turn out for the best. Steve was very *optimistic* about his chances of getting a summer job.
op·ti·mis·tic (op′tə mis′tik) *adjective.*

optional   Left to one's choice; not required. Going to the class party is *optional.*
op·tion·al (op′shən əl) *adjective.*

or   Is your new coat blue *or* green? We didn't know whether to stay *or* leave. We saw a cougar, *or* mountain lion, at the zoo. You should eat lunch *or* you will be hungry. ▲ Other words that sound like this are **oar** and **ore.**
or (ôr) *conjunction.*

-or   A *suffix* that means "a person or thing that does something." *Inventor* means "a person that invents." *Elevator* means "a thing that elevates."

oral   **1.** Not written; using speech; spoken. Each student must give an *oral* report on the book he reads. **2.** Having to do with the mouth. Brushing your teeth after every meal is good *oral* hygiene.
o·ral (ôr′əl) *adjective.*

orange   **1.** A round fruit that has a thick orange or yellow skin and a sweetish juice. Oranges grow on evergreen trees in warm climates. **2.** A reddish-yellow color. *Noun.*
—Having the color orange; reddish-yellow. *Adjective.*
or·ange (ôr′inj *or* or′inj) *noun, plural* **oranges;** *adjective.*

Oranges

orangeade   A drink made of orange juice and water and sweetened with sugar.
or·ange·ade (ôr′in jād′ *or* or′in jād′) *noun, plural* **orangeades.**

orangutan   A large ape that lives in trees in certain parts of Asia. Orangutans have very long, strong arms, short legs, and a shaggy coat of reddish-brown hair.
o·rang·u·tan (ô rang′oo tan′) *noun, plural* **orangutans.**

Orangutan

orbit   **1.** The path that a planet or other heavenly body follows as it moves in a circle around another heavenly body. The *orbit* of the earth around the sun takes about 365 days. **2.** One complete trip of a spacecraft or man-made satellite along such a path. The spacecraft made three *orbits* around the moon before it landed. *Noun.*

—To move in an orbit around a heavenly body. The planet Mercury *orbits* the sun. *Verb.*

or·bit (ôr′bit) *noun, plural* **orbits;** *verb,* **orbited, orbiting.**

orchard An area where fruit trees are grown.

or·chard (ôr′chərd) *noun, plural* **orchards.**

orchestra **1.** A group of musicians playing together on various instruments. **2.** The violins, horns, drums, and other instruments played by such a group of musicians. **3.** The main floor of a theater. **4.** The area just in front of the stage in which the orchestra sits to play.

or·ches·tra (ôr′kis trə) *noun, plural* **orchestras.**

orchid A plant that has flowers that grow in various shapes and colors. The flowers are usually white, but they may also be found in yellow, purple, green, or blue.

or·chid (ôr′kid) *noun, plural* **orchids.**

ordain **1.** To decide or order by law or authority. The law *ordains* the punishment a convicted criminal will receive. **2.** To admit formally to the ministry or other religious office. He was *ordained* as a priest.

or·dain (ôr dān′) *verb,* **ordained, ordaining.**

Orchids

ordeal A very hard or painful experience or test. Living through the earthquake was quite an *ordeal.*

or·deal (ôr dēl′) *noun, plural* **ordeals.**

order **1.** A command to do something. A soldier must obey *orders.* **2.** The way in which things are arranged; position in a series. The teacher called the students' names in alphabetical *order.* **3.** A condition in which laws or rules are obeyed. The police restored *order* after the riot. **4.** Clean, neat, or proper condition. Tom kept his room in *order.* The telephone is out of *order.* **5.** A request for goods. Father called the grocery store and gave them our *order.* **6.** A group of persons who live under the same rules or belong to the same organization. He joined an *order* of monks. *Noun.*

—**1.** To tell to do something; give an order to; command. The policeman *ordered* the thief to put up his hands. **2.** To place an order for; ask for. We *ordered* eggs and bread from the grocery store. **3.** To put into proper order; arrange neatly or properly. Jill *ordered* the books on her shelves. *Verb.*

or·der (ôr′dər) *noun, plural* **orders;** *verb,* **ordered, ordering.**

in order to. So as to be able to. He stood on a chair *in order to* see better.

orderly **1.** Arranged in a certain way or order; having order. The children marched in an *orderly* line. She kept her room *orderly.* **2.** Not causing or making trouble or noise. An *orderly* crowd of people waited outside of the theater for the actress to come out.

or·der·ly (ôr′dər lē) *adjective.*

ordinal number A number that shows position in a series. First, second, and third are ordinal numbers.

or·di·nal number (ôrd′ən əl).

ordinarily In most cases; usually. *Ordinarily,* the museum is open on Sundays.

or·di·nar·i·ly (ôrd′ən er′ə lē) *adverb.*

ordinary **1.** Commonly used; regular; usual. Her *ordinary* tone of voice is very soft. **2.** Not different in any way from others. That new western movie is very *ordinary.*

or·di·nar·y (ôrd′ən er′ē) *adjective.*

ore A rock or other mineral found in the earth and containing enough of a metal or of a useful mineral to make mining it worthwhile. ▲ Other words that sound like this are **oar** and **or.**

ore (ôr) *noun, plural* **ores.**

Oregon A state in the northwestern United States, on the Pacific. Its capital is Salem.

Or·e·gon (ôr′ə gon′ *or* ôr′ə gən) *noun.*

▲ The name **Oregon** may have come from a mapmaker's mistake. Somehow, the Indian name for the Wisconsin River was changed on a map to *Oregon.* People in the East used this name for a river that they had heard about in the West. Later, explorers found a river that they thought was this Oregon River they had heard stories about. The river's name was later changed to the Columbia River, but Oregon was kept as the name of the state that lies south of this river.

at; āpe; cär; end; mē; it; īce; hot; ōld; fôrk; wood; fōol; oil; out; up; turn; sing; thin; this; hw in white; zh in treasure. ə stands for a in about, e in taken i in pencil, o in lemon, and u in circus.

organ **1.** A musical instrument made up of pipes of different lengths which are sounded by air blown from a bellows. The organ is played by means of one or more keyboards. **2.** A part of an animal or plant that is made up of several kinds of tissues and that does a particular job. The heart, liver, and eyes are *organs* of the body.
or·gan (ôr′gən) *noun, plural* **organs.**

Organ

organic **1.** Having to do with or coming from living things. Decaying leaves, grass, vegetables, and other *organic* matter can be used to make soil fertile. **2.** Using or grown by farming or gardening methods in which chemicals are not used. Organic farming does not use chemical fertilizers to grow food.
or·gan·ic (ôr gan′ik) *adjective.*

organism A living animal or plant.
or·gan·ism (ôr′gə niz′əm) *noun, plural* **organisms.**

organization **1.** The act of organizing. The class president was in charge of the *organization* of the school dance. **2.** The state or way of being organized. In our library, the *organization* of books is by subject. **3.** A group of people joined together for a particular purpose. Her mother belongs to an *organization* that does work for charity.
or·gan·i·za·tion (ôr′gə ni zā′shən) *noun, plural* **organizations.**

organize **1.** To arrange or put together in an orderly way. He *organized* the stamps in his collection according to what country they were from. Who is in charge of *organizing* the class trip? **2.** To cause to join together in a labor union or other organization.
or·gan·ize (ôr′gə nīz′) *verb,* **organized, organizing.**

Orient The countries of Asia. China and Japan are countries of the Orient.
O·ri·ent (ôr′ē ənt) *noun.*

Oriental Having to do with or belonging to the Orient. *Adjective.*
—A member of one of the groups of people native to the Orient. *Noun.*
O·ri·en·tal (ôr′ē ent′əl) *adjective; noun, plural* **Orientals.**

origin **1.** The cause or source of something; what something begins or comes from. The *origin* of the fire was in the basement. **2.** Parents; ancestry. Brian is of Irish *origin.*
or·i·gin (ôr′ə jin *or* or′ə jin) *noun, plural* **origins.**

original **1.** That has not been made, done, thought of, or used before; new. The idea for his story was *original.* **2.** Able to do, make, or think of something new or different; creative. An inventor must be an *original* thinker. **3.** Having to do with or belonging to the origin or beginning of something; first. The *original* owner of the house still lives there. *Adjective.*
—Something that is original. That painting is an *original* by a famous artist. *Noun.*
o·rig·i·nal (ə rij′ən əl) *adjective; noun, plural* **originals.**

originally At or from the start; at first. Basketball was *originally* played in the United States.
o·rig·i·nal·ly (ə rij′ən əl ē) *adverb.*

originate **1.** To bring into being; start. He *originated* the design for the new airplane. **2.** To come into being; begin. The fire *originated* in an old deserted building.
o·rig·i·nate (ə rij′ə nāt′) *verb,* **originated, originating.**

oriole Any of various songbirds that are related to the crow and are found in most parts of the world. The male is usually bright orange or yellow with black markings on the head, tail, and wings.
o·ri·ole (ôr′ē ōl′) *noun, plural* **orioles.**

Oriole

ornament A small object that is used as a decoration. Christmas tree *ornaments* are usually brightly colored. *Noun.*

—To decorate with ornaments. Mother used pearl buttons to *ornament* the dress she had made. *Verb.*

or·na·ment (ôr′nə mənt *for noun;* ôr′nə ment′ *for verb*) *noun, plural* **ornaments;** *verb,* **ornamented, ornamenting.**

ornate Having much decoration. The palace was filled with *ornate* furniture.

or·nate (ôr nāt′) *adjective.*

orphan A child whose parents are dead. *Noun.*

—To make an orphan of. The war *orphaned* hundreds of children. *Verb.*

or·phan (ôr′fən) *noun, plural* **orphans;** *verb,* **orphaned, orphaning.**

orphanage A place that takes in and cares for orphans.

or·phan·age (ôr′fə nij) *noun, plural* **orphanages.**

orthodontist A dentist whose work is straightening the teeth.

or·tho·don·tist (ôr′thə don′tist) *noun, plural* **orthodontists.**

orthodox **1.** Accepted by most people; widely held to be true. His opinions on politics are very *orthodox.* **2.** Holding or following widely accepted beliefs or views. She is very *orthodox* in her religious beliefs.

or·tho·dox (ôr′thə doks′) *adjective.*

ostrich A large two-toed bird that has a long neck, long strong legs, and a small flat head. The male ostrich has large, white feathers on the wings and tail that are used for ornaments. The ostrich is the largest of all living birds. It cannot fly, but it can run very fast. Ostriches are found in Africa.

os·trich (ôs′trich *or* os′trich) *noun, plural* **ostriches.**

Ostrich

other If you don't help me, some *other* person will. The *other* guests haven't arrived yet. I spoke to her the *other* day. I don't know any *others* at the party. I could not feel *other* than surprised.

oth·er (uth′ər) *adjective; pronoun; adverb.*

every other. Every second or alternate. That magazine comes out *every other* week.

otherwise The food ran out early, but *otherwise* the picnic was a success. Fortunately we had an umbrella; *otherwise* we would have gotten wet. His story of what happened sounds true, but the facts are *otherwise.* The roof must be fixed; *otherwise,* it will leak.

oth·er·wise (uth′ər wīz′) *adverb; adjective; conjunction.*

otter A water animal that looks like a weasel. Otters have webbed feet, long, slightly flattened tails, and brown, shiny fur.

ot·ter (ot′ər) *noun, plural* **otters** or **otter.**

Otter

ouch A sound used to express sudden pain. *Ouch!* I burned my finger on the stove!

ouch (ouch) *interjection.*

ought You *ought* to thank her for her help. We *ought* to obey the law. Dinner *ought* to be ready by now. ▲ Another word that sounds like this is **aught.**

ought (ôt) *verb.*

ounce **1.** A unit of weight equal to 1/16 of a pound. **2.** A unit of measure for liquids. Sixteen ounces equal one pint. **3.** A small bit. The hikers didn't have an *ounce* of energy left when they reached the end of the climb.

ounce (ouns) *noun, plural* **ounces.**

our *Our* house is on Oak Street. That is *our* dog. ▲ Another word that sounds like this is **hour.**

our (our) *adjective.*

ours Their dog is older than *ours.*

ours (ourz) *pronoun.*

ourselves We *ourselves* made the tree house. We took it upon *ourselves* to tell you.

our·selves (our selvz′) *pronoun plural.*

at; āpe; cär; end; mē; it; īce; hot; ōld; fôrk; wood; fōol; oil; out; up; turn; sing; thin; this; hw in white; zh in treasure. ə stands for a in about, e in taken i in pencil, o in lemon, and u in circus.

441

-ous A *suffix* that means "full of." *Dangerous* means "full of danger." *Ambitious* means "full of ambition."

out The water flowed *out*. The doctor is *out* for the day. The children went *out* to play. He put *out* his hand for the candy. The firemen put *out* the fire. We are *out* of butter. The sun came *out* after the rain. The dress is made *out* of silk. She looked *out* the window.
out (out) *adverb; adjective; preposition.*

outboard motor A motor attached to the outside of the stern of a small boat.
out·board motor (out′bôrd′).

outbreak A breaking out of something. There was an *outbreak* of flu last winter.
out·break (out′brāk′) *noun, plural* **outbreaks.**

outburst A bursting forth of something. We were surprised by her *outburst* of anger.
out·burst (out′burst′) *noun, plural* **outbursts.**

outcome A result; end. We are waiting to hear the *outcome* of the election.
out·come (out′kum′) *noun, plural* **outcomes.**

outdo To do better than. Jane tried to *outdo* the rest of the class in geography.
out·do (out′dōō′) *verb,* **outdid, outdone, outdoing.**

outdoor Used or done out in the open instead of inside a house or other building. Baseball is an *outdoor* game.
out·door (out′dôr′) *adjective.*

outdoors Not in a house or other building; out under the sky. We ate *outdoors* under a tree. *Adverb.*
—The world that is outside houses or other buildings; the open air. We took a walk in the *outdoors. Noun.*
out·doors (out′dôrz′) *adverb; noun.*

outer On the outside. We wear warm *outer* clothes in the winter.
out·er (ou′tər) *adjective.*

outer space The space beyond the earth's atmosphere. The planet Mars is in outer space.

outfield The part of a baseball field beyond the infield and between the foul lines.
out·field (out′fēld′) *noun.*

outfit **1.** All the articles or pieces of equipment needed for doing something. I bought a skiing *outfit*. **2.** A set of clothes. The hat, shoes, and rest of her *outfit* were red. **3.** A group of people who work or belong together. What army *outfit* was his father in during the war? *Noun.*
—To give articles or equipment needed for doing something. They *outfitted* the mountain climbers. *Verb.*

out·fit (out′fit) *noun, plural* **outfits;** *verb,* **outfitted, outfitting.**

outgoing Friendly and liking to talk. An *outgoing* person makes friends easily.
out·go·ing (out′gō′ing) *adjective.*

outgrow **1.** To grow too big for. The baby will soon *outgrow* his clothes. **2.** To leave behind or lose as one grows older. She *outgrew* her fear of the dark.
out·grow (out′grō′) *verb,* **outgrew, outgrown, outgrowing.**

outing A short trip for pleasure. All the students enjoyed the school *outing* to the state park.
out·ing (ou′ting) *noun, plural* **outings.**

outlaw A person who constantly breaks the law; criminal. The police searched for the *outlaws. Noun.*
—To make illegal; prohibit. The state *outlawed* the sale of fireworks. *Verb.*
out·law (out′lô′) *noun, plural* **outlaws;** *verb,* **outlawed, outlawing.**

outlet **1.** A place at which something comes out. Dead leaves clogged the *outlets* of the drainpipes. **2.** A means of expressing or getting rid of something. Playing tennis is a good *outlet* for a person's energy. **3.** A place in an electric wiring system for plugging in appliances. The toaster was plugged into the *outlet.*
out·let (out′let) *noun, plural* **outlets.**

outline **1.** The shape of an object formed by following along its outer edges. Through the fog, we saw the *outline* of a passing ship. **2.** A summary of a story, speech, or other writing. He made a brief *outline* of his book report before he began to write it. *Noun.*
—To give a summary of. The general *outlined* his plan of attack. *Verb.*
out·line (out′līn′) *noun, plural* **outlines;** *verb,* **outlined, outlining.**

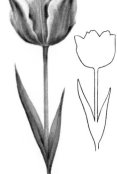

A Flower and Its **Outline**

outlook A view into the future. The weather *outlook* for tomorrow is not good.
out·look (out′look′) *noun, plural* **outlooks.**

outlying Located far from the center of something. The zoo is located in an *outlying* district of the city.
out·ly·ing (out′lī′ing) *adjective.*

outnumber To be greater in number than.

The home team's fans *outnumbered* the visiting team's at the football game.

out·num·ber (out′num′bər) *verb*, **outnumbered, outnumbering.**

out-of-date No longer in style or use; old-fashioned. She wore some old *out-of-date* clothes she found in the attic to the costume party.

out-of-date (out′əv dāt′) *adjective.*

out-of-doors Done, used, or living outside; outdoor. We have *out-of-doors* furniture for the backyard. *Adjective.*
—Not inside. We built a fire *out-of-doors. Adverb.*
—The open air. Football is played in the *out-of-doors. Noun.*

out-of-doors (out′əv dôrz′) *adjective; adverb; noun.*

outpost A small military station that keeps control over an area and guards against attack.

out·post (out′pōst′) *noun, plural* **outposts.**

output The amount of something produced. All the employees increased their work *output* during the rush at Christmas time.

out·put (out′poot′) *noun.*

outrage **1.** An act of great violence or cruelty. The dictator committed many *outrages* against the people of the country. **2.** Great anger. The people of the country felt *outrage* at the enemy's secret attack. *Noun.*
—To cause to feel great anger. The man's cruelty to his dog *outraged* his neighbors. *Verb.*

out·rage (out′rāj′) *noun, plural* **outrages;** *verb,* **outraged, outraging.**

outrageous Shocking; shameful. Insulting her in front of all her friends was an *outrageous* thing to do.

out·ra·geous (out rā′jəs) *adjective.*

outrigger A frame ending in a float that is attached to the outside of a canoe. It keeps the canoe from turning over.

out·rig·ger (out′rig′ər) *noun, plural* **outriggers.**

Outrigger

outright Complete; total. Saying he was home when he was not is an *outright* lie. *Adjective.*
—**1.** In a direct or honest way; openly. Please say *outright* what you think about my idea. **2.** Completely and all at once. We paid for the bicycle *outright. Adverb.*

out·right (out′rīt′) *adjective; adverb.*

outrun To run faster or farther than. Our horse *outran* all the others in the race.

out·run (out′run′) *verb,* **outran, outrun, outrunning.**

outside The outer side, surface, or part. The *outside* of the house was painted white. *Noun.*
—**1.** On the outside; outer. The *outside* layer of paint was peeling. **2.** Extremely slight; not likely. There is only an *outside* chance that we will be able to go to the movies. *Adjective.*
—On or to the outside; outdoors. Do you want to go *outside* for some fresh air? We played *outside* all day. *Adverb.*
—Beyond the limits or range of. They live just *outside* Philadelphia. *Preposition.*

out·side (out′sīd′ *or* out′sīd′) *noun, plural* **outsides;** *adjective; adverb; preposition.*

outskirts The region or area that is outside or at the edge of a town or city. They live in a house on the *outskirts* of town.

out·skirts (out′skurts′) *noun plural.*

outsmart To get the better of; be cleverer than. Jane always *outsmarts* her brother at games.

out·smart (out′smärt′) *verb,* **outsmarted, outsmarting.**

outspoken Honest or open. She was very *outspoken* in her criticism of our plan.

out·spo·ken (out′spō′kən) *adjective.*

outstanding **1.** So good as to stand out from others of its kind. He is an *outstanding* football player. She wrote an *outstanding* book report. **2.** Not paid or settled. He has an *outstanding* debt of $100.

out·stand·ing (out′stan′ding) *adjective.*

outward From the inside toward the outside. The gate opens *outward.* We passed the *outward* bound train.

out·ward (out′wərd) *adverb; adjective.*

outwit To get the better of; be more clever

at; āpe; cär; end; mē; it; īce; hot; ōld;
fôrk; wood; fool; oil; out; up; turn; sing;
thin; this; hw in white; zh in treasure.
ə stands for a in about, e in taken
i in pencil, o in lemon, and u in circus.

443

than. The rabbit *outwitted* the fox that was chasing him.
out·wit (out′wit′) *verb,* **outwitted, outwitting.**

oval Shaped like an egg or an ellipse. The turkey was served on an *oval* platter. *Adjective.*
—Something shaped like an egg or an ellipse. *Noun.*
o·val (ō′vəl) *adjective; noun, plural* **ovals.**

ovary **1.** The part of a female animal that produces eggs. **2.** The part of a plant in which seeds are formed.
o·va·ry (ō′vər ē) *noun, plural* **ovaries.**

oven An enclosed space that is used to heat, bake, or roast food that is placed inside. A stove has an oven. Mother put the turkey in the *oven* to roast.
ov·en (uv′ən) *noun, plural* **ovens.**

The mirror has an **oval** shape.

over The roof of the building stuck out *over* the street. Mother put a blanket *over* the sleeping baby. The horse jumped *over* the fence. School is closed *over* the Christmas holidays. She spent *over* twenty dollars on groceries. He gets upset *over* silly things. The water in the pot boiled *over.* The cat knocked the lamp *over.* Come *over* for dinner tonight. If you make a mistake, you'll have to write the sentence *over.* The summer will soon be *over.*
o·ver (ō′vər) *preposition; adverb; adjective.*

▲ There are many words beginning with **over-** that you will not find in this dictionary. You can find the meaning of most of these words either by putting the words "too much" after the part of the word that follows *over-* or by putting the word "too" in place of *over-.* For example, *overcook* means "to cook too much," and *overactive* means "too active."

overalls Loose-fitting trousers worn by farmers and workmen. Overalls usually have a piece that covers the chest.
o·ver·alls (ō′vər ôlz′) *noun plural.*

overboard Over the side of a ship into the water. The sailor slipped and fell *overboard.*
o·ver·board (ō′vər bôrd′) *adverb.*

overcame He *overcame* his fear of the water and learned to swim.
o·ver·came (ō′vər kām′) *verb.*

overcast Clouded over; cloudy. There was an *overcast* sky before the storm.
o·ver·cast (ō′vər kast′) *adjective.*

overcoat A man's heavy outer coat worn over a suit or other clothing for warmth.
o·ver·coat (ō′vər kōt′) *noun, plural* **overcoats.**

overcome **1.** To get the better of; beat or conquer. He tried to *overcome* the others in the race. Our soldiers *overcame* the enemy. **2.** To get over or deal with. He finally *overcame* his fear of flying by learning all he could about airplanes. **3.** To make tired or helpless. Many people in the crowd were *overcome* by the smoke from the fire.
o·ver·come (ō′vər kum′) *verb,* **overcame, overcome, overcoming.**

overdo **1.** To do or use too much. Don't *overdo* your exercises or you will get too stiff. **2.** To cook food too much. Be careful not to *overdo* the steak. ▲ Another word that sounds like this is **overdue.**
o·ver·do (ō′vər doo′) *verb,* **overdid, overdone, overdoing.**

overdue **1.** Not paid past the date when payment is due. The rent is *overdue.* **2.** Not on time; late. The plane from New York is twenty minutes *overdue.* ▲ Another word that sounds like this is **overdo.**
o·ver·due (ō′vər doo′ *or* ō′vər dyoo′) *adjective.*

overflow **1.** To flow beyond the usual limits. Water from the kitchen sink *overflowed* onto the floor. **2.** To be so full that the contents flow over. The bathtub *overflowed.* **3.** To flow over the top edge of. The water *overflowed* the glass. **4.** To flow or spread over; flood. When the dam burst, water *overflowed* the town. *Verb.*
—Something that flows over. We mopped up the *overflow* of water from the bathtub. *Noun.*
o·ver·flow (ō′vər flō′ *for verb;* ō′vər flō′ *for noun*) *verb,* **overflowed, overflown, overflowing;** *noun.*

overgrow To grow over. The garden of the old house was *overgrown* with weeds.
o·ver·grow (ō′vər grō′) *verb,* **overgrew, overgrown, overgrowing.**

overhand With the hand raised above the elbow or the arm raised above the shoulders. He threw the ball with an *overhand* pitch. That pitcher throws *overhand.*
o·ver·hand (ō′vər hand′) *adjective; adverb.*

overhaul 1. To examine completely and make needed repairs or changes. The mechanic *overhauled* the car's engine. 2. To catch up with. The large boat quickly *overhauled* the small fishing boat. *Verb.*
—The act of overhauling. The car's engine needs an *overhaul. Noun.*
o·ver·haul (ō′vər hôl′ *for verb;* ō′vər hôl′ *for noun*) *verb,* **overhauled, overhauling;** *noun,* plural **overhauls.**

overhead Above the head. Birds flew *overhead.* A light was burning *overhead. Adverb.*
—The general expenses of running a business. Money spent for rent, taxes, heating, and lighting is part of the overhead. *Noun.*
—Above the head. Please turn on the *overhead* lights. *Adjective.*
o·ver·head (ō′vər hed′ *for adverb;* ō′vər hed′ *for noun and adjective*) *adverb; noun,* plural **overheads;** *adjective.*

overhear To hear something one is not supposed to hear. I *overheard* the conversation of the people sitting behind me on the train.
o·ver·hear (ō′vər hēr′) *verb,* **overheard, overhearing.**

overjoy To make very happy. We were *overjoyed* when we heard that our team won the championship.
o·ver·joy (ō′vər joi′) *verb,* **overjoyed, overjoying.**

overlap To rest on top of something and partly cover it up. She arranged the magazines on the table so that one *overlapped* the other.
o·ver·lap (ō′vər lap′) *verb,* **overlapped, overlapping.**

overlook 1. To not see, notice, or think of. The thief *overlooked* the possibility that the house had a burglar alarm. 2. To think of as never having happened; ignore. She *overlooked* his rudeness because she knew he was angry. 3. To have a view of. The house on the hill *overlooks* a river.
o·ver·look (ō′vər look′) *verb,* **overlooked, overlooking.**

overnight 1. During or through the night. A storm struck the town *overnight.* 2. Very quickly; suddenly. The town seemed to grow into a city *overnight. Adverb.*
—1. For one night. We had an *overnight* guest. 2. Lasting through or happening during the night. We took an *overnight* train trip to New York from Chicago. 3. Used or made for short trips. I packed everything I needed for my weekend visit in an *overnight* bag. *Adjective.*
o·ver·night (ō′vər nīt′ *for adverb;* ō′vər nīt′ *for adjective*) *adverb; adjective.*

overpass A bridge or road that crosses above another roadway.
o·ver·pass (ō′vər pas′) *noun,* plural **overpasses.**

overpower 1. To beat or conquer by greater strength or power. The prisoner *overpowered* the guard and escaped. 2. To make helpless. He was *overpowered* by sadness when his dog died.
o·ver·pow·er (ō′vər pou′ər) *verb,* **overpowered, overpowering.**

overrun 1. To spread over or throughout. Weeds *overran* the flower garden. 2. To flow over. The river *overran* the banks. 3. To run beyond. The baseball player *overran* second base.
o·ver·run (ō′vər run′) *verb,* **overran, overrun, overrunning.**

overseas Over, across, or beyond the sea; abroad. We plan to travel *overseas* this summer, visiting France and Italy. *Adverb.*
—1. Working, located, or serving overseas. That company has an *overseas* office. 2. Having to do with countries across the sea; foreign. His company does a lot of *overseas* business. *Adjective.*
o·ver·seas (ō′vər sēz′) *adverb; adjective.*

overshoe A shoe or boot that is worn over an ordinary shoe to protect against cold, snow, water, or mud. Overshoes are usually made of rubber.
o·ver·shoe (ō′vər shoo′) *noun,* plural **overshoes.**

oversight A careless mistake that was not made on purpose. Leaving her name off the list of people I invited to the party was an *oversight.*
o·ver·sight (ō′vər sīt′) *noun,* plural **oversights.**

overtake To catch up with. The police car tried to *overtake* the car that the bank robbers had escaped in.
o·ver·take (ō′vər tāk′) *verb,* **overtook, overtaken, overtaking.**

overtime Time worked beyond the regular working hours. Susan will be paid extra for the *overtime* she worked this week. *Noun.*

at; āpe; cär; end; mē; it; īce; hot; ōld;
fôrk; wood; fool; oil; out; up; turn; sing;
thin; this; hw in white; zh in treasure.
ə stands for a in about, e in taken
i in pencil, o in lemon, and u in circus.

—Beyond regular working hours. Pat worked three hours *overtime. Adverb.*

—Of or for overtime. Robin gets *overtime* pay at her job. *Adjective.*

o·ver·time (ō′vər tīm′) *noun; adverb; adjective.*

overture **1.** A musical composition played by an orchestra to introduce an opera, ballet, or other larger musical work. **2.** An offer to begin something; suggestion or proposal. Joan made *overtures* of friendship to the new girl in her class.

o·ver·ture (ō′vər chər) *noun, plural* **overtures.**

overweight Having more than the normal or needed weight. She dieted because she was *overweight.*

o·ver·weight (ō′vər wāt′) *adjective.*

overwhelm To overcome completely; overpower or make helpless. The enemy soldiers *overwhelmed* our men.

o·ver·whelm (ō′vər hwelm′) *verb,* **overwhelmed, overwhelming.**

overwork To cause to work too much. The farmer *overworked* his mule. *Verb.*

—Too much work. *Overwork* was the cause of his illness. *Noun.*

o·ver·work (ō′vər wurk′ *for verb;* ō′vər-wurk′ *for noun) verb,* **overworked, overworking;** *noun.*

owe **1.** To have to pay. She *owes* Jim two dollars. **2.** To have to give. She *owes* us an apology for being so late. **3.** To be indebted for. I *owe* a great deal to my brother for all the help he gave me with my report. ▲ Another word that sounds like this is **oh.**

owe (ō) *verb,* **owed, owing.**

owl A bird that has a round head with large staring eyes and a hooked bill, a short square tail, and soft feathers. Owls usually hunt for food at night, and they live on mice, frogs, snakes, and insects.

owl (oul) *noun, plural* **owls.**

own The accident was her *own* fault. Even my *own* brother wouldn't help me. *Adjective.*

—Something that belongs to one. That bicycle is my *own. Noun.*

Owl

—**1.** To have as belonging to one; possess. That farmer *owns* all the land between here and the river. **2.** To admit doing something; confess. The suspect *owned* up to the robbery. *Verb.*

own (ōn) *adjective; noun; verb,* **owned, owning.**

owner A person who owns something. Who is the *owner* of the blue car parked in front of the house?

own·er (ō′nər) *noun, plural* **owners.**

ox **1.** The adult male of domestic cattle. It is used as a work animal or for beef. **2.** Any of various animals related to the ox. Buffaloes, bison, and yaks are also called oxen.

ox (oks) *noun, plural* **oxen.**

oxen More than one ox.

ox·en (ok′sən) *noun plural.*

oxford A shoe that laces over the top of the foot and comes up to just below the ankle.

ox·ford (oks′fərd) *noun, plural* **oxfords.**

oxide A compound of oxygen and one other chemical element.

ox·ide (ok′sīd) *noun, plural* **oxides.**

oxidize To combine a chemical substance with oxygen.

ox·i·dize (ok′sə dīz′) *verb,* **oxidized, oxidizing.**

oxygen A gas that has no color or smell. Oxygen makes up about one-fifth of the air. People, animals, and plants must have oxygen to live. Oxygen is a chemical element.

ox·y·gen (ok′sə jən) *noun.*

Oxfords

oyster An animal that has a soft body and a rough, hinged shell. Oysters are found in shallow waters along coasts. Some kinds of oysters are eaten as food, while other kinds are raised for the fine pearls they produce.

oys·ter (ois′tər) *noun, plural* **oysters.**

Oyster

P

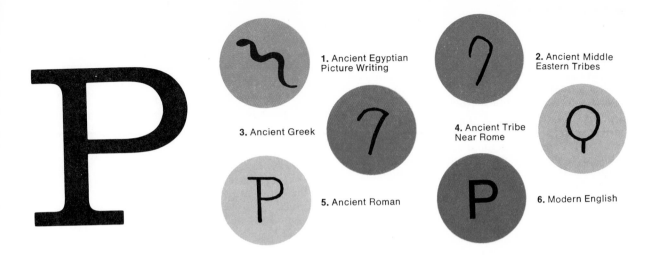

1. Ancient Egyptian Picture Writing
2. Ancient Middle Eastern Tribes
3. Ancient Greek
4. Ancient Tribe Near Rome
5. Ancient Roman
6. Modern English

P is the sixteenth letter of the alphabet. The oldest form of the letter **P** was a drawing that the ancient Egyptians (**1**) used in their picture writing nearly 5000 years ago. This drawing, which looked like a hook, was borrowed by several ancient tribes (**2**) in the Middle East. The ancient Greeks (**3**) borrowed a form of this letter about 3000 years ago. This letter was then borrowed by an ancient tribe (**4**) that settled north of Rome about 2800 years ago. They changed the shape of the letter by adding a closed loop at the top. The Romans (**5**) borrowed this letter about 2400 years ago. They wrote it in almost the same way that we write the capital letter **P** today (**6**).

p, P   The sixteenth letter of the alphabet.
   p, P (pē) *noun, plural* **p's, P's.**

pace   **1.** A single step. The troops took two *paces* forward. **2.** The length of a single step. I was about six *paces* away from him before I recognized him. **3.** The rate of speed in walking, running, or moving. The hungry boy quickened his *pace* as he neared home. Alice did the work at a fast *pace*. **4.** A way of stepping or moving. The trot and the gallop are two of the *paces* of a horse. *Noun.*
   —**1.** To walk back and forth across. Jan *paced* the room. **2.** To measure by taking paces. Herb *paced* off five feet from the tree and began to dig. *Verb.*
   pace (pās) *noun, plural* **paces;** *verb,* **paced, pacing.**

pacemaker   An electronic device put into the body by surgery. A pacemaker gives the heart regular, mild, electric shocks to make it beat normally. It is used in the treatment of diseases of the heart.
   pace·mak·er (pās′mā′kər) *noun, plural* **pacemakers.**

Pacific   The ocean that separates North America and South America from Asia and Australia. *Noun.*
   —Of the Pacific Ocean. *Adjective.*
   Pa·cif·ic (pə sif′ik) *noun; adjective.*

pacifist   A person who is against war and fighting. Fran's older brother would not join the army because he is a *pacifist*.

pac·i·fist (pas′ə fist) *noun, plural* **pacifists.**

pack   **1.** A group of things wrapped or tied together so that they can be carried easily; bundle. Each camper carried a *pack* on his back. **2.** A set or group of things that are alike. Dolores bought a *pack* of cards. A large *pack* of wolves lives in those mountains. **3.** A large amount of something. The stories he told are just a *pack* of lies. *Noun.*
   —**1.** To place in something for storing or carrying. We had to *pack* all our dishes in boxes when we moved. **2.** To fill something up with other things. Karen *packed* her suitcases for the trip. **3.** To press together tightly. Terry *packed* the snow into a large ball. **4.** To fill by crowding together. The audience *packed* the theater. *Verb.*
   pack (pak) *noun, plural* **packs;** *verb,* **packed, packing.**

package   **1.** A thing or group of things packed, wrapped up, or tied together; bundle. Jennifer received a large *package* on her birthday. **2.** A box, case, or other thing in which something is packed. Follow the directions on the *package* to make the soup. *Noun.*
   —To make or put into a package. That cereal is *packaged* in a bright red box. *Verb.*
   pack·age (pak′ij) *noun, plural* **packages;** *verb,* **packaged, packaging.**

pack animal   An animal used for carrying loads. Horses and mules are used as pack animals.

447

pact A promise made by countries or people to follow a particular course of action; agreement or treaty. The two nations that were at war finally signed a peace *pact*. The boys made a *pact* never to tell anyone their secret.
pact (pakt) *noun, plural* **pacts.**

pad **1.** A soft piece of thick material. Pads are used as stuffing or for protection or comfort. The football player put on his shoulder *pads*. **2.** A number of sheets of paper that are fastened together along one side. We leave a *pad* and pencil by the telephone for messages. **3.** A part like a small, soft cushion that is on the bottom side of the feet of dogs, foxes, and some other animals. **4.** A block of cloth that is soaked with ink. It is used to put ink on a rubber stamp. *Noun.*
—To cover, stuff, or line with a pad. The chair was *padded* so that it would be more comfortable. *Verb.*
pad (pad) *noun, plural* **pads;** *verb,* **padded, padding.**

Paddle

paddle **1.** A short oar that is used to move and steer a canoe or other small boat. **2.** A small, broad board with a short handle. It is used to hit the ball in table tennis and other games. **3.** A flat, wooden tool. Paddles are used for beating, stirring, or mixing things. *Noun.*
—**1.** To move a canoe or other boat with a paddle or paddles. Barbara *paddled* across the lake in fifteen minutes. **2.** To hit with a paddle or with the hand; spank. Joe's father told him he would *paddle* him if he caught him playing with firecrackers again. *Verb.*
pad·dle (pad′əl) *noun, plural* **paddles;** *verb,* **paddled, paddling.**

paddle tennis A game that is similar to tennis. It is played with wooden paddles and a rubber ball.

paddle wheel A large wheel with broad boards, or paddles, fixed around it. Paddle wheels are used to move steamboats.

paddock A small field or area that is fenced in. Animals can graze or exercise in a paddock.
pad·dock (pad′ək) *noun, plural* **paddocks.**

paddy A field where rice is grown.
pad·dy (pad′ē) *noun, plural* **paddies.**

padlock A lock that can be put on and taken off. It has a curved bar that is hinged on one end. The other end of the bar can be put through an opening or link and then snapped shut. *Noun.*
—To fasten or lock with a padlock. Hank *padlocked* the barn door. *Verb.*
pad·lock (pad′lok′) *noun, plural* **padlocks;** *verb,* **padlocked, padlocking.**

pagan A person who is not a Christian, Jew, or Muslim. A pagan believes in many gods or no god at all. The ancient Greeks and Romans were pagans.
pa·gan (pā′gən) *noun, plural* **pagans.**

page¹ **1.** One side of a sheet of paper in a book, newspaper, or magazine. Find the exact *page* where the lesson begins. **2.** An important event or period. The Civil War was a sad *page* in American history.
page (pāj) *noun, plural* **pages.**

page² A boy or young man who runs errands. In times long ago, pages were attendants at a royal court or in training to be knights. Today, there are pages who work in hotels and run errands for the guests. *Noun.*
—To try to find someone by calling out his name. They *paged* the doctor in the hospital by calling him over the loudspeaker. *Verb.*
page (pāj) *noun, plural* **pages;** *verb,* **paged, paging.**

pageant **1.** A kind of play that is about events in history or legend. Our school gave a *pageant* about the first Thanksgiving. **2.** A

Paddle Wheel

colorful parade or ceremony for an important event. The wedding of the king and queen was a magnificent *pageant.*

pag·eant (paj′ənt) *noun, plural* **pageants.**

pagoda A temple or tower that is many stories high. The roof of each story usually curves upward. There are pagodas in China, Japan, and other countries in the East.

pa·go·da (pə·gō′də) *noun, plural* **pagodas.**

Pagoda

paid He *paid* his friend a visit. Look up **pay** for more information.

paid (pād) *verb.*

pail A round, open container with a flat bottom and a curved handle; bucket. It is used for carrying sand, water, or other things. ▲ Another word that sounds like this is **pale.**

pail (pāl) *noun, plural* **pails.**

pain 1. A feeling of being hurt; suffering. The *pain* in Sam's tooth became so bad that he went to the dentist. The neighbors tried to ease the old woman's *pain* after her husband died. 2. **pains.** Care or effort. Lou took great *pains* to put the model airplane together neatly. *Noun.*
—To cause pain to. Ted's sprained ankle *pained* him. His unkind remarks *pained* her very much. *Verb.* ▲ Another word that sounds like this is **pane.**

pain (pān) *noun, plural* **pains;** *verb,* **pained, paining.**

painful 1. Causing pain. Victor's broken arm was very *painful.* 2. Very difficult or unpleasant. It was a *painful* task for the coach to tell the boy he was not good enough to make the team.

pain·ful (pān′fəl) *adjective.*

paint A mixture of coloring matter and water, oil, or some other liquid. Paint is spread on a surface to color it or protect it. *Noun.*
—1. To cover with paint. The workmen *painted* the kitchen walls. 2. To make a picture or design of something by using paint; make with paint. This artist was famous for *painting* mountain scenes. 3. To tell about or

describe clearly. The reporter *painted* a sad picture of the city's slums in his articles. *Verb.*

paint (pānt) *noun, plural* **paints;** *verb,* **painted, painting.**

painter 1. A person who paints pictures; artist. Rembrandt was a famous *painter.* 2. A person whose work is painting things like walls and houses. The landlord sent the *painters* over to paint our apartment.

paint·er (pān′tər) *noun, plural* **painters.**

painting 1. Something painted; picture. A *painting* of the family's two children hung over the sofa. 2. The act or art of using paints. June's older sister went to Paris to study *painting.*

paint·ing (pān′ting) *noun, plural* **paintings.**

pair 1. A set of things meant to be used together. Jesse got a new *pair* of shoes. 2. A single thing made up of two parts. You will find a *pair* of scissors in the top drawer. 3. Two persons or animals that are alike or that go together. A *pair* of black horses were pulling the wagon. *Noun.*
—1. To join or match in a pair. They *paired* the two tallest boys to lead the march. 2. To form into pairs. The whole class *paired* off for the square dance. *Verb.* ▲ Other words that sound like this are **pare** and **pear.**

pair (per) *noun, plural* **pairs** or **pair;** *verb,* **paired, pairing.**

pajamas A set of clothes to sleep in. They are usually made up of a shirt and trousers.

pa·ja·mas (pə jä′məz *or* pə jam′əz) *noun plural.*

pal A close friend. Fred and his *pals* play softball every day after school.

pal (pal) *noun, plural* **pals.**

palace A very large, grand building where a king or other ruler lives.

pal·ace (pal′is) *noun, plural* **palaces.**

▲ The word **palace** goes back to the Latin word for the *Palatine.* The Palatine is a hill in Rome where the first Roman emperor, Augustus, built his palace.

palate The roof of the mouth. The bony part in the front is called the **hard palate,** and the fleshy part in the back is called the **soft**

at; āpe; cär; end; mē; it; īce; hot; ōld; fôrk; wood; fool; oil; out; up; turn; sing; thin; this; hw in white; zh in treasure. ə stands for a in about, e in taken i in pencil, o in lemon, and u in circus.

palate. ▲ Another word that sounds like this is **palette.**

pal·ate (pal′it) *noun, plural* **palates.**

pale **1.** Not having much color. Richard is blond and has a *pale* complexion. **2.** Not bright in color. The apples we used for the pie were a *pale* green. The lake glimmered in the *pale* moonlight. *Adjective.*

—To turn pale. Her face *paled* when she heard that her brother had been hurt during the football game. *Verb.* ▲ Another word that sounds like this is **pail.**

pale (pāl) *adjective,* **paler, palest;** *verb,* **paled, paling.**

Palette

palette A thin, oval board with a hole for the thumb at one end. Artists place and mix their paints on palettes. ▲ Another word that sounds like this is **palate.**

pal·ette (pal′it) *noun, plural* **palettes.**

palisades A line of steep cliffs that rise along a river.

pal·i·sades (pal′i sādz′) *noun plural.*

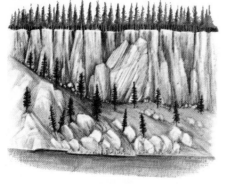
Palisades

palm¹ The inside of the hand between the wrist and the fingers. *Noun.*

—**1.** To hold or hide in the hand. The magician *palmed* the cards so that everyone would think they had disappeared. **2.** To get rid of by fooling someone. The crook *palmed* off the cheap stone as a diamond to the old woman. *Verb.*

palm (päm) *noun, plural* **palms;** *verb,* **palmed, palming.**

palm² Any of a number of trees that grow in warm climates. They have large leaves like feathers or fans that grow at the very top of a tall trunk.

palm (päm) *noun, plural* **palms.**

palmetto A palm tree that grows in the southern United States. It has leaves shaped like fans.

pal·met·to (pal met′ō) *noun, plural* **palmettos** or **palmettoes.**

Palmetto

Leaf

palomino A light tan horse having a cream-colored or white mane and tail.

pal·o·mi·no (pal′ə mē′nō) *noun, plural* **palominos.**

pampas Wide grassy plains in Argentina and other countries of South America.

pam·pas (pam′-pəz) *noun plural.*

pamper To treat too well; spoil. The parents *pampered* their only child.

pam·per (pam′-pər) *verb,* **pampered, pampering.**

Palomino

pamphlet A small book that has a paper cover. The board game came with a *pamphlet* of instructions telling how to play it.

pam·phlet (pam′flit) *noun, plural* **pamphlets.**

pan **1.** A metal dish used for cooking or baking. Pans are usually broad and shallow and do not have a cover. **2.** Anything like a pan. Pans are used to wash gold ore from gravel. *Noun.*

—To wash soil or gravel in a pan to separate the gold in it. The prospector *panned* for gold. *Verb.*

pan (pan) *noun, plural* **pans;** *verb,* **panned, panning.**

pancake   A flat, thin cake made of batter. It is cooked in a pan or on a griddle.
pan·cake (pan′kāk′) *noun, plural* **pancakes.**

pancreas   A gland near the stomach that helps digestion.
pan·cre·as (pan′krē əs) *noun.*

panda   **1.** A large animal that looks like a bear. It has long white fur with black patches and lives in southern China. It is also called the **giant panda.** **2.** A reddish-brown animal that is something like a raccoon. It has short legs, a long bushy tail, and a white face. It is also called the **lesser panda.**
pan·da (pan′də) *noun, plural* **pandas.**

Panda

pane   A sheet of glass in a window or door.
▲ Another word that sounds like this is **pain.**
pane (pān) *noun, plural* **panes.**

panel   **1.** A part or section of something that is set off in some way from what is around it. Panels may be in a door or a wall, on a piece of furniture, or in a dress. They may be higher or lower than the rest of a surface, or may have a border around them or be of another color. **2.** A group of persons gathered together to talk about or judge something. The *panel* of judges for the baking contest awarded first prize to Mrs. Thompson for her chocolate cake. **3.** A board containing the dials, instruments, and controls for running something. Sally knows how to work the control *panel* on her set of electric trains. *Noun.*
—To arrange in panels; decorate with panels. The walls of the living room were *paneled* in walnut. *Verb.*
pan·el (pan′əl) *noun, plural* **panels;** *verb,* **paneled, paneling.**

pang   A sudden, sharp pain or feeling. The boys began to feel *pangs* of hunger after they had been hiking for a few hours. He felt *pangs* of guilt after he lied to his friend.
pang (pang) *noun, plural* **pangs.**

panic   A feeling of fear that is so great it makes a person lose control of himself and want to run away. When the theater caught fire, *panic* spread through the crowd. *Noun.*
—To fill with or have a feeling of great fear. The lightning *panicked* the horses. *Verb.*

pan·ic (pan′ik) *noun, plural* **panics;** *verb,* **panicked, panicking.**

panorama   A wide or complete view of an area. You can see a *panorama* of the whole valley from the mountaintop.
pan·o·ram·a (pan′ə ram′ə) *noun, plural* **panoramas.**

pansy   A flower having five flat petals that overlap each other. Pansies grow in many colors.
pan·sy (pan′zē) *noun, plural* **pansies.**

Pansies

pant   **1.** To breathe quickly and hard; gasp for breath. Louise *panted* as she ran up the stairs. **2.** To say while gasping for breath. "Help me," he *panted.*
pant (pant) *verb,* **panted, panting.**

panther   A large leopard with a black coat.
pan·ther (pan′thər) *noun, plural* **panthers** or **panther.**

Panther

pantomime   **1.** The telling of a story without talking, through the use of gestures, body movements, and facial expressions. **2.** A play acted in this way. The class put on a *pantomime* of the first meeting between the Indians and the Pilgrims. *Noun.*
—To act or show in pantomime. The clown *pantomimed* baking a cake. *Verb.*
pan·to·mime (pan′tə mīm′) *noun, plural* **pantomimes;** *verb,* **pantomimed, pantomiming.**

at; āpe; cär; end; mē; it; īce; hot; ōld;
fôrk; wood; fōol; oil; out; up; turn; sing;
thin; this; hw in white; zh in treasure.
ə stands for a in about, e in taken
i in pencil, o in lemon, and u in circus.

pantry   A small room for storing food, dishes, or silver.
   pan·try (pan′trē) *noun, plural* **pantries.**

▲ The word **pantry** comes from an old French word that meant "a place for keeping bread." The French word goes back to the Latin word for bread.

---

pants   Clothes for the part of the body below the waist. Pants are divided so that they cover each leg separately. They usually reach from the waist to the ankles.
   pants (pants) *noun plural.*

papaya   A yellowish-orange fruit that grows on a tropical American tree. It looks like a melon and has a sweet taste.
   pa·pa·ya (pə pä′yə) *noun, plural* **papayas.**

Whole Fruit

Split Fruit

Papaya Tree

paper   **1.** A material that is used for writing, printing, wrapping things, covering walls, and many other purposes. Paper is made from wood, rags, or certain grasses. It is usually made in thin pieces called sheets. **2.** A piece or sheet of paper. Stuart wrote his name at the top of the *paper.* **3.** A piece of paper with writing or printing on it; document. These *papers* prove that he is the owner of the house. **4.** A written report or essay on a particular topic. My brother's history *paper* is ten pages long. **5.** A newspaper. Dad always reads the evening *paper* right before dinner. *Noun.*
—To cover with wallpaper. The workmen *papered* the hall. *Verb.*
   pa·per (pā′pər) *noun, plural* **papers;** *verb,* **papered, papering.**

▲ The word **paper** goes back to the Greek word for the *papyrus* plant. This is because the earliest writing material that was at all like the paper we use was made from the papyrus plant and was called papyrus.

---

paperback   A book that has a soft paper cover.
   pa·per·back (pā′pər bak′) *noun, plural* **paperbacks.**

paper clip   A small piece of bent wire that is used to hold sheets of paper together.

papoose   A North American Indian baby or small child.
   pa·poose (pa poos′) *noun, plural* **papooses.**

paprika   A reddish-orange powder used as a spice and to add color to food. It is made from sweet red peppers.
   pap·ri·ka (pa prē′kə *or* pap′ri kə) *noun, plural* **paprikas.**

papyrus   **1.** A tall plant that grows in swamps and along rivers in parts of Africa and Europe. **2.** A material like paper that is made from this plant. The ancient Egyptians and other peoples used this material to write on.
   pa·py·rus (pə pī′rəs) *noun, plural* **papyri.**

parachute   A large device made of fabric that is shaped like an umbrella. A parachute is attached to something to slow it down as it falls through the air. Parachutes are used to drop people or things safely to the ground from an airplane. *Noun.*
—To come or send down by parachute. The pilot *parachuted* from the burning plane. The air force *parachuted* supplies to the soldiers who were surrounded by the enemy. *Verb.*
   par·a·chute (par′ə-shoot′) *noun, plural* **parachutes;** *verb,* **parachuted, parachuting.**

Parachute

parade   A march or procession in honor of a person or event. Every year my father takes us downtown to watch the Fourth of July *parade. Noun.*
—**1.** To march in a parade. The soldiers *paraded* through town. **2.** To make a great show of; show off. That man likes to *parade* his knowledge before everyone that he meets. *Verb.*
   pa·rade (pə rād′) *noun, plural* **parades;** *verb,* **paraded, parading.**

paradise **1.** Heaven. **2.** A place or state of great happiness. The island where they spent their vacation was a *paradise* of peace and beauty.
  par·a·dise (par′ə dīs′) *noun.*

paraffin A white substance like wax. It is used for making candles and waxed paper, and for sealing jars.
  par·af·fin (par′ə fin) *noun.*

paragraph A group of sentences on one particular subject or idea. A paragraph is a small part of something written. It begins on a new line and is set in from the rest of the lines.
  par·a·graph (par′ə graf′) *noun, plural* **para-graphs.**

▲ The word **paragraph** goes back to two Greek words that mean "to write beside." The first meaning of *paragraph* was a symbol drawn beside some writing to show that the writer was starting to write about a new idea.

parakeet A small parrot. It has a slender body, a long, pointed tail, and brightly colored feathers. Parakeets are often kept as pets.
  par·a·keet (par′ə kēt′) *noun, plural* **parakeets.**

parallel **1.** Going in the same direction and always being the same distance apart. If lines are parallel, they never meet or cross each other. The two rails of a railroad track are *parallel.* **2.** That are alike; similar. Even though these children live in different parts of the world, they have had *parallel* experiences at school. *Adjective.*

Parakeet

—**1.** A parallel line or surface. The teacher drew a line connecting two points and then drew a *parallel.* **2.** A being alike; a similarity. There are many *parallels* in the personalities of those two sisters. **3.** Any of the imaginary lines that circle the earth in the same direction as the equator. They are used to mark off latitude. The ship was near the twenty-eighth *parallel. Noun.*
—**1.** To be or lie in the same direction and always the same distance apart. The railroad tracks *parallel* the highway. **2.** To be similar to. The growth of the small town *paralleled* the growth of the large city nearby. *Verb.*

—In the same direction and always the same distance apart. The road runs *parallel* to the river. *Adverb.*
  par·al·lel (par′ə lel′) *adjective; noun, plural* **parallels;** *verb,* **paralleled, paralleling;** *adverb.*

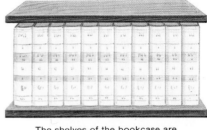
The shelves of the bookcase are
parallel to each other.

paralysis A loss of the power to move or feel in a part of the body.
  pa·ral·y·sis (pə ral′ə sis) *noun, plural* **paraly-ses.**

paralyze **1.** To take away the power to move or feel in a part of the body. His right arm was *paralyzed.* **2.** To make unable to act or do anything; make helpless. The bus strike *paralyzed* the city.
  par·a·lyze (par′ə līz′) *verb,* **paralyzed, para-lyzing.**

paramecium A very tiny water animal made up of only one cell. It can be seen only through a microscope.
  par·a·me·ci·um (par′ə mē′shē əm) *noun, plural* **paramecia.**

Paramecium

paraprofessional A person who works with and helps a teacher, nurse, or other professional worker.
  par·a·pro·fes·sion·al (par′ə prə fesh′ən əl) *noun, plural* **paraprofessionals.**

at; āpe; cär; end; mē; it; īce; hot; ōld;
fôrk; wood; fōōl; oil; out; up; turn; sing;
thin; this; hw in white; zh in treasure.
ə stands for a in about, e in taken
i in pencil, o in lemon, and u in circus.

parasite An animal or plant that lives on or in another animal or plant and gets its food from it. Fleas and tapeworms are parasites on animals. Mistletoe is a parasite on trees.
par·a·site (par′ə sīt′) *noun, plural* **parasites.**

▲ The word **parasite** goes back to two Greek words that mean "beside" and "food." In Greek, a parasite was a person who ate beside someone else or at someone else's table. The word was used especially for a person who flattered another person so that he would be invited to stay for dinner.

parasol A small, light umbrella. Parasols are used as a protection against the sun.
par·a·sol (par′ə sôl′) *noun,*
plural **parasols.**

paratrooper A soldier who is trained to parachute from an airplane into an area of battle.
par·a·troop·er (par′ə-trōō′pər) *noun, plural* **paratroopers.**

parcel 1. Something wrapped up; bundle or package. We received many *parcels* in the mail around Christmas. 2. A piece or section. They bought the *parcel* of land next to ours. *Noun.*
—To divide into sections; give out in parts. The guide *parceled* out supplies to the campers. *Verb.*
par·cel (pär′səl) *noun,*
plural **parcels;** *verb,* **parceled, parceling.**

Parasol

parch 1. To make very dried up. The summer sun *parched* the lawn. 2. To make very hot and thirsty. Hiking on the hot day *parched* the campers.
parch (pärch) *verb,* **parched, parching.**

parchment The skin of sheep, goats, or other animals prepared so that it can be written on, or paper made to look like this skin. Diplomas and other important documents are often written on parchment.
parch·ment (pärch′mənt) *noun, plural* **parchments.**

pardon 1. To free a person from punishment. The governor *pardoned* the prisoner. 2. To not have hard feelings about; not want to blame or punish. Please *pardon* his rude remark. *Verb.*
—1. A freeing from punishment. The pris-

oner received a *pardon* from the state after the real thief gave himself up. 2. A refusal to blame or punish; forgiveness. I beg your *pardon* if I hurt your feelings. *Noun.*
par·don (pärd′ən) *verb,* **pardoned, pardoning;** *noun, plural* **pardons.**

pare 1. To cut or peel off the outer part of something. Charlie *pared* the apple with a knife. 2. To make less little by little; cut down. The family tried to *pare* expenses in order to save money. ▲ Other words that sound like this are **pair** and **pear.**
pare (per) *verb,* **pared, paring.**

parent 1. A father or mother. 2. An animal or plant that produces another animal or plant.
par·ent (per′ənt) *noun, plural* **parents.**

parenthesis Either or both of two curved lines ( ). A parenthesis is used to set off a word or phrase within a sentence in order to explain or add to what is said.
pa·ren·the·sis (pə ren′thə sis) *noun, plural* **parentheses.**

parish 1. An area that has its own church and clergyman. 2. The people who live in this area and belong to this church.
par·ish (par′ish) *noun, plural* **parishes.**

park 1. A piece of land with benches, trees, paths, and playgrounds that is set apart for the pleasure of the public. 2. A large area of land that is left in its natural state by the government. In California, there are many *parks* where people can camp out. *Noun.*
—To leave an automobile or other vehicle in a place where it can stay for a time. He *parked* his car near the house. *Verb.*
park (pärk) *noun, plural* **parks;** *verb,* **parked, parking.**

parka A warm fur or cloth jacket with a hood. Eskimos often wear fur parkas.
par·ka (pär′kə) *noun, plural* **parkas.**

parking meter A kind of clock or timer mounted on a pole near a parking space. It has a slot where people can put in coins to pay for the use of parking space for a limited amount of time.

parkway A highway or wide road with trees, bushes, or grass planted in certain areas.
park·way (pärk′wā′) *noun, plural* **parkways.**

parliament 1. A group of people who have the duty and the power to make the laws of a country. 2. **Parliament.** A group like this in England. It is made up of the House of Commons and the House of Lords.
par·lia·ment (pär′lə mənt) *noun, plural* **parliaments.**

parlor **1.** A room in a house used for entertaining guests. **2.** A room or group of rooms used as a shop. A new ice-cream *parlor* just opened down the street.
par·lor (pär′lər) *noun, plural* **parlors.**

▲ The word **parlor** was first used for a place in a monastery where a monk could talk to a visitor from outside the monastery. This led to the meaning "a small room in a house that is used for entertaining guests."

parochial Having to do with a parish or with any other religious group. Hal goes to a *parochial* school.
pa·ro·chi·al (pə rō′kē əl) *adjective.*

parole The release of a person from prison before his full sentence has been served. People are usually put on parole for good behavior, and they must then obey certain rules for a time. *Noun.*
—To release a person from prison before his full sentence is served. The man was *paroled* after four years in prison. *Verb.*
pa·role (pə rōl′) *noun, plural* **paroles;** *verb,* **paroled, paroling.**

parrot A bird with a wide curved bill, a long pointed tail, and glossy, brightly colored feathers. Some parrots can imitate speech and other sounds. Parrots are sometimes kept as pets. *Noun.*
—To repeat or imitate what someone else has said without thinking about it or understanding it. The little boy *parroted* everything his older sister said. *Verb.*
par·rot (par′ət) *noun, plural* **parrots;** *verb,* **parroted, parroting.**

Parrot

parsley A small plant that has many tiny leaves on each branch. It is used to flavor and decorate food.
pars·ley (pärs′lē) *noun, plural* **parsleys.**

parsnip The thick, white root of a plant that is related to the carrot. This root is cooked and eaten as a vegetable.
pars·nip (pärs′nip) *noun, plural* **parsnips.**

parson A clergyman in charge of a parish.
par·son (pär′sən) *noun, plural* **parsons.**

part **1.** Something less than the whole. We liked the last *part* of the movie the best. Jack ate only *part* of his dinner. **2.** A piece that

helps make up a whole. The repairman took the back off the television set and spread its *parts* all over his work table. **3.** A share. They all did their *part* to make the picnic a success. **4.** One of the sides in an argument or contest. Kate always takes her mother's *part* in any disagreement. **5.** A line made to divide one's hair when combing it, so that it will fall a certain way. Ned always wears his hair in a side *part.* **6.** A character or role in a movie, play, or other entertainment. Neil played the *part* of a cowboy in the school play. *Noun.*
—**1.** To separate by coming between; force or hold apart. The referee *parted* the two boxers. **2.** To go in different directions; separate. They shook hands and *parted* at the corner. **3.** To comb the hair so as to make it fall along a dividing line. Sherry *parted* her hair in the middle. *Verb.*
—In some degree; not completely. The sled is *part* mine and *part* my sister's. *Adverb.*
—Not full or complete; partial. Mr. Dempsey is *part* owner of the store. *Adjective.*
part (pärt) *noun, plural* **parts;** *verb,* **parted, parting;** *adverb; adjective.*
to part with. To give up. Billy refused *to part with* the stray kitten he had found.
to take part. To take or have a share. Everyone should *take part* in the project to clean up the town park.

partial **1.** Not complete; not total. He made only a *partial* recovery from the accident and always walked with a limp. **2.** Showing more favor than is fair to one side, person, or group. The umpire was *partial* to our team.
par·tial (pär′shəl) *adjective.*

participate To take part or have a share with others. Everyone *participated* in making decorations for the party.
par·tic·i·pate (pär tis′ə pāt′) *verb,* **participated, participating.**

participle The form of a verb that is used with a helping verb to form certain tenses. A participle can sometimes act as a noun or adjective. In the sentence *She has studied all day, studied* is a past participle. In the sentence *He is studying in his room, studying* is a present participle.
par·ti·ci·ple (pär′tə sip′əl) *noun, plural* **participles.**

at; āpe; cär; end; mē; it; īce; hot; ōld;
fôrk; wood; fōōl; oil; out; up; turn; sing;
thin; this; hw in white; zh in treasure.
ə stands for a in about, e in taken
i in pencil, o in lemon, and u in circus.

particle A very small bit or piece of something. A *particle* of dirt flew into my eye.
par·ti·cle (pär′ti kəl) *noun, plural* **particles.**

particular 1. Taken by itself; apart from others. At this *particular* moment, he is taking a shower and cannot come to the phone. 2. Having to do with some one person or thing. Erica's *particular* talent is drawing pictures of children. 3. Unusual in some way; special. That book is of *particular* interest to anyone who owns a dog. 4. Very careful about details; hard to please; fussy. She is very *particular* about keeping her room neat. *Adjective.*
—A single and separate fact or part; detail. All the *particulars* of the robbery were in the morning paper. *Noun.*
par·tic·u·lar (pər tik′yə lər) *adjective; noun, plural* **particulars.**

partition A wall or panel that divides up space. The horse reared up in the stable and kicked at the *partition* of his stall. *Noun.*
—1. To divide into shares or parts. The large farm was *partitioned* into small lots for houses. 2. To separate by a wall or panel. The workmen *partitioned* off a small room in the basement for the washing machine and dryer. *Verb.*
par·ti·tion (pär tish′ən) *noun, plural* **partitions;** *verb,* **partitioned, partitioning.**

partly In some degree; not wholly or completely; in part. He is only *partly* to blame for the accident because the other driver was speeding.
part·ly (pärt′lē) *adverb.*

partner 1. A person who runs a business with one or more other people and who shares the profits and losses of the business. My mother and my aunt are *partners* in a beauty parlor. 2. A person who plays with another person on the same side in a game. Mickey and Betty were tennis *partners* during the school tournament. 3. A person who dances with another. He asked Joan to be his *partner* for the first dance.
part·ner (pärt′nər) *noun, plural* **partners.**

partnership A business that is run by two or more people who share the profits and losses. The bakery on the corner is a *partnership* that is run by three brothers.
part·ner·ship (pärt′nər ship′) *noun, plural* **partnerships.**

part of speech One of the classes into which the words of a language are divided. The eight parts of speech into which the English language is divided are noun, pronoun, adjective, verb, adverb, preposition, conjunction, and interjection.

partridge A bird that is hunted as game. Partridges have plump bodies with gray, brown, and white feathers.
par·tridge (pär′trij) *noun, plural* **partridges** or **partridge.**

Partridge

part-time For only part of the usual working time. Harry got a *part-time* job for Saturdays at the grocery store. *Adjective.*
—On a part-time schedule. My brother works *part-time* after school. *Adverb.*
part-time (pärt′tīm′) *adjective; adverb.*

party 1. A gathering of people to have a good time. Sue invited all her friends to her birthday *party.* 2. A group of people who are doing something together. A search *party* went through the woods looking for the lost child. 3. An organization working to gain political power or control. Each political *party* chose a candidate to run for President. 4. A person who takes part in an action or plan. Jill refused to be a *party* to the practical joke they played on the new girl. 5. A person. The *party* I called on the telephone was not there.
par·ty (pär′tē) *noun, plural* **parties.**

pass 1. To go past; move or go by. I *pass* the park on my way to school. The hours *passed* slowly. 2. To go from one place or state to another; move. Many thoughts *passed* through his mind as he waited. 3. To hand or move from one person to another. Please *pass* the salt. Herb *passed* the ball to Eric, who took a shot and made a basket. 4. To complete a test or course of study with success. Stan always *passes* all his subjects. 5. To come to an end; die. Mary's grandfather *passed* away when she was a baby. 6. To use or spend time. Ellen *passed* the hour she had to wait by reading a newspaper. 7. To approve or make into law. The Senate *passed* the bill quickly. *Verb.*

—1. A written permission. No one was allowed to enter the building without showing a *pass*. **2.** A free ticket. My uncle's boss gave him five *passes* to the baseball game. **3.** A way or opening through which to go. A gap or passage in a mountain range is a pass. **4.** A moving or throwing of a ball from one player to another. The quarterback made a long *pass* to another player on his team. *Noun.*

pass (pas) *verb*, **passed, passing;** *noun, plural* **passes.**

to pass out. 1. To give out. The teacher *passed out* books to everyone in the class. **2.** To lose consciousness; faint. Several marchers in the parade *passed out* from the heat.

passage **1.** A short part of a piece of music or writing. The teacher read a *passage* from the story. **2.** A route, path, or other way by which a person or thing can pass. The prisoners escaped by using an underground *passage*. **3.** A trip or voyage. The ship's *passage* across the Atlantic was rough. **4.** A passing or moving. The *passage* of time in the play was shown by dimming the lights. **5.** A making into law; approval. *Passage* of the bill in Congress seemed certain.

pas·sage (pas′ij) *noun, plural* **passages.**

passageway A way along which a person or thing can pass. The *passageway* from the basement of the building leads to an alley.

pas·sage·way (pas′ij wā′) *noun, plural* **passageways.**

passenger A person who travels in an automobile, bus, train, airplane, or boat.

pas·sen·ger (pas′ən jər) *noun, plural* **passengers.**

passing **1.** Going or moving by. The boy watched the *passing* parade. The family grew richer with the *passing* years. **2.** Not lasting; brief. David had a *passing* fancy for collecting stamps. **3.** Given or done in passing. When she was angry at Joel, she wouldn't even give him a *passing* glance. **4.** Allowing one to pass a test or course of study. Ricky got a *passing* grade on the arithmetic test. *Adjective.*

—A going by or past. We noticed the *passing* of summer as the leaves started to turn brown. *Noun.*

pass·ing (pas′ing) *adjective; noun, plural* **passings.**

passion **1.** A very strong feeling. Love, hate, and anger are passions. **2.** A very strong liking. My sister has a *passion* for baseball.

pas·sion (pash′ən) *noun, plural* **passions.**

Passover A Jewish holiday that celebrates the escape of the Jews from slavery in Egypt long ago.

Pass·o·ver (pas′ō′vər) *noun.*

passport A document given to a person by the government of his country. It proves that a person is a citizen of a country and gives him official permission to travel to other countries.

pass·port (pas′pôrt′) *noun, plural* **passports.**

password A secret word or phrase that identifies the speaker or allows him to pass a guard.

pass·word (pas′wurd′) *noun, plural* **passwords.**

past **1.** Gone by; ended; over. Vacation is *past. Past* events have shown that he can be trusted. **2.** Gone by just before the present time; just ended. She saw three movies in the *past* week. **3.** Of time gone by; former. He is a *past* mayor of our town. *Adjective.*

—A time that has gone by. Dinosaurs lived in the distant *past. Noun.*

—Beyond in place, time, or amount. He threw the ball *past* the catcher. My grandfather is *past* seventy. *Preposition.*

—So as to pass or go by. We watched the train roll *past. Adverb.*

past (past) *adjective; noun; preposition; adverb.*

paste **1.** A mixture used to stick things together. Paste is usually made of flour and water. **2.** Any soft, smooth, very thick mixture. Mother put tomato *paste* into the spaghetti sauce. *Noun.*

—1. To stick with paste. Joyce *pasted* the photographs into her album. **2.** To cover with something stuck on with paste. Jimmy *pasted* the walls of his room with posters. *Verb.*

paste (pāst) *noun, plural* **pastes;** *verb*, **pasted, pasting.**

pastel **1.** A crayon like chalk. Pastels are used in drawing. **2.** A picture drawn with such crayons.

pas·tel (pas tel′) *noun, plural* **pastels.**

pasteurize To heat milk or other food hot enough to kill certain germs. Milk is pasteurized so that people will not get certain diseases from drinking it.

pas·teur·ize (pas′chə rīz′) *verb*, **pasteurized, pasteurizing.**

at; āpe; cär; end; mē; it; īce; hot; ōld;
fôrk; wood; fōōl; oil; out; up; turn; sing;
thin; **th**is; hw in white; zh in treasure.
ə stands for a in about, e in taken
i in pencil, o in lemon, and u in circus.

▲ The word **pasteurize** comes from the name of Louis *Pasteur*. Louis Pasteur was a French scientist who found this way to kill certain germs in milk.

pastime Something that makes time pass in a pleasant and happy way. Riding her bicycle is one of Pat's favorite *pastimes*.
pas·time (pas′tīm′) *noun, plural* **pastimes.**

pastor A minister in charge of a parish or church.
pas·tor (pas′tər) *noun, plural* **pastors.**

past participle A form of a verb showing an action or state that happened or existed in the past. In the sentence *Jack has worked all day, worked* is a past participle.

pastry 1. Pies, tarts, and other sweet baked goods. 2. Crust made of dough. The meat pie was topped with a layer of *pastry*.
pas·try (pās′trē) *noun, plural* **pastries.**

past tense A form of a verb showing an action or state that happened or existed in the past. In the sentence *The cat jumped off the fence, jumped* is in the past tense.

pasture 1. A field or other piece of land on which cows, horses, sheep, or other animals graze. 2. Grass and other growing plants that animals feed on. This valley provides excellent *pasture* for livestock. *Noun.*
—To put animals in a pasture to graze. The farmer *pastured* the ponies. *Verb.*
pas·ture (pas′chər) *noun, plural* **pastures;** *verb,* **pastured, pasturing.**

pat 1. To tap or stroke gently with the hand. People pat dogs to show them love or to let them know that they have been good. 2. To shape or smooth by tapping or hitting gently. Mother took off her hat and *patted* her hair into place. *Verb.*
—1. A gentle tap or stroke. Jackie finished the mud pie with three *pats*. 2. A small, flat slice. He topped the stack of pancakes with a *pat* of butter. *Noun.*
pat (pat) *verb,* **patted, patting;** *noun, plural* **pats.**

patch 1. A small piece of material. Patches are often used to cover holes or worn spots in clothing. They are also used as decorations, badges, or bandages. Tim's mother sewed a *patch* over the hole in his blue jeans. The pirate captain wore a *patch* over one eye. 2. A small area that is different from what is around it. The car skidded on a *patch* of ice in the road. 3. A small piece of ground where something grows. The children went out to pick berries in the strawberry *patch*. *Noun.*
—1. To put a patch on something. Diane

patched the hole in the elbow of her sweater. 2. To fix or put together in a hasty or careless way. The man tried to *patch* the roof before the rain could leak in. 3. To make by joining pieces together. My grandmother used to *patch* quilts as a hobby. *Verb.*
patch (pach) *noun, plural* **patches;** *verb,* **patched, patching.**

patchwork Pieces of cloth of different colors and shapes that are sewed together. The quilt was a *patchwork*.
patch·work (pach′wurk′) *noun.*

Patchwork Quilt

patent A piece of paper given to a person or company by the government. It gives someone the right to be the only one to make, use, or sell a new invention for a certain number of years. The engineer took out a *patent* on the new kind of movie camera that she invented. *Noun.*
—To get a patent for. The scientist *patented* his new machine so that no one else would be able to use it. *Verb.*
pat·ent (pat′ənt) *noun, plural* **patents;** *verb,* **patented, patenting.**

patent leather A leather with a very smooth and shiny surface. Linda's shoes were made of black *patent leather*.

paternal 1. Of or like a father. The old man had *paternal* feelings for the little boy. 2. Related through one's father. Michael's *paternal* grandfather comes from Ireland.
pa·ter·nal (pə turn′əl) *adjective.*

path 1. A trail or way on which people or animals may walk. The *path* in the woods leads to the lake. Sam shoveled a *path* through the snow. 2. The line along which a person or thing moves. The scientist traced the *path* of the rocket.
path (path) *noun, plural* **paths.**

pathetic Causing pity or sorrow. The wet, frightened puppy was a *pathetic* sight.
pa·thet·ic (pə thet′ik) *adjective.*

patience A being able to put up with hardship, pain, trouble, or delay without getting angry or upset. The crowd showed great *patience* as they waited in the rain to buy tickets to the movie.

pa·tience (pā′shəns) *noun.*

patient Having or showing patience. A patient person is able to put up with hardship, pain, trouble, or delay without getting angry or upset. Larry was very *patient* with his baby brother whenever he had to watch him. *Adjective.*

—A person who is under the care or treatment of a doctor. *Noun.*

pa·tient (pā′shənt) *adjective; noun, plural* **patients.**

patio **1.** A paved outdoor space for cooking, eating, and relaxing. Our neighbors have a barbecue on their *patio* every weekend. **2.** An inner court or yard that has no roof and is open to the sky. Many houses in Spain or Latin America are built around patios.

pat·i·o (pat′ē ō′) *noun, plural* **patios.**

patriot A person who loves his country and defends or supports it with loyalty. We studied the lives of many American *patriots* in school.

pa·tri·ot (pā′trē ət) *noun, plural* **patriots.**

patriotic Showing or feeling love and loyal support of one's country. The Fourth of July is a *patriotic* holiday.

pa·tri·ot·ic (pā′trē ot′ik) *adjective.*

patrol To go through or around an area to guard it or make sure that everything is all right. The mayor promised that extra police cars would *patrol* the neighborhood. *Verb.*

—**1.** A going through or around an area to guard it or make sure that everything is all right. The scouts were sent out on *patrol* to see if enemy troops were in sight. **2.** One or more people who do this. The night *patrol* of the building is made up of two watchmen. **3.** A group of soldiers, ships, or airplanes that are sent out to fight or find out about the enemy. *Noun.*

pa·trol (pə trōl′) *verb,* **patrolled, patrolling;** *noun, plural* **patrols.**

patron **1.** A person who regularly buys at a particular store or regularly goes to a particular restaurant. Some of this store's *patrons* have been customers for more than twenty years. **2.** A person who supports or helps a person, group, or cause with his money or power. That rich businessman who gave money to build the new concert hall is a *patron* of the arts.

pa·tron (pā′trən) *noun, plural* **patrons.**

pattern **1.** The way in which colors, shapes, or lines are arranged or repeated in some

order; design. The wallpaper was printed with a pretty flower *pattern*. **2.** A guide or model that is to be followed. Joan sewed the dress according to a *pattern*. **3.** A set of actions or qualities that is repeated or that does not change. The scientist studied the *pattern* of the monkey's behavior. *Noun.*

—To make according to a pattern. Eddie always *patterned* his behavior after that of his older brother. *Verb.*

pat·tern (pat′ərn) *noun, plural* **patterns;** *verb,* **patterned, patterning.**

pause To stop for a short time. The rider *paused* to let his horse rest. *Verb.*

—A short stop or rest. After a *pause* because of rain, the game continued. *Noun.*

pause (pôz) *verb,* **paused, pausing;** *noun, plural* **pauses.**

pave To cover a road or street with pavement. The workmen *paved* the road with concrete.

pave (pāv) *verb,* **paved, paving.**

pavement A covering or surface for a street, road, or sidewalk. A pavement is usually made from concrete or asphalt.

pave·ment (pāv′mənt) *noun, plural* **pavements.**

pavilion **1.** A building or other structure that is used for a show or exhibit, or for recreation. The dance was held at a *pavilion* in the park. **2.** One of a group of buildings that make up a hospital.

pa·vil·ion (pə vil′yən) *noun, plural* **pavilions.**

Pavilion

paw The foot of a four-footed animal having nails or claws. Dogs and cats have paws. *Noun.*

at; āpe; cär; end; mē; it; īce; hot; ōld; fôrk; wood; fool; oil; out; up; turn; sing; thin; this; hw in white; zh in treasure. ə stands for a in about, e in taken i in pencil, o in lemon, and u in circus.

—**1.** To strike or scrape something with the paws or feet. The angry bull *pawed* the ground and then charged toward us. **2.** To touch or handle roughly, clumsily, or without care. The shoppers *pawed* the fruit that was on sale. *Verb.*

paw (pô) *noun, plural* **paws;** *verb,* **pawed, pawing.**

pawn¹ To leave something valuable with a lender of money in order to get a loan. The valuable object is left as a pledge that the money that is loaned will be paid back by the borrower.

pawn (pôn) *verb,* **pawned, pawning.**

pawn² **1.** One of the pieces used in the game of chess. The pawn is the piece of lowest value used in the game. **2.** A person or thing used by someone to gain some advantage. The robbers used their hostage as a *pawn* to bargain for a safe escape.

pawn (pôn) *noun, plural* **pawns.**

pawnbroker A person whose business is lending money to people who leave valuable things with him in return. Ray left his typewriter with a *pawnbroker* to get money to pay off some bills.

pawn·bro·ker (pôn′brō′kər) *noun, plural* **pawnbrokers.**

pay **1.** To give money to someone in return for things or work. He had to *pay* fifteen dollars to have the radio fixed. *Pay* the saleslady for the dress. This job *pays* two hundred dollars a week. **2.** To give money in order to settle. He had to *pay* a fine for breaking the traffic laws. **3.** To be worthwhile or good for someone. It will *pay* him to plan now for the future. It *pays* to get plenty of sleep. **4.** To give or suffer something in return. The man *paid* for his bad eating habits by having poor health. **5.** To make or give. Jonathan *paid* his aunt a visit in the hospital. Robin was very surprised when Jack *paid* her a compliment. *Verb.*
—Money given in return for things or work. The men went on strike because they wanted higher *pay.* Larry's boss gave him a raise in *pay. Noun.*

pay (pā) *verb,* **paid, paying;** *noun.*

payment **1.** The act of paying. The company demanded that *payment* for the television set be made when it was delivered. **2.** Something that is paid. The *payments* on his new car are one hundred dollars per month.

pay·ment (pā′mənt) *noun, plural* **payments.**

payroll **1.** A list of people to be paid and the amount that each one is to receive. The

company added her name to the *payroll* as soon as she was hired. **2.** The total amount of money to be paid. The robbers got away with the store's entire *payroll.*

pay·roll (pā′rōl′) *noun, plural* **payrolls.**

pea A small, round green vegetable. It is the seed of a kind of plant.

pea (pē) *noun, plural* **peas.**

peace **1.** Freedom from fighting. The conference was held to work toward world *peace.* **2.** A lack of noise or disorder; quiet or calm. He loves the *peace* and quiet of the country. ▲ Another word that sounds like this is **piece.**

peace (pēs) *noun.*

Pea

peaceful **1.** Free from war or disorder; quiet and calm. Everyone who visited the *peaceful* valley never forgot its beauty. **2.** Liking peace; avoiding fights and disorder. The people of that country are very *peaceful.*

peace·ful (pēs′fəl) *adjective.*

peace pipe A long pipe for smoking tobacco. It was used by North American Indians as a symbol of peace or friendship.

peach **1.** A round, sweet, juicy fruit. It has smooth yellow or yellow-red skin and grows on a tree that has pink flowers. **2.** A yellowish-pink color. *Noun.*
—Having a yellowish-pink color. *Adjective.*

peach (pēch) *noun, plural* **peaches;** *adjective.*

Blossom

Nut

Peach

▲ The word **peach** goes back to a Latin word that means "Persian." The Romans called this fruit a "Persian apple" because they first brought peaches to Rome from a country in western Asia called Persia.

peacock A large bird with a beautiful tail

and shiny blue feathers on its head, neck, and body. The peacock's tail has bright green and gold feathers with spots like eyes on them. When the peacock raises its tail, its feathers spread out like a fan.

pea·cock (pē′kok′) *noun, plural* **peacocks** or **peacock.**

Peacock

peak **1.** The pointed top of a mountain or hill. We could see the snow-covered *peaks* in the distance. **2.** A sharp or pointed end or top. The workmen started putting on new shingles at the *peak* of the roof. **3.** The highest point. Traffic reached its *peak* during the afternoon rush hour. The football star was at the *peak* of his career. **4.** The brim or front part of a cap that sticks out. A baseball player's cap has a peak. ▲ Another word that sounds like this is **peek.**

peak (pēk) *noun, plural* **peaks.**

peal A loud, long sound or series of sounds. A *peal* of thunder frightened the puppy. *Peals* of laughter greeted the clown as he skipped toward the audience. *Noun.*
—To sound or ring out in a peal. The church bells *pealed* loudly on Sunday morning. The big clock in the tower *pealed* twelve o'clock. *Verb.* ▲ Another word that sounds like this is **peel.**

peal (pēl) *noun, plural* **peals;** *verb,* **pealed, pealing.**

peanut A seed like a nut that grows in a pod under the ground. Peanuts are eaten for food, and are also used to make peanut butter. The oil from peanuts is used for cooking. Peanuts are also used to feed hogs and other livestock.

pea·nut (pē′nut′) *noun, plural* **peanuts.**

peanut butter A soft, creamy food made from ground, roasted peanuts. Peanut butter is used as a spread on crackers and in sandwiches.

pear A sweet, juicy fruit that grows on trees. Pears are shaped like bells and usually have a smooth yellow or brown skin. ▲ Other words that sound like this are **pair** and **pare.**

pear (per) *noun, plural* **pears.**

Pears

pearl **1.** A small, round, white or cream-colored gem that has a soft, glowing shine. Pearls are formed inside the shells of certain kinds of oysters. **2.** Something like a pearl. *Pearls* of dew covered the flowers.

pearl (purl) *noun, plural* **pearls.**

peasant A person who works on or owns a small farm.

peas·ant (pez′ənt) *noun, plural* **peasants.**

peat A kind of soil made up of decayed plants. It is found in swampy areas and is used as a fertilizer and as fuel.

peat (pēt) *noun.*

pebble A small stone that is usually round and smooth.

peb·ble (peb′əl) *noun, plural* **pebbles.**

pecan A nut that has a sweet taste. It grows on a large tree and has a thin shell.

pe·can (pi kän′ *or* pi kan′) *noun, plural* **pecans.**

Nut

Kernel

Pecan Tree in Autumn

at; āpe; cär; end; mē; it; īce; hot; ōld; fôrk; wood; fōol; oil; out; up; turn; sing; thin; this; hw in white; zh in treasure.
ə stands for a in about, e in taken i in pencil, o in lemon, and u in circus.

peck¹ **1.** A unit of measure used for fruits, vegetables, grains, and other dry things. A peck is equal to eight quarts, or one-fourth of a bushel. **2.** A large amount. The boy got into a *peck* of trouble when he broke the window.
peck (pek) *noun, plural* **pecks.**

peck² **1.** To strike something with the beak in a short, quick movement. The parakeet *pecked* the bars of its cage. The hen *pecked* at my finger. **2.** To strike at and pick up with the beak. The chicken *pecked* the corn. *Verb.*
—**1.** A short, quick stroke made with the beak. The canary gave me a *peck* on the finger. **2.** A quick kiss. He gave his mother a *peck* on the cheek as he ran out. *Noun.*
peck (pek) *verb,* **pecked, pecking;** *noun, plural* **pecks.**

peculiar **1.** Not usual; strange; queer. She had a *peculiar* habit of snapping her fingers while she was talking to people. **2.** Belonging to a certain person, group, place, or thing. The kangaroo is *peculiar* to Australia.
pe·cul·iar (pi kyōōl′yər) *adjective.*

peculiarity **1.** Something that is peculiar. The many *pecularities* about the accident made the police suspicious. **2.** The state or quality of being peculiar. The *peculiarity* of her behavior made them think that she wasn't feeling well.
pe·cu·li·ar·i·ty (pi kyōō′lē ar′ə tē) *noun, plural* **peculiarities.**

pedal A lever or part that is moved by the foot to run or control something. The pedals on a bicycle make it go. The pedals on a piano change the tone of the notes played. *Noun.*
—To work or use the pedals of something. Joey *pedaled* his bicycle down the block. *Verb.* ▲ Another word that sounds like this is **peddle.**
ped·al (ped′əl) *noun, plural* **pedals;** *verb,* **pedaled, pedaling.**

peddle To carry goods from place to place and offer them for sale. The old man *peddled* vegetables from door to door. ▲ Another word that sounds like this is **pedal.**
ped·dle (ped′əl) *verb,* **peddled, peddling.**

peddler A person who travels around selling goods which he carries from place to place.
ped·dler (ped′lər) *noun, plural* **peddlers.**

pedestal **1.** A base on which a column or statue stands. The bust of George Washington stood upon a marble *pedestal* in the museum. **2.** The base or other part of something that supports it. The *pedestal* of the lamp was cracked.
ped·es·tal (ped′əs təl) *noun, plural* **pedestals.**

pedestrian A person who travels on foot; walker. Sidewalks are for the use of *pedestrians.*
ped·es·tri·an (pə des′trē ən) *noun, plural* **pedestrians.**

pediatrician A doctor who takes care of and treats babies and children.
pe·di·a·tri·cian (pē′dē ə trish′ən) *noun, plural* **pediatricians.**

pedigree A line of ancestors; descent. This dog's *pedigree* includes many prize-winning champions.
ped·i·gree (ped′ə grē′) *noun, plural* **pedigrees.**

peek To look quickly or secretly. Dorothy tried to *peek* into the box holding her present even though she knew it was to be a surprise. *Verb.*
—A quick or secret look. Ron took a *peek* in the oven to see what was for dinner. *Noun.*
▲ Another word that sounds like this is **peak.**
peek (pēk) *verb,* **peeked, peeking;** *noun, plural* **peeks.**

peel The skin or outer covering of certain fruits and vegetables. Don't slip on that banana *peel. Noun.*
—**1.** To take off the skin or outer covering of something. Sam *peeled* a pound of potatoes. **2.** To remove or strip. Harriet *peeled* the stamp off the envelope so that she could save it for her collection. **3.** To come off in pieces or strips. The paint is *peeling* from the walls. **4.** To lose or shed an outer covering or layer. His sunburned back is *peeling. Verb.* ▲ Another word that sounds like this is **peal.**
peel (pēl) *noun, plural* **peels;** *verb,* **peeled, peeling.**

peep¹ **1.** To look secretly or quickly through a narrow opening or from a hiding place. Maria *peeped* through a crack in the curtain to see how many people were in the audience. **2.** To come slowly or partly into view; show slightly. The moon *peeped* through the clouds. *Verb.*
—A secret or quick look. The boys took a *peep* at the rabbit through the grass so they would not frighten it. *Noun.*
peep (pēp) *verb,* **peeped, peeping;** *noun, plural* **peeps.**

peep² A short, sharp sound like that made by a young bird or chicken. We could hear the *peep* of the chicks as we got nearer to the barn. *Noun.*
—To make a peep. The chicks *peeped* as we let them out of the box. *Verb.*
peep (pēp) *noun, plural* **peeps;** *verb,* **peeped, peeping.**

peer¹　**1.** A person who is equal to another. As a baseball player, Joe has few *peers*. **2.** A man who has a title; nobleman. Dukes and earls are peers. ▲ Another word that sounds like this is **pier**.
　peer (pēr) *noun, plural* **peers.**

peer²　**1.** To look hard or closely, as if trying to see something clearly. The old woman *peered* at me through her glasses, but she didn't recognize me. **2.** To come into view. The sun *peered* over the mountain. ▲ Another word that sounds like this is **pier**.
　peer (pēr) *verb,* **peered, peering.**

peg　A piece of wood, metal, or other material that can be fitted or driven into a surface. Pegs are used to fasten parts together, to hang things on, or to mark the score in a game. *Noun.*
　—To fasten with pegs. We watched the workmen *peg* down the circus tents. *Verb.*
　peg (peg) *noun, plural* **pegs;** *verb,* **pegged, pegging.**

Pekingese　A small dog with a long, silky coat. It has a flat, wrinkled face.
　Pe·king·ese (pē′kə nēz′ *or* pē′king ēz′) *noun, plural* **Pekingese.**

pelican　A big bird that has a very large bill and webbed feet. Pelicans eat fish and have a large pouch under their bills that is used for storing food.
　pel·i·can (pel′i-kən) *noun, plural* **pelicans.**

pellet　A small, hard piece of something that is shaped like a bullet or ball. Linda put food *pellets* in the cage for her pet mice. *Pellets* of ice hit the windshield as we drove on through the storm.
　pel·let (pel′it) *noun, plural* **pellets.**

Pelican

pell-mell　In a jumbled or confused way. The crowd ran *pell-mell* from the burning building.
　pell-mell (pel′mel′) *adverb.*

pelt¹　**1.** To attack or strike with something over and over. The children *pelted* each other with snowballs. **2.** To beat against heavily over and over. Hail *pelted* the roof.
　pelt (pelt) *verb,* **pelted, pelting.**

pelt²　The skin of an animal with its fur or hair still on it. Pelts are used to make things like clothing and rugs.
　pelt (pelt) *noun, plural* **pelts.**

pen¹　A long, thin tool for writing or drawing with ink. A fountain pen and a ball-point pen are kinds of pens.
　pen (pen) *noun, plural* **pens.**

pen²　**1.** A small, closed yard for cows, pigs, sheep, or other animals. **2.** Any small, closed-off area. *Noun.*
　—To hold or shut up in a pen. The farmer *penned* the horses. *Verb.*
　pen (pen) *noun, plural* **pens;** *verb,* **penned, penning.**

penalize　To give a penalty or punishment to. One of the players was *penalized* for tripping a player on the other team.
　pe·nal·ize (pēn′əl īz′) *verb,* **penalized, penalizing.**

penalty　**1.** A punishment. There is a *penalty* for illegal parking in this city. **2.** A disadvantage or punishment placed on a player or team for breaking the rules of some sport or game. The referee called a *penalty* of five yards for their team.
　pen·al·ty (pen′əl tē) *noun, plural* **penalties.**

pencil　A long, thin tool for writing or drawing. It is usually made of a stick of graphite that is enclosed in a covering of wood. *Noun.*
　—To write, draw, or mark with a pencil. The artist drew a man's face and then *penciled* in a mustache on it. *Verb.*
　pen·cil (pen′səl) *noun, plural* **pencils;** *verb,* **penciled, penciling.**

pendulum　A weight that is hung from a fixed point in such a way that it can swing back and forth. Pendulums are often used as part of grandfather clocks and other clocks.
　pen·du·lum (pen′jə ləm) *noun, plural* **pendulums.**

penetrate　**1.** To go into or pass through. The sword *penetrated* the knight's shield. The headlights of the car could not *penetrate* the fog. **2.** To find the meaning of; understand. Science tries to *penetrate* the mysteries of nature.
　pen·e·trate (pen′ə trāt′) *verb,* **penetrated, penetrating.**

at; āpe; cär; end; mē; it; īce; hot; ōld;
fôrk; wood; fōol; oil; out; up; turn; sing;
thin; this; hw in white; zh in treasure.
ə stands for a in about, e in taken
i in pencil, o in lemon, and u in circus.

penguin A sea bird whose feathers are black or gray on the back and white on the chest. Penguins cannot fly. Their wings look like flippers and are used for swimming. They live in and near Antarctica.
pen·guin (pen′gwin) *noun, plural* **penguins.**

penicillin A powerful drug that destroys bacteria and is used to treat many diseases. It is made from a kind of fungus mold.
pen·i·cil·lin (pen′ə-sil′ən) *noun.*

peninsula A piece of land that sticks out from a larger body of land and is almost entirely surrounded by water. Florida is a peninsula.
pen·in·su·la (pə nin′sə lə *or* pə nin′syə lə) *noun, plural* **peninsulas.**

Penguin

▲ The word **peninsula** goes back to two Latin words that mean "almost" and "island."

penitentiary A prison for people who have been found guilty of a serious crime.
pen·i·ten·tia·ry (pen′ə ten′shər ē) *noun, plural* **penitentiaries.**

penmanship The art or way of writing. Children begin to learn *penmanship* in the first grade.
pen·man·ship (pen′mən ship′) *noun.*

pen name A made-up name that an author uses instead of his real name when he writes. The *pen name* of Samuel Clemens is Mark Twain.

pennant A long, narrow flag that is shaped like a triangle. Pennants are used for signaling. They are also often used as school emblems. In some sports contests, the winning team gets a pennant.
pen·nant (pen′ənt) *noun, plural* **pennants.**

Pennsylvania A state in the eastern United States. Its capital is Harrisburg.
Penn·syl·va·nia (pen′səl vān′yə) *noun.*

▲ The word **Pennsylvania** once meant "Penn's woods." It was made from the last name of William *Penn* and a Latin word meaning "woods." King Charles II of England gave this name to the colony when he gave it to William Penn.

penny 1. A coin that is worth one cent. It is used in the United States and Canada. One hundred pennies equal one dollar. 2. A British coin. One hundred pennies equal one pound.
pen·ny (pen′ē) *noun, plural* **pennies** or **pence** *(for definition 2).*

pension A sum of money other than wages that is paid regularly to someone. Many companies pay pensions to people who retire after working for them for a long time.
pen·sion (pen′shən) *noun, plural* **pensions.**

pentagon A figure that has five sides.
pen·ta·gon (pen′tə gon′) *noun, plural* **pentagons.**

penthouse An apartment or house built on the roof of a building.
pent·house (pent′hous′) *noun, plural* **penthouses.**

peony A large pink, red, or white flower.
pe·o·ny (pē′ə nē) *noun, plural* **peonies.**

people 1. Men, women, and children; persons. This theater can seat 500 *people.* 2. All of the persons making up a nation, race, tribe, or group. The museum exhibit shows the crafts of African *peoples.* Many of the *people* of Israel originally came from other lands. 3. The public; persons in general. This country was founded on a belief in government by the *people. Noun.*
—To fill with people. A great number of human beings *people* the earth. *Verb.*
peo·ple (pē′pəl) *noun, plural* **people** or **peoples** *(for definition 2); verb,* **peopled, peopling.**

Peonies

pepper 1. A hot spice that is used to flavor foods. Black pepper is made from the whole, ground dried berries of a tropical plant. White pepper comes from the seeds inside these berries. 2. The red or green fruit of a group of plants. The fruit can be sweet or hot and can be eaten raw or cooked. *Noun.*
—1. To flavor with pepper. Carol salted and *peppered* the fried eggs. 2. To cover or sprinkle. Father *peppered* the ground with grass seed in the fall. *Verb.*
pep·per (pep′ər) *noun, plural* **peppers;** *verb,* **peppered, peppering.**

peppermint   **1.** A plant that looks, smells, and tastes like mint. The oil from the peppermint is used to flavor candy, chewing gum, and toothpaste. **2.** A candy that is flavored with peppermint oil.
pep·per·mint (pep′ər mint′) *noun, plural* **peppermints.**

per   For each. My brother earns sixty dollars *per* week on his summer job.
per (pur *or* pər) *preposition.*

perceive   **1.** To become aware of through seeing, hearing, tasting, smelling, or feeling. I could barely *perceive* the figure of a man through the fog. **2.** To understand; comprehend. The teacher soon *perceived* that the students did not understand her explanation.
per·ceive (pər sēv′) *verb,* **perceived, perceiving.**

percent   The number of parts in every hundred. Two *percent* of fifty is one. Twenty *percent* of the class was out sick with the chicken pox. The symbol for percent when it is written with a number is %. For example, five percent is also written 5%.
per·cent (pər sent′) *noun.*

percentage   **1.** The proportion of something to every hundred. What *percentage* of the class passed the arithmetic test? **2.** A part of a whole; portion. A large *percentage* of the students ride the bus to school.
per·cent·age (pər sen′tij) *noun, plural* **percentages.**

perch¹   **1.** A bar, branch, or anything else a bird can come to rest on. Our pet canary uses a swinging bar in its cage as a *perch.* **2.** Any raised place for sitting or standing. The lifeguard watched the swimmer from his *perch* above the pool. *Noun.*
—**1.** To sit or rest on. The bird *perched* on the fence. **2.** To set on a high place. The cat loved to *perch* itself on a window ledge in the sun. *Verb.*
perch (purch) *noun, plural* **perches;** *verb,* **perched, perching.**

perch²   A small fish that is found in fresh water in North America and most parts of Europe. It is used for food.
perch (purch) *noun, plural* **perches** or **perch.**

Perch

percussion instrument   A musical instrument that is played by striking one thing against another. The drum, cymbal, xylophone, and piano are percussion instruments.
per·cus·sion instrument (pər kush′ən).

perfect   **1.** Without a mistake or fault. Alice's spelling test was *perfect.* This is a *perfect* apple because it doesn't have one bruise or bad spot. **2.** Fully formed; complete; exact. Jim drew a *perfect* circle with the use of a compass. The picture the artist drew was a *perfect* likeness of my mother. **3.** Very great. My mother told me that I was making a *perfect* nuisance of myself. *Adjective.*
—To make or complete without any mistakes or faults. Scientists finally *perfected* a rocket for space travel. *Verb.*
per·fect (pur′fikt *for adjective;* pər fect′ *for verb*) *adjective; verb,* **perfected, perfecting.**

perfection   **1.** The condition of being perfect or without fault; excellence. It does not surprise me that my brother gets good grades in school because he always works for *perfection* in anything he does. **2.** The act of making perfect. The *perfection* of a ballet dancer's style takes many years of practice.
per·fec·tion (pər fek′shən) *noun.*

perfectly   **1.** In an excellent way; without fault. That dress fits you *perfectly.* **2.** Completely; entirely. I had a *perfectly* wonderful time at the party.
per·fect·ly (pur′fikt lē) *adverb.*

perforate   To make a hole or holes through. Jan *perforated* the box with a knife so the kitten could breathe more easily. Sheets of stamps are *perforated* to make it easy to tear off one or two at a time.
per·fo·rate (pur′fə rāt′) *verb,* **perforated, perforating.**

perform   **1.** To carry out; do. A soldier is trained to *perform* his duties. The doctor *performed* a difficult operation. **2.** To sing, act, or do something in public that requires skill. Our class is going to *perform* a play this Saturday. A magician *performed* tricks at the birthday party. Tom will *perform* on the piano at the school concert.
per·form (pər fôrm′) *verb,* **performed, performing.**

at; āpe; cär; end; mē; it; īce; hot; ōld; fôrk; wood; fool; oil; out; up; turn; sing; thin; this; hw in white; zh in treasure.
ə stands for a in about, e in taken i in pencil, o in lemon, and u in circus.

465

performance 1. A play, musical program, or something else that is done in public to entertain. The audience enjoyed last night's *performance* of the school play. The show closed after ten *performances.* 2. The act of carrying out an action. The worker wasted no time in the *performance* of his job. 3. The way in which something works; operation. The advertisement said that the *performance* of the car had been tested on rough country roads.
per·form·ance (pər fôr′məns) *noun, plural* **performances.**

performer A person who sings, acts, or does some form of entertainment in public. A singer, a dancer, and a juggler are performers.
per·form·er (pər fôr′mər) *noun, plural* **performers.**

perfume 1. A liquid that has a sweet, pleasant smell. Mother put on some *perfume* behind her ears. 2. A sweet, pleasant smell. The *perfume* from the flowers filled the room. *Noun.*
—To fill with a sweet, pleasant smell. The roses *perfumed* the air. *Verb.*
per·fume (pur′fyo͞om *or* pər fyo͞om′ *for noun;* pər fyo͞om′ *for verb*) *noun, plural* **perfumes;** *verb,* **perfumed, perfuming.**

perhaps Maybe; possibly. *Perhaps* we should go shopping with Mother so we can help her carry the packages home.
per·haps (pər haps′) *adverb.*

peril A chance or risk of harm or loss; danger. Icy roads are a *peril* to drivers.
per·il (per′əl) *noun, plural* **perils.**

perimeter The boundary of a figure or an area. The *perimeter* of a square is equal to four times the length of one side.
per·rim·e·ter (pə rim′ə tər) *noun, plural* **perimeters.**

period 1. A portion of time. A day is a *period* of twenty-four hours. He made a goal in the second *period* of the hockey game. 2. A mark of punctuation (.). A period shows the end of a sentence or of an abbreviation.
per·ri·od (pēr′ē əd) *noun, plural* **periods.**

periodic Happening now and again at regular times. Mother makes sure that everyone in our family makes *periodic* visits to the dentist.
per·ri·od·ic (pēr′ē od′ik) *adjective.*

periodical A magazine that is printed at regular times. Periodicals usually come out every two weeks or every month.
per·ri·od·i·cal (pēr′ē od′i kəl) *noun, plural* **periodicals.**

periscope An instrument on a submarine that is used to see ships, land, or other things above the surface of the water.
per·i·scope (per′ə skōp′) *noun, plural* **periscopes.**

perish To be destroyed; die. Many people *perished* when the ship sank.
per·ish (per′ish) *verb,* **perished, perishing.**

perishable Likely to spoil or decay quickly. Milk, meat, and other *perishable* foods should be kept in a refrigerator.
per·ish·a·ble (per′i shə bəl) *adjective.*

perjury The act or crime of swearing under oath that something is true which one knows to be not true.
per·ju·ry (pur′jər ē) *noun, plural* **perjuries.**

permanent Lasting or meant to last; enduring. When Carol graduated from high school, she started looking for a *permanent* job.
per·ma·nent (pur′mə nənt) *adjective.*

permission A consent from someone in authority. Nick asked his parents for *permission* to stay overnight at his friend's house. Jill asked the teacher for *permission* to leave early.
per·mis·sion (pər mish′ən) *noun.*

permit To allow or let. My mother will not *permit* me to play outside after it is dark. That state *permits* people to drive automobiles when they are sixteen years old. *Verb.*
—A written order giving permission to do something. You must have a *permit* to fish in this stream. *Noun.*
per·mit (pər mit′ *for verb;* pur′mit *or* pər·mit′ *for noun*) *verb,* **permitted, permitting;** *noun, plural* **permits.**

perpendicular 1. Straight up and down; upright. Only an expert mountain climber could climb the *perpendicular* face of those cliffs. 2. At right angles to a given line or surface. The sides of a square are *perpendicular* to the base. The telephone pole is *perpendicular* to the road. *Adjective.*
—A line or surface that is at right angles. The crossing of these two lines forms a *perpendicular. Noun.*

The poles are **perpendicular** to the ground.

per·pen·dic·u·lar (pur′pən dik′yə lər) *adjective; noun, plural* **perpendiculars.**

perpetual **1.** Lasting for a very long time or forever. Some of the highest mountains in the world are covered by *perpetual* snow. **2.** Continuing without stopping. The *perpetual* rise and fall of the tides is influenced by the moon and sun.
per·pet·u·al (pər pech′ $\overline{oo}$ əl) *adjective.*

perplex To confuse; puzzle. Janet was *perplexed* by her friend's sudden unfriendly behavior. Frank was *perplexed* by the arithmetic problem and asked the teacher to explain it.
per·plex (pər pleks′) *verb,* **perplexed, perplexing.**

persecute To treat in a cruel and unjust way. The early Christians were *persecuted* by the ancient Romans.
per·se·cute (pur′sə kyo͞ot′) *verb,* **persecuted, persecuting.**

persecution The act of persecuting or the state of being persecuted. The *persecution* of the early Christians for their religious beliefs forced them to meet in secret.
per·se·cu·tion (pur′sə kyo͞o′shən) *noun, plural* **persecutions.**

persimmon A fruit that has thin orange or yellow skin. Persimmons are sweet when they are fully ripe.
per·sim·mon (pər sim′ən) *noun, plural* **persimmons.**

▲ The word **persimmon** comes from a word used by Indians in North America. The Indian word meant "dried fruit."

Persimmons

persist To continue firmly and stubbornly. The teacher warned Martha that if she *persisted* in passing notes in class she would have to stay after school. The rainy weather *persisted* all week.
per·sist (pər sist′) *verb,* **persisted, persisting.**

persistent **1.** Continuing firmly and stubbornly. A persistent person does not give up when he is faced with trouble or disapproval. My brother is *persistent* in trying out for the basketball team every year, even though he is always turned down. **2.** Lasting; continuing. Sally has had a *persistent* cough for a month.
per·sist·ent (pər sis′tənt) *adjective.*

person **1.** A man, woman, or child; human being. Every ten years, the government takes an official count of every *person* living in this country. **2.** The body of a human being. The police searched the man suspected of robbing the store but could find no money on his *person.*
per·son (pur′sən) *noun, plural* **persons.**
in person. Physically present. The movie star looked more handsome when I saw him *in person.*

personal **1.** Private; not public. My diary is *personal,* and other people should not read it without permission. **2.** Done or made in person. The famous actress made a *personal* appearance at the first showing of her new movie. **3.** Having to do with a person's body. In health class, we learned the importance of *personal* cleanliness.
per·son·al (pur′sən əl) *adjective.*

personality **1.** All of a person's characteristics, habits, behavior, and other qualities. A person's personality makes him or her different from everybody else. Ron is very easy to get along with because he has such a friendly *personality.* **2.** A well-known person. At dinner last night we sat next to a famous television *personality.*
per·son·al·i·ty (pur′sə nal′ə tē) *noun, plural* **personalities.**

personally **1.** Not with the help of others; by oneself. The senator answered my letter *personally.* **2.** As far as oneself is concerned; for oneself. *Personally,* I am in favor of going camping. **3.** As a person or individual. I don't like him *personally.*
per·son·al·ly (pur′sən əl ē) *adverb.*

personnel The group of people working for a company or other organization. The *personnel* in this company are given two weeks of vacation a year.
per·son·nel (pur′sə nel′) *noun.*

at; āpe; cär; end; mē; it; īce; hot; ōld;
fôrk; wood; fo͞ol; oil; out; up; turn; sing;
thin; **th**is; **hw** in white; **zh** in treasure.
ə stands for **a** in about, **e** in taken
i in pencil, **o** in lemon, and **u** in circus.

perspective   1. The art of painting or drawing objects on a flat surface in a way that gives the appearance of distance and depth. 2. A point of view. Maybe we can solve this problem if we look at it from a different *perspective.*

per·spec·tive (pər spek′tiv) *noun, plural* **perspectives.**

Perspective makes it appear that the railroad tracks meet in the distance.

perspiration   1. Moisture that is given off through the pores of the skin; sweat. The basketball player was dripping with *perspiration* by the end of the game. 2. The act or process of giving off moisture through the pores of the skin; sweating. When a person's body gets too hot, it cools off through *perspiration.*

per·spi·ra·tion (pur′spə rā′shən) *noun.*

perspire   To give off perspiration; sweat. I always *perspire* when I play tennis on a hot day.

per·spire (pər spīr′) *verb,* **perspired, perspiring.**

persuade   To cause to do or believe something by argument; convince. John *persuaded* me to go to the movies with him even though I didn't like the picture that was playing.

per·suade (pər swād′) *verb,* **persuaded, persuading.**

pertain   To be related to or connected with. We spent this month studying the events that *pertain* to the American Revolution.

per·tain (pər tān′) *verb,* **pertained, pertaining.**

peso   A coin that is used in Mexico, the Philippines, and several Latin American countries.

pe·so (pā′sō) *noun, plural* **pesos.**

pessimistic   Looking on the bad side of things; expecting the worst. Since our best player was out sick, we were all *pessimistic* about winning the game.

pes·si·mis·tic (pes′ə mis′tik) *adjective.*

pest   A person or thing that is troublesome or annoying; nuisance. My little brother can be such a *pest* when he follows me around. Ants are *pests* at a picnic.

pest (pest) *noun, plural* **pests.**

pester   To trouble or bother; annoy. Mother does not like us to *pester* her with silly questions when she is making dinner.

pes·ter (pes′tər) *verb,* **pestered, pestering.**

pestle   A tool that is shaped like a club. It is used for pounding, grinding, or mixing something in a bowl called a mortar.

pes·tle (pes′əl *or* pest′əl) *noun, plural* **pestles.**

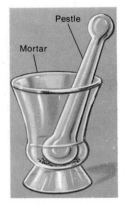

Pestle

Mortar

pet   1. An animal that is kept in a person's home for fun and companionship. Dogs, cats, and birds are the most common pets. 2. Any person who is treated with special kindness or favor; favorite. All the students tease him because he is the teacher's *pet. Noun.*
—Kept or treated as a pet. My sister has a *pet* rabbit. *Adjective.*
—To stroke or pat gently and lovingly. The cat purrs whenever we *pet* it. *Verb.*

pet (pet) *noun, plural* **pets;** *adjective; verb,* **petted, petting.**

petal   One of the parts of a flower. Petals come in many colors and shapes. The petals of a daisy are usually white and are arranged in a circle.

pet·al (pet′əl) *noun, plural* **petals.**

petition   A formal request that is made to a person in authority. All the people on our street signed a *petition* asking the city to put a stop sign on the corner. *Noun.*
—To make a formal request to. The students in our school *petitioned* the principal to do away with the rule of wearing uniforms to class. *Verb.*

pe·ti·tion (pə tish′ən) *noun, plural* **petitions;** *verb,* **petitioned, petitioning.**

petrify   1. To turn into stone. Petrified wood was formed when water seeped through the dead wood of fallen trees and left minerals inside the wood cells. The minerals eventually took the place of the wood cells when they decayed. **2.** To make helpless with fear. The child was *petrified* by the loud thunder.

> **pet·ri·fy** (pet′rə fī′) *verb*, **petrified, petrifying.**

petroleum An oily liquid that is found beneath the surface of the earth. Petroleum is made into gasoline, kerosene, oil for heating buildings, and many other products.

> **pe·tro·le·um** (pə trō′lē əm) *noun*.

petticoat A skirt that is made to be worn under a dress or outer skirt.

> **pet·ti·coat** (pet′ē kōt′) *noun, plural* **petticoats.**

petunia A garden plant that has white, pink, or purple flowers shaped like trumpets.

> **pe·tu·nia** (pə tōōn′yə *or* pə tyōōn′yə) *noun, plural* **petunias.**

pew A long bench in church for people to sit on. Pews are usually made out of wood. They are arranged in rows.

> **pew** (pyōō) *noun, plural* **pews.**

Petunias

pewter A metal that is made by combining tin, copper, and other metals. Pewter is used to make plates, pitchers, mugs, and candlesticks.

> **pew·ter** (pyōō′tər) *noun*.

Pharaoh The title of the kings of ancient Egypt.

> **Phar·aoh** (fer′ō) *noun, plural* **Pharaohs.**

pharmacist A person whose job is to prepare drugs and medicines.

> **phar·ma·cist** (fär′mə sist) *noun, plural* **pharmacists.**

pharmacy A store where drugs and medicines are sold; drugstore.

> **phar·ma·cy** (fär′mə sē) *noun, plural* **pharmacies.**

phase **1.** A stage of development of a person or thing. Every baby goes through a *phase* when it tries to put everything in its mouth. **2.** One side or view. Bob was interested in all *phases* of stamp collecting. **3.** The appearance and shape of the moon or a planet as it is seen at a particular time, which depends on how much of its lighted side can be seen from the earth.

> **phase** (fāz) *noun, plural* **phases.**

pheasant A bird that has a long tail and brightly colored feathers. Pheasants are hunted for sport and for food.

> **pheas·ant** (fez′ənt) *noun, plural* **pheasants.**

Pheasant

▲ The word **pheasant** goes back to the Greek name for this bird, which meant "of *Phasis*." The Phasis is a river in the part of Asia where this bird came from.

phenomenon **1.** A fact or event that can be seen. Snow is a *phenomenon* of the weather. **2.** A person or thing that is extraordinary or remarkable. The election of a woman as governor was a *phenomenon* in our state because only men had been governor before.

> **phe·nom·e·non** (fə nom′ə non′) *noun, plural* **phenomena** or **phenomenons.**

philodendron A plant that has shiny, heart-shaped leaves. The philodendron is widely grown as a house plant.

> **phil·o·den·dron** (fil′ə den′drən) *noun, plural* **philodendrons.**

philosopher A person who knows a great deal about philosophy. Philosophers generally try to answer questions about the nature of man and man's search for meaning in life.

> **phi·los·o·pher** (fə los′ə fər) *noun, plural* **philosophers.**

philosophy **1.** The study of the basic nature and purpose of man, the universe, and life itself. **2.** A person's principles and beliefs. My father's *philosophy* is to be kind to others.

> **phi·los·o·phy** (fə los′ə fē) *noun, plural* **philosophies.**

at; āpe; cär; end; mē; it; īce; hot; ōld;
fôrk; wood; fōol; oil; out; up; turn; sing;
thin; this; hw in white; zh in treasure.
ə stands for a in about, e in taken
i in pencil, o in lemon, and u in circus.

phlox A plant that has groups of small white, pink, red, purple, or blue flowers.
phlox (floks) *noun*, *plural* **phloxes.**

phone A telephone. *Noun.*
—To call on the telephone. Will you *phone* me tomorrow? *Verb.*
phone (fōn) *noun*, *plural* **phones;** *verb*, **phoned, phoning.**

Phlox

phonetic Having to do with or representing speech sounds. We use the *phonetic* symbol ô to show how to pronounce the sound of "o" in "fork."
pho·net·ic (fə net′ik) *adjective.*

phonograph An instrument that reproduces sound from records. The needle of a phonograph picks up the sounds that have been recorded on a record as the record turns. It plays them through loudspeakers so we can hear them.
pho·no·graph (fō′nə graf′) *noun*, *plural* **phonographs.**

phosphorus A substance that looks like yellow wax. Phosphorus glows faintly in the dark and is very poisonous. Phosphorus is a chemical element.
phos·pho·rus (fos′fər əs) *noun.*

photo A photograph.
pho·to (fō′tō) *noun*, *plural* **photos.**

photograph A picture that is made by using a camera. *Noun.*
—To take a picture of. We *photographed* the beautiful sunset. *Verb.*
pho·to·graph (fō′tə graf′) *noun*, *plural* **photographs;** *verb*, **photographed, photographing.**

photographer A person who takes pictures for fun or as a job. Robin is learning how to become a good *photographer* in her spare time.
pho·tog·ra·pher (fə tog′rə fər) *noun*, *plural* **photographers.**

photography The art of taking pictures with a camera. In photography, light from an object passes through the lens of a camera. The light reproduces a picture of the object on special film inside the camera that is sensitive to light.
pho·tog·ra·phy (fə tog′rə fē) *noun.*

phrase 1. A group of words expressing a single thought. A phrase is not a complete sentence. In the sentence *Hank is in the garage, in the garage* is a phrase. 2. A short expression. "Lower taxes!" was the *phrase* that the marchers chanted. *Noun.*
—To express in a particular way. The teacher *phrased* his questions very carefully so everyone would understand. *Verb.*
phrase (frāz) *noun*, *plural* **phrases;** *verb*, **phrased, phrasing.**

physical 1. Having to do with the body. A weight lifter has great *physical* strength. 2. Having to do with matter and energy. Physics is a *physical* science. 3. Having to do with things that we see in nature. The map shows mountains, lakes, and other *physical* features of the country.
phys·i·cal (fiz′i kəl) *adjective.*

physician A person who is trained and licensed to treat sickness or injury; doctor.
phy·si·cian (fə zish′ən) *noun*, *plural* **physicians.**

physicist A person who knows a great deal about physics.
phys·i·cist (fiz′ə sist) *noun*, *plural* **physicists.**

physics The science that deals with matter and energy and the laws governing them. Physics studies motion, light, heat, sound, and electricity and force.
phys·ics (fiz′iks) *noun plural.*

pi The symbol π that represents the ratio of the circumference of a circle to its diameter. Pi is equal to about 3.1416. ▲ Another word that sounds like this is **pie.**
pi (pī) *noun*, *plural* **pis.**

pianist A person who plays the piano.
pi·an·ist (pē an′ist *or* pē′ə nist) *noun*, *plural* **pianists.**

piano A musical instrument. The keys of the piano control little felt-covered hammers that strike metal strings and thus produce tones.
pi·an·o (pē an′ō) *noun*, *plural* **pianos.**

Piano

piccolo A small flute. The piccolo has a higher pitch than an ordinary flute.
   pic·co·lo (pik′ə lō′) *noun, plural* **piccolos.**

pick¹ **1.** To select or choose. He *picked* a card from the deck. I *picked* out a new dress at the store. **2.** To gather with the fingers. Mother *picked* flowers from our garden. We *picked* wild blueberries for a pie. **3.** To remove with the fingers or something pointed. Our dog loves to *pick* the meat off a bone. **4.** To play a musical instrument by plucking. Nancy *picked* the strings of her guitar. **5.** To cause on purpose. The bully *picked* a fight with Ron on the way to school. **6.** To steal the contents of. The thief *picked* the man's pocket. **7.** To open with a wire or something pointed instead of a key. The burglar *picked* the lock on the front door. **8.** To eat in a small amount. Tom *picked* at his food because he wasn't hungry. *Verb.*
   —**1.** The best part. That puppy is the *pick* of the litter. **2.** A small, thin piece of plastic or other material. It is used to pluck the strings of a guitar or similar musical instrument. *Noun.*
   pick (pik) *verb,* **picked, picking;** *noun, plural* **picks.**
   to pick on. To find fault with; criticize or annoy. The older boys *picked on* the new student.
   to pick up. 1. To take or lift up. We *picked up* pebbles and shells as we walked along the beach. **2.** To get by chance. The boy next door *picks up* extra money on weekends by doing odd jobs around the neighborhood. **3.** To learn. Ruth *picked up* Italian after living in Italy for only a few months.

pick² **1.** A tool with a wooden handle and a metal head that is pointed at two ends. A pick is used for breaking rocks and loosening dirt. It is also called a **pickax. 2.** A pointed tool. An ice pick can be used to break up ice.
   pick (pik) *noun, plural* **picks.**

pickerel A freshwater fish that has a thin body and a pointed head. Pickerels live in North America and are used for food.
   pick·er·el (pik′ər əl) *noun, plural* **pickerels** or **pickerel.**

picket **1.** A pointed stake that is driven into the ground to hold something in place or to build a fence. **2.** A person who stands or walks outside a factory or office to protest something. The *pickets* outside the governor's office wanted him to vote for the new education bill. *Noun.*
   —To stand in front of or walk about as a picket. The workers *picketed* the steel factory to demand better pay. *Verb.*

pick·et (pik′it) *noun, plural* **pickets;** *verb,* **picketed, picketing.**

pickle Any food that has been preserved in a mixture of salt water or vinegar. Cucumbers are very often prepared in this way. *Noun.*
   —To preserve in a mixture of salt water or vinegar. My grandmother *pickles* beets every summer. *Verb.*
   pick·le (pik′əl) *noun, plural* **pickles;** *verb,* **pickled, pickling.**

pickpocket A person who steals from other people's pockets or purses.
   pick·pock·et (pik′pok′it) *noun, plural* **pickpockets.**

pickup **1.** The act of picking up for the moving or delivery of something. There is a *pickup* of mail this afternoon. **2.** The ability to start to go faster quickly. This old car doesn't have much *pickup*. **3.** A small truck with an open back that is used for carrying light loads. The farmer uses a *pickup* to carry grain for his chickens from the store to the farm.
   pick·up (pik′up′) *noun, plural* **pickups.**

picnic A party or trip for which food is taken along and eaten outside. Mother made sandwiches and we all drove to the beach for a *picnic* on Sunday afternoon. *Noun.*
   —To go on or have a picnic. We *picnicked* in the park. *Verb.*
   pic·nic (pik′nik) *noun, plural* **picnics;** *verb,* **picnicked, picnicking.**

picture **1.** A painting, drawing, or photograph that represents a person or thing. This book has a beautiful *picture* of an old New England town in the winter. **2.** An image that

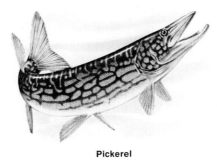

Pickerel

at; āpe; cär; end; mē; it; īce; hot; ōld;
fôrk; wood; fōol; oil; out; up; turn; sing;
thin; this; hw in white; zh in treasure.
ə stands for a in about, e in taken
i in pencil, o in lemon, and u in circus.

is seen on a television or motion-picture screen. This television set's *picture* is not very clear. **3.** A description in words. A German boy visited our class and gave us a very good *picture* of life in his country. **4.** A likeness or perfect example. John is the *picture* of his father. Nancy looks the *picture* of health. **5.** A motion picture; movie. Have you seen the *picture* that is playing downtown? *Noun.*
—**1.** To draw or paint a picture of. The artist *pictured* an old man sitting in a chair. **2.** To give a description of. The writer *pictured* the horrors of war. **3.** To imagine. It is hard for me to *picture* my grandmother as a young girl. *Verb.*

pic·ture (pik′chər) *noun, plural* **pictures;** *verb,* **pictured, picturing.**

picturesque Pretty and interesting enough to be the subject of a painting, drawing, or photograph. A cottage by the sea is *picturesque.*

pic·tur·esque (pik′chə resk′) *adjective.*

pie A pastry shell that is filled with fruit, meat, or other foods. Pies are baked in an oven and can be eaten for dessert or for a main course. ▲ Another word that sounds like this is **pi.**

pie (pī) *noun, plural* **pies.**

piece **1.** A part that has been broken, cut, or torn from something; fragment. There are *pieces* of broken glass all over the floor. **2.** A single thing that is part of a whole, group, or set. How big a *piece* of cake would you like? We took three *pieces* of luggage on our trip. When we play chess, you play with the black *pieces,* and I'll play with the white. **3.** An artistic or literary work. Jack is learning a new *piece* of music for the piano. **4.** An example or instance. It was a *piece* of luck that she found her watch. **5.** A coin. A dime is a ten-cent *piece. Noun.*
—To join the parts or pieces of. It was hard to *piece* the jigsaw puzzle together. The police were able to *piece* together the evidence and figure out who had committed the crime. *Verb.* ▲ Another word that sounds like this is **peace.**

piece (pēs) *noun, plural* **pieces;** *verb,* **pieced, piecing.**

pier **1.** A structure built out over the water. It is used as a landing place for boats or ships. **2.** A pillar or other kind of support that is used to hold up a bridge. Modern bridges have steel piers to support them. ▲ Another word that sounds like this is **peer.**

pier (pēr) *noun, plural* **piers.**

pierce To pass through; go into. A huge nail *pierced* the tire of my bicycle. A shrill cry suddenly *pierced* the stillness of the night.

pierce (pērs) *verb,* **pierced, piercing.**

pig An animal that has a roundish body, short legs with hooves, a short snout, and a short, curly tail. Some pigs are raised for their meat, which is called pork.

pig (pig) *noun, plural* **pigs.**

pigeon A bird that has a plump body, a small head, and thick soft feathers. Pigeons live in the wild, but are also found in nearly every city of the world.

pi·geon (pij′ən) *noun, plural* **pigeons.**

Pigeon

piggyback On the back or shoulders. My little brother loves to have Father give him a *piggyback* ride. He carried the little boy *piggyback.*

pig·gy·back (pig′ē bak′) *adjective; adverb.*

pigment A substance that is used for coloring or dyeing. Pink paint is made by mixing red and white *pigments.*

pig·ment (pig′mənt) *noun, plural* **pigments.**

pigtail A braid of hair hanging down from the back of either side of the head.

pig·tail (pig′tāl′) *noun, plural* **pigtails.**

pike A large freshwater fish that has a long, thin body and a large mouth with many sharp teeth.

Piggyback

pike (pīk) *noun, plural* **pikes.**

pile¹ **1.** A number of things lying one on top of the other; heap. There is a *pile* of newspapers on the floor. We keep a *pile* of wood in the backyard to burn in our fireplace. **2.** A large amount. Jim has to finish a *pile* of homework before he goes to bed. *Noun.*
—**1.** To form or put into a heap or mass. Every fall we *pile* up the dead leaves in one corner of the yard and burn them. **2.** To cover with a large amount. The librarian always has her desk *piled* with books, magazines, and papers. *Verb.*

pile (pīl) *noun, plural* **piles;** *verb,* **piled, piling.**

pile² A beam of wood, steel, or concrete that is used to support a bridge or pier.
pile (pīl) *noun, plural* **piles.**

pile³ The soft, thick fibers on the surface of a carpet, or of velvet or other material.
pile (pīl) *noun.*

pilgrim **1.** A person who travels to a sacred place for a religious purpose. During the Middle Ages, *pilgrims* went to the city of Jerusalem to see where Jesus lived. **2. Pilgrim.** One of a group of English settlers who founded Plymouth, Massachusetts, the first permanent settlement in New England.
pil·grim (pil′grəm) *noun, plural* **pilgrims.**

▲ The word **pilgrim** goes back to a Latin word that means "foreigner." A pilgrim often wanders far from his home, so he is a foreigner in the places he travels to.

pill A small tablet or ball of medicine. A pill is made either to be swallowed whole or to be chewed up.
pill (pil) *noun, plural* **pills.**

pillar A column that is used as support for a building or that stands alone as a monument. The roof of the porch is supported by *pillars.*
pil·lar (pil′ər) *noun, plural* **pillars.**

pillory A frame of wood with holes for a person's head and hands. A pillory used to be set up in a public place, and people who had done something wrong were put in it as a punishment.
pil·lo·ry (pil′ər ē) *noun, plural* **pillories.**

pillow A bag or case that is filled with feathers or other soft material. Pillows are used to support the head when resting or sleeping.
pil·low (pil′ō) *noun, plural* **pillows.**

pilot **1.** A person who operates an aircraft or spacecraft. **2.** A person who steers large ships into and out of a harbor. *Noun.*
—To act as a pilot. The captain *piloted* the airplane safely through the storm. *Verb.*
pi·lot (pī′lət) *noun, plural* **pilots;** *verb,* **piloted, piloting.**

pimple A small raised bump on the skin. Pimples are often red and painful.
pim·ple (pim′pəl) *noun, plural* **pimples.**

pin **1.** A short, straight piece of wire with a point at one end and a head at the other. A pin is used for holding cloth, paper, and other materials together. **2.** An ornament or badge that has a pin or clasp for attaching it to clothing. Janet wore a *pin* in the shape of a butterfly on the collar of her blouse. **3.** Any long piece of wood, metal, or plastic that is used to hold things together or in place. My sister sets her hair with *pins* after she washes it. **4.** One of the ten pieces of wood in the shape of a bottle that is used as a target in bowling. The object is to knock the pins down with a ball. *Noun.*
—**1.** To hold together or attach with a pin or pins. Sandy *pinned* the hem of her dress up. **2.** To hold fast in one position. The wrestler *pinned* his opponent to the mat. *Verb.*
pin (pin) *noun, plural* **pins;** *verb,* **pinned, pinning.**

pinafore A sleeveless piece of clothing that looks like an apron. Pinafores are worn by little girls over their dresses.
pin·a·fore (pin′ə fôr′) *noun, plural* **pinafores.**

pinch **1.** To squeeze between the finger and thumb or between any other surfaces. Mary sneaked up behind me and *pinched* my arm. I *pinched* my finger in the drawer when I closed it. **2.** To make thin or wrinkled. His face was *pinched* from the cold. *Verb.*
—**1.** A sharp squeeze. My sister gave me a *pinch* to keep me awake during the movie. **2.** A very small amount. The recipe called for a *pinch* of salt. **3.** A time of need or emergency. I can loan you money if you are in a *pinch. Noun.*
pinch (pinch) *verb,* **pinched, pinching;** *noun, plural* **pinches.**

pinch hitter A person who bats in place of another player in baseball.

Needles and Cone

Pine Tree

pine An evergreen tree that has cones and

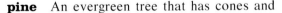

at; āpe; cär; end; mē; it; īce; hot; ōld;
fôrk; wood; fo͞ol; oil; out; up; turn; sing;
thin; this; hw in white; zh in treasure.
ə stands for a in about, e in taken
i in pencil, o in lemon, and u in circus.

leaves that look like needles. The wood from the pine is used in building and in making turpentine.

pine (pīn) *noun, plural* **pines.**

pineapple A large, oval fruit. The outside of a pineapple is hard and prickly, but the yellow meat inside is juicy and good to eat.

pine·ap·ple (pīn′-ap′əl) *noun, plural* **pineapples.**

Pineapple

▲ The word **pineapple** was first used for *pine cone* and meant "fruit of the pine tree." The name was given to this fruit because it looks something like a big pine cone.

Ping-Pong The trademark for the game of table tennis. Look up **table tennis** for more information.

Ping-Pong (ping′pong′) *noun.*

pink **1.** A light red color. It is made by mixing red and white. **2.** A garden plant that has sweet-smelling pink, red, or white flowers. *Noun.*
—Having the color pink. *Adjective.*

pink (pingk) *noun, plural* **pinks;** *adjective,* **pinker, pinkest.**

pinpoint To locate or fix exactly. The rescue team used a helicopter to *pinpoint* the place where the airplane had crashed.

pin·point (pin′point′) *verb,* **pinpointed, pinpointing.**

pint A unit of measurement. It is equal to half a quart.

pint (pīnt) *noun, plural* **pints.**

pinto A horse or pony that has spots or patches of two or more colors.

pin·to (pin′tō) *noun, plural* **pintos.**

pinwheel A toy made of colored paper or plastic that is pinned to a stick. It spins when the wind blows it.

pin·wheel (pin′hwēl′) *noun, plural* **pinwheels.**

pioneer **1.** A person who is the first to explore and settle a region. *Pioneers* opened up the American West. **2.** A person who is the first to open up or develop an area of thought or research. That doctor was a *pioneer* in heart disease. *Noun.*
—To be the first to explore or open up for others. American scientists *pioneered* in sending men to the moon. *Verb.*

pi·o·neer (pī′ə nēr′) *noun, plural* **pioneers;** *verb,* **pioneered, pioneering.**

pipe **1.** A tube of metal, glass, or other material used for carrying a gas or liquid. The water in our house flows through copper *pipes.* **2.** A tube with a bowl of wood or clay at one end that is used for smoking tobacco. **3.** A musical instrument that is in the shape of a tube. A person plays a pipe by blowing into it at one end. *Noun.*
—**1.** To carry by means of a pipe or pipes. The farmer *piped* water to his fields. The company *pipes* oil from the oil wells to a factory where it is made into gasoline. **2.** To put in or supply with pipes. The builders *piped* the new house for gas. **3.** To play on a pipe. The man in the parade *piped* a tune. *Verb.*

pipe (pīp) *noun, plural* **pipes;** *verb,* **piped, piping.**

pirate A person who robs ships at sea.

pi·rate (pī′rit) *noun, plural* **pirates.**

pistil The part of a flower where seeds are made. ▲ Another word that sounds like this is **pistol.**

pis·til (pist′əl) *noun, plural* **pistils.**

pistol A small gun that is held and fired with one hand. ▲ Another word that sounds like this is **pistil.**

pis·tol (pist′əl) *noun, plural* **pistols.**

piston A cylinder that fits closely inside a tube or hollow cylinder where it moves back and forth. The movement of the pistons in an automobile turns the wheels of the car.

pis·ton (pis′tən) *noun, plural* **pistons.**

pit¹ **1.** A hole in the ground that is natural or man-made. The workmen dug a deep *pit* in the back yard for the pool. **2.** A hollow place in the surface of anything. A woodpecker made small *pits* in the trunk of the tree. *Noun.*
—**1.** To make small holes in. Pebbles thrown against the window *pitted* the glass. **2.** To match in a race or contest. The young racing car driver *pitted* his daring against the experience and skill of the champion. *Verb.*

pit (pit) *noun, plural* **pits;** *verb,* **pitted, pitting.**

pit² The hard stone that is in the middle of some fruits. Peaches and plums have pits.

pit (pit) *noun, plural* **pits.**

pitch¹ **1.** To throw or toss. The boys spent the afternoon trying to *pitch* horseshoes around a stake. The baseball team had their best player *pitching* in the opening game. **2.** To set up. The boys *pitched* their tents in a little clearing. **3.** To fall or plunge forward.

The painter lost his balance and *pitched* off the ladder. The ship tossed and *pitched* in the rough seas. *Verb.*
—**1.** A throw to a batter in baseball. The umpire ruled that the *pitch* had gone right over home plate. **2.** A high point or degree. Mary worked herself up to a *pitch* of excitement just before her birthday. **3.** The highness or lowness of a sound in music. The music director hummed the *pitch* for the chorus before each song. *Noun.*
  pitch (pich) *verb,* **pitched, pitching;** *noun,* *plural* **pitches.**

pitch² A dark, sticky substance that is made from tar. Pitch is used to make the roofs of houses waterproof and to pave streets.
  pitch (pich) *noun.*

pitcher¹ A container with a handle and a lip or spout. A pitcher is used for holding and pouring milk, water, and other liquids.
  pitch·er (pich′ər) *noun,* *plural* **pitchers.**

pitcher² A person in a baseball game who throws the ball to the batter.
  pitch·er (pich′ər) *noun,* *plural* **pitchers.**

pitchfork A tool that looks like a large fork. It is used to lift and throw hay.
  pitch·fork (pich′fôrk′) *noun,* *plural* **pitchforks.**

Pitchfork

pith **1.** The soft, spongy tissue in the center of the stems of certain plants. The pith is important in carrying food and water from the soil up to the leaves of the plant. **2.** Any soft tissue that is like this. The pith of an orange is the soft white part that sometimes sticks to the fruit when you try to peel it.
  pith (pith) *noun.*

pitiful Arousing sorrow and sympathy. The lost puppy dog looked so *pitiful* that we took it home and kept it as a pet.
  pit·i·ful (pit′i fəl) *adjective.*

pity **1.** A feeling of sorrow and sympathy for the unhappiness of another. We felt *pity* for our friends who lost everything when their house burned down. **2.** A cause for regret. What a *pity* you have a cold and can't come to the party. *Noun.*
—To feel sorrow and sympathy for. We *pity* the people who lost their homes in the flood. *Verb.*
  pit·y (pit′ē) *noun,* *plural* **pities;** *verb,* **pitied, pitying.**

pivot A point, shaft, or pin that something turns on. The hands of a clock turn on a *pivot. Noun.*
—To turn on a pivot or as if on a pivot. The gun on that tank can *pivot* around and fire in any direction. Alan *pivoted* around and passed the ball to another player on his team. *Verb.*
  piv·ot (piv′ət) *noun,* *plural* **pivots;** *verb,* **pivoted, pivoting.**

pizza An Italian dish that is made of a flat baked crust topped with tomato sauce and cheese and sometimes also with mushrooms or sausages.
  piz·za (pēt′sə) *noun,* *plural* **pizzas.**

place **1.** A part of space; location; area. Here is a *place* to hang your coat. We visited many interesting *places* on our trip to Chicago. The *place* where I hit my elbow is still sore. **2.** A house. Ann's parents have rented a *place* in the country for the summer. **3.** A passage in a book or other writing. Sam lost his *place* when he dropped the book. **4.** A space or seat for a person. Would you save my *place* in line? **5.** A rank or standing. George Washington will always have an important *place* in the history of our country. **6.** Duty or business. It is not your *place* to criticize her work. *Noun.*
—**1.** To put or be in a particular spot or location. *Place* the napkin beside the plate. Helen *placed* third in the swimming race. **2.** To identify by connecting with the correct time and location. I've seen that boy before, but I can't *place* him. *Verb.*
  place (plās) *noun,* *plural* **places;** *verb,* **placed, placing.**
to take place. To happen. The band concert *took place* in the park.

at; āpe; cär; end; mē; it; īce; hot; ōld;
fôrk; wood; fōol; oil; out; up; turn; sing;
thin; this; hw in white; zh in treasure.
ə stands for a in about, e in taken
i in pencil, o in lemon, and u in circus.

placid Calm and peaceful. The lake was *placid*. Alice has a *placid* disposition.
plac·id (plas′id) *adjective*.

plague **1.** A very serious disease that spreads quickly among the people in an area. A plague often causes death. **2.** Anything that causes great misfortune. The trees were destroyed by a *plague* of caterpillars. *Noun*.
—To trouble or annoy. The new pupil *plagued* the teacher with silly questions. *Verb*.
plague (plāg) *noun, plural* **plagues;** *verb,* **plagued, plaguing.**

▲ The word **plague** used to mean "a blow or a wound." For example, a soldier could give a *plague* to another soldier with his sword. This led to the meaning "a great evil" and later that led to the meaning "a serious disease that affects many people."

plaid A pattern of stripes of different colors and widths crossing each other. Cloth with a pattern of plaid is used to make clothing and many other things.
plaid (plad) *noun, plural* **plaids.**

Plaid

plain **1.** Clearly seen, heard, or understood. As the airplane descended for a landing, the people and houses on the ground came into *plain* view. My friend made it *plain* that she did not agree with me. **2.** Straightforward; direct; frank. I will be *plain* with you and tell you the truth. **3.** Without decoration. Mother wore a *plain* black dress with a silver necklace. **4.** Not rich or highly seasoned. I like *plain* food. **5.** Common or ordinary. The people in this town are *plain*, honest folk. **6.** Not beautiful. That girl has a *plain* but sweet face. *Adjective.*
—An area of flat or almost flat land. Buffaloes used to roam the Western *plains*. *Noun*. ▲ Another word that sounds like this is **plane.**
plain (plān) *adjective,* **plainer, plainest;** *noun, plural* **plains.**

plan **1.** A way of doing something that has been thought out ahead of time. Do you have any *plans* for this weekend? The generals had a *plan* of attack. **2.** A drawing that shows how the parts of something are arranged. The

plans of the house show that there are three bedrooms on the second floor. *Noun*.
—**1.** To think out a way of doing something ahead of time. The political candidate hired someone to help him *plan* his campaign. **2.** To make a drawing of. The town hired an architect to *plan* the new school. *Verb*.
plan (plan) *noun, plural* **plans;** *verb,* **planned, planning.**

plane¹ **1.** A level or grade. Sam reached a high *plane* of success in his work. **2.** An aircraft that is driven by an engine. This is also called an **airplane.** Look up **airplane** for more information. *Noun*.
—Level or flat. This highway has a *plane* surface. *Adjective*. ▲ Another word that sounds like this is **plain.**
plane (plān) *noun, plural* **planes;** *adjective*.

plane² A hand tool with a sharp blade that sticks out from the bottom. A plane is used for smoothing wood and making it flat. *Noun*.
—To smooth with a plane. The carpenter *planed* the door down a little so it fit the door opening exactly. *Verb*. ▲ Another word that sounds like this is **plain.**
plane (plān) *noun, plural* **planes;** *verb,* **planed, planing.**

Plane

planet One of nine large bodies that move around the sun. The planets are Mercury, Venus, Earth, Mars, Jupiter, Saturn, Uranus, Neptune, and Pluto.
plan·et (plan′it) *noun, plural* **planets.**

▲ The word **planet** goes back to a Greek word meaning "wandering star." Long ago, when people looked up at the sky, it looked to them as if the other stars were standing still while the planets moved between them.

planetarium A building in which there is a device that shows the movements of the sun, moon, planets, and stars by projecting their images on a curved ceiling.
plan·e·tar·i·um (plan′ə ter′ē əm) *noun, plural* **planetariums.**

plank A long, flat piece of sawed wood that is thicker than a board.
plank (plangk) *noun, plural* **planks.**

plankton Very small plants and animals that float in the sea or another body of water. Plankton is the basic food for all animals that live in the sea.
plank·ton (plangk′tən) *noun.*

plant **1.** Any living thing that is not an animal. Plants cannot move around and are not able to smell, hear, see, or touch. Some plants can make their own food. Trees, flowers, grasses, and seaweeds are plants. **2.** The buildings, machinery, and tools that are used in making or manufacturing something. Automobiles are manufactured in *plants. Noun.*
—**1.** To set or place in the ground so that it will take root and grow. We *planted* our tomato seeds in May. Our neighbor *planted* a small maple tree in the front of his house. **2.** To place or set firmly in position. David *planted* his feet on the ground and refused to move. *Verb.*
plant (plant) *noun, plural* **plants;** *verb,* **planted, planting.**

plantation A large estate or farm where one crop is grown. Most of the plantations in the South before the Civil War grew either cotton, tobacco, or rice.
plan·ta·tion (plan tā′shən) *noun, plural* **plantations.**

planter **1.** A person or machine that plants. After plowing the soil to break up the ground, farmers use a planter to scatter the seeds. **2.** A person who owns or manages a plantation. **3.** A container for growing plants.
plant·er (plan′tər) *noun, plural* **planters.**

plasma The liquid part of the blood. The blood cells are suspended in the plasma.
plas·ma (plaz′mə) *noun, plural* **plasmas.**

plaster A mixture of lime, sand, and water that becomes hard when dry. Plaster is used for covering walls and ceilings. *Noun.*
—**1.** To cover with plaster. Tom *plastered* the ceiling to repair the damage done by the leak. **2.** To cover thoroughly. The men *plastered* the sides of buildings with posters advertising the circus. *Verb.*
plas·ter (plas′tər) *noun; verb,* **plastered, plastering.**

plastic A man-made material that can be molded and shaped when heated. The cellophane that candy is wrapped in is a plastic. *Noun.*
—**1.** Able to be molded and shaped. Wax is a *plastic* material when it is heated. **2.** Made of plastic. The radio has a *plastic* case. The *plastic* seats in this car are made to look like leather. *Adjective.*
plas·tic (plas′tik) *noun, plural* **plastics;** *adjective.*

plate **1.** A flat or shallow dish. Food is served or eaten from *plates.* The ushers at church pass the *plate* for the collection just before the sermon. **2.** A flat, thin piece of metal. Modern warships are covered with *plates* of steel. A knight's armor was made out of metal *plates* hinged together. **3.** A piece of metal on which something is or can be engraved. A car can be identified by the number on its license *plate.* In printing, the words or pictures to be printed are copied onto metal *plates* that fit into a printing press. **4.** Home plate in a baseball game. The umpire ruled that the runner had touched the *plate* before he was tagged with the ball. *Noun.*
—To cover with a coat of silver, gold, or other metal. The jewelry store *plated* the old silver box and made it look like new again. *Verb.*
plate (plāt) *noun, plural* **plates;** *verb,* **plated, plating.**

plateau An area of flat land that is raised above the surrounding country.
pla·teau (pla tō′) *noun, plural* **plateaus.**

platform **1.** A raised, flat surface. The speaker stood on a *platform.* We waited on the *platform* for the train. **2.** A statement of the principles or beliefs of a group. The political party adopted a *platform* that called for lowering the voting age.
plat·form (plat′fôrm′) *noun, plural* **platforms.**

platinum A soft metal that looks like silver but does not tarnish. It is more expensive than silver and is used in making jewelry and watches. Platinum is a chemical element.
plat·i·num (plat′ən əm) *noun.*

platter A large, oval dish. It is used for serving fish or meat.
plat·ter (plat′ər) *noun, plural* **platters.**

platypus An animal that has a wide flat bill, webbed feet, and soft brown fur. A platypus lays eggs. It is found in Australia.
plat·y·pus (plat′ə pəs) *noun, plural* **platypuses.**

play **1.** Something that is done for fun or pleasure; sport. The children spent several hours at *play.* **2.** A move or turn in a game. The quarterback made a great *play.* It is

at; āpe; cär; end; mē; it; īce; hot; ōld;
fôrk; wood; fōōl; oil; out; up; turn; sing;
thin; this; hw in white; zh in treasure.
ə stands for a in about, e in taken
i in pencil, o in lemon, and u in circus.

Susan's *play* next. **3.** A story that is written to be acted out on stage. We saw a *play* about Robin Hood. **4.** A way of acting or behaving. Tom is well liked for his sense of fair *play*. *Noun.*
—**1.** To do something for fun or pleasure. The children *played* all morning in the backyard. Carl *played* a trick on Pat. **2.** To act carelessly with something. Don't *play* with matches. **3.** To act the part of. He *played* an old sailor in the movie. The children *played* cowboys and Indians. **4.** To make or cause to make music. My sister is learning how to *play* the piano. Bill likes to *play* his radio when he studies. **5.** To act or behave. Ted's mother told him not to *play* so rough with the baby. **6.** To be in a game. Linda *played* for the first quarter of the basketball game. Our baseball team *played* Lincoln School for the city championship. *Verb.*

play (plā) *noun, plural* **plays**; *verb,* **played, playing.**

player **1.** A person who plays in a sport or game. My father was a good football *player* in college. **2.** A person who performs. That restaurant has a piano *player* every night. **3.** A machine that gives out music. The neighbors complained that our record *player* was too loud.

play·er (plā′ər) *noun, plural* **players.**

playmate A person who plays with another.

play·mate (plā′māt′) *noun, plural* **playmates.**

playpen A small pen that folds up easily. It is used for a baby or small child to play in.

play·pen (plā′pen′) *noun, plural* **playpens.**

Playpen

playwright A person who writes plays. William Shakespeare is the most famous English *playwright* who ever lived.

play·wright (plā′rīt′) *noun, plural* **playwrights.**

plaza A public square or open space in a city or town. There is a *plaza* with benches

and a large fountain in the middle of the shopping center.

pla·za (plä′zə *or* plaz′ə) *noun, plural* **plazas.**

plea **1.** A sincere request. The Red Cross made a *plea* for money to aid the victims of the flood. **2.** An answer given to a charge in a court of law. The prisoner gave a *plea* of not guilty at the start of his trial.

plea (plē) *noun, plural* **pleas.**

plead **1.** To make a sincere request; beg. The prisoner *pleaded* for mercy. **2.** To give as an excuse. She *pleaded* illness when they asked her why she was not coming to the party. **3.** To speak in defense of someone in a court of law. The lawyer agreed to *plead* the accused man's case. **4.** To give as an answer to a charge in a court of law. The accused thief will *plead* guilty.

plead (plēd) *verb,* **pleaded** or **pled, pleading.**

pleasant **1.** Giving pleasure. It was cool and *pleasant* by the lake. **2.** Having good manners; behaving in a pleasing way. She is a *pleasant* person.

pleas·ant (plez′ənt) *adjective,* **pleasanter, pleasantest.**

please **1.** To give pleasure to. The cool swim on such a hot day *pleased* him. My shiny new bicycle really *pleases* me. **2.** To choose. The children may buy whatever they *please*. **3.** *Please* is also used to ask politely for something. *Please* give me some more ice cream. Close the door, *please*.

please (plēz) *verb,* **pleased, pleasing.**

pleasure **1.** A feeling of delight and happiness. The circus clowns gave *pleasure* to the children in the audience. Carol takes *pleasure* in helping others. **2.** Something that gives a feeling of joy and happiness. It is a *pleasure* to see you again.

pleas·ure (plezh′ər) *noun, plural* **pleasures.**

pleat A flat fold made by doubling cloth upon itself and fastening it into place. Sally's skirt has *pleats*. *Noun.*
—To make pleats in. Mother *pleated* the skirt she was making. *Verb.*

pleat (plēt) *noun, plural* **pleats**; *verb,* **pleated, pleating.**

pled The injured boy *pled* for help. Look up **plead** for more information.

pled (pled) *verb.*

pledge **1.** A serious promise. The boys made a *pledge* to keep the secret. The man made a *pledge* to give money to the hospital fund drive. **2.** Something given as security. He gave the storekeeper his watch as a *pledge* that he would come back and pay what he owed. *Noun.*

—**1.** To promise. The children *pledge* allegiance to the flag each morning. **2.** To give something as security. The woman *pledged* her jewelry for the loan. *Verb.*

pledge (plej) *noun, plural* **pledges;** *verb,* **pledged, pledging.**

plentiful In a large amount; more than enough; abundant. Food was *plentiful* on the farm. We have a *plentiful* supply of wood for our fireplace.

plen·ti·ful (plen′ti fəl) *adjective.*

plenty A large amount; as much as is needed of something. There is *plenty* of milk left. She has *plenty* of money.

plen·ty (plen′tē) *noun.*

pliers A tool made for gripping or bending things. Some pliers can also cut wire.

pli·ers (plī′ərz) *noun plural.*

plod **1.** To move in a slow, heavy way. The children *plodded* through the deep snow. **2.** To work in a slow, steady way. My brother always *plods* through his homework.

plod (plod) *verb,* **plodded, plodding.**

plot **1.** A secret plan. The outlaws formed a *plot* to rob the stagecoach. **2.** The main story. That movie has an exciting *plot.* **3.** A small piece of ground. He lay down on a grassy *plot* in the shade. Mother prepared a *plot* of ground for her rose bush. *Noun.*

—**1.** To make a secret plan. The thieves *plotted* to rob the store. **2.** To make a chart or map of. The captain will *plot* the ship's course. *Verb.*

plot (plot) *noun, plural* **plots;** *verb,* **plotted, plotting.**

plover A bird with a straight, pointed bill. Plovers live on beaches or other open areas.

plo·ver (pluv′ər or plō′vər) *noun, plural* **plovers.**

plow **1.** A heavy farm tool for breaking up soil. A farmer uses a plow to prepare soil for planting seeds. A plow is usually drawn by a tractor or by animals. **2.** Something like a plow. A snowplow is a plow for removing snow from roads and other surfaces. *Noun.*

Plover

—**1.** To turn over with a plow. The farmer *plowed* the field for planting corn. **2.** To move ahead in a steady, strong way, as a plow does. The ship *plowed* through the waves. *Verb.*

plow (plou) *noun, plural* **plows;** *verb,* **plowed, plowing.**

pluck **1.** To pull off; pick. She *plucked* the feathers from the chicken. Ann *plucked* a rose from the rose bush. **2.** To pull off hair or feathers from. Grandmother *plucked* the chicken. **3.** To give a pull; tug. The child *plucked* at her mother's skirt for attention. *Verb.*

—**1.** The act of pulling. The musician gave a *pluck* to the strings of the guitar. **2.** Courage. The boy showed *pluck* when he stood up to the school bully. *Noun.*

pluck (pluk) *verb,* **plucked, plucking;** *noun, plural* **plucks.**

plug **1.** A piece of rubber, wood, or some other thing used to stop up a hole. She pulled out the *plug* to let the water out of the bathtub. **2.** A device with prongs, placed on the end of a cord or wire. It is used to make an electrical connection when put into an electrical outlet. *Noun.*

—**1.** To stop up. He *plugged* up the barrel with a wooden stopper. Grease *plugged* up the kitchen drain. **2.** To put the electrical plug of a machine or appliance into an outlet. *Plug* in the radio. **3.** To work in a slow, steady way. Tom always *plugs* away at his schoolwork. *Verb.*

plug (plug) *noun, plural* **plugs;** *verb,* **plugged, plugging.**

plum A soft, juicy fruit with red or purple skin and a pit. It grows on a tree that has oval leaves and small white or pink flowers. Dried plums are called prunes. ▲ Another word that sounds like this is **plumb.**

plum (plum) *noun, plural* **plums.**

plumage The feathers of a bird. The male cardinal has bright red *plumage.*

plum·age (plōō′mij) *noun.*

plumb To test or measure by means of a line with a weight at one end. He will *plumb* the well to see how deep the water is. *Verb.*

—A weight at the end of a line. It is used to test whether something is straight up and down, or to measure how deep something is. *Noun.* ▲ Another word that sounds like this is **plum.**

plumb (plum) *verb,* **plumbed, plumbing;** *noun, plural* **plumbs.**

at; āpe; cär; end; mē; it; īce; hot; ōld; fôrk; wood; fōōl; oil; out; up; turn; sing; thin; this; hw in white; zh in treasure. ə stands for a in about, e in taken i in pencil, o in lemon, and u in circus.

plumber   A person who puts in and repairs water pipes.
plumb·er (plum′ər) *noun, plural* **plumbers.**

plumbing   The pipes for bringing water in or taking water out of a building. The *plumbing* in that old house leaks.
plumb·ing (plum′ing) *noun.*

plume   **1.** A large, fluffy feather. Ostriches have long *plumes* on their tails and wings. **2.** A decoration made of a feather or feathers. It is sometimes worn on a hat or helmet.
plume (plo͞om) *noun, plural* **plumes.**

plump   Full and round; nicely fat. That healthy baby has *plump*, rosy cheeks.
plump (plump) *adjective,* **plumper, plumpest.**

plunder   To steal from; rob. The soldiers *plundered* the town. *Verb.*
—Something stolen. The outlaws hid their *plunder* in an old shed. *Noun.*
plun·der (plun′dər) *verb,* **plundered, plundering;** *noun.*

plunge   **1.** To put in suddenly. Jack *plunged* his hand into the water to try to catch the fish. **2.** To dive or fall suddenly. The swimmer *plunged* into the pool. The kite *plunged* to the ground. *Verb.*
—The act of plunging. Becky enjoys an early morning *plunge* in the lake. *Noun.*
plunge (plunj) *verb,* **plunged, plunging;** *noun, plural* **plunges.**

plural   Of or showing more than one. A *plural* noun is a noun that refers to more than one person or thing. A *plural* verb refers to the action of more than one person or thing. *Adjective.*
—The form of a word showing more than one. "Doors" is the *plural* of "door." "Children" is the *plural* of "child." "Are" is the *plural* of the verb "to be." *Noun.*
plu·ral (ploor′əl) *adjective; noun, plural* **plurals.**

plus   With the addition of. Two *plus* two is four. Dinner *plus* dessert cost eight dollars at that restaurant. *Preposition.*
—Somewhat higher than. His grade was A *plus. Adjective.*
—A sign (+) showing that something is to be added. *Noun.*
plus (plus) *preposition; adjective; noun, plural* **pluses.**

Pluto   The furthest planet from the sun.
Plu·to (plo͞o′tō) *noun.*

plutonium   A silvery, radioactive metal. It is used in splitting the atom and as a fuel in producing atomic energy. Plutonium is a man-made chemical element.
plu·to·ni·um (plo͞o tō′nē əm) *noun.*

plywood   A strong board made of thin layers of wood glued together. Plywood is used for building.
ply·wood (plī′wood′) *noun.*

P.M.   The time of day between noon and midnight. We get out of school at 3:00 *P.M.*

▲ **P.M.** comes from the first letters of the Latin words *post meridiem. Post meridiem* means "after noon."

pneumonia   A disease in which the lungs become inflamed.
pneu·mo·nia (no͞o mōn′yə *or* nyo͞o mōn′yə) *noun.*

pocket   **1.** A small bag or pouch. Pockets are sewn on or into clothes to hold pens, money, keys, and other small things. Pockets are also sewn inside suitcases or purses to carry things. **2.** A hole in the earth that contains gold or other ore. The miners drilled until they hit a *pocket* of iron ore. *Noun.*
—Small enough to be carried in the pocket. My father has a *pocket* watch. *Adjective.*
—To put in a pocket. Dan *pocketed* the coins. *Verb.*
pock·et (pok′it) *noun, plural* **pockets;** *adjective; verb,* **pocketed, pocketing.**

pocketbook   A bag used by a woman to carry money, keys, and other small things; handbag; purse.
pock·et·book (pok′it book′) *noun, plural* **pocketbooks.**

pocketknife   A small knife with one or more blades that fold into the handle.
pock·et·knife (pok′it nīf′) *noun, plural* **pocketknives.**

pod   The part of certain plants that holds the seeds. A pod splits open along the side when it is ripe. Beans and peas have pods.
pod (pod) *noun, plural* **pods.**

poem   A form of writing that is in verse and expresses imaginative thought or strong feeling. A poem is usually written with a rhythmic arrangement of words and often with rhyme.
po·em (pō′əm) *noun, plural* **poems.**

poet   A person who writes poetry.
po·et (pō′it) *noun, plural* **poets.**

poetic   Of or like poetry. Have you read the *poetic* writings of Robert Louis Stevenson?
po·et·ic (pō et′ik) *adjective.*

poetry   **1.** Poems. He likes to read *poetry.* **2.** The art of writing poems. She studied *poetry* in school.
po·et·ry (pō′i trē) *noun.*

poinsettia A plant with small flowers and large, bright-red leaves that look like flower petals. Poinsettias are used for decoration during Christmas.

poin·set·ti·a (poin set′ē-ə *or* poin set′ə) *noun, plural* **poinsettias.**

Poinsettia

point 1. A fine, sharp end. The knife has a *point.* You write with the *point* of your pencil. 2. A piece of land with a sharp end sticking out into the water. A light-house was built on the *point.* 3. A dot; mark. We use a *point* to separate dollars and cents when we write $3.50. A period is a *point.* 4. A place, position, step, or degree. Tourists visit the *points* of interest in our town. The chapter ended at an exciting *point* in the story. The plane was at the *point* of taking off. 5. The main part, idea, or purpose. What is the *point* of that joke? I don't see the *point* in eating if you are not hungry. 6. A special quality; trait. Honesty is one of her good *points.* 7. A score in a game. Our football team is ahead by six *points.* 8. One of the thirty-two marks that show direction on a compass. *Noun.*
—1. To show; indicate. Tim *pointed* at the bicycle he liked best. The road sign *points* in the direction of town. The teacher *pointed* out his mistakes to him. 2. To aim. The policeman *pointed* his gun at the thief. *Verb.*
point (point) *noun, plural* **points;** *verb,* **pointed, pointing.**

pointer 1. Something that points or is used to point. A long stick that is used by teachers to point out things on blackboards, maps, and charts is called a pointer. 2. A dog with short hair and long ears. Pointers are used to hunt birds. 3. A piece of advice; hint. Dad gave me some *pointers* on fishing.
point·er (poin′tər) *noun, plural* **pointers.**

Pointer

point of view A way of thinking about something; attitude. From my *point of view,* hockey is a more exciting game to watch than football.

poise 1. Calmness and confidence. Ed kept his *poise,* and was not nervous or confused when he spoke in front of the class. 2. Balance. The acrobat walked across the tightrope with perfect *poise. Noun.*
—To be or keep in balance. Sally *poised* on the edge of the diving board. *Verb.*
poise (poiz) *noun; verb,* **poised, poising.**

poison A drug or other substance that causes sickness or death by chemical action. Arsenic is a poison. *Noun.*
—1. To give poison to. The farmer *poisoned* the insect pests that damaged his crops. 2. To put poison in. Dangerous germs *poisoned* the canned soup. 3. To have a bad effect on. The woman *poisoned* the minds of others with lies and gossip. *Verb.*
poi·son (poi′zən) *noun, plural* **poisons;** *verb,* **poisoned, poisoning.**

poison ivy A plant that has shiny leaves with three leaflets. It is a vine that climbs on things or grows along the ground like ivy. It causes an itchy rash if you touch it.

poisonous Causing sickness or death by poison. The dog was bitten by a *poisonous* snake.
poi·son·ous (poi′zə nəs) *adjective.*

Poison Ivy

poke 1. To push against or into something. John *poked* his brother in the back with his finger. Mark *poked* the frog with a stick to make it jump. 2. To push. She *poked* her head out the window. 3. To move slowly. He just *pokes* along and never hurries. *Verb.*
—A pushing with something. He gave his friend a *poke* in the ribs with his finger. *Noun.*
poke (pōk) *verb,* **poked, poking;** *noun, plural* **pokes.**

poker¹ A metal rod for stirring a fire.
pok·er (pō′kər) *noun, plural* **pokers.**

at; āpe; cär; end; mē; it; īce; hot; ōld;
fôrk; wood; fool; oil; out; up; turn; sing;
thin; this; hw in white; zh in treasure.
ə stands for a in about, e in taken
i in pencil, o in lemon, and u in circus.

poker² A card game in which the players bet on cards that they hold.
  pok·er (pō′kər) *noun, plural* **pokers.**

polar Of or having to do with the North Pole or the South Pole. That explorer has led many *polar* expeditions.
  po·lar (pō′lər) *adjective.*

polar bear A large white bear that lives in the Arctic.

Polar Bear

pole¹ A long, thin piece of wood, metal, or other hard material. Jeff has a new fishing *pole.* ▲ Another word that sounds like this is **poll.**
  pole (pōl) *noun, plural* **poles.**

pole² **1.** Either end of the earth's axis. The North Pole is opposite the South Pole. **2.** Either end of a magnet or battery where the force is strongest. ▲ Another word that sounds like this is **poll.**
  pole (pōl) *noun, plural* **poles.**

polecat **1.** A small animal found in Europe. It has long, soft, gray fur. Polecats spray a bad-smelling liquid when attacked or frightened. **2.** The skunk of North America.
  pole·cat (pōl′kat′) *noun, plural* **polecats.**

pole vault A contest in which a person leaps over a bar raised above the ground with the aid of a long pole.
  pole vault (vôlt).

police A group of persons given power by a government to keep order and to enforce the law. *Noun.*
  —To keep order in. Patrolmen *policed* the city streets. The boys *policed* the summer camp by picking up trash and litter. *Verb.*
  po·lice (pə lēs′) *noun; verb,* **policed, policing.**

policeman A man who is a member of the police.
  po·lice·man (pə lēs′mən) *noun, plural* **policemen.**

policewoman A woman who is a member of the police.
  po·lice·wom·an (pə lēs′woom′ən) *noun, plural* **policewomen.**

policy¹ A guiding belief or plan for doing something. What is the school's *policy* about pets in class? We studied the government's economic *policy.* It is a good *policy* to always be polite to others.
  pol·i·cy (pol′ə sē) *noun, plural* **policies.**

policy² A written contract that is an agreement between an insurance company and the person being insured.
  pol·i·cy (pol′ə sē) *noun, plural* **policies.**

polio A disease that can cause paralysis; poliomyelitis.
  po·li·o (pō′lē ō′) *noun.*

poliomyelitis A disease that can cause paralysis by attacking the spinal cord. It affects mainly children. A vaccine now helps to prevent the disease. This disease is also called **infantile paralysis.**
  po·li·o·my·e·li·tis (pō′lē ō mī′ə lī′tis) *noun.*

polish **1.** The smoothness or shine of something. The waxed floor had a bright *polish.* **2.** A substance used to give a shine to something. He uses *polish* on his shoes whenever they look dirty. *Noun.*
  —To shine. Jim *polished* his shoes. *Verb.*
  pol·ish (pol′ish) *noun, plural* **polishes;** *verb,* **polished, polishing.**

polite Having good manners; showing a consideration for others; courteous. Carol is always *polite,* and says "thank you" and "please."
  po·lite (pə līt′) *adjective,* **politer, politest.**

political Of or having to do with politics, politicians, or government. She belongs to a *political* party. Democracy is one kind of *political* system.
  po·lit·i·cal (pə lit′i kəl) *adjective.*

politician A person who holds or seeks public office.
  pol·i·ti·cian (pol′ə tish′ən) *noun, plural* **politicians.**

politics **1.** The profession of holding public office; the managing of government. She went into *politics* and ran for Congress. **2.** Opinions or beliefs about government. Dad is conservative in his *politics.*
  pol·i·tics (pol′ə tiks) *noun plural.*

polka A lively dance.
  pol·ka (pōl′kə *or* pō′kə) *noun, plural* **polkas.**

polka dot A round dot placed over and over again to form a pattern on cloth or other material. This pattern is used on scarves, ties, blouses, and other things.
  pol·ka dot (pō′kə).

poll **1.** A collecting of votes or opinions. An election poll is the casting and recording of votes for persons who are running for pub-

lic office. A public opinion poll is the collecting of answers to questions about important issues or happenings. **2. polls.** A place where votes are cast and recorded. *Noun.*
—**1.** To receive votes. The winner of the election *polled* twice as many votes as the loser. **2.** To question a group of people to get their opinions about important issues or happenings. The newspaper reporter *polled* the town to find out how many people supported the President's decision. *Verb.* ▲ Another word that sounds like this is **pole.**
poll (pōl) *noun, plural* **polls;** *verb,* **polled, polling.**

pollen A yellowish powder made in the anthers of flowers. Pollen is made up of the male reproductive cells of flowering plants and fertilizes the female reproductive cells to form seeds.
pol·len (pol′ən) *noun.*

pollute To make dirty or impure. Smoke and the exhaust from automobiles *pollute* the air we breathe. Waste and garbage *pollute* our rivers and lakes.
pol·lute (pə lo͞ot′) *verb,* **polluted, polluting.**

polo A game played on horseback with long-handled mallets. The object of the game is to hit a wooden ball through the other team's goal posts.
po·lo (pō′lō) *noun.*

polygon A figure that has three or more straight sides. A square is a polygon.
pol·y·gon (pol′ē gon′) *noun, plural* **polygons.**

polyp A small animal that lives in the sea and has a body shaped like a bag or cup. The polyp's mouth has many tentacles around it that catch food. Some polyps are joined to other polyps in a colony. Corals are polyps.
pol·yp (pol′ip) *noun, plural* **polyps.**

pomegranate A round reddish-yellow fruit that has a tough skin, a juicy red pulp, and many seeds.
pome·gran·ate (pom′gran′it) *noun, plural* **pomegranates.**

Whole Fruit

Split Fruit

Pomegranate

poncho A cloak made of one piece of cloth or other material. It has a hole in the middle for the head. A cloth poncho looks like a blanket and is often worn for warmth. A waterproof poncho is worn by soldiers and hikers to keep dry.
pon·cho (pon′chō) *noun, plural* **ponchos.**

Poncho

pond A body of water surrounded by land. It is smaller than a lake.
pond (pond) *noun, plural* **ponds.**

ponder To think about something carefully. The two friends *pondered* over the arithmetic problem.
pon·der (pon′dər) *verb,* **pondered, pondering.**

pony A small horse. The children rode on the *pony* at the fair.
po·ny (pō′nē) *noun, plural* **ponies.**

poodle A dog with thick curly hair. Its hair is sometimes cut in a fancy way.
poo·dle (po͞od′əl) *noun, plural* **poodles.**

pool¹ **1.** A tank of water to swim in. Pools can be either indoors or outdoors. Our school has a *pool.* **2.** A small body of water. **3.** A small amount of any liquid. A *pool* of gravy spilled on the tablecloth.
pool (po͞ol) *noun, plural* **pools.**

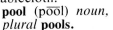

Poodle

pool² **1.** A game played with hard balls and a long stick called a cue. The game is played on a large table that has six pockets. The object of the game is to hit the balls into the pockets by striking one ball against another with the cue. **2.** Things shared by a

at; āpe; cär; end; mē; it; īce; hot; ōld;
fôrk; wood; fo͞ol; oil; out; up; turn; sing;
thin; **th**is; hw in white; zh in treasure.
ə stands for a in about, e in taken
i in pencil, o in lemon, and u in circus.

group of people. Dad belongs to a car *pool* in which each person takes a turn driving the others to work. *Noun.*
—To put together for a group to share. The children *pooled* their money to buy a present for their mother. *Verb.*
pool (pool) *noun, plural* **pools**; *verb,* **pooled, pooling.**

poor 1. Having little money. She is too *poor* to buy a new dress. 2. Below standard; less than needed; bad. He has *poor* health. The farmer had a *poor* wheat crop. He is a *poor* student. 3. Unfortunate. The *poor* boy lost his pet dog.
poor (poor) *adjective,* **poorer, poorest.**

pop 1. To make or cause to make a short, sharp sound. The balloon will *pop* if you squeeze it. He blew into the paper bag and then *popped* it between his hands. 2. To move or appear quickly or without being expected. Aunt Mary *popped* in to see us. He *popped* his head out the window. *Verb.*
—1. A short, sharp sound. The firecracker exploded with a loud *pop.* 2. A soft drink. Jean drank a bottle of *pop. Noun.*
pop (pop) *verb,* **popped, popping;** *noun, plural,* **pops.**

popcorn A kind of corn having kernels that burst open with a pop when heated. The kernels become white and fluffy, and can be eaten.
pop·corn (pop'kôrn') *noun.*

pope The head of the Roman Catholic Church.
pope (pōp) *noun, plural* **popes.**

poplar A tall, fast-growing tree. It has wide leaves and long, hanging stalks of flowers. The wood of the poplar is soft and is used to make pulp for paper and cardboard.
pop·lar (pop'lər) *noun, plural* **poplars.**

poppy A plant with round, red or yellow flowers. Opium comes from one kind of poppy.
pop·py (pop'ē) *noun, plural* **poppies.**

popular 1. Pleasing to very many people. Baseball is a *popular* sport. The beach is a *popular* place to go on summer afternoons. 2. Having many friends; well-liked. Bill is *popular* at school. 3. Of or for the people. Our country has a *popular* government. 4. Accepted by many people; widespread. It

Poppy

is a *popular* belief that a four-leaf clover will bring good luck.
pop·u·lar (pop'yə lər) *adjective.*

popularity The state of being popular. Gail's *popularity* at school was due to her friendly, happy nature.
pop·u·lar·i·ty (pop'yə lar'ə tē) *noun.*

population 1. The number of people who live in a place. What is the *population* of your city? 2. People. The entire *population* was forced to leave the town because of the flood.
pop·u·la·tion (pop'yə lā'shən) *noun.*

populous Having many people. New York is a *populous* city.
pop·u·lous (pop'yə ləs) *adjective.*

porcelain A kind of pottery. It is very hard, and is thin enough to see through when held to the light. Cups, plates, and other dishes are sometimes made of porcelain.
por·ce·lain (pôr'sə lin) *noun.*

porch A roofed area built onto a house. Grandmother's house has a large front *porch.*
porch (pôrch) *noun, plural* **porches.**

porcupine An animal whose body is covered with sharp quills.
por·cu·pine (pôr'kyə pīn') *noun, plural* **porcupines.**

Porcupine

▲ The word **porcupine** was made from two Latin words that meant "pig" and "thorn."

pore[1] A very small opening in the skin or other surface. Perspiration passes through the *pores* in our skin. ▲ Another word that sounds like this is **pour.**
pore (pôr) *noun, plural* **pores.**

pore[2] To look at, study, or think about carefully. John *pored* over his homework. ▲ Another word that sounds like this is **pour.**
pore (pôr) *verb,* **pored, poring.**

pork The meat of a pig used as food.
pork (pôrk) *noun.*

porpoise An animal that is warm-blooded and lives in the ocean. A porpoise has a round head with a short, blunt beak. Porpoises are very intelligent animals.
por·poise (pôr′pəs) *noun, plural* **porpoises** or **porpoise.**

Porpoise

porridge A soft food made by boiling ground grains in water or milk. It is usually eaten for breakfast. Oatmeal is a porridge.
por·ridge (pôr′ij) *noun, plural* **porridges.**

port **1.** A place where boats and ships can anchor and be safe from storms; harbor. **2.** A city with a harbor. New York City is an important *port.*
port (pôrt) *noun, plural* **ports.**

portable Easy to carry from place to place. Sarah took a *portable* radio to the beach.
port·a·ble (pôr′tə bəl) *adjective.*

porter **1.** A person who carries baggage. The *porter* at the hotel carried our suitcases to our room. **2.** A person who waits on people on a passenger train.
por·ter (pôr′tər) *noun, plural* **porters.**

porthole A small round opening in the side of a boat or ship. It lets in air and light.
port·hole (pôrt′hōl′) *noun, plural* **portholes.**

portico A porch or covered walkway. A portico usually has columns supporting its roof. Some churches, courthouses, and large homes have porticoes at the entrance.
por·ti·co (pôr′ti kō′) *noun, plural* **porticoes** or **porticos.**

Portico

portion A part. Mother gave Joan a small *portion* of potatoes. *Noun.*
—To divide something into portions. Jack *portioned* out the food among the boys on the camping trip. *Verb.*
por·tion (pôr′shən) *noun, plural* **portions;** *verb,* **portioned, portioning.**

portrait A picture of someone. The artist painted a *portrait* of the little girl with her dog.
por·trait (pôr′trit *or* pôr′trāt) *noun, plural* **portraits.**

portray **1.** To make a picture of someone or something. The artist *portrayed* the king in a painting. **2.** To picture in words; describe. In the book, the author *portrays* a girl's life in a small town. **3.** To play the part of. The boy *portrayed* a sheriff in the school play.
por·tray (pôr trā′) *verb,* **portrayed, portraying.**

pose **1.** A position of the body. She took a sitting *pose* for the picture. **2.** A way of behaving for effect. That boy's tough manner is just a *pose. Noun.*
—**1.** To hold a position for a picture. The children *posed* for the class photograph. **2.** To take on a false manner or appearance. The thief *posed* as a repairman to get into the house. *Verb.*
pose (pōz) *noun, plural* **poses;** *verb,* **posed, posing.**

position **1.** The place where a person or thing is. From his *position* at the window, Ken could see the whole parade. **2.** A way of being placed. He was seated in a comfortable *position.* **3.** A way of thinking about something; point of view. What is the senator's *position* on the proposal to increase taxes? **4.** Rank; standing. That judge has been a woman of high *position* for many years.
po·si·tion (pə zish′ən) *noun, plural* **positions.**

positive **1.** Certain; sure. The lawyer gave *positive* proof that the prisoner was guilty. I am *positive* that I just saw Ann walk by outside. **2.** Helpful or favorable. The teacher made some *positive* comments about my work. **3.** More than zero. Five is a *positive* number. **4.** Having a certain kind of electric charge. Magnets have a positive pole at one end and a negative pole at the other.
pos·i·tive (poz′ə tiv) *adjective.*

at; āpe; cär; end; mē; it; īce; hot; ōld;
fôrk; wood; fōōl; oil; out; up; turn; sing;
thin; **th**is; hw in white; zh in treasure.
ə stands for a in about, e in taken
i in pencil, o in lemon, and u in circus.

posse A group of men gathered by a sheriff to help him capture a criminal.
pos·se (pos′ē) *noun, plural* **posses.**

▲ The word **posse** goes back to the Latin word for "power." In the Middle Ages, the word was used as part of a phrase that meant "the force or power of a county." This force was all the men in a county that the sheriff could call out to help him.

possess **1.** To have or own. Johnny *possesses* a good singing voice. That man *possesses* great wealth. **2.** To have an influence over. What *possessed* him to be so mean to his little brother?
pos·sess (pə zes′) *verb,* **possessed, possessing.**

possession **1.** The owning of something. The two men fought for *possession* of the gold. **2.** Something owned. The family lost all their *possessions* in the fire. **3.** A place under the control of a foreign country. The Philippine Islands were once a *possession* of the United States.
pos·ses·sion (pə zesh′ən) *noun, plural* **possessions.**

possessive **1.** Showing that something belongs to someone. In the sentence *This is my book,* my is a possessive word showing that the book belongs to me. In the sentence *The pencil is yours, yours* is a possessive word showing that the pencil belongs to you. **2.** Showing a strong desire to keep something owned. Christopher is very *possessive* about his toys and won't let anyone else play with them. *Adjective.*
—A word showing that something belongs to someone. In the sentence *I met Karen's brother, Karen's* is a possessive. *Noun.*
pos·ses·sive (pə zes′iv) *adjective; noun, plural* **possessives.**

possibility **1.** The fact of being possible. There is a *possibility* that our team may win the championship. The *possibility* that friends might come to visit made Nancy clean up her room. **2.** Something possible. Snow is a *possibility* on Christmas.
pos·si·bil·i·ty (pos′ə bil′ə tē) *noun, plural* **possibilities.**

possible **1.** Capable of being, being done, or happening. It is not *possible* to be in two places at the same time. Learning French is *possible* if you study hard. It is *possible* that Grandmother may visit us this weekend. **2.** Able to be used or considered. The park is a *possible* place for our picnic. Jack is a *possible* choice for class president.
pos·si·ble (pos′ə bəl) *adjective.*

possum A small furry animal. The female carries its young in a pouch on its stomach. This animal is usually called an **opossum.** Look up **opossum** for more information.
pos·sum (pos′əm) *noun, plural* **possums.**

post[1] A piece of wood or other hard material that is set upright to support something. The boys helped their father set up the fence *posts.* The player kicked the football between the goal *posts. Noun.*
—To put up a notice of something. The teacher *posted* the names of the winners of the drawing contest. The sheriff *posted* a reward for the outlaw's capture. *Verb.*
post (pōst) *noun, plural* **posts;** *verb,* **posted, posting.**

post[2] **1.** A place where a soldier, policeman, or guard must be to do his duty. The policeman did not leave his *post.* **2.** A place where soldiers work or are trained. There is an army *post* near our town. **3.** A job; position. He has been named to the *post* of Secretary of State. *Noun.*
—To assign to a post. The police *posted* guards around the museum to protect the valuable painting. *Verb.*
post (pōst) *noun, plural* **posts;** *verb,* **posted, posting.**

post[3] **1.** A system for picking up and delivering mail. I will send the letter by *post.* **2.** A delivery of mail. The letter came in today's *post. Noun.*
—**1.** To put in a mailbox. I will *post* the package right away. **2.** To let know; keep informed. Sally will keep her friends *posted* about what she does at summer camp. *Verb.*
post (pōst) *noun, plural* **posts;** *verb,* **posted, posting.**

post- A *prefix* that means "after." *Postwar* means "after a war."

postage The amount of money charged for sending something by mail.
post·age (pōs′tij) *noun.*

postage stamp A small printed piece of paper put out by a government. It is placed on mail to show that postage has been paid.

postal Of or having to do with mail or delivering mail. The *postal* service in our town is good. A mailman is a *postal* worker.
post·al (pōst′əl) *adjective.*

post card A card that can be sent through the mail without an envelope. Some post cards have a picture on one side.

poster A large printed sign. A poster usually has a notice or advertisement for the public to see.
post·er (pōs′tər) *noun, plural* **posters.**

postman A person who delivers mail. This person is usually called a **mailman.**
   post·man (pōst′mən) *noun, plural* **postmen.**

postmark An official mark stamped on mail. A postmark cancels the postage stamp and shows the place and date of mailing.
   post·mark (pōst′märk′) *noun, plural* **postmarks.**

postmaster The person in charge of a post office.
   post·mas·ter (pōst′mas′tər) *noun, plural* **postmasters.**

post office A place where mail is brought and made ready for delivery and stamps are sold.

postpone To put off until later; delay. The baseball game was *postponed* until next Sunday because of rain.
   post·pone (pōst pōn′) *verb,* **postponed, postponing.**

posture The way you hold your body when you sit, stand, or walk. Tim's *posture* is good, because he stands straight and tall.
   pos·ture (pos′chər) *noun, plural* **postures.**

pot A round container for holding things. It is made of baked clay, metal, glass, or another hard material. Sue put the plant in a clay *pot.* Mother makes coffee in a large metal *pot* with a spout and a handle.
   pot (pot) *noun, plural* **pots.**

potassium A soft, silvery metal. It is a chemical element. Compounds that contain potassium are used to make soap, fertilizers, explosives, and other things.
   po·tas·si·um (pə tas′ē əm) *noun.*

potato The thick, rounded, underground stem of a leafy plant. Potatoes are eaten as a vegetable.
   po·ta·to (pə tā′tō) *noun, plural* **potatoes.**

potential Able to exist or happen; possible. That popular girl is a *potential* leader in our class. A board with rusty nails sticking out is a *potential* danger.
   po·ten·tial (pə ten′shəl) *adjective.*

Potato

potter A person who makes pottery.
   pot·ter (pot′ər) *noun, plural* **potters.**

pottery Pots, bowls, dishes, and other things made from clay and hardened by heat.
   pot·ter·y (pot′ər ē) *noun.*

Pottery

pouch 1. A bag; sack. The mailman took the letters out of his *pouch.* 2. A part like a bag. Kangaroos and opossums have *pouches* to carry their young in.
   pouch (pouch) *noun, plural* **pouches.**

poultry Chickens, turkeys, geese, and other birds raised for their eggs or meat.
   poul·try (pōl′trē) *noun.*

pounce To come down on suddenly and take hold of; leap on and attack suddenly. The eagle *pounced* on the small rabbit. The kitten *pounced* on the rubber ball. *Verb.*
—The act of leaping on and attacking something. *Noun.*
   pounce (pouns) *verb,* **pounced, pouncing;** *noun, plural* **pounces.**

pound[1] 1. A unit of weight. A pound is equal to sixteen ounces. 2. A unit of money in Great Britain and certain other countries.
   pound (pound) *noun, plural* **pounds** or **pound.**

pound[2] 1. To hit with heavy blows. Jack *pounded* the stakes of the tent into the ground. He *pounded* on the table to get attention. The waves *pounded* against the rocks during the storm. 2. To beat heavily. His heart *pounded* with fright.
   pound (pound) *verb,* **pounded, pounding.**

pound[3] A place where stray dogs and other animals are kept.
   pound (pound) *noun, plural* **pounds.**

pour 1. To flow or cause to flow. The milk *poured* on the floor when I knocked the glass over. He *poured* water into a pail. The crowd *poured* out of the theater. 2. To rain hard. It *poured* all day. ▲ Another word that sounds like this is **pore.**
   pour (pôr) *verb,* **poured, pouring.**

at; āpe; cär; end; mē; it; īce; hot; ōld;
fôrk; wood; fool; oil; out; up; turn; sing;
thin; this; hw in white; zh in treasure.
ə stands for a in about, e in taken
i in pencil, o in lemon, and u in circus.

pout To thrust out the lips to show displeasure. The little boy *pouted* because his mother had scolded him.

pout (pout) *verb*, **pouted, pouting.**

poverty 1. A lack of money; being poor. That family lives in *poverty*. 2. The lack of what is needed. The *poverty* of the soil caused the farmer to give up his farm.

pov·er·ty (pov′ər tē) *noun*.

powder 1. Fine bits made by grinding, crushing, or crumbling something. The plaster figure turned into *powder* when Jack hit it with a hammer. 2. Anything in the form of fine bits. Mother uses a face *powder*. He washed his clothes with soap *powder*. 3. Something in this form that explodes when set on fire and is used in guns and explosives; gunpowder. *Noun*.
—1. To make into fine bits. The glass *powdered* when it was crushed. 2. To cover with fine bits. She *powdered* her face. The baker *powdered* the rolling pin with flour. The light snow *powdered* the streets. *Verb*.

pow·der (pou′dər) *noun, plural* **powders;** *verb*, **powdered, powdering.**

power 1. The ability or right to do or cause something; strength or authority. Man has the *power* of speech. The motor has much *power* and can run the large machine. The Congress has the *power* to declare war. In olden days, people thought that witches had evil *powers*. 2. A person or thing that has strength or authority. The king's friend was the real *power* behind the throne. 3. Energy that can do work. Scientists are studying ways to use nuclear *power* in place of electricity. 4. The product of a number that is multiplied by itself a given number of times. 5 to the second *power* is 25. 27 is the third *power* of 3. *Noun*.
—To provide with power. That lawn mower is *powered* by a motor. *Verb*.

pow·er (pou′ər) *noun, plural* **powers;** *verb*, **powered, powering.**

powerful Having great power. That king is a *powerful* ruler. This big car has a *powerful* engine.

pow·er·ful (pou′ər fəl) *adjective*.

practical 1. Having to do with real life; coming from experience. John gained much *practical* knowledge of farming while visiting on a farm. 2. That can be used or done. Those heavy clothes are not *practical* for a hike on a hot summer's day. 3. Sensible; down to earth. She told her friend to be *practical* and save his money.

prac·ti·cal (prak′ti kəl) *adjective*.

practical joke A prank or trick. John's favorite *practical joke* was putting salt in the sugar bowl.

practically 1. Nearly; almost. My homework is *practically* finished. It is *practically* time for us to leave. 2. Truly; really. That player *practically* won the game by himself.

prac·ti·cal·ly (prak′ti kə lē *or* prak′tik lē) *adverb*.

practice 1. The doing of some action over and over again to gain skill. He needs more *practice* before he can be a good tennis player. *Practice* will help you to play the piano well. 2. The usual way of doing something; habit. She makes a *practice* of being polite to people. 3. Profession. Jack's older sister chose the *practice* of medicine as a career. *Noun*.
—1. To do some action over and over again to gain skill. He *practices* the violin every day. 2. To do as a habit. He should *practice* doing good instead of just talking about it. 3. To work at a profession. Phil's father *practices* law. *Verb*.

prac·tice (prak′tis) *noun, plural* **practices;** *verb*, **practiced, practicing.**

prairie Flat or rolling land covered with grass. A prairie has very few trees.

prai·rie (prer′ē) *noun, plural* **prairies.**

prairie dog An animal like a squirrel that lives in the prairie in underground dens. The prairie dog is a small, plump animal with short, round ears, short legs, and a short tail. It has a yellowish-brown coat.

Prairie Dog

praise Words that show high regard and approval. Gene's good work at school deserves much *praise*. *Noun*.
—1. To show high regard and approval of. The teacher *praised* Sue's good drawing. 2. To worship. "*Praise* ye the Lord." *Verb*.

praise (prāz) *noun, plural* **praises;** *verb*, **praised, praising.**

prance 1. To move in a proud, happy way. The boy *pranced* around the house in his new baseball uniform. 2. To spring forward on the hind legs. The horse *pranced* and leaped about the field.

prance (prans) *verb*, **pranced, prancing.**

prank A teasing trick; practical joke. Greg played a *prank* on his older brother.
　prank (prangk) *noun, plural* **pranks.**

pray **1.** To speak to God to give thanks or to appeal for something; worship God. Dad *prays* before each meal, thanking God for the food. **2.** To ask earnestly from God. All the people *prayed* for the safe return of the lost child. **3.** To be so kind as to; please. *Pray* be quiet. ▲ Another word that sounds like this is **prey.**
　pray (prā) *verb,* **prayed, praying.**

prayer **1.** The act of praying to God. The child was on his knees in *prayer.* **2.** The words said when praying. She says a *prayer* every night. **3.** Something prayed for. All her *prayers* were granted.
　prayer (prer) *noun, plural* **prayers.**

praying mantis A long insect having front legs that can grasp things.
　praying man·tis (man′tis).

▲ This insect is called a **praying mantis** because it holds its front legs in a way that looks like hands folded in prayer. *Mantis* comes from a Greek word that means "religious teacher" or "prophet."

---

pre- A *prefix* that means "before." *Prewar* means "before a war." *Preschool* means "before school."

preach **1.** To give a talk on a religious subject; give a sermon. The new minister will *preach* next Sunday. **2.** To give advice; urge. Father is always *preaching* about saving money.
　preach (prēch) *verb,* **preached, preaching.**

preacher A person who preaches.
　preach·er (prē′chər) *noun, plural* **preachers.**

precaution Something done beforehand to prevent harm or danger. Frank takes *precautions* before crossing a busy street by looking both ways.
　pre·cau·tion (pri kô′shən) *noun, plural* **precautions.**

precede To go ahead of. Gail *preceded* Tom through the door. The number 3 *precedes* the number 7.
　pre·cede (pri sēd′) *verb,* **preceded, preceding.**

preceding That goes before; earlier. In this dictionary, you will find the entry word **prairie** on the *preceding* page.
　pre·ced·ing (pri sē′ding) *adjective.*

precinct A part of a town or city. Each police *precinct* in our city has a police station.
　pre·cinct (prē′singkt′) *noun, plural* **precincts.**

precious **1.** Having great value. Gold is a precious metal. Pearls are *precious.* **2.** Dear; beloved. She lost her *precious* dog.
　pre·cious (presh′əs) *adjective.*

precipitate **1.** To make something happen suddenly. The boy's unkind remark to his friend *precipitated* an argument. **2.** To change vapor in the air into rain, sleet, hail, or snow.
　pre·cip·i·tate (pri sip′ə tāt′) *verb,* **precipitated, precipitating.**

precipitation The falling of water in the form of rain, sleet, hail, or snow. The weather forecast warned of some *precipitation* during the day.
　pre·cip·i·ta·tion (pri sip′ə tā′shən) *noun.*

precise **1.** Definite; exact. We had no trouble putting the model car together because the instructions were very *precise.* Jan measured out the *precise* amount of flour for the cake. **2.** Strict or careful. Walter speaks in a clear and *precise* way.
　pre·cise (pri sīs′) *adjective.*

precision Accuracy; exactness. This watch keeps time with great *precision.*
　pre·ci·sion (pri sizh′ən) *noun.*

predator An animal that lives by hunting other animals for food. Lions, wolves, and sharks are predators.
　pred·a·tor (pred′ə tər) *noun, plural* **predators.**

predecessor A person who held an office or position before another person. President Franklin Roosevelt was President Harry Truman's *predecessor* in the White House.
　pred·e·ces·sor (pred′ə ses′ər) *noun, plural* **predecessors.**

predicate The part of a sentence that shows what the subject is or what the subject does. In the sentence *Betty is pretty,* the words *is pretty* form the predicate. In the sentence *The dog ran home quickly,* the words *ran home quickly* form the predicate.
　pred·i·cate (pred′i kit) *noun, plural* **predicates.**

predict To tell beforehand. The fortune-teller claimed to be able to *predict* the future.
　pre·dict (pri dikt′) *verb,* **predicted, predicting.**

prediction **1.** The act of predicting something. The weatherman's job is the *prediction*

at; āpe; cär; end; mē; it; īce; hot; ōld;
fôrk; wood; fool; oil; out; up; turn; sing;
thin; this; hw in white; zh in treasure.
ə stands for a in about, e in taken
i in pencil, o in lemon, and u in circus.

of the weather. **2.** Something predicted. My *prediction* that our team would win has come true.

pre·dic·tion (pri dik′shən) *noun, plural* **predictions.**

preface An introduction to a book or speech. Our spelling book has a short *preface* written by the author in the front of the book.

pref·ace (pref′is) *noun, plural* **prefaces.**

prefer To like better. Sam *prefers* football to baseball. I *prefer* to study in the library.

pre·fer (pri fur′) *verb,* **preferred, preferring.**

preference Something liked better; first choice. Jane's *preference* is to go to the seashore rather than to the mountains this summer.

pref·er·ence (pref′ər əns) *noun, plural* **preferences.**

prefix A syllable or group of syllables added to the front of the word. A prefix can change the meaning of the word or form a new word. In the word *dislike*, *dis-* is a prefix. *Post-* in *postwar* is a prefix.

pre·fix (prē′fiks′) *noun, plural* **prefixes.**

pregnant Having one or more unborn young developing within the body. A woman is pregnant for about nine months before she has a baby.

preg·nant (preg′nənt) *adjective.*

prehistoric Belonging to a time before people started writing history. Dinosaurs were *prehistoric* animals.

pre·his·tor·ic (prē′his tôr′ik) *adjective.*

prejudice An opinion that has been formed in a hasty way without careful thought; bias. People show prejudice when they dislike other people because they belong to a different religion or a different race. *Noun.*
—To cause to have prejudice. The mean boy tried to *prejudice* people against the girl by telling untrue stories. Being hurt once by a dentist *prejudiced* Steve against all dentists. *Verb.*

prej·u·dice (prej′ə dis) *noun, plural* **prejudices;** *verb,* **prejudiced, prejudicing.**

preliminary Coming before the main part. The players took part in a *preliminary* warm-up before the game began. Mother bought food and made other *preliminary* arrangements for the party.

pre·lim·i·nar·y (pri lim′ə ner′ē) *adjective.*

premier A person who is the chief minister in a government; prime minister.

pre·mier (pri mēr′ *or* prim yer′) *noun, plural* **premiers.**

premise **1.** A fact that is thought to be true without needing proof. A premise is used as a starting point for a line of reasoning or argument. **2. premises.** Land and the buildings on it. The owner of the warehouse hired a watchman to guard the *premises* at night.

prem·ise (prem′is) *noun, plural* **premises.**

preparation **1.** The act of making something ready; being made ready. The cook was busy with the *preparation* of dinner. **2.** An action needed to make something ready. Ruth had to make many *preparations* for the party. **3.** Something put together for a purpose. That medicine is a *preparation* to help stop coughing.

prep·a·ra·tion (prep′ə rā′shən) *noun, plural* **preparations.**

prepare To make or get ready. Bill *prepared* himself for the game by practicing. We will *prepare* lunch.

pre·pare (pri per′) *verb,* **prepared, preparing.**

preposition A word that shows the relation between a noun or pronoun and another word. *By, into,* and *on* are prepositions. In the sentence "The cat climbed up the tree," the word "up" is a preposition.

prep·o·si·tion (prep′ə zish′ən) *noun, plural* **prepositions.**

prepositional Having a preposition; serving as a preposition. In the sentence *He is in the house, in the house* is a prepositional phrase.

prep·o·si·tion·al (prep′ə zish′ən əl) *adjective.*

prescription An order written by a doctor for medicine. The doctor gave Mrs. Brown a *prescription* for cough medicine.

pre·scrip·tion (pri skrip′shən) *noun, plural* **prescriptions.**

presence **1.** The fact of being in a place at a certain time. The *presence* of the growling dog in the room made me nervous. **2.** The area around or near a person. He signed his will in the *presence* of a lawyer.

pres·ence (prez′əns) *noun.*

present¹ **1.** In a place at a certain time. Were you *present* at the party? **2.** Going on at this time; being or happening now. Do you know who the *present* mayor is in your town? My older sister likes her *present* job. *Adjective.*
—The present time. He is not home at *present. Noun.*

pres·ent (prez′ənt) *adjective; noun.*

present² **1.** To introduce a person to another person. Brenda *presented* her friend to her parents. **2.** To bring or place before another person. Jeff *presented* himself at the teacher's office. **3.** To give. The principal

presented the awards to the students with the highest marks. The company *presented* Mr. Brown with a watch when he retired. **4.** To display; show. The class will *present* a puppet show. The theater will *present* a new movie. *Verb.*
—Something given. Joyce received many *presents* for Christmas. *Noun.*

pre·sent (pri zent′ *for verb;* prez′ənt *for noun*) *verb,* **presented, presenting;** *noun,* *plural* **presents.**

presentation The act of presenting something. The students went to the assembly for the *presentation* of the awards.

pres·en·ta·tion (prez′ən tā′shən *or* prē′zən-tā′shən) *noun, plural* **presentations.**

present participle A form of a verb showing an action or state that is happening or exists at the present time. In the sentence *I am reading, reading* is a present participle.

present tense A form of a verb showing an action or state that is happening or exists at the present time. In the sentence *He reads well, reads* is in the present tense.

preservative Anything that preserves things. Salt is used as a *preservative* for meat.

pre·serv·a·tive (pri zur′və tiv) *noun, plural* **preservatives.**

preserve **1.** To keep or protect. Dad *preserves* the wood of the old table by waxing it. It is important that we *preserve* our freedoms in America. **2.** To fix food so that it won't spoil. Mother will *preserve* the tomatoes by canning them. *Verb.*
—**1.** An area set aside for the protection of plants and animals. People cannot hunt in a game *preserve.* **2. preserves.** Fruit that has been boiled with sugar and then put in glass jars for later use. Grandmother made some strawberry *preserves. Noun.*

pre·serve (pri zurv′) *verb,* **preserved, preserving;** *noun, plural* **preserves.**

president **1.** A person who is in charge; head. Colleges, universities, governments, and large companies have presidents. **2. President.** The person who is the head of the United States government.

pres·i·dent (prez′ə dənt) *noun, plural* **presidents.**

press **1.** To use force on something; push on something. Jerry *pressed* the button to start the machine. She *pressed* the doorbell. **2.** To push forward; go on. Dad *pressed* through the crowd of people. **3.** To squeeze. Mother *pressed* juice from the grapefruit. **4.** To iron. Bill has to *press* his pants. **5.** To hold close; hug. Brenda *pressed* the kitten to her. *Verb.*

—**1.** A pushing on something. A *press* of the button started the elevator. **2.** A tool or machine for pressing. The factory has a large *press* for shaping metal. **3.** A machine for printing things; printing press. **4.** Newspapers and magazines and the people who write them. The President's speech was described the next day in the *press. Noun.*

press (pres) *verb,* **pressed, pressing;** *noun, plural* **presses.**

Printing Press

pressure **1.** Force caused by one thing pushing against another thing. The *pressure* of steam makes a steam engine work. The *pressure* of the man's foot on the gas pedal made the car go faster. The *pressure* of the atmosphere at sea level is about fifteen pounds per square inch. **2.** Strong demand; pressing influence. The parents put *pressure* on their children to do well in school. **3.** A burden; strain. The man went on a vacation to get away from the *pressure* of city life. *Noun.*
—To urge strongly. The salesman tried to *pressure* people into buying things they didn't need. *Verb.*

pres·sure (presh′ər) *noun, plural* **pressures;** *verb,* **pressured, pressuring.**

prestige Respect; high regard. Betty's winning of the state scholarship brought *prestige* to the school.

pres·tige (pres tēzh′) *noun.*

at; āpe; cär; end; mē; it; īce; hot; ōld; fôrk; wood; fool; oil; out; up; turn; sing; thin; this; hw in white; zh in treasure. ə stands for a in about, e in taken i in pencil, o in lemon, and u in circus.

pretend **1.** To claim. He likes to play chess, but he does not *pretend* to be an expert at the game. **2.** To give a false show. Joel *pretended* to be asleep. She *pretends* to like school, but she really doesn't. **3.** To make believe. The little boy *pretended* he was a pirate.
   pre·tend (pri tend′) *verb*, **pretended, pretending.**

pretty Sweetly pleasing; attractive; charming. His sister is very *pretty*. The artist painted a *pretty* picture. The teacher read a *pretty* poem about spring. *Adjective.*
   —Fairly; quite. It is raining *pretty* hard. *Adverb.*
   pret·ty (prit′ē) *adjective*, **prettier, prettiest;** *adverb.*

pretzel A crisp food baked in the shape of a knot or stick and salted on the outside.
   pret·zel (pret′səl) *noun, plural* **pretzels.**

prevent **1.** To keep something from happening. Dressing warmly may *prevent* a cold. Putting out campfires helps *prevent* forest fires. **2.** To keep from doing something; hinder. The noise outside his window *prevented* him from sleeping.
   pre·vent (pri vent′) *verb*, **prevented, preventing.**

prevention The preventing of something. The policeman's work was the *prevention* of crime.
   pre·ven·tion (pri ven′shən) *noun.*

preview A showing of something ahead of time. Mother and Dad went to a *preview* of the new film a week before it opened in the theaters.
   pre·view (prē′vyōō) *noun, plural* **previews.**

previous Coming before; earlier. Our team lost today's game, but has won all its *previous* games this year.
   pre·vi·ous (prē′vē əs) *adjective.*

prey **1.** An animal that is hunted by another animal for food. Rabbits, birds, and snakes are the *prey* of foxes. **2.** A person or thing that is a victim. The woman was the *prey* of a dishonest salesman. **3.** The habit of hunting animals for food. A tiger is a beast of *prey*. *Noun.*
   —**1.** To hunt for food. Owls *prey* on mice and other small animals. **2.** To trouble; distress. Worry about failing the test *preyed* on the student's mind. *Verb.* ▲ Another word that sounds like this is **pray.**
   prey (prā) *noun, plural* **preys;** *verb*, **preyed, preying.**

price **1.** The amount of money for which something is bought or sold. What is the *price* of that radio? **2.** The cost at which something is gained. The country won the war, but paid a great *price* in lives lost. *Noun.*
   —**1.** To set a price on. The bicycle is *priced* at $40. **2.** To find out the price of. Jan and her mother are going downtown to *price* the new spring coats. *Verb.*
   price (prīs) *noun, plural* **prices;** *verb*, **priced, pricing.**

prick To make a small hole with a sharp point. She *pricked* her finger with a pin. *Verb.*
   —A small hole in something. There were several *pricks* on her fingers from the thorns. *Noun.*
   prick (prik) *verb*, **pricked, pricking;** *noun, plural* **pricks.**

prickly **1.** Having small, sharp thorns or points. We planted *prickly* rose bushes along the fence. **2.** Stinging or tingling. She had a *prickly* rash from the heat.
   prick·ly (prik′lē) *adjective*, **pricklier, prickliest.**

prickly pear A cactus that has red or purple pear-shaped fruit.

pride **1.** The feeling a person has of his own worth and importance; self-respect. Although he was very poor, the man never lost his *pride*. **2.** Too high an opinion of oneself. He knew he was wrong, but his foolish *pride* kept him from apologizing to her. **3.** Pleasure or satisfaction in something that one does or is connected with. The mechanic took *pride* in his work. ▲ Another word that sounds like this is **pried.**
   pride (prīd) *noun.*

Prickly Pear

pried[1] He was unpopular because he always *pried* into other people's business. Look up **pry** for more information. ▲ Another word that sounds like this is **pride.**
   pried (prīd) *verb.*

pried[2] We *pried* the cover off the jar. Look up **pry** for more information. ▲ Another word that sounds like this is **pride.**
   pried (prīd) *verb.*

priest A clergyman of the Roman Catholic, Orthodox, and other Christian churches.
   priest (prēst) *noun, plural* **priests.**

primary **1.** First or greatest in importance; main. The travelers' *primary* concern was finding a place to stay for the night. **2.** First in order or in time. The first three or four grades of school are called *primary* school. Digging a foundation is one of the *primary* stages of building a house. *Adjective.*
—An election in which members of the same political party run against one another to be elected as their party's candidate. *Noun.*
 pri·ma·ry (prī′mer′ē) *adjective; noun, plural* **primaries.**

primary color One of the basic colors from which all other colors can be made. In mixing paint, red, yellow, and blue are the primary colors.

primate A man, an ape, or a monkey. Primates are the highest order of mammals.
 pri·mate (prī′māt) *noun, plural* **primates.**

prime **1.** The first or greatest in importance or value; main. His *prime* concern at the moment was passing the test. **2.** Of the best quality; excellent. We get *prime* beef from the butcher. *Adjective.*
—The best stage or condition. The trees were cut down before they reached their *prime*. *Noun.*
 prime (prīm) *adjective; noun.*

prime minister The leader of a parliamentary government. Both Great Britain and Canada have prime ministers.

primer A beginning book on a subject. That reading *primer* has short stories in it.
 prim·er (prim′ər) *noun, plural* **primers.**

primitive **1.** Having to do with an early or first stage in the development of something. A worm is a *primitive* form of life. The cave men were *primitive* people. **2.** Very simple or crude. A stone ax is a *primitive* tool.
 prim·i·tive (prim′ə tiv) *adjective.*

primrose A flower that is shaped like a trumpet. It grows in clusters on a garden plant.
 prim·rose (prim′-rōz′) *noun, plural* **primroses.**

prince **1.** The son of a king or queen. **2.** A nobleman of very high rank.
 prince (prins) *noun, plural* **princes.**

princess **1.** The daughter of a king or queen. **2.** The wife of a prince.

Primrose

prin·cess (prin′sis *or* prin′ses) *noun, plural* **princesses.**

principal The greatest or first; chief. Our *principal* task this weekend is to weed the garden. *Adjective.*
—**1.** The person who is the head of a school. **2.** A person who leads or plays an important role in some activity. *Noun.* ▲ Another word that sounds like this is **principle.**
 prin·ci·pal (prin′sə pəl) *adjective; noun, plural* **principals.**

principle **1.** A basic truth, law, or belief. Our government is based on the *principle* that all men are created equal. **2.** A rule of behavior that a person chooses to live by. It is against my *principles* to be late for an appointment. He made it a *principle* to answer all his letters promptly. ▲ Another word that sounds like this is **principal.**
 prin·ci·ple (prin′sə pəl) *noun, plural* **principles.**

print **1.** To put letters, words, or a picture on paper, cloth, or some other surface. The poem she wrote was *printed* in the town newspaper. We learned to *print* designs on silk. **2.** To write in letters like those made by type, instead of script. We learn to *print* our names before we learn to write them in script. *Verb.*
—**1.** Letters that are made by printing, not by writing in script. That book has large *print*. **2.** A mark that is made by pressing into something. There were *prints* in the snow where the birds had hopped around. **3.** A photograph made from a negative. We had *prints* made of the class picture to give to each member of the class. **4.** Cloth with a design on it. Ruth bought two new dresses in bright *prints*. *Noun.*
 print (print) *verb,* **printed, printing;** *noun, plural* **prints.**

printer A person or company whose business it is to print books, magazines, or other material.
 print·er (prin′tər) *noun, plural* **printers.**

printing press A machine that prints letters or words on paper.

prism A solid object that is transparent. A prism can break up a ray of light into the colors of the rainbow. A prism has three

at; āpe; cär; end; mē; it; īce; hot; ōld;
fôrk; wood; fo͞ol; oil; out; up; turn; sing;
thin; this; hw in white; zh in treasure.
ə stands for **a** in about, **e** in taken
i in pencil, **o** in lemon, and **u** in circus.

sides that are rectangular and equal and two ends that are parallel to one another.

prism (priz′əm) *noun, plural* **prisms.**

prison A building or other place where a person who is accused or convicted of a crime is forced to stay.

pris·on (priz′ən) *noun, plural* **prisons.**

prisoner 1. A person who is forced to stay in a prison. 2. Any person who is captured by someone else; captive. The kidnapers kept the boy a *prisoner* in the basement of the old house.

pris·on·er (priz′ə nər) *noun, plural* **prisoners.**

privacy The condition of being alone or private. The writer went to his cabin in the mountains so that he could have *privacy* to finish his novel.

pri·va·cy (prī′və sē) *noun, plural* **privacies.**

private 1. Belonging to a particular person or group. That is a *private* driveway, not a town road. 2. Not meant to be shared with others; not public. Our telephone conversation was *private.* 3. Not holding a public office. The senator retired and became a *private* citizen. *Adjective.*
—A soldier of the lowest rank. A private is next below a corporal. *Noun.*

pri·vate (prī′vit) *adjective; noun, plural* **privates.**

privilege A special right given to a person or group. We were given the *privilege* to stay up late on Friday night to watch television.

priv·i·lege (priv′ə lij) *noun, plural* **privileges.**

privileged Having special rights or advantages. The seniors are a *privileged* group, because they are the only class that is allowed to eat lunch outside school.

priv·i·leged (priv′ə lijd) *adjective.*

prize¹ Something that is won in a contest or game. The blue ribbon was the top *prize* in the dog show. *Noun.*
—That has won or is good enough to win a prize. Jack raised a *prize* calf for the state competition. *Adjective.*

prize (prīz) *noun, plural* **prizes;** *adjective.*

prize² To think very highly of. They *prize* Susan's advice about gardening because she knows a great deal about it.

prize (prīz) *verb,* **prized, prizing.**

pro A person who is a professional, not an amateur. Brad took lessons from a tennis *pro* at the town tennis courts.

pro (prō) *noun, plural* **pros.**

probability 1. The condition of being almost sure to happen; likelihood. Bad weather increases the *probability* of accidents on the roads. 2. A thing that is likely to happen. Rain today is a strong *probability.*

prob·a·bil·i·ty (prob′ə bil′ə tē) *noun, plural* **probabilities.**

probable Likely to happen or be true. It is *probable* that the governor will be elected for another term because he is very popular with the voters.

prob·a·ble (prob′ə bəl) *adjective.*

probably Almost surely; most likely. We will *probably* go on a trip this summer.

prob·a·bly (prob′ə blē) *adverb.*

probation A period of time for testing a person's ability, behavior, or qualifications for something. When John joined the company, he had three months' *probation* to see if he could do his new job. When a convict is let out of prison on *probation,* he is supposed to prove that he can act properly in society.

pro·ba·tion (prō bā′shən) *noun, plural* **probations.**

probe 1. A thorough investigation of something. The newspaper report led to a *probe* of prison conditions. 2. A tool or device used to test or explore. Surgeons use a *probe* to make sure a wound is clean. A space *probe* is a spacecraft with scientific instruments used to gather information about outer space. *Noun.*
—To investigate or explore thoroughly. The police *probed* the details of the prisoner's alibi. The doctors *probed* into the causes of the disease. *Verb.*

probe (prōb) *noun, plural* **probes;** *verb,* **probed, probing.**

problem A question or condition that is difficult to deal with or that has not been solved. There were ten *problems* on the arithmetic test. Rising prices are a serious *problem* in our country today.

prob·lem (prob′ləm) *noun, plural* **problems.**

procedure A proper way of doing something. A procedure is a definite order of steps that should be followed. We were told the *procedure* for leaving the building in case of fire.

pro·ce·dure (prə sē′jər) *noun, plural* **procedures.**

proceed To move on or continue something that is being done. The speaker waited for the applause to stop and then *proceeded* with his speech.

pro·ceed (prə sēd′) *verb,* **proceeded, proceeding.**

proceeds Money that is raised for a special purpose by selling something. The *proceeds* from the cake sale will pay for the class trip.

pro·ceeds (prō′sēdz) *noun plural.*

process A series of things that are done in making or doing something. The *process* of making bread is simple but takes time. He is now in the *process* of changing to a new job. *Noun.*
—To do or make something by a special series of steps. We read an article about how cheese is *processed. Verb.*
proc·ess (pros′es) *noun, plural* **processes;** *verb,* **processed, processing.**

procession 1. A continuous forward movement of something or someone. We followed the *procession* of the parade along the avenue. 2. A group of persons moving forward in a line or in order. The wedding *procession* started down the aisle.
pro·ces·sion (prə sesh′ən) *noun, plural* **processions.**

proclaim To announce publicly. The mayor *proclaimed* a town holiday when the President came to visit.
pro·claim (prə klām′) *verb,* **proclaimed, proclaiming.**

proclamation An official announcement of something. Abraham Lincoln made a *proclamation* in 1863 that freed slaves in many states.
proc·la·ma·tion (prok′lə mā′shən) *noun, plural* **proclamations.**

prod 1. To push or jab with something sharp or pointed. My friend *prodded* me with his elbow to get my attention. 2. To make do something. She tried to *prod* him into helping her wash the dishes. *Verb.*
—1. A push or jab. She gave her friend a *prod* to get her to move over. 2. Something pointed. The men used long poles as *prods* to keep the sheep moving through the gates. *Noun.*
prod (prod) *verb,* **prodded, prodding;** *noun, plural* **prods.**

produce 1. To make or create something. That factory *produces* automobiles. A cow *produces* milk. 2. To bring forth; show. The lawyer *produced* new evidence at the trial. *Verb.*
—Something that is made or yielded. They sell lettuce, tomatoes, carrots, and other garden *produce. Noun.*
pro·duce (prə dōōs′ *or* prə dyōōs′ *for verb;* prod′ōōs *or* prod′yōōs *or* prō′dōōs *or* prō′dyōōs *for noun*) *verb,* **produced, producing;** *noun.*

producer A person, company, or thing that makes or creates something. The United States is the leading *producer* of automobiles in the world. That man is the *producer* of a new movie.

pro·duc·er (prə dōō′sər *or* prə dyōō′sər) *noun, plural* **producers.**

product 1. Anything that is made or created. That farm sells dairy *products.* The story he told me was a *product* of his imagination. 2. A number that is gotten by multiplying two other numbers. When you multiply 3 times 4, the *product* is 12.
pro·duct (prod′əkt) *noun, plural* **products.**

production 1. The act of making or creating something. The *production* of steel is an important industry in that town. 2. Something that is made or created. The musical show was an elaborate *production.*
pro·duc·tion (prə duk′shən) *noun, plural* **productions.**

productive Making or yielding large amounts of something. Farmers today use many methods for making their land *productive.*
pro·duc·tive (prə duk′tiv) *adjective.*

profession 1. A job that requires special education and training. Law and medicine are two *professions* that require years of education. 2. The act of declaring something or stating a belief in something. The knight made a *profession* of his loyalty to the king.
pro·fes·sion (prə fesh′ən) *noun, plural* **professions.**

professional 1. Having to do with a job that requires special education. An architect is a *professional* person. 2. Making money from doing something that other people do for fun. Once the athlete played *professional* basketball he couldn't be in the Olympic games, which is only for people who are amateurs. *Adjective.*
—1. A person who has a job that requires special education. 2. A person who works for money doing something that other people do for fun. After many years of being an amateur golfer, he decided to try to become a *professional. Noun.*
pro·fes·sion·al (prə fesh′ən əl) *adjective; noun, plural* **professionals.**

professor A teacher having a high rank in a college or university.
pro·fes·sor (prə fes′ər) *noun, plural* **professors.**

at; āpe; cär; end; mē; it; īce; hot; ōld;
fôrk; wood; fōol; oil; out; up; turn; sing;
thin; this; hw in white; zh in treasure.
ə stands for a in about, e in taken
i in pencil, o in lemon, and u in circus.

profile 1. A side view or outline of a person's head or of something else. There is a *profile* of George Washington on a quarter. 2. A short description of someone or something. The newspaper printed a *profile* of the new mayor.

Profiles

pro·file (prō′fīl) *noun, plural* **profiles.**

profit 1. The amount of money left after all the costs of running a business or making or selling something have been paid. We bought the old boat for $100, spent $50 fixing it up, and sold it for $200, which gave us a *profit* of $50. 2. Anything that is gained by doing something. It will be to his *profit* to study hard for the test. *Noun.*
—To gain or benefit in some way. It will *profit* you to go to summer school to be better prepared for next year. *Verb.* ▲ Another word that sounds like this is **prophet.**
prof·it (prof′it) *noun, plural* **profits;** *verb,* **profited, profiting.**

profitable Giving a profit. The dry cleaner has a very *profitable* business.
prof·it·a·ble (prof′i tə bəl) *adjective.*

profound 1. Showing great understanding or knowledge. That book contains a *profound* analysis of man's feelings about death. 2. Very great or deep. We felt *profound* sorrow when we heard of his death.
pro·found (prə found′) *adjective.*

program 1. A list telling what will be done and who will do it in a play, concert, or other presentation. The names of the players on the baseball team appeared in the *program* sold at the stadium. 2. A play or other presentation or performance. The class planned an interesting *program* for their parents. What is your favorite television *program*? 3. A plan of what will be done. We have a new *program* to fight crime in our city.
pro·gram (prō′gram) *noun, plural* **programs.**

progress A forward movement. Heavy seas slowed the ship's *progress* through the ocean. Are you making any *progress* with your book report? *Noun.*
—To move forward. The building of the new house *progressed* rapidly. *Verb.*
prog·ress (prog′res *for noun;* prə gres′ *for verb*) *noun; verb,* **progressed, progressing.**

progressive 1. Moving forward. In science class, we followed the *progressive* growth of a lima bean from a seed to a full-grown plant. 2. In favor of reform or improvement. The

new senator had many *progressive* ideas for protecting against pollution. *Adjective.*
—A person who favors improvement or reform in politics or some other area. *Noun.*
pro·gres·sive (prə gres′iv) *adjective; noun, plural* **progressives.**

prohibit To not allow; forbid or prevent. Smoking is *prohibited* in the classrooms.
pro·hib·it (prō hib′it) *verb,* **prohibited, prohibiting.**

project 1. A plan or activity to be done. Harry's *project* for the weekend was to clean the basement. Our *project* for science class was to raise a baby chicken. 2. A group of apartment buildings that are designed as a unit. That is the site for the new housing *project. Noun.*
—1. To throw forward. A slingshot *projects* stones into the air. 2. To cause light, a shadow, or an image to fall on a surface. The movie was *projected* on a screen. The house *projected* a shadow over the garden. 3. To imagine or predict what will happen. The newspapers took polls to *project* the winner of the election. *Verb.*
proj·ect (proj′ekt *for noun;* prə jekt′ *for verb*) *noun, plural* **projects;** *verb,* **projected, projecting.**

projectile Any object that can be thrown or shot through the air. A bullet is a projectile.
pro·jec·tile (prə jek′tīl) *noun, plural* **projectiles.**

projector A machine that is used to show a movie or photographic slides on a screen or other surface.
pro·jec·tor (prə jek′tər) *noun, plural* **projectors.**

prominent 1. Well-known or important. The mayor was a *prominent* citizen of the town. 2. Very easy to see because it stands out in some way; noticeable. The tall tree was a *prominent* feature in the grassy field.
prom·i·nent (prom′ə nənt) *adjective.*

promise 1. Words given by a person, saying that something will or will not be done or happen. I gave my mother a *promise* that I would clean my room today. 2. Something that gives a reason for expecting success or progress in the future. He shows great *promise* as a writer. *Noun.*
—1. To give one's word that something will or will not be done or happen. I *promise* to be home by 5:30. 2. To give reason to expect something. The beautiful red sunset *promises* a sunny day for tomorrow. *Verb.*
prom·ise (prom′is) *noun, plural* **promises;** *verb,* **promised, promising.**

promontory A high piece of land that sticks out into a body of water. There was an old lighthouse on the *promontory.*
prom·on·to·ry (prom′ən tôr′ē) *noun, plural* **promontories.**

Promontory

promote 1. To give a higher rank or importance to. The store *promoted* him from clerk to manager. Everyone in the class will be *promoted* from third to fourth grade next year. 2. To help in doing or contribute to something. Eating too much sugar *promotes* tooth decay. Advertising *promotes* the sale of products.
pro·mote (prə mōt′) *verb,* **promoted, promoting.**

prompt Quick or on time. The restaurant gave very *prompt* service. It is good to be *prompt* when you have a date with someone. *Adjective.*
—1. To cause someone to do something. The sound of thunder *prompted* me to close the windows. 2. To remind an actor or speaker of what he is supposed to say if he forgets. Sally's job was to *prompt* the actress if she forgot her lines. *Verb.*
prompt (prompt) *adjective,* **prompter, promptest;** *verb,* **prompted, prompting.**

prone 1. Lying flat with the face downward. He stretched out *prone* on the floor and fell asleep. 2. Having the wish or tendency to do something. He is *prone* to eat too much.
prone (prōn) *adjective.*

prong One of the pointed ends of an antler, or a fork or other tool.
prong (prông) *noun, plural* **prongs.**

pronoun A word used instead of a noun to refer to a person, place, or thing without naming it. *I, you, he, who, what,* and *this* are pronouns. In the sentence "Patrick said he would water the flowers," "he" is the pronoun used to refer to "Patrick."
pro·noun (prō′noun′) *noun, plural* **pronouns.**

pronounce 1. To make the sound of a letter or word. People from different parts of the country *pronounce* certain words differently. If you look up the word "adult," you will see that there are two ways to *pronounce* this word, and both ways are correct. 2. To say or declare something to be so. The judge *pronounced* him not guilty.
pro·nounce (prə nouns′) *verb,* **pronounced, pronouncing.**

pronounced Strongly or clearly seen or heard. Claire has a *pronounced* British accent.
pro·nounced (prə nounst′) *adjective.*

pronunciation A way of making the sound of a letter, a word, or words. In this dictionary, the *pronunciation* of each word is shown after all the definitions.
pro·nun·ci·a·tion (prə nun′sē ā′shən) *noun, plural* **pronunciations.**

proof Facts or evidence showing that something is true. The lawyer had *proof* of the woman's innocence.
proof (pro͞of) *noun, plural* **proofs.**

proofread To read over written material to find and correct mistakes. You should *proofread* a paper you have written before you hand it in to the teacher.
proof·read (pro͞of′rēd′) *verb,* **proofread, proofreading.**

prop To hold up or hold in place by putting something under or against. He *propped* up the sagging roof with some lumber. Pillows helped *prop* the sick boy up in bed. *Verb.*
—A thing used to hold something in a position. He used a large stone as a *prop* to keep the door open. *Noun.*
prop (prop) *verb,* **propped, propping;** *noun, plural* **props.**

propaganda Ideas or information that a group of people deliberately spread to try to influence the thinking of other people. Often propaganda is not completely true or fair. The government published *propaganda* criticizing the way of life in other countries.
prop·a·gan·da (prop′ə gan′də) *noun.*

propel To cause to move forward or onward. The plane was *propelled* by jet engines.
pro·pel (prə pel′) *verb,* **propelled, propelling.**

at; āpe; cär; end; mē; it; īce; hot; ōld; fôrk; wo͝od; fo͞ol; oil; out; up; turn; sing; thin; this; hw in white; zh in treasure.
ə stands for a in about, e in taken
i in pencil, o in lemon, and u in circus.

propeller A device that is made up of blades mounted at an angle around a hub. When a propeller turns, it moves air or water and provides the force to drive a boat or aircraft forward.

Propeller

pro·pel·ler (prə pel′ər) *noun, plural* propellers.

proper **1.** Correct or suitable for a certain purpose or occasion. A carpenter must have the *proper* tools to do his work. **2.** Thought of in a strict sense. The village we live in is not part of the city *proper*. **3.** Having to do with a particular person, place, or thing. A *proper* noun usually begins with a capital letter. "Mary," "Friday," and "Boston" are *proper* nouns.
prop·er (prop′ər) *adjective*.

properly **1.** In a correct or suitable way. The dentist showed us how to brush our teeth *properly*. **2.** In a strict sense. *Properly* speaking, that book is not a novel, it is a biography.
prop·er·ly (prop′ər lē) *adverb*.

property **1.** Anything that is owned by a person. The school building was town *property*. That coat is my *property*. **2.** A piece of land. We bought some *property* near the ocean. **3.** A characteristic of something. Heat is a *property* of fire.
prop·er·ty (prop′ər tē) *noun, plural* properties.

prophecy Something that a person says will happen in the future. There was a *prophecy* that there would be a great flood in ten years.
proph·e·cy (prof′ə sē) *noun, plural* prophecies.

prophet **1.** A person who tells others a message he thinks he has from God. **2.** A person who tells what will happen in the future. ▲ Another word that sounds like this is **profit**.
proph·et (prof′it) *noun, plural* prophets.

proportion **1.** The relation of one thing to another with regard to size, number, or amount. The *proportion* of boys to girls in the class is two to one. **2.** **proportions.** The size or dimensions of something. He measured the *proportions* of the room.
pro·por·tion (prə pôr′shən) *noun, plural* proportions.

proposal **1.** A plan or suggestion that is presented to others for consideration. The student committee wrote a *proposal* to reorganize the rules of the school. **2.** An offer of marriage. He chose the night of the dance to make his *proposal* to her.
pro·pos·al (prə pō′zəl) *noun, plural* proposals.

propose **1.** To suggest something to other people for their consideration. Henry *proposed* Jill for class president. **2.** To intend or plan to do something. Jack *proposes* to study to be a doctor. **3.** To make an offer of marriage. Phil planned to *propose* to Jane that weekend.
pro·pose (prə pōz′) *verb,* proposed, proposing.

proprietor A person who owns a business or other property. The angry customer said she would complain to the *proprietor* of the restaurant.
pro·pri·e·tor (prə prī′ə tər) *noun, plural* proprietors.

propulsion The force that moves something forward or onward. The spacecraft was launched by means of rocket *propulsion*.
pro·pul·sion (prə pul′shən) *noun*.

prose Written or spoken language that is like everyday or normal speech, not like poetry.
prose (prōz) *noun*.

prosecute To bring a person or case to trial in a court of law. They *prosecuted* the man for theft.
pros·e·cute (pros′ə kyo͞ot′) *verb,* prosecuted, prosecuting.

prospect **1.** Something that is looked forward to or expected. Herb was excited at the *prospect* of owning a racing bike. Her *prospects* for success in her new job are very good. **2.** A person who will probably do something that is expected of him. The salesman thought the woman was a good *prospect* for buying the vacuum cleaner he was selling. *Noun.*
—To search or explore. The man went *prospecting* for gold in Alaska. *Verb.*
pros·pect (pros′pekt) *noun, plural* prospects; *verb,* prospected, prospecting.

prospector A person who explores for gold or other minerals.
pros·pec·tor (pros′pek tər) *noun, plural* prospectors.

prosper To be successful; do very well. The town *prospered* when several companies moved their factories there.
pros·per (pros′pər) *verb,* prospered, prospering.

prosperity Success, wealth, or good fortune in life. Since it had been a good season for crops, the farmers enjoyed great *prosperity*.

pros·per·i·ty (pros per′ə tē) *noun.*

prosperous Having success, wealth, or good fortune. The *prosperous* man tried to help others less fortunate than he.

pros·per·ous (pros′pər əs) *adjective.*

protect To keep from harm; defend. Football players wear helmets to *protect* their heads. That law is intended to *protect* the right of citizens to vote.

pro·tect (prə tekt′) *verb,* **protected, protecting.**

protection 1. The keeping of someone or something from harm. Our state has game preserves for the *protection* of wild animals. 2. A person or thing that protects. Susan put on a lotion as a *protection* against sunburn.

pro·tec·tion (prə tek′shən) *noun.*

protective Keeping from harm; protecting. A turtle has a *protective* shell. We put a *protective* coating of wax on the floors.

pro·tec·tive (prə tek′tiv) *adjective.*

protein A substance that is found in all living cells of animals and plants. Proteins contain nitrogen, carbon, hydrogen, and oxygen, and are necessary to life. Meat, fish, eggs, and milk contain much protein.

pro·tein (prō′tēn) *noun, plural* **proteins.**

protest An objection or complaint against something. The people of the town made a *protest* against the building of the new highway. The parents ignored the little boy's *protests* about going to bed early. *Noun.*
—To make a protest; object to. The students *protested* against closing the library on Sundays. *Verb.*

pro·test (prō′test *for noun;* prə test′ *for verb*) *noun, plural* **protests;** *verb,* **protested, protesting.**

Protestant A member of any Christian church other than the Roman Catholic Church or the Orthodox Church.

Prot·es·tant (prot′is tənt) *noun, plural* **Protestants.**

proton A particle found in the nucleus of an atom. A proton has a positive electric charge that is equal to the negative electric charge of an electron in the atom.

pro·ton (prō′ton) *noun, plural* **protons.**

protoplasm A substance that is like a jelly and is the living matter of every plant and animal cell.

pro·to·plasm (prō′tə plaz′əm) *noun.*

protozoan A tiny, one-celled animal that can be seen only through a microscope. An ameba is one kind of protozoan.

pro·to·zo·an (prō′tə zō′ən) *noun, plural* **protozoans.**

protrude To stick out. Rocks *protruded* from the snow.

pro·trude (prō trood′) *verb,* **protruded, protruding.**

proud 1. Having a strong sense of satisfaction in a person or thing. She was *proud* of the bookcase she had made. 2. Having a sense of one's own dignity and value. She was too *proud* to ask her friends for money.

proud (proud) *adjective,* **prouder, proudest.**

prove To show that something is what it is supposed to be, or does what it is supposed to do. They asked the salesman to *prove* that the washing machine would really get clothes cleaner. The lawyer *proved* the innocence of the prisoner. The new play *proved* to be a great success.

prove (proov) *verb,* **proved, proved** or **proven, proving.**

proven She has *proven* that she is a loyal friend.

prov·en (proo′vən) *verb.*

proverb A short saying that is used by many people because it expresses something that is believed to be true. "Haste makes waste" is a proverb.

prov·erb (prov′ərb) *noun, plural* **proverbs.**

provide 1. To give what is needed or wanted; supply. The art teacher *provided* paper, brushes, and paint for the students. Trees *provide* a shade from the sun. 2. To set as a condition. The law *provides* that a person is innocent until proven guilty. 3. To get ready for a future need. Her parents had *provided* for their children's college education by saving money every year.

pro·vide (prə vīd′) *verb,* **provided, providing.**

provided On the condition that; if. We're going on a picnic, *provided* it doesn't rain.

pro·vid·ed (prə vī′did) *conjunction.*

providing If; provided. I can go, *providing* my parents say it is all right.

pro·vid·ing (prə vī′ding) *conjunction.*

province 1. One of the parts that some countries are divided into. Canada is made up of ten provinces that are similar to the states

at; āpe; cär; end; mē; it; īce; hot; ōld;
fôrk; wood; fool; oil; out; up; turn; sing;
thin; this; hw in white; zh in treasure.
ə stands for a in about, e in taken
i in pencil, o in lemon, and u in circus.

of the United States. **2.** An area of activity or authority. Representing a person in a court of law is within the *province* of a lawyer.
　prov·ince (prov′ins) *noun, plural* **provinces.**

provision **1.** The act of giving something that is needed. The coach was responsible for the *provision* of equipment to the team. **2.** The act of planning ahead for a future need. Has any *provision* been made for holding the party indoors if it rains? **3.** A condition or requirement. One of the *provisions* for voting is the ability to read. **4. provisions.** A supply of food. The ship has *provisions* for one month.
　pro·vi·sion (prə vizh′ən) *noun, plural* **provisions.**

provoke **1.** To make angry. His rude reply *provoked* her. **2.** To stir up; excite. He *provoked* the cat into scratching him when he pulled its tail. **3.** To bring out; arouse. The newspaper article *provoked* much discussion.
　pro·voke (prə vōk′) *verb,* **provoked, provoking.**

prow The front part of a boat or ship; bow.
　prow (prou) *noun, plural* **prows.**

prowl To move or roam quietly or secretly. The tiger *prowled* through the forest. The thief *prowled* the streets at night.
　prowl (proul) *verb,* **prowled, prowling.**

Prow

prudence Good judgment and caution. He showed *prudence* in spending his money.
　pru·dence (prōod′əns) *noun.*

prune[1] A plum that has been dried for eating.
　prune (prōōn) *noun, plural* **prunes.**

prune[2] To cut off or cut out unwanted parts from something. We *pruned* dead branches off the tree. Mother *prunes* her rose bushes.
　prune (prōōn) *verb,* **pruned, pruning.**

pry[1] To look closely or curiously. He told her not to *pry* when she kept asking him why he had quit his job.
　pry (prī) *verb,* **pried, prying.**

pry[2] **1.** To move or raise by force. He *pried* off the top of the crate with a crowbar. **2.** To get with much effort. He tried to *pry* information about the accident from her, but she wouldn't tell him anything.
　pry (prī) *verb,* **pried, prying.**

psalm A sacred song or poem. There is a Book of *Psalms* in the Old Testament.
　psalm (säm) *noun, plural* **psalms.**

psychiatrist A doctor who treats mental illness.
　psy·chi·a·trist (si kī′ə trist *or* sī kī′ə trist) *noun, plural* **psychiatrists.**

psychologist A person who knows a great deal about psychology.
　psy·chol·o·gist (sī kol′ə jist) *noun, plural* **psychologists.**

psychology The study of the mind and of the way people behave.
　psy·chol·o·gy (sī kol′ə jē) *noun.*

public **1.** Having to do with or for all the people. The mayor made a *public* announcement that he was retiring from office. A *public* beach is for anybody to use. **2.** Working for the government of a town, city, or country. A judge is a *public* official. *Adjective.*
—All the people of a town, city, or country. The museum is open to the *public* every day. *Noun.*
　pub·lic (pub′lik) *adjective; noun.*

publication A magazine, newspaper, book, or any other printed material that is published. We subscribe to several *publications* about nature and natural history.
　pub·li·ca·tion (pub′li kā′shən) *noun, plural* **publications.**

public school A free school that is supported by people's taxes.

publish To print a newspaper, magazine, book, or other material and offer for sale. The boy wrote a short article that he hoped to have *published* in a magazine.
　pub·lish (pub′lish) *verb,* **published, publishing.**

publisher A person or company that publishes books, magazines, newspapers, or other material.
　pub·lish·er (pub′li shər) *noun, plural* **publishers.**

puck A black disk made of hard rubber. A puck is used in playing ice hockey.
　puck (puk) *noun, plural* **pucks.**

pucker To gather into folds; wrinkle. She *puckered* the sleeve of the blouse as she sewed it on.
　puck·er (puk′ər) *verb,* **puckered, puckering.**

pudding A sweet, soft dessert that is cooked.
　pud·ding (pood′ing) *noun, plural* **puddings.**

puddle A small pool of water or other liquid that is not very deep. There were *puddles* in the road after the rain. There was a *puddle* of milk on the floor where the glass had spilled.

pud·dle (pud′əl) *noun, plural* **puddles.**

pueblo An American Indian village made up of adobe and stone houses joined together in groups.

pueb·lo (pweb′lō) *noun, plural* **pueblos.**

Puerto Rican **1.** A person who was born or is living in Puerto Rico. **2.** Having to do with Puerto Rico or its people.

Puer·to Ri·can (pwer′tō rē′kən).

Puerto Rico An island in the West Indies. The people of Puerto Rico are United States citizens. The capital of Puerto Rico is San Juan.

Puer·to Ri·co (pwer′tō rē′kō).

puff **1.** A short, sudden blast of air, breath, smoke, or something like this. A *puff* of wind rippled the pond. A *puff* of smoke came out of the chimney. **2.** Anything soft, round, and fluffy. Mother gave me a big, pink powder *puff. Noun.*
—**1.** To blow or breathe in a puff or puffs. The engine *puffed* smoke. We *puffed* from climbing all the stairs. **2.** To swell up. His finger *puffed* up from the bee sting. *Verb.*

puff (puf) *noun, plural* **puffs;** *verb,* **puffed, puffing.**

puffin A sea bird that lives in northern regions. Puffins have black and white feathers, a plump body, and a large, brightly colored bill.

puf·fin (puf′in) *noun, plural* **puffins.**

pull **1.** To grab or hold something and move it forward or toward oneself. Two horses *pulled* the wagon. She *pulled* the closet door open. **2.** To remove or tear out something. The dentist had to *pull* my tooth. He *pulled* the weeds from his vege-

Puffin

table garden. **3.** To go or move. The policeman told us to *pull* the car over to the side of the road. The rowboat *pulled* away from the shore. *Verb.*
—**1.** The work done or the force used in moving something by pulling it. It was a long, hard *pull* to the top of the hill when his brother was on the sled. The strong *pull* of the magnet attracted the ring that had fallen in the drain. **2.** The act of pulling something.

Give a *pull* on the rope and the bell will ring. *Noun.*

pull (pool) *verb,* **pulled, pulling;** *noun, plural* **pulls.**

pulley A wheel with a groove around it that a rope or chain can be pulled over. Pulleys are used to lift heavy weights.

pul·ley (pool′ē) *noun, plural* **pulleys.**

pulp **1.** The soft, juicy part of fruits and vegetables. **2.** Any soft, wet mass of material. Wood pulp is used to make paper.

pulp (pulp) *noun, plural* **pulps.**

pulpit A platform in a church from which a minister gives a sermon.

pul·pit (pool′pit) *noun, plural* **pulpits.**

Pulley

pulse **1.** The rhythmic movement of the arteries caused by the beating of the heart. **2.** Any regular, rhythmic beat. We heard the steady *pulse* of the train engine.

pulse (puls) *noun, plural* **pulses.**

puma A wild cat that lives in North and South America. This animal is usually called a **cougar.** Look up **cougar** for more information.

pu·ma (pyoo′mə) *noun, plural* **pumas.**

pump A machine that is used to move water or other liquids or a gas from one place to another. The car drew up to the gasoline *pump. Noun.*
—**1.** To move a liquid or gas from one place to another with a pump. We *pumped* water into the swimming pool. My brother *pumps* gas at the gas station on weekends. **2.** To fill with air or other gas. Don *pumped* up the flat tire. **3.** To get or try to get information from by questioning closely. The police *pumped* the suspect about his friends. *Verb.*

pump (pump) *noun, plural* **pumps;** *verb,* **pumped, pumping.**

at; āpe; cär; end; mē; it; īce; hot; ōld; fôrk; wood; fool; oil; out; up; turn; sing; thin; this; hw in white; zh in treasure. ə stands for a in about, e in taken i in pencil, o in lemon, and u in circus.

pumpkin A large, yellowish-orange fruit with a hard outer rind and a soft pulp inside. Pumpkins grow on vines.

Pumpkin

pump·kin (pump′kin or pung′kin) *noun, plural* **pumpkins.**

pun A joking way of saying something by using a word that has two different meanings or two words that sound the same but have different meanings. For example: "The robbers sat in their prison cell talking about old *crimes*" (*times*).

pun (pun) *noun, plural* **puns.**

punch¹ **1.** To hit a person or thing with the fist or part of the hand. The man *punched* him and gave him a black eye. She *punched* the elevator button for the eighth floor. **2.** To herd or drive cattle. The cowboy *punched* cattle to earn some money. *Verb.*
—A blow with the fist or part of the hand. He knocked out his opponent with one powerful *punch. Noun.*

punch (punch) *verb,* **punched, punching;** *noun, plural* **punches.**

punch² A tool for making holes in or putting a design on a surface. You can use a paper *punch* to fix plain paper so that it will fit in your notebook. *Noun.*
—To make holes in or press a design on with a punch. The man *punched* another hole in the belt so he could tighten it. *Verb.*

punch (punch) *noun, plural* **punches;** *verb,* **punched, punching.**

punch³ A drink made by mixing different fruit juices, sodas, or other ingredients.

punch (punch) *noun, plural* **punches.**

punctual On time; prompt. He always tried to be *punctual* for his appointments.

punc·tu·al (pungk′choo əl) *adjective.*

punctuate To mark written material with periods, commas, and other punctuation marks to make the meaning clear.

punc·tu·ate (pungk′choo āt′) *verb,* **punctuated, punctuating.**

punctuation The use of periods, commas, and other marks to make the meaning of written material clear. Her spelling was excellent, but she was poor at *punctuation*.

punc·tu·a·tion (pungk′choo ā′shən) *noun.*

punctuation mark Any of a group of marks used to make the meaning of written material clear. Periods, commas, semicolons, hyphens, quotation marks, and question marks are punctuation marks.

puncture To make a hole in something with a sharp object. We *punctured* the balloons with pins. The nail *punctured* the left front tire. *Verb.*
—A hole made by a sharp object. The man at the garage fixed the *puncture* in the tire. *Noun.*

punc·ture (pungk′chər) *verb,* **punctured, puncturing;** *noun, plural* **punctures.**

punish **1.** To make a person suffer for a wrong he has done. The law *punishes* criminals. She was *punished* for lying by being ignored by her friends. **2.** To treat or handle roughly. The bumpy dirt road really *punished* the car.

pun·ish (pun′ish) *verb,* **punished, punishing.**

punishment **1.** The act of punishing. The *punishment* of criminals is left to the courts. **2.** The penalty for a crime or wrong. His *punishment* for robbery was five years in prison.

pun·ish·ment (pun′ish mənt) *noun, plural* **punishments.**

pup **1.** A young dog; puppy. **2.** A young fox, wolf, or seal.

pup (pup) *noun, plural* **pups.**

pupa An insect at the stage after it is a larva and before it is an adult. A caterpillar in its cocoon is a pupa.

pu·pa (pyo͞o′pə) *noun, plural* **pupas.**

pupil¹ A person who is studying in school or with a teacher; student.

pu·pil (pyo͞o′pəl) *noun, plural* **pupils.**

pupil² The opening in the center of the iris of the eye. Light enters the eye through the pupil. The pupil gets smaller in bright light and larger in darkness.

pu·pil (pyo͞o′pəl) *noun, plural* **pupils.**

Puppets

puppet A small doll that is made to look like a person or animal and has parts that can be moved. Some puppets fit over a person's hand and are made to move by the fingers.

Other puppets have strings attached to parts of their bodies and are moved by a person pulling the strings.

pup·pet (pup′it) *noun, plural* **puppets.**

puppy   A young dog.

pup·py (pup′ē) *noun, plural* **puppies.**

purchase   To get something by paying money; buy. We *purchased* our train ticket at the station. *Verb.*

—Something that is gotten by being paid for. She walked into the house and piled her *purchases* on the table. *Noun.*

pur·chase (pur′chəs) *verb,* **purchased, purchasing;** *noun, plural* **purchases.**

pure   **1.** Not mixed with anything else. I bought a scarf of *pure* silk. We drank *pure* water from a mountain stream. **2.** Nothing but. It was *pure* luck that I won the game.

pure (pyoor) *adjective,* **purer, purest.**

purify   To make pure or clean. The filter will *purify* the air.

pu·ri·fy (pyoor′ə fī′) *verb,* **purified, purifying.**

Puritan   A person who was a member of a group of Protestants in England during the 1500s and 1600s. The Puritans wanted simpler forms of worship and stricter morals than those of the Church of England. Some Puritans fled England and settled in America.

Pu·ri·tan (pyoor′it ən) *noun, plural* **Puritans.**

purity   The condition of being pure or clean. We tested the *purity* of the water in the swimming pool.

pu·ri·ty (pyoor′ə tē) *noun.*

purple   The color that is made by mixing red and blue. *Noun.*

—Having the color purple. *Adjective.*

pur·ple (pur′pəl) *noun, plural* **purples;** *adjective.*

purpose   The reason for which something is made or done. What is the *purpose* of that hook on the wall? What is your *purpose* in going to college?

pur·pose (pur′pəs) *noun, plural* **purposes.**

on purpose. Not by accident; deliberately. He spilled the milk *on purpose* because he was mad.

purposely   On purpose; deliberately. He *purposely* left the ball park before the game was over to get out ahead of the crowd.

pur·pose·ly (pur′pəs lē) *adverb.*

purr   A soft, murmuring sound like the one made by a cat when it's happy. *Noun.*

—To make a soft, murmuring sound. The kitten *purred* when I petted it. *Verb.*

purr (pur) *noun, plural* **purrs;** *verb,* **purred, purring.**

purse   A woman's handbag that is used to carry money, keys, and other small things. *Noun.*

—To draw together. She *pursed* her lips in anger. *Verb.*

purse (purs) *noun, plural* **purses;** *verb,* **pursed, pursing.**

pursue   **1.** To follow in order to catch up to or capture. The police *pursued* the thief down the street. **2.** To follow or carry out. Wes *pursues* his hobby of stamp collecting very seriously.

pur·sue (pər soo′) *verb,* **pursued, pursuing.**

pursuit   **1.** The act of pursuing. The police were in *pursuit* of the speeding car. **2.** A hobby or other interest a person has. Making model cars is one of Bob's *pursuits*.

pur·suit (pər soot′) *noun, plural* **pursuits.**

pus   A thick, yellowish fluid that collects in a sore or other infection in a person's body.

pus (pus) *noun.*

push   **1.** To press on something in order to move it. He *pushed* the shopping cart through the market. You have to *push* hard against that door to open it. **2.** To move forward with effort. We had to *push* through the crowd. **3.** To work hard to do or sell something. The senator *pushed* for tax reform. The store is *pushing* canned soup this week. *Verb.*

—A shove or strong effort to move forward. She gave him a *push* that almost knocked him down. They made a big *push* to finish the work by five o'clock. *Noun.*

push (poosh) *verb,* **pushed, pushing;** *noun, plural* **pushes.**

Pushcart

pushcart   A small cart that is meant to be

---

at; āpe; cär; end; mē; it; īce; hot; ōld;
fôrk; wood; fōol; oil; out; up; turn; sing;
thin; this; hw in white; zh in treasure.
ə stands for a in about, e in taken
i in pencil, o in lemon, and u in circus.

pushed by a person instead of pulled by a horse. We saw peddlers with *pushcarts* full of fresh fruit and vegetables on the streets of the town.

push·cart (poosh′kärt′) *noun, plural* **push-carts.**

push-up An exercise in which a person lies face down and raises and lowers himself by straightening and bending his arms while keeping the rest of his body straight.

push-up (poosh′up′) *noun, plural* **push-ups.**

pussy willow A shrub that has silvery, furry catkins that grow on long straight branches.

pus·sy willow (poos′ē).

Pussy Willow

put 1. To cause something or someone to be in a certain place, condition, or position; place; set. *Put* the box on the table. Her friendly smile *put* him at ease. You *put* them to a lot of trouble by being late. The boy *put* the blame on his friend. 2. To say; state. *Put* your question clearly.

put (poot) *verb,* **put, putting.**

to put off. To delay or postpone. She *put off* going to the dentist.

to put on. To present or perform. The class *put on* a Christmas play.

to put out. 1. To extinguish. The firemen *put out* the fire. **2.** To annoy. She was *put out* that they didn't ask her to go with them to the movies.

to put up. To build. There is a new shopping center being *put up* down the road.

to put up with. To bear patiently; endure. I *put up with* his rudeness for one day, and then told him that he was behaving very badly.

Python

putt To hit a golf ball with a gentle stroke when it is near the hole so it will go into the cup.

putt (put) *verb,* **putted, putting.**

putty A soft, claylike material used to fill cracks in wood, or to fasten panes of glass to window frames.

put·ty (put′ē) *noun, plural* **putties.**

puzzle Something that is confusing or is difficult to do. It is fun to put together a jigsaw *puzzle* on a rainy day. The solution to the mystery was a *puzzle. Noun.*
—**1.** To confuse or be hard to understand. The arithmetic problem *puzzled* him. Her unfriendly behavior *puzzled* her friends. **2.** To be confused by something. He *puzzled* over the answer to the problem. *Verb.*

puz·zle (puz′əl) *noun, plural* **puzzles;** *verb,* **puzzled, puzzling.**

pygmy 1. A very small person or thing. 2. Pygmy. A member of a dark-skinned tribe of people living in Africa. Pygmies are usually less than five feet tall.

pyg·my (pig′mē) *noun, plural* **pygmies.**

Pyramid

pyramid 1. Pyramid. A huge stone structure that is square at the bottom and has four sides shaped like triangles with the points meeting at the top. The Pyramids were built as tombs in ancient Egypt. 2. A solid object or other thing shaped like a Pyramid.

pyr·a·mid (pir′ə mid′) *noun, plural* **pyra-mids.**

python A large snake that coils around its prey and crushes or suffocates it.

py·thon (pī′thon) *noun, plural* **pythons.**

at; āpe; cär; end; mē; it; īce; hot; ōld;
fôrk; wood; fool; oil; out; up; turn; sing;
thin; this; hw in white; zh in treasure.
ə stands for a in about, e in taken
i in pencil, o in lemon, and u in circus.

504

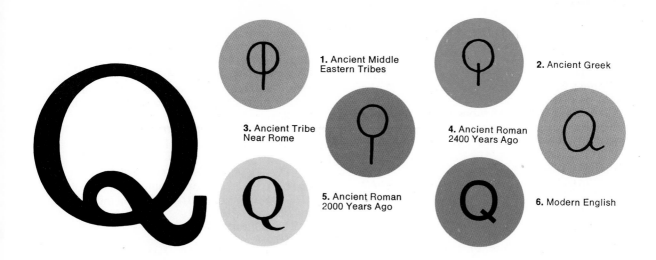

1. Ancient Middle Eastern Tribes

2. Ancient Greek

3. Ancient Tribe Near Rome

4. Ancient Roman 2400 Years Ago

5. Ancient Roman 2000 Years Ago

6. Modern English

Q is the seventeenth letter of the alphabet. It is one of very few letters whose shape has hardly changed throughout the entire history of the alphabet. The oldest form of the letter **Q** was a letter used in the alphabet of several ancient tribes (**1**) in the Middle East. They used this letter to stand for a *k* sound made at the back of the throat. The ancient Greeks (**2**) borrowed this letter about 3000 years ago. The Greek letter was borrowed by an ancient tribe (**3**) that settled north of Rome about 2800 years ago. Their alphabet had three different letters that stood for the *k* sound. These three letters were old forms of our modern letters **C**, **K**, and **Q**. They used their form of **C** before the letters **E** and **I**, and their form of **K** before the letter **A**. Their form of **Q** was used only before the letter **U**. When the Romans (**4**) borrowed these letters, they used them in the same special ways. Several hundred years later, the Romans stopped using all these letters to stand for the same sound. They used their form of **Q** only before the letter **U** to stand for the *kw* sound. Our spelling rule that **Q** is followed by **U** comes from this old Roman spelling rule. By about 2000 years ago (**5**), the Romans were writing and pronouncing the letter **Q** in the same way that we write and pronounce the letter **Q** today (**6**).

q, Q   The seventeenth letter of the alphabet.
   q, Q (kyo͞o) *noun, plural* **q's, Q's.**

quack   The harsh, flat sound that a duck makes. *Noun.*
—To make the sound that a duck makes. *Verb.*
   quack (kwak) *noun, plural* **quacks;** *verb,* **quacked, quacking.**

quadrilateral   A design or figure having four sides and four angles. A square is a quadrilateral.
   quad·ri·lat·er·al (kwod′rə lat′ər əl) *noun, plural* **quadrilaterals.**

quadruped   An animal that has four feet. A cat is a quadruped.
   quad·ru·ped (kwod′rə ped′) *noun, plural* **quadrupeds.**

quail   A bird that has a plump body and brown or gray feathers that are often dotted with white.
   quail (kwāl) *noun, plural* **quails** or **quail.**

quaint   Pleasant or attractive in an old-fashioned or amusing way. We walked down the *quaint*, narrow streets of the old seaport.
   quaint (kwānt) *adjective,* **quainter, quaintest.**

quake   To shake or tremble. The boy *quaked* with terror when the man threatened to hurt him. The thunder made the house *quake.* *Verb.*
—A trembling or shaking. *Noun.*
   quake (kwāk) *verb,* **quaked, quaking;** *noun, plural* **quakes.**

qualification   **1.** Something that makes a person or thing fit for a job or task. Jerry's ability to swim well was one of his *qualifications* for the job of lifeguard. **2.** Something that limits or restricts. Jan is, without *qualification,* the best tennis player I know.

Quail

505

qual·i·fi·ca·tion (kwol'ə fi kā'shən) *noun,* *plural* **qualifications.**

qualify 1. To make or become fit for something. Her years of experience as a teacher *qualified* her for the job of principal. 2. To limit or restrict. Eric *qualified* his statement that men are taller than women with the word "usually."
qual·i·fy (kwol'ə fī') *verb,* **qualified, qualifying.**

quality 1. Something that makes a person or thing what it is. George has all the *qualities* of a successful businessman. The most obvious *quality* of water is wetness. 2. Degree of excellence. That market sells meat of the highest *quality.*
qual·i·ty (kwol'ə tē) *noun,* *plural* **qualities.**

qualm 1. A feeling that something is bad or wrong. The suspect had no *qualms* about lying to the police. 2. A sudden feeling of doubt or uneasiness. Susan had *qualms* about being away from home for the first time.
qualm (kwäm) *noun,* *plural* **qualms.**

quantity 1. A number or amount. The recipe calls for a small *quantity* of milk. 2. A large number or amount. That restaurant buys food in *quantity.*
quan·ti·ty (kwon'tə tē) *noun,* *plural* **quantities.**

quarantine The keeping of a person or thing away from others to stop the spreading of a disease. The boy at camp who had chicken pox was put in *quarantine* to keep him from giving the disease to anyone else. *Noun.*
—To put a person or thing in quarantine. The passengers with smallpox were *quarantined* on the ship. *Verb.*
quar·an·tine (kwôr'ən tēn') *noun,* *plural* **quarantines;** *verb,* **quarantined, quarantining.**

▲ In the past, ships that came from foreign lands and might be bringing diseases were often made to wait forty days before landing in a port and unloading. At the end of forty days, if no disease had broken out on the ships, the ships were allowed to dock. The word **quarantine** comes from the Italian word for "forty," because of this forty-day waiting period.

quarrel An angry argument or disagreement. Michael had a *quarrel* with his sister about whose turn it was to wash the dishes. *Noun.*
—1. To have an angry argument or disagreement. The children *quarreled* about who would ride the bicycle first. 2. To find fault. I won't *quarrel* with your decision. *Verb.*
quar·rel (kwôr'əl) *noun,* *plural* **quarrels;** *verb,* **quarreled, quarreling.**

quarry A place where stone is cut or blasted out. Quarries supply stone for use in building.
quar·ry (kwôr'ē) *noun,* *plural* **quarries.**

quart A unit of measure. It is equal to two pints.
quart (kwôrt) *noun,* *plural* **quarts.**

quarter 1. One of four equal parts. Bob divided the pie into *quarters.* Fifteen minutes is a *quarter* of an hour. Three months is a *quarter* of a year. 2. A coin of the United States and Canada equal to twenty-five cents or one-quarter of a dollar. 3. One of four periods of about seven days each that together make up the time it takes for the moon to revolve around the earth. 4. One of the four equal time periods into which basketball, football, and certain other games are divided. 5. A section or district. Their house was in the old *quarter* of the city. 6. **quarters.** A place to live or stay. The soldiers had their *quarters* in tents. *Noun.*
—To divide into four equal units. Molly *quartered* the pie. *Verb.*
quar·ter (kwôr'tər) *noun,* *plural* **quarters;** *verb,* **quartered, quartering.**

Quarter of a Pie

quarterly Happening or done once every three months. The bank pays *quarterly* interest on my savings account. *Adjective.*
—Once every three months. The magazine was published *quarterly. Adverb.*
quar·ter·ly (kwôr'tər lē) *adjective; adverb.*

quartet 1. A musical piece written for four singers or musicians. 2. A group of four singers or musicians performing together. This word is also spelled **quartette.**
quar·tet (kwôr tet') *noun,* *plural* **quartets.**

quartz A kind of clear, hard rock. There are many different colors of quartz. It is the most common mineral and is the main ingredient of sand.
quartz (kwôrts) *noun.*

quasar A starlike heavenly body. Quasars send out huge quantities of light or of very powerful radio waves. Quasars are thought to be at very great distances from the earth.
qua·sar (kwā'sär) *noun,* *plural* **quasars.**

quay A landing place for boats or ships. Quays are usually made of stone. ▲ Another word that sounds like this is **key**.
quay (kē) *noun, plural* **quays.**

Quay

queen 1. The wife or widow of a king. 2. A woman who rules a kingdom. 3. A woman or thing that is beautiful or important. The new ocean liner is the *queen* of the seas. 4. A female bee or other insect that lays eggs. 5. The most powerful piece in the game of chess.
queen (kwēn) *noun, plural* **queens.**

queer Different from what is normal or usual; strange; peculiar. He behaved in a *queer* way yesterday. Her voice sounded *queer* on the phone.
queer (kwēr) *adjective,* **queerer, queerest.**

quench 1. To put an end to by satisfying. Bill *quenched* his thirst with a long drink of water. 2. To put out. The firemen *quenched* the fire.
quench (kwench) *verb,* **quenched, quenching.**

query A question. Any *queries* from the audience should be put to the speaker after he has finished his speech. *Noun.*
—1. To ask about. My friend *queried* my reasons for quitting my summer job. 2. To express doubt about. The teacher *queried* some of the facts in my history report. *Verb.*
que·ry (kwēr′ē) *noun, plural* **queries;** *verb,* **queried, querying.**

quest A search or pursuit. The explorers went in *quest* of gold. The team's *quest* for victory failed.
quest (kwest) *noun, plural* **quests.**

question 1. Something asked in order to get an answer or find out something. Mickey answered the stranger's *question* about which road to take to get to the highway. I didn't know the answer to the last *question* on the history test. 2. A matter to be talked over. The meeting dealt with the *question* of who would be the next president of the club. 3. Doubt; uncertainty. Susan is, without *question*, the best student in the class. *Noun.*
—To ask questions of or about. The police *questioned* the witness to the robbery. *Verb.*
ques·tion (kwes′chən) *noun, plural* **questions;** *verb,* **questioned, questioning.**
beside the question. Off the subject. Your comment is *beside the question.*
out of the question. Not to be considered or thought about. My parents said that my driving the car was *out of the question* until I was old enough to get a license.

question mark A punctuation mark (?) that is put at the end of a question.

quetzal A bird of Central America that has shiny green and bright red feathers.
quet·zel (ket säl′) *noun, plural* **quetzals.**

quick 1. Done or happening in a short time; fast. Leslie made a *quick* trip to the store. Norman gave the letter a *quick* glance. 2. Thinking, learning, or reacting easily and rapidly. My little brother Charles has a very *quick* mind. *Adjective.*
—Tender, sensitive flesh. The flesh beneath the fingernail or toenail is called the quick. *Noun.*
quick (kwik) *adjective,* **quicker, quickest;** *noun.*

quicksand Very deep, wet sand. A person or thing that moves or stands on quicksand will sink into it.
quick·sand (kwik′sand′) *noun.*

quiet 1. Making little or no noise; without noise. We were all *quiet* while the teacher read us the exciting story. It is always very *quiet* in the library. 2. With little or no disturbance or motion; not busy; peaceful. Our family spent a *quiet* weekend at home. *Adjective.*
—A being quiet. Andrew enjoyed the peace and *quiet* of his own room. *Noun.*
—To make or become quiet. The mother *quieted* the crying baby. Vicky went on with her story after the laughter *quieted* down. *Verb.*
qui·et (kwī′it) *adjective,* **quieter, quietest;** *noun; verb,* **quieted, quieting.**

at; āpe; cär; end; mē; it; īce; hot; ōld; fôrk; wood; fo͞ol; oil; out; up; turn; sing; thin; this; hw in white; zh in treasure. ə stands for a in about, e in taken i in pencil, o in lemon, and u in circus.

quill **1.** A large, stiff feather. **2.** A pen made from the hollow stem of a feather. **3.** One of the sharp spines of a porcupine or other animal.
quill (kwil) *noun, plural* **quills.**

Quill

quilt A bed covering made of two pieces of cloth that are stuffed with soft material. The two pieces of cloth are held together by lines of stitching that are sewn all over the surface of the cloth. *Noun.*
—To make a quilt or quilts. *Verb.*
quilt (kwilt) *noun, plural* **quilts;** *verb,* **quilted, quilting.**

quinine A bitter drug used to treat malaria and some other diseases.
qui·nine (kwī′nīn) *noun.*

quintet **1.** A musical piece written for five singers or musicians. **2.** A group of five singers or musicians performing together. This word is also spelled **quintette.**
quin·tet (kwin tet′) *noun, plural* **quintets.**

quirt A riding whip made of knotted rawhide thongs and having a short handle.
quirt (kwurt) *noun, plural* **quirts.**

quit **1.** To stop doing something. Kevin *quit* reading to go outside for a walk. **2.** To go away from; leave. The guard would not *quit* his post. My father may *quit* his job and look for a new one. **3.** To give up or stop trying. Jeff refused to *quit,* even though he knew he couldn't win the race.
quit (kwit) *verb,* **quit or quitted, quitting.**

quite **1.** Very much or completely. The sign made it *quite* clear which road we should take. It is *quite* warm today. **2.** Really; actually. Climbing the mountain was *quite* an achievement.
quite (kwīt) *adverb.*

quiver[1] To shake slightly; shiver. The leaves *quivered* in the breeze.
quiv·er (kwiv′ər) *verb,* **quivered, quivering.**

quiver[2] A case for holding arrows.
quiv·er (kwiv′ər) *noun, plural* **quivers.**

quiz A short or informal test. The teacher gave us a spelling *quiz* today. *Noun.*
—To question. The class was *quizzed* on last week's work. The police *quizzed* the man they thought had committed the crime. *Verb.*
quiz (kwiz) *noun, plural* **quizzes;** *verb,* **quizzed, quizzing.**

Quiver

▲ Probably the first meaning of **quiz** was "to make fun of." Someone could *quiz* a person by asking him questions he could not answer. This made him seem foolish to other people. That may be how we came to use quiz to mean "to test by asking questions."

quota A share of a total due to or from a person, group, or organization. Each soldier received his daily *quota* of rations.
quo·ta (kwō′tə) *noun, plural* **quotas.**

quotation A person's words repeated exactly by another person. The book began with a *quotation* from the Bible.
quo·ta·tion (kwō tā′shən) *noun, plural* **quotations.**

quotation mark One of a pair of punctuation marks (" ") used to show the beginning and end of a quotation.

quote To repeat the exact words of. The newspaper *quoted* parts of the President's speech. *Verb.*
—A quotation. *Noun.*
quote (kwōt) *verb,* **quoted, quoting;** *noun, plural* **quotes.**

quotient A number obtained by dividing one number by another.
quo·tient (kwō′shənt) *noun, plural* **quotients.**

at; āpe; cär; end; mē; it; īce; hot; ōld;
fôrk; wood; fo͞ol; oil; out; up; turn; sing;
thin; this; hw in white; zh in treasure.
ə stands for a in about, e in taken
i in pencil, o in lemon, and u in circus.

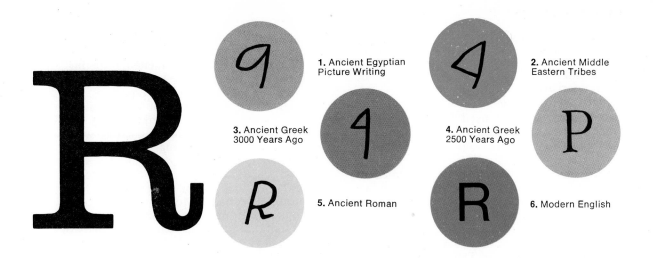

1. Ancient Egyptian Picture Writing

2. Ancient Middle Eastern Tribes

3. Ancient Greek 3000 Years Ago

4. Ancient Greek 2500 Years Ago

5. Ancient Roman

6. Modern English

R is the eighteenth letter of the alphabet. The oldest form of the letter **R** was a drawing that the ancient Egyptians (**1**) used in their picture writing nearly 5000 years ago. This Egyptian drawing stood for the word "mouth." Several ancient tribes (**2**) in the Middle East borrowed this drawing. They called this letter *resh,* meaning "head," and drew it to look something like a side view of a person's head. The ancient Greeks (**3**) borrowed this letter about 2000 years ago. Several hundred years later, the Greeks (**4**) changed the letter's shape by turning it around. This new form of **R** looked like a modern capital letter **P**. The Romans (**5**) borrowed this new form of **R** from the Greeks. By about 2400 years ago, the Romans had added a line to this letter, making it look very much like our modern capital letter **R** (**6**).

r, R The eighteenth letter of the alphabet.
r, R (är) *noun, plural* **r's, R's.**

rabbi A teacher of the Jewish religion. A rabbi is usually the leader of a congregation.
rab·bi (rab′ī) *noun, plural* **rabbis.**

rabbit A small animal that has long ears, a short tail, and soft fur. Rabbits live in burrows that they dig in the ground.
rab·bit (rab′it) *noun, plural* **rabbits.**

Rabbit

rabies A disease that can affect people, dogs, bats, and all other warm-blooded animals. A person almost always dies of it if he is not treated. Rabies is caused by a virus. People get rabies if they are bitten by an animal that already has the disease.
ra·bies (rā′bēz) *noun.*

raccoon A small animal with brownish-gray fur. It has a pointed face with black masklike markings and a long, bushy tail marked with black rings.
rac·coon (ra·kōōn′) *noun, plural* **raccoons.**

Raccoon

race[1] A contest to find out who is fastest. Donna won the *race* because she is the best swimmer on the team. Ted and Sam had a *race* to see who could finish his homework first. *Noun.*
—**1.** To take part in a contest of speed; be in a race against. The two boys *raced* each other to school. **2.** To move or go very fast. Richard *raced* down the stairs to answer the door. *Verb.*
race (rās) *noun, plural* **races;** *verb,* **raced, racing.**

race[2] A very large group of people having

509

certain physical characteristics in common. These characteristics are passed on from one generation to another. Dark skin, black curly hair, and broad features are considered to be characteristics of the Negro *race*.

> **race** (rās) *noun, plural* **races.**

racetrack An area used for racing. Most racetracks are round or oval.

> **race·track** (rās′trak′) *noun, plural* **race-tracks.**

racial Of or having to do with a race of human beings. *Racial* prejudice is prejudice against people because of the race they belong to.

> **ra·cial** (rā′shəl) *adjective.*

rack 1. A frame or stand for hanging, storing, or showing things. The store had many *racks* of men's suits. 2. An instrument of torture used to stretch a victim's body. *Noun.*
—To cause great pain or suffering. The injured man was *racked* with pain. *Verb.*

> **rack** (rak) *noun, plural* **racks;** *verb,* **racked, racking.**

racket¹ 1. A loud or confusing noise. I could hardly hear what Sarah was saying because of the *racket* in the train station. 2. A dishonest plan or way to get money from someone.

> **rack·et** (rak′it) *noun, plural* **rackets.**

racket² A round or oval frame with a network of strings and a thin handle. Rackets are usually made of wood or metal and are used to strike the ball in tennis and other games.

> **rack·et** (rak′it) *noun, plural* **rackets.**

radar A device used to find and track distant objects by the reflection of radio waves.

> **ra·dar** (rā′dar) *noun.*

▲ The word **radar** is short for *radio detecting and ranging.* It is made up of the first two letters of *radio* and the beginning letter of each of the other three words.

radiant 1. Shining brightly; beaming. Fred shielded his eyes from the *radiant* summer sun. Ethel's face was *radiant* from the excitement of winning the contest. 2. Given off in waves or made up of waves. The warmth we get from the sun is *radiant* heat.

> **ra·di·ant** (rā′dē ənt) *adjective.*

radiant energy Energy that is sent off in waves. Heat, radio waves, light, and X rays are kinds of radiant energy.

radiate 1. To give off rays. The lamp *radiated* light through the room. 2. To be given off in rays. Heat and light *radiate* from the sun. 3. To move or branch outward from a center. Many spokes *radiated* from the hub of the bicycle wheel.

> **ra·di·ate** (rā′dē āt′) *verb,* **radiated, radiating.**

radiator 1. A device for heating a room. It is made up of a series of pipes or coils through which steam or hot water passes. 2. A device for cooling something. The radiator in a car engine holds and cools water which is then passed through the engine.

> **ra·di·a·tor** (rā′dē ā′tər) *noun, plural* **radiators.**

radical 1. Going to or affecting the most important part; basic. Moving from the country to the city caused a *radical* change in Mary's life. 2. Favoring extreme changes or reforms. The man did not agree with his son's *radical* political beliefs. *Adjective.*
—A person who favors extreme changes or reforms. *Noun.*

> **rad·i·cal** (rad′i kəl) *adjective; noun, plural* **radicals.**

radii More than one radius. Look up **radius** for more information.

> **ra·di·i** (rā′dē ī′) *noun plural.*

radio 1. A way of sending messages, music, or other sounds by electric waves. 2. A device for receiving or sending such sounds. *Noun.*
—To send a message by radio. The pilot *radioed* the airport for permission to land. *Verb.*

> **ra·di·o** (rā′dē ō′) *noun, plural* **radios;** *verb,* **radioed, radioing.**

radioactive Of, caused by, or having radioactivity. Uranium is a *radioactive* element.

> **ra·di·o·ac·tive** (rā′dē ō ak′tiv) *adjective.*

radioactivity The giving off of energy in the form of certain rays. The rays are given off during a process in which atoms of one element are changed into atoms of another element.

> **ra·di·o·ac·tiv·i·ty** (rā′dē-ō ak tiv′ə tē) *noun.*

radish The small red or white root of a plant. Radishes have a strong, sharp taste and are usually eaten raw in salads.

> **rad·ish** (rad′ish) *noun, plural* **radishes.**

radium A white metal that is highly radioactive. Radium is used in the treatment of cancer. It is a chemical element.

> **ra·di·um** (rā′dē əm) *noun.*

Radish

radius   **1.** A line going from the center to the outside of a circle or sphere. **2.** A circular area that is measured by the length of its radius. There are no other houses within a *radius* of three miles of the farm.
ra·di·us (rā′dē əs) *noun, plural* **radii** or **radiuses.**

raft   A kind of flat boat made of logs or boards that have been fastened together.
raft (raft) *noun, plural* **rafts.**

Raft

rag   **1.** A small piece of cloth. It is usually made of worn or torn material. **2. rags.** Old clothing that is torn or worn out.
rag (rag) *noun, plural* **rags.**

rage   Violent or great anger. He attacked the man in a fit of *rage. Noun.*
—To talk or act in a violent way. He *raged* at the people who had hurt his friend. The storm *raged* along the coast. *Verb.*
rage (rāj) *noun, plural* **rages;** *verb,* **raged, raging.**

ragged   **1.** Worn or torn into rags. After a few years, his jacket became stained and *ragged.* **2.** Wearing tattered clothing. The *ragged* man begged for money to get some food. **3.** Rough and uneven. *Ragged* cliffs rose over the beach.
rag·ged (rag′id) *adjective.*

raid   A sudden, surprise attack. The police planned a *raid* on the house where the thieves were hiding. *Noun.*
—To make a raid on. Burglars *raided* the jewelry store. *Verb.*
raid (rād) *noun, plural* **raids;** *verb,* **raided, raiding.**

rail   **1.** A long, narrow bar of wood, metal, or other material. It is used as a guard or support. The long metal bars on which a train rides are rails. **2.** A railroad. Jim preferred traveling by *rail* to driving a car.
rail (rāl) *noun, plural* **rails.**

railing   A fence or barrier made of a rail or rails. She held onto the *railing* as she went down the steep staircase.
rail·ing (rā′ling) *noun, plural* **railings.**

railroad   **1.** The metal tracks on which a train runs. **2.** All the tracks, stations, and cars that are part of a system of transportation by rail. My grandfather worked for the *railroad.* Another word for this is **railway.**
rail·road (rāl′rōd′) *noun, plural* **railroads.**

rain   **1.** Water that falls in drops from clouds to the earth. *Rain* came through the open window and soaked the curtains. **2.** A falling of rain; storm or shower. Andrea was caught in the *rain* without an umbrella. **3.** A heavy or rapid fall of anything. A *rain* of rice hit the bride and groom as they left the church. *Noun.*
—**1.** To fall in drops of water. We put off our picnic because it *rained.* **2.** To fall or pour like rain. Bullets *rained* on the soldiers. *Verb.* ▲ Other words that sound like this are **reign** and **rein.**
rain (rān) *noun, plural* **rains;** *verb,* **rained, raining.**

rainbow   An arc of colored light seen in the sky. It is caused by the sun's rays being seen through tiny drops of water in the air. A rainbow is made up of seven colors: red, orange, yellow, green, blue, indigo, and violet.
rain·bow (rān′bō′) *noun, plural* **rainbows.**

Rainbow

at; āpe; cär; end; mē; it; īce; hot; ōld;
fôrk; wood; fōol; oil; out; up; turn; sing;
thin; this; hw in white; zh in treasure.
ə stands for a in about, e in taken
i in pencil, o in lemon, and u in circus.

raincoat A waterproof coat that keeps a person dry when it is raining.
rain·coat (rān′kōt′) *noun, plural* **raincoats.**

raindrop A drop of rain.
rain·drop (rān′drop′) *noun, plural* **raindrops.**

rainfall The amount of rain, snow, sleet, or hail that falls on an area in a certain period of time. The yearly *rainfall* in that city is over thirty inches.
rain·fall (rān′fôl′) *noun, plural* **rainfalls.**

rainy Having much rain. It's dangerous to drive fast in *rainy* weather.
rain·y (rā′nē) *adjective,* **rainier, rainiest.**

raise 1. To move or cause to move to a higher position, place, degree, or amount. The boy *raised* his arm above his head. The young soldier was *raised* from private to corporal. On my birthday, my parents *raised* my allowance. Joan *raised* her voice as she became more angry. 2. To cause to rise or appear. The bee sting *raised* a bump on Tim's arm. 3. To gather together; collect. The town *raised* the money to build a new school. 4. To take care of and help to grow. That rancher *raises* horses and cattle. 5. To ask or bring up. Ellen *raised* an interesting question about the story we were reading. 6. To build. A new house was *raised* on the lot where the old house had stood. *Verb.*
—An increase in amount. Pat received a *raise* in pay of five dollars a week. *Noun.*
raise (rāz) *verb,* **raised, raising;** *noun, plural* **raises.**

raisin A sweet, dried grape.
rai·sin (rā′zin) *noun, plural* **raisins.**

rake A tool that has a long handle with teeth or prongs attached at one end. It is used to gather leaves or hay together or to smooth down earth. *Noun.*
—To gather or smooth with a rake. Ted *raked* the fallen leaves from the grass. *Verb.*
rake (rāk) *noun, plural* **rakes;** *verb,* **raked, raking.**

rally 1. To bring or come together for some purpose. The general tried to *rally* his scattered troops. The people of the town *rallied* to help the family rebuild their burned house. 2. To come to help. His friends *rallied* behind the boy who had been teased by the bully. 3. To recover strength or health; get better. With the doctor's help, the patient began to *rally. Verb.*
—A meeting for a particular purpose. Hundreds of people were at the political *rally* for the man who was running for senator. *Noun.*
ral·ly (ral′ē) *verb,* **rallied, rallying;** *noun, plural* **rallies.**

ram 1. A male sheep. 2. A device or part of a machine used to batter, crush, or force something. *Noun.*
—1. To strike against with great force. The train wreck happened when one train *rammed* into the back of another. 2. To force or drive down. The farmer *rammed* the fence post into the ground. *Verb.*
ram (ram) *noun, plural* **rams;** *verb,* **rammed, ramming.**

Ram

ramble 1. To wander about; roam. We *rambled* through the fields before having our picnic. 2. To talk or write in a confused way. The speaker *rambled* on and never came to the point of his story.
ram·ble (ram′bəl) *verb,* **rambled, rambling.**

ramp A sloping passageway connecting two different levels. The movable staircase for getting on and off an airplane is a ramp.
ramp (ramp) *noun, plural* **ramps.**

ramrod 1. A rod used to ram the charge down the barrel of a gun that is loaded through the muzzle. 2. A rod used to clean the barrel of a gun.
ram·rod (ram′rod′) *noun, plural* **ramrods.**

ran Steve was so late that he *ran* all the way to school. Look up **run** for more information.
ran (ran) *verb.*

ranch A large farm on which large herds of cattle, sheep, and horses are raised. *Noun.*
—To manage or work on a ranch. *Verb.*
ranch (ranch) *noun, plural* **ranches;** *verb,* **ranched, ranching.**

random With no clear plan or purpose; not planned. The teacher made a *random* choice of three students to help pass out the new books. Howard

Ramrod

picked a magazine at *random* from the pile.
ran·dom (ran′dəm) *adjective.*

▲ The first meaning of **random** was "great speed or force," and people used "at *random*" to mean "at full speed." When people do things very fast, they often do them without thinking or planning. So *random* came to mean "without a plan or purpose."

rang Dan *rang* the doorbell twice, but there was no answer. Look up **ring** for more information.
rang (rang) *verb.*

range 1. The distance between certain limits. There is a wide *range* in prices for a television set. This dress is sold in a large *range* of sizes. The airplane flew out of our *range* of vision. 2. The greatest distance at which something can work or go. A rifle has a greater *range* than a bow and arrow. 3. A place set aside for shooting practice or for testing rockets. Bob did some target shooting on the pistol *range*. 4. A large area of land on which livestock roam and graze. The cowboys rounded up the cattle on the open *range*. 5. A row or series of mountains. 6. A large stove having burners and an oven. *Noun.*
—1. To go between certain limits. The price for that bicycle *ranges* between forty and fifty dollars in different stores. 2. To wander or roam. Cattle *ranged* over the prairie. *Verb.*
range (rānj) *noun, plural* **ranges;** *verb,* **ranged, ranging.**

ranger 1. A person whose work is looking after and guarding a forest. 2. A member of a group of armed men who patrol an area to keep law and order.
ran·ger (rān′jər) *noun, plural* **rangers.**

rank¹ 1. A position, grade, or standing. The soldier was promoted from corporal to the *rank* of sergeant. Carol has a high *rank* in her class at school. 2. High position or standing. The governor of the state is a man of *rank*. 3. **ranks.** The common soldiers of an army. *Noun.*
—1. To arrange in a row or rows. The teacher *ranked* the students for the fire drill. 2. To have or give a position. The students were *ranked* according to their grades. Diane *ranks* high in her science class. *Verb.*
rank (rangk) *noun, plural* **ranks;** *verb,* **ranked, ranking.**

rank² 1. Having a strong, bad smell or taste. The old cheese gave off a *rank* odor. 2. Complete; extreme. He was accused of being a *rank* coward.
rank (rangk) *adjective,* **ranker, rankest.**

ransom 1. The release of a captive for a price. The police received a note saying the man was being held for *ransom*. 2. The price paid or demanded before a captive is set free. The parents of the kidnaped child had to pay a *ransom* of $10,000. *Noun.*
—To get a captive set free by paying a price. *Verb.*
ran·som (ran′səm) *noun, plural* **ransoms;** *verb,* **ransomed, ransoming.**

rap A quick, sharp knock or tap. We heard a *rap* on the window. *Noun.*
—To knock or tap sharply. He *rapped* on the door but there was no answer. *Verb.* ▲ Another word that sounds like this is **wrap.**
rap (rap) *noun, plural* **raps;** *verb,* **rapped, rapping.**

rapid Very quick. The train went at a *rapid* pace. Tom is a *rapid* worker. *Adjective.*
—**rapids.** A part of a river where the water flows very fast. It was dangerous to go over the *rapids* in a canoe. *Noun.*
rap·id (rap′id) *adjective; noun plural.*

rare¹ 1. Not often happening, seen, or found. Thunder storms are *rare* during the winter in this part of the country. 2. Unusually fine or valuable. That man has some *rare* stamps in his collection.
rare (rer) *adjective,* **rarer, rarest.**

rare² Cooked for only a short time. Mike likes his hamburgers *rare*.
rare (rer) *adjective,* **rarer, rarest.**

rascal A mischievous person. My little brother is a *rascal*.
ras·cal (ras′kəl) *noun, plural* **rascals.**

rash¹ Too hasty; not careful. Helen made a *rash* decision that she was sorry about afterwards.
rash (rash) *adjective,* **rasher, rashest.**

rash² A breaking out of red spots on the skin. Measles and poison ivy cause a *rash*.
rash (rash) *noun, plural* **rashes.**

rasp To make a harsh, grating sound. The iron gate *rasped* because the hinges were rusty. *Verb.*
—A harsh, grating sound. Harriet spoke with a *rasp* because she had a sore throat. *Noun.*
rasp (rasp) *verb,* **rasped, rasping;** *noun, plural* **rasps.**

at; āpe; cär; end; mē; it; īce; hot; ōld;
fôrk; wood; fōōl; oil; out; up; turn; sing;
thin; **th**is; hw in white; zh in treasure.
ə stands for a in about, e in taken
i in pencil, o in lemon, and u in circus.

raspberry   A small, sweet fruit of a prickly plant. Raspberries are usually red or black. **rasp·ber·ry** (raz′ber′ē) *noun, plural* **rasp-berries.**

rat   An animal that is like a mouse, but is larger. It has a long nose, round ears, and a long, thin tail. **rat** (rat) *noun, plural* **rats.**

Raspberries

rate   **1.** An amount or number measured against the amount or number of something else. The car was going at a *rate* of more than sixty miles per hour. **2.** The price or charge for something. Telephone *rates* went up last year. **3.** A rank or class. Maureen's school work has always been of the first *rate. Noun.*
—**1.** To consider; regard. Don *rated* the movie as very good. **2.** To place in or have a certain class or rank. Our school is *rated* first among the local baseball teams. *Verb.*
rate (rāt) *noun, plural* **rates;** *verb,* **rated, rating.**

rather   **1.** More willingly. I would *rather* stay home than go out tonight. **2.** More properly; instead. Patricia, *rather* than Cindy, deserved to win. **3.** More correctly. The airplane is landing at about noon or, *rather,* at 12:10 P.M. **4.** Somewhat. It is *rather* cold today.
rath·er (rath′ər) *adverb.*

ratio   A comparison in number or quantity between two things. The ratio is the number of times the second thing can be divided into the first thing. If there are 12 girls and 6 boys in a class, the *ratio* of girls to boys is 2 to 1.
ra·ti·o (rā′shē ō′) *noun, plural* **ratios.**

ration   A fixed portion or share of food for the day. Each mountain climber carried his *rations* in the pack on his back. *Noun.*
—**1.** To give out in portions. Food and clothing were *rationed* to people whose homes had been damaged in the fire. **2.** To limit to fixed portions. The government *rationed* meat during World War II. *Verb.*
ra·tion (rash′ən *or* rā′shən) *noun, plural* **rations;** *verb,* **rationed, rationing.**

rational   **1.** Based on reason; sensible. William used *rational* arguments to support his ideas. **2.** Able to think clearly. Even during an emergency, Ed thinks in a *rational* way.
ra·tion·al (rash′ən əl) *adjective.*

rattle   **1.** To make a series of short, sharp sounds. The doors and windows *rattled* when the wind blew against the house. **2.** To talk or say quickly. Cathy *rattled* off the answers. **3.** To confuse or embarrass. Gary was *rattled* by the mistake he made in answering the teacher's question. *Verb.*
—**1.** A series of short, sharp sounds. He could tell by the *rattle* of the doorknob that someone was trying to get into the room. **2.** A baby's toy or other thing that makes a rattling noise when it is shaken. *Noun.*
rat·tle (rat′əl) *verb,* **rattled, rattling;** *noun, plural* **rattles.**

rattlesnake   A poisonous American snake. A rattlesnake has a number of horny rings at the end of its tail that rattle when it shakes its tail.
rat·tle·snake (rat′əl snāk′) *noun, plural* **rattlesnakes.**

Rattlesnake

ravel   To separate into loose threads; fray. Pulling the piece of yarn made the cuff of the sweater *ravel.*
rav·el (rav′əl) *verb,* **raveled, raveling.**

raven   A bird that looks very much like a crow but is larger. It has shiny black feathers and a harsh cry.
ra·ven (rā′vən) *noun, plural* **ravens.**

Raven

ravine   A deep, narrow valley. Ravines are often formed by a river or stream flowing through and wearing down a space between two hills.
ra·vine (rə vēn′) *noun, plural* **ravines.**

raw **1.** Not cooked. Carrots may be cooked or eaten *raw.* **2.** Not treated or processed; natural. Milk as it comes from the cow and before it is pasteurized is *raw.* **3.** Not trained or experienced. The *raw* recruits in the army were given six weeks of basic training. **4.** Having the skin rubbed off. Fred's heel was *raw* where the new shoe had pinched it. **5.** Damp and cold. The November night was *raw* and chilling.
  raw (rô) *adjective,* **rawer, rawest.**

rawhide The hide of cattle or other animals that has not been tanned. The cowboy wore boots made of *rawhide.*
  raw·hide (rô′hīd′) *noun.*

raw material A substance that has not been treated, processed, or prepared. Wood is the *raw material* used in making paper.

ray¹ **1.** A narrow beam of light or other radiant energy. The sun's *rays* brightened the room. **2.** One of a group of lines or parts coming from a center. The arms of a starfish are *rays.* **3.** A very small amount. There was still a *ray* of hope that the lost sailors would be found.
  ray (rā) *noun, plural* **rays.**

ray² A fish that has a broad, flat body and broad fins.
  ray (rā) *noun, plural* **rays.**

Ray

rayon A fiber or cloth made from cellulose.
  ray·on (rā′on) *noun.*

razor A device with a sharp blade used for shaving or cutting off hair.
  ra·zor (rā′zər) *noun, plural* **razors.**

re- A *prefix* that means "again."

▲ There are many words beginning with **re-** that you will not find in this dictionary. You can understand the meaning of these words by adding the word "again" to the part of the word that follows *re-.* For example, the word *rebuild* means "to build again," and the word *reheat* means "to heat again."

reach **1.** To arrive at; come to. We *reached* the cabin after walking for two miles through the woods. **2.** To touch or grasp. Unless I stand on my toes, I can't *reach* the top shelf of the bookcase. **3.** To stretch or extend. The draperies *reached* from the ceiling to the floor. **4.** To stretch the arm or hand out. Fred *reached* across the table for the salt. **5.** To try to grasp something. Walter *reached* into his pocket for his keys. **6.** To get in touch with someone; contact. I tried to *reach* Jill by telephone, but she wasn't home. *Verb.*
  —**1.** The distance covered in reaching. A person would have to have a long *reach* to get that box off the shelf in the closet. **2.** As much as a person is able to do or understand. The boy knew that winning the race was within his *reach.* **3.** The act of reaching. With a *reach* of his arm Tom pulled the apple from the tree. *Noun.*
  reach (rēch) *verb,* **reached, reaching;** *noun, plural* **reaches.**

react To act because something has happened or has been done; respond. Judy *reacted* to the good news by smiling. Ted *reacted* against his parents' strictness by being very naughty.
  re·act (rē akt′) *verb,* **reacted, reacting.**

reaction An action in response to something that has happened or has been done. What was his mother's *reaction* when she saw his report card?
  re·ac·tion (rē ak′shən) *noun, plural* **reactions.**

reactor A device that produces controlled atomic energy. It splits atoms without causing an atomic explosion.
  re·ac·tor (rē ak′tər) *noun, plural* **reactors.**

read **1.** To look at and understand the meaning of something that is written. I learned to *read* when I was in first grade. Dick *read* an article about football in the newspaper. **2.** To say aloud something that is written. Todd sometimes *reads* bedtime stories to his little brother. **3.** To learn about by reading. Helene likes to *read* about horses. **4.** To get the meaning of; understand. Sometimes my parents seem to be able to *read* my thoughts. **5.** To give or show information. The thermometer *read* seventy degrees this morn-

at; āpe; cär; end; mē; it; īce; hot; ōld; fôrk; wood; fōol; oil; out; up; turn; sing; thin; this; hw in white; zh in treasure.
ə stands for a in about, e in taken
i in pencil, o in lemon, and u in circus.

ing. ▲ Another word that sounds like this is **reed**.

read (rēd) *verb*, **read** (red), **reading**.

▲ The first meaning of **read** was "to have an idea" or "to think." For example, someone might have said, "I *read* that this story is not true." This use of *read* led to the meaning "to guess," and then "to figure out the meaning of." Now we use *read* especially to mean "to look at something written to find out what it means."

---

reader 1. A person who reads. 2. A schoolbook that helps to teach reading.

read·er (rē′dər) *noun*, *plural* **readers**.

readily 1. In a willing way. Peter *readily* followed his friend's advice. 2. Without difficulty; easily. The story was *readily* understood by everyone in the class.

read·i·ly (red′ə lē) *adverb*.

reading 1. The act of looking at and understanding something that is written. Gary preferred *reading* to playing baseball. 2. The act of saying aloud something that is written. The writer gave a *reading* of his newest poem. 3. Something read or to be read. This book on sailing is interesting *reading*.

read·ing (rē′ding) *noun*, *plural* **readings**.

ready 1. Prepared for use or action. When I finish packing my suitcase I'll be *ready* for the trip. 2. Willing. Charles was *ready* to work hard to make the money for the bicycle he wanted. 3. Likely. The dynamite was *ready* to explode any minute. 4. Quick; prompt. The politician had a *ready* answer for any question he was asked. 5. Easy to get at. My father keeps some *ready* cash around the house in case of an emergency. *Adjective*.
—To make ready; prepare. The mechanics have to *ready* the plane before it can take off. We *readied* the house before the guests came. *Verb*.

read·y (red′ē) *adjective*, **readier**, **readiest**; *verb*, **readied**, **readying**.

real 1. Actual or true; not imagined. The man's adventures were *real;* he did not make them up. 2. Genuine; not imitation. These flowers are *real*, not plastic.

re·al (rē′əl *or* rēl) *adjective*.

real estate Land together with the buildings, trees, water, and other things on it.

reality 1. The state or quality of being real. Some people doubted the *reality* of his story. 2. Something that is real. Jean could hardly believe that her dream of owning a horse had become a *reality*.

re·al·i·ty (rē al′ə tē) *noun*, *plural* **realities**.

realize 1. To understand completely. Chuck didn't *realize* how late it was because his watch had stopped. 2. To make something real. Years of practice helped Mike to *realize* his dream of becoming a baseball player.

re·al·ize (rē′ə līz′) *verb*, **realized**, **realizing**.

really 1. In fact; actually. The man told the police what had *really* caused the accident. Although Johnny and Susan argue sometimes, they are *really* good friends. 2. Truly; very. Andrew and Paul spent a *really* pleasant afternoon together in the park.

re·al·ly (rē′ə lē *or* rē′lē) *adverb*.

realm 1. A kingdom. The king chose the bravest knights in the *realm*. 2. An area or field of interest, knowledge, or power. Betty likes to read about almost anything in the *realm* of science.

realm (relm) *noun*, *plural* **realms**.

reap 1. To gather grain or a crop by cutting it down. 2. To cut down or harvest a crop from. The farmer *reaped* his fields in the autumn. 3. To get as a reward. Barbara's kindness *reaped* many good friendships for her.

reap (rēp) *verb*, **reaped**, **reaping**.

rear[1] The part that is behind or in the back. My parents sat in the front seat, and my brother and I sat in the *rear* of the car. *Noun*.
—At or in the back. We left the house by the *rear* door. *Adjective*.

rear (rēr) *noun*, *plural* **rears**; *adjective*.

rear[2] 1. To take care of and help to grow up. My grandparents *reared* my father and his brothers and sisters. 2. To go up on the back legs. The frightened horse *reared* and threw its rider.

rear (rēr) *verb*, **reared**, **rearing**.

reason 1. A cause or motive. There is no *reason* to doubt her word. I wonder what *reason* he had for getting so angry. 2. A statement that explains something; excuse. Bob could give no *reason* for being late. 3. The ability to think clearly. The sudden shock made him lose all *reason* for a few minutes. *Noun*.
—1. To think clearly. Amy was able to *reason* the answer to the arithmetic problem. 2. To try to change a person's mind. He was so stubborn that it was useless to *reason* with him. *Verb*.

rea·son (rē′zən) *noun*, *plural* **reasons**; *verb*, **reasoned**, **reasoning**.

reasonable 1. Showing or using good sense and thinking; not foolish. A *reasonable* person will always listen to both sides of an argument. 2. Not asking too much; fair. My brother's asking to borrow my bicycle be-

cause his was broken was a *reasonable* request. **3.** Not too expensive. The grocery store sold tomatoes at a *reasonable* price.
　rea·son·a·ble (rē′zə nə bəl *or* rēz′nə bəl) *adjective.*

reasoning　**1.** The process of drawing conclusions from facts; logical thinking. To do well in mathematics, you must be good at *reasoning.* **2.** Reasons or arguments. I didn't agree with his *reasoning.*
　rea·son·ing (rē′zə ning *or* rēz′ning) *noun.*

rebel　**1.** A person who fights against or will not obey authority. The *rebels* attacked the king's palace in an attempt to take control of the government. **2. Rebel.** A Southerner who fought against the North in the Civil War. *Noun.*
　—**1.** To fight against authority. The man *rebelled* at being ordered to do something he thought was wrong. **2.** To feel or show great dislike. The sick boy *rebelled* against taking the medicine because it tasted bad. *Verb.*
　reb·el (reb′əl *for noun;* ri bel′ *for verb*) *noun, plural* **rebels;** *verb,* **rebelled, rebelling.**

▲　The word **rebel** goes back to a Latin word that means "to make war again." The word was used to talk about people who had been conquered in war and started another war against the people who had beaten them.

rebellion　**1.** An armed fight against one's government. The Revolutionary War was a *rebellion* by the American colonists against the British. **2.** A fighting against any authority.
　re·bel·lion (ri bel′yən) *noun, plural* **rebellions.**

recall　**1.** To bring back to mind; remember. That man's face is familiar to me, but I don't *recall* his name. **2.** To take or order back. The auto manufacturer *recalled* the cars because there was a defect in the engine.
　re·call (ri kôl′) *verb,* **recalled, recalling.**

receipt　**1.** A written statement showing that a package, mail, or money has been received. The man in the store gave Patricia a *receipt* to show that she had paid for the coat. **2. receipts.** The amount of money that has been received. The store's *receipts* for the week were over $1000.
　re·ceipt (ri sēt′) *noun, plural* **receipts.**

receive　**1.** To take or get something. Jan *received* a watch for her birthday. I *received* a letter from Jack today. **2.** To greet or welcome. The host of the party *received* his guests at the door.
　re·ceive (ri sēv′) *verb,* **received, receiving.**

receiver　**1.** A person or thing that receives. **2.** A device that changes electrical impulses or radio waves into pictures or sounds. The part of a telephone that you hold to your ear is a receiver.
　re·ceiv·er (ri sē′vər) *noun, plural* **receivers.**

recent　Done, made, or happening not long ago. The radio program reported the most *recent* news about the election. The landing of men on the moon is one of the most exciting events of *recent* times.
　re·cent (rē′sənt) *adjective.*

Receiver

reception　**1.** The act or way of receiving. The play got a warm *reception* from everyone in the audience. **2.** A party or gathering where guests are received. **3.** The quality of the sound of a radio or the sound and picture of a television. Putting an antenna on the roof of our house greatly improved the television *reception.*
　re·cep·tion (ri sep′shən) *noun, plural* **receptions.**

recess　**1.** A time during which work or other activity stops. We played baseball during *recess* at school. **2.** A part of a wall that is set back from the rest; niche. *Noun.*
　—To stop work or other activity for a time. The trial started again after the court had *recessed* for lunch. *Verb.*
　re·cess (rē′ses *or* ri ses′) *noun, plural* **recesses;** *verb,* **recessed, recessing.**

recipe　A list of instructions for making something to eat or drink.
　rec·i·pe (res′ə pē′) *noun, plural* **recipes.**

▲　The word **recipe** comes from a Latin word that means "take!" Doctors used to use the Latin word when they wrote prescriptions. They would tell the druggist to "take" certain drugs and put them together to make the medicine.

at; āpe; cär; end; mē; it; īce; hot; ōld;
fôrk; wood; fōōl; oil; out; up; turn; sing;
thin; this; hw in white; zh in treasure.
ə stands for a in about, e in taken
i in pencil, o in lemon, and u in circus.

recital 1. A performance or concert of music or dance. All of the teacher's students played in the piano *recital*. 2. A story or account. Mr. Simpson's *recital* of his experiences in Africa was very interesting.
re·cit·al (ri sīt′əl) *noun, plural* **recitals.**

recite 1. To repeat from memory. Beth can *recite* the names of all the fifty states and their capitals. 2. To tell the story of. Edward *recited* his adventures at camp to the class.
re·cite (ri sīt′) *verb,* **recited, reciting.**

reckless Not careful. It was *reckless* of John to have skated out onto the thin ice.
reck·less (rek′lis) *adjective.*

reckon 1. To count or calculate. Taxes are *reckoned* according to the amount of money a person makes. 2. To think or consider. They *reckon* her to be the prettiest girl in the class.
reck·on (rek′ən) *verb,* **reckoned, reckoning.**

recognition 1. A recognizing or being recognized. The criminal escaped *recognition* by wearing a mask. 2. An accepting of something as being true, right, or valid. The young man demanded *recognition* of his rights as a citizen. 3. Favorable attention or notice. That singer has gained *recognition* for his records.
rec·og·ni·tion (rek′əg nish′ən) *noun.*

recognize 1. To know that you have seen or heard about a person or thing before. I hardly *recognized* that boy because he had grown so much taller since I last saw him. 2. To understand and accept something to be true, right, or valid. Michael *recognized* that it was his duty to report the crime to the police.
rec·og·nize (rek′əg nīz′) *verb,* **recognized, recognizing.**

recommend 1. To speak in favor of. The librarian *recommended* this book to me. 2. To advise; suggest. The nurse *recommended* that Tim stay home from school until his cold was better.
rec·om·mend (rek′ə mend′) *verb,* **recommended, recommending.**

record 1. A written account of something. The school keeps a *record* of the number of days each student is absent. The story the witness told was in the *record* of the trial. 2. All the facts about what a person, group, or thing has done. Daniel's school *record* is excellent. The football team had a *record* of seven wins and two losses. 3. A performance or act that is better than all others. The runner set a new school *record* for the 100-yard dash. 4. A disk on which music or other sounds have been recorded to be played back on a phonograph. *Noun.*
—1. To set down in writing. Jim *recorded* his feelings about his new home in a letter to a friend. 2. To indicate or show. This thermometer *records* temperatures up to 120 degrees. 3. To put music or other sounds on a phonograph record or a magnetic tape. *Verb.*
rec·ord (rek′ərd *for noun;* ri kôrd′ *for verb*) *noun, plural* **records;** *verb,* **recorded, recording.**

recorder 1. A person whose job is taking notes and keeping records. 2. A machine that records sound on magnetic tape. 3. A musical instrument that is something like a flute.
re·cord·er (ri kôr′dər) *noun, plural* **recorders.**

recording A phonograph record or magnetic tape. Kevin owns a beautiful *recording* of that song.
re·cord·ing (ri kôr′ding) *noun, plural* **recordings.**

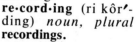

Recorder

recover 1. To get back something that was lost or stolen. The police *recovered* all the jewelry that the thieves had taken. 2. To make up for. We took a short cut to *recover* the time we had lost in changing the flat tire. 3. To get back to a normal condition or position. My brother *recovered* from the measles faster than I did.
re·cov·er (ri kuv′ər) *verb,* **recovered, recovering.**

recovery The act of recovering. Tom was given a reward for his *recovery* of the lost wallet. The patient's speedy *recovery* was due to good medical care.
re·cov·er·y (ri kuv′ər ē) *noun, plural* **recoveries.**

recreation Something that is done for amusement or relaxation. Sports, games, and hobbies are kinds of recreation.
rec·re·a·tion (rek′rē ā′shən) *noun, plural* **recreations.**

recruit A newly enlisted soldier or sailor. The *recruits* went through six weeks of basic training. *Noun.*
—To get someone to join. The coach *recruited* nine boys for the baseball team. *Verb.*
re·cruit (ri krōōt′) *noun, plural* **recruits;** *verb,* **recruited, recruiting.**

rectangle A four-sided figure that has four right angles. A square is a kind of rectangle.
rec·tan·gle (rek′tang′gəl) *noun, plural* **rectangles.**

red **1.** The color of blood. **2.** Something having this color. The artist used a bright *red* to paint a picture of the fire engine. *Noun.* —Having the color red. *Adjective.*
red (red) *noun, plural* **reds;** *adjective,* **redder, reddest.**

red blood cell A blood cell that carries oxygen to the cells and tissues of the body. Man and all other animals with backbones have red blood cells.

Red Cross An international organization whose main purpose is to take care of victims of war and of floods, fires, and earthquakes.

Red Deer

red deer A reddish-brown deer that is found in Europe and Asia.

reduce To make or become less or smaller in size, number, or degree. When the road got slippery the driver *reduced* his speed. Mike *reduced* by going on a diet. After Christmas, the store *reduced* the price of many items. The forest was *reduced* to ashes by the fire.
re·duce (ri d$\overline{oo}$s′ *or* ri dy$\overline{oo}$s′) *verb,* **reduced, reducing.**

reduction **1.** The act of reducing or the state of being reduced. The *reduction* of the speed limit resulted in fewer traffic accidents. **2.** The amount that something is reduced. The store is offering a ten percent *reduction* on the price of summer clothes.
re·duc·tion (ri duk′shən) *noun, plural* **reductions.**

Red-winged Blackbird

red-winged blackbird A blackbird that lives in America. The male bird has a bright red patch at the shoulder of each wing.
red-winged blackbird (red′wingd′).

redwood A very tall evergreen tree that has thick reddish-brown bark. It grows along the western coast of North America. Redwoods may grow from 300 to 340 feet tall, and some are probably more than 2000 years old.
red·wood (red′-wood′) *noun, plural* **redwoods.**

reed **1.** A tall grass having long, narrow leaves and jointed stems. Reeds usually grow in marshes and other wet places. **2.** A thin piece of wood, reed, metal, or plastic that is used in the mouthpieces of some musical instruments. A reed makes a musical sound when air passes over it and makes it vibrate. **3.** A musical wind instrument whose tone is produced by a vibrating reed. This is also called a **reed instrument.** ▲ Another word that sounds like this is **read.**
reed (rēd) *noun, plural* **reeds.**

Redwood Tree

reef A ridge of sand, rock, or coral that lies at or near the surface of the ocean or another body of water.
reef (rēf) *noun, plural* **reefs.**

reel¹ A spool or similar device on which something is wound. Fishing line, motion picture film, and magnetic tape are wound on reels. *Noun.*
—**1.** To wind on a reel. The sailor *reeled* the rope. **2.** To pull by winding a line on a reel. The fisherman *reeled* in a huge swordfish. *Verb.*
reel (rēl) *noun, plural* **reels;** *verb,* **reeled, reeling.**

reel² **1.** To be thrown off balance; stagger. Jack *reeled* when Larry accidentally ran into him. **2.** To turn or seem to turn round and

at; āpe; cär; end; mē; it; īce; hot; ōld;
fôrk; wood; fōol; oil; out; up; turn; sing;
thin; this; hw in white; zh in treasure.
ə stands for a in about, e in taken
i in pencil, o in lemon, and u in circus.

round. The ride on the merry-go-round made him so dizzy that his head began to *reel*.
reel (rēl) *verb*, **reeled, reeling.**

reel³   A lively folk dance. It is performed by two or more couples who form two lines facing each other.
reel (rēl) *noun, plural* **reels.**

reelect   To elect again. The President was *reelected* and served another four years.
re·e·lect (rē'i lekt') *verb*, **reelected, reelecting.**

reentry   1. An entering again. 2. The return of a spacecraft or missile to the earth.
re·en·try (rē en'trē) *noun, plural* **reentries.**

refer   1. To send or direct a person to someone or something. The doctor *referred* his patient to a surgeon for an operation. 2. To turn to for help or information. The speaker *referred* to his notes every few minutes. 3. To direct attention to. When she spoke of her home town, she *referred* to the town where she grew up, not the town where she was born. 4. To turn something over to someone else. The teacher *referred* the problem to the principal.
re·fer (ri fur') *verb*, **referred, referring.**

referee   An official in certain sports and games who enforces the rules. The *referee* in the basketball game called a foul on a player on the home team. *Noun.*
—To act as a referee. Our teacher *refereed* the hockey game. *Verb.*
ref·er·ee (ref'ə rē') *noun, plural* **referees;** *verb*, **refereed, refereeing.**

reference   1. A statement that calls or directs attention to something. The author of the book made a *reference* to another book he had written. 2. A person or thing that is referred to; source of information or help. The encyclopedia was the *reference* for his report. 3. A statement about a person's ability or character. The baby-sitter had very good *references* written by the people for whom she had worked the summer before.
ref·er·ence (ref'ər əns) *noun, plural* **references.**

refill   To fill again. The hiker *refilled* his canteen with water. *Verb.*
—Something that replaces the material that first filled a container. Ted had to buy a *refill* for his ballpoint pen when it ran out of ink. *Noun.*
re·fill (rē fil' *for verb;* rē'fil' *for noun*) *verb*, **refilled, refilling;** *noun, plural* **refills.**

refine   To make fine and pure. Crude oil is *refined* before it can be used for gasoline.
re·fine (ri fīn') *verb*, **refined, refining.**

refinery   A place where crude oil, sugar, or some other substance is refined.
re·fin·er·y (ri fī'nər ē) *noun, plural* **refineries.**

reflect   1. To turn or throw back. The sand at the beach *reflects* the light and heat of the sun. 2. To give back an image of something. The water of the lake *reflected* the trees along its banks. 3. To think seriously or carefully. Penny often *reflects* on what she will do when she grows up. 4. To bring blame or discredit. His cowardice *reflects* on his character.
re·flect (ri flekt') *verb*, **reflected, reflecting.**

reflection   1. An image given back by a reflecting surface. The boy looked at his *reflection* in the water. 2. Something that is reflected. The *reflection* of the sun in the car windshield blinded the driver for a moment. 3. Serious or careful thinking. Upon *reflection*, my mother decided to take the new job. 4. Something that shows or expresses something else. His smile was a *reflection* of his happiness. 5. Something that causes blame or discredit. The parents thought that their child's bad behavior was a *reflection* on them.
re·flec·tion (ri flek'shən) *noun, plural* **reflections.**

Reflection

reform   1. To make a change for the better; correct; improve. The government tried to *reform* the prison system. 2. To become better. The criminal promised to *reform* and live an honest life. *Verb.*
—A change for the better. The town planned several *reforms* in the schools. *Noun.*
re·form (ri fôrm') *verb*, **reformed, reforming;** *noun, plural* **reforms.**

reformatory   A special school to which young people are sent who have broken the law.

re·form·a·to·ry (ri fôr′mə tôr′ē) *noun, plural* **reformatories.**

refrain A part of a song or poem that is repeated several times.
re·frain (ri frān′) *noun, plural* **refrains.**

refresh To make or become fresh again. The cold drinks of lemonade *refreshed* us after the long, hot hike.
re·fresh (ri fresh′) *verb,* **refreshed, refreshing.**

refreshment Food or drink. The *refreshments* at the birthday party were ice cream and cake.
re·fresh·ment (ri fresh′mənt) *noun, plural* **refreshments.**

refrigerate To make or keep cool or cold. Tony *refrigerated* the meat to keep it from spoiling.
re·frig·er·ate (ri frij′ə rāt′) *verb,* **refrigerated, refrigerating.**

refrigerator A box or room with a cooling system. Refrigerators are used to keep food and other things from spoiling.
re·frig·er·a·tor (ri frij′ə rā′tər) *noun, plural* **refrigerators.**

refuge A shelter or protection from danger or trouble. The frightened puppy took *refuge* under the bed.
ref·uge (ref′yōoj) *noun, plural* **refuges.**

refugee A person who flees from a place to find safety or protection. The *refugees* had to leave their own country because of the war and find homes in another place.
ref·u·gee (ref′yōo jē′) *noun, plural* **refugees.**

refund To give or pay back. The salesman *refunded* Mary's money when she returned the dress she had bought. *Verb.*
—The return of money that has been paid. When Mrs. White's new skirt faded, she took it back to the store and asked for a *refund. Noun.*
re·fund (ri fund′ *for verb;* rē′fund *for noun*) *verb,* **refunded, refunding;** *noun, plural* **refunds.**

refuse[1] To say no to; reject. Betsy *refused* their offer of help. His father *refused* to let him stay up late.
re·fuse (ri fyōoz′) *verb,* **refused, refusing.**

refuse[2] Anything thrown away as useless or worthless; trash or rubbish. The street was littered with *refuse* after the parade.
ref·use (ref′yōos) *noun.*

regain 1. To get back again; recover. Steve quickly *regained* his health after being sick. 2. To get back to. We *regained* the highway after a short detour.
re·gain (rē gān′) *verb,* **regained, regaining.**

regard 1. To think of; consider. Robin *regards* Jack as her best friend. 2. To look at closely. The stranger *regarded* us with suspicion. 3. To show respect or consideration for. Sarah always *regards* other people's feelings. *Verb.*
—1. Careful thought, attention, or consideration. Jack always has *regard* for the feelings of others. 2. Respect or affection. Ruth held her uncle in the highest *regard.* 3. **regards.** Best wishes. Please give my *regards* to your family. *Noun.*
re·gard (ri gärd′) *verb,* **regarded, regarding;** *noun, plural* **regards.**

regardless In spite of. I'm buying the book, *regardless* of the cost.
re·gard·less (ri gärd′lis) *adjective.*

regime A system of government. The people suffered under the *regime* of the cruel dictator.
re·gime (rə zhēm′ *or* rā zhēm′) *noun, plural* **regimes.**

regiment A military unit made up of several battalions. It is usually commanded by a colonel.
reg·i·ment (rej′ə mənt) *noun, plural* **regiments.**

region Any large area or territory. This plant grows in desert *regions.*
re·gion (rē′jən) *noun, plural* **regions.**

register 1. A written list or record. Every guest had to write his name in the hotel *register.* 2. A machine that automatically records and counts. A cash *register* records money that is taken in. 3. An opening or a similar device that controls the passage of air in a heating or ventilating system. *Noun.*
—1. To write in a list or record. The teacher *registered* the names of students who were absent. Voters must *register* before they can vote. 2. To show or express. Her face *registered* her disappointment. 3. To show or record, as on a scale or meter. The temperature *registered* fifty degrees today. 4. To have mail officially recorded by paying a fee. If a letter or package has been *registered,* there is less chance that it will be lost, stolen, or damaged. *Verb.*
reg·is·ter (rej′is tər) *noun, plural* **registers;** *verb,* **registered, registering.**

at; āpe; cär; end; mē; it; īce; hot; ōld;
fôrk; wood; fōol; oil; out; up; turn; sing;
thin; this; hw in white; zh in treasure.
ə stands for a in about, e in taken
i in pencil, o in lemon, and u in circus.

521

regret To feel sorry about. Debbie *regretted* having said unkind things about her friends. *Verb.*
—A feeling of sadness or sorrow. Mr. Wilson felt no *regret* about his decision to move to another city. *Noun.*
re·gret (ri gret′) *verb,* **regretted, regretting;** *noun, plural* **regrets.**

regular 1. Normal; usual. Our *regular* teacher was absent today. Six o'clock is our *regular* dinner time. 2. Happening again and again at the same time. We went to Canada as part of our *regular* summer vacation. 3. According to habit or usual behavior. My father is a *regular* customer at that store.
reg·u·lar (reg′yə lər) *adjective.*

regulate 1. To control, manage, or set. Laws are made to *regulate* people's behavior. Valves *regulate* the flow of blood in your heart. 2. To put or keep in good working order or at some standard. The jeweler *regulated* my watch so it would be more accurate. Turn the dial to *regulate* the temperature of the room.
reg·u·late (reg′yə lāt′) *verb,* **regulated, regulating.**

regulation 1. A law, rule, or order. One of our school *regulations* forbids smoking. 2. The act of regulating or the state of being regulated. A thermostat was used for the *regulation* of the temperature in the building.
reg·u·la·tion (reg′yə lā′shən) *noun, plural* **regulations.**

rehearsal A practicing in order to prepare for a performance. The actors had many *rehearsals* before the play opened.
re·hears·al (ri hur′səl) *noun, plural* **rehearsals.**

rehearse To practice or train in order to prepare for a performance. The dancers *rehearsed* their parts in the ballet. The director *rehearsed* the actors until they knew all their lines.
re·hearse (ri hurs′) *verb,* **rehearsed, rehearsing.**

reign 1. The period of time that a monarch rules. That building was designed during the *reign* of Queen Victoria. 2. The power or rule of a monarch. The people were unhappy under the *reign* of the cruel king. *Noun.*
—1. To hold or have the power of a monarch. The king *reigned* for nearly sixty years. 2. To be widespread; exist everywhere. Disease and starvation *reigned* throughout the country after the terrible flood. *Verb.* ▲ Other words that sound like this are **rain** and **rein.**
reign (rān) *noun, plural* **reigns;** *verb,* **reigned, reigning.**

rein 1. One of two or more narrow straps that are attached to a bridle or bit. Reins are used to guide and control a horse or other animal. 2. Any means of control. Harvey kept a tight *rein* on his temper. *Noun.*
—To guide and control. Marjorie *reined* the horse in when he started to gallop too fast. *Verb.* ▲ Other words that sound like this are **rain** and **reign.**
rein (rān) *noun, plural* **reins;** *verb,* **reined, reining.**

reindeer A large deer that has a white, gray, or brown coat and branching antlers. It is found in northern regions.
rein·deer (rān′dēr′) *noun, plural* **reindeer.**

Reindeer

reinforce To give more strength to by adding new or extra parts, materials, or people. The workers *reinforced* the dam with sandbags. The general *reinforced* the fort with more troops.
re·in·force (rē′in fôrs′) *verb,* **reinforced, reinforcing.**

reject To refuse to accept, allow, or approve. My father *rejected* the man's offer to buy our house. The government *rejected* the plan to lower taxes.
re·ject (ri jekt′) *verb,* **rejected, rejecting.**

rejoice To show or feel great joy. The soldier's parents *rejoiced* at the news of his safe return from the war.
re·joice (ri jois′) *verb,* **rejoiced, rejoicing.**

relapse A falling or slipping back into a former condition. We thought he was over the flu, but he has had a *relapse.*
re·lapse (rē′laps′) *noun, plural* **relapses.**

relate 1. To tell the story of. The witness *related* what he had seen. 2. To connect in thought or meaning. The teacher *related* his improved grades to better study habits.
re·late (ri lāt′) *verb,* **related, relating.**

related Belonging to the same family. My sister's husband is *related* to me by marriage.
re·lat·ed (ri lā′tid) *adjective.*

relation 1. A connection in thought or meaning between two or more things. The doctor explained the *relation* between a good diet and a healthy body. 2. A connection or dealings between one person or thing and another. The two countries broke off *relations* when the war began. 3. A person who belongs to the same family as another; relative. The young woman sent wedding invitations to all her close *relations*.
re·la·tion (ri lā′shən) *noun, plural* **relations.**

relationship The state of being related; connection. There was a *relationship* between the number of times the actors rehearsed the play and how well they performed it.
re·la·tion·ship (ri lā′shən ship′) *noun, plural* **relationships.**

relative Having meaning only in relation or comparison to something else. The words "right" and "left" are *relative* because their meaning depends on which way a person looks at something. *Adjective.*
—A person who belongs to the same family as someone else. *Noun.*
rel·a·tive (rel′ə tiv) *adjective; noun, plural* **relatives.**

relax 1. To make or become less tense. A hot bath helped to *relax* the athlete's sore leg muscles. My father likes to *relax* by reading the newspaper when he comes home from work. 2. To make less strict. The coach *relaxed* the rules so that girls could try out for the team.
re·lax (ri laks′) *verb,* **relaxed, relaxing.**

relay A fresh set, team, or supply that replaces or relieves another. The drivers of the stagecoaches used several *relays* of horses on the long journey. *Noun.*
—To pass along. My brother answered the telephone and *relayed* my friend's message to me. *Verb.*
re·lay (rē′lā′ *for noun;* rē′lā′ *or* ri lā′ *for verb*) *noun, plural* **relays;** *verb,* **relayed, relaying.**

relay race A race between two or more teams. Each team member goes a certain distance, and then another team member takes his place.

release To set free; let go. The man was *released* after being held prisoner for ten days. My father *released* me from the promise I had made. *Verb.*
—The act of releasing or the state of being released. The man's *release* from prison came after two years. *Noun.*
re·lease (ri lēs′) *verb,* **released, releasing;** *noun, plural* **releases.**

relevant Having to do with the matter at hand; appropriate. His question about Christopher Columbus was *relevant* to our discussion of explorers.
rel·e·vant (rel′ə vənt) *adjective.*

reliable That can be depended on and trusted. Caroline is a *reliable* person who always has her work finished on time.
re·li·a·ble (ri lī′ə bəl) *adjective.*

relic A thing from the past. We found arrowheads and other Indian *relics.*
rel·ic (rel′ik) *noun, plural* **relics.**

relief¹ 1. Comfort or help. The medicine gave her *relief* from her headache. We got *relief* from the heat by going into an air-conditioned room. It was a great *relief* to all of us when our lost dog came home. The government sent *relief* for the victims of the flood. 2. Freedom from a job or duty. The night watchman will not get *relief* until seven o'clock in the morning.
re·lief (ri lēf′) *noun, plural* **reliefs.**

relief² A standing out of a figure or design from a flat background.
re·lief (ri lēf′) *noun, plural* **reliefs.**

Relief

relieve 1. To free from discomfort or pain; comfort or help. The doctor gave her medicine to *relieve* her cough. The good news *relieved* him of his worries. 2. To free from a job or duty. The lifeguard couldn't leave the pool until he was *relieved* by another lifeguard.
re·lieve (ri lēv′) *verb,* **relieved, relieving.**

at; āpe; cär; end; mē; it; īce; hot; ōld;
fôrk; wood; fool; oil; out; up; turn; sing;
thin; this; hw in white; zh in treasure.
ə stands for a in about, e in taken
i in pencil, o in lemon, and u in circus.

religion **1.** Belief in or worship of God, or a god or gods. **2.** A particular system of belief and worship. Christianity and Buddhism are two of the world's major *religions*.
re·li·gion (ri lij′ən) *noun, plural* **religions.**

religious **1.** Showing devotion to a religion. She belongs to a very *religious* family. **2.** Of or having to do with religion. Henry's *religious* beliefs are not the same as mine.
re·li·gious (ri lij′əs) *adjective.*

relish A mixture of spices, pickles, olives, chopped vegetables, and the like. It is used as a side dish and to flavor food.
rel·ish (rel′ish) *noun, plural* **relishes.**

reluctant Unwilling. Billy is *reluctant* to lend Jim a book because he never returns what he borrows.
re·luc·tant (ri luk′tənt) *adjective.*

rely To trust; depend. You can *rely* on Carol to be of help when you need her.
re·ly (ri lī′) *verb,* **relied, relying.**

remain **1.** To stay behind or in the same place. Dick *remained* at home while the rest of us went to the party. **2.** To go on being. Ellen and I *remained* friends in spite of our quarrel. **3.** To be left. All that *remains* of the ancient city is ruins.
re·main (ri mān′) *verb,* **remained, remaining.**

remainder **1.** A remaining part. I wasn't hungry any more, so Ben ate the *remainder* of my sandwich. **2.** The number found when one number is subtracted from another. If you subtract 3 from 10, the *remainder* is 7. **3.** The number left over when a number cannot be divided evenly. If you divide 3 into 10, the answer is 3 with a *remainder* of 1.
re·main·der (ri mān′dər) *noun, plural* **remainders.**

remains **1.** Something that is left. The explorer found the *remains* of an ancient city. **2.** A dead body.
re·mains (ri mānz′) *noun plural.*

remark A short statement or comment. The farmer made a few *remarks* about the weather. *Noun.*
—To say; mention. Nancy *remarked* that she liked the sweater I was wearing. *Verb.*
re·mark (ri märk′) *noun, plural* **remarks;** *verb,* **remarked, remarking.**

remarkable Worthy of being noticed; not ordinary; unusual. Elizabeth's science project is *remarkable*.
re·mark·a·ble (ri mär′kə bəl) *adjective.*

remedy Something that heals, improves, or gets rid of a bad condition. The scientist hoped to discover a *remedy* for the common cold. *Noun.*

—To heal, improve, or get rid of a bad condition. The city government hoped to *remedy* the air pollution in the town. *Verb.*
rem·e·dy (rem′ə dē) *noun, plural* **remedies;** *verb,* **remedied, remedying.**

remember **1.** To bring back or recall to the mind. Do you *remember* where you left your jacket? **2.** To keep in mind carefully. Please *remember* that you have an appointment with the dentist today. **3.** To reward or present with a gift. The old man *remembered* his favorite charities in his will. **4.**
re·mem·ber (ri mem′bər) *verb,* **remembered, remembering.**

remind To make a person think of someone or something; cause to remember. The girl I met yesterday *reminds* me of you. Harriet *reminded* David that it was time to go home for dinner.
re·mind (ri mīnd′) *verb,* **reminded, reminding.**

remote **1.** Not near; far away. The explorer traveled to *remote* regions. **2.** Out of the way. The *remote* mountain village was visited by very few tourists. **3.** Small; slight. There was only a *remote* possibility that our team would win.
re·mote (ri mōt′) *adjective,* **remoter, remotest.**

remote control The controlling of a machine or device from a distance. Guided missiles and some televisions are run by remote control.

removal The act of removing or the state of being removed. The *removal* of the books from the shelf took only a few minutes.
re·mov·al (ri moo′vəl) *noun, plural* **removals.**

remove **1.** To take or move away or off. The waiter *removed* the dishes from the table. Martin *removed* his sweater because the room was warm. **2.** To do away with; get rid of. The pilot's calm words *removed* the passengers' fear. **3.** To dismiss from an office or position. The politician was *removed* from office for having taken money dishonestly.
re·move (ri moov′) *verb,* **removed, removing.**

render **1.** To cause to be or become; make. The surprise gift *rendered* Joan speechless. **2.** To give or present. He *rendered* an apology for his rude behavior. The jury *rendered* a verdict of not guilty. The musician *rendered* the song beautifully.
ren·der (ren′dər) *verb,* **rendered, rendering.**

rendezvous An appointment to meet at a certain place at a certain time. The boy scouts made a *rendezvous* to meet at the camp at noon.

ren·dez·vous (rän′də voo′) *noun, plural* **rendezvous.**

renew 1. To make new or as if new again. The carpenter *renewed* the finish on the scratched table. 2. To begin again. After being separated for several years, they *renewed* their friendship. 3. To cause to continue for a period of time. Francis *renewed* his subscription to the magazine. 4. To replace with more. The ship *renewed* its supply of food before sailing again.
re·new (ri noo′ *or* ri nyoo′) *verb,* **renewed, renewing.**

rent A payment for the use of something. My father pays the *rent* for our apartment every month. *Noun.*
—1. To get the right to use something in return for paying rent. We do not own this car; we have only *rented* it for the weekend. 2. To give the right to use something in return for the paying of rent. The store *rents* out bicycles. 3. To be for rent. The apartment *rents* for two hundred dollars a month. *Verb.*
rent (rent) *noun, plural* **rents;** *verb,* **rented, renting.**

repaid Patrick *repaid* the money he borrowed. Look up **repay** for more information.
re·paid (ri pād′) *verb.*

repair To put into good condition again; fix; mend. The carpenter *repaired* the broken leg of the table. *Verb.*
—1. The act of repairing. The damaged chair was beyond *repair.* 2. The condition that something is in. Eric keeps his bicycle in good *repair. Noun.*
re·pair (ri per′) *verb,* **repaired, repairing;** *noun, plural* **repairs.**

repay 1. To pay or give back. Sarah promised to *repay* the loan quickly. 2. To pay or give back to a person. He forgot to *repay* me for the money he borrowed. 3. To give, make, or do in return. I hope that I will be able to *repay* your kindness to me someday.
re·pay (ri pā′) *verb,* **repaid, repaying.**

repeal To do away with officially. Congress voted to *repeal* the old law. *Verb.*
—The act of repealing. The President supported the *repeal* of the law. *Noun.*
re·peal (ri pēl′) *verb,* **repealed, repealing;** *noun, plural* **repeals.**

repeat To say, do, or make again. The teacher *repeated* the question to the class. When he copied the letter over, he *repeated* the mistake he had made the first time.
re·peat (ri pēt′) *verb,* **repeated, repeating.**

repel 1. To drive back or away. The soldiers *repelled* the enemy's attack. 2. To cause to feel dislike or disgust. When they saw how dirty the kitchen of the restaurant was, the thought of eating there *repelled* them. 3. To keep off or out. This raincoat *repels* water.
re·pel (ri pel′) *verb,* **repelled, repelling.**

repetition The act of repeating. His *repetition* of the telephone number helped him to remember it.
rep·e·ti·tion (rep′ə tish′ən) *noun, plural* **repetitions.**

replace 1. To take or fill the place of. Richard will *replace* John as the president of the club. 2. To get or give something that takes the place of something else. We bought a new pane for the window to *replace* the one that had been broken. 3. To put back. Christine decided not to buy the magazine, and *replaced* it in the rack.
re·place (ri plās′) *verb,* **replaced, replacing.**

reply To answer in speech, writing, or action. Steve did not *reply* to Judy's question. Sue *replied* that she liked the movie very much. When we waved to David, he *replied* with a friendly smile. *Verb.*
—Something said, written, or done in answer. Terry gave the correct *reply* to the teacher's question. *Noun.*
re·ply (ri plī′) *verb,* **replied, replying;** *noun, plural* **replies.**

report An account of or statement about something. The weather *report* said that it might snow today. Edith wrote a book *report* for the teacher. *Noun.*
—1. To make or give a report. My father *reported* the crime to the police. The newspaper *reported* the news of the fire. 2. To present oneself. He was asked to *report* to the principal's office. *Verb.*
re·port (ri pôrt′) *noun, plural* **reports;** *verb,* **reported, reporting.**

report card A written report of a student's grades and behavior.

reporter A person whose job is to gather and report news for a newspaper, magazine, television or radio show, or the like.
re·port·er (ri pôr′tər) *noun, plural* **reporters.**

represent 1. To be a sign or symbol of; stand for. The dots on the map *represent* towns and cities. The letters of the alphabet

at; āpe; cär; end; mē; it; īce; hot; ōld; fôrk; wood; fool; oil; out; up; turn; sing; thin; this; hw in white; zh in treasure. ə stands for a in about, e in taken i in pencil, o in lemon, and u in circus.

represent the sounds of our language. **2.** To speak or act for. Two senators *represent* the citizens of each state.

rep·re·sent (rep′ri zent′) *verb,* **represented, representing.**

representative   A person who is chosen to speak or act for others. The members of the Congress are our elected *representatives* in the federal government. The company had sales *representatives* in all the large cities in our state. *Noun.*
—**1.** Characteristic of a group or kind. The museum had a *representative* collection of modern art. **2.** Made up of representatives. The Congress is a *representative* body. *Adjective.*

rep·re·sent·a·tive   (rep′ri zen′tə tiv)   *noun, plural* **representatives;** *adjective.*

reproduce   **1.** To produce, form, or bring about again. The tape recorder *reproduced* their conversation. **2.** To produce offspring. Most plants *reproduce* by means of seeds.

re·pro·duce (rē′prə do͞os′ *or* rē′prə dyo͞os′) *verb,* **reproduced, reproducing.**

reproduction   **1.** The process by which living things produce offspring or others like themselves. **2.** Something that is reproduced. That picture is a *reproduction* of a famous painting.

re·pro·duc·tion (rē′prə duk′shən) *noun, plural* **reproductions.**

reptile   A cold-blooded animal that has a backbone. Reptiles have dry, scaly skin. They move by crawling on their stomachs or creeping on short legs. Most reptiles reproduce by laying eggs. Lizards, snakes, alligators, and turtles are reptiles.

rep·tile (rep′təl *or* rep′tīl) *noun, plural* **reptiles.**

republic   **1.** A form of government in which the authority belongs to the people. The people elect representatives to manage the government. A republic is headed by a president, rather than a king or other royal ruler. **2.** A country that has such a form of government. The United States is a republic.

re·pub·lic (ri pub′lik) *noun, plural* **republics.**

▲   The word **republic** goes back to two Latin words that mean "public thing." Since citizens in a republic vote for their rulers, the government is a thing that belongs to the public.

---

republican   Of or like a republic. The rebels overthrew the king and set up a *republican* government. *Adjective.*

—**1.** A person who believes in or supports a republic as a form of government. **2. Republican.** A person who is a member of the Republican Party. *Noun.*

re·pub·li·can (ri pub′li kən) *adjective; noun, plural* **republicans.**

Republican Party   One of the two main political parties of the United States.

reputation   What most people think of a person or thing. That judge has a *reputation* for always being fair and honest. That restaurant has a bad *reputation*. Cheating on the test ruined the girl's *reputation*.

rep·u·ta·tion (rep′yə tā′shən) *noun, plural* **reputations.**

request   To ask or ask for. Joe *requested* permission to leave school early today. She *requested* us to be on time for her party. *Verb.*

—**1.** The act of asking for something. The teacher's *request* for attention made the class quiet down. **2.** Something that is asked for. His father felt that three dollars more allowance a week was too large a *request*. *Noun.*

re·quest (ri kwest′) *verb,* **requested, requesting;** *noun, plural* **requests.**

require   **1.** To have need of. The cut on his arm *required* medical attention. Sewing a dress *requires* skill and patience. **2.** To force someone to do something. The law *requires* that people stop their cars at a red light.

re·quire (ri kwīr′) *verb,* **required, requiring.**

requirement   Something that is necessary; demand or need. Good grades are a *requirement* for getting into that college. Eating properly is a *requirement* for good health.

re·quire·ment (ri kwīr′mənt) *noun, plural* **requirements.**

rescue   To save or free. The lifeguard *rescued* the drowning woman. *Verb.*
—The act of rescuing. The policeman got a medal for his *rescue* of the man from his attackers. *Noun.*

res·cue (res′kyo͞o) *verb,* **rescued, rescuing;** *noun, plural* **rescues.**

research   A careful study or investigation in order to find and learn facts. She did much *research* in the library before writing her report on life in ancient Egypt. *Noun.*
—To do research for. She used books from the library to *research* her book report. *Verb.*

re·search (ri surch′ *or* rē′surch′) *noun, plural* **researches;** *verb,* **researched, researching.**

resemblance   A likeness in appearance. There is a close *resemblance* between the two brothers.

re·sem·blance (ri zem′bləns) *noun, plural* **re-semblances.**

resemble To be like or similar to. That blue hat *resembles* mine.
re·sem·ble (ri zem′bəl) *verb,* **resembled, re-sembling.**

resent To feel anger or bitterness at or toward. I *resent* your unkind remark.
re·sent (ri zent′) *verb,* **resented, resenting.**

resentment A feeling of anger or bitterness. He felt *resentment* at being called a coward.
re·sent·ment (ri zent′mənt) *noun, plural* **re-sentments.**

reservation **1.** An arrangement that is made to have something set aside for a particular person. We made *reservations* for five people for dinner at the new restaurant. **2.** Land set aside by the government for a special purpose. Reservations have been set aside for Indian tribes to live on. Places where wild animals can live without danger of being killed are called reservations. **3.** Something that limits or causes doubt. She had some *reservations* about walking home alone at night.
res·er·va·tion (rez′ər vā′shən) *noun, plural* **reservations.**

reserve **1.** To set aside or have set aside for a particular person or purpose. Her parents *reserved* rooms at the hotel for the family. He *reserves* his weekends for working in the garden. **2.** To save until a later time. The athlete *reserved* his strength for the race. **3.** To keep for oneself. I *reserve* the right to make up my mind about whether I'll go or not. *Verb.*
—**1.** Something that is set aside; store; supply. The woodsman had a large *reserve* of food for the winter. **2.** The habit of keeping one's feelings or thoughts to oneself. Her *reserve* makes it hard for her to make friends easily. **3. reserves.** The part of the armed forces that is kept ready for service in an emergency. *Noun.*
re·serve (ri zurv′) *verb,* **reserved, reserving;** *noun, plural* **reserves.**

reservoir A place used to store water.
res·er·voir (rez′ər vwär′) *noun, plural* **reservoirs.**

residence **1.** A place where a person lives or resides. His business office is in town, but his *residence* is in the suburbs. **2.** A period of time spent living in a place. After ten years' *residence* in the city, her family moved.
res·i·dence (rez′ə dəns) *noun, plural* **resi-dences.**

resident A person who lives in a particular place. She is a *resident* of this town.
res·i·dent (rez′ə dənt) *noun, plural* **residents.**

residential Having to do with or suitable for residences. A *residential* neighborhood does not have factories or office buildings.
res·i·den·tial (rez′ə den′shəl) *adjective.*

resign To give up a job, position, or office. Jack *resigned* as captain of the team so he would have more time to study.
re·sign (ri zīn′) *verb,* **resigned, resigning.**

resignation The act of resigning. We were surprised by the club treasurer's *resignation.*
res·ig·na·tion (rez′ig nā′shən) *noun, plural* **resignations.**

resin A yellow or brown sticky substance that comes from pine, balsam, and certain other trees. Resin is used especially in paints and plastics and in making linoleum, glue, and rubber.
res·in (rez′in) *noun, plural* **resins.**

resist **1.** To keep from giving into. Peter found it hard to *resist* telling me the secret. **2.** To fight against or overcome. The little country *resisted* the enemy invasion. **3.** To overcome the effect or action of. This metal *resists* rusting.
re·sist (ri zist′) *verb,* **resisted, resisting.**

resistance **1.** The act of resisting. The store owner made no *resistance* to the thief when he saw that he had a gun. **2.** The ability to overcome something. Sally caught a cold because she's been working too hard and her *resistance* is low. **3.** A force that opposes or works against the motion of another. Automobiles are built so that they can overcome air *resistance.*
re·sist·ance (ri zis′təns) *noun.*

resolution **1.** Something that is decided upon. She made a *resolution* to go on a diet. The town council passed a *resolution* to make the town's park larger. **2.** The state or quality of being very determined. No one could overcome his *resolution* once his mind was made up.
res·o·lu·tion (rez′ə loo′shən) *noun, plural* **resolutions.**

resolve **1.** To decide to do something; de-termine. June *resolved* to go to college. **2.** To

at; āpe; cär; end; mē; it; īce; hot; ōld;
fôrk; wood; fool; oil; out; up; turn; sing;
thin; this; hw in white; zh in treasure.
ə stands for a in about, e in taken
i in pencil, o in lemon, and u in circus.

settle, explain, or solve. She *resolved* the argument by giving proof that what she had said was true.

re·solve (ri zolv´) *verb,* **resolved, resolving.**

resonant **1.** Able to increase or prolong sounds. The wood of a guitar is *resonant.* **2.** Having a full, rich sound. The famous actor had a *resonant* voice.

res·o·nant (rez´ə nənt) *adjective.*

resort To use or go to for help or protection. He *resorts* to his family whenever he's in trouble. *Verb.*

—**1.** A place where people go for fun or relaxation. We are going to a *resort* in the mountains to ski. **2.** A person or thing that is used or gone to for help or protection. The police are your best *resort* when something has been stolen. *Noun.*

re·sort (ri zôrt´) *verb,* **resorted, resorting;** *noun, plural* **resorts.**

resound **1.** To be filled with sound. The stadium *resounded* with cheers when the home team scored a touchdown. **2.** To make a loud, long, or echoing sound. Thunder *resounded* in the air.

re·sound (ri zound´) *verb,* **resounded, resounding.**

resource **1.** A person or thing that is used or gone to for help or protection. His friends were his *resource* when he needed to borrow money. **2. resources.** The wealth of a country or its way of producing wealth. Oil is one of that country's largest natural *resources.* **3.** Skill and cleverness in dealing with situations. The prisoner showed great *resource* in escaping from his cell. **4.** The action or means used in an emergency or a difficult time. When caught, the spy's only *resource* was to lie.

re·source (rē´sôrs´ *or* ri sôrs´) *noun, plural* **resources.**

respect **1.** High regard or consideration. It is important to have *respect* for the rights and opinions of others. **2.** A favorable opinion; admiration. The mayor had won the *respect* of everyone in the town. **3.** A special way; particular point. In some *respects,* she is a better student than her sister. **4.** Relation; reference. He showed an improvement with *respect* to grades. **5. respects.** Regards or greetings. Please give my *respects* to your family. *Noun.*

—To have or show honor or consideration for. We *respect* his honesty. She *respected* my privacy and didn't bother me while I was working. *Verb.*

re·spect (ri spekt´) *noun, plural* **respects;** *verb,* **respected, respecting.**

respectable **1.** Honest and decent; having a good reputation. He is a *respectable* member of the community. **2.** Better than average; pretty good or large. His marks in school are *respectable.*

re·spect·a·ble (ri spek´tə bəl) *adjective.*

respectful Having or showing respect. She was always *respectful* when she talked to her teachers.

re·spect·ful (ri spekt´fəl) *adjective.*

respective Belonging to each. The children went to their *respective* homes after school.

re·spec·tive (ri spek´tiv) *adjective.*

respectively Regarding each in the order given. Mrs. Gordon and Mr. Lane are, *respectively,* the principal and assistant principal of the school.

re·spec·tive·ly (ri spek´tiv lē) *adverb.*

respiration The act or process of breathing. *Respiration* is more difficult at high altitudes because the air has less oxygen.

res·pi·ra·tion (res´pə rā´shən) *noun.*

respiratory Having to do with respiration or the organs used in respiration. A disease that affects the lungs is a *respiratory* disease.

res·pi·ra·to·ry (res´pər ə tôr´ē) *adjective.*

respond **1.** To give an answer. He did not *respond* to my question. **2.** To act in return; react. She *responded* to the sudden flash of light by blinking her eyes. The patient *responded* well to the medicine.

re·spond (ri spond´) *verb,* **responded, responding.**

response Something said or done in answer. What was his *response* to your question?

re·sponse (ri spons´) *noun, plural* **responses.**

responsibility **1.** The quality or condition of being responsible. He felt a great deal of *responsibility* for his younger brother. **2.** Something for which a person is responsible; job or duty. Setting the table for dinner is your *responsibility.*

re·spon·si·bil·i·ty (ri spon´sə bil´ə tē) *noun, plural* **responsibilities.**

responsible **1.** Having as a job, duty, or concern. Tom is *responsible* for collecting the class dues. **2.** Able to be trusted; trustworthy; reliable. Allison is a very *responsible* baby-sitter. **3.** Being the main cause. Carelessness is *responsible* for many accidents. **4.** Involving important duties. Being president of that bank is a very *responsible* job.

re·spon·si·ble (ri spon´sə bəl) *adjective.*

rest¹ **1.** A time of ease or relaxation; stopping of work or activity. The plumber took a *rest* before finishing the job. **2.** Freedom from

work or anything that troubles or disturbs; quiet. Sunday is the family's day of *rest*. **3.** Sleep. She did not get enough *rest* last night. **4.** The state of not being in motion. The butterfly came to *rest* on the flower. **5.** Something that acts as a stand or support for something else. The chair has a head *rest* on the back. **6.** A silence in music. *Noun.*
—**1.** To stop work or activity; take a rest. The children *rested* on the porch after their softball game. **2.** To be quiet or at ease. She couldn't *rest* until she knew that everyone was home safely. **3.** To support or be supported. Jane's hands *rested* in her lap. Jim *rested* his arm on the table. **4.** To give rest to. He *rested* his horse after the race. **5.** To be directed or fixed. The hungry boy's eyes *rested* on the cake on the table. *Verb.*
    rest (rest) *noun, plural* **rests;** *verb,* **rested, resting.**

rest² **1.** Something that is left; remainder. I ate the *rest* of the cake after everyone left. **2.** Those people or things remaining; others. The *rest* will meet us in the park after lunch. *Noun.*
—To continue to be; remain. The responsibility for the money *rests* with him. *Verb.*
    rest (rest) *noun; verb,* **rested, resting.**

restaurant A place where food is prepared and served to customers at tables by a waiter or waitress.
    res·tau·rant (res′tər ənt) *noun, plural* **restaurants.**

restless **1.** Not able to rest. The audience got *restless* because the speech was so long. **2.** Not giving rest; not restful. The patient spent a *restless* night.
    rest·less (rest′lis) *adjective.*

restore **1.** To bring back; establish again. The police tried to *restore* order in the crowd after the fight broke out. **2.** To bring back to a former or original state or condition. The old house has been *restored* by its new owners. **3.** To return something lost, stolen, or taken. The police *restored* the jewels to their owner.
    re·store (ri stôr′) *verb,* **restored, restoring.**

restrain **1.** To hold in. He tried to *restrain* his laughter. **2.** To keep from doing something. We *restrained* him from throwing the ball out the window.
    re·strain (ri strān′) *verb,* **restrained, restraining.**

restrict To keep within certain limits. Use of the swimming pool is *restricted* to club members.
    re·strict (ri strikt′) *verb,* **restricted, restricting.**

restriction **1.** Something that restricts. There are no *restrictions* on who can use the gym during school hours. **2.** The act of restricting or the state of being restricted. Club membership is open to students of all ages without *restriction*.
    re·stric·tion (ri strik′shən) *noun, plural* **restrictions.**

result Something that happens or is caused by something else. The bicycle accident was a *result* of carelessness. He won the race as a *result* of his greater speed. *Noun.*
—**1.** To be a result. Her high grades *result* from her good study habits. **2.** To have as a result. The lack of rain *resulted* in a poor corn crop for the farmers. *Verb.*
    re·sult (ri zult′) *noun, plural* **results;** *verb,* **resulted, resulting.**

resume **1.** To go on again after stopping. She *resumed* talking after answering the doorbell. **2.** To take again. The children *resumed* their places after recess.
    re·sume (ri zo̅o̅m′) *verb,* **resumed, resuming.**

retail The sale of goods in small amounts directly to customers. Her father's store deals in the *retail* of sporting equipment. *Noun.*
—Having to do with the selling of goods at retail. That is a *retail* dress shop. *Adjective.*
    re·tail (rē′tāl) *noun; adjective.*

retain **1.** To continue to have or hold; keep. Her family *retained* ownership of their house even after they moved away. **2.** To keep in mind; remember. She *retained* all the important dates and battles of the Revolutionary War. **3.** To hire the services of by paying a fee. The accused murderer *retained* a lawyer to defend him.
    re·tain (ri tān′) *verb,* **retained, retaining.**

retina The lining of the back of the eyeball. It is made up of several layers of cells that are sensitive to light. These cells send the images of things seen to the brain.
    ret·i·na (ret′ən ə) *noun, plural* **retinas.**

▲ The word **retina** probably comes from a Latin word that means "net." The people who first used the word probably thought that the retina looked like a net.

---

at; āpe; cär; end; mē; it; īce; hot; ōld; fôrk; wood; fo̅o̅l; oil; out; up; turn; sing; thin; this; hw in white; zh in treasure. ə stands for a in about, e in taken i in pencil, o in lemon, and u in circus.

retire 1. To take oneself away from a business, job, or office. My grandfather *retired* as president of the company when he was 65. 2. To go to bed. We *retired* early last night.
re·tire (ri tīr′) *verb,* **retired, retiring.**

retirement The act of retiring or the state of being retired. He took up gardening after his *retirement* from business.
re·tire·ment (ri tīr′mənt) *noun, plural* **retirements.**

retiring Avoiding people or publicity; shy. He has a very *retiring* nature and isn't comfortable in large crowds of people.
re·tir·ing (ri tīr′ing) *adjective.*

retreat To draw or move back. The defeated enemy soldiers *retreated. Verb.*
—1. The act of retreating. The soldiers surrendered soon after their *retreat.* 2. A place in which to rest or relax. We have a summer *retreat* in the mountains. 3. A signal for soldiers to retreat. The *retreat* was sounded by the bugler. *Noun.*
re·treat (ri trēt′) *verb,* **retreated, retreating;** *noun, plural* **retreats.**

retrieve 1. To get back; recover. He *retrieved* the ball from the pond. 2. To find and bring back dead or wounded game. Our dog is trained to *retrieve.*
re·trieve (ri trēv′) *verb,* **retrieved, retrieving.**

retriever A dog that is trained to retrieve game for a hunter.
re·triev·er (ri trē′vər) *noun, plural* **retrievers.**

Retriever

return 1. To come or go back. He *returned* home to get the book he had forgotten. She will *return* in an hour. 2. To happen or take place again. Winter *returns* every year. 3. To take, bring, send, give, or put back. She *returned* the book to the library. 4. To give or put back in the same way. I *returned* her visit. She *returned* his love. 5. To report in an official way. The jury *returned* a verdict of not guilty. *Verb.*
—1. The act of returning. We will call you after our *return* from vacation. 2. **returns.** An amount of money made as a profit. The *returns* from the cake sale were more than fifty dollars. *Noun.*
re·turn (ri turn′) *verb,* **returned, returning;** *noun, plural* **returns.**

reunion A coming or bringing together again of family, friends, or other groups of people. Mother's college class is holding its tenth *reunion* this year.
re·un·ion (rē yo̅o̅n′yən) *noun, plural* **reunions.**

reveal 1. To make known. If you *reveal* my secret, I will be very angry. 2. To show; display. He opened the lid to *reveal* what was in the box.
re·veal (ri vēl′) *verb,* **revealed, revealing.**

reveille A signal played on a bugle to wake up soldiers.
rev·eil·le (rev′ə lē) *noun.*

▲ The word **reveille** comes from a French word that means "Wake up!"

revenge Injury, harm, or punishment done to pay back a wrong. The man swore to get *revenge* on those who had attacked him. *Noun.*
—To cause injury, harm, or punishment in order to pay back a wrong. I will *revenge* his insults. *Verb.*
re·venge (ri venj′) *noun; verb,* **revenged, revenging.**

revenue 1. Money that is made from property or other investments. The company's *revenues* rose last year. 2. The money that is made by a government from taxes and other sources.
rev·e·nue (rev′ə no̅o̅′ *or* rev′ə nyo̅o̅′) *noun, plural* **revenues.**

reverence A feeling of deep love and respect. All the people of the town had *reverence* for the old doctor.
rev·er·ence (rev′ər əns *or* rev′rəns) *noun.*

reverent Feeling or showing deep love and respect. The man gave the old lady a *reverent* bow when he was introduced to her.
rev·er·ent (rev′ər ənt *or* rev′rənt) *adjective.*

reverse 1. Something that is the direct opposite of something else; contrary. Tom did the *reverse* of what he was supposed to do. 2. The position of gears in a machine that makes them move in a direction that is opposite to the usual direction. You have to put the car in *reverse* in order to back up. 3. The back side of something. The song I like is on the *reverse* of that record. 4. A change of luck from good to bad; setback. The man had many *reverses* in the first year of his business. *Noun.*

—Opposite in position or direction. The king's picture is on the *reverse* side of the coin. He put the car in *reverse* gear. *Adjective.*

—**1.** To turn something around, upside down, or inside out. She *reversed* the sock to mend the hole. **2.** To change to the opposite. He *reversed* his opinion once he had heard all the facts. *Verb.*

re·verse (ri vurs′) *noun, plural* **reverses;** *adjective; verb,* **reversed, reversing.**

review **1.** To study, go over, or examine again. John *reviewed* his notes in studying for the test. The higher court *reviewed* the decision of the lower court. **2.** To go over in one's mind; look back on. Phyllis *reviewed* the day's events with a smile. **3.** To give an account of a movie, play, book, or other work to praise or criticize it. She *reviews* new movies for the local newspaper. **4.** To make a formal or official inspection of. The general *reviewed* the troops. *Verb.*

—**1.** A studying, going over, or examining again. She made a quick *review* of her notes before the test. **2.** A looking back. A *review* of the events of the past year was very interesting. **3.** An account of a movie, play, book, or other work given to praise or criticize it. The author's latest book got a very good *review.* **4.** A formal or official inspection. There was a *review* of the troops before the parade. *Noun.*

re·view (ri vyo͞o′) *verb,* **reviewed, reviewing;** *noun, plural* **reviews.**

revise **1.** To change in order to correct or make better. She *revised* what she had written in order to make it easier to understand. **2.** To make different. I *revised* my bad opinion of him after talking to him for a while.

re·vise (ri vīz′) *verb,* **revised, revising.**

revive **1.** To bring back to consciousness. The fireman *revived* the unconscious woman. **2.** To bring back into use, interest, or notice. The old movie was *revived* with great success. **3.** To give new strength or freshness to. A good meal *revived* the hungry children.

re·vive (ri vīv′) *verb,* **revived, reviving.**

revoke To cancel or make no longer good or useful. The motor vehicle bureau *revoked* his driver's license after his third conviction for speeding.

re·voke (ri vōk′) *verb,* **revoked, revoking.**

revolt An uprising or rebellion against a government or other authority. The citizens took part in the *revolt* against the cruel ruler. *Noun.*

—**1.** To rebel against a government or other authority. The prisoners *revolted.* **2.** To cause

to feel sick or disgusted. The smell of the garbage *revolted* him. *Verb.*

re·volt (ri vōlt′) *noun, plural* **revolts;** *verb,* **revolted, revolting.**

revolution **1.** The overthrow of a system of government and the setting up of a new or different system of government. Revolutions are often carried out through the use of force. The *revolution* in that country got rid of the dictator and set up a democratic form of government. **2.** A sudden or complete change. The development of modern machines brought about a *revolution* in industry. **3.** Movement in a circle around a central point or object. The spacecraft made three *revolutions* around the moon before landing.

rev·o·lu·tion (rev′ə lo͞o′shən) *noun, plural* **revolutions.**

revolutionary Having to do with or tending to bring about a revolution. The *revolutionary* leaders formed a new government. The steam engine was a *revolutionary* invention.

rev·o·lu·tion·ar·y (rev′ə lo͞o′shə ner′ē) *adjective.*

revolve **1.** To move in a circle around a central point or object. The planets *revolve* around the sun. **2.** To spin or turn around a central point. Wheels *revolve* when in motion. **3.** To depend on. His whole life *revolves* around his family and his work.

re·volve (ri volv′) *verb,* **revolved, revolving.**

revolver A pistol that can be fired several times without reloading. The bullets are held in a cylinder that revolves with each shot.

re·volv·er (ri vol′vər) *noun, plural* **revolvers.**

reward **1.** Something given or received in return for something done. The student received a medal as a *reward* for getting the best marks in English. **2.** Money offered or given for the return of lost property or the capture of criminals. She offered a fifty dollar *reward* for the return of her lost dog. *Noun.*

—**1.** To give a reward to. The man *rewarded* Betty with twenty dollars for finding his watch. **2.** To give a reward for. The woman *rewarded* Linda for returning the wallet she had found. *Verb.*

re·ward (ri wôrd′) *noun, plural* **rewards;** *verb,* **rewarded, rewarding.**

at; āpe; cär; end; mē; it; īce; hot; ōld; fôrk; wood; fo͞ol; oil; out; up; turn; sing; thin; this; hw in white; zh in treasure. ə stands for a in about, e in taken i in pencil, o in lemon, and u in circus.

rhea A bird that cannot fly. The rhea looks like an ostrich but is smaller. It is found in South America.
  rhe·a (rē′ə) *noun, plural* **rheas.**

rhesus monkey A very small yellowish-brown monkey with a short tail. It is found in India. The rhesus monkey is widely used in medical research.
  rhe·sus monkey (rē′səs).

rheumatism A disease that is marked by painful stiffness of the joints and muscles, swelling, and inflammation.
  rheu·ma·tism (rōō′ mə tiz′əm)

Rhea

rhinoceros A very large animal having a thick skin and one or two horns rising from the snout. Rhinoceroses are found in Africa and Asia.
  rhi·noc·er·os (rī nos′ər əs) *noun, plural* **rhinoceroses** or **rhinoceros.**

▲ The word **rhinoceros** comes from the Greek name for this animal. It was made by putting together two Greek words that mean "nose" and "horn."

Rhinoceros

Rhode Island A state in the northeastern United States. It is the smallest state in the union. Its capital is Providence.
  Rhode Island (rōd).

▲ The name **Rhode Island** comes from the island of *Rhodes* in the Aegean Sea. An Italian sailor gave this name to an island near the colony of Rhode Island, because he thought it looked like Rhodes. After a while, the name was used for the whole colony and later for the state.

rhododendron An evergreen shrub that has clusters of bell-shaped flowers and shiny leaves.
  rho·do·den·dron (rō′də den′drən) *noun, plural* **rhododendrons.**

rhubarb A plant with reddish stalks that have a slightly sour taste. The stalks are cooked in pies, sauces, and other dishes.
  rhu·barb (rōō′bärb) *noun, plural* **rhubarbs.**

Rhododendron

rhyme 1. The sounding alike of sounds at the ends of lines of verse. For example: Humpty Dumpty sat on a wall, Humpty Dumpty had a great fall. 2. A word that has a sound that is like or the same as another. "Mail" is a *rhyme* for "pail." 3. Verse or poetry having sounds at the ends of lines that are alike or the same. *Noun.*
—To make a rhyme. "Wide" *rhymes* with "side." *Verb.*
  rhyme (rīm) *noun, plural* **rhymes;** *verb,* **rhymed, rhyming.**

rhythm A regular or orderly repeating of sounds or movements. We could hear the *rhythm* of drumbeats from the parade.
  rhythm (rith′əm) *noun, plural* **rhythms.**

rib 1. One of the curved bones that are attached to the backbone and curve around to enclose the chest cavity. 2. Something like a rib. An umbrella has ribs to which the material is attached.
  rib (rib) *noun, plural* **ribs.**

ribbon 1. A band of cloth, paper, or other material that is used for decoration. Jane wore a long yellow *ribbon* in her hair. The present was tied with green and yellow *ribbons.* 2. A band of material that is like a ribbon. I need a new typewriter *ribbon.*
  rib·bon (rib′ən) *noun, plural* **ribbons.**

rice The grains of a grass plant that is grown in many warm areas of the world. Rice is an important food in India, China, and many other parts of the world.
  rice (rīs) *noun.*

rich 1. Having much money, land, or other valuable things. His grandmother was a very *rich* woman. 2. Having a lot of something. Our country is *rich* in natural resources. 3. Able to produce much; fertile. The soil on this farm is very *rich.* 4. Deep and full. He has a *rich,* baritone voice. 5. Having a heavy, strong taste or having large amounts of butter, eggs, sugar, and flavoring. This is a very *rich* sauce.
  rich (rich) *adjective,* **richer, richest.**

riches Much money, land, and other valuable things; wealth. Her family has great *riches*.
rich·es (rich′iz) *noun plural.*

ricksha A small carriage with two wheels and a hood. It is pulled by one or two men. The ricksha is used in Asian countries.
rick·sha (rik′shô′) *noun, plural* **rickshas.**

Ricksha

rid To clear or free of something that is not wanted. What can we do to *rid* the house of ants?
rid (rid) *verb,* **rid** or **ridded, ridding.**

ridden Has he ever *ridden* a horse? Look up **ride** for more information.
rid·den (rid′ən) *verb.*

riddle¹ A question or problem that is hard to figure out or understand; puzzling question or problem. For example: What has four wheels and flies? Answer: A garbage truck.
rid·dle (rid′əl) *noun, plural* **riddles.**

riddle² To make holes in many places. He *riddled* the target with bullets.
rid·dle (rid′əl) *verb,* **riddled, riddling.**

ride 1. To sit on something and make it move in order to be carried by it. He *rides* to school every day on his bicycle. She likes to *ride* horses. 2. To be carried on or in a car, train, or other vehicle. We *rode* through the town on the bus. I'm going to *ride* the train to New York. 3. To be carried along. The sailboat *rode* over the waves. *Verb.*
—1. A short trip on an animal or in a car, train, or other vehicle. We took a *ride* around the block on our bicycles. 2. A merry-go-round or other device on which people ride for amusement. We tried all the *rides* at the amusement park. *Noun.*
ride (rīd) *verb,* **rode, ridden, riding;** *noun, plural* **rides.**

rider A person who rides. There were a number of horseback *riders* in the park.
rid·er (rī′dər) *noun, plural* **riders.**

ridge 1. The long and narrow upper part of something. The animal had a black and white spot on the *ridge* of its back. 2. A raised,

narrow strip. Corduroy has *ridges.* 3. A long and narrow chain of hills or mountains.
ridge (rij) *noun, plural* **ridges.**

ridicule To make fun of a person or thing. That mean girl often *ridicules* her little brother. *Verb.*
—Words or actions that make fun of a person or thing. His strange way of dressing leaves him open to *ridicule. Noun.*
rid·i·cule (rid′ə kyo̅o̅l′) *verb,* **ridiculed, ridiculing;** *noun.*

ridiculous Very silly or foolish. She wore a *ridiculous* hat with fruit and flowers on it to the costume party.
ri·dic·u·lous (ri dik′yə ləs) *adjective.*

rifle A firearm that is meant to be fired from the shoulder. A rifle has special grooves cut into its barrel to cause the bullet to spin as it is fired.
ri·fle (rī′fəl) *noun, plural* **rifles.**

rig 1. To fit a boat or ship with masts, sails, lines, and the like. The shipbuilder *rigged* the boat. 2. To fit out; equip. Tom *rigged* his car with a special rack for carrying skis. 3. To make or build in a hurry or by using odd bits and pieces of material. The boy *rigged* up a record player from old used parts. *Verb.*
—1. An arrangement of masts, sails, lines, and the like on a boat or ship. 2. Equipment used for a special purpose. We bought new fishing *rig* for our trip. The field is filled with oil drilling *rigs. Noun.*
rig (rig) *verb,* **rigged, rigging;** *noun, plural* **rigs.**

rigging 1. All the lines of a boat or ship. The rigging includes such things as ropes, chains, and wires. It is used for supporting the masts or working the sails. 2. Equipment used for a special purpose. The workmen set up the *rigging* for drilling the oil well.
rig·ging (rig′ing) *noun, plural* **riggings.**

right 1. Correct or true; free from mistakes. She gave the *right* answer to the arithmetic problem. 2. Just, moral, or good. Telling the truth was the *right* thing to do. 3. On or toward the side of the body that is to the east when one is facing north. He writes with his *right* hand. She sat on the *right* side of the room. 4. Proper; suitable. She is the *right* person to head the committee. *Adjective.*

at; āpe; cär; end; mē; it; īce; hot; ōld;
fôrk; wood; fo̅o̅l; oil; out; up; turn; sing;
thin; this; hw in white; zh in treasure.
ə stands for **a** in about, **e** in taken
i in pencil, **o** in lemon, and **u** in circus.

—**1.** Something that is just, moral, or good. The parents tried to teach their children to do *right*. **2.** A just, moral, or lawful claim. Every citizen is guaranteed the *right* to free speech. **3.** The right side or direction. Our house is on your *right* when you come down the street. *Noun.*

—**1.** Correctly. John didn't spell my name *right*. **2.** According to that which is just, moral, or good. You must act *right* and return the wallet you found to its owner. **3.** In a proper way; suitably. This telephone doesn't work *right*. **4.** Exactly. Put the book *right* here on the table. **5.** Without delay; immediately. Let's leave *right* after breakfast. **6.** To. or toward the right. Turn *right* at the next corner. *Adverb.*

—**1.** To make good, just, or correct. He *righted* the wrong he had done his friend and apologized. **2.** To put back into a proper or normal position. We *righted* the raft after it had flipped over. *Verb.* ▲ Another word that sounds like this is **write.**

right (rīt) *adjective; noun, plural* **rights;** *adverb; verb,* **righted, righting.**

right away. At once; immediately. I'll be there *right away.*

right angle An angle of 90 degrees. It is formed by two lines that are perpendicular to each other.

right-hand **1.** On or toward the right. We drive on the *right-hand* side of the street. **2.** For the right hand. I have lost my *right-hand* glove. **3.** Most trusted and helpful. Jim is the coach's *right-hand* man.

right-hand (rīt′hand′) *adjective.*

right-handed **1.** Using the right hand more often and more easily than the left hand. She is *right-handed.* **2.** Done with the right hand. Al made a *right-handed* throw to the catcher.

right-hand·ed (rīt′han′did) *adjective.*

rigid **1.** Not bending or giving; stiff. *Rigid* steel beams are used in building. **2.** Not changing; fixed. Our school has *rigid* rules against smoking.

rig·id (rij′id) *adjective.*

rim The outer edge or border of something. There was a chip on the *rim* of the glass. *Noun.*

—To form a rim around. The mountains *rimmed* the valley. *Verb.*

rim (rim) *noun, plural* **rims;** *verb,* **rimmed, rimming.**

rind A firm outer covering or skin. Oranges, lemons, and watermelons have rinds. Some cheeses also have rinds.

rind (rīnd) *noun, plural* **rinds.**

ring¹ **1.** A closed, curved line; circle. The children arranged their chairs in a *ring* around the teacher. **2.** A band of metal or other material in the shape of a circle. She wore a *ring* of gold on her finger. Put all the keys on a *ring*. **3.** An enclosed area. Rings are used for circus performances or for sport events, such as boxing. *Noun.*

—To form a ring around. Trees *ringed* the pond. *Verb.* ▲ Another word that sounds like this is **wring.**

Ring

ring (ring) *noun, plural* **rings;** *verb,* **ringed, ringing.**

ring² **1.** To make a clear sound like that of a bell. Did you hear the telephone *ring?* **2.** To cause something to make a clear sound. The visitor *rang* the doorbell twice. **3.** To be full of loud and clear sounds; echo. The room *rang* with laughter. **4.** To have a ringing or buzzing sound in the ear or ears. My ears *rang* from the shrill noise. *Verb.*

—**1.** A clear sound like that made by a bell. The loud *ring* of the alarm clock woke me up. **2.** A telephone call. I'll give you a *ring* tomorrow. *Noun.* ▲ Another word that sounds like this is **wring.**

ring (ring) *verb,* **rang, rung, ringing;** *noun, plural* **rings.**

rink A place that has a surface for ice skating or roller skating.

rink (ringk) *noun, plural* **rinks.**

Rink

rinse **1.** To use clear water to take out soap or other matter from something. She *rinsed* the blouse before hanging it up to dry. She *rinsed* the soap off her hands. **2.** To wash lightly. Please *rinse* the glass before you put it in the dishwasher. *Verb.*

—The act of rinsing. She gave her hair a *rinse* after she got out of the pool. *Noun.*

rinse (rins) *verb*, **rinsed, rinsing;** *noun.*

riot A noisy and violent disorder caused by a group or crowd of people. Several people were hurt in the *riot* at the prison. *Noun.*

—To take part in a noisy and violent disorder. The prisoners threatened to *riot. Verb.*

ri·ot (rī′ət) *noun, plural* **riots;** *verb,* **rioted, rioting.**

rip To tear or pull apart something. The boy *ripped* his pants on the fence. She *ripped* the paper into little pieces. *Verb.*

—A torn place; tear. You have a *rip* in your shirt. *Noun.*

rip (rip) *verb,* **ripped, ripping;** *noun, plural* **rips.**

ripe Fully grown and ready to be eaten. The tomatoes in the garden are *ripe* now.

ripe (rīp) *adjective,* **riper, ripest.**

ripen To become ripe. The tomatoes *ripened* on the vine.

rip·en (rī′pən) *verb,* **ripened, ripening.**

ripple 1. A very small wave. The breeze made *ripples* on the surface of the pond. 2. Anything that is like a ripple. This cotton material has *ripples* in it. 3. A sound that is like the sound made by the flowing of very small waves. There was a *ripple* of applause when the speaker finished. *Noun.*

—To cause ripples in. The stone he threw in the pond *rippled* the water. *Verb.*

rip·ple (rip′əl) *noun, plural* **ripples;** *verb,* **rippled, rippling.**

rise 1. To get up from a sitting, kneeling, or lying position; stand up. Everyone had to *rise* when the judge entered the courtroom. 2. To get out of bed. We *rise* at 7:00 every morning. 3. To move from a lower to a higher place; go upward. Smoke *rose* from the chimney. We watched the balloon *rise* and float away. The sun *rises* in the east. 4. To reach upward. The new building *rises* above all the others on the street. 5. To become greater or higher. The cost of living *rose* last month. 6. To go upward in position, rank, or importance. He *rose* to the presidency of his company. 7. To start; begin. That river *rises* in the mountains. Their ill feeling toward each other *rose* from a misunderstanding. 8. To rebel; revolt. The people *rose* against the cruel dictator. *Verb.*

—1. A moving upward. There was a *rise* in temperature during the day. 2. An upward slope. He was so tired that he could not even climb the *rise* of the hill. *Noun.*

rise (rīz) *verb,* **rose, risen, rising;** *noun, plural* **rises.**

risk A chance of loss or harm; danger. There is *risk* involved in riding a bicycle without holding onto the handlebars. *Noun.*

—1. To put in danger of loss or harm. The girl *risked* her life to save her baby sister from the burning house. 2. To take the risk of. He *risked* losing all his money when he bought the store. *Verb.*

risk (risk) *noun, plural* **risks;** *verb,* **risked, risking.**

ritual A system or body of special ceremonies. Baptism is part of the *ritual* of most churches.

rit·u·al (rich′o͞o əl) *noun, plural* **rituals.**

rival A person who is or tries to be as good as or better than another. The two girls were *rivals* for class president. John has no *rival* as a chess player. *Noun.*

—1. To try to be as good as or better than another. The two schools *rival* each other in football. 2. To be the equal of. Joan *rivals* her sister in getting good marks. *Verb.*

—Trying to get the same thing as another; competing. The two *rival* teams both practiced hard before the game. *Adjective.*

ri·val (rī′vəl) *noun, plural* **rivals;** *verb,* **rivaled, rivaling;** *adjective.*

river 1. A large stream of water that flows naturally and empties into a lake, ocean, or other river. 2. Anything that is like a river. A *river* of oil spilled from the truck when it was turned over in the accident.

riv·er (riv′ər) *noun, plural* **rivers.**

rivet A metal bolt that is used to fasten pieces of metal together. A rivet has a head on one end, and after it has been put in place between the pieces of metal, the other end is hammered flat to make another head. *Noun.*

—1. To fasten with a rivet. The workmen *riveted* the steel beams together. 2. To hold or fasten firmly. The children's attention was *riveted* on the puppet show. *Verb.*

riv·et (riv′it) *noun, plural* **rivets;** *verb,* **riveted, riveting.**

roach A brown or black insect. This insect is also called a **cockroach.** Look up **cockroach** for more information.

roach (rōch) *noun, plural* **roaches.**

road 1. A strip of pavement or cleared ground used for going from one place to

at; āpe; cär; end; mē; it; īce; hot; ōld;
fôrk; wo͝od; fo͞ol; oil; out; up; turn; sing;
thin; this; hw in white; zh in treasure.
ə stands for a in about, e in taken
i in pencil, o in lemon, and u in circus.

another. Roads are used by people, cars, and trucks. There was only a dirt *road* between the two mountain villages. We passed Jane riding her bicycle on the *road* to town. **2.** A way for going or moving toward something wanted. Many people helped the actor on his *road* to success. ▲ Another word that sounds like this is **rode.**

road (rōd) *noun, plural* **roads.**

roadrunner A bird that has brownish-black streaked feathers, a long tail tipped with white, and a shaggy crest on top of its head. Roadrunners usually run very fast instead of flying. They are found in the southwestern United States.

road·run·ner (rōd′run′ər) *noun, plural* **road-runners.**

Roadrunner

roadside An area along the side of a road. We pulled the car up on the *roadside* to rest. *Noun.*

—Along the side of the road. They have very good vegetables at that *roadside* stand. *Adjective.*

road·side (rōd′sīd′) *noun, plural* **roadsides;** *adjective.*

roam To go or move about without any particular place to go; wander. We *roamed* through the woods.

roam (rōm) *verb,* **roamed, roaming.**

roar **1.** To make a loud, deep sound or cry. The lion *roared.* The motor *roared* when it was started. The car *roared* down the street. **2.** To laugh loudly. Everyone at the party *roared* at his jokes. *Verb.*

—A loud, deep sound or cry. We could hear the *roar* of the ocean waves. *Noun.*

roar (rôr) *verb,* **roared, roaring;** *noun, plural* **roars.**

roast **1.** To cook in an oven or over an open fire or hot coals. We *roasted* a chicken for dinner. The children *roasted* marshmallows over the campfire. **2.** To dry and brown by heat. Coffee beans are *roasted* and ground before they are used to make coffee. **3.** To be very hot or too hot. I'm *roasting* in my heavy winter coat. *Verb.*

—A piece of meat that has been roasted or is ready to be roasted. We had a *roast* of beef for dinner. *Noun.*

roast (rōst) *verb,* **roasted, roasting;** *noun, plural* **roasts.**

rob To take away from by using force or violence; steal from. Two men *robbed* the jewelry store in broad daylight.

rob (rob) *verb,* **robbed, robbing.**

robber A person who robs.

rob·ber (rob′ər) *noun, plural* **robbers.**

robbery The act of taking something by the use of force or violence; theft. Did you read about the bank *robbery* on Tuesday?

rob·ber·y (rob′ər ē) *noun, plural* **robberies.**

robe **1.** A loose piece of clothing that is worn as a covering. Susan got a very pretty yellow *robe* for Christmas to wear over her pajamas. **2.** A piece of clothing that is worn to show one's office, profession, or rank. Priests and judges wear robes. *Noun.*

—To put a robe on. The priest *robed* himself before the church service. *Verb.*

robe (rōb) *noun, plural* **robes;** *verb,* **robed, robing.**

robin A bird that lives in North America and Europe. The robin that lives in North America has a reddish-orange breast and a black head and tail.

rob·in (rob′in) *noun, plural* **robins.**

robot A machine that looks somewhat like a person. It can do some of the same things that a human being can do.

ro·bot (rō′bət) *noun, plural* **robots.**

Robin

robust Having strength and energy; in good health. The star of the football team was a *robust* young man.

ro·bust (rō bust′ *or* rō′bust) *adjective.*

▲ The word **robust** goes back to a Latin word that means "oak." Oak is a strong, hard wood, so the Latin word meaning "oak" developed into a word meaning "strong."

rock[1] **1.** A piece of stone. The children threw *rocks* at the cans lined up on the fence. **2.** A large mass of stone forming a cliff or peak. The boat was thrown against the *rocks* by the large waves. **3.** A mass of mineral

matter that is formed naturally and is part of the earth's crust. Granite, limestone, and slate are rocks. **4.** Something that is like a rock in hardness or strength; strong support. Mother was our *rock* during the family crisis.
rock (rok) *noun, plural* **rocks.**

rock² **1.** To move back and forth or from side to side. The mother *rocked* the baby in her arms. **2.** To cause to shake violently. The explosion *rocked* the building. *Verb.*
—A rocking motion. She gave the baby a *rock* in the cradle. *Noun.*
rock (rok) *verb,* **rocked, rocking;** *noun, plural* **rocks.**

rocker **1.** A rocking chair. **2.** One of the two curved pieces on which a cradle, rocking chair, or other object rocks.
rock·er (rok′ər) *noun, plural* **rockers.**

rocket A device that is driven forward by a stream of hot gases that are released from the rear. Rockets are used as fireworks and weapons and to propel spacecraft. *Noun.*
—To move or rise very quickly. The price of food is *rocketing* upward. *Verb.*
rock·et (rok′it) *noun, plural* **rockets;** *verb,* **rocketed, rocketing.**

Rocking Chair

rocking chair A chair that is mounted on rockers or springs, so that it can rock back and forth.

rocking horse A toy horse mounted on rockers. It is large enough for a child to ride.

Rocking Horse

rock 'n' roll A kind of popular music that has a strong, steady beat and fairly simple words.
rock 'n' roll (rok′ən rōl′).

rocky¹ Full of rocks. The *rocky* beach was hard to walk on.
rock·y (rok′ē) *adjective,* **rockier, rockiest.**

rocky² Likely to fall or sway. Don't sit in that *rocky* old chair because one of its legs is broken.
rock·y (rok′ē) *adjective,* **rockier, rockiest.**

rod **1.** A thin, straight piece of metal, wood, or other material. The curtains were hung from metal *rods.* **2.** A long pole used for fishing. This is also called a **fishing rod.** Look up **fishing rod** for more information. **3.** A stick or bundle of sticks used to beat or punish. **4.** A unit for measuring. It is equal to 5½ yards or 16½ feet.
rod (rod) *noun, plural* **rods.**

rode She *rode* her bicycle over to my house. Look up **ride** for more information. ▲ Another word that sounds like this is **road.**
rode (rōd) *verb.*

rodent Any of a number of animals that have a pair of large front teeth used for gnawing. Rats, mice, squirrels, guinea pigs, and beavers are rodents.
ro·dent (rōd′ənt) *noun, plural* **rodents.**

rodeo A show in which cowboys compete with one another in horseback riding, calf roping, steer wrestling, and other similar events.
ro·de·o (rō′dē ō′ *or* rō dā′ō) *noun, plural* **rodeos.**

roe¹ The eggs of fish. ▲ Another word that sounds like this is **row.**
roe (rō) *noun.*

roe² A small deer that has a reddish-brown coat. It is found in the forests of Europe and northern Asia. ▲ Another word that sounds like this is **row.**
roe (rō) *noun, plural* **roes** or **roe.**

rogue **1.** A person who is dishonest; cheat. **2.** A person who is playful or mischievous.
rogue (rōg) *noun, plural* **rogues.**

role **1.** A character or part played by an actor. He tried out for the *role* of the hero in the school play. **2.** A part played by a person or thing; position. She took on the *role* of guide on our tour through the museum. ▲ Another word that sounds like this is **roll.**
role (rōl) *noun, plural* **roles.**

at; āpe; cär; end; mē; it; īce; hot; ōld; fôrk; wood; fōol; oil; out; up; turn; sing; thin; this; hw in white; zh in treasure. ə stands for a in about, e in taken i in pencil, o in lemon, and u in circus.

▲ The word **role** comes from a French word that was first used to mean "a roll of paper on which an actor's part or lines are written."

roll **1.** To move by turning over and over. The ball *rolled* off the table. He *rolled* the hoop. **2.** To move or be moved on wheels or rollers. The wagon *rolled* down the hill. She *rolled* the cart down the street. **3.** To turn over many times. The dog *rolled* in the mud. **4.** To move in an up and down motion or from side to side. The fog *rolled* in from the water. The ship *rolled* in the storm. **5.** To make a deep, continuous sound; rumble. The drums *rolled*. **6.** To wrap something around on itself or on something else. *Roll* up the blanket. She *rolled* the clay into a ball. **7.** To wrap in a covering. She *rolled* the old clothes in a newspaper. **8.** To spread out or make flat with a roller. He *rolled* out the dough for the cookies. **9.** To pronounce an *r* or other speech sound with a trill. Scottish people *roll* their r's. *Verb.*
—**1.** Something that is rolled up. Please buy me a *roll* of stamps at the post office. **2.** A list of names of people belonging to a group. The teacher called the *roll* and checked off the names of the students present. **3.** A piece of baked bread dough. I put the hamburger on a *roll*. **4.** A rolling or swaying motion. The *roll* of the boat in the rough waves was making us dizzy. **5.** A quick, continuous series of short sounds, as those made by beating on a drum. *Noun.* ▲ Another word that sounds like this is **role.**

roll (rōl) *verb*, **rolled, rolling;** *noun, plural* **rolls.**

roller **1.** A cylinder on which something is rolled or wound up. A window shade is on a *roller.* Hair *rollers* are made of wire mesh or plastic. **2.** A cylinder that smooths, spreads out, flattens, or crushes. We painted the walls with a paint *roller.* **3.** A small wheel on which something is rolled or moved. The moving men put the piano on *rollers* so they could move it. **4.** A long, swelling wave that breaks on the shoreline.

Roller

roll·er (rō′lər) *noun, plural* **rollers.**

roller coaster A ride in an amusement park. A roller coaster is like a small railroad that moves very fast over a track having sharp turns and sudden, steep inclines.

roller-skate To skate on roller skates. The children *roller-skated* down the street. **roll·er-skate** (rō′lər-skāt′) *verb*, **roller-skated, roller-skating.**

roller skate A skate that has small wheels on the bottom. Roller skates are used for skating on flat surfaces, such as sidewalks.

rolling pin A smooth cylinder used to roll out dough. Rolling pins are usually made of wood and have a handle at each end.

Roller Skates

Roman **1.** Of or having to do with ancient or modern Rome, its people, or their culture. **2.** Of or having to do with the style of type most widely used in printing. The letters of Roman type are upright. This sentence is printed in Roman type. *Adjective.*
—**1.** A person who was born or is living in Rome. **2.** A person who lived in ancient Rome. **3.** Roman type or lettering. *Noun.*
Ro·man (rō′mən) *adjective; noun, plural* **Romans.**

Roman Catholic **1.** Having to do with or like the Roman Catholic Church. **2.** A member of the Roman Catholic Church.

Roman Catholic Church The Christian church that recognizes the Pope as its supreme head.

romance **1.** A love affair. The story of Sleeping Beauty is about a *romance* that she has with a prince. **2.** A quality of love, excitement, mystery, or adventure. The dim lights gave a sense of *romance* to the room. **3.** A story or poem that tells of heroes and their deeds, of adventure, and of love.
ro·mance (rō mans′ *or* rō′mans) *noun, plural* **romances.**

▲ The word **romance** comes from an old French word that meant "something written in a *Romance* language." In the Middle Ages, stories of love and adventure were usually written in one of these Romance languages, instead of in Latin, which was used in more serious writings.

Romance languages The languages that developed from Latin. French, Spanish, Italian, and Portuguese are Romance languages.

Roman numeral Any one of the letters used in a numbering system based on that used by the ancient Romans. In this system I = 1, V = 5, X = 10, L = 50, C = 100, D = 500, and M = 1,000.

romantic 1. Having to do with or marked by romance. My older sister likes to read *romantic* novels. 2. Having thoughts and feelings of love and adventure. She is a very *romantic* person. 3. Suitable for love or romance. The candles gave the room a *romantic* atmosphere.
ro·man·tic (rō man′tik) *adjective.*

Rome The capital of Italy, in the central part of the country. An ancient city in the same place was the capital and center of the Roman Empire.
Rome (rōm) *noun.*

romp To play in a lively and noisy way. The children *romped* in the waves at the seashore. *Verb.*
—Lively and noisy play. The boy and his dog went for a *romp* in the woods. *Noun.*
romp (romp) *verb,* **romped, romping;** *noun, plural* **romps.**

rompers A loose, one-piece garment worn by young children.
romp·ers (rom′pərz) *noun plural.*

roof 1. The outer covering of the top of a building. The cat climbed up on the *roof* of the house. 2. Something that is like a roof in position or use. She burned the *roof* of her mouth on the hot chocolate. The *roof* of the car is blue. *Noun.*
—To cover with a roof. Our new house will be *roofed* this week. *Verb.*
roof (roof *or* roof) *noun, plural* **roofs;** *verb,* **roofed, roofing.**

rook[1] A European bird that is like a crow. It lives in large groups.
rook (rook) *noun, plural* **rooks.**

rook[2] A piece that is used in the game of chess. The rook can move any number of spaces across or up and down the board, parallel to the sides.
rook (rook) *noun, plural* **rooks.**

rookie 1. A person who has just joined a group and has had no experience. The new policeman in our neighborhood is a *rookie*. 2. An athlete with no experience in the major leagues.
rook·ie (rook′ē) *noun, plural* **rookies.**

room 1. An area that is or may be taken up by something; space. There was no *room* to park the car in the lot. Is there *room* for this book in the suitcase? 2. An area in a house or other building that is separated or set off by walls. Our house has seven *rooms*. 3. A chance or opportunity to do something. There is *room* for improvement in his schoolwork. *Noun.*
—To live in a room or rooms. Rick and Jack *roomed* together at college. *Verb.*
room (room *or* room) *noun, plural* **rooms;** *verb,* **roomed, rooming.**

roommate A person with whom one shares a room or rooms. She was my *roommate* in college.
room·mate (room′māt′ *or* room′māt′) *noun, plural* **roommates.**

roomy Having plenty of room; large. They live in a *roomy* old house at the end of the street.
room·y (roo′mē *or* room′ē) *adjective,* **roomier, roomiest.**

roost 1. A perch on which birds rest or sleep. 2. A building or other place for birds to rest or sleep for the night. *Noun.*
—To rest or sleep on a roost as a bird does. *Verb.*
roost (roost) *noun, plural* **roosts;** *verb,* **roosted, roosting.**

rooster A male chicken.
roost·er (roos′tər) *noun, plural* **roosters.**

root[1] 1. The lower part of a plant that grows down into the ground. Roots hold the plant in the soil and take in water and minerals to feed the plant. 2. A part that is like a root. Teeth and hair have *roots*. 3. A part where something begins; origin. The *root* of his problem in meeting with people is his shyness. 4. A word to which a prefix or suffix is added to make other words. "Faith" is the

Rooster

at; āpe; cär; end; mē; it; īce; hot; ōld; fôrk; wood; fool; oil; out; up; turn; sing; thin; this; hw in white; zh in treasure. ə stands for a in about, e in taken i in pencil, o in lemon, and u in circus.

root of "faithful," "faithless," and "unfaithful." *Noun.*
—**1.** To develop roots and begin to grow. These plants will not *root* in this soil. **2.** To fix or establish firmly. Fear *rooted* him to the spot. **3.** To pull, tear, or get rid of completely. We *rooted* up the weeds in the garden. *Verb.* ▲ Another word that sounds like this is **route.**

root (rōōt *or* root) *noun, plural* **roots;** *verb,* **rooted, rooting.**

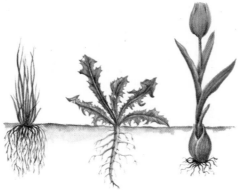

Roots

root² **1.** To dig in the earth with the snout. The pig *rooted* about for food. **2.** To search for something; rummage. We *rooted* through all the closets looking for the missing baseball glove. ▲ Another word that sounds like this is **route.**

root (root *or* root) *verb,* **rooted, rooting.**

root³ To support a team or a person in a contest. Everyone was *rooting* for our team to win. ▲ Another word that sounds like this is **route.**

root (rōōt *or* root) *verb,* **rooted, rooting.**

rope **1.** A strong cord made of twisted or woven strands of wire, fiber, or other material. Ropes are used for pulling, lifting, or hanging objects. **2.** A number of things joined together by twisting or stringing. Jane wore a *rope* of pearls around her neck. *Noun.*
—**1.** To tie, bind, or fasten with a rope. He *roped* the boxes together to make them easier to carry. **2.** To separate or enclose with a rope or ropes. The police *roped* off the street for the parade. **3.** To catch with a lasso or rope. The cowboy *roped* the calf for branding. *Verb.*

rope (rōp) *noun, plural* **ropes;** *verb,* **roped, roping.**

to know the ropes. To be familiar with or experienced in some activity. Now that he *knows the ropes,* his job is much easier.

▲ Sailors who have spent most of their lives working on a sailing ship have come to know what all the different ropes are used for and which ropes to pull to raise the different sails. The idea of these sailors' knowledge of the ropes led people to say that anyone who is experienced at anything "**knows the ropes.**"

rose¹ **1.** A flower that grows on a bush or vine with thorns. Roses are usually red, pink, yellow, or white, and have a sweet smell. **2.** A pinkish-red color. *Noun.*
—Having the color rose. *Adjective.*

rose (rōz) *noun, plural* **roses;** *adjective.*

rose² Everyone *rose* when the judge entered the courtroom. Look up **rise** for more information.

rose (rōz) *verb.*

Roses

rosebud The bud of a rose.

rose·bud (rōz′bud′) *noun, plural* **rosebuds.**

rosy **1.** Having the color rose; pinkish-red. The baby's cheeks were *rosy* from the cold. **2.** Full of hope; bright; cheerful. He has a *rosy* outlook on his future.

ros·y (rō′zē) *adjective,* **rosier, rosiest.**

rot To make or become rotten; decay. The apples will *rot* on the tree. The damp air in the basement will *rot* the old wooden chest. *Verb.*
—**1.** The process of rotting. *Rot* ruined the books in the damp basement. **2.** A disease of plants. It is caused by any of various fungi or bacteria. *Noun.*

rot (rot) *verb,* **rotted, rotting;** *noun.*

rotary Having a part or parts that turn. A *rotary* engine has cylinders that turn.

ro·ta·ry (rō′tər ē) *adjective.*

rotate **1.** To turn or cause to turn around on an axis. The earth *rotates* from west to east. Electricity *rotates* the wheel of the machine. **2.** To change in a fixed order; take turns regularly. The guards will *rotate* every four hours. The farmer *rotates* the kinds of crops he grows in this field every year to keep the soil fertile.

ro·tate (rō′tāt) *verb,* **rotated, rotating.**

▲ The word **rotate** comes from a Latin word that means "wheel."

rotation The act or process of turning on an axis. The *rotation* of the earth takes twenty-four hours.

ro·ta·tion (rō tā′shən) *noun, plural* **rotations.**

rotor **1.** The part of a motor or other machine that turns or rotates. **2.** A set of large, turning blades that lifts and moves a helicopter or other aircraft.

ro·tor (rō′tər) *noun, plural* **rotors.**

rotten **1.** Decayed; spoiled. That is a *rotten* apple. This meat is *rotten.* **2.** Likely to break, crack, or give way; weak. The wood in this old floor is *rotten.* **3.** Very bad. That was a *rotten* movie.

rot·ten (rot′ən) *adjective,* **rottener, rottenest.**

rouge A red or pink cosmetic used to color the cheeks.

rouge (rōozh) *noun, plural* **rouges.**

rough **1.** Having an uneven surface; not smooth or level. The bark of the tree is *rough.* Our car bounced over the *rough* country road. **2.** Marked by or showing force, violence, or ruggedness. Football is a *rough* game. The little boat tossed on the *rough* waters. **3.** Not having or showing gentleness or politeness; rude. He spoke to her in a very *rough* way. **4.** Not completely or perfectly done or made. She made a *rough* sketch of the flowers on the table. He gave us a *rough* estimate of how long it would take to fix the car. **5.** In a natural or unfinished state. The jeweler cut the *rough* diamond into smaller stones. **6.** Hard or unpleasant. She had a *rough* day at work because her assistant was sick. *Adjective.*

—**1.** To treat in a violent or rugged way. The bully *roughed* up the little boy. **2.** To plan, sketch, or shape in an incomplete way. The builder *roughed* out a plan for the house. She *roughed* in the details of the drawing. *Verb.*

▲ Another word that sounds like this is **ruff.**

rough (ruf) *adjective,* **rougher, roughest;** *verb,* **roughed, roughing.**

round **1.** Shaped like a ball or globe. Grapefruits are *round.* She shaped the clay into a *round* mass. **2.** Shaped like a circle; circular. The table is *round.* Tires and hoops are *round.* **3.** Having a curved outline or surface. He has *round* shoulders. The chair has a *round* back. *Adjective.*

—**1.** Something that has a round shape. She cut the cookie dough into *rounds.* **2.** Movement in a circle or about an axis; revolution. The spacecraft made two *rounds* of the moon before it landed. **3. rounds.** A fixed or regular course or route. The guard made his *rounds* of the property every hour. **4.** A series of happenings or actions. There is always a *round* of parties to go to over the Christmas holidays. **5.** A single outburst. There was a *round* of applause when the actress appeared. **6.** A complete game or a section of a game or contest. There are ten *rounds* in the boxing match. We played a *round* of golf this afternoon. **7.** A short song that is sung by three or more voices. Each voice begins the song in turn at a different time. "Row, Row, Row, Your Boat" is a round. **8.** A single discharge of a gun or other firearm or the ammunition needed for this. The policeman fired three *rounds* at the target. *Noun.*

—**1.** To make or become round. Dad *rounded* the corners of the table he was making. **2.** To pass or travel to the other side of; go around. The car *rounded* the corner just as we stepped out of the house. *Verb.*

—Around. The top spun *round* and *round.* The children gathered *round* the teacher. *Adverb, Preposition.*

round (round) *adjective,* **rounder, roundest;** *noun, plural* **rounds;** *verb,* **rounded, rounding;** *adverb; preposition.*

to round up. To drive or gather together. The farmer *rounded up* the stray cows.

roundhouse A round building with a turntable inside. A roundhouse is used to store or repair locomotives.

round·house (round′hous′) *noun, plural* **roundhouses.**

Roundhouse

at; āpe; cär; end; mē; it; īce; hot; ōld;
fôrk; wood; fōol; oil; out; up; turn; sing;
thin; this; hw in white; zh in treasure.
ə stands for a in about, e in taken
i in pencil, o in lemon, and u in circus.

round number   A number given in terms of the nearest whole number or in tens, hundreds, thousands, and the like. 500 is the *round number* for 498. 6 is the *round number* for 5⅞.

round trip   A trip to a place and back to the starting point. She took a *round trip* from Chicago to New York and back to Chicago.

roundup   1. The act of driving or gathering scattered cattle together for counting, branding, or selling. 2. A gathering together of people or things. There was a *roundup* of suspects after the latest robbery.
   round·up (round′up′) *noun, plural* **roundups.**

rouse   1. To awaken from sleep, rest, or the like. The loud banging on the door *roused* us. 2. To stir up; excite. The touchdown by the home team *roused* the crowd.
   rouse (rouz) *verb,* **roused, rousing.**

rout¹   A complete defeat, or a disorderly retreat following such a defeat. There was much celebrating after the *rout* of the enemy soldiers. *Noun.*
   —1. To beat completely. Our football team *routed* theirs in the championship game by twenty-one points. 2. To force to retreat. Our soldiers *routed* the enemy. *Verb.*
   rout (rout) *noun, plural* **routs;** *verb,* **routed, routing.**

rout²   1. To find or uncover by sending; discover. He *routed* out his old baseball glove from the closet. 2. To drive out; make leave. They *routed* us from our tents at seven o'clock each morning at camp.
   rout (rout) *verb,* **routed, routing.**

route   1. A road or other way for traveling on. We drove along the ocean *route* to the beach. 2. A regular course or territory covered by a salesman or delivery man. John has a newspaper *route. Noun.*
   —1. To arrange the route for. The woman at the travel agency *routed* our trip across the country. 2. To send by a certain route. The company *routes* its products through New York. *Verb.* ▲ Another word that sounds like this is **root.**
   route (ro͞ot *or* rout) *noun, plural* **routes;** *verb,* **routed, routing.**

routine   1. A regular way of doing something. Shopping for groceries is part of my weekly *routine.* 2. Sameness of actions or ways of doing things. The boys became bored with the *routine* of camp life. *Noun.*
   —According to routine; regular. Making my bed is one of my *routine* chores. *Adjective.*
   rou·tine (ro͞o tēn′) *noun, plural* **routines;** *adjective.*

row¹   1. A series of people or things arranged in a line. A *row* of trees was planted in front of the house. 2. A line of chairs or seats. We sat in the last *row* to watch the movie. ▲ Another word that sounds like this is **roe.**
   row (rō) *noun, plural* **rows.**

row²   1. To use oars to make a boat move. We *rowed* across the lake. Only one person is needed to *row* the boat. 2. To carry in a rowboat. Will you *row* me across the lake? *Verb.*
   —A trip in a rowboat. It is a long *row* across the river. *Noun.* ▲ Another word that sounds like this is **roe.**
   row (rō) *verb,* **rowed, rowing;** *noun, plural* **rows.**

row³   A noisy quarrel or fight. They had a *row* over who would use the bathroom first.
   row (rou) *noun, plural* **rows.**

rowboat   A boat that is moved by oars.
   row·boat (rō′bōt′) *noun, plural* **rowboats.**

Rowboat

royal   1. Of or having to do with a king or queen. The *royal* family lives in the palace. 2. Belonging to or serving a king or queen. The king and queen live in the *royal* palace. He is a member of the *royal* navy. 3. Coming from or by a king or queen. The king issued a *royal* command. 4. Suitable for or like a king or queen. We were given a *royal* welcome when we arrived at our friend's house.
   roy·al (roi′əl) *adjective.*

royalty   1. A royal person or persons. Kings, queens, princes, and princesses are royalty. 2. The position or power of a king or queen. The crown is a symbol of *royalty.*
   roy·al·ty (roi′əl tē) *noun, plural* **royalties.**

rub   1. To press along or put pressure on the surface of. The swimmer *rubbed* his leg to ease the cramp. The kitten *rubbed* against my leg. 2. To put or spread on or over. Jean *rubbed* lotion on her sunburned arms. 3. To move one thing against another or two things against each other. He *rubbed* his cold hands together to make them warm. 4. To apply pressure to in order to clean, polish, or make smooth. I *rubbed* the table with wax until it shone. **5.** To take away by applying pressure. Carol *rubbed* out with her foot what she had written in the sand. *Verb.*

—The act of rubbing. Mom gave my sore shoulder a good *rub. Noun.*

rub (rub) *verb,* **rubbed, rubbing;** *noun, plural* **rubs.**

rubber **1.** A strong, elastic, waterproof substance that is gotten from the milky liquid in certain tropical trees. Rubber is used to make tires. **2.** Something made of rubber. Overshoes that are worn in the rain are called *rubbers.*

rub·ber (rub′ər) *noun, plural* **rubbers.**

▲ The word **rubber** comes from the word *rub.* This material was first used to rub out, or erase, pencil marks.

rubber band An elastic loop of rubber. It is used to hold things together.

rubber stamp A stamp made of rubber, with raised printing or a design. It is pressed on a pad containing ink and is used to print dates, names, and the like.

rubbish **1.** Useless waste material; trash. Put all the *rubbish* in a pile by the back door. **2.** Worthless talk or thoughts; nonsense. Those rumors were just a lot of *rubbish.*

rub·bish (rub′ish) *noun.*

rubble Rough, broken pieces of stone, rock, or other solid material. The rescue workers searched through the *rubble* of the bombed building.

rub·ble (rub′əl) *noun.*

ruby **1.** A clear, red precious stone. **2.** A deep red color. *Noun.*

—Having the color ruby; deep red. *Adjective.*

ru·by (rōo′bē) *noun, plural* **rubies;** *adjective.*

rudder **1.** A broad, flat, movable piece of wood, metal, or other material that is attached to the rear of a boat or ship. It is used in steering. **2.** A piece that is like the rudder of a boat or ship, attached at the tail of an aircraft.

rud·der (rud′ər) *noun, plural* **rudders.**

ruddy Having a healthy redness. He has a *ruddy* complexion.

rud·dy (rud′ē) *adjective,* **ruddier, ruddiest.**

rude **1.** Having or showing bad manners; not polite. She gave a very *rude* answer to my question. I've never met such a *rude* person. **2.** Roughly made or done; crude. Cave men used *rude* tools made of stone.

rude (rōod) *adjective,* **ruder, rudest.**

ruff **1.** A ring of feathers or hairs growing around the neck of a bird or other animal. **2.** A stiff, round frill, worn as a collar by men and women in former times. ▲ Another word that sounds like this is **rough.**

ruff (ruf) *noun, plural* **ruffs.**

ruffed grouse A North American game bird that has brownish feathers and a fan-shaped tail. The male has a tuft of black feathers on each side of the neck.

ruffed grouse (ruft).

ruffle **1.** To disturb the smoothness or calmness of something. The wind *ruffled* the water. The bird *ruffled* its feathers. **2.** To disturb or upset. Nothing can *ruffle* that man. *Verb.*

—A strip of ribbon, lace, or other material gathered along one edge. It is used for trimming or decoration on clothes, curtains, bedspreads, and other things. *Noun.*

ruf·fle (ruf′əl) *verb,* **ruffled, ruffling;** *noun, plural* **ruffles.**

Ruffle

rug A piece of heavy fabric, used to cover part of a floor. There was a small *rug* in front of the fireplace.

rug (rug) *noun, plural* **rugs.**

rugged **1.** Having a sharp, rough outline or surface; rough and uneven. The mountain has many *rugged* peaks. It is hard to land a boat on this *rugged* coastline. **2.** Very strong and sturdy. Our school has a *rugged* football team. **3.** Hard to do or put up with; harsh. Life on the frontier was very *rugged.*

rug·ged (rug′id) *adjective.*

ruin **1.** Destruction, damage, or collapse. The storekeeper faced financial *ruin* if his business didn't improve soon. **2. ruins.** The remains of something destroyed or decayed. There are many *ruins* of ancient temples in Greece and Italy. **3.** Something that causes destruction, damage, or collapse. All that money and fame will be the *ruin* of him if he's not careful. *Noun.*

at; āpe; cär; end; mē; it; īce; hot; ōld;
fôrk; wood; fōol; oil; out; up; turn; sing;
thin; this; hw in white; zh in treasure.
ə stands for a in about, e in taken
i in pencil, o in lemon, and u in circus.

—To bring to ruin; harm or damage greatly. The earthquake *ruined* the town. The lack of rain *ruined* the crops. Her sprained ankle *ruined* her chances of making the basketball team. *Verb.*

ru·in (rōo′in) *noun, plural* **ruins;** *verb,* **ruined, ruining.**

rule **1.** A direction or principle that serves as a guide for behavior or action. Baseball, football, and other games have rules. Clubs and other organizations have rules for members to follow. One of the *rules* of good manners is not to speak when your mouth is full of food. **2.** Control or government. The people of the country were happy under the *rule* of the king. **3.** Something that usually or normally happens or is done. Long hair is no longer the *rule* among the boys in my school. *Noun.*

—**1.** To have power or control over; govern. The king *rules* his subjects fairly. **2.** To make a decision with authority. The club *ruled* against accepting new members until next year. *Verb.*

rule (rōol) *noun, plural* **rules;** *verb,* **ruled, ruling.**

ruler **1.** A person who rules. The queen was a just *ruler.* **2.** A strip of wood, plastic, metal, or other material that is marked off in measuring units. It is used for drawing straight lines and for measuring.

rul·er (rōo′lər) *noun, plural* **rulers.**

rum An alcoholic liquor made from the juice of sugar cane or from molasses.

rum (rum) *noun, plural* **rums.**

rumble To make a heavy, deep, rolling sound. Thunder *rumbled* in the distance. The tanks *rumbled* down the road. *Verb.*

—A heavy, deep, rolling sound. We were awakened in the middle of the night by the *rumble* of thunder. *Noun.*

rum·ble (rum′bəl) *verb,* **rumbled, rumbling;** *noun, plural* **rumbles.**

ruminant An animal that has hooves and chews the cud. Cows, sheep, deer, giraffes, and camels are ruminants.

ru·mi·nant (rōo′mə nənt) *noun, plural* **ruminants.**

rummage To search through something completely by moving things around. He *rummaged* in the closet for his missing shoe. *Verb.*

—A complete search made by moving things around. Her *rummage* through her bureau drawers did not turn up her missing glove. *Noun.*

rum·mage (rum′ij) *verb,* **rummaged, rummaging;** *noun, plural* **rummages.**

▲ The word **rummage** comes from an early French word that means "to put cargo on a ship." Our meanings of the word come from the idea of the confusion and mess that there is on a ship when all the cargo is piled around to be put away below the deck.

rummage sale A sale of used furniture, old clothes, and other things. Rummage sales are usually held to raise money for some charity.

rumor **1.** A story or statement that is passed from one person to another as truth without anything to prove it. Someone started a *rumor* that the game next Saturday had been canceled. **2.** What people are saying; general talk. *Rumor* has it that he will be named captain of the team. *Noun.*

—To spread or tell by rumor. It is *rumored* that our teacher is getting married. *Verb.*

ru·mor (rōo′mər) *noun, plural* **rumors;** *verb,* **rumored, rumoring.**

rump The part of an animal's body where the back and legs are joined. A cut of meat from this part is also called a rump.

rump (rump) *noun, plural* **rumps.**

run **1.** To go or cause to go quickly; move at a faster pace than a walk. John had to *run* to catch the bus. The little boy *ran* for help when he saw the fire break out. The dog slipped out of his leash and *ran* across the street. The rider *ran* the horse until it was exhausted. **2.** To do by or as if by running. Joan *ran* the race in three minutes and forty seconds. Bob went to *run* an errand for his mother. **3.** To go or travel regularly. A bus *runs* every hour from Boston to New York. **4.** To move or cause to move freely and easily. We always let our cats *run* in the house. Al oiled the electric can opener so it would *run* better. Dad had to stop the water from *running* through the pipes while he fixed the leak. The road *runs* north about ten miles before coming to a town. The newspaper company couldn't *run* the printing presses because the workers were on strike. Mother went into the bathroom to *run* the water for her bath. **5.** To take part in or enter a race or contest. Seven horses *ran* in the fifth race. The Democrats haven't decided who will *run* for mayor yet. **6.** To pass into or bring to a particular place or condition. If you *run* into any trouble, just call me. The theater only *ran* the movie for one week. **7.** To be in effect or force. The sale will *run* for one week. Blond hair *runs* in her family. **8.** To expose oneself to. Pat *ran* the risk of catching

cold by going out in the pouring rain without a raincoat. **9.** To be in charge of. The vice-president of our club *ran* the meeting because the president was on vacation. A good friend of ours *runs* the local grocery store. **10.** To spread when exposed to water. The colors in this shirt *ran* after the first washing. **11.** To suffer from; have. The sick man was *running* a high fever. **12.** To have the stitches break at some point and come undone. Ruth's stocking *ran* as she bent down to pick up her pen. **13.** To get past or through. The ship tried to *run* the enemy blockade in the fog. *Verb.*
—**1.** The act of running. Dick took his dog for a *run* around the block. The children broke into a *run* as they neared the park. **2.** A trip. We took a *run* into town this afternoon. This train makes four *runs* a day. **3.** The freedom to move about or use. Karen's mother gave us the *run* of the house, telling us that we could help ourselves to anything we wanted in the refrigerator. **4.** A period of time during which something continues to happen. We had a *run* of rainy days during July. The play has a six-month *run* at this theater. **5.** A place where stitches have broken and come undone. Janet got a *run* in her stocking. **6.** In baseball, a score that is made by touching home plate after touching the three bases. *Noun.*

run (run) *verb*, **ran, run, running;** *noun, plural* **runs.**

to run across. To meet or come upon by chance. On her way home, Mary *ran across* a friend she hadn't seen in a couple of years.

to run down. 1. To make or become weak in strength or health. Phil was *run down* from not getting enough sleep at night. **2.** To knock down. The driver accidentally *ran down* the skunk as it ran out from the bushes. **3.** To find by searching. The plumbers *ran down* the source of the leak.

to run into. 1. To meet by chance. I *ran into* Betty when I was downtown shopping. **2.** To crash into. The car *ran into* a telephone pole.

to run out. To come to an end; be used up. The time *ran out* and the teacher asked that all the tests be passed in. I couldn't have cereal this morning because I *ran out* of milk.

runaway A person or animal that runs away. A horse that has broken away from the rider's control is a runaway. *Noun.*
—Running away; fleeing; escaping. We finally caught the *runaway* horse. *Adjective.*

run·a·way (run′ə wā′) *noun, plural* **runa-ways;** *adjective.*

run-down **1.** Having bad health; tired or sick. She felt *run-down* after working so hard. **2.** In need of repair; falling apart. They bought a large, *run-down* house.

run-down (run′doun′) *adjective.*

rung[1] The telephone has *rung* three times. Look up **ring** for more information. ▲ Another word that sounds like this is **wrung.**

rung (rung) *verb.*

rung[2] **1.** A piece that forms a step of a ladder. **2.** A piece that is placed between the legs of a chair or forms part of the back of a chair. ▲ Another word that sounds like this is **wrung.**

Rungs

rung (rung) *noun, plural* **rungs.**

runner **1.** A person or animal that runs. He is a fast *runner.* **2.** One of the long narrow parts or blades on which a sled or an ice skate moves. **3.** A narrow strip of rug, carpet, or other material. We have a *runner* on the floor in the hall. **4.** The thin stem of certain plants that trails along the ground and puts down roots to produce new plants. Strawberry plants have runners.

run·ner (run′ər) *noun, plural* **run-ners.**

runner-up A person, group, or team that finishes in second place in a contest.

Runner

run·ner-up (run′ər up′) *noun, plural* **runners-up.**

running The act of a person or thing that runs. The *running* of the horse race took two minutes. *Noun.*
—That runs. We could hear *running* water. The mechanic checked the *running* parts of the

at; āpe; cär; end; mē; it; īce; hot; ōld;
fôrk; wood; fool; oil; out; up; turn; sing;
thin; this; hw in white; zh in treasure.
ə stands for a in about, e in taken
i in pencil, o in lemon, and u in circus.

engine. *Adjective.*

run·ning (run′ing) *noun, plural* **runnings;** *adjective.*

running mate A person who is a candidate for office from the same political party as another. A running mate is a candidate for the less important of two offices. A Presidential candidate's running mate is the candidate for the office of Vice-President.

runway A long, narrow area where an airplane can take off and land.
run·way (run′wā′) *noun, plural* **runways.**

rupture The act of breaking open or bursting. The *rupture* of the main water pipe caused flooding in the street. *Noun.*
—To break open or off. She *ruptured* a tiny blood vessel in her leg when she bumped it. *Verb.*
rup·ture (rup′chər) *noun, plural* **ruptures;** *verb,* **ruptured, rupturing.**

rural In, having to do with, or like the country. He lives in a *rural* part of the state. The *rural* population lives mainly on farms.
ru·ral (roor′əl) *adjective.*

rush[1] **1.** To move, go, or come quickly. We'll have to *rush* or we'll miss the bus. Water *rushed* out of the broken pipe. The police *rushed* the injured man to the hospital. **2.** To act or do in a quick or hasty manner. Don't *rush* your work or you will make a mistake. *Verb.*
—**1.** The act of rushing; sudden, quick movement. There was a *rush* of water from the broken dam. **2.** Busy or hurried activity. There was such a *rush* in the department store on Christmas Eve that I couldn't find a salesclerk to help me. **3.** A busy or hurried state. He was in such a *rush* to leave that he didn't even say good-bye. *Noun.*
—Needing to be done quickly; urgent. Typing this letter is a *rush* job. *Adjective.*
rush (rush) *verb,* **rushed, rushing;** *noun, plural* **rushes;** *adjective.*

rush[2] A plant that looks like grass. It has slender, hollow stems and bunches of small green or brown flowers. Rushes are found in marshy places. The stems are used to weave mats, baskets, and chair seats.
rush (rush) *noun, plural* **rushes.**

Russia A country in eastern Europe and in Asia. This country is usually called the **Soviet Union.** Look up **Soviet Union** for more information.
Rus·sia (rush′ə) *noun.*

Russian **1.** A person who was born or is living in Russia. **2.** The language of Russia. *Noun.*

—Of or having to do with Russia, its people, or their language. *Adjective.*
Rus·sian (rush′ən) *noun, plural* **Russians;** *adjective.*

rust **1.** A reddish-brown or orange coating that forms on iron when it is exposed to moisture or air. **2.** A plant disease that causes reddish-brown or orange spots and streaks to appear on the plant. **3.** A reddish-brown or orange color. *Noun.*
—To become covered with rust. The hinges on the old gate *rusted. Verb.*
—Having the color rust. *Adjective.*
rust (rust) *noun, plural* **rusts;** *verb,* **rusted, rusting;** *adjective.*

rustle **1.** To make or cause to make soft, fluttering sounds. The leaves *rustled* in the wind. **2.** To steal cattle. *Verb.*
—A soft, fluttering sound of things being rubbed together or stirred about. We heard the *rustle* of papers in the next room. *Noun.*
rus·tle (rus′əl) *verb,* **rustled, rustling;** *noun, plural* **rustles.**

rusty **1.** Covered with rust. He replaced the *rusty* nails in the fence. **2.** Made by rust. There are *rusty* spots on these metal chairs. **3.** Not as good as it used to be because of not being used. My piano playing is a bit *rusty* because I haven't practiced for a long time.
rust·y (rus′tē) *adjective,* **rustier, rustiest.**

rut **1.** A track or groove made in the ground by a wheel or by constant use. The tractor left *ruts* in the dirt road. **2.** A fixed way of living, thinking, or acting; boring routine or sameness. He was in a *rut*, doing the same things every day. *Noun.*
—To make ruts in. The heavy trucks *rutted* the road. *Verb.*
rut (rut) *noun, plural* **ruts;** *verb,* **rutted, rutting.**

ruthless Not having pity or mercy. The dictator was a *ruthless* ruler.
ruth·less (rooth′lis) *adjective.*

rye A plant that is like a grass and has slender stems. The grain of this plant is used as food for animals and in making flour and whiskey and other alcoholic liquors. ▲ Another word that sounds like this is **wry.**
rye (rī) *noun, plural* **ryes.**

at; āpe; cär; end; mē; it; īce; hot; ōld;
fôrk; wood; fool; oil; out; up; turn; sing;
thin; this; hw in white; zh in treasure.
ə stands for a in about, e in taken
i in pencil, o in lemon, and u in circus.

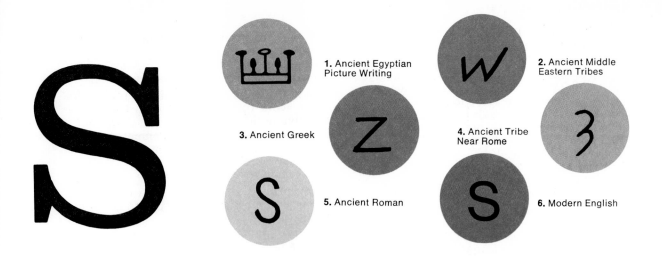

1. Ancient Egyptian Picture Writing

2. Ancient Middle Eastern Tribes

3. Ancient Greek

4. Ancient Tribe Near Rome

5. Ancient Roman

6. Modern English

S is the nineteenth letter of the alphabet. The oldest form of the letter **S** was a drawing that the ancient Egyptians (**1**) used in their picture writing nearly 5000 years ago. This drawing represented teeth. Several ancient tribes in the Middle East (**2**) borrowed this drawing. They made the Egyptian drawing simpler, writing it very much like a modern letter **W**. When the ancient Greeks (**3**) borrowed this letter, they changed its shape and wrote it more like a modern letter **Z**. This letter was borrowed by an ancient tribe (**4**) that settled north of Rome about 2800 years ago. They rounded the corners of the letter, making it look something like the number *3*. The Romans (**5**) borrowed the letter from them. By about 2400 years ago the Romans were writing this letter in almost the same way that we write the capital letter **S** today (**6**).

s, S   The nineteenth letter of the alphabet.
s, S (es) *noun, plural* **s's, S's.**

-s   A *suffix* that shows that a noun is plural. The word *horses* is the plural of *horse.*

Sabbath   The day of the week that is used for worship. Sunday is the Sabbath for Christians. Saturday is the Sabbath for Jews.
Sab·bath (sab′əth) *noun, plural* **Sabbaths.**

saber   A sword with a long, curved blade.
sa·ber (sā′bər) *noun, plural* **sabers.**

Saber-toothed Tiger

saber-toothed tiger   A large animal related to the cat. Saber-toothed tigers lived millions of years ago. They had long, curved teeth in the upper jaw.
sa·ber-toothed tiger (sā′bər to͞otht′).

sable   A small animal that has a bushy tail and round ears. Its soft, brown fur is very valuable and is used for making coats.
sa·ble (sā′bəl) *noun, plural* **sables.**

sac   A part in a plant or animal that is shaped like a bag and usually holds liquid. Bees and wasps store their poisons in sacs. ▲ Another word that sounds like this is **sack.**
sac (sak) *noun, plural* **sacs.**

sack   A large bag that is made of coarse, strong material. Post office workers put mail into *sacks* for mailmen to deliver. We bought a *sack* of potatoes at the market. ▲ Another word that sounds like this is **sac.**
sack (sak) *noun, plural* **sacks.**

sacred   Belonging to God or a god; having to do with religion. Every Sunday morning our church choir sings *sacred* music.
sa·cred (sā′krid) *adjective.*

sacrifice   **1.** The ceremony of offering something to a god as an act of worship. The ancient Greeks often killed a sheep on the

Sable

547

altar as a *sacrifice* to a god. **2.** The giving up of something that is wanted for the sake of something else. The parents made many *sacrifices* in order to save enough money to give their children a college education. *Noun.*
—**1.** To offer as a sacrifice to a god. Ancient peoples *sacrificed* animals to their gods. **2.** To give up for the sake of something else. Diane *sacrificed* a chance to go skiing to take care of her little brother. *Verb.*
sac·ri·fice (sak′rə fīs′) *noun, plural* **sacrifices;** *verb,* **sacrificed, sacrificing.**

sad 1. Unhappy or sorrowful. I was *sad* when my friend moved to another city. **2.** Causing unhappiness or sorrow. The wet and hungry dog was a *sad* sight. It was a *sad* day when our team lost the championship game.
sad (sad) *adjective,* **sadder, saddest.**

saddle A seat for a rider on the back of a horse, donkey, or similar animal. A saddle for a horse is usually made out of leather. *Noun.*
—To put a saddle on. The cowboy *saddled* his horse and went for a ride. *Verb.*
sad·dle (sad′əl) *noun, plural* **saddles;** *verb,* **saddled, saddling.**

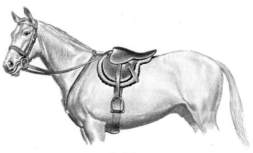

Saddle

safari A long hunting trip. Years ago many hunters went on *safaris* in Africa.
sa·fa·ri (sə fär′ē) *noun, plural* **safaris.**

safe 1. Free from harm or danger. It is not *safe* to skate on thin ice. The spy found a *safe* place to hide the secret paper. **2.** Without a chance of failure or error. It is a *safe* guess that it will rain today. **3.** Careful. My mother is a very *safe* driver. **4.** Having reached a base in baseball without being put out. *Adjective.*
—A strong metal box or other container. It is used to keep money, jewelry, or other things of value safe. *Noun.*
safe (sāf) *adjective,* **safer, safest;** *noun, plural* **safes.**

safeguard Something that protects. We put a screen in front of the fireplace as a *safeguard* against escaping sparks. *Noun.*

—To protect or guard. The dam *safeguarded* the town against a flood. *Verb.*
safe·guard (sāf′gärd) *noun, plural* **safeguards;** *verb,* **safeguarded, safeguarding.**

safety Freedom from harm or danger. The police work for the *safety* of all the people who live in this city. *Noun.*
—Giving safety. The government requires car makers to put seat belts in new cars as a *safety* measure. *Adjective.*
safe·ty (sāf′tē) *noun; adjective.*

safety pin A pin that is bent so as to form a spring. It has a guard at one end to cover the point.

sag To sink or hang down. The old bed *sagged* in the middle because the springs were too loose.
sag (sag) *verb,* **sagged, sagging.**

sagebrush A plant that has silvery white leaves and small yellow or white flowers. Sagebrush grows on the dry plains of western North America.
sage·brush (sāj′brush′) *noun.*

said Lucy *said* "hello" to the mailman. Look up **say** for more information.
said (sed) *verb.*

sail 1. A piece of material that is attached to a boat or ship. It is used to catch the wind and move the boat forward in the water. **2.** Something that is like a sail in shape or use. The flat part of the arm of a windmill is called a *sail.* **3.** A trip or ride in a boat. It is a beautiful day for a *sail. Noun.*
—**1.** To move through or travel over the water. The boat *sailed* out of the harbor. **2.** To begin a trip by water. The ship will *sail* for Hawaii in two weeks. **3.** To steer or run a boat. I am going to learn how to *sail.* **4.** To move smoothly and without difficulty. The acrobat *sailed* through the air. *Verb.* ▲ Another word that sounds like this is **sale.**
sail (sāl) *noun, plural* **sails;** *verb,* **sailed, sailing.**

sailboat A boat that is moved by the wind blowing against its sail or sails.
sail·boat (sāl′bōt′) *noun, plural* **sailboats.**

sailor A person whose work is sailing a boat. A sailor may work for a steamship company or be in the navy.
sail·or (sā′lər) *noun, plural* **sailors.**

saint 1. A very holy person. The Roman Catholic Church publicly declares such holy people to be saints after their death. **2.** A person who is very kind and patient. The sick man thought his nurse was a *saint.*
saint (sānt) *noun, plural* **saints.**

Saint Bernard A large, reddish-brown and white dog that has a big head and thick fur. **Saint Ber·nard** (bər närd′).

Saint Bernard

▲ This kind of dog is called a **Saint Bernard** after the monastery of *Saint Bernard* in the mountains of Switzerland. Monks in this monastery used these dogs to rescue people who were lost in the snow of the mountains.

sake **1.** Benefit or advantage; good. My grandfather moved to a warmer climate for the *sake* of his health. **2.** Purpose or reason. Diane took the new job for the *sake* of making more money.
sake (sāk) *noun, plural* **sakes.**

salad A cold dish that is made with lettuce, tomatoes, or other vegetables and often served with a dressing. Meat, fish, or fruit are also used in salads.
sal·ad (sal′əd) *noun, plural* **salads.**

salamander An animal that looks like a small lizard. They live in or near fresh water. **sal·a·man·der** (sal′ə man′dər) *noun, plural* **salamanders.**

Salamander

salary A fixed amount of money that is paid to someone for work done. It is paid at regular times. My brother's summer job pays a *salary* of seventy dollars a week.
sal·a·ry (sal′ə rē) *noun, plural* **salaries.**

▲ The word **salary** comes from the Latin word for "pay" or "allowance," which came from the Latin word for "salt." The Romans first used this word for "pay" for money that was paid to soldiers to buy salt.

sale **1.** An exchange of goods or property for money. A real estate agent arranged for the *sale* of our house. **2.** The selling of something for less than it usually costs. The store is having a *sale* on bathing suits. ▲ Another word that sounds like this is **sail.**
sale (sāl) *noun, plural* **sales.**

salesman A man whose job is selling things. Frank works as a car *salesman.*
sales·man (sālz′mən) *noun, plural* **salesmen.**

saliva A clear liquid that is given off into the mouth by glands. It keeps the mouth moist, helps in chewing, and starts digestion.
sa·li·va (sə lī′və) *noun.*

salmon **1.** A large fish with a silvery body. It is used for food. Most salmon live in salt water but swim to fresh water to lay their eggs. **2.** A yellowish-pink color like the color of the salmon's flesh. *Noun.*
—Having the color salmon; yellowish-pink. *Adjective.*
sal·mon (sam′ən) *noun, plural* **salmon** or **salmons;** *adjective.*

Salmon

saloon A place where alcoholic drinks are served; bar.
sa·loon (sə loon′) *noun, plural* **saloons.**

salt **1.** A white substance that is found in sea water and in the earth. Salt is used to season and preserve foods. **2.** A chemical substance that is formed by the reaction of an acid with a base. *Noun.*
—Containing salt. The *salt* water in the ocean is not good to drink. *Adjective.*
—To season or preserve with salt. Mother *salted* the meat before she cooked it. *Verb.*
salt (sôlt) *noun, plural* **salts;** *adjective; verb,* **salted, salting.**

at; āpe; cär; end; mē; it; īce; hot; ōld; fôrk; wood; fōōl; oil; out; up; turn; sing; thin; <u>th</u>is; **hw** in white; **zh** in treasure. ə stands for **a** in about, **e** in taken **i** in pencil, **o** in lemon, and **u** in circus.

saltwater Having to do with or living in salt water or the sea. A shark is a *saltwater* fish.
salt·wa·ter (sôlt′wô′tər) *adjective.*

salute 1. To show formal respect by raising the right hand to the forehead. The sailor *saluted* when the flag was raised. 2. To greet with friendly or respectful words or actions. Grandfather *saluted* the ladies by tipping his hat to them. *Verb.*
—The act or gesture of saluting. The President was greeted by a twenty-one gun *salute. Noun.*
sa·lute (sə loot′) *verb,* **saluted, saluting;** *noun, plural* **salutes.**

Salute

▲ The word **salute** comes from a Latin word that means "to wish good health to."

salvage To save from being lost or destroyed. Our neighbor was able to *salvage* a few pieces of furniture from his burning house. *Verb.*
—The rescue of a ship or its cargo or crew from being lost or destroyed. *Noun.*
sal·vage (sal′vij) *verb,* **salvaged, salvaging;** *noun.*

salvation 1. The saving or freeing from difficulty, danger, or evil. The people in the town prayed for the *salvation* of the miners who had been trapped by the rock slide. 2. A person or thing that saves or frees. The only *salvation* for the men lost in the desert was a small container of water they had brought with them.
sal·va·tion (sal vā′shən) *noun.*

salve A soft substance that heals or soothes wounds or sores. Mother put some *salve* on the spot where I scraped my knee.
salve (sav) *noun, plural* **salves.**

same 1. Like another in every way. The two girls wore the *same* dress to the dance. 2. Being the very one; not another; identical. That is the *same* man I sat next to on the bus yesterday. 3. Not changed. Ann is the *same* kind, friendly person she was a year ago. *Adjective.*
—A person or thing that is alike or identical. Dave ordered cherry pie for dessert, and I asked for the *same. Noun.*
same (sām) *adjective; noun.*

sample A small part or piece of anything that shows what the whole is like. Mother brought home a *sample* of the wallpaper she had picked out. *Noun.*
—To test or judge a part of. The judges *sampled* each pie in the contest. *Verb.*
sam·ple (sam′pəl) *noun, plural* **samples;** *verb,* **sampled, sampling.**

sanctuary 1. Safety or protection. The escaped prisoners found *sanctuary* deep in the woods. 2. A natural area where birds and animals are protected. The land in back of our house is part of a bird *sanctuary.*
sanc·tu·ar·y (sangk′choo er′ē) *noun, plural* **sanctuaries.**

sand Tiny, loose grains of crushed or worn-down rocks. Sand is found on beaches and in deserts. *Noun.*
—1. To scrape and smooth with sandpaper or sand. Tom *sanded* down the edges of the bird house he was making. 2. To sprinkle or cover with sand. The city *sanded* the roads after the snowstorm. *Verb.*
sand (sand) *noun; verb,* **sanded, sanding.**

sandal A shoe with a sole that is held to the foot by one or more straps.
san·dal (sand′əl) *noun, plural* **sandals.**

sandbox A large, low box filled with sand for children to play in.
sand·box (sand′boks′) *noun, plural* **sandboxes.**

sandpaper A strong, heavy paper with a rough coating of sand on one side. It is used for smoothing and cleaning wood and other surfaces. *Noun.*
—To smooth and clean by rubbing with sandpaper. Joe *sandpapered* the surface of the old door until it was smooth. *Verb.*
sand·pa·per (sand′pā′pər) *noun; verb,* **sandpapered, sandpapering.**

sandpiper A bird that has a long, thin bill, long legs, and brown or grayish feathers. Sandpipers live along the seashore.
sand·pip·er (sand′pi′pər) *noun, plural* **sandpipers.**

Sandpiper

sandstone A kind of rock that is made up mainly of grains of sand.
sand·stone (sand′stōn′) *noun.*

sandwich Two or more slices of bread with meat, cheese, or some other filling between them. *Noun.*
—To fit or squeeze in tightly. I found the book I wanted *sandwiched* in between two other books on the shelf. *Verb.*
sand·wich (sand′wich) *noun, plural* **sandwiches;** *verb,* **sandwiched, sandwiching.**

▲ The word **sandwich** comes from the name of the Earl of *Sandwich.* It is said that he invented the sandwich so that he would not have to leave the gambling table in the middle of a card game to eat a regular meal.

sandy 1. Containing or like sand. The road to the beach is *sandy* and full of bumps. The cactus is a plant that grows in *sandy* soil. 2. Yellowish-red in color. Ted has *sandy* hair.
sand·y (san′dē) *adjective,* **sandier, sandiest.**

sane 1. Having a healthy mind; not crazy. 2. Having or showing good sense. Jane gave me some *sane* advice. ▲ Another word that sounds like this is **seine.**
sane (sān) *adjective,* **saner, sanest.**

sang Debbie *sang* a cheerful song. Look up **sing** for more information.
sang (sang) *verb.*

sanitation The protection of people's health by keeping living conditions clean. Sanitation includes getting rid of garbage and keeping drinking water clean.
san·i·ta·tion (san′ə tā′shən) *noun.*

sank The ship *sank* during a hurricane. Look up **sink** for more information.
sank (sangk) *verb.*

sap A liquid that flows through a plant. Sap carries water and food from one part of a plant to another.
sap (sap) *noun, plural* **saps.**

sapphire A precious stone that is a clear, deep-blue color.
sap·phire (saf′īr) *noun, plural* **sapphires.**

sarcastic Using sharp, bitter remarks that are meant to hurt or make fun of someone or something. Joan's *sarcastic* answer hurt her friend's feelings.
sar·cas·tic (sär kas′tik) *adjective.*

sardine A fish that lives in salt water and is used for food. Sardines are usually caught when they are young and small. They are packed tightly in oil in flat cans.
sar·dine (sär dēn′) *noun, plural* **sardines** or **sardine.**

sari A piece of clothing worn by Hindu women.
sa·ri (sär′ē) *noun, plural* **saris.**

sash¹ A broad piece of cloth that is worn around the waist or over one shoulder. Amy's new dress came with a bright pink *sash* instead of a belt.
sash (sash) *noun, plural* **sashes.**

sash² The frame that holds the glass in a window or door.
sash (sash) *noun, plural* **sashes.**

sat Father *sat* in his favorite chair. Look up **sit** for more information.
sat (sat) *verb.*

Satan The chief spirit of evil; the Devil.
Sa·tan (sāt′ən) *noun.*

Sari

satellite 1. A heavenly body that moves around another body larger than itself. 2. A man-made object that moves around the earth, the moon, or other bodies in space. Satellites are used to forecast the weather, to connect radio and television communications around the world, and to provide information about conditions in space. 3. A country that is dependent upon or controlled by another more powerful country.
sat·el·lite (sat′əl īt′) *noun, plural* **satellites.**

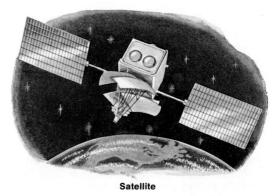
Satellite

at; āpe; cär; end; mē; it; īce; hot; ōld;
fôrk; wood; fōōl; oil; out; up; turn; sing;
thin; this; hw in white; zh in treasure.
ə stands for a in about, e in taken
i in pencil, o in lemon, and u in circus.

551

satin A fabric that has a smooth, shiny surface. It is made of silk or similar materials. **sat·in** (sat′in) *noun, plural* **satins.**

satisfaction The state of being satisfied. Ron gets a lot of *satisfaction* from doing his school work well. **sat·is·fac·tion** (sat′is fak′shən) *noun.*

satisfy **1.** To meet the needs and desires of. The sandwich was enough to *satisfy* Ellen's hunger until dinner. The team's performance in the game did not *satisfy* the coach. **2.** To make free from doubt; convince. Elizabeth's explanation of why she was late *satisfied* her parents. **sat·is·fy** (sat′is fī′) *verb,* **satisfied, satisfying.**

saturate To soak or fill completely. The spilled milk *saturated* the rug. **sat·u·rate** (sach′ə rāt′) *verb,* **saturated, saturating.**

Saturday The seventh day of the week. **Sat·ur·day** (sat′ər dē *or* sat′ər dā′) *noun, plural* **Saturdays.**

▲ The word **Saturday** comes from "Saturn's day". The Romans named the day *Saturn's day* in honor of their god of farming, who was called Saturn.

Saturn The second largest planet. It is the sixth closest planet to the sun. Saturn is surrounded by rings. **Sat·urn** (sat′ərn) *noun.*

satyr A god of the countryside in the stories of ancient times. A satyr was supposed to have the body of a man and the horns, tail, and legs of a goat. **sat·yr** (sat′ər *or* sā′tər) *noun, plural* **satyrs.**

sauce A liquid or creamy mixture that is served with food to make it taste better. Norman served the chicken with a wine *sauce.* Mother made a delicious dessert of peaches covered with a raspberry *sauce.* **sauce** (sôs) *noun, plural* **sauces.**

saucer A small, shallow dish that is used for holding a cup. **sau·cer** (sô′sər) *noun, plural* **saucers.**

sausage Finely chopped meat that is mixed with spices and stuffed into a thin case like a tube. A frankfurter is a sausage. **sau·sage** (sô′sij) *noun, plural* **sausages.**

▲ The word **sausage** goes back to a Latin word for this food, which meant "seasoned with salt." Salt was often put into meat that was fixed in this way so that the meat would not spoil so soon.

savage **1.** Cruel or fierce. There was *savage* fighting all day on the battlefield. **2.** Not tamed; wild. The leopard is a *savage* animal. *Adjective.*
—A person who is cruel, fierce or brutal. *Noun.*
sav·age (sav′ij) *adjective; noun, plural* **savages.**

save **1.** To free from harm; make safe. The firemen *saved* the woman from the burning house. **2.** To set aside money or anything else for use in the future. Dick is *saving* part of his allowance every week to buy a new baseball mitt. Mother *saved* the leftover food from the party. **3.** To keep from being lost, spent, or damaged; preserve. Laura *saved* time by shopping at the store on the corner. **4.** To avoid expense or waste. One way to *save* on food is to buy what is on sale. The man found it hard to *save* because of his low salary. **save** (sāv) *verb,* **saved, saving.**

savings Money that is saved. Donna took all of her *savings* out of the bank and bought a camera. **sav·ings** (sā′vingz) *noun plural.*

saw¹ A tool or machine that has a sharp metal blade with teeth on one edge. It is used for cutting wood, metal, or other hard materials. *Noun.*
—To cut or be cut with a saw. Phil *sawed* the log in half. This wood *saws* more easily than I thought it would. *Verb.*
saw (sô) *noun, plural* **saws;** *verb,* **sawed, sawed** or **sawn, sawing.**

Sawhorse

saw² Anne *saw* a plane overhead. Look up **see** for more information. **saw** (sô) *verb.*

sawdust The fine particles that fall from wood as it is being sawed. **saw·dust** (sô′dust′) *noun.*

sawhorse A wooden frame that is made up of a plank with two legs at each end. It is used to support boards while they are being sawed. **saw·horse** (sô′hôrs′) *noun, plural* **sawhorses.**

sawmill A place where machines saw logs into lumber. **saw·mill** (sô′mil′) *noun, plural* **sawmills.**

saxophone A musical instrument that has a curved metal body with keys fitted along it. It is played by blowing into the mouthpiece and pushing down the various keys with the fingers.
sax·o·phone (sak′sə-fōn′) *noun, plural* **saxophones.**

Saxophone

say **1.** To speak or pronounce words. What did you *say?* He *said* "Hello" when we met him on the street. **2.** To make known or express in words; declare. John *said* that he enjoyed meeting you. It is hard to *say* how long this job will take. *Verb.*
—The right or chance to speak. Everyone had his *say* at the meeting. *Noun.*
say (sā) *verb,* **said, saying;** *noun.*

saying A familiar statement that contains some truth or common sense; proverb. "A stitch in time saves nine" is a saying.
say·ing (sā′ing) *noun, plural* **sayings.**

says Janet *says* she doesn't want to go.
says (sez) *verb.*

scab A crust that forms over a sore or wound to protect it as it heals.
scab (skab) *noun, plural* **scabs.**

scaffold A platform that is used to hold workers during work on a building.
scaf·fold (skaf′əld) *noun, plural* **scaffolds.**

scale¹ A device used to find out how heavy something is. It works by balancing the thing to be weighed against another weight or against the force of a spring.
scale (skāl) *noun, plural* **scales.**

scale² One of the hard, flat structures that cover the body of fish, snakes, and lizards. *Noun.*
—To take off the scales from. The man in the fish store *scaled* the fish for us. *Verb.*
scale (skāl) *noun, plural* **scales;** *verb,* **scaled, scaling.**

scale³ **1.** A series of

Scale

steps or degrees. The pay *scale* for that job is from $100 per week to $175 per week. **2.** The size of a plan, map, or model compared with what it represents. The *scale* of the map is one inch for every 200 miles. **3.** A series of marks made along a line at regularly spaced points. A scale is used on a measuring device. The *scale* of that ruler is inches and fractions of an inch. **4.** Relative size or extent. The artist worked on a large *scale.* **5.** A series of musical tones that go up or down in pitch. A scale is usually made up of the eight notes in an octave. *Noun.*
—**1.** To climb up. The mountain climbers *scaled* the steep cliff. **2.** To change by a fixed amount. The two warring countries *scaled* down the level of fighting during the peace talks. *Verb.*
scale (skāl) *noun, plural* **scales;** *verb,* **scaled, scaling.**

scallop **1.** A sea animal that is enclosed by two ridged shells. These shells close to protect the soft body inside, and open to let in food and water. The body of the scallop is good to eat. **2.** One of a series of curves that look like the edge of a scallop shell. Martha's new dress had *scallops* along the bottom instead of a straight hem. *Noun.*
—To shape or make with a series of curves. The edges of the tablecloth were *scalloped.* *Verb.*
scal·lop (skol′əp *or* skal′əp) *noun, plural* **scallops;** *verb,* **scalloped, scalloping.**

scalp The skin that covers the head. It is usually covered with hair.
scalp (skalp) *noun, plural* **scalps.**

scamper To run or move quickly. The rabbit *scampered* off into the woods. The children *scampered* about the yard.
scam·per (skam′pər) *verb,* **scampered, scampering.**

scan To look at closely and carefully. Eleanor *scanned* her father's face to see if he was angry with her. The sailor *scanned* the horizon for land.
scan (skan) *verb,* **scanned, scanning.**

scandal **1.** Something that shocks people's sense of right and wrong and disgraces those who are involved in it. There was a *scandal* when it was discovered that the mayor had

at; āpe; cär; end; mē; it; īce; hot; ōld;
fôrk; wood; fōōl; oil; out; up; turn; sing;
thin; this; hw in white; zh in treasure.
ə stands for a in about, e in taken
i in pencil, o in lemon, and u in circus.

stolen city funds. **2.** Talk that harms a person's good name; harmful gossip. The old man enjoyed hearing the *scandal* about his neighbor.
scan·dal (skand′əl) *noun, plural* **scandals.**

scant Not enough or barely enough. The boys brought only *scant* food supplies for the camping trip. The recipe calls for a *scant* teaspoon of salt.
scant (skant) *adjective,* **scanter, scantest.**

scar **1.** A mark on the skin left by a cut or burn that has healed. The cut left a *scar* on his knee. **2.** Any mark that is like this. The burning cigarette left an ugly *scar* on the top of the table. *Noun.*
—To mark with a scar or scars. The little boy *scarred* the chair by hitting it with a hammer. *Verb.*
scar (skär) *noun, plural* **scars;** *verb,* **scarred, scarring.**

scarce Difficult to get or find. Water is *scarce* in the desert.
scarce (skers) *adjective,* **scarcer, scarcest.**

scarcely **1.** Barely or hardly. I had *scarcely* come in when the phone rang. **2.** Certainly not. She would *scarcely* go back to visit them again after the unfriendly way they treated her.
scarce·ly (skers′lē) *adverb.*

scare To frighten or become afraid. The loud thunder *scared* the children. My older sister doesn't *scare* easily. *Verb.*
—**1.** A sudden fear or fright. The sound of the explosion gave Mark quite a *scare*. **2.** A condition of widespread fear or fright; panic. There was a bomb *scare* in the department store. *Noun.*
scare (sker) *verb,* **scared, scaring;** *noun, plural* **scares.**

scarecrow The figure of a person dressed in old clothes. A scarecrow is used to scare crows and other birds away from corn and other crops.
scare·crow (sker′-krō′) *noun, plural* **scarecrows.**

scarf A piece of cloth worn about the neck or head. A scarf is worn for warmth or decoration.
scarf (skärf) *noun, plural* **scarfs** or **scarves.**

Scarecrow

scarlet A bright red color. *Noun.*
—Having the color scarlet. Carol is wearing a *scarlet* blouse. *Adjective.*
scar·let (skär′lit) *noun, plural* **scarlets;** *adjective.*

scatter **1.** To spread or throw about here and there. The wind *scattered* the leaves all over the yard. **2.** To separate or cause to separate. The crowd *scattered* when the police arrived. The loud crash of thunder *scattered* the herd of cattle.
scat·ter (skat′ər) *verb,* **scattered, scattering.**

scene **1.** The place where something happens. The police arrived on the *scene* just as the bank robbers were escaping. **2.** A part of an act in a play or movie. The play was so bad that we left after the first *scene* of the second act. **3.** View; sight. The *scene* from the porch, overlooking the valley, was quite beautiful. **4.** A show of strong feeling in front of others. The little boy made a *scene* when he couldn't have his own way. ▲ Another word that sounds like this is **seen.**
scene (sēn) *noun, plural* **scenes.**

scenery **1.** The general appearance of a place. They drove to the mountains to look at the *scenery*. **2.** The painted screens or pictures that are used to make the setting of a play or movie. The *scenery* for the first act set the play at a seaport.
scen·er·y (sē′nər ē) *noun, plural* **sceneries.**

scent **1.** A smell. The *scent* of lilacs was in the air. Hunting dogs are able to track down foxes by their *scent*. **2.** The trail or tracks by which someone or something can be traced or found. Some false clues threw the detective off the *scent* of the robbers. **3.** The sense of smell. Bloodhounds are known for their keen *scent*. ▲ Other words that sound like this are **cent** and **sent.**
scent (sent) *noun, plural* **scents.**

scepter A rod or staff that is carried by a king or queen. A scepter is used as a symbol of royal office or power.
scep·ter (sep′tər) *noun, plural* **scepters.**

schedule **1.** A list of times, events, things to do, or any other kind of information. Do you have a television *schedule* for this week? The candidate's *schedule* shows that he will campaign at the shopping center this morning. **2.** The time at which something is supposed to happen. The train

Scepter

was running behind *schedule* because of an accident. *Noun.*

—To put in or on a schedule. I *scheduled* an appointment with my dentist for Friday. *Verb.*

sched·ule (skej′ool) *noun, plural* **schedules;** *verb,* **scheduled, scheduling.**

scheme **1.** A plan or plot for doing something. The thieves had a *scheme* for robbing the bank. **2.** An orderly arrangement of related things; design. Helen chose the color *scheme* for her room. *Noun.*

—To plan or plot. The man *schemed* to cheat his business partner out of thousands of dollars. *Verb.*

scheme (skēm) *noun, plural* **schemes;** *verb,* **schemed, scheming.**

scholar A person who has much knowledge. My grandfather was a history *scholar.*

schol·ar (skol′ər) *noun, plural* **scholars.**

scholarship **1.** Money that is given to a student to help him continue his studies. The girl received a *scholarship* to college. **2.** Knowledge or learning. That book on the life of George Washington showed the author's fine *scholarship.*

schol·ar·ship (skol′ər ship′) *noun, plural* **scholarships.**

school¹ **1.** A place for teaching and learning. I walk to *school* every morning. Mary goes to dancing *school* on Friday afternoons. **2.** A department of a college or university for teaching in a particular field. My brother was accepted at the state university's *school* of medicine. **3.** A period or time of teaching at a school. There is no *school* today because of the snowstorm. **4.** The process of being educated at a school. My father says he found *school* very difficult when he was my age. *Noun.*

—To train or teach. Doctors must *school* themselves to be calm during emergencies. *Verb.*

school (skool) *noun, plural* **schools;** *verb,* **schooled, schooling.**

▲ The word **school** goes back to a Greek word that first meant "free time in which people can do whatever they wish." Later, the Greek word was used especially for free time that people used for learning. Finally, the word came to mean "a place for learning."

---

school² A large group of fish or water animals swimming together. The fishermen saw a large *school* of tuna just ahead of them.

school (skool) *noun, plural* **schools.**

schooner A ship that has two or more masts and sails that are set lengthwise.

schoon·er (skoo′nər) *noun, plural* **schooners.**

Schooner

schwa The symbol (ə) used in English for a vowel sound that is spoken without any force. The *a* in *ago* and the *o* in *lemon* are represented by a schwa.

schwa (shwä) *noun, plural* **schwas.**

science **1.** Knowledge about things in nature and the universe. Science is based on facts that are learned from experiments and careful study. **2.** Any particular branch of such knowledge. Biology, chemistry, and physics are sciences.

sci·ence (sī′əns) *noun, plural* **sciences.**

scientific Having to do with or used in science. Some of the *scientific* theories about the moon have been changed by the information brought back by astronauts who walked on the moon.

sci·en·tif·ic (sī′ən tif′ik) *adjective.*

scientist A person who knows a great deal about some branch of science.

sci·en·tist (sī′ən tist) *noun, plural* **scientists.**

scissors A tool used for cutting. It has two blades held together in the middle. When these two blades are closed over each other, they form a double cutting edge. Scissors are used to cut paper, thread, cardboard, cloth, and many other kinds of material.

scis·sors (siz′ərz) *noun plural.*

---

at; āpe; cär; end; mē; it; īce; hot; ōld; fôrk; wood; fool; oil; out; up; turn; sing; thin; this; hw in white; zh in treasure.
ə stands for a in about, e in taken i in pencil, o in lemon, and u in circus.

---

scold To find fault with; speak sharply to. Bill's mother *scolded* him for tracking mud into the house.

scold (skōld) *verb*, **scolded, scolding.**

scoop **1.** A tool that is shaped like a small shovel. It is used for taking up flour, sugar, or other soft substances. **2.** The large bucket of a steam shovel. It is used for taking up dirt, sand, or other material from the ground. **3.** A tool shaped like a cup attached to a handle. It is used to take up portions of food. Dave asked for a *scoop* of chocolate ice cream. *Noun.*

—To take up with a scoop, or as if with a scoop. Susan *scooped* a cup of sugar and added it to the cake batter. Linda *scooped* up her books and ran off to school. *Verb.*

scoop (skōōp) *noun, plural* **scoops;** *verb,* **scooped, scooping.**

scope The range or extent of an idea, action, or a person's understanding. Landing a spacecraft on Mars is within the *scope* of modern science. The lecture on nuclear energy was beyond my *scope.*

scope (skōp) *noun.*

scorch **1.** To burn slightly on the surface. Lucy *scorched* the tablecloth with the iron. **2.** To dry up with heat. The hot summer sun *scorched* the grass. *Verb.*

—A slight burn. Your necktie will cover the *scorch* on the front of your shirt. *Noun.*

scorch (skôrch) *verb,* **scorched, scorching;** *noun, plural* **scorches.**

score **1.** A record of points made in a game or on a test. The *score* after six innings of the baseball game was 5 to 4. What was your *score* on the spelling test? **2.** A set or group of twenty. More than a *score* of people came to the meeting last night. **3.** A debt or wrong to be settled. When the prisoner got out of jail, he felt he had a *score* to settle with the judge who had sentenced him. **4.** Written or printed music. A score shows all the parts for instruments and voices. *Noun.*

—**1.** To make points in a game or test. Dave *scored* twenty points in the basketball game. **2.** To keep a record of points made in a game or test. The teacher *scored* our arithmetic tests. *Verb.*

score (skôr) *noun, plural* **scores;** *verb,* **scored, scoring.**

scorn A feeling of hatred for someone or something thought of as low or bad. The students in the class had nothing but *scorn* for the boy who cheated on the test. *Noun.*

—To treat as low or bad. The whole town *scorned* the mayor when they learned that he was taking money dishonestly. *Verb.*

scorn (skôrn) *noun; verb,* **scorned, scorning.**

scorpion An animal that is like a spider. It has a long tail with a poisonous stinger on the end.

scor·pi·on (skôr′-pē ən) *noun, plural* **scorpions.**

Scorpion

scout **1.** A soldier, ship, or plane sent out to find out and bring back information. The *scout* brought back word that the enemy was camped five miles ahead. **2.** A person who belongs to the Boy Scouts or Girl Scouts. *Noun.*

—To look at or explore in order to find out and bring back information. The two soldiers went ahead to *scout* the trail. *Verb.*

scout (skout) *noun, plural* **scouts;** *verb,* **scouted, scouting.**

scoutmaster A man who leads a troop of Boy Scouts.

scout·mas·ter (skout′mas′tər) *noun, plural* **scoutmasters.**

scowl An angry frown. Father had a *scowl* on his face when he came in to tell us to clean up our room. *Noun.*

—To frown in an angry way. The mother *scowled* at her son's rude behavior. *Verb.*

scowl (skoul) *noun, plural* **scowls;** *verb,* **scowled, scowling.**

scramble **1.** To mix together; mix up. We *scrambled* the pieces of the jigsaw puzzle before starting to put it together. **2.** To cook eggs with the whites and yolks mixed together. **3.** To move or climb quickly. The children *scrambled* down the rocks along the stream. **4.** To struggle or compete with others. The players *scrambled* for the ball. *Verb.*

—**1.** The act of moving or climbing quickly. The *scramble* up the hill left everyone out of breath. **2.** A struggle or competition. There was a *scramble* for the best seats in the theater. *Noun.*

scram·ble (skram′bəl) *verb,* **scrambled, scrambling;** *noun, plural* **scrambles.**

scrap **1.** A small piece or little bit of something. Dan wrote down the telephone number on a *scrap* of paper. The butcher fed *scraps* of meat to his dog. **2.** Worn or used material that has been thrown away but can be used again. My brother was able to sell his old car for *scrap. Noun.*

—**1.** To throw away or give up as useless. The family decided to *scrap* the idea of going on a picnic because it looked like rain. **2.** To break up into scrap. The navy decided to *scrap* the old battleship. *Verb.*

scrap (skrap) *noun, plural* **scraps;** *verb,* **scrapped, scrapping.**

scrapbook A book with blank pages on which pictures, newspaper clippings, and other items may be pasted.

scrap·book (skrap′book′) *noun, plural* **scrapbooks.**

scrape **1.** To injure or scratch by rubbing against something sharp or rough. John fell and *scraped* his knee. My mother *scraped* the fender of the car against the wall of the garage. **2.** To rub or move with a harsh, grating sound. He *scraped* his chair on the floor as he stood up. **3.** To clean or smooth by rubbing. We *scraped* the dinner plates before putting them in the dishwasher. **4.** To get or collect with difficulty. The two boys *scraped* up enough money to go on a bicycle trip around the state. *Verb.*
—**1.** A mark made on a surface by rubbing or scratching against something sharp or rough. There is a big *scrape* on one of the desks. **2.** A harsh, grating sound. We heard the *scrape* of sleds on the pavement where the snow had melted. **3.** A difficult, unpleasant situation. Tom was in a *scrape* when the ball he threw broke the window. *Noun.*

scrape (skrāp) *verb,* **scraped, scraping;** *noun, plural* **scrapes.**

scraper A tool used for scraping off paint or for smoothing a surface.

scrap·er (skrā′pər) *noun, plural* **scrapers.**

scratch **1.** To scrape or cut with nails, claws, or anything else that is sharp and pointed. Al's cat *scratched* him. The broken glass *scratched* the top of the table. **2.** To rub or scrape in order to stop itching. Herb *scratched* his arm where he had a mosquito bite. **3.** To rub with a harsh, grating sound. We could hear the puppy *scratch-ing* at the door. **4.** To cancel or strike out. *Scratch* my name off the list. *Verb.*

Scraper

—**1.** A mark made by scraping or cutting. Linda got *scratches* on her leg from the thorns on the rose bushes. **2.** A harsh, grating sound. The *scratch* of the branch against the window startled us. *Noun.*

scratch (skrach) *verb,* **scratched, scratching;** *noun, plural* **scratches.**

scream To make a loud, shrill, piercing cry or sound. People scream when they are very frightened or in pain. The woman *screamed* when she saw a robber in the apartment. The frightened child *screamed* for help. *Verb.*
—A loud, shrill, piercing cry or sound. There were *screams* of terror when fire broke out in the crowded store. The *scream* of a train whistle broke the silence of the night. *Noun.*

scream (skrēm) *verb,* **screamed, screaming;** *noun, plural* **screams.**

screech To make a shrill, harsh cry or sound. The monkeys *screeched* to each other as they swung through the trees. *Verb.*
—A shrill, harsh sound. We heard the *screech* of brakes as the speeding car came to a stop. *Noun.*

screech (skrēch) *verb,* **screeched, screeching;** *noun, plural* **screeches.**

A Screen for Showing Movies

screen **1.** Wire mesh or netting in a frame. We use *screens* on the windows in the summer to keep out the flies. **2.** A covered frame that is used to hide or divide. In our house, there is a *screen* that separates the dining area from the kitchen. **3.** Anything like a screen. The soldiers used a smoke *screen* to sneak up on the enemy. **4.** A surface that reflects light, on which motion pictures or slides are projected. **5.** The front surface of the picture tube of a television set on which the image is shown. *Noun.*
—To hide or protect with a screen. Dad *screened* in the porch to keep out the mosquitoes. She *screened* her eyes from the sun with her hands. *Verb.*

screen (skrēn) *noun, plural* **screens;** *verb,* **screened, screening.**

at; āpe; cär; end; mē; it; īce; hot; ōld;
fôrk; wood; fool; oil; out; up; turn; sing;
thin; **this;** **hw** in **white;** **zh** in treasure.
ə stands for **a** in about, **e** in taken
i in pencil, **o** in lemon, and **u** in circus.

screw A kind of nail with ridges cut along its length. It is used for holding things together. It is twisted or turned into place with a screwdriver. *Noun.*
—**1.** To attach or fasten with a screw or screws. The workmen *screwed* a lock to the door. **2.** To fix in place by twisting or turning. Allison *screwed* a new light bulb into the socket. *Screw* the cap back on the tube of toothpaste. *Verb.*

Screwdriver

screw (skroo) *noun, plural* **screws;** *verb,* **screwed, screwing.**

screwdriver A tool for turning screws. It fits into the slot on the head of a screw.
screw·driv·er (skroo′drī′vər) *noun, plural* **screwdrivers.**

scribble To write or draw quickly or carelessly. Jack *scribbled* a note to his friend. *Verb.*
—Writing or a drawing that is made by scribbling. The piece of paper was covered with messy *scribbles. Noun.*
scrib·ble (skrib′əl) *verb,* **scribbled, scribbling;** *noun, plural* **scribbles.**

scribe A person who wrote down or copied letters, books, and other kinds of written materials before the invention of printing.
scribe (skrīb) *noun, plural* **scribes.**

script **1.** Handwriting in which the letters are joined together. After we learned to print, our teacher taught us how to write *script.* **2.** The written text of a play, movie, or television or radio show. We are supposed to be able to say our lines without looking at the *script* at this Friday's rehearsal of the play.
script (skript) *noun, plural* **scripts.**

scroll **1.** A roll of paper, parchment, or other material with writing on it. Each end of a scroll is often rolled around a rod. **2.** A design or ornament that looks like a partly unrolled scroll.
scroll (skrōl) *noun, plural* **scrolls.**

scrub To rub in order to wash or clean. Pam had to *scrub* her hands to get the dirt out from under her fingernails. *Verb.*
—The act of scrubbing. He gave the kitchen floor a good *scrub. Noun.*
scrub (skrub) *verb,* **scrubbed, scrubbing;** *noun.*

scuff To scratch the surface of by scraping or wear. Donna *scuffed* her new shoes on the gravel.
scuff (skuf) *verb,* **scuffed, scuffing.**

scuffle A confused struggle or fight. The robber and the policeman had a *scuffle. Noun.*
—To struggle or fight in a confused way. The boys *scuffled* on the stairs. *Verb.*
scuf·fle (skuf′əl) *noun, plural* **scuffles;** *verb,* **scuffled, scuffling.**

sculptor A person who makes or carves figures in stone, clay, metal, or any other material. The famous *sculptor* made a statue of the President.
sculp·tor (skulp′tər) *noun, plural* **sculptors.**

sculpture **1.** The art of carving or making figures or designs. Sculpture is done by carving stone, modeling in clay, or casting in bronze or another metal. **2.** The figure or design that is made in this way. That statue is a beautiful piece of *sculpture. Noun.*
—To carve, model, or cast figures or designs. The artist *sculptured* the figure of a lion. *Verb.*
sculp·ture (skulp′chər) *noun, plural* **sculptures;** *verb,* **sculptured, sculpturing.**

scurry To go or move in a hurry. The little boy *scurried* after his father.
scur·ry (skur′ē) *verb,* **scurried, scurrying.**

scurvy A disease that is caused by a lack of vitamin C. A person with scurvy feels very weak and has bleeding gums. Scurvy can be prevented by eating fruits that contain a large amount of vitamin C, such as lemons, oranges, and limes.
scur·vy (skur′vē) *noun.*

scythe A tool with a long curved blade and a long bent handle. It is used for mowing or cutting grasses and other crops.
scythe (sīth) *noun, plural* **scythes.**

Scythe

sea   **1.** The large body of salt water that covers almost three-fourths of the earth's surface; ocean. **2.** A large part of this body of salt water that is partly enclosed by land. The Mediterranean *Sea* is between southern Europe, western Asia, and northern Africa. **3.** The movement of the waves of the ocean. The ship struggled to remain afloat in the rough *seas*. ▲ Another word that sounds like this is **see.**
  sea (sē) *noun, plural* **seas.**

seaboard   The land on or near the sea. New York City is on the Atlantic *seaboard.*
  sea·board (sē′bôrd′) *noun, plural* **seaboards.**

seafood   A saltwater fish or shellfish used for food.
  sea·food (sē′food′) *noun, plural* **seafoods.**

sea gull   A bird with long wings that lives near the sea. Look up **gull** for more information.

sea horse   A kind of fish with a head that looks like that of a horse. It uses its tail to hold onto underwater plants.

seal¹   A sea animal that lives in cold regions and has flippers instead of feet. Seals spend some of their time on land, especially when they have their young. The fur of the seal is very valuable and is used to make coats and hats.
  seal (sēl) *noun, plural* **seals** or **seal.**

Sea Horse

seal²   **1.** A design that is stamped on wax, paper, or other soft material. A seal is used to show ownership or authority. The important government document had the *seal* of the United States on it. **2.** Something that closes tightly and completely. The *seal* on the jar was so tight we had to run the top under hot water to loosen it. **3.** A stamp or sticker. Mother buys Christmas *seals* and puts them on the backs of envelopes. *Noun.*
  —**1.** To close tightly and completely. Linda *sealed* the envelope. The workman *sealed* the cracks in the wall with plaster before painting. **2.** To settle or decide. The two men *sealed* their agreement by shaking hands. **3.** To place a seal on. The diploma was stamped and *sealed* by the college. *Verb.*
  seal (sēl) *noun, plural* **seals;** *verb,* **sealed, sealing.**

sea lion   A large seal that is found in the Pacific Ocean.

Sea Lion

seam   **1.** A line formed by sewing together the edges of two or more pieces of cloth, leather, or other material. One of the *seams* in this dress is coming apart. **2.** Any mark or line like a seam. Water leaked into the rowboat because the *seams* were no longer tight. *Noun.*
  —To join together in a seam. Mary *seamed* the two parts of the skirt together. *Verb.* ▲ Another word that sounds like this is **seem.**
  seam (sēm) *noun, plural* **seams;** *verb,* **seamed, seaming.**

seaman   A sailor of the lowest rank.
  sea·man (sē′mən) *noun, plural* **seamen.**

seamstress   A woman whose job is sewing.
  seam·stress (sēm′stris) *noun, plural* **seamstresses.**

seaport   A port or harbor, or a town or city with a harbor that is used by ships. New York City is one of the busiest *seaports* in the country.
  sea·port (sē′pôrt′) *noun, plural* **seaports.**

search   To look carefully in order to find something. I've *searched* all my drawers, but my notebook is still missing. John *searched* through his pockets for his keys. *Verb.*
  —The act of searching. The police led the *search* for the missing child. *Noun.*
  search (surch) *verb,* **searched, searching;** *noun, plural* **searches.**

searchlight   A special light that gives off a very strong beam of light. The navy boat used a *searchlight* on the deck to patrol the harbor.

search·light (surch′līt′) *noun, plural* **searchlights.**

seashell The shell of an oyster, clam, or other sea animal. When we went for a walk on the beach, we collected different *seashells.*

sea·shell (sē′shel′) *noun, plural* **seashells.**

Kinds of Seashells

seashore The land near or on the sea.

sea·shore (sē′shôr′) *noun, plural* **seashores.**

seasick Sick and dizzy because of the rolling motion of a boat or ship.

sea·sick (sē′sik′) *adjective.*

season **1.** One of the four parts of the year; spring, summer, fall, or winter. **2.** Any special part of the year. There is almost no rain during the dry *season* in parts of Asia and Africa. Father watches a game every weekend during the football *season. Noun.*
—To add seasoning to food in order to bring out the flavor. Mother *seasoned* the steak with salt and pepper. *Verb.*

sea·son (sē′zən) *noun, plural* **seasons;** *verb,* **seasoned, seasoning.**

seasoning Something that is used to bring out the flavor of food. Salt, pepper, and herbs are seasonings.

sea·son·ing (sē′zə ning) *noun, plural* **seasonings.**

seat **1.** Something to sit on. A chair, stool, or bench is a seat. Bring two more chairs so we will have enough *seats* for everyone. **2.** A place to sit. I couldn't get a *seat* on the bus. The children found *seats* on the floor. **3.** The part of the body that one sits on, or the clothes covering it. His pants have a rip in the *seat.* **4.** A membership or position. Mother has a *seat* on the town council. The senator has a *seat* in Congress. **5.** A center. A college is a *seat* of learning. *Noun.*
—**1.** To place on or lead to a seat. Janet *seated* her little brother in the chair. The usher *seated* the wedding guests. **2.** To have seats for. That theater *seats* 500 people. *Verb.*

seat (sēt) *noun, plural* **seats;** *verb,* **seated, seating.**

seat belt A strap that is fastened to hold a person in the seat of an automobile or airplane in case of a crash, bump, or jolt.

seaweed A plant that grows in the sea. Seaweeds are green, brown, or red in color. All seaweeds need sunlight to make their own food.

sea·weed (sē′wēd′) *noun, plural* **seaweeds.**

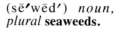

Seat Belt

secede To withdraw from a group or organization. South Carolina was the first southern state to *secede* from the Union before the Civil War.

se·cede (si sēd′) *verb,* **seceded, seceding.**

second¹ **1.** Next after the first. Sally lives on the *second* floor of the building. I liked the movie better the *second* time I saw it. Gail was the *second* person to arrive at the party. **2.** Below the first or best. Bill is the *second* pitcher on the baseball team. **3.** Another. May I have a *second* helping of potatoes, please? *Adjective.*
—In second place; after the first. Maria finished the test first, and I finished *second. Adverb.*
—**1.** A person or thing that is next after the first. Lois was the *second* in line. **2.** Something lower in quality. The shirts were sold as *seconds* because some buttons were missing. **3.** A person who helps or supports another. In olden days, when a person went to fight a duel, he took a friend along as a *second. Noun.*
—To help or support. Walt *seconded* the motion to end the meeting. *Verb.*

sec·ond (sek′ənd) *adjective; adverb; noun, plural* **seconds;** *verb,* **seconded, seconding.**

second² One of sixty parts of a minute.

sec·ond (sek′ənd) *noun, plural* **seconds.**

secondary After the first or main thing; not as important. The bus had to take a *secondary* road because the main road was closed.

sec·ond·ar·y (sek′ən der′ē) *adjective.*

secondary school A school that is attended after elementary or grade school.

secondhand Already used or owned by someone else; gotten from another. My brother bought a *secondhand* bicycle. He has only *secondhand* knowledge of how the accident happened because he was not there.

sec·ond·hand (sek′ənd hand′) *adjective.*

secrecy The condition of being secret or being kept secret. The rebels made their plans in *secrecy*.
se·cre·cy (sē′krə sē) *noun*.

secret **1.** Known only to oneself or a few; hidden. The pirate buried his treasure in a *secret* place. The club members use a *secret* password. **2.** Acting in a hidden way. The *secret* agent spied on the enemy. *Adjective.*
—**1.** Something secret. He told her a *secret*. **2.** A hidden reason or cause. Hard work is the *secret* of her success. The scientist sought to learn the *secrets* of nature. *Noun.*
se·cret (sē′krit) *adjective; noun, plural* **secrets.**

secretary **1.** A person whose work is writing letters and keeping records for another person, a business, or an organization. Ellen was elected *secretary* of the stamp club. **2.** A person who is the head of a department of a government. The *Secretary* of State heads the State Department. **3.** A piece of furniture. It has a writing surface, several drawers, and sometimes also shelves.
sec·re·tar·y (sek′-rə ter′ē) *noun, plural* **secretaries.**

Secretary

section **1.** A part taken from a whole; portion. Dad cut the apple into four *sections*. Mother planted vegetables in one *section* of the garden. **2.** A part of something written. Ben always reads the sports *section* of the newspaper. **3.** A part of an area or group. We visited the old *section* of the city. The trumpet player plays in the brass *section* of the orchestra. *Noun.*
—To cut into parts; divide. Henry *sectioned* the watermelon so everyone could have a slice. *Verb.*
sec·tion (sek′shən) *noun, plural* **sections;** *verb,* **sectioned, sectioning.**

secular Of or having to do with the world; not religious. The public schools give a secular education.
sec·u·lar (sek′yə lər) *adjective.*

secure **1.** Safe from harm or loss. The basement was a *secure* place to be during the wind storm. The jewels were *secure* in a safe. **2.** Firm; steady; sound. The old ladder is not *secure* enough to climb. *Adjective.*
—**1.** To get. He *secured* a ticket to the baseball game. **2.** To fasten firmly. Dorothy *secured* the lock on her suitcase. **3.** To make safe. The guards *secured* the gold against robbers in an armored truck. *Verb.*
se·cure (si kyoor′) *adjective,* **securer, securest;** *verb,* **secured, securing.**

security **1.** Protection from harm or loss; safety. The golfers ran to the *security* of the clubhouse during the lightning storm. Money in the bank gave Mother a feeling of *security*. **2.** Something that protects. A burglar alarm is our *security* against thieves entering our home.
se·cu·ri·ty (si kyoor′ə tē) *noun, plural* **securities.**

sedan An automobile with a roof. It has two or four doors, and a seat in both the front and the back.
se·dan (si dan′) *noun, plural* **sedans.**

sedan chair A closed chair on poles. It is carried by two men. Sedan chairs were much used in the 1600s and 1700s.

Sedan Chair

sediment Small pieces of matter that settle at the bottom of a liquid. Dead leaves and other *sediment* lay at the bottom of the pond.
sed·i·ment (sed′ə mənt) *noun.*

see **1.** To look at with the eyes; view. We could *see* thousands of stars on the clear night. When your eyes are closed, you cannot

at; āpe; cär; end; mē; it; īce; hot; ōld;
fôrk; wood; fōol; oil; out; up; turn; sing;
thin; **th**is; **hw** in white; **zh** in treasure.
ə stands for **a** in about, **e** in taken
i in pencil, **o** in lemon, and **u** in circus.

see. Do you want to go *see* a movie? **2.** To understand. I don't *see* why you have to leave now. **3.** To find out. *See* who is at the door. **4.** To make sure. *See* that you finish your homework. **5.** To visit or meet with. The dentist does not *see* people on Saturdays. **6.** To experience. Those old shoes have *seen* much wear. ▲ Another word that sounds like this is **sea.**

see (sē) *verb,* **saw, seen, seeing.**

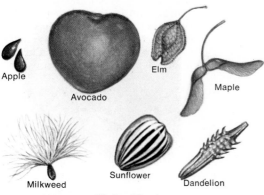

Apple
Avocado
Elm
Maple
Milkweed
Sunflower
Dandelion

Kinds of Seeds

seed The part of a plant from which a new plant will grow. Tom has planted the *seeds* for his vegetable garden. *Noun.*
—**1.** To plant land with seeds. Fred *seeded* the lawn. **2.** To take seeds out of. Jean *seeded* the watermelon. *Verb.*

seed (sēd) *noun, plural* **seeds** or **seed;** *verb,* **seeded, seeding.**

seedling A young plant grown from a seed.
seed·ling (sēd′ling) *noun, plural* **seedlings.**

seek **1.** To try to find; go in search of. The police were *seeking* a stolen car. **2.** To try. Every candidate in the election will *seek* to win. **3.** To try to get; ask for. The flood victims *sought* help.
seek (sēk) *verb,* **sought, seeking.**

seem To appear to be. The tall boy *seems* older than he really is. That book *seems* easy to read. It *seems* to be raining outside. ▲ Another word that sounds like this is **seam.**
seem (sēm) *verb,* **seemed, seeming.**

seen I have not *seen* that movie yet. Look up **see** for more information. ▲ Another word that sounds like this is **scene.**
seen (sēn) *verb.*

seep To flow or spread slowly. Water *seeped* into the ground after the rain.
seep (sēp) *verb,* **seeped, seeping.**

seesaw A device used by children for play. It is made of a long board with a support in the middle. When a child is seated on either end of the board, one end goes up as the other end goes down. *Noun.*
—To move up and down on a seesaw. *Verb.*
see·saw (sē′sô′) *noun, plural* **seesaws;** *verb,* **seesawed, seesawing.**

segment One of the parts into which a whole is divided; section. Johnny cut the string into small *segments.* You can separate the *segments* of a grapefruit with a spoon.
seg·ment (seg′mənt) *noun, plural* **segments.**

segregation The setting apart of one racial group from another racial group. Laws have been passed against the *segregation* of black children and white children in the public schools.
seg·re·ga·tion (seg′rə gā′shən) *noun.*

seine A fishing net. It hangs down in the water and has floats on the top edge and weights on the bottom edge. ▲ Another word that sounds like this is **sane.**
seine (sān) *noun, plural* **seines.**

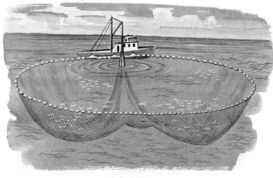

Seine

seismograph An instrument that tells when an earthquake happens, where it happens, and how powerful it is.
seis·mo·graph (sīz′mə graf′) *noun, plural* **seismographs.**

seize **1.** To take hold of; grab. The dog *seized* the bone. **2.** To get control of; capture. The soldiers *seized* the fort.
seize (sēz) *verb,* **seized, seizing.**

seldom Not often; rarely. I *seldom* see my friend now that he has moved to another city.
sel·dom (sel′dəm) *adverb.*

select To pick out; choose. Nancy *selected* a red dress to wear to the party.
se·lect (si lekt′) *verb,* **selected, selecting.**

selection The selecting of something. Jan spent the afternoon in the *selection* of gifts for his friends.
se·lec·tion (si lek′shən) *noun, plural* **selections.**

self One's own person apart from all other persons. I know my own *self* best.
self (self) *noun, plural* **selves.**

self- A *prefix* that means "for, by, or to oneself or itself." *Self-addressed* means "addressed to oneself." *Self-respect* means "respect for oneself."

self-conscious Very shy and embarrassed around other people. The *self-conscious* boy did not like to speak in front of the class.
self-con·scious (self′kon′shəs) *adjective.*

selfish Thinking only of oneself; not thinking of others. A selfish person is not interested in the wishes and feelings of other people.
self·ish (sel′fish) *adjective.*

sell **1.** To give something in return for money. Richard wants to *sell* his old bicycle for twenty-five dollars. **2.** To deal in. That store *sells* shoes. **3.** To be offered for sale. This candy *sells* for fifteen cents. ▲ Another word that sounds like this is **cell.**
sell (sel) *verb,* **sold, selling.**

selves More than one self. Look up **self** for more information.
selves (selvz) *noun plural.*

semaphore A post with movable arms used to give signals to railroad trains.
sem·a·phore (sem′ə fôr′) *noun, plural* **semaphores.**

semicircle Half a circle. The children sat in a *semicircle* around the campfire.
sem·i·cir·cle (sem′ē sur′kəl) *noun, plural* **semicircles.**

Semicircle

semicolon A mark of punctuation (;). A semicolon shows a greater break in thought than that shown by a comma, but not as great as that shown by a period. For example: Ten runners began the race; only two finished.
sem·i·co·lon (sem′ē kō′lən) *noun, plural* **semicolons.**

seminary A school that trains students to be priests, ministers, or rabbis.
sem·i·nar·y (sem′ə ner′ē) *noun, plural* **seminaries.**

senate The upper and smaller branch of an assembly that makes laws. The legislatures of most states of the United States have senates. The Congress of the United States is made up of the Senate and the House of Representatives.
sen·ate (sen′it) *noun, plural* **senates.**

▲ The word **senate** comes from a Latin word that means "old man." In Rome, the government council known as the senate was made up of the heads of noble families, who were old men.

These **semaphore** signals mean "stop," "slow," and "go ahead."

senator A member of a senate.
sen·a·tor (sen′ə tər) *noun, plural* **senators.**

send **1.** To cause to go from one place to another. Mary *sends* birthday cards to her friends. *Send* Jeff to buy some milk. The batter *sent* the ball into left field. **2.** To cause to go, come, or be. The soft music *sent* me to sleep. His rude remark *sent* her into a rage. *Send* a reply to his letter right away.
send (send) *verb,* **sent, sending.**

senior **1.** The older of two. "Senior" is used after the name of a father whose son has the same name. William Lawrence, *Senior,* is the father of William Lawrence, Junior. **2.** Higher in rank, longer in service, or older in age. A general is a *senior* officer. Senator

at; āpe; cär; end; mē; it; īce; hot; ōld; fôrk; wood; fool; oil; out; up; turn; sing; thin; this; hw in white; zh in treasure. ə stands for a in about, e in taken i in pencil, o in lemon, and u in circus.

Martin is a *senior* member of Congress. My grandfather has joined a club for *senior* citizens. **3.** Of or having to do with the last year of high school or college. My older sister is in her *senior* year in high school. *Adjective.*
—**1.** A person who is older than another or higher in rank than another. My sister is my *senior* by five years. **2.** A student who is in the last year of high school or college. *Noun.*
  sen·ior (sēn′yər) *adjective; noun, plural* **seniors.**

señor The Spanish form of address for a man.
  se·ñor (sen yôr′) *noun, plural* **senores.**

señora The Spanish form of address for a married woman.
  se·ño·ra (sen yôr′ə) *noun, plural* **senoras.**

señorita The Spanish form of address for an unmarried girl or woman.
  se·ño·ri·ta (sen′yə rē′tə) *noun, plural* **senoritas.**

sensation **1.** The power or ability to see, hear, smell, taste, or touch. **2.** A being aware; feeling. We had a *sensation* of warmth when we sat near the campfire. The little boy felt a *sensation* of fear when he saw the big dog. **3.** Great excitement; strong feeling. The baseball player caused a *sensation* when he hit the winning home run.
  sen·sa·tion (sen sā′shən) *noun, plural* **sensations.**

sensational Causing great excitement or strong feeling. The football player made a *sensational* run to score a touchdown.
  sen·sa·tion·al (sen sā′shən əl) *adjective.*

sense **1.** A power of a living being to know about its surroundings and about changes in its own body. Sight, hearing, smell, taste, and touch are the five senses. **2.** Feeling. He had a *sense* of failure after losing the race. **3.** Understanding or appreciation. Greg has a good *sense* of humor. **4.** Intelligence; good judgment. The puppy hasn't *sense* enough to come in out of the rain. **5.** Use; reason. What is the *sense* of keeping that old radio that doesn't work? **6.** Meaning. The word "run" has many different *senses. Noun.*
—To feel; understand. We could *sense* that Jill was glad to be home. *Verb.*
  sense (sens) *noun, plural* **senses;** *verb,* **sensed, sensing.**

sensible Having or showing good sense; wise. It is *sensible* to look both ways before crossing the street.
  sen·si·ble (sen′sə bəl) *adjective.*

sensitive **1.** Easily affected or hurt. A baby's skin is very *sensitive.* That *sensitive* boy becomes very upset if he is criticized. **2.** Having deep feelings; very aware. A poet must be a *sensitive* person.
  sen·si·tive (sen′sə tiv) *adjective.*

sent Edna *sent* a package to her uncle. Look up **send** for more information. ▲ Other words that sound like this are **cent** and **scent.**
  sent (sent) *verb.*

sentence **1.** A group of words that gives a complete thought. A sentence states something or asks a question. "The dog and cat" is not a sentence. "The dog and cat are fighting" is a sentence. **2.** A punishment for crime set by a court. The judge gave the thief a *sentence* of three years in prison. *Noun.*
—To set the punishment of. The judge *sentenced* the man to thirty days in jail. *Verb.*
  sen·tence (sen′təns) *noun, plural* **sentences;** *verb,* **sentenced, sentencing.**

sentiment Feeling or emotion. There is much *sentiment* in our town against closing the park on Sundays.
  sen·ti·ment (sen′tə mənt) *noun, plural* **sentiments.**

sentimental Having or showing tender feeling. The orchestra played a *sentimental* song.
  sen·ti·men·tal (sen′tə ment′əl) *adjective.*

sentry A person stationed to keep watch and warn others of danger; guard.
  sen·try (sen′trē) *noun, plural* **sentries.**

sepal One of the leaflike parts that form the calyx, or outer covering, of a flower. Sepals are usually green, but in some flowers, like the tulip, they are the same color as the petals.
  se·pal (sē′pəl) *noun, plural* **sepals.**

Sentry

separate **1.** To keep apart; be in between; divide. A fence *separates* our yard from our neighbor's. **2.** To set apart; place apart. Jean *separated* her books from her sister's. **3.** To go apart; come apart. The two friends *separated* and went home. *Verb.*
—Set apart; not joined. Jan and her sister have *separate* rooms. *Adjective.*

sep·a·rate (sep′ə rāt′ *for verb;* sep′ər it *for adjective*) *verb,* **separated, separating;** *adjective.*

separation 1. The separating of things. The *separation* of the jigsaw puzzle was easy. 2. The condition of being separated. The two sisters were happy to see each other again after a year's *separation.*
sep·a·ra·tion (sep′ə rā′shən) *noun, plural* **separations.**

September The ninth month of the year. September has thirty days.
Sep·tem·ber (sep tem′bər) *noun.*

▲ The word **September** comes from the Latin word for "seven." The early Roman calendar began with March, and September was the seventh month.

sequence 1. The coming of one thing after another in a fixed order. Winter, spring, summer, and fall follow each other in *sequence* each year. 2. A series of connected things. The boy took a *sequence* of pictures with his camera.
se·quence (sē′kwəns) *noun, plural* **sequences.**

sequoia A huge evergreen tree. It has thick, reddish-brown bark and sharply pointed leaves. Sequoias grow in California and Oregon.
se·quoi·a (si kwoi′ə) *noun, plural* **sequoias.**

Leaves and Cone
Sequoia Tree

▲ The word **sequoia** comes from the name of *Sequoya,* a chief of a tribe of American Indians. The tree was named in honor of this chief, who thought of a way to write the language spoken by this Indian tribe.

serene Calm and peaceful; quiet. The lake was *serene* after the storm had passed.
se·rene (sə rēn′) *adjective,* **serener, serenest.**

serf In olden times, a person who was like a slave. A serf was forced to stay on the land where he lived and was sold along with the land. ▲ Another word that sounds like this is **surf.**
serf (surf) *noun, plural* **serfs.**

sergeant An army officer. A sergeant is below a lieutenant but above a corporal.
ser·geant (sär′jənt) *noun, plural* **sergeants.**

serial A long story broken up into parts. The parts of a serial are shown on television or published in a magazine or newspaper one at a time. ▲ Another word that sounds like this is **cereal.**
se·ri·al (sēr′ē əl) *noun, plural* **serials.**

series A number of similar things coming one after another. A *series* of small shops lined the main street of town. The famous explorer gave a *series* of talks at the school. We have had a *series* of bright, sunny days this month.
se·ries (sēr′ēz) *noun, plural* **series.**

serious 1. Having a thoughtful, solemn manner; grave. Judge Matthews is a *serious* person. 2. Not joking; sincere. Was he *serious* when he said he had lost his watch? 3. Important. This is a *serious* matter. 4. Dangerous. Cancer is a *serious* illness.
se·ri·ous (sēr′ē əs) *adjective.*

sermon 1. A public talk about religion or morals. It is given by a clergyman. 2. Any serious talk. The mother gave the selfish boy a *sermon* about sharing with others.
ser·mon (sur′mən) *noun, plural* **sermons.**

serpent A very large snake.
ser·pent (sur′pənt) *noun, plural* **serpents.**

serum 1. A thin, clear liquid that separates from blood when a clot forms. 2. A liquid used to prevent or cure a disease. It is taken from the blood of an animal that has been made immune to the disease.
se·rum (sēr′əm) *noun, plural* **serums.**

servant A person hired to do certain duties. Maids and cooks are servants in the home. Policemen and firemen are public servants.
serv·ant (sur′vənt) *noun, plural* **servants.**

at; āpe; cär; end; mē; it; īce; hot; ōld; fôrk; wood; fool; oil; out; up; turn; sing; thin; this; hw in white; zh in treasure. ə stands for a in about, e in taken i in pencil, o in lemon, and u in circus.

serve **1.** To set food before; place food on a table. The waiter *served* us quickly. Mother *serves* dinner at six o'clock. **2.** To supply. The bakery *serves* its customers with fresh bread daily. That stew will *serve* ten people. **3.** To be a servant to; do certain duties for; work. The maid *served* the family for many years. **4.** To be of use. This sofa can *serve* as a bed. **5.** In some games, to put a ball into play. John *served* first in our tennis match. **6.** To give; present. He was *served* with a summons for speeding. *Verb.*
—In some games, the putting of a ball into play. The tennis player's *serve* was good. *Noun.*
serve (surv) *verb,* **served, serving;** *noun, plural* **serves.**

service **1.** A helpful act; useful work. That woman spends much time in *service* to the poor. The girl did a *service* for the old man when she ran an errand for him. The sick man needs the *services* of a doctor. **2.** Employment as a servant. The maid has been in the *service* of the family for many years. **3.** A system or way of giving something needed by the public. Mail *service* is good in our town. Train *service* is slow today. **4.** A branch of the armed forces. Mr. Jones spent three years in the *service.* **5.** A religious ceremony. We went to *services* at our church. **6.** A set of things needed for use while eating. Mother has a china *service* for eight people. *Noun.*
—To make or keep ready for use. The repairman *serviced* the washing machine. *Verb.*
serv·ice (sur′vis) *noun, plural* **services;** *verb,* **serviced, servicing.**

serviceman **1.** A member of a branch of the armed forces. **2.** A person whose work is to repair and service something. The *serviceman* came to fix our television.
serv·ice·man (sur′vis man′) *noun, plural* **servicemen.**

session **1.** A meeting. While in Washington, D.C., we attended a *session* of the Supreme Court. The musicians went to a recording *session.* **2.** A series of meetings. This *session* of Congress will last until summer. **3.** A time or period when classes are given at a school or college.
ses·sion (sesh′ən) *noun, plural* **sessions.**
in session. In the act of meeting. Court is now *in session.*

set **1.** To place; put. Dan *set* his books on the table. Carol *set* the toy horse on its feet. **2.** To put in the correct order; arrange; fix. Charlie will *set* the table. Mother *set* the mousetrap. *Set* your watch by the kitchen clock. The doctor *set* Andy's broken arm. **3.** To cause to be; put in some condition. Ruth *set* her pet canary free from its cage. Dad *set* the logs on fire. **4.** To begin; start. The children *set* out on their hike. Jan *set* to work on her book report. **5.** To fix or arrange. Have they *set* a date for the party? The runner *set* a new record in the race. **6.** To go down. The sun will *set* at eight o'clock. *Verb.*
—**1.** Fixed or decided. That restaurant charges a *set* price for lunch. Most games have *set* rules you must learn. **2.** Fixed in a certain position. The old man is *set* in his ways. **3.** Ready; prepared. We are all *set* to leave. *Adjective.*
—**1.** A group of things or persons. Mother bought a new *set* of dishes. We have a *set* of books on science. **2.** An apparatus for sending out or receiving by radio, television, telephone, or telegraph. Is the television *set* working? **3.** The scenery for a play. **4.** One part of a match in tennis. *Noun.*
set (set) *verb,* **set, setting;** *adjective; noun, plural* **sets.**

setter A long-haired hunting dog. A setter has large, drooping ears and a soft, silky coat.
set·ter (set′ər) *noun, plural* **setters.**

Setter

settle **1.** To agree about something; decide. The two brothers could not *settle* their argument. **2.** To come to rest. She *settled* in the comfortable chair. The bird *settled* on the branch. **3.** To make a home in a place. English colonists *settled* New England. **4.** To sink. The pebble *settled* to the bottom of the pond. **5.** To calm or become calm. The medicine *settled* my stomach. It took the class a long time to *settle* down after the fire drill.
set·tle (set′əl) *verb,* **settled, settling.**

settlement **1.** The act of settling or the condition of being settled. The *settlement* of Jamestown, Virginia took place in 1607. **2.** A small village or group of houses. During the 1800s, pioneers built many *settlements* in the

American West. **3.** A colony. A part of Canada was at one time a French *settlement*.
set·tle·ment (set′əl mənt) *noun, plural* **settlements.**

settler A person who settles in a new land or country. The first *settlers* of Florida were from Spain.
set·tler (set′lər) *noun, plural* **settlers.**

seven One more than six; 7.
sev·en (sev′ən) *noun, plural* **sevens;** *adjective.*

seventeen Seven more than ten; 17.
sev·en·teen (sev′ən tēn′) *noun, plural* **seventeens;** *adjective.*

seventeenth **1.** Next after the sixteenth. **2.** One of seventeen equal parts; 1/17.
sev·en·teenth (sev′ən tēnth′) *adjective; noun, plural* **seventeenths.**

seventh **1.** Next after the sixth. **2.** One of seven equal parts; 1/7.
sev·enth (sev′ənth) *adjective; noun, plural* **sevenths.**

seventieth **1.** Next after the sixty-ninth. **2.** One of seventy equal parts; 1/70.
sev·en·ti·eth (sev′ən tē ith) *adjective; noun, plural* **seventieths.**

seventy Seven times ten; 70.
sev·en·ty (sev′ən tē) *noun, plural* **seventies;** *adjective.*

several More than two, but not many. They played baseball for *several* hours. I ate *several* cookies. I saw *several* of my classmates at the ball game.
sev·er·al (sev′ər əl) *adjective; noun.*

severe **1.** Very strict; harsh. That country has *severe* laws. **2.** Dangerous; serious. The soldier had a *severe* wound. **3.** Violent or sharp. The *severe* storm blew down many trees.
se·vere (sə vēr′) *adjective,* **severer, severest.**

sew To make or fasten things with a needle and thread. A person can sew by hand or with a sewing machine. Mother often *sews* clothes for us. John will *sew* the button on his shirt. ▲ Other words that sound like this are **so** and **sow.**
sew (sō) *verb,* **sewed, sewed** or **sewn, sewing.**

sewage Waste matter that is carried off by sewers and drains.
sew·age (soo′ij) *noun.*

sewer A pipe or channel under the ground for carrying off waste matter.
sew·er (soo′ər) *noun, plural* **sewers.**

sewing Work done with a needle and thread. The tailor is busy with his *sewing*.
sew·ing (sō′ing) *noun.*

sewing machine A machine for sewing things. Most sewing machines are run by electric motors.

Sewing Machine

sewn The tailor has *sewn* the rip in my coat. Look up **sew** for more information. ▲ Another word that sounds like this is **sown.**
sewn (sōn) *verb.*

sex **1.** One of the two divisions, male or female, that people and animals are divided into. **2.** The fact or character of being male or female. The club is open to all children, regardless of *sex*.
sex (seks) *noun, plural* **sexes.**

shabby Worn-out and faded. The boy wore a *shabby* coat.
shab·by (shab′ē) *adjective,* **shabbier, shabbiest.**

shack A small, roughly built hut or cabin.
shack (shak) *noun, plural* **shacks.**

shad A fish related to the herring. Shad are good to eat. They live along the coasts of Europe and North America.
shad (shad) *noun, plural* **shad** or **shads.**

Shad

at; āpe; cär; end; mē; it; īce; hot; ōld;
fôrk; wood; fool; oil; out; up; turn; sing;
thin; this; hw in white; zh in treasure.
ə stands for a in about, e in taken
i in pencil, o in lemon, and u in circus.

shade　**1.** A place sheltered from the sun; place darker than the area around it. Bill rested in the *shade* of a tree. **2.** Something that shuts out or cuts down on light. He pulled down the window *shades.* Mother bought a new *shade* for the lamp. **3.** The amount of darkness of a color. The dress was a deep *shade* of green. **4.** A small amount or difference. Jeff is a *shade* taller than his brother. The word "run" has many *shades* of meaning. *Noun.*
—**1.** To shelter from heat or light. The large umbrella *shaded* her from the hot sun. **2.** To mark with darkness. The artist *shaded* the faces in his picture. *Verb.*
　shade (shād) *noun, plural* **shades;** *verb,* **shaded, shading.**

shadow　**1.** A dark area or figure made when rays of light are blocked by a person or thing. The boy cast a *shadow* behind him as he walked. **2.** A slight amount; suggestion. There is not a *shadow* of a doubt that he is lying. *Noun.*
—To follow and watch another person closely and secretly. The detective *shadowed* the suspected criminal. *Verb.*
　shad·ow (shad′ō) *noun, plural* **shadows;** *verb,* **shadowed, shadowing.**

Shadow

shady　**1.** Full of or giving shade. We sat in a *shady* part of the yard. A big *shady* tree is next to the house. **2.** Not completely honest. The dishonest shopkeeper tried to carry out a *shady* business deal.
　shad·y (shā′dē) *adjective,* **shadier, shadiest.**

shaft　**1.** A long, thin part connected to the head of an arrow or spear. **2.** The long handle of a hammer, golf club, hockey stick, or the like. **3.** A bar in a machine that supports parts or carries motion to other parts. **4.** A ray or beam. *Shafts* of light came through the window. **5.** A deep passage that goes straight down. An elevator goes up and down an elevator *shaft.* A coal mine uses a *shaft* to reach the coal.
　shaft (shaft) *noun, plural* **shafts.**

shaggy　**1.** Covered with long, rough hair or something like hair. Pete's dog is large and *shaggy.* **2.** Long and bushy. The boy's hair is *shaggy.*
　shag·gy (shag′ē) *adjective,* **shaggier, shaggiest.**

shake　**1.** To move up and down or from side to side. *Shake* the bottle to mix the salad dressing. The house *shakes* when the trains go by. **2.** To tremble or cause to tremble. The icy wind made him *shake* with cold. **3.** To weaken. Nothing will *shake* my trust in my friends. **4.** To upset. The terrible news has *shaken* us all. *Verb.*
—The act of shaking. The boy scared the dog away with a *shake* of a big stick. *Noun.*
　shake (shāk) *verb,* **shook, shaken, shaking;** *noun, plural* **shakes**

shaky　**1.** Trembling; shaking. The frightened boy answered in a *shaky* voice. **2.** Not firm; unsound. The old bridge is *shaky.*
　shak·y (shā′kē) *adjective,* **shakier, shakiest.**

shale　A rock formed from mud that has hardened. Shale is found in thin layers.
　shale (shāl) *noun.*

shall　I *shall* be home tomorrow.
　shall (shal) *verb.*

shallow　Not deep. The water in the pond is *shallow.*
　shal·low (shal′ō) *adjective,* **shallower, shallowest.**

shame　**1.** A painful feeling caused by having done something wrong or foolish. He felt much *shame* for having lied to his friend. **2.** Dishonor; disgrace. His arrest for robbery brought *shame* to his family. **3.** A thing to be sorry for. It is a *shame* that our team lost. *Noun.*
—To cause to feel shame. She was *shamed* by her foolish mistake. *Verb.*
　shame (shām) *noun; verb,* **shamed, shaming.**

shampoo　To wash the hair. I *shampoo* my hair twice a week. *Verb.*
—A special soap used to wash the hair. *Noun.*
　sham·poo (sham poo′) *verb,* **shampooed, shampooing;** *noun, plural* **shampoos.**

shamrock　A leaf with three parts or leaflets. A three-leaf clover is a shamrock.
　sham·rock (sham′rok′) *noun, plural* **shamrocks.**

shape　**1.** Form; figure. All circles have the same *shape.* A lion has a different *shape* from a bear. **2.** Condition. He was in bad *shape* after his fall. Martha exercises every day to keep in *shape*. **3.** Definite or good form; order. Get the room in *shape* before company comes. *Noun.*

—**1.** To give form to. Joey *shaped* the wire into the figure of a man. A baker *shapes* dough into loaves. **2.** To take on a form; develop. Our plans for the party are *shaping* up well. *Verb.*

> **shape** (shāp) *noun, plural* **shapes**; *verb,* **shaped, shaping.**

share **1.** The part that is given or belongs to one person. The boy ate his *share* of the candy. Joan's *share* of the closet space is smaller than her sister's. **2.** One of the equal parts into which the ownership of a company or business is divided. Mother owns ten *shares* of stock in a large company. *Noun.*

—**1.** To use with another or others. The two friends *shared* a tent on their camping trip. **2.** To divide into portions and give to others as well as to oneself. Jerry *shared* his lunch with two friends. **3.** To have a share. We all *shared* in the fun at the party. *Verb.*

> **share** (sher) *noun, plural* **shares**; *verb,* **shared, sharing.**

shark A fish that lives in the sea. A shark has gray scales and a large mouth with sharp teeth. Sharks eat other fish. Some kinds of sharks will attack people.

> **shark** (shärk) *noun, plural* **sharks.**

Shark

sharp **1.** Having an edge or point that cuts or pierces easily. That knife has a *sharp* blade. A needle has a *sharp* point. **2.** Having a pointed end; not rounded. That mountain has a *sharp* peak. This table has *sharp* edges. **3.** Harsh or biting. The strong cheese had a *sharp* taste. The winter wind is very *sharp*. **4.** Having a sudden change in direction. The road ahead has a *sharp* curve. **5.** Clear. Your camera takes *sharp* pictures. **6.** Watchful; alert. Keep a *sharp* lookout. The dog has *sharp* ears. *Adjective.*

—Promptly; exactly. We must leave at ten o'clock *sharp*. *Adverb.*

—**1.** A tone or note in music that is one half note above its natural pitch. **2.** A symbol (#) that shows this tone or note. *Noun.*

> **sharp** (shärp) *adjective,* **sharper, sharpest;** *adverb; noun, plural* **sharps.**

sharpen To make or become sharp. *Sharpen* the knife. Jack *sharpened* his pencil.

> **sharp·en** (shär′pən) *verb,* **sharpened, sharpening.**

shatter To break into pieces. The glass *shattered* when I dropped it. The ball *shattered* the window.

> **shat·ter** (shat′ər) *verb,* **shattered, shattering.**

shave **1.** To remove hair with a razor. My older brother *shaved* off his beard. Dad *shaves* with an electric razor. **2.** To cut off in thin strips. The carpenter *shaved* the edge of the board with a plane. *Verb.*

—**1.** The removing of hair with a razor. Dad went to the barbershop for a *shave*. **2.** A narrow escape. We had a close *shave* today when a car almost hit us. *Noun.*

> **shave** (shāv) *verb,* **shaved, shaved** or **shaven, shaving;** *noun, plural* **shaves.**

shaving A thin piece or slice. The floor of the carpenter's shop was covered with wood *shavings*.

> **shav·ing** (shā′ving) *noun, plural* **shavings.**

shawl A piece of cloth that is worn over the shoulders or head.

> **shawl** (shôl) *noun, plural* **shawls.**

she Betty told us *she* would come to our party. Is your kitten a *she* or a *he*?

> **she** (shē) *pronoun; noun, plural* **shes.**

Shawl

shear **1.** To cut or clip with shears or scissors. Bill *sheared* the hedge. **2.** To cut off; remove. The farmer *sheared* wool from his sheep. The side of the building was *sheared* off by the explosion. ▲ Another word that sounds like this is **sheer.**

> **shear** (sher) *verb,* **sheared, sheared** or **shorn, shearing.**

shears A cutting instrument like scissors.

at; āpe; cär; end; mē; it; īce; hot; ōld;
fôrk; wood; fōōl; oil; out; up; turn; sing;
thin; this; hw in white; zh in treasure.
ə stands for a in about, e in taken
i in pencil, o in lemon, and u in circus.

There are shears for cutting grass and cutting metal.

shears (shērz) *noun plural.*

shed¹ A small building used for storing wood and other things.

shed (shed) *noun, plural* **sheds.**

shed² **1.** To let fall. The lost child *shed* tears. **2.** To throw off. A dog *sheds* hair. Many trees *shed* their leaves in the fall. My waterproof coat *sheds* rain. **3.** To send out. The moon *shed* little light last night.

shed (shed) *verb,* **shed, shedding.**

she'd *She'd* better do her homework. *She'd* come if she could.

she'd (shēd) contraction for "she had" and "she would."

sheep An animal that is related to the goat. Many kinds of sheep are raised for their wool, meat, milk, and skin. Other kinds live wild in mountain regions.

sheep (shēp) *noun, plural* **sheep.**

Sheep

sheer **1.** Very fine and thin. The window has *sheer* curtains. She wore a *sheer* blouse. **2.** Total; utter. It was *sheer* stupidity to drive in that snowstorm. **3.** Steep. There is a *sheer* drop of 400 feet from the edge of the cliff. ▲ Another word that sounds like this is **shear.**

sheer (shēr) *adjective,* **sheerer, sheerest.**

sheet **1.** A large piece of cotton, linen, or other cloth. It is used to cover a bed. **2.** A thin, broad piece of something. He bought a *sheet* of plywood. Jan drew a picture on a *sheet* of paper. **3.** A flat, broad area or surface. A *sheet* of ice covered the sidewalk in front of the house.

sheet (shēt) *noun, plural* **sheets.**

sheik A leader or chief of a group of Arabs.

sheik (shēk) *noun, plural* **sheiks.**

shelf **1.** A thin piece of wood or metal fastened to a wall or frame. It is used to hold books, dishes, and other things. **2.** Anything like a shelf. The ship was stuck on a *shelf* of sand.

shelf (shelf) *noun, plural* **shelves.**

shell **1.** A hard outer covering. Turtles, lobsters, snails, and beetles have shells. Eggs and nuts also have shells. **2.** Something like a shell. Mother filled the pastry *shell* with custard. The framework of a building is called a *shell.* **3.** A case of metal or cardboard filled with explosives or bits of metal. It is fired from a cannon or gun. *Noun.*
—**1.** To take off the shell of something. The boys *shelled* peanuts for the party. **2.** To bombard with shells. The army *shelled* the city. *Verb.*

shell (shel) *noun, plural* **shells;** *verb,* **shelled, shelling.**

she'll *She'll* come tomorrow. *She'll* take good care of that dog.

she'll (shēl) contraction for "she will" and "she shall."

shellac A liquid used as a varnish on floors and furniture to protect them and make them shine. *Noun.*
—To coat with shellac. Dan will *shellac* the table. *Verb.*

shel·lac (shə lak′) *noun, plural* **shellacs;** *verb,* **shellacked, shellacking.**

shellfish An animal with a shell that lives in water. Shrimps, crabs, and oysters are shellfish.

shell·fish (shel′fish′) *noun, plural* **shellfish** or **shellfishes.**

shelter Something that covers or protects. The hikers used an old barn as a *shelter* during the rainstorm. *Noun.*
—To give shelter to. The tent *sheltered* the campers from the rain. The family *sheltered* the poor, hungry puppy. *Verb.*

shel·ter (shel′tər) *noun, plural* **shelters;** *verb,* **sheltered, sheltering.**

shelve **1.** To place on a shelf. We helped the librarian *shelve* the new books. **2.** To put aside. The club *shelved* the plan to have a party. **3.** To furnish with shelves. The builder will *shelve* the walls of the kitchen.

shelve (shelv) *verb,* **shelved, shelving.**

shelves More than one shelf. Look up **shelf** for more information.

shelves (shelvz) *noun plural.*

shepherd A person who takes care of sheep. *Noun.*
—**1.** To tend as a shepherd. The boy will *shepherd* the flock of sheep. **2.** To watch over or guide. The teacher *shepherded* the class through the museum. *Verb.*

shep·herd (shep′ərd) *noun, plural* **shepherds;** *verb,* **shepherded, shepherding.**

sherbet A frozen dessert. It is made of fruit juices, water, sugar, and a small amount of egg whites or milk.
sher·bet (shur′bit) *noun, plural* **sherbets.**

sheriff The main law officer of a county. The sheriff is in charge of keeping order and taking care of the jails.
sher·iff (sher′if) *noun, plural* **sheriffs.**

she's *She's* late this morning. *She's* been doing her homework.
she's (shēz) contraction for "she is" and "she has."

shied The horse *shied* at the loud noise. Look up **shy** for more information.
shied (shīd) *verb.*

shield 1. A piece of armor used in olden times. It was carried on the arm to protect the body or head during a battle. 2. A person or thing that defends or protects. Ann stood as a *shield* between her little brother and the growling dog. The umbrella was a *shield* against the rain. 3. Something shaped like a shield. A policeman's badge is called a shield. *Noun.*
—To defend or protect. He *shielded* his eyes with his hand in the bright sunshine. *Verb.*
shield (shēld) *noun, plural* **shields;** *verb,* **shielded, shielding.**

Shield

shift To move or change. John helped to *shift* the heavy table to the other side of the room. She *shifted* her position in the chair. The driver of the car *shifted* from first gear into second gear. *Verb.*
—1. A movement or change. The boy's sudden *shift* in position from one side of the canoe to the other almost made it tip over. 2. A group of workers, or the time that they work. My sister is on the day *shift* at the factory. *Noun.*
shift (shift) *verb,* **shifted, shifting;** *noun, plural* **shifts.**

shilling A coin that was once used in Great Britain. Twenty shillings were equal to one pound.
shil·ling (shil′ing) *noun, plural* **shillings.**

shimmer To shine with a faint light; glimmer. The lake *shimmered* in the moonlight.
shim·mer (shim′ər) *verb,* **shimmered, shimmering.**

shin The front part of the leg from the knee to the ankle. *Noun.*
—To climb by using the arms and legs. Billy likes to *shin* up trees. *Verb.*
shin (shin) *noun, plural* **shins;** *verb,* **shinned, shinning.**

shine 1. To give forth light; be bright; glow. The stars *shine* at night. Jean's face *shone* with happiness. 2. To make bright or gleaming. Jack *shined* his shoes. 3. To do very well. Ann *shines* in arithmetic at school. *Verb.*
—Light or brightness. The *shine* from the lamp hurts my eyes. The polished floor has a nice *shine. Noun.*
shine (shīn) *verb,* **shone** or **shined, shining;** *noun.*

shingle A thin piece of wood or other material. Shingles are placed in overlapping rows on roofs and sometimes on walls of buildings. *Noun.*
—To cover with shingles. The workmen will *shingle* the roof. *Verb.*
shin·gle (shing′gəl) *noun, plural* **shingles;** *verb,* **shingled, shingling.**

Shingles

shiny Shining; bright. We polished the floor and made it *shiny.*
shin·y (shī′nē) *adjective,* **shinier, shiniest.**

ship 1. A large boat. 2. An airplane or spacecraft. *Noun.*
—1. To send by ship, train, truck, or airplane. The factory will *ship* the furniture by truck. 2. To go on a ship as a member of the crew. Jim *shipped* as cabin boy on the voyage. *Verb.*
ship (ship) *noun, plural* **ships;** *verb,* **shipped, shipping.**

-ship A *suffix* that means "the state of being." *Friendship* means "the state of being a friend."

at; āpe; cär; end; mē; it; īce; hot; ōld;
fôrk; wood; fo͞ol; oil; out; up; turn; sing;
thin; this; hw in white; zh in treasure.
ə stands for **a** in about, **e** in taken
i in pencil, **o** in lemon, and **u** in circus.

shipment 1. The shipping of goods. The farmer's crops were loaded for *shipment* to market. 2. Something shipped. Several *shipments* of books arrived at the library.
ship·ment (ship′mənt) *noun, plural* **shipments.**

shipping 1. The sending of goods by ship, train, truck, or airplane. That company's business is *shipping.* 2. Ships. New York City's harbor is open to the world's *shipping.*
ship·ping (ship′ing) *noun, plural* **shippings.**

shipwreck The destruction or loss of a ship at sea. All the passengers and crew were saved from the *shipwreck. Noun.*
—To cause to be destroyed or lost. The storm *shipwrecked* the ocean liner. *Verb.*
ship·wreck (ship′rek′) *noun, plural* **shipwrecks;** *verb,* **shipwrecked, shipwrecking.**

shipyard A place where ships are built or repaired.
ship·yard (ship′yärd′) *noun, plural* **shipyards.**

shirt A piece of clothing worn on the upper part of the body. One kind of shirt has a collar and sleeves, and buttons down the front.
shirt (shurt) *noun, plural* **shirts.**

shiver To shake; tremble. Bill *shivered* in the cold room. *Verb.*
—The act or instance of shivering. The ghost story sent *shivers* up my back. *Noun.*
shiv·er (shiv′ər) *verb,* **shivered, shivering;** *noun, plural* **shivers.**

shoal A place in a river, lake, or ocean where the water is shallow.
shoal (shōl) *noun, plural* **shoals.**

shock[1] 1. A sudden, violent upsetting of the mind or emotions. The father never got over the *shock* of his son's death. 2. A sudden, violent blow or jolt. The *shock* caused by the explosion broke windows in nearby buildings. 3. A feeling caused by electricity passing through the body. I felt a *shock* when I touched a wire at the back of the radio. 4. A serious weakening of the body or mind caused by injury. The passengers of the wrecked automobile suffered *shock. Noun.*
—To disturb the mind or emotions of. My friend's rudeness *shocked* me. *Verb.*
shock (shok) *noun, plural* **shocks;** *verb,* **shocked, shocking.**

shock[2] A bundle of wheat, corn, or other grain stalks set up on end in a field.
shock (shok) *noun, plural* **shocks.**

shock[3] A thick, bushy mass of hair. Tim has a *shock* of blond hair over his forehead.
shock (shok) *noun, plural* **shocks.**

shocking Causing horror, surprise, or disgust. We heard the *shocking* news of the accident.
shock·ing (shok′ing) *adjective.*

shoe An outer covering for the foot. Shoes are usually made of leather.
shoe (sho͞o) *noun, plural* **shoes.**

shone The light *shone* in the window. Look up **shine** for more information.
shone (shōn) *verb.*

shook She *shook* her head. Look up **shake** for more information.
shook (shook) *verb.*

shoot 1. To hit with a bullet, arrow, or the like. Hunters *shoot* deer with rifles. 2. To send forth from a weapon. Ann *shot* an arrow at the target. 3. To cause to send forth; fire. Soldiers *shoot* cannons. The sheriff *shot* at the escaping outlaw. 4. To move or cause to move fast. The train will *shoot* by any minute. The snake *shot* out its tongue. 5. To come forth; sprout; grow. The bean plants are *shooting* up from the ground. 6. To photograph. That movie was *shot* in Rome. *Verb.*
—A new or young plant; sprout. *Noun.* ▲ Another word that sounds like this is **chute.**
shoot (sho͞ot) *verb,* **shot, shooting;** *noun, plural* **shoots.**

shop 1. A place where goods are sold. Kate went to the pet *shop* to look at puppies. 2. A place where a particular kind of work is done. Dad took the broken radio to the repair *shop. Noun.*
—To visit stores in order to look at and buy goods. Fran and her mother will *shop* for clothes. *Verb.*
shop (shop) *noun, plural* **shops;** *verb,* **shopped, shopping.**

shore 1. The land along the edge of an ocean, lake, or large river. We walked along the *shore.* 2. Land. The sailors were glad to be back on *shore* after the long voyage.
shore (shôr) *noun, plural* **shores.**

short 1. Not long or tall. Rick has *short* hair. It's a *short* trip to the store. She is a *short* girl. 2. Not having enough. The hikers were *short* of food, so they came home a day early. 3. To take less time to pronounce. The "i" in "bit" is a *short* vowel. *Adjective.*
—1. Suddenly; abruptly. The horse stopped *short* and the rider fell out of the saddle. 2. Not quite up to. The football player kicked the ball *short* of the goal line. *Adverb.*
—**shorts.** 1. Pants that are worn above the knee. Men, women, and children wear shorts in warm weather for comfort and for sports. 2. Men's underpants. *Noun.*

short (shôrt) *adjective*, **shorter, shortest;** *adverb; noun plural.*

shortage Too small an amount or supply; lack. There was a water *shortage* last summer because so little rain fell.
  short·age (shôr′tij) *noun, plural* **shortages.**

short circuit An electric circuit that has too much current flowing through it. A short circuit may blow a fuse or cause a fire. It is usually formed accidentally.

shortening Any of various fats that are used in cooking. Butter, lard, and vegetable oil are kinds of shortening.
  short·en·ing (shôrt′ən ing) *noun.*

shorthand A method of rapid handwriting that uses symbols or letters to take the place of words. The woman asked her secretary to take down a letter in *shorthand.*
  short·hand (shôrt′hand′) *noun.*

shorthorn A kind of cattle with short horns. It is raised for beef.
  short·horn (shôrt′hôrn′) *noun, plural* **short-horns.**

Shorthorn

shortly In a short time; soon. The doctor will see you *shortly.*
  short·ly (shôrt′lē) *adverb.*

shortstop A baseball player whose position is between second and third base.
  short·stop (shôrt′stop′) *noun, plural* **short-stops.**

shot¹ **1.** The firing of a gun or other weapon. Did you hear a *shot?* **2.** A person who fires a gun or other weapon. Jerry is a good *shot.* **3.** A ball or balls of lead or steel that are fired from a gun or cannon. **4.** The sending off of a rocket or missile. We watched the moon *shot* on television. **5.** The distance over which something can travel; range. The general gave the command not to fire until the enemy was within rifle *shot.* **6.** An injection of medicine. Everyone in the school got a free measles *shot.* **7.** An aim or stroke in certain games. The basketball team took practice *shots* before the game.

shot (shot) *noun, plural* **shots** or *(for definition 3)* **shot.**

shot² The policeman *shot* his gun in the air as a warning. Look up **shoot** for more information.
  shot (shot) *verb.*

should You *should* put a bandage on that cut. If anyone *should* call while I'm out, say that I'll be back in an hour. He *should* be here by five o'clock.
  should (shood) *verb.*

shoulder **1.** The part on either side of the body to which the arms are attached. **2.** The part of a shirt, dress, or other piece of clothing that covers the shoulder. I ripped my sweater at the *shoulder.* **3.** The edge or border on either side of a road or highway. Father pulled onto the *shoulder* of the road to change the flat tire. *Noun.*
—To push with the shoulder or shoulders. Susan *shouldered* her way through the crowd to see what was going on. *Verb.*
  shoul·der (shōl′dər) *noun, plural* **shoulders;** *verb,* **shouldered, shouldering.**

shouldn't She *shouldn't* eat so much candy.
  should·n't (shood′ənt) contraction for "should not."

shout To cry out loudly. The boys *shouted* for help when their canoe overturned. *Verb.*
—A loud cry or yell. The little girl gave a *shout* when she found the hidden Easter basket. *Noun.*
  shout (shout) *verb,* **shouted, shouting;** *noun, plural* **shouts.**

shove To push forward from behind. She *shoved* the chair closer to the table and sat down. *Verb.*
—A strong push. Joan's mother gave her a *shove* on the swing to get her started. *Noun.*
  shove (shuv) *verb,* **shoved, shoving;** *noun, plural* **shoves.**

shovel A tool or machine with a broad scoop. A shovel is used for digging and moving dirt, snow, and other loose material. *Noun.*
—**1.** To dig up and move with a shovel. The man *shoveled* dirt into the back of the truck. Dad *shoveled* a path through the snow. **2.** To

at; āpe; cär; end; mē; it; īce; hot; ōld; fôrk; wood; fōōl; oil; out; up; turn; sing; thin; this; hw in white; zh in treasure. ə stands for a in about, e in taken i in pencil, o in lemon, and u in circus.

move or throw in large amounts. Ted's mother told him to stop *shoveling* food into his mouth. *Verb.*

    shov·el (shuv′əl) *noun, plural* **shovels;** *verb,* **shoveled, shoveling.**

show **1.** To bring to sight or view. Please *show* your ticket at the gate of the ball park. The theater *showed* that same movie last week. **2.** To be able to be seen; be in sight. Ann's slip *showed* under her dress. **3.** To make or be made known. Betsy *showed* her anger by stamping her foot. Mother's worry *showed* on her face. **4.** To point out. Carl *showed* the man the way to the bus station. **5.** To explain to. Bob *showed* his sister how to change a tire. Mike asked Jane if she could *show* him how to do the arithmetic problem. **6.** To grant or give. The judge *showed* mercy in his decision. *Verb.*
—**1.** Something that is seen in public; display. We get tickets to see the horse *show* every year. **2.** Any program of entertainment in the theater or on radio or television. Did you watch that special *show* about animals on television last night? **3.** A display meant to attract or give a false impression. All the boys put up a *show* of bravery, but none wanted to be the first to dive off the high diving board. *Noun.*

    show (shō) *verb,* **showed, shown** or **showed, showing;** *noun, plural* **shows.**

shower **1.** A short fall of rain. The forecast is for *showers* this afternoon. **2.** A fall of anything in large numbers. There was a *shower* of sparks when the firecrackers went off. **3.** A bath in which water is sprayed on a person from an overhead fixture. *Noun.*
—**1.** To fall or make fall in a shower. It *showered* all day long, so we played inside. The wedding guests *showered* rice on the bride and groom. **2.** To bathe by taking a shower. Janet *showered* and dressed to go out to dinner. **3.** To give freely and in large amounts. Grandmother always *showers* us with presents when she comes to visit. *Verb.*

    show·er (shou′ər) *noun, plural* **showers;** *verb,* **showered, showering.**

shown We were *shown* many sights in Arizona by our friends there. Look up **show** for more information. ▲ Another word that sounds like this is **shone.**

    shown (shōn) *verb.*

shrank My new shirt *shrank* when I washed it. Look up **shrink** for more information.

    shrank (shrangk) *verb.*

shred **1.** A small piece or narrow strip torn or cut off. Janet put *shreds* of paper in the

bottom of the puppies' box. **2.** A small amount; bit. Joe said that there was not a *shred* of truth in his friend's story. *Noun.*
—To tear or cut into small pieces or narrow strips. Mother *shredded* cabbage for the salad. *Verb.*

    shred (shred) *noun, plural* **shreds;** *verb,* **shredded** or **shred, shredding.**

shrew A small animal that looks something like a mouse. A shrew has a long, pointed nose and short, rounded ears.

    shrew (shr$\overline{oo}$) *noun, plural* **shrews.**

Shrew

shrewd Clever and sharp. Mr. Johnson is a *shrewd* businessman.

    shrewd (shr$\overline{oo}$d) *adjective,* **shrewder, shrewdest.**

shriek A loud, sharp cry or sound. We could hear *shrieks* of laughter coming from the birthday party next door. *Noun.*
—To make a loud, sharp cry or sound. Jill *shrieked* with laughter when she saw her brother fall into the swimming pool with all his clothes on. *Verb.*

    shriek (shrēk) *noun, plural* **shrieks;** *verb,* **shrieked, shrieking.**

shrill Having a sharp, high sound. The policeman used a *shrill* whistle to direct traffic.

    shrill (shril) *adjective,* **shriller, shrillest.**

shrimp A sea animal that is covered with a thin shell and has a long tail. Shrimps are used for food.

    shrimp (shrimp) *noun, plural* **shrimps** or **shrimp.**

Shrimp

shrine A holy place for worship. A shrine often marks the tomb of a saint, contains a holy object, or is in memory of a religious person or event.

    shrine (shrīn) *noun, plural* **shrines.**

shrink **1.** To become smaller because of heat, cold, or wetness. That wool sweater will *shrink* if it's washed in hot water. **2.** To draw back in fear or horror. The woman *shrank* from the terrible sight of the car accident.
　shrink (shringk) *verb*, **shrank** or **shrunk**, **shrunk** or **shrunken**, **shrinking**.

shrub A woody plant that is smaller than a tree. A shrub has many stems that branch out at or near the ground.
　shrub (shrub) *noun*, *plural* **shrubs**.

shrug To raise or draw up the shoulders to show doubt or lack of interest. When Dan asked Martha if she wanted to go to the movies, she just *shrugged*. *Verb*.
—The act of raising or drawing up the shoulders to show doubt or lack of interest. *Noun*.
　shrug (shrug) *verb*, **shrugged**, **shrugging**; *noun*, *plural* **shrugs**.

shrunk My sweater *shrunk* in the wash. Look up **shrink** for more information.
　shrunk (shrungk) *verb*.

shudder To tremble suddenly from fear or cold. The strange sounds in the cave made Liz *shudder*. *Verb*.
—The act of trembling suddenly from fear or cold. The lost little boy felt a *shudder* of fear at every sound he heard in the woods. *Noun*.
　shud·der (shud′ər) *verb*, **shuddered**, **shuddering**; *noun*, *plural* **shudders**.

shuffle **1.** To walk by dragging the feet. The old man *shuffled* up the street. John *shuffles* his feet when he walks. **2.** To mix playing cards to change the order. When we play cards, the winner gets to *shuffle* for the next game. **3.** To move from one place to another. She *shuffled* the papers on her desk. *Verb*.
—The act of dragging the feet. The tired man walked with a *shuffle*. *Noun*.
　shuf·fle (shuf′əl) *verb*, **shuffled**, **shuffling**; *noun*, *plural* **shuffles**.

Sickle

shut **1.** To move something so as to block or cover up an entrance or opening; close. John *shut* the window. *Shut* your eyes and count to ten. **2.** To become closed. The door *shut* behind Alice as she left the room. **3.** To stop the working or flow of. We *shut* off the electricity in the cabin for the winter.
　shut (shut) *verb*, **shut**, **shutting**.

shutter **1.** A movable cover for a window. Shutters are used to shut out light and to keep people from look-ing in. **2.** A cover over a camera lens. A shutter lets in light when a pic-ture is taken.
　shut·ter (shut′ər) *noun*, *plural* **shut-ters**.

Shutters

shuttle **1.** A de-vice on a loom. It carries the yarn back and forth through the yarn strung on the loom. **2.** A train, airplane, or bus that runs back and forth be-tween two places.
　shut·tle (shut′əl) *noun*, *plural* **shuttles**.

shy **1.** Bashful. A shy person is uncomfort-able around other people. The *shy* little boy hid behind his mother's skirts. **2.** Easily frightened; timid. Animals that live in the woods are usually too *shy* to get close to people. *Adjective*.
—To move back suddenly in fear. Robin's horse *shied* at the loud noise. *Verb*.
　shy (shī) *adjective*, **shyer** or **shier**, **shyest** or **shiest**; *verb*, **shied**, **shying**.

sick **1.** Suffering from a disease or having poor health; ill. Robert isn't coming to school today because he is *sick*. **2.** Tired or dis-gusted. Louise bought new curtains because she was *sick* of the old ones.
　sick (sik) *adjective*, **sicker**, **sickest**.

sickle A tool having a sharp, curved blade that is attached to a short handle. A sickle is used for cutting grass or grain.
　sick·le (sik′əl) *noun*, *plural* **sickles**.

at; āpe; cär; end; mē; it; īce; hot; ōld;
fôrk; wood; fōol; oil; out; up; turn; sing;
thin; **th**is; **hw** in white; **zh** in treasure.
ə stands for **a** in about, **e** in taken
i in pencil, **o** in lemon, and **u** in circus.

sickness Illness or poor health. There has been quite a lot of *sickness* in our family this year.
sick·ness (sik′nis) *noun, plural* **sicknesses.**

side **1.** A line or surface that encloses something. A triangle has three *sides*. Father painted one *side* of the house last week. **2.** One of the two surfaces of a piece of paper or cloth, or any other flat object. One *side* of the cloth is shinier than the other. **3.** The place or space away from a central line or point. Put the chairs on the left *side* of the room. **4.** The right or left part of the body of a person or animal. Bobby got a pain in his *side* from running too much. **5.** One of two opposing groups or persons. Which *side* is winning the game? Henry was on his friend's *side* during the argument. **6.** A point of view or position. You should look at all *sides* of the question before making up your mind. *Noun.*
—**1.** At or near one side. The boys tried to sneak in the *side* door of the theater without paying. **2.** Coming from or directed toward one side. The army surprised the enemy with a *side* attack. **3.** Less important. The governor said he would discuss the *side* issues concerning the new law after the meeting. *Adjective.*
side (sīd) *noun, plural* **sides;** *adjective.*

sideshow A small show that is part of a larger show or entertainment. I like to see the *sideshows* at the circus.
side·show (sīd′shō′) *noun, plural* **sideshows.**

sidewalk A place by the side of the street where people can walk.
side·walk (sīd′wôk′) *noun, plural* **sidewalks.**

sideways **1.** Toward or from one side. The man moved *sideways* so that I could get past him. **2.** With one side forward. Susan had to walk *sideways* through the narrow door in order to fit through it with all her packages. *Adverb.*
—Moving or directed toward one side. Carolyn gave her sister a *sideways* glance to see what she was doing. *Adjective.*
side·ways (sīd′wāz′) *adverb; adjective.*

siege The surrounding of an enemy fort or position for a long time in order to cut off food and other supplies and force surrender. The soldiers carried on a *siege* of the fort for four months before the enemy finally surrendered.
siege (sēj) *noun, plural* **sieges.**

siesta An afternoon nap or rest. Siestas are taken especially in Spain and some other hot countries.
si·es·ta (sē es′tə) *noun, plural* **siestas.**

sieve A utensil that has a bottom with many holes in it. A sieve is used for sifting or draining. Jane sifted the flour through a *sieve* to get out all the lumps.
sieve (siv) *noun, plural* **sieves.**

Sieve

sift **1.** To separate large pieces from small pieces by using a sieve. Peggy helped *sift* the stones and pebbles out of the garden soil. **2.** To put through a sieve to take out lumps or make lighter. The recipe said to *sift* the flour before using it. **3.** To fall loosely as if through a sieve. Snow *sifted* through the cracks in the window of the cabin. **4.** To look at closely. The police *sifted* the evidence carefully to try to solve the crime.
sift (sift) *verb,* **sifted, sifting.**

sigh **1.** To make a long, deep breathing sound because of sadness, tiredness, or relief. Doug *sighed* with relief when he learned that someone had found the watch he had lost. **2.** To make a sound like this. The wind *sighed* through the trees. *Verb.*
—The act or sound of sighing. The mother uttered a *sigh* of relief when she learned her son had not been hurt in the fire. *Noun.*
sigh (sī) *verb,* **sighed, sighing;** *noun, plural* **sighs.**

sight **1.** The power or ability to see. Joe's *sight* improved when he started wearing glasses. **2.** The act of seeing. The *sight* of the strangers frightened the baby and she began to cry. **3.** The range or distance a person can see. We kept the candy out of the children's *sight* until after dinner. **4.** Something that is worth seeing. The sunset was a beautiful *sight*. **5.** Something on a gun or other object that helps in aiming or seeing. In shooting a rifle, a person must first line up the target in the sight. **6.** Something that is unpleasant or odd to look at. The room was a *sight* after the party. *Noun.*
—To see with the eyes. After hiking for hours, the group finally *sighted* the cabin. *Verb.* ▲ Other words that sound like this are **cite** and **site.**
sight (sīt) *noun, plural* **sights;** *verb,* **sighted, sighting.**

sign **1.** Something that stands for, shows, or suggests something else. A fever is a *sign* of

illness. The dark clouds were a *sign* of an approaching storm. ÷ is a *sign* for division. Father nodded as a *sign* that he agreed with what I said. **2.** A notice or board with writing on it that gives information. The *sign* on the door of the shop said "Closed on Sundays." **3.** Something that warns or points out what is to come. Some people believe that breaking a mirror is a *sign* of bad luck. **4.** A trace. There was no *sign* of Robin's pet cat. *Noun.*
—To write one's name on. Margaret *signed* her name at the bottom of the letter. *Verb.*
sign (sīn) *noun, plural* **signs;** *verb,* **signed, signing.**

signal **1.** Something that warns, directs, or informs. The flashing light was a *signal* that a train was coming. **2.** A sign or action that brings about something. One shot was fired in the air as the *signal* for the race to begin. *Noun.*
—**1.** To make a signal to. The men on the sinking ship *signaled* a passing ship for help. **2.** To make known by a signal or signals. A whistle *signals* the end of the working day at the factory. *Verb.*
sig·nal (sig′nəl) *noun, plural* **signals;** *verb,* **signaled, signaling.**

signature **1.** The name of a person written in his own handwriting. The museum has letters with Abraham Lincoln's *signature* **2.** A sign at the beginning of each section of music. The signature shows the pitch and time of a piece of music.
sig·na·ture (sig′nə chər) *noun, plural* **signatures.**

significance Special value or meaning; importance. The election of a new President is an event of great *significance* in the United States.
sig·nif·i·cance (sig nif′i kəns) *noun.*

significant Having special value or meaning; important. July 20, 1969 was a *significant* date in the history of space travel because that was the day of the first moon landing.
sig·nif·i·cant (sig nif′i kənt) *adjective.*

silence A lack of sound; complete quiet. The audience listened to the concert in *silence. Noun.*
—To make or keep silent. The teacher banged a book on the desk to *silence* the noisy students. *Verb.*
si·lence (sī′ləns) *noun, plural* **silences;** *verb,* **silenced, silencing.**

silent **1.** Completely quiet; still. We crept through the *silent* house. **2.** Not speaking or saying little. The children remained *silent* during the church service. He is a shy, *silent*

boy. **3.** Not spoken or expressed; not said out loud. The "k" in "know" is *silent.*
si·lent (sī′lənt) *adjective.*

silhouette **1.** A picture or drawing showing the outline of a figure or object filled in with black or another solid color. **2.** A dark outline seen against a lighter background. From our window at dusk, you can see the *silhouette* of the mountains against the sky. *Noun.*
—To show as a dark outline against a lighter background. The horse standing on the hill was *silhouetted* against the sky. *Verb.*
sil·hou·ette (sil′o͞o et′) *noun, plural* **silhouettes;** *verb,* **silhouetted, silhouetting.**

silk **1.** A soft, shiny cloth that is made from threads that are spun by silkworms. Silk is used to make scarves, ties, blouses, and many other pieces of clothing. **2.** Anything that is like silk. The tassels on an ear of corn are called silk.
silk (silk) *noun, plural* **silks.**

▲ The word **silk** goes back to the Greek word for this cloth. The Greeks named this cloth from the word meaning "Chinese," because the Chinese people were famous for the silk cloth they made.

---

silkworm A caterpillar that makes silk thread to spin its cocoon. The silkworm was originally found in China.
silk·worm (silk′-wurm′) *noun, plural* **silkworms.**

sill The piece of wood or stone at the bottom of a door or window.
sill (sil) *noun, plural* **sills.**

Cocoon

Silkworm

silly Without judgment or common sense; foolish. Don't be *silly,* you can't drive home in this snowstorm. Before the airplane was invented, some people thought that flying was a *silly* idea.
sil·ly (sil′ē) *adjective,* **sillier, silliest.**

at; āpe; cär; end; mē; it; īce; hot; ōld; fôrk; wood; fo͞ol; oil; out; up; turn; sing; thin; this; hw in white; zh in treasure. ə stands for a in about, e in taken i in pencil, o in lemon, and u in circus.

silo A tall, round tower that is used to store foods for farm animals. Silos are made out of metal, concrete, or other material.
si·lo (sī′lō) *noun, plural* **silos.**

Silo

silt Fine particles of sand, clay, dirt, and other material. Silt is carried by flowing water, as in a river, and eventually it settles to the bottom.
silt (silt) *noun.*

silver **1.** A shiny, white metal that is soft and easily shaped. It is used to make coins, jewelry, and spoons, forks, and other things for the table. Silver is a chemical element. **2.** Coins that are made from silver; change. Dad always carries some *silver* in his pocket. **3.** Spoons, forks, or other things made of or coated with silver. **4.** The color of silver. *Noun.*
—**1.** Made of or coated with silver. Mother polished the *silver* tray. **2.** Having the color of silver. *Adjective.*
—To coat with silver. Amy took the old bowl to a jeweler to have it *silvered. Verb.*
sil·ver (sil′vər) *noun, plural* **silvers;** *adjective; verb,* **silvered, silvering.**

silversmith A person who makes or repairs pieces of silver.
sil·ver·smith (sil′vər smith′) *noun, plural* **silversmiths.**

silverware **1.** Spoons, forks, dishes, or anything else for the table that is made of or coated with silver. **2.** Spoons, forks, or knives made out of a metal other than silver.
sil·ver·ware (sil′vər wer′) *noun.*

similar Much the same; alike. The two dresses I bought today are very *similar.*
sim·i·lar (sim′ə lər) *adjective.*

similarity Likeness or resemblance. There

is a strong *similarity* between you and your older brother.
sim·i·lar·i·ty (sim′ə lar′ə tē) *noun, plural* **similarities.**

simmer To cook just below the boiling point. The recipe says to *simmer* the soup in a covered pot for two hours.
sim·mer (sim′ər) *verb,* **simmered, simmering.**

simple **1.** Easy to understand or do. That history test was really *simple.* Jane thought that learning to ride a two-wheeled bicycle was *simple.* **2.** Without ornament; plain. The architect made a *simple* design for the building. **3.** Natural and honest. Ruth is a *simple,* fun-loving person.
sim·ple (sim′pəl) *adjective,* **simpler, simplest.**

simplify To make easier. The teacher *simplified* the arithmetic problem so the class could understand it better.
sim·pli·fy (sim′plə fī′) *verb,* **simplified, simplifying.**

simply **1.** In a natural and honest way. The lecturer spoke *simply* and to the point. **2.** Without decoration; plainly. The girl dressed *simply.* **3.** Merely; only. Saying "hello" to friends you meet on the street is *simply* a matter of politeness.
sim·ply (sim′plē) *adverb.*

simultaneously At the same time. The doorbell and the telephone rang *simultaneously.*
si·mul·ta·ne·ous·ly (sī′məl tā′nē əs lē) *adverb.*

sin **1.** An act that goes against the will of God. In many religions, murder is a *sin.* **2.** Any wrong or bad act. It's a *sin* to be cruel to animals. *Noun.*
—To go against the will of God. The man confessed in his prayers that he had *sinned. Verb.*
sin (sin) *noun, plural* **sins;** *verb,* **sinned, sinning.**

since John left last week and has been away ever *since.* Ted was sick last month but has *since* recovered. Joyce has been gone *since* five o'clock. There have been many changes in this town *since* my father was a boy. I haven't seen Gregory *since* we went to camp together two years ago. *Since* the car isn't working, we'll have to take the bus.
since (sins) *adverb; preposition; conjunction.*

sincere Not false or pretended; honest and true. Debbie gave us her *sincere* thanks for a wonderful weekend.
sin·cere (sin sēr′) *adjective,* **sincerer, sincerest.**

sinew A strong cord or band of tissue that

joins a muscle to a bone. The sinews make it possible for the muscles to move an arm, leg, finger, or other part of the body.

sin·ew (sin′yo͞o) *noun, plural* **sinews.**

sing   **1.** To make words or sounds with musical tones. The school choir *sings* beautifully. The whole class *sang* a Christmas carol. The birds *sang* in the trees. **2.** To make a whistling or humming sound. The tea kettle *sang* when the water started boiling.

sing (sing) *verb,* **sang** or **sung, sung, singing.**

singer   A person or bird that sings. My mother is one of the *singers* in the church choir. My friend's canary is a good *singer.*

sing·er (sing′ər) *noun, plural* **singers.**

single   **1.** Only one. The little girl wore a *single* flower in her hair. Jim tore a *single* sheet of paper from his notebook. **2.** To be used by one person only. The woman asked for a *single* room at the hotel. **3.** Not married. My older brother is *single. Adjective.*
—A hit in baseball that allows the batter to reach first base safely. *Noun.*
—To pick or choose from others. Mary *singled* out the black cat as her favorite. *Verb.*

sin·gle (sing′gəl) *adjective; noun, plural* **singles;** *verb,* **singled, singling.**

singular   Showing only one person or thing. "Girl" is a *singular* noun; "girls" is a plural noun. "Am" is a *singular* verb; "are" is a plural verb. *Adjective.*
—The form of a word that shows only one person or thing. "Boy" is the *singular* of "boys." "Woman" is the *singular* of "women." *Noun.*

sin·gu·lar (sing′gyə lər) *adjective; noun, plural* **singulars.**

sinister   Evil or suggesting evil. The dark old house looked *sinister* at night. In the story, the witch gave a *sinister* laugh and disappeared.

sin·is·ter (sin′is tər) *adjective.*

sink   **1.** To go down partly or completely. The wheels of the car *sank* into the mud. The ship *sank* after hitting the rocks. **2.** To become less. The children's voices *sank* to a whisper when the teacher entered the room. **3.** To fall into a certain state. Tom was so tired he *sank* into a deep sleep as soon as his head hit the pillow. **4.** To dig. The workmen *sank* a well behind the house. **5.** To go through or into deeply. The light rain *sank* into the dry ground. *Verb.*
—A basin of metal or porcelain that is used for washing. A sink has faucets to turn water on and off and a drain to take water away. *Noun.*

sink (singk) *verb,* **sank** or **sunk, sunk** or **sunken, sinking;** *noun, plural* **sinks.**

sip   To drink little by little. George *sipped* the hot tea. *Verb.*
—A little drink. Can I have a *sip* of your soda? *Noun.*

sip (sip) *verb,* **sipped, sipping;** *noun, plural* **sips.**

siphon   A bent tube with one side longer than the other. A siphon is used to move a liquid from one container to another one that is placed below it. The liquid is drawn off by air pressure.

si·phon (sī′fən) *noun, plural* **siphons.**

Siphon

sir   **1.** A title used in place of a man's name. The sales clerk said to the man, "May I help you, *sir?*" **2. Sir.** A title used in front of the name of a knight. *Sir* Lancelot was the bravest knight in King Arthur's Court.

sir (sur) *noun, plural* **sirs.**

Sire   A title used when speaking to a king or noble. "I beg your forgiveness, *Sire,*" said the man to the king.

Sire (sīr) *noun, plural* **Sires.**

siren   A kind of whistle with a loud, shrill sound. It is used as a signal or warning. Ambulances and police cars have sirens.

si·ren (sī′rən) *noun, plural* **sirens.**

sister   A girl or woman with the same mother and father as another person.

sis·ter (sis′tər) *noun, plural* **sisters.**

sister-in-law   **1.** The sister of a husband or wife. **2.** The wife of a brother.

sis·ter-in-law (sis′tər in lô′) *noun, plural* **sisters-in-law.**

sit   **1.** To be in a position in which the weight of the body rests on the lower back part and not the feet. Bob *sat* in a chair. **2.** To cause to sit; seat. Mother *sat* the children around the table for the birthday party. **3.** To rest on a perch; roost. The bird *sat* on a branch. **4.** To

at; āpe; cär; end; mē; it; īce; hot; ōld;
fôrk; wood; fo͞ol; oil; out; up; turn; sing;
thin; this; hw in white; zh in treasure.
ə stands for a in about, e in taken
i in pencil, o in lemon, and u in circus.

cover eggs in order to hatch them. Chickens *sit* on their eggs.

sit (sit) *verb,* **sat, sitting.**

site   The position or location of something. Our house is in a mountain *site* with a beautiful view. That town is the *site* of one of the major battles in the Civil War. ▲ Other words that sound like this are **cite** and **sight.**

site (sīt) *noun, plural* **sites.**

Skating

situate   To give a position to; place. A large flower garden was *situated* alongside of the house.

sit·u·ate (sich′o͞o āt′) *verb,* **situated, situating.**

situation   A condition or state of affairs; circumstance. Ted found himself in a difficult *situation* when his car ran out of gas on a deserted country road.

sit·u·a·tion (sich′o͞o ā′shən) *noun, plural* **situations.**

six   One more than five; 6.

six (siks) *noun, plural* **sixes;** *adjective.*

sixteen   Six more than ten; 16.

six·teen (siks′tēn′) *noun, plural* **sixteens;** *adjective.*

sixteenth   **1.** Next after the fifteenth. **2.** One of sixteen equal parts; 1/16.

six·teenth (siks′tēnth′) *adjective; noun, plural* **sixteenths.**

sixth   **1.** Next after the fifth. **2.** One of six equal parts; 1/6.

sixth (siksth) *adjective; noun, plural* **sixths.**

sixtieth   **1.** Next after the fifty-ninth. **2.** One of sixty equal parts; 1/60.

six·ti·eth (siks′tē ith) *adjective; noun, plural* **sixtieths.**

sixty   Six times ten; 60.

six·ty (siks′tē) *noun, plural* **sixties;** *adjective.*

size   **1.** The amount of space something takes up; the length, width, and height of something. The *size* of the living room in our new house is twice as large as the one in our old house. **2.** Amount or number. John asked his father to increase the *size* of his allowance. Our dancing class has increased in *size* since last year. **3.** A series of measurements used for shoes, clothing, and other things sold in stores. What *size* shirt do you wear?

size (sīz) *noun, plural* **sizes.**

sizzle   To make a hissing sound. The bacon *sizzled* as it cooked in the pan.

siz·zle (siz′əl) *verb,* **sizzled, sizzling.**

skate¹   **1.** A special shoe with a metal runner attached to the sole; ice skate. It is used for moving over ice. **2.** A skate with small wheels attached to the sole; roller skate. It is used for moving over a flat surface, like a sidewalk. *Noun.*
—To glide or move along on skates. The children *skate* when the pond freezes over. *Verb.*

skate (skāt) *noun, plural* **skates;** *verb,* **skated, skating.**

skate²   A broad, flat fish that is related to the shark.

skate (skāt) *noun, plural* **skates** or **skate.**

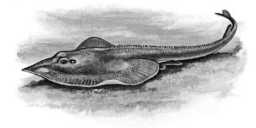

Skate

skeleton   **1.** A framework of bones that supports the body of all animals with backbones. Birds, fish, and man have a skeleton. **2.** Any framework or structure that is used as a support. Workmen build the *skeleton* of a building before they put up the inside and outside walls.

skel·e·ton (skel′ət ən) *noun, plural* **skeletons.**

sketch   **1.** A rough, quick drawing. The artist made several *sketches* of the model before starting his painting. **2.** A short description, story, or play. That play is made up of five short *sketches* about different people in history. *Noun.*
—To make a sketch of; draw roughly and quickly. Jim *sketched* the old barn for his art class. *Verb.*

sketch (skech) *noun, plural* **sketches;** *verb,* **sketched, sketching.**

ski **1.** One of a pair of long, narrow runners that curve upward at the front. Skis are usually made of wood or metal and are made to be attached to boots. They are used for gliding over snow. **2.** One of a pair of similar wooden runners that are used for gliding over water. *Noun.*
—To travel on skis. Debbie *skied* down the mountain. *Verb.*

  ski (skē) *noun, plural* **skis** or **ski;** *verb,* **skied, skiing.**

Skiing

skid A sideways slide or slip on an icy or wet surface. The *skid* of the car on the wet road warned Tim to drive slowly. *Noun.*
—To slide or slip sideways on an icy or wet surface. The truck *skidded* on the icy road. *Verb.*

  skid (skid) *noun, plural* **skids;** *verb,* **skidded, skidding.**

skill The power or ability to do something. Skill comes from practice, study, or experience. Mark shows great *skill* in playing the piano. My mother works with children who have poor reading *skills.*

  skill (skil) *noun, plural* **skills.**

skilled **1.** Having or showing skill and ability. My uncle is a *skilled* craftsman who repairs old clocks. **2.** Requiring special ability or training. The factory is trying to hire experienced workers for some *skilled* jobs.

  skilled (skild) *adjective.*

skillet A shallow pan with a handle. A skillet is used for frying.

  skil·let (skil′it) *noun, plural* **skillets.**

skim **1.** To remove something that is floating from the surface of a liquid. The cook *skimmed* the fat from the soup while it cooked. **2.** To read quickly. Mother likes to *skim* the morning paper while she eats break-

fast. **3.** To move or glide lightly and swiftly. The sailboat *skimmed* easily across the lake. **4.** To throw so as to bounce lightly across a surface. The two boys had a contest to see who could *skim* a stone the farthest across the pond.

  skim (skim) *verb,* **skimmed, skimming.**

skim milk Milk from which the cream has been removed. Another name for this is **skimmed milk.**

skin **1.** The outer covering of the body of a person or animal. The skin protects the organs inside the body from disease or injury. **2.** The outer covering or hide that is removed from an animal with fur. The *skin* of a calf is used to make shoes, handbags, and clothing. **3.** Anything that is like skin. This apple has a bright red *skin. Noun.*
—To take off the skin from. Jack *skinned* his knees when he fell off his bicycle. The early trappers in America made a living by *skinning* animals and selling the hides. *Verb.*

  skin (skin) *noun, plural* **skins;** *verb,* **skinned, skinning.**

skin diving Swimming underwater for long periods of time. A face mask and flippers, and sometimes an oxygen tank or a snorkel, are used in skin diving.

skinny Very thin. She was very *skinny* as a child.

  skin·ny (skin′ē) *adjective,* **skinnier, skinniest.**

skip **1.** To spring or bound along, hopping lightly on one foot and then on the other. The children *skipped* down the path. **2.** To jump or leap over. The children *skipped* rope in the playground. **3.** To pass by or leave out. The teacher told the students they could *skip* over pages 112 to 116. Ron *skipped* the arithmetic problems he couldn't do. **4.** To throw in order to bounce across a surface. The boys liked to *skip* stones across the pond. *Verb.*
—A light springing or jumping step. The girl

Skin Diving

at; āpe; cär; end; mē; it; īce; hot; ōld;
fôrk; wood; fōōl; oil; out; up; turn; sing;
thin; this; hw in white; zh in treasure.
ə stands for a in about, e in taken
i in pencil, o in lemon, and u in circus.

gave a *skip* to avoid the puddle. *Noun.*

skip (skip) *verb*, **skipped, slipping;** *noun, plural* **skips.**

skirt **1.** A piece of clothing that is worn by women or girls. It hangs down from the waist. Skirts are worn with some kind of blouse or sweater on top. **2.** The part of a dress or similar piece of clothing that hangs down from the waist. *Noun.*
—To move along the border or edge of. The highway *skirted* the town. *Verb.*

skirt (skurt) *noun, plural* **skirts;** *verb*, **skirted, skirting.**

skull The bony framework of the head in animals that have a backbone. The skull protects the brain.

skull (skul) *noun, plural* **skulls.**

skunk A black animal that has a bushy tail and white stripes along its back. A skunk sprays a strong, bad-smelling liquid when it is frightened or attacked.

skunk (skungk) *noun, plural* **skunks.**

Skunk

sky The upper space or air beyond the earth. On clear days, the sky has a light-blue color. Today's weather forecast is for sunshine and blue *skies.*

sky (skī) *noun, plural* **skies.**

skydiving The act or sport of parachuting from an airplane and falling as far as safely possible before opening the parachute.

sky·div·ing (skī′dī′ving) *noun.*

skylark A small European bird that sings a beautiful song while it is flying. The skylark has brown feathers with marks of black and white.

sky·lark (skī′lärk′) *noun, plural* **skylarks.**

skyline **1.** The outline of buildings, mountains, or other objects as seen against the sky. We saw the city's *skyline* as we drove over the bridge. **2.** The line at which the earth and

Skylark

sky seem to come together; horizon. The sunset turned the *skyline* into beautiful shades of red and orange.

sky·line (skī′līn′) *noun, plural* **skylines.**

Skyline

skyrocket A kind of firecracker that goes off high in the air and gives off a shower of colored sparks. *Noun.*
—To rise suddenly and quickly. The cost of food has *skyrocketed* during the past year. *Verb.*

sky·rock·et (skī′rok′it) *noun, plural* **skyrockets;** *verb*, **skyrocketed, skyrocketing.**

skyscraper A very tall building. New York City has many *skyscrapers.*

sky·scrap·er (skī′skrā′pər) *noun, plural* **skyscrapers.**

slab A broad, flat, thick piece of stone or other material. The workmen had to lift up big *slabs* of concrete to reach the broken water pipe under the sidewalk.

slab (slab) *noun, plural* **slabs.**

slack **1.** Not tight or firm; loose. The sailor tightened the *slack* rope because the boat was drifting too far from the dock. **2.** Slow and unhurried; not lively. Bill left the house early so he could walk to school at a *slack* pace. *Adjective.*
—A part that hangs loose. The cowboy took up the *slack* in the rope. *Noun.*

slack (slak) *adjective*, **slacker, slackest;** *noun, plural* **slacks.**

slacks Trousers for casual or informal wear.

slacks (slaks) *noun plural.*

slain In the story, the people lived in fear for their lives until the dragon was *slain.* Look up **slay** for more information.

slain (slān) *verb.*

slam **1.** To close with force and a loud noise. The driver *slammed* the car door behind him. **2.** To throw or put with force and a loud noise. The angry girl *slammed* the phone down. **3.** To strike or hit with force and a loud noise. The shutters *slammed* against the side of the house in the wind. *Verb.*
—A forceful and noisy closing or striking. Bruce closed the door with a *slam. Noun.*
   slam (slam) *verb,* **slammed, slamming;** *noun,* *plural* **slams.**

slang An informal kind of language used in everyday conversation. Slang uses new words and new and different meanings for old words. The use of slang helps to keep language lively and interesting.
   slang (slang) *noun.*

▲ Most **slang** is used for only a short time, and then it disappears from the language. Some slang words and phrases that people once said but we no longer use today are *skiddoo,* meaning "go away," and *the cat's pajamas,* meaning "wonderful." There are other words, however, that were slang at first and are now part of our standard language. *Kidnap, skyscraper,* and *jazz* were all considered slang at one time. Slang words do make our language interesting, but in most cases you should use slang only in everyday conversation, not in writing and formal speaking.

slant To run or slope away from a straight line. The barn roof *slants* toward the ground so the rain can run off. He *slanted* the ladder against the wall. *Verb.*
—A sloping direction or line. Make sure you hang the picture straight, not on a *slant. Noun.*
   slant (slant) *verb,* **slanted, slanting;** *noun,* *plural* **slants.**

slap A sharp, quick blow with the open hand or something flat. He greeted his friend with a *slap* on the back. *Noun.*
—**1.** To hit with a sharp, quick blow. Pam *slapped* the fly with a rolled-up newspaper. **2.** To put or throw noisily and forcefully. Dick *slapped* his books down on the desk and ran out the door. *Verb.*
   slap (slap) *noun, plural* **slaps;** *verb,* **slapped, slapping.**

slash **1.** To cut with a sweeping stroke of a knife or another sharp object. The robbers had *slashed* the tires of the policemen's car so they couldn't follow them. **2.** To lower sharply. The store *slashed* its prices when it was going out of business. *Verb.*
—**1.** A sweeping stroke with great force. The lion trainer made the animals obey him by a *slash* of his whip on the floor. **2.** A cut made by a forceful, sweeping stroke. The woman had a *slash* over her eye where she had been hit by broken glass. **3.** A sharp lowering. The store advertised a *slash* in the prices of all its clothing. *Noun.*
   slash (slash) *verb,* **slashed, slashing;** *noun,* *plural* **slashes.**

slat A thin, flat strip of wood, metal, or other material. The *slats* on the back of the chair are coming loose.
   slat (slat) *noun, plural* **slats.**

slate A bluish-gray rock that splits easily into thin layers. Slate is used to make blackboards and garden walks, and to cover roofs.
   slate (slāt) *noun.*

slaughter **1.** The act of killing an animal or animals for food. The farmer fattened his pigs before *slaughter.* **2.** A brutal killing; massacre. The army was responsible for the *slaughter* of hundreds of innocent men, women, and children. *Noun.*
—To kill for food. The farmer *slaughtered* one of his turkeys for Thanksgiving dinner. *Verb.*
   slaugh·ter (slô′tər) *noun, plural* **slaughters;** *verb,* **slaughtered, slaughtering.**

slave **1.** A person who is owned by another person. Before the Civil War, Southern whites used Negro *slaves* to work on their plantations. **2.** A person who works or is made to work hard and long. Those people are *slaves* of the company and make very little money for all the work they do. *Noun.*
—To work hard and long. The writer *slaved* away at his desk for hours. *Verb.*
   slave (slāv) *noun, plural* **slaves;** *verb,* **slaved, slaving.**

▲ The word **slave** comes from a Latin word that means "Slav." The Slavs are a group of people who live in eastern and central Europe. In the Middle Ages, many Slavs were captured by the Germans and made to work as servants and slaves.

slavery **1.** The practice of owning slaves. Abraham Lincoln outlawed *slavery* in the

at; āpe; cär; end; mē; it; īce; hot; ōld;
fôrk; wood; fool; oil; out; up; turn; sing;
thin; this; hw in white; zh in treasure.
ə stands for a in about, e in taken
i in pencil, o in lemon, and u in circus.

United States during the Civil War. **2.** The condition of being a slave. During the first part of the 1800s, many Africans were sold into *slavery* and sent to America.

slav·er·y (slā′vər ē) *noun.*

slay To kill in a violent way. The brave knight went out to *slay* the dragon. ▲ Another word that sounds like this is **sleigh**.

slay (slā) *verb,* **slew, slain, slaying.**

Dog Sled

sled A wooden framework mounted on metal runners. A sled is used to carry people or loads over the snow. *Noun.*
—To ride on a sled. All the children were *sledding* down the hill. *Verb.*

sled (sled) *noun, plural* **sleds;** *verb,* **sledded, sledding.**

sledgehammer A heavy hammer with a long handle that is usually held with both hands.

sledge·ham·mer (slej′-ham′ər) *noun, plu-ral* **sledgehammers.**

sleek **1.** Smooth and shiny. That cat has *sleek* black fur. **2.** Looking healthy and well taken care of. Ellen owns a *sleek*, dark-brown horse.

sleek (slēk) *adjective,* **sleeker, sleekest.**

sleep A time of rest that occurs naturally for man and animals at regular times. During sleep, the body regains its strength and energy. I got eight hours' *sleep* last night. Did you have a good night's *sleep? Noun.*

Sledgehammer

—To be in a state of sleep; be asleep. A baby *sleeps* a large part of the day. *Verb.*

sleep (slēp) *noun; verb,* **slept, sleeping.**

sleeping bag A long, warmly-lined or pad-ded bag. It is used for sleeping outdoors.

sleepy **1.** Ready for or needing sleep. If Amy stays up past her bedtime, she gets very *sleepy.* **2.** Dull or quiet. We take our summer vacation in a *sleepy* little town way up in the mountains.

sleep·y (slē′pē) *adjective,* **sleepier, sleepiest.**

sleet Frozen or partly frozen rain. *Noun.*
—To shower sleet. The roads were very slippery because it had *sleeted* all day. *Verb.*

sleet (slēt) *noun; verb,* **sleeted, sleeting.**

sleeve The part of a piece of clothing that covers all or part of the arm.

sleeve (slēv) *noun, plural* **sleeves.**

sleigh A carriage on metal runners that is drawn by a horse. A sleigh is used for travel-ing over snow or ice. ▲ Another word that sounds like this is **slay**.

sleigh (slā) *noun, plural* **sleighs.**

Sleigh

slender **1.** Not big around; thin. Everyone in my family is very *slender* because we get a lot of exercise. The new dining room chairs have *slender* legs. **2.** Small in size or amount. The candidate won the election by only a *slender* margin.

slen·der (slen′dər) *adjective,* **slenderer, slenderest.**

slept Steve *slept* until about noon on Satur-day. Look up **sleep** for more information.

slept (slept) *verb.*

slew The hunter *slew* the deer. Look up **slay** for more information.

slew (slo̅o̅) *verb.*

slice A thin, flat piece cut from something larger. Would you put a *slice* of bread in the toaster for me? *Noun.*
—**1.** To cut into a thin, flat piece or pieces. Bobby *sliced* the cake and gave everyone a piece. **2.** To move through like a knife. The fin of the shark *sliced* the water. *Verb.*

slice (slīs) *noun, plural* **slices;** *verb,* **sliced, slicing.**

slick **1.** Smooth and shiny. The horse had a *slick* brown coat. **2.** Smooth and slippery. A freshly waxed floor is *slick. Adjective.*
—A smooth or slippery place on a surface.

The boat left a *slick* of oil on the water. *Noun.*

slick (slik) *adjective,* **slicker, slickest;** *noun, plural* **slicks.**

slid The boy fell and *slid* down the steep hill.

slid (slid) *verb.*

slide **1.** To move or cause to move smoothly. The wet bar of soap *slid* across the floor. Ken *slid* into the seat next to me. **2.** To fall or move suddenly from a position. As the woman crossed the icy walk, her feet *slid* out from under her and she fell. *Verb.*
—**1.** The act of sliding. Harry took a *slide* down the hill on his new sled. **2.** A smooth surface for sliding. The children played on the *slide* in the playground. **3.** A small sheet of glass or plastic. Objects are put on a glass *slide* and looked at under a microscope. *Slides* with pictures on them are put in a projector and shown on a screen. **4.** The fall of a mass of rock, snow, or other material down a slope. The road was closed because of rock *slides. Noun.*

slide (slīd) *verb,* **slid, slid** or **slidden, sliding;** *noun, plural* **slides.**

slight **1.** Not much or not important; small. There is only a *slight* chance that it will rain today. **2.** Not big around; thin. My mother is very *slight* and weighs only about one hundred pounds. *Adjective.*
—To treat as unimportant; not pay enough attention to. The girl felt she had been *slighted* when she was not invited to her friend's picnic. *Verb.*

slight (slīt) *adjective,* **slighter, slightest;** *verb,* **slighted, slighting.**

slim **1.** Small in thickness; thin. The fashion model had a very *slim* figure. **2.** Small in amount; slight. The team felt it had only a *slim* chance of winning the game. *Adjective.*
—To become slim. The boy *slimmed* down by going on a diet. *Verb.*

slim (slim) *adjective,* **slimmer, slimmest;** *verb,* **slimmed, slimming.**

sling **1.** A device for throwing stones. A sling is usually made of a piece of leather with a string fastened to each end. **2.** A loop of cloth hanging down from the neck to support an injured arm or hand. When Mary broke her arm, she had to wear a *sling* for a few months. *Noun.*
—**1.** To hang with a sling or strap. The hunter *slung* his gun over his shoulder. **2.** To hang or throw loosely. Jeff *slung* the hammock between two trees. *Verb.*

sling (sling) *noun, plural* **slings;** *verb,* **slung, slinging.**

slingshot A Y-shaped piece of wood or metal with an elastic band fastened to the tips of two prongs. A slingshot is used to shoot stones or other small objects.

Slingshot

sling·shot (sling'shot') *noun, plural* **slingshots.**

slip¹ **1.** To move or slide suddenly out of place or out of control. The man *slipped* on the icy sidewalk. The soapy glass *slipped* out of her hands. **2.** To move or go quietly. The thief *slipped* out of the apartment without a sound. **3.** To cause to move smoothly and easily. Susan *slipped* the ring from her finger. **4.** To put or give quietly and quickly. Judy *slipped* me a note during class. **5.** To fail to be noticed or remembered. My summer vacation always seems to *slip* by, and it's time for school again before I know it. I know I've met that man somewhere before, but his name *slips* my mind. **6.** To put on or take off clothing quickly and easily. Rick *slipped* into his pajamas and went to bed. **7.** To make a mistake. Dan *slipped* up on the last word of the spelling test. *Verb.*
—**1.** The act of slipping. The woman took a *slip* on the icy sidewalk and broke her hip. **2.** A piece of clothing worn under a woman's dress or skirt. A slip is made out of a light material like cotton or nylon. **3.** A mistake or error. The robbery would have been a perfect crime, except for one little *slip* that gave the thieves away. *Noun.*

slip (slip) *verb,* **slipped, slipping;** *noun, plural* **slips.**

slip² **1.** A small piece of paper, cloth, or any other material. Joan wrote her friend's telephone number on a *slip* of paper. **2.** A small shoot or twig cut from a plant. Dave cut a *slip* from the plant to grow a new plant.

slip (slip) *noun, plural* **slips.**

slipper A light, low shoe that is easily slipped on or off the foot. Slippers are worn indoors.

slip·per (slip'ər) *noun, plural* **slippers.**

at; āpe; cär; end; mē; it; īce; hot; ōld;
fôrk; wood; fool; oil; out; up; turn; sing;
thin; this; hw in white; zh in treasure.
ə stands for a in about, e in taken
i in pencil, o in lemon, and u in circus.

slippery **1.** Causing or likely to cause slipping or sliding. Freezing rain made the roads *slippery*. **2.** Slipping or sliding away easily. The wet fish was too *slippery* to hold.
slip·per·y (slip′ər ē) *adjective,* **slipperier, slipperiest.**

slit A long, narrow cut or opening. There was a *slit* up one side of the long dress. There is a *slit* in the mailbox to drop in letters. *Noun.*
—To cut or make a slit or slits in. Allison *slit* open the envelope with a knife and read the letter. *Verb.*
slit (slit) *noun, plural* **slits;** *verb,* **slitted, slitting.**

sliver A thin, pointed piece that has been broken or torn off; splinter. Ruth got a *sliver* of wood stuck in her foot from walking barefoot on the floor.
sliv·er (sliv′ər) *noun, plural* **slivers.**

slogan A phrase or motto. Slogans are used by a person, a group, or a business. "No taxation without representation" was a *slogan* used by American colonists who were against English rule.
slo·gan (slō′gən) *noun, plural* **slogans.**

▲ The word **slogan** comes from a call to battle that was used by people living in the highlands of Scotland.

---

sloop A sailboat with one mast and sails that run from front to rear.
sloop (slo͞op) *noun, plural* **sloops.**

slope To lie or cause to lie at an angle. The road *slopes* toward the river. *Verb.*
—**1.** A line, piece of ground, or any surface that is not flat or level. The house was built on a *slope*. **2.** The amount of slope or slant. The river bank has a steep *slope* at this point. *Noun.*
slope (slōp) *verb,* **sloped, sloping;** *noun, plural* **slopes.**

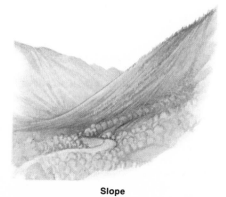

Slope

sloppy **1.** Very wet or slushy. The roads are *sloppy* from the snow and rain today. **2.** Not neat; messy. His clothes looked very *sloppy* after he had slept overnight in them.
slop·py (slop′ē) *adjective,* **sloppier, sloppiest.**

slot A narrow, straight opening. A mailbox has a *slot* for letters.
slot (slot) *noun, plural* **slots.**

sloth A slow-moving animal that lives in the forests of South America. Sloths use their long arms and legs and their curved claws to hang upside down from trees.
sloth (slôth *or* slōth) *noun, plural* **sloths.**

Sloth

slouch **1.** To sit, stand, or walk in a loose, drooping way. Mother always tells us to stand up straight and not *slouch*. **2.** To hang or bend down. That boy *slouches* his shoulders when he walks. *Verb.*
—A drooping of the head and shoulders while sitting, standing, or walking. The tired man walked with a *slouch. Noun.*
slouch (slouch) *verb,* **slouched, slouching;** *noun, plural* **slouches.**

slow **1.** Acting, moving, or happening with little speed; not fast or quick. She was *slow* to answer the teacher's question. It was a *slow* climb up the steep mountain. **2.** Behind the correct time. My watch is always *slow*. **3.** Not quick to learn or understand. I am *slow* in arithmetic. **4.** Not easily excited or moved. My father is *slow* to anger. *Adjective.*
—In a slow manner. The sign warns drivers to drive *slow* through the town. *Adverb.*
—To make or become slow. The car *slowed* down at the flashing yellow light. *Verb.*
slow (slō) *adjective,* **slower, slowest;** *adverb; verb,* **slowed, slowing.**

slug¹ **1.** An animal that looks like a snail, but either has a very small shell or none at all. Some slugs eat plants and can become harmful pests in gardens. **2.** A piece of lead or other metal that is fired from a gun. **3.** A round, flat piece of metal. A slug is used in a candy machine or similar machine in place of a coin. It is against the law to use slugs.
slug (slug) *noun, plural* **slugs.**

slug² To strike or hit hard. The batter *slugged* the ball over the fence for a home run. *Verb.*
—A hard or heavy strike or hit. Larry gave

the bully a *slug* and told him to stop bothering the other boys. *Noun.*

slug (slug) *verb,* **slugged, slugging;** *noun, plural* **slugs.**

sluice 1. A man-made channel for water that has a gate or valve for controlling the amount of flow. 2. A long, sloping trough through which water is run. A sluice is often used for separating gold ore from dirt.

sluice (slo̅o̅s) *noun, plural* **sluices.**

Sluice

slum A poor, crowded section of a city. Bad housing and dirty living conditions are some of the problems that slums have.

slum (slum) *noun, plural* **slums.**

slumber 1. To sleep or spend in sleeping. The baby *slumbered* peacefully. Dave *slumbered* away the afternoon on a blanket in the back yard. 2. To be quiet or calm. The town *slumbered* under the afternoon sun. *Verb.*

—A sleep. In the fairy tale, the prince woke the princess from her long *slumber,* and they lived happily ever after. *Noun.*

slum·ber (slum′bər) *verb,* **slumbered, slumbering;** *noun.*

slump To fall or sink suddenly or heavily. Father *slumped* in his favorite chair after a hard day at the office. *Verb.*

—A sharp, sudden fall or decline. This store has a *slump* in sales every summer when most customers are away on vacation. The baseball team was in a *slump* and had lost six of its last seven games. *Noun.*

slump (slump) *verb,* **slumped, slumping;** *noun, plural* **slumps.**

slung The boy *slung* the book bag over his shoulder. Look up **sling** for more information.

slung (slung) *verb.*

slush Partly melted snow or ice.

slush (slush) *noun.*

sly 1. Clever and shrewd; crafty. The thief was very *sly* and avoided being caught. 2. Mischievous in a playful way. The little girl gave her friend a *sly* glance.

sly (slī) *adjective,* **slier** or **slyer, sliest** or **slyest.**

smack 1. To press together and open quickly so as to make a sharp sound. The boy *smacked* his lips when he saw the chocolate cake. 2. To strike or hit sharply. Joe *smacked* the rolled-up newspaper on the picnic table to scare the flies away. The car skidded and *smacked* into the fence. 3. To kiss loudly. Ed *smacked* his mother on the cheek. *Verb.*

—A loud slap or kiss. The boy got a *smack* on his cheek from his sister for the birthday present he had given her. *Noun.*

—Directly or squarely. The boy rode his bicycle *smack* into a tree. *Adverb.*

smack (smak) *verb,* **smacked, smacking;** *noun, plural* **smacks;** *adverb.*

small 1. Not large; little. A mouse is a *small* animal. Peter lives in a *small* town. A *small* crowd started to gather in front of the theater. 2. Not important. We had a *small* problem trying to decide who should give Jan the present. 3. Soft or weak. The shy girl replied in a *small* voice. *Adjective.*

—A small or narrow part. Dad sometimes gets pains in the *small* of his back if he lifts something heavy. *Noun.*

small (smôl) *adjective,* **smaller, smallest;** *noun.*

small intestine A part of the digestive system that is between the stomach and the large intestine. The small intestine helps to break down food particles and to absorb what the body needs into the bloodstream.

small letter A letter that is not a capital letter. "a" is a *small letter;* "A" is a capital letter.

smallpox A very contagious disease. People with smallpox have a high fever and bumps on the skin that can leave permanent scars.

small·pox (smôl′poks′) *noun.*

smart 1. Clever or intelligent; bright. Linda is a *smart* girl who always does well in school. It was very *smart* of him to figure out the answer to the riddle. 2. Neat and trim. The children looked very *smart* in their school uniforms. 3. Stylish or fashionable. My sister bought a *smart* new dress for the

at; āpe; cär; end; mē; it; īce; hot; ōld; fôrk; wood; fo̅o̅l; oil; out; up; turn; sing; thin; this; hw in white; zh in treasure.
ə stands for a in about, e in taken i in pencil, o in lemon, and u in circus.

party. **4.** Quick or brisk; lively. The soldiers marched down the road at a *smart* pace. *Adjective.*
—**1.** To cause or feel a sharp, stinging pain. The soap *smarted* when it got in my eyes. My face *smarted* from the icy cold wind. **2.** To feel hurt. The boy *smarted* from the scolding his mother gave him in front of his friends. *Verb.*

smart (smärt) *adjective,* **smarter, smartest;** *verb,* **smarted, smarting.**

smash **1.** To break violently into pieces. The boys accidentally *smashed* the window with the baseball. The plate slipped from my hand and *smashed* on the floor. **2.** To hit with a hard blow. The car rolled down the hill and *smashed* into a tree. *Verb.*
—The act of breaking violently. We heard the *smash* of glass from the other room. *Noun.*

smash (smash) *verb,* **smashed, smashing;** *noun, plural* **smashes.**

smear **1.** To cover or make dirty with something wet, sticky, or greasy. The little girl *smeared* her dress with mud. **2.** To spread something wet, sticky, or greasy on something else. He *smeared* paint all over his clothes. **3.** To become or cause to become blurred or messed up. The wet paint *smeared* when he touched it. **4.** To harm a person's reputation. The candidate for governor *smeared* his opponent by saying that he was dishonest. *Verb.*
—A mark or stain made by smearing. There was a *smear* of dirt on the little girl's cheek. *Noun.*

smear (smēr) *verb,* **smeared, smearing;** *noun, plural* **smears.**

smell **1.** To know or become aware of an odor by using the nose. I think I *smell* rubber burning. **2.** To test or sample by smelling; sniff. Mother told us it wasn't polite to *smell* our food before eating it. Our dog *smells* every stranger that comes into the house. **3.** To have or give off an odor that is very often bad. The trash can *smelled* of garbage. *Verb.*
—**1.** The sense by which odors are recognized. Dogs have a better *smell* than cats. **2.** An odor or scent. The old sailor said he loved to wake up in the morning to the *smell* of the sea. *Noun.*

smell (smel) *verb,* **smelled** or **smelt, smelling;** *noun, plural* **smells.**

smelt[1] To melt ore to separate the metal from it. The first step in making steel is to *smelt* iron ore.

smelt (smelt) *verb,* **smelted, smelting.**

smelt[2] A small, thin silvery fish found in waters of the Northern Hemisphere. It is used for food.

smelt (smelt) *noun, plural* **smelts** or **smelt.**

smile An expression of the face that is made by turning up the corners of the mouth. A smile can show that a person is happy, amused, or being friendly. *Noun.*
—To have or give a smile. The boy *smiled* with delight when he saw the new baseball mitt. *Verb.*

smile (smīl) *noun, plural* **smiles;** *verb,* **smiled, smiling.**

smock A loose garment that looks like a long shirt. A smock is worn over other clothing to protect it. The art teacher makes us all wear *smocks* when we paint.

Smock

smock (smok) *noun, plural* **smocks.**

smog A combination of smoke and fog in the air. Smog is found especially over cities or areas where there are factories.

smog (smog) *noun.*

▲ The word **smog** was made up of the first two letters of *smoke* and the last two letters of *fog.*

smoke A gas that is given off from something that is burning. Smoke can be seen in the air because of the carbon particles in it. *Noun.*
—**1.** To send out or produce smoke. We could see a chimney *smoking* in the distance. **2.** To draw in and breathe out smoke from tobacco. Dad *smokes* a pipe. **3.** To preserve by using smoke. We had a delicious ham this Christmas that was *smoked* in Virginia. *Verb.*

smoke (smōk) *noun, plural* **smokes;** *verb,* **smoked, smoking.**

Smelt

smokestack   A tall chimney from which smoke escapes. Smokestacks are used on factories and big ships.
smoke·stack   (smōk′stak′)   *noun, plural* **smokestacks.**

smoky   **1.** Giving off too much smoke. We had to move back from the campfire because it was *smoky*. **2.** Filled with smoke. The room was so *smoky* that you could barely see who was standing a few feet from you. **3.** Like the color or taste of smoke. She owns a beautiful *smoky* gray cat.
smok·y   (smō′kē)   *adjective,* **smokier, smokiest.**

smooth   **1.** Having a surface that is not uneven or rough. The baby has such *smooth* skin. This new section of the highway is very *smooth*. **2.** Even or gentle. The pilot made a *smooth* landing. **3.** Free from difficulties or trouble. We are making *smooth* progress in our plans to set up a stamp club. **4.** Able and skillful. That salesman is a *smooth* talker. *Adjective.*
—**1.** To make even or level. Larry *smoothed* the wrinkles out of his sweater before folding it. **2.** To free from difficulty; make easy. The club president *smoothed* the way for the vice-president to take over as president the following year. *Verb.*
smooth   (smo͞oth)   *adjective,* **smoother, smoothest;** *verb,* **smoothed, smoothing.**

smother   **1.** To keep from taking in air; kill by taking away air. The skier was almost *smothered* by the snow slide. **2.** To make go out or die down by covering. The campers used dirt to *smother* their fire. **3.** To cover thickly. The cook *smothered* the steak with onions. **4.** To hide or hold back. Dan *smothered* a yawn.
smoth·er   (smuth′ər)   *verb,* **smothered, smothering.**

smudge   To make or become dirty or smeared. The boy *smudged* the white towel with his dirty hands. Wet ink *smudges* easily. *Verb.*
—A dirty mark or stain. The child's dirty hand had left a *smudge* on the white wall. *Noun.*
smudge   (smuj)   *verb,* **smudged, smudging;** *noun, plural* **smudges.**

smuggle   **1.** To take in or out of a country secretly and against the law. The man tried to *smuggle* stolen jewels out of the country. **2.** To take or carry secretly. Someone *smuggled* a gun to one of the prisoners in the jail.
smug·gle   (smug′əl)   *verb,* **smuggled, smuggling.**

snack   A small amount of food or drink eaten in between regular meals.
snack   (snak)   *noun, plural* **snacks.**

snail   A slow-moving animal that is found in water and on land. Snails have soft bodies that are protected by a spiral-shaped shell.
snail   (snāl)   *noun, plural* **snails.**

Snail

snake   A kind of animal that has a long body covered with scales and no legs, arms, or wings. Snakes move by curving and then straightening out their bodies. Some snakes have a poisonous bite.
snake   (snāk)   *noun, plural* **snakes.**

snap   **1.** To make or cause to make a sudden, sharp sound. The dry wood *snapped* as it burned. Henry *snapped* his fingers and his dog ran over to him. **2.** To break suddenly and sharply. The twig *snapped* when I stepped on it. The strong wind *snapped* the string of the kite. **3.** To move, act, or speak quickly and sharply. Mary closed the door and the lock *snapped* shut. The soldiers *snapped* to attention as the general walked by. Jane said she was sorry for having *snapped* at me when I asked her to help. **4.** To seize or snatch suddenly or eagerly. The fish *snapped* at the bait. **5.** To take a photograph. Ruth *snapped* a picture of her sister. *Verb.*
—**1.** A sudden, sharp sound or action. The stem of the glass broke with a *snap*. **2.** A fastener or clasp. Sue replaced the *snap* on the front of her dress. **3.** A sudden bite or snatch. The dog took a *snap* at the mailman. **4.** A short period of cold weather. We had a cold *snap* about a week ago. **5.** A thin, crisp cookie. Bob helped his mother make lemon *snaps* for dessert. *Noun.*
—Made or done quickly and with little thought. Bill takes his time about things and never makes a *snap* decision about anything. *Adjective.*
snap   (snap)   *verb,* **snapped, snapping;** *noun, plural* **snaps;** *adjective.*

at; āpe; cär; end; mē; it; īce; hot; ōld;
fôrk; wood; fo͞ol; oil; out; up; turn; sing;
thin; this; hw in white; zh in treasure.
ə stands for a in about, e in taken
i in pencil, o in lemon, and u in circus.

snapdragon A garden flower that can be yellow, red, white, or many other colors.
snap·dra·gon (snap′drag′ən) *noun, plural* **snapdragons.**

snapshot An informal photograph that is taken with a small, inexpensive camera.
snap·shot (snap′shot′) *noun, plural* **snapshots.**

snare A trap for catching small animals. A *snare* is made up of a noose that jerks tight around the animal when the trap is set off. *Noun.*
—To catch with or as if with a snare. The boy *snared* a rabbit. The police *snared* the thief just as he was trying to leave the country. *Verb.*
snare (sner) *noun, plural* **snares;** *verb,* **snared, snaring.**

Snapdragons

snarl¹ 1. To growl while showing the teeth. The dog *snarled* at the stranger. 2. To speak in an angry way. The grocer *snarled* at the clumsy delivery boy. *Verb.*
—An angry growl. The two dogs gave each other a *snarl. Noun.*
snarl (snärl) *verb,* **snarled, snarling;** *noun, plural* **snarls.**

snarl² 1. A tangled or knotted mass. Susan tried to brush the *snarls* out of her long hair. 2. A confused condition. The accident caused a traffic *snarl* on the highway. *Noun.*
—1. To make tangled or knotted. The wind and rain *snarled* Mary's hair. 2. To make confused. The snowstorm *snarled* traffic. *Verb.*
snarl (snärl) *noun, plural* **snarls;** *verb,* **snarled, snarling.**

snatch To seize or grab suddenly or quickly. Dick's mother scolded him for *snatching* the candy from his sister. *Verb.*
—1. The act of seizing or grabbing suddenly and quickly. The thief made a *snatch* at the woman's purse. 2. A small amount. We could hear *snatches* of the conversation at the next table. *Noun.*
snatch (snach) *verb,* **snatched, snatching;** *noun, plural* **snatches.**

sneak To move, act, or take in a secret or sly way. The boys *sneaked* into the theater by a side door. Ken *sneaked* an extra cookie from the jar when his mother wasn't looking. *Verb.*

—A person who is sly and dishonest. That girl is such a *sneak* I wouldn't trust her to tell the truth about anything. *Noun.*
sneak (snēk) *verb,* **sneaked, sneaking;** *noun, plural* **sneaks.**

sneakers Canvas shoes with rubber soles.
sneak·ers (snē′kərz) *noun plural.*

sneer An expression of the face that shows hatred or scorn. The rude boy answered our question with a nasty *sneer. Noun.*
—To have or say with a sneer. She *sneered* an answer to his insult. *Verb.*
sneer (snēr) *noun, plural* **sneers;** *verb,* **sneered, sneering.**

sneeze To put forth air from the nose and mouth in a sudden, violent way. Ever since I caught this cold I have been *sneezing* and blowing my nose all day long. *Verb.*
—The act of sneezing. Lucy found her handkerchief just in time to cover her *sneeze. Noun.*
sneeze (snēz) *verb,* **sneezed, sneezing;** *noun, plural* **sneezes.**

snicker A sly, disrespectful laugh. Jack heard *snickers* from his friends when he tried to chin himself and couldn't do it. *Noun.*
—To laugh in a sly, disrespectful way. *Verb.*
snick·er (snik′ər) *noun, plural* **snickers;** *verb,* **snickered, snickering.**

sniff 1. To take in air through the nose in a short, quick breath. The kitten *sniffed* at her food. We *sniffed* the clean mountain air. 2. To smell by sniffing. Ann *sniffed* the flower. *Verb.*
—Something that is sniffed; scent; smell. I uncovered the stew cooking on the stove and took a *sniff. Noun.*
sniff (snif) *verb,* **sniffed, sniffing;** *noun, plural* **sniffs.**

sniffle To breathe through the nose or sniff again and again. The unhappy boy sat in the corner and *sniffled*, trying not to cry. *Verb.*
—the sniffles. A slight cold in the head. Andy got *the sniffles* from walking around in the rain without his rubbers. *Noun.*
snif·fle (snif′əl) *verb,* **sniffled, sniffling;** *noun plural.*

snip To cut with scissors in short, quick strokes. Robin *snipped* off some threads that were hanging from her dress. *Verb.*
—1. The act of snipping. The barber took a few last *snips* to finish the haircut. 2. A small piece that is snipped off. Pat took a *snip* of the skirt material to see if she could find a blouse to match. *Noun.*
snip (snip) *verb,* **snipped, snipping;** *noun, plural* **snips.**

snipe A bird with a long bill and brown feathers that are spotted with black and white. A snipe lives in marshes and swamps.
snipe (snīp) *noun, plural* **snipes** or **snipe.**

Snipe

snob A person who feels he is better than others and cares too much about money and social position.
snob (snob) *noun, plural* **snobs.**

snore To make harsh breathing sounds while sleeping. I don't like to sleep in the same room as my brother because he *snores* so loudly.
snore (snôr) *verb,* **snored, snoring.**

snorkel A tube through which a person can breathe while swimming with the face held underwater.
snor·kel (snôr′kəl) *noun, plural* **snorkels.**

Snorkel

snort To force air through the nose noisily and with great force. The horse *snorted* and threw back its head.
snort (snôrt) *verb,* **snorted, snorting.**

snout The front part of an animal's head, including the nose, mouth, and jaws.
snout (snout) *noun, plural* **snouts.**

snow **1.** Soft, white crystals or flakes of ice formed by water vapor that freezes in the air. **2.** A fall of snow. We had a heavy *snow* last night. *Noun.*
—**1.** To fall as snow. It *snowed* all day. **2.** To cover or shut in with snow. The farm was *snowed* in for two days. *Verb.*
snow (snō) *noun, plural* **snows;** *verb,* **snowed, snowing.**

snowflake One of the small ice crystals that fall as snow.
snow·flake (snō′flāk′) *noun, plural* **snow-flakes.**

snowman A figure of a person made by shaping a mass of snow.
snow·man (snō′man′) *noun, plural* **snowmen.**

snowmobile A vehicle for travel on the snow. It has runners or skis.
snow·mo·bile (snō′mō bēl′) *noun, plural* **snowmobiles.**

snowplow A machine having a wide, curved metal blade that pushes snow off a road or other surface.
snow·plow (snō′plou′) *noun, plural* **snow-plows.**

snowshoe A flat, webbed frame that is attached to boots for walking over deep snow without sinking into it.
snow·shoe (snō′shoo͞′) *noun, plural* **snow-shoes.**

snowy **1.** Covered with or having a lot of snow. The *snowy* streets looked clean and beautiful. It was a lovely, *snowy* evening. **2.** White like snow. The tree was covered with *snowy* blossoms.
snow·y (snō′ē) *adjective,* **snowier, snowiest.**

snug **1.** Comfortable, warm, and cozy. It is nice to get into a *snug* bed on a cold night.
Snowshoes
2. Fitting very closely or tightly. The sweater was a bit *snug,* but he could still wear it.
snug (snug) *adjective,* **snugger, snuggest.**

snuggle To lie close to or hold closely for warmth or protection, or to show love. The lion cubs *snuggled* together against their mother.
snug·gle (snug′əl) *verb,* **snuggled, snuggling.**

so Don't talk *so* fast; I can't understand you. It was *so* cold out that we had to come in. Alan was tired, *so* he went to bed early. Susan likes to read, and *so* does her brother.

at; āpe; cär; end; mē; it; īce; hot; ōld;
fôrk; wood; fōōl; oil; out; up; turn; sing;
thin; **th**is; **hw** in white; **zh** in treasure.
ə stands for **a** in about, **e** in taken
i in pencil, **o** in lemon, and **u** in circus.

Please turn out the light *so* that I can sleep. It will take an hour or *so* to finish dinner. ▲ Other words that sound like this are **sew** and **sow**.

so (sō) *adverb; conjunction; pronoun.*

soak **1.** To make very wet. We were *soaked* in the sudden rainstorm. **2.** To take in; absorb. The sponge *soaked* up the spilled juice. **3.** To let something stay in water or other liquid. We left the dirty clothes to *soak* overnight.

soak (sōk) *verb,* **soaked, soaking.**

soap A substance used for washing and cleaning. Soap is usually made with fats and lye. Soaps are made in the form of bars, powders, and liquids. *Noun.*
—To rub or cover with soap. She *soaped* her hands well before she rinsed them. *Verb.*

soap (sōp) *noun, plural* **soaps;** *verb,* **soaped, soaping.**

soar **1.** To fly high in the air. The birds *soared* in the sky. **2.** To go very high. The buildings *soared* overhead. The price of food *soared* this year. ▲ Another word that sounds like this is **sore.**

soar (sôr) *verb,* **soared, soaring.**

sob To cry with short gasps of breath. The little boy *sobbed* when he was told he couldn't go with his friends. *Verb.*
—The act or sound of crying with short gasps of breath. *Noun.*

sob (sob) *verb,* **sobbed, sobbing;** *noun, plural* **sobs.**

sober **1.** Not drunk. A person should not drive a car when he is not *sober.* **2.** Very serious and solemn. The room was decorated in a *sober* way, with no bright colors.

so·ber (sō'bər) *adjective,* **soberer, soberest.**

soccer A game in which the players try to move a round ball into a goal by kicking it or striking it with any part of their bodies except the hands and arms. Soccer is played by two teams of eleven players each.

soc·cer (sok'ər) *noun.*

▲ The word **soccer** comes from the letters *s-o-c* in *association.* This game was called "association football" when it was first played in England.

---

sociable Liking to be with other people; friendly. Sarah is a very *sociable* girl and loves to give parties.

so·cia·ble (sō'shə bəl) *adjective.*

social **1.** Having to do with people as a group. A family is a *social* unit. Geography and history are *social* studies. **2.** Having to do with people being together in a friendly way. We paid a *social* visit to our neighbor. **3.** Having to do with ants, bees, or other animals that live together in organized communities. A bee is a *social* insect. **4.** Having to do with fashionable society. The wedding was written about in the *social* pages of the newspapers. *Adjective.*
—A party or other friendly get-together. We are going to a church *social* tonight. *Noun.*

so·cial (sō'shəl) *adjective; noun, plural* **socials.**

socialism An economic system in which the major businesses, factories, farms, and other means of production are owned and run by the people as a whole or by the government, rather than by individuals.

so·cial·ism (sō'shə liz'əm) *noun.*

socialist A person who believes in socialism.

so·cial·ist (sō'shə list) *noun, plural* **socialists.**

society **1.** Human beings as a group; all people. Having enough food to go around will be one of *society's* biggest problems in years to come. **2.** A particular group of people. In its early years, this country had an agricultural *society.* **3.** A club or other group of people who join together because of an interest they all share. My aunt belongs to a literary *society.* **4.** The wealthy or fashionable people of a group or community.

so·ci·e·ty (sə sī'ə tē) *noun, plural* **societies.**

sock A knitted cloth covering for the foot and the lower leg.

sock (sok) *noun, plural* **socks.**

socket An opening into which something fits. We screwed the light bulb into the *socket.* The plug from the lamp was plugged into a wall *socket.* Our eyes are set in *sockets.*

sock·et (sok'it) *noun, plural* **sockets.**

Soccer

sod The top layer of soil that has grass growing on it. People who do not want to plant grass seed to start a lawn buy pieces of sod. *Noun.*
—To plant with sod. We *sodded* our front yard. *Verb.*
sod (sod) *noun; verb,* **sodded, sodding.**

soda **1.** A sweet soft drink made with soda water, flavoring, and sometimes ice cream. **2.** A white powder made with sodium that is used in cooking, medicine, and in making soaps and other cleaners.
so·da (sō′də) *noun, plural* **sodas.**

soda fountain A counter where ice cream, ice cream sodas, and soft drinks are served.

soda water A bubbly drink made of water that has been mixed with carbon dioxide gas.

sodium A soft, silvery metal. Salt contains sodium. Sodium is a chemical element.
so·di·um (sō′dē əm) *noun.*

sofa A long seat that has a back and arms and is upholstered; couch. A sofa has room for two or more people.
so·fa (sō′fə) *noun, plural* **sofas.**

Sofa

soft **1.** Easy to shape; not hard. The *soft* clay was easy to mold. I like a *soft* pillow to put my head on. **2.** Smooth to the touch; not rough. A baby has very *soft* skin. **3.** Gentle or light; not harsh or sharp. She has a *soft* voice. The *soft* breeze felt good. The room was lit with *soft* lights. **4.** Weak. His muscles were *soft* because he had been sick in bed for months.
soft (sôft) *adjective,* **softer, softest.**

softball **1.** A game that is like baseball, but is played on a smaller field with a larger, softer ball that is pitched underhand. **2.** The ball used in this game.
soft·ball (sôft′bôl′) *noun, plural* **softballs.**

soft drink A sweet drink that is made with soda water. It has no alcohol in it.

soften To make or become soft or softer. We *soften* our skin with lotions. Butter will *soften* in a warm room.
soft·en (sô′fən) *verb,* **softened, softening.**

soggy Very wet or damp; soaked. The ground was *soggy* for days after the heavy rain.
sog·gy (sog′ē) *adjective,* **soggier, soggiest.**

soil¹ **1.** The top part of the ground in which plants grow; dirt; earth. There is very sandy *soil* along the seacoast. **2.** A country or land. The United States has fought in many wars on foreign *soil.*
soil (soil) *noun, plural* **soils.**

soil² To make or become dirty. Steve *soiled* his jacket getting out of the car. White clothes *soil* easily.
soil (soil) *verb,* **soiled, soiling.**

solar Having to do with or coming from the sun. A *solar* eclipse happens when the sun's light is blocked by the moon passing between the sun and the earth. *Solar* energy may be used to heat our homes in the future.
so·lar (sō′lər) *adjective.*

solar system The sun and all the planets, satellites, and comets that revolve around it.

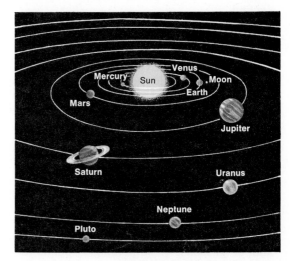
Solar System

at; āpe; cär; end; mē; it; īce; hot; ōld;
fôrk; wood; fōōl; oil; out; up; turn; sing;
thin; **th**is; hw in white; zh in treasure.
ə stands for **a** in about, **e** in taken
i in pencil, **o** in lemon, and **u** in circus.

sold We *sold* our house last week. Look up **sell** for more information.
　　sold (sōld) *verb.*

solder Any metal that can be melted and used to join two other metal surfaces together. A mixture of tin and lead is often used as solder. *Noun.*
—To fasten together with solder. The electrician *soldered* the wires together. *Verb.*
　　sol·der (sod′ər) *noun, plural* **solders;** *verb,* **soldered, soldering.**

soldier A person who is a member of an army.
　　sol·dier (sōl′jər) *noun, plural* **soldiers.**

▲ The word **soldier** goes back to the Latin name for a gold coin in Roman money. The word for *soldier* was taken from the word for this coin because soldiers used to join the army in return for money.

sole¹ The bottom part of the foot or of a covering for the foot. The skin on the *soles* of your feet gets tougher when you walk barefoot. The *soles* of shoes are made of leather or rubber. *Noun.*
—To put a sole on a shoe or other foot covering. *Verb.* ▲ Another word that sounds like this is **soul.**
　　sole (sōl) *noun, plural* **soles;** *verb,* **soled, soling.**

sole² 1. Being the only one or ones; only. Jeffrey was the *sole* person from our class who went to the meeting. Those two people were the *sole* survivors of the fire. 2. Belonging to a single person or group. The company has *sole* rights to make that machine. ▲ Another word that sounds like this is **soul.**
　　sole (sōl) *adjective.*

sole³ A kind of flatfish that is good to eat. ▲ Another word that sounds like this is **soul.**
　　sole (sōl) *noun, plural* **soles** or **sole.**

solemn Very serious; grave. They made a *solemn* promise never to reveal the secret.
　　sol·emn (sol′əm) *adjective.*

solid 1. Having shape and hardness; not liquid or gaseous. If something is solid, it is completely filled and does not have empty spaces inside. Melted wax becomes *solid* when it cools. Water in its *solid* form is ice. 2. Of one material, color, or kind; not mixed. The ring is made of *solid* gold. The carpet is *solid* green. 3. Very strong and reliable; not weak. The foundation of the old house is still *solid.* 4. Not interrupted or broken. Sue slept for twelve *solid* hours. *Adjective.*

—A form of matter that has shape and hardness. A solid is not a liquid or a gas. Ice is a *solid. Noun.*
　　sol·id (sol′id) *adjective; noun, plural* **solids.**

solitary 1. Alone. We saw a *solitary* hiker on the trail ahead. 2. Single. Not a *solitary* person came into the store while I was there.
　　sol·i·tar·y (sol′i ter′ē) *adjective.*

solo Music for one person to sing or play on an instrument by himself. The drummer had a *solo* in the concert. *Noun.*
—1. Made for one instrument or one person singing alone. There are three *solo* parts in the concert. 2. Made or done by one person alone. Patricia was nervous before her first *solo* airplane flight. *Adjective.*
　　so·lo (sō′lō) *noun, plural* **solos;** *adjective.*

▲ The word **solo** comes from an Italian word that means "alone."

soluble Able to be dissolved in a liquid. Soap is *soluble* in water.
　　sol·u·ble (sol′yə bəl) *adjective.*

solution 1. The answer to a problem. We tried to find the *solution* to the puzzle. 2. A mixture formed by a substance dissolved in a liquid. Salt mixed in water makes a *solution.*
　　so·lu·tion (sə loo′shən) *noun, plural* **solutions.**

solve To find the answer to. She *solved* all the arithmetic problems correctly.
　　solve (solv) *verb,* **solved, solving.**

somber Dark and gloomy. Ralph was in a *somber* mood after he failed the test. It was a gray, *somber* sky that looked like rain.
　　som·ber (som′bər) *adjective.*

Sombrero

sombrero A hat with a broad brim that is worn in Mexico.
　　som·brer·o (som brer′ō) *noun, plural* **sombreros.**

▲ The word **sombrero** comes from the Spanish word for this hat. The Spaniards named the hat from their word for "shade" because the hat shades a person's face from the sun.

some *Some* birds cannot fly. *Some* friends of mine are coming to visit. Please have *some* potatoes. *Some* of the girls want to start a

softball team. He kept *some* of his books in the attic. ▲ Another word that sounds like this is **sum.**
some (sum) *adjective; pronoun.*

somebody *Somebody* took my raincoat by mistake.
some·bod·y (sum′bod′ē) *pronoun.*

someday We must get this grate fixed *someday* soon.
some·day (sum′dā′) *adverb.*

somehow In a way not known or stated. *Somehow* we must get this work finished today. Don't worry, we'll do it *somehow.*
some·how (sum′hou′) *adverb.*

someone *Someone* left the front door wide open.
some·one (sum′wun′) *pronoun.*

somersault To roll by turning the body heels over head. Alex can *somersault* ten times without stopping. *Verb.*
—A roll of the body done by turning heels over head. *Noun.*
som·er·sault (sum′ər sôlt′) *verb,* **somersaulted, somersaulting;** *noun, plural* **somersaults.**

something I saw *something* moving in the bushes. *Something* is wrong with the car. He looks *something* like his cousin.
some·thing (sum′thing) *pronoun; adverb.*

sometime I saw that movie *sometime* last year.
some·time (sum′tīm′) *adverb.*

sometimes *Sometimes* we spend a weekend in the country.
some·times (sum′tīmz′) *adverb.*

somewhat She was *somewhat* upset that you could not come to the party. That movie was *somewhat* of a disappointment.
some·what (sum′hwut′) *adverb; noun.*

somewhere We will stop for dinner *somewhere* along the highway. This book costs *somewhere* around ten dollars. We will find *somewhere* to stay when we get to the lake.
some·where (sum′hwer′) *adverb; noun.*

son A male child. A man or a boy is the son of his mother and father. ▲ Another word that sounds like this is **sun.**
son (sun) *noun, plural* **sons.**

sonar An instrument used to discover objects under the water and show where they are.
so·nar (sō′när) *noun, plural* **sonars.**

sonata A piece of music that is written for one or two instruments. A sonata usually has three or four movements in different rhythms.
so·na·ta (sə nä′tə) *noun, plural* **sonatas.**

song 1. A piece of music that is sung. 2. The musical call of a bird.
song (sông) *noun, plural* **songs.**

songbird A bird that has a musical call. The canary and the lark are songbirds.
song·bird (sông′burd′) *noun, plural* **songbirds.**

son-in-law The husband of one's daughter.
son-in-law (sun′in lô′) *noun, plural* **sons-in-law.**

sonnet A poem that has fourteen lines and a set pattern of rhyme.
son·net (son′it) *noun, plural* **sonnets.**

soon 1. In a short time. Come to visit us again *soon.* 2. Ahead of time; early. The guests arrived too *soon,* and we weren't ready. 3. Quickly. I'll be there as *soon* as I can. 4. Readily; willingly. I would just as *soon* do it now as later.
soon (soon) *adverb.*

soot A black, greasy, powdery substance. Soot forms when wood, coal, or oil is burned.
soot (soot *or* soot) *noun.*

soothe To quiet, calm, or ease. The mother *soothed* the crying child by holding him. The lotion *soothed* his sunburn.
soothe (sooth) *verb,* **soothed, soothing.**

sophisticated Having much knowledge and experience of the world; cultured. She had developed *sophisticated* tastes from living in many different countries during her life.
so·phis·ti·cat·ed (sə fis′tə kā′tid) *adjective.*

sophomore A student in the second year of a four-year high school or college.
soph·o·more (sof′ə môr′) *noun, plural* **sophomores.**

soprano 1. The highest singing voice of women and boys. 2. A singer who has such a voice. 3. A musical instrument that has the range of a soprano voice.
so·pran·o (sə pran′ō) *noun, plural* **sopranos.**

sore 1. Painful; hurting. Randy's back was *sore* from lifting so many heavy boxes. 2. Feeling anger; annoyed. Don't be *sore* just because he forgot your birthday. *Adjective.*
—A place on the body that has been hurt. There was a *sore* on his arm where he had scratched himself on the branch. *Noun.*

at; āpe; cär; end; mē; it; īce; hot; ōld;
fôrk; wood; fool; oil; out; up; turn; sing;
thin; **this**; **hw** in white; **zh** in treasure.
ə stands for **a** in about, **e** in taken
i in pencil, **o** in lemon, and **u** in circus.

▲ Another word that sounds like this is **soar.**
sore (sôr) *adjective,* **sorer, sorest;** *noun, plural* **sores.**

sorrel A plant that has long clusters of small, green flowers and heart-shaped leaves.
sor·rel (sôr′əl) *noun, plural* **sorrels.**

sorrow Sadness or grief. People feel deep *sorrow* when someone they love dies.
sor·row (sor′ō) *noun, plural* **sorrows.**

sorrowful Very sad; feeling or showing sorrow. She had a very *sorrowful* look on her face, but she wouldn't tell us what was wrong.
sor·row·ful (sor′ō fəl) *adjective.*

Sorrel

sorry 1. Feeling sadness, sympathy, or regret. She was *sorry* to hear that he had been so sick. 2. Not very good; poor. The broken-down old car was a *sorry* sight.
sor·ry (sor′ē) *adjective,* **sorrier, sorriest.**

sort A group of people or things that are alike in some way; kind; type. This *sort* of plant grows best in the shade. A remark of that *sort* makes me angry. *Noun.*
—To place or separate according to kind or type. We *sorted* the socks by color. It is your job to *sort* the mail today. *Verb.*
sort (sôrt) *noun, plural* **sorts;** *verb,* **sorted, sorting.**
out of sorts. Slightly ill or cross. We all felt *out of sorts* because the rainy weather kept us indoors.

SOS A call or signal for help. The ship sent out an *SOS* when the engines broke down.
SOS (es′ō′es′).

sought I *sought* help from the librarian in finding the book I wanted. Look up **seek** for more information.
sought (sôt) *verb.*

soul 1. The part of a person that is thought to control what he thinks, feels, and does. Many people believe that a person's soul never dies. 2. A person. Don't tell another *soul* what I just told you. ▲ Another word that sounds like this is **sole.**
soul (sōl) *noun, plural* **souls.**

sound¹ 1. What can be heard. Sounds are vibrations that move through the air and produce sensation in the ear. 2. One of the noises that make up human speech. The word "cat" begins with a "k" *sound. Noun.*
—1. To make or cause to make a noise that can be heard. The bell *sounded* at nine o'clock. The driver of the car *sounded* the horn. 2. To seem to be. His excuse for being late *sounds* reasonable. 3. To pronounce or be pronounced. "Doe" and "dough" *sound* alike. *Verb.*
sound (sound) *noun, plural* **sounds;** *verb,* **sounded, sounding.**

sound² 1. Strong and healthy. The doctor said Fred's arm had healed and was perfectly *sound.* 2. Free from damage or injury. The old house was built on a *sound* foundation. 3. Sensible. The teacher gave him some *sound* advice. *Adjective.*
—Deeply and completely. He is *sound* asleep. *Adverb.*
sound (sound) *adjective,* **sounder, soundest;** *adverb.*

sound³ 1. To measure how deep water is. One way to *sound* water is to drop a line or rope with a weight on the end until it touches bottom. 2. To try to learn what a person thinks about something. I *sounded* out Father about my going to the party. 3. To dive deeply and quickly. Whales *sound* when they sense danger.
sound (sound) *verb,* **sounded, sounding.**

sound⁴ A long, narrow passage of water between two larger bodies of water, or between the mainland and an island.
sound (sound) *noun, plural* **sounds.**

soundproof Not letting sound pass in or out. The singing star recorded his new song in a *soundproof* studio. *Adjective.*
—To make soundproof. The workmen *soundproofed* the new gym. *Verb.*
sound·proof (sound′proof′) *adjective; verb,* **soundproofed, soundproofing.**

soup A liquid food made by boiling meat, fish, or vegetables in water.
soup (sōop) *noun, plural* **soups.**

sour 1. Having a sharp taste. Lemons and green apples are *sour.* 2. Bad or unpleasant. He had a *sour* look on his face because he was in a bad mood. *Adjective.*
—To make or become sharp-tasting. The milk *soured* when we left it out all day. *Verb.*
sour (sour *or* sou′ər) *adjective,* **sourer, sourest;** *verb,* **soured, souring.**

source The place or thing from which something comes or begins. A mountain lake is the *source* of this river. Newspapers are a *source* of information about current events.
source (sôrs) *noun, plural* **sources.**

south 1. The direction to your left as you watch the sun set in the evening. South is one of the four main points of the compass. It is located directly opposite north. **2. South.** Any region or place that is in this direction. **3. the South.** The region of the United States that is south of Pennsylvania, the Ohio River, and Missouri. *Noun.*

—**1.** Toward or in the south. The *south* side of the street is usually sunny during the daytime. **2.** Coming from the south. A *south* wind was blowing. *Adjective.*

—Toward the south. Most birds travel *south* in the winter. *Adverb.*

south (south) *noun; adjective; adverb.*

South America A continent in the Western Hemisphere. It is southeast of North America. It is the fourth largest continent.

South American **1.** A person who was born or is living in South America. **2.** Having to do with South America or its people.

South Carolina A state in the southeastern United States. Its capital is Columbia.
South Car·o·li·na (kar′ə lī′nə).

▲ **South Carolina** used to be the southern part of the colony of Carolina. King Charles I of England named this colony *Carolana,* which means "from Charles" or "belonging to Charles." King Charles II later changed the name to *Carolina.*

South Dakota A state in the north-central United States. Its capital is Pierre.
South Da·ko·ta (də kō′tə).

▲ **South Dakota** used to be the southern part of the Dakota Territory. The territory was named after the *Dakota* Indians, who lived there. Their name is an Indian word that means "friendly tribes."

---

southeast **1.** The direction halfway between south and east. **2.** The point of the compass showing this direction. *Noun.*

—**1.** Toward or in the southeast. The bus stops at the *southeast* corner of the street. **2.** Coming from the southeast. A *southeast* wind was blowing. *Adjective.*

—Toward the southeast. The plane was traveling *southeast. Adverb.*

south·east (sou*th*′ēst′) *noun; adjective; adverb.*

southern **1.** In or toward the south. Florida is a *southern* state. **2.** Coming from the south. A *southern* breeze was blowing. **3.** Of or in the part of the United States that is in the south.

south·ern (su*th*′ərn) *adjective.*

southerner **1.** A person who was born or is

living in the southern part of a country or region. **2. Southerner.** A person living in the southern part of the United States.

south·ern·er (su*th*′ər nər) *noun, plural* **southerners.**

South Pole The point on the earth that is farthest south. The South Pole is the southern end of the earth's axis.

southward Toward the south. The wind blew *southward* from the mountains.

south·ward (south′wərd) *adverb; adjective.*

southwest **1.** The direction halfway between south and west. **2.** The point of the compass showing this direction. *Noun.*

—**1.** Toward or in the southwest. That house is on the *southwest* corner of the street. **2.** Coming from the southwest. A *southwest* wind was blowing. *Adjective.*

—Toward the southwest. The ship sailed *southwest. Adverb.*

south·west (south′west′) *noun; adjective; adverb.*

southwester A waterproof hat with a wide brim. It is worn to cover the back of the neck as well as the head.

south·west·er (south′-wes′tər *or* sou′wes′-tər) *noun, plural* **southwesters.**

souvenir Something that is kept as a reminder of a person, place, or event. Joan bought a flag as a *souvenir* of the World Series.

Southwester

sou·ve·nir (soo′və nēr′ *or* soo′və nēr′) *noun, plural* **souvenirs.**

sovereign A king or queen.

sov·er·eign (sov′ər ən *or* sov′rən) *noun, plural* **sovereigns.**

Soviet Union A country in eastern Europe and in Asia. Its capital is Moscow.

So·vi·et Union (sō′vē et′).

sow¹ To scatter seeds over the ground. The farmer *sowed* the field. ▲ Other words that sound like this are **sew** and **so.**

sow (sō) *verb,* **sowed, sown** or **sowed, sowing.**

sow² A full-grown female pig.

sow (sou) *noun, plural* **sows.**

---

at; āpe; cär; end; mē; it; īce; hot; ōld; fôrk; wood; fool; oil; out; up; turn; sing; thin; this; hw in white; zh in treasure.
ə stands for a in about, e in taken
i in pencil, o in lemon, and u in circus.

soybean A seed that is used as food. Soybeans are rich in oil and protein. They grow in pods on bushy plants.
soy·bean (soi′-bēn′) *noun, plural* **soybeans.**

Pods

Beans

Soybeans

space 1. The area in which the whole universe exists. It has no limits. The planet earth and everything and everyone on it exist in space. 2. The region beyond the earth's atmosphere; outer space. The rocket was launched into *space.* 3. A distance or area between things. There is not much *space* between our house and the house next door. We had a hard time finding a parking *space* downtown. 4. A period of time. *Noun.*
—To put spaces in between. The builders *spaced* the houses far apart. *Verb.*
space (spās) *noun, plural* **spaces;** *verb,* **spaced, spacing.**

spacecraft A vehicle used for flight in outer space. This is also called a **spaceship.**
space·craft (spās′kraft′) *noun, plural* **space-craft.**

spade[1] A tool used for digging. It has a long handle and a flat blade that can be pressed into the ground with the foot. *Noun.*
—To dig with a spade. We *spaded* the garden and then raked it. *Verb.*
spade (spād) *noun, plural* **spades;** *verb,* **spaded, spading.**

spade[2] 1. A playing card marked with one or more figures shaped like this: (♠) 2. **spades.** The suit of cards marked with this figure.
spade (spād) *noun, plural* **spades.**

spaghetti A white food that is shaped into long thin strings. It is made of a mixture of flour and water. It is cooked by boiling.
spa·ghet·ti (spə get′ē) *noun.*

Spain A country in southwestern Europe. Its capital is Madrid.
Spain (spān) *noun.*

span 1. The distance or part between two supports. The *span* of that bridge is very wide. 2. The full reach or length of anything.

Some people accomplish a great deal in the *span* of their lives.
span (span) *noun, plural* **spans.**

Spaniard A person who was born or is living in Spain.
Span·iard (span′yərd) *noun, plural* **Span-iards.**

spaniel A small or medium-sized dog with long, drooping ears, a silky, wavy coat, and short legs.
span·iel (span′yəl) *noun, plural* **spaniels.**

Spaniel

Spanish 1. The people of Spain. 2. The language spoken in Spain. It is also spoken in Mexico and many other countries south of the United States. *Noun.*
—Of or having to do with Spain, its people, or their language. *Adjective.*
Span·ish (span′ish) *noun; adjective.*

spank To hit with the open hand or something flat as punishment. Her mother *spanked* her for kicking her younger sister.
spank (spangk) *verb,* **spanked, spanking.**

spare 1. To not hurt or injure; show mercy to. He tried to *spare* her feelings by not telling her what a poor job she had done. 2. To do without; give away or give up. Can you *spare* a dollar? He said he could *spare* a few minutes to help them. *Verb.*
—1. More than is needed; extra. We have a *spare* tire in the trunk. 2. Small in amount or quantity. He followed a *spare* diet in order to lose weight. *Adjective.*
—1. Something extra. In case you get a flat tire, it is wise to always carry a *spare.* 2. The knocking down of all the pins in bowling in two rolls of the ball. *Noun.*
spare (sper) *verb,* **spared, sparing;** *adjective,* **sparer, sparest;** *noun, plural* **spares.**

spark 1. A small bit of burning material. Sparks fly off burning logs. 2. A small flash of light caused by electricity passing through the air. 3. A small amount; trace. The boys showed a *spark* of interest when someone suggested a canoe trip. *Noun.*

—To send out sparks. The burning logs hissed and *sparked*. *Verb.*

spark (spärk) *noun, plural* **sparks;** *verb,* **sparked, sparking.**

sparkle 1. To shine in quick, bright flashes. The diamonds *sparkled* in the sun. His eyes *sparkled* with laughter. 2. To bubble like champagne. The soda *sparkled* as we poured it into the glass. *Verb.*

—A bright, shiny look. The *sparkle* of the water in the sun was beautiful. *Noun.*

spar·kle (spär′kəl) *verb,* **sparkled, sparkling;** *noun, plural* **sparkles.**

sparrow A small bird with brown, white, and gray feathers and a short bill.

spar·row (spar′ō) *noun, plural* **sparrows.**

sparse Thinly spread out; not crowded or full. The population in the desert area was *sparse.*

sparse (spärs) *adjective,* **sparser, sparsest.**

Sparrow

spat[1] A small argument or disagreement. They had a *spat* about which television program they would watch.

spat (spat) *noun, plural* **spats.**

spat[2] The cat *spat* angrily. Look up **spit** for more information.

spat (spat) *verb.*

spatter To splash or fall in drops or small bits. Mud *spattered* on his boots.

spat·ter (spat′ər) *verb,* **spattered, spattering.**

spatula A small tool with a flat blade. Spatulas are used to lift and turn over foods like eggs, and also to spread thick, soft foods, like icing for a cake.

spat·u·la (spach′ə lə) *noun, plural* **spatulas.**

spawn The eggs of fish, frogs, and some other animals that live in water. *Noun.*

—To produce eggs. *Verb.*

spawn (spôn) *noun; verb,* **spawned, spawning.**

speak To say words; talk. The baby cannot

Spatula

speak yet. Did you *speak* to John about going fishing? Edith *speaks* French very well.

speak (spēk) *verb,* **spoke, spoken, speaking.**

speaker 1. A person who speaks. People who give speeches are called speakers. 2. A device that changes electrical signals into sounds; loudspeaker.

speak·er (spē′kər) *noun, plural* **speakers.**

spear 1. A weapon with a sharp, pointed head attached to a long shaft. 2. A long, thin stalk of a plant. Asparagus grows in spears. *Noun.*

—To stab with something sharp. She *speared* the piece of meat with her fork. *Verb.*

spear (spēr) *noun, plural* **spears;** *verb,* **speared, spearing.**

spearmint A plant whose leaves are used to flavor foods.

spear·mint (spēr′mint′) *noun, plural* **spearmints.**

special Different from others in a certain way; not ordinary; unusual. Jack has a *special* interest in hockey. My birthday is a *special* day to me.

spe·cial (spesh′əl) *adjective.*

specialist A person who knows a great deal about something. A veterinarian is a *specialist* in the treatment and care of animals.

spe·cial·ist (spesh′ə list) *noun, plural* **specialists.**

Spearmint

specialize To learn a great deal about a special thing or area. In her study of medicine, she decided to *specialize* in surgery.

spe·cial·ize (spesh′ə līz′) *verb,* **specialized, specializing.**

specialty 1. A special thing that a person knows a great deal about. That doctor's *specialty* is heart disease. 2. A special product or service. Italian food is the *specialty* of this restaurant.

spe·cial·ty (spesh′əl tē) *noun, plural* **specialties.**

at; āpe; cär; end; mē; it; īce; hot; ōld; fôrk; wood; fōōl; oil; out; up; turn; sing; thin; **th**is; hw in white; zh in treasure. ə stands for **a** in about, **e** in taken **i** in pencil, **o** in lemon, and **u** in circus.

599

species   A group of animals or plants that have certain characteristics in common. Lions and tigers are two different *species* of cat.
    spe·cies (spē′shēz) *noun, plural* **species.**

specific   Definite; particular. Nine hundred dollars was the *specific* amount of money he needed to buy that used car.
    spe·cif·ic (spi sif′ik) *adjective.*

specimen   A single person or thing that shows what the whole group is like; sample. Bob collects *specimens* of different kinds of insects.
    spec·i·men (spes′ə mən) *noun, plural* **specimens.**

speck   A very small bit or part. There is not a *speck* of dust in the house.
    speck (spek) *noun, plural* **specks.**

spectacle   **1.** A very unusual sight or show. The sunrise over the ocean was a magnificent *spectacle.* **2. spectacles.** A pair of eyeglasses.
    spec·ta·cle (spek′tə kəl) *noun, plural* **spectacles.**

spectacular   Very unusual or impressive. There is a *spectacular* view from that mountaintop.
    spec·tac·u·lar (spek tak′yə lər) *adjective.*

spectator   A person who watches something but does not take part; observer. There were many *spectators* at the football game.
    spec·ta·tor (spek′tā′tər) *noun, plural* **spectators.**

spectrum   A band of colors into which white light is separated by being passed through a prism, or by other means. A rainbow is a spectrum caused by sunlight passing through raindrops. The colors of the spectrum are red, orange, yellow, green, blue, indigo, and violet.
    spec·trum (spek′trəm) *noun, plural* **spectrums.**

Spectrum

speculate   To think of reasons or answers for something. It was fun for the children to *speculate* about what was in the boxes under the Christmas tree.
    spec·u·late (spek′yə lāt′) *verb,* **speculated, speculating.**

sped   Christopher *sped* down the hill on his bicycle. Look up **speed** for more information.
    sped (sped) *verb.*

speech   **1.** The ability to use spoken words to express ideas, thoughts, and feelings. Animals do not have the power of *speech.* **2.** Something that is spoken; talk. The President's *speech* was broadcast on television.
    speech (spēch) *noun, plural* **speeches.**

speechless   Not able to say anything. She sat *speechless* when she heard she had won the contest.
    speech·less (spēch′lis) *adjective.*

speed   **1.** Quick or fast motion; swiftness. Jim ran with great *speed* and won the race. **2.** The rate of motion. She drove the car at a *speed* of forty miles per hour. *Noun.*
    —1. To move quickly or rapidly. We *sped* down the hill on our sleds. **2.** To drive faster than is safe or lawful. He was arrested because he was *speeding. Verb.*
    speed (spēd) *noun, plural* **speeds;** *verb,* **sped** or **speeded, speeding.**

speedometer   A device that shows how fast a car or other vehicle is moving.
    speed·om·e·ter (spē dom′ə ter) *noun, plural* **speedometers.**

spell¹   To write or say the letters of a word in the right order. You *spell* "speak" s-p-e-a-k.
    spell (spel) *verb,* **spelled** or **spelt, spelling.**

spell²   **1.** A word or words supposed to have magic power. The wicked witch cast a *spell* that put the princess to sleep for many years. **2.** Charm or fascination. He was caught in the *spell* of the beautiful music.
    spell (spel) *noun, plural* **spells.**

spell³   A period of time. She sat and rested for a short *spell.* We have had a long *spell* of hot weather. *Noun.*
    —To take a person's place at doing something for a time. If you're tired, I'll *spell* you at mowing the lawn for a while. *Verb.*
    spell (spel) *noun, plural* **spells;** *verb,* **spelled, spelling.**

speller   **1.** A person who spells words. Pamela is the best *speller* in my class. **2.** A book used to teach spelling. We had many lists of words to learn in our *speller.*
    spell·er (spel′ər) *noun, plural* **spellers.**

spelling   **1.** The way a word is spelled. We all have to study to learn *spelling.* **2.** The

writing or saying of the letters of a word in the right order. "Catsup" and "ketchup" are two correct *spellings* of the same word.
spell·ing (spel′ing) *noun, plural* **spellings.**

spend　**1.** To pay out money. Harriet said she could *spend* ten dollars on a scarf. **2.** To pass time. We *spent* the weekend in the country. **3.** To use up. Karl *spends* a lot of energy working on his car.
spend (spend) *verb,* **spent, spending.**

spent　We *spent* the day swimming.
spent (spent) *verb.*

sperm　The male cell of reproduction.
sperm (spurm) *noun, plural* **sperms.**

Sperm Whale

sperm whale　A large whale with a square head.

sphere　**1.** A round body like a ball. All the points on the surface of a sphere are the same distance from its center. **2.** An area of interest, knowledge, or activity. Chemistry is outside my *sphere* of knowledge.
sphere (sfēr) *noun, plural* **spheres.**

sphinx　A kind of statue of ancient Egypt. It has the head of a man and the body of a lion.
sphinx (sfingks) *noun, plural* **sphinxes.**

Sphinx

spice　The seeds or other parts of certain plants that are used to flavor food. Pepper, cloves, and cinnamon are spices. *Noun.*

—To flavor with a spice or spices. I *spiced* the hamburgers with pepper. *Verb.*
spice (spīs) *noun, plural* **spices;** *verb,* **spiced, spicing.**

spider　A small animal with four pairs of legs, a body that is divided into two parts, and no wings. Spiders spin webs to catch insects for food.
spi·der (spī′dər) *noun, plural* **spiders.**

spied　The secret agent *spied* on the enemy. Look up **spy** for more information.
spied (spīd) *verb.*

spike¹　**1.** A large, heavy nail. Spikes are used to hold railroad ties together. **2.** Any sharp, pointed object or projection. Baseball shoes have *spikes* on the bottom of the soles.
spike (spīk) *noun, plural* **spikes.**

spike²　**1.** An ear of grain. Wheat has spikes. Corn ears are spikes. **2.** A long cluster of flowers.
spike (spīk) *noun, plural* **spikes.**

Spikes

spill　**1.** To make or let something fall, run out, or flow. Ralph *spilled* his milk on the tablecloth. **2.** To fall or flow out. Water *spilled* from the glass onto the floor.
spill (spil) *verb,* **spilled** or **spilt, spilling.**

spin　**1.** To make thin fibers into thread. Cotton fibers are *spun* into thread. **2.** To make a web or cocoon by giving off a sticky substance that hardens into thread. Spiders *spin* webs. Silkworms *spin* cocoons. **3.** To turn quickly in a circle. She *spun* the top. **4.** To tell. Uncle Dan is good at *spinning* ghost stories. **5.** To feel dizzy. The hot sun made my head *spin. Verb.*

—**1.** A quick turning motion. Give the wheel a *spin.* **2.** A quick ride. He took a *spin* on his bicycle. *Noun.*
spin (spin) *verb,* **spun, spinning;** *noun, plural* **spins.**

spinach　The dark green leaves of a garden plant. They are eaten as a vegetable.
spin·ach (spin′ich) *noun.*

at; āpe; cär; end; mē; it; īce; hot; ōld; fôrk; wood; fo͞ol; oil; out; up; turn; sing; thin; this; hw in white; zh in treasure.
ə stands for a in about, e in taken i in pencil, o in lemon, and u in circus.

spinal column   The column of bones in the back; backbone.
spi·nal column (spīn′əl).

spinal cord   A band of nerve tissue running through the center of the backbone.

spindle   A stick or rod on which or with which something is turned. Fibers of cotton are spun into thread from a spindle.
spin·dle (spind′əl) *noun, plural* **spindles.**

spine   1. The series of bones in the back. Look up **backbone** for more information. 2. A sharp, pointed growth on a plant or animal. The quills of a porcupine are spines.
spine (spīn) *noun, plural* **spines.**

Spinning Wheel

spinning wheel
A large wheel and a spindle on a stand. It is used to spin thread. A spinning wheel is run by hand.

spiral   A curve that keeps winding. A spring is a spiral. *Noun.*
—To move in or take the shape of a spiral. The staircase *spirals* to the second floor. *Verb.*
spi·ral (spī′rəl) *noun, plural* **spirals;** *verb,* **spiraled, spiraling.**

spire   A tall, narrow structure that tapers to a point at the top. Spires are built on top of towers.
spire (spīr) *noun, plural* **spires.**

spirit   1. The part of a person that is thought to control what he thinks, feels, and does; soul. 2. A supernatural being; ghost. 3. Enthusiasm or liveliness. He danced with *spirit.* 4. **spirits.** The way a person thinks or feels. She was in good *spirits* after winning the election.
spir·it (spir′it) *noun, plural* **spirits.**

spiritual   Having to do with religion. A priest and a rabbi are *spiritual* leaders. *Adjective.*
—A religious folk song. Spirituals were originally sung by the Negroes of the southern United States. *Noun.*

Spire

spir·i·tu·al (spir′i choo əl) *adjective; noun, plural* **spirituals.**

spit   To force out saliva or food from the mouth. He *spit* out the fish bone.
spit (spit) *verb,* **spit** or **spat, spitting.**

spite   A feeling of ill will toward another. The little boy broke the dish out of *spite* because his mother would not let him have more candy. *Noun.*
—To show ill will toward someone. Lou let the air out of Harry's bicycle tires to *spite* him. *Verb.*
spite (spīt) *noun; verb,* **spited, spiting.**
in spite of. Even though; regardless. We are going on the hike *in spite of* the rain.

splash   To throw water or other liquid about. The children had fun *splashing* in the pool. The passing car *splashed* mud on her coat. *Verb.*
—1. The sound made by something hitting water or other liquid. When she dove, she hit the water with a loud *splash.* 2. A spot of water or other liquid, or of color. The race horse had a *splash* of white on his nose. *Noun.*
splash (splash) *verb,* **splashed, splashing;** *noun, plural* **splashes.**

splendid   1. Very beautiful or magnificent. A peacock's tail has a *splendid* display of colors. 2. Very good; excellent. Having a party was a *splendid* idea.
splen·did (splen′did) *adjective.*

splendor   Great beauty or magnificence. The boy had never seen anything like the *splendor* of the royal palace.
splen·dor (splen′dər) *noun, plural* **splendors.**

splint   A piece of wood or other material that is used to hold a broken bone in place. If a person breaks a bone in his arm, someone might tie splints to the arm to hold it straight until a cast is put on.
splint (splint) *noun, plural* **splints.**

splinter   A thin, sharp piece broken off from something hard or brittle. Eddie got a *splinter* in his foot from walking on the boardwalk in bare feet. *Noun.*
—To break into thin, sharp pieces. The glass in the window *splintered* when the ball hit it. *Verb.*
splin·ter (splin′tər) *noun, plural* **splinters;** *verb,* **splintered, splintering.**

split   To break apart or divide into parts or layers. Her jacket *split* at the seam. The search party *split* into two groups. *Verb.*
—1. A break or division in something. The heavy wind made a *split* in the sail. There was a *split* in the political party over whether to

support the new candidate for mayor. **2.** An exercise in which a person lets his body slide to the floor with the legs spread out in opposite directions. *Noun.*

split (split) *verb*, **split, splitting;** *noun, plural* **splits.**

spoil **1.** To damage or hurt in some way. Too much salt *spoiled* the taste of the soup. The child was *spoiled* by getting too much attention from the rest of the family. **2.** To become so bad it cannot be eaten. The meat *spoiled* when we left it out of the refrigerator overnight. *Verb.*
—**spoils.** Property seized by force. The soldiers carried away jewels and art works as *spoils* from the conquered city. *Noun.*

spoil (spoil) *verb*, **spoiled** or **spoilt, spoiling;** *noun plural.*

spoke[1] I *spoke* to her yesterday. Look up **speak** for more information.

spoke (spōk) *verb.*

spoke[2] One of the rods or bars that connect the rim of a wheel to the hub.

spoke (spōk) *noun, plural* **spokes.**

spoken Have you *spoken* to your neighbor lately? Look up **speak** for more information. *Verb.*
—Said in speech; not written; oral. People communicate with one another by the *spoken* word. *Adjective.*

spo·ken (spō′kən) *verb; adjective.*

sponge **1.** A water animal that lives attached to rocks. A sponge has a body that is full of holes and absorbs water easily. The dried skeletons of some sponges are used instead of cloth for cleaning and washing. **2.** A cleaning pad made to look like the skeleton of a sponge. *Noun.*
—To clean with a wet sponge. We *sponged* off the table. *Verb.*

sponge (spunj) *noun, plural* **sponges;** *verb,* **sponged, sponging.**

sponsor A person who is responsible in some way for another person or a thing. That senator is the *sponsor* of the bill. The *sponsors* of a television program pay the costs of making the program. *Noun.*
—To act as a sponsor for. The church *sponsored* the fair to raise money for elderly people. *Verb.*

spon·sor (spon′sər) *noun, plural* **sponsors;** *verb,* **sponsored, sponsoring.**

spontaneous Not planned or forced. There was a *spontaneous* burst of applause from the crowd when the batter hit a home run to win the game.

spon·ta·ne·ous (spon tā′nē əs) *adjective.*

spool A piece of wood or other material shaped like a cylinder. Wire, thread, and tape are wound around spools.

spool (spool) *noun, plural* **spools.**

Spools of Thread

spoon A utensil with a small, shallow bowl at one end of a handle. A spoon is used for eating, measuring, or stirring. *Noun.*
—To lift up or move with a spoon. The father *spooned* the food into the baby's mouth. *Verb.*

spoon (spoon) *noun, plural* **spoons;** *verb,* **spooned, spooning.**

spore A tiny body that can grow into a new plant or animal. Ferns and mushrooms grow from spores.

spore (spôr) *noun, plural* **spores.**

sport **1.** A game in which a person is physically active and often is competing with someone else. Baseball, bowling, swimming, and sailing are kinds of sports. **2.** Amusement; fun. Vincent thought collecting butterflies was great *sport.* **3.** A person who plays fair and is a good loser. Ann is always a good *sport* when she plays cards.

sport (spôrt) *noun, plural* **sports.**

sportsmanship Fair play. The losing team showed good *sportsmanship* by congratulating the winners.

sports·man·ship (spôrts′mən ship′) *noun.*

spot **1.** A mark or stain left by dirt, food, or other matter. Dad got a *spot* of gravy on his necktie. **2.** A mark or part on something that is different from the rest. My dog is white with black *spots.* **3.** A place. That park is a pleasant *spot* for a picnic. *Noun.*
—**1.** To mark or be marked with a stain or blot. The paint *spotted* the floor. **2.** To see; recognize. I *spotted* Susan in the crowd. *Verb.*

spot (spot) *noun, plural* **spots;** *verb,* **spotted, spotting.**

at; āpe; cär; end; mē; it; īce; hot; ōld; fôrk; wood; fool; oil; out; up; turn; sing; thin; this; hw in white; zh in treasure. ə stands for a in about, e in taken i in pencil, o in lemon, and u in circus.

spout To force out water or other liquid through a narrow opening. The elephant *spouted* water from its trunk. Water *spouted* from the fire hydrant. *Verb.*
—A narrow opening or part through which water or other liquid flows or is poured. The teapot has a curved *spout.* At a water fountain, the water comes up out of a *spout. Noun.*

Spout

spout (spout) *verb,* spouted, spouting; *noun, plural* spouts.

sprain To injure part of the body by twisting or straining it in a violent way. My little sister *sprained* her arm when she fell out of the tree.
sprain (sprān) *verb,* sprained, spraining.

sprang He *sprang* out of the chair suddenly when the phone rang. Look up **spring** for more information.
sprang (sprang) *verb.*

sprawl 1. To lie or sit with the body stretched out in an awkward or careless manner. She *sprawled* in the chair with one leg hooked over the arm. 2. To spread out in a way that is not regular or organized. New houses *sprawled* over the countryside outside the city.
sprawl (sprôl) *verb,* sprawled, sprawling.

spray Water or other liquid in tiny drops. The *spray* from the ocean waves felt nice and cool. We bought some poison *spray* to kill mosquitoes. *Noun.*
—To put on in a spray. He *sprayed* paint on the wall. *Verb.*
spray (sprā) *noun, plural* sprays; *verb,* sprayed, spraying.

spread 1. To open wide or stretch out. We *spread* the blanket on the sand. The bird *spread* its wings and flew away. 2. To put or make a thin layer or covering on. Jay *spread* peanut butter on his bread. 3. To scatter or reach out over an area; extend. The farmer *spread* fertilizer over his fields. The fire *spread* through the house. 4. To make or become known by more people. News of the accident *spread* quickly. Who *spread* the rumor that school would be closed tomorrow? *Verb.*
—1. The amount or extent to which something opens wide. The *spread* of the robin's wings was eight inches from the tip of one wing to the other. 2. A cloth covering for a

bed. 3. Food that is soft enough to be spread in a thin layer. For lunch we had sandwiches made with chicken *spread. Noun.*
spread (spred) *verb,* spread, spreading; *noun, plural* spreads.

spring 1. To move forward or jump up quickly; leap. She had to *spring* out of the way to avoid being hit by the car. 2. To move or snap quickly like a rubber band. The door *sprang* shut behind him. 3. To come or appear suddenly. Weeds seemed to *spring* up everywhere in our garden. 4. To cause to happen suddenly. She hoped to *spring* a surprise on him and have the new bicycle delivered for his birthday. *Verb.*
—1. A jump or leap. The acrobat made a beautiful *spring* from one trapeze to the next. 2. An elastic device that can be stretched or bent and will move back to its original shape when it is released. Some beds have spiral-shaped metal *springs* inside. 3. A place where underground water comes out of the earth. We drank from a cool mountain *spring.* 4. The season of the year that comes between winter and summer. *Noun.*
spring (spring) *verb,* sprang or sprung, sprung, springing; *noun, plural* springs.

Springboard

springboard A board that helps a person who is diving or tumbling to spring higher in the air.
spring·board (spring′bôrd′) *noun, plural* springboards.

sprinkle 1. To scatter something in small drops or bits. Mother *sprinkled* sugar on the cookies. 2. To rain gently. It *sprinkled* for a few minutes, and then the sun came out again.
sprin·kle (spring′kəl) *verb,* sprinkled, sprinkling.

sprinkler A device that is used to water gardens or lawns.
sprin·kler (spring′klər) *noun, plural* **sprinklers.**

Sprinkler

sprint To run a short, fast race. We *sprinted* across the football field. *Verb.*
—A short, fast race. The sixty-yard dash is a *sprint. Noun.*
sprint (sprint) *verb,* **sprinted, sprinting;** *noun, plural* **sprints.**

sprout To begin to grow. The seeds that I planted are starting to *sprout. Verb.*
—A new growth on a plant. The *sprouts* on the plant grew into new leaves. *Noun.*
sprout (sprout) *verb,* **sprouted, sprouting;** *noun, plural* **sprouts.**

spruce An evergreen tree with cones and short needle-shaped leaves. Its wood is used in making pulp for paper.
spruce (sprōōs) *noun, plural* **spruces.**

Needles

Cone

Spruce Tree

sprung The front door of the house had been *sprung* open by the thieves. Look up **spring** for more information.
sprung (sprung) *verb.*

spun The football player *spun* around quickly and caught the ball. Look up **spin** for more information.
spun (spun) *verb.*

spur A sharp metal piece worn on the heel of a rider's boot. A spur is used to make a horse go faster. *Noun.*
—**1.** To prick a horse with a spur or spurs. The cowboy *spurred* his horse so it would run faster. **2.** To urge on. The crowd's cheers *spurred* the home team to victory. *Verb.*
spur (spur) *noun, plural* **spurs;** *verb,* **spurred, spurring.**

Spurs

spurt To pour out suddenly in a stream. Water *spurted* from the broken pipe. *Verb.*
—A sudden pouring out or bursting forth. A *spurt* of water came out of the hose. *Spurts* of flame shot out of the burning building. *Noun.*
spurt (spurt) *verb,* **spurted, spurting;** *noun, plural* **spurts.**

sputter **1.** To make popping or spitting noises. The motor *sputtered* and stopped. **2.** To speak quickly in a confused way. He *sputtered* with anger.
sput·ter (sput′ər) *verb,* **sputtered, sputtering.**

spy A person who watches others secretly. A person is sometimes hired as a spy by the government of one country to try to discover secret information about another country. *Noun.*
—**1.** To watch others secretly; act as a spy. The submarine was sent to *spy* on enemy ships. **2.** To catch sight of; see. The sailor *spied* another ship on the horizon. *Verb.*
spy (spī) *noun, plural* **spies;** *verb,* **spied, spying.**

squad **1.** A small group of soldiers who work, drill, or fight together. **2.** A small group of people working together. The counselor picked a clean-up *squad* to make sure our campsite was neat.
squad (skwod) *noun, plural* **squads.**

at; āpe; cär; end; mē; it; īce; hot; ōld;
fôrk; wood; fōol; oil; out; up; turn; sing;
thin; this; hw in white; zh in treasure.
ə stands for a in about, e in taken
i in pencil, o in lemon, and u in circus.

squadron   A group of airplanes, ships, or other military units.

   squad·ron (skwod′rən) *noun, plural* **squadrons.**

square   **1.** A figure having four sides that are all the same length. **2.** Something having the shape of a square. A checkerboard is covered with light and dark *squares.* **3.** An open space in a city or town that has streets on all sides. Squares are often planted with grass, trees, or flowers, and used as parks. **4.** The number obtained when a number is multiplied by itself. Twenty-five is the *square* of five. *Noun.*
—**1.** Having four sides that are all the same length; square in shape. The hat came in a *square* box. **2.** Forming a right angle. This desk has *square* corners. **3.** Measuring things in terms of an area shaped like a square. Our back yard is 50 feet wide and 100 feet long, so its total area is 5000 *square* feet. **4.** Fair or just; honest. That used-car dealer promises all his customers a *square* deal. *Adjective.*
—**1.** To bring into the form of a right angle; make look like part of a square. The carpenter *squared* the door frame so the door would close easily. **2.** To mark in a square or squares. The children *squared* off part of the playing field for their game. **3.** To fit or match with something else; agree. The witness's story doesn't *square* with the facts. **4.** To multiply a number by itself. Two *squared* equals four. *Verb.*
—Directly and firmly. The truck hit the car *square* on its fender. *Adverb.*

   square (skwer) *noun, plural* **squares;** *adjective,* **squarer, squarest;** *verb,* **squared, squaring;** *adverb.*

The windowpanes have a **square** shape.

square dance   A dance performed by groups of couples who are arranged in a square at the start of the dance.

Square Dance

square root   A number that, when multiplied by itself, will produce a certain number. The *square root* of 36 is 6.

squash¹   To squeeze or press into a soft or flat mass; crush. Michael *squashed* the flower when he accidentally stepped on it. Pam *squashed* her clothes into a small suitcase. *Verb.*
—A game somewhat like tennis and handball. It is played in a walled court with rackets and a rubber ball. *Noun.*

   squash (skwosh) *verb,* **squashed, squashing;** *noun.*

squash²   Any of several vegetables of various shapes that are usually yellow or green in color.

   squash (skwosh) *noun, plural* **squashes.**

Kinds of Squash

squat   **1.** To crouch or sit with the knees bent and drawn close to the body. Keith *squatted* down to pet the cat. **2.** To settle on land that one does not own without having a

right to it. **3.** To settle on public land in order to become its owner. When the American frontier was being settled, the government encouraged people to be pioneers by saying that they could keep land that they had *squatted* on. *Verb.*
—Short and thick; low and broad. That round, *squat* teapot was a present from my aunt. *Adjective.*

squat (skwot) *verb,* **squatted** or **squat, squatting;** *adjective.*

squawk To make a shrill, harsh cry like that of a frightened hen. *Verb.*
—A shrill, harsh cry, such as one made by a frightened hen. We could hear the *squawks* of the chickens in the barnyard. *Noun.*

squawk (skwôk) *verb,* **squawked, squawking;** *noun, plural* **squawks.**

squeak A short, thin, high sound or cry. We heard the *squeak* of the rusty hinges as someone opened the gate. *Noun.*
—To make a short, thin, high sound or cry. The mouse *squeaked* and ran when it saw the cat. *Verb.*

squeak (skwēk) *noun, plural* **squeaks;** *verb,* **squeaked, squeaking.**

squeal To make a loud, shrill cry or sound. Amy *squealed* with delight when she saw all her presents. *Verb.*
—A loud, shrill cry or sound. There was a *squeal* of brakes as the speeding car came to a stop. *Noun.*

squeal (skwēl) *verb,* **squealed, squealing;** *noun, plural* **squeals.**

squeeze **1.** To press hard. *Squeeze* the tube of toothpaste from the bottom. **2.** To get by squeezing or by putting on pressure of some kind. Kitty *squeezed* the juice from the orange. **3.** To hug or clasp in affection. Peggy *squeezed* the child in her arms. **4.** To force by pushing or shoving. Jack *squeezed* his shirts into the drawer. Sue could barely *squeeze* through the small opening in the fence. *Verb.*
—The act of squeezing. She gave his hand a gentle *squeeze. Noun.*

squeeze (skwēz) *verb,* **squeezed, squeezing;** *noun, plural* **squeezes.**

squid An animal that is like an octopus and lives in the sea. A squid has ten arms and a body shaped like a tube.

squid (skwid) *noun, plural* **squids** or **squid.**

squint To partly close the eyes. The bright sunlight made me *squint.*

squint (skwint) *verb,* **squinted, squinting.**

squire **1.** A gentleman or landowner in Great Britain who lives in the country and owns land there. **2.** A young man who was a knight's attendant in order to prepare himself for becoming a knight. The knight's *squire* rode behind him, carrying his armor and shield.

squire (skwīr) *noun, plural* **squires.**

squirm **1.** To turn or twist the body; wriggle. The little boy was bored and began to *squirm* in his seat. **2.** To feel uncomfortable or nervous. The lawyer's clever questions made the witness *squirm. Verb.*
—A turn or twist of the body. With a *squirm,* the puppy jumped out of her arms. *Noun.*

squirm (skwurm) *verb,* **squirmed, squirming;** *noun, plural* **squirms.**

squirrel A small animal with a long, bushy tail. Squirrels live in trees and feed mainly on nuts.

squir·rel (skwur′-əl) *noun, plural* **squirrels.**

Squirrel

squirt **1.** To force out liquid in a thin stream through a narrow opening. The workman *squirted* some oil on the rusty hinge. **2.** To wet a person or thing by squirting with a liquid. He *squirted* his sisters with water from the hose. **3.** To come out in a thin stream. Ink *squirted* from the fountain pen. *Verb.*
—The act of squirting or the amount squirted. She put a few *squirts* of chocolate syrup in a glass to make a chocolate soda. *Noun.*

squirt (skwurt) *verb,* **squirted, squirting;** *noun, plural* **squirts.**

stab **1.** To wound or make a hole in with a pointed weapon. At the end of the movie, the

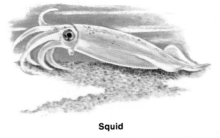
Squid

at; āpe; cär; end; mē; it; īce; hot; ōld;
fôrk; wood; fōōl; oil; out; up; turn; sing;
thin; this; hw in white; zh in treasure.
ə stands for a in about, e in taken
i in pencil, o in lemon, and u in circus.

villain almost *stabs* the hero with his sword.
2. To stick or drive something pointed into something. Matt *stabbed* a fork into the meat and began to cut it. *Verb.*
—**1.** A blow or thrust made with a pointed weapon or as if with a pointed weapon. Lee made a *stab* at the piece of cake with her fork. **2.** A sharp but brief feeling; pang. Nick felt a *stab* of pain when he tried to move his sprained ankle. **3.** An attempt; try. Skiing looked hard to Jill, but she decided to take a *stab* at it. *Noun.*
   stab (stab) *verb*, **stabbed, stabbing;** *noun*, *plural* **stabs.**

stable¹ A building where horses or cattle are kept and fed. *Noun.*
—To put or keep in a stable. Vince *stabled* his horse at his uncle's farm. *Verb.*
   sta·ble (stā′bəl) *noun, plural* **stables;** *verb*, **stabled, stabling.**

stable² Not easily moved, shaken, or changed; firm; steady. The wooden bridge over the river is *stable* and can hold a lot of weight. That new country does not have a *stable* government.
   sta·ble (stā′bəl) *adjective.*

stack A number of things piled up one on top of the other; pile. Roy had a big *stack* of pancakes for breakfast. *Stacks* of books covered the floor of her room. *Noun.*
—To pile or arrange in a stack. Teddy *stacked* the records neatly in the corner. *Verb.*
   stack (stak) *noun, plural* **stacks;** *verb*, **stacked, stacking.**

stadium A structure made up of rows of seats built around an open field. People sit in stadiums to watch such things as sports contests and concerts.
   sta·di·um (stā′dē əm) *noun, plural* **stadiums.**

staff **1.** A stick, rod, or pole. The boy scouts hung the flag on its *staff.* **2.** A group of people who work somewhere or for somebody. A hospital *staff* includes doctors and nurses. A school *staff* includes the principal and the teachers. **3.** The five lines and the four spaces between them on which music is written.
   staff (staf) *noun, plural* **staffs.**

stag A full-grown male deer.
   stag (stag) *noun, plural* **stags.**

stage **1.** The raised platform in a theater on which actors perform. **2.** A place where something important takes place. Europe was the *stage* of World War I. **3.** A single step, period, or degree in a process or development. During the last *stages* of their journey, the explorers found that they were low on food. **4.** A stagecoach. **5.** A section of a rocket

that has its own engine and fuel. It is usually separated from the rest of the rocket at a point when its fuel is used up. The first *stage* of the missile fell away shortly after takeoff. *Noun.*
—To plan, carry on, or present. The children in the class *staged* a play for Thanksgiving. The striking workers *staged* a protest in front of the factory. *Verb.*
   stage (stāj) *noun, plural* **stages;** *verb*, **staged, staging.**

stagecoach A large, closed coach that was drawn by horses. Stagecoaches were used for carrying passengers, mail, and baggage throughout the western United States.
   stage·coach (stāj′kōch′) *noun, plural* **stage-coaches.**

Stagecoach

stagger **1.** To move or cause to move with a swaying motion. Sally *staggered* because she was dizzy from spinning around and around. The punch *staggered* the boxer, and he fell back against the ropes. **2.** To stun; shock. She was *staggered* by the news of his illness. **3.** To arrange to be at different times. The school *staggered* the lunch hours so that not all the students would be in the cafeteria at the same time. *Verb.*
—An unsteady or swaying motion. Jack walked with a *stagger* after his ride on the merry-go-round. *Noun.*
   stag·ger (stag′ər) *verb*, **staggered, staggering;** *noun, plural* **staggers.**

stain **1.** A mark or spot. The spilled ink left a large *stain* on the rug. **2.** A cause of shame or dishonor. The man vowed to wipe out the *stain* on his family name. **3.** A dye or other substance used to color something. Lois put a brown *stain* on the bookcase she had built. *Noun.*
—**1.** To spot or soil. He *stained* the towels when he wiped his greasy hands on them. **2.** To color with a dye or anything like it.

They *stained* the wooden bookcase. **3.** To bring shame or dishonor upon. The dishonesty of one man *stained* the reputation of the entire company. *Verb.*

    stain (stān) *noun, plural* **stains;** *verb,* **stained, staining.**

stair **1. stairs.** A set of steps for going from one level or floor to another. We climbed the *stairs* to the attic. **2.** A step in such a set. I tripped on the bottom *stair* and almost fell. ▲ Another word that sounds like this is **stare.**

    stair (ster) *noun, plural* **stairs.**

staircase A set of stairs with the railing and framework that support it. This is also called a **stairway.**

    stair·case (ster′kās′) *noun, plural* **staircases.**

stake **1.** A stick or post pointed at one end so that it can be driven into the ground. The campers drove *stakes* into the ground and tied the corners of the tent to them. **2.** Money or anything else that is risked in a bet or gamble. The men played poker for high *stakes.* **3.** An interest or share in something. She has a large *stake* in the business and will lose a lot of money if it fails. *Noun.*
—**1.** To fasten or hold up with a stake. The workmen *staked* down the circus tent. **2.** To mark the boundaries of a piece of land; claim. Each of the miners *staked* out his claim. **3.** To risk something in a bet or gamble. He *staked* all his savings on the machine he had invented. *Verb.* ▲ Another word that sounds like this is **steak.**

    stake (stāk) *noun, plural* **stakes;** *verb,* **staked, staking.**

stalactite A piece of stone that looks like an icicle and hangs from the roof of a cave. A stalactite is formed by the dripping of water that contains lime.

    sta·lac·tite (stə-lak′tīt) *noun, plural* **stalactites.**

stalagmite A piece of stone that is shaped like a cone and is built up on the floor of a cave. A stalagmite is formed by water that contains lime dripping from above.

    sta·lag·mite (stə-lag′mīt) *noun, plural* **stalagmites.**

Stalactites and Stalagmites

stale **1.** Not fresh. The old bread was so *stale* that we couldn't eat it. **2.** Not new or interesting. The audience was bored with his *stale* jokes. **3.** Not in shape or condition; out of practice. Her tennis game was *stale* because she hadn't played for a while.

    stale (stāl) *adjective,* **staler, stalest.**

stalk¹ The main stem of a plant. The flower and leaves of the rose grow on the stalk.

    stalk (stôk) *noun, plural* **stalks.**

stalk² **1.** To follow quietly and carefully so as to catch. The lion *stalked* the antelope. **2.** To walk in a stiff, proud manner. She got up and *stalked* out of the room in anger.

    stalk (stôk) *verb,* **stalked, stalking.**

stall **1.** A place in a barn or stable for a horse, cow, or other animal. **2.** A counter or booth where things are shown for sale. Mary was in charge of the *stall* that sold cakes and cookies at the school fair. *Noun.*
—To stop running. The motor of our old car sometimes *stalls* on cold days. *Verb.*

    stall (stôl) *noun, plural* **stalls;** *verb,* **stalled, stalling.**

stallion A male horse.

    stal·lion (stal′yən) *noun, plural* **stallions.**

stamen The part of a flower that produces pollen. The stamens of a flower are usually surrounded by the petals.

    sta·men (stā′mən) *noun, plural* **stamens.**

Stamen

stammer **1.** To speak with difficulty. A person who stammers might repeat the same sound several times when trying to say a word. **2.** To say in a confused or nervous way. The embarrassed girl *stammered* an excuse for being late for class. *Verb.*
—A stammering. He sometimes speaks with a *stammer* when he's tired or nervous. *Noun.*

    stam·mer (stam′ər) *verb,* **stammered, stammering;** *noun, plural* **stammers.**

stamp **1.** A small piece of paper with a sticky back; postage stamp. Stamps are put

at; āpe; cär; end; mē; it; īce; hot; ōld; fôrk; wood; fōōl; oil; out; up; turn; sing; thin; this; hw in white; zh in treasure. ə stands for a in about, e in taken i in pencil, o in lemon, and u in circus.

out by the government and are pasted on letters or packages to show that a mailing fee has been paid. **2.** A bringing down of one's foot with force. With a *stamp* of her foot, the child refused to go to her room. **3.** A tool for cutting, shaping, or pressing a design or letters on something like paper, wax, or metal. He used a rubber *stamp* to put the date on the library card. *Noun.*
—**1.** To bring down one's foot or feet with force. The spoiled child *stamped* his feet angrily. **2.** To put out, stop, or do away with. The new police chief promised to *stamp* out crime. **3.** To mark with a tool that makes or prints a design or letters. The salesman *stamped* the bill to show it had been paid. The secretary *stamped* the date on the letter and filed it. **4.** To put a postage stamp on. Donna sealed the envelope and *stamped* it. *Verb.*
stamp (stamp) *noun, plural* **stamps;** *verb,* **stamped, stamping.**

Stamps

stampede **1.** A sudden, wild running or rush of a frightened herd of animals. The thunderstorm frightened the cattle and caused a *stampede.* **2.** A sudden, wild rush of many people. There was a *stampede* toward the exit when the fire broke out in the theater. *Noun.*
—To make a sudden, wild rush. The horses *stampeded* when they heard the gunfire. *Verb.*
stam·pede (stam pēd′) *noun, plural* **stampedes;** *verb,* **stampeded, stampeding.**

stand **1.** To be upright on one's feet. We had to *stand* in the back of the room because there were no seats. **2.** To get up on one's feet. The crowd *stood* to sing the national anthem. **3.** To be or put upright. A ladder *stood* against the side of the barn. Kevin *stood* the barrel on its end. **4.** To be in a particular place, condition, or situation. The village *stands* at the foot of the hill. The door at the end of the hall *stood* open. He *stood* trial and was found guilty. **5.** To stay the same; be in force. The rule against chewing gum in class still *stands.* **6.** To put up with; bear. I can't *stand* all this noise. **7.** To take a

position or have an opinion. How does the mayor *stand* on that issue? *Verb.*
—**1.** A position or opinion. What is the candidate's *stand* on lowering taxes? **2.** A stop or halt for battle. The troops made their last *stand* by the river. **3.** A place where someone or something should be or usually is. The guard took his *stand* at the door. **4.** A rack or something like it to put things on or in. There's an umbrella *stand* in the hall. **5.** A booth, counter, or other small place where things are sold. You can get a magazine or newspaper at the *stand* on the corner. **6.** A raised place where people can sit or stand. The mayor watched the parade from the reviewing *stand.* We sat in the *stands* at the baseball game. *Noun.*
stand (stand) *verb,* **stood, standing;** *noun, plural* **stands.**

standard **1.** Anything used to set an example or serve as something to be copied. These cars must meet strict safety *standards* before they are allowed to be sold. **2.** A flag or emblem. Tom carried his school's *standard* in the parade. *Noun.*
—**1.** Used as a standard. A pound is a *standard* measure of weight. **2.** Widely used; usual. It's *standard* practice to send people their bills on the first of the month. **3.** Thought of as excellent or as an authority. This is the *standard* book on gardening. *Adjective.*
stand·ard (stan′dərd) *noun, plural* **standards;** *adjective.*

stanza A group of lines in poetry that are arranged in a particular pattern. A stanza forms one of the parts of a poem or song.
stan·za (stan′zə) *noun, plural* **stanzas.**

staple[1] A piece of wire or metal that is bent into the shape of a U. Small staples are used to hold papers, fabrics, and other thin materials together. Large staples are used to fasten wire, hooks, and other heavy materials to wood or some other surface. *Noun.*
—To hold together or attach with a staple. Ron *stapled* the pages of his book report together before handing it in. *Verb.*
sta·ple (stā′pəl) *noun, plural* **staples;** *verb,* **stapled, stapling.**

staple[2] **1.** A very important product that everyone needs and uses. Flour, salt, and sugar are staples. **2.** A very important crop or product of a country or region. Rice is a *staple* of China.
sta·ple (stā′pəl) *noun, plural* **staples.**

star **1.** A heavenly body that looks like a bright point of light in the night sky. A star shines by its own light. **2.** A figure that has five or more points. A starfish has the shape

of a five-pointed *star*. **3.** A person who is very good or outstanding in some field. My brother is the basketball *star* in our school. **4.** An actor or actress who plays the lead role in a play, movie, or television show. *Noun.*
—**1.** To mark with a star. Frank *starred* the words on his vocabulary list that he still needed to study. **2.** To play a leading role. My favorite actor *stars* in this movie. *Verb.*
—Leading; best. Janet is the *star* speller in our class. *Adjective.*
> **star** (stär) *noun, plural* **stars;** *verb,* **starred, starring;** *adjective.*

starboard The right side of a boat or ship when a person on deck faces forward. The sailor saw land off the *starboard. Noun.*
—On the right side of a boat or ship. The tugboat moved toward the *starboard* bow of the ship. *Adjective.*
> **star·board** (stär′bərd) *noun; adjective.*

starch **1.** A white food substance that is made and stored in most plants. It has no taste or smell. Potatoes, wheat, corn, and rice contain starch. **2.** A substance used to stiffen clothes or cloth. My mother uses *starch* to make the curtains stiff. *Noun.*
—To make stiff by using starch. The laundry *starched* my father's shirts. *Verb.*
> **starch** (stärch) *noun, plural* **starches;** *verb,* **starched, starching.**

stare To look very hard or very long with the eyes wide open. Nicky *stared* at the bicycles in the store window. *Verb.*
—A long, fixed look with the eyes wide open. She sat with a blank *stare* on her face and didn't seem to hear what he said. *Noun.* ▲ Another word that sounds like this is **stair.**
> **stare** (ster) *verb,* **stared, staring;** *noun, plural* **stares.**

starfish An animal that lives in the sea and has a flat body that is shaped like a star.
> **star·fish** (stär′fish′) *noun, plural* **starfish** or **starfishes.**

starling A bird with a plump body, pointed wings, and a short tail. Starlings are found in most parts of the world.
> **star·ling** (stär′ling) *noun, plural* **starlings.**

Star of David A star with six points. It is the symbol of the Jewish religion and of the country of Israel.

starry **1.** With many stars in the sky; lighted by stars. It was a cold, *starry* night. **2.** Shining like a star; bright. Angela's eyes

Starling

were *starry* when she received the award.
> **star·ry** (stär′ē) *adjective,* **starrier, starriest.**

Stars and Stripes The flag of the United States. It is made up of red and white stripes with a blue square with white stars on it in the upper left corner. The stripes stand for the thirteen original colonies, and the fifty stars on the blue square stand for the fifty states of the union.

Star-Spangled Banner The national anthem of the United States.
> **Star-Span·gled Banner** (stär′spang′gəld).

start **1.** To set out or make a beginning on something. What time does the game *start?* The family *started* their trip. **2.** To put into action or set going. Joel turned the key and *started* the car's engine. My father has *started* a new insurance business in town. **3.** To move suddenly from surprise or fear. Louise *started* when Ted tapped her on the shoulder. *Verb.*
—**1.** The act of starting; beginning. We got an early *start* this morning and reached the lake before noon. **2.** A sudden movement; jerk. Al woke up with a *start* when the phone rang. *Noun.*
> **start** (stärt) *verb,* **started, starting;** *noun, plural* **starts.**

starve **1.** To suffer from or die of hunger. The little lost puppy would have *starved* if we had not found it and given it food. **2.** To be very hungry. It's almost time for lunch, and I'm *starving.*
> **starve** (stärv) *verb,* **starved, starving.**

state **1.** The condition of a person or thing. She was very upset after the accident and was in no *state* to see anyone. Water in its solid *state* is ice. **2.** A group of people living together under one government; nation. The continent of Africa has many new, independent *states.* **3.** A group of people living in a political unit that is part of a larger government. Hawaii is a *state* of the United States. **4. the States.** The United States. *Noun.*
—To show or explain in words; express. The test question asked everyone to *state* the causes of the Civil War. The witness *stated* his name before testifying. *Verb.*

> at; āpe; cär; end; mē; it; īce; hot; ōld;
> fôrk; wood; fōōl; oil; out; up; turn; sing;
> thin; <u>th</u>is; hw in white; zh in treasure.
> ə stands for a in about, e in taken
> i in pencil, o in lemon, and u in circus.

—**1.** Having to do with a state. Their *state* highway system is one of the best in the country. **2.** Having to do with a ceremony; formal. A *state* dinner was held for the visiting diplomat. *Adjective.*

state (stāt) *noun, plural* **states;** *verb,* **stated, stating;** *adjective.*

stately Grand and graceful in appearance or manner; dignified; majestic. The orchestra played a *stately* march as the king and queen entered.

state·ly (stāt′lē) *adjective,* **statelier, stateliest.**

statement Something stated. The police took the witness' *statement* of what had happened during the robbery. Every month my parents get a *statement* from the bank telling how much money they have in their checking account.

state·ment (stāt′mənt) *noun, plural* **statements.**

statesman A person skilled in carrying out public or national affairs. George Washington and Benjamin Franklin were great American *statesmen.*

states·man (stāts′mən) *noun, plural* **statesmen.**

static Without growth, change, or movement; staying the same. The town's population has remained *static* for the last year. *Adjective.*
—Electrical charges in the air. Static causes the noisy crackling or hissing sounds that sometimes interfere with radio broadcasts. *Noun.*

stat·ic (stat′ik) *adjective; noun.*

station **1.** A regular stopping place along a route or way. Many stations are set up along railroad and bus lines to take on and let off passengers. **2.** A building or place set up for a certain purpose. There is a police *station* on the next block. They brought the boy to the first-aid *station* after he fell off his bike. **3.** The place or position in which a person or thing stands or is supposed to stand. The guard could not leave his *station.* **4.** A channel that sends out radio or television programs. *Noun.*
—To place in a post or position. Lenny *stationed* himself by the door so he could see everyone who entered. *Verb.*

sta·tion (stā′shən) *noun, plural* **stations;** *verb,* **stationed, stationing.**

stationary **1.** Standing still; not moving. During the rush hour, traffic was *stationary* for blocks. **2.** Not able to be moved. The desks in the old classroom were *stationary* because they were bolted to the floor. **3.** Staying the same; not changing. The price

of eggs has been *stationary* for months. ▲ Another word that sounds like this is **stationery.**

sta·tion·ar·y (stā′shə ner′ē) *adjective.*

stationery Paper, envelopes, and other materials used for writing. ▲ Another word that sounds like this is **stationary.**

sta·tion·er·y (stā′shə ner′ē) *noun.*

station wagon An automobile that has one or more rows of seats in the rear that can be folded down or taken out. A station wagon has a door across the back that can be used for loading and unloading things.

statistics Figures and facts that are collected to get information about a particular subject. *Statistics* show that there are fewer farmers in this country today than there were thirty years ago.

sta·tis·tics (stə tis′tiks) *noun plural.*

statue A likeness of a person or animal that is made out of stone, bronze, clay, or some other solid material.

stat·ue (stach′oo) *noun, plural* **statues.**

status **1.** The position or rank of someone when compared with other people. That judge has much *status* in our town. **2.** The condition or situation of a person or thing; state. Where the form asked for job *status,* the man marked "unemployed," because he did not have a job.

sta·tus (stā′təs *or* stat′əs) *noun.*

stave One of the long, narrow strips of wood that make up the sides of a barrel or keg.

stave (stāv) *noun, plural* **staves.**

stay¹ **1.** To wait in one place; not leave; remain. *Stay* where you are so that you don't get lost in the crowd. **2.** To keep on being; continue. We *stayed* friends for many years after she moved. **3.** To live for a short time. We *stayed* at a hotel during our vacation. *Verb.*
—A visit or stop. After a brief *stay* at the seashore, they returned home. *Noun.*

Staves

stay (stā) *verb,* **stayed, staying;** *noun, plural* **stays.**

stay² A strong rope or wire used to support the mast of a ship.
stay (stā) *noun, plural* **stays.**

steadfast Not changing or moving. She was *steadfast* in her determination to become a doctor.
stead·fast (sted′fast′) *adjective.*

Steamboat

steady 1. Firm in movement or position; not shaky. Make sure the ladder is *steady* before you climb up. 2. Going at an even rate. The hikers walked at a *steady* pace. The patient has shown *steady* progress ever since he began taking that medicine. 3. Not changing; regular. This drugstore has many *steady* customers. She began to look for a *steady* job when she finished school. 4. Not easily upset; calm. When the fire broke out, the students showed courage and *steady* nerves. *Adjective.*
—To make or become steady. Jack *steadied* himself on the end of the diving board before diving into the pool. *Verb.*
stead·y (sted′ē) *adjective,* **steadier, steadiest;** *verb,* **steadied, steadying.**

steak A slice of meat or fish for broiling or frying. ▲ Another word that sounds like this is **stake.**
steak (stāk) *noun, plural* **steaks.**

steal 1. To take something that does not belong to one. The police arrested the man for *stealing* television sets. 2. To take in a secret or tricky way. The children *stole* a glance at the Christmas presents. 3. To get, take, or win by surprise or charm. The kitten *stole* my mother's heart, and she agreed to let us keep it. 4. To move or pass secretly, quietly, or without being noticed. He *stole* out of the room before the class was over. 5. To get to the next base in baseball without advancing by a hit or error. ▲ Another word that sounds like this is **steel.**

steal (stēl) *verb,* **stole, stolen, stealing.**

steam Water in the form of a gas or vapor. Water gives off steam when it is heated to the boiling point. Steam is often used to heat buildings and to run engines. *Noun.*
—1. To cook, soften, or work on with steam. My mother *steamed* the clams. He *steamed* the wrinkles out of his shirt. 2. To give off steam. The boiling water *steamed.* 3. To be covered with steam or mist. The bathroom mirror *steamed* up when he turned on the hot water. 4. To move by steam. The boat *steamed* into port. *Verb.*
steam (stēm) *noun; verb,* **steamed, steaming.**

steamboat A boat moved by steam. *Steamboats* were once used to carry cargo on the Mississippi River.
steam·boat (stēm′bōt′) *noun, plural* **steamboats.**

steam engine An engine run by steam.

steamer 1. A boat moved by steam; steamboat or steamship. 2. A clam with a soft shell. It is usually cooked by steaming.
steam·er (stē′mər) *noun, plural* **steamers.**

steamroller A large engine on wide, heavy rollers. It is used to press down and smooth out the material used in making roads.
steam·roll·er (stēm′rō′lər) *noun, plural* **steamrollers.**

This type of **steamroller** was used years ago.

steamship A large ship that is driven by steam.
steam·ship (stēm′ship′) *noun, plural* **steamships.**

at; āpe; cär; end; mē; it; īce; hot; ōld;
fôrk; wood; fool; oil; out; up; turn; sing;
thin; this; hw in white; zh in treasure.
ə stands for a in about, e in taken
i in pencil, o in lemon, and u in circus.

steam shovel A large machine that is used for digging. It has a large bucket or scoop on the end of a long beam.

steed A horse. The knight rode a beautiful *steed.*
  steed (stēd) *noun, plural* **steeds.**

steel A metal made of iron mixed with carbon. It is hard and strong. Steel is used to make machines, tools, automobiles, and many other things. ▲ Another word that sounds like this is **steal.**
  steel (stēl) *noun.*

steel wool A pad that is made of fine threads of steel. It is used for cleaning or polishing things.

steep¹ Having a very sharp slope; rising sharply. The hill was so *steep* that none of us could ride up it on our bicycles.
  steep (stēp) *adjective,* **steeper, steepest.**

steep² **1.** To soak in water or another liquid. They *steeped* the tea leaves to get the full flavor out of them. **2.** To be full of something. The disappearance of the famous painting was *steeped* in mystery.
  steep (stēp) *verb,* **steeped, steeping.**

steeple A high tower with a top part that narrows to a point. Steeples are often built on the roofs of churches.
  stee·ple (stē′pəl) *noun, plural* **steeples.**

steer¹ **1.** To guide the course of. John carefully *steered* his bicycle around the hole in the road. **2.** To be guided. A large truck does not *steer* as easily as a car. **3.** To follow or direct one's course. The boys in the sailboat *steered* a course for the dock on the other side of the lake.
  steer (stēr) *verb,* **steered, steering.**

steer² A bull that is raised for meat.
  steer (stēr) *noun, plural* **steers.**

stem¹ **1.** The main part of a plant that supports the leaves and flowers. Water and food travel through the stem to all parts of the plant. **2.** Anything that is like the stem of a plant in shape or purpose. The long thin part of a pipe through which the smoke travels is called the stem. The *stem* of the wine glass broke while Mother was washing it.
  stem (stem) *noun, plural* **stems.**

stem² To stop or check. We called in a plumber because Dad had not been able to *stem* the flow of water from the leaky pipe.
  stem (stem) *verb,* **stemmed, stemming.**

step **1.** The movement of lifting the foot and putting it down again in a new position. Dick had trouble learning the new dance *step.* Nancy had only taken two *steps* from the door when she realized she had forgotten her wallet. **2.** A short distance. The store is only a few *steps* from our house. **3.** Any place to put the foot in going up or coming down. A stair or the rung of a ladder is a step. **4.** An action or stage in a series. Learning the rules is one of the first *steps* in learning to play a game. **5.** The sound made by putting the foot down. Our dog starts barking whenever he hears *steps* in the hall. *Noun.*
  —**1.** To move by taking a step or steps. The driver asked everyone to *step* to the rear of the bus. **2.** To put or press the foot. Be careful you don't *step* on a piece of broken glass. *Verb.* ▲ Another word that sounds like this is **steppe.**
  step (step) *noun, plural* **steps;** *verb,* **stepped, stepping.**

stepfather A man who has married a person's mother after the death or divorce of the real father.
  step·fa·ther (step′fä′thər) *noun, plural* **stepfathers.**

stepmother A woman who has married a person's father after the death or divorce of the real mother.
  step·moth·er (step′muth′ər) *noun, plural* **stepmothers.**

steppe A large grassy plain. Steppes are found in southeastern Europe and parts of Asia. ▲ Another word that sounds like this is **step.**
  steppe (step) *noun, plural* **steppes.**

stereo A record player that reproduces sound using two or more sets of speakers, microphones, and other equipment. A stereo makes sound seem more natural and lifelike.
  ster·e·o (ster′ē ō′ *or* stēr′ē ō′) *noun, plural* **stereos.**

sterilize To free from dirt or germs. In science class, we *sterilized* the test tubes by boiling them in water.
  ster·i·lize (ster′ə līz′) *verb,* **sterilized, sterilizing.**

sterling **1.** A metal that is made of 92.5 percent pure silver. It is silver of fine quality. It is also called **sterling silver. 2.** The British system of money. *Noun.*
  —**1.** Made of sterling silver. Jan's sister got a *sterling* tea set for a wedding present. **2.** Of very fine quality; excellent. He's known for his honesty and *sterling* character. *Adjective.*
  ster·ling (stur′ling) *noun; adjective.*

stern¹ **1.** Harsh or strict. Mother was *stern* when she realized that we had lied to her. **2.** Not wavering or giving in; firm; hard. The *stern* determination of the settlers helped them bear the hardships of the icy winter.
  stern (sturn) *adjective,* **sterner, sternest.**

stern² The rear part of a boat or ship.
 stern (sturn) *noun, plural* **sterns.**

stethoscope An instrument used by doctors to listen to heartbeats and other sounds in the body.
 steth·o·scope (steth'ə skōp') *noun, plural* **stethoscopes.**

Stethoscope

stew A dish made of pieces of meat or fish and vegetables cooked together in a liquid. We had beef *stew* for dinner. *Noun.*
—To cook food slowly in a liquid. She let the prunes *stew* on the stove. *Verb.*
 stew (stoo *or* styoo) *noun, plural* **stews;** *verb,* **stewed, stewing.**

steward 1. A man in charge of food and other services for passengers on ships, airplanes, and trains. 2. Someone who takes care of the property of another. The duke's *steward* is in charge of the estate when the duke is away.
 stew·ard (stoo'ərd *or* styoo'ərd) *noun, plural* **stewards.**

stewardess A woman who serves passengers on an airplane.
 stew·ard·ess (stoo'ər dis *or* styoo'ər dis) *noun, plural* **stewardesses.**

stick¹ 1. A long thin piece of wood. The girls played ball and used a *stick* for a bat. 2. Something shaped like a stick. We bought some peppermint *sticks* at the candy store.
 stick (stik) *noun, plural* **sticks.**

stick² 1. To push something pointed or sharp into something else; pierce; stab. Jack *stuck* the knife into the pie and cut it into eight pieces. 2. To make something stay on or hold fast to something else; fasten; attach. *Stick* a stamp on the envelope before you mail it. 3. To hold fast or close. The wet shirt *stuck* to his back. 4. To be or become set or fixed in place. The splinter *stuck* in her foot. 5. To put in a place or position. He *stuck* his hand in the bathtub to see if the water was too hot. 6. To extend out from something else. Harry's comb *stuck* out of his pocket. 7. To keep from moving. They were *stuck* in traffic for half an hour. 8. To continue something; keep on. If you don't *stick* to practicing, you'll never learn how to play the piano.
 stick (stik) *verb,* **stuck, sticking.**

sticky 1. That sticks. This glue is *sticky.*
2. Covered with something sticky. The little boy's hands were *sticky* after he ate his jelly sandwich.
 stick·y (stik'ē) *adjective,* **stickier, stickiest.**

stiff 1. Not easily bent. The new leather belt was very *stiff.* 2. Not able to move easily. My back was *stiff* after working in the garden all morning. 3. Not natural or easy in manner; formal. The guard made a *stiff* bow as the king and queen passed. 4. Hard to deal with or bear up under. There was *stiff* competition for the position of quarterback on the football team. The judge gave the thief a *stiff* sentence. 5. Greater, stronger, or larger than usual. They're asking a *stiff* price for their house. *Adjective.*
—Completely; extremely. Roger was bored *stiff* by the movie. *Adverb.*
 stiff (stif) *adjective,* **stiffer, stiffest;** *adverb.*

stifle 1. To hold back; stop. Paula *stifled* a yawn. 2. To make breathing difficult for; smother. The extreme heat and smoke from the fire *stifled* the people in the building. 3. To be unable to breathe freely; feel smothered. I opened the window because I was *stifling.*
 sti·fle (stī'fəl) *verb,* **stifled, stifling.**

still 1. Without motion. The water was *still* after the storm. 2. Without sound; silent. The house was *still* after everyone went to bed. *Adjective.*
—To make or become quiet or calm. Sharon rocked the baby in her arms to *still* his crying. *Verb.*
—Quiet and calm; silence. In the *still* of the night an owl hooted in the distance. *Noun.*
—1. Without motion; not moving. The little boy could hardly sit *still* while his mother washed his ears. 2. Up to this or that time; as before. They *still* live down the block from us. 3. Beyond this; even; yet. After Rose fell off the bicycle, she tried *still* harder to learn how to ride it. 4. All the same; nevertheless. Ernie's the shortest boy on the school basketball team, but he's *still* the best player. *Adverb.*
—In spite of that. The children were tired; *still* they wanted to wait up for their father to come home. *Conjunction.*
 still (stil) *adjective,* **stiller, stillest;** *verb,* **stilled, stilling;** *noun; adverb; conjunction.*

at; āpe; cär; end; mē; it; īce; hot; ōld;
fôrk; wood; fōol; oil; out; up; turn; sing;
thin; this; hw in white; zh in treasure.
ə stands for a in about, e in taken
i in pencil, o in lemon, and u in circus.

stilt   One of a pair of long sticks with a small block on which the foot can rest. By using stilts, a person can stand or walk several feet above the ground. Stilts are worn by clowns in circuses and are also used by children to play with.
   stilt (stilt) *noun, plural* **stilts.**

stimulate   To make more active or excited. A visit from the librarian *stimulated* the class's interest in books. This drug *stimulates* the heart.
   stim·u·late (stim′yə lāt′) *verb,* **stimulated, stimulating.**

stimulus   **1.** Something that causes a living thing to react. The plant grew toward the *stimulus* of the light. **2.** Anything that causes action or excites. The coach's speech before the game acted as a *stimulus* to the team.
   stim·u·lus (stim′yə ləs) *noun, plural* **stimuli.**

sting   **1.** To stick or wound with a small, sharp point. A bee is one kind of insect that *stings.* **2.** To cause or have a sharp, burning pain or hurt. Iodine *stings* when you put it on a cut. My finger *stings* where I cut it. *Verb.*
   —**1.** A sharp, pointed part of an insect or animal; stinger. **2.** A wound made by this. The bee *sting* on her arm is red and swollen. **3.** A sharp, burning pain. His mother rubbed lotion on his back to ease the *sting* of his sunburn. *Noun.*
   sting (sting) *verb,* **stung, stinging;** *noun, plural* **stings.**

stinger   A sharp, pointed part of an insect or animal. It is used to stick or wound.
   sting·er (sting′ər) *noun, plural* **stingers.**

stingray   A broad, flat fish that lives in the ocean. It has a long tail with stingers that can cause painful wounds.
   sting·ray (sting′rā′) *noun, plural* **stingrays.**

stingy   Not willing to give or share money or other things; not generous. The *stingy* boy wouldn't give his brother any of his candy.
   stin·gy (stin′jē) *adjective,* **stingier, stingiest.**

stink   A strong, bad smell. As we drove past the city dump, we could smell the *stink* of burning garbage. *Noun.*
   —To give off or have a strong, bad smell. Those rotten eggs *stink. Verb.*
   stink (stingk) *noun, plural* **stinks;** *verb,* **stank** or **stunk, stunk, stinking.**

stir   **1.** To mix something by moving it around in a circular motion with a spoon, stick, or similar object. Jerry *stirred* his tea after he added sugar. **2.** To move or cause to move about. Tony could hear someone *stirring* in the kitchen. The wind *stirred* the leaves. **3.** To bring about or urge on. She's

always starting rumors and *stirring* up trouble. **4.** To move the feelings of. The lawyer's plea for mercy *stirred* the jury. **5.** To excite; awake. Grandfather's stories of faraway places *stirred* my imagination. *Verb.*
   —**1.** A burst of activity or excitement. The news that the money was missing caused quite a *stir.* **2.** The act of stirring. Give the soup a *stir* every few minutes. *Noun.*
   stir (stur) *verb,* **stirred, stirring;** *noun, plural* **stirs.**

stirrup   One of a pair of metal or leather loops that hang from either side of a saddle to hold a rider's foot.
   stir·rup (stur′əp) *noun, plural* **stirrups.**

stitch   **1.** One complete movement made by a needle and thread. Stitches are made by people in sewing and by doctors in closing up wounds or cuts. **2.** Any similar movement made with a needle and thread or yarn in knitting, crocheting, and embroidering. *Noun.*
   —To make, fasten, or mend with stitches; sew. Rick *stitched* up the tear in his football uniform. My mother *stitched* a name tag on the jacket that I took to camp. *Verb.*
   stitch (stich) *noun, plural* **stitches;** *verb,* **stitched, stitching.**

Stirrup

stock   **1.** A supply of things kept to be sold or used. This store has a large *stock* of fishing rods. The squirrel put away a *stock* of nuts for the winter. **2.** Cattle, sheep, and other animals raised or kept on a farm or ranch; livestock. **3.** Family or race; descent. Her aunt comes from German *stock.* **4.** Shares in a company. My grandfather owns some *stock* in an automobile company. **5. stocks.** A wooden frame with holes for a person's ankles and, sometimes, hands. People used to be put in the stocks as a punishment for certain crimes. **6.** A liquid in which meat, poultry, or fish has been cooked. It is often used in making soup or gravy. **7.** The part of something that is used as a handle or support. The soldier placed the *stock* of the rifle against his shoulder and then aimed. *Noun.*
   —**1.** To fill or supply something with a stock. They *stocked* the cabin with enough food for a week. **2.** To put in, have, or keep a stock or

supply of something. The hardware store *stocks* all kinds of tools. We *stocked* up on soda and potato chips for the picnic. *Verb.*
—**1.** Kept in stock or on hand. Greeting cards are a *stock* item in that candy store. **2.** Taking care of stock. He worked his way up from *stock* clerk to store manager. *Adjective.*
stock (stok) *noun, plural* **stocks;** *verb,* **stocked, stocking;** *adjective.*

stockade **1.** An area closed off by a fence made of strong posts that are set upright in the ground. A stockade serves as a barrier for defense against an attack. **2.** A military jail for soldiers or sailors.
stock·ade (sto kād′) *noun, plural* **stockades.**

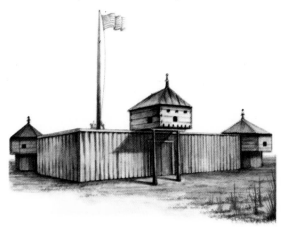

Stockade

stock exchange A place where stocks and bonds are bought and sold.

stocking A close-fitting covering for the foot and leg. Stockings are usually made of nylon, cotton, or wool.
stock·ing (stok′ing) *noun, plural* **stockings.**

stock market **1.** A place where stocks and bonds are bought and sold; stock exchange. **2.** The business carried on in such a place. Prices on the *stock market* went down when news of the war got out.

stocky Having a solid, sturdy form or build. Eddie is tall and thin, but his brother Dennis is short and *stocky.*
stock·y (stok′ē) *adjective,* **stockier, stockiest.**

stockyard A place with pens and sheds where livestock is kept before being shipped to market.
stock·yard (stok′yärd′) *noun, plural* **stockyards.**

stoke To tend or feed fuel to a fire or furnace. The engineer's helper *stoked* the furnace of the old steam locomotive.
stoke (stōk) *verb,* **stoked, stoking.**

stole The robbers *stole* thousands of dollars from the bank. Look up **steal** for more information.
stole (stōl) *verb.*

stolen A number of books have been *stolen* from the library. Look up **steal** for more information.
sto·len (stō′lən) *verb.*

stomach **1.** The part of the body that receives and begins to digest food that has been swallowed. The stomach is like a large muscular bag. **2.** The part of the body containing the stomach; belly. *Noun.*
—To put up with; bear. I just can't *stomach* the way she makes fun of people. *Verb.*
stom·ach (stum′ək) *noun, plural* **stomachs;** *verb,* **stomached, stomaching.**

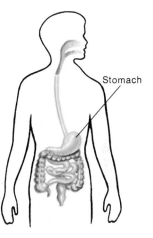

Stomach

stomp **1.** To walk heavily or violently on the floor. The angry girl *stomped* out of the room. **2.** To bring down the foot or feet heavily and with force; stamp. He *stomped* his feet on the floor in anger.
stomp (stomp) *verb,* **stomped, stomping.**

stone **1.** The hard material that rocks are made of. Stone is used for building. **2.** A piece of this material. **3.** A valuable jewel; gem. The *stones* in her diamond necklace are beautiful. **4.** The hard pit or seed of cherries, peaches and some other fruits. *Noun.*
—To throw stones at. The angry mob tried to *stone* the thief. *Verb.*
stone (stōn) *noun, plural* **stones;** *verb,* **stoned, stoning.**

Stone Age The earliest period of human culture. During the Stone Age, people used mostly stone tools and weapons.

stood Fred *stood* at the window. Look up **stand** for more information.
stood (sto͞od) *verb.*

at; āpe; cär; end; mē; it; īce; hot; ōld;
fôrk; wood; fo͞ol; oil; out; up; turn; sing;
thin; **th**is; **hw** in white; **zh** in treasure.
ə stands for **a** in about, **e** in taken
i in pencil, **o** in lemon, and **u** in circus.

stool **1.** A seat without a back or arms. We sat on *stools* at the soda fountain. **2.** A low bench used to rest the feet on.
   stool (stool) *noun, plural* **stools**.

stoop¹ **1.** To bend forward and downward. Ed *stooped* to pick up the pencil. **2.** To stand or walk with the head and shoulders bent forward. The old woman *stoops* when she walks. **3.** To lower oneself to do something. He *stooped* to stealing from his friends. *Verb.*
   —A bending forward of the head and shoulders. He walked with a *stoop*. *Noun.*
   stoop (stoop) *verb,* **stooped, stooping;** *noun, plural* **stoops**.

stoop² A small porch with stairs at the entrance of a house or other building.
   stoop (stoop) *noun, plural* **stoops**.

Stoop

stop **1.** To keep from moving or doing something. The driver tried to *stop* the car. Mother told us to *stop* making so much noise. **2.** To keep from continuing; end. The firemen *stopped* the spread of the fire. **3.** To come to an end or halt. The snow may *stop* soon. **4.** To close up. She used a cork to *stop* up the bottle. *Verb.*
   —**1.** The act of stopping or the state of being stopped. The car made a *stop* at the traffic light. **2.** A place where a stop is made. The bus *stop* is at the corner. **3.** Something that stops. He put the rubber *stop* back in the bottle. **4.** A part that regulates or controls the pitch or tone of a musical instrument. *Noun.*
   stop (stop) *verb,* **stopped, stopping;** *noun, plural* **stops**.

stopper Something used to stop up the opening of a bottle or other container.
   stop·per (stop′ər) *noun, plural* **stoppers**.

stopwatch A watch used to time races or contests. It has a button that can be pressed to stop or start a hand at a split second.
   stop·watch (stop′woch′) *noun, plural* **stop-watches**.

storage **1.** The act of storing things or the state of being stored. The furniture was picked up for *storage* today. **2.** A place for storing things. The chest is used as a *storage* for all our toys.
   stor·age (stôr′ij) *noun.*

store **1.** A place where goods are sold. Mother went to the grocery *store*. **2.** A supply of things put away for future use. There was a *store* of wood in the cellar for use during the winter. *Noun.*
   —To put away for future use. The farmer and his wife *stored* food and supplies for the winter. *Verb.*
   store (stôr) *noun, plural* **stores;** *verb,* **stored, storing.**
   in store. Set aside; waiting. There is a surprise *in store* for her when she gets home.

storehouse **1.** A place or building where things are stored. **2.** A large supply. Our teacher is a *storehouse* of information.
   store·house (stôr′hous′) *noun, plural* **store-houses**.

stork A bird with long legs, a long neck, and a long bill.
   stork (stôrk) *noun, plural* **storks** or **stork**.

Stork

storm **1.** A strong wind with heavy rain, hail, sleet, or snow. Storms may also have thunder and lightning. **2.** A sudden, strong outburst. The little boy's *storm* of tears showed that he was very unhappy. **3.** A sudden, violent attack. The soldiers took the town by *storm*. *Noun.*
   —**1.** To blow hard with rain, hail, sleet, or snow. It *stormed* all day. **2.** To rush violently and angrily. The man *stormed* out of the house. **3.** To attack violently. Troops *stormed* the fort. *Verb.*

storm (stôrm) *noun, plural* **storms;** *verb,* **stormed, storming.**

stormy **1.** Of or having to do with storms. We had *stormy* weather all day. **2.** Violent and angry. The two brothers had a *stormy* argument.

storm·y (stôr′mē) *adjective,* **stormier, stormiest.**

story[1] **1.** An account of something that happened. The newspaper has a *story* about the circus parade. **2.** An account that has been made up to entertain people. We listened to the scary ghost *stories.* Dad read us a *story* about dragons. **3.** A lie. She told a *story* about why she was late.

sto·ry (stôr′ē) *noun, plural* **stories.**

story[2] A floor of a building with its set of rooms. That office building has twenty-five *stories.*

sto·ry (stôr′ē) *noun, plural* **stories.**

stout **1.** Thick and heavy; fat. The *stout* woman found it hard to climb stairs. **2.** Having courage; brave. The *stout* soldier wasn't afraid of the fighting. **3.** Having strength; strong. *Stout* beams held up the roof.

stout (stout) *adjective,* **stouter, stoutest.**

stove A large object made of metal, used for cooking or heating. Some stoves burn wood, coal, or gas, and others work by electricity.

stove (stōv) *noun, plural* **stoves.**

stovepipe A metal pipe used to carry smoke and fumes away from a stove.

stove·pipe (stōv′pīp′) *noun, plural* **stove-pipes.**

Stovepipe

stow **1.** To put away; pack. The boys *stowed* their camping gear in the empty tent. **2.** To fill; load. Dad *stowed* the trunk of the car with suit-cases.

stow (stō) *verb,* **stowed, stowing.**

stowaway A person who hides on a ship or airplane in order to get a free ride.

stow·a·way (stō′ə-wā′) *noun, plural* **stowaways.**

straggle To wander or stray. The tired hikers *straggled* back to camp.

strag·gle (strag′əl) *verb,* **straggled, straggling.**

straight **1.** Not bent, curved, or crooked. Jean drew a *straight* line. The tree grew *straight* and tall. **2.** In proper order. Gail always keeps her closet *straight.* **3.** Direct and truthful; honest; upright. She gave a *straight* answer to the question. *Adjective.*
—**1.** In a straight way. Stand up *straight.* **2.** Without delay; immediately. He went *straight* home after the ball game. *Adverb.*
▲ Another word that sounds like this is **strait.**

straight (strāt) *adjective,* **straighter, straightest;** *adverb.*

straighten **1.** To make or become straight. She *straightened* the ruler and drew a line across the paper. **2.** To put into proper order. Joan *straightened* up her room.

straight·en (strāt′ən) *verb,* **straightened, straightening.**

straightforward Honest; truthful. She is a *straightforward* person who never tries to deceive people. He gave a *straightforward* answer.

straight·for·ward (strāt′fôr′wərd) *adjective.*

strain[1] **1.** To draw or pull tight; pull with force. The weight of the heavy crate *strained* the ropes. The large dog *strained* at the leash. **2.** To hurt or weaken. He *strained* his back lifting the heavy weight. She *strained* her eyes reading in dim light. **3.** To use or drive to the utmost. He *strained* every muscle to lift the heavy trunk. **4.** To press or pour through a strainer. Mother always *strains* the fresh orange juice she makes. *Verb.*
—**1.** Great force or weight. The *strain* on the wire made it snap. **2.** A hurt; injury. The boy suffered muscle *strain* after the long race. **3.** Harmful pressure caused by worry or overwork. Her head aches from nervous *strain. Noun.*

strain (strān) *verb,* **strained, straining;** *noun, plural* **strains.**

strain[2] **1.** Line of descent; ancestry. That dog has a collie *strain.* **2.** A characteristic or tendency that is inherited. Jane's family has a musical *strain.* **3.** A melody; tune. We listened to the familiar *strains* of the national anthem.

strain (strān) *noun, plural* **strains.**

strait **1.** A narrow channel between two larger bodies of water. **2. straits.** Distress or

at; āpe; cär; end; mē; it; īce; hot; ōld;
fôrk; wood; fōōl; oil; out; up; turn; sing;
thin; this; hw in white; zh in treasure.
ə stands for **a** in about, **e** in taken
i in pencil, **o** in lemon, and **u** in circus.

difficulty. The poor family was in terrible *straits* for money. ▲ Another word that sounds like this is **straight**.

strait (strāt) *noun, plural* **straits.**

strand¹ To leave in a helpless position. The travelers were *stranded* on the desert when their car broke down.

strand (strand) *verb,* **stranded, stranding.**

strand² **1.** One of the threads or wires twisted together to form a rope, cord, or cable. **2.** A hair or thread. *Strands* of hair fell across his forehead.

strand (strand) *noun, plural* **strands.**

strange **1.** Odd or unusual. Jean painted a *strange* animal with green hair and purple eyes. **2.** Not familiar. We stopped in a *strange* town overnight. I heard a *strange* voice on the telephone. **3.** Ill at ease; uncomfortable. He felt *strange* being away from home for the first time.

strange (strānj) *adjective,* **stranger, strangest.**

stranger **1.** A person whom one does not know. *Strangers* moved into the house next door to ours. **2.** A person from another place or country. We were *strangers* when we first moved to the town.

stran·ger (strān′jər) *noun, plural* **strangers.**

strangle **1.** To kill by squeezing the throat to stop the breath. **2.** To choke. He loosened his tie because it *strangled* him.

stran·gle (strang′gəl) *verb,* **strangled, strangling.**

strap A long strip of leather, cloth, or other material. It is used to hold things together or in place. The girl's bag hung by a *strap* from her shoulder. *Noun.*
—To fasten or hold with a strap. Henry *strapped* his knapsack to his back for the hike. *Verb.*

strap (strap) *noun, plural* **straps;** *verb,* **strapped, strapping.**

strategic **1.** Of or having to do with strategy. The general has a *strategic* plan for capturing the enemy's fort. **2.** Important to strategy. The island was *strategic* because it was located at the entrance to the river.

stra·te·gic (strə tē′jik) *adjective.*

strategy **1.** The planning and directing of the movements of troops and ships during a war. **2.** A plan for achieving a goal. What is the team's *strategy* for winning the game?

strat·e·gy (strat′ə jē) *noun, plural* **strategies.**

straw **1.** A long tube made of paper or plastic. It is used to suck up a liquid. **2.** The dry stalks of rye, oat, wheat, or other grains after they have been cut and threshed.

straw (strô) *noun, plural* **straws.**

strawberry The sweet red fruit of a plant that grows low to the ground.

straw·ber·ry (strô′- ber′ē) *noun, plural* **strawberries.**

stray To wander away. The kitten *strayed* from the yard. *Verb.*
—**1.** Wandering or lost. A *stray* dog followed me home. **2.** Found here and there; scattered. A few *stray* flowers grew in the yard. *Adjective.*
—A lost or homeless animal. The cowboys rounded up some *strays* on the range. *Noun.*

Strawberries

stray (strā) *verb,* **strayed, straying;** *adjective; noun, plural* **strays.**

streak **1.** A long, thin mark. The woman has *streaks* of gray in her hair. *Streaks* of lightning flashed across the sky. **2.** A trace of anything. That bully has a mean *streak*. *Noun.*
—**1.** To mark with streaks. His face was *streaked* with dirt. **2.** To move at great speed. The ambulance *streaked* down the street. *Verb.*

streak (strēk) *noun, plural* **streaks;** *verb,* **streaked, streaking.**

stream **1.** A body of flowing water. We went wading in the *stream*. **2.** A steady flow or movement. A *stream* of tears came from her eyes. A *stream* of people came out of the theater. *Noun.*
—**1.** To move steadily; flow. Light *streamed* into the room. Students *streamed* from the school after classes were over. **2.** To wave or float. The school banners *streamed* in the wind at the stadium. *Verb.*

stream (strēm) *noun, plural* **streams;** *verb,* **streamed, streaming.**

streamer A long, narrow flag or strip. We decorated the room with paper *streamers* hung from the ceiling.

stream·er (strē′mər) *noun, plural* **streamers.**

streamline **1.** To design and build something so that it has the least possible resistance to air or water. Cars and boats are *streamlined*. **2.** To make something more modern or work better. The new mayor *streamlined* the city government.

stream·line (strēm′līn′) *verb,* **streamlined, streamlining.**

street A public way in a town or city. A street usually has sidewalks and buildings on both sides.

street (strēt) *noun, plural* **streets.**

streetcar A vehicle for carrying passengers. It looks somewhat like a bus. Streetcars are powered by electricity and run on rails through city streets.

   street·car (strēt′kär′) *noun, plural* **streetcars.**

strength **1.** The quality of being strong; energy, power, or force. The man had to build up his *strength* after his illness. That honest girl has great *strength* of character. **2.** The ability to take much strain; firmness. Mother tested the *strength* of the clothesline before hanging the blanket on it. **3.** The degree of power or force; intensity. This medicine does not have much *strength*.

   strength (strength) *noun, plural* **strengths.**

strengthen To make or become strong. Jerry *strengthened* his muscles by lifting weights.

   strength·en (streng′thən) *verb,* **strengthened, strenghtening.**

strenuous **1.** Needing much effort. Cutting down the big tree was *strenuous* work. **2.** Very active; energetic. There was *strenuous* opposition to the plan to build a new school.

   stren·u·ous (stren′yoo əs) *adjective.*

stress **1.** The force, pressure, or strain put on one thing by another. The rocket was designed to withstand the *stress* of leaving the earth's atmosphere. **2.** A special importance. Mother puts much *stress* on good table manners. **3.** A stronger tone of voice given to a word or syllable of a word; accent. In the word "brother," the *stress* is on the first syllable. In the word "tonight," the *stress* is on the second syllable. *Noun.*
—**1.** To give special importance to. The teacher *stressed* the need for good study habits. **2.** To pronounce a word or syllable of a word with stress. When you say the word "begin," you *stress* the second syllable. *Verb.*

   stress (stres) *noun, plural* **stresses;** *verb,* **stressed, stressing.**

stretch **1.** To spread out one's arms, legs, or body to full length. Jean *stretched* her arms above her head. Billy *stretched* himself out on the sofa. **2.** To reach; extend. She *stretched* out her hand for the candy. The road *stretches* for miles. **3.** To pull; strain. Rubber *stretches* easily. *Verb.*
—**1.** An unbroken space or area. The boys rowed their boat along a *stretch* of the river. **2.** The act of stretching. My older brother could touch the ceiling with a *stretch* of his arms. *Noun.*

   stretch (strech) *verb,* **stretched, stretching;** *noun, plural* **stretches.**

stretcher A piece of canvas stretched across a frame. A stretcher is used to carry a sick or injured person.

   stretch·er (strech′ər) *noun, plural* **stretchers.**

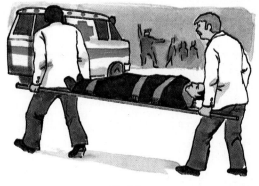

Stretcher

stricken He was *stricken* by a disease. Look up **strike** for more information. *Verb.*
—Hurt by something. Help was sent to *stricken* towns after the flood. *Adjective.*

   strick·en (strik′ən) *verb; adjective.*

strict **1.** Following a rule or making others follow a rule in a careful, exact way. The teacher is very *strict* about correct spelling. **2.** To be followed in a careful, exact way; carefully enforced. That school has *strict* rules. **3.** Complete; absolute. She told her friend the secret in *strict* confidence.

   strict (strikt) *adjective,* **stricter, strictest.**

stride **1.** To walk with long steps. That long-legged boy always *strides* down the street. **2.** To pass over with a long step. She tried to *stride* over the mud puddle in the road. *Verb.*
—**1.** A long step. My friend's *stride* is longer than mine. **2.** Progress or improvement. Science has made great *strides* in fighting disease. *Noun.*

   stride (strīd) *verb,* **strode, stridden, striding;** *noun, plural* **strides.**

strike **1.** To give a blow to; hit. She *struck* her brother for his insulting remark. The car *struck* the tree. **2.** To make an impression on. She *strikes* me as a nice person. What he said *struck* me as funny. **3.** To give the time by sounding. The clock *struck* twelve. **4.** To find or discover suddenly. The men hope to *strike*

at; āpe; cär; end; mē; it; īce; hot; ōld;
fôrk; wood; fool; oil; out; up; turn; sing;
thin; this; hw in white; zh in treasure.
ə stands for **a** in about, **e** in taken
i in pencil, **o** in lemon, and **u** in circus.

621

oil. **5.** To stop work in order to get higher pay, shorter hours, or better working conditions. The workers plan to *strike* if they are not given more money. *Verb.*
—**1.** The stopping of work. The mailmen went on *strike* for higher pay. **2.** A sudden discovery. His gold *strike* made him very rich. **3.** A pitched ball that the batter swings at and misses, or that is within the strike zone. *Noun.*
  strike (strīk) *verb,* **struck, struck** or **stricken, striking;** *noun, plural* **strikes.**
  to strike out. To put out or be put out in baseball. The pitcher *struck out* the batter.

strike zone An area in baseball that is over home plate and between the batter's knees and armpits.

string **1.** A thin line of twisted threads or wire. He held the kite by a *string.* She tied the package with a *string.* **2.** Something like a string. The violinist needs new *strings* for his violin. We gave mother a *string* of pearls. **3.** A series or row of persons, things, or events. There has been a *string* of robberies in the town. **4. strings.** Musical instruments that have strings and are played with a bow. *Noun.*
—**1.** To put on a string. Jill and Ann like to *string* beads. **2.** To provide with strings. Marty had his tennis racket *strung.* **3.** To stretch from one place to another. Mother *strung* the clothesline from the back of the house to a tree. **4.** To arrange in a row or series. We *strung* lights on the Christmas tree. *Verb.*
  string (string) *noun, plural* **strings;** *verb,* **strung, stringing.**

string bean A long green bean that is eaten as a vegetable.

Pod

Seed

String Beans

strip¹ **1.** To take off the clothing or covering; undress. **2.** To pull off. Jack's mother told him not to *strip* the bark from the tree.
  strip (strip) *verb,* **stripped, stripping.**

strip² A long, narrow piece of something. He tore the paper into *strips.*
  strip (strip) *noun, plural* **strips.**

stripe A long, narrow band. Phil's shirt had red and white *stripes.* Zebras have *stripes. Noun.*
—To mark with a stripe or stripes. Alan *striped* the model racing car with paint. *Verb.*
  stripe (strīp) *noun, plural* **stripes;** *verb,* **striped, striping.**

strive To make a great effort; try hard. Alice always *strives* to win in tennis.
  strive (strīv) *verb,* **strove** or **strived, striven, striving.**

The cat has **striped** fur.

strode The two friends *strode* through the park together. Look up **stride** for more information.
  strode (strōd) *verb.*

stroke¹ **1.** The act of striking. My brother can split a log with one *stroke* of an ax. **2.** An unexpected event. Winning that money was a *stroke* of good luck! **3.** A mark made by a pen, pencil, or brush. Bill finished the drawing with a few *strokes* of the crayon. **4.** A sudden weakness or sickness caused by the breaking or blocking of a blood vessel in the brain. A stroke often causes paralysis.
  stroke (strōk) *noun, plural* **strokes.**

stroke² To rub gently. Ken *stroked* the puppy's head.
  stroke (strōk) *verb,* **stroked, stroking.**

stroll To walk in a slow, relaxed way. We *strolled* through the park on the way home. *Verb.*
—A slow, relaxed walk. Let's take a *stroll. Noun.*
  stroll (strōl) *verb,* **strolled, strolling;** *noun, plural* **strolls.**

strong **1.** Having much power, force, or energy; full of strength. The *strong* boy helped his father move the large table. The storm had *strong* winds that damaged trees and buildings. That country has a *strong* leader. **2.** Able to resist; firm. The house has *strong* walls. She is *strong* in her beliefs.
  strong (strông) *adjective,* **stronger, strongest.**

strove He *strove* to do better in school. Look up **strive** for more information.
  strove (strōv) *verb.*

struck He *struck* his head on the table when he fell. Look up **strike** for more information.
  struck (struk) *verb.*

structure **1.** Anything that is built. A house, church, or bridge is a structure. **2.** An

622

arrangement of parts, or the way parts are arranged. The flood weakened the *structure* of the house. We studied the *structure* of a plant cell by looking at it through a microscope.

struc·ture (struk′chər) *noun, plural* **structures.**

struggle **1.** To make a great effort. The children *struggled* through the heavy snow. Sara *struggled* to finish the arithmetic problem. **2.** To fight; battle. The soldiers *struggled* bravely with the enemy. *Verb.*
—**1.** A great effort. It was a *struggle* for him to learn French. **2.** A fight; battle. The thief gave himself up to the police without a *struggle. Noun.*

strug·gle (strug′əl) *verb,* **struggled, struggling;** *noun, plural* **struggles.**

strum To play in an easy, relaxed, or unskilled way. Bill likes to *strum* on his guitar.

strum (strum) *verb,* **strummed, strumming.**

strung Karen *strung* the beads. Look up **string** for more information.

strung (strung) *verb.*

stub A short part that remains after the rest has been used up, or broken or torn off. He tried to write with the *stub* of a pencil. *Noun.*
—To strike one's toe or foot against something. She *stubbed* her toe on the table leg. *Verb.*

stub (stub) *noun, plural* **stubs;** *verb,* **stubbed, stubbing.**

stubble **1.** Short stalks of grain left standing after the crop has been cut. A low *stubble* covered the field. **2.** A short, rough growth. The man's face had a *stubble* of a beard.

stub·ble (stub′əl) *noun.*

stubborn **1.** Not giving in; not yielding. The *stubborn* girl would not admit that she was wrong. **2.** Hard to overcome or deal with. He has a *stubborn* cold.

stub·born (stub′ərn) *adjective.*

stuck He *stuck* himself with a pin. Look up **stick** for more information.

stuck (stuk) *verb.*

student **1.** A person who is going to a school. The fourth grade has thirty *students.* My older brother is a *student* in college. **2.** A person who studies something. That scientist is a *student* of the ways animals behave.

stu·dent (stōōd′ənt *or* styōōd′ənt) *noun, plural* **students.**

studio **1.** A place where a painter or other artist works. We went to the photographer's *studio* to have our pictures taken. Jean goes to the dancer's *studio* for dancing lessons. **2.** A place where motion pictures are filmed.

3. A place where radio or television programs are broadcast.

stu·di·o (stōō′dē ō′ *or* styōō′dē ō′) *noun, plural* **studios.**

study **1.** To try to learn by reading or thinking about something. Our class *studied* the planets of the solar system. Bill wants to *study* law when he goes to college. **2.** To look at closely; examine. He *studied* her face to see if he knew her. *Verb.*
—**1.** The act of studying. Many hours of *study* are needed to learn French well. **2.** A close look at something; examination. Make a careful *study* of the photograph to see if you know any of the people in it. **3.** A thing studied; subject. How is your brother doing in his *studies* at college? **4.** A room used for studying. My father uses the extra bedroom as his *study. Noun.*

stud·y (stud′ē) *verb,* **studied, studying;** *noun, plural* **studies.**

stuff **1.** Something that a thing or person is made of. What kind of *stuff* is in this pillow? **2.** Useless matter or things. There is some black *stuff* on your shirt. The box was full of *stuff* to be thrown away. *Noun.*
—**1.** To pack full. She *stuffed* her suitcase with clothes. **2.** To force in. He *stuffed* the papers into his notebook. **3.** To fill. I *stuffed* myself with pie at dinner. **4.** To fill the skin of a dead animal in order to make it look natural or alive. **5.** To put stuffing into a chicken, turkey, fish, or other food to be cooked. *Verb.*

stuff (stuf) *noun; verb,* **stuffed, stuffing.**

stuffing Something used to fill or pack another thing. A mixture of bread crumbs and other food is used as *stuffing* for turkey, duck, or chicken. Feathers are sometimes used as *stuffing* for pillows.

stuff·ing (stuf′ing) *noun, plural* **stuffings.**

stuffy **1.** Without fresh air; close. The room is *stuffy;* please open a window. **2.** Dull and uninteresting; boring. The professor gave a *stuffy* talk.

stuff·y (stuf′ē) *adjective,* **stuffier, stuffiest.**

stumble **1.** To lose one's balance; trip. I *stumbled* over the rake in the yard. **2.** To move or speak in a clumsy way. She *stumbled* around in the dark room until she found

at; āpe; cär; end; mē; it; īce; hot; ōld; fôrk; wood; fōōl; oil; out; up; turn; sing; thin; this; hw in white; zh in treasure.
ə stands for a in about, e in taken
i in pencil, o in lemon, and u in circus.

623

the lamp. **3.** To discover by chance. The detective *stumbled* on an important clue.

stum·ble (stum′bəl) *verb*, **stumbled, stumbling.**

stump **1.** The lower part of a tree trunk. When a tree is cut down, only the stump is left above the ground. **2.** The part of anything left after the main part is gone. The boy tried to write with the *stump* of a pencil. *Noun.*

—To puzzle; confuse. This arithmetic problem has *stumped* me. *Verb.*

stump (stump) *noun, plural* **stumps;** *verb,* **stumped, stumping.**

stun **1.** To make unconscious. The blow on the head *stunned* him. **2.** To shock. We were *stunned* by the terrible news.

stun (stun) *verb,* **stunned, stunning.**

stung I was *stung* by a bee. Look up **sting** for more information.

stung (stung) *verb.*

stunt[1] To check or hinder growth. Lack of light and water *stunted* the plant's growth.

stunt (stunt) *verb,* **stunted, stunting.**

stunt[2] An act that shows skill or strength. The acrobat performed many *stunts* on the high trapeze.

stunt (stunt) *noun, plural* **stunts.**

stupid Lacking common sense or intelligence. He is *stupid* to drive home in this snowstorm. She gave a *stupid* answer.

stu·pid (stoo′pid *or* styoo′pid) *adjective.*

sturdy **1.** Strong; hardy. Heavy trucks drove on the *sturdy* bridge. He is a *sturdy* boy. **2.** Hard to overcome; unyielding. Their football team put up a *sturdy* defense, but our team won anyway.

stur·dy (stur′dē) *adjective,* **sturdier, sturdiest.**

Sturgeon

sturgeon A fish that is good to eat. Sturgeons have rows of bony, pointed scales on their sides.

stur·geon (stur′jən) *noun, plural* **sturgeons** or **sturgeon.**

stutter To repeat sounds when speaking. Many people who stutter repeat such letters as "d" and "b" at the beginning of a word. *Verb.*

—The act of stuttering. He has a bad *stutter*. *Noun.*

stut·ter (stut′ər) *verb,* **stuttered, stuttering;** *noun.*

style **1.** A particular way of saying or doing something. That author has a clear and simple *style* of writing. Our house is built in the modern *style*. **2.** Fashion; elegance. She wears clothes in the latest *style*. That rich family always travels in *style*. **3.** The part of the pistil of a flower shaped like a stalk. *Noun.*

—**1.** To name; call. George Washington has been *styled* the "Father of His Country." **2.** To design. Gail *styled* the dress that her sister made. *Verb.*

style (stīl) *noun, plural* **styles;** *verb,* **styled, styling.**

subject **1.** Something thought or talked about. The *subject* of Tim's report is "My Hobbies." Ann's favorite *subjects* in school are arithmetic and spelling. **2.** A person or thing that experiences something. The scientist used mice as *subjects* of an experiment. **3.** A person or thing that is under the control of another. The people were loyal *subjects* of the king. **4.** A word or group of words that does the action of the verb in a sentence. In the sentence "John ran fast," "John" is the subject. *Noun.*

—**1.** Under the control of another. The members are *subject* to the club's rules. **2.** Likely to be affected; liable to have. He is *subject* to sore throats. **3.** Depending on. She may go on the trip, *subject* to her parents' approval. *Adjective.*

—**1.** To bring under control. The strong nation tried to *subject* the weak nation to its will. **2.** To cause to experience. That boy *subjects* himself to much teasing because he wears such funny clothes. *Verb.*

sub·ject (sub′jikt *for noun and adjective;* səb jekt′ *for verb*) *noun, plural* **subjects;** *adjective; verb,* **subjected, subjecting.**

Submarine

submarine A ship that can go under water.

Submarines are used to look for and attack enemy ships during wartime. They are also used to explore the depths of the sea. *Noun.* —Under water. Seaweed is a *submarine* plant. *Adjective.*

sub·mar·ine (sub′mə rēn′ *for noun;* sub′mə rēn′ *for adjective*) *noun, plural* **submarines;** *adjective.*

submerge **1.** To cover with a liquid. The river almost *submerged* the house during the flood. **2.** To go beneath the surface of water or another liquid. The diver *submerged* to look for the sunken ship.

sub·merge (səb murj′) *verb,* **submerged, submerging.**

submit **1.** To yield to some power or authority. The children *submitted* to their parents' wishes. **2.** To present. Sally will *submit* her book report on Monday.

sub·mit (səb mit′) *verb,* **submitted, submitting.**

subordinate Lower in rank or importance. Sailors are *subordinate* to the captain on a ship. *Adjective.* —A person or thing that is lower in rank or importance. The president of that company always listens to the advice of his *subordinates. Noun.*

sub·or·di·nate (sə bôr′də nit) *adjective; noun, plural* **subordinates.**

subscribe **1.** To agree to take and pay for. Dad *subscribes* to the local newspaper. **2.** To give or show one's agreement or approval. He *subscribes* to the belief that there will be lasting peace on earth someday.

sub·scribe (səb skrīb′) *verb,* **subscribed, subscribing.**

subscription **1.** The subscribing to something. *Subscription* to that stamp magazine is expensive. **2.** Something subscribed to. My parents gave me a magazine *subscription* for my birthday.

sub·scrip·tion (səb skrip′shən) *noun, plural* **subscriptions.**

subsequent Happening after; coming as a result. *Subsequent* experiments showed that the scientist's theory was correct.

sub·se·quent (sub′sə kwənt) *adjective.*

subside **1.** To sink to a lower level. The flood waters *subsided.* **2.** To become less. After a short while, Jeff's anger *subsided.*

sub·side (səb sīd′) *verb,* **subsided, subsiding.**

substance **1.** The material that something is made of. Wood is the main *substance* of paper. Diamonds and the graphite in your pencil are different forms of the same *substance.* **2.** The important part of something;

meaning. The *substance* of his letter is that he is homesick.

sub·stance (sub′stəns) *noun, plural* **substances.**

substantial **1.** Large in amount; ample. We ate a *substantial* dinner. Jack earned a *substantial* amount of money as a writer. **2.** Strong; firm. That *substantial* bridge can support heavy trucks and buses. **3.** Real; not imaginary. Rocks, trees, and rivers are all *substantial* things.

sub·stan·tial (səb stan′shəl) *adjective.*

substitute A person who does something in place of another; a thing used in place of another. The baker used margarine as a *substitute* for butter in the rolls. *Noun.* —**1.** To put in place of another. The coach *substituted* the new player for Bill in the seventh inning. **2.** To take the place of another. Miss Jones *substituted* for our regular teacher, who was sick. *Verb.*

sub·sti·tute (sub′stə tōot′ *or* sub′stə tyoot′) *noun, plural* **substitutes;** *verb,* **substituted, substituting.**

subtle Faint and delicate. That flower has a *subtle* smell.

sub·tle (sut′əl) *adjective,* **subtler, subtlest.**

subtract To take away from. If you *subtract* 3 from 7, you have 4.

sub·tract (səb trakt′) *verb,* **subtracted, subtracting.**

subtraction The subtracting of one number from another number to find the difference. $5 - 2 = 3$ is an example of subtraction.

sub·trac·tion (səb trak′shən) *noun, plural* **subtractions.**

subtrahend The number to be subtracted from another number. When you subtract 4 from 11, the number 4 is the subtrahend.

sub·tra·hend (sub′trə hend′) *noun, plural* **subtrahends.**

suburb An area with homes and stores next to or near a city. We live in the *suburbs,* so Father has to drive to work in the city.

sub·urb (sub′urb) *noun, plural* **suburbs.**

suburban Of or having to do with a suburb. There are many nice homes in the *suburban* community where Nancy lives.

sub·ur·ban (sə bur′bən) *adjective.*

at; āpe; cär; end; mē; it; īce; hot; ōld; fôrk; wood; fōol; oil; out; up; turn; sing; thin; this; hw in white; zh in treasure. ə stands for a in about, e in taken i in pencil, o in lemon, and u in circus.

subway A railroad under the ground. Subways run under the streets and buildings of a city. They are powered by electricity.
sub·way (sub′wā′) *noun, plural* **subways.**

succeed **1.** To turn out well; do well. The team *succeeded* in winning the championship. We know that she will *succeed* when she grows up. **2.** To come next. After the king died, his son *succeeded* to the throne.
suc·ceed (sək sēd′) *verb,* **succeeded, succeeding.**

success **1.** A result that has been hoped for; a turning out well or doing well. The coach was pleased with the *success* of the team. The young woman had much *success* as a writer. **2.** A person or thing that succeeds. The party was a big *success.*
suc·cess (sək ses′) *noun, plural* **successes.**

successful Having success. The writer's book was *successful* and sold many copies. My aunt is a *successful* lawyer.
suc·cess·ful (sək ses′fəl) *adjective.*

succession **1.** A group of persons or things following one after another. The football team has had a *succession* of victories. **2.** The coming of one person or thing after another. There has been a peaceful *succession* of rulers in England for many years. The two rifle shots came in quick *succession.*
suc·ces·sion (sək sesh′ən) *noun, plural* **successions.**

successive Following one after another. Our team has had three *successive* defeats.
suc·ces·sive (sək ses′iv) *adjective.*

such **1.** Of the same kind; of that kind. I have never seen *such* rainy weather. How could he have done *such* a thing? **2.** Similar; like. Mother bought tomatoes, lettuce, and other *such* vegetables for a salad. **3.** So much of. It is *such* a surprise to see you again. *Adjective.*
—A person or thing of that kind. We need hot dogs and *such* for the picnic. *Pronoun.*
such (such) *adjective; pronoun.*

suck **1.** To draw something into the mouth. I like to *suck* chocolate milk through a straw. **2.** To draw liquid from something with the mouth. She *sucked* an orange. **3.** To hold in the mouth and lick. He *sucked* on a piece of hard candy. **4.** To draw in. The vacuum cleaner *sucked* in dust.
suck (suk) *verb,* **sucked, sucking.**

suction The drawing of a gas or liquid into a space from which part or all of the air has been removed. A vacuum cleaner works by means of suction.
suc·tion (suk′shən) *noun.*

sudden **1.** Happening without warning; not expected. A *sudden* snowstorm trapped many cars on the highway. **2.** Hasty; quick. He made a *sudden* decision. The car made a *sudden* turn to the left.
sud·den (sud′ən) *adjective.*

suds Soapy water with foam or bubbles on top.
suds (sudz) *noun plural.*

sue To start a case against in a court of law. She will *sue* the store where she fell and hurt herself.
sue (sōō) *verb,* **sued, suing.**

suede Leather with a soft, fuzzy feel to it. It is used to make clothes, handbags, belts, and other articles.
suede (swād) *noun.*

suet The hard fat from cattle and sheep. It is used in cooking.
su·et (sōō′it) *noun.*

suffer **1.** To have pain or sorrow. She has *suffered* from a sore throat all week. The little boy *suffers* from his brother's mean teasing. **2.** To have or feel. She *suffered* much pain from her broken leg. **3.** To be harmed or damaged. His schoolwork *suffers* when he doesn't study.
suf·fer (suf′ər) *verb,* **suffered, suffering.**

suffering The feeling of pain or sorrow. The doctor gave the hurt child some medicine to ease his *suffering.*
suf·fer·ing (suf′ər ing) *noun, plural* **sufferings.**

sufficient As much as is necessary or needed; enough. Do we have *sufficient* supplies for our camping trip?
suf·fi·cient (sə fish′ənt) *adjective.*

suffix A syllable or group of syllables added to the end of a word. A suffix can change the meaning of the word or form a new word. The ending "-ness" in the word "badness" is a suffix. The ending "-er" in the word "painter" is a suffix.
suf·fix (suf′iks) *noun, plural* **suffixes.**

suffocate **1.** To kill by keeping from breathing. Some of the miners were *suffocated* by the cave-in at the mine. **2.** To die from a lack of air. The turtle may *suffocate* if you keep it in a box with no holes to let air in. **3.** To keep from breathing easily. The small, crowded room *suffocated* me.
suf·fo·cate (suf′ə kāt′) *verb,* **suffocated, suffocating.**

sugar A white or brown sweet substance. It is usually in the form of small crystals or powder. Sugar comes mainly from sugar beets and sugarcane. *Noun.*

—To sweeten with or sprinkle with sugar. Dad always *sugars* his coffee. Mother *sugared* the cookies. *Verb.*

sug·ar (shoog′ər) *noun, plural* **sugars;** *verb,* **sugared, sugaring.**

sugar beet A plant whose long, thick roots are a source of sugar.

sugarcane A tall grass. The sweet juice in its stem is a source of sugar.

sug·ar·cane (shoog′ər kān′) *noun.*

Sugarcane

suggest 1. To offer as something to think about. Bill *suggests* that we play baseball. The salesclerk *suggested* a blue tie to the customer. 2. To call to mind. The color red *suggests* warmth. 3. To hint. Her smile *suggests* that she is happy.

sug·gest (səg jest′) *verb,* **suggested, suggesting.**

suggestion 1. The act of suggesting something. We went to the movies at Mother's *suggestion.* 2. Something suggested. He took his friend's *suggestion* and bought a lock for his bicycle. 3. A hint; trace. There is a *suggestion* of roses in that perfume.

sug·ges·tion (səg jes′chən) *noun, plural* **suggestions.**

suicide The taking of one's own life on purpose.

su·i·cide (soo′ə sīd′) *noun, plural* **suicides.**

suit 1. A set of clothes made to be worn together. A man's suit has trousers and a jacket and sometimes a vest. 2. A case brought to a court of law. The woman brought *suit* against the store where she fell and broke her hip. 3. Any of the four sets of playing cards in a deck. The four suits are spades, hearts, diamonds, or clubs. *Noun.*
—1. To meet the needs of; be right for. A small house will not *suit* a large family. The lively music *suits* my happy mood. 2. To be convenient to; please; satisfy. Stay as long as it *suits* you. 3. To be becoming to. The yellow dress *suits* her perfectly. *Verb.*

suit (soot) *noun, plural* **suits;** *verb,* **suited, suiting.**

suitable Right; proper. The soil in our backyard is *suitable* for growing tomatoes.

suit·a·ble (soo′tə bəl) *adjective.*

suitcase A flat bag for carrying clothes when traveling.

suit·case (soot′kās′) *noun, plural* **suitcases.**

suite 1. A group of rooms that are connected. The family took a *suite* at the hotel. 2. A set of matching or similar things. Mother and Dad bought a new *suite* of furniture for the dining room. ▲ Another word that sounds like this is **sweet.**

suite (swēt) *noun, plural* **suites.**

suitor A man who courts a woman. Jack's older sister has many *suitors.*

suit·or (soo′tər) *noun, plural* **suitors.**

sulfur A yellow substance that is used to make matches, fertilizers, and explosives. Sulfur is a chemical element. This word is also spelled **sulphur.**

sul·fur (sul′fər) *noun.*

sulky A light carriage for one person. It has two wheels and is drawn by one horse. Sulkies are used in horse racing.

sulk·y (sul′kē) *noun, plural* **sulkies.**

Sulky

sullen 1. Gloomy and silent from anger. The boy was *sullen* after he was scolded by the teacher. 2. Gloomy; dismal. It was a *sullen,* rainy morning.

sul·len (sul′ən) *adjective.*

sultan In former times, a ruler of certain Muslim countries.

sul·tan (sult′ən) *noun, plural* **sultans.**

sultry Very hot and damp. The explorer went into the *sultry* jungle.

sul·try (sul′trē) *adjective,* **sultrier, sultriest.**

sum 1. The number that results from adding two or more numbers together. The sum of 6 plus 8 is 14. 2. An amount of money. Dean was paid the *sum* of three dollars for mowing

at; āpe; cär; end; mē; it; īce; hot; ōld; fôrk; wood; fool; oil; out; up; turn; sing; thin; this; hw in white; zh in treasure. ə stands for a in about, e in taken i in pencil, o in lemon, and u in circus.

the lawn. ▲ Another word that sounds like this is **some.**

sum (sum) *noun, plural* **sums.**

to sum up. To tell briefly; give a summary of. The news reporter *summed up* the main events of the day.

sumac A tree or shrub that has pointed leaves and clusters of flowers and berries. Some kinds of sumacs have leaves that cause an itchy rash when touched.

su·mac (shŏŏ′mak *or* sŏŏ′mak) *noun, plural* **sumacs.**

Sumac

summarize To make a summary of. The teacher asked the student to *summarize* the story.

sum·ma·rize (sum′ə-rīz′) *verb,* **summarized, summarizing.**

summary A brief account that has the main points of something. The radio announcer gave a *summary* of the day's news.

sum·ma·ry (sum′ər ē) *noun, plural* **summaries.**

summer The season of the year that comes between spring and autumn. *Noun.*
—To spend the summer. The family will *summer* in the mountains. *Verb.*

sum·mer (sum′ər) *noun, plural* **summers;** *verb,* **summered, summering.**

summit The highest point or level. The men climbed to the *summit* of the mountain.

sum·mit (sum′it) *noun, plural* **summits.**

summon 1. To send for; call for. Mrs. Hughes *summoned* the police after she had discovered the robbery. 2. To stir up; arouse. She *summoned* up her courage and dove off the high diving board.

sum·mon (sum′ən) *verb,* **summoned, summoning.**

summons A notice or command to appear somewhere or do something. He was given a *summons* to appear in court.

sum·mons (sum′ənz) *noun, plural* **summonses.**

sun 1. The star around which the earth and other planets revolve. The sun gives light and heat. 2. Light and heat from the sun. The plants in my room need plenty of *sun.* Her face was red from too much *sun. Noun.*
—To be in the light and heat of the sun. My sister likes to *sun* herself on the beach. *Verb.*

▲ Another word that sounds like this is **son.**

sun (sun) *noun; verb,* **sunned, sunning.**

sunbathe To lie in the sun. Sue likes to *sunbathe* in her back yard.

sun·bathe (sun′bāth) *verb,* **sunbathed, sunbathing.**

sunburn A redness or burn on the skin caused by too much sun.

sun·burn (sun′burn′) *noun, plural* **sunburns.**

sundae Ice cream served with syrup, fruit, or nuts on top.

sun·dae (sun′dē *or* sun′dā) *noun, plural* **sundaes.**

Sunday The first day of the week.

Sun·day (sun′dē *or* sun′dā) *noun, plural* **Sundays.**

▲ The ancient Romans' name for this day meant "day of the sun." The word **Sunday** comes from an Old English word that meant "sun's day."

sundown The setting of the sun.

sun·down (sun′doun′) *noun, plural* **sundowns.**

sunflower A large flower that grows on a tall plant. A sunflower has a brown center and yellow petals.

sun·flow·er (sun′flou′ər) *noun, plural* **sunflowers.**

sung The choir has *sung* many songs. Look up **sing** for more information.

sung (sung) *verb.*

sunglasses Eyeglasses with colored lenses to protect the eyes from the glare of the sun.

sun·glass·es (sun′glas′iz) *noun plural.*

sunk The rock has *sunk* to the bottom of the pond. Look up **sink** for more information.

sunk (sungk) *verb.*

Sunflower

sunken 1. Having sunk below the surface. The divers found *sunken* treasure. 2. Placed below the area around it. Our house has a *sunken* garden in the back yard. 3. Hollow. The thin boy had *sunken* cheeks.

sunk·en (sung′kən) *adjective.*

sunlight The light of the sun.

sun·light (sun′līt′) *noun.*

sunny 1. Full of sunlight; warmed by sunlight. It is a *sunny* day today. We sat on the *sunny* porch. 2. Cheerful; happy. Ruth has a *sunny* nature. The child has a *sunny* smile.

sun·ny (sun′ē) *adjective,* **sunnier, sunniest.**

sunrise   The rising of the sun at the start of the day.
sun·rise (sun′rīz′) *noun, plural* **sunrises.**

sunset   The setting of the sun at the end of the day.
sun·set (sun′set′) *noun, plural* **sunsets.**

Sunset

sunshine   The light from the sun. The *sunshine* came through the window.
sun·shine (sun′shīn′) *noun.*

superb   Very fine; excellent. The actress gave a *superb* performance.
su·perb (soo purb′) *adjective.*

superhighway   A highway for traveling at high speeds.
su·per·high·way (soo′pər hī′wā′) *noun, plural* **superhighways.**

superintendent   A person who directs or manages something. The *superintendent* of police is the head of the police department. The *superintendent* of an apartment house sees that the building is kept clean, heated, and in good condition.
su·per·in·tend·ent   (soo′pər in ten′dənt) *noun, plural* **superintendents.**

superior   1. Higher or greater. Our baseball team has *superior* pitching. Fran does *superior* work at school. The soldier saluted his *superior* officer. 2. Proud; haughty. That boy has a *superior* attitude because his father is a famous man. *Adjective.*
—A person who is higher. The principal of a school is the teacher's *superior. Noun.*
su·pe·ri·or (sə pēr′ē ər) *adjective; noun, plural* **superiors.**

superiority   The state or quality of being superior. The football team showed its *superiority* by winning the state championship.
su·pe·ri·or·i·ty (sə pēr′ē ôr′ə tē) *noun.*

superlative   Of the highest sort; above all others. Landing men on the moon was a *superlative* achievement. *Adjective.*

—The form of an adjective or adverb that gives the idea of "most." "Best" is the *superlative* of "good." "Highest" is the *superlative* of "high." *Noun.*
su·per·la·tive (sə pur′lə tiv) *adjective; noun, plural* **superlatives.**

supermarket   A large store that sells food and household goods. Customers serve themselves in a supermarket.
su·per·mar·ket (soo′pər mär′kit) *noun, plural* **supermarkets.**

supernatural   Beyond the natural world. Ghosts and demons are *supernatural* creatures.
su·per·nat·u·ral (soo′pər nach′ər əl) *adjective.*

superstition   A belief based on ignorance and fear. The belief that a black cat will bring bad luck is a *superstition.* Many people will not open umbrellas indoors or walk under ladders because of their *superstitions.*
su·per·sti·tion (soo′pər stish′ən) *noun, plural* **superstitions.**

superstitious   Having or showing superstition. The *superstitious* boy carries a rabbit's foot for good luck.
su·per·sti·tious (soo′pər stish′əs) *adjective.*

supervise   To watch over and direct. The foreman *supervised* the workers at the automobile factory.
su·per·vise (soo′pər vīz′) *verb,* **supervised, supervising.**

supper   The last meal of the day. It is eaten in the evening.
sup·per (sup′ər) *noun, plural* **suppers.**

supple   Easy to bend; not stiff. The *supple* branch can be bent without breaking it.
sup·ple (sup′əl) *adjective,* **suppler, supplest.**

supplement   Something added to complete or improve another thing. My history book has a *supplement* in the back that lists all the presidents of the United States. Jean takes vitamins as a *supplement* to her diet. *Noun.*
—To add as a supplement. Fred *supplements* his allowance by earning money mowing lawns. *Verb.*
sup·ple·ment (sup′lə mənt *for noun;* sup′lə ment′ *for verb*) *noun, plural* **supplements;** *verb,* **supplemented, supplementing.**

at; āpe; cär; end; mē; it; īce; hot; ōld;
fôrk; wood; fool; oil; out; up; turn; sing;
thin; this; hw in white; zh in treasure.
ə stands for a in about, e in taken
i in pencil, o in lemon, and u in circus.

supply To provide with something needed or wanted. Rain *supplies* water for the garden. The newspaper *supplies* news. *Verb.*
—A quantity of something that is needed or ready for use. The store has a new *supply* of crayons and paints. We have bought the *supplies* for our camping trip. *Noun.*
   sup·ply (sə plī′) *verb,* **supplied, supplying;** *noun, plural* **supplies.**

support **1.** To hold up. These book shelves can *support* heavy books. The columns *support* the roof of the porch. **2.** To provide for. Jane's mother *supports* her family by working in a bank. Scientists do not believe that the planet Venus can *support* life. **3.** To help or back. Many people will *support* him as a candidate for mayor. **4.** To show to be true. The facts *support* the prisoner's story. *Verb.*
—**1.** The supporting of something or someone. The builder used heavy beams for the *support* of the roof. His friends gave him *support* when he ran for club president. **2.** A person or thing that supports. The center pole is the main *support* of the tent. *Noun.*
   sup·port (sə pôrt′) *verb,* **supported, supporting;** *noun, plural* **supports.**

suppose **1.** To imagine to be possible. Just *suppose* that we were able to fly. **2.** To believe. I *suppose* that I'll be finished with my homework soon. **3.** To expect or require. She is *supposed* to be here now.
   sup·pose (sə pōz′) *verb,* **supposed, supposing.**

supreme **1.** Greatest in power or authority; most important. The king was *supreme* in his country. **2.** Highest; utmost. He made a *supreme* effort to lift the heavy box.
   su·preme (sə prēm′) *adjective.*

Supreme Court The highest court in the United States.

sure **1.** Having no doubt; confident. He is *sure* that he is right. Are you *sure* you locked the front door? **2.** Certain to be; dependable. Our team is a *sure* winner. **3.** Steady; firm. Jerry had a *sure* grip on the bat when he swung at the ball. *Adjective.*
—Surely; certainly. *Sure,* I'm going to the game. *Adverb.*
   sure (shoor) *adjective,* **surer, surest;** *adverb.*

surely Without doubt; truly. He will *surely* be there.
   sure·ly (shoor′lē) *adverb.*

surf The rise and splash of the waves of the sea on the shore. ▲ Another word that sounds like this is **serf.**
   surf (surf) *noun.*

surface **1.** The outside or top part of a thing. The *surface* of the stone is rough. The as-tronauts explored the *surface* of the moon. **2.** Outer look or appearance. The problem seemed simple on the *surface. Noun.*
—Of or having to do with a surface; on a surface. He scraped off the *surface* rust from the metal. *Adjective.*
—**1.** To come to the surface. The submarine *surfaced.* **2.** To cover the surface of. The workmen *surfaced* our driveway with gravel. *Verb.*
   sur·face (sur′fis) *noun, plural* **surfaces;** *adjective; verb,* **surfaced, surfacing.**

surfboard A long, flat board used to ride on the crest of a wave.
   surf·board (surf′bôrd′) *noun, plural* **surf-boards.**

Surfboard

surfing A sport in which a person rides on the crest of a wave into the shore on a surfboard.
   surf·ing (sur′fing) *noun.*

surge To swell and move with force like a wave. The flood waters *surged* over the river banks. The crowd *surged* forward. *Verb.*
—**1.** A swelling movement. The *surge* of the waves tossed the ship. **2.** A sudden rise. He felt a *surge* of anger. *Noun.*
   surge (surj) *verb,* **surged, surging;** *noun, plural* **surges.**

surgeon A doctor who operates on people.
   sur·geon (sur′jən) *noun, plural* **surgeons.**

surgery The treatment of diseases or injuries by operations.
   sur·ger·y (sur′jər ē) *noun.*

surname A last name; family name. Linda's *surname* is Banks.
   sur·name (sur′nām′) *noun, plural* **surnames.**

surplus An amount greater than what is used or needed; quantity left over. The family has a *surplus* of furniture stored in the attic. *Noun.*
—Greater than what is needed; left over. The

farmer sold his *surplus* vegetables at a road-side stand. *Adjective.*

sur·plus (sur′plus′) *noun; adjective.*

surprise **1.** To cause to feel sudden wonder or amazement. Dad *surprised* us with gifts. Ann *surprised* her mother by cleaning her room. **2.** To come upon suddenly and unexpectedly. Mr. Smith *surprised* a burglar in his store. *Verb.*

—**1.** A feeling of wonder or amazement caused by something unexpected. Winning the contest filled him with *surprise.* **2.** Something that causes surprise. The birthday party was a complete *surprise* to her. **3.** The act of coming upon someone suddenly and unexpectedly. We caught Tim by *surprise. Noun.*

sur·prise (sər prīz′) *verb,* **surprised, surprising;** *noun, plural* **surprises.**

surrender To give up; yield. The outlaw *surrendered* to the sheriff. *Verb.*

—The act of surrendering. The *surrender* of the city took place after the army's defeat. *Noun.*

sur·ren·der (sə ren′dər) *verb,* **surrendered, surrendering;** *noun, plural* **surrenders.**

surround To be on all sides of; form a circle around. A crowd *surrounded* the famous baseball player to get his autograph. A fence *surrounds* our yard.

sur·round (sə round′) *verb,* **surrounded, surrounding.**

surroundings The things or conditions that surround a person. We moved from the city to the country because we wanted quieter *surroundings.*

sur·round·ings (sə roun′dingz) *noun plural.*

survey **1.** To look at or study in detail. The mayor *surveyed* the damage to the city after the bad storm. **2.** To measure land to find out its boundaries, shape, or size. The men *surveyed* the property before it was divided into lots for building. *Verb.*

—**1.** A detailed study. The company made a *survey* of how many people bought their product. **2.** A measuring of land. Mr. Thomas had a *survey* made of his property. *Noun.*

sur·vey (sər vā′ *for verb;* sur′vā *or* sər vā′ *for noun*) *verb,* **surveyed, surveying;** *noun, plural* **surveys.**

surveyor A person whose work is surveying land.

sur·vey·or (sər vā′ər) *noun, plural* **surveyors.**

survival **1.** The act of surviving. The *survival* of all the passengers in the bus accident was a miracle. **2.** A person or thing that survives. The custom of throwing rice at a wedding is a *survival* from olden times.

sur·viv·al (sər vī′vəl) *noun, plural* **survivals.**

survive **1.** To live longer than; live through. She *survived* her husband by ten years. All the passengers and the crew *survived* the plane crash. **2.** To continue to exist. These plants won't *survive* unless you water them.

sur·vive (sər vīv′) *verb,* **survived, surviving.**

suspect **1.** To think that something is possible or true. I *suspect* that she has already gone. Dave *suspected* that a trick was being played on him. **2.** To think someone is guilty without proof. The sheriff *suspected* the stranger of the crime. **3.** To doubt; distrust. We *suspected* his honesty. *Verb.*

—A person who is suspected. The sheriff put the *suspect* in jail. *Noun.*

sus·pect (sə spekt′ *for verb;* sus′pekt′ *for noun*) *verb,* **suspected, suspecting;** *noun, plural* **suspects.**

suspend **1.** To attach so as to hang down. Dad *suspended* the swing from a tree branch. **2.** To hold in place. Bits of lemon were *suspended* in the glass of lemonade. **3.** To stop or cause to stop for a time. She *suspended* payments on her car. **4.** To keep from using. The judge *suspended* the man's driver's license. **5.** To keep out for a time. The principal *suspended* the boy from school for breaking the rules.

sus·pend (sə spend′) *verb,* **suspended, suspending.**

suspenders Two straps worn over the shoulders to hold up trousers or a skirt.

sus·pend·ers (sə spen′dərz) *noun plural.*

suspense The state of being in doubt and worried about what will happen. The exciting mystery program on television kept me in *suspense.*

sus·pense (sə spens′) *noun.*

suspension The act of suspending. Bits of dirt are held in *suspension* in muddy water. The principal ordered the girl's *suspension* from school.

sus·pen·sion (sə spen′shən) *noun, plural* **suspensions.**

Suspenders

at; āpe; cär; end; mē; it; īce; hot; ōld; fôrk; wood; fōol; oil; out; up; turn; sing; thin; this; hw in white; zh in treasure. ə stands for a in about, e in taken i in pencil, o in lemon, and u in circus.

suspension bridge A bridge suspended from cables or chains between towers.

Suspension Bridge

suspicion **1.** The act or instance of suspecting. My *suspicions* that he was the one who was stealing the food turned out to be true. **2.** The state of being suspected. The police arrested him on *suspicion* of murder.
sus·pi·cion (sə spish′ən) *noun, plural* suspicions.

suspicious **1.** Causing suspicion. The man waiting outside the bank acted in a *suspicious* manner. **2.** Feeling or showing suspicion. The old farmer is *suspicious* of strangers. The sheriff gave the stranger a *suspicious* glance.
sus·pi·cious (sə spish′əs) *adjective.*

swallow[1] **1.** To cause food to pass from the mouth to the stomach. **2.** To take in and cover over. During the earthquake, the ground opened up and *swallowed* the village. **3.** To take or keep back. She *swallowed* her pride and apologized for being rude. *Verb.*
—The act of swallowing. With a quick *swallow* Ruth finished her milk. *Noun.*
swal·low (swol′ō) *verb,* swallowed, swallowing; *noun, plural* swallows.

swallow[2] A small bird with long wings and a forked tail. Swallows are black, brown, or dark blue.
swal·low (swol′ō) *noun, plural* swallows.

swam Gail *swam* across the pool. Look up **swim** for more information.
swam (swam) *verb.*

swamp Soft, wet land. Swamps have trees and shrubs growing in them. *Noun.*
—To fill with water. The high waves *swamped* the ship and made it sink. *Verb.*
swamp (swomp) *noun, plural* swamps; *verb,* swamped, swamping.

swan A large water bird that has a long, graceful neck and webbed feet. Swans are related to ducks and geese.
swan (swon) *noun, plural* swans.

Swan

swarm **1.** A group of bees that fly off together to start a new colony. **2.** A large group of people or animals. *Swarms* of people filled the sidewalks. *Noun.*
—**1.** To fly off together to start a new colony. The bees *swarmed.* **2.** To move in a large group. People *swarmed* out of the theater. **3.** To be filled. The river *swarmed* with alligators. *Verb.*
swarm (sworm) *noun, plural* swarms; *verb,* swarmed, swarming.

sway **1.** To move or cause to move back and forth. The dancers *swayed* to the music. The wind *swayed* the trees. **2.** To change the thinking of; influence. Nothing he said could *sway* her from giving up her job. *Verb.*
—**1.** The act of swaying. We could feel the *sway* of the bus as it turned. **2.** Influence or control. The country was under the *sway* of a dictator. *Noun.*
sway (swā) *verb,* swayed, swaying; *noun, plural* sways.

swear **1.** To make a solemn statement by calling on God or another sacred being or thing. Witnesses in a trial have to *swear* on a Bible that they will tell the truth. Mr. Holt was *sworn* in as mayor. **2.** To promise in a solemn way. I *swear* that I'm telling the truth. **3.** To use bad language; curse.
swear (swer) *verb,* swore, sworn, swearing.

sweat **1.** A salty fluid given off through the skin. After playing ball, his face was covered with *sweat.* **2.** A moisture formed in drops on a surface. *Sweat* formed on the outside of the glass filled with cold water. *Noun.*
—**1.** To give off sweat. He *sweated* in the hot sun. **2.** To gather moisture in drops from the surrounding air. The glass of cold lemonade *sweated* in the warm room. *Verb.*
sweat (swet) *noun; verb,* sweated, sweating.

sweater A warm knitted piece of clothing worn over the upper part of the body. Sweaters are often made of wool. You pull a sweater on over your head or button it like a jacket.

sweat·er (swet′ər) *noun, plural* **sweaters.**

sweep 1. To clean with a broom or brush. Please *sweep* the floor. 2. To clear away or take up. We *swept* up the crumbs from the floor. She *swept* up her change and left the store. 3. To move or carry quickly and with force. The wind *swept* the leaves from the sidewalk. The fire *swept* through the old barn. 4. To pass over with a quick, steady motion. The sailor's eyes *swept* the horizon for a sign of land. *Verb.*
—1. Any quick, sweeping motion. He knocked the books off the table with a *sweep* of his hand. 2. Reach or range. From the mountain you can see a *sweep* of flat land that goes on for miles. *Noun.*

sweep (swēp) *verb,* **swept, sweeping;** *noun, plural* **sweeps.**

sweet 1. Having a pleasant taste like that of sugar or honey. This apple is *sweet* and juicy. 2. Pleasing to the smell. A rose has a *sweet* odor. 3. Not sour or salted; fresh. Dad uses *sweet* cream in his coffee. 4. Pleasing and kindly; good-natured. Beth is a *sweet* person. Carol said some *sweet* things about you in her letter. *Adjective.*
—Something that is sweet. We ate cookies, cakes, and other *sweets* for dessert. *Noun.* ▲ Another word that sounds like this is **suite.**

sweet (swēt) *adjective,* **sweeter, sweetest;** *noun, plural* **sweets.**

sweetheart A person who is loved by and loves another.

sweet·heart (swēt′härt′) *noun, plural* **sweet-hearts.**

sweet pea A sweet-smelling flower. Sweet peas may be purple, pink, red, or white. They grow on climbing plants.

sweet potato The soft, sweet orange root of a vine. The sweet potato is cooked and eaten as a vegetable.

swell 1. To grow or cause to grow in size. The sponge *swelled* as it absorbed the water. The sprain *swelled* my wrist. 2. To rise above a level.

Sweet Peas

become filled with emotion. Her heart *swelled* with happiness when she was given the puppy. Pride *swelled* his head. *Verb.*
—A wave or series of waves. The ship rose and fell in the *swell* of the sea. *Noun.*
—Fine; excellent. You look *swell* in your new clothes. ▲ This meaning is used mostly in everyday conversation. *Adjective.*

swell (swel) *verb,* **swelled, swelled** or **swollen, swelling;** *noun, plural* **swells;** *adjective,* **sweller, swellest.**

swelling A swollen part. Bob has a *swelling* on his leg where the baseball hit him.

swell·ing (swel′ing) *noun, plural* **swellings.**

swept Jack *swept* the floor of the cabin. Look up **sweep** for more information.

swept (swept) *verb.*

swift 1. Moving very quickly; able to move very quickly. The cowboy has a *swift* horse. 2. Happening quickly; quick. The frog made a *swift* leap into the pond. Pat gave a *swift* reply to the teacher's question. *Adjective.*
—A bird with narrow wings and dark gray, brown, or bluish feathers. *Noun.*

swift (swift) *adjective,* **swifter, swiftest;** *noun, plural* **swifts.**

swim 1. To move in the water by using arms or legs, or fins and tail. I learned to *swim* at camp last summer. We watched the fish *swim* in the pond. 2. To move across something in this way. Florence tried to *swim* the lake. 3. To be in a liquid or be covered with a liquid. The ice cream was *swimming* in chocolate syrup. Her eyes *swam* with tears. 4. To have a dizzy feeling. The rocking of the boat made my head *swim. Verb.*
—The act, time, or distance of swimming. Fran took a quick *swim* before lunch. *Noun.*

swim (swim) *verb,* **swam, swum, swimming;** *noun, plural* **swims.**

swimmer A person who swims.

swim·mer (swim′ər) *noun, plural* **swimmers.**

swindle To take someone's money or property in a dishonest way; cheat. The salesman *swindled* the old woman. *Verb.*
—The act of swindling. *Noun.*

swin·dle (swind′əl) *verb,* **swindled, swindling;** *noun, plural* **swindles.**

swine A pig or hog.

swine (swīn) *noun, plural* **swine.**

at; āpe; cär; end; mē; it; īce; hot; ōld;
fôrk; wood; fool; oil; out; up; turn; sing;
thin; this; hw in white; zh in treasure.
ə stands for a in about, e in taken
i in pencil, o in lemon, and u in circus.

swing **1.** To move back and forth with a steady motion. Bill likes to *swing* on an old tire that hangs by a rope from a tree. **2.** To move or turn in a curved motion. Charlie *swung* the baseball bat. The driver had to *swing* his car off the road to keep from hitting the truck. *Verb.*
—**1.** The swinging of something. He hit the ball with a *swing* of his golf club. **2.** A seat hung by chains or ropes in which a person can sit and swing. We enjoy the *swings* in playground. *Noun.*
  swing (swing) *verb,* **swung, swinging;** *noun, plural* **swings.**

Swing

swirl To move around and around. The water *swirled* as it went down the drain. The wind *swirled* the dry leaves. *Verb.*
—**1.** A spinning or twisting motion. I could see the *swirl* of smoke rising from the campfire. **2.** Something shaped like a curl. Mother put chocolate *swirls* on the cake. *Noun.*
  swirl (swurl) *verb,* **swirled, swirling;** *noun, plural* **swirls.**

swish To move with a soft, rustling sound. The woman's long dress *swished* as she walked. *Verb.*
—A rustling movement or sound. The cat showed her anger with a *swish* of her tail. *Noun.*
  swish (swish) *verb,* **swished, swishing;** *noun, plural* **swishes.**

switch **1.** A long, thin stick or rod used for whipping. **2.** A stroke or lash. The cow brushed flies off with a *switch* of its tail. **3.** A change. The coach made a *switch* to a new pitcher in the ninth inning of the game. **4.** A device used to open or close an electric circuit. Where is the *switch* to turn on the bedroom light? **5.** A device by which a train can change from one track to another. *Noun.*
—**1.** To strike or whip with a switch. The man *switched* the horse. **2.** To move or swing with a quick motion. The cat *switched* its tail. **3.** To change. Jack *switched* records on the phonograph. Bill and Fred *switched* seats.

4. To turn on or off by means of an electrical switch. Mary *switched* on the light. **5.** To move a train from one track to another. *Verb.*
  switch (swich) *noun, plural* **switches;** *verb,* **switched, switching.**

switchboard A panel with openings for plugs. It is used to connect and disconnect telephone lines.
  switch·board (swich′bôrd′) *noun, plural* **switchboards.**

swollen Her sore toe has *swollen*. Look up **swell** for more information. *Verb.*
—Made larger by swelling. He has a *swollen* finger. *Adjective.*
  swol·len (swō′lən) *verb; adjective.*

swoop **1.** To rush down suddenly. The hawk *swooped* down on the rabbit. Outlaws *swooped* down from the hills to attack the stagecoach. **2.** To take suddenly; seize. Kate *swooped* up the kitten into her arms. *Verb.*
—The act of swooping. With a *swoop*, the eagle caught the squirrel. *Noun.*
  swoop (swo͞op) *verb,* **swooped, swooping;** *noun, plural* **swoops.**

sword A weapon that has a long, sharp blade set in a handle or hilt.
  sword (sôrd) *noun, plural* **swords.**

swordfish A large saltwater fish with a long, flat, bony part like a sword that sticks out from the upper jaw. People catch swordfish for food and for sport.
  sword·fish (sôrd′fish′) *noun, plural* **swordfish** or **swordfishes.**

Swordfish

swore He *swore* he was telling the truth. Look up **swear** for more information.
  swore (swôr) *verb.*

sworn Mr. Chandler was *sworn* in as mayor. Look up **swear** for more information.
  sworn (swôrn) *verb.*

swum She has *swum* in the lake all day. Look up **swim** for more information.
  swum (swum) *verb.*

swung Jerry *swung* the bat at the ball. Look up **swing** for more information.
swung (swung) *verb.*

sycamore A tree with smooth, brown bark that peels off in thin layers.
syc·a·more (sik′ə môr′) *noun, plural* **sycamores.**

Leaf

Sycamore Tree

syllabify To divide a word into syllables.
syl·lab·i·fy (si lab′ə fī′) *verb,* **syllabified, syllabifying.**

syllable **1.** A single spoken sound that forms a word or part of a word. The word "break" is said in one *syllable.* The word "important" is said in three *syllables.* **2.** A letter or group of letters used in writing to represent a syllable. A syllable shows where a word may be divided at the end of a line.
syl·la·ble (sil′ə bəl) *noun, plural* **syllables.**

symbol Something that stands for or represents something else. The dove is a *symbol* of peace. The mark + is the *symbol* for addition. ▲ Another word that sounds like this is **cymbal.**
sym·bol (sim′bəl) *noun, plural* **symbols.**

symbolize To be a symbol of; stand for. The owl *symbolizes* wisdom.
sym·bol·ize (sim′bə līz′) *verb,* **symbolized, symbolizing.**

symmetry A balanced arrangement of parts on either side of a line or around a center. A snowflake has *symmetry.*
sym·me·try (sim′ə trē) *noun, plural* **symmetries.**

sympathetic **1.** Feeling or showing kindness and pity toward others. A sympathetic person shares and understands the sorrow or trouble of others. A *sympathetic* neighbor brought flowers to the sick woman. **2.** In favor of. Dad is *sympathetic* to our plans for a picnic.

sym·pa·thet·ic (sim′pə thet′ik) *adjective.*

sympathy **1.** The ability to share and understand the sorrow or trouble of others. Frank had *sympathy* for the hurt dog. Everyone felt *sympathy* for the people who had lost their homes in the flood. **2.** Favor; support. The teacher is in *sympathy* with our plan for a science project.
sym·pa·thy (sim′pə thē) *noun, plural* **sympathies.**

symphony **1.** A long musical composition written for an orchestra. A symphony usually has four parts. **2.** A large orchestra that plays symphonies.
sym·pho·ny (sim′fə nē) *noun, plural* **symphonies.**

symptom A sign of something. A sore throat often is a *symptom* of a cold.
symp·tom (simp′təm) *noun, plural* **symptoms.**

synagogue A building that is used by Jews for worship and religious instruction.
syn·a·gogue (sin′ə gog′) *noun, plural* **synagogues.**

synonym A word that has the same or almost the same meaning as another word. "Large" is a *synonym* of "big."
syn·o·nym (sin′ə nim) *noun, plural* **synonyms.**

synonymous Having the same or almost the same meaning. The words "leap" and "jump" are *synonymous.*
syn·on·y·mous (sin on′ə məs) *adjective.*

synthetic Made by people; not found in nature. Plastic is a *synthetic* material.
syn·thet·ic (sin thet′ik) *adjective.*

syrup A thick, sweet liquid. Some syrups are made by boiling sugar with water or fruit juice.
syr·up (sir′əp *or* sur′əp) *noun, plural* **syrups.**

system **1.** A group of things that form a whole. Our state has a good *system* of roads. The Rockies are a main mountain *system* of North America. **2.** A group of laws, beliefs, or facts. In school we learned about the American *system* of government. **3.** An orderly method. Steve has a good *system* for studying.
sys·tem (sis′təm) *noun, plural* **systems.**

at; āpe; cär; end; mē; it; īce; hot; ōld;
fôrk; wood; fōol; oil; out; up; turn; sing;
thin; this; hw in white; zh in treasure.
ə stands for a in about, e in taken
i in pencil, o in lemon, and u in circus.

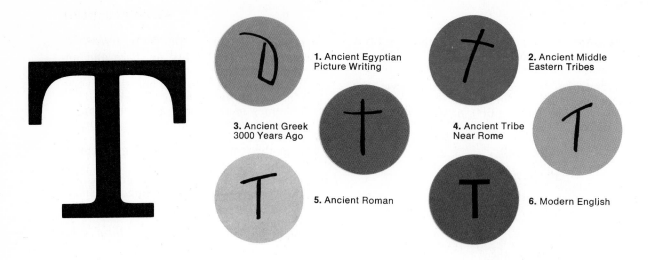

1. Ancient Egyptian Picture Writing

2. Ancient Middle Eastern Tribes

3. Ancient Greek 3000 Years Ago

4. Ancient Tribe Near Rome

5. Ancient Roman

6. Modern English

T is the twentieth letter of the alphabet. The oldest form of the letter **T** was a drawing that the ancient Egyptians (**1**) used in their picture writing nearly 5000 years ago. This drawing was borrowed by several ancient tribes (**2**) in the Middle East. They wrote it very much like a modern lower case **t**. The ancient Greeks (**3**) borrowed this letter and continued to write it as earlier people had. This letter was borrowed by an ancient tribe (**4**) that settled north of Rome about 2800 years ago. They changed its shape by drawing the short line at the top, rather than in the middle, of the letter. The Romans (**5**) borrowed this new form of **T.** By about 2400 years ago the Romans were writing this letter in almost the same way that we write the capital letter **T** today (**6**).

t, T   The twentieth letter of the alphabet.
　　t, T (tē) *noun, plural* **t's, T's.**

tab   A small flap that sticks out from something. She opened the can of soda by pulling the *tab*.
　　tab (tab) *noun, plural* **tabs.**

table   **1.** A piece of furniture with a flat top supported by one or more legs. The *table* in the dining room can seat eight people. **2.** The food served at a table or any other place. My mother always sets a good *table*. **3.** A list of facts or information. The *table* of contents is always in the front of a book.
　　ta·ble (tā′bəl) *noun, plural* **tables.**

tablespoon   A large spoon that is used to serve and measure food. A tablespoon holds the same amount as three teaspoons.
　　ta·ble·spoon (tā′bəl spoon′) *noun, plural* **tablespoons.**

tablet   **1.** A number of sheets of paper held together at one edge; pad. Pat bought a *tablet* of writing paper at the stationery store. **2.** A small, flat piece of medicine or candy. He took some *tablets* to help get rid of his cold. **3.** A thin, flat slab of wood or stone. Before paper was invented, the ancient Egyptians used to write on stone *tablets*.
　　tab·let (tab′lit) *noun, plural* **tablets.**

table tennis   A game that is similar to tennis. It is played on a table with a small plastic ball and wooden paddles.

tack   **1.** A small nail that has a sharp point and a broad, flat head. **2.** A course of action. We decided to take a new *tack* in trying to solve the problem. *Noun.*
　　—1. To fasten with a tack or tacks. Chris *tacked* posters to the walls of his room. **2.** To attach or add. I think you should *tack* a bow onto the dress right here. *Verb.*
　　tack (tak) *noun, plural* **tacks;** *verb,* **tacked, tacking.**

tackle   **1.** The equipment used for some activity or sport. Ron asked his sister if she knew where his fishing *tackle* was. **2.** A system of ropes and pulleys used for raising and lowering heavy loads. Tackle is used for raising and lowering the sails on a ship. **3.** The act of stopping and bringing to the ground. Eddie's *tackle* of the player who was running for a touchdown saved the game for his team. *Noun.*
　　—1. To deal with; work on. How do you think we should *tackle* this problem? **2.** To stop and bring to the ground. The policeman *tackled* the fleeing burglar. *Verb.*
　　tack·le (tak′əl) *noun, plural* **tackles;** *verb,* **tackled, tackling.**

tact   The ability to say or do the right thing when dealing with people or difficult situations. When Jack asked me if I liked his awful new purple and green tie, I tried to use *tact* when I answered that it was very colorful.
　　tact (takt) *noun.*

tadpole A very young frog or toad when it still lives under water and has gills, a tail, and no legs.

tad·pole (tad′pōl′) *noun, plural* tadpoles.

Tadpole

taffy A chewy candy made out of brown sugar or molasses mixed with butter. Taffy is pulled until it holds its shape.

taf·fy (taf′ē) *noun, plural* taffies.

tag¹ A piece of paper, plastic, or other material that is attached to or hanging from something. The price *tag* says this shirt costs ten dollars. *Noun.*
—**1.** To attach a tag to. My suitcases are *tagged* with my name and address so I won't lose them. **2.** To follow closely. The dog *tagged* along wherever the boys went. *Verb.*

tag (tag) *noun, plural* tags; *verb,* tagged, tagging.

tag² A game in which one player, called "it," chases the other players until he touches one. The player who is touched then becomes "it" and must chase the others. *Noun.*
—To touch or tap. Peter *tagged* his sister, so she was "it." *Verb.*

tag (tag) *noun; verb,* tagged, tagging.

tail **1.** The part of an animal's body that sticks out from the back end. Our dog wags his *tail* when he sees us coming home from school. **2.** Anything that is shaped like a tail. The *tail* of a comet is made up of gases and solid material. **3.** The end or rear part of anything. The airplane had an exit in the *tail* that could be used in case of emergency. *Noun.*
—To follow closely and secretly. The secret agent *tailed* the spy. *Verb.*
—At or coming from the rear. That bird has beautiful blue *tail* feathers. *Adjective.* ▲ Another word that sounds like this is **tale.**

tail (tāl) *noun, plural* tails; *verb,* tailed, tailing; *adjective.*

tailor A person who makes, alters, or repairs clothing. *Noun.*
—To make as a tailor does. He *tailored* the suit so that it would fit the customer perfectly. *Verb.*

tai·lor (tā′lər) *noun, plural* tailors; *verb,* tailored, tailoring.

take **1.** To get hold of. The mother reached down to *take* her child's hand as they crossed the street. Andy *took* a book from the shelf. **2.** To capture or win by using force or skill.

The invading army *took* many prisoners. John's painting *took* first prize. **3.** To get, use, or carry something. Jill *took* a seat near the front of the bus. My parents only *took* two suitcases on their trip. My sister *takes* the bus home from work. **4.** To move or remove. *Take* the trash to the town dump. If you *take* 3 from 5, you get 2. **5.** To lead or conduct. This staircase will *take* you to the street. Fred *took* Mary to the party. **6.** To receive or accept. Mother makes us *take* our vitamins every day. *Take* my advice and don't bother Dad about that right now. Our team really *took* a beating in that game. **7.** To make or do. Let's *take* a walk. I have to *take* a history test this morning. Dick *took* a photograph of our house. **8.** To need or require. It *takes* practice to learn how to play the guitar. **9.** To have a sense of; feel. Frank *takes* great pride in his coin collection.

take (tāk) *verb,* took, taken, taking.

to take after. To be like or resemble. Johnny *takes after* his father.

to take off. **1.** To remove. It is proper for a man to *take off* his hat when he is indoors. **2.** To rise up in flight. The airplane *took off* on time.

to take over. To assume control of. Sam is *taking over* his father's business.

to take up. **1.** To make shorter or smaller. Ruth *took up* the hem of her dress. **2.** To begin to do something. Martha decided to *take up* tennis. **3.** To occupy. Going to work and caring for her family *takes up* all of that woman's time.

taken Is this seat *taken?* Look up **take** for more information.

tak·en (tā′kən) *verb.*

takeoff The act of rising up in flight. We fastened our seat belts during *takeoff.*

take·off (tāk′ôf′) *noun, plural* takeoffs.

tale **1.** A story. The old sailor told the children a *tale* about his life at sea. **2.** A story that is not true; lie. The boy told the teacher a *tale* when she asked if he had broken the window. ▲ Another word that sounds like this is **tail.**

tale (tāl) *noun, plural* tales.

talent **1.** A natural ability or skill. Tom has a real *talent* for playing the piano. **2.** A person

at; āpe; cär; end; mē; it; īce; hot; ōld;
fôrk; wood; fōōl; oil; out; up; turn; sing;
thin; **this**; hw in white; zh in treasure.
ə stands for a in about, e in taken
i in pencil, o in lemon, and u in circus.

or persons who have talent. That movie producer is always looking for new acting *talent*.

tal·ent (tal'ənt) *noun, plural* **talents.**

talented Having or showing talent. That man is a very *talented* dancer.

tal·ent·ed (tal'ən tid) *adjective.*

talk **1.** To express ideas by using speech; speak. The baby cannot *talk* yet. **2.** To discuss. Joan *talked* with the doctor about the pain in her back. My grandmother loves to *talk* politics. **3.** To bring or persuade by speech. Jane *talked* us out of leaving early. *Verb.*
—**1.** An expression of ideas; conversation. The two friends had a long *talk*. **2.** An informal speech or lecture. The professor gave a *talk* about his trip to Africa. *Noun.*

talk (tôk) *verb,* **talked, talking;** *noun, plural* **talks.**

tall **1.** Higher than average; not short or low. My father is a *tall* man. That is a *tall* building. **2.** Having a certain height. My sister is five feet *tall*. **3.** Hard to believe; exaggerated. My uncle is always telling *tall* stories so that I never know when to believe him.

tall (tôl) *adjective,* **taller, tallest.**

tallow The fat from cattle and sheep. Tallow is used in making candles, soap, and margarine.

tal·low (tal'ō) *noun.*

talon The strong, sharp claw of an eagle or other bird of prey.

tal·on (tal'ən) *noun, plural* **talons.**

tambourine A small drum that has metal disks attached loosely around the rim. A person plays a tambourine by shaking it or hitting it with the knuckles.

tam·bou·rine (tam'bə rēn') *noun, plural* **tambourines.**

tame **1.** Taken from a wild or natural state by man and made gentle or obedient. The elephants in the circus are quite *tame*. **2.** Not fearful or shy. The deer was *tame* enough to let us feed it. *Adjective.*
—To take from a wild or natural state and make gentle or obedient. The cowboy's job was to *tame* wild horses. *Verb.*

tame (tām) *adjective,* **tamer, tamest;** *verb,* **tamed, taming.**

Tambourine

tan **1.** To make into leather by soaking in a special solution. That company *tans* cow hides for leather to make purses and belts. **2.** To make or become brown by exposure to the sun. Sun had *tanned* the mountain climber's face. *Verb.*
—**1.** A yellowish-brown color. **2.** The brown color given to a person's skin by exposure to the sun. Phyllis gets a beautiful *tan* at the beach every summer. *Noun.*
—Having the color tan. *Adjective.*

tan (tan) *verb,* **tanned, tanning;** *noun, plural* **tans;** *adjective,* **tanner, tannest.**

tangerine A small, sweet juicy fruit that is like an orange. A tangerine has a reddish-orange skin that peels easily.

tan·ge·rine (tan'jə rēn') *noun, plural* **tangerines.**

▲ The word **tangerine** comes from the French name for *Tangier*, which is a city in northern Africa. Tangerines were first brought to Europe from the city of Tangier.

---

tangle To twist together in a confused mass; snarl. The strong wind *tangled* her hair. *Verb.*
—A twisted, confused mass. The yarn was in a *tangle* after the kitten finished playing with it. *Noun.*

tan·gle (tang'gəl) *verb,* **tangled, tangling;** *noun, plural* **tangles.**

tank **1.** A large container for holding liquid or gas. The driver backed his car closer to the gas pump so the hose could reach his gas *tank*. Skin divers carry *tanks* of air on their backs so they can stay under water longer. **2.** An enclosed, armored vehicle that is used in combat. A tank has machine guns and a cannon, and moves on two continuous metal belts.

tank (tangk) *noun, plural* **tanks.**

tanker A ship, truck, or airplane that has tanks for carrying oil or other liquid.

tank·er (tang'kər) *noun, plural* **tankers.**

tanner A person whose job is making animal hides or skins into leather.

tan·ner (tan'ər) *noun, plural* **tanners.**

tantrum An outburst of bad temper or anger. The child had a *tantrum* when he didn't get what he wanted.

tan·trum (tan'trəm) *noun, plural* **tantrums.**

tap¹ **1.** To hit or strike lightly. The teacher *tapped* on the desk with a ruler for attention. **2.** To make or do by striking or hitting lightly again and again. Ted *tapped* out the beat of the music with his foot. *Verb.*

—A light or gentle blow. Ruth turned around when she felt a *tap* on her shoulder. *Noun.*
tap (tap) *verb,* **tapped, tapping;** *noun, plural* **taps.**

tap² A device for turning water or another liquid on or off; faucet. The kitchen sink has a *tap. Noun.*
—**1.** To put a hole in to draw liquid from. The farmers in Vermont *tap* the trunks of sugar maple trees to collect sap for making maple syrup. **2.** To cut into and connect with secretly in order to get information. The secret agent *tapped* the enemy's telephones. *Verb.*

Tap

tap (tap) *noun, plural* **taps;** *verb,* **tapped, tapping.**

tape A long narrow strip of cloth, paper, plastic, or some other material. Bob used *tape* to repair the tear on the page of his book. A specially-treated plastic *tape* is used to record sounds. *Noun.*
—**1.** To fasten with a tape. Nick *taped* the two pieces of paper together. **2.** To record on a specially-treated plastic tape. The television station *taped* the President's speech. *Verb.*
tape (tāp) *noun, plural* **tapes;** *verb,* **taped, taping.**

taper **1.** To make or become gradually smaller at one end. The tailor *tapered* the legs of Tom's slacks. The candle *tapers* to a point. **2.** To become less and less. Store sales *tapered* off after the Christmas holiday. ▲ Another word that sounds like this is **tapir.**
ta·per (tā′pər) *verb,* **tapered, tapering.**

tape recorder A machine that records sound on a specially-treated plastic tape. A tape recorder can then play back the sound that has been recorded.

tapestry A heavy woven fabric that is decorated with designs and pictures. Tapestries are used to hang on walls and to cover floors.
tap·es·try (tap′is trē) *noun, plural* **tapestries.**

tapeworm A long, flat worm that lives in the intestines of man and other animals.
tape·worm (tāp′wurm′) *noun, plural* **tapeworms.**

tapir A large animal that has a long nose and looks like a pig. Tapirs live in tropical America and parts of Asia. ▲ Another word that sounds like this is **taper.**
ta·pir (tā′pər) *noun, plural* **tapirs.**

Tapir

taps A bugle call that is played at the end of the day as a signal that all lights must be put out. It is also played at military funerals.
taps (taps) *noun plural.*

tar A dark sticky substance that is made from coal or wood. Tar is used to pave roads and to waterproof roofs and sheds. *Noun.*
—To cover or coat with tar. The workmen *tarred* the new highway. *Verb.*
tar (tär) *noun; verb,* **tarred, tarring.**

tarantula A hairy spider that is found in tropical areas of the world. Tarantulas have a bite that is painful but usually not dangerous.
ta·ran·tu·la (tə ran′chə lə) *noun, plural* **tarantulas.**

target **1.** A mark or object that is aimed at. He shot an arrow into the center of the *target.* The plane dropped its bombs directly on *target.* **2.** A person or thing that is made fun of or criticized. He was the *target* for the other boys' teasing after he struck out four times in the baseball game.
tar·get (tär′git) *noun, plural* **targets.**

tariff A duty or tax that a government puts on goods coming into a country. There was a high *tariff* on foreign cars.
tar·iff (tar′if) *noun, plural* **tariffs.**

tarnish **1.** To dull the shine or color of. Too much heat *tarnishes* silver. **2.** To lose shine or color. The candlesticks have *tarnished. Verb.*
—A surface coating that results from tarnishing. Some polish will take the *tarnish* off that silver platter. *Noun.*
tar·nish (tär′nish) *verb,* **tarnished, tarnishing;** *noun.*

at; āpe; cär; end; mē; it; īce; hot; ōld;
fôrk; wood; fool; oil; out; up; turn; sing;
thin; **th**is; **hw** in white; **zh** in treasure.
ə stands for **a** in about, **e** in taken
i in pencil, **o** in lemon, and **u** in circus.

tarpon   A large, silvery fish that lives along the coast of the Atlantic Ocean.
   tar·pon (tär′pən) *noun, plural* **tarpons** or **tarpon.**

Tarpon

tart[1]   **1.** Sharp in taste; not sweet. This apple is crisp and *tart*. **2.** Sharp in tone or meaning. The clerk in the store gave a *tart* answer to the customer's question.
   tart (tärt) *adjective,* **tarter, tartest.**

tart[2]   A pastry shell containing a custard, fruit, or other filling.
   tart (tärt) *noun, plural* **tarts.**

tartan   A woolen cloth with a plaid pattern. Each Scottish clan has its own special tartan.
   tar·tan (tärt′ən) *noun, plural* **tartans.**

tartar   A brownish substance that forms on the teeth. Tartar will form into a hard crust unless it is taken off by brushing the teeth.
   tar·tar (tär′tər) *noun.*

task   A piece of work to be done. Writing that long book report was quite a *task*.
   task (task) *noun, plural* **tasks.**

Tartan

tassel   **1.** A hanging group of threads or cords that are tied together at one end. The cord on the bottom of our window shade ends in a *tassel*. **2.** Anything that is like this in shape. An ear of corn has a silky *tassel* at one end.
   tas·sel (tas′əl) *noun, plural* **tassels.**

taste   **1.** The sense by which the flavor of something in the mouth is no-

Tassel

ticed. **2.** A particular flavor of food or anything else that is taken into the mouth. The four basic tastes are sweet, bitter, sour, and salty. This ham has a very salty *taste*. **3.** A small amount; sample. May I have a *taste* of your pie? The hot weather these last few days gives us a *taste* of what summer will be like. **4.** A liking or preference. I found a dress that was just the right color, but the style was not to my *taste*. **5.** A feeling of appreciation for what is good or beautiful. My brother has good *taste* in music. *Noun.*
   —**1.** To get the flavor of something by means of the sense of taste. I can *taste* the pepper in this stew. **2.** To have a particular flavor. The sauce *tastes* too sweet. **3.** To get the flavor of. *Taste* the soup to see if it needs salt. *Verb.*
   taste (tāst) *noun, plural* **tastes;** *verb,* **tasted, tasting.**

tasty   Pleasing to the sense of taste. This is a very *tasty* dessert.
   tast·y (tās′tē) *adjective,* **tastier, tastiest.**

tattered   Torn or hanging in shreds. We passed an old man in *tattered* clothes who was begging for food.
   tat·tered (tat′ərd) *adjective.*

tattle   To tell secrets. Mike's little sister always *tattles* on him.
   tat·tle (tat′əl) *verb,* **tattled, tattling.**

tattletale   A person who tells the secrets of others. My little brother is such a *tattletale* that I never tell him anything I don't want my parents to know.
   tat·tle·tale (tat′əl tāl′) *noun, plural* **tattle-tales.**

tattoo   To mark the skin with colored figures or designs. The skin is tattooed by pricking it with needles that have been dipped in colors. *Verb.*
   —A figure or design that is made by tattooing. The sailor had a *tattoo* of a ship on his arm. *Noun.*
   tat·too (ta to̅o̅′) *verb,* **tattooed, tattooing;** *noun, plural* **tattoos.**

taught   My older sister *taught* school before taking a job with the airline company. Look up **teach** for more information. ▲ Another word that sounds like this is **taut.**
   taught (tôt) *verb.*

taut   **1.** Tightly drawn or stretched; not loose. The boys made sure the ropes on the tent were *taut*. **2.** Showing tension or strain; tight. The mother's nerves were *taut* while she waited for the doctor to look at her sick child. ▲ Another word that sounds like this is **taught.**
   taut (tôt) *adjective,* **tauter, tautest.**

tavern 1. A place where alcoholic beverages are sold and drunk; bar. 2. A place where travelers can stay overnight; inn. On our trip to Virginia, we stayed in an old *tavern* that had been built in 1789.
tav·ern (tav′ərn) *noun, plural* **taverns.**

tax 1. Money that people must pay for the support of the government. Most people pay the government some part of the money they earn each year as a *tax.* 2. A heavy burden or demand; strain. The illness was a *tax* on his strength. *Noun.*
—1. To put a tax on. Our city *taxes* its citizens and uses the money to run schools, pay policemen and firemen, collect garbage, and give many other services. 2. To make a heavy demand on; strain. Nancy *taxed* her brain for hours until she solved the arithmetic problem. *Verb.*
tax (taks) *noun, plural* **taxes;** *verb,* **taxed, taxing.**

taxation The system of taxing. Taxation gives the government money to provide schools, hospitals, clean water, and many other services.
tax·a·tion (tak sā′shən) *noun.*

taxi An automobile that can be hired to take a person somewhere; taxicab. *Noun.*
—1. To ride in a taxicab. We *taxied* to the train station. 2. To move slowly along the ground or over the surface of the water. The airplane *taxied* out to the runway to take off. *Verb.*
tax·i (tak′sē) *noun, plural* **taxis;** *verb,* **taxied, taxiing** or **taxying.**

taxicab An automobile that can be hired to take a person somewhere. A taxicab usually has a meter that records the fare to be paid.
tax·i·cab (tak′sē kab′) *noun, plural* **taxicabs.**

tea 1. A drink that is made by pouring boiling water over the dried leaves of a shrub that is grown in China, Japan, and India. 2. A party that is held in the late afternoon. Tea, sandwiches, cookies, and other light refreshments are served.
tea (tē) *noun, plural* **teas.**

teach 1. To help a person to learn; show how. Mrs. Cameron *teaches* us reading and spelling. 2. To give lessons or classes in. My older sister has a summer job *teaching* swimming in a camp.
teach (tēch) *verb,* **taught, teaching.**

teacher A person who gives lessons or classes. My father is an English *teacher.*
teach·er (tē′chər) *noun, plural* **teachers.**

teakettle A small covered kettle with a spout and handle. It is used to boil water.

tea·ket·tle (tē′ket′əl) *noun, plural* **teakettles.**

teal A small duck with a short neck. Teals live in rivers and swampy areas.
teal (tēl) *noun, plural* **teals** or **teal.**

Teal

team 1. A group that plays or acts together. Our school has a good hockey *team* this year. A *team* of scientists worked on the new missile project. 2. Two or more horses or other animals that are harnessed together to do work. In many parts of the world, a *team* of oxen is still used to pull a plow. *Noun.*
—To work together; form a team. The children *teamed* up to collect money to buy the teacher a Christmas present. *Verb.* ▲ Another word that sounds like this is **teem.**
team (tēm) *noun, plural* **teams;** *verb,* **teamed, teaming.**

tear¹ 1. To pull or become pulled apart. Jill made a mistake and had to *tear* up the report she was writing and start over again. I *tore* a hole in my coat when I caught it on a nail. 2. To cut or wound. The thorn from the rose *tore* Bob's finger. 3. To move quickly or by force. When Margo noticed how late it was, she *tore* out of the house. 4. To divide or split into sides. The country was *torn* by a civil war. *Verb.*
—A torn part or place. The tailor sewed the *tear* in my coat. *Noun.*
tear (ter) *verb,* **tore, torn, tearing;** *noun, plural* **tears.**

tear² 1. A drop of clear, salty liquid that

at; āpe; cär; end; mē; it; īce; hot; ōld;
fôrk; wood; fōōl; oil; out; up; turn; sing;
thin; **th**is; **hw** in white; **zh** in treasure.
ə stands for **a** in about, **e** in taken
i in pencil, **o** in lemon, and **u** in circus.

comes from the eye. Tears form when you cry, or when you get something in your eye. **2. tears.** The act of crying. Joe burst into *tears* when he cut his finger. ▲ Another word that sounds like this is **tier.**

　tear (tēr) *noun, plural* **tears.**

tease　To annoy or make fun of in a playful way. John *teased* his little sister by pulling her braids. *Verb.*

　—A person who annoys or makes fun of people. Ann is a *tease,* but she doesn't mean any harm by it. *Noun.*

　tease (tēz) *verb,* **teased, teasing;** *noun, plural* **teases.**

teaspoon　A spoon that is used to eat with and measure food. Three teaspoons hold the same amount as one tablespoon.

　tea·spoon (tē′spo͞on′) *noun, plural* **teaspoons.**

technical　**1.** Having to do with a science, art, or profession. The judge explained the case in the *technical* language of the law. **2.** Having to do with engineering or any of the mechanical or industrial arts. My brother goes to a *technical* school where he is learning to be an electrician.

　tech·ni·cal (tek′ni kəl) *adjective.*

technique　A method or way of bringing about a desired result in a science, art, sport, or profession. My sister is learning the *techniques* of painting at art school. Jack is practicing a new *technique* for pitching the ball in baseball.

　tech·nique (tek nēk′) *noun, plural* **techniques.**

technology　The science that has to do with engineering or the mechanical or industrial arts.

　tech·nol·o·gy (tek nol′ə jē) *noun.*

tedious　Long and tiring; boring. Helping Dad wash the windows in our house is a *tedious* job.

　te·di·ous (tē′dē əs *or* tē′jəs) *adjective.*

teem　To be full; swarm. The creek near our house *teems* with fish. By noon the beach was *teeming* with people. ▲ Another word that sounds like this is **team.**

　teem (tēm) *verb,* **teemed, teeming.**

teenager　A person who is between the ages of thirteen and nineteen.

　teen·ag·er (tēn′ā′jər) *noun, plural* **teenagers.**

teens　The years of one's life between thirteen and nineteen. When I was still in my *teens,* our family moved to Chicago.

　teens (tēnz) *noun plural.*

teeth　More than one tooth. Look up **tooth** for more information.

　teeth (tēth) *noun plural.*

telegram　A message that is sent by telegraph.

　tel·e·gram (tel′ə gram′) *noun, plural* **telegrams.**

telegraph　The system or equipment used for sending messages over a long distance. The message is sent in code over wires by means of electricity. *Noun.*

　—To send by telegraph. Friends and relatives who could not come to the wedding *telegraphed* good wishes to the couple. *Verb.*

　tel·e·graph (tel′ə graf′) *noun, plural* **telegraphs;** *verb,* **telegraphed, telegraphing.**

telephone　**1.** The system for sending sound or speech over wires by means of electricity. **2.** An instrument used to send sound or speech over a distance. A telephone has two parts. You speak into one part and hear with the other. There is also a dial to signal the person you want to talk to. *Noun.*

　—**1.** To talk with someone by telephone. I will *telephone* you tomorrow. **2.** To send by telephone. My aunt *telephoned* her love and good wishes on my birthday. *Verb.*

　tel·e·phone (tel′ə fōn′) *noun, plural* **telephones;** *verb,* **telephoned, telephoning.**

▲ The word **telephone** comes from two Greek words that mean "far away" and "sound or voice." A telephone lets someone hear sounds from far away.

telescope　An instrument that makes distant objects seem larger and nearer. A telescope uses a system of lenses or mirrors to make things look bigger. Telescopes are very useful for studying the stars and other bodies in outer space.

　tel·e·scope (tel′ə skōp′) *noun, plural* **telescopes.**

Telescope

televise　To send by television. All the major stations *televised* man's first walk on the moon.

　tel·e·vise (tel′ə vīz′) *verb,* **televised, televising.**

television　**1.** A system for sending and receiving pictures and sound over long distances by means of electricity. **2.** A set or device on which these pictures are seen and the sound is heard.

　tel·e·vi·sion (tel′ə vizh′ən) *noun, plural* **televisions.**

tell　**1.** To put in words; say. When we were little, Mother used to *tell* us a story before we went to sleep. *Tell* us about your vacation. **2.** To give an order to; command. Mother *told* us to stop making so much noise.

tell (tel) *verb,* **told, telling.**

teller **1.** A person who tells or relates. The old sea captain is a wonderful *teller* of tales of adventure. **2.** A person who works in a bank giving out and receiving money.

tell·er (tel′ər) *noun, plural* **tellers.**

temper **1.** A tendency to become angry or irritated. My sister has quite a *temper* when she does not get her own way. **2.** A usual state of mind. Father has an even *temper,* and few things really upset him. **3.** Control over the emotions. Dan lost his *temper* and stormed out of the house. *Noun.*
—To lessen the harshness of; soften. The teacher *tempered* her criticism of the student's work by saying that she thought it was getting better. *Verb.*

tem·per (tem′pər) *noun, plural* **tempers;** *verb,* **tempered, tempering.**

temperate Not too hot and not too cold. Most areas of the United States have a *temperate* climate.

tem·per·ate (tem′pər it) *adjective.*

temperature The degree of heat or coldness. The temperature of a person's body or of the weather outdoors is measured by a thermometer. The nurse sent Mark home from school today with a *temperature* of 102 degrees. The radio announcer says the *temperature* will drop to fifteen degrees before morning.

tem·per·a·ture (tem′pər ə chər) *noun, plural* **temperatures.**

temple¹ A building that is used for the worship of a god or gods. When we were in Greece, we saw the ruins of the ancient *temples.* People of the Jewish religion worship in *temples.*

tem·ple (tem′pəl) *noun, plural* **temples.**

Temple

temple² The flattened part on either side of the forehead. The temple is above the cheekbone and in front of the ear.

tem·ple (tem′pəl) *noun, plural* **temples.**

temporary Lasting or used for a short time only. Phil tried to find a *temporary* job for the summer until school started in September.

tem·po·rar·y (tem′pə rer′ē) *adjective.*

tempt **1.** To persuade to do something that is wrong or foolish. The fear of getting a poor mark *tempted* the girl to cheat on the final test. **2.** To appeal strongly to; attract. The chocolate cake *tempted* him. **3.** To act in a bold way toward. The woman *tempted* fate by swimming alone in the ocean at night.

tempt (tempt) *verb,* **tempted, tempting.**

ten One more than nine; 10.

ten (ten) *noun, plural* **tens;** *adjective.*

tenant A person who pays money to use a house, apartment, office, or land that belongs to someone else.

ten·ant (ten′ənt) *noun, plural* **tenants.**

tend¹ **1.** To be likely or apt. My sister has to be careful not to eat too much because she *tends* to gain weight easily. **2.** To lead to or be directed to. Unclean living conditions *tend* to produce disease. The road *tends* to the left just ahead.

tend (tend) *verb,* **tended, tending.**

tend² To take care of or look after. Our neighbor *tended* our plants while we were away on vacation.

tend (tend) *verb,* **tended, tending.**

tendency A natural or usual leaning or inclination. My brother has a *tendency* to get angry if he is criticized.

tend·en·cy (ten′dən sē) *noun, plural* **tendencies.**

tender **1.** Not tough or hard; soft. This steak is very *tender.* **2.** Not strong; delicate. The *tender* leaves of the young plant became limp in the hot sun. **3.** Kind or loving. The mother gave her child a *tender* look. **4.** Very sensitive; painful. Lucy's arm was still *tender* after the cut had healed. Yesterday's baseball game is a *tender* subject with Ted because he played so badly.

ten·der (ten′dər) *adjective.*

tendon A strong cord or band of tissue that

at; āpe; cär; end; mē; it; īce; hot; ōld;
fôrk; wood; fool; oil; out; up; turn; sing;
thin; this; hw in white; zh in treasure.
ə stands for a in about, e in taken
i in pencil, o in lemon, and u in circus.

attaches a muscle to a bone or other part of the body.

ten·don (ten′dən) *noun, plural* **tendons.**

tenement An old apartment building in a poor section of a city. A tenement is usually in bad condition and has too many people living in it.

ten·e·ment (ten′ə mənt) *noun, plural* **tenements.**

Tennessee A state in the southeastern United States. Its capital is Nashville.

Ten·nes·see (ten′ə sē′) *noun.*

▲ **Tennessee** comes from the name that the Cherokee Indian tribe had for their ancient capital city. The name is so old that we do not know what the word meant before it became the name of this city. The name was used for a stream near the city, and the river that the stream runs into soon was also called Tennessee. The name of the state came from the Tennessee River.

Tennis

tennis A game in which two or four players hit a ball over a net with a racket. Tennis is played on courts of grass, clay, concrete, or other material.

ten·nis (ten′is) *noun.*

tenor **1.** A man's singing voice that is lower than an alto and higher than a bass. **2.** A singer who has such a voice. **3.** A musical instrument that has the range of a tenor voice.

ten·or (ten′ər) *noun, plural* **tenors.**

tense¹ **1.** Stretched or drawn tight; strained. Peter's muscles were *tense* as he tried to lift the heavy trunk. **2.** Showing or causing strain or suspense. Linda gave her mother a *tense* look before going into the dentist's office. *Adjective.*

—To make or become tense. Michael *tensed* when he heard that the principal wanted to see him. *Verb.*

tense (tens) *adjective,* **tenser, tensest;** *verb,* **tensed, tensing.**

tense² The form of a verb that shows the time of its action or its state of being. He *sits* is in the present tense. He *sat* is in the past tense. He *will sit* is in the future tense.

tense (tens) *noun, plural* **tenses.**

tent A moveable shelter that is made out of canvas or nylon. A tent is held up by one or more poles and tied with cord to pegs in the ground.

tent (tent) *noun, plural* **tents.**

tentacle A long, thin growth of certain animals. Tentacles are used to feel, grasp, and move. An octopus has eight tentacles. A jellyfish uses its tentacles to draw food into its mouth.

ten·ta·cle (ten′tə kəl) *noun, plural* **tentacles.**

tenth **1.** Next after the ninth. **2.** One of ten equal parts; ¹/₁₀.

tenth (tenth) *adjective; noun, plural* **tenths.**

tepee A cone-shaped tent that is made of animal skins stretched over poles. Tepees were used by some tribes of North American Indians.

te·pee (tē′pē′) *noun, plural* **tepees.**

▲ The word **tepee** comes from a word that Indians who lived on the plains of North America used for this kind of tent. This word was made up of two other Indian words that meant "to be used for living."

Tepee

term **1.** A word or group of words that has a specific meaning. "Pneumonia" is a medical

term. "Serve," "set," and "racket" are *terms* used in tennis. **2.** A definite or limited period of time. The *term* of office for the President of the United States is four years. During the spring *term* at school, everyone is busy studying for final tests. **3. terms.** A relationship between people. We are on good *terms* with our neighbors. **4. terms.** The conditions under which something is to be done. The *terms* of the peace treaty were accepted by all the countries that had fought in the war. *Noun.*
—To call or name. Sandra is *termed* beautiful by everyone who knows her. *Verb.*

term (turm) *noun, plural* **terms;** *verb,* **termed, terming.**

terminal A station at either end of a railroad, bus, air, or other transportation line. When Grandma comes to visit, we meet her at the bus *terminal.*

ter·mi·nal (tur′mən əl) *noun, plural* **terminals.**

termite An insect that has a white body and a dark head. Termites live in large groups and eat wood, paper, and other similar material. Termites can cause great damage to buildings, furniture, and some crops.

ter·mite (tur′mīt) *noun, plural* **termites.**

terrace **1.** A paved outdoor space next to a house that is used for lounging and eating. **2.** A balcony of an apartment house. **3.** A raised level of earth with sides that are either straight up and down or sloping. Farmers often build terraces on hillsides to make more flat space for growing crops.

ter·race (ter′is) *noun, plural* **terraces.**

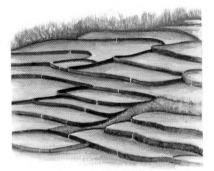

Terraces

terrible **1.** Causing fear or terror; awful. The volcano erupted with a *terrible* roar. **2.** Very bad. We had *terrible* weather on our vacation.

ter·ri·ble (ter′ə bəl) *adjective.*

terrier One of various lively, small dogs that can have either a smooth or wiry coat. Terriers were once used to hunt animals that burrow in the ground.

ter·ri·er (ter′ē ər) *noun, plural* **terriers.**

Terrier

terrific **1.** Unusually great or severe. That family has had to undergo *terrific* difficulties ever since their home was washed away in the flood. **2.** Extremely good; wonderful. That's a *terrific* idea!

ter·rif·ic (tə rif′ik) *adjective.*

terrify To fill with terror; frighten greatly. The child was *terrified* by the bad dream she had.

ter·ri·fy (ter′ə fī′) *verb,* **terrified, terrifying.**

territory **1.** Any large area of land; region. The plane was shot down over enemy *territory.* **2.** Land that is under the control of a distant government. A territory does not have the full rights of a state or province. Hawaii was a *territory* of the United States until it became a state in 1959.

ter·ri·to·ry (ter′ə tôr′ē) *noun, plural* **territories.**

terror **1.** Great fear. The child was filled with *terror* when she got lost in the woods. **2.** A person or thing that causes great fear. The cruel dictator was a *terror* to the people of the country.

ter·ror (ter′ər) *noun, plural* **terrors.**

test **1.** A set of problems or exercises; examination. A test is used to determine a person's knowledge or skill. The teacher announced that there would be a spelling *test* on Friday. **2.** Any method of finding out the nature or quality of something. The doctor did a blood *test* on the patient. *Noun.*
—To put to a test of any kind. The teacher *tested* the class in arithmetic. *Verb.*

at; āpe; cär; end; mē; it; īce; hot; ōld;
fôrk; wood; fōōl; oil; out; up; turn; sing;
thin; **th**is; hw in white; zh in treasure.
ə stands for a in about, e in taken
i in pencil, o in lemon, and u in circus.

test (test) *noun, plural* **tests;** *verb,* **tested, testing.**

Testament Either of two main divisions of the Bible. The Old Testament deals with the time before the birth of Jesus. The New Testament deals with the time after the birth of Jesus.
Tes·ta·ment (tes′tə mənt) *noun, plural* **Testaments.**

testify To give evidence or proof. I can *testify* to his honesty. The man *testified* that the defendant was innocent.
tes·ti·fy (tes′tə fī′) *verb,* **testified, testifying.**

testimony 1. A statement made under oath by a witness in a court of law. The *testimony* of people who saw the crime led the jury to find the accused man guilty. 2. Proof or evidence. The students bought their teacher a present at the end of school as *testimony* of their appreciation for her.
tes·ti·mo·ny (tes′tə mō′nē) *noun, plural* **testimonies.**

test tube A thin glass tube that is closed at one end. A test tube is used in scientific experiments.

tetanus A serious disease that is caused by a germ that enters the body through a deep, narrow wound. Tetanus causes extreme stiffness of some muscles. A person can be protected from tetanus by getting a shot from a doctor. This disease is also called **lockjaw.**
tet·a·nus (tet′ən əs) *noun.*

Test Tubes

Texas A state in the south-central United States. Its capital is Austin.
Tex·as (tek′səs) *noun.*

▲ **Texas** comes from an Indian word that means "friends." Spanish explorers used the name for Indians who lived in part of the land that is now Texas. These Spaniards also heard Indian tales of an area called "the great kingdom of Texas." This led Spanish settlers to name their territory *Texas*, and the name was kept by the state.

text 1. The main body of reading matter in a book. The *text* in each chapter of this book is followed by homework questions. 2. The original or actual words of a writer or speaker. The newspaper printed the full *text* of the President's speech. 3. Any subject on which a person writes or speaks. The *text* for the minister's sermon was taken from a recent newspaper headline.
text (tekst) *noun, plural* **texts.**

textbook A book that is used in school for the study of a particular subject. Alice lost her history *textbook.*
text·book (tekst′book′) *noun, plural* **textbooks.**

textile A fabric that is made by weaving or knitting. Cotton and wool are textiles. *Noun.* —Having to do with textiles or their manufacture. Our class visited a *textile* factory to see how cotton is made into cloth. *Adjective.*
tex·tile (teks′tīl *or* teks′til) *noun, plural* **textiles;** *adjective.*

texture The look and feel of something. Silk has a smooth *texture.* Sandpaper has a rough *texture.*
tex·ture (teks′chər) *noun, plural* **textures.**

than A cow is bigger *than* a rabbit. I would rather play outside *than* do my homework.
than (than *or* thən) *conjunction.*

thank 1. To say that one is pleased or grateful. *Thank* you for your help. Bob *thanked* his brother for the birthday present. 2. To hold responsible; blame. He has only himself to *thank* for failing the test.
thank (thangk) *verb,* **thanked, thanking.**

thankful Feeling or expressing thanks; grateful. Mike was *thankful* for his father's help with his homework.
thank·ful (thangk′fəl) *adjective.*

thanks I thank you. *Thanks* for the help. *Interjection.* —An expression or feeling of gratitude. The family gave *thanks* that no one had been hurt in the fire. *Noun.*
thanks (thangks) *interjection; noun plural.*

Thanksgiving A holiday in the United States celebrated as a day of thanksgiving and feasting. It observes the memory of the harvest feast celebrated by the Pilgrims in 1621. It falls on the fourth Thursday in November.
Thanks·giv·ing (thangks′giv′ing) *noun, plural* **Thanksgivings.**

that *That* girl won the prize. I want to wear this coat instead of *that* one. *That* is the same boy I sat next to on the bus yesterday. I prefer this dress to *that.* The boy *that* lives next door is in my class at school. I'm sorry *that* you can't come to the party. He stayed up so late *that* he was tired the next day.
that (that) *adjective; pronoun, plural* **those;** *conjunction; adverb.*

thatch   Straw, reeds, or similar material that is used to cover a roof. *Noun.*
—To cover a roof with thatch. The farmer *thatched* the roof of his house with straw. *Verb.*
thatch (thach) *noun; verb,* **thatched, thatching.**

A House With a Thatched Roof

that's   *That's* the book I left here yesterday.
that's (th<u>a</u>ts) contraction for "that is."

thaw   **1.** To free or become free of frost or ice; melt. The sun *thawed* the snow on the roof. The ice on the road *thawed* from the heat of the sun. **2.** To become warm. The ice skaters *thawed* out in front of a large fire. The unfriendly relations between the two countries began to *thaw. Verb.*
—Weather that is warm enough to melt ice and snow. When the spring *thaw* came, water from melting snow flooded the river. *Noun.*
thaw (thô) *verb,* **thawed, thawing;** *noun, plural* **thaws.**

the¹   Close *the* door. *The* moon is full tonight. *The* lion is found in Africa. A stone hit him on *the* arm. *The* President will give a very important speech today.
the (th<u>ə</u> *or* th<u>ē</u>) *definite article.*

the²   *The* sooner you finish your homework, *the* more time you will have to play outside.
the (th<u>ə</u> *or* th<u>ē</u>) *adverb.*

theater   A building or other place where plays or motion pictures are presented. This word is also spelled **theatre.**
the·a·ter (thē′<u>ə</u> tər) *noun, plural* **theaters.**

thee   An old form of the word "you." "May no harm come to *thee*," said the king.
thee (th<u>ē</u>) *pronoun.*

theft   The act of stealing. The man was arrested by the police for auto *theft.*
theft (theft) *noun, plural* **thefts.**

their   *Their* house is the white one at the end of the road. Were any of *their* friends at the party? ▲ Other words that sound like this are **there** and **they're.**
their (ther) *adjective.*

theirs   Our car is new; *theirs* is old. After Susan and her brother came to my house, I went to *theirs.*
theirs (th<u>e</u>rz) *pronoun.*

them   Rick knew which train his grandparents were taking, and he met *them* at the station.
them (<u>th</u>em *or* <u>th</u>əm) *pronoun.*

theme   **1.** The main subject or idea of something. The *theme* of the book was the loyalty of a dog to his master. **2.** The main tune from a piece of music.
theme (th<u>ē</u>m) *noun, plural* **themes.**

themselves   The children built the tree house *themselves.* The dinner guests seated *themselves* around the table. The players on the losing team were not *themselves* today.
them·selves (<u>th</u>em selvz′ *or* <u>th</u>əm selvz′) *pronoun.*

then   The play ended and *then* the curtain went down. If you don't think you'll read the book, *then* give it back to me. I hope we will finish the work before *then.*
then (<u>th</u>en) *adverb; noun.*

theory   **1.** A group of ideas or principles that explain why something happens. The *theory* of gravity explains why a leaf falls to the ground when it comes off a tree. The fire department has a *theory* about how the fire started. **2.** The rules or methods of an art or science, rather than its practice. His courses at college gave Doug a good understanding of the *theory* of how an airplane flies, but he had never actually flown one himself.
the·o·ry (thē′ər ē) *noun, plural* **theories.**

there   Just put the packages down *there.* We had wanted to see the new park, so we walked *there* after lunch. *There* is no more milk. Hello *there;* how are you today? Do you know the way home from *there? There, there!* Don't worry. ▲ Other words that sound like this are **their** and **they're.**
there (ther) *adverb; noun; interjection.*

thereafter   The sun shone the first day of

at; āpe; cär; end; mē; it; īce; hot; ōld;
fôrk; wood; fōōl; oil; out; up; turn; sing;
thin; <u>th</u>is; hw in white; zh in treasure.
ə stands for a in about, e in taken
i in pencil, o in lemon, and u in circus.

their vacation, but it rained every day *there-after.*

there·af·ter (<u>th</u>er af′tər) *adverb.*

thereby Larry won the race, *thereby* winning the championship for his school.

there·by (<u>th</u>er bī′) *adverb.*

therefore Nancy hurt her leg in gym class and *therefore* had to go to the nurse.

there·fore (<u>th</u>er′fôr′) *adverb.*

there's *There's* some sliced ham and cheese in the refrigerator if you are hungry.

there's (<u>th</u>erz) contraction for "there is."

thermometer A device for measuring temperature. Most thermometers are thin glass tubes that contain mercury or alcohol. The column of mercury or alcohol rises or falls as the temperature changes.

ther·mom·e·ter (thər mom′ə tər) *noun, plural* **thermometers.**

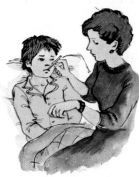

Thermometer

thermos bottle A container made to keep liquids hot or cold for many hours.

ther·mos bottle (thur′məs).

thermostat A device that automatically controls temperature. Thermostats control the temperature in furnaces, ovens, and refrigerators.

ther·mo·stat (thur′mə stat′) *noun, plural* **thermostats.**

these The plural of **this.** Look up **this** for more information.

these (<u>th</u>ēz) *adjective; pronoun plural.*

they Susan and Bob were late because *they* missed the train.

they (<u>th</u>ā) *pronoun plural.*

they'd *They'd* better leave now or they will be late for the show. *They'd* be too polite to leave without saying good-by.

they'd (<u>th</u>ād) contraction for "they had" and "they would."

they'll *They'll* be back before you know it. *They'll* somehow manage to come for a visit this summer.

they'll (<u>th</u>āl) contraction for "they will" and "they shall."

they're *They're* supposed to be in school by nine o'clock. ▲ Other words that sound like this are **their** and **there.**

they're (<u>th</u>er) contraction for "they are."

they've *They've* played this game before, so they know what to do.

they've (<u>th</u>āv) contraction for "they have."

thick **1.** Having much space between one side or surface and the other; not thin. The outside walls of this old building are very *thick.* **2.** Measured from one side or surface to the other. That stone wall is three feet *thick.* **3.** That does not flow or pour easily. Mother makes delicious *thick* pea soup. **4.** Growing or being close together; dense. The hikers had trouble making their way through the *thick* forest. *Adjective.*
—So as to be thick. Dad asked the butcher to cut the steaks *thick. Adverb.*
—The part or place of greatest activity or danger. The brave soldier was in the *thick* of the fight. *Noun.*

thick (thik) *adjective,* **thicker, thickest;** *adverb; noun.*

thicken To make or become thick or thicker. Mother *thickened* the gravy.

thick·en (thik′ən) *verb,* **thickened, thickening.**

thicket A thick growth of shrubs or bushes.

thick·et (thik′it) *noun, plural* **thickets.**

thickness **1.** The state of being thick. The *thickness* of the trees around our house makes it impossible to see any of the other houses near ours. **2.** The distance between two sides or surfaces of something; the measurement other than the length or width. The *thickness* of this piece of wood is one inch.

thick·ness (thik′nis) *noun, plural* **thicknesses.**

thief A person who steals; robber. The *thief* broke into the house and stole a fur coat.

thief (thēf) *noun, plural* **thieves.**

thieves More than one thief.

thieves (thēvz) *noun plural.*

thigh The part of the leg between the hip and the knee.

thigh (thī) *noun, plural* **thighs.**

thimble A small metal cap that is worn on the finger to protect it when pushing the needle through material in sewing.

thim·ble (thim′bəl) *noun, plural* **thimbles.**

thin **1.** Having little space between one side or surface and the other; not thick. The *thin* wrapping paper did not hide the title of the book Susan was giving as a

Thimble

present. **2.** Not fat; slender or lean. Horses have *thin*, long faces. **3.** That flows or pours easily; watery. Mother served the lamb with a *thin* sauce. **4.** Easily seen through; flimsy. Peter gave his teacher a *thin* excuse for being late to class. **5.** Not dense. It is sometimes harder to breathe on top of mountains because the air is *thin*. Father's hair is getting *thin* on the top of his head. **6.** Having a faint, shrill sound; weak. The sick woman answered the doctor's questions in a *thin* voice. *Adjective.*
—So as to be thin. I like my roast beef sliced *thin*. *Adverb.*
—To make or become thin. Mother *thinned* the gravy with a little water. Men's hair sometimes *thins* as they get older. *Verb.*
   thin (thin) *adjective,* **thinner, thinnest;** *adverb;* *verb,* **thinned, thinning.**

thing   **1.** Whatever is spoken of, thought of, or done. That was an unkind *thing* to say. A mother's love for her children is a *thing* that cannot be put into words. **2.** Something that can be touched, seen, heard, smelled, or tasted but is not alive. A book is a *thing*. The *things* on the top floor were all that was not damaged by the flood. **3.** A person or animal. The lost child was a sad *thing*. A young kitten is a soft little *thing*. **4.** Affair; matter. *Things* haven't changed since you've been gone. How are *things* at school? **5. things.** Belongings. I packed my *things* for the trip in two suitcases.
   thing (thing) *noun, plural* **things.**

think   **1.** To use the mind to form ideas or to make decisions. *Think* it over carefully before you give me your final answer. **2.** To have or form in the mind as an opinion, belief, or idea. She *thought* we were sisters. It's getting late; I *think* we should go home. Who *thought* of the first alphabet? **3.** To call to mind or remember. Robin often *thought* of her wonderful summer vacation. **4.** To have care or consideration. A person who is selfish always *thinks* of himself first.
   think (thingk) *verb,* **thought, thinking.**

third   **1.** Next after the second. **2.** One of three equal parts; $1/3$.
   third (thurd) *adjective; noun, plural* **thirds.**

thirst   **1.** An uncomfortable feeling of dryness in the mouth and throat. Thirst is caused by the need to drink water or other liquids. **2.** The desire or need for something to drink or for anything else. John satisfied his *thirst* by drinking a large glass of water. The people who went on the mountain climbing trip had a *thirst* for adventure and excitement.
   thirst (thurst) *noun, plural* **thirsts.**

thirsty   **1.** Feeling the need to drink something. Could I have some more water; I'm *thirsty*. **2.** Lacking water or moisture. The plants in the garden were *thirsty* after five days in the hot sun.
   thirst·y (thurs′tē) *adjective,* **thirstier, thirstiest.**

thirteen   Three more than ten; 13.
   thir·teen (thur′tēn′) *noun, plural* **thirteens;** *adjective.*

thirteenth   **1.** Next after the twelfth. **2.** One of thirteen equal parts; $1/13$.
   thir·teenth (thur′tēnth′) *adjective; noun, plural* **thirteenths.**

thirtieth   **1.** Next after the twenty-ninth. **2.** One of thirty equal parts; $1/30$.
   thir·ti·eth (thur′tē ith) *adjective; noun, plural* **thirtieths.**

thirty   Three times ten; 30.
   thir·ty (thur′tē) *noun, plural* **thirties;** *adjective.*

this   *This* house is ten years old. *This* dress is cheaper than that one. Is *this* your coat? *This* is mine; that is hers. Is it *this* hot here every day?
   this (<u>th</u>is) *adjective; pronoun, plural* **these;** *adverb.*

thistle   A prickly plant that has red or purple flowers.
   this·tle (this′əl) *noun, plural* **thistles.**

thong   A narrow strip of leather or other material that is used for fastening. Some sandals are held on the foot by a *thong* that fits between the first two toes.
   thong (thông) *noun, plural* **thongs.**

Thistle

thorax   **1.** The part of the body between the neck and the abdomen. The thorax includes the heart, lungs, and ribs. **2.** The part of an insect's body between the head and abdomen. The thorax includes the wings and legs.
   tho·rax (thôr′aks) *noun, plural* **thoraxes.**

at; āpe; cär; end; mē; it; īce; hot; ōld;
fôrk; wood; fo͞ol; oil; out; up; turn; sing;
thin; <u>th</u>is; hw in white; zh in treasure.
ə stands for a in about, e in taken
i in pencil, o in lemon, and u in circus.

thorn **1.** A sharp point on a branch or stem. Roses have thorns. **2.** A tree or shrub that has thorns.

thorn (thôrn) *noun, plural* **thorns.**

thorny **1.** Full of thorns; prickly. Rose bushes are very *thorny*. **2.** Causing trouble; difficult. This is going to be a very *thorny* problem to solve.

thorn·y (thôr′nē) *adjective,* **thornier, thorniest.**

thorough Leaving nothing out; careful and complete. The police made a *thorough* search for the escaped prisoners.

thor·ough (thur′ō) *adjective.*

Thorns

those The plural of **that.** Look up **that** for more information.

those (th̄oz) *adjective; pronoun plural.*

thou An old form of the word "you." "*Thou* shalt not steal" is one of the Ten Commandments in the Bible.

thou (thou) *pronoun.*

though I was late for school, *though* I got up earlier than usual. The meal was good, *though* the vegetables were cooked a little too much. Bill won't help us; you can count on Jim, *though*.

though (th̄o) *conjunction; adverb.*

thought I *thought* Dad was going to take us to the zoo this afternoon. Look up **think** for more information. *Verb.*
—**1.** The act of thinking. Jill was lost in *thought* when the teacher called on her. **2.** Ideas or opinions. What are your *thoughts* on how to solve this problem? **3.** Careful attention or consideration. The teacher warned us to give some *thought* to the questions on the test before writing the answers. *Noun.*

thought (thôt) *verb; noun, plural* **thoughts.**

thoughtful Showing or having concern and care for other people and their feelings. A thoughtful person does not do or say things that make other people unhappy. June had a *thoughtful* look on her face.

thought·ful (thôt′fəl) *adjective.*

thousand Ten times a hundred; 1000.

thou·sand (thou′zənd) *noun, plural* **thousands;** *adjective.*

thousandth **1.** Next after the 999th. **2.** One of a thousand equal parts: $1/1000$.

thou·sandth (thou′zəndth) *adjective; noun, plural* **thousandths.**

thrash **1.** To give a beating to. The farmer warned that he would *thrash* any boy he caught stealing cherries from his trees. **2.** To make wild movements; toss violently. The animal *thrashed* about trying to escape from its cage.

thrash (thrash) *verb,* **thrashed, thrashing.**

thread **1.** A very thin cord that is used in sewing and in weaving cloth. Threads can be made out of cotton, wool, silk, or any other similar material. **2.** Anything that is thin and long like a thread. A *thread* of paint dripped down the wall. **3.** The main idea or thought that connects the different parts of a story or speech. The *thread* of the story was the lost dog's struggle to find its way home again. **4.** A winding ridge that twists around a screw or nut. The threads of a screw make it hold tightly to a piece of wood or whatever it is driven into. *Noun.*
—**1.** To pass a thread through. Mother taught me how to *thread* a needle and knot the thread at one end. **2.** To make one's way in a winding or twisting manner. The newspaper reporter *threaded* his way through the crowd to see what all the excitement was about. *Verb.*

thread (thred) *noun, plural* **threads;** *verb,* **threaded, threading.**

threat **1.** A statement of something that will be done to hurt or punish. Under the *threat* of being killed, the captured soldiers told the enemy what they wanted to know. **2.** A person or thing that is the cause of danger or harm. The murderer was a *threat* to society. The outbreak of polio was a *threat* to everyone in the community. **3.** A sign or possibility of some danger or harm that might happen. The country lived under the constant *threat* of war.

threat (thret) *noun, plural* **threats.**

threaten **1.** To say what will be done to hurt or punish; make a threat of or against. The robber *threatened* the bank teller's life if she didn't hand over the money he wanted. The shop owner *threatened* to call the police if the men didn't leave his store. **2.** To be the cause of danger or harm. The lack of rain *threatened* the farmer's crops. **3.** To be a sign or possibility of. The dark clouds *threaten* rain.

threat·en (thret′ən) *verb,* **threatened, threatening.**

three One more than two; 3.

three (thrē) *noun, plural* **threes;** *adjective.*

thresh To separate grain or seeds from grass or cereal plants. Farmers today use machines to thresh their crops.

thresh (thresh) *verb,* **threshed, threshing.**

threshold 1. A piece of wood, stone, or metal that forms the bottom of a door frame. 2. A point of entering or beginning. The scientist was on the *threshold* of an important discovery.
thresh·old (thresh′ōld) *noun, plural* **thresholds.**

threw Lucy *threw* the ball back to her friend. Look up **throw** for more information. ▲ Another word that sounds like this is **through.**
threw (thrōō) *verb.*

thrifty Very careful in the use of money. Mother is very *thrifty* and tries to buy everything she can on sale.
thrift·y (thrif′tē) *adjective,* **thriftier, thriftiest.**

thrill 1. A sudden feeling of pleasure or excitement. Cindy remembered the *thrill* of getting a horse of her very own. 2. Something that gives such a sudden feeling of pleasure or excitement. Mike's first airplane ride was a *thrill* for him. *Noun.*
—To fill with pleasure or excitement. The home team's victory *thrilled* the crowd. *Verb.*
thrill (thril) *noun, plural* **thrills;** *verb,* **thrilled, thrilling.**

▲ The first meaning of **thrill** was "to pierce or pass through quickly." A knight might have *thrilled* someone with his sword, or the sound of a horn might have *thrilled* the quiet night. The idea of moving through quickly and sharply led to the meaning "to give a sudden feeling of excitement."

thrive To be successful; do well. The little plant is *thriving* in the sun.
thrive (thrīv) *verb,* **throve** or **thrived, thrived** or **thriven, thriving.**

throat 1. The passage in the body between the mouth and the stomach. All food taken in through the mouth must pass through the throat. 2. The front of the neck. Ann's new summer dress had short sleeves and was open at the *throat.* 3. Any narrow opening that is like the throat. Tom held the bottle by the *throat* and twisted off the cap.
throat (thrōt) *noun, plural* **throats.**

throb To beat or pound heavily and fast. Tim could feel his heart *throbbing* with excitement. *Verb.*
—A heavy, fast beat. A *throb* of pain shot through Robin's finger. *Noun.*
throb (throb) *verb,* **throbbed, throbbing;** *noun, plural* **throbs.**

throne 1. The chair that a king or queen sits on during ceremonies and other special occa-sions. 2. Royal power or authority. The young prince came to the *throne* after his father died. ▲ Another word that sounds like this is **thrown.**
throne (thrōn) *noun, plural* **thrones.**

throng A large number of people; crowd. A *throng* of people crowded around the movie star. *Noun.*
—To move in a large group; crowd. People from all over *thronged* to the county fair. *Verb.*
throng (thrông) *noun, plural* **throngs;** *verb,* **thronged, thronging.**

throttle A valve that controls the amount of steam or gasoline that flows to an engine. The railroad engineer opened up the *throttle* to make the train go faster.
throt·tle (throt′əl) *noun, plural* **throttles.**

through 1. From one end or side to the other. Linda read *through* the book in one day. Rick hammered the nails *through* the piece of wood. 2. To various parts or places in. Our family plans to travel *through* New England this summer. 3. By means of. We heard the news *through* our next door neighbor. *Preposition.*
—1. From one side or end to the other. The farmer opened the barnyard gate and the cattle went *through.* 2. Throughout; completely. Sarah was soaked *through* from the rain. *Adverb.*
—1. Going the whole distance with no changes and few or no stops. We got plane reservations on a *through* flight to Chicago. 2. That allows free passage. This is a dead-end street, but I think the next one is a *through* street. 3. Finished. Are you *through* with your homework yet? *Adjective.*
▲ Another word that sounds like this is **threw.**
through (thrōō) *preposition; adverb; adjective.*

throughout That man is a famous lawyer who is known *throughout* the state. Ann visited her friend *throughout* her summer vacation.
through·out (thrōō out′) *preposition.*

throw 1. To send up into or through the air. Jim and Mike *threw* a ball back and forth. *Throw* me the magazine that's on the table. 2. To bring or make fall to the ground. The

at; āpe; cär; end; mē; it; īce; hot; ōld;
fôrk; wood; fōol; oil; out; up; turn; sing;
thin; **th**is; hw in white; zh in treasure.
ə stands for a in about, e in taken
i in pencil, o in lemon, and u in circus.

horse reared and *threw* its rider. **3.** To put quickly and carelessly. Alice *threw* a coat on and ran out to play. **4.** To put or place in a certain position or condition. The fire alarm *threw* the crowd into a panic. *Verb.*
—The act of throwing; toss. That was a good *throw. Noun.*
> **throw** (thrō) *verb,* **threw, thrown, throwing;** *noun, plural* **throws.**

thrown I think Mother has finally *thrown* out those old clothes that were in the attic. Look up **throw** for more information. ▲ Another word that sounds like this is **throne.**
> **thrown** (thrōn) *verb.*

thrush One of many kinds of birds that are known for their song. A robin is a thrush.
> **thrush** (thrush) *noun, plural* **thrushes.**

thrust To push or shove suddenly or with force. Ted *thrust* some money into his pocket and hurried to meet his friends. *Verb.*
—A sudden, strong drive or push. The army made a *thrust* into enemy territory. *Noun.*
> **thrust** (thrust) *verb,* **thrust, thrusting;** *noun, plural* **thrusts.**

thumb **1.** The short, thick finger on the hand. The thumb makes it easier to pick things up with the hand. **2.** The part of a glove or mitten that covers the thumb. I have a hole in the *thumb* of my glove. *Noun.*
—To turn and look through the pages of. Bob *thumbed* through a magazine while he was waiting to see the dentist. *Verb.*
> **thumb** (thum) *noun, plural* **thumbs;** *verb,* **thumbed, thumbing.**

thumbtack A tack with a flat, round head that can be pressed into a wall or board with the thumb. Notices and other pieces of paper are usually posted on bulletin boards with thumbtacks.
> **thumb·tack** (thum′tak′) *noun, plural* **thumb·tacks.**

thump A dull, heavy sound. Pat dropped the heavy suitcase with a *thump. Noun.*
—**1.** To beat or hit so as to make a dull, heavy sound. Jim *thumped* his head on the floor when he fell out of bed. **2.** To beat rapidly. Her heart *thumped* when the judges prepared to announce the winner of the contest. *Verb.*
> **thump** (thump) *noun, plural* **thumps;** *verb,* **thumped, thumping.**

thunder **1.** A loud rumbling or cracking sound that follows lightning. Thunder is caused when a lightning discharge heats the air in its path. **2.** Any noise that is like thunder. The soldiers could hear the *thunder* of cannon in the distance. *Noun.*

—To make thunder or a noise that is like thunder. It stopped *thundering* as the storm moved away from our area. The express train *thundered* through the station. *Verb.*
> **thun·der** (thun′dər) *noun; verb,* **thundered, thundering.**

thunderstorm A storm that has thunder and lightning.
> **thun·der·storm** (thun′dər stôrm′) *noun, plural* **thunderstorms.**

Thursday The fifth day of the week.
> **Thurs·day** (thurz′dē *or* thurz′dā) *noun, plural* **Thursdays.**

▲ The word **Thursday** comes from an Old English word that meant "Thor's day." This day was named after *Thor,* who was the god of thunder in the religion of people who lived in England long ago.

---

thus **1.** In this way. Written *thus,* the directions are hard to understand. **2.** As a result; therefore. He did not study and *thus* failed the test. **3.** To this extent or degree. I'm sure they arrived safely, but we have not heard from them *thus* far.
> **thus** (thus) *adverb.*

thy An old form of the word "your." "Honor *thy* father and *thy* mother" is one of the Ten Commandments in the Bible.
> **thy** (thī) *pronoun.*

thyme A small plant that is related to the mint. Thyme leaves are used to flavor foods. ▲ Another word that sounds like this is **time.**
> **thyme** (tīm) *noun, plural* **thymes.**

thyroid gland A gland in the neck that controls the body's rate of growth.
> **thy·roid gland** (thī′roid).

tiara A band for the head that looks like a crown. Tiaras are worn by women and are often decorated with jewels.
> **ti·ar·a** (tē ar′ə *or* tē är′ə) *noun, plural* **tiaras.**

tick¹ A light, clicking sound. A clock makes a tick. *Noun.*
—**1.** To make a light, clicking sound. Tom wound the clock because it had stopped *ticking.* **2.** To pass. The minutes *ticked* away as Chris waited for the bus. **3.** To mark with a dot, slash, or other mark; check. Mother *ticked* off each item on her grocery list as she bought it.
> **tick** (tik) *noun, plural* **ticks;** *verb,* **ticked, ticking.**

Tiara

tick²   A tiny animal that looks like a spider. Ticks attach themselves to the skin of man and other animals to suck their blood. Some ticks carry diseases.
tick (tik) *noun, plural* **ticks.**

ticket   **1.** A card or piece of paper that gives the person who holds it certain rights or services. You need a *ticket* to get into the movies and to ride a train. **2.** A tag or label that is attached to something to show its price, tell who owns it, or give some other information. The *ticket* on the sweater said that it cost twenty dollars. **3.** A summons that orders a person to come to court. Policemen often give *tickets* to drivers for parking in the wrong place, driving too fast, or breaking other traffic laws. *Noun.*
—**1.** To attach a tag or label to. The men at the airport *ticketed* our suitcases for the flight to Los Angeles. **2.** To give a summons to. The policeman *ticketed* Mr. James for driving through a red light. *Verb.*
tick·et (tik′it) *noun, plural* **tickets;** *verb,* **ticketed, ticketing.**

tickle   **1.** To touch a part of the body to cause a tingling feeling. It makes me laugh when my sister *tickles* my foot. **2.** To have a tingling feeling. The dust in the air made my nose *tickle.* **3.** To please or delight. The children were *tickled* by the clowns. *Verb.*
—A tingling feeling. The *tickle* in his throat made him cough. *Noun.*
tick·le (tik′əl) *verb,* **tickled, tickling;** *noun, plural* **tickles.**

tidal wave   A huge, powerful ocean wave that is caused by an underwater earthquake. Tidal waves can destroy buildings and kill many people.
tid·al wave (tīd′əl).

tide   **1.** The regular rise and fall of the oceans and other large bodies of water. High tide and low tide each occur about twice a day. The movement of the tides is caused by the attraction or pull of the sun and moon on the earth. **2.** Anything that rises and falls. The *tide* of the battle turned against the invading army.
tide (tīd) *noun, plural* **tides.**

tidy   **1.** Clean and neat. My brother's closet is not very *tidy.* She is a very *tidy* person. **2.** Quite large. Janet managed to save quite a *tidy* sum from her summer job. *Adjective.*
—To make clean and neat. Bob's mother asked him to *tidy* up his room. *Verb.*
ti·dy (tī′dē) *adjective,* **tidier, tidiest;** *verb,* **tidied, tidying.**

tie   **1.** To fasten or attach with a bow or knot.

Carla *tied* her hair with a ribbon. My little brother is learning how to *tie* his own shoes. **2.** To draw together or join closely. A common interest in football *tied* the two boys together. **3.** To equal the score or total of. The two baseball teams were *tied* at five to five. *Verb.*
—**1.** A cord, string, or anything that ties or joins things together. This skirt has a *tie* in front. There are very strong *ties* of friendship between Ellen and Nancy. **2.** A strip of cloth that is worn around the neck; necktie. **3.** An equal score. The game ended in a *tie.* **4.** A timber or rod that holds together and strengthens other parts. The rails of a railroad are attached to wooden *ties. Noun.*
tie (tī) *verb,* **tied, tying;** *noun, plural* **ties.**

tier   One of a series of layers or rows that are arranged one above another. The cake had three *tiers.* The football stadium has *tiers* of seats for the spectators. ▲ Another word that sounds like this is **tear.**
tier (tēr) *noun, plural* **tiers.**

Tiers

tiger   A large animal that is a member of the cat family. A tiger has an orange or yellow coat with black or brown stripes.
ti·ger (tī′gər) *noun, plural* **tigers.**

Tiger

tight   **1.** Held firmly; secure. Make a *tight* knot so the string won't come loose. **2.** Made so that the parts are close together. This sweater is very warm because it has such a *tight* knit. **3.** Fitting the body closely. My belt

at; āpe; cär; end; mē; it; īce; hot; ōld;
fôrk; wood; fool; oil; out; up; turn; sing;
thin; this; hw in white; zh in treasure.
ə stands for a in about, e in taken
i in pencil, o in lemon, and u in circus.

653

was *tight* after I ate that big dinner. **4.** Having little time or space to spare. Donna has a very *tight* schedule at school this year. **5.** Hard to deal with; difficult. The boy knew that if he were caught sneaking into the theater he would be in a *tight* spot. **6.** Not generous; stingy. That old man is very *tight* with his money. **7.** Evenly matched; close. The race is very *tight;* it's hard to tell who will win. *Adjective.*
—Firmly; securely. The boy closed the jar *tight. Adverb.*
  tight (tīt) *adjective,* **tighter, tightest;** *adverb.*

tightrope A wire or rope that is stretched tightly and placed high above the ground. Acrobats perform on a tightrope.
  tight·rope (tīt′rōp′) *noun, plural* **tightropes.**

tile A thin piece of baked clay or porcelain. Tiles are used for covering roofs, floors, or walls. *Noun.*
—To cover with tiles. Father *tiled* the bathroom. *Verb.*
  tile (tīl) *noun, plural* **tiles;** *verb,* **tiled, tiling.**

till¹ If you wait *till* tomorrow to go to the library I'll go with you. We don't expect Grandfather to arrive *till* Sunday. Wait *till* you hear from me before making up your mind. We didn't see Joe *till* after the meeting.
  till (til) *preposition; conjunction.*

till² To prepare and use land for growing crops. Farmers use a plow to *till* the soil.
  till (til) *verb,* **tilled, tilling.**

till³ A drawer where money is kept. The cashier put the money in the *till.*
  till (til) *noun, plural* **tills.**

tiller A bar or handle used to turn the rudder of a boat.
  till·er (til′ər) *noun, plural* **tillers.**

Tiller

tilt To raise one end or side of; tip. Don't *tilt* your chair so far back or you will fall. *Verb.*
—A sloping or slanting position. The *tilt* of her head suggested that she was listening very carefully to what he was saying. *Noun.*
  tilt (tilt) *verb,* **tilted, tilting;** *noun, plural* **tilts.**

timber **1.** Wood that is used in building houses, boats, and many other structures. **2.** A large, heavy piece of wood; beam. Each floor in our house is held up with *timbers* that run from side to side. **3.** Trees; forest. When settlers first came to America, a large part of this country was covered with *timber.*
  tim·ber (tim′bər) *noun, plural* **timbers.**

time **1.** The period during which events, conditions, or actions happen or continue. The changing of summer into fall shows the passing of *time.* Dinosaurs lived a long *time* ago. **2.** An exact point in time. What *time* is it? It's *time* for lunch. **3.** A portion of time available or taken for some purpose. I have no *time* to help you with that work. The runner's *time* for the mile was four minutes. **4.** A portion of time in history. William Shakespeare lived during the *time* of Queen Elizabeth I of England. **5.** A person's experience. Bill had a terrible *time* trying to get the model plane to fly. **6.** One of a number of actions or happenings that is repeated. We saw that movie four *times. Noun.*
—**1.** To arrange or set according to time. The bomb was *timed* to go off at midnight. **2.** To measure the time or rate of. The coach *timed* the runners. *Verb.* ▲ Another word that sounds like this is **thyme.**
  time (tīm) *noun, plural* **times;** *verb,* **timed, timing.**
  in time. 1. Before it is too late. We got to the station *in time* to catch the train. **2.** In the correct rhythm or tempo. The children clapped their hands *in time* to the music.
  on time. At the correct time. Did you get to school *on time?*

times Multiplied by. Two *times* two equals four.
  times (tīmz) *preposition.*

timid Easily frightened; lacking courage or boldness; shy. The little boy was *timid* about meeting people for the first time. Betsy gave a *timid* reply to the teacher because she wasn't sure her answer was correct.
  tim·id (tim′id) *adjective.*

tin **1.** A soft, silver-white metal that does not rust easily. Tin is often used over steel as a coating for cans. Tin is a metallic element. **2.** Something that is made out of tin. Helen buttered the muffin *tin* before putting in the batter. *Noun.*
—Made out of tin. Mike kicked a *tin* can down the street on his way home from school. *Adjective.*
  tin (tin) *noun, plural* **tins;** *adjective.*

tinfoil A very thin sheet of tin, aluminum, or other metal that is used as a wrapping.

Mother wrapped the leftover chicken in *tinfoil* and put it in the refrigerator.

tin·foil (tin′foil′) *noun.*

tingle To have a slight stinging feeling. Mary's face *tingled* from the cold. *Verb.*

—A slight stinging feeling. Joe felt a *tingle* of excitement when he took his first airplane ride. *Noun.*

tin·gle (ting′gəl) *verb,* **tingled, tingling;** *noun,* plural **tingles.**

tinkle To make a light, ringing sound. Lucy's charm bracelet *tinkled* whenever she moved her arm. *Verb.*

—A light, ringing sound. We heard the *tinkle* of sleigh bells in the distance. *Noun.*

tin·kle (ting′kəl) *verb,* **tinkled, tinkling;** *noun,* plural **tinkles.**

tint A shade of a color. There were *tints* of red in her hair. *Noun.*

—To give a slight color to. Anne *tinted* the Easter eggs yellow, pink, blue, and purple. *Verb.*

tint (tint) *noun,* plural **tints;** *verb,* **tinted, tinting.**

tiny Very small. Babies are *tiny* when they are first born.

ti·ny (tī′nē) *adjective,* **tinier, tiniest.**

tip¹ **1.** The end part or point. Jack hit the *tip* of his toe against the chair. **2.** A small piece that forms the end of something. Put the *tip* back on the pen so you don't get ink all over your shirt.

tip (tip) *noun,* plural **tips.**

tip² **1.** To raise one end or side; tilt. Tom *tipped* the bowl to get out the last few drops of soup. **2.** To upset; overturn. I accidentally *tipped* over the chair. Her glass of milk *tipped* over when she reached out for some salt. **3.** To raise or touch one's hat as a greeting. Grandfather *tips* his hat to friends he meets on the street.

tip (tip) *verb,* **tipped, tipping.**

tip³ **1.** A gift of money that is given in return for some service. Mother gave the doorman a *tip* for helping her with her packages. **2.** A piece of useful information. The salesman gave Donna a *tip* about the care of her new car. *Noun.*

—**1.** To give a gift of money for some service. Father *tipped* the waiter as we left the restaurant. **2.** To give a piece of useful information. A secret telephone call *tipped* off the police about the plan to rob the bank. *Verb.*

tip (tip) *noun,* plural **tips;** *verb,* **tipped, tipping.**

tiptoe To move or walk on the tips of one's toes; walk quietly. The mother *tiptoed* out of the room so she wouldn't wake up the baby.

tip·toe (tip′tō′) *verb,* **tiptoed, tiptoeing.**

tire¹ To make or become weak. Reading in the dim light *tired* Tim's eyes. After being sick for so long she *tired* more easily.

tire (tīr) *verb,* **tired, tiring.**

tire² A band of rubber that fits around a wheel. Some rubber tires surround an inner tube that contains air, and other tires contain the air themselves.

tire (tīr) *noun,* plural **tires.**

tired Worn-out; weary. Ruth was *tired* after playing tennis for an hour in the hot sun.

tired (tīrd) *adjective.*

tissue **1.** A group of cells in a plant or animal that are similar in form and in function. The protective tissue in plants covers the entire surface and guards against disease or other injury. In animals, the nervous tissue sends messages from the brain to other parts of the body. **2.** A soft, thin paper that easily absorbs moisture. A tissue is used in place of a handkerchief.

tis·sue (tish′oo) *noun,* plural **tissues.**

tissue paper A very thin paper that is used for wrapping or packing.

title **1.** The name of a book, painting, song, or other similar thing. **2.** A word or group of words used with a person's name to show rank, occupation, or position. The *title* of "Sir" before a man's name means that he has received the rank of knighthood. **3.** A championship. That man once held the heavyweight boxing *title.* **4.** The right a person has to ownership of property. My parents own *title* to our house.

ti·tle (tīt′əl) *noun,* plural **titles.**

to Turn *to* the left at the bottom of the hill. The tree fell *to* the ground. The glass was smashed *to* bits when it fell. The police came *to* our aid. The store is open from nine *to* six. Joan gave the letter *to* her sister. I learned *to* swim last summer. ▲ Other words that sound like this are **too** and **two.**

to (tōō *or* tŏŏ *or* tə) *preposition.*

toad An animal that is like a frog. A toad has rough, dry skin and spends most of its time on land rather than in water.

toad (tōd) *noun,* plural **toads.**

at; āpe; cär; end; mē; it; īce; hot; ōld;
fôrk; wood; fōōl; oil; out; up; turn; sing;
thin; this; hw in white; zh in treasure.
ə stands for a in about, e in taken
i in pencil, o in lemon, and u in circus.

toast¹ Sliced bread that has been browned by heat. Toast is often eaten at breakfast with butter spread on it. *Noun.*
—**1.** To brown by heating. Mother *toasted* some bread for breakfast. **2.** To warm thoroughly. We *toasted* our cold feet before a roaring fire. *Verb.*
  toast (tōst) *noun; verb,* **toasted, toasting.**

toast² The act of drinking in honor of or to the health of a person or thing. There were several *toasts* to the bride and groom at the wedding party. *Noun.*
—To drink in honor of or to the health of. Father *toasted* Grandfather on his ninetieth birthday. *Verb.*
  toast (tōst) *noun, plural* **toasts;** *verb,* **toasted, toasting.**

tobacco The leaves of a plant that are used for smoking and chewing. Cigarettes and cigars are made with tobacco.
  to·bac·co (tə bak′ō) *noun, plural* **tobaccos** or **tobaccoes.**

Toboggan

toboggan A long, flat sled without runners. A toboggan has a curled up front end. They are used to travel over snow. *Noun.*
—To ride on a toboggan. The children *tobogganed* down the hill. *Verb.*
  to·bog·gan (tə bog′ən) *noun, plural* **toboggans;** *verb,* **tobogganed, tobogganing.**

today The present day or time. *Today* is my birthday. *Noun.*
—**1.** On or during the present day. Do you want to go ice skating *today?* **2.** At the present time. *Today* people in this country light their houses with electricity. *Adverb.*
  to·day (tə dā′) *noun; adverb.*

toe **1.** One of the five end parts of the foot. **2.** The part of a sock, shoe, or stocking that covers the toes. The *toe* of my sock has a big hole in it. ▲ Another word that sounds like this is **tow.**
  toe (tō) *noun, plural* **toes.**

toga A loose outer piece of clothing worn by the men of ancient Rome.
  to·ga (tō′gə) *noun, plural* **togas.**

together **1.** With one another. Jane and Alice went to the store *together.* **2.** Into one gathering or mass. Mix the butter and sugar *together.* **3.** In agreement or cooperation. Let's try to get *together* on this problem, so we can solve it. **4.** Considered as a whole. Edward knows more about collecting stamps than all the rest of us *together.*
  to·geth·er (tə geth′ər) *adverb.*

toilet A bowl that is filled with water and has a seat attached to it. A toilet flushes away body wastes and then fills up with clean water.
  toi·let (toi′lit) *noun, plural* **toilets.**

token **1.** Something that is a sign of something else; symbol. We gave a gift to our teacher at the end of the year as a *token* of our appreciation. **2.** A piece of metal that looks like a coin and is used in place of money. You need a *token* to get a ride on a subway.
  to·ken (tō′kən) *noun, plural* **tokens.**

told Jane *told* me her new telephone number. Look up **tell** for more information.
  told (tōld) *verb.*

tolerant Willing to respect or try to understand customs, ideas, or beliefs that are different from one's own. A person who is tolerant will not dislike someone just because he thinks or acts differently from that person.
  tol·er·ant (tol′ər ənt) *adjective.*

tolerate To be able to put up with; endure; stand. Jack *tolerated* the noise as long as he could, but finally he asked the other boys to be quiet.
  tol·er·ate (tol′ə rāt′) *verb,* **tolerated, tolerating.**

toll¹ To sound with slow, regular strokes. The church bells *toll* every Sunday morning. *Verb.*
—The stroke or sound of a bell tolling. The *toll* of the church bell signaled the beginning of the service. *Noun.*
  toll (tōl) *verb,* **tolled, tolling;** *noun, plural* **tolls.**

toll² A tax or fee paid for the right to do or use something. Some highways, bridges, and tunnels charge a *toll* to drivers.
  toll (tōl) *noun, plural* **tolls.**

tomahawk A small ax. It was once used as a tool or weapon by certain Indians in North America.
  tom·a·hawk (tom′ə hôk′) *noun, plural* **tomahawks.**

tomato A round, juicy fruit that is usually red. It is eaten as a vegetable, either raw or cooked. Tomatoes grow on vines.
to·ma·to (tə mā′tō or tə-mä′tō) *noun, plural* to-matoes.

tomb A grave or building in which a dead body is placed.
tomb (to͞om) *noun, plural* tombs.

tomboy A young girl who likes to do things that are usually thought to be preferred by boys.
tom·boy (tom′boi′) *noun, plural* tomboys.

tomcat A male cat.
tom·cat (tom′kat′) *noun, plural* tomcats.

Tomatoes

tomorrow 1. The day after today. If today is Saturday, then *tomorrow* is Sunday. 2. The future. I wonder if people will live in outer space in the world of *tomorrow. Noun.*
—On the day after today. We are going on a trip *tomorrow. Adverb.*
to·mor·row (tə môr′ō or tə mor′ō) *noun; adverb.*

tom-tom A small drum. Tom-toms are usually played by being beaten with the hands.
tom-tom (tom′tom′) *noun, plural* tom-toms.

ton A measure of weight equal to 2000 pounds in the United States and Canada, and 2240 pounds in Great Britain.
ton (tun) *noun, plural* tons.

tone 1. Any sound thought of in terms of its quality, length, pitch, or loudness. The musician produced soft, beautiful *tones* on his violin. Judy answered the phone in an angry *tone* of voice. 2. The difference in pitch between two musical notes. The notes F and G are one *tone* apart. 3. The main style or character of something. Although he made several jokes, the *tone* of his speech was serious. 4. A shade of color. The artist used several *tones* of red to paint the flowers.
tone (tōn) *noun, plural* tones.

Tom-tom

tongs A tool used to pick up things. It usually has two connected, curved arms.
tongs (tongz or tôngz) *noun plural.*

tongue 1. A movable piece of flesh in the mouth. It is used for tasting and swallowing. People also use their tongues to speak. 2. An animal's tongue cooked and used as food. 3. A language. My mother is from Puerto Rico, and Spanish is her native *tongue.* 4. The ability to speak. Steve was so surprised by what happened that he lost his *tongue* for a moment. 5. Something that is shaped like a tongue. The narrow piece of material under the laces of a shoe is called a *tongue.*
tongue (tung) *noun, plural* tongues.

Tongs

tonight The night of this day. The rain should stop by *tonight. Noun.*
—On or during this night. I am going to go to sleep early *tonight. Adverb.*
to·night (tə nīt′) *noun; adverb.*

tonsil Either of two small, oval pieces of flesh in the throat. The tonsils are located just behind a person's mouth.
ton·sil (ton′səl) *noun, plural* tonsils.

too She is a good student and a very kind person, *too.* There are *too* many people in this small room. Ted has grown *too* tall to wear the clothes he had last year. ▲ Other words that sound like this are **to** and **two.**
too (to͞o) *adverb.*

took Jim *took* the book off the shelf. Look up **take** for more information.
took (took) *verb.*

tool 1. A device that is used in doing work. Tools are held in the hand. A hammer, a saw, and a screwdriver are tools. 2. A person or thing that is used like a tool. A good memory is a useful *tool* for learning. *Noun.*
—To work, shape, or mark with a tool or tools. Edward *tooled* his initials in the leather belt he had made. *Verb.*

at; āpe; cär; end; mē; it; īce; hot; ōld;
fôrk; wood; fo͞ol; oil; out; up; turn; sing;
thin; this; hw in white; zh in treasure.
ə stands for a in about, e in taken
i in pencil, o in lemon, and u in circus.

tool (tool) *noun, plural* **tools;** *verb,* **tooled, tooling.**

toot The short, quick noise that a horn or whistle makes. *Noun.*
—To make or cause to make a short, quick blast of sound. Dad *tooted* the car horn when he was ready to leave. *Verb.*
toot (toot) *noun, plural* **toots;** *verb,* **tooted, tooting.**

tooth **1.** One of the hard, white bonelike parts in the mouth. Teeth are used for biting and chewing. A tooth is set in the jaw and supported by the gum. **2.** Something that is shaped or used like a tooth. The thin pieces that stick out on a comb are called teeth.
tooth (tooth) *noun, plural* **teeth.**

toothbrush A small, narrow brush with a long handle. It is used to clean the teeth.
tooth·brush (tooth'brush') *noun, plural* **toothbrushes.**

toothpaste A paste for cleaning the teeth.
tooth·paste (tooth'pāst') *noun, plural* **toothpastes.**

toothpick A small, narrow piece of wood or other material that is used to remove food from between the teeth.
tooth·pick (tooth'pik') *noun, plural* **toothpicks.**

top **1.** The highest or upper part of something. Greg wrote his name at the *top* of the page. A bird built a nest near the *top* of the tree. Ellen's high marks put her at the *top* of her class at school. **2.** A piece of clothing for the upper half of the body. Jill was wearing a blue skirt and a white *top.* **3.** The highest pitch or degree. Frank sang at the *top* of his voice. *Noun.*
—**1.** Of or at the top. Richard kept his socks in the *top* drawer of his bureau. **2.** Highest or greatest. Steve drove the car at *top* speed. *Adjective.*
—**1.** To put a top on. Jane *topped* the dessert with whipped cream. **2.** To be on or from the top of something. A tall steeple *topped* the church. **3.** To be or do better than. The singer's new record *topped* all the ones he had made before. *Verb.*
top (top) *noun, plural* **tops;** *adjective; verb,* **topped, topping.**

topaz A precious stone. Most topazes are light brown or yellow.
to·paz (tō'paz) *noun, plural* **topazes.**

topic What something is about. The subject of a book, talk, or discussion is its topic. The senator spoke on the *topic* "How to Save Our Forests."
top·ic (top'ik) *noun, plural* **topics.**

topography A description or drawing of the hills, valleys, lakes, roads, bridges, and other things found on the surface of a place.
to·pog·ra·phy (tə pog'rə fē) *noun, plural* **topographies.**

topple To fall or make fall forward. The bookcase *toppled* over.
top·ple (top'əl) *verb,* **toppled, toppling.**

tops The very best. Jerry was *tops* on the basketball team.
tops (tops) *adjective.*

topsoil The top part of the soil that has most of the foods that plants need to grow.
top·soil (top'soil') *noun.*

torch **1.** A flaming light. Castles used to be lighted with torches which were heavy sticks of wood soaked in oil at one end. **2.** A tool that shoots flames out at one end. Welders use torches to burn through or soften metal.
torch (tôrch) *noun, plural* **torches.**

Torch

tore He *tore* his trousers when he climbed over the fence. Look up **tear** for more information.
tore (tôr) *verb.*

toreador The man who fights and kills the bull in a bullfight.
tor·e·a·dor (tôr'ē ə dôr') *noun, plural* **toreadors.**

torment To cause someone great pain or suffering. He was *tormented* by guilt for having lied. *Verb.*
—Great pain or suffering. The bad burn caused him *torment. Noun.*
tor·ment (tôr'ment' *for verb;* tôr'ment *for noun*) *verb,* **tormented, tormenting;** *noun.*

Toreador

torn The sheet was *torn* in two places. Look up **tear** for more information.
torn (tôrn) *verb.*

658

tornado A dark column of wind that whirls around at a very high speed. A tornado can suck up and destroy almost anything on the ground that is in its path.
tor·na·do (tôr nā′dō) *noun, plural* **tornadoes** or **tornados.**

torpedo A large cigar-shaped metal shell that is filled with a material that explodes when it hits something. It moves underwater and is used to blow up enemy ships. *Noun.*
—To hit with a torpedo. The submarine *torpedoed* the enemy battleship. *Verb.*
tor·pe·do (tôr pē′dō) *noun, plural* **torpedoes;** *verb,* **torpedoed, torpedoing.**

torrent A fast flowing, heavy stream of water or other liquid. When the dam broke, *torrents* of water flowed over the land.
tor·rent (tôr′ənt) *noun, plural* **torrents.**

tortoise A turtle that lives on land.
tor·toise (tôr′təs) *noun, plural* **tortoises** or **tortoise.**

torture To cause very great or severe pain or suffering to. He was *tortured* by his memories of the accident. *Verb.*
—A cause of very great pain or suffering. Wearing the tight shoes was *torture* for her. *Noun.*
tor·ture (tôr′chər) *verb,* **tortured, torturing;** *noun.*

Tortoise

toss 1. To throw lightly into or through the air. Please *toss* me a towel. 2. To move back and forth. The waves *tossed* the little boat. 3. To throw a coin into the air so as to decide something by the side that lands upward. Let's *toss* a coin to see who has to wash the dishes. *Verb.*
—A throw or fling. We decided which team was going to bat first by a *toss* of a coin. *Noun.*
toss (tôs) *verb,* **tossed, tossing;** *noun, plural* **tosses.**

total Being all there is; making up the whole; entire; complete. I paid the *total* amount of the bill. The experiment was a *total* failure. *Adjective.*
—The whole amount. The cost of repairing the television set came to a *total* of forty dollars. *Noun.*
—1. To find the sum of; add up. The waiter *totaled* the bill for us. 2. To amount to. The bill *totaled* ten dollars. *Verb.*
to·tal (tōt′əl) *adjective; noun, plural* **totals;** *verb,* **totaled, totaling.**

totally Completely; entirely. It was *totally* dark by the time we got home.
to·tal·ly (tōt′əl ē) *adverb.*

tote To carry or haul. The woman *toted* the heavy packages home from the store.
tote (tōt) *verb,* **toted, toting.**

totem An animal, plant, or object that is the symbol of a family of North American Indians. The Indians carved these symbols on poles that stood outside their homes.
to·tem (tō′təm) *noun, plural* **totems.**

toucan A bird that has a heavy body, a very large beak, and brightly colored feathers. Toucans are found in tropical America.
tou·can (tōō′kan) *noun, plural* **toucans.**

Totem Pole

Toucan

touch 1. To put a hand or other part of the body on or against something. I *touched* the hot stove and burned my finger. 2. To bring something against something else. Bob *touched* the match to the paper to start the fire. 3. To come or be against. Our hands *touched.* 4. To affect a person's feelings or emotions. She was *touched* that her old friend still remembered her birthday. *Verb.*
—1. The sense by which a person becomes aware of things by putting a part of the body on or against them. Babies learn about ob-

at; āpe; cär; end; mē; it; īce; hot; ōld;
fôrk; wood; fōōl; oil; out; up; turn; sing;
thin; this; hw in white; zh in treasure.
ə stands for **a** in about, **e** in taken
i in pencil, **o** in lemon, and **u** in circus.

659

jects by *touch*. **2.** The act of touching. The balloon burst at the *touch* of a pin. **3.** A small amount; little bit. The salad needs a *touch* of salt. With a couple of *touches* of paint, the table looked like new. **4.** Communication between people by talking or writing. My best friend moved to another city, but we try to keep in *touch*. *Noun.*
> **touch** (tuch) *verb*, **touched, touching;** *noun,* *plural* **touches.**

touchdown A score made in football by getting the ball across the other team's goal line. It counts six points.
> **touch·down** (tuch′doun′) *noun, plural* **touch·downs.**

tough **1.** Not easy to break, cut, or damage; strong. Canvas is a *tough* cloth. The *tough* piece of meat was hard to chew. **2.** Able to put up with difficulty, strain, or hardship. The early pioneers in the West had to be *tough*. **3.** Rough; violent. Gordie is a *tough* hockey player. That is a *tough* neighborhood. **4.** Hard to deal with or do. Clearing the field for planting was a *tough* job.
> **tough** (tuf) *adjective*, **tougher, toughest.**

tour A trip or journey in which many places are visited or many things are seen. On their *tour* of the United States they traveled in thirty states. We made a *tour* of the museums in the city. *Noun.*
—To travel in or through a place. We hope to *tour* Europe this summer. *Verb.*
> **tour** (toor) *noun, plural* **tours;** *verb*, **toured, touring.**

tourist A person who travels on a vacation. There are many *tourists* in Florida in the winter.
> **tour·ist** (toor′ist) *noun, plural* **tourists.**

tournament A contest between two or more people or teams. People from all over the world competed in the chess *tournament*.
> **tour·na·ment** (toor′nə mənt *or* tur′nə mənt) *noun, plural* **tournaments.**

tourniquet Something used to stop bleeding by pressing on a blood vessel. A tourniquet is usually made of a strip of cloth that is wrapped around a part of the body and twisted tight with a stick.
> **tour·ni·quet** (tur′nə kit) *noun, plural* **tourni·quets.**

tow To pull or drag behind. They tied a rope between their boat and ours and *towed* us into the harbor. ▲ Another word that sounds like this is **toe.**
> **tow** (tō) *verb*, **towed, towing.**

toward The dog ran *toward* the house. What are your feelings *toward* her? The snow stopped *toward* morning. He was saving part of his allowance *toward* a new bicycle. This word is also spelled **towards.**
> **to·ward** (tə wôrd′ *or* tôrd) *preposition.*

towboat A boat used to pull barges or other boats; tugboat.
> **tow·boat** (tō′bōt′) *noun, plural* **towboats.**

towel A piece of paper or cloth that is used for wiping or drying something. *Noun.*
—To wipe or dry with a towel. He *toweled* himself after he went swimming. *Verb.*
> **tow·el** (tou′əl) *noun, plural* **towels;** *verb*, **tow·eled, toweling.**

tower A tall and narrow structure or part of a building. The church had a high *tower* with bells. *Noun.*
—To rise high up in the air. The skyscraper *towered* above the other buildings. *Verb.*
> **tow·er** (tou′ər) *noun, plural* **towers;** *verb*, **towered, towering.**

towering **1.** Very tall. *Towering* palm trees grew along the beach. **2.** Very great. He was in a *towering* rage.
> **tow·er·ing** (tou′ər ing) *adjective.*

town An area in which people live and work. A town has houses and other buildings. It is smaller than a city.
> **town** (toun) *noun, plural* **towns.**

Tower

toy Something for a child to play with. A doll, a kite, and a ball are toys. *Noun.*
—To play with. The nervous girl *toyed* with the button on her jacket as she talked. *Verb.*
> **toy** (toi) *noun, plural* **toys;** *verb*, **toyed, toying.**

trace A small bit left behind showing that something was there. They found arrowheads, bowls, and other *traces* of an Indian village when they dug in the field. There were *traces* of sugar at the bottom of the cup. *Noun.*
—**1.** To follow the trail, course, or path of someone or something. We *traced* the route we had followed on the map. The police *trace* missing persons. **2.** To copy by following lines as seen through a piece of paper. I *traced* the picture by placing a thin piece of paper over it. *Verb.*
> **trace** (trās) *noun, plural* **traces;** *verb*, **traced, tracing.**

trachea The tube in the body that is between the throat and the lungs; windpipe.
tra·che·a (trā′kē ə) *noun, plural* **tracheae.**

track **1.** A mark or marks left by a person, animal, or object as it moves over a surface. We saw deer *tracks* in the snow. The tire *tracks* on the road showed where the car had skidded. **2.** A path, race course, or other trail. The horses raced around the *track.* **3.** A set of rails on which trains move. It is dangerous to walk along the railroad *track.* **4.** The continuous metal belts that tractors move on. *Noun.*
—**1.** To follow the marks or path left by a person, animal, or thing. The dogs *tracked* the fox. **2.** To make marks on something. I forgot to wipe my feet and *tracked* mud on the carpet. *Verb.*
track (trak) *noun, plural* **tracks;** *verb,* **tracked, tracking.**

track and field A group of contests in running, jumping, and throwing.

tract **1.** A piece of land; area. There is a *tract* of wooded land for sale near our house. **2.** A group of parts or organs in the body that work together. The stomach and the intestines are part of the digestive *tract.*
tract (trakt) *noun, plural* **tracts.**

traction The force of friction that holds a moving body to a surface. Deep tire treads provide *traction* for wheels moving on a snowy road.
trac·tion (trak′shən) *noun.*

tractor A vehicle with heavy tires or a chain of continuous metal tracks. Tractors are used to pull heavy loads over rough ground.
trac·tor (trak′tər) *noun, plural* **tractors.**

Tractor

trade **1.** The business of buying and selling goods; commerce. The United States engages in much foreign *trade.* **2.** The giving of one thing in exchange for something else. I made a *trade* of my ham sandwich for her chicken sandwich. **3.** A kind of job or work. My uncle is an electrician by *trade. Noun.*
—**1.** To buy or sell as a business. He *trades* in fishing and boat supplies. **2.** To give one thing in exchange for something else. I *traded* four of my baseball cards for three of his. David *traded* seats with his sister so that she could see better. *Verb.*
trade (trād) *noun, plural* **trades;** **trading.**

trademark A picture, word, or mark that a manufacturer uses to show that it made a product.
trade·mark (trād′märk′) *noun, plural* **trademarks.**

trader A person who buys and sells things as a business.
trad·er (trā′dər) *noun, plural* **traders.**

trading post A store set up in a frontier region. At trading posts people get food or supplies in exchange for things like hides or furs.

tradition Customs, beliefs, or other knowledge that is passed down from parents to their children. It is a *tradition* in our family to exchange Christmas presents on Christmas Eve.
tra·di·tion (trə dish′ən) *noun, plural* **traditions.**

traditional According to tradition. Turkey is the *traditional* Thanksgiving dinner.
tra·di·tion·al (trə dish′ən əl) *adjective.*

traffic **1.** Automobiles, airplanes, ships, or people moving along a route. There is heavy *traffic* in and out of the airports during the holidays. **2.** A buying and selling or exchange of goods. The police work to stop *traffic* in drugs. *Noun.*
—To buy or sell; deal in. The police knew the man was *trafficking* in stolen goods. *Verb.*
traf·fic (traf′ik) *noun; verb,* **trafficked, trafficking.**

tragedy **1.** A story in which life is treated in a serious way and which usually has a sad ending. **2.** A sad or dreadful event. The explosion in the coal mine was a great *tragedy.*
trag·e·dy (traj′ə dē) *noun, plural* **tragedies.**

▲ The word **tragedy** goes back to the Greek word for a serious play with an unhappy ending. The Greek word means "goat song," but no one knows exactly why the Greeks called this kind of play a "goat song." One idea is that this kind of play was at first just a song that was sung when a goat was killed in a Greek religious ceremony.

tragic **1.** Having to do with a story that is a tragedy. The play had a *tragic* ending. **2.** Very sad or dreadful. The plane crash was a *tragic* accident.
trag·ic (traj′ik) *adjective.*

trail **1.** A path through an area that is wild or not lived in. The hikers followed the *trail* through the woods. **2.** A mark, scent, or path made by a person or animal. The hunters followed the bear's *trail.* **3.** Something that follows along behind. The airplane left a *trail* of smoke. *Noun.*
—**1.** To follow behind. The boys *trailed* the parade down the street. **2.** To follow the scent or path of. The police *trailed* the bank robbers to an old house. **3.** To drag or be dragged behind. The children *trailed* their kites on the ground. Her long dress *trailed* along the floor. **4.** To be behind or losing in a game or contest. Our team *trailed* by ten points. **5.** To grow over or along a surface. Ivy *trailed* over the wall. *Verb.*
trail (trāl) *noun, plural* **trails;** *verb,* **trailed, trailing.**

trailer A vehicle that is pulled by a car or a truck. Some trailers are used to carry goods, and some are made for people to live in.
trail·er (trā′lər) *noun, plural* **trailers.**

train **1.** A line of railroad cars connected together. Some trains carry passengers; other trains carry only freight. **2.** A group of people, animals, or vehicles traveling together in a long line. Wagon *trains* crossed the prairie. Mule *trains* carried supplies into the hills. **3.** Any connected series of events, ideas, or parts of a thing. It was hard for me to follow the writer's *train* of thought. **4.** The part of a dress or robe that trails on the ground behind the person who wears it. The bride's gown had a long *train. Noun.*
—**1.** To develop or influence a person's thoughts, behavior, or character. The parents *trained* their children to respect the rights and feelings of others. **2.** To teach or learn how to do something. My grandfather was *trained* to be a carpenter. We *trained* the dog to bark when it wants to go out. **3.** To get ready for something by practicing, exercising, or teaching. Boxers have to *train* for a fight. **4.** To

make something go a certain way. Jeanette *trained* her hair to curl under. *Verb.*
train (trān) *noun, plural* **trains;** *verb,* **trained, training.**

trainer A person who trains an athlete, race horse, or the like. The boxer's *trainer* helped him get ready for the championship fight.
train·er (trā′nər) *noun, plural* **trainers.**

training **1.** Teaching; education. The sergeant took charge of the *training* of the new soldiers. **2.** Good physical condition that athletes work to keep in. The football players kept in *training* by practicing every day.
train·ing (trā′ning) *noun, plural* **trainings.**

trait A quality or characteristic of a person or animal. Bravery and chivalry were *traits* that knights were supposed to have.
trait (trāt) *noun, plural* **traits.**

traitor A person who betrays his country or the trust of another person or group. The *traitor* fought on the side of the enemy against his own country.
trai·tor (trā′tər) *noun, plural* **traitors.**

tramp **1.** To walk or step heavily. The workmen *tramped* into the house in their boots. Don't *tramp* on the flowers! **2.** To travel on foot; walk or hike. They spent the day *tramping* through the woods. *Verb.*
—**1.** A person who wanders from place to place and has no home or job. The *tramp* went to the farmer's door and begged for food. **2.** The sound of a heavy step. We heard the *tramp* of the marchers coming down the street. *Noun.*
tramp (tramp) *verb,* **tramped, tramping;** *noun, plural* **tramps.**

trample To step on heavily and crush. Do not *trample* the new grass.
tram·ple (tram′pəl) *verb,* **trampled, trampling.**

Trampoline

trampoline A piece of canvas attached by

springs to a metal frame. People do tumbling exercises on trampolines.

tram·po·line (tram′pə lēn′ *or* tram′pə lēn′) *noun, plural* **trampolines.**

transcribe To make a written copy of something. The class secretary *transcribes* the minutes of each meeting.

tran·scribe (tran skrīb′) *verb,* **transcribed, transcribing.**

transfer To move from one person or place to another. Ed *transferred* his wallet from his jacket to his slacks. Next year we have to *transfer* to a new school. *Verb.*
—**1.** A move from one person or place to another. Dad's *transfer* to the company's office in New York takes place in June. **2.** A ticket that lets a person change from one bus, train, or plane to another without paying more money. *Noun.*

trans·fer (trans fur′ *or* trans′fər *for verb;* trans′fər *for noun*) *verb,* **transferred, transferring;** *noun, plural* **transfers.**

transform To change in shape, appearance, or nature. The yellow paint *transformed* the dark room into a bright one. You can *transform* water into ice by freezing it. In science class, we learned how a caterpillar *transforms* into a butterfly.

trans·form (trans fôrm′) *verb,* **transformed, transforming.**

transfusion The transfer of blood from one person to another.

trans·fu·sion (trans fyōō′zhən) *noun, plural* **transfusions.**

transistor A very small electronic device that controls the electric current in television sets, radios, computers, and other equipment.

tran·sis·tor (tran zis′tər) *noun, plural* **transistors.**

transition The change or movement from one place or condition to another. The *transition* from high school to college is difficult for some people.

tran·si·tion (tran zish′ən) *noun, plural* **transitions.**

translate To say in or change into another language. The class had to *translate* the short story from English to French.

trans·late (trans lāt′) *verb,* **translated, translating.**

translation A changing of something into another language. We read an English *translation* of the Spanish story.

trans·la·tion (trans lā′shən) *noun, plural* **translations.**

translucent Allowing some light to pass through. Frosted window glass is *translucent;*

you can see light through it but cannot see objects clearly.

trans·lu·cent (trans lōō′sənt) *adjective.*

transmission **1.** The act of sending or passing from one person or place to another. Insects cause the *transmission* of some diseases. **2.** The broadcasting of radio or television waves. **3.** A series of gears in an automobile that causes power to be transferred from the engine to the wheels.

trans·mis·sion (trans mish′ən) *noun, plural* **transmissions.**

transmit **1.** To send, pass, or cause to go from one person or place to another. My father works for a business that *transmits* freight from city to city by airplane and railroad. **2.** To send out signals by radio or television. That station *transmits* the news twenty-four hours a day.

trans·mit (trans mit′) *verb,* **transmitted, transmitting.**

transmitter A device that sends out radio or television signals.

trans·mit·ter (trans mit′ər) *noun, plural* **transmitters.**

transom A small window above a door or another window.

tran·som (tran′səm) *noun, plural* **transoms.**

transparent **1.** Allowing light to pass through so that things on the other side can be clearly seen. The lenses in eyeglasses are *transparent.* **2.** Easy to understand; obvious. His excuse for not doing his homework was a *transparent* lie.

trans·par·ent (trans per′ənt *or* trans par′ənt) *adjective.*

transplant **1.** To take from one place and put in another. We *transplanted* the bush from the front yard to the back yard. **2.** To transfer skin or an organ from one person or animal to another, or from one part of the body to another.

trans·plant (trans plant′) *verb,* **transplanted, transplanting.**

transport To bring or carry from one place to another. The new automobiles were *transported* across the ocean by ship. *Verb.*
—**1.** The act of transporting. Ships are used for *transport* of oil. **2.** A ship or airplane that

at; āpe; cär; end; mē; it; īce; hot; ōld; fôrk; wood; fōōl; oil; out; up; turn; sing; thin; this; hw in white; zh in treasure. ə stands for a in about, e in taken i in pencil, o in lemon, and u in circus.

is used to carry people or freight from one place to another. *Noun.*

trans·port (trans pôrt′ *for verb;* trans′pôrt *for noun*) *verb,* **transported, transporting;** *noun, plural* **transports.**

transportation The act or means of carrying or moving something from one place to another. A bus provides my *transportation* to school.

trans·por·ta·tion (trans′pər tā′shən) *noun.*

trap **1.** A device that catches animals that step in or on it. Mice are caught in *traps.* **2.** A trick used to catch a person or get him to admit something. The lawyer's question was a *trap* to get the man to confess to the robbery. *Noun.*
—To catch in a trap. The hunter *trapped* a lion. The lawyer *trapped* the accused man with his questions. *Verb.*

trap (trap) *noun, plural* **traps;** *verb,* **trapped, trapping.**

trap door A door in a ceiling or floor. In the old farm house there was a *trap door* in the kitchen floor that led to a small cellar.

trapeze A short bar hung between two ropes, used to swing from in gymnastics. The circus acrobat performed on a *trapeze.*

tra·peze (tra pēz′) *noun, plural* **trapezes.**

Trapeze

trapper A person who traps wild animals for their fur.

trap·per (trap′ər) *noun, plural* **trappers.**

trash Worthless objects or stuff that is thrown away. We cleared the garage of old newspapers and other *trash.*

trash (trash) *noun.*

travel **1.** To go from one place to another; make a trip for business or pleasure. Jennifer *traveled* through England last summer. **2.** To

pass or move from one point to another. Sound *travels* in waves.

trav·el (trav′əl) *verb,* **traveled, traveling.**

▲ The word **travel** comes from another English word that means "hard and very tiring work." Taking a trip may have been connected with the word for hard work because long ago traveling was very dangerous and uncomfortable.

traveler A person who travels. We met many fellow *travelers* while visiting Rome.

trav·el·er (trav′ə lər) *noun, plural* **travelers.**

trawl A net or long line that is dragged slowly over the ocean bottom to catch fish. *Noun.*
—To fish with a trawl. They *trawled* for flounder. *Verb.*

trawl (trôl) *noun, plural* **trawls;** *verb,* **trawled, trawling.**

tray A flat dish made of wood, metal, or china, used to carry or display things. Waiters carry food on large *trays.*

tray (trā) *noun, plural* **trays.**

treacherous Disloyal or dangerous. The *treacherous* man betrayed his country to the enemy.

treach·er·ous (trech′ər əs) *adjective.*

tread **1.** To walk on or along. We heard someone *tread* down the hall. **2.** To step on heavily; trample. The dog *trod* on the flowers and broke their stems. *Verb.*
—**1.** The way or sound of walking; footstep. She heard his *tread* as he came up the stairs. **2.** The outer, grooved surface of a tire. The *tread* on those old tires is quite worn. **3.** The top surface of a step in a staircase. *Noun.*

tread (tred) *verb,* **trod, trodden** or **trod, treading;** *noun, plural* **treads.**

treason The betraying of one's country by helping an enemy. Giving the army's battle plans to the enemy was an act of *treason.*

trea·son (trē′zən) *noun.*

treasure Money, jewels, or other things that are valuable. A chest of gold coins was part of the pirate's *treasure. Noun.*
—To think of as being of great value or importance; cherish. Judy *treasured* the memory of her grandparents. *Verb.*

treas·ure (trezh′ər) *noun, plural* **treasures;** *verb,* **treasured, treasuring.**

treasurer A person who is responsible for taking care of the money of a club or business.

treas·ur·er (trezh′ər ər) *noun, plural* **treasurers.**

treasury **1.** The money or other funds of a business, government, or other group. The club members paid for the tickets to the play out of the club *treasury.* **2. Treasury.** A department of the government that is in charge of the country's finances.
treas·ur·y (trezh′ər ē) *noun, plural* **treasuries.**

treat **1.** To behave toward or deal with in a certain way. The police *treated* the prisoner fairly. **2.** To give medical care to. The doctor *treated* her burned hand with an ointment. **3.** To pay for the entertainment of another person. I will *treat* you to the movie. *Verb.*
—Something that is a special pleasure. Going to the circus was a *treat* for all of us. *Noun.*
treat (trēt) *verb,* **treated, treating;** *noun, plural* **treats.**

treatment The way something or someone is treated. Rest in bed was the doctor's *treatment* for a bad cold. Her mother scolded her for her unfair *treatment* of her little brother.
treat·ment (trēt′mənt) *noun, plural* **treatments.**

treaty A formal agreement between countries. A peace *treaty* was signed to end the war.
trea·ty (trē′tē) *noun, plural* **treaties.**

tree A plant with a single main stem or trunk that is made up of solid, woody tissue. Trees have branches and leaves at a distance above the ground. *Noun.*
—To chase up a tree. The dog *treed* the cat. *Verb.*
tree (trē) *noun, plural* **trees;** *verb,* **treed, treeing.**

trellis A frame of crossed strips of wood or metal that a plant can grow on.
trel·lis (trel′is) *noun, plural* **trellises.**

tremble **1.** To shake with cold, fear, weakness, or anger. The kitten *trembled* as the sound of thunder grew louder. **2.** To move or vibrate. The building *trembled* from the explosion.
trem·ble (trem′bəl) *verb,* **trembled, trembling.**

Trellis

tremendous Very large or great; enormous. A *tremendous* clap of thunder shook the house.
tre·men·dous (tri men′dəs) *adjective.*

tremor A shaking or trembling. Earthquakes cause great *tremors* in the earth. Her nervousness caused a *tremor* in her voice.
trem·or (trem′ər) *noun, plural* **tremors.**

trench A long, narrow ditch. The soldiers fought from *trenches* in the battlefield.
trench (trench) *noun, plural* **trenches.**

trend A direction or course that seems to be followed. There is a *trend* toward higher prices in this country.
trend (trend) *noun, plural* **trends.**

trespass To go on or enter another person's property unlawfully or without permission. The hunters *trespassed* on private property and were arrested. *Verb.*
—A sin. We prayed that our *trespasses* would be forgiven. *Noun.*
tres·pass (tres′pəs *or* tres′pas′) *verb,* **trespassed, trespassing;** *noun, plural* **trespasses.**

Trestle

trestle A framework used to hold up a railroad bridge or other raised structure.
tres·tle (tres′əl) *noun, plural* **trestles.**

trial **1.** The examining and deciding of a case that is brought to a court of law. **2.** A trying or testing of anything. The mechanic made some adjustments and then gave the

at; āpe; cär; end; mē; it; īce; hot; ōld;
fôrk; wood; fōol; oil; out; up; turn; sing;
thin; this; hw in white; zh in treasure.
ə stands for a in about, e in taken
i in pencil, o in lemon, and u in circus.

665

car another *trial* to see if it would run better.

tri·al (trī′əl) *noun, plural* **trials.**

triangle **1.** A figure or object with three sides and three angles. **2.** A musical instrument made of a metal bar bent in the shape of a triangle. A triangle sounds like a bell when it is hit.

tri·an·gle (trī′ang′gəl) *noun, plural* **triangles.**

triangular Having to do with or looking like a triangle. The tent had a *triangular* shape.

tri·an·gu·lar (trī ang′yə-lər) *adjective.*

tribal Having to do with a tribe. She studied the *tribal* customs of the Indians of North America in a course at her college.

trib·al (trī′bəl) *adjective.*

Triangle

tribe A group of people who are joined because they have the same ancestors, social customs, and other characteristics. There are many *tribes* of American Indians.

tribe (trīb) *noun, plural* **tribes.**

tribesman A member of a tribe.

tribes·man (trībz′mən) *noun, plural* **tribesmen.**

tributary A river or stream that flows into a larger body of water. The Tennessee River is a main *tributary* of the Ohio River.

trib·u·tar·y (trib′yə ter′ē) *noun, plural* **tributaries.**

tribute Anything done or given to show thanks or respect. The applause was a *tribute* to the singer's performance. The statue was erected as a *tribute* to the soldiers who had died in the war.

trib·ute (trib′yo͞ot) *noun, plural* **tributes.**

trick **1.** Something done to fool or cheat. The slamming of the door was only a *trick* to make the others think he had left. **2.** A clever or skillful act. The magician pulled a rabbit out of a hat and did many other *tricks.* The boy taught his dog the *trick* of opening a door. **3.** A joke or prank. Jerry enjoys playing *tricks* on his friends. *Noun.*

—To fool or cheat with a trick. The salesman tried to *trick* us into buying a used car that was falling apart. *Verb.*

trick (trik) *noun, plural* **tricks;** *verb,* **tricked, tricking.**

trickle **1.** To flow or fall drop by drop or in a thin stream. The rain *trickled* down the window. **2.** To move very slowly or one by one. The children *trickled* back into the classroom after lunch. *Verb.*

—A small flow or thin stream. There was a *trickle* of milk down the side of the pitcher. *Noun.*

trick·le (trik′əl) *verb,* **trickled, trickling;** *noun, plural* **trickles.**

tricky **1.** Using or marked by tricks. The magician could do some *tricky* things with cards. **2.** Hard in an unexpected way; needing careful handling. The first question on the test was *tricky* and I had to read it over several times.

trick·y (trik′ē) *adjective,* **trickier, trickiest.**

tricycle A vehicle with two wheels in the back and one in front. It is moved by pedaling and steered with handlebars. Children often learn to ride tricycles before they ride bicycles.

tri·cy·cle (trī′si kəl *or* trī′sik′əl) *noun, plural* **tricycles.**

tried I *tried* to get home before it was dark. Look up **try** for more information.

tried (trīd) *verb.*

Tricycle

trifle Something that is small in amount or importance. Let's not argue over such a *trifle* as whether to eat now or twenty minutes from now. This dress is just a *trifle* more expensive than the other one. *Noun.*

—To treat something in a careless way. Don't *trifle* with the camera; you could break it. *Verb.*

tri·fle (trī′fəl) *noun, plural* **trifles;** *verb,* **trifled, trifling.**

trigger A small lever that is pulled or pressed to shoot a gun. *Noun.*

—To start or cause something. A spark from a campfire *triggered* the forest fire. *Verb.*

trig·ger (trig′ər) *noun, plural* **triggers;** *verb,* **triggered, triggering.**

trim **1.** To cut away or remove parts to make something neat and orderly. I need to *trim* my hair. Ben tried to *trim* the hedge evenly. **2.** To add ornaments or decorations to. It's fun to *trim* a Christmas tree. *Verb.*

—**1.** Something that decorates or ornaments. June put white lace *trim* on her dress. **2.** A good, fit condition. The boxer worked to stay in *trim* for the fight. *Noun.*

trim (trim) *verb,* **trimmed, trimming;** *noun, plural* **trims.**

trimming   1. Anything used as a decoration or ornament. The dress had velvet *trimming* on the sleeves. 2. **trimmings.** Things that usually go with something. At the party we had ice cream, cake, and all the *trimmings*.
trim·ming (trim′ing) *noun, plural* **trimmings.**

trio   1. A musical piece written for three singers or musicians. 2. A group of three singers or musicians performing together.
tri·o (trē′ō) *noun, plural* **trios.**

trip   The act of traveling or going from one place to another. His *trip* to Chicago was for business. *Noun.*
—1. To catch one's foot on something and stumble or fall. He *tripped* on the edge of the rug. 2. To cause someone to stumble or fall. The wire on the ground *tripped* her. 3. To make or cause to make a mistake. He *tripped* up on the third question on the test. *Verb.*
trip (trip) *noun, plural* **trips;** *verb,* **tripped, tripping.**

triple   1. Made up of three parts. There was a special *triple* feature at the movies. A *triple* play in baseball is a play during which three outs are made. 2. Three times as much or as many. Bob ordered a *triple* scoop of ice cream. *Adjective.*
—To make or become three times as much or as many. The population of our town *tripled* in ten years. *Verb.*
tri·ple (trip′əl) *adjective; verb,* **tripled, tripling.**

triplet   One of three children born at the same time to the same mother.
trip·let (trip′lit) *noun, plural* **triplets.**

Tripod

tripod   A three-legged stand for holding up a telescope or some other instrument. The camera was mounted on a *tripod*.
tri·pod (trī′pod′) *noun, plural* **tripods.**

triumph   1. A great success or victory. The discovery of polio vaccine was a medical *triumph*. 2. Great happiness caused by success or victory. She grinned in *triumph* when she heard she had won the contest. *Noun.*
—To succeed or win. Our soldiers *triumphed* over the enemy. *Verb.*
tri·umph (trī′umf) *noun, plural* **triumphs;** *verb,* **triumphed, triumphing.**

triumphant   Successful or victorious. Our team was *triumphant* in the championship match.
tri·um·phant (trī um′fənt) *adjective.*

trivial   Of little or no importance. The teacher said Barbara's report was very good and she had made only one or two *trivial* mistakes.
triv·i·al (triv′ē əl) *adjective.*

trod   The girls *trod* wearily home after a day of shopping. Look up **tread** for more information.
trod (trod) *verb.*

trodden   The path through the woods had been well *trodden*. Look up **tread** for more information.
trod·den (trod′ən) *verb.*

Trolley

trolley   1. A small wheel that moves along an overhead wire and picks up electricity to run a streetcar, train, or bus. 2. A kind of streetcar that runs on tracks and gets its power from a trolley.
trol·ley (trol′ē) *noun, plural* **trolleys.**

at; āpe; cär; end; mē; it; īce; hot; ōld;
fôrk; wood; fōol; oil; out; up; turn; sing;
thin; this; hw in white; zh in treasure.
ə stands for a in about, e in taken
i in pencil, o in lemon, and u in circus.

trombone   A brass musical instrument. A trombone is made up of two long, U-shaped tubes. One tube has a flaring end and the other tube may be slid back and forth to change the pitch of the tones.

Trombone

trom·bone (trom-bōn′ *or* trom′bōn) *noun, plural* **trombones.**

troop   1. A group of persons doing something together. Ellen and Joan are in the same Girl Scout *troop*. 2. **troops.** Soldiers. The enemy *troops* surrendered. *Noun.*
—To walk or march in a group. When recess was over, the students *trooped* back into the classroom. *Verb.*
troop (trōōp) *noun, plural* **troops;** *verb,* **trooped, trooping.**

trooper   A policeman. The state *trooper* patrolled the highway.
troop·er (trōō′pər) *noun, plural* **troopers.**

trophy   A cup, small statue, or other object given to someone as an award for winning some contest or doing something outstanding. The captain of the basketball team accepted the championship *trophy*.
tro·phy (trō′fē) *noun, plural* **trophies.**

tropical   Having to do with or found in the tropics. Orchids are *tropical* plants.
trop·i·cal (trop′i kəl) *adjective.*

tropics   A region of the earth that is near the equator. It is always hot in the tropics.
trop·ics (trop′iks) *noun plural.*

trot   The gait of an animal that is between a walk and a run or gallop. *Noun.*
—1. To move or ride at a trot. When a horse trots, the left hind foot and the right forefoot are lifted together, and the right hind foot and the left forefoot are lifted together. 2. To move quickly; hurry. The little boy *trotted* after his big brother. *Verb.*
trot (trot) *noun, plural* **trots;** *verb,* **trotted, trotting.**

trouble   1. A difficult or dangerous situation. The people in the valley will be in *trouble* if the dam breaks. 2. Extra work or effort. Jane went to a lot of *trouble* to make this dinner a success. *Noun.*
—1. To disturb or make uncomfortable. The fact that Phil was late *troubled* his mother. Does your headache still *trouble* you? 2. To cause someone to make an extra effort. May I *trouble* you for a glass of water? *Verb.*
trou·ble (trub′əl) *noun, plural* **troubles;** *verb,* **troubled, troubling.**

trough   A long, deep, narrow box or other container. Farmers use troughs to hold food and water for animals.
trough (trôf) *noun, plural* **troughs.**

trousers   A piece of clothing that is worn over the lower part of the body and covers each leg separately.
trou·sers (trou′zərz) *noun plural.*

trout   A fish that lives in fresh water and is good to eat. Some trout have speckles on their bodies.
trout (trout) *noun, plural* **trouts** or **trout.**

Trout

truce   A short stop in fighting. A truce is agreed to by both sides in order to try to reach a peace agreement.
truce (trōōs) *noun, plural* **truces.**

truck   A large motor vehicle that is made to carry heavy loads. Some trucks have an open area in the back to put things in, and others have a closed trailer behind. *Noun.*
—To move something by truck. When we moved, all our furniture was *trucked* to the new house. *Verb.*
truck (truk) *noun, plural* **trucks;** *verb,* **trucked, trucking.**

trudge   To walk slowly and with an effort. The tired boys *trudged* up the hill. The soldiers *trudged* the last mile in the rain. *Verb.*
—A slow, tiring walk. The campers had a long *trudge* back to their camp. *Noun.*
trudge (truj) *verb,* **trudged, trudging;** *noun, plural* **trudges.**

true   1. Agreeing with the facts; not false, wrong, or made-up. The movie was based on a *true* story. Everything he said was *true;* he didn't lie. 2. Faithful to someone or something; loyal. She is a *true* friend. 3. Genuine; real. That drink is made with *true* chocolate flavoring.
true (trōō) *adjective,* **truer, truest.**

truly In a real, genuine, or honest way; sincerely. I am *truly* sorry I forgot to call you. He did a *truly* good job of building the model airplane.
tru·ly (trōō′lē) *adverb*.

trumpet **1.** A brass musical instrument. A trumpet is made up of a long tube coiled into a loop with a flared end. **2.** A sound like the sound made with a trumpet. The cry of an elephant is called a trumpet. *Noun.*
—To make a sound like a trumpet. The elephant *trumpeted*. *Verb.*
trum·pet (trum′pit) *noun, plural* **trumpets;** *verb,* **trumpeted, trumpeting.**

Trumpet

trunk **1.** The main stem of a tree. The branches grow out from the trunk. **2.** A large box used for carrying and storing things. **3.** The part of an automobile where suitcases and other things are stored and carried. **4.** The long snout of an elephant. **5. trunks.** Short pants. Trunks are worn by men for swimming, boxing, and other sports.
trunk (trungk) *noun, plural* **trunks.**

trust To believe or have confidence in. We should not have *trusted* the weather report. I *trust* her to keep a secret. I *trust* that you will be on time. *Verb.*
—**1.** Belief or confidence in someone or something. I have complete *trust* in his honesty. Donny's parents have *trust* in him. **2.** The care or keeping of someone. Her niece was left in her *trust* for the week. *Noun.*
trust (trust) *verb,* **trusted, trusting;** *noun.*

truth **1.** Something that is true. She taught her children to tell the *truth*. **2.** The quality of being true, honest, or sincere. The jury doubted the *truth* of the witness's statement.
truth (trōōth) *noun, plural* **truths.**

truthful Telling the truth. The newspaper gave a *truthful* picture of conditions in the jail.
truth·ful (trōōth′fəl) *adjective*.

try **1.** To make an effort to do something. He *tried* moving the box alone, but it was too heavy. Please *try* not to be late. **2.** To make a test of. *Try* out the bicycle's brakes before you start down the hill. **3.** To examine or investigate in a court of law. He was *tried* for robbery and found guilty. *Verb.*

—An effort or attempt. We each have one more *try* to hit the target. *Noun.*
try (trī) *verb,* **tried, trying;** *noun, plural* **tries.**

tryout A test to see if a person can do something well. The *tryouts* for parts in the new play will be held this afternoon.
try·out (trī′out′) *noun, plural* **tryouts.**

T-shirt A light, close-fitting shirt with short sleeves and no collar.
T-shirt (tē′shurt′) *noun, plural* **T-shirts.**

tub **1.** A large open container used for taking a bath; bathtub. **2.** A round container used to hold butter, honey, or other foods.
tub (tub) *noun, plural* **tubs.**

tuba A very large brass musical instrument that has a deep, mellow tone.
tu·ba (tōō′bə *or* tyōō′bə) *noun, plural* **tubas.**

Tuba

tube **1.** A hollow piece of glass, rubber, plastic, or metal in the shape of a long pipe. Tubes are used to carry or hold liquids or gases. A garden hose is a long tube. **2.** Anything like a tube in shape or use. A tunnel under a river or the ground is a tube. Lipstick comes in a tube. **3.** A container of soft metal or plastic that has a cap that screws on. It is used for holding toothpaste, shampoo, medicine, and other products.
tube (toob *or* tyoob) *noun, plural* **tubes.**

tuberculosis A disease that is caused by bacteria and usually affects the lungs. It can be passed from one person to another.

at; āpe; cär; end; mē; it; īce; hot; ōld; fôrk; wood; fōol; oil; out; up; turn; sing; thin; this; hw in white; zh in treasure.
ə stands for a in about, e in taken
i in pencil, o in lemon, and u in circus.

tu·ber·cu·lo·sis (tōō bur'kyə lō'sis *or* tyōō-bur'kyə lō'sis) *noun.*

tuck 1. To push or fold the edge or ends of something in place. He *tucked* his shirt in. Mother *tucked* the blanket around me. 2. To put into a hidden, safe, or covered space. There is a wasp's nest *tucked* under the window ledge. She *tucked* the secret message between the pages of the book. *Verb.*
—A fold sewed in a piece of clothing to make it fit better or to decorate it. Jane made a *tuck* in the waist of the skirt. *Noun.*
tuck (tuk) *verb,* **tucked, tucking;** *noun, plural* **tucks.**

Tuesday The third day of the week.
Tues·day (tōōz'dē *or* tōōz'dā *or* tyōōz'dē *or* tyōōz'dā) *noun, plural* **Tuesdays.**

▲ The Romans' name for **Tuesday** meant "day of Mars." *Mars* was the Roman god of war. Some early English people had a god of war who was named *Tiw,* so they changed the name from "Mars' day" to "Tiw's day." The word *Tuesday* comes from an Old English word that meant "Tiw's day."

tuft A bunch of feathers, hair, grass, threads, or other things that is fastened or growing together at one end and loose at the other. *Tufts* of grass grew up between the stones. The bird had a *tuft* of feathers on its head.
tuft (tuft) *noun, plural* **tufts.**

tug To give a pull on something. He *tugged* at his mother's sleeve to get her attention. The horses *tugged* the heavy wagon. *Verb.*
—A hard pull. Alan felt a *tug* on his fishing line. *Noun.*
tug (tug) *verb,* **tugged, tugging;** *noun, plural* **tugs.**

tugboat A small, powerful boat that is used to push or pull barges or other boats.
tug·boat (tug'bōt') *noun, plural* **tugboats.**

Tugboat

tuition Money paid for instruction or teaching. My parents pay my sister's *tuition* at college.
tu·i·tion (tōō ish'ən *or* tyōō ish'ən) *noun, plural* **tuitions.**

tulip A cup-shaped flower that grows on the end of a long stem. The tulip plant grows from a bulb and has long, spear-shaped leaves.
tu·lip (tōō'lip *or* tyōō'lip) *noun, plural* **tulips.**

Tulips

tumble 1. To fall in a helpless or clumsy way. He *tumbled* down the icy hill. The apples *tumbled* off the cart. 2. To roll or toss about. We could hear the pail *tumbling* around in the trunk of the car. 3. To do somersaults, headstands, or other acrobatics. *Verb.*
—A fall. Jack took a *tumble* when he tripped on the branch. *Noun.*
tum·ble (tum'bəl) *verb,* **tumbled, tumbling;** *noun, plural* **tumbles.**

tuna A large fish found in warm seas all over the world. Tuna is used for food.
tu·na (tōō'nə) *noun, plural* **tunas** *or* **tuna.**

tundra A huge, treeless plain in arctic regions.
tun·dra (tun'drə) *noun, plural* **tundras.**

tune 1. A series of notes that make up a song or the melody of a piece of music. We hummed the *tune* when we couldn't remember the words. 2. The right pitch or key. The old piano was out of *tune.* 3. Agreement or harmony. The old man's opinions were not in *tune* with modern ideas. *Noun.*
—To put or bring into tune. Eric *tuned* his guitar. The orchestra *tuned* up before it played. *Verb.*
tune (tōōn *or* tyōōn) *noun, plural* **tunes;** *verb,* **tuned, tuning.**

tunic 1. A piece of clothing that looks like a shirt and reaches to the knees. Men in ancient Greece and Rome wore tunics. 2. A uniform jacket that fits closely. Tunics are often worn as part of a military or police uniform.
tu·nic (tōō'nik *or* tyōō'nik) *noun, plural* **tunics.**

tunnel A long passage built underneath the ground or water. There is a subway *tunnel* under the river. *Noun.*

—To make a tunnel under or through something. The prisoners *tunneled* under the wall to escape. *Verb.*

tun·nel (tun′əl) *noun, plural* **tunnels;** *verb,* **tunneled, tunneling.**

turban A long scarf that is wound around the head and worn like a hat. Men in India and Arab countries wear turbans.

tur·ban (tur′bən) *noun, plural* **turbans.**

turbine An engine that is run by a stream of gas or liquid that moves against its blades and turns them.

tur·bine (tur′bin *or* tur′bīn) *noun, plural* **turbines.**

Turban

turf The top part of the soil that is covered with small plants and grass.

turf (turf) *noun.*

turkey A large bird with reddish-brown feathers that is raised as food.

tur·key (tur′kē) *noun, plural* **turkeys.**

Turkey

Turkey A country in western Asia and southeastern Europe. Its capital is Ankara.

Tur·key (tur′kē) *noun.*

Turkish The language of Turkey. *Noun.*
—Of or having to do with Turkey, its people, or their language. *Adjective.*

Turk·ish (tur′kish) *noun; adjective.*

turmoil Great confusion or disorder. The airport was in a *turmoil* during the bad snowstorm.

tur·moil (tur′moil) *noun.*

turn 1. To move or cause to move around in a circle or part of a circle; rotate or revolve. The earth *turns.* The key *turned* in the lock. Power from the car engine *turns* the wheels. 2. To go or make go a certain or different way. The river *turns* south after the bridge. Pam *turned* the car left at the corner. *Turn*

the pancakes over before they burn. 3. To change or cause to change in nature or condition. Leaves *turn* brown in the fall. The milk *turned* sour. 4. To have or cause to have different feelings about. His old friends *turned* against him when he was in trouble. 5. To make or become sick. His stomach *turned* when the roller coaster went down the big hill. *Verb.*
—1. A movement around in a circle or part of a circle. She had to make a quick *turn* to catch the ball. 2. A change in position or direction. Make a left *turn* after you pass the church. There is a sharp *turn* in the road just ahead. 3. A time, occasion, or chance at something. It's Mike's *turn* at bat. She said it was his *turn* to wash the dishes. *Noun.*

turn (turn) *verb,* **turned, turning;** *noun, plural* **turns.**

to turn down. To refuse. I had to *turn down* his invitation to go to the movies.

to turn out. 1. To make. The machine *turns out* twenty copies a minute. 2. To show up; appear. A huge crowd *turned out* for the game.

turnip A round, white or yellow vegetable that is the root of a certain plant. The turnip plant has soft, prickly leaves and clusters of bright yellow flowers.

tur·nip (tur′nip) *noun, plural* **turnips.**

turnpike A large road or highway. People have to pay a toll to ride on some turnpikes.

turn·pike (turn′pīk′) *noun, plural* **turnpikes.**

turnstile A revolving gate or movable bar at an exit or entrance. People pass through a turnstile one at a time.

Turnstile

turn·stile (turn′stīl′) *noun, plural* **turnstiles.**

turntable A round platform that turns

at; āpe; cär; end; mē; it; īce; hot; ōld;
fôrk; wood; fool; oil; out; up; turn; sing;
thin; this; hw in white; zh in treasure.
ə stands for a in about, e in taken
i in pencil, o in lemon, and u in circus.

things around. Record players have turn-tables that turn the records.

turn·ta·ble (turn′tā′bəl) *noun, plural* **turnta-bles.**

turpentine A liquid that is mixed with paints and other substances to make them thinner. Turpentine is made from the sticky resin of pine trees. It burns easily.

tur·pen·tine (tur′pən tīn′) *noun.*

turquoise **1.** A greenish-blue mineral that is used as a gem stone. **2.** A greenish-blue color. *Noun.*
—Of the color turquoise. *Adjective.*

tur·quoise (tur′kwoiz *or* tur′koiz) *noun, plural* **turquoises;** *adjective.*

turret **1.** A small tower on a building. Some castles have *turrets* at each corner. **2.** A structure on top of a military tank or ship within which guns or cannons are mounted.

tur·ret (tur′it) *noun, plural* **turrets.**

Turret

turtle An animal with a low, wide body covered by a hard shell. Turtles have a sharp-edged jaw but no teeth. They live on land and in salt and fresh water.

tur·tle (turt′əl) *noun, plural* **turtles.**

Turtle

tusk A long, pointed tooth that sticks out of the side of the mouth of certain animals. Elephants, walruses, and wild boars have tusks.

tusk (tusk) *noun, plural* **tusks.**

tutor A teacher who gives private lessons to a pupil. When Stuart was sick for three months, he had a *tutor* at home. *Noun.*
—To teach privately; act as a tutor. Lisa

made extra money by *tutoring* French at night. *Verb.*

tu·tor (too′tər *or* tyoo′tər) *noun, plural* **tu-tors;** *verb,* **tutored, tutoring.**

TV Television. We watched *TV* for an hour.

tweed A rough wool cloth woven with two or more different colors of yarn. Tweed is used to make jackets, slacks, and other clothes.

tweed (twēd) *noun, plural* **tweeds.**

▲ The word **tweed** comes from the Scottish word *tweel,* which is the name of a kind of cloth. The word was changed to *tweed* because of the name of the Tweed River, which runs through the part of Scotland that is famous for making tweed cloth.

twelfth **1.** Next after the eleventh. **2.** One of twelve equal parts; $\frac{1}{12}$.

twelfth (twelfth) *adjective; noun, plural* **twelfths.**

twelve Two more than ten; 12.

twelve (twelv) *noun, plural* **twelves;** *adjective.*

twentieth **1.** Next after the nineteenth. **2.** One of twenty equal parts; $\frac{1}{20}$.

twen·ti·eth (twen′tē ith) *adjective; noun, plural* **twentieths.**

twenty Two times ten; 20.

twen·ty (twen′tē) *noun, plural* **twenties;** *adjective.*

twice Two times. I called him *twice* today but he doesn't answer.

twice (twīs) *adverb.*

twig A small branch of a tree or other woody plant.

twig (twig) *noun, plural* **twigs.**

twilight The time just after sunset or just before sunrise when there is a soft, hazy light reflected from the sun.

twi·light (twī′līt′) *noun.*

twin One of two children or animals born at the same time to the same mother. Some twins look exactly alike. *Noun.*
—**1.** Being a twin. Rhoda is Ruth's *twin* sister. **2.** Being identical or being very much alike. We could see the *twin* mountain peaks in the distance. *Adjective.*

twin (twin) *noun, plural* **twins;** *adjective.*

twine A strong string made of two or more strands twisted together. *Noun.*
—To wind or coil one thing around another. Ivy *twined* around the gate post. She *twined* a ribbon through the lace. *Verb.*

twine (twīn) *noun, plural* **twines;** *verb,* **twined, twining.**

twinge A sudden, sharp pain. Paul felt a *twinge* in his sore tooth.
twinge (twinj) *noun, plural* **twinges.**

twinkle To shine with flashes of light. Stars *twinkle* in the sky at night. His eyes *twinkled* with laughter. *Verb.*
—A flash of light or brightness. We saw the *twinkle* of the lights down below as the airplane flew over the city. *Noun.*
twin·kle (twing′kəl) *verb,* **twinkled, twinkling;** *noun, plural* **twinkles.**

twirl To spin around quickly. Susie learned to *twirl* a baton at school. The dancers *twirled* around the floor.
twirl (twurl) *verb,* **twirled, twirling.**

twist **1.** To wind or turn around something. The dog's chain was *twisted* around the tree. The road *twisted* around the mountain. **2.** To change the natural or usual shape of. He *twisted* his face into an angry look. **3.** To change the meaning of. She *twisted* my words when she told you that I didn't want to come to your party. **4.** To hurt a part of the body by turning from its natural shape or position. Mother *twisted* her ankle when she slipped off the ladder. *Verb.*
—A turn or bend in something. There is a *twist* in the wire that I can't straighten out. *Noun.*
twist (twist) *verb,* **twisted, twisting;** *noun, plural* **twists.**

twitch To move or pull with a sudden jerk or tug. The rabbit's nose *twitched.*
twitch (twich) *verb,* **twitched, twitching.**

twitter **1.** A series of short, light chirping sounds made by a bird or birds. We heard the *twitter* of birds in the trees outside our window. **2.** A nervous or excited state. Everyone was in a *twitter* on the last day of school before summer vacation. *Noun.*
—To make short, light chirping sounds. The sparrows *twittered* in the trees. *Verb.*
twit·ter (twit′ər) *noun, plural* **twitters;** *verb,* **twittered, twittering.**

two One more than one; 2. ▲ Other words that sound like this are **to** and **too.**
two (to͞o) *noun, plural* **twos;** *adjective.*

tying She is *tying* a bow with the ribbon. Look up **tie** for more information.
ty·ing (tī′ing) *verb.*

type **1.** A kind or group of things that are the same in some way. A collie is a *type* of dog. What *type* of sports do you like? **2.** A piece of metal with a raised letter, number, or figure on the surface that is used in printing. *Noun.*
—**1.** To write with a typewriter. I *typed* a letter to my brother at college. **2.** To find out

what group a person or thing belongs to. The hospital *typed* his blood. *Verb.*
type (tīp) *noun, plural* **types;** *verb,* **typed, typing.**

typewriter A machine that prints letters. It has keys for each letter of the alphabet, for numbers, and for punctuation marks. When you hit a key, the letter hits an inked ribbon and is printed on a piece of paper.
type·writ·er (tīp′rī′tər) *noun, plural* **typewriters.**

Typewriter

typhoid fever A serious disease that people get from bacteria in their food or drink. It causes a very high fever and infection of the intestines. It can be passed from one person to another.
ty·phoid fever (tī′foid).

typhoon A tropical storm with violent winds.
ty·phoon (tī fo͞on′) *noun, plural* **typhoons.**

▲ The word **typhoon** comes from two Chinese words that mean "great wind."

typical Showing the qualities or characteristics of a certain type. The picture shows the inside of a *typical* modern house. On a *typical* summer's day we go to the beach and then come home to cook dinner outside.
typ·i·cal (tip′i kəl) *adjective.*

typist A person who types letters or other papers.
typ·ist (tī′pist) *noun, plural* **typists.**

tyranny The cruel use of force or authority. The dictator ruled his country with *tyranny.*
tyr·an·ny (tir′ə nē) *noun.*

tyrant A person who uses force or his authority in a cruel or unjust way. The *tyrant* had any person who disagreed with him put in jail.
ty·rant (tī′rənt) *noun, plural* **tyrants.**

at; āpe; cär; end; mē; it; īce; hot; ōld;
fôrk; wood; fo͞ol; oil; out; up; turn; sing;
thin; this; hw in white; zh in treasure.
ə stands for a in about, e in taken
i in pencil, o in lemon, and u in circus.

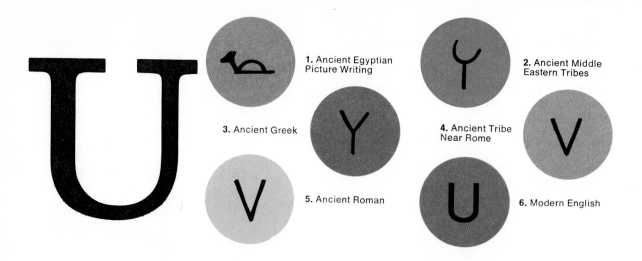

1. Ancient Egyptian Picture Writing

2. Ancient Middle Eastern Tribes

3. Ancient Greek

4. Ancient Tribe Near Rome

5. Ancient Roman

6. Modern English

U is the twenty-first letter of the alphabet. The oldest form of the letter **U** was a drawing that the ancient Egyptians (**1**) used in their picture writing nearly 5000 years ago. This drawing was borrowed by several ancient tribes (**2**) in the Middle East. They used it to stand for both the vowel sound *u*, as the *u* in *rude*, and the consonant sound *w*, as the *w* in *water*. The ancient Greeks (**3**) borrowed this letter, writing it very much like a modern capital letter **Y**. They used it to stand for the *u* sound only. This letter was then borrowed by an ancient tribe (**4**) that settled north of Rome about 2800 years ago. They changed its shape so that it looked like a modern capital letter **V**. The Romans (**5**) borrowed this letter about 2400 years ago. By about 1000 years ago, two forms of this V-shaped letter were being used in writing: **V** at the beginning of a word, and a new letter, **U**, in the middle of a word. In the following years, the letter **U**, which was used for only the *u* sound, was written almost exactly as we write it today (**6**).

u, U The twenty-first letter of the alphabet.
u, U (yo͞o) *noun, plural* **u's, U's.**

ugly **1.** Not nice or pleasing to look at. He has an *ugly* scar on his arm. That is an *ugly* painting. **2.** Likely to cause trouble or harm. He is in an *ugly* mood today.
ug·ly (ug′lē) *adjective,* **uglier, ugliest.**

ukulele A small guitar that has four strings. It is played by plucking the strings.
u·ku·le·le (yo͞o′kə lā′lē) *noun, plural* **ukuleles.**

ultimate **1.** Coming at the end; final. The *ultimate* cost of building that highway was forty million dollars. The team's *ultimate* victory resulted from much training and work. **2.** Most basic. Scientists have several different theories about the *ultimate* beginnings of life.
ul·ti·mate (ul′tə mit) *adjective.*

umbrella A circular piece of cloth or plastic stretched on a framework that can be folded up when it is not needed. An umbrella is used to give protection from the rain or sun.
um·brel·la (um-brel′ə) *noun, plural* **umbrellas.**

umpire A person who rules on plays in baseball or certain other sports. *Noun.*
—To act as an umpire. Jeff's dad will *umpire* our softball game on Saturday. *Verb.*

Ukulele

Umbrella

674

um·pire (ŭm′pīr) *noun, plural* **umpires**; *verb,* **umpired, umpiring.**

un- A *prefix* that means "not."

▲ There are many words beginning with **un-** that you will not find in this dictionary. You can understand the meaning of these words by putting the word "not" in front of the part of the word that follows *un-*. For example, the word *unexpected* means "not expected," the word *unclear* means "not clear," and the word *unsuccessful* means "not successful."

unaccented Not accented. In the word "ago," the "a" is unaccented.
un·ac·cent·ed (un ak′sen tid) *adjective.*

unanimous In or showing total agreement. The family was *unanimous* in wanting to go on a picnic. Jack was elected club president by a *unanimous* vote.
u·nan·i·mous (yо̄о̄ nan′ə məs) *adjective.*

▲ The word **unanimous** comes from a Latin word that means "of one mind." When people are *unanimous* about something, they have all made up their mind in the same way about it.

unbelievable That cannot be believed; hard to believe. She told an *unbelievable* story about seeing a ghost. The circus acrobats did *unbelievable* tricks.
un·be·liev·a·ble (un′bi lē′və bəl) *adjective.*

unbroken 1. Not broken. There was not an *unbroken* piece of china left in the box after it crashed to the floor. 2. Not interrupted. We drove through miles of *unbroken* desert. The football team has had an *unbroken* series of victories. 3. Not beaten; not surpassed. The athlete's swimming record is still *unbroken*. 4. Not weakened or tamed. He could not handle the *unbroken* horse.
un·bro·ken (un brō′kən) *adjective.*

uncanny Strange and mysterious. We heard *uncanny* sounds coming from the deserted house. She has an *uncanny* ability to know what other people are thinking.
un·can·ny (un kan′ē) *adjective.*

uncertain 1. Not known for sure; not certain. It is still *uncertain* whether our team will win the game. 2. Not dependable; changing. The weather was *uncertain*, so we called off the picnic.
un·cer·tain (un surt′ən) *adjective.*

unchanged Not changed. The sick man's condition was *unchanged*.
un·changed (un chānjd′) *adjective.*

uncle 1. The brother of one's mother or father. 2. The husband of one's aunt.
un·cle (ung′kəl) *noun, plural* **uncles.**

uncomfortable 1. Causing discomfort. That chair is hard and *uncomfortable*. 2. Feeling discomfort. He is *uncomfortable* in his tight shoes.
un·com·fort·a·ble (un kum′fər tə bəl *or* un-kumf′tə bəl) *adjective.*

uncommon Unusual; rare. That bird is *uncommon* in this part of the country.
un·com·mon (un kom′ən) *adjective.*

unconscious 1. Not conscious. He was knocked *unconscious* when he fell out of the tree and hit his head. 2. Not knowing; unaware. He was *unconscious* of how sloppy he looked. 3. Not done on purpose. She made an *unconscious* mistake when she called him by his brother's name.
un·con·scious (un kon′shəs) *adjective.*

unconstitutional Not in keeping with the constitution of a state or country. The Supreme Court declared the new state law *unconstitutional*.
un·con·sti·tu·tion·al (un′kon stə то̄о̄′shən əl *or* un′kon stə tyо̄о̄′shən əl) *adjective.*

uncover 1. To make known. The detective *uncovered* some new clues. 2. To take away something that covers. The cook *uncovered* the pan.
un·cov·er (un kuv′ər) *verb,* **uncovered, uncovering.**

undecided 1. Not having one's mind made up. Sally is still *undecided* about what she wants for her birthday. 2. Not yet settled. The result of the school election is still *undecided*.
un·de·cid·ed (un′di sī′did) *adjective.*

under The kitten crawled *under* the sofa. John is wearing a blue shirt *under* his coat. I want to spend *under* $5.00 for the present. Dad drove five miles *under* the speed limit. The fire is *under* control. *Under* the new rules, the swimming pool is open one night a week. The country grew rich and strong *under* the king. The damaged boat slowly went *under*. Jeff scooped mud off the *under* part of his shoe.
un·der (un′dər) *preposition; adverb; adjective.*

at; āpe; cär; end; mē; it; īce; hot; ōld;
fôrk; wood; fо̄о̄l; oil; out; up; turn; sing;
thin; this; hw in white; zh in treasure.
ə stands for a in about, e in taken
i in pencil, o in lemon, and u in circus.

underbrush Bushes and other plants growing beneath big trees in a forest or woods.
un·der·brush (un′dər brush′) *noun.*

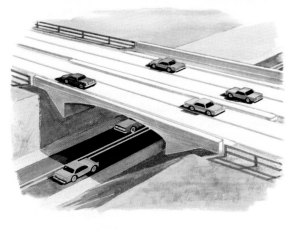

Underpass

underdeveloped 1. Not fully developed. The boy's muscles are *underdeveloped*. 2. Behind in growth or development. The rich country sent aid to the *underdeveloped* country.
un·der·de·vel·oped (un′dər di vel′əpt) *adjective.*

underfoot 1. In the way. The baby's toys are always *underfoot*. 2. Beneath the feet; on the ground. Because of the rain it was wet *underfoot*.
un·der·foot (un′dər foot′) *adverb.*

undergo To go through; experience. The street will *undergo* repairs. The early settlers of America had to *undergo* many hardships.
un·der·go (un′dər gō′) *verb,* **underwent, undergone, undergoing.**

undergraduate A student in a college or university who has not yet graduated.
un·der·grad·u·ate (un′dər graj′o͞o it) *noun, plural* **undergraduates.**

underground 1. Below the earth's surface. The workers built an *underground* passage for the subway. 2. Secret; hidden. The spies belonged to an *underground* organization. *Adjective.*
—1. A place below the earth's surface. 2. A group working in secret. The *underground* in the country continued to fight against the government. *Noun.*
—Below the earth's surface. Miners work *underground. Adverb.*
un·der·ground (un′dər ground′ *for adjective and adverb;* un′dər ground′ *for noun) adjective; noun, plural* **undergrounds;** *adverb.*

undergrowth Small bushes and plants growing under the large trees in a forest.
un·der·growth (un′dər grōth′) *noun.*

underline To draw a line under. The teacher *underlined* the words that I had spelled wrong on the test.
un·der·line (un′dər līn′) *verb,* **underlined, underlining.**

underneath Bill found the missing shoe *underneath* his bed. She packed the records on top and the books *underneath.*
un·der·neath (un′dər nēth′) *preposition; adverb.*

underpass A road that goes under a bridge or another road.
un·der·pass (un′dər pas′) *noun, plural* **underpasses.**

underprivileged Lacking the advantages that others have because one is poor.
un·der·priv·i·leged (un′dər priv′ə lijd) *adjective.*

undersea Lying, done, or used under the surface of the sea. The wreck of the old ship was found during an *undersea* exploration.
un·der·sea (un′dər sē′ *or* un′dər sē′) *adjective.*

undershirt A shirt with short sleeves or no sleeves that is worn under a person's clothing.
un·der·shirt (un′dər shurt′) *noun, plural* **undershirts.**

underside The bottom side or surface of something. The bird had brown wings and a red *underside.*
un·der·side (un′dər sīd′) *noun, plural* **undersides.**

understand 1. To get the meaning of. I didn't *understand* the teacher's question. 2. To know very well. My parents *understand* French because they lived for a time in France. 3. To be in sympathy or agreement with. The two friends are very close and *understand* each other completely. 4. To be told something; learn. I *understand* that you hope to go to college. 5. To take as a fact; assume. I *understand* that I can return the tickets before the game and get my money back.
un·der·stand (un′dər stand′) *verb,* **understood, understanding.**

understanding 1. A grasping of the meaning of something. Paul has a good *understanding* of arithmetic. 2. Opinion; belief. It was Sam's *understanding* that we would meet at three o'clock. 3. Sympathy or agreement. Mary always shows *understanding* when people bring her their problems. The two

friends reached an *understanding* that ended their quarrel. *Noun.*
—Feeling or showing sympathy. The teacher gave the nervous girl an *understanding* look as she got up to read in front of the class. *Adjective.*
    un·der·stand·ing (un′dər stan′ding) *noun, plural* **understandings;** *adjective.*

understood Joan *understood* the meaning of the poem. Look up **understand** for more information.
    un·der·stood (un′dər stood′) *verb.*

undertake **1.** To try to do; attempt. The explorers planned to *undertake* a journey over the mountain ridge. **2.** To agree to do something; accept a job or task. The nurse will *undertake* the patient's care when the doctor is away.
    un·der·take (un′dər tāk′) *verb,* **undertook, undertaken, undertaking.**

undertaker A person whose job is arranging funerals and preparing dead people for burial.
    un·der·tak·er (un′dər tā′kər) *noun, plural* **undertakers.**

undertook The explorers *undertook* the trip on horseback. Look up **undertake** for more information.
    un·der·took (un′dər took′) *verb.*

underwater Lying, used, or done below the surface of the water. An *underwater* tunnel connected the island and the mainland. The book had photographs of *underwater* plants. *Adjective.*
—Below the surface of the water. Jack likes to swim *underwater. Adverb.*
    un·der·wa·ter (un′dər wô′tər) *adjective; adverb.*

underwear Clothing worn under a person's outer clothing.
    un·der·wear (un′dər wer′) *noun.*

underweight Having less than the normal or needed weight. Fred was a little *underweight* after he was sick.
    un·der·weight (un′dər wāt′) *adjective.*

underwent Howard *underwent* an operation to have his tonsils removed. Look up **undergo** for more information.
    un·der·went (un′dər went′) *verb.*

undid Peter *undid* the laces of his shoes. Look up **undo** for more information.
    un·did (un did′) *verb.*

undisturbed Not disturbed or bothered. Bob was *undisturbed* by the noise.
    un·dis·turbed (un′dis turbd′) *adjective.*

undo **1.** To loosen or unfasten something; untie. This is a hard knot to *undo.* Steve

helped his little sister *undo* the package. **2.** To do away with something that has been done. The tornado *undid* the farmer's hard work of planting his crops.
    un·do (un doo′) *verb,* **undid, undone, undoing.**

undoing Ruin or downfall. Carelessness was the thief's *undoing.*
    un·do·ing (un doo′ing) *noun.*

undone¹ Not finished or done. Tony left the last question on the test *undone.*
    un·done (un dun′) *adjective.*

undone² He felt more comfortable when his necktie was *undone.* Look up **undo** for more information.
    un·done (un dun′) *verb.*

undress To take one's clothes off. The tired boy *undressed* and went to bed.
    un·dress (un dres′) *verb,* **undressed, undressing.**

unearth **1.** To dig up out of the earth. The dog *unearthed* a bone it had buried. **2.** To search for and find; deliver. My grandmother *unearthed* some old family photographs.
    un·earth (un urth′) *verb,* **unearthed, unearthing.**

uneasy **1.** Worried; nervous. Jane's father was *uneasy* about her staying out so late. **2.** Uncomfortable. She dropped off into an *uneasy* sleep. His rude remark was followed by an *uneasy* silence in the group.
    un·eas·y (un ē′zē) *adjective,* **uneasier, uneasiest.**

unemployed Not having a job; out of work. The closing of the factory left many people *unemployed.*
    un·em·ployed (un′em ploid′) *adjective.*

unequal **1.** Not the same; uneven. The boys complained that Ted had divided the cake into *unequal* pieces. The sleeves of the sweater Jean knitted were of *unequal* length. **2.** Not well matched; unfair. When the older boys played the younger boys in football, it was an *unequal* contest. **3.** Not strong or able enough. He proved *unequal* to the difficult job of taking care of his younger brothers.
    un·e·qual (un ē′kwəl) *adjective.*

uneven **1.** Not straight, smooth, or regular. The hem of the dress was *uneven.* The car

at; āpe; cär; end; mē; it; īce; hot; ōld; fôrk; wood; fool; oil; out; up; turn; sing; thin; this; hw in white; zh in treasure.
ə stands for a in about, e in taken i in pencil, o in lemon, and u in circus.

bounced along the *uneven* road. **2.** Being an odd number. 1, 3, and 5 are *uneven*. **3.** Not well matched; unfair. There was no way our team could win the *uneven* contest.

un·e·ven (un ē′vən) *adjective,* **unevener, unevenest.**

unexpected Coming or happening without warning; not expected. The train was late because of an *unexpected* delay.

un·ex·pect·ted (un′iks pek′tid) *adjective.*

unfair Not fair or just. The older boy had an *unfair* advantage over the younger boy in the fight.

un·fair (un fer′) *adjective.*

unfamiliar **1.** Not well known or easily recognized; strange. The handwriting on the envelope is *unfamiliar* to me. **2.** Not acquainted. The librarian was *unfamiliar* with the book I wanted.

un·fa·mil·iar (un′fə mil′yər) *adjective.*

unhappy Without happiness or joy; sad. Victor was *unhappy* about having to move to a different town.

un·hap·py (un hap′ē) *adjective,* **unhappier, unhappiest.**

unicorn An imaginary animal that looks like a white horse with a long pointed horn in the middle of its forehead.

u·ni·corn (yōō′nə kôrn′) *noun, plural* **unicorns.**

Unicorn

unicycle A vehicle that is like a bicycle but has only one wheel. It is used mostly by acrobats and other entertainers.

u·ni·cy·cle (yōō′nə sī′kəl) *noun, plural* **unicycles.**

uniform **1.** Always the same; not changing. All the rooms in the building are painted a *uniform* color. **2.** Showing little or no difference; all alike. The houses on that street are of *uniform* design. *Adjective.*
—The special or official clothes that the members of a particular group wear. Soldiers, policemen, postmen, and students at some schools wear uniforms. *Noun.*

un·i·form (yōō′nə fôrm′) *adjective; noun, plural* **uniforms.**

unimportant With no special value, meaning, or interest; not important. The newspaper didn't bother to print a story on the *unimportant* incident. It is *unimportant* what color car we buy as long as we get one that runs well.

un·im·por·tant (un′im pôrt′ənt) *adjective.*

union **1.** A joining together of two or more people or things. The new town was formed by the *union* of three small villages. **2. the Union. a.** The United States of America. **b.** The states that stayed loyal to the Federal government during the Civil War. **3.** A group of workers joined together to protect their interests and improve their working conditions.

un·ion (yōōn′yən) *noun, plural* **unions.**

unique Not having an equal; being the only one of its kind. Being the first person to set foot on the moon was a *unique* achievement.

u·nique (yoo nēk′) *adjective.*

unison Complete agreement. The students answered the teacher's question in *unison.*

u·ni·son (yōō′nə sən *or* yōō′nə zən) *noun, plural* **unisons.**

unit **1.** A single person, thing, or group that is part of a larger group. That apartment building contains fifty *units.* **2.** A piece of equipment having a special purpose. The builder installed an air-conditioning *unit* in the house. **3.** A fixed quantity or amount that is used as a standard of measurement. An hour is a *unit* of time. **4.** The smallest whole number; one.

u·nit (yōō′nit) *noun, plural* **units.**

unite To bring or join together; make or become one. The two families were *united* by marriage. All the people in the country *united* in the battle against the enemy.

u·nite (yoo nīt′) *verb,* **united, uniting.**

United Nations An international organization that includes most of the countries of the world as its members. It was founded in 1945 to keep world peace. Its headquarters are in New York City.

United States A country that is mainly in

North America. It is made up of fifty states. Its capital is Washington, D. C. This country is also called the **United States of America.**

universal 1. Of, for, or shared by all. There was *universal* joy when the war ended. 2. Being everywhere. Disease is *universal* in the world.
u·ni·ver·sal (yo͞o′nə vur′səl) *adjective.*

universe Everything that exists, including the earth, the heavens, and all of space.
u·ni·verse (yo͞o′nə vurs′) *noun, plural* **universes.**

▲ The word **universe** comes from a Latin word that means "the whole world."

university A school of higher learning. It is usually made up of one or more colleges.
u·ni·ver·si·ty (yo͞o′nə vur′sə tē) *noun, plural* **universities.**

unjust Not fair or just. The man complained that the judge's decision had been *unjust.*
un·just (un just′) *adjective.*

unkind Not kind; cruel. His *unkind* remark hurt her feelings.
un·kind (un kīnd′) *adjective,* **unkinder, unkindest.**

unknown Not known; not familiar. That man's name is *unknown* to me. The sailors were shipwrecked on an *unknown* island.
un·known (un nōn′) *adjective.*

unless *Unless* you return all the library books you borrowed, you cannot borrow any more.
un·less (un les′) *conjunction.*

unlike Different from. *Unlike* most of his friends, he enjoys dancing. *Preposition.*
—Not the same; different. A deer and a mouse are *unlike* animals. *Adjective.*
un·like (un līk′) *preposition; adjective.*

unlikely 1. Not likely or probable. It is *unlikely* that it will rain today. 2. Not likely to succeed. The two men had an *unlikely* plan for making money.
un·like·ly (un līk′lē) *adjective,* **unlikelier, unlikeliest.**

unlimited Without any limits. This card will give you *unlimited* use of the town library.
un·lim·it·ed (un lim′ə tid) *adjective.*

unload 1. To take off a load. The men *unloaded* the cargo from the ship. 2. To remove a load from. We *unloaded* the car when we got home. 3. To remove ammunition from. The soldier *unloaded* his gun.
un·load (un lōd′) *verb,* **unloaded, unloading.**

unlock 1. To open the lock of. Bill *unlocked* the front door with his key. 2. To make known. The detective *unlocked* the mystery of the strange crime.
un·lock (un lok′) *verb,* **unlocked, unlocking.**

unlucky 1. Not having good luck. The *unlucky* man had his wallet stolen for the third time. 2. Causing bad luck. Some people believe that thirteen is an *unlucky* number.
un·luck·y (un luk′ē) *adjective,* **unluckier, unluckiest.**

unmanned Without a crew. The *unmanned* spacecraft landed on the planet Mars.
un·manned (un mand′) *adjective.*

unmistakable That cannot be mistaken; plain; clear. There was an *unmistakable* note of anger in her voice.
un·mis·tak·a·ble (un′mis tā′kə bəl) *adjective.*

unnatural Going against or different from what is usual or normal in nature; not natural. The cat grew to an *unnatural* size.
un·nat·u·ral (un nach′ər əl) *adjective.*

unnecessary Not necessary; needless. It was *unnecessary* for him to repeat his question, because I heard it the first time.
un·nec·es·sar·y (un nes′ə ser′ē) *adjective.*

unpleasant Not pleasing; disagreeable. There was an *unpleasant* odor coming from the sewer.
un·pleas·ant (un plez′ənt) *adjective.*

unpopular Not generally liked or accepted. He was afraid he might be *unpopular* at his new school. The politician had a number of ideas that were *unpopular* with the voters.
un·pop·u·lar (un pop′yə lər) *adjective.*

unreasonable 1. Not showing or using good sense; not reasonable. He is being *unreasonable* in wanting his own way all the time. 2. Too great. The prices at that restaurant were *unreasonable.*
un·rea·son·a·ble (un rē′zə nə bəl *or* un·rēz′nə bəl) *adjective.*

unreliable Not to be trusted. That boy is *unreliable* and never keeps his promise.
un·re·li·a·ble (un′ri lī′ə bəl) *adjective.*

unrest An uneasy or discontented state. There was political *unrest* in the country under the dictator's rule.
un·rest (un rest′) *noun.*

at; āpe; cär; end; mē; it; īce; hot; ōld;
fôrk; wood; fo͞ol; oil; out; up; turn; sing;
thin; this; hw in white; zh in treasure.
ə stands for a in about, e in taken
i in pencil, o in lemon, and u in circus.

unruly Hard to control or manage. The police tried to control the *unruly* mob. After he washes his hair, it is *unruly* and hard to comb.
un·ru·ly (un r o͞o′lē) *adjective,* **unrulier, unruliest.**

unsettled **1.** Not peaceful, calm, or orderly. There were still *unsettled* conditions in the country following the war. **2.** Not decided. The question of how much the club should charge new members for dues is still *unsettled*. **3.** Not paid. The old man died and left behind a lot of *unsettled* doctor bills. **4.** Not being lived in; not inhabited. Many areas of Alaska remain largely *unsettled*.
un·set·tled (un set′əld) *adjective.*

unskilled **1.** Not having skill, training, or experience. An *unskilled* worker generally gets paid less than a skilled worker does. **2.** Not needing special skills, training, or experience. The new factory will provide many *unskilled* jobs for the town.
un·skilled (un skild′) *adjective.*

unsound **1.** Not strong or solid; weak. That old wooden bridge is *unsound*. **2.** Not based on truth or good judgment. He gave you *unsound* advice when he told you to buy that old bicycle.
un·sound (un sound′) *adjective.*

unstable **1.** Not firmly fixed; easily moved. That chair is *unstable* because one leg is broken. **2.** Liable to change. A group of army officers tried to overthrow the *unstable* government of that country.
un·sta·ble (un stā′bəl) *adjective.*

unsteady Not firm; shaky. This ladder is *unsteady* because it is not standing on level ground. Diane fought back her tears and answered in an *unsteady* voice.
un·stead·y (un sted′ē) *adjective,* **unsteadier, unsteadiest.**

untie To loosen or undo; free. The little boy asked his sister to help him *untie* the knot in his shoelace.
un·tie (un tī′) *verb,* **untied, untying.**

until Wait *until* eight o'clock before you telephone home. Tickets for the baseball game will not go on sale *until* Wednesday. Wait here *until* I get back. We couldn't take the car out of the garage *until* we cleared the snow from the driveway.
un·til (ən til′ *or* un til′) *preposition; conjunction.*

unused **1.** Not in use; not put to use. I think that there is room for the books on the *unused* shelf in the bookcase. **2.** Never having been used; new. I have an *unused* toothbrush I could give you. **3.** Not accustomed. Robert came from a small town and was *unused* to the noise of the city.
un·used (un yo͞ozd′) *adjective.*

unusual Not usual, common, or ordinary; rare. It is very *unusual* for Andy not to want to go to the hockey game with us.
un·u·su·al (un yo͞o′zhoo əl) *adjective.*

up Jack climbed *up* to the top of the ladder. We looked *up* to see the airplane. Jane turned the sound *up* on the television. The sun came *up* at five o'clock. Stand *up* straight. Take the *up* escalator to the fourth floor. Food prices were *up* again this month. My brother didn't get *up* until nine o'clock this morning. The house next door is *up* for sale. The spider climbed *up* the wall. The boys rowed *up* the river.
up (up) *adverb; adjective; preposition.*

upholster To fit with padding, cushions, or coverings. The cat tore up our couch so badly that it had to be *upholstered* again.
up·hol·ster (up hōl′stər) *verb,* **upholstered, upholstering.**

upkeep The keeping of something in good condition; maintenance. Much money is needed for the *upkeep* of the city's parks.
up·keep (up′kēp′) *noun.*

upon He lay with his head *upon* the pillow. Bill and his friends came *upon* a bird's nest with four eggs in it.
up·on (ə pôn′ *or* ə pon′) *preposition.*

upper Higher. The people who live in the *upper* stories of that building have a beautiful view of the city.
up·per (up′ər) *adjective.*

upper hand A position of control; advantage. Our team gained the *upper hand* in the last half of the basketball game.

upright **1.** Straight up; erect. The front porch was supported by four *upright* pillars. **2.** Good; honest. That *upright* man would never lie or cheat. *Adjective.*
—In a straight up and down position. Joe placed the chair *upright* after the dog knocked it over. *Adverb.*
up·right (up′rīt′) *adjective; adverb.*

uprising A revolt against a government or other authority; rebellion. The dictator used troops to put down the people's *uprising*.
up·ris·ing (up′rī′zing) *noun, plural* **uprisings.**

uproar A noisy and excited disturbance. The crowd was in an *uproar* when the player hit a home run to win the game.
up·roar (up′rôr′) *noun, plural* **uproars.**

uproot **1.** To tear or pull up by the roots. The bulldozers *uprooted* bushes and trees to make way for the new highway. **2.** To cause to leave. The flood *uprooted* many families from their homes.

    up·root (up r$\overline{oo}$t$'$ *or* up root$'$) *verb,* **uprooted, uprooting.**

upset **1.** To turn or knock over. I accidentally *upset* the glass of milk. **2.** To interfere with. The rain *upset* our plans for a picnic. **3.** To make nervous and worried; disturb. The news of his cousin's accident *upset* him greatly. **4.** To make sick. Eating all that candy will *upset* your stomach. **5.** To defeat unexpectedly. The young tennis player *upset* the city champion. *Verb.*

—**1.** Turned or knocked over. The *upset* glass of milk spilled all over me. **2.** Nervous and worried. Don was *upset* about missing his plane. **3.** Sick. My sister got an *upset* stomach from eating too much. *Adjective.*

    up·set (up set$'$) *verb,* **upset, upsetting;** *adjective.*

upside down **1.** So that the top side or part becomes the bottom side or part. You're holding the book *upside down.* **2.** In or into complete disorder or confusion. I turned my room *upside down* looking for the missing keys.

upstairs **1.** Up the stairs. Dick ran *upstairs* to get his baseball glove. **2.** On or to an upper floor. Fran is watching television *upstairs.*

    up·stairs (up$'$sterz$'$) *adverb.*

upstream Toward or at the source of a stream; against the current. The boys rowed *upstream.* The *upstream* fishing is good today.

    up·stream (up$'$str$\overline{e}$m$'$) *adverb; adjective.*

Salmon Swimming Upstream

up-to-date Using or showing the latest developments or style. You can tell this is an *up-to-date* map because it shows the new highway. The fashion model always wore the most *up-to-date* clothes.

    up-to-date (up$'$tϑ d$\overline{a}$t$'$) *adjective.*

upward From a lower to a higher place. The people on the street looked *upward* to see the plane fly overhead. The cost of food has climbed steadily *upward.* This word is also spelled **upwards.** *Adverb.*

—Moving from a lower place to a higher place. There is a constant *upward* trend in the birth rate for many countries of the world. *Adjective.*

    up·ward (up$'$wϑrd) *adverb; adjective.*

uranium A silver-colored metal that is used as a source of nuclear energy. Uranium is a chemical element.

    u·ra·ni·um (yoo r$\overline{a}'$n$\overline{e}$ ϑm) *noun.*

▲ Scientists named **uranium** after the planet *Uranus.* Uranus was discovered a short while before the element was named, and so the most recently discovered element was named after the most recently discovered planet.

Uranus The third largest planet. It is the seventh closest planet to the sun.

    U·ra·nus (yoor$'$$\vartheta$ nϑs *or* yoo r$\overline{a}'$nϑs) *noun.*

urban Having to do with a city or city life. In this country the *urban* population is much larger than the number of people who live on farms.

    ur·ban (ur$'$bϑn) *adjective.*

urge **1.** To try to convince or persuade. Jim *urged* his friend to try out for the football team. We *urged* Mary to come to the movies with us. **2.** To drive or force on. The rider *urged* his horse on to win the race. **3.** To speak or argue strongly for. The group of citizens *urged* better conditions in the city's prisons. *Verb.*

—A strong desire or impulse. Jane had a sudden *urge* for a chocolate bar. *Noun.*

    urge (urj) *verb,* **urged, urging;** *noun, plural* **urges.**

urgent Needing or demanding immediate action or attention. The man left the country on *urgent* business. The hospital made an *urgent* request for people to give blood.

    ur·gent (ur$'$jϑnt) *adjective.*

urine A clear, yellow-colored fluid containing waste material given off by the kidneys and discharged from the body.

    u·rine (yoor$'$in) *noun.*

at; $\overline{a}$pe; c$\ddot{a}$r; end; m$\overline{e}$; it; $\overline{i}$ce; hot; $\overline{o}$ld; f$\hat{o}$rk; wood; f$\overline{oo}$l; oil; out; up; turn; sing; thin; <u>th</u>is; **hw** in white; **zh** in treasure. ϑ stands for **a** in about, **e** in taken **i** in pencil, **o** in lemon, and **u** in circus.

urn 1. A vase set on a base. In ancient Greece and Rome, urns were used to hold the ashes of the dead. Today, urns are used for decoration or to hold plants. 2. A container with a faucet that is used to serve coffee or tea. ▲ Another word that sounds like this is **earn**.
urn (urn) *noun, plural* **urns.**

Urn

us We called to him, but he didn't see *us*. Our teacher gave *us* a party at the end of the school year.
us (us *or* əs) *pronoun.*

U. S. An abbreviation for **United States.**

U.S.A. An abbreviation for **United States of America.**

usage 1. A way of handling something. The kitchen floor gets such hard *usage* it never stays shiny for more than a day after it's waxed. 2. The usual way in which people use words in speaking or writing.
us·age (yo͞o′sij *or* yo͞o′zij) *noun, plural* **usages.**

use 1. To put into service for a particular purpose. May I *use* your scissors? John *uses* a dictionary to find out the meanings of words he does not know. 2. To finish completely. We *used* up all the butter at breakfast. *Verb.*
—1. The act of using or the state of being used. Tom made the bookcase with the *use* of a saw and a hammer and nails. The auditorium is in *use* until later this afternoon. 2. The quality of being useful or helpful. There's no *use* worrying about something until you know whether it's going to happen or not. 3. A need or purpose for which something is used. Do you have any *use* for these empty bottles? 4. The right or ability to use something. My brother gave me the *use* of his bicycle while he was away. When Jan broke her leg, she lost the *use* of it for a few months. 5. The way of using. My older brother taught me the proper *use* of that tool. *Noun.*
use (yo͞oz *for verb;* yo͞os *for noun*) *verb,* **used, using;** *noun, plural* **uses.**
used to. 1. Did at a time in the past. We *used to* be good friends. We *used to* take a vacation in the mountains. 2. Familiar with; accustomed to. The boy from the city was not *used to* life on the farm.

used That has been used by someone else; not new. Steve is saving his money to buy a *used* car.
used (yo͞ozd) *adjective.*

useful Serving a good use or purpose; helpful. A pocketknife can be very *useful* on a camping trip. He gave us several *useful* ideas about how to raise money for our club.
use·ful (yo͞os′fəl) *adjective.*

usher A person who leads people to their seats in a church, theater, stadium, or other place. *Noun.*
—To act as an usher. The waiter *ushered* us to a table. *Verb.*
ush·er (ush′ər) *noun, plural* **ushers;** *verb,* **ushered, ushering.**

usual Common or expected. Hot weather is *usual* for July and August.
u·su·al (yo͞o′zho͞o əl) *adjective.*

Utah A state in the western United States. Its capital is Salt Lake City.
U·tah (yo͞o′tô *or* yo͞o′tä) *noun.*

▲ **Utah** comes from the way Spanish explorers said the name of a tribe that lived where Colorado and Utah are now. The Indian word means "people who live in high places." Congress took this name when it named the territory of Utah, and the name was later given to the state.

utensil An object or tool that is useful or necessary in doing or making something. Mother keeps all her cooking *utensils* in a drawer in the kitchen.
u·ten·sil (yo͞o ten′sil) *noun, plural* **utensils.**

utility 1. The quality of being useful. Scientists are looking into the *utility* of the sun's rays as a source of energy on earth. 2. A company that provides service to the public. Telephone companies are *utilities.*
u·til·i·ty (yo͞o til′ə tē) *noun, plural* **utilities.**

utmost Greatest or highest. Everyone in school has the *utmost* respect for our principal. *Adjective.*
—The most or greatest possible. The coach did his *utmost* to make us into a winning team. *Noun.*
ut·most (ut′mōst′) *adjective; noun.*

utter¹ To give voice to; express out loud. Helen *uttered* a sigh of relief when she found out she had passed the test.
ut·ter (ut′ər) *verb,* **uttered, uttering.**

utter² Complete or perfect; total. When the light bulb blew out, Dick found himself in *utter* darkness.
ut·ter (ut′ər) *adjective.*

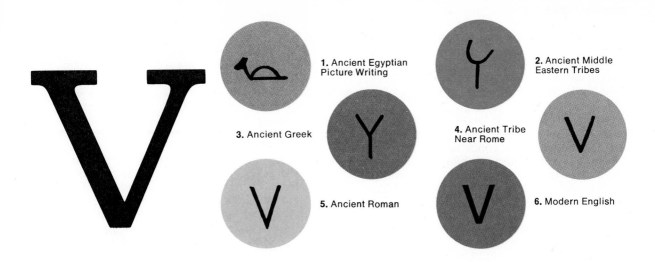

1. Ancient Egyptian Picture Writing
2. Ancient Middle Eastern Tribes
3. Ancient Greek
4. Ancient Tribe Near Rome
5. Ancient Roman
6. Modern English

V is the twenty-second letter of the alphabet. The oldest form of the letter **V** was a drawing that the ancient Egyptians (**1**) used in their picture writing nearly 5000 years ago. This drawing was borrowed by several ancient tribes (**2**) in the Middle East. They used it to stand for both the vowel sound *u*, as the *u* in *rude,* and the consonant sound *w*, as the *w* in *water.* The ancient Greeks (**3**) borrowed this letter, writing it very much like a modern capital letter **Y.** They used it to stand for the *u* sound only. This letter was borrowed by an ancient tribe (**4**) that settled north of Rome about 2800 years ago. They changed its shape so that it looked like a modern capital letter **V.** The Romans (**5**) borrowed this letter about 2400 years ago, writing it in exactly the same way that we write the capital letter **V** today (**6**). By about 1000 years ago, two forms of this V-shaped letter were being used in writing: **V** at the beginning of a word, and a new letter, **U,** in the middle of a word. In the following years the letter **V** came to be used more and more for the *v* sound, which, although it did not exist in the language of the Romans, was used in such languages as English, French, and Italian.

v, V The twenty-second letter of the alphabet.

   v, V (vē) *noun, plural* **v's, V's.**

vacant Not having anyone or anything in it; empty. You can sit in the *vacant* chair.

   va·cant (vā′kənt) *adjective.*

vacation A period of rest or freedom from school, business, or other activity.

   va·ca·tion (vā kā′shən) *noun, plural* **vacations.**

vaccinate To inoculate with a vaccine.

   vac·ci·nate (vak′sə nāt′) *verb,* **vaccinated, vaccinating.**

vaccine The dead or weakened germs of certain diseases that are used to inoculate people to prevent or lessen the effect of those diseases. Vaccines can protect people against such diseases as smallpox and polio.

   vac·cine (vak sēn′ *or* vak′sēn) *noun, plural* **vaccines.**

vacuum A space that is completely empty of matter. Science has not yet been able to make a perfect vacuum. Therefore, the word *vacuum* usually refers to space with most but not all of the matter removed. *Noun.*
—To clean with a vacuum cleaner. Mother *vacuumed* the rug before the party. *Verb.*

   vac·u·um (vak′yōō əm *or* vak′yōōm) *noun, plural* **vacuums;** *verb,* **vacuumed, vacuuming.**

Vacuum Cleaner

vacuum cleaner A machine that is used for cleaning carpets, floors, and pieces of furniture. A vacuum cleaner works by suction.

vague Not clear or definite. John only had a *vague* idea of how to get to the movie theater. We could see only the *vague* outline of the building in the fog.

vague (vāg) *adjective*, **vaguer, vaguest.**

vain **1.** Too proud of one's looks, abilities, or accomplishments; conceited. The *vain* boy spent a lot of time combing his hair and looking in the mirror. **2.** Not successful. The man at the garage made a *vain* effort to fix our car. ▲ Other words that sound like this are **vane** and **vein.**

vain (vān) *adjective*, **vainer, vainest.**

in vain. Without success. The captain's attempt to keep the ship from sinking was *in vain.*

valentine **1.** A greeting card sent on Valentine's Day to one's sweetheart. **2.** A sweetheart chosen on Valentine's Day. Bob asked Pauline to be his *valentine.*

val·en·tine (val′ən tīn′) *noun, plural* **valentines.**

Valentine's Day The day named in honor of Saint Valentine, an early Christian saint. It is celebrated by the sending of valentines. It falls on February 14.

valiant Full of or showing courage; brave. The knights of olden times were *valiant* men. The small group of soldiers put up a *valiant* fight against the enemy.

val·iant (val′yənt) *adjective.*

valid **1.** Soundly based on facts or evidence; true. The experiment proved that the scientist's theory was *valid.* Does she have a *valid* reason for not doing her homework? **2.** Having force under the law. The policeman told the woman that her driver's license was not *valid* because it was out-of-date.

val·id (val′id) *adjective.*

valley An area of low land between hills or mountains. Valleys often have rivers flowing through them.

val·ley (val′ē) *noun, plural* **valleys.**

valuable **1.** Having great value; worth much money. John has a very *valuable* coin collection. **2.** Having great use or importance. Tim's summer job was a *valuable* experience for him. *Adjective.*

—**valuables.** Things that have great value. The robbers broke in and stole grandmother's jewelry and other *valuables. Noun.*

val·u·a·ble (val′yōō ə bəl *or* val′yə bəl) *adjective; noun plural.*

value The worth, usefulness, or importance of something. Jim places great *value* on

Sara's friendship. The *value* of land in this area has gone up in recent years. *Noun.*

—**1.** To think of as being worth; set a price for. The jeweler *valued* the diamond necklace at three thousand dollars. **2.** Think highly of. Frank has always *valued* his parents' advice. *Verb.*

val·ue (val′yōō) *noun, plural* **values;** *verb,* **valued, valuing.**

valve **1.** A device that controls the flow of liquid or gases. The faucet on a sink works a *valve* that turns the water on and off. The *valves* of the heart control the flow of blood into and out of the heart. **2.** One of the pair of hinged shells of an oyster, clam, or similar animal.

valve (valv) *noun, plural* **valves.**

van A large, covered truck that is used to move furniture, animals, or other large items.

van (van) *noun, plural* **vans.**

vane A flat or curved metal blade. The *vanes* of a windmill catch the wind and provide force to do work. ▲ Other words that sound like this are **vain** and **vein.**

vane (vān) *noun, plural* **vanes.**

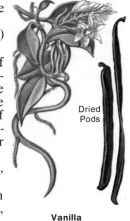

Vane

vanilla A flavoring that is used in candies, ice cream, and cookies. Vanilla comes from the seed pods of a tropical plant that is a type of orchid.

va·nil·la (və nil′ə) *noun.*

vanish To go out of sight or existence; disappear. The airplane *vanished* above the clouds. All hope of winning the game *vanished* when our star player was injured.

van·ish (van′ish) *verb,* **vanished, vanishing.**

Dried Pods

vanity Too much pride in one's looks, abilities, or accomplishments; conceit. Ted's *vanity* made him

Vanilla

think he was the best football player the school had ever had.

van·i·ty (van′i tē) *noun, plural* **vanities.**

vanquish To defeat or overcome. Our soldiers *vanquished* the enemy in battle.

van·quish (vang′kwish) *verb,* **vanquished, vanquishing.**

vapor Small particles of mist, steam, or smoke that can be seen in the air. When water boils in a pot, you can see the *vapor* rising into the air.

va·por (vā′pər) *noun.*

variable Likely to change. The weather is so *variable* at this time of year that I don't know whether to pack cool summer clothes or wool slacks and sweaters for my trip. *Adjective.*
—Something that changes or is likely to change. The temperature is a *variable* at this time of the year. *Noun.*

var·i·a·ble (ver′ē ə bəl) *adjective; noun, plural* **variables.**

variation 1. A change. Sunsets have so many *variations* of color that each sunset looks different. The weather forecaster reported a temperature *variation* of fifteen degrees from yesterday. 2. A different form of something. Jane told the children a story that was a *variation* of one of her earlier ones.

var·i·a·tion (ver′ē ā′shən) *noun, plural* **variations.**

variety 1. Change or difference; lack of sameness. A job that has no *variety* can become boring. 2. A number of different things. The woman bought a *variety* of foods at the grocery store. 3. A different kind or form of something. This rose is a new *variety.*

va·ri·e·ty (və rī′ə tē) *noun, plural* **varieties.**

various 1. Different from one another; of different kinds. Students of *various* backgrounds and nationalities go to our school. 2. More than one; many. We spent the night in *various* towns on our motor trip.

var·i·ous (ver′ē əs) *adjective.*

varnish A liquid that gives a hard, clear coating to wood, metal, or other materials. *Noun.*
—To put varnish on; cover with varnish. The workmen *varnished* the floor. *Verb.*

var·nish (vär′nish) *noun, plural* **varnishes;** *verb,* **varnished, varnishing.**

vary 1. To make or become different; change. Mother tries to *vary* the meals she cooks from night to night. 2. To be different; differ. The flowers in our garden *vary* widely in color.

var·y (ver′ē) *verb,* **varied, varying.**

vase A container that is usually higher than it is wide. Vases are mostly used for holding flowers.

vase (vās *or* vāz *or* väz) *noun, plural* **vases.**

vassal A person in the Middle Ages who received land and protection from a lord in return for his loyalty and service.

vas·sal (vas′əl) *noun, plural* **vassals.**

vast Very great in size or amount. A *vast* number of people came to watch the football game. The rancher raises cattle on a *vast* area.

vast (vast) *adjective,* **vaster, vastest.**

vat A large tank or container used for holding liquids.

vat (vat) *noun, plural* **vats.**

vault A safe room or compartment that is used to store money, jewels, or other things of value. Banks keep their money in steel *vaults.*

vault (vôlt) *noun, plural* **vaults.**

veal The meat of a calf.

veal (vēl) *noun.*

vegetable A plant whose roots, leaves, or other parts are used as food. Carrots, spinach, potatoes, lettuce, and beans are vegetables. *Noun.*
—Having to do with or made from vegetables. On our way back from the country, we stopped at a *vegetable* stand and bought fresh corn. I had *vegetable* soup for lunch. *Adjective.*

veg·e·ta·ble (vej′ə tə bəl *or* vej′tə bəl) *noun, plural* **vegetables;** *adjective.*

vegetation Plant life. Jungles have very thick *vegetation.* A desert has very little *vegetation.*

veg·e·ta·tion (vej′ə tā′shən) *noun.*

vehicle A means of carrying or transporting people or goods. Automobiles, ships, and airplanes are vehicles.

ve·hi·cle (vē′ə kəl) *noun, plural* **vehicles.**

Vase

at; āpe; cär; end; mē; it; īce; hot; ōld;
fôrk; wood; fōol; oil; out; up; turn; sing;
thin; this; hw in white; zh in treasure.
ə stands for a in about, e in taken
i in pencil, o in lemon, and u in circus.

veil **1.** A very thin material that is worn by women over the head and shoulders. The bride's *veil* was made out of lace. **2.** Something that hides. A *veil* of secrecy surrounded the army's plans for the coming attack. *Noun.*
—To cover or hide with a veil. Some women in countries of the Middle East *veil* their faces. She tried to *veil* her anger with a smile. *Verb.*
   veil (vāl) *noun, plural* **veils;** *verb,* **veiled, veiling.**

Veil

vein **1.** One of the blood vessels that carries blood from all parts of the body to the heart. **2.** One of the ribs that form the framework of a leaf or an insect's wing. The veins in a leaf carry food and water to the cells in the leaf. The veins in an insect's wing make the wing strong and firm. **3.** A mineral deposit that forms in rock. The miners found a *vein* of silver in the mine. **4.** A marking of a different color in marble or other stone, or in wood. This slab of marble is completely white except for a few black veins. **5.** A quality or mood. There was a humorous *vein* in everything that the man said. ▲ Other words that sound like this are **vain** and **vane.**
   vein (vān) *noun, plural* **veins.**

Vein

velocity The rate of motion; speed. Light has a *velocity* of about 186,000 miles per second.
   ve·loc·i·ty (və los'ə tē) *noun, plural* **velocities.**

velvet A fabric with a soft, thick pile. Velvet can be made out of silk, nylon, or other materials. *Noun.*
—**1.** Made of or covered with velvet. Susan wore a red *velvet* dress to the school dance. **2.** That is like velvet in smoothness or softness. My little black kitten has *velvet* fur. *Adjective.*
   vel·vet (vel'vit) *noun; adjective.*

vending machine A machine that is worked by putting a coin into a slot. Vending machines are used to sell candy, cigarettes, and many other small things.
   vend·ing machine (ven'ding).

Vending Machine

vendor A person who sells something. Jim bought an apple from the fruit *vendor* on the corner.
   ven·dor (ven'dər) *noun, plural* **vendors.**

Venetian blind A window shade that has a series of wooden or metal slats that run side to side. The slats can be opened or closed, and the shade can be raised or lowered by using cords attached to the side.
   Ve·ne·tian blind (vi nē'shən).

▲ This kind of shade may be called a **Venetian blind** because it was first made and used in the Italian city of *Venice.*

venom The poison of some snakes, spiders, and other animals. The venom can be passed to a person by a bite or sting.
   ven·om (ven'əm) *noun, plural* **venoms.**

vent **1.** A hole or other opening through which gas or liquid passes. We have a *vent* above the stove that draws air out of the kitchen. **2.** A means of escape; way out. He gave *vent* to his anger by shouting. *Noun.*
—To let out. The boy *vented* his anger at his brother by kicking the door. *Verb.*
   vent (vent) *noun, plural* **vents;** *verb,* **vented, venting.**

ventilation The circulation or change of air. This room gets very good *ventilation* when both the front and back windows are open.
   ven·ti·la·tion (vent'əl ā'shən) *noun.*

ventricle Either of the two lower chambers of the heart. The ventricles receive blood from the auricles and pump it into the arteries.
   ven·tri·cle (ven'tri kəl) *noun, plural* **ventricles.**

venture A task or job that involves risk or danger. The plan to get behind the enemy line was a *venture* that called for great courage. *Noun.*

—**1.** To put in danger; risk. The firemen *ventured* their lives by entering the burning building to save those trapped by the fire. **2.** To express at the risk of criticism. If I had to *venture* a guess, I would say it won't rain today. *Verb.*

ven·ture (ven′chər) *noun, plural* **ventures;** *verb,* **ventured, venturing.**

Venus The sixth largest planet. It is the second planet in order of distance from the sun.

Ve·nus (vē′nəs) *noun.*

veranda An open porch that runs along one or more sides of a house. A veranda usually has a roof.

ve·ran·da (və ran′də) *noun, plural* **verandas.**

Veranda

verb A word that expresses action or state of being. *Run, think, buy, go,* and *be* are verbs.

verb (vurb) *noun, plural* **verbs.**

verbal In words; spoken. Nancy gave us a *verbal* description of what her missing bracelet looked like.

ver·bal (vur′bəl) *adjective.*

verdict The decision of a jury in a trial. The jurors agreed on a *verdict* of "guilty."

ver·dict (vur′dikt) *noun, plural* **verdicts.**

Vermont A state in the northeastern United States. Its capital is Montpelier.

Ver·mont (vər mont′) *noun.*

▲ The area where **Vermont** is once was known by English settlers as Green Mountain. The name *Vermont* probably comes from the French words for "green mountain." The French name became popular, and the territory chose this as its official name in 1777.

versatile **1.** Able to do many different things well. The young man was a *versatile*

athlete who could play most games with skill. **2.** Having many uses. A hammer is a *versatile* tool to have around the house.

ver·sa·tile (vur′sə til) *adjective.*

verse **1.** Words that are written in a particular pattern and often in rhyme; poetry. **2.** A section of a poem or song; stanza. I only know the first *verse* of that song. **3.** One of the short parts into which the chapters of the Bible are divided.

verse (vurs) *noun, plural* **verses.**

version **1.** An account or description given from a particular point of view. Each boy had his own *version* of who had started the fight. **2.** A translation from one language into another. I read the English *version* of the French story.

ver·sion (vur′zhən) *noun, plural* **versions.**

vertebra One of the small bones that make up the backbone.

ver·te·bra (vur′tə brə) *noun, plural* **vertebras.**

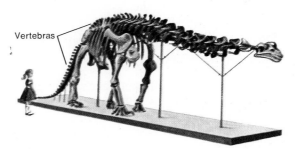

Vertebras

vertebrate Having a backbone. Man is a *vertebrate* animal. *Adjective.*
—One of a large group of animals that have a backbone. Fish, amphibians, reptiles, birds, and mammals are vertebrates. *Noun.*

ver·te·brate (vur′tə brāt′ *or* vur′tə brit) *adjective; noun, plural* **vertebrates.**

vertical Straight up and down; upright. The walls of a building are in a *vertical* position.

ver·ti·cal (vur′ti kəl) *adjective.*

very That boy is *very* strong for his age. I am *very* sorry to hear that you are not feeling well. That woman is the *very* best dancer I have ever seen. The *very* idea of having to get up so early made him groan. Your gift was

at; āpe; cär; end; mē; it; īce; hot; ōld;
fôrk; wood; fōōl; oil; out; up; turn; sing;
thin; this; hw in white; zh in treasure.
ə stands for **a** in about, **e** in taken
i in pencil, **o** in lemon, and **u** in circus.

687

the *very* thing I have been wanting. That actor is at the *very* top of his career.
ver·y (ver'ē) *adverb; adjective.*

vessel **1.** A ship or large boat. Both passenger ships and *vessels* carrying freight were docked at the pier. **2.** A hollow container or holder. Vases, cups, and bowls are vessels.
ves·sel (ves'əl) *noun, plural* **vessels.**

vest A short, sleeveless piece of clothing that is worn over a man's shirt or a woman's blouse. *Noun.*
—To give authority or power to. The new President was *vested* with all the rights and powers of his office. *Verb.*
vest (vest) *noun, plural* **vests;** *verb,* **vested, vesting.**

Vest

veteran **1.** A person who has had a lot of experience. The actor was a *veteran* of the stage and screen. **2.** A person who has served in the armed forces. My older brother is an Army *veteran. Noun.*
—Having had a lot of experience. The newspaper sent a *veteran* reporter to cover the important story. *Adjective.*
vet·er·an (vet'ər ən) *noun, plural* **veterans;** *adjective.*

veterinarian A doctor who treats animals.
vet·er·i·nar·i·an (vet'ər ə ner'ē ən) *noun, plural* **veterinarians.**

veto The power of a president, governor, or official group to stop the passing of an act or measure. The President has the power of *veto* over any bill that is passed by Congress. *Noun.*
—To refuse to approve; stop or prevent by a veto. The governor *vetoed* the bill passed by the legislature. Mother *vetoed* our idea of going swimming right after we had eaten. *Verb.*
ve·to (vē'tō) *noun, plural* **vetoes;** *verb,* **vetoed, vetoing.**

▲ The word **veto** comes from a Latin word that means "I forbid." In ancient Rome, there was a government official who was supposed to speak for the common people and protect them from unfair laws. If he did not like a law that the Senate was trying to pass, he would say *"veto"*—"I forbid."

---

via By way of. Sally drove home *via* the highway.
vi·a (vī'ə *or* vē'ə) *preposition.*

vibrate To move rapidly back and forth or up and down. The strings of a guitar *vibrate* when they are plucked.
vi·brate (vī'brāt) *verb,* **vibrated, vibrating.**

vibration Rapid movement back and forth or up and down. People many miles away could feel the *vibration* from the earthquake.
vi·bra·tion (vī brā'shən) *noun, plural* **vibrations.**

vice-president An officer who ranks second to a president. A vice-president takes the place of a president when necessary.
vice-pres·i·dent (vīs'prez'ə dənt) *noun, plural* **vice-presidents.**

vice versa The other way around. My brother helps me with my homework, and *vice versa.*
vi·ce ver·sa (vī'sə vur'sə).

vicinity The area near or surrounding a particular place; neighborhood. There are several parks and playgrounds in the *vicinity* of our house.
vi·cin·i·ty (vi sin'ə tē) *noun, plural* **vicinities.**

vicious **1.** Wicked; evil. The kidnapers planned a *vicious* crime. **2.** Full of spite. The boy told *vicious* lies to try to put the blame on someone else. **3.** Fierce or savage. The hungry wolves were *vicious.*
vi·cious (vish'əs) *adjective.*

victim **1.** A person who is injured, killed, or ruined. A friend of ours was the *victim* of an automobile accident. **2.** A person who is cheated or tricked. My friend lost twenty dollars as the *victim* of a dishonest storekeeper.
vic·tim (vik'təm) *noun, plural* **victims.**

victorious **1.** Having won a victory. The *victorious* army was welcomed home. **2.** Having to do with victory. The general mapped out his plan for a *victorious* end of the war.
vic·to·ri·ous (vik tôr'ē əs) *adjective.*

victory The defeat of an enemy or opponent. Our team gained its first *victory* of the season in yesterday's game.
vic·to·ry (vik'tər ē) *noun, plural* **victories.**

video Having to do with the picture part of television. *Adjective.*
—The picture part of television. *Noun.*
vid·e·o (vid'ē ō') *adjective; noun, plural* **videos.**

view **1.** The act of looking or seeing; sight. The sailors got their first *view* of land after many weeks at sea. **2.** The range or extent of

seeing. The airplane soon passed out of *view*. **3.** Something that is seen or can be seen. We have a lovely *view* of the lake from our window. **4.** A particular way of thinking about something; opinion. The two friends had different *views* on who would make the best class president. *Noun.*
—**1.** To look at or see. Many people *viewed* the exhibit at the museum. **2.** To think about; consider. The people *viewed* the President's new education bill with approval. *Verb.*
view (vyoo) *noun, plural* **views;** *verb,* **viewed, viewing.**

vigor Active power or force; strength. Janice campaigned for class president with great *vigor*. Even though Grandfather is over eighty, he is still full of *vigor*.
vig·or (vig′ər) *noun.*

vigorous Full of or done with vigor. Our dog is still just as *vigorous* as she was when she was a puppy.
vig·or·ous (vig′ər əs) *adjective.*

village A small group of houses. A village is usually smaller than a town.
vil·lage (vil′ij) *noun, plural* **villages.**

villain A wicked or evil person. In the story, the *villain* tried to trick the beautiful princess into going away with him.
vil·lain (vil′ən) *noun, plural* **villains.**

vine A plant with a long, thin stem that grows along the ground or climbs on trees, fences, or other supports. Grapes, melons, and squash grow on vines.
vine (vīn) *noun, plural* **vines.**

Vine

vinegar A sour liquid that is made by fermenting cider, wine, or other liquids. Vinegar is used in salad dressing and to flavor and preserve food.
vin·e·gar (vin′ə gər) *noun, plural* **vinegars.**

vineyard An area where grapes are grown.
vine·yard (vin′yərd) *noun, plural* **vineyards.**

viola A musical instrument that looks like a violin but is a little larger.
vi·o·la (vē ō′lə) *noun, plural* **violas.**

violate To fail to obey or keep; break. The driver *violated* the law by going through a red light.
vi·o·late (vī′ə lāt′) *verb,* **violated, violating.**

violence Strong physical force. The robbers threatened to use *violence* if the banker did not open the vault.
vi·o·lence (vī′ə ləns) *noun.*

violent **1.** Acting with or coming from strong physical force. The thief gave the watchman a *violent* blow on the head. **2.** Caused by or showing strong feeling or emotion. My friend has a *violent* temper.
vi·o·lent (vī′ə lənt) *adjective.*

violet A small purple, white, or pink flower. Many violets grow wild, while others are grown in gardens and indoors.
vi·o·let (vī′ə lit) *noun, plural* **violets.**

Violets

violin A musical instrument that has four strings and is played with a bow.
vi·o·lin (vī′ə lin′) *noun, plural* **violins.**

virgin Not yet used or touched; unmarked. We made footprints in the *virgin* snow. The early settlers in America cut down *virgin* forests to make way for farm land.
vir·gin (vur′jin) *adjective.*

Violin

Virginia A state in the eastern United States. Its capital is Richmond.
Vir·gin·ia (vur jin′yə) *noun.*

at; āpe; cär; end; mē; it; īce; hot; ōld;
fôrk; wood; fool; oil; out; up; turn; sing;
thin; this; hw in white; zh in treasure.
ə stands for a in about, e in taken
i in pencil, o in lemon, and u in circus.

689

▲ **Virginia** was named by Queen Elizabeth I of England. She named the colony Virginia because she was called "the Virgin Queen."

virtually In almost every way; practically. The tornado *virtually* destroyed the town and the surrounding area.
vir·tu·al·ly (vur′cho͞o ə lē) *adverb.*

virtue **1.** Moral goodness in one's thinking and behavior. Sarah's *virtue* is shown in the thoughtful things she does for other people. Honesty is a *virtue*. **2.** Any good quality or characteristic. He has the *virtue* of being sympathetic to other people's problems. Vaccines have the *virtue* of preventing disease.
vir·tue (vur′cho͞o) *noun, plural* **virtues.**

virus A tiny form of living matter that grows only in living tissue. Viruses cause many diseases in man, animals, and plants. Polio and measles are caused by viruses.
vi·rus (vī′rəs) *noun, plural* **viruses.**

vise A tool with two jaws that are opened and closed by turning a screw. A vise is used to hold an object firmly in place while it is being worked on.
vise (vīs) *noun, plural* **vises.**

Vise

visible **1.** Able to be seen. Their house is *visible* from the road. **2.** Easily seen or understood. The new mayor made many promises, but there has been no *visible* improvement in the city government since he took office.
vis·i·ble (viz′ə bəl) *adjective.*

vision **1.** The act or power of seeing; sense of sight. The man's *vision* weakened as he grew older. **2.** The ability to plan ahead; foresight. The writers of the United States Constitution had great *vision* to write a document that still meets the country's needs after two hundred years. **3.** Something that is imagined or dreamed. The young writer had *visions* of success and fame.
vi·sion (vizh′ən) *noun, plural* **visions.**

visit To go or come to see. We *visited* Grandmother last Sunday. Friends from Boston *visited* us for the weekend. *Verb.*
—A short stay or call. Ellen paid a *visit* to her friend last night. *Noun.*

vis·it (viz′it) *verb,* **visited, visiting;** *noun, plural* **visits.**

visitor A person who visits; guest. We have to clean up our rooms because Mom is expecting *visitors* this afternoon.
vis·i·tor (viz′i tər) *noun, plural* **visitors.**

visor The brim that sticks out on the front of a cap. A visor is made to shade the eyes from the sun.
vi·sor (vī′zər) *noun, plural* **visors.**

Visor

visual Having to do with or used in seeing. Eyeglasses are used to correct nearsightedness and other *visual* defects. The teacher used charts, slides, and other *visual* aids to help explain how the heart works.
vis·u·al (vizh′o͞o əl) *adjective.*

vital **1.** Having to do with or necessary to life. The wounded man's heartbeat and other *vital* signs began to weaken. The liver is a *vital* organ. **2.** Full of life and energy. Liz has a *vital* personality and is interested in everything that goes on around her. **3.** Very important or necessary. That star player is *vital* to our basketball team.
vi·tal (vīt′əl) *adjective.*

vitamin One of a group of substances that are needed in small amounts for the health and the normal working of the body. We get most of the vitamins we need from eating the right kinds of food.
vi·ta·min (vī′tə min) *noun, plural* **vitamins.**

vivid **1.** Bright and strong; brilliant. The room was painted a *vivid* yellow. **2.** Clear and sharp. My mother has a *vivid* memory of her childhood. The witness gave a *vivid* description of the robber. **3.** Active; lively. Susan must have a *vivid* imagination to be able to write so many good stories.
viv·id (viv′id) *adjective.*

vocabulary **1.** All the words used or understood by a person or group. The English vocabulary is one of the largest of all languages. Dick has increased his *vocabulary* by

looking up words that he doesn't know in a dictionary. Doctors use a special *vocabulary* when they talk to each other about medical matters. **2.** A list of words and their meanings in alphabetical order.
vo·cab·u·lar·y (vō kab′yə ler′ē) *noun, plural* **vocabularies.**

vocal Having to do with or expressed by the voice. A baby produces *vocal* sounds long before he really learns how to talk.
vo·cal (vō′kəl) *adjective.*

vocal cords Either of the two pairs of membranes in the larynx. Air from the lungs passes through the lower pair of vocal cords and causes them to vibrate. This makes the sound of the voice.

voice **1.** The sound that is produced through the mouth by speaking, singing, or shouting. Sandy knew her father was home from work because she could hear his *voice* downstairs. **2.** The ability to produce sound through the mouth; speech. The singer lost his *voice* because of a sore throat. **3.** The right to express a view, opinion, or choice. The people must have a *voice* in the running of their government. *Noun.*
—To express or utter. The teacher encouraged the students to *voice* their opinions in class. *Verb.*
voice (vois) *noun, plural* **voices;** *verb,* **voiced, voicing.**

Volcano

volcano An opening in the surface of the earth through which lava, gases, and ashes are forced out. One of the world's active volcanoes is in Hawaii.

vol·ca·no (vol kā′nō) *noun, plural* **volcanoes** or **volcanos.**

▲ The word **volcano** comes from an Italian word that means the same thing. The Italians took the word from the name of *Vulcan.* Vulcan was the god of fire in Roman religion.

volleyball **1.** A game in which two teams stand on either side of a high net and hit a large ball back and forth. Each side tries not to let the ball touch the ground. **2.** The ball that is used in this game.
vol·ley·ball (vol′ē bôl′) *noun, plural* **volleyballs.**

Volleyball

volt A unit for measuring the force of an electric current.
volt (vōlt) *noun, plural* **volts.**

▲ The word **volt** comes from the name of Alessandro *Volta.* He was an Italian scientist who invented a device that was the earliest kind of electric battery.

voltage The force of an electric current measured in volts.
vol·tage (vōl′tij) *noun, plural* **voltages.**

volume **1.** A collection of written or printed pages bound together; book. Our school has a library of 10,000 *volumes.* **2.** One of a set or series of related books, newspapers, or mag-

at; āpe; cär; end; mē; it; īce; hot; ōld;
fôrk; wood; fool; oil; out; up; turn; sing;
thin; this; hw in white; zh in treasure.
ə stands for **a** in about, **e** in taken
i in pencil, **o** in lemon, and **u** in circus.

azines. The first *volume* of that encyclopedia has a long article on Africa. **3.** The amount of space occupied. The *volume* of a room can be found by multiplying the height by the length by the width. **4.** The amount of sound. Please turn up the *volume* on the television set.

vol·ume (vol′yoom) *noun, plural* **volumes.**

voluntary **1.** Done, made, or acting of one's own free will; not forced. The man made a *voluntary* confession of his crime. There are many *voluntary* workers in that hospital. **2.** Controlled by the will. Raising an arm is done by *voluntary* muscles, but digesting food in the stomach is not.

vol·un·tar·y (vol′ən ter′ē) *adjective.*

volunteer **1.** A person who offers to help or does something of his own free will without pay. Jane asked for *volunteers* for the decorating committee. The candidate for mayor has many *volunteers* who are helping in his campaign. **2.** A person who joins the military service of his own free will. *Noun.*
—**1.** To offer to help or do something of one's own free will. Robert's father *volunteered* to coach the boy's baseball team. **2.** To give or offer readily. Linda *volunteered* an answer to the question. *Verb.*
—Having to do with or serving as a volunteer. My father is a *volunteer* fireman in our town. *Adjective.*

vol·un·teer (vol′ən tēr′) *noun, plural* **volunteers;** *verb,* **volunteered, volunteering;** *adjective.*

vote **1.** The formal expression of a wish or choice. A vote can be taken by ballot, by voice, or by a show of hands. Each citizen has one *vote* in the election for President. **2.** The right of expressing such a wish or choice. In some countries women still have not been given the *vote. Noun.*
—**1.** To express one's wish or choice by a vote. We *vote* for President by secret ballot. At our club meetings, we *vote* by a show of hands. **2.** To give by a vote. The school board *voted* money for a new library. *Verb.*

vote (vōt) *noun, plural* **votes;** *verb,* **voted, voting.**

vow A solemn promise or pledge. The knight took a *vow* of loyalty to his lord. *Noun.*
—To promise or pledge solemnly. The bride and groom *vowed* to love and be faithful to each other. *Verb.*

vow (vou) *noun, plural* **vows;** *verb,* **vowed, vowing.**

vowel A voiced speech sound made by not blocking the flow of air through the mouth. *A, e, i, o, u,* and sometimes *y* are the letters that represent such a sound.

vow·el (vou′əl) *noun, plural* **vowels.**

voyage A journey by water or through space. Our friends came to the ship to wish us a pleasant *voyage. Noun.*
—To journey by water or through space. It was just a few years ago that man first *voyaged* to the moon. *Verb.*

voy·age (voi′ij) *noun, plural* **voyages;** *verb,* **voyaged, voyaging.**

vulgar Showing or marked by a lack of good manners, breeding, or taste. The boy told a *vulgar* joke.

vul·gar (vul′gər) *adjective.*

Vulture

vulture A large bird that has dark, dull feathers and a bald head and neck. Vultures feed on the meat of dead animals.

vul·ture (vul′chər) *noun, plural* **vultures.**

at; āpe; cär; end; mē; it; īce; hot; ōld;
fôrk; wood; fool; oil; out; up; turn; sing;
thin; this; hw in white; zh in treasure.
ə stands for a in about, e in taken
i in pencil, o in lemon, and u in circus.

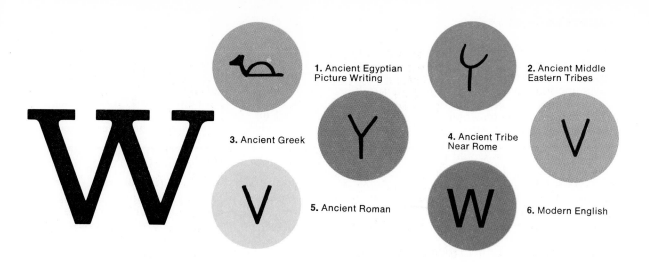

1. Ancient Egyptian Picture Writing
2. Ancient Middle Eastern Tribes
3. Ancient Greek
4. Ancient Tribe Near Rome
5. Ancient Roman
6. Modern English

W is the twenty-third letter of the alphabet. It is one of only three letters that we use today that was not used in the Roman alphabet or an earlier alphabet. Because **W** began as a form of the letter **V**, they have the same early history. The oldest form of the letter **W** was a drawing that the ancient Egyptians (**1**) used in their picture writing nearly 5000 years ago. This drawing was borrowed by several ancient tribes (**2**) in the Middle East. They used it to stand for both the vowel sound *u,* as the *u* in *rude,* and the consonant sound *w,* as the *w* in *water.* The ancient Greeks (**3**) borrowed this letter, writing it very much like a modern capital letter **Y.** They used it to stand for the *u* sound only. This letter was borrowed by an ancient tribe (**4**) that settled north of Rome about 2800 years ago. They changed its shape so that it looked like a modern capital letter **V.** The Romans (**5**) borrowed this letter about 2400 years ago. By about 1000 years ago, two forms of this V-shaped letter were being used in writing: **V** at the beginning of a word, and a new letter, **U,** in the middle of a word. The letter **V** began to be used for the *v* sound only, rather than the *u* sound. Because the letter **V** had originally stood for the *w* sound, there was no longer a letter in the alphabet that stood for this sound. At first, the problem was solved by writing two **V**'s or two **U**'s to stand for the *w* sound. These pairs of letters were soon joined into a new letter that, because of the way it had been made up, was called "double U." This letter was written in almost exactly the way that we write the capital letter **W** today (**6**).

w, W The twenty-third letter of the alphabet.
w, W (dub′əl yo͞o′) *noun, plural* **w's, W's.**

wad **1.** A small, tightly packed lump of soft material. The nurse cleaned my cut with a *wad* of cotton. I stepped on a *wad* of chewing gum. **2.** A tight roll of paper money. He had a large *wad* of one dollar bills in his pocket. *Noun.*
—To roll, press, or pack into a wad. She *wadded* up the letter and threw it away. *Verb.*
wad (wod) *noun, plural* **wads;** *verb,* **wadded, wadding.**

waddle To walk or move with short steps, swaying the body from side to side. The duck *waddled* across the yard. *Verb.*
—A swaying or rocking walk. A duck walks with a *waddle. Noun.*
wad·dle (wod′əl) *verb,* **waddled, waddling;** *noun, plural* **waddles.**

wade **1.** To walk in or through water or mud. Christopher *waded* into the ocean up to his knees. **2.** To move or make one's way slowly and with difficulty. She had to *wade* through a pile of papers to find the missing letter.
wade (wād) *verb,* **waded, wading.**

wafer A thin, crisp cookie or cracker.
wa·fer (wā′fər) *noun, plural* **wafers.**

waffle A crisp cake made of batter. Waffles have square-shaped markings on them that are made by the special cooking utensil they are cooked in.
waf·fle (wof′əl) *noun, plural* **waffles.**

wag To cause to move quickly from side to side or up and down. The friendly dog *wagged* its tail at the visitors. *Verb.*
—The act of wagging; wagging motion. The puppy greeted us with a *wag* of its tail. *Noun.*
wag (wag) *verb,* **wagged, wagging;** *noun, plural* **wags.**

wage Payment for work done. Jack got a weekly *wage* of thirty dollars for working at the grocery store after school. *Noun.*
—To carry on or take part in. The rebel leaders are *waging* a war against the government soldiers. *Verb.*

693

wage (wāj) *noun, plural* **wages;** *verb,* **waged, waging.**

wager An agreement or promise to give or pay something to another person if he is right about something and you are wrong; bet. They made a *wager* on which team would win the football game. *Noun.*
—To make a wager; bet. He *wagered* two dollars that his team would win. *Verb.*
wa·ger (wā′jər) *noun, plural* **wagers;** *verb,* **wagered, wagering.**

wagon **1.** A vehicle that has four wheels. It is used for carrying heavy loads. Wagons are usually drawn by a horse or horses. **2.** A child's low, four-wheeled vehicle. Peggy pulled her little brother Michael along the street in his *wagon.*
wag·on (wag′ən) *noun, plural* **wagons.**

Wagon

wail **1.** To make a long, sad cry to show sadness or pain. The sick baby *wailed.* **2.** To make a sound that sounds like a long, sad cry. The wind *wailed* all through the stormy night. *Verb.*
—A long, sad cry or a sound that sounds like this. The children were frightened by the *wail* of the wind. *Noun.*
wail (wāl) *verb,* **wailed, wailing;** *noun, plural* **wails.**

waist **1.** The part of the human body between the ribs and the hips. **2.** A piece of clothing or part of a piece of clothing that covers this part of the body. The dress had a belt at the *waist.* ▲ Another word that sounds like this is **waste.**
waist (wāst) *noun, plural* **waists.**

wait **1.** To stay in a place until someone comes or something happens. *Wait* until it stops raining before you leave. You must *wait* your turn to use the sled. **2.** To put off; delay. Mother will *wait* dinner for us if we're late. **3.** To be put off or delayed. The job of cleaning out the garage can *wait* until next week. *Verb.*

—The act of waiting, or the amount of time spent waiting. There will be a two-hour *wait* before the next plane. *Noun.* ▲ Another word that sounds like this is **weight.**
wait (wāt) *verb,* **waited, waiting;** *noun.*
to wait on. To serve or help. She could not find a clerk to *wait on* her when she wanted to pay for the book.

waiter A man whose job is serving food and drink in a restaurant or other place.
wait·er (wā′tər) *noun, plural* **waiters.**

waitress A woman whose job is serving food or drink in a restaurant or other place.
wait·ress (wā′tris) *noun, plural* **waitresses.**

wake¹ **1.** To stop sleeping. What time did you *wake* up this morning? **2.** To stop from sleeping. Be quiet or you will *wake* the baby. *Verb.*
—A watch over the body of a dead person before burial. *Noun.*
wake (wāk) *verb,* **waked** or **woke, waked, waking;** *noun, plural* **wakes.**

wake² The track left by a boat, ship, or other thing moving through water.
wake (wāk) *noun, plural* **wakes.**

waken **1.** To stop from sleeping; wake. If you're not quiet, you will *waken* him. **2.** To stop sleeping. He *wakened* when the telephone rang. **3.** To make active; stir up. Visiting the art museum *wakened* Larry's interest in learning how to paint.
wak·en (wā′kən) *verb,* **wakened, wakening.**

walk **1.** To move or travel on foot. A person walks by placing one foot on the ground before lifting the other. **2.** To move through, over, or across on foot. Let's *walk* the beach after we swim. **3.** To go with on foot. I'll *walk* you to the corner. **4.** To make or help to walk. John will *walk* the dog after dinner. **5.** To allow a batter in baseball to go to first base by pitching four balls. *Verb.*
—**1.** The act of walking. We took a *walk* around the park. **2.** The distance to be walked. This is often measured by the time that it takes to walk a certain distance. The beach is only a ten-minute *walk* from here. It's a long *walk* to your house. **3.** A place set apart for walking. The *walk* through the park was covered with leaves. **4.** A particular social position or occupation. People from all *walks* of life live in this neighborhood. *Noun.*
walk (wôk) *verb,* **walked, walking;** *noun, plural* **walks.**

wall **1.** A structure made of stone, plaster, wood, brick, or other material. Walls form the sides of buildings or rooms. Walls also can be built to divide or protect an area. Many cities of long ago were surrounded

by walls for protection against attack. **2.** Something that looks like or serves the same purpose as a wall. A *wall* of fire kept the firemen from getting near the burning house. *Noun.*
—To divide, protect, or block with a wall or walls. The workmen *walled* up the old entrance to the building. Mr. Wilson *walled* in his garden. *Verb.*
wall (wôl) *noun, plural* **walls;** *verb,* **walled, walling.**

wallet A flat, folding case for holding money, cards, or photographs.
wal·let (wol′it *or* wô′lit) *noun, plural* **wallets.**

wallpaper Paper that is used to decorate the walls of a room. Wallpaper is colored or has designs or patterns printed on it. *Noun.*
—To put wallpaper on the walls of. Mother wants to *wallpaper* the kitchen. *Verb.*
wall·pa·per (wôl′pā′pər) *noun, plural* **wallpapers;** *verb,* **wallpapered, wallpapering.**

Kernel

Nut

Walnut Tree

walnut A sweet, oily nut that has a hard shell. Walnuts grow on tall trees. The wood of this tree is used to make furniture.
wal·nut (wôl′nut′) *noun, plural* **walnuts.**

walrus A large animal that lives in water in the Arctic regions. The walrus looks like a seal but is larger. It has a thick neck, a pair of long ivory tusks, and a tough hide.
wal·rus (wôl′rəs *or* wol′rəs) *noun, plural* **walruses** *or* **walrus.**

Walrus

▲ The word **walrus** comes from the Dutch name for this animal. The Dutch word means "whale horse."

waltz **1.** A dance that is performed by two people who whirl and glide across the dance floor. **2.** The music for this dance. *Noun.*
—To dance a waltz. *Verb.*
waltz (wôlts) *noun, plural* **waltzes;** *verb,* **waltzed, waltzing.**

wampum Small, polished beads made from shells and strung together or woven into belts, collars, and necklaces. Wampum was used by certain tribes of North American Indians as money.
wam·pum (wom′pəm *or* wôm′pəm) *noun.*

wand A thin rod or stick. The magician waved his *wand* and made flowers appear in the glass.
wand (wond) *noun, plural* **wands.**

Wand

wander **1.** To go or move about with no particular place to go. We *wandered* all through the woods looking for wild flowers. **2.** To lose one's way; stray. The small child *wandered* off from his mother in the store. **3.** To not pay attention or stay on the right subject. His thoughts *wandered* and he didn't hear the teacher's question.
wan·der (won′dər) *verb,* **wandered, wandering.**

want **1.** To have a desire or wish for. Nancy *wants* a new bicycle. **2.** To have need of; be without. The stew *wants* salt. He was not hired for the job because he is so young and *wants* experience. *Verb.*
—A need; lack. She comes from a rich family and has no *want* of money. *Noun.*
want (wont *or* wônt) *verb,* **wanted, wanting;** *noun, plural* **wants.**

at; āpe; cär; end; mē; it; īce; hot; ōld; fôrk; wood; fool; oil; out; up; turn; sing; thin; this; hw in white; zh in treasure.
ə stands for a in about, e in taken
i in pencil, o in lemon, and u in circus.

695

wanting **1.** Missing; lacking. *The only thing* wanting *is the mustard for the hot dogs.* **2.** Not having something needed. *He was* wanting *in experience for the job.*
want·ing (won′ting *or* wôn′ting) *adjective.*

war **1.** An armed fight between countries or different groups within a country. *The Revolutionary* War *between England and the American colonies ended in 1783.* **2.** Any struggle or fight. *Millions of dollars are spent each year in the* war *against cancer.* *Noun.*
—To carry on a war; fight. *The two countries* warred *for many years before a peace treaty was finally signed.* *Verb.* ▲ Another word that sounds like this is **wore.**
war (wôr) *noun, plural* **wars;** *verb,* **warred, warring.**

warbler A small songbird that often has brightly colored feathers.
war·bler (wôr′-blər) *noun, plural* **warblers.**

Warbler

ward **1.** A room or division of a hospital. *A number of patients are taken care of in a ward. The children's* ward *has one hundred beds.* **2.** A person who is under the care or control of a court or another person acting as guardian. **3.** A division of a city or town. *Cities and towns are divided into wards for purposes of local government.*
ward (wôrd) *noun, plural* **wards.**
to ward off. To turn back or aside. *Our soldiers* warded off *the enemy attack.*

warden A person whose job is taking care of or guarding a person or thing. *A person who is in charge of a prison is called a warden.*
ward·en (wôrd′ən) *noun, plural* **wardens.**

wardrobe **1.** All of a person's clothes. *That actress has a beautiful* wardrobe. **2.** A piece of furniture or a closet for keeping clothes. *Sue hung her dress in the* wardrobe.

▲ The word **wardrobe** comes from a word that was used long ago in France for a place to keep clothes. The French word was made up of a word that meant "to guard" and another word that meant "a piece of clothing."

ware **1. wares.** Things for sale. *Each person at the county fair had his* wares *on display.* **2.** Pots and other things made of baked clay; pottery. *Mother bought a new piece of ceramic* ware *at the fair.* ▲ Another word that sounds like this is **wear.**
ware (wer) *noun, plural* **wares.**

warehouse A building where merchandise is stored. *The new sofa we ordered will be sent from the* warehouse.
ware·house (wer′hous′) *noun, plural* **warehouses.**

warfare The act of fighting a war. *Soldiers are trained in* warfare.
war·fare (wôr′fer′) *noun.*

warlike **1.** Favoring war; quick to go to war. *That is a very* warlike *country.* **2.** Threatening war; hostile. *Sinking the foreign ship was a* warlike *act.*
war·like (wôr′līk′) *adjective.*

warm **1.** Somewhat hot; not cold. *The fire made the room* warm. *I'm going to take a* warm *bath after our hike.* **2.** Having a feeling of heat. *His forehead is* warm *from the fever.* **3.** Giving off or holding in heat. *The sun is* warm. *We all wore* warm *clothing on the camping trip.* **4.** Full of or showing kind feelings. *She gave us her* warm *thanks for helping her when she was in need. He is a very* warm *person who makes friends easily wherever he goes.* *Adjective.*
—**1.** To make or become warm or heated. *Please* warm *the milk for the baby. The soup will* warm *quickly on the stove.* **2.** To fill or be filled with kind, friendly thoughts and feelings. *The sight of home* warmed *their hearts. The whole family* warmed *to the friendly little puppy.* *Verb.*
warm (wôrm) *adjective,* **warmer, warmest;** *verb,* **warmed, warming.**
to warm up. 1. To make warm. *Please* warm up *the rolls in the oven for dinner.* **2.** To get ready by practicing or exercising. *The team* warmed up *before the game.* **3.** To make or become more friendly or enthusiastic. *The shy girl finally* warmed up *to her new classmates.*

warm-blooded Having blood that stays at almost the same temperature, even when the temperature of the air or of other surroundings changes. *Birds, human beings, and other mammals are warm-blooded. Snakes and turtles are cold-blooded.*
warm-blood·ed (wôrm′blud′id) *adjective.*

warmth The state or quality of being warm. *We felt the* warmth *of the sun on our faces. The actor was pleased by the* warmth *of the* audience's applause. The *warmth* of her smile made us feel at ease right away.

    warmth (wôrmth) *noun.*

warn **1.** To put on guard by giving notice beforehand; caution. The news on the radio *warned* the townspeople of the coming storm. **2.** To give advice or notice to. Jack's mother *warned* him not to eat too much candy. The flashing yellow light *warned* of danger ahead.

    warn (wôrn) *verb,* **warned, warning.**

warning Notice or advice given beforehand. The teacher gave her a *warning* not to copy her friend's homework again.

    warn·ing (wôr′ning) *noun, plural* **warnings.**

warrant **1.** A thing that gives a good reason for doing something. There was no *warrant* for his rude behavior. **2.** An official paper that gives authority for an arrest, payment of money, or other such thing. The police had a *warrant* to search the house for stolen property. *Noun.*

    —**1.** To give good reason for. Her behavior *warranted* the punishment she got. **2.** To guarantee. The car dealer *warranted* the new car for one year. *Verb.*

    war·rant (wôr′ənt *or* wor′ənt) *noun, plural* **warrants;** *verb,* **warranted, warranting.**

warrior A person who fights or is experienced in fighting battles.

    war·ri·or (wôr′ē ər *or* wor′ē ər) *noun, plural* **warriors.**

warship A ship built and armed for use in war.

    war·ship (wôr′ship′) *noun, plural* **warships.**

wart **1.** A small, hard lump that grows on the skin. **2.** A similar lump that grows on a plant.

    wart (wôrt) *noun, plural* **warts.**

wary **1.** Always on the alert; watchful. She is very *wary* when walking home alone. **2.** Showing caution; guarded. He gave a *wary* answer to the question asked by the police about his friend.

    war·y (wer′ē) *adjective,* **warier, wariest.**

was I *was* at home yesterday. He *was* taking a bath when the phone rang.

    was (wuz *or* woz *or* wəz) *verb.*

wash **1.** To make something free of dirt, germs, or the like by using water or soap and water on it. He *washed* his face. She *washed* the dishes. **2.** To take out or away by using water or soap and water. I *washed* the gravy stain out of the tablecloth. **3.** To clean oneself. Did you *wash* before dinner? **4.** To carry away, wear away, or destroy by water. The rain *washed* away the grass seed on the lawn. The flood *washed* out the bridge. *Verb.*

—**1.** The act of washing. We gave the car a quick *wash.* **2.** The amount of clothes or other things washed at one time. I hung the *wash* on the line to dry. **3.** A flow or rush of water, or the sound made by this. We could hear the *wash* of the waves on the beach. **4.** A liquid that is used for a special purpose. The doctor gave her a *wash* for her infected eye. *Noun.*

    wash (wôsh *or* wosh) *verb,* **washed, washing;** *noun, plural* **washes.**

washer **1.** A person who washes. **2.** A machine for washing. A washing machine is one kind of washer. **3.** A flat ring of metal, rubber, or other material. It is placed between a nut and a bolt to give a tighter fit.

    wash·er (wô′shər *or* wosh′ər) *noun, plural* **washers.**

washing machine A machine for washing clothes and other things.

Washington A state in the northwestern United States. Its capital is Olympia.

    Wash·ing·ton (wô′shing tən *or* wosh′ing tən) *noun.*

▲ **Washington** was named after George Washington. It is the only state that is named for a President.

Washington The capital of the United States. It lies between Maryland and northern Virginia, and includes all of the District of Columbia. Another name for this is **Washington, D. C.**

wasn't She *wasn't* home when I called.

    was·n't (wuz′ənt *or* woz′ənt) contraction for "was not."

wasp An insect that has wings and a thin body with a narrow waist. Wasps can give a painful sting.

    wasp (wosp) *noun, plural* **wasps.**

waste **1.** To use or spend in a careless or useless way. He *wasted* his money when he bought that broken-down old bicycle. She sat there *wasting* her time daydreaming. **2.** To

Wasp

at; āpe; cär; end; mē; it; īce; hot; ōld;
fôrk; wood; fo͞ol; oil; out; up; turn; sing;
thin; **th**is; hw in white; zh in treasure.
ə stands for **a** in about, **e** in taken
i in pencil, **o** in lemon, and **u** in circus.

use up, wear away, or exhaust. The long sickness *wasted* the old man's strength. **3.** To destroy; ruin. The army *wasted* everything in its path as it marched forward. **4.** To lose energy, strength, or health. The homeless kitten would have *wasted* away from lack of food if we hadn't found it and taken it in. *Verb.*
—**1.** The act of wasting or the state of being wasted. It's a *waste* of time trying to convince her to go to the party if she does not want to go. **2.** Worthless material; garbage or refuse. There was a lot of *waste* floating in the dirty river. *Noun.*
—**1.** Left over or thrown away as worthless. She had a pile of *waste* material after she finished making the dress. **2.** Having to do with or used for waste. A garbage can is a *waste* container. *Adjective.* ▲ Another word that sounds like this is **waist.**
waste (wāst) *verb,* **wasted, wasting;** *noun; adjective.*

wastebasket A basket or other container used for scraps of paper or other things to be thrown away.
waste·bas·ket (wāst′bas′kit) *noun, plural* **wastebaskets.**

wasteful Using or spending something in a careless or useless way. People should try not to be *wasteful* of our country's natural resources.
waste·ful (wāst′fəl) *adjective.*

wasteland A piece of land or an area where there are few or no living things. A desert is a wasteland.
waste·land (wāst′land′) *noun, plural* **wastelands.**

watch **1.** To look at a person or thing carefully. The little boy *watched* television all afternoon. *Watch* closely while I show you how to run the washing machine. **2.** To keep guard over; take care of. The mother *watched* the children as they played in the swimming pool. The shepherd *watched* his flock of sheep. **3.** To be on the alert; wait. The prisoner *watched* for a chance to try to escape from his cell. *Verb.*
—**1.** The act of watching closely; close attention. Will you keep *watch* for the bus while I go and get a newspaper? **2.** One or more persons whose work is protecting or guarding something. The night *watch* at the museum comes on duty at 9:00. **3.** A small device that is used for telling time. Watches are usually worn on the wrist or carried in the pocket. *Noun.*
watch (woch) *verb,* **watched, watching;** *noun, plural* **watches.**

▲ The first meaning of **watch** was "to be awake." If someone had trouble sleeping he might have said, "I *watched* all night." This idea of being awake led to the meaning of staying awake on purpose in order to look out for something. From this meaning the word came to mean "to look at with attention."

watchdog A dog that is kept to guard a house or property.
watch·dog (woch′dôg′) *noun, plural* **watch-dogs.**

watchful On the alert. The teacher is very *watchful* for mistakes in spelling when she checks our reports.
watch·ful (woch′fəl) *adjective.*

watchman A man whose work is guarding a building or property. A watchman usually works during the night when a place or building is empty.
watch·man (woch′mən) *noun, plural* **watch-men.**

water The liquid that is found over the earth in the form of oceans, lakes, rivers, and ponds. Water has no color, smell, or taste in its pure form. We use water for washing and drinking. *Noun.*
—**1.** To put water into or on. She *watered* the plants every day. **2.** To give water to for drinking. We stopped to *water* the horses. **3.** To give forth water from the body. The smoke made my eyes *water. Verb.*
wa·ter (wô′tər) *noun, plural* **waters;** *verb,* **watered, watering.**

water buffalo A black buffalo of Asia that has long horns that curve backward. The water buffalo is used for carrying or pulling heavy loads.

Water Buffalo

water color **1.** A paint that is made by mixing pigment with water. **2.** The art of painting with water colors. **3.** A picture or design made with water colors.

watercress A plant that grows in water. It has sharp tasting leaves that are used in salads.

wa·ter·cress (wô′tər kres′) *noun, plural* **watercresses.**

waterfall A flow of water falling from a high place.
wa·ter·fall (wô′tər fôl′) *noun, plural* **waterfalls.**

waterfront **1.** The part of a city or town that is beside the harbor of a river or ocean. The waterfront often has docks for ships. **2.** Land next to a lake, river, or other body of water. Our cottage at the lake is right on the *waterfront.*
wa·ter·front (wô′tər frunt′) *noun, plural* **waterfronts.**

water lily A plant that grows in freshwater ponds and lakes. The leaves and flowers of water lilies float on top of the water.

watermelon A large, juicy fruit that has a thick green rind and a watery pulp that is pink or red. Watermelons grow on vines.
wa·ter·mel·on (wô′tər mel′ən) *noun, plural* **watermelons.**

Watermelon

waterproof Not letting water pass through. Material for clothing and other things is often treated or coated with a substance that will make it waterproof. She made sure she bought a *waterproof* tent. *Adjective.*
—To make waterproof. My raincoat has been *waterproofed. Verb.*
wa·ter·proof (wô′tər pro͞of′) *adjective; verb,* **waterproofed, waterproofing.**

watershed **1.** A ridge or other high land area that separates two different river basins. **2.** The total land area from which water drains into a stream or river.
wa·ter·shed (wô′tər shed′) *noun, plural* **watersheds.**

water-ski To glide over the surface of the water on water skis while being pulled by a towing rope attached to a boat.
water-ski (wô′tər skē′) *verb,* **water-skied, water-skiing.**

water ski One of a pair of short, wide skis used in water-skiing.

waterway A river, canal, or other body of water that is used as a route for ships.
wa·ter·way (wô′tər wā′) *noun, plural* **waterways.**

water wheel A wheel that is turned by the weight or pressure of water falling on it. Water wheels are used to provide power.

Water Wheel

waterworks **1.** The entire system for supplying water to a city or town. Reservoirs, machinery, pipes, and buildings are part of a waterworks. **2.** A building in which the machinery for pumping water to a city or town is located.
wa·ter·works (wô′tər wurks′) *noun plural.*

watery **1.** Having to do with or containing water. The ground was *watery* after the heavy rains. **2.** Containing too much water. This gravy is *watery.*
wa·ter·y (wô′tər ē) *adjective,* **waterier, wateriest.**

watt A unit for measuring electrical power.
watt (wot) *noun, plural* **watts.**

▲ The word **watt** comes from the name of James *Watt.* He was a Scottish engineer and inventor.

at; āpe; cär; end; mē; it; īce; hot; ōld;
fôrk; wood; fo͞ol; oil; out; up; turn; sing;
thin; this; hw in white; zh in treasure.
ə stands for a in about, e in taken
i in pencil, o in lemon, and u in circus.

wave **1.** To move freely back and forth or up and down; move with a swaying motion. The stalks of wheat *waved* in the wind. The children *waved* their flags as the parade passed by. **2.** To show or signal by waving the hand or something else. Father *waved* good-by to us as the train pulled out. She *waved* for us to stop. **3.** To have or give a curving form or appearance to. She *waves* her hair by setting it in curlers. *Verb.*
—**1.** A curving or rippling movement on the surface of the ocean or another body of water. The ship rode gently over the *waves.* **2.** Anything like a wave in movement or shape. Sound, heat, and light move in waves. **3.** The act of waving with the hand or with something held in the hand. He signaled for us to come in with a *wave* of his hand. **4.** A sudden rush or increase. We had a heat *wave* last week with temperatures rising into the high 90s. **5.** A curve or series of curves. She has many *waves* in her hair. *Noun.*

wave (wāv) *verb*, **waved, waving;** *noun, plural* **waves.**

wave-length The distance between any two points that are on the same wave. For example, the distance between the two highest points of a wave is one wave-length.

wave-length (wāv′lengkth′ *or* wāv′length′) *noun, plural* **wave-lengths.**

waver **1.** To move in an unsteady way up and down or from side to side; sway. The ladder *wavered* and fell over. **2.** To flicker; quiver. The candle flame *wavered* in the breeze. **3.** To show doubt; be uncertain. He *wavered* between spending the money on a new bicycle or saving it.

wa·ver (wā′vər) *verb*, **wavered, wavering.**

wavy Having a curving movement or shape; full of waves. He has *wavy* hair.

wav·y (wā′vē) *adjective*, **wavier, waviest.**

wax¹ **1.** Any of various fatty substances that come from plants or animals. Bees make a wax called beeswax that is used in making their honeycombs. Wax also forms inside the ear. **2.** A substance that is like or contains wax. Wax is used to polish furniture and cars. *Noun.*
—To cover or polish with wax. We *waxed* the floors this afternoon. *Verb.*

wax (waks) *noun, plural* **waxes;** *verb*, **waxed, waxing.**

wax² **1.** To become larger in size, brightness, or strength. The moon *waxes* as it gets nearer to the full moon. **2.** To become. John *waxed* enthusiastic when he spoke about the plans for the camping trip.

wax (waks) *verb*, **waxed, waxing.**

way **1.** A method for doing or getting something. She thought of a *way* to solve the puzzle. Being kind to others is a good *way* to make friends. **2.** A road or path that leads from one place to another. That road is the quickest *way* to town. **3.** A direction. The storm is heading this *way.* **4.** A moving along a particular route or in a particular direction. We passed John on his *way* to school. **5.** Distance. They walked a long *way* before finding the right house. **6.** Something that a person wants to have or do; wish. He becomes angry if he cannot have his *way.* **7.** A particular detail or feature. In many *ways,* the plan is a good one. *Noun.*
—At or to a distance; far. The water from the breaking waves came *way* up the beach. *Adverb.* ▲ Another word that sounds like this is **weigh.**

way (wā) *noun, plural* **ways;** *adverb.*

we *We* are going to go home. *We* won the baseball game. ▲ Another word that sounds like this is **wee.**

we (wē) *pronoun plural.*

weak **1.** Liable to fall or give way. The legs of the old chair are *weak.* **2.** Not having strength, force, or power. Lack of food made the lost hikers *weak.* The light is too *weak* to read by. ▲ Another word that sounds like this is **week.**

weak (wēk) *adjective*, **weaker, weakest.**

weaken To make or become weak or weaker. She *weakened* the tea by adding water. The runner *weakened* as he neared the finish line.

weak·en (wē′kən) *verb*, **weakened, weakening.**

weakly In a weak manner. The shy girl answered the question *weakly. Adverb.*
—Not healthy or strong; weak. He has been a *weakly* boy since childhood. *Adjective.* ▲ Another word that sounds like this is **weekly.**

weak·ly (wēk′lē) *adverb; adjective*, **weaklier, weakliest.**

weakness **1.** The state or quality of being weak. His *weakness* from the illness kept him in bed. **2.** A weak point. His biggest *weakness* is that he won't ever listen to other people's ideas. **3.** A special liking; fondness. Sally has a *weakness* for ice cream.

weak·ness (wēk′nis) *noun, plural* **weaknesses.**

wealth **1.** A great amount of money or valuable things; riches. He is a man of great *wealth.* **2.** A great amount of anything. She has a *wealth* of ideas for the class science project.

wealth (welth) *noun.*

wealthy Having wealth; rich. She comes from a *wealthy* family.
wealth·y (wel′thē) *adjective,* **wealthier, wealthiest.**

weapon **1.** Anything used in a fight to attack or defend. Guns and knives are weapons. **2.** Any means used to attack or defend. The cruel ruler used the threat of prison as a *weapon* against anyone who would criticize his policies.
weap·on (wep′ən) *noun, plural* **weapons.**

wear **1.** To carry or have on the body. We *wear* warm clothes in the winter. She *wore* a silver bracelet on her wrist. **2.** To have or show. She *wears* her hair long. He *wore* a big smile. **3.** To damage or use up. We *wore* the rug in the hall after walking on it for so many years. **4.** To cause or make. He *wore* holes in his socks. **5.** To last or hold out. The material of the trousers did not *wear* well. *Verb.*
—**1.** The act of wearing or the state of being worn. This suit has had five years of *wear.* **2.** Clothing. This store only sells women's *wear.* **3.** Damage caused by use or age. This chair shows signs of *wear. Noun.* ▲ Another word that sounds like this is **ware.**
wear (wer) *verb,* **wore, worn, wearing;** *noun.*
to wear out. 1. To use until no longer fit or able to be used. She *wore out* the soles of her shoes after only two months. **2.** To make tired; exhaust. He was *worn out* from the long hike.

weary Very tired. He was *weary* after the hard day's work. *Adjective.*
—To make or become weary; tire. The long walk *wearied* her. *Verb.*
wea·ry (wēr′ē) *adjective,* **wearier, weariest;** *verb,* **wearied, wearying.**

weasel A small animal that has a slender body, short legs, a long neck, and soft, thick brownish fur. Weasels eat rabbits and other small animals, snakes, and small birds.
wea·sel (wē′zəl) *noun, plural* **weasels** or **weasel.**

Weasel

weather The condition of the air or atmosphere at a particular time and place. The *weather* has been cold and rainy for the past week. *Noun.*
—To cause to be dried, bleached, or aged by the weather. The salt air and sun *weathered* the shingles of our house at the beach. **2.** To come safely through. The little boat *weathered* the storm. *Verb.*
weath·er (weth′ər) *noun; verb,* **weathered, weathering.**

weathercock A weather vane that is in the shape of a rooster.
weath·er·cock (weth′ər-kok′) *noun, plural* **weathercocks.**

weatherman A person who studies and forecasts the weather.
weath·er·man (weth′ər-man′) *noun, plural* **weathermen.**

weather vane A device that is moved by the wind. It shows the direction in which the wind is blowing.

Weathercock

weave **1.** To lace or put together. She is *weaving* the yarn into cloth. She *wove* a basket out of straw. He *weaves* rugs out of old yarn. **2.** To spin a web or cocoon. Spiders *weave* webs. **3.** To move or make by turning and twisting. The policeman had to *weave* his way through the crowd to reach the sick woman. *Verb.*
—A way or kind of weaving. The rug has a loose *weave. Noun.* ▲ Another word that sounds like this is **we've.**
weave (wēv) *verb,* **wove** or **weaved** *(for definition 3),* **woven** or **wove** or **weaved** *(for definition 3),* **weaving;** *noun, plural* **weaves.**

weaver A person who weaves or whose job is weaving.
weav·er (wē′vər) *noun, plural* **weavers.**

web **1.** A network of fine threads that are spun by a spider; cobweb. **2.** Anything that is like a spider's web. We got lost in the *web* of streets in the old part of town. **3.** The skin

at; āpe; cär; end; mē; it; īce; hot; ōld;
fôrk; wood; fo͞ol; oil; out; up; turn; sing;
thin; this; hw in white; zh in treasure.
ə stands for a in about, e in taken
i in pencil, o in lemon, and u in circus.

between the toes of ducks, geese, and other birds that swim.

web (web) *noun, plural* **webs.**

webbed Having or joined by a web or webbing. A duck has *webbed* feet.

webbed (webd) *adjective.*

web-footed Having the toes joined by a web. Ducks are *web-footed.*

web-foot·ed (web′-foot′id) *adjective.*

wed **1.** To take a husband or wife; marry. John and Barbara will *wed* next Saturday. **2.** To join as husband and wife. My parents were *wedded* by a clergyman.

wed (wed) *verb,* **wedded, wedded** or **wed, wedding.**

Webbed Feet

we'd *We'd* be happy to drive you home. *We'd* just left when the rain began. He said *we'd* get the package tomorrow. ▲ Another word that sounds like this is **weed.**

we'd (wēd) contraction for "we would," "we had," and "we should."

wedding **1.** A marriage ceremony. We are going to my cousin's *wedding* tomorrow. **2.** The anniversary of a marriage. A golden wedding is a celebration of fifty years of marriage.

wed·ding (wed′ing) *noun, plural* **weddings.**

wedge **1.** A piece of wood or metal that is shaped like a triangle or is tapered at one end. It is pounded or driven into or between objects to separate, split, or lift them. Bill drove a *wedge* into the logs to split them for firewood. **2.** Something that has the shape of a wedge. She put a *wedge* of cheese out for snacks. *Noun.*
—**1.** To separate or split by driving a wedge into. The workmen *wedged* the floor boards

Wedge

apart. **2.** To fasten or fix in place with a wedge. Margaret *wedged* the door open with a piece of wood. **3.** To drive, push, or crowd. He *wedged* the book into place on the crowded shelf. *Verb.*

wedge (wej) *noun, plural* **wedges;** *verb,* **wedged, wedging.**

Wednesday The fourth day of the week.

Wednes·day (wenz′dē *or* wenz′dā) *noun, plural* **Wednesdays.**

▲ The word **Wednesday** comes from an Old English word that meant "Woden's day." Long ago, certain people in England believed in Woden, who they thought was the king of the gods. They named this day in his honor.

---

wee **1.** Very small; tiny. The *wee* baby was asleep in the cradle. **2.** Early. The milkman makes his deliveries in the *wee* hours of the morning. ▲ Another word that sounds like this is **we.**

wee (wē) *adjective,* **weer, weest.**

weed A plant that is useless or harmful and grows where it is not wanted. We pulled the *weeds* out of our vegetable garden. *Noun.*
—**1.** To take out the weeds from. John is *weeding* the lawn. **2.** To take out what is harmful or not wanted. The coach *weeded* out the boys who were troublemakers from the baseball team. *Verb.* ▲ Another word that sounds like this is **we'd.**

weed (wēd) *noun, plural* **weeds;** *verb,* **weeded, weeding.**

week **1.** A period of seven days. A week is usually thought of as starting with Sunday. **2.** The part of a seven-day period during which a person works or goes to school. Bill doesn't watch television much during the *week* because he has to study. Her work *week* is thirty-five hours. ▲ Another word that sounds like this is **weak.**

week (wēk) *noun, plural* **weeks.**

weekday Any day of the week except Saturday and Sunday.

week·day (wēk′dā′) *noun, plural* **weekdays.**

weekend The period of time from Friday night or Saturday morning until Sunday night or Monday morning. We went to the country for the *weekend.*

week·end (wēk′end′) *noun, plural* **weekends.**

weekly **1.** For or having to do with a week or weekdays. She is doing her *weekly* laundry. **2.** Done, happening, or published once a week. Our school has a *weekly* newspaper. *Adjective.*
—A newspaper or magazine published once a week. *Noun.*

—Once each week; every week. He shops for groceries *weekly. Adverb.* ▲ Another word that sounds like this is **weakly.**

week·ly (wēk′lē) *adjective; noun, plural* **weeklies;** *adverb.*

weep To show sorrow, joy, or other strong emotion by crying. The sad story made us *weep.*

weep (wēp) *verb,* **wept, weeping.**

weevil A beetle that destroys and eats cotton, grain, and other crops.

wee·vil (wē′vəl) *noun, plural* **weevils.**

weigh 1. To find out the weight or heaviness of a person or thing. The grocer *weighed* the tomatoes. The doctor put the baby on the scale to *weigh* him. 2. To have, amount to, or be equal to a specified weight. The car *weighs* 3744 pounds. She *weighs* exactly the same as her sister. 3. To think about or examine carefully. He *weighed* his chances of winning the race. She *weighed* her words before answering. 4. To lie heavily on; burden. The heavy snowfall *weighed* down the branches of the trees. His guilt about having lied to his mother *weighed* on his conscience. ▲ Another word that sounds like this is **way.**

weigh (wā) *verb,* **weighed, weighing.**

weight 1. The amount of heaviness of a person or thing. Her *weight* is 100 pounds. 2. The quality of a thing that comes from the pull of gravity upon it. Weight tends to pull things toward the center of the earth. The *weight* of helium is less than the *weight* of air, so a balloon filled with helium will rise in the air. 3. A system of units for expressing weight. Troy *weight* is used for gems and precious metals, such as gold and silver. 4. Something heavy. He used a rock as a *weight* to put on the tablecloth to keep it from blowing off. 5. A burden or load. The *weight* of his debts worried him. 6. Strong influence; importance. Her advice carries much *weight* with her friends. ▲ Another word that sounds like this is **wait.**

weight (wāt) *noun, plural* **weights.**

weightless 1. Having little or no weight. The little baby was practically *weightless.* 2. Not influenced by the pull of gravity. An object in outer space is *weightless.*

weight·less (wāt′lis) *adjective.*

weird Strange or mysterious; odd. *Weird* sounds came from the deserted old house.

weird (wērd) *adjective,* **weirder, weirdest.**

welcome 1. To greet someone in a pleasant and friendly way. My father *welcomed* the guests when they arrived at the party. 2. To receive or accept with pleasure or gladness.

My father works so hard that he *welcomes* a summer vacation. *Verb.*

—A glad and friendly greeting. We received a very nice *welcome* at their house. *Noun.*

—1. Received kindly and with pleasure. You are always a *welcome* visitor to our house. 2. Free to use, have, or enjoy. Anyone is *welcome* to the newspaper when I've finished reading it. "You are welcome" or "You're welcome" are used in answering someone who has thanked you. *Adjective.*

wel·come (wel′kəm) *verb,* **welcomed, welcoming;** *noun, plural* **welcomes;** *adjective.*

weld To join pieces of metal or plastic by heating until soft enough to be hammered and pressed together. The plumber *welded* the broken pieces of pipe together.

weld (weld) *verb,* **welded, welding.**

welfare 1. The condition of being happy and healthy. He wrote a letter to us because he was concerned about Grandfather's *welfare.* 2. Money or other aid given by the government to people who are in need.

wel·fare (wel′fer′) *noun.*

well¹ 1. In a good or satisfactory way. Robert plays the bugle *well.* I did not sleep *well* last night. 2. In a complete way; thoroughly. Be sure to mix the flour and salt *well.* 3. To a considerable degree. The piano weighs *well* over 300 pounds. She walked *well* ahead of us. 4. In a close or personal way. Do you know your neighbors *well? Adverb.*

—1. In good health; healthy. Everyone in our family is *well.* 2. Good; fortunate. It is *well* that you called now because we were just leaving. *Adjective.*

—*Well* is used to show surprise or to bring in another idea or thought. *Well!* How nice to see you. *Well,* I think that it's time to leave now. *Interjection.*

well (wel) *adverb,* **better, best;** *adjective; interjection.*

well² 1. A hole or pit made in the ground to get water, oil, or gas. 2. A natural spring or fountain. 3. Something that is like a well in shape or use. The old desk has a *well* for ink. An encyclopedia is a *well* of information. *Noun.*

—To rise or fill. Tears *welled* in her eyes when she had to leave. *Verb.*

at; āpe; cär; end; mē; it; īce; hot; ōld;
fôrk; wood; fōōl; oil; out; up; turn; sing;
thin; **th**is; **hw** in white; **zh** in treasure.
ə stands for **a** in about, **e** in taken
i in pencil, **o** in lemon, and **u** in circus.

well (wel) *noun, plural* **wells;** *verb,* **welled, welling.**

we'll *We'll* see you at the party. *We'll* go to the picnic if it doesn't rain.
we'll (wēl) contraction for "we shall" and "we will."

well-balanced Nicely or evenly balanced. He eats *well-balanced* meals every day.
well-bal·anced (wel′bal′ənst) *adjective.*

well-behaved Having or showing good conduct or manners. All the children were *well-behaved.*
well-be·haved (wel′bi hāvd′) *adjective.*

well-being Health and happiness; welfare. The parents were only concerned for the *well-being* of their children.
well-be·ing (wel′bē′ing) *noun.*

well-known Known to many people; generally or widely known. He is a *well-known* movie actor.
well-known (wel′nōn′) *adjective.*

well-mannered Having or showing good manners; polite. It was not very *well-mannered* of him to stare at the stranger.
well-man·nered (wel′man′ərd) *adjective.*

went He *went* to the grocery store. I *went* to bed early last night.
went (went) *verb.*

wept She *wept* when she heard the sad story. Look up **weep** for more information.
wept (wept) *verb.*

were We *were* at home all day. They *were* glad to see him.
were (wur) *verb.*

we're *We're* going home now.
we're (wēr) contraction for "we are."

weren't They *weren't* home this afternoon.
weren't (wurnt *or* wur′ənt) contraction for "were not."

west 1. The direction you face when you watch the sun set in the evening. West is one of the four main points of the compass. It is located directly opposite east. 2. **West.** Any region or place that is in this direction. 3. **the West.** The region of the United States that is west of the Mississippi River. *Noun.*
—1. Toward or in the west. The grocery store is on the *west* side of the street. 2. Coming from the west. A *west* wind was blowing. *Adjective.*
—Toward the west. We sailed *west* to cross the lake. *Adverb.*
west (west) *noun; adjective; adverb.*

western 1. In or toward the west. California is a *western* state. 2. Coming from the west. A *western* breeze was blowing.

3. **Western.** Of or in the part of the United States that is in the west. *Adjective.*
—A story, book, or motion picture about frontier life in the western United States. Westerns are usually about cowboys and the early settlers. *Noun.*
west·ern (wes′tərn) *adjective; noun, plural* **westerns.**

westerner 1. A person who was born or is living in the western part of a country or region. 2. **Westerner.** A person living in the western part of the United States.
west·ern·er (wes′tər nər) *noun, plural* **westerners.**

Western Hemisphere The western half of the earth. It includes North and South America.

West Virginia A state in the eastern United States. Its capital is Charleston.

▲ **West Virginia** used to be the western part of the colony of Virginia. Queen Elizabeth I of England named the colony *Virginia* because she was called "the Virgin Queen."

westward Toward the west. The airplane flew *westward* into the sunset.
west·ward (west′wərd) *adverb; adjective.*

wet 1. Covered, soaked, or moist with water or other liquid. Her bathing suit was still *wet* from her morning swim. The little boy's eyes were *wet* with tears. 2. Not yet dry. A footprint was made in the *wet* cement. 3. Having rainfall; rainy. April is often a *wet* month. *Adjective.*
—To make wet. The directions said to *wet* the ground before planting the seeds. *Verb.*
wet (wet) *adjective,* **wetter, wettest;** *verb,* **wet** or **wetted, wetting.**

we've *We've* enjoyed seeing you. ▲ Another word that sounds like this is **weave.**
we've (wēv) contraction for "we have."

Whale

whale A large animal that has a body like a fish. Whales are found in all oceans and in certain fresh waters. A whale is a mammal. Some whales are hunted for their oil, meat, and bone.

whale (hwāl) *noun, plural* **whales** or **whale.**

whaler **1.** A person whose job is hunting and killing whales. **2.** A ship or boat used in whaling.

whal·er (hwā′lər) *noun, plural* **whalers.**

whaling The act or work of hunting and killing whales for their oil, meat, and bone.

whal·ing (hwā′ling) *noun.*

wharf A structure that is built along a shore. It is used as a landing place for boats and ships; dock.

wharf (hworf) *noun, plural* **wharves** or **wharfs.**

what *What* do you want to do? *What* day is the party? They knew *what* he was thinking. Choose *what* you want for dinner. *What* books are missing from the shelf? Take *what* food you need for the picnic. *What* does it matter? *What* did you do that for? *What* a silly thing to say!

what (hwut *or* hwot *or* hwət) *pronoun; adjective; adverb; interjection.*

whatever Take *whatever* you want to eat from the refrigerator. *Whatever* you say, he still won't come to the party. *Whatever* is that noise? Take *whatever* books you want to read.

what·ev·er (hwət ev′ər) *pronoun; adjective.*

what's *What's* his name? *What's* happened?

what's (hwuts *or* hwots) *contraction for* "what is" and "what has."

wheat A grass that has thin, hollow stems and long, thin leaves. The tiny grains of wheat are used to make flour and other foods. Wheat is a very important food for human beings and animals.

wheat (hwēt) *noun.*

wheel **1.** A round frame that has a middle part that is connected to the outside rim by spokes. A wheel turns on its center and is used on cars, wagons, and other vehicles and on certain machines. **2.** Any machine or other thing that has or uses a wheel. A spinning *wheel* is used for making thread. *Noun.*

Wheat

—**1.** To turn. He *wheeled* around when I called his name. **2.** To move or roll on wheels. I *wheeled* the cart around the grocery store. *Verb.*

wheel (hwēl) *noun, plural* **wheels;** *verb,* **wheeled, wheeling.**

wheelbarrow A small vehicle with one or two wheels at the front end and two handles at the back. Wheelbarrows are used to move sand, dirt, bricks, or other small loads.

wheel·bar·row (hwēl′bar′ō) *noun, plural* **wheelbarrows.**

Wheelbarrow

wheeze To breathe with a hoarse, whistling sound. He is *wheezing* because he has a bad cold.

wheeze (hwēz) *verb,* **wheezed, wheezing.**

whelk A large snail that lives in salt water. Whelks have spiral shells.

whelk (hwelk) *noun, plural* **whelks.**

Whelk

when *When* did you arrive at school? I'll come *when* you call me. The children played until noon, *when* they had lunch. He wore only a shirt *when* he should have worn a sweater. Since *when* have you liked to take long walks?

when (hwen) *adverb; conjunction; pronoun.*

whenever You may come *whenever* you like.

when·ev·er (hwen ev′ər) *adverb; conjunction.*

where *Where* did you put the camera? *Where* does he live? *Where* did you buy that book? The keys are still *where* you left them last night.

where (hwer) *adverb; conjunction.*

at; āpe; cär; end; mē; it; īce; hot; ōld; fôrk; wood; fōōl; oil; out; up; turn; sing; thin; <u>th</u>is; hw in white; zh in treasure. ə stands for a in about, e in taken i in pencil, o in lemon, and u in circus.

whereabouts   *Whereabouts* did you last see him? The police established the *whereabouts* of the suspect at the time of the crime.
where·a·bouts (hwer′ə bouts′) *adverb; noun.*

whereupon   They waited for him to finish speaking, *whereupon* they left.
where·up·on (hwer′ə pôn′ *or* hwer′ə pon′) *conjunction.*

wherever   *Wherever* did you buy that hat? I will go *wherever* you go.
where·ev·er (hwer ev′ər) *adverb; conjunction.*

whether   *Whether* is used to show that there is a choice between things. You must decide *whether* to take the bus or the train. Write to us *whether* you will come to visit next month.
wheth·er (hwe<u>th</u>′ər) *conjunction.*

whew   A word used to show relief, surprise, or dismay. "*Whew!* We just made the train," she said.
whew (hwyo͞o) *interjection.*

whey   The watery part of milk that separates from the curd when milk turns sour.
whey (hwā) *noun.*

which   *Which* of the books did you like best? This jacket, *which* I bought last year, is my favorite. You are late, *which* reminds me that you were late yesterday too. *Which* girl is your sister?
which (hwich) *pronoun; adjective.*

whichever   You can have *whichever* picture you like best.
which·ev·er (hwich ev′ər) *pronoun.*

whiff   A sudden light puff, breath, or smell. A *whiff* of smoke rose from the fire. The *whiff* of bacon made him hungry.
whiff (hwif) *noun, plural* **whiffs.**

while   We stopped walking and rested for a *while*. It seemed a long *while* before she answered the question. *Noun.*
—Did anyone call *while* I was away? *While* they are our neighbors, we don't know them well. *Conjunction.*
—To spend time in a relaxed, pleasant way. We *whiled* away the afternoon listening to records. *Verb.*
while (hwīl) *noun; conjunction; verb,* **whiled, whiling.**

whim   A sudden idea or wish to do something. Rosemary had a *whim* to go for a walk in the rain.
whim (hwim) *noun, plural* **whims.**

whimper   To cry with weak, broken sounds. The puppy *whimpered* for its mother.
whim·per (hwim′pər) *verb,* **whimpered, whimpering.**

whine   To cry in a low, complaining way. The tired child *whined* that she wanted to go home.
whine (hwīn) *verb,* **whined, whining.**

whinny   To neigh in a low, gentle way. My horse *whinnied* when he saw me coming. *Verb.*
—A soft neigh. We heard the *whinnies* of the horses. *Noun.*
whin·ny (hwin′ē) *verb,* **whinnied, whinnying;** *noun, plural* **whinnies.**

whip   **1.** To hit with a strap, rod, or something similar. The driver of the carriage *whipped* the horses to make them go faster. **2.** To beat eggs, cream, or the like until foamy. Joan *whipped* cream for the cake. **3.** To move, take, or throw suddenly and quickly. The cowboy *whipped* his gun out of its holster. Tony *whipped* around when he heard the explosion. *Verb.*
—A rod or strap that bends easily and has a handle. Whips are usually used for driving horses or other animals. *Noun.*
whip (hwip) *verb,* **whipped, whipping;** *noun, plural* **whips.**

whippoorwill   A plump bird with brown and black feathers. The whippoorwill lives in North America. Its call sounds like its name.
whip·poor·will (hwip′ər wil′) *noun, plural* **whip-poorwills.**

Whippoorwill

whir   To move or turn with a whizzing or buzzing sound. The helicopter *whirred* overhead. *Verb.*
—A whizzing or buzzing sound. *Noun.*
whir (hwur) *verb,* **whirred, whirring;** *noun, plural* **whirs.**

whirl   **1.** To turn or cause to turn quickly in a circle. The blades of a fan whirl. The breeze *whirled* the bits of paper around in the air. **2.** To move or turn around suddenly or quickly. The guard *whirled* when he heard the noise. *Verb.*
—**1.** A quick turn in a circle; whirling movement. We watched the skaters make graceful leaps and *whirls* on the ice. **2.** A confused or dizzy condition. His head was in a *whirl* after he was hit by the ball. *Noun.*
whirl (hwurl) *verb,* **whirled, whirling;** *noun, plural* **whirls.**

whirlpool A current of water that moves quickly in a circle. The small boat was caught in a *whirlpool.*
  whirl·pool (hwurl′pool′) *noun, plural* **whirlpools.**

whisk **1.** To brush lightly. Sarah *whisked* the crumbs off the table with a napkin. **2.** To move or cause to move quickly. Bob *whisked* out the door. The taxi *whisked* us to the airport.
  whisk (hwisk) *verb,* **whisked, whisking.**

whisker **1.** **whiskers.** The hair growing on a man's face; a beard or part of a beard. **2.** A stiff hair that grows on the face. Cats and dogs have whiskers.
  whisk·er (hwis′kər) *noun, plural* **whiskers.**

whiskey A strong alcoholic drink made from rye, corn, or other grains.
  whis·key (hwis′kē) *noun, plural* **whiskeys.**

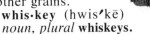
Whiskers

▲ The word **whiskey** comes from a word in a language that was spoken by people in Scotland and Ireland. In the language of these people, the word meant "water of life."

whisper To speak or say very softly. People whisper when they tell secrets. Ruth *whispered* the answer to the question to me. *Verb.*
—A very soft sound. The teacher heard *whispers* from the back of the room. *Noun.*
  whis·per (hwis′pər) *verb,* **whispered, whispering;** *noun, plural* **whispers.**

whistle **1.** To make a clear, sharp sound by forcing air out through closed lips or through the teeth. **2.** To make or move with a sound like this. The kettle *whistled* when the water boiled. The wind *whistled* through the trees. **3.** To call or signal by whistling. The policeman *whistled* for us to stop. *Verb.*
—**1.** A device that makes a clear, sharp sound when air is blown through it. The lifeguard blew his *whistle* to warn the swimmers who were too close to the rocks. **2.** A whistling sound. The dog came when he heard my *whistle. Noun.*
  whis·tle (hwis′əl) *verb,* **whistled, whistling;** *noun, plural* **whistles.**

white **1.** Having the lightest of all colors; having the color of fresh snow; opposite of black. **2.** Light in color. I like the *white* meat of turkey better than the dark. His face was *white* with fear. **3.** Pale gray; silvery. Grandfather has *white* hair. **4.** Belonging to a race of people having light skin. **5.** Not harmful. He has a habit of telling *white* lies. **6.** Snowy. He likes a *white* Christmas. *Adjective.*
—**1.** The lightest of all colors; the opposite of black. White is the color of fresh snow. **2.** Something that is white or light-colored. The recipe called for the *whites* of four eggs. **3.** A member of a race of people that has light skin. *Noun.*
  white (hwīt) *adjective,* **whiter, whitest;** *noun, plural* **whites.**

white blood cell A colorless cell found in the blood. White blood cells protect the body against infection by destroying germs that carry disease.

White House **1.** The official home of the President of the United States. The White House is in Washington, D.C. **2.** The authority of the President of the United States. The *White House* said that the peace negotiations were going well.

whiten To make or become white. Bleach *whitens* clothes. Charlie's face *whitened* in fear when he heard the strange noises.
  whit·en (hwīt′ən) *verb,* **whitened, whitening.**

whitewash A watery, white paint used on walls, wood fences, and other surfaces.
  white·wash (hwīt′wôsh′ *or* hwīt′wosh′) *noun.*

whittle **1.** To cut small bits or pieces from wood, soap, or the like with a knife. Harry *whittled* some wood while he waited for dinner. **2.** To make or shape by cutting away small bits with a knife. Grandfather *whittled* a dog from a piece of wood.
  whit·tle (hwit′əl) *verb,* **whittled, whittling.**

whiz To make a buzzing sound while moving quickly. The plane

Whittle

at; āpe; cär; end; mē; it; īce; hot; ōld; fôrk; wood; fool; oil; out; up; turn; sing; thin; <u>th</u>is; **hw** in white; **zh** in treasure. ə stands for **a** in about, **e** in taken **i** in pencil, **o** in lemon, and **u** in circus.

whizzed over the rooftops. The train *whizzed* by.
whiz (hwiz) *verb*, **whizzed, whizzing.**

who *Who* gave you that pen? The woman *who* wrote that story has a good sense of humor.
who (hoo͞) *pronoun.*

whoa Stop. *Whoa* is usually used as a command to a horse.
whoa (hwō *or* wō) *interjection.*

who'd *Who'd* say such a thing about you? William knew someone *who'd* climbed that mountain.
who'd (hoo͞d) contraction for "who would" and "who had."

whoever *Whoever* wants to come along is welcome. *Whoever* wrote this poem is very clever. *Whoever* told you such a silly story?
who·ev·er (hoo͞ ev′ər) *pronoun.*

whole Having all its parts; entire; complete. Have you read the *whole* book already? Fifty-two cards make a *whole* deck. *Adjective.*
—All the parts that make up a thing. Margaret spent the *whole* of her allowance on a present for her friend. *Noun.* ▲ Another word that sounds like this is **hole.**
whole (hōl) *adjective; noun.*

whole number A number that tells how many complete things there are. 0, 1, 2 and 21 are whole numbers; $^3/_4$, $^7/_8$, and other fractions are not whole numbers.

wholesome 1. Good for the health. Exercise and a proper diet are *wholesome.* 2. Showing good health. June is a *wholesome* young girl.
whole·some (hōl′səm) *adjective.*

who'll *Who'll* bake the cake? *Who'll* call Susan tomorrow to remind her?
who'll (hool͞) contraction for "who will" and "who shall."

wholly Entirely; completely. I am *wholly* to blame for what happened. ▲ Another word that sounds like this is **holy.**
whol·ly (hōl′lē) *adverb.*

whom She is the girl for *whom* the party is being given. To *whom* am I speaking?
whom (hoom͞) *pronoun.*

whoop A loud cry or shout. Alan gave a *whoop* of joy when he caught the fish. *Noun.*
—To give a loud cry or shout. Steve *whooped* with laughter when he heard what had happened. *Verb.* ▲ Another word that sounds like this is **hoop.**
whoop (hoop͞ *or* woop) *noun, plural* **whoops;** *verb,* **whooped, whooping.**

whooping crane A crane that has a white body, wings with black tips, and a red face. It is the tallest of all North American birds. It is nearly extinct.

who's *Who's* going to be at the meeting? ▲ Another word that sounds like this is **whose.**
who's (hooz͞) contraction for "who is."

whose *Whose* house is that? That big tree *whose* branches droop to the ground is a willow. ▲ Another word that sounds like this is **who's.**
whose (hooz͞) *pronoun.*

Whooping Crane

why *Why* are you laughing? I don't know the reason *why* Carolyn can't come with us.
—"Why" is used to show surprise or other feelings. *Why,* look who's here!
why (hwī) *adverb; interjection.*

wick A cord in an oil lamp, candle, or cigarette lighter that soaks up the fuel and burns when it is lit.
wick (wik) *noun, plural* **wicks.**

wicked Evil or very bad. The witch in the story was a *wicked* woman.
wick·ed (wik′id) *adjective.*

wicker Thin twigs that are easily bent and are woven together to make baskets and furniture.
wick·er (wik′ər) *noun.*

wide 1. Made up of or covering a large area from side to side. There is a *wide* porch across the back of the house. 2. Having a certain distance from side to side. The room is twelve feet *wide.* 3. Large in amount. This store carries a *wide* selection of furniture. 4. Far away from a specific place. His arrow was *wide* of the target. *Adjective.*
—1. Over a large area. The writer traveled far and *wide* to learn about different countries. 2. To a large or full extent. He opened his mouth *wide* and yawned. Please open the window *wide* because it's too hot in here. *Adverb.*
wide (wīd) *adjective,* **wider, widest;** *adverb.*

widen To make or become wide or wider. The road *widens* just ahead.
wid·en (wīd′ən) *verb,* **widened, widening.**

widespread 1. Happening over a large area or to many people. The flu epidemic was *widespread* in the country. 2. Fully open. He greeted her with *widespread* arms.
wide·spread (wīd′spred′) *adjective.*

widow A woman whose husband is dead and who has not married again.
wid·ow (wid′ō) *noun, plural* **widows.**

widower A man whose wife is dead and who had not married again.
wid·ow·er (wid′ō ər) *noun, plural* **widowers.**

width The distance from one side of something to the other side. The *width* of the room is fifteen feet.
width (width) *noun, plural* **widths.**

wife A married woman.
wife (wīf) *noun, plural* **wives.**

▲ The word **wife** did not originally refer to a married woman. At first it simply meant "a woman," whether or not she was married.

wig A covering for the head made of real or man-made hair.
wig (wig) *noun, plural* **wigs.**

wiggle To move from side to side in short, jerky movements. The little boy *wiggled* his toes in the sand.
wig·gle (wig′əl) *verb,* **wiggled, wiggling.**

Wig

wigwam A hut made of poles covered with bark, leaves, or hides. Some North American Indian tribes built wigwams to live in.
wig·wam (wig′wom) *noun, plural* **wigwams.**

Wigwam

wild 1. Not controlled by people; living or growing naturally. There are *wild* ponies on that island. *Wild* flowers grew along the road. 2. Not disciplined or orderly. He is a *wild* boy who always plays rough. 3. Crazy or fantastic. Betty has a *wild* idea for Dad's surprise party. *Adjective.*
—Not under control. Blueberries grow *wild* in the wood behind our house. *Adverb.*
wild (wīld) *adjective;* **wilder, wildest;** *adverb.*

wildcat A bobcat, lynx, or other small cat that is not tamed. A wildcat is larger than a domestic cat but smaller than a lion.
wild·cat (wīld′kat′) *noun, plural* **wildcats.**

wilderness A place where no people live. In a wilderness there may be dense forests and many wild animals.
wil·der·ness (wil′dər nis) *noun, plural* **wildernesses.**

wildlife Wild animals that live naturally in an area.
wild·life (wīld′līf′) *noun.*

will[1] She *will* visit you tonight. I *will* help you paint the house. He *will* do as he is told. This camera *will* not work.
will (wil) *verb.*

will[2] 1. The power of a person's mind to make a choice or to control what he does. Do you have the *will* to say no when you know you should not do something? Her *will* to succeed was strong. 2. A legal document that says what a person wants to have done with everything he owns when he dies. *Noun.*
—1. To use the power of the mind to decide what to do. The runner *willed* himself to keep going when he was so tired he wanted to give up. 2. To give away what one owns by a will. The wealthy man *willed* all his money to charity. *Verb.*
will (wil) *noun, plural* **wills;** *verb,* **willed, willing.**

willing Wanting or ready to. He was *willing* to do any job if it would help the project to be a success.
will·ing (wil′ing) *adjective.*

willow A tree or bush that has long, thin branches that bend easily, and tiny flowers that grow in furry spikes.
wil·low (wil′ō) *noun, plural* **willows.**

at; āpe; cär; end; mē; it; īce; hot; ōld;
fôrk; wood; fōol; oil; out; up; turn; sing;
thin; this; hw in white; zh in treasure.
ə stands for a in about, e in taken
i in pencil, o in lemon, and u in circus.

wilt To become limp; droop. The flowers *wilted* soon after they were cut.
  wilt (wilt) *verb,* **wilted, wilting.**

win **1.** To do better than any other person in a race or contest; be successful or victorious. Don is a very good card player and *wins* often. The black horse *won* the race. **2.** To get by effort; gain. He *won* fame as an author. *Verb.*
—A victory or success. The school football team had ten *wins* and no losses this season. *Noun.*
  win (win) *verb,* **won, winning;** *noun, plural* **wins.**

wince To draw back slightly from something painful, dangerous, or unpleasant. Phyllis *winced* when the doctor gave her the injection.
  wince (wins) *verb,* **winced, wincing.**

winch A machine for lifting or pulling something. A winch is made up of a large spool or pulley with a rope or chain around it. Ships' anchors are hoisted on a winch. Matt turned the *winch* to lift the bucket out of the well.
  winch (winch) *noun, plural* **winches.**

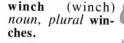
Winch

wind¹ **1.** Air that is moving over the earth. The *wind* blew his hat off. The strong *winds* knocked the tree down. **2.** Breath. The hard blow knocked the *wind* out of him. *Noun.*
—To cause someone to be out of breath. Climbing the long flight of stairs *winded* her. *Verb.*
  wind (wind) *noun, plural* **winds;** *verb,* **winded winding.**

wind² **1.** To wrap in a circle. Judy *wound* the yarn into a ball before she started knitting. Mike *wound* the wool scarf around his neck. The ivy *wound* around the pole. **2.** To move or cause to move in one direction and then another. The road *winds* around the mountain. The policeman *wound* his car through the traffic. *Verb.*
  wind (wīnd) *verb,* **wound, winding.**

wind instrument A musical instrument that is played by blowing into it. A trumpet and a flute are wind instruments.

windmill A machine that uses the power of the wind to turn large vanes at the top. Windmills are usually used to pump water or grind grain.
  wind·mill (wind′mil′) *noun, plural* **windmills.**

Windmill

window An opening in a wall or roof that lets in air and light. Panes of glass fill the opening of most windows.
  win·dow (win′dō) *noun, plural* **windows.**

windowpane A single pane of glass in a window.
  win·dow·pane (win′dō pān′) *noun, plural* **windowpanes.**

windpipe A tube that goes from the throat to the lungs. It carries air to and from the lungs.
  wind·pipe (wind′pīp′) *noun, plural* **windpipes.**

windshield A glass or plastic screen attached near the front of an automobile, motorcycle, or other vehicle. A windshield protects the driver and riders from the windw.
  wind·shield (wind′shēld′) *noun, plural* **windshields.**

windy Having or swept by strong winds. We need a *windy* day for flying our kites.
  wind·y (win′dē) *adjective,* **windier, windiest.**

wine The juice of grapes or other fruits that is fermented and made into an alcoholic drink.
  wine (wīn) *noun, plural* **wines.**

wing **1.** A movable part of the body of a bird, insect, or other animal that is used in flying. **2.** A structure located on either side of an airplane. Wings lift the airplane and support it during flight. **3.** A part that is attached to and sticks out from the main part of a structure. We added a new *wing* with two bedrooms to our house. The actors who were supposed to go on stage next waited in the *wings. Noun.*
—**1.** To fly. The bird *winged* its way home.

2. To wound slightly. The bullet *winged* him in the arm. *Verb.*

wing (wing) *noun, plural* **wings;** *verb,* **winged, winging.**

winged Having wings. Bats are *winged* animals.

winged (wingd *or* wing′id) *adjective.*

wingspread The distance between the tip of one wing and the tip of another when they are opened wide. Eagles have a very wide *wingspread.*

wing·spread (wing′spred′) *noun, plural* **wingspreads.**

wink To close and open one or both eyes quickly. People usually wink as a sign or signal. Mother *winked* at me to show me she knew the secret. *Verb.*

—1. A quick closing and opening of one or both eyes. She gave me a *wink* to tell me to keep quiet about the party. **2.** A very short time. I didn't get a *wink* of sleep last night. *Noun.*

wink (wingk) *verb,* **winked, winking;** *noun, plural* **winks.**

winner A person or thing that wins. John was the *winner* of the contest.

win·ner (win′ər) *noun, plural* **winners.**

winning 1. That wins; victorious or successful. Who has the *winning* ticket? **2.** Charming or attractive. She has a very *winning* smile. *Adjective.*

—winnings. Something that is won. My father and I play cards for pennies and I get to keep my *winnings. Noun.*

win·ning (win′ing) *adjective; noun, plural* **winnings.**

winter The season of the year between fall and spring.

win·ter (win′tər) *noun, plural* **winters.**

wintergreen A plant whose oil is used in medicine or for flavoring.

win·ter·green (win′tər grēn′) *noun, plural* **wintergreens.**

wintry Having to do with or like winter. It was a cold, *wintry* day with gray skies overhead.

win·try (win′trē) *adjective,* **wintrier, wintriest.**

wipe 1. To clean or dry by rubbing with or on some-

Wintergreen

thing. If you wash the dishes, I will *wipe* them dry. Please *wipe* your shoes on the mat before coming into the house. **2.** To take away by cleaning or drying. Please *wipe* up the spilled milk.

wipe (wīp) *verb,* **wiped, wiping.**

to wipe out. To destroy totally. The epidemic *wiped out* the population of the village.

wire 1. A thin metal thread. Wire is made by stretching a rod of metal until it is thin. **2.** A telegram. He sent a *wire* to the hotel to reserve a room. *Noun.*

**—Made of wire. We put the eggs into a *wire* basket. *Adjective.*

—1. To put in wires for electricity. The new house was *wired* but the plumbing was not in yet. **2.** To fasten with a wire. Bob *wired* the broken gate together. **3.** To send a telegram. She *wired* to tell them what time she would arrive. *Verb.*

wire (wīr) *noun, plural* **wires;** *adjective; verb,* **wired, wiring.**

wireless Having or using no wires. Radio is a form of *wireless* communication. *Adjective.*

**—A radio. In England people say they listen to the *wireless* instead of to the radio. *Noun.*

wire·less (wīr′lis) *adjective; noun, plural* **wirelesses.**

wiring A system of wires that carry electric current. The *wiring* in our house is connected to a fuse box. The *wiring* for the car radio came loose and Don had to fix it.

wir·ing (wīr′ing) *noun.*

Wisconsin A state in the north-central United States. Its capital is Madison.

Wis·con·sin (wis kon′sən) *noun.*

▲ **Wisconsin** was named after the *Wisconsin* River, which is the main river in the state. This name is the English form of an earlier French name. The French name probably came from an Indian word that means "at the big river" or "the place where the waters come together."

wisdom Good judgment and intelligence in knowing what is right, good, and true. We grow in wisdom as we gain more experience as well as knowledge.

wis·dom (wiz′dəm) *noun.*

at; āpe; cär; end; mē; it; īce; hot; ōld; fôrk; wood; fool; oil; out; up; turn; sing; thin; this; hw in white; zh in treasure.
ə stands for a in about, e in taken
i in pencil, o in lemon, and u in circus.

wise Having or showing good judgment and intelligence in making decisions about what is right or wrong, good or bad, and true or false. The club members made a *wise* choice when they elected Tim president.
wise (wīz) *adjective,* **wiser, wisest.**

wish A strong need or desire. When Phil was ten years old his only *wish* was to be a fireman when he grew up. Carla stayed out late against her mother's *wishes. Noun.*
—**1.** To want something very much; have a wish for. Ruth *wished* she had more money. I *wish* summer would last longer. I *wish* you good luck. **2.** To make a wish. When you blow out the birthday candles, don't forget to *wish. Verb.*
wish (wish) *noun, plural* **wishes;** *verb,* **wished, wishing.**

wishbone A forked bone in front of the breastbone of chickens and other birds. Some people make wishes on wishbones. One person holds one end and another person holds the other end and they pull to break the bone. The person with the longer piece is supposed to get his wish.
wish·bone (wish′bōn′) *noun, plural* **wish-bones.**

wisp A small bit or piece of something. Dan brushed *wisps* of hay off his shirt. *Wisps* of smoke drifted up from the chimney.
wisp (wisp) *noun, plural* **wisps.**

wisteria A vine with a woody stem that has long, drooping clusters of white, pink, blue, or purple flowers.
wis·te·ri·a (wi-stēr′ē ə) *noun.*

wistful Sadly wishful. The little girl was *wistful* as she looked at all the clothes she couldn't buy.
wist·ful (wist′fəl) *adjective.*

wit **1.** The ability to make clever, amusing, and unusual comments about people, things, and life. **2.** A person who has this ability. Janice was the class *wit.* **3.** The ability to think and reason; understanding. He kept his *wits* about him when the fire started and saved the little children's lives.
wit (wit) *noun, plural* **wits.**

Wisteria

witch A woman who is thought to have magic powers.
witch (wich) *noun, plural* **witches.**

with We went to the circus *with* our friends. We mixed chocolate syrup *with* the milk. The girl *with* the umbrella is my sister. He chopped down the tree *with* an ax. We had milk *with* dinner. Are you pleased *with* your gift? He trembled *with* fear. She fought *with* her brother about which television show to watch.
with (with *or* with) *preposition.*

withdraw **1.** To take away; remove. The captain *withdrew* his troops from the battle. Alan will have to *withdraw* money from the bank to pay for the car. **2.** To take back. She *withdrew* her offer to buy the house.
with·draw (with drô′ *or* with drô′) *verb,* **withdrew, withdrawn, withdrawing.**

withdrawn The soldiers were *withdrawn* from the patrol. Look up **withdraw** for more information. *Verb.*
—Very shy or quiet. He was a *withdrawn* boy who did not enjoy being with large groups of people. *Adjective.*
with·drawn (with drôn′ *or* with drôn′) *verb; adjective.*

wither To dry up or shrivel. The flowers *withered* soon after they were cut. The hot sun *withered* the crops.
with·er (with′ər) *verb,* **withered, withering.**

within The troops camped *within* the walls of the fort. I will return *within* the hour. It is not *within* his power to help us.
with·in (with in′ *or* with in′) *preposition.*

without He was exhausted after a night *without* sleep. She ordered a hamburger *without* onions. It was rude to leave *without* saying thank you.
with·out (with out′ *or* with out′) *preposition; adverb.*

withstand To hold out against; not give in to. He *withstood* the temptation to eat another piece of cake.
with·stand (with stand′ *or* with stand′) *verb,* **withstood, withstanding.**

witness A person who has seen or heard something. We were *witnesses* to the accident and had to testify in court. *Noun.*
—**1.** To be present to see or hear something. Who *witnessed* the fight? **2.** To sign a will or other document as a witness. *Verb.*
wit·ness (wit′nis) *noun, plural* **witnesses;** *verb,* **witnessed, witnessing.**

witty Clever and amusing; having wit. She made a *witty* remark and we all laughed.
wit·ty (wit′ē) *adjective,* **wittier, wittiest.**

wives More than one wife. Look up **wife** for more information.
wives (wīvz) *noun plural.*

wizard **1.** A man who is thought to have magic powers. **2.** A person who is very clever and skillful. Marsha is a *wizard* at arithmetic.
wiz·ard (wiz′ərd) *noun, plural* **wizards.**

wobble To move from side to side in an unsteady or shaky way. The old chair *wobbled* because the legs were loose.
wob·ble (wob′əl) *verb,* **wobbled, wobbling.**

woe Great sadness or suffering. The story told of the hunger, sickness, and other *woes* of the early settlers in America.
woe (wō) *noun, plural* **woes.**

woke I *woke* when the alarm went off at seven o'clock this morning. Look up **wake** for more information.
woke (wōk) *verb.*

Wolf

wolf A wild animal that looks like a dog. Wolves have gray fur, a pointed muzzle, and a bushy tail. They live in cold, northern areas. *Noun.*
—To eat very quickly and hungrily. The boys *wolfed* down their lunch so they could get back outside to play ball. *Verb.*
wolf (woolf) *noun, plural* **wolves;** *verb,* **wolfed, wolfing.**

wolverine A small, strong animal that looks like a large weasel. It has dark-brown fur and a long, bushy tail.
wol·ver·ine (wool′və rēn′) *noun, plural* **wolverines.**

Wolverine

wolves More than one wolf. Look up **wolf** for more information.
wolves (woolvz) *noun plural.*

woman **1.** An adult female person. **2.** Adult female people as a group.
wom·an (woom′ən) *noun, plural* **women.**

▲ The word **woman** comes from two Old English words. The first word meant "wife" and the second meant "man."

womb The organ in a female body that holds and nourishes a baby until it is born.
womb (woom) *noun, plural* **wombs.**

wombat A stout animal that has coarse black or brownish-yellow fur. The female wombat has a pouch in which she carries her young. Wombats are found in Australia.
wom·bat (wom′bat) *noun, plural* **wombats.**

women More than one woman. Look up **woman** for more information.
wom·en (wim′ən) *noun plural.*

won Who *won* the first prize? Look up **win** for more information. ▲ Another word that sounds like this is **one.**
won (wun) *verb.*

wonder **1.** An unusual, surprising, or very impressive thing. The pyramids in Egypt are one of the *wonders* of the world. **2.** The feeling caused by something unusual, surprising, or very impressive. We watched with *wonder* as the strong man lifted the car off the ground. *Noun.*
—**1.** To want to know or learn; be curious about. I *wonder* why the sky is blue. **2.** To feel or be surprised or impressed. We *wondered* at the man's enormous strength. *Verb.*
won·der (wun′dər) *noun, plural* **wonders;** *verb,* **wondered, wondering.**

wonderful Very good or amazing. The bicycle was a *wonderful* gift.
won·der·ful (wun′dər fəl) *adjective.*

won't He *won't* be able to finish the work today.
won't (wōnt) contraction for "will not."

wood **1.** The hard material that makes up the trunk and branches of a tree or bush. Wood is cut and prepared for use as building material and fuel. **2. woods.** An area of trees growing naturally; forest. ▲ Another word that sounds like this is **would.**
wood (wood) *noun, plural* **woods.**

at; āpe; cär; end; mē; it; īce; hot; ōld;
fôrk; wood; fōōl; oil; out; up; turn; sing;
thin; **th**is; **hw** in white; **zh** in treasure.
ə stands for **a** in about, **e** in taken
i in pencil, **o** in lemon, and **u** in circus.

713

woodchuck A stout, short-legged animal that has coarse, brown fur. Woodchucks live underground in holes which they dig. They eat leaves and grass and sleep in the winter. This animal is also called a **groundhog.**
  wood·chuck (wood′chuk′) *noun, plural* **woodchucks.**

Woodchuck

woodcutter A person whose work is cutting down trees or chopping wood.
  wood·cut·ter (wood′kut′ər) *noun, plural* **woodcutters.**

wooded Having trees or woods. We had a picnic in a *wooded* area near our house.
  wood·ed (wood′id) *adjective.*

wooden Made of wood. The books are stored in *wooden* boxes in the attic.
  wood·en (wood′ən) *adjective.*

woodpecker A bird that has a strong, pointed bill. The woodpecker uses its bill to make holes in trees in order to get insects to eat. It is found in forests throughout the world.
  wood·peck·er (wood′pek′ər) *noun, plural* **woodpeckers.**

Woodpecker

woodsman A woodcutter, hunter, or other man who lives or works in the woods.
  woods·man (woodz′mən) *noun, plural* **woodsmen.**

woodwind A musical instrument that is played by blowing air into it. It is made of a tube with holes along its length. The holes are opened or closed to change the pitch of the tones. The flute, oboe, clarinet, and saxophone are woodwinds.
  wood·wind (wood′wind′) *noun, plural* **woodwinds.**

woodwork Parts or things that are made out of wood. Window and door frames are parts of the woodwork of a house.
  wood·work (wood′wurk′) *noun.*

woodworking The art of making things out of wood.
  wood·work·ing (wood′wur′king) *noun.*

woody 1. Containing wood. *Woody* plants have wood branches rather than soft green stems. 2. Having many trees. We sailed to one of the small, *woody* islands in the bay.
  wood·y (wood′ē) *adjective,* **woodier, woodiest.**

wool The soft, thick, curly hair of sheep and some other animals like the llama and alpaca. Wool is spun into yarn which is made into cloth.
  wool (wool) *noun, plural* **wools.**

woolen Made of wool. I have a red *woolen* coat.
  wool·en (wool′ən) *adjective.*

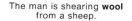
The man is shearing **wool** from a sheep.

word 1. A sound or group of sounds having meaning and forming part of a language. 2. A written or printed letter or group of letters standing for such a sound. The *word* "house" has five letters. 3. A short conversation or statement. I'd like a *word* with you before you leave. 4. A promise or vow. Gary gave Pat his *word* that he would be there. 5. A message or news. Have you had any *word* from your brother since he left? *Noun.*
—To put into words. He *worded* his question carefully. *Verb.*
  word (wurd) *noun, plural* **words;** *verb,* **worded, wording.**

wording The way of saying or writing something in words. The teacher said that the *wording* of his answer was not clear.
  word·ing (wur′ding) *noun.*

wordy Using too many words. The man was a very *wordy* speaker and we lost interest in what he was saying.
  word·y (wur′dē) *adjective,* **wordier, wordiest.**

wore I *wore* my new coat last Sunday. Look up **wear** for more information. ▲ Another word that sounds like this is **war.**
  wore (wôr) *verb.*

work 1. An effort made to do or get something. Work can be done by the mind, as in writing a paper, or by the body, as in digging a garden. 2. What a person does to earn money; a job or occupation. What kind of *work* does your father do? 3. Something that is done or is to be done. Each man was told what his *work* for the week would be. The painting was a beautiful *work* of art. 4. **works.** The moving parts of a machine, watch, or other device. *Noun.*

—**1.** To put forth effort in order to do or get something. Bill *worked* hard to finish his boat in time for the race. **2.** To have a job. She *works* in a business office. **3.** To act or make act properly; operate. Can you *work* the tape recorder? Did the medicine *work?* **4.** To solve. I couldn't *work* the last math problem. *Verb.*

   work (wurk) *noun, plural* **works;** *verb,* **worked, working.**

   out of work. Without a job. That man lost his job last month and has been *out of work* ever since.

   to make short work of. To do quickly. Once Jim started his homework he *made short work of* it.

workbench A strong table used for working. Carpenters use workbenches.
   work·bench (work′bench′) *noun, plural* **workbenches.**

workbook A book that has questions and exercises to be answered or done by a student. A workbook is used as a guide to the student in studying a certain subject.
   work·book (wurk′book′) *noun, plural* **workbooks.**

worker **1.** A person who works. There were over one hundred *workers* in the factory. Many students volunteered as *workers* to clean up after the dance. **2.** A female bee, ant, termite, or other insect that cannot reproduce and does most of the work in a colony.
   work·er (wur′kər) *noun, plural* **workers.**

working **1.** In operation; that works. Is that telephone *working?* **2.** Having to do with or doing a job. Our *working* hours are 9:00 A.M. to 5:00 P.M. My sister graduated from college and is a *working* girl now.
   work·ing (wur′king) *adjective.*

workman A man who works with his hands or with machines. Many *workmen* have been hired to build the new office building.
   work·man (wurk′mən) *noun, plural* **workmen.**

workmanship The skill with which a thing is made. The beautifully carved cabinet showed excellent *workmanship.*
   work·man·ship (wurk′mən ship′) *noun.*

workshop **1.** A room or building in which work is done by hand or with machines. Dad has a *workshop* in the basement. The garage has a *workshop* where cars are repaired. **2.** A group of people who are studying or working together on a special subject. The school has a *workshop* in child care this summer.
   work·shop (wurk′shop′) *noun, plural* **workshops.**

world **1.** The earth. Dick dreamed of sailing around the *world* in a huge ship. **2.** A part of the earth. The United States is in the western *world.* **3.** All the people who live on the earth. The *world* waited for news of the first men to land on the moon. **4.** Any activity, interest, or part of life which people or other living things share. We studied the *world* of fish and the sea. Most people who work are part of the business *world.* **5.** A large amount; great deal. The rain did the corn crop a *world* of good.
   world (wurld) *noun, plural* **worlds.**

worldwide All over the world. That movie actress has won *worldwide* fame.
   world·wide (wurld′wīd′) *adjective.*

worm A long, thin animal with a soft body and no legs. Worms crawl or creep. *Noun.*
—**1.** To move by wiggling or creeping like a worm. It took him ten minutes to *worm* his way through the crowd to the door. **2.** To get in a sneaky way. She tried to *worm* the secret out of him. *Verb.*
   worm (wurm) *noun, plural* **worms;** *verb,* **wormed, worming.**

worn I have *worn* this coat for three years. Look up **wear** for more information. *Verb.*
—Damaged by use or wear. His pants are *worn* at the knees. *Adjective.*
   worn (wôrn) *verb; adjective.*

worn-out **1.** Used or worn so much that it should not or cannot be used any more. These shoes are *worn-out.* **2.** Very tired. The hikers were *worn-out* by the time they reached their campsite.
   worn-out (wôrn′out′) *adjective.*

worry **1.** To feel or cause to feel uneasy or troubled about something. Her parents *worry* when she is out too late. The arithmetic problem *worried* her. **2.** To pull or bite at something with the teeth. The puppy *worried* at the rug. *Verb.*
—Something that causes an uneasy or troubled feeling; anxiety. Their biggest *worry* was that it might rain on the day of the picnic. *Noun.*
   wor·ry (wur′ē) *verb,* **worried, worrying;** *noun, plural* **worries.**

worse I am a bad speller, but my brother is *worse.* The weather was *worse* yesterday

at; āpe; cär; end; mē; it; īce; hot; ōld;
fôrk; wood; fool; oil; out; up; turn; sing;
thin; **th**is; **hw** in white; **zh** in treasure.
ə stands for **a** in about, **e** in taken
i in pencil, **o** in lemon, and **u** in circus.

than it is today. She sings *worse* now than she did before the lessons. The soup was not great, but I have tasted *worse*. The doctor said that his patient was *worse*.

worse (wurs) *adjective; adverb; noun.*

worship Prayer, religious services, and other acts done in honor of God. A church is a place of *worship. Noun.*
—**1.** To pay honor to God. We *worship* God in prayer. **2.** To give great love or devotion to. The children *worshipped* their grandparents. *Verb.*

wor·ship (wur′ship) *noun; verb,* **worshiped** or **worshipped, worshiping** or **worshipping.**

worst That was the *worst* movie I ever saw. That was the *worst* car accident that the policeman had ever seen. His sore throat hurts *worst* in the morning. None of the photographs are good, but the one of you and me is the *worst.*

worst (wurst) *adjective; adverb; noun.*

worth **1.** Good enough for; deserving of. That movie was *worth* seeing. Do you think it's *worth* the trouble to fix the old clock? **2.** Having the same value as. This old coin is *worth* thirty dollars today. **3.** Having wealth that amounts to. That famous movie star is supposed to be *worth* millions of dollars. *Preposition.*
—**1.** The quality that makes a person or thing good or important; excellence. That old painting has great *worth.* **2.** The value of something in money. That diamond's *worth* is said to be $50,000. **3.** The amount that a certain sum of money will buy. Joe asked for fifty cents' *worth* of chocolate candy. We put three dollars' *worth* of gasoline in the tank. *Noun.*

worth (wurth) *preposition; noun.*

worthless Not good or valuable. Her advice about fixing the car is *worthless* since she doesn't really know anything about cars. The basement was full of *worthless* old furniture.

worth·less (wurth′lis) *adjective.*

worthwhile Good enough or important enough to spend time, effort, or money on. Doing volunteer work at the hospital is a *worthwhile* activity.

worth·while (wurth′hwīl′) *adjective.*

worthy Good or important; worthwhile. He wanted to give the money he won to a *worthy* charity.

wor·thy (wur′thē) *adjective,* **worthier, worthiest.**

would If you *would* help, we would finish sooner. We wondered if Don *would* be on

time. They said they *would* return tonight. During the summer we *would* sit on the beach for hours. *Would* you please help me carry this heavy box upstairs? ▲ Another word that sounds like this is **wood.**

would (wood) *verb.*

wouldn't She *wouldn't* tell me who had called her.

would'nt (wood′ənt) contraction for "would not."

wound[1] A cut or other injury to a part of the body. *Noun.*
—**1.** To hurt or injure by cutting, piercing, or tearing the skin. The policeman's bullet *wounded* the bank robber. **2.** To hurt a person's feelings. His pride was *wounded* when he didn't get the job. *Verb.*

wound (woond) *noun, plural* **wounds;** *verb,* **wounded, wounding.**

wound[2] I *wound* the clock before I went to bed. Look up **wind** for more information.

wound (wound) *verb.*

wove The driver *wove* the fire truck through the traffic. Look up **weave** for more information.

wove (wōv) *verb.*

woven The robin had *woven* twigs together to make a nest. Look up **weave** for more information.

wo·ven (wō′vən) *verb.*

wow A word that is used to express surprise, wonder, or pleasure. "*Wow,* did you see how far he hit that ball?" asked Peter.

wow (wou) *interjection.*

wrap **1.** To fold or put a cover around someone or something. Ruth enjoys *wrapping* presents. Dad *wrapped* a blanket around the baby. **2.** To hide by covering. The top of the mountain was *wrapped* in fog. **3.** To clasp or fold. The little boy *wrapped his arms around his mother's neck.* ▲ Another word that sounds like this is **rap.**

wrap (rap) *verb,* **wrapped** or **wrapt, wrapping.**

wrapper **1.** A piece of paper or other covering for something. He threw away the candy *wrapper.* **2.** A person who wraps packages in a store. Susan worked as a *wrapper* during Christmas vacation.

wrap·per (rap′ər) *noun, plural* **wrappers.**

wrapping Paper or other covering for something. We burned the *wrappings* from the Christmas presents in the fireplace.

wrap·ping (rap′ing) *noun, plural* **wrappings.**

wrath Very great anger. His rude behavior aroused his father's *wrath.*

wrath (rath) *noun.*

wreath A circle of leaves or flowers woven together. We hung a Christmas *wreath* on the front door.
  wreath (rēth) *noun, plural* **wreaths.**

wreck To destroy or ruin. The builders *wrecked* the old house to clear the land. His dishonesty will *wreck* his career. *Verb.*
—What is left of something that has been ruined or damaged. There are many automobile *wrecks* in the junkyard. The room was a *wreck* after the party. *Noun.*
  wreck (rek) *verb,* **wrecked, wrecking;** *noun, plural* **wrecks.**

Wreath

wreckage What is left of something that has been ruined or destroyed. We went to look at the *wreckage* after the building burned.
  wreck·age (rek′ij) *noun.*

wren A songbird with a narrow bill, a short tail and wings, and brown feathers with black or white markings.
  wren (ren) *noun, plural* **wrens.**

wrench 1. A very hard, sharp twist or pull. He gave the doorknob *wrench* but the door was stuck and would not open. 2. A tool with jaws that is used to grip and to turn a nut or bolt. *Noun.*
—To twist or pull with a hard, sharp motion. He *wrenched* the gun out of the man's hand. *Verb.*
  wrench (rench) *noun, plural* **wrenches;** *verb,* **wrenched, wrenching.**

Wren

wrestle 1. To force or try to force a person to the ground in a hand to hand struggle. The champion *wrestled* his opponent to the mat. The boys *wrestled* on the lawn. 2. To struggle very hard. She *wrestled* with the last problem on the test.
  wres·tle (res′əl) *verb,* **wrestled, wrestling.**

wrestling A sport in which two people struggle hand to hand and try to force each other to the ground.
  wres·tling (res′ling) *noun.*

Wrestling

wretched 1. Very unhappy, poor, or uncomfortable. Her toothache made her feel *wretched.* 2. Very bad or evil. The cruel soldiers were *wretched* people.
  wretch·ed (rech′id) *adjective.*

wriggle 1. To twist or turn from side to side with short, quick moves; squirm. The bored children *wriggled* in their seats. The snake *wriggled* through the grass. 2. To get into or out of a position by tricky means. Harry always tries to *wriggle* out of helping with the dishes.
  wrig·gle (rig′əl) *verb,* **wriggled, wriggling.**

wring 1. To squeeze or twist or force water or other liquid out. You must *wring* the wet clothes before hanging them up to dry. 2. To force out liquid by squeezing or twisting. She *wrung* the water from her bathing suit. 3. To get by force. He said he would *wring* the truth out of his brother. 4. To hold tightly and press or twist. The man *wrung* his hands nervously.
▲ Another word that sounds like this is **ring.**
  wring (ring) *verb,* **wrung, wringing.**

wrinkle A small fold, ridge, or line in a smooth surface. Mary ironed the *wrinkles* out of her dress. He had small *wrinkles* at the corners of his eyes. *Noun.*
—To make or have a fold, ridge, or line in a smooth surface. He *wrinkled* his forehead when he frowned. The skirt *wrinkled* after she sat in it. *Verb.*
  wrin·kle (ring′kəl) *noun, plural* **wrinkles;** *verb,* **wrinkled, wrinkling.**

at; āpe; cär; end; mē; it; īce; hot; ōld;
fôrk; wood; fo͞ol; oil; out; up; turn; sing;
thin; this; hw in white; zh in treasure.
ə stands for a in about, e in taken
i in pencil, o in lemon, and u in circus.

wrist The joint between the hand and the arm.
　wrist (rist) *noun, plural* **wrists.**

wristwatch A watch that is worn on a strap around the wrist.
　wrist·watch (rist′woch′) *noun, plural* **wrist-watches.**

writ A written legal paper that orders a person to do or not to do something.
　writ (rit) *noun, plural* **writs.**

write **1.** To form the letters, words, or symbols of something on paper or some other surface. The teacher *wrote* his name on the blackboard. *Write* the answers to the questions in blue ink. **2.** To make up stories, poems, or articles; be the author of. Jane's aunt *writes* children's stories. **3.** To send a letter. Please *write* us when you are on vacation. ▲ Another word that sounds like this is **right.**
　write (rīt) *verb,* **wrote, written, writing.**

writer A person who writes stories, poems, or articles; author.
　writ·er (rī′tər) *noun, plural* **writers.**

writing **1.** Letters, words, or symbols that are written by hand. Her *writing* is neat and easy to read. Do you know whose *writing* this is? **2.** A book, play, or other thing that has been written. We study the *writings* of many authors in English class.
　writ·ing (rī′ting) *noun, plural* **writings.**

written Joan has *written* her book report. Look up **write** for more information.
　writ·ten (rit′ən) *verb.*

wrong **1.** Not correct or true. Her answer to the question was *wrong.* **2.** Not moral or good; bad. It was *wrong* of him to steal. **3.** Not proper; unsuitable. A heavy sweater is the *wrong* thing to wear on a hot day. **4.** Out of order; not working. Something is *wrong* with my watch. *Adjective.*
—Something that is not moral or good. He did his friend a great *wrong* by not telling him the truth. *Noun.*
—In a way that is not right; incorrectly. She spelled several words *wrong* in her report. *Adverb.*
—To treat in an unjust or bad way. She *wronged* us by lying to us. *Verb.*
　wrong (rông) *adjective; noun, plural* **wrongs;** *adverb; verb,* **wronged, wronging.**

wrote He *wrote* down what the teacher said. Look up **write** for more information.
　wrote (rōt) *verb.*

wrung She *wrung* out the wet shirt and hung it up to dry. Look up **wring** for more information. ▲ Another word that sounds like this is **rung.**
　wrung (rung) *verb.*

wry Twisted to one side. He gave her a *wry* smile. ▲ Another word that sounds like this is **rye.**
　wry (rī) *adjective,* **wrier, wriest.**

Wyoming A state in the western United States. Its capital is Cheyenne.
　Wy·o·ming (wī ō′ming) *noun.*

▲ The name **Wyoming** comes from an Indian word that means "the end of the plains" or "on the great plain." The Indians used this name for a valley in Pennsylvania, but it fit the new western territory well, so Congress made it the official name in 1868. The name was kept when the territory became a state.

---

at; āpe; cär; end; mē; it; īce; hot; ōld;
fôrk; wood; fōol; oil; out; up; turn; sing;
thin; this; hw in white; zh in treasure.
ə stands for a in about, e in taken
i in pencil, o in lemon, and u in circus.

X

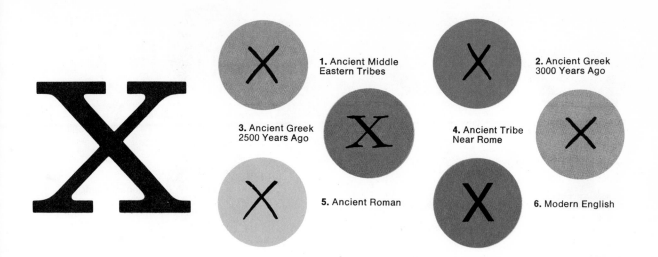

1. Ancient Middle Eastern Tribes

2. Ancient Greek 3000 Years Ago

3. Ancient Greek 2500 Years Ago

4. Ancient Tribe Near Rome

5. Ancient Roman

6. Modern English

X is the twenty-fourth letter of the alphabet. The oldest form of this letter was used in the alphabet of several ancient tribes (**1**) in the Middle East. It was written as either a plus sign or a modern letter **X**. The form of this letter that looked like the modern letter **X** is often called a "cross sign." When the ancient Greeks (**2**) borrowed the "cross sign" letter they used it to stand for two different sounds: a *kh* sound in the Eastern Greek alphabet, and a *ks* sound in the Western Greek alphabet. Several hundred years after the Greeks first borrowed this letter, they were writing it (**3**) very much like a modern capital letter **X**. The Western Greek form of the "cross sign" letter was borrowed by an ancient tribe (**4**) that settled north of Rome about 2800 years ago. The Romans (**5**) borrowed this letter and, by about 2400 years ago, were writing it in almost exactly the same way that we write the capital letter **X** today (**6**).

x, X The twenty-fourth letter of the alphabet.

    x, X (eks) *noun, plural* **x's, X's.**

Xerox A trademark for a process for making photographic copies of written or printed matter.

    Xe·rox (zēr′oks) *noun.*

Xmas Christmas. Look up **Christmas** for more information.

    X·mas (kris′məs *or* eks′məs) *noun.*

▲ The word **Xmas** is made up of the letter "X" and the ending *mas* from *Christmas.* "X" was the first letter of the ancient Greek word meaning "Christ" and was used as a symbol for *Christ.*

X-ray To examine, photograph, or treat with X rays. The doctor *X-rayed* the boy's arm to see if any bones had been broken.

    X-ray (eks′rā′) *verb,* **X-rayed, X-raying.**

X ray **1.** A kind of radiation that can pass through substances that ordinary rays of light cannot pass through. Doctors use X rays to take pictures of parts inside the body that cannot be seen from outside. X rays can be used to see if a bone has been broken or to see if there is a cavity inside a tooth. **2.** A photograph made with X rays. The doctor looked at the *X ray* of the woman's injured wrist.

xylophone A musical instrument that is made up of one or two rows of wooden bars. The bars are of different lengths, and they are sounded by hitting them with small wooden hammers.

    xy·lo·phone (zī′lə fōn′) *noun, plural* **xylophones.**

Xylophone

▲ The word **xylophone** comes from two Greek words meaning "wood" and "sound" or "voice."

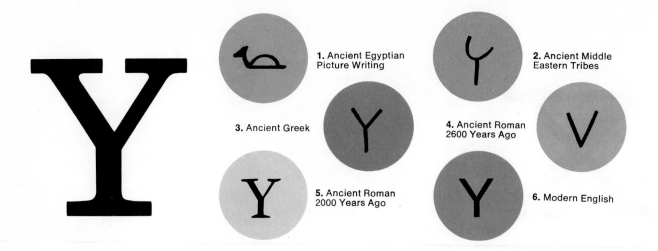

1. Ancient Egyptian Picture Writing

2. Ancient Middle Eastern Tribes

3. Ancient Greek

4. Ancient Roman 2600 Years Ago

5. Ancient Roman 2000 Years Ago

6. Modern English

Y is the twenty-fifth letter of the alphabet. The oldest form of the letter **Y** was a drawing that the ancient Egyptians (**1**) used in their picture writing nearly 5000 years ago. This drawing was borrowed by several ancient tribes (**2**) in the Middle East. They used it to stand for both the vowel sound *u,* as the *u* in *rude,* and the consonant sound *w,* as the *w* in *water.* The ancient Greeks (**3**) borrowed this letter, writing it very much like a modern capital letter **Y**. They used it to stand for the *u* sound only. The Romans borrowed this letter twice from the ancient Greeks. The first time (**4**), about 2600 years ago, they used it to form the letter **V**. About 2000 years ago, the Romans borrowed the letter for a second time (**5**), so that they could write certain words that they had borrowed from the Greek language. This later form of **Y** was written in almost the same way that we write the capital letter **Y** today (**6**).

The letter **Y** is the only letter of the alphabet that is often used as a vowel, as in "funny" and "cry," and as a consonant, as in "yes" and "you."

y, Y The twenty-fifth letter of the alphabet.
y, Y (wī) *noun, plural* **y's, Y's.**

-y A *suffix* that means: **1.** "Having." *Rainy* means "having rain." **2.** "Full of." *Juicy* means "full of juice."

yacht A small ship used for pleasure trips.
yacht (yot) *noun, plural* **yachts.**

▲ The word **yacht** comes from an old Dutch word that meant "ship for chasing."

---

yak A long-haired ox that is found in Asia. Yaks are raised for their meat and milk. They are also used to carry heavy loads.
yak (yak) *noun, plural* **yaks.**

Yak

yam **1.** The root of a trailing tropical vine. It is ground into flour or eaten baked or broiled. **2.** A kind of sweet potato. Look up **sweet potato** for more information.
yam (yam) *noun, plural* **yams.**

yank To pull something in a sharp, sudden way; jerk; tug. The selfish boy *yanked* the toy truck away from his little brother. *Verb.*
—A sharp, sudden pull. With one *yank* on the ribbon, she untied the bow on her birthday present. *Noun.*
yank (yangk) *verb,* **yanked, yanking;** *noun, plural* **yanks.**

Yams

yard¹ An area of ground next to or surrounding a house, school, or other building. I'm going outside to play in the *yard.*
yard (yärd) *noun, plural* **yards.**

yard² **1.** A measure of length equal to thirty-six inches, or three feet. **2.** A long rod fastened across the mast of a ship to support a sail.

yard (yärd) *noun, plural* **yards.**

yarn **1.** Thread used in knitting or weaving. It is spun from cotton, wool, silk, nylon, or other material. **2.** A long or made-up story. Joan listened while her grandfather told *yarns* of his experiences as a sailor.

yarn (yärn) *noun, plural* **yarns.**

yawn **1.** To open the mouth wide and take a deep breath. People yawn because they are tired, sleepy, or bored. **2.** To be wide open. The entrance to the huge cave *yawned* in front of them. *Verb.*

—The act of opening the mouth wide and taking a deep breath. The bored woman tried to hide a *yawn* as the speaker went on and on. *Noun.*

yawn (yôn) *verb,* **yawned, yawning;** *noun, plural* **yawns.**

ye You. ▲ This word was common in olden times, but it is not often used today.

ye (yē) *pronoun.*

year **1.** A period of time made up of the twelve months from January 1 to December 31. A year contains 365 days. There are 366 days in a leap year. **2.** Any period of twelve months. We moved to our new house a *year* ago last May. **3.** A part of a year spent in a particular activity. During the school *year* my sister and I get up at 7:30 in the morning.

year (yēr) *noun, plural* **years.**

yearly **1.** Happening or returning once a year. We made our *yearly* trip to my uncle's house at Christmas time. **2.** Measured by the year. Mrs. Green's *yearly* salary at her new job is $10,000.

year·ly (yēr′lē) *adjective.*

yeast A substance that is used in baking to make dough rise. It is made up of tiny cells of fungus plants.

yeast (yēst) *noun, plural* **yeasts.**

yell To cry out loudly. Barbara got mad and *yelled* at me for taking her bicycle. *Verb.*

—A loud, strong cry. Give a *yell* if you need any help. *Noun.*

yell (yel) *verb,* **yelled, yelling;** *noun, plural* **yells.**

yellow **1.** The color of gold, butter, or ripe lemons. **2.** The yolk of an egg. *Noun.*

—**1.** Having the color yellow. **2.** Having a yellowish skin. *Adjective.*

—To make or become yellow. The old newspaper had *yellowed* with age. *Verb.*

yel·low (yel′ō) *noun, plural* **yellows;** *adjective,* **yellower, yellowest;** *verb,* **yellowed, yellowing.**

yellow jacket A kind of wasp that has yellow markings.

Yellow Jacket

yes *Yes,* you are right. *Yes,* you may borrow ten cents.

yes (yes) *noun, plural* **yeses.**

yesterday The day before today. *Yesterday* was sunny, but by this morning it had begun to rain. *Noun.*

—On the day before today. Ben started to read the book *yesterday* and finished it by this afternoon. *Adverb.*

yes·ter·day (yes′tər dē *or* yes′tər dā′) *noun, plural* **yesterdays;** *adverb.*

yet Judy is not *yet* old enough to drive a car. Sarah has never *yet* broken a promise she has made to me. The farmer went to the fields early and is working *yet.* The police will solve the mystery *yet.* Aren't you finished eating *yet?* There are three days *yet* to go until the holiday. The teacher is strict, *yet* completely fair. Fred said he knew the way, *yet* he soon got lost.

yet (yet) *adverb; conjunction.*

yew An evergreen tree that has reddish-brown bark and flat, needle-shaped leaves. It grows in Europe and Asia. The wood of this tree is used to make bows for archery. ▲ Other words that sound like this are **ewe** and **you.**

yew (yōō) *noun, plural* **yews.**

Needles
Yew Tree

at; āpe; cär; end; mē; it; īce; hot; ōld; fôrk; wood; fōōl; oil; out; up; turn; sing; thin; this; hw in white; zh in treasure. ə stands for a in about, e in taken i in pencil, o in lemon, and u in circus.

yield **1.** To give forth; produce. The field *yielded* a large crop of wheat. **2.** To give up or in; surrender. The defeated army *yielded* the town to the enemy. We *yielded* to his argument and let him have his own way. **3.** To give way to force or pressure. The lock on the door was broken and it *yielded* when we pushed against it. *Verb.*
—An amount produced. The farm's *yield* of corn was greater this year than last. *Noun.*
   yield (yēld) *verb,* **yielded, yielding;** *noun, plural* **yields.**

yoke **1.** A wooden frame used to join together two work animals. **2.** A pair of animals joined by a yoke. The wagon was pulled by a *yoke* of oxen. **3.** The part of a shirt, dress, or other piece of clothing that fits around the shoulders and neck. *Noun.*
—To join with a yoke. The farmer *yoked* the oxen to the plow. *Verb.* ▲ Another word that sounds like this is **yolk.**
   yoke (yōk) *noun, plural* **yokes** *for definitions 1 and 3)* or yoke *(for definition 2); verb,* **yoked, yoking.**

Yoke

yolk The yellow part of an egg. ▲ Another word that sounds like this is **yoke.**
   yolk (yōk) *noun, plural* **yolks.**

yonder In that place; over there. *Yonder* stands the castle of the king. *Adverb.*
—Being at a distance, but within sight. Wildflowers are blooming in *yonder* field. *Adjective.*
   yon·der (yon′dər) *adverb; adjective.*

you Do *you* want to go? We will meet *you* at six o'clock. *You* must be at least eighteen years old to be able to vote. ▲ Other words that sound like this are **ewe** and **yew.**
   you (yōō *or* yə) *pronoun.*

you'd *You'd* better not forget to lock the door. *You'd* have liked the movie we saw last night.

you'd (yōōd) contraction for "you had" and "you would."

you'll *You'll* probably grow up to be nearly as tall as your father. *You'll* have to explain why you were absent from school.
   you'll (yōōl *or* yool) contraction for "you will" and "you shall."

young **1.** Having lived or existed for a short time. A lamb is a *young* sheep. The age of space travel is still *young.* **2.** Having the look or qualities of a young person. My grandmother is a very active woman and is quite *young* for her age. **3.** Of or belonging to the early part of life. Mr. Gordon spent his *young* years in England. *Adjective.*
—Young offspring. The lion caught an antelope to feed her *young. Noun.*
   young (yung) *adjective,* **younger, youngest;** *noun.*

youngster A young person. Many of the *youngsters* in the neighborhood helped to clean up the vacant lot.
   young·ster (yung′stər) *noun, plural* **youngsters.**

your Is it true that Tom is *your* brother? Let's meet tomorrow at *your* house. Philip agrees with *your* opinion. ▲ Another word that sounds like this is **you're.**
   your (yoor *or* yər) *adjective.*

you're *You're* almost as tall as I am. ▲ Another word that sounds like this is **your.**
   you·re (yoor *or* yôr *or* yər) contraction for "you are."

yours Is this coat *yours?* The picture Ed painted is good, but *yours* is even better.
   yours (yoorz) *pronoun.*

yourself You *yourself* know that what you did was wrong. Be careful of the fire, or you will burn *yourself.* After a good night's sleep you will feel like *yourself* again.
   your·self (yoor self′ *or* yər self′) *pronoun, plural* **yourselves.**

youth **1.** The condition or quality of being young. Mrs. Armstrong still has the bright, fresh look of *youth.* **2.** The time of life between childhood and adulthood. In his *youth,* my father wanted to be a soldier. **3.** The beginning or early stage of something. Aviation was still in its *youth* when my grandfather first flew in an airplane. **4.** A young man. The car was driven by a *youth* of about eighteen years of age.
   youth (yōōth) *noun, plural* **youths** *or* **youth.**

you've *You've* been talking on the telephone for nearly half an hour.
   you've (yōōv *or* yoov) contraction for "you have."

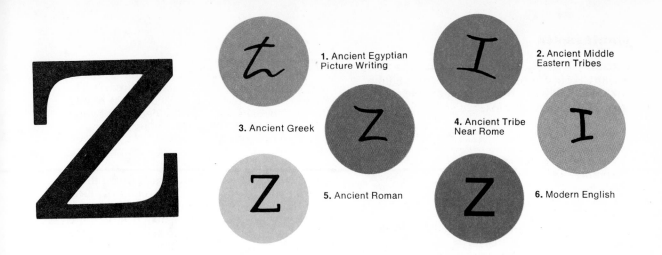

1. Ancient Egyptian Picture Writing

2. Ancient Middle Eastern Tribes

3. Ancient Greek

4. Ancient Tribe Near Rome

5. Ancient Roman

6. Modern English

Z is the twenty-sixth and last letter of the alphabet. The oldest form of the letter **Z** was a drawing that the ancient Egyptians (**1**) used in their picture writing nearly 5000 years ago. This drawing was borrowed by several ancient tribes (**2**) in the Middle East. They wrote this letter very much like a modern capital letter **I**. When the ancient Greeks (**3**) borrowed this letter they changed its shape so that it looked like a modern capital letter **Z**. The older form of this letter, which looked like a capital letter **I** was used by an ancient tribe (**4**) that settled north of Rome about 2800 years ago. But the Romans (**5**) borrowed the Greek form of the letter. By about 2400 years ago, the Romans were writing this letter in almost the same way that we write the capital letter **Z** today (**6**).

The letter **Z** is used less often in our language than any other letter of the alphabet. Most of the words that we use that contain **Z** come from either Greek, which gave us the words "zoo" and "zone," or from Arabic, which gave us the word "zero." In everyday speaking and writing we use **Z** in many words that imitate sound or imitate the sound that something makes, such as "buzz," "fizz," and "sizzle."

z, Z   The twenty-sixth and last letter of the alphabet.
  z, Z (zē) *noun, plural* **z's, Z's.**

zebra   A wild animal that has a light-colored coat with black stripes. It looks like a horse. Zebras come from southern and eastern Africa.
  ze·bra (zē′brə) *noun, plural* **zebras** or **zebra.**

Zebra

zenith   **1.** The point in the heavens directly above the place where a person stands. **2.** The highest or greatest point. The musician's recent concert was the *zenith* of her career.
  ze·nith (zē′nith) *noun, plural* **zeniths.**

▲   The word **zenith** goes back to an Arabic word meaning "way." It was used in an Arabic phrase that meant "way overhead."

zero   **1.** The number that leaves any number the same when it is added to it; 0. **2.** A point on a thermometer or other scale from which something is measured. The temperature outside is ten degrees above *zero*. **3.** Nothing. The business did not lose money, but its profit was *zero. Noun.*
  —1. Of, being, or at zero. The temperature was *zero* degrees last night. **2.** None at all; not any. The team had *zero* victories last season. *Adjective.*
  ze·ro (zēr′ō) *noun, plural* **zeros** or **zeroes;** *adjective.*

zigzag   A line, pattern, or course that has or moves in a series of short, sharp turns from one side to the other. *Noun.*
  —To move in or form a zigzag. Chuck *zigzagged* through the crowd. *Verb.*
  zig·zag (zig′zag′) *noun, plural* **zigzags;** *verb,* **zigzagged, zigzagging.**

zinc   A grayish-white metal. It is used to make alloys and in electric batteries. Zinc is a chemical element.
  zinc (zingk) *noun.*

zinnia A kind of flower that grows in many colors. It is often grown as a garden plant.
zin·ni·a (zin′ē ə) *noun, plural* **zinnias.**

zip To fasten or close with a zipper. Larry *zipped* up his jacket before going outside.
zip (zip) *verb,* **zipped, zipping.**

Zip Code A number that identifies a U.S. postal delivery area. The Zip Code is written after the state in an address on a letter, package, or other piece of mail.

Zinnias

zipper A fastener made up of two rows of interlocking teeth. The teeth may be joined or separated by pulling a sliding device up or down. Zippers are used on clothing, suitcases, and other articles.
zip·per (zip′ər) *noun, plural* **zippers.**

zither A musical instrument made up of a shallow, wooden sound box with thirty to forty-five strings stretched across it. It is played by plucking the strings.
zith·er (zith′ər *or* zi<u>th</u>′ər) *noun, plural* **zithers.**

zodiac An imaginary belt in the heavens. It is divided into twelve parts which are called signs.
zo·di·ac (zō′dē ak′) *noun.*

Zither

▲ The word **zodiac** comes from a Greek word meaning "of animal figures." The Greeks called the zodiac a "circle of animal figures" because it was divided into twelve parts, and each part had a picture of an animal as its symbol.

zone **1.** Any of the five regions into which the earth's surface is divided according to the climate found there. **2.** Any region or area that has some special quality, condition, or use. Cars are not allowed to go more than fifteen miles per hour in the school *zone.* The area at the end of a football field is called the end *zone. Noun.*
—To divide into zones. That part of the city is *zoned* for private houses, and no apartment buildings can be built there. *Verb.*
zone (zōn) *noun, plural* **zones;** *verb,* **zoned, zoning.**

zoo A park or other place where animals are kept for exhibition.
zoo (zo͞o) *noun, plural* **zoos.**

zoology The science that deals with the study of all forms of animal life.
zo·ol·o·gy (zō ol′ə jē) *noun.*

zoom To move or climb suddenly and quickly. The airplane *zoomed* into the clouds. Judy *zoomed* down the hall to answer the telephone.
zoom (zo͞om) *verb,* **zoomed, zooming.**

at; āpe; cär; end; mē; it; īce; hot; ōld; fôrk; wood; fo͞ol; oil; out; up; turn; sing; thin; <u>th</u>is; hw in white; zh in treasure. ə stands for a in about, e in taken i in pencil, o in lemon, and u in circus.